MATTHEW

Zondervan Exegetical Commentary Series: New Testament

MATTHEW

ZONDERVAN
Exegetical Commentary
ON THE
New Testament

GRANT R. OSBORNE

CLINTON E. ARNOLD
General Editor

ZONDERVAN.com/
AUTHORTRACKER
follow your favorite authors

For my wife, Nancy
Her faithful love and patience with me
are a treasure beyond compare.

ZONDERVAN

Matthew

This title is also available as a Zondervan ebook.
Visit www.zondervan.com/ebooks.

Requests for information should be addressed to:

Zondervan, *Grand Rapids, Michigan 49530*

Library of Congress Cataloging-in-Publication Data

Osborne, Grant R.
Matthew / Grant R. Osborne ; Clinton E. Arnold, general editor.
p. cm. — (Zondervan exegetical commentary series on the New Testament ; v. 1)
Includes bibliographical references and indexes.
ISBN 978-0-310-24357-1 (hardcover, printed)
1. Bible. N.T. Matthew—Commentaries. I. Arnold, Clinton E. II. Title.
BS2575.53.O83 2009
226.2'07—dc22 2009043783

Interior design: Beth Shagene

Printed in the United States of America

12 13 14 15 16 17 18 /DCI/ 27 26 25 24 23 22 21 20 19 18 17 16 15 14 13 12 11 10 9 8 7 6 5 4 3 2

Contents

Series Introduction

This generation has been blessed with an abundance of excellent commentaries. Some are technical and do a good job of addressing issues that the critics have raised; other commentaries are long and provide extensive information about word usage and catalog nearly every opinion expressed on the various interpretive issues; still other commentaries focus on providing cultural and historical background information; and then there are those commentaries that endeavor to draw out many applicational insights.

The key question to ask is: What are you looking for in a commentary? This commentary series might be for you if

- you have taken Greek and would like a commentary that helps you apply what you have learned without assuming you are a well-trained scholar.
- you would find it useful to see a concise, one- or two-sentence statement of what the commentator thinks the main point of each passage is.
- you would like help interpreting the words of Scripture without getting bogged down in scholarly issues that seem irrelevant to the life of the church.
- you would like to see a visual representation (a graphical display) of the flow of thought in each passage.
- you would like expert guidance from solid evangelical scholars who set out to explain the meaning of the original text in the clearest way possible and to help you navigate through the main interpretive issues.
- you want to benefit from the results of the latest and best scholarly studies and historical information that help to illuminate the meaning of the text.
- you would find it useful to see a brief summary of the key theological insights that can be gleaned from each passage and some discussion of the relevance of these for Christians today.

These are just some of the features that characterize the new Zondervan Exegetical Commentary on the New Testament series. The idea for this series was refined over time by an editorial board who listened to pastors and teachers express what they wanted to see in a commentary series based on the Greek text. That board consisted of myself, George H. Guthrie, William D. Mounce, Thomas R. Schreiner, and Mark L. Strauss along with Zondervan senior editor at large, Verlyn Verbrugge, and former Zondervan senior acquisitions editor, Jack Kuhatschek. We also enlisted a board of consulting editors who are active pastors, ministry leaders, and seminary professors to help in the process of designing a commentary series that will be useful to the church. Zondervan senior acquisitions editor David Frees has now been shepherding the process to completion.

We arrived at a design that includes seven components for the treatment of each biblical passage. What follows is a brief orientation to these primary components of the commentary.

Literary Context

In this section, you will find a concise discussion of how the passage functions in the broader literary context of the book. The commentator highlights connections with the preceding and following material in the book and makes observations on the key literary features of this text.

Main Idea

Many readers will find this to be an enormously helpful feature of this series. For each passage, the commentator carefully crafts a one- or two-sentence statement of the big idea or central thrust of the passage.

Translation and Graphical Layout

Another unique feature of this series is the presentation of each commentator's translation of the Greek text in a graphical layout. The purpose of this diagram is to help the reader visualize, and thus better understand, the flow of thought within the text. The translation itself reflects the interpretive decisions made by each commentator in the "Explanation" section of the commentary. Here are a few insights that will help you to understand the way these are put together:

1. On the far left side next to the verse numbers is a series of interpretive labels that indicate the function of each clause or phrase of the biblical text. The corresponding portion of the text is on the same line to the right of the label. We have not used technical linguistic jargon for these, so they should be easily understood.
2. In general, we place every clause (a group of words containing a subject and a predicate) on a separate line and identify how it is supporting the principal assertion of the text (namely, is it saying when the action occurred, how it took place, or why it took place). We sometimes place longer phrases or a series of items on separate lines as well.

3. Subordinate (or dependent) clauses and phrases are indented and placed directly under the words that they modify. This helps the reader to more easily see the nature of the relationship of clauses and phrases in the flow of the text.
4. Every main clause has been placed in bold print and pushed to the left margin for clear identification.
5. Sometimes when the level of subordination moves too far to the right — as often happens with some of Paul's long, involved sentences! — we reposition the flow to the left of the diagram, but use an arrow to indicate that this has happened.
6. The overall process we have followed has been deeply informed by principles of discourse analysis and narrative criticism (for the gospels and Acts).

Structure

Immediately following the translation, the commentator describes the flow of thought in the passage and explains how certain interpretive decisions regarding the relationship of the clauses were made in the passage.

Exegetical Outline

The overall structure of the passage is described in a detailed exegetical outline. This will be particularly helpful for those who are looking for a way to concisely explain the flow of thought in the passage in a teaching or preaching setting.

Explanation of the Text

As an exegetical commentary, this work makes use of the Greek language to interpret the meaning of the text. If your Greek is rather rusty (or even somewhat limited), don't be too concerned. All of the Greek words are cited in parentheses following an English translation. We have made every effort to make this commentary as readable and useful as possible even for the nonspecialist.

Those who will benefit the most from this commentary will have had the equivalent of two years of Greek in college or seminary. This would include a semester or two of working through an intermediate grammar (such as Wallace, Porter, Brooks and Winberry, or Dana and Mantey). The authors use the grammatical language that is found in these kinds of grammars. The details of the grammar of the passage, however, are only discussed when it has a bearing on the interpretation of the text.

The emphasis on this section of the text is to convey the meaning. Commentators examine words and images, grammatical details, relevant OT and Jewish background to a particular concept, historical and cultural context, important text-critical issues, and various interpretational issues that surface.

Theology in Application

This, too, is a unique feature for an exegetical commentary series. We felt it was important for each author not only to describe what the text means in its various details, but also to take a moment and reflect on the theological contribution that it makes. In this section, the theological message of the passage is summarized. The authors discuss the theology of the text in terms of its place within the book and in a broader biblical-theological context. Finally, each commentator provides some suggestions on what the message of the passage is for the church today. At the conclusion of each volume in this series is a summary of the whole range of theological themes touched on by this book of the Bible.

Our sincere hope and prayer is that you find this series helpful not only for your own understanding of the text of the New Testament, but as you are actively engaged in teaching and preaching God's Word to people who are hungry to be fed on its truth.

Clinton E. Arnold, general editor

Author's Preface

On my very first sabbatical, in Fall 1979–80, I spent a semester at Tyndale House working on the gospel of Matthew in the hopes of writing a commentary. The commentary did not work out at that time, but since then I have been waiting for an opportunity to do so. I have also taught Matthew for over thirty years in my Gospels class at Trinity Evangelical Divinity School and have done two editions of extended class notes for the students. Needless to say, when the chance to produce a commentary on Matthew for the Zondervan Exegetical Commentary series arrived, I rejoiced at the opportunity. I can honestly say it was a labor of love, and the deeper I have gone into this wondrous gospel, the more I have marveled at the intricacy of its structure, the depth of its insight, and the practical value of its theological message. I pray I have somehow been able to communicate that message for the reader.

In addition, I cannot think of a format with more value for the busy pastor who wishes to do justice to the text for the church. If I were to dedicate the rest of my life to one single thing, it would be bringing the Bible back into the center of the church's life. One of my greatest worries is the "dumbing down" of the church, and in my forty-plus years of ministry I have seen biblical preaching receive less and less place in the life of the church. I cannot help but wonder if some actually believe the Bible is the Word of God when they do not care what it means and do not want to proclaim its truths to their congregations. My "life verse" is 2 Tim 2:15, "Do your best to present yourself to God as one approved, a worker who does not need to be ashamed and who correctly handles the word of truth." This means that when I stand before God and give account for my ministry (Heb 13:17), I will stand in shame if I have not had a Bible-centered ministry. Thanks be to God that there are many pastors who are standing sure on the Word and proclaiming it to the best of their abilities. This commentary is for them.

The problem for the busy pastor is finding the time for the exegetical analysis necessary for expository preaching or for a topical series that is biblical and asks, "What does the Word of God have to say on this issue?" Enter the Zondervan Exegetical Commentary series, with its discussion of literary context, main idea (perfect for the proposition or "big idea" in the sermon), and the structural analysis (perfect for the sermon outline). When I saw how the exegetical analysis was to be done point-by-point through the text, I was especially excited, for the criteria for deciding what to cover was always, "What does the pastor need?" rather than "What do the scholars want to see?" Having been pastor of two churches and interim pastor of two others, that was music to my ears. Also, the final section on "Theology in Application" fits exactly with what overwhelmed pastors need for the biblical theology and application side of their message. Finally, this commentary uses others more than most because as a pastor I had always wanted to know which scholars held the various positions on a problem I was studying. So there are longer lists of "who holds what" in this commentary.

Finally, one goal in this commentary series is to summarize briefly the current state of scholarship on key issues; thus on debated passages, I usually list scholars on the various sides of the point. In doing so, I avoid laborious, complicated details that satisfy the scholar but are too much detail for the busy pastor. Instead, I summarize the sides as simply and practically as possible so that the pastor can decide which of the possibilities to choose on the issue. In other words, every aspect of this project got my juices flowing, and I feel that it is at a perfect level for someone preaching through Matthew and wanting to know what the issues are, how to solve the interpretive problems, and how to develop a series of messages through Matthew's gospel.

There are so many people to thank on a project such as this. First, I want to express my appreciation to Trinity Evangelical Divinity School for the sabbatical I received to devote to this commentary. I also want to thank two research assistants, Justin Fuhrmann and especially Stephen Smith, for their invaluable help with bibliography and the line diagrams. Stephen deserves special thanks for compiling the indices as well. Thanks are also due my administrative assistant, Jessica Langenhahn. Then there are the helpful critiques of the series editor, Clint Arnold; the associate editor, Mark Strauss; and the even more detailed reading of my Zondervan editor, Verlyn Verbrugge. Without their thoughtful readings and suggestions, there would be many more errors than there are now. The entire Zondervan team deserves my gratitude for a job well done. Any mistakes are mine and mine alone.

Most of all, I want to thank the Lord for using this undeserving servant and for giving me the most wonderful calling I could possibly have. To spend my life proclaiming, teaching, and writing on the Word of God is a privilege beyond compare, and I wake up every morning so grateful to the Lord for allowing me to share the only reliable and final truth this world will ever know, his inspired Word. May this commentary play some small part in encouraging pastors and teachers to fall in love with his Word and to experience, as I do, the joy of preaching its unbelievably deep truths.

Abbreviations

1 En.	*1 Enoch*
2 Bar.	*2 Baruch*
2 Clem.	*2 Clement*
3 Bar.	*3 Baruch*
4 Bar.	*4 Baruch*
AB	Anchor Bible
ABD	*Anchor Bible Dictionary*. Edited by David Noel Freedman. 6 vols. New York: Doubleday, 1992.
Adv. Haer.	*Against Heresies* (Irenaeus)
AnBib	Analecta biblica
Ant.	*Antiquities* (Josephus)
ANTC	Abingdon New Testament Commentaries
Apoc. Abr.	*Apocalypse of Abraham*
Apoc. Elijah	*Apocalypse of Elijah*
ASTI	*Annual of the Swedish Theological Institute*
AUSS	Andrews University Seminary Studies
b. Bat.	*Babylonian Talmud: Baba Batra*
b. Ber.	*Babylonian Talmud: Berakot*
b. ᶜErub.	*Babylonian Talmud: ᶜErubin*
b. Ḥag.	*Babylonian Talmud: Ḥagigah*
b. Ketub.	*Babylonian Talmud: Ketubbot*
b. Mak.	*Babylonian Talmud: Makkot*
b. Menaḥ.	*Babylonian Talmud: Menaḥ*
b. Qidd.	*Babylonian Talmud: Qiddušin*
b. Pesaḥ	*Babylonian Talmud: Pesaḥim*
b. Sanh.	*Babylonian Talmud: Sanhedrin*
b. Šabb.	*Babylonian Talmud: Šabbat*
b. Soṭah	*Babylonian Talmud: Soṭah*
b. Taᶜan	*Babylonian Talmud: Taᶜanit*
b. Yoma	*Babylonian Talmud: Yoma (= Kippurim)*
BA	*Biblical Archaeologist*

BAGD	Bauer, W., W. F. Arndt, F. W. Gingrich, and F. W. Danker. *A Greek-English Lexicon of the New Testament and Other Early Christian Literature*, 2nd ed. Chicago, 1979.
BAR	*Biblical Archaeology Review*
BBR	*Bulletin for Biblical Research*
BDF	Blass, F., A. Debrunner, and R. W. Funk. *A Greek Grammar of the New Testament and Other Early Christian Literature*. Chicago, 1961.
BECNT	Baker Exegetical Commentary on the New Testament
Bib	*Biblica*
BibInt	*Biblical Interpretation*
BibOr	Biblica et orientalia
BJRL	*Bulletin of the John Rylands University Library of Manchester*
BK	*Bibel und Kirche*
BNTC	Black's New Testament Commentaries
BR	*Biblical Research*
BRev	*Bible Review*
BSac	*Bibliotheca Sacra*
BT	*Bible Translator*
BTB	*Biblical Theology Bulletin*
BurH	*Buried History*
Byz.	Byzantine
BZ	*Biblische Zeitschrift*
BZNW	Beihefte zur Zeitschrift für die neutestamentliche Wissenschaft
CBQ	*Catholic Biblical Quarterly*
ChrTo	*Christianity Today*
ConBNT	Coniectanea biblica: New Testament Series
CurTM	*Currents in Theology and Missions*
Did.	*Didache*
DJG	*Dictionary of Jesus and the Gospels*. Edited by Joel B. Green, Scot McKnight, and I. Howard Marshall. Downers Grove, IL: IVP, 1992.
DNTB	*Dictionary of New Testament Background*. Edited by Craig A. Evans and Stanley E. Porter. Downers Grove, IL: IVP, 2000.
DOTP	*Dictionary of Old Testament: Pentateuch*. Edited by David W. Baker and T. Desmond Alexander. Downers Grove, IL: IVP, 2003.
DPL	*Dictionary of Paul and His Letters*. Edited by Gerald F. Hawthorne, Ralph P. Martin, and Daniel G. Reid. Downers Grove, IL: IVP, 1993.
DRev	*Downside Review*
DSD	*Dead Sea Discoveries*
Dt. Rab.	*Deuteronomy Rabbah*
EDNT	*Exegetical Dictionary of the New Testament*. Edited by H. Balz, G. Schneider. English translation. Grand Rapids, 1990–1993.

EstBib	*Estudios bíblicos*
ETL	*Ephemerides theologicae lovanienses*
ETR	*Etudes theologiques et religieuses*
EvT	*Evangelische Theologie*
EvQ	*Evangelical Quarterly*
Exod. Rab.	*Exodus Rabbah*
ExpTim	*Expository Times*
FiloNT	*Filología Neotestamentaria*
FoiVie	*Foi et vie*
FS	Festschrift
Gen. Rab.	*Genesis Rabbah*
GTJ	*Grace Theological Journal*
HeyJ	*Heythrop Journal*
Hist. Eccl.	*Historia ecclesiastica* (Eusebius)
HTR	*Harvard Theological Review*
IBS	*Irish Biblical Studies*
ICC	International Critical Commentary
Int	*Interpretation*
IVP	InterVarsity Press
JBL	*Journal of Biblical Literature*
JETS	*Journal of the Evangelical Theological Society*
JJS	*Journal of Jewish Studies*
JosAsen	*Joseph and Asenath*
JQR	*Jewish Quarterly Review*
JSNT	*Journal for the Study of the New Testament*
JSNTSup	Journal for the Study of the New Testament Supplement Series
JSOT	*Journal for the Study of the Old Testament*
JSP	*Journal for the Study of the Pseudepigrapha*
JTS	*Journal of Theological Studies*
Jub.	*Jubilees*
J.W.	*Jewish War* (Josephus)
KJV	King James Version
LB	Living Bible
LTJ	*Lutheran Theological Journal*
LXX	Septuagint
m. ʾAbot	*Mishnah: ʾAbot*
m. Ber.	*Mishnah: Berakot*
m. Demai	*Mishnah: Demai*
m. Giṭ.	*Mishnah: Giṭṭin*
m. Ḥag.	*Mishnah: Ḥagigah*
m. Ker.	*Mishnah: Kerithot*

m. Ketub.	*Mishnah: Ketubbot*
m. Maʿaś.	*Mishnah: Maʿaśerot*
m. Neg.	*Mishnah: Negaʿim*
m. Pesaḥ	*Mishnah: Pesaḥim*
m. Sanh.	*Mishnah: Sanhedrin*
m. Šabb.	*Mishnah: Šabbat*
m. Šeb.	*Mishnah: Šebiʿit*
m. Šeqal.	*Mishnah: Šeqalim*
m. Soṭah	*Mishnah: Soṭah*
m. Yeb.	*Mishnah: Yebamot*
m. Yoma	*Mishnah: Yoma (= Kippurim)*
Midr. Cant.	*Midrash on Canticles*
Midr. Pss.	*Midrash on Psalms*
MSJ	*Master's Seminary Journal*
MT	Masoretic Text
NASB	New American Standard Bible
NCBC	New Century Bible Commentary
NEB	New English Bible
NET	New English Translation
NICNT	New International Commentary on the New Testament
NICOT	New International Commentary on the Old Testament
NIDNTT	*New International Dictionary of New Testament Theology*. Edited by C. Brown. 4 vols. Grand Rapids, 1986.
NIGTC	New International Greek Testament Commentary
NIV	New International Version
NIVAC	NIV Application Commentary
NJB	New Jerusalem Bible
NLT	New Living Translation
NovT	*Novum Testamentum*
NovTSup	Novum Testamentum Supplements
NRSV	New Revised Standard Version
NRTh	*La nouvelle revue théologique*
n.s.	new series
NSBT	New Studies in Biblical Theology
NTL	New Testament Library
NTS	*New Testament Studies*
Num. Rab.	*Numbers Rabbah*
PNTC	Pillar New Testament Commentary
Prot. Jas.	*Protoevangelium of James*
Pss. Sol.	*Psalms of Solomon*
Qoh. Rab.	*Qohelet Rabbah*

RB	*Revue biblique*
RelS	*Religious Studies*
RelStTh	*Religious Studies and Theology*
ResQ	*Restoration Quarterly*
RevExp	*Review and Expositor*
RevQ	*Revue de Qumran*
RHPR	*Revue d'histoire et de philosophie religieuses*
RRelRes	*Review of Religious Research*
RSR	*Recherches de science religieuse*
RSV	Revised Standard Version
RR	*Review of Religion*
SBL	Society of Biblical Literature
SBLDS	Society of Biblical Literature Dissertation Series
SBLMS	Society of Biblical Literature Monograph Series
SBLSymS	Society of Biblical Literature Symposium Studies
SBLSP	*Society of Biblical Literature Seminar Papers*
Scr	*Scripture*
SE	*Studia evangelica*
Sib. Or.	*Sibylline Oracles*
SJT	*Scottish Journal of Theology*
SNT	Studien zum Neuen Testament
SNTSMS	Society for New Testament Studies Monograph Series
SNTSSup	Society for New Testament Studies Supplement Series
SNTSU	*Studien zum Neuen Testament und seiner Umwelt*
SP	Sacra pagina
ST	*Studia theologica*
Str-B	Strack, H. L., and P. Billerbeck, *Kommentar zum Neuen Testament aus Talmud und Midrasch.* 6 vols. Munich, 1922 – 1961.
t. Ber.	*Tosefta Berakot*
t. Soṭah	*Tosefta Soṭah*
T. Abr.	*Testament of Abraham*
T. Benj.	*Testament of Benjamin*
T. Isaac	*Testament of Isaac*
T. Iss.	*Testament of Issachar*
T. Jac.	*Testament of Jacob*
T. Job	*Testament of Job*
T. Jos.	*Testament of Joseph*
T. Jud.	*Testament of Judah*
T. Levi	*Testament of Levi*
T. Mos.	*Testament of Moses*

T. Sol.	*Testament of Solomon*
TBei	*Theologische Beiträge*
TBT	*The Bible Today*
TDNT	*Theological Dictionary of the New Testament*. Edited by Gerhard Kittel and Gerhard Friedrich. Translated by Geoffrey W. Bromiley. 10 vols. Grand Rapids: Eerdmans, 1964–1976.
Tg. Isa.	*Targum of Isaiah*
Tg. Neof.	*Targum Neofiti*
Tg. Zech.	*Targum of Zechariah*
TGl	*Theologie und Glaube*
Them	*Themelios*
ThSt	Theologische Studiën
ThTo	*Theology Today*
TJ	*Trinity Journal*
TNIV	Today's New International Version
TNTC	Tyndale New Testament Commentary
TR	Textus Receptus
TS	*Theological Studies*
TTZ	*Trierer theologische Zeitschrift*
TynBul	*Tyndale Bulletin*
TZ	*Theologische Zeitschrift*
USQR	*Union Seminary Quarterly Review*
VC	*Vigiliae christianae*
WBC	Word Biblical Commentary
Wallace	Daniel B. Wallace, *Greek Grammar beyond the Basics*, Grand Rapids: Zondervan, 1996.
WTJ	*Westminster Theological Journal*
WUNT	Wissenschaftliche Untersuchungen zum Neuen Testament und die Kunde der älteren Kirche
WW	*Word and World*
y. Ber.	*Jerusalem Talmud: Berakot*
y. Qidd.	*Jerusalem Talmud: Qiddušin*
ZDPV	*Zeitschrift des deutschen Palästina-Vereins*
ZNW	*Zeitschrift für die neutestamentliche Wissenschaft*

Introduction

Matthew has always been the gospel most widely read and the one first consulted for details about the life of Christ. It has been considered "the church's gospel" from the time of Augustine. Until the nineteenth century it was thought to be the first gospel written, the one that provided the material behind Mark and Luke (see further below). There are several reasons for this popularity. Matthew (along with Luke) contains the most stories and the most famous discourses, especially the Sermon on the Mount (chs. 5 – 7) but also the longer versions of the Mission Discourse (ch. 10), the Parable Discourse (ch. 13), and the Olivet Discourse (chs. 24 – 25). So Matthew centers on Jesus' teaching and his ethical mandate, and there are key messages for the life of the church. People have always gravitated to the Jesus who says, "God blesses the poor in spirit" (5:3), and "I will give you the keys of the kingdom of heaven" (16:19).

How to Study and Preach the Gospel of Matthew

I pastored my first church in Ohio between my college and seminary years. I was a young twenty-two-year-old preacher and enjoyed the pulpit ministry more than I can say. However, while I had good success with the OT, especially with the poets and prophecy, and dearly loved to preach the NT epistles, I had virtually no success with the gospels. Every time I tried, my preaching seemed to fall flat. In seminary I gravitated to the narrative portions of the OT and especially to the gospels, wanting to fill my gaps. There I discovered my basic mistake. I was preaching the gospels similar to how my high school history teacher taught me history — names, dates, places, brute facts. What I needed to realize was my weakness in understanding history and especially the gospels — they are not just brute history; they are history seen through theological eyes.

The word "gospel" is not just "good news"; the verb used (*euaggelizomai*) means to "preach the good news." They are "history with a message," carefully crafted stories to bring out the heavenly truths embedded into the earthly events. Now the gospels are my favorite passages to preach and teach! In the gospels (and the narrative portions of the OT) theology comes alive and is dramatized in story form. Let me say here explicitly that the details I chose to include in this commentary, both exegetical and theological, were chosen on the basis of one major question: What would I want to know as a pastor preparing a sermon on this passage? But how do we do that? What is the process for preaching a sermon series through Matthew? Here I will sum up the principles of general and special hermeneutics.[1]

First, we must utilize the basic hermeneutical principles of grammatical-historical exegesis to understand what Matthew was trying to say. General or basic hermeneutics for every type of biblical text have been attempted in the commentary proper in order to ascertain the essential message Matthew was trying to give when he produced his form of the gospel vis-à-vis the other sacred evangelists. This process consists of studying the context (the developing themes Matthew was presenting as he organized his story of Jesus), grammar (the way he worded his sentences and organized his thoughts), semantics (the words he chose to produce the meaning he intended to communicate), syntax (the whole of his thought development in uttering his message to his readers), background (the customs and cultures that he was assuming and within which he presented his story), and theology (the themes he was communicating by the way he organized his material).

Second, special hermeneutics recognizes the elements of narrative that go into understanding how Matthew's stories function.[2] Literary theorists realize that stories contain point of view (the perspective taken by the author, the "shape" given to the story, and the intended effect on the readers), narrative or story time (not chronological because it relates to the order of events in the developing work as a whole rather than the historical progression of them in the life of Christ),[3] plot development (the sequence of events in terms of conflict and climax), characterization and dialogue (the way the characters in a story relate to each other and to the events of the story), and the implied reader (the original audience the author had in mind when writing the story). The goal of analyzing biblical narrative is to see how the stories function at each of these levels and then to put them together in terms of their message and effect on the reader.

Study the Plot at the Macro Level

Each gospel has its own unique metanarrative and plot development. One of the difficult tasks in any serious study is to determine the major and minor points of the plot, ascertain the structural development, and decide on the plot of the major

1. See my *The Hermeneutical Spiral: A Comprehensive Introduction to Biblical Interpretation* (2nd ed.; Downers Grove, IL: IVP, 2006), passim, for this approach.

2. The following will be drawn from my "Literary Theory and Biblical Interpretation," in *Words and the Word: Exploration in Biblical Interpretation and Literary Theory,* ed David G. Firth and Jamie A. Grant (Nottingham, Eng: IVP, 2008), 17–50.

3. A comparison of the four Gospels shows that they all have a different order of events, demonstrating that their purpose was to show the impact and meaning of Jesus' life rather than a day-by-day tracing of events. This is not problematic for historical veracity because ancient historians did not take a detailed chronological approach in telling history. This will be discussed further later.

sections. The difficulty is shown by the fact that if you consult ten commentaries, you will on the average discover six to seven different structures among them. So in the end you must do the work yourself and see which outline fits best.

The most helpful tool for doing this is text-linguistics, which is part of discourse analysis and studies the way the author has stylistically developed his narrative. By looking at the text in terms of its macro level (changes of genre and boundaries in the text as a whole) and its micro level (the structure and communication within each discourse unit within the larger structure), one can see how the author has organized and presented his or her developing argument.[4] This is accomplished by considering introductory particles, changes of verbal aspect or mood, and shifts of focus, by which we try to demarcate the author's developing emphases. Then we look at the major section as a whole and map these changes into a literary structure, tracing the plot of the whole.

Matthew has structured his gospel very differently from the others and organized it around the five discourse units (chs. 5 – 7; 10; 13; 18; 23 – 35), interspersing carefully planned narrative units between each of the discourses. For instance, chs. 8 – 9 form the first extended narrative in Matthew and take place between the Sermon on the Mount (chs. 5 – 7) and Missionary Discourse (ch. 10). An analysis of this section finds three blocks of three miracles each (8:1 – 17; 8:23 – 9:8; 9:18 – 34), broken by discipleship sections (8:18 – 22; 9:9 – 13, 14 – 17). The first set concerns authority over illness, the second set authority over nature, demons, and paralysis, and the third set authority over disabilities and death.[5] The primary thrust is Jesus' all-embracing power and authority, with a second theme being the place of faith in the process, as seen in the leper, the centurion, the woman with the hemorrhage, and the two blind men. With this analysis, each pericope or episode/section is seen in its place as contributing to the overall effect of the Matthean narrative.

Study the Plot at the Micro Level

Here we do the same type of structural analysis, but of the individual story. The same text-linguistic principles are used but in the smaller passage. We are looking for the primary sections where the focus changes to a new unit and then determine the plot of the individual story. An excellent example here would be the parable of the wedding banquet in 22:1 – 14, the third of a triad of parables (21:28 – 22:14) detailing God's gracious invitation to Israel, their refusal to respond, and the judgment that resulted. There are three parts, each with its own individual emphasis — the first (the original invitation, its rejection, and the punishment meted out by the king, vv.

4. See George Guthrie, "Discourse Analysis," *Interpreting the New Testament: Essays on Methods and Issues*, ed. D. A. Black and D. S. Dockery (Nashville: Broadman & Holman, 2001), 260.

5. Craig Keener, *A Commentary on the Gospel of Matthew* (Grand Rapids: Eerdmans, 1999), 258.

1–7) centers on Israel's rejection of Jesus; the second (the invitation and its acceptance by "the bad and good," vv. 8–10) turns to the Gentiles; and the third (the guest who tries to enter the banquet dressed inappropriately along with his punishment by the king, vv. 11–13) turns to the church. So this becomes a salvation-historical parable tracing the movement of God's salvation and the resultant responsibility to respond from Israel to the church.

Study the Redactional (Editorial) Changes

Redaction criticism, which developed in the 1960s and 1970s, centers on the way the gospels used their sources. By noting the changes between Matthew, Mark, and Luke, we can see more clearly how they organized their individual works and the theological intentions they had in doing so. Of course, the theology flows out of the whole of the literary passage, but the changes guide us in seeing how they structured their material. Robert Stein suggests looking at the seams between episodes, insertions, arrangement, introductions, vocabulary, christological titles, selection or omission of material, and conclusions.[6] The student studies what the author selected for his rendition of the story, how he organized it, what context he placed it in, and what the theological implications are.

As the example of this, let us consider the walking on the water miracle in Mark 6:45–52 and Matt 14:22–33. Both follow the feeding of the five thousand, which demonstrates that "God will provide" for his people; yet when the disciples are sent across the lake and the storm arises, they forget all about that and fear for their lives (see on 6:30–44). In Mark 6:48 (only in Mark) we are told that Jesus "was about to pass by them," which demonstrates that Christ is Lord of the water; that is, as Yahweh passed by at Mount Sinai (Exod 33:18ff.) and Mount Horeb (1 Kgs 19:11ff.), so Jesus does likewise.[7] His purpose is to ensure them that God is with them and will care for them. Yet the disciples miss the signal entirely, look at Jesus walking on the water, and think he is a ghost. They are probably thinking, "What he is, is what we are going to be in another minute—ghosts!!" Mark stops the story right there and deliberately (most likely) draws his conclusion—the disciples fail because "they had not understood about the loaves; their hearts were hardened" (Mark 6:52).

Matthew follows Mark to that point and denotes their failure but goes on. He like many newscasters adds "the rest of the story." After the episode of Peter walking on the water and failing, the disciples then conclude, "Truly you are the Son of God!" (Matt 14:33). There could not be a greater polarity than the conclusions of Mark and Matthew, from hardened hearts to a christological affirmation greater than the disciples ever do in Mark (they never get beyond Messiah)! Yet the conclusions do

6. Robert Stein, "Interpreting the Synoptic Gospels," in *Interpreting the New Testament: Essays on Methods and Issues* (ed. D. A. Black and D. S. Dockery; Nashville: Broadman & Holman, 2001), 349–51.

7. Joel Marcus, *Mark 1–8* (AB; New York: Doubleday, 2000), 426.

not contradict one another, for Matthew recognizes the failure but passes on to the later victory. The difference is in the theological purposes of each author. Mark for the rest of his gospel centers on the disciples' repeated failures (true discipleship is seen in "the little people"—see on discipleship below) while Matthew recognizes failure but wants to show that the presence of Jesus makes the difference and allows the disciples to find victory. This is seen also after the feeding of the four thousand in both gospels; Mark ends with "Do you still not understand?" (Mark 8:21), while Matthew ends with "Then they understood...." (Matt 16:12). This is in keeping with the discipleship themes in their respective gospels, as Mark centers on the disciples' failure while Matthew centers on their growing understanding.[8]

Study the Characters and Dialogue

As shown above, characterization is essential to all biblical narrative. As we see the interaction between the characters and between the characters and God/Jesus, the themes come to the fore. In all four gospels, the basic story centers on the impact between Jesus and four groups—the disciples, the crowds, the leaders, and the demons—in a descending order of growing opposition to Jesus. Let me give two examples of this. The first is the cosmic encounter with the two demon-possessed men in Gedara in Matt 8:28–34. The dialogue with Jesus and the demon is critical. While some think the demon's "What is it to us and to you, Son of God?" (lit. trans.) is just supernatural knowledge of Jesus on the part of the demon, it is more likely that this is spiritual warfare. The first part is an idiom meaning "We have nothing in common" and "leave us alone" (cf. Judg 11:12; 2 Sam 16:10; Mark 1:24) and is an attempt to gain control over Jesus. Marcus says that in ancient magical texts a magician says "I know you" to a god in order to gain control over it.[9] Jesus' "Be silent" then forces the submission of the demonic realm to himself. The dialogue shows that spiritual warfare is taking place, and the exorcism is a "tying up" of Satan (cf. Mark 3:27).

Study the Implied Reader and Perform Reader Identification

The significance of narrative texts for us cannot be understood until we have studied how the author intended to draw his original readers into the story (the illocutionary aspect) and what he wanted them to do with it (the perlocutionary aspect).[10] We then consciously align ourselves with that original message and

8. For Matthew's discipleship theme, see Jeannine K. Brown, *The Disciples in Narrative Perspective: The Portrayal and Function of the Matthean Disciples* (Academia Biblica 9; Boston: Brill, 2002).

9. Ibid, 193.

10. This language stems from "speech act theory." This approach involves three levels of communication—the locutionary (the propositional meaning in the communication), the illocutionary (the actions performed in it), and the perlocutionary (the effects it intends to have on the reader). See Osborne, *Hermeneutical Spiral*, 119–20, 502–3.

ascertain what the parallel situation is with that today; in other words, "if the author were here in my congregation, what issues would he address in this text?" (reader identification).

To illustrate this, let us consider the temptation narrative (Matt 4:1 – 11/Luke 4:1 – 13). This used to be a sermon I had my students write in my course on the gospels until I realized that hardly any of them got it right. Now I use it as my example in class. They made two mistakes: first, they had always heard this taught as a discipleship passage, i.e., if we memorize Scripture, we can defeat the devil any time. Second, they neglected to study seriously the passages Jesus quoted against the devil.

Let us take these one at a time. (1) If we look at this passage in context, it is the final preparatory event in Jesus' ministry (after his baptism), and the major theme is Jesus as Son of God. Luke 4 demonstrates this best; Jesus is proclaimed God's "Son, whom I love" at his baptism (3:22), and then Luke inserts the genealogy here, running in opposite order to the genealogy in Matthew and going all the way to Adam, who is called finally "the son of God" (3:38). These passages prepare for the temptations, with the first being, "If [a condition of fact, meaning virtually 'since'] you are the Son of God" (4:3). Satan knows Jesus is Son of God and tempts him to selfishly prove it to the world.

(2) All three of Jesus' quotes stem from Deut 6 – 8, and each time the quote occurs at that place in Deuteronomy where Israel failed in the very test Jesus is enduring. In other words, Jesus is saying to Satan, "I know what you are doing; it worked with Israel, but it will not work with me." So the thrust of the temptation is clear; it is Christology, not discipleship. Jesus begins his ministry by taking on Satan in open combat and defeating him, thereby proving himself to be Son of God. The reader is called to worship, to recognize Jesus as Son of God. There may be a secondary application as the reader says, "I will not fail as Israel did," but the primary thrust is that victory comes through recognizing Jesus to be Son of God.

The purpose of this commentary is to aid in the task of proclaiming the truths of Matthew to the church and world of our day. The basic process is quite simple.[11]

1. Do a structural analysis, noting its place in the developing story of Matthew and then the "actantial" units of the story itself, i.e., the story line of the pericope and the development of its plot within its setting.
2. Consider the style by which Matthew tells the story (inclusion, repetition, symbolic language, irony, antitheses, etc.) to ascertain the way he has colored the narrative.
3. Do a redactional analysis by comparing it with the same story in other

11. See ibid., 216 – 21.

gospels in order to see additions and omissions that will give clues to Matthew's major emphases.

4. Exegete the details both syntactically (how the various grammatical and semantic components add meaning) and historically (the customs and cultural background to the story) to unlock the deep meaning of the passage.
5. Perform a theological analysis, discovering which aspects of Matthean theology are highlighted in the passage. There are two aspects — the propositional (= biblical theology) and the dramatic or commissive (= the praxis demanded by the passage). The commentary discusses these aspects in the final section on each passage ("Theology in Application").
6. Develop the contextualization of the passage for today. The sermon must build a bridge from the message of Matthew for his day (what it meant) to its significance for our day (what it means). We can perform a deep and accurate study of its original meaning, but if it is not applied carefully, our detailed analysis is wasted. God's Word is meant to change lives, not just lead to head knowledge, but that application must be tied closely to the meaning of the text. We should ask, "If Matthew was standing in my pulpit, what would he ask my congregation to do as a result of this passage?"

The Historical Trustworthiness of Matthew's Gospel

There has been a huge debate over the last two centuries over the veracity of the gospel stories about Jesus. In my recent "History and Theology in the Synoptic Gospels,"[12] I delineate three stages in the debate.

1. *History or Theology (1900 – 1970).* This is the period of radical skepticism, as Bultmann and others assumed a complete break between the history behind the gospels and the theological portrait within them. For them the historic Christ was a product of the early church and the Jesus of history a mere presupposition of NT theology.[13] R. H. Lightfoot said the gospels "yield little more than a whisper of his voice; we trace in them but the outskirts of his ways."[14] The "quest" of the recent Jesus Seminar is a throwback to the radical doubt period.
2. *History and Theology (1970 – 85).* This is a period of reappraisal as a set of works on each gospel argued for the interdependence of history and theology, with I. H. Marshall asserting that Luke followed historical sources and combined history and theology in a faithful portrait of the historical Jesus;[15]

12. Grant R. Osborne, "History and Theology in the Synoptic Gospels," *TJ* 24 n.s. (2003): 5 – 22.

13. R. Bultmann, *Theology of the New Testament* (trans. K. Grobel; New York: Scribner's, 1951), 1:3.

14. R. H. Lightfoot, *History and Interpretation in the Gospels* (New York: Hodder & Stoughton, 1934), 225.

15. I. H. Marshall, *Luke: Historian and Theologian* (Grand Rapids: Zondervan, 1970).

he was followed by Ralph Martin on Mark, Stephen Smalley on John, and R. T. France on Matthew.[16] Then the six-volume Gospel Perspective series (1980 – 1986) was summed up in Craig Blomberg's *Historical Reliability of the Gospels* (1987),[17] showing in great depth the basic validity of the gospels' historical portraits. Ben Meyer's *Aims of Jesus* argued that both the events and their significance are valid goals of the historian in Jesus study.[18]

3. *Theologically Motivated History (1985 to the present).* The "third quest" for the historical Jesus now recognizes that theology is a partner and a path to history, an essential aspect of all historical enquiry into the life of Jesus. E. P. Sanders argued that the historical Jesus can be found by situating Jesus within the Judaism of his day and by explaining how his movement eventually broke with Judaism.[19] J. P. Meier is even more open and seeks objectivity with the evidence, impossible in a final sense but somewhat possible by bracketing one's worldview and presuppositions.[20] Then N. T. Wright states that the gospels were indeed ancient biographies and for the most part were reliable documents. He seeks what is "real" in the narrative and subjects it to "critical examination" to determine what is a valid reflection of the historical record, both factual event and theological reflection.[21] This is a huge step forward in historical Jesus studies.

In terms of genre, we can differentiate historical writing from fictive writing[22] by considering the "authorial stance," i.e., the fictive stance of the novelist and the assertive stance of the historian, as "the historian claims — asserts — that the projected world (the story) of the text together with the authorial point of view counts as a story and an interpretation of events as they actually occurred."[23] Anthony Thiselton speaks of "extratextual factors," especially the illocutionary stance of the author that either creates an imaginary world or ties the reader to the real world implied in the text.[24] Walhout provides three criteria for doing so: (1) The world

16. Ralph Martin, *Mark: Evangelist and Theologian* (Exeter: Paternoster, 1972); Stephen Smalley, *John: Evangelist and Interpreter* (London: Paternoster, 1978); R. T. France, *Matthew — Evangelist and Teacher* (London: Paternoster, 1989).

17. Craig Blomberg, *The Historical Reliability of the Gospels* (Downers Grove, IL: IVP, 1987).

18. Ben F. Meyer, *The Aims of Jesus* (London: SCM, 1979). See also A. E. Harvey, *Jesus and the Constraints of History: The Bampton Lectures 1980* (London: Duckworth, 1982).

19. E. P. Sanders, *Jesus and Judaism* (Philadelphia: Fortress, 1985), 18.

20. J. P. Meier, *A Marginal Jew: Rethinking the Historical Jesus, Vol. 1: The Roots of the Problem and the Person* (New York: Doubleday, 1991), 4 – 6.

21. N. T. Wright, *The New Testament and the People of God* (Minneapolis: Fortress, 1992), 32 – 37.

22. See Osborne, "Literary Theory and Biblical Interpretation," in *Words and the Word: Exploration in Biblical Interpretation and Literary Theory,* ed David G. Firth and Jamie A. Grant (Nottingham, Eng: IVP, 2008), 17 – 50.

23. Clarence Walhout, "Texts and Actions," in *The Responsibility of Hermeneutics* (ed. R. Lundin, A. C. Thiselton, C. Walhout; Grand Rapids: Eerdmans, 1985), 69. John Searle says, "roughly speaking, whether or not a work is literature is for the readers to decide, whether or not it is fiction is for the author to decide" (*Expression and Meaning: Studies in the Theory of Speech Acts* [Cambridge: Cambridge Univ. Press, 1979], 59).

24. Anthony Thiselton, *New Horizons in Hermeneutics* (Grand Rapids: Zondervan, 1992), 372 – 73, building on Searle.

behind the text is factually accurate, presenting events it claims actually occurred; (2) the author's "techniques of presentation" (e.g., phrasing, genealogies, etc.) fit the state of affairs at that time; (3) there is an atmosphere of history (factually conceived) behind the details.[25]

In short, historical narrative will "tell it like it was" and interpret events written as they happened, while fiction will build an imaginary world, often with background details that fit the period but with a quite different stance. In fact, one can disagree with the interpretive stance of the historian and yet recognize the historical facts behind the narration. While there is theological assertion in the biblical narratives, that does not obviate their basic historical stance.

Biblical narratives contain both narrative and historical elements. As narrative, they exemplify real/implied author and reader, point of view, story time, plot, characterization, and dialogue. As history, they attempt to trace what actually happened. A good definition will help:

> "Narrative history" involves an attempt to express through language ... the meaning ... that is, a particular understanding/explanation ... of the relationship of a selected sequence of actual events from the past ... and to convince others through various means, including the theological force and aesthetic appeal of the rendering ... that the sequence under review has meaning and that this meaning has been rightly perceived.[26]

Our task, then, is to compare the historical story to external data on the event in history and to evaluate the event portrayed in terms of its contribution to historical knowledge. By ascertaining the implicit commentary and point of view, one can see how the author is not only telling what happened but also developing the significance and moral content of the story. "It is clear that in the historical narratives of the Scriptures, the authors believed they were retelling the historical past of Israel and the early church so as to solidify the self-conscious identity of the people in their present time. In other words, there was a historical purpose throughout."[27]

The reader attempts to enter the world of the story and reconstruct the historical nucleus as well as to evaluate the original theological interpretation. The story has a performative function and draws the reader into its narrative world, thereby communicating the intended meaning, i.e., either an imaginary fictive world or a reconstructed historical world. The historical narrative in Scripture (and the early church) claims to proclaim events that actually happened (Luke 1:1 – 4; John 19:35; 21:24; 1 Cor 15:6; 2 Pe 1:16 – 18), and these claims should be taken seriously. There is no theoretical reason why literary and historical interests cannot coincide in the gospels and

25. Walhout, "Texts," 72 – 73.

26. I. Provan, V. P. Long, and T. Longman III, *A Biblical History of Israel* (Louisville: Westminster John Knox, 2003), 84.

27. Grant R. Osborne, "Historical Narrative and Truth in the Bible," *JETS* 48 (2005): 684.

why the stories cannot be trustworthy representations of what really happened. One of the purposes of this commentary is to show how this is so in Matthew.[28]

The Genre of Matthew

Primarily, of course, Matthew is a "gospel" (lit., "good news") about Jesus the Messiah, but as a genre a gospel refers to a theological biography of the life of Christ. There has been much debate regarding the exact genre of Matthew and the other gospels. Gundry has argued that Matthew is creative midrash (referring to Jewish theological interpretations of OT texts), with ancient readers able to distinguish between the historical parts and the nonhistorical midrash.[29] However, while there is midrashic use of OT texts in Matthew, his gospel is more of a hermeneutical appropriation of the OT than a genre seen in his stories as a whole (a use not seen until the fourth century AD).[30] The current consensus is that the closest parallel is Greco-Roman biography,[31] but that should probably be widened to include Jewish as well as Hellenistic biographies. Aune argues, in fact, that no parallel is sufficient and that the evangelists reworked the forms of their day to produce a new type of biography, the gospel.[32]

Keener does a fine job of discussing the similarities and differences.[33] Like the evangelists, ancient biographers did not try to cover the whole life of the person and often used a topical rather than chronological order. They were free to expand or shorten stories (Matthew normally abbreviates Mark) but still for the most part sought to present accurate history (especially historians like Tacitus and Suetonius). Jewish biographies were often novel-type expansions of OT stories (*1 Enoch*, *Assumption of Moses*, *Testament of the Twelve Patriarchs*), and the closest Jewish parallels for the historiography of Matthew are indeed the OT stories (books like Esther, Job, Ruth, Jonah, Daniel; cf. also Judith, Tobit). Parallel to the differ-

28. D. A. Carson, "Matthew," *Expositor's Bible Commentary* (ed. Frank E. Gaebelein; Grand Rapids: Zondervan, 1984), 8, in his section on "History and Theology," argues that Matthew (1) wants to tell us about Jesus rather than the problems in his own community; (2) does indeed represent kerygma but centered on the church's desire to know about the historical Jesus; (3) draws his themes from Jesus and not just from the later church; (4) and does indeed provide his own theology but still tells about Jesus of Nazareth. Therefore (5) it is erroneous to assume that the themes stem from the post-80 church since all could fit a much earlier period, including the time of Jesus.

29. Robert H. Gundry, *Matthew: A Commentary on His Literary and Theological Art* (Grand Rapids: Eerdmans, 1982), 26–28; see also M. D. Goulder, *Midrash and Lection in Matthew* (London: SPCK, 1974).

30. See Carson, "Matthew," 39–41; Douglas J. Moo, "Matthew and Midrash: An Evaluation of Robert H. Gundry's Approach," *JETS* 26 (1983): 31–39.

31. P. L. Shuler, *A Genre for the Gospels: The Biographical Character of Matthew* (Philadelphia: Fortress, 1982), calls it an "encomium" or "laudatory biography." Most (e.g., Hagner, Blomberg) prefer to be more general on this. See also Richard A. Burridge, *What Are the Gospels? A Comparison with Graeco-Roman Biography* (SNTSMS 70; Cambridge: Cambridge Univ. Press, 1992).

32. David E. Aune, *The New Testament in Its Literary Environment* (Philadelphia: Westminster, 1987), 17–76. See also Robert A. Guelich, "The Gospel Genre," in *The Gospel and the Gospels* (ed. P. Stuhlmacher; Grand Rapids: Eerdmans, 1991), 173–208.

33. Keener, *Matthew*, 16–24.

ences in the four gospels would be the differences in Samuel-Kings/Chronicles. The gospels combined this with Hellenistic patterns (it was common for Jewish works in Greek to adopt Greek style: cf. Philo). Keener concludes (italics his):

> Matthew did not write his Gospel without forethought; he was a historian-biographer and interpreter and not just a storyteller.... Like other writers, Matthew would follow one main source (in this case Mark) and weave his other sources around it.... If Matthew's basic genre suggests historical *intention*, his relatively conservative use of sources ... indicates that Matthew's other purposes did not obscure an essential historical intention.[34]

The Purpose and Audience of Matthew's Gospel

It has been common for scholars to argue for one purpose for Matthew's gospel. This is a mistake; few books have a single purpose. Matthew is a multifaceted work, and there are several purposes. (1) Perhaps the major one has already been discussed — to tell the story of Jesus. Moreover, when the gospel is seen as a whole, Matthew is telling the impact of Jesus on four groups — the leaders, the crowds, the disciples, and the demons. In doing so he asks the reader to identify herself with each and ask, "Which group am I?" Am I opposed to Jesus like the leaders, excited on the surface but refusing to commit like the crowds, committed and growing in spite of repeated failures like the disciples, or being influenced in the cosmic war by the demonic forces? Jesus confronts each group at their own level and displays the authority and wisdom of the Son of God.

(2) The second purpose is apologetic and evangelistic. One major consensus is that Matthew writes a Jewish gospel. It has been a mainstay of gospel studies for the last fifty years to assume they were written to particular communities led by the author, and so the primary historical dimension is not the historical Jesus but uncovering the life of that community (this is called the *Sitz im Leben* approach or "the situation in the life" of the [later] church). This is now widely regarded as erroneous, for the gospels were written for the whole church as well as for unbelievers.[35] Matthew especially had the Jewish Christian church and the Jewish people in mind. With the preponderance of OT fulfillment quotations ("in order to fulfill what was spoken by the Lord through the prophet"), the rabbinic style of the reasoning in several passages (e.g., 15:1 – 20; 19:1 – 9), the centrality of Jesus' fulfilling the law in the Sermon on the Mount (5:17 – 19), and the way Jesus relates to the Jewish people throughout, it seems clear that Jewish issues are uppermost.

Moreover, there is a strong apologetic air to the whole. Jesus is in constant debate with the leaders, and it is clear that he, not they, is the final interpreter of

34. Ibid, 23 – 24.

35. See Bauckham, "For Whom Were the Gospels Written?" in *The Gospel for All Christians* (ed. Richard Bauckham; Grand Rapids: Eerdmans, 1998), 9 – 48.

Torah, as seen in 7:28 – 29: "The crowds were amazed at his teaching, for he was teaching as one who had great authority, not like their teachers of law." Throughout the first gospel it is "your synagogues" (23:34) or "their synagogues" (4:23; 9:35; 10:17; 12:9; 13:54) and "the Jews until this very day" (28:15), reflecting ongoing debates between Jews and Christians right up to Matthew's time. The conflict is especially keen between Jesus and the Pharisees/scribes. This is evident in 21:23 – 22:46, a series of controversies between Jesus and the leaders in the temple court. In them Jesus' messianic teaching authority is seen in contrast to the growing rejection of the leaders. In each debate Jesus demonstrates his superiority to the religious experts as he takes them on in rabbinic fashion and decimates them with his handling of Torah.

At the same time it is clear that Matthew wants to evangelize the Jewish people, not just prove them wrong. Jesus is presented as Messiah and Son of God, the one whose mission is to present himself as the atoning sacrifice and "ransom" for the people (20:28; 26:28). Jesus restricts his and the disciples' mission to "the lost sheep of the house of Israel" (10:5 – 6; 15:24; more on this below). Clearly his primary desire is to see the Jewish people repent and become his followers. At the same time, Matthew shows that the Jewish people for the most part rejected his call and followed the leaders in their opposition to Jesus. This is seen especially in chs. 11 – 12 and throughout Passion Week.

There are two results of this theme of Jewish rejection. First, there is an emphasis on the judgment of the Jewish people. In 11:22, 24 Jesus says, "God will be more tolerant toward Tyre and Sidon [and Sodom] on the day of judgment than to you" (cf. 10:15) because they repented. In 12:32 he warns them about committing the unpardonable sin; in 12:35 – 37 he warns that they will be condemned at the final judgment for their evil; and in 12:39, 41 – 42 he calls them a "evil and adulterous generation" who will be condemned by Nineveh and the Queen of the South for their refusal to repent. The rejection theme comes to a head in the parables of the wicked tenants (21:41, "He will destroy those evil people in an evil way") and the wedding banquet (22:13, "throw him out into the outermost darkness") and in the woes against the leaders (23:33, "Snakes! Offspring of vipers! How will you escape from the judgment of Gehenna?").

Second, the kingdom promises are taken from the Jewish people and given to the righteous remnant (the few who believe) and to the Gentiles. The first glimpse of this theme is remarkably at Jesus' first miracle, the healing of the centurion's servant, when Jesus lauded the centurion's faith and then said, "Many from the east and the west will come and will sit down at the feast ... but the children of the kingdom will be thrown into outermost darkness" (8:11 – 12). Then in 21:43 he says that "the kingdom of God will be taken away from you and given to a people who will produce its fruit"; and in 22:9 – 10 the wedding invitation is extended to "everyone they found, the bad and the good." This theme of the Gentile mission will be explored further later.

(3) Matthew wants to explore the true meaning of the reality of the kingdom that has been inaugurated by Jesus. All three Synoptic Gospels present the kingdom as coming in the incarnation, life, death, and resurrection of Jesus; but Matthew especially centers on the ethical implications of this. The church is the kingdom community, and the Sermon on the Mount is the final Torah of the kingdom reality. For Matthew "righteousness" is a life lived in accordance with these kingdom demands (a life lived by the will of God), and every citizen of the kingdom will be judged according to the way they have lived their lives (16:27, "the Son of Man ... will reward each one on the basis of their deed"). The parables of 24:45 – 25:46 develop this theme, centering on the punishment of those who had not lived according to God's commands and, therefore, were not prepared for the Master's return.

(4) There is a catechetical aspect to this gospel. Although Stendahl went too far in positing the genesis of this work in a "school of Matthew,"[36] it is probably true that the centrality of the five discourses does likely relate to the catechetical needs of the church. Matthew centers on the teaching discourses of Jesus and their ethical implications, and this redactional choice likely arises in part from catechetical interests.

Authorship and Date

Like all four gospels, the first gospel never names its author, probably to give all the glory to Jesus. Yet the unanimous witness of the church fathers (e.g., Papias, Irenaeus, Clement of Alexandria, Eusebius, Origen) is that the apostle Matthew was the author. In this gospel the name is found in 9:9; 10:3, where he is a tax collector whom Jesus calls to follow him; then he becomes one of the Twelve. Interestingly, in Mark 2:14 he is called Levi (though he is called "Matthew" in Mark 3:18). Two names were common in the ancient world (e.g., Simon Peter, Thomas called Didymus), sometimes from birth and other times a Christian addition. The only actual incident recorded of Matthew is the banquet he gave in Mark 2/Matt 9/Luke 5.

Papias (bishop of Hierapolis in the province of Asia) said early in the second century:[37] "Matthew compiled the oracles [*logia*] in the Hebrew dialect, and everyone translated them as he was able" (Eusebius, *Eccl. Hist.* 3.39.16). Needless to say, there is considerable debate over the meaning and significance of this statement. Some think that *logia* refers to Q (written originally in the Aramaic), others that it signifies the OT quotations (perhaps a *testimonia* source) in Matthew. It is also thought by some that "Hebrew dialect" refers to Semitic style in Matthew rather

36. Krister Stendahl, *The School of St. Matthew and Its Use of the Old Testament* (Philadelphia: Fortress, 1968).

37. See Robert W. Yarborough, "The Date of Papias: A Reassessment," *JETS* 26 (1983): 181 – 91.

than an original Aramaic version of the gospel. Another option is that Papias did mean Matthew originally wrote an Aramaic Ur-Gospel but was wrong. It is difficult to know what Papias actually meant, but any deep study of Matthew makes it difficult to surmise how it could have been translated from a Hebrew/Aramaic original. Whether Papias was referring to a sayings collection or a *testimonia* source cannot be proven, and it is probably best to withhold judgment. The major point is that Papias is the earliest source for Matthew writing a gospel (or Ur-Gospel).

The current consensus among critical scholars is that Matthew did not write this gospel.[38] One major reason is the even greater consensus that Mark was first (see below); this leads to the conclusion that an apostle, one of the Twelve and an eyewitness of the Jesus-event, would not depend on a nonwitness like Mark. There are two responses to this: (1) Papias (Eusebius, *Eccl. Hist.* 3.39.15) said that Mark wrote Peter's gospel, and Matthew would definitely have accepted material stemming from Peter. (2) There is no valid reason for supposing Matthew would refuse material from Mark on any account. Matthew undoubtedly knew Mark (his mother Mary had the main house church in Jerusalem in her home, Acts 12:12) and would certainly have used material from the widely accepted first gospel he penned; to assume otherwise is to give Matthew a higher degree of pride than is warranted. The same is true of Matthew's use of Q; he would have no problem using authentic *logia* of Jesus, whatever the source.

Another reason for rejecting Matthean authorship is the good Greek he used; it is thought that a Palestinian first-century Jew would not know Greek that well. This too is a mistake, for most Jews were trilingual (Aramaic, Greek, and Latin), and especially Galilean Jews like Matthew would have grown up with Gentiles constantly around. Moreover, as a tax/toll collector Matthew would have been required to know Greek well. Connected to this is the view that the anti-Semitism of this gospel fits a later period than that of Matthew, namely, the period reflecting a distinct break between Judaism and Christianity, the early to mid 80s. Against this is the unanimous view of all four gospels that there were distinct tensions between Jesus and Judaism, and that the rejection of Jesus by the leaders is now seen as a given in historical Jesus studies. As will be argued throughout this commentary, passages reflecting a strong denunciation of the leaders by Jesus (e.g., ch. 23) can be seen as historically accurate.

The unanimous acceptance of Matthean authorship in the early church cannot be so easily dismissed. The level of Greek, the literary qualities of the book, and the whole Jewish Christian orientation of it fit closely the ascription of it to Matthew. Why would the church so quickly forget (within fifty to sixty years of its writing) the person who wrote it, and why would it be ascribed to a minor (so far as we know)

38. See the chart in W. D. Davies and Dale C. Allison Jr., *The Gospel according to Matthew* (ICC; Edinburgh: T&T Clark, 1988), 1:10–11.

apostle like Matthew if that were not true. We can never know for certain who wrote it, but there is little reason to doubt the witness of the early church fathers.

The date is more difficult. The one thing certain is that it was written in the first century. The earliest allusions are found in Ignatius's *Epistle to the Smyrneans* 1.1 (AD 110) and in the *Didache* (written towards the beginning of the second century). The primary debate is whether Matthew was written before AD 70 (Carson, Gundry, France, Morris, Blomberg, Wilkins) or after AD 70, perhaps in the 80s (Bruce, Davies and Allison, Hagner, Luz, Keener). In favor of a post-70 date are these considerations:[39]

1. Matthew's diatribe against the Pharisees fits the later date, as in the 60s they may have been somewhat tolerant of "law-keeping Jewish Christians."
2. The Jewish worldview of Matthew fits the rabbinic movement of the 70s and 80s.
3. Mark probably dates in the mid 60s, which would place Matthew in the 70s.
4. Matthew separates the disciples' question in 24:3 unlike Mark 13:2 – 4 and points to further reflection on the scene.
5. The arguments of some that the explicit reference to the destruction of Jerusalem in ch. 24 demands a late date depends entirely on one's view of prophecy. If we posit that Jesus could foretell the future (and there is no reason to think otherwise if we accept Jesus as the Son of God), then that argument disappears.

The above are strong arguments, and the position is tenable. However, I still believe that it is slightly more likely that Matthew was written before AD 70. For one thing, there is no major break with Judaism reflected in Matthew, and it is likely that most of the readers were Jewish Christians still living in Jewish circles.[40] Moreover, I would personally date Mark in the mid to late 50s (especially if one dates Luke in AD 61 – 62, when the book of Acts ends).[41] Why would Matthew mention so many Jewish rituals (washing of hands, temple tax, offerings in the temple) and center so often on the Sadducees (who disappeared after AD 70), unless he was writing before the destruction of the temple? Therefore, a date of AD 65 – 67 is somewhat preferable, though I recognize certainty is not possible.

Sources

The so-called "Synoptic problem" centers on the literary relationship of Matthew, Mark, and Luke, called the "Synoptic Gospels" because they have the "same look" (*syn-optic*). This is a reflection of the fact that many passages have similar wording

39. Keener, *Matthew*, 42 – 43.
40. See Carson, "Matthew," 20 – 21.
41. See William F. Larkin, *Acts* (IVPNTC; Downers Grove, IL: IVP, 1995).

(e.g., Matt 19:13 – 15 = Mark 10:13 – 16 = Luke 18:15 – 17) or a similar order of events (e.g., Matt 12:46 – 13:58 = Mark 3:31 – 6:6 = Luke 8:19 – 56). Something has to account for this literary connection, and the majority of scholars accept some type of interdependence between the three. From the time of Augustine it was thought that Matthew was first, followed by Mark (who abbreviated Matthew) and Luke (who used Mark), following the canonical order. But in the eighteenth and nineteenth century dissenting voices began appearing, so that now there are two major camps. The first of these, the "Griesbach hypothesis" (J. J. Griesbach proposed this in 1783, 1789), argues that Matthew was first, Luke used Matthew, and Mark abbreviated both. This is indeed viable, following early church tradition regarding Matthean priority and explaining when two of the Synoptists agree against another (e.g., Mark and Luke against Matthew).

However, there are stronger arguments for Markan priority, especially the form called the "two- or four-source" hypothesis formulated by B. H. Streeter,[42] which says that Matthew and Luke used Mark and Q as well as their own special material (M and L).[43] Let me provide four basic arguments for this.

(1) The linguistic argument recognizes that Mark uses more primitive and awkward language than Matthew and Luke, leading them at times to smooth out the phrases, as when Mark speaks of the disciples' "hardened heart" (6:52; 8:17, omitted by the others) or when Mark has Jesus challenge the rich young ruler, "Why do you call me good?"(10:18) while Matthew has "Why are you asking me about what is good?" (19:17) to avoid the possible misunderstanding that Jesus is denying his goodness. Several have noted that this is similar to the text-critical "least likely reading," since the question is which reading would more likely give rise to the other.[44]

(2) As to theological differences, Mark also is the more difficult. One of the best examples is Mark's theme of discipleship failure. Consider Mark 6:51 – 52, where Mark ends the walking on the water pericope with, "They were completely amazed, for they had not understood about the loaves; their hearts were hardened." Matthew omits this and concludes the same episode with the worship of the disciples, who say, "Truly you are the Son of God." It is hard to conceive of a more polar-opposite ending. The same is true of Mark 8:21, "Do you still not understand?" where Matt

42. B. H. Streeter, *The Four Gospels: A Study of Origins Treating of the Manuscript Tradition, Sources, Authorship, and Dates* (New York: Macmillan, 1925).

43. In the following I will be utilizing Grant R. Osborne and Matthew C. Williams, "The Case for the Markan Priority View of Gospel Origins: The Two-/Four-Source View," in *Three Views on the Origins of the Synoptic Gospels*, ed. R. L. Thomas (Grand Rapids: Kregel, 2002), 19 – 96; as well as my "Response" in *Rethinking the Synoptic Problem* (ed. D. A. Black and D. R. Beck; Grand Rapids: Baker, 2001), 137 – 51. In that work see also Scot McKnight, "A Generation Who Knew Not Streeter: The Case for Markan Priority," 65 – 96. For a major and refreshing new take on Markan priority, see Matthew C. Williams, *Two Gospels from One: A Comprehensive New Analysis of the Synoptic Gospels* (Grand Rapids: Kregel, 2006).

44. McKnight, "Generation Who Knew Not Streeter," 82; D. A. Carson and Douglas Moo, *Introduction to the New Testament* (2nd ed.: Grand Rapids: Zondervan, 2005), 97; Matthew C. Williams, *Two Gospels from One*, 41 – 47.

16:12 has, "Then they understood." Once more, which direction is the more likely? Certainly from Mark to Matthew fits better.

(3) The redactional phenomena favor Markan priority. Mark 6:5 – 6 after the rejection of Jesus at Nazareth reads, "He could not do any miracles there, except lay his hands on a few sick people and heal them." Matthew 13:58 replaces "any" with "many" and drops the second half, providing a simpler summary, "he did not do many miracles there." Is it likely that Mark would take Matthew's clear statement and turn it into a difficult, seemingly inconsistent narration? Matthew tends to shorten Mark whenever he uses it as a source.

(4) Matthew and Luke reproduce nearly all of Mark, yet add a significant number of stories. This is easier to conceive if Mark were written first. If Matthew were first, it is harder to conceive of Mark omitting so much material from Jesus, especially discourses like the Sermon on the Mount or the Church Discourse of ch. 18 or the parables in the Olivet Discourse (ch. 13). Would Mark have omitted "the Son of the living God" from Peter's confession (Mark 8:29 = Matt 16:16) in light of the centrality of that title for Mark's gospel (Mark 1:1 NRSV)?

All of this makes it likely that Mark was the first gospel, and that Matthew and Luke used Mark as well as Q.[45] There is no evidence that such a text existed (though the *Gospel of Thomas* does show that collections of Jesus' sayings did occur), but it is a viable hypothesis to explain why 235 or so verses containing sayings of Jesus parallel one another in Matthew and Luke but are not found in Mark. The question is how so many sayings would be found in both Matthew and Luke merely by chance. At one level, the many fanciful and erroneous theories that have developed on the basis of so-called Q (e.g., the Jesus Seminar, who use it to reconstruct Jesus as a sage and cynic philosopher) make one reluctant to propound such a source at all.

Nevertheless, recent work has made the likelihood of Q more viable,[46] and Blomberg comments that the prevalence of collected wisdom sayings like Q in the ancient world would make it strange if early Christians had failed to develop just such a collection.[47] I have gone back and forth on the question whether Q was an oral tradition or a written document, and until such a manuscript is found we will never know. Also, it is true that many sayings attributed to Q probably came from different sources in Matthew and Luke, as will be seen from time to time in the commentary that follows.

Finally, a word should be said about M (material common only to Matthew) and L (material common only to Luke) sources. Luke 1:2 says clearly that Luke used several sources in constructing his gospel, so L becomes a convenient symbol for

45. Q (from the German *Quelle* or "source") is a hypothetical document proposed to explain the number of sayings of Jesus (235 verses) that are found in Matthew and Luke but not Mark.

46. E.g., Charles E. Carlston and Dennis Norlin, "Statistics and Q — Some Further Observations," *NovT* 41 (1999): 108 – 23.

47. Craig L. Blomberg, "The Synoptic Problem: Where We Stand at the Start of a New Century," *Rethinking the Synoptic Problem* (ed. D. A. Black and D. R. Beck; Grand Rapids: Baker, 2001), 28 – 29 (cf. 17 – 40).

what he gathered in writing his work. M is more difficult to prove, but if Matthew wrote this work (as we have argued), then much (if not most) of it is due to his own memory. This does not preclude that he used other sources in addition to Mark, but many (if not most) of these stories were events he himself had experienced.

The Use of the Old Testament in Matthew[48]

The first gospel contains sixty quotations from the OT and numerous allusions and echoes, making the OT more central than in any other gospel, in terms of both frequency and emphasis. Stanton says it well: "The OT is woven into the warp and woof of this gospel: the evangelist uses Scripture to underline some of his most prominent and distinctive theological concerns."[49]

Of the sixty quotes, there are ten fulfillment (*plēroun*) passages (1:22 – 23; 2:15, 17 – 18, 23; 4:14 – 16; 8:17; 12:17 – 21; 13:35; 21:4 – 5; 27:9 – 10) along with one *anaplēroun* formula passage (13:14 – 15), all commentary on the part of the evangelist. In addition, several fulfillment passages lack the *plēroun* formula introduction (2:5; 3:3; 9:13; 11:10; 12:7; 15:8 – 9; 26:31, 56). The emphasis is on the sovereign control of history by God, who governs all of human history to fulfill his will. Half of the quotations occur in the introductory chapters to establish just this point. The life of Jesus fulfills or completes all the promises of God found in the Scriptures. The meaning of *plēroun* is found in the programmatic 5:17 – 20, "I have not come to destroy but to fulfill [the law and the prophets]." Here *plēroun* implies that the OT is completed by being fulfilled in Jesus; in both his deeds and his teaching he lifted the OT to a higher plane. There are two ideas — he has completed or "filled up" the meaning of the OT, and he is the final interpreter of Torah.

The problem is that few if any of the fulfillment passages were intended originally as messianic prophecies. So in what way were they fulfilled? The answer is typology. Typology is "analogous fulfillment," not direct prophecy but indirect, centering on Jesus as the Messiah reliving or "fulfilling" the experiences of Israel. With respect to this another concept is crucial — corporate identity. As Ellis says, "the individual (male) person may be viewed as extending beyond himself to include those who 'belong' to him. Thus, the husband (at the family level) and the king (at the national level) both have an individual and a corporate existence encompassing, respectively, the household and the nation."[50]

The king (or high priest) represents the nation before God, but the Messiah rep-

48. This is taken from my *Hermeneutical Spiral*, 333 – 34.

49. Graham Stanton, *A Gospel for a New People: Studies in Matthew* (Edinburgh: T&T Clark, 1992), 146.

50. E. Earle Ellis, *The Old Testament in Early Christianity: Canon and Interpretation in Light of Modern Research* (Grand Rapids: Baker, 1992), 110 (cf. 110 – 16). Richard N. Longenecker, *Biblical Exegesis in the Apostolic Period* (Grand Rapids: Eerdmans, 1999), 93 – 95, brings together the four aspects of typology — corporate solidarity, correspondence in history, eschatological fulfillment, and messianic presence.

resents the whole history of the nation, so Jesus is corporately identified with (and relives) the history of Israel, that is, the whole OT. In this way:

- Jesus relives the exile, both going in (2:17 – 18) and returning from it (2:15)
- Jesus fulfills the Isaianic longing for both salvation for the Gentiles (in his Galilean ministry, 4:14 – 16) and healing (the work of the suffering Servant in Isa 53:4; see Matt 8:17) as well as the promise of the suffering Servant in Isa 42:1 – 4 (Matt 12:17 – 21)
- Jesus fulfills the opposite promises of judgment on those who reject God (13:14 – 15) and of God's mysteries spoken in parables to those who are open (13:35)
- Jesus fulfills the Zech 9:9 promise of the Messiah riding into Jerusalem on a donkey (Matt 21:4 – 5)
- Judas fulfills the pattern of rejection seen in Jer 19 and Zech 11 (Matt 27:9 – 10).

In so doing, Matthew sees all three sections of the OT — the Law, the Prophets, and the Writings — fulfilled in Jesus. He has completed their expectations and fully interpreted their meaning.

The major debate concerns the nature of these quotations. The fulfillment quotations (often called "reflection quotations" because they reflect on the prophetic nature of the fulfillment) seem to be Matthew's own translation of the Hebrew mixed with the LXX;[51] and the other quotations, taken from Mark, Q, or M material, are woven into the narrative and taken from the LXX. Several hypotheses have been suggested. (1) Matthew was utilizing a *testimonia* collection of messianic proof texts (this is doubtful because of the distinctive nature of these texts and their close fit in Matthew's gospel). (2) They are the product of a "school of Matthew" that utilized the pesher exegesis of Qumran,[52] though Qumran used an ongoing interpretation of a continuous text rather than the sporadic use as in Matthew.[53] (3) They stem from the missionary preaching of the church. This is the most likely hypothesis, though with their appropriateness in Matthew, several probably stemmed from Matthew's own study of the OT background to the life of Jesus.[54]

The main point is that all the quotations present Jesus and the church/kingdom community he founded as fulfilling the prophetic expectations of the OT. Stanton adds that Matthew's redaction is also highly christological and reflects his distinctive themes. The use of *huios* in 1:23; 2:15 emphasizes Jesus as Son of God; in 1:23

51. Robert Gundry, *The Use of the Old Testament in St. Matthew's Gospel with Specific Reference to the Messianic Hope* (NovTSup 18; Leiden: Brill, 1967).

52. Krister Stendahl, *School of St. Matthew*, passim. Longenecker, *Biblical Exegesis*, 142 – 43, also sees a pesher style of exegesis in Matthew.

53. B. Gärtner, "The Habakkuk Commentary (DSH) and the Gospel of Matthew," *ST* (1954): 1 – 24.

54. So Donald A. Hagner, *Matthew 1 – 13* (WBC; Dallas: Word, 1993), lvi – lvii. G. M. Soares-Prabhu, *The Formula Quotations in the Infancy Narratives of Matthew* (AnBib 63; Rome: Pontifical Biblical Press, 1976), 104, calls them "free Targumic translations made from the original Hebrew by Matthew, in view of the context into which he has inserted them."

Jesus is Immanuel — God with us, echoed in 28:20; at 2:6 he is the shepherd of Israel; in 2:17 – 18 Jesus relives the exodus and exile; in 2:23 he is the messianic "branch" and "holy one" of God; in 8:17; 13:35 he is the lowly servant; in 21:4 – 5 the two animals at the triumphal entry stress Jesus as the humble king (cf. 5:5; 11:29).[55]

Structure

Most biblical books have almost as many positions on structure as there are scholars working on them. There are probably two reasons for this: (1) ancient writers rarely thought in terms of structure like we do, so their books are open to many different patterns; (2) scholars are like the Athenians in Acts 17:21 in that they spend a great deal of time searching for "something new" (NRSV), and this is a good place to start. Still, most NT books do have a basic structure, and it is important to see how the plot ideas develop.

The classic work on Matthew's structure was that of Benjamin W. Bacon, who centered on the five discourse units and believed Matthew was a rabbi who organized his gospel into a "new Pentateuch":

Prologue (1:1 – 2:23)
Book I (3:1 – 7:29)
Book II (8:1 – 11:1)
Book III (11:2 – 13:53)
Book IV (13:54 – 19:1)
Book V (19:2 – 26:2)
Epilogue (26:3 – 28:20)[56]

The other well-known format is the threefold outline of Jack Dean Kingsbury, who builds on the clause "From that time Jesus began to" in 4:17 and 16:21, which yields as follows:

I. The Person of Jesus (1:1 – 4:16)
II. The Proclamation of Jesus Messiah (4:17 – 16:20)
III. The Suffering, Death, and Resurrection of Jesus Messiah (16:21 – 28:20).[57]

Third, some organize Matthew on the basis of Mark's outline because Matthew is generally following Mark, resulting in the following structure:

I. Introduction (1:1 – 4:11)
II. Galilean Ministry (4:12 – 16:20)

55. Stanton, *Studies in Matthew*, 360 – 62.

56. Benjamin W. Bacon, "The Five Books of Moses against the Jews," *Expositor* 15 (1918): 56 – 66.

57. Jack Dean Kingsbury, *Matthew: Structure, Christology, Kingdom* (Philadelphia: Fortress, 1975). See also Blomberg, *Matthew* (NAC; Nashville: Broadman, 1992), 22 – 25, 49, who follows Kingsbury but still tries to keep the narrative/discourse pattern.

III. The Journey from Galilee to Jerusalem (16:21 – 20:34)
IV. Confrontation with the Leaders in Jerusalem (21:1 – 25:46)
V. Passion and Resurrection (26:1 – 28:20).[58]

A fourth outline is the chiastic one presented by C. H. Lohr:[59]

Narrative	The Beginnings (chs. 1 – 4)	= Death and Resurrection (chs. 26 – 28)
Discourse	Kingdom and Blessings (chs. 5 – 7)	= Woes and Kingdom (chs. 23 – 25)
Narrative	Authority and Invitation (chs. 8 – 9)	= Authority and Invitation (chs. 19 – 22)
Discourse	Mission Discourse (ch. 10)	= Community Discourse (ch. 18)
Narrative	Rejection by This Generation (chs. 11 – 12)	= Accepted by the Disciples (chs. 14 – 17)
	Parable Discourse (ch. 13)	

While each of these structures has certain strengths, each also has certain weaknesses. Bacon and Lohr recognize the incontrovertible fact that Matthew's structure centers on his alteration of narrative and discourse, but both add another twist that is not truly warranted. Kingsbury has made too much of a statement repeated only twice. Better is Davies and Allison, who simply follow the discourse and narrative pattern, but they make too much of Matthew's tendency to arrange material in triads,[60] which works in several places but not in all. Best is D. A. Carson, who simply follows the narrative-discourse pattern.[61] Mine is closest to his:

I. Jesus' Origin and Preparation for Ministry (1:1 – 4:11)
   A. The Birth and Infancy of Jesus (1:1 – 2:23)
      1. The Genealogy of Jesus the Messiah (1:1 – 17)
      2. The Virginal Conception (1:18 – 25)
      3. The Visit of the Magi (2:1 – 12)
      4. The Evil Actions of Herod and Flight to Egypt (2:13 – 23)
   B. Inaugural Events in Jesus' Ministry (3:1 – 4:11)
      1. John the Baptist (3:1 – 12)
      2. The Baptism of Jesus (3:13 – 17)
      3. The Testing/Temptation of Jesus (4:1 – 11)
II. The Kingdom Message Goes Out (4:12 – 7:29)
   A. Early Galilean Ministry (4:12 – 25)
      1. Beginning the Capernaum Ministry (4:12 – 17)
      2. The Call of the Disciples (4:18 – 22)
      3. Summary of His Ministry (4:23 – 25)
   B. First Discourse: The Sermon on the Mount (5:1 – 7:29)
      1. The Setting of the Sermon (5:1 – 2)

58. R. T. France, *The Gospel of Matthew* (NICNT; Grand Rapids: Eerdmans, 2007), 2 – 5.

59. C. H. Lohr, "Oral Techniques in the Gospel of Matthew," *CBQ* 23 (1961): 403 – 35. See also H. J. B. Combrink, "The Structure of the Gospel of Matthew as Narrative," *TynBul* 34 (1983): 61 – 90.

60. Davies and Allison, *Matthew,* 1:58 – 72.

61. Carson, "Matthew," 50 – 57.

2. Introduction (5:3 – 16)
    a. The Beatitudes (5:3 – 12)
    b. The Salt and Light Sayings (5:13 – 16)
3. The Relationship of the Law to the New Covenant in Jesus (5:17 – 48)
    a. Jesus and the Law — Continuity (5:17 – 20)
    b. Examples — Six Antitheses on the New Righteousness (5:21 – 48)
        (1) Murder = Anger (5:21 – 26)
        (2) Adultery = Lust (5:27 – 30)
        (3) Divorce/Remarriage = Adultery (5:31 – 32)
        (4) Oaths Are Unnecessary (5:33 – 37)
        (5) Retaliation Is Wrong (5:38 – 42)
        (6) Love for Enemies (5:43 – 48)
4. Inward Righteousness (6:1 – 18)
    a. Almsgiving (6:1 – 4)
    b. Prayer (6:5 – 15)
    c. Fasting (6:16 – 18)
5. Social Ethics (6:19 – 7:12)
    a. God and Possessions (6:19 – 34)
        (1) Kingdom Priorities and the Two Masters (6:19 – 24)
        (2) Anxiety and Trust (6:25 – 34)
    b. Social Relationships (7:1 – 12)
        (1) Prohibition against Judging Others (7:1 – 5)
        (2) The Need for Discernment (7:6)
        (3) A Prayer for Help (7:7 – 8)
        (4) God Answers Prayer (7:9 – 11)
        (5) The Golden Rule (7:12)
6. Conclusion — The Two Paths (7:13 – 27)
    a. The Two Ways (7:13 – 14)
    b. False Prophets (7:15 – 23)
    c. The Two Builders (7:24 – 27)
7. Conclusion to the Sermon — Jesus' Authority (7:28 – 29)

III. The Kingdom Comes with Authority (8:1 – 11:1)

A. Authority and Discipleship in Jesus' Ministry (8:1 – 9:34)

1. Three Healing Miracles (8:1 – 17)
    a. Healing the Leper (8:1 – 4)
    b. Healing the Centurion's Servant (8:5 – 13)
    c. Healing Peter's Mother-In-Law (8:14 – 17)
2. The Demands of Discipleship (8:18 – 22)
3. Three Miracles Showing His Authority (8:23 – 9:8)
    a. Calming of the Storm (8:23 – 27)
    b. Exorcism of Two Demon-Possessed Men (8:28 – 34)

c. Healing of the Paralytic (9:1 – 8)
4. Discipleship and the Reality of the New Kingdom (9:9 – 17)
a. The Call of Matthew (9:9 – 13)
b. Fasting and the Reality of the New Kingdom (9:14 – 17)
5. Three Healing Miracles Showing Compassion (9:18 – 34)
a. Healing a Woman and Raising a Young Girl (9:18 – 26)
b. Healing Two Blind Men (9:27 – 31)
c. Exorcizing a Young Man (9:32 – 34)
B. Second Discourse: Mission and Opposition (9:35 – 11:1)
1. Introduction (9:35 – 10:4)
a. The Call for Workers (9:35 – 38)
b. The Commissioning of the Twelve (10:1 – 4)
2. Instructions for the Jewish Mission (10:5 – 15)
3. Persecution in the Mission (10:16 – 23)
4. Sharing in Jesus' Mission (10:24 – 42)
a. No Need to Fear (10:24 – 31)
b. Confession and Conflict in Discipleship (10:32 – 42)
(1) Fearless Confession (10:32 – 33)
(2) Conflicts Produced (10:34 – 36)
(3) Counting the Cost (10:37 – 39)
(4) Results — Oneness (10:40 – 42)
5. Conclusion (11:1)
IV. Preaching and Teaching in the Midst of Opposition (11:2 – 13:53)
A. Jesus' Deeds: Revelation and Rejection (11:2 – 12:50)
1. Revelation and Rejection Begun (11:2 – 30)
a. Jesus and John the Baptist (11:2 – 19)
(1) John's Doubts and Jesus' Response (11:2 – 6)
(2) Jesus' Testimony about John (11:7 – 15)
(3) Rejection by Israel (11:16 – 19)
b. Woes on Unrepentant Towns (11:20 – 24)
c. The Father Reveals the Son (11:25 – 30)
2. Rejection of the Humble Servant (12:1 – 21)
a. Harvesting Grain on the Sabbath (12:1 – 8)
b. Healing the Man with the Withered Hand (12:9 – 14)
c. The Humble Servant (12:15 – 21)
3. Controversy and Community (12:22 – 50)
a. Confrontation over Beelzebul (12:22 – 37)
(1) The Healing of the Demon-Possessed Man (12:22 – 23)
(2) The Conflict with the Pharisees (12:24 – 30)
(3) The Unforgivable Sin (12:31 – 32)
(4) Good and Evil Speech (12:33 – 37)

b. Controversy over the Sign of Jonah (12:38 – 45)
c. Family and Community (12:46 – 50)
B. Third Discourse: Kingdom Parables (13:1 – 53)
1. Parable of the Soils (13:1 – 23)
a. The Parable Presented (13:1 – 9)
b. The Purpose of Parables (13:10 – 17)
c. Interpretation of the Soils (13:18 – 23)
2. Parables of the Kingdom Growing (13:24 – 43)
a. Parable of the Weeds (13:24 – 30)
b. Parable of the Mustard Seed (13:31 – 32)
c. Parable of the Yeast (13:33)
d. Parables Fulfilling Prophecy (13:34 – 35)
e. Parable of the Weeds Explained (13:36 – 43)
3. Final Parables for the Disciples (13:44 – 52)
a. The Hidden Treasure (13:44)
b. The Costly Pearl (13:45 – 46)
c. The Dragnet (13:47 – 50)
d. The Scribe Trained for the Kingdom (13:51 – 52)
4. Conclusion (13:53)
V. Rejection, Suffering, and Glory (13:54 – 18:35)
A. Jesus' Deeds: Rejection, Discipleship, and Glory (13:54 – 17:27)
1. Rejection and Discipleship (13:54 – 16:20)
a. Teaching and Rejection at Nazareth (13:54 – 58)
b. Herod, Jesus, and the Baptist (14:1 – 12)
c. Feeding of the 5,000 (14:13 – 21)
d. Walking on the Water (14:22 – 33)
e. Healings at Gennesaret (14:34 – 36)
f. Jesus and Tradition (15:1 – 20)
(1) The Leaders — The Tradition of the Elders (15:1 – 9)
(2) The Crowd Called to Understanding (15:10 – 11)
(3) The Message Explained to the Disciples (15:12 – 20)
g. Further Healings (15:21 – 31)
(1) The Faith of the Canaanite Woman (15:21 – 28)
(2) Summary Healings (15:29 – 31)
h. Feeding of the 4,000 (15:32 – 39)
i. Demand for a Sign (16:1 – 4)
j. Warning about the Leaders (16:5 – 12)
k. Peter's Confession and Jesus' Blessing (16:13 – 20)
2. The Movement to the Cross (16:21 – 17:27)
a. First Passion Prediction and Discipleship (16:21 – 28)
(1) Jesus Predicts His Death (16:21)

(2) Peter and Jesus Rebuke One Another (16:22 – 23)
(3) The Path of Discipleship (16:24 – 28)
b. Transfiguration (17:1 – 13)
c. Healing of the Epileptic Child (17:14 – 21)
d. Second Passion Prediction and Temple Tax (17:22 – 27)
B. Fourth Discourse: Life and Relationships in the Community (18:1 – 35)
1. Relationships in the Community (18:1 – 14)
a. The Greatest in the Kingdom (18:1 – 4)
b. Warning against Causing Others to Sin (18:5 – 9)
c. The Problem of Wandering Sheep (18:10 – 14)
2. Discipline and Forgiveness (18:15 – 35)
a. Discipline and Reconciliation (18:15 – 20)
b. The Absolute Need for Forgiveness (18:21 – 35)
(1) Introduction — The Need for Forgiveness (18:21 – 22)
(2) The Parable of the Unmerciful Slave (18:23 – 34)
(3) Conclusion — A Warning on the Necessity of Forgiveness (18:35)
VI. The Movement to the Cross (19:1 – 25:46)
A. Jesus' Deeds: Opposition and Discipleship (19:1 – 22:46)
1. The Road to Jerusalem (19:1 – 20:34)
a. The Question on Divorce (19:1 – 12)
b. Blessing the Children (19:13 – 15)
c. Wealth and Kingdom Rewards (19:16 – 30)
(1) Encounter with the Rich Young Man (19:16 – 22)
(2) The Difficulty for the Rich to Enter the Kingdom (19:23 – 26)
(3) The Rewards for Leaving All (19:27 – 30)
d. Parable of Workers in the Vineyard (20:1 – 16)
e. Third Passion Prediction and Kingdom Honor (20:17 – 28)
(1) Jesus' Passion Prediction (20:17 – 19)
(2) The Ambitious Request for Honor and Power (20:20 – 23)
(3) Jesus' Teaching about True Greatness (20:24 – 28)
f. Healing of the Two Blind Men (20:29 – 34)
2. Beginning Events of Passion Week (21:1 – 22:46)
a. The Messiah Enters Jerusalem (21:1 – 22)
(1) The Lowly King in His Humble Entry (21:1 – 11)
(2) Judgment on the Temple (21:12 – 17)
(3) Judgment Parable: Cursing the Fig Tree (21:18 – 22)
b. Controversies in the Temple Court (21:23 – 22:46)
(1) The Question about Jesus' Authority (21:23 – 27)
(2) The Parable of the Two Sons (21:28 – 32)
(3) The Parable of the Wicked Tenants (21:33 – 46)
(4) The Parable of the Wedding Banquet (22:1 – 14)

(5) Paying Tribute Taxes to Caesar (22:15 – 22)
(6) Marriage in the Resurrection (22:23 – 33)
(7) The Greatest Commandment (22:34 – 40)
(8) Son of David and Lord of David (22:41 – 46)

B. Fifth Discourse: Guilt and Judgment of Israel (23:1 – 25:46)
1. Guilt — Woes upon the Leaders (23:1 – 39)
a. Warning and Humility (23:1 – 12)
(1) Warning about the Deeds of the Scribes and Pharisees (23:1 – 7)
(2) Admonition for Proper Behavior (23:8 – 12)
b. The Seven Woes (23:13 – 36)
(1) Woes on the Negative Effect They Have on Others (23:13 – 15)
(a) Judgment for Closing the Kingdom to Others (23:13)
(b) Judgment for Leading Proselytes to Gehenna (23:15)
(2) Woes on the Misleading Effect of Their Teaching and Conduct (23:16 – 24)
(a) Judgment for Their False Teaching on Oaths and the Temple (23:16 – 22)
(b) Judgment for Their False Teaching on Tithing While Ignoring Mercy (23:23 – 24)
(3) Woes on Their External Religion (23:25 – 32)
(a) Judgment for Their Ritual Cleanliness Yet Unclean Hearts (23:25 – 26)
(b) Judgment for Their Self-Righteous Exterior Yet Wicked Interior (23:27 – 28)
(4) Woe for Participating in the Sins of Their Ancestors (23:29 – 32)
(5) Conclusion — Judgment Coming (23:33 – 36)
c. Lament over Jerusalem (23:37 – 39)
2. Judgment — Olivet Discourse (24:1 – 25:46)
a. Destruction of Jerusalem and the Events of the End Time (24:1 – 35)
(1) Prophecy on the Destruction (24:1 – 3)
(2) The Destruction and the End-Time Events (24:4 – 28)
(a) Signs That Are Not the End (24:4 – 14)
(i) Great Deception and Great Travail (24:4 – 8)
(ii) Great Apostasy and the Great Mission (24:9 – 14)
(b) Signs That Point to the End (24:15 – 28)
(i) The Abomination and the Need to Flee (24:15 – 22)
(ii) The Speculations of the False Messiahs vs. the True Parousia (24:23 – 28)
(3) The Parousia (24:29 – 31)
(4) The Nearness of the Day (24:32 – 35)
b. Parables on Readiness (24:36 – 25:30)
(1) The Need for Spiritual Vigilance (24:36 – 44)
(2) The Parable of the Faithful and Wicked Slaves (24:45 – 51)
(3) The Parable of the Ten Bridesmaids (25:1 – 13)
(4) The Parable of the Talents (25:14 – 30)
c. Teaching on the Final Judgment (25:31 – 46)

VII. The Passion and Resurrection of Jesus (26:1 – 28:20)

- A. The Passion Narrative (26:1 – 27:61)
  - 1. Preliminary Events (26:1 – 16)
    - a. Introduction — Plot to Kill Jesus (26:1 – 5)
    - b. Anointing of Jesus (26:6 – 13)
    - c. Judas' Betrayal (26:14 – 16)
  - 2. The Last Supper/Passover (26:17 – 30)
    - a. Preparation for the Supper (26:17 – 19)
    - b. Prediction of Judas's Betrayal (26:20 – 25)
    - c. Words of Institution (26:26 – 30)
  - 3. Events in Gethsemane (26:31 – 56)
    - a. Jesus Predicts the Failure of His Disciples (26:31 – 35)
    - b. The Prayer of Victory at Gethsemane (26:36 – 46)
    - c. The Arrest of Jesus (26:47 – 56)
  - 4. The Trials of Jesus and Peter's Denials (26:57 – 27:26)
    - a. The Sanhedrin Trial and Peter's Denials (26:57 – 75)
    - b. The Trial before Pilate (27:1 – 26)
      - (1) The Delivery of Jesus to Pilate (27:1 – 2)
      - (2) The Suicide of Judas (27:3 – 10)
      - (3) Interrogation by Pilate (27:11 – 14)
      - (4) The Barabbas Incident (27:15 – 23)
      - (5) The Verdict Is Rendered (27:24 – 26)
  - 5. The Crucifixion and Death of Jesus (27:27 – 50)
    - a. Mockery by the Roman Soldiers (27:27 – 31)
    - b. The Crucifixion of Jesus (27:32 – 38)
    - c. Mockery by the Jews (27:39 – 44)
    - d. The Death of Jesus (27:45 – 50)
  - 6. Events Following Jesus' Death (27:51 – 61)
    - a. The Incredible After-Events — The Curtain and the Raised Saints (27:51 – 53)
    - b. Witnesses to the Events — The Soldiers and the Women (27:54 – 56)
    - c. The Burial of Jesus (27:57 – 61)
- B. The Resurrection Narrative (27:62 – 28:20)
  - 1. Preparatory Events (27:62 – 28:1)
  - 2. Reactions to the Resurrection (28:2 – 10)
  - 3. Results of the Resurrection (28:11 – 20)

Select Bibliography on Matthew

Albright, W. F. and C. S. Mann. *Matthew.* Anchor Bible. Garden City, NY: Doubleday, 1971.

Allen, Willoughby C. *A Critical and Exegetical Commentary on the Gospel according to St. Matthew.* International Critical Commentary. Edinburgh: T&T Clark, 1912.

Allison, Dale C. *The New Moses: A Matthean Typology.* Minneapolis: Fortress, 1993.

Aune, David E. *The New Testament in Its Literary Environment.* Philadelphia: Westminster, 1987.

Bacon, Benjamin W. "The Five Books of Moses against the Jews." *The Expositor* 15 (1918): 56 – 66.

Bailey, Kenneth E. *Poet and Peasant.* Grand Rapids: Eerdmans, 1976.

———. *Through Peasant Eyes: More Lucan Parables, Their Culture and Style.* Grand Rapids: Eerdmans, 1980.

Baltensweiler, H. *Die Ehe im Neuen Testament.* Zurich: Zwingli, 1967.

Banks, Robert. *Jesus and the Law in the Synoptic Tradition.* Society for New Testament Studies Monograph Series 28. Cambridge: Cambridge University Press, 1975.

Bauckham, Richard. "For Whom Were the Gospels Written?" Pages 9 – 48 in *The Gospel for All Christians.* Edited by Richard Bauckham. Grand Rapids: Eerdmans, 1998.

Beare, Francis Wright. *The Gospel according to Matthew: Translation, Introduction and Commentary.* Philadelphia: Harper & Row, 1981.

———. "The Mission of the Twelve and the Mission Charge: Matthew 10 and Parallels." *Journal of Biblical Literature* 89 (1970): 1 – 13.

Beasley-Murray, George R. *Baptism in the New Testament.* Grand Rapids: Eerdmans, 1962.

———. *John.* Word Biblical Commentary 36. Waco, TX: Word, 1987.

Berger, Klaus. "Die königlichen Messiastraditionen des Neuen Testaments." *New Testament Studies* 20 (1973 – 1974): 3 – 9.

Betz, Hans-Dieter. *Essays on the Sermon on the Mount.* Philadelphia: Fortress, 1985.

Block, Dan. *The Book of Ezekiel, Chapters 1 – 24.* New International Commentary on the Old Testament. Grand Rapids: Eerdmans, 1997.

Blomberg, Craig L. *The Historical Reliability of the Gospels.* Downers Grove, IL: IVP, 1987.

———. *Interpreting the Parables.* Downers Grove, IL: IVP, 1990.

Bock, Darrell L. *Luke.* IVP New Testament Commentary. Downers Grove, IL: IVP, 1994.

———. *Luke 1:1 – 9:50.* Baker Exegetical Commentary on the New Testament. Grand Rapids: Baker, 1994.

———. *Luke 9:51 – 24:53.* Baker Exegetical Commentary on the New Testament. Grand Rapids: Baker, 1996.

Bonhoeffer, Dietrich. *Discipleship.* Translated by B. Green and R. Krauss. Minneapolis: Fortress, 2001.

Bonnard, Pierre. *L'évangile selon Saint Matthieu.* Neuchâtel: Delachaux & Niestlé, 1963.

Booth, R. P. *Jesus and the Laws of Purity: Tradition History and Legal History in Mark 7.* Journal for the Study of the New Testament Supplement Series 13. Sheffield: JSOT Press, 1986.

Bornkamm, Günther, Gerhard Barth, and Heinz Joachim Held. *Tradition and Interpretation in Matthew.* The New Testament Library. Philadelphia: Westminster Press, 1963.

Brandon, S. G. F. *Jesus and the Zealots.* New York: Scribner's, 1967.

Broadus, John A. *Commentary on the Gospel of Matthew.* Philadelphia: American Baptist Publication Society, 1886.

Brown, Jeannine K. *The Disciples in Narrative Perspective: The Portrayal and Function of the Matthean Disciples.* Academic Biblica 9. Boston: Brill, 2002.

Brown, Raymond E. *The Birth of the Messiah: A Commentary on the Infancy Narratives in the Gospels of Matthew and Luke.* 2nd ed. New York: Doubleday, 1993.

———. *The Death of the Messiah: From Gethsemane to Grave. A Commentary on the Passion Narratives of the Four Gospels.* 2 vols. New York: Doubleday, 1994.

———. *The Semitic Background of the Term "Mystery" in the New Testament.* Philadelphia: Fortress, 1968.

Brown, Schuyler. "The Twofold Representation of the Mission in Matthew's Gospel." *Studia Theologica* 31 (1977): 21 – 32.

Bruner, F. Dale. *Matthew: The Christbook.* 2 vols. Dallas: Word, 1987, 1990.

Buchanan, George W. "Matthean Beatitudes and Traditional Problems." *Journal from the Radical Reformation* 3 (1993): 45 – 69.

Bultmann, Rudolf. *The History of the Synoptic Tradition.* 2nd ed. Translated by J. Marsh. Oxford: Blackwell, 1968.

———. *Theology of the New Testament.* 2 vols. Translated by K. Grobel. New York: Charles Scribner's Sons, 1951.

Caragounis, Chrys C. *Peter the Rock.* Beihefte zur Zeitschrift für die neutestamentliche Wissenschaft 58. Berlin: de Gruyter, 1990.

Carson, D. A. "Matthew." Pages 1 – 599 in vol. 8 of *The Expositor's Bible Commentary.* Edited by Frank E. Gaebelein. 12 vols. Grand Rapids: Zondervan, 1984.

———. *The Sermon on the Mount: An Evangelical Exposition of Matthew 5 – 7.* Grand Rapids: Baker, 1978.

———. *When Jesus Confronts the World.* Grand Rapids: Baker, 1987.

Carter, Warren. *Households and Discipleship: A Study of Matthew 19 – 20.* Journal for the Study of the New Testament Supplement Series 103. Sheffield: JSOT Press, 1994.

Casey, Maurice. "General, Generic, and Indefinite: The Use of the Term 'Son of Man' in Jewish Sources and the Teaching of Jesus." *Journal for the Study of the New Testament* 29 (1987): 21 – 56.

Cassidy, Richard J. "Matthew 17:24 – 27 — A Word on Civil Taxes." *Catholic Biblical Quarterly* 41 (1979): 571 – 80.

Charette, Blaine. *The Theme of Recompense in Matthew's Gospel.* Journal for the Study of the New Testament Supplement Series 79. Sheffield: JSOT Press, 1992.

Cope, O. Lamar. *Matthew: A Scribe Trained for the Kingdom of Heaven.* New York: Ktav, 1977.

Crossan, John Dominic. *Cliffs of Fall: Paradox and Polyvalence in the Parables of Jesus.* New York: Seabury, 1980.

———. *The Historical Jesus: The Life of a Mediterranean Jewish Peasant.* San Francisco: Harper, 1991.

Cullmann, Oscar. *The Christology of the New Testament.* Philadelphia: Westminster, 1959.

Daube, David. *The New Testament and Rabbinic Judaism*. London: University of London Press, 1956.

Davies, W. D., and Dale C. Allison Jr. *The Gospel According to Matthew*. 3 vols. International Critical Commentary. Edinburgh: T&T Clark, 1988.

Derrett, J. D. M. *Law in the New Testament*. London: Dartman, Longman, & Todd, 1970.

———. "Two 'Harsh' Sayings of Christ Explained." *Downside Review* 103 (1985): 218 – 29.

Deutsch, Celia. *Hidden Wisdom and the Easy Yoke: Wisdom, Torah and Discipleship in Matthew 11.25 – 30*. Journal for the Study of the New Testament Supplement Series 18. Sheffield: JSOT Press, 1987.

Dibelius, Martin. *From Tradition to Gospel*. Translated by B. L. Woolf. Cambridge: James Clarke & Company, 1971.

Dodd, C. H. *According to the Scriptures*. London: Nisbet, 1952.

Donaldson, Terence L. *Jesus on the Mountain: A Study in Matthean Theology*. Journal for the Study of the New Testament Supplement Series 8. Sheffield: JSOT Press, 1985.

Dunn, J. D. G. *Jesus and the Spirit: A Study of the Religious and Charismatic Experience of Jesus and the First Christians as Reflected in the New Testament*. London: SCM, 1975.

Edwards, James R. *The Gospel according to Mark*. Pillar New Testament Commentary. Grand Rapids: Eerdmans, 2002.

Edwards, Richard A. *Matthew's Narrative Portrait of the Disciples*. Valley Forge, PA: Trinity Press International, 1997.

Ferguson, Everett. *Backgrounds of Early Christianity*. Grand Rapids: Eerdmans, 1987.

Filson, Floyd V. *The Gospel according to St. Matthew*. 2nd ed. Black's New Testament Commentaries. London: Adam & Charles Black, 1971.

Fitzmyer, Joseph A. "The Use of Explicit Old Testament Quotations in Qumran Literature and in the New Testament." *New Testament Studies* 7 (1960 – 1961): 362 – 63.

Fowler, Robert M. *Loaves and Fishes: The Function of the Feeding Stories in the Gospel of Mark*. Chico, CA: Scholars Press, 1981.

France, R. T. *The Gospel of Matthew*. New International Commentary on the New Testament. Grand Rapids: Eerdmans, 2007.

———. *Jesus and the Old Testament*. Grand Rapids: Baker, 1982.

———. *Matthew*. Tyndale New Testament Commentaries. Grand Rapids: Eerdmans, 1985.

———. *Matthew: Evangelist and Teacher*. London: Paternoster, 1989.

Funk, R. W., et. al. *The Five Gospels: The Search for the Authentic Words of Jesus*. New York: Macmillan, 1993.

Garland, David E. *The Intention of Matthew 23*. Novum Testamentum Supplement 52. Leiden: Brill, 1979.

———. *Reading Matthew: A Literary and Theological Commentary on the First Gospel*. New York: Crossroad, 1993.

Gench, Frances Taylor. *Wisdom in the Christology of Matthew*. New York: University Press of America, 1997.

Gerhardsson, Birger. *The Testing of God's Son (Matt 4:11 & Par.): An Analysis of an Early Christian Midrash*. Coniectanea Biblica New Testament Series 2.1. Lund: Gleerup, 1966.

Gnilka, Joachim. *Das Matthäusevangelium*. 2 vols. Herders theologischer Kommentar zum Neuen Testament. Freiburg: Herder, 1986, 1988.

Goulder, M. D. *Midrash and Lection in Matthew*. London: SPCK, 1974.

Grimm, W. *Weil ich dich liebe: Die Verkündigung Jesu und Deutereojesaja*. Frankfurt am Main: Peter Lang, 1976.

Grundmann, Walter. *Das Evangelium nach Matthäus*. Berlin: Evangelische Verlagsanstalt, 1981.

Guelich, Robert A. *Mark 1 – 8:26*. Word Biblical Commentary 34A. Dallas: Word Books, 1989.

———. *The Sermon on the Mount: A Foundation for Understanding*. Waco, TX: Word, 1982.

Gundry, Robert H. *Mark: A Commentary on His Apology for the Cross*. Grand Rapids: Eerdmans, 1992.

———. *Matthew: A Commentary on His Literary and Theological Art*. Grand Rapids: Eerdmans, 1982.

———. *The Use of the Old Testament in St. Matthew's Gospel with Specific Reference to the Messianic Hope*. Novum Testamentum Supplements 18. Leiden: Brill, 1967.

Hagner, Donald A. *Matthew*. 2 vols. Word Biblical Commentary 33A-B. Dallas: Word, 1993, 1995.

Hare, Douglas R. A. *The Theme of Jewish Persecution of Christians in the Gospel according to St. Matthew*. Cambridge: Cambridge University Press, 1967.

Harrington, Daniel J. *The Gospel of Matthew*. Sacra Pagina 1. Collegeville, MN: Liturgical Press, 1991.

Hauerwas, Stanley, *Matthew*. Brazos Theological Commentary. Grand Rapids: Baker, 2006.

Held, Hans-Joachim. "Matthew as Interpreter of the Miracle Stories." Pages 165 – 299 in *Tradition and Interpretation in Matthew*. Edited by Günther Bornkamm et al. Philadelphia: Westminster, 1963.

Hengel, Martin. *The Charismatic Leader and His Followers*. Translated by J. Greig. New York: Crossroad, 1981.

Hill, David. *The Gospel of Matthew*. New Century Bible. Greenwood, SC: Attic, 1972.

Hoehner, Harold W. *Chronological Aspects of the Life of Christ*. Grand Rapids: Zondervan, 1977.

Hooker, Morna. *Jesus and the Servant*. London: SPCK, 1959.

Horsley, Richard A. *Galilee: History, Politics, People*. Valley Forge, Pa.: Trinity Press International, 1995.

Hubbard, Benjamin J. *The Matthean Redaction of a Primitive Apostolic Commissioning: An Exegesis of Matthew 28:16 – 20*. Society of Biblical Literature Dissertation Series 19. Missoula, MT: Society of Biblical Literature, 1974.

Jeremias, Joachim. *New Testament Theology: The Proclamation of Jesus*. Translated by J. Bowden. New York: Scribner's, 1971.

———. *The Parables of Jesus*. 2nd ed. New York: Scribner's, 1972.

———. *The Sermon on the Mount*. Translated by N. Perrin. Philadelphia: Fortress, 1963.

Jones, Ivor H. *The Matthean Parables: A Literary and Historical Commentary*. Studien zum Neuen Testament 80. New York: Brill, 1995.

Keener, Craig S. *A Commentary on the Gospel of Matthew*. Grand Rapids: Eerdmans, 1999.

Kingsbury, Jack Dean. *Matthew as Story*. 2nd ed. Philadelphia: Fortress, 1988.

———. *Matthew: Structure, Christology, Kingdom*. Philadelphia: Fortress, 1975.

———. "Observations on the 'Miracle Chapters' of Matthew 8 – 9." *Catholic Biblical Quarterly* 40 (1978): 559 – 73.

———. *The Parables of Jesus in Matthew 13: A Study in Redaction Criticism*. London: SPCK, 1969.

Knowles, Michael. *Jeremiah in Matthew's Gospel: The Rejected-Prophet Motif in Matthean Redaction*. Journal for the Study of the New Testament Supplement Series 68. Sheffield: Sheffield Academic Press, 1993.

Lagrange. M.-J. *Évangile selon Saint Matthieu*. Paris: Lecoffre, 1948.

Lambrecht, Jan. *The Sermon on the Mount: Proclamation and Exhortation.* Wilmington, DE: Michael Glazier, 1985.

Lane, William L. *The Gospel according to Mark.* New International Commentary on the New Testament. Grand Rapids: Eerdmans, 1974.

Lightfoot, R. H. *History and Interpretation in the Gospels.* New York: Hodder & Stoughton, 1934.

Loader, W. R. G. "Son of David, Blindness, Possession, and Duality in Matthew." *Catholic Biblical Quarterly* 44 (1982): 570 – 85.

Longenecker, Richard N. *The Christology of Early Jewish Christianity.* Grand Rapids: Baker, 1981.

Louw, Johannes P., and Eugene A. Nida. *Greek-English Lexicon of the New Testament Based on Semantic Domains.* 2nd ed. New York: United Bible Societies, 1989.

Luther, Martin. *Luther's Works.* 15 vols. Edited and translated by J. J. Pelikan and H. T. Lehmann. St. Louis: Concordia, 1955 – 1960.

Luz, Ulrich. *Matthew: A Commentary.* 3 vols. Translated by W. C. Linss. Minneapolis, MN: Augsburg, 1989 – 2005.

———. *Studies in Matthew.* Grand Rapids: Eerdmans, 2005.

———. *The Theology of the Gospel of Matthew.* Translated by J. Bradford Robinson. Cambridge: Cambridge University Press, 1995.

Malina, B. J. *The New Testament World: Insights from Cultural Anthropology.* Atlanta: John Knox, 1981.

Manson, T. W. *The Sayings of Jesus.* London: SCM, 1949.

Marcus, Joel. *Mark 1 – 8.* Anchor Bible Commentary 27. New York: Doubleday, 2000.

Marshall, I. Howard. *Commentary on Luke.* New International Greek Testament Commentary. Grand Rapids: Eerdmans, 1978.

———. *Luke: Historian and Theologian.* Grand Rapids: Zondervan, 1970.

———. *New Testament Theology: Many Witnesses, One Gospel.* Downers Grove, IL: IVP, 2004.

McKnight, Scot. *Jesus and His Death: Historiography, the Historical Jesus, and Atonement Theory.* Waco, TX: Baylor University Press, 2005.

———. *A Light Among the Gentiles: Jewish Missionary Activity in the Second Temple Period.* Minneapolis: Fortress, 1991.

McNeile, Alan Hugh. *The Gospel according to Matthew.* Grand Rapids: Baker, 1980, originally 1915.

Meier, J. P. *Law and History in Matthew's Gospel: A Redactional Study of Mt. 5:17 – 48.* Rome: Biblical Institute Press, 1976.

———. *A Marginal Jew: Rethinking the Historical Jesus.* Volume 1: *The Roots of the Problem and the Person.* New York: Doubleday, 1991.

———. *Matthew.* Wilmington: Glazier, 1980.

———. *The Vision of Matthew: Christ, Church, and Morality in the First Gospel.* New York: Paulist, 1979.

Metzger, Bruce. *A Textual Commentary on the Greek New Testament.* New York: United Bible Societies, 1971.

Meyer, Ben F. *The Aims of Jesus.* London: SCM, 1979.

Moo, Douglas J. *The Old Testament in the Gospel Passion Narratives.* Sheffield: Almond Press, 1983.

Morosco, Robert E. "Redaction Criticism and the Evangelical: Matthew 10 as a Test Case." *Journal of the Evangelical Theological Society* 22 (1979): 323 – 31.

Morris, Leon. *The Gospel according to Matthew.* Grand Rapids: Eerdmans, 1992.

Mounce, Robert H. *Matthew.* Good News Commentaries. New York: Harper & Row, 1985.

Nolland, John. *The Gospel of Matthew: A Commentary on the Greek Text.* New International Greek Testament Commentary. Grand Rapids: Eerdmans, 2005.

Olmstead, Wesley G. *Matthew's Trilogy of Parables: The Nation, the Nations and the Reader in Matthew 21:28 – 22:14*. Society for New Testament Studies Monograph Series 127. Cambridge: Cambridge University Press, 2003.

Orton, David E. *The Understanding Scribe: Matthew and the Apocalyptic Ideal*. Journal for the Study of the New Testament Supplement Series 25. Sheffield: JSOT Press, 1989.

Osborne, Grant R. *The Hermeneutical Spiral: A Comprehensive Introduction to Biblical Interpretation*. 2nd ed. Downers Grove, IL: IVP, 2006.

———. "History and Theology in the Synoptic Gospels." *Trinity Journal* 24 (2003): 5 – 22.

———. "Historical Narrative and Truth in the Bible." *Journal of the Evangelical Theological Society* 48 (2005): 673 – 88.

———. "John." Cornerstone Biblical Commentary. Carol Stream, IL: Tyndale, 2007.

———. *Revelation*. Baker Exegetical Commentary on the New Testament. Grand Rapids: Baker, 2002.

———. *Romans*. IVP New Testament Commentary. Downers Grove, IL: IVP, 2004.

Osborne, Grant R., and Matthew C. Williams, "The Case for the Markan Priority View of Gospel Origins: The Two-/Four-Source View." Pages 19 – 96 in *Three Views on the Origins of the Synoptic Gospels*. Edited by R. L. Thomas. Grand Rapids: Kregel, 2002.

Oswalt, John. *The Book of Isaiah, Chapters 40 – 66*. New International Commentary on the Old Testament. Grand Rapids: Eerdmans, 1998.

Overman, J. Andrew. *Church and Community in Crisis: The Gospel according to Matthew*. Valley Forge, PA: Trinity Press International, 1996.

Patte, Daniel. *The Gospel according to Matthew: A Structural Commentary on Matthew's Faith*. Philadelphia: Fortress, 1987.

Plummer, Alfred. *An Exegetical Commentary on the Gospel according to St. Matthew*. Grand Rapids: Eerdmans, 1956.

Porter, Stanley E. *Idioms of the Greek New Testament*. Sheffield: Sheffield Academic Press, 1992.

Pregeant, Russell. *Matthew*. Chalice Commentaries. St. Louis: Chalice, 2004.

Przybylski, Benno. *Righteousness in Matthew and His World of Thought*. Cambridge: Cambridge University Press, 1980.

Rhoads, David, and Donald Michie. *Mark as Story: An Introduction to the Narrative of a Gospel*. Philadelphia: Fortress, 1982.

Ridderbos. Herman N. *Matthew*. Bible Student's Commentary. Grand Rapids: Zondervan, 1987.

Riesner, Rainer. "Der Afbau der Reden im Matthäus-Evangelium." *Theologische Beiträge* 9 (1978): 177 – 78.

Safrai, S., and M. Stern, eds. *The Jewish People in the First Century*. 2 vols. Philadelphia: Fortress, 1976.

Saldarini, Anthony. *Matthew's Christian-Jewish Community*. Chicago: University of Chicago Press, 1994.

Sanders, E. P. *Jesus and Judaism*. Philadelphia: Fortress, 1985.

Schlatter, Adolf. *Der Evangelist Matthäus*. Stuttgart: Calwer, 1929.

Schnabel, Eckhard J. *Early Christian Mission*. 2 vols. Downers Grove, IL: IVP, 2004.

Schnackenburg, Rudolf. *The Gospel of Matthew*. Grand Rapids: Eerdmans, 2002.

Schweizer, Eduard. *The Good News according to Matthew*. Translated by David E. Green. Atlanta: John Knox, 1975.

———. "Matthew's Church." Pages 129 – 55 in *The Interpretation of Matthew*. Edited by G. Stanton. Philadelphia: Fortress, 1983.

Scott, Bernard B. *Hear Then the Parable: A Commentary on the Parables of Jesus*. Minneapolis: Fortress, 1989.

Senior, Donald P. *Matthew*. Abingdon New Testament Commentaries. Nashville: Abingdon, 1998.

———. *The Passion Narrative according to Matthew: A Redactional Study*. Leuven: Leuven University Press, 1982.

Shuler, P. L. *A Genre for the Gospels: The Biographical Character of Matthew*. Philadelphia: Fortress, 1982.

Sim, David C. *The Gospel of Matthew and Christian Judaism: The History and Social Setting of the Matthean Community*. Edinburgh: T&T Clark, 1998.

Soares-Prabhu, George M. *The Formula Quotations in the Infancy Narrative of Matthew*. Rome: Biblical Institute Press, 1976.

Stanton, Graham. *A Gospel for a New People: Studies in Matthew*. Edinburgh: T&T Clark, 1992.

Stein, Robert H. *An Introduction to the Parables of Jesus*. Philadelphia: Westminster, 1981.

Stendahl, Krister. *The School of St. Matthew and Its Use of the Old Testament*. Philadelphia: Fortress, 1968.

Strack, H. L., and P. Billerbeck. *Kommentar zum Neuen Testament aus Talmud und Midrash*. 6 vols. Munich: C. H. Beck, 1922 – 1961.

Strecker, Georg. *The Sermon on the Mount: An Exegetical Commentary*. Translated by O. C. Dean Jr. Nashville: Abingdon, 1988 (orig. 1985).

Suggs, M. J. *Wisdom, Christology, and Law in Matthew's Gospel*. Cambridge, MA: Harvard University Press, 1970.

Tannehill, Robert C. *The Sword of His Mouth*. Society for New Testament Studies Supplement 1. Philadelphia: Fortress, 1975.

Tasker, R. V. G. *The Gospel according to St. Matthew*. Tyndale New Testament Commentary. Grand Rapids: Eerdmans, 1961.

Taylor, Vincent. *The Formation of the Gospel Tradition*. London: Macmillan, 1935.

Theissen, Gerd. *The Gospels in Context: Social and Political History in the Synoptic Tradition*. Translated by L. M. Maloney. Minneapolis: Fortress, 1991.

———. *The Miracle Stories of the Early Christian Tradition*. Edinburgh: T&T Clark, 1983.

Theissen, Gerd, and Annette Merz, *The Historical Jesus: A Comprehensive Guide*. Minneapolis, Fortress, 1997.

Thielmann, Frank. *Theology of the New Testament: A Canonical and Synthetic Approach*. Grand Rapids: Zondervan, 2005.

Thompson, William G. *Matthew's Advice to a Divided Community: Matt 17, 22 – 18, 35*. Analecta Biblica 44. Rome: Pontifical Biblical Institute, 1970.

Tolbert, Mary Ann. *Perspectives on the Parables: An Approach to Multiple Interpretations*. Philadelphia: Fortress, 1979.

Tournay, R. J. "Ne nous laisse pas entrer en tentation." *La nouvelle revue théologique* 120 (1998): 440 – 43.

Trotter, Andrew H. "Understanding and Stumbling: A Study of the Disciples' Understanding of Jesus and His Teaching in the Gospel of Matthew." PhD diss., Cambridge University, 1986.

Turner, David L. "The Gospel of Matthew." Cornerstone Biblical Commentary. Carol Stream, IL: Tyndale, 2006.

Twelftree, Graham H. *Jesus the Miracle Worker*. Downers Grove, IL: IVP, 1999.

Vanhoozer, Kevin J. *Is There a Meaning in This Text?: The Bible, the Reader, and the Morality of Literary Knowledge*. Grand Rapids: Zondervan, 1998.

Verseput, Donald J. "The Faith of the Reader and the Narrative of Matthew 13:53 – 16:20." *Journal for the Study of the New Testament* 46 (1992): 3 – 24.

———. *The Rejection of the Humble Messianic King: A Study of Matthew 11 – 12*. Europäische Hochschulschriften 23. Frankfurt: Peter Lang, 1986.

Viviano, Benedict T. "Social World and Community Leadership: The Case of Matthew 23:1 – 12, 34." *Journal for the Study of the New Testament* 39 (1990): 3 – 21.

Wang, Emily. "The Humbleness Motif in the Gospel of Matthew." PhD diss., Trinity Evangelical Divinity School, 2005.

Warfield, Benjamin B. *Selected Shorter Writings*. Nutley, NJ: Presbyterian & Reformed, 1970.

Weaver, Dorothy J. *Matthew's Missionary Discourse: A Literary Critical Analysis*. Journal for the Study of the New Testament Supplement Series 38. Sheffield: JSOT Press, 1990.

Wiebe, Philip H. "Jesus' Divorce Exception." *Journal of the Evangelical Theological Society* 32 (1989): 327 – 33.

Wilkens, W. "Die Versuchung Jesus nach Matthäus." *New Testament Studies* 28 (1982): 481 – 83.

Wilkins, Michael J. *The Concept of Disciple in Matthew's Gospel as Reflected in the Use of the Term Mathētēs*. Novum Testamentum Supplements. Leiden: Brill, 1988.

———. *Discipleship in the Ancient World and in Matthew's Gospel*. Grand Rapids: Baker, 1995.

———. *Matthew*. NIV Application Commentary. Grand Rapids: Zondervan, 2004.

Williams, Matthew C. *Two Gospels from One: A Comprehensive New Analysis of the Synoptic Gospels*. Grand Rapids: Kregel, 2006.

Willis, Wendell L., ed. *The Kingdom of God in Twentieth-Century Interpretation*. Peabody, MA: Hendrickson, 1987.

Winterhalter, Roger, and George W. Fisk. *Jesus' Parables: Finding Our God Within*. New York: Paulist, 1993.

Witherington, Ben III. *The Christology of Jesus*. Minneapolis: Augsburg/Fortress, 1990.

———. *Jesus the Sage: The Pilgrimage of Wisdom*. Minneapolis: Fortress, 1994.

———. *Matthew*. Smith & Helwys Bible Commentary. Macon, GA: Smith & Helwys, 2006.

Wrede, Wilhelm. *The Messianic Secret*. Translated by J. C. G. Greig. Cambridge: James Clarke & Company, 1971.

Wright, N. T. *Jesus and the Victory of God*. Christian Origins and the Question of God 2. Minneapolis: Fortress, 1996.

———. *The New Testament and the People of God*. Christian Origins and the Question of God 1. Minneapolis: Fortress, 1992.

Yang, Yong-Eui. *Jesus and the Sabbath in Matthew's Gospel*. Journal for the Study of the New Testament Supplement Series 138. Sheffield: Sheffield Academic Press, 1997.

Young, Edward J. *The Book of Isaiah*. Vol. 1. New International Commentary on the Old Testament. Grand Rapids: Eerdmans, 1965.

Zahn, Theodor. *Introduction to the New Testament*. 3 vols. Edinburgh: T&T Clark, 1909.

Zerwick, Maximilian. *Biblical Greek*. Rome: Pontifical Biblical Institute, 1963.

Matthew 1:1 – 17

CHAPTER 1

Literary Context

Matthew begins with genealogical proof that Jesus is indeed the Davidic Messiah and that God has sovereignly controlled his ancestry. This proves that Jesus is the son of Abraham and of David and sets the tone for the rest of the book. As Bruner says, Matthew "turns dull genealogy into evangelism and a birth story into a lexicon for the names of God."[1]

- **I. Jesus' Origin and Preparation for Ministry (1:1 – 4:11)**
  - **A. The Birth and Infancy of Jesus (1:1 – 2:23)**
    - ➦ **1. The Genealogy of Jesus the Messiah (1:1 – 17)**
    - 2. The Virginal Conception (1:18 – 25)
    - 3. The Visit of the Magi (2:1 – 12)

Main Idea

Matthew shows that Jesus is the expected Davidic Messiah, whose pedigree demonstrates his claim. At the same time he shows that the lineage of Jesus goes beyond Jewish heritage to embrace the Gentiles as well, thereby preparing for his theme of universal mission.

1. F. Dale Bruner, *The Christbook: A Historical/Theological Commentary, Matthew 1 – 12* (Waco, TX: Word, 1987), 1.

Translation

Matthew 1:1-17

1a	Introduction	**This is a record of the genealogy of Jesus**
b	Identification #1	[1] the Messiah
c	Identification #2	[2] the son of David
d	Identification #3	[3] the son of Abraham.
2a	Series #1	**Abraham was the father of Isaac**
b		**Isaac the father of Jacob**
c		**Jacob the father of Judah and his brothers**
3a		**Judah the father of Perez and Zerah,**
b	Description	whose mother was Tamar
c		**Perez the father of Hezron**
d		**Hezron the father of Ram**
4a		**Ram the father of Amminadab**
b		**Amminadab the father of Nahshon**
c		**Nahshon the father of Salmon**
5a		**Salmon the father of Boaz,**
b	Description	whose mother was Rahab
c		**Boaz the father of Obed,**
d	Description	whose mother was Ruth
e		**Obed the father of** Jesse
6a		and **Jesse the father of King David.**
b	Series #2	**David was the father of Solomon,**
c	Description	whose mother was the wife of Uriah
7a		**Solomon the father of Rehoboam**
b		**Rehoboam the father of Abijah**
c		**Abijah the father of Asa**
8a		**Asa the father of Jehoshaphat**
b		**Jehoshaphat the father of Jehoram**
c		**Jehoram the father of Uzziah**
9a		**Uzziah the father of Jotham**
b		**Jotham the father of Ahaz**
c		**Ahaz the father of Hezekiah**
10a		**Hezekiah the father of Manasseh**
b		**Manasseh the father of Amon**
c		**Amon the father of Josiah**
11a		and **Josiah was the father of Jeconiah and his brothers**
b	Setting (Temporal)	at the time of the exile to Babylon.
12a	Setting (Temporal)	After the exile to Babylon
b	Series #3	**Jeconiah was the father of Shealitiel**
c		**Shealitiel the father of Zerubbabel**
13a		**Zerubbabel the father of Abiud**
b		**Abiud the father of Eliakim**
c		**Eliakim the father of Azor**

14a		**Azor the father of Zadok**
b		**Zadok the father of Akim**
c		**Akim the father of Eliud**
15a		**Eliud the father of Eleazar**
b		**Eleazar the father of Matthan**
c		**Matthan the father of Jacob**
16a		and **Jacob the father of Joseph,**
b	Identification	the husband of Mary,
c		from whom is born Jesus
d	Identification	who is called the Christ.
17a	Summary	So **there were fourteen generations between Abraham and David**
b		fourteen between David and the Babylonian exile and
c		fourteen between the exile and the Messiah.

Structure and Literary Form

These verses parallel Luke 3:23 – 38, but the two probably do not have a common source (Q), for they go in two directions with quite different names from David to Christ. There were two types of genealogies: ascending (cf. Luke), moving from the birth of the individual to the ancestors, containing common names not found elsewhere; and descending (cf. Matthew), moving from the ancestors to the person; the latter type normally had more elaboration, as is the case with Matthew, with famous biblical ancestors named. Matthew shows the direct royal line only from Abraham up to Christ, whereas Luke goes through David's son Nathan (Matthew has Solomon) down through Abraham to Adam in order to stress Jesus as "Son of God" (cf. Luke 3:22, 38; 4:3).

It has often been argued that Matthew provides Joseph's line and Luke gives Mary's; but this is doubtful because Matthew, not Luke, stresses the women; and Luke 3:23 begins with Joseph, not Mary. Both center on Joseph's line, with Matthew showing the legal throne succession and Luke the actual line. The names in the two lists are the same from Abraham to David but diverge greatly from David to Joseph, again because Matthew centers on the royal line and Luke on the common line.[2]

Matthew's list consists of a heading (1:1) followed by three sections of fourteen names each (cf. 1:17), although in reality only the second set has fourteen. The three are:

vv. 2 – 6a: Abraham to David — thirteen names

2. See the excellent chart in Douglas S. Huffman, "Genealogy," *DJG*, 257. For a good discussion of the two genealogies that harmonizes them and shows the historicity of both, see Darrell Bock, *Luke 1:1–9:50* (BECNT; Grand Rapids: Baker, 1994), 918 – 23.

vv. 6b – 11: David to the exile — fourteen names
vv. 12 – 16: the exile to Christ — thirteen names

There are fourteen names in the first series if David is counted. The problem is that there are only thirteen generations (periods between names). This is resolved by simply assuming that Matthew is counting the generation leading to Abraham. In the second series, there are fourteen names only if David is not counted, so there are fourteen full generations (periods between names). In the third series, there are fourteen names if you count Christ, so like the first series, you have to count the generation leading up to Jeconiah as the first. The importance of this is seen in v. 17, which claims fourteen names for each list.

The question is the meaning of the number fourteen. A couple of interesting theories posit that Matthew measures fourteen generations (of thirty-five years each = 490 years) from the captivity to Jesus, thus reenacting Daniel's seventy weeks of years (= 490 years, cf. Dan 9:24 – 27) or that the 3 x 14 = 6 x 7, with Jesus beginning the seventh seven or "the dawn of the eternal Sabbath."[3] However, the most likely explanation for a Jewish gospel like Matthew's finds the key in *gematria*, stemming from the practice of using letters of the alphabet for numbers. Thus every name or phrase also had a numerical significance by adding up the letters. For our purposes the name David (*dwd* in Hebrew [vowels were introduced later]) added up to fourteen ($d = 4$, $w = 6$, so $4 + 6 + 4 = 14$). The only drawback is that Matthew is writing in Greek, not Hebrew,[4] but since this is meant mainly for Christian Jews, the approach is still valid. Matthew is thus suggesting by this arrangement of the genealogy that Jesus is the Son of David or the royal Messiah.

Exegetical Outline

I. The Birth and Infancy of Jesus (1:1 – 2:23)

➦ **A. The Genealogy of Jesus (1:1 – 17)**

1. The heading (1:1)

2. The genealogy (1:2 – 16)

a. From Abraham to David (vv. 2 – 6a)

b. From David to the exile (vv. 6b – 11)

c. From the exile to Jesus the Christ (vv. 12 – 16)

3. Summary (1:17)

3. See Davies and Allison, *Matthew*, 1:161 – 62. They discuss eight views of this arrangement.

4. So Hagner, *Matthew 1 – 13*, 7. France, *Gospel of Matthew*, 31 – 32, finds *gematria* doubtful because there is no explcit indication of such in the text. He believes the fourteen is best seen as twice seven, thus making six sevens here and hinting that a seventh seven is coming, marking the end of days. Yet this seems far more complex than the *gematria*, and such is often suggested in the NT without comments indicating such (e.g., 666 in Rev 13:18).

Explanation of the Text

Genealogies had many uses in the ancient world. Since society was organized as a whole around kinship patterns, lists that describe actual kinship relationships were central as "the basis for regulating social interaction, marriage, and inheritance," with both horizontal (those on the same genealogical level considered social equals) and vertical (their status in society determined by the level of ancestry they occupy).[5] The genealogy here is a linear type used by rulers to justify their power, rank, and status. At the same time it is used to state political relationships between families by noting a common ancestor (Abraham, the father of the nation) and at the same time the three groups of fourteen (*gematria* for "David," see above) showing the special status of the ruler (the royal Messiah descending from David).[6]

These verses also function as the prologue for Matthew's gospel, and the purpose of the prologue in every gospel (e.g., Mark 1:1 – 15; John 1:1 – 18) is to tell the reader who this Jesus really is; in the rest of the book we then see the participants (the leaders, the crowds, the disciples, and the demons) wrestling with these truths. The genealogy sets the tone for the book but especially for the birth of Jesus in the next scene, telling us that it is no ordinary event but the birth of the expected Messiah (1:18 – 25), the Anointed One in the line of ancestry from Abraham and David. Thus it is no wonder that the Magi make a state visit to this King of kings and that they bear royal gifts (2:1 – 12); it is also natural that Herod is so threatened by this God-sent Messiah that he tries to kill him before his reign can replace Herod's (2:13 – 23). Yet in it all God is sovereign and supernaturally intervenes in world history to protect his Chosen One (2:12, 13 – 15, 22). This basic theme (to be seen again in the resurrection narratives) will dominate the opening and closing scenes of Matthew's gospel.

1:1 This is a record of the genealogy (Βίβλος γενέσεως). This can be translated in different ways[7] depending on whether it refers to the whole book ("record of the history," so Zahn, Davies and Allison, Morris), to the first unit of the book, namely 1:1 – 4:16 ("record of the origins," so Kingsbury), to the first two chapters ("record of the birth," so Carson, Blomberg),[8] or to this section itself ("record of the genealogy," so Brown, Gundry, Hagner, Nolland).[9] A great deal can be said for a reference to the birth narratives (chs. 1 – 2) as a whole, since *genesis* is used in 1:18 for the conception of Jesus; but it is probably best to restrict it to the genealogy itself (still, there is double meaning, with "genealogy" primary here but still connoting the "origin" as well).

Vv. 1 and 17 frame the genealogy and center on the three names in a chiastic arrangement (Christ/David/Abraham in v. 1; Abraham/David/Christ in v. 17; see Hagner, 5). The phrase in 1:1a is taken from Gen 2:4; 5:1 (cf. Gen 6:1; 10:1; 11:10, 27 etc.), where it introduces genealogies or historical narrative and hints here that Jesus fulfills

5. Robert R. Wilson, "Genealogy, Genealogies," *ABD*, 2:931. See also J. J. McDermott, "Multipurpose Genealogies," *TBT* 35 (1997): 382 – 86.

6. See Wilson, "Genealogy, Genealogies," 2:931. John Nolland, *The Gospel of Matthew: A Commentary on the Greek Text* (NIGTC; Grand Rapids: Eerdmans, 2005), 70, believes Matthew builds the genealogy on a core of ten generations in Ruth 4:18 – 22 plus sixteen names derived from 1 Chr 3:10 – 19.

7. The one thing all have in common is considering *geneseōs* to be an objective genitive, i.e., the object of the verbal idea expressed in the governing noun (see BDF §163; Wallace, 116 – 19), "this records the genealogy."

8. Craig Blomberg, *Matthew*, 52.

9. John Nolland, "What Kind of Genesis Do We Have in Matt 1.1?" *NTS* 42 (1996): 463 – 71.

these events and brings a new beginning or new creation.[10]

1:1 ... of Jesus the Messiah (Ἰησοῦ Χριστοῦ). Matthew actually has "of Jesus Christ" (without the article, which often is a proper name rather than a title). However, Matthew uses *Christos* only sixteen times ("Jesus" appears 150 times), usually with titular force (except possibly 1:18, though as continuing this verse the force may be there), and here its coupling with "Son of David" demands a messianic thrust.[11]

The "Messiah," or "Anointed One," was the subject of great speculation in the first century. Evans shows that many later ideas were not found prior to AD 70, such as that the Messiah would perform miracles, be preexistent, or suffer death. The Jews expected a victorious, conquering Messiah, with a wide variety of images, such as an anointed figure (*1 En.* 48:10, 52:4; *4 Ezra* 7:28 – 9; CD 12:23 – 13:1, 14:19), a prince (CD 7:19 – 20; 1QM 3:16; *Sib. Or.* 3:460), a branch of David (4Q161 frags. 7 – 10 iii 22; 4Q1174 frags. 1 – 3 i 11), the scepter (1QSb 5:27 – 8, 4Q 161 frags. 2 – 6 ii 17), Son of God (4Q246 1:9, 2:1), and Son of Man (*1 En.* 46:11 – 5, 52:4, 62:1 – 15; *4 Ezra* 13:3). Of special interest are the priestly and royal figures of Qumran (1QS 9:11; CD 12:23 – 13:1, 14:19, 19:10 – 11, 20:1).[12] However, the one thing they all had in common was that he would liberate Israel from her enemies.[13]

1:1 ... the son of David (υἱοῦ Δαυίδ). This is certainly a messianic title (though the anarthrous form stresses more the theological [qualitative] aspect than the titular), developing during the exilic period to explain how the promise to David of an eternal throne would be kept (2 Sam 7:10 – 16; cf. Ps 89:3 – 4; 132:11 – 12; Isa 9:7) and how God would send a "righteous Branch" to remove foreign oppressors from the land and return it to Israel (Jer 23:5 – 8; Ezek 17:22; 37:21 – 28). This expectation continued in the intertestamental period (*Pss Sol* 17 – 18; 1QM 11:1 – 18; 4QFlor 1:11 – 14). Jesus' disciples held that view, as seen in James and John wanting the seats of power in Jesus' kingdom (Matt 20:21) and Peter cutting the ear off the high priest's slave (John 18:10 – 11; cf. Acts 1:6). In Matthew, however, the emphasis is obviously not on destroying Israel's enemies but on the fulfillment of prophecy. The deliverance Jesus offers is not political but spiritual (and physical via healing, cf. 9:27; 15:22; 20:31). Matthew mentions David seventeen times, five times in this section alone; and the title occurs ten times, six of which are specific to Matthew. Jesus' fulfilling Davidic expectations is critical to this gospel.

1:1 ... the son of Abraham (υἱοῦ Ἀβραάμ). This is not a messianic title here, though in some Jewish circles it may have been (cf. *T. Levi* 8:15). First, it means Jesus is a true Israelite who can trace his ancestry back to Abraham. Yet also he fulfills the promise of Abraham, who was given the great covenant, and in him "all peoples on earth will be blessed" (Gen 12:3; 15:5; 18:18; 22:18).[14] The two great covenants, that of Abraham and of David, come to full expression in Jesus, and the purpose of this genealogy is to make this evident. Matthew

10. See R. T. France, *Matthew* (TNTC; Grand Rapids: Eerdmans, 1985), 73.

11. Stanley Hauerwas, *Matthew* (BTCB; Grand Rapids: Baker, 2006), 27, asks why this is out of chronological order, with "son of David" before "son of Abraham." He believes Matthew is describing one "born a king, yet a king to be sacrificed." The royal Messiah (David) was to "end up on the cross" (Abraham, who was asked to sacrifice his son).

12. Craig A. Evans, "Messianism," in *Dictionary of New Testament Backgrounds*, ed. C. A. Evans and S. E. Porter (Downers Grove, IL: IVP, 2000), 698 – 707.

13. So Blomberg, *Matthew*, 52, from R. A. Horsley, *The Liberation of Christmas* (New York: Crossroad, 1989).

14. See Joachim Gnilka, *Das Matthäusevangelium* (2 vols.; HTKNT; Freiburg: Herder, 1986, 1988), 1:7, who sees in this the fulfillment of the Abrahamic blessing to the nations.

will emphasize the Abraham theme often (3:9; 8:11; 22:32, cf. 21:33 – 44; 25:31 – 46), and he is likely presenting Jesus as the one who fulfills the Abrahamic promise to bring God's blessing to the nations.

1:2 Abraham was the father of Isaac, Isaac the father of Jacob (Ἀβραὰμ ἐγέννησεν τὸν Ἰσαάκ, Ἰσαὰκ δὲ ἐγέννησεν τὸν Ἰακώβ). "Was the father of" (ἐγέννησεν, lit., "gave birth to") here refers to the father's role in the birth process for the purpose of the genealogy. Matthew begins with Abraham because he is the father of the nation, and through him God elected his covenant people.

1:2 Jacob the father of Judah and his brothers (Ἰακὼβ δὲ ἐγέννησεν τὸν Ἰούδαν καὶ τοὺς ἀδελφοὺς αὐτοῦ). Judah is singled out from the patriarchs because the royal line ascends through him, and the "scepter" and "ruler's staff" belonged to him (Gen 49:10; cf. Heb 7:14; Rev 5:5). The added "and his brothers" (nowhere else in the genealogy) points to the centrality of the twelve tribes as the covenant people. Jesus' choice of twelve disciples (see below) fulfills this symbolism as the new covenant people.[15] Christ has come to bring deliverance to all Israel.

1:3 Judah the father of Perez and Zerah (Ἰούδας δὲ ἐγέννησεν τὸν Φάρες καὶ τὸν Ζάρα). Matthew mentions both Perez and Zerah because they were twins (Gen 38:27 – 30). The book of Ruth ends with the genealogy of Perez to David (Ruth 4:18 – 22), showing that a major purpose of that book was to trace the Davidic line and to show that Ruth through her faithful devotion was a worthy ancestress to David.

1:3 ... whose mother was Tamar (ἐκ τῆς Θαμάρ). ἐκ (lit., "out of") connotes origin, and with a woman this preposition means "whose mother was." Matthew mentions four women in the list — Tamar, Rahab (v. 5a), Ruth (v. 5b), and the wife of Uriah (Bathsheba, v. 6). This is unusual in Jewish genealogies,[16] and several explanations are possible. (1) The emphasis could be on the illegitimacy and sexual sin connected with them (Tamar's incest with her father-in-law Judah, Rahab's prostitution, Ruth a Moabitess who may have seduced Boaz, and Bathsheba's adultery with David); if so, the message is Christ's power to forgive and perhaps also on their foreshadowing the scandal of Mary's illegitimate pregnancy and shame before outsiders (showing how God overcomes such).[17]

(2) All four women were foreigners and Gentiles (Tamar the Canaanite or from Aram,[18] Rahab from Jericho, Ruth the Moabitess, and Bathsheba the wife of a Hittite). This along with the appearance of the Magi stresses at the outset the Gentile mission toward which Matthew is building (28:18 – 20) and shows that all humanity is involved in the birth of the Messiah.[19]

(3) All four are present as a result of divine providence; God works his will in the most

15. Gundry, *Matthew*, 14, 17, believes Matthew wants to stress the people of God as a "brotherhood," prefiguring the church as the family of God.

16. Though see the genealogies of Gen 11:27 – 29; 22:20 – 24; 35:22 – 26; 1 Chr 2:18 – 20 for exceptions.

17. First suggested by Jerome; see Blomberg, *Matthew*, 55 – 56, and his "The Liberation of Illegitimacy: Women and Rulers in Matthew 1 – 2," *BTB* (1991): 145 – 50, as well as Floyd V. Filson, *The Gospel according to St. Matthew* (BNTC; 2nd ed.; London: Adam & Charles Black, 1971), 52 – 53.

18. See Nolland, *Matthew*, 74; Richard Bauckham, "Tamar's Ancestry and Rahab's Marriage: Two Problems in the Matthean Genealogy," *NovT* 37 (1995): 313 – 29.

19. Supported by Luther; see Hauerwas, *Matthew*, 32; Eduard Schweizer, *The Good News according to Matthew* (trans. David E. Green; Atlanta: John Knox, 1975), 24 – 25, though he adds that the choice of minor women shows "the strange righteousness of God, which does not choose what is great in the eyes of men."

unlikely ways, and that is exactly what has led to the birth of Jesus.[20]

None of the these explanations is without objection (there is little concrete evidence for Ruth's sexual sin or for the foreign birth of Tamar or Bathsheba), but a growing number of scholars consider all viable.[21] Putting them together, God in his providence saw fit to include women who were foreigners and sinners in the royal lineage of Jesus so as to show that he is God not only of righteous Jews but of all humanity and that he has come to bring salvation to the whole world of humanity. Moreover, they foreshadow Mary and provide a rationale for God's choice of an unwed mother to bear the Messiah.[22]

1:3 Perez the father of Hezron, Hezron the father of Ram (Φάρες δὲ ἐγέννησεν τὸν Ἑσρώμ, Ἑσρὼμ δὲ ἐγέννησεν τὸν Ἀράμ). Hezron, grandson of Judah by Tamar (Gen 38:29), was part of the seventy who migrated with Jacob to Egypt (46:12) and lent his name to the Hezronites, an important clan in southern Judea (Num 26:6), from which came David's family through his son Ram (1 Chr 2:9 – 15; cf. Ruth 4:18 – 19).

1:4 Ram the father of Amminadab, Amminadab the father of Nahshon, Nahshon the father of Salmon (Ἀρὰμ δὲ ἐγέννησεν τὸν Ἀμιναδάβ, Ἀμιναδὰβ δὲ ἐγέννησεν τὸν Ναασσών, Ναασσὼν δὲ ἐγέννησεν τὸν Σαλμών). Approximately four hundred years are covered from Perez to Amminadab, demanding the omission of several names from the list.[23] This follows the genealogical lists in 1 Chr 2:10 – 11; Ruth 4:19 – 20. Amminadab not only fathered Nahshon, chief of the tribe of Judah in the wilderness (Num 2:3), but also Elishebah, the wife of Aaron (Exod 6:23). Nahshon helped conduct the census in Num 1:7 and led Judah to its place at the head of the tribes at the departure from Mount Sinai (Num 10:14). Nothing is said of Salmon apart from his name in genealogies. Mainly he is the father of Boaz (next verse).

1:5 Salmon the father of Boaz, whose mother was Rahab (Σαλμὼν δὲ ἐγέννησεν τὸν Βόες ἐκ τῆς Ῥαχάβ). Rahab was the prostitute who saved the spies at Jericho by hiding them in her house (Josh 2; 6), and this is almost certainly the same Rahab.[24] The problem is that she lived two hundred years earlier, but as in vv. 3 – 4 there are likely several generations omitted from the list. It means she is the ancestress of Boaz. Later Rahab was considered a proselyte who married Joshua and was the ancestress of Jeremiah and Ezekiel (*b. Meg.* 14b, 15a). In the NT she is seen as a woman of faith in Heb 11:31 and an example of faith leading to works in Jas 2:25.

1:5 Boaz the father of Obed, whose mother was Ruth (Βόες δὲ ἐγέννησεν τὸν Ἰωβὴδ ἐκ τῆς Ῥούθ). Boaz was the wealthy landowner who rescued Ruth from poverty and became her "kinsman-redeemer" by purchasing the property from Naomi (Ruth 4:3) and marrying Ruth, thereby "maintaining the name" of her deceased husband Mahlon (Ruth 4:10). He was an example of covenant faithfulness and a worthy progenitor of David (seventh in the genealogical list of Ruth

20. See David Hill, *The Gospel of Matthew* (NCBC; Greenwood, SC: Attic, 1972), 74; Raymond E. Brown, *The Birth of the Messiah: A Commentary on the Infancy Narratives in the Gospels of Matthew and Luke* (2nd ed.; New York: Doubleday, 1993), 73 – 74; Hagner, *Matthew 1 – 13*, 10 – 11.

21. So Carson, "Matthew," 8:66; Bruner, *Christbook*, 5 – 7; Davies and Allison, *Matthew*, 170 – 72; Leon Morris, *The Gospel according to Matthew* (Grand Rapids: Eerdmans, 1992), 23.

22. See also Brown, *Birth of the Messiah*, 69 – 71.

23. Carson, "Matthew," 65. He notes that "was the father of" does not demand immediate relationship but can cover several generations, as in "was the ancestor of" or "became the progenitor of."

24. See Raymond E. Brown, "*Rachab* in Matt 1,5 Probably Is Rahab of Jericho," *Bib* 63 (1982): 79 – 80.

4:18 – 22). Obed was the son given to the couple to reward their faithfulness and was thereby the grandfather of David.

1:5 – 6 Obed the father of Jesse, and Jesse the father of King David (Ἰωβὴδ δὲ ἐγέννησεν τὸν Ἰεσσαί, Ἰεσσαὶ δὲ ἐγέννησεν τὸν Δαυὶδ τὸν βασιλέα). Jesse lived in Bethlehem and had eight sons, with David the youngest (1 Sam 16:1 – 13). His primary role in the narrative of David's life was to send David to Saul and his brothers (16:14 – 23; 17:12 – 18). Still, his name is used in a messianic context in "a shoot will come up from the stump of Jesse" and "the root of Jesse will stand" in Isa 11:1, 10. "King David" brings out a major purpose of the list in Matthew, to trace the royal line of Jesus. This is one of the major differences with the genealogical list in Luke 3:23 – 31. Matthew moves from Abraham to Christ and traces the succession of the royal throne while Luke moves from Christ clear down to Adam and traces his common roots.[25] This ends the first list of fourteen names in Matthew's genealogy.

1:6 David was the father of Solomon, whose mother was the wife of Uriah (Δαυὶδ δὲ ἐγέννησεν τὸν Σολομῶνα ἐκ τῆς τοῦ Οὐρίου). It is interesting that Bathsheba is not named but called simply "the wife of Uriah." This contrasts David's adulterous liaison over against Uriah, the rightful husband, and probably also calls attention to Uriah the Hittite, so as to highlight the presence of Gentiles in Jesus' origins.

1:7 Solomon the father of Rehoboam (Σολομὼν δὲ ἐγέννησεν τὸν Ῥοβοάμ). The list in vv. 7 – 10 is drawn from 1 Chr 3:10 – 14. These verses especially demonstrate God's providential leading, for many of the kings mentioned were evil (Rehoboam, Abijah, Joram), yet they were part of the messianic line. God is completely sovereign, yet people are responsible for their choices. These kings came to evil ends due to their sin, but God used them to produce the messianic line.

1:7 Rehoboam the father of Abijah (Ῥοβοὰμ δὲ ἐγέννησεν τὸν Ἀβιά). Rehoboam inherited his father Solomon's love of luxury and an extensive harem (he had eighteen wives and sixty concubines, 2 Chr 11:18 – 23). To support his lavish lifestyle he overtaxed the people, so that the northern ten tribes revolted and forced the divided monarchy.

1:7 Abijah the father of Asa (Ἀβιὰ δὲ ἐγέννησεν τὸν Ἀσάφ). Rehoboam's son Abijah began well but went the way of his father and reigned only three years (negative in 1 Kgs 15:1 – 8, positive in 2 Chr 12:16 – 14:1). Asa,[26] however, was a good king who removed the altars and high places and brought the nation back to God, thus ensuring peace for the first thirty-five years of his reign (2 Chr 14 – 15).

1:8 Asa the father of Jehoshaphat (Ἀσὰφ δὲ ἐγέννησεν τὸν Ἰωσαφάτ). These followed the pattern established. Jehoshaphat was known for godliness like his father and brought further reform and even sent out priests to teach the people the ways of the Lord. Even the surrounding nations began to fear the Lord (2 Chr 17; 19 – 20).

25. The two lists are similar from Abraham to David but diverge greatly after that. The other option (Luther, Bengel et al.) is to say that Luke traces Mary's descent while Matthew traces Joseph's, but Luke 3:23 clearly begins with Joseph, not Mary, so that is unlikely.

26. An interesting phenomenon occurs in vv. 7, 10 where the Greek has Ἀσάφ for "Asa" and Ἀμώς for "Amon." Some consider these errors, but it is more likely that they are deliberate and introduce a wisdom (Asaph wrote several of the psalms [e.g., Ps 50; 73 – 83] and prophetic (Amos the eighth-century prophet) theme into the genealogy, so Gundry, *Matthew*, 15; Davies and Allison, *Matthew*, 1: 175, 177; contra Hagner, *Matthew 1 – 13*, 11.

1:8 Jehoshaphat the father of Jehoram (Ἰωσαφὰτ δὲ ἐγέννησεν τὸν Ἰωράμ). Jehoram (*Joram* in the Greek) was evil, probably because his father foolishly allied with Ahab and married his son to Athaliah, daughter of Ahab and Jezebel. Jehoram murdered his brothers to eliminate rivals and had a terrible reign (2 Chr 21).

1:8 Jehoram the father of Uzziah (Ἰωρὰμ δὲ ἐγέννησεν τὸν Ὀζίαν). Three kings are omitted between Jehoram and Uzziah (Ahaziah, Jehoash, Amaziah). All three were evil kings, and Matthew probably felt they were unnecessary (several evil kings are recorded) and dropped them to make his list fourteen. Uzziah began well and won many victories, strengthening the kingdom (2 Kgs 14; 2 Chr 26). But he fell into sin and pride late in life and died a leper.

1:9 Uzziah the father of Jotham (Ὀζίας δὲ ἐγέννησεν τὸν Ἰωαθάμ). These also stem from 1 Chr 3 (see on v. 7). Jotham, like Hezekiah, was a good king. A ruler during the time of Isaiah, Hosea, and Micah, Jotham was victorious over the Ammonites and did much good, though he failed to remove the high places (2 Kgs 15:32 – 38).

1:9 Jotham the father of Ahaz (Ἰωαθὰμ δὲ ἐγέννησεν τὸν Ἀχάζ). In contrast with Jotham, Ahaz refused to listen to Isaiah and brought unbelief into the land, even sacrificing children to the "sacred" fires (2 Chr 28:3). During his significant reign Judah became a vassal of Assyria and lost once for all its freedom (2 Kgs 16).

1:9 Ahaz the father of Hezekiah (Ἀχὰζ δὲ ἐγέννησεν τὸν Ἑζεκίαν). Hezekiah is one of the well-known kings, cleansing the temple and destroying the high places (2 Chr 30). God told him that he was going to die, but Hezekiah prayed for more time and God granted him fifteen more years. Despite a warning from God, however, he made a secret pact with Babylon, leading to such heavy tribute from Assyria that he even had to remove the gold plates from the temple doors and pillars (2 Kgs 20).

1:10 Hezekiah the father of Manasseh (Ἑζεκίας δὲ ἐγέννησεν τὸν Μανασσῆ). Manasseh is described in 2 Kgs 21:11 – 18 as one of the most wicked kings in the history of Judah, rebuilding the altars and high places, practicing sorcery, and even sacrificing his own son in the fire. Yet in 2 Chr 33:10 – 20 he repented, removed the altars, and reinstituted temple worship.

1:10 Manasseh the father of Amon (Μανασσῆς δὲ ἐγέννησεν τὸν Ἀμώς). Manasseh's son Amon returned to the abominations and in his two-year reign returned to idol worship (2 Chr 33:21 – 25).

1:10 Amon the father of Josiah (Ἀμὼς δὲ ἐγέννησεν τὸν Ἰωσίαν). Josiah was the greatest of the reformers. Crowned while just eight years old, he brought a measure of independence to the land and removed all the idolatrous images. While renovating the temple, he rediscovered the Book of the Law and renewed the Passover celebration (2 Chr 34 – 35).

1:11 And Josiah was the father of Jeconiah and his brothers at the time of the exile to Babylon (Ἰωσίας δὲ ἐγέννησεν τὸν Ἰεχονίαν καὶ τοὺς ἀδελφοὺς αὐτοῦ ἐπὶ τῆς μετοικεσίας Βαβυλῶνος). Josiah was actually succeeded by his sons Jehoahaz (who reigned three months) and Jehoiakim (who reigned eleven years). Jehoahaz was taken captive to Egypt, and Jehoiakim was taken bound to Babylon. Matthew omits both and instead names Jehoiakim's son Jeconiah (better known as Jehoiachin, cf. 2 Kgs 24:8 – 17; 2 Chr 36:9 – 10), probably because the Babylonian exile began with him and his uncle Zedekiah (not in the royal line of Jesus), who succeeded him. His was a three-month evil reign, and during that time Nebuchadnezzar came and took all the treasures from the temple and royal palace.

The added phrase "and his brothers" probably refers to Zedekiah, who was the brother of Jehoiakim and succeeded Jehoiachin, thus leading the nation into the exile. But the text says "brothers," while 1 Chr 3:16 only mentions this one. Gundry has an interesting solution, arguing that the "brothers" are not siblings but his fellow Jews who are led away with him into captivity.[27] Either is possible. The Babylonian captivity ends the second list of fourteen names.

1:12 After the exile to Babylon (Μετὰ δὲ τὴν μετοικεσίαν Βαβυλῶνος). The final list of fourteen names begins with an emphasis on the Babylonian exile, a major break in Israelite history. The use of "exile" (μετοικεσία) may well be due to the view that divine providence was at work in the exile; God was punishing Israel for her sins to cleanse the nation (2 Chr 36:15 – 21).[28] "To Babylon" (Βαβυλῶνος) is another objective genitive (see on 1:1), meaning "after they were exiled to Babylon."

1:12 Jeconiah was the father of Shealitiel (Ἰεχονίας ἐγέννησεν τὸν Σαλαθιήλ). Shealtiel was the son of Jeconiah/Jehoiachin (1 Chr 3:17) and is mentioned only as the father of Zerubbabel (Ezra 3:2, 8; Neh 12:1). Nothing else is known about him. Shealtiel bridges the legal ancestry from before the exile until after it (cf. 1 Chr 3:17 – 18).

1:12 Shealtiel the father of Zerubbabel (Σαλαθιὴλ δὲ ἐγέννησεν τὸν Ζοροβαβέλ). Zerubbabel was the Persian-appointed governor of Jerusalem and became a messianic figure, called Yahweh's "signet ring" and "chosen" one in Hag 2:23 and both "lampstand" and "anointed" in Zech 4:2, 14.

1:13 – 15 Zerubbabel the father of Abiud, Abiud the father of Eliakim, Eliakim the father of Azor, Azor the father of Zadok, Zadok the father of Akim, Akim the father of Eliud, Eliud the father of Eleazar, Eleazar the father of Matthan, Matthan the father of Jacob (Ζοροβαβὲλ δὲ ἐγέννησεν τὸν Ἀβιούδ, Ἀβιοὺδ δὲ ἐγέννησεν τὸν Ἐλιακίμ, Ἐλιακὶμ δὲ ἐγέννησεν τὸν Ἀζώρ, Ἀζὼρ δὲ ἐγέννησεν τὸν Σαδώκ, Σαδὼκ δὲ ἐγέννησεν τὸν Ἀχίμ, Ἀχὶμ δὲ ἐγέννησεν τὸν Ἐλιούδ, Ἐλιοὺδ δὲ ἐγέννησεν τὸν Ἐλεάζαρ, Ἐλεάζαρ δὲ ἐγέννησεν τὸν Ματθάν, Ματθὰν δὲ ἐγέννησεν τὸν Ἰακώβ). These nine names are unknown to us, and Matthew probably got them from the same kind of traditional list as he used from Chronicles in constructing the list thus far. Gundry provides a conjectural solution by saying Matthew constructed it from lists in the OT,[29] but that explanation is unlikely. Gaps are indicated by the fact that these nine names cover a period of nearly five hundred years. Again the emphasis is on the royal line and divine guidance in preparing for the Davidic Messiah.

1:16 And Jacob the father of Joseph, the husband of Mary (Ἰακὼβ δὲ ἐγέννησεν τὸν Ἰωσὴφ τὸν ἄνδρα Μαρίας). While the line of descent is patriarchal (the line of Joseph), in keeping with Jewish genealogies, it is clear that the emphasis is on "the husband of Mary." The central figure is Mary, who according to 1:18 is "with child by means of the Holy Spirit." The other four women in the list (1:3, 5, 6) lead up to the main figure, the mother of the Messiah. Yet this is still the official line of Jesus from the standpoint that he is undoubtedly adopted by Joseph. Davies and Allison state, "Matthew has in mind legal, not necessarily physical, descent, that is, the transmission

27. Gundry, *Matthew*, 16 – 17.

28. See Davies and Allison, *Matthew*, 1:179. They add (p. 180) that Matthew's message may well be that the lost kingdom that ceased at the exile is being restored to Israel by the coming of the Messiah.

29. Gundry, *Matthew*, 17 – 19.

of legal heirship; and the idea of paternity on two levels — divine and human, with position in society being determined by the mother's husband."[30]

1:16 From whom is born Jesus who is called the Christ (ἐξ ἧς ἐγεννήθη Ἰησοῦς ὁ λεγόμενος Χριστός). The genealogy ends on this critical note. Mary (not Joseph) conceives and delivers the Messiah. At first glance "Messiah" (Χριστός) seems to be anarthrous, but actually it belongs with the participle and is governed by the article (ὁ) and is a messianic title. The climax of the genealogy is threefold: the coming of the Messiah, the woman who bears him, and the sovereign control of God who directs the process (seen in the divine passive "is born" [ἐγεννήθη], meaning the Holy Spirit is behind the birth).

1:17 So there were fourteen generations between Abraham and David, fourteen between David and the Babylonian exile, and fourteen between the exile and the Messiah (Πᾶσαι οὖν αἱ γενεαὶ ἀπὸ Ἀβραὰμ ἕως Δαυὶδ γενεαὶ δεκατέσσαρες, καὶ ἀπὸ Δαυὶδ ἕως τῆς μετοικεσίας Βαβυλῶνος γενεαὶ δεκατέσσαρες, καὶ ἀπὸ τῆς μετοικεσίας Βαβυλῶνος ἕως τοῦ Χριστοῦ γενεαὶ δεκατέσσαρες). Matthew summarizes the basic message of his genealogy, seen in the cryptic "fourteen generations." As already stated (see the Introduction), this is *gematria* for the name "David," so the emphasis is on Jesus as the Davidic Messiah. The son of David (1:1) has arrived, and God's kingdom is about to break into human history.

Theology in Application

The main idea is the arrival of the royal Messiah. We must realize that this is Matthew's prologue, similar to those in Mark (Mark 1:1 – 15) and John (John 1:1 – 18). In this Jewish gospel, a royal genealogy is the perfect way to begin, since genealogies indicated one's position in society. The Davidic Messiah was the subject of much longing in Jesus' day, so Matthew wants to tell his readers the major thing he is saying in his gospel, that in Jesus God's promises in the OT have come true. We will see this time and again in Matthew's gospel, especially in the early chapters. Within this there are several subthemes that stand out.

1. The Messiah Is Now Here

For the Jewish people (and the disciples during Jesus' life) that meant he would come as a conquering king. David was the great warrior-king who won great battles for his people. So when they thought of the royal Messiah, what they contemplated was the destruction of the Romans with the Jewish people as the new world rulers. Yet for Matthew this is not the main point; Jesus would first come as suffering Servant, dying for the sins of humankind (the Jews understood Isaiah 52 – 53 as referring to the nation rather than the Messiah), and would not return to defeat his enemies until his second coming (Rev 19:11 – 21).

30. Davies and Allison, *Matthew*, 1:185.

The genealogy here has both aspects in mind. The Christ has arrived, and the time of fulfillment is here. At the same time, Matthew has a great interest in the return of Christ (cf. 13:24 – 30, 36 – 43; 20:1 – 16; 22:1 – 14; 25:1 – 46). For the church today this means that we are living in the last days. Our Messiah, the divine warrior, is near, and the great victory is coming soon.

2. The Kingdom Is Here

The entire hope for the Jewish people centered on the Davidic reign. Since David's actual reign ceased, they were awaiting the coming of God's Messiah to fulfill the promise of an eternal Davidic reign (2 Sam 7:11 – 16). This is fulfilled in the presence of the kingdom that Jesus has inaugurated, and that is a major Matthean theme. "Kingdom" means simply "God reigns," and the purpose of the church today is to allow God to reign in every aspect of its life — its mission, its community, its ethics. We celebrate in every aspect of church life the reign of God, and Jesus' teaching in Matthew can be called "the ethics of the kingdom." More than anything else we are the children of the kingdom, citizens of heaven and resident aliens in our earthly home (cf. Eph 2:19; Phil 3:20; 1 Pet 1:1, 17; 2:11).

3. Divine Providence at Work

Matthew is interested in salvation history and wants to show how God is in sovereign control of world history and guides it for his own purposes.[31] This will be carried out in the infancy narratives, when every attempt to thwart God's will (e.g., by Herod) is overturned as God supernaturally intervenes, first in the dream to the Magi (2:12) and then in the angelic messages to Joseph in the dreams of 2:13, 19. This, of course, is one of the primary messages of Scripture, but the average Christian shows all too little awareness of this in his or her daily life. For example, consider trials and faith. Most of the time we trust ourselves more than God to take care of life's difficulties, yet we claim to believe that he is sovereign. The same God who has guided the process of the coming of the Messiah guides the progress of our lives.

4. God's Focus on the Outcasts and Downtrodden

The four women mentioned in 1:3, 5, 6 prepared for God's choice of Mary to bear his Son. All were outsiders, many encased in scandal, yet all were chosen by God and made an essential part of the greatest story in all of history. This same

31. Bruner, *Christbook*, 13, makes this the prime message of the genealogy, saying, "To the human participants in this history, things didn't look too orderly. But when one looks back on Old Testament history through the lens that the history of Jesus Christ offers, one sees that God's hand was steady and sure, that the historical 'N-shape' had a draftsman, that God was in control."

truth was evident in Jesus' choice of his twelve disciples; he did not select the great teachers like Gamaliel or leaders like Nicodemus. He turned to peasant fishermen (Simon and Andrew, James, and John), despised tax collectors (Levi), and insurrectionists (Simon the Zealot). For the mother of the Messiah, God chose a peasant in a small town, and then had her give birth in suspicious (scandalous) circumstances as an unwed mother. This genealogy tells us that God has worked in this way throughout history. Paul catches it well: "If I must boast, I will boast of the things that show my weakness" (2 Cor 11:30). The point is that when God works through our low status and weakness, the glory goes to him. None of us should ever feel inferior or inadequate. Rather, we should rejoice in such, for God turns human weakness into divine strength.

5. A Worldwide Mission

The four women were all Gentiles or related to Gentiles, and this leads into a major motif in the first gospel, the preparation of the new community of God to fulfill the Abrahamic covenant (to be a blessing to all nations) by taking the gospel directly to the Gentiles. The Jewish people had no concept of direct mission to the Gentiles. When they "travel[ed] over sea and land" to make converts (23:15), they went only to the synagogues to talk God-fearers into becoming full proselytes.[32] Jesus introduced a whole new movement in salvation history, the universal mission to all nations (28:19). Yet it took a decade for the disciples to understand its implications, and only after the lengthy process of Spirit-inspired events in the steps to the Gentile mission of Acts 7 – 11. In our time this lesson has been learned, but it is still a lengthy process in turning believers today into "world Christians."

32. See McKnight, *A Light Among the Gentiles: Jewish Missionary Activity in the Second Temple Period* (Minneapolis: Fortress, 1991) for the history of the Jewish mission to the Gentiles.

CHAPTER 2

Matthew 1:18 – 25

Literary Context

The infancy narratives of Matthew center clearly on the theme of divine providence, as God supernaturally controls all events so as to accomplish his will.[1] Thus it is natural that after using the genealogy to state that the time of fulfillment is at hand and that the expected royal Messiah is to appear, Matthew chronicles the birth of that very messianic figure.

I. Jesus' Origin and Preparation for Ministry (1:1 – 4:11)

A. The Birth and Infancy of Jesus (1:1 – 2:23)

1. The Genealogy of Jesus the Messiah (1:1 – 17)
2. ➦ **The Virginal Conception (1:18 – 25)**
3. The Visit of the Magi (2:1 – 12)

Main Idea

There are two major ideas here — the sovereign control of all history by God, who works out his plan of salvation in history "when the set time had fully come" (Gal 4:4), and the virgin birth of Jesus as the typological fulfillment of Isa 7:14.

1. See Kenneth R. R. Gros Louis, "Different Ways of Looking at the Birth of Jesus," *BRev* 1 (1985): 33 – 40, who argues that Matthew centers on God's providential control while Luke centers on people in the midst of history.

Translation

Matthew 1:18-25

18a	Introduction	Now **the origins of Jesus Messiah occurred in this way:**
b		**His mother Mary was pledged in marriage to Joseph.**
c	Setting (Temporal)	Before the marriage could be consummated,
d	Problem	**she was found to be with child by means of the Holy Spirit**
19a	Solution #1	**[1] Now Joseph, her husband . . . planned to divorce her privately**
b	Basis for 19a	because he was righteous and was not willing to cause her public disgrace.
20a	Setting (Temporal)	Now while he was reflecting on this,
b	Solution #2	**[2] look, the angel of the Lord appeared to him in a dream saying**
c		*"Joseph, son of David,* *do not be afraid to take Mary as your wife,*
d	Basis for 20c	for *that which is conceived in her is from the Holy Spirit.*
21a		And *she will give birth to a son,*
b		and *you are to call his name Jesus*
c	Basis for 21b	for *he will save his people from their sins."*
22a	Fulfillment Formula for 21c	**This all took place in order to fulfill what the Lord had said through the prophet:**
23a		*"Look, a virgin will conceive and give birth to a son.*
b		And *they will call his name 'Immanuel,'* (Isa 7:14)
c	Explanation	*which means, 'God with us.'"*
24a	Setting (Temporal)	So when Joseph arose from his sleep,
b	Resolution of 18d	**he did what the angel of the Lord had commanded him and took Mary as his wife.**
25a		And **he did not have sexual relations with her**
b		until she had given birth to a son,
c		And **he called his name Jesus.**

Structure and Literary Form

This material stems from Matthew's special sources (M). It is certainly traditional material (as nearly all agree)[2] and is a different tradition from Luke 2:1 – 20. This story comprises two major elements: the angelic announcement of vv. 20 – 21

2. For the historicity of the incarnation, see Blomberg, *Historical Reliability*, 163 – 64; on 1:18 – 2:23 as a whole, including the virgin birth, see Keener, *Matthew*, 81 – 86.

and the fulfillment quotation of vv. 22 – 23. The angelic feature follows similar stories in the OT (e.g., Gen 16; 17 – 18; Judg 13; 1 Kgs 13) and Matthew's infancy narrative (Matt 2:13 – 15, 19 – 21). The general pattern is the description of the situation (1:18 – 19), the appearance of an angel (1:20a), an angelic prophecy (1:20b – 21), and the positive results (1:22 – 25).[3]

Exegetical Outline

➦ I. The Virginal Conception (1:18 – 25)

- **A. The problem (v. 18)**
  1. Introduction
  2. Mary engaged to Joseph
  3. Mary conceives by the Holy Spirit
- **B. The solution (vv. 19 – 21)**
  1. The false one: Joseph's decision (v. 19)
  2. The correct one: God's decision (vv. 20 – 21)
     - a. Angel's message: the Holy Spirit behind the conception (v. 20)
     - b. Angel's message: name the child Jesus (v. 21)
- **C. The results (vv. 22 – 25)**
  1. Scripture fulfilled (vv. 22 – 23)
  2. Joseph obeys (vv. 24 – 25)
     - a. Married Mary (v. 24)
     - b. Mary remains a virgin until Jesus is born (v. 25a)
     - c. Named the child Jesus (v. 25b)

Explanation of the Text

What is unusual is that the actual birth of Jesus is not really told. Rather, Isa 7:14 and the virgin birth as well as Joseph's acceptance of that miraculous event is narrated, and the birth itself is replaced with a record of Jesus' conception.[4] Matthew's purpose is to give a theological perspective on the birth from the standpoint of Isa 7:14 (see below). The genealogy tells the significance of the birth, this paragraph the miraculous nature of it, and the following section the royal overtones as the Magi bring royal gifts (2:1 – 12). We could not do better than to quote the conclusion of Kingsbury:

> Jesus, the son born to Mary, is the kingly Messiah of Israel in whom Israel's entire history, begun in Abraham, reaches its eschatological conclusion. Adopted by Joseph into the line of

3. See Davies and Allison, *Matthew*, 1:196 – 97.

4. For the historicity of the scene, see R. T. France, "Scripture, Tradition, and History in the Infancy Narratives of Matthew," *Gospel Perspectives: Studies of History and Tradition in the Four Gospels* (ed. R. T. France and David Wenham; Sheffield: JSOT Press, 1981), 239 – 66; and Carson, "Matthew," 71 – 73; contra Brown, *Birth of the Messiah*, 138 – 43, who believes the divine sonship of Jesus was first connected to his resurrection and gradually moved back to his conception via the virgin birth.

> David, Jesus can legitimately be called the Son of David and the Son of Abraham. Ultimately, however, Jesus has his origin in God, which means he is the Son of God, for he was conceived in Mary, a virgin, by the creative act of God's Holy Spirit. As Messiah, Son of David, Son of Abraham, and Son of God, Jesus' mission will be to save his people, the disciples who will constitute his Church, from their sins. By so doing, Jesus will inaugurate the eschatological age of salvation.[5]

Here Matthew is clarifying further the meaning of his genealogy. Every aspect of Jesus' origin is under the sovereign hand of God, who superintends each step. In so doing, Scripture is being fulfilled, as the virginal conception reenacts Isa 7:14, "Therefore, the Lord himself will give you a sign: The virgin will conceive and give birth to a son, and will call him Immanuel." The typological correspondence means that God continues to act in divinely set patterns as he does his will. As R. T. France says, this entails "correspondence between New and Old Testament events, based on a conviction of the unchanging character of the principles of God's working, and a consequent understanding and description of the New Testament event in terms of the Old Testament model"[6]

As for the fulfillment emphasis, the whole paragraph can be called a "haggadic midrash" on Isa 7:14, that is, an explanation of the meaning and significance of the Isaiah text (midrash) in order to show the theological significance of Jesus fulfilling it (haggadic).[7] As Knowles points out, the formula quotations provide a basic outline of Jesus' life and ministry and "show that the basic elements of Jesus' origin, identity, ministry — even his betrayal — were already providentially set out in the inspired text and so conform to 'the divinely ordained plan for the Messiah.' "[8] The historical events (the virginal conception and Joseph's decision directed by angelic revelation not to divorce her) are interpreted via the prophetic material. These are not two separate traditions conflated by Matthew (as some have suggested) but two sides of the same coin, namely, the sovereign control of God over salvation history. Matthew wants to tell us that the conception of the Davidic Messiah was the result of divine providence from start to finish (a major theme of the genealogy as well).

1:18 Now the origins of Jesus Messiah[9] occurred in this way (Τοῦ δὲ Ἰησοῦ Χριστοῦ ἡ γένεσις οὕτως ἦν). "Jesus Messiah" (a simple possessive genitive) is located first for emphasis and connects clearly to "the Messiah" (τοῦ Χριστοῦ) in 1:17, thereby linking this section closely to the genealogy above. Some see a chiastic pattern, with the order of the names of the key figures in 1:1 – 17 (Joseph, Mary, Christ) reversed in 1:18 – 25 (Christ, Mary, Joseph).[10] If this is intentional, the central pair would be Jesus Messiah, and this would be describing his origins. The debated word is "origins" (γένεσις), which has a wide range of meanings from creation to birth to origins. In a real sense all three apply here, yet while most

5. Jack Dean Kingsbury, "The Birth Narrative of Matthew," *The Gospel of Matthew in Current Study* (ed. David E. Aune; Grand Rapids: Eerdmans, 2001), 164 – 65. Ben Witherington III, *Matthew* (Smith & Helwys Bible Commentary; Macon, GA: Smith & Helwys, 2006), 43, gives a "sapiential reading" in seeing the virgin birth and "Immanuel" title as highlighting Jesus as Wisdom come in the flesh, the Son of David/Solomon who is Wisdom Incarnate. This is interesting but unlikely (see on 11:19 for the wisdom theme in Matthew).

6. France, *Matthew* (TNTC), 40. See also Osborne, *Hermeneutical Spiral*, 328 – 29.

7. See Hagner, *Matthew 1 – 13*, 15 – 16. For passages on a virgin birth from targumic and midrashic material, see J. D. M. Derrett, "Shared Themes: The Virgin Birth (Matthew 1:18 – 2:12), *Journal of Higher Criticism* 4 (1997): 57 – 67.

8. Michael Knowles, *Jeremiah in Matthew's Gospel: The Rejected-Prophet Motif in Matthean Redaction* (JSNTSup 68; Sheffield: Sheffield Academic Press, 1993), 26 – 27.

9. For arguments in behalf of seeing this not as a proper name but as a title, see on 1:1.

10. Davies and Allison, *Matthew*, 1:197.

choose "birth" to translate it, that may be too narrow. As Kingsbury notes,[11] "birth" would fit Luke 2 but not Matthew 1, which centers on the conception and repeats the same word from 1:1. As "origin," this then refers to Jesus' relationship to Mary and Joseph as well as to his lineage (1:1 – 17) and to God.[12]

1:18 His mother Mary was pledged in marriage to Joseph (μνηστευθείσης τῆς μητρὸς αὐτοῦ Μαρίας τῷ Ἰωσήφ). This is the first of many genitive absolutes in Matthew,[13] separate grammatically and introducing an adverbial idea (probably temporal — "after she was betrothed and before the marriage was consummated"). The key term is "pledged in marriage" (μνηστευθείσης), which means a great deal more than the "engagement" today. It was legally binding (a contract signed by witnesses) and could be broken only by a writ of divorce. If the "husband" (he was considered such) were to die, the engaged woman would be considered a widow. Still, the marriage was not consummated until the wedding night, when the bride ritually went from her parent's home to her husband's home. Betrothal usually happened about the age of twelve (arranged by the two sets of parents), with the wedding a year later. The husbands were usually about eighteen (in order to be established financially).[14]

1:18 Before the marriage could be consummated, she was found to be with child by means of the Holy Spirit (πρὶν ἢ συνελθεῖν αὐτοὺς εὑρέθη ἐν γαστρὶ ἔχουσα ἐκ πνεύματος ἁγίου). This means that Mary was discovered to be pregnant during the engagement period, with "to come together" (συνελθεῖν) a frequent Greek term for sexual intercourse that consummated the marriage. As Carson notes, this does not mean they tried to hide the truth but were found out; rather, it refers to the simple fact that her condition became known.[15] The Holy Spirit is the creative agent, the source (ἐκ) of the conception. Matthew wants to be certain the reader does not entertain for a moment the possibility of an illicit event. It is the Spirit, not any human agent, who is responsible for the conception. So the true origin of Jesus is divine. Hill sees in this a "new creation" theme; as the Spirit was present in the original creation (Gen 1 – 2), he is now recreating in the messianic era.[16]

1:19 Now Joseph her husband, because he was righteous (Ἰωσὴφ δὲ ὁ ἀνὴρ αὐτῆς, δίκαιος ὤν). The causal participial clause gives us a glimpse into Joseph's character. The term δίκαιος has both a spiritual ("righteous") and a legal ("just") connotation. Both are probably intended here.[17] As a person he was righteous or faithful to God and

11. Kingsbury, "Birth Narrative," 155 – 57.

12. France, *Gospel of Matthew*, 411 – 42, sees an apologetic purpose, with ch. 1 supporting *who* Jesus is and ch. 2 telling *where* he is from.

13. See Gundry, *Matthew*, 649; Wallace, 655.

14. An ancient tradition says Joseph was older. In the apocryphal Christian gospels, Joseph was older with children (*Prot. Jas.* 9.2), living to 111 years after marrying at forty with six children, his first marriage lasting forty-nine years, then dying when Jesus was in his twenties (*History of Joseph the Carpenter*). See Stanley E. Porter, "Joseph, Husband of Mary," *ABD*, 3:974. But this cannot be proven. In the four gospels, he is not mentioned after Jesus' visit to the temple at age twelve in Luke 2:41 – 52. Likely he died during the intervening years before Jesus began his ministry. Mark does not mention Joseph at all, probably because Mark begins with the baptism of Jesus after Joseph had died.

15. Carson, "Matthew," 74.

16. Hill, *Matthew*, 78. Davies and Allison, *Matthew*, 1:201, add several other possibilities: the Spirit as the giver of life (Gen 6:3; Ps 33:6); Jesus as Davidic Messiah and Suffering Servant connected with the Spirit (Isa 11:2; 42:1); the Spirit as the power behind miracles (the virgin birth, cf. Matt 12:28; Acts 2:4); the Spirit linked to eschatological sonship (John 3:5; Rom 8:9 – 17); the fresh and full coming of the Holy Spirit as a sign of the messianic age (Isa 44:3 – 4; Ezek 37:1 – 14). These are possible, but it is difficult to know how much is intended here.

17. Bruner, *Christbook*, 22, talks of whether the righteousness of Joseph is merciful (taking the καί as "and unwilling") or strictly legal (taking the καί as "but unwilling"), opting for the possibility that it is a mixture of both.

his laws; as a husband (betrothal was legally binding, cf. 1:18) he acted with justice toward Mary.[18] Matthew wants the reader to know how pious Jesus' parents are: "Matthew invites his audience to learn from Joseph's character about fidelity, discipline, and preferring God's honor above one's own."[19]

1:19 . . . and was not willing to cause her public disgrace,[20] planned to divorce her privately (καὶ μὴ θέλων αὐτὴν δειγματίσαι, ἐβουλήθη λάθρᾳ ἀπολῦσαι αὐτήν). Joseph's righteous character placed him in a dilemma: he had to divorce Mary because of her pregnancy,[21] yet he did not "want" (a second causal participle) to "disgrace" her (δειγματίζω means to make an example by disgracing her publicly, often used of an adulteress, see BAGD, 172). So he compromised by deciding to do so privately. According to Jewish tradition, this would be done by giving her a writ of divorce (see Deut 24:1) privately in front of two witnesses rather than in front of the whole town.

1:20 Now while he was reflecting on this (ταῦτα δὲ αὐτοῦ ἐνθυμηθέντος). Another genitive absolute, "while he was reflecting" (αὐτοῦ ἐνθυμηθέντος, used temporally), depicts Joseph as "thinking" or "reflecting" about what to do. He could not think of any alternative but a private divorce. He probably did not know Mary very well, and they had little opportunity to converse.[22] The only conclusion he could make is that she had relations with another man, so he was doing the most merciful thing he knew.

1:20 . . . look, the angel of the Lord appeared to him in[23] a dream, saying (ἰδοὺ ἄγγελος κυρίου κατ' ὄναρ ἐφάνη αὐτῷ λέγων). At the critical time (for the dramatic use of "look" [ἰδού],[24] see on 19:16), God himself intervenes by sending "the[25] angel of the Lord" (only in Matthew in the NT — 1:20, 24; 2:13, 19) in a dream (six times, cf. 2:12 – 13, 19, 22; 27:19). It was common for God to send revelatory messages via dreams (Gen 28:12; 37:5 – 9; Num 12:6; Judg 7:13; Dan 2:3; 4:5; 7:1).[26] Clearly, dreams are a primary form for God's

18. France, *Gospel of Matthew*, 51, thinks this describes not so much Joseph acting graciously toward Mary as that Joseph sought to keep the law "righteously" and therefore terminate the marriage on the grounds of adultery. In the context, both aspects fit. Richard J. Erickson, "Joseph and the Birth of Jesus in Matthew 1," *BBR* 10 (2000): 35 – 51, sees Joseph as an Abraham figure, with Jesus as an antitype of Isaiah, thereby preparing for the fulfillment of the Abrahamic covenant (Gen 12:3, 18:18 et al.) in becoming a source of blessing for the nations (the Gentile mission).

19. Keener, *Matthew*, 90. B. Orchard, "The Betrothal and Marriage of Mary to Joseph (Part 1)," *Homiletical and Pastoral Review* 102 (2001): 7 – 14, takes their marriage as the first "sacramental union" and argues that they remained celibate for the rest of their lives.

20. There is debate over the two participles: either they are contrast ("though righteous, he did not want to disgrace her," so Brown, Davies and Allison, Hagner) or in agreement ("because he was righteous and therefore not willing to disgrace her" (so A. Tosato, "Joseph, Being a Just Man [Matt. 1:19]," *CBQ* 41 (1979): 547 – 51; Carson, Blomberg). The latter is more likely in light of the "and" (καί) as well as the tone of the passage. Moreover, it is best to see the participles as causal, providing the reason for Joseph's action.

21. As Keener shows (*Matthew*, 91), there was no real option in the first century. Jewish law virtually demanded that a husband expose a wife who by infidelity had so diminished his honor (*m. Ketub.* 1:4).

22. Keener, *Matthew*, 92, points out that betrothed couples in Jewish society were allowed little privacy, and Joseph had probably never gotten to know Mary very well. So he would have had little reason to believe her protestations of innocence.

23. κατά used distributively can mean "in" (BAGD, 406, 1d).

24. This is a favorite dramatic particle of Matthew (62 times, but also 57 times in Luke) to point to a message of particular importance.

25. Wallace, 252, has a good discussion of why these anarthrous nouns should be translated: *the* angel of *the* Lord," following the LXX practice (see also Turner, *Syntax*, 180).

26. For the biblical use of dreams in Matthew as a fulfillment of dream patterns in the OT, see Robert K. Gnuse, "Dream Genre in the Matthean Infancy Narrative," *NovT* 32 (1990): 97 – 120.

sovereign control as he reveals his will and guides human actions in accordance with his will.

1:20 "Joseph, son of David, do not be afraid to take Mary as your wife" (Ἰωσὴφ υἱὸς Δαυίδ, μὴ φοβηθῇς παραλαβεῖν Μαριὰν τὴν γυναῖκά σου). Joseph is called "son of David," linking him with Jesus the Davidic Messiah (cf. 1:1, 17) and looking forward to his legal adoption of Jesus (as well as bringing Jesus into the Davidic line). The reference to his fear is natural in light of his situation vis-à-vis the community. He is in difficult straits, since failure to divorce Mary will also dishonor him (see above). God, however, makes clear the divine will: he must take Mary as his wife.

1:20 "For that which is conceived[27] in her is from the Holy Spirit" (τὸ γὰρ ἐν αὐτῇ γεννηθὲν ἐκ πνεύματός ἐστιν ἁγίου). The reason is taken from v. 18. The child was conceived by the direct work of the Holy Spirit. It is clear that the Spirit is a major emphasis of this section, indicating divine providence at work.

1:21 "... and she will give birth to a son, and you are to call[28] his name Jesus" (τέξεται δὲ υἱόν, καὶ καλέσεις τὸ ὄνομα αὐτοῦ Ἰησοῦν). The first half reflects Isa 7:14 LXX (see v. 23) and continues the emphasis on the virgin birth from vv. 18, 20. In Luke 1:31 Mary is told "to call him Jesus" (undoubtedly both passages are correct). Here the emphasis is on Joseph. The name was officially given on the eighth day after birth, when the male child was circumcised (Luke 2:21 – 38). By giving him the name, Joseph was making the baby Jesus his child (Isa 43:1, "I have called you by name, you are mine," NRSV). The Greek here is Semitic, and the future tense "you are to call" (καλέσεις) gives it imperatival force; thus, as the TNIV reads, "you are to give him the name Jesus."[29]

The Greek name "Jesus" (Ἰησοῦς) reflects the Hebrew *Yehoshua*/*Yeshua* (Joshua, "Yahweh saves"). In the Jewish world names were not just marks of identification but were symbols containing the hopes and prayers of the parents for their children. "Jesus" means that through him[30] God promises that salvation will come to his people, though the Jewish people mistakenly interpreted it in terms of the other meaning of "save," that God would "deliver" his people by destroying their enemies.

1:21 For he will save his people from their sins (αὐτὸς γὰρ σώσει τὸν λαὸν αὐτοῦ ἀπὸ τῶν ἁμαρτιῶν αὐτῶν). God had a different kind of salvation in mind, as seen in the added "from their sins." "People" (λαός) is the term used in the gospels for the people of God,[31] here indicating those who will respond to the salvation Jesus brings. It is clear that Jesus has come to bring spiritual salvation rather than political deliverance. "Sin"[32] refers to that basic self-centered aversion toward God's laws, and sin clearly throughout the OT was the cause of God's wrath poured out on the nation of Israel. Christ alone has provided the antidote for sin once-for-all (cf. Matt 3:6; 9:9 – 13; 11:19; 20:28; 26:28; Heb 7:27; 9:12, 26, 28; 10:10).

27. τό with the participle γεννηθέν is used substantivally and is equivalent to a clause, "what is conceived."

28. Three times (vv. 21, 23, 25), "to call" (καλέω) will have a double accusative, with the second telling what the name will be (this double object works in English as well as Greek).

29. See Carson, *Matthew*, 75.

30. The emphatic "he" (αὐτός) in the next part of this verse means that Jesus alone can bring eschatological salvation to humankind.

31. Nolland, *Matthew*, 98, states that this does not refer to "a new Christian people of God, but to the historic people of God."

32. "Sin" (ἁμαρτία) here, the basic New Testament term (48 times in Romans alone), means a failure to keep God's standard and contains also the result, the "guilt" that one has before God. See Peter Fiedler, "ἁμαρτία," *EDNT*, 1:66.

1:22 This all took place in order to fulfill what the Lord had said through the prophet[33] (Τοῦτο δὲ ὅλον γέγονεν ἵνα πληρωθῇ τὸ ῥηθὲν ὑπὸ κυρίου διὰ τοῦ προφήτου λέγοντος). There is emphasis upon ὅλον, the "whole" set of events that surrounded the birth of the Messiah. God controlled every aspect of the situation to fulfill his will. The use of "to fulfill" (πληρωθῇ) is Matthean, found in ten particular fulfillment passages (1:22; 2:15, 17, 23; 4:14; 8:17; 12:17; 13:35; 21:4; 27:9).[34] Four are in the infancy narratives and establish the theme for the rest of the book, namely, that God sovereignly controls all events in conformity with his plan. The primary method Matthew uses is typology (see the introduction to this section); that is, the events of Jesus' birth are analogous to the way God has worked during the old covenant. Yet there is also a direct relationship between promise and fulfillment here (see below on v. 23). God has sovereignly controlled salvation history in order to prepare for his Messiah.

1:23 "Look, a virgin will conceive and give birth to a son" (Ἰδοὺ ἡ παρθένος ἐν γαστρὶ ἕξει καὶ τέξεται υἱόν). For dramatic "look" (ἰδού) see v. 20; 19:16. An enormous amount has been written about the use of Isa 7:14 here in Matthew.[35] The problem is the Hebrew *ʿalmâ* (Isa 7:14 MT) and the Greek παρθένος (Isa 7:14 LXX as well as Matthew here); the Hebrew term mainly refers to a young woman able to bear children,[36] while the Greek term denotes a virgin.[37] Two poles can be detected: some believe the Isaiah passage was a messianic prophecy not meant to be fulfilled in Isaiah's day but only in the virgin birth of Jesus.[38] Others argue that there is no messianic component whatsoever and Isaiah's prophecy was fulfilled in the birth of Hezekiah or Maher-Shalal-Hash-Baz (Isa 8:3–4) to a "young woman" in Ahaz's day.[39]

However, a growing consensus prefers a view between these extremes.[40] The prophecy was given to Ahaz and introduced by "Therefore, the Lord himself will give you a sign." In other words, it was mainly intended for Ahaz that God would destroy the kings he dreaded (Isa 7:14–17). So at least a partial fulfillment is indicated for Ahaz's time. Yet the larger Isaianic context indicates also that a greater picture was envisaged as well. This promised "Immanuel" would bring a dawning of a great light (9:2–3) and would be called "Wonderful Counselor, Mighty God, Everlasting Father, Prince of Peace" (9:6). He is the "shoot from the stump of Jesse," the "Branch" on which the Spirit rests (11:1–11), showing a distinct messianic longing.

The LXX recognized this greater thrust and chose to interpret *ʿalmâ* with the narrower

33. It is debated whether the angel's message ends with v. 21 (with the Isa. 7:14 quote added by Matthew, so Hagner, *Matthew 1–13*, 20; Brown, *Birth of the Messiah*, 144) or with v. 23 (so Carson, "Matthew," 76). While the latter is certainly possible, there are ten formula quotations in Matthew (see below), and they all seem the editorial comment of the evangelist (so France, *Matthew* [TNTC], 38–40; Blomberg, *Matthew*, 30–32).

34. Matt 26:54, 56 also contain "to be fulfilled" (πληρωθῆναι), yet these are not fulfillment passages, but rather contain general emphases on fulfillment. In addition, 13:14–15 uses "fulfill" (ἀναπληρόω) in a fulfillment sense.

35. George Soares-Prabhu, *The Formula Quotations*, 229–31, points out that Matthew is following the LXX here except for his switch from the singular to the plural "they will call" (καλέσουσιν), which he believes is a redactional (targumic) change to an impersonal plural to show Jesus was not specifically called "Immanuel" but in a general way fulfilled it.

36. John Walton, "עַלְמָה," *NIDOTTE*, 3:416–18.

37. Joseph A. Fitzmyer, "παρθένος," *EDNT*, 3:40.

38. Edward J. Young, *The Book of Isaiah* (NICOT; Grand Rapids: Eerdmans, 1965), 1:288–94.

39. Hill, *Matthew*, 79–80; Brown, *Birth of the Messiah*, 147–49.

40. See John N. Oswalt, *The Book of Isaiah, Chapters 1–39* (NICOT; Grand Rapids, Eerdmans, 1986), 207–13; France, *Matthew*, 79–80; Carson, "Matthew," 79–80; Hagner, *Matthew 1–13*, 20; Blomberg, *Matthew*, 59–60; Keener, *Matthew*, 87.

"virgin" (παρθένος), thus emphasizing the supernatural manifestations of the child's birth. Matthew utilized this Septuagintal emphasis and applied it to the virgin birth of Jesus. As Blomberg says, "So it is best to see a partial, proleptic fulfillment of Isaiah's prophecy in his time, with the complete and more glorious fulfillment in Jesus' own birth."[41]

1:23 "... and they will call his name 'Immanuel'" (καὶ καλέσουσιν τὸ ὄνομα αὐτοῦ Ἐμμανουήλ). In further fulfillment of Isa 7:14, "Immanuel" (Ἐμμανουήλ) was not the literal name of Jesus but became his name metaphorically by describing his messianic work, namely, establishing the presence of God with his people (a major Matthean theme, cf. 18:20; 28:20). In fact, Jesus is the presence of God in a sense similar to John 1:14, in which Jesus is the incarnate Shekinah; that is, in Jesus God is once again walking planet Earth. "Shekinah" comes from the Hebrew *šākan*, which means "to live, dwell," and in the OT the word referred to God's actually dwelling in the Most Holy Place. It came to mean that the glory of God was dwelling on planet Earth. While Isaiah has "you will call," Matthew has "they will call," namely, those who join the messianic community.

1:23 "... which means, 'God with us'" (ὅ ἐστιν μεθερμηνευόμενον Μεθ' ἡμῶν ὁ θεός). J. C. Fenton[42] links this with "I am with you always" in 28:20 and concludes that here Matthew uses "God" (ὁ θεός) as a Christological title. M. J. Harris[43] qualifies this by saying that the meaning is, "in Jesus God is present to bring salvation to his people" rather than that Jesus is indeed God dwelling among his people. Still, this comes close to using "God" (θεός) as a title for Christ. This promise of omnipresence is part of a Matthean christological theme found at the beginning (here), in the middle (18:20), and at the end (28:20) of Matthew's gospel.

1:24 So when Joseph arose[44] from his sleep, he did what the angel of the Lord had commanded him and took Mary as his wife (ἐγερθεὶς δὲ ὁ Ἰωσὴφ ἀπὸ τοῦ ὕπνου ἐποίησεν ὡς προσέταξεν αὐτῷ ὁ ἄγγελος κυρίου καὶ παρέλαβεν τὴν γυναῖκα αὐτοῦ). The "righteous" character of Joseph (1:19) is further shown in his immediate obedience to the angel's command. When the revelatory dream ends, Joseph awakes and instantly does the Lord's bidding. Mary's obedience in Luke 1 is the same, so we see what kind of pious, God-fearing parents Jesus had, who are models for us all. "Took as his wife" means he officially married her.

1:25 And he did not have sexual relations with her until she had given birth to a son, and he called his name Jesus (καὶ οὐκ ἐγίνωσκεν αὐτὴν ἕως οὗ ἔτεκεν υἱόν· καὶ ἐκάλεσεν τὸ ὄνομα αὐτοῦ Ἰησοῦν). The verb "have sexual relations" (γινώσκω, lit., "know," imperfect tense to place this in the foreground for emphasis) is an ancient euphemism for sexual relations, and Matthew says this to emphasize further the virgin birth; the imperfect tense denotes that Joseph at no time had sexual intercourse with his wife "until" after the

41. Blomberg, *Matthew*, 60. See also Warren Carter, "Evoking Isaiah: Matthean Soteriology and an Intertextual Reading of Isaiah 7 – 9 and Matthew 1:23 and 4:15 – 16," *JBL* 119 (2000): 503 – 20, who sees the whole context of Isa 7 – 9 intended and thus a message of how God will overcome the worldly powers and bring salvation to the nations through Jesus.

42. J. C. Fenton, "Matthew and the Divinity of Jesus: Three Questions concerning Matthew 1:20 – 23," in *Studia Biblica 1978, Vol 2: Papers on the Gospels* (ed. E. A. Livingstone; Sheffield: JSOT Press, 1980), 79 – 82.

43. Murray J. Harris, *Jesus as God: The New Testament Use of Theos in Reference to Jesus* (Grand Rapids: Baker, 1992), 258.

44. "When he arose" (ἐγερθείς) is another temporal participle, see 1:18.

birth of Jesus. In light of the Roman Catholic doctrine of Mary's perpetual virginity, it is common to deny that this implies sexual relations afterward.[45] However, the context makes the renewal of conjugal relations likely, and the fact that Jesus had brothers (e.g., Matt 12:46; Mark 6:3 also mentions sisters) also makes perpetual virginity difficult to sustain. The main point is that the virgin birth occurred and Joseph officially adopted Jesus as his son and heir on the eighth day.

Theology in Application

Many of the themes in 1:1 – 17 are continued here, such as divine providence and the messianic nature of Jesus. Many further themes are introduced. This is not quite a Christmas story, centering on the conception of Jesus more than his birth, but it still has important repercussions as it teaches the important doctrine of the virgin birth and the even more critical issue of Jesus' divine origin. So it still is extremely relevant for Christmas.

1. God's Control of World History

This theme carries over from the first section and is certainly one of the controlling motifs of the Bible as a whole, not just Matthew. It is clear here that when needed, God supernaturally intervenes in human affairs. Joseph was about to divorce Mary, and so God sent an angel in a dream-vision to tell him God's intentions and to give him God's orders. We could all wish God would do so in our lives and guide us that directly. However, God did not always use miraculous means to make his will known, even in biblical times. For instance, in Acts 16:6 – 7, it says twice that on Paul's second missionary journey the Holy Spirit twice "kept" the apostle and the others from going south to Asia (Ephesus) and north to Bithynia but led them instead to Troas, where they received the vision from the man of Macedonia. Note that Luke does not say they had a dream or direct message. I believe it was a growing conviction through their own prayer and decision that that was not God's will. As God guides our decision process (via prayer), he is working with us in ways analogous to the way he led Joseph here.

2. God's Desire for "Righteous" Followers

When one closely follows the Lord and seeks to obey his commands (cf. 28:20b), that "righteous" lifestyle is what God honors. Forensic righteousness (= justification) occurs when God declares us right with him as a result of Jesus'

45. See Davies and Allison, *Matthew*, 1:219, who point out the Greek expression makes no statement about what happened afterward. Brown, *Birth of the Messiah*, 132, concurs but admits that Matthew was also making no statement about perpetual virginity. Morris, *Matthew*, 32, argues that the construction does imply resumption of sexual relations.

atoning sacrifice, but that must always lead to moral righteousness, as we live rightly before him.[46] When we center on obedience, the life that results is especially blessed by God. The result is that we, like Joseph, become "just" in our relationship with others. Justice all too seldom occurs in the world as a whole. In America our litigious society means that the one with the best lawyer wins, and justice too often occurs only by chance. In much of the world the strong dominate the weak, and justice is not a consideration. But the "righteous" person is always just and merciful, as Joseph was toward Mary.

3. Jesus as Messiah and Son of God

Jesus is the God-man, born of Mary (the human side) and the Holy Spirit (the divine side). We can never fully understand how Jesus can be fully human and fully divine, but this passage tells us at least the means by which this was accomplished. As stated above, this is the primary thrust of the passage, and much of the gospel flows out of the truth presented here. Jesus is our friend who understands our weaknesses and can "sympathize" with our plight (Heb 4:14 – 16). At the same time he is our sovereign Lord, the object of our worship. Plummer has an interesting discussion of the meaning of the virgin birth for Jesus' life and mission:

> The Messiah was born *in* the flesh, not *of* the flesh ... and therefore was able to vanquish sin and death in the region in which they had done their victories. He was not born of the flesh but of the Spirit; and therefore He did not share in that innate proneness towards evil which all other human beings exhibit. It was possible for Him to pass the whole of His life without sin.[47]

4. The Holy Spirit at Work

The Spirit is not a major theme in Matthew, unlike Luke and John. However, here the Spirit is central, and Matthew does want his readers to realize his presence in Jesus' birth and in our world. While simplistic, there is truth in the Trinitarian saying, "The Father proclaims, the Son performs, the Spirit perfects." The Spirit is the presence of the Father and the Son in this world. Jesus makes clear in John's Farewell Discourse (John 14 – 17) that he must depart so the Spirit may come (John 16:7). This is the age of the Spirit, the final stage in God's plan to prepare this world for the eschaton, when the eternal age will be inaugurated. Bruner says:

> The Holy Spirit is the one who brings Jesus to birth in persons, the one who makes Jesus alive in human life, who makes Jesus historical and real. The Genesis of

46. See Douglas J. Moo, *The Epistle to the Romans* (NICNT; Grand Rapids: Eerdmans, 1996), 79 – 89; Grant R. Osborne, *Romans* (IVPNTC; Downers Grove, IL: IVP, 2004), 42 – 43.

47. Alfred Plummer, *An Exegetical Commentary on the Gospel according to St. Matthew* (Grand Rapids: Eerdmans, 1956), 6 – 7.

Jesus inside human life is the exclusive work of the Holy Spirit, the *Creator Spiritus*, who began the world's *creation* (Gen 1:2) and now generates the world's *salvation*.[48]

5. Fulfillment of Scripture

This is a major Matthean theme and centers on the truth behind the birth of Jesus as a salvation-historical event. The whole OT in a sense prepared for his coming, and he fulfilled both direct prophecies and the history of the nation (typology).

6. Salvation Has Come through Jesus

Matthew is not as well known as Luke and John for his soteriology. Still, "to save" (σῴζω) is found fifteen times (fourteen in Mark, seventeen in Luke, only six in John), and in a healing context (9:21, 22: "your faith has healed [saved] you") it is generally agreed that the use of this verb indicates holistic salvation, spiritual as well as physical. Here in 1:21 it is salvation "from their sins," and that is a major theme. The Baptist's preaching led people to confess their sins and be baptized (3:6; cf. 3:5 – 12), and Jesus' healing ministry was associated with authority to "forgive sins" (9:2, 5 – 6).

Further, Jesus says that his "blood of the covenant" is to be "poured out for many for the forgiveness of sins" (26:28), which clearly states Jesus' self-awareness that his death will be vicarious, a substitutionary atonement for sins. Finally, Jesus twice says that believers who "stand firm to the end will be saved" (10:22; 24:13), meaning that final salvation goes to those who remain true in spite of persecution and trauma.

7. God's New Presence through Jesus

Jesus is never called "Immanuel" (1:23) as a proper name; rather, the term is a metaphor for the fact that in Jesus God is present "with" his people in a whole new way. There are four stages biblically: (1) God is present via his "Shekinah," or dwelling via the pillar of fire and cloud in the exodus and his throne at the midpoint where the wings of the seraphim meet above the ark, i.e., in the Most Holy Place throughout the OT. (2) God is present via his Son, who was in a sense a walking Most Holy Place during his life on this earth. (3) God is present via the Holy Spirit during the church age. (4) God is present physically and in full reality throughout eternity (Rev 21:1 – 22:5).

48. Bruner, *Christbook*, 20 – 21 (italics his).

CHAPTER 3

Matthew 2:1 – 12

Literary Context

Matthew 2 continues some of the themes in ch. 1 (Jesus the kingly Messiah, the providential hand of God), elaborates on others (the inclusion of the Gentiles, the fulfillment of Scripture), and introduces still others (conflict, persecution).

I. Jesus' Origin and Preparation for Ministry (1:1 – 4:11)

A. The Birth and Infancy of Jesus (1:1 – 2:23)

1. The Genealogy of Jesus the Messiah (1:1 – 17)
2. The Virginal Conception (1:18 – 25)
3. **The Visit of the Magi (2:1 – 12)**
4. The Evil Actions of Herod and Flight to Egypt (2:13 – 23)

Main Idea

This pericope presents contrasting reactions to the birth of the messianic king from the Magi (who want to worship him and are part of the Gentile mission theme in Matthew) and from the existing king, Herod, who perceives in him a threat and wants to kill him. This antithesis carries through the gospel: the redemptive influence of Jesus will extend far beyond the confines of Jerusalem to the far corners of the earth, yet those closest to Jesus will reject him.

Translation

Matthew 2:1-12

1a Setting — After Jesus had been born
in Bethlehem of Judea
in the days of Herod the king,

b Scene #1 — **[1] look, Magi from the East arrived in Jerusalem saying,**
2a Question — *"Where is the one born King of the Jews?*
b Basis for 2a — For *we have seen his star when it rose and*
have come to worship him."

3a — When King Herod heard this,
b Result of 2a-b — **he was deeply disturbed and all Jerusalem with him.**
4a Question — **He called together the chief priests and the teachers of law**
for the people and
asked them where the Messiah was to be born.
5a Answer to 4a — And **they said to him,**
b — *"In Bethlehem of Judea, for this is how it has been written*
by the prophet:
6a — *'And you, Bethlehem in the land of Judah, are by no*
means least among the rulers of Judah.
b — *Because from you will come a ruler who will shepherd*
my people, Israel.'" (Mic 5:2; 2 Sam 5:2)

7a Scene #2 — **[2] Then Herod secretly called the magi and**
ascertained from them exactly the time
the star had appeared.
8a — So, **he sent them to Bethlehem and said,**
b Command — *"Go and search very carefully for the infant.*
c — *When you have found him,*
d — *report back to me so that I can also come and worship him."*

9a — After listening to the king,
b Response — **they departed.**
c — And **look, the star they had seen when it rose, went before them**
d — until it came and
stood
before the the place where
the infant was.

10a Result of 9c-d — When they saw the star,
b — **they were filled with great joy.**

11a — When they came into the house,
b — **they saw the infant with his mother Mary**
c Result #1 of 11a-b — [1] and **they fell on their knees and**
worshiped him.

d	Result #2 of 11a-b	[2] And	**opening their treasure chests,**
			they offered him gifts: gold, frankincense, and myrrh.
12a	Conclusion		After they were warned in a dream not to return to Herod,
b			**they went back to their country another way.**

Structure and Literary Form

This story is peculiar to Matthew (M material), but several have supposed that Matthew has created a haggadic midrash around a *testimonia* collection of OT passages used here (in order: Mic 5:1 – 3; Ps 72:10 – 11; Hos 11:1; Jer 31:15; Isa 11:1) and constructed the story himself.[1] But there is no valid reason for denying the historical basis of the story.[2] There is a certain geographical structure here,[3] with two main scenes: (1) In vv. 1 – 6 the Magi come from the east to Jerusalem, where they meet Herod and are informed of the details of the prophetic fulfillment. (2) In vv. 7 – 12 the star lights the way as they go to Bethlehem to the very birthplace of the messianic king. After worshiping him and giving gifts, they return to the east by another route, having been warned in a dream against going back to Herod. Like 1:18 – 25, this constitutes haggadic midrash, this time on Mic 5:2 and Ps 72:10 – 11, as the writer does not just tell of the fulfillment but draws out the theological implications.

Exegetical Outline

➡ **I. The Magi Come to Jerusalem (2:1 – 6)**

A. Their question: Where do we go to give him homage (vv. 1 – 2)

B. Herod's consternation and question — where is he to be born (vv. 3 – 4)

C. The scribes' answer — in Bethlehem (vv. 5 – 6)

II. The Magi Go to Bethlehem (2:7 – 11)

A. Herod's request — tell me (vv. 7 – 8)

B. The star guides the Magi (vv. 9 – 10)

C. They give gifts to the child-king (v. 11)

II. The Magi Return Home by Another Route (1:12)

1. Hill, *Matthew*, 80 – 81; Schweizer, *Matthew*, 36 – 37; Brown, *Birth of the Messiah*, 188 – 96. Gundry, *Matthew*, 26 – 27, thinks this is also a midrashic reworking of the shepherd story in Luke 2:8 – 20.

2. This haggadic style does not mean the story is unhistorical, contra Gundry, *Matthew*, 26 – 27, who believes this is creative midrash to turn the story of the Jewish shepherds (Luke 2) into an adoration by Gentile Magi. On the historicity of the scene, see Carson, "Matthew," 82 – 83; Hagner, *Matthew 1 – 13*, 25; Keener, *Matthew*, 98. See Craig Blomberg, *Historical Reliability*, 43 – 53, on midrash as interpretive technique and not unhistorical genre.

3. See Brown, *Birth of the Messiah*, 178 – 79.

Explanation of the Text

The Magi were Gentiles who came from the far east to pay homage to the messianic king. They typify the nations in Isaiah's "procession of the nations to Zion" theme (Isa 2:2 – 5; 11:10, 12; 14:1; 49:22; 56:3, 6; 60:3, 6, 11) and reenact the Queen of Sheba's visit to Solomon with royal gifts (1 Kgs 10:1 – 10).[4] They also show that indeed the whole world will worship the Messiah and declare him King (cf. Rev 21:24, 26).

At the same time, it is clear that God's sovereign hand is evident. He reveals the reality of the royal birth to the Magi and guides them via a star. All this fulfills the prophetic mandate in Mic 5:2 (cf. 2 Sam 5:2) regarding the royal king born in Bethlehem and Ps 72:10 – 11 (cf. Isa 60:6) about kings bringing gifts of gold and frankincense to the king.

Finally, there is Herod's tragic attempt to destroy the Christ child, which introduces the central theme of conflict and God's triumph over opposition.[5] As Witherington says, "The issue here is in part who is the real king of the Jews — the pretender who liked to call himself king of the Jews even though he was an Idumenean (see Josephus, *Ant.* 15.373; 16.311) or the one born King of the Jews?"[6]

2:1 After Jesus had been born in Bethlehem of Judea (Τοῦ δὲ Ἰησοῦ γεννηθέντος ἐν Βηθλέεμ τῆς Ἰουδαίας). A genitive absolute ("after Jesus had been born" [τοῦ Ἰησοῦ γεννηθέντος]) is used temporally (see 1:18, 20). This contains a twofold connection to 1:18 – 25: the name Jesus and the fact of his birth. The events of ch. 2 are the follow-up to the primary event — the birth of the One who brings salvation. Bethlehem of Judea anticipates the messianic fulfillment of v. 6 and is written this way to distinguish this Bethlehem (five miles south of Jerusalem) from the Bethlehem of Zebulun (Josh 19:15) further north. This is David's home ("the town of David," Luke 2:4), the long-awaited birthplace of the Davidic Messiah (Mic 5:2, cf. v. 6).

2:1 ... in the days of Herod the king (ἐν ἡμέραις Ἡρῴδου τοῦ βασιλέως). King Herod was Herod the Great, born in 73 BC, the son of the Idumean Arab Antipater, head of the police force who kept order for Rome. He not only took over for his father but was named king of Judea by Rome in 37 BC. Known for his paranoia and jealousy, he killed his wife Mariamne and two of his sons. Herod died in 4 BC, so Jesus must have been born some time before that, perhaps as early as 6 BC, since he had been in Bethlehem for some time and also sojourned in Egypt for a while before Herod died.

2:1 Look, Magi from the East arrived in Jerusalem (ἰδοὺ μάγοι ἀπὸ ἀνατολῶν παρεγένοντο εἰς Ἱεροσόλυμα). Magi in the ancient world were a priestly caste of magicians and astrologers who were wise in interpreting the stars (hence "wise men").[7] Simon "Magus" in Acts 8 was one such. There are four possible source countries for the Magi[8] — Arabia, Babylon, Persia, Egypt — and it

4. For this see Steve Willis, "Matthew's Birth Narratives: Prophecy and the Magi," *ExpTim* 105 (1993): 43 – 45.

5. See E. Cuvillier, "La visite des mages dans l'évangile de Matthieu (Matthieu 2, 1 – 12)," *FoiVie* 98 (1999): 75 – 85, who notes the centrality of this theme.

6. Witherington, *Matthew*, 57.

7. Later legends that there were three (from the three gifts) and they were kings (from Tertullian c. 200 AD) cannot be verified, for Matthew is silent. However, from history they were probably priestly, and from the value of the gifts they were wealthy, possibly court astrologers.

8. Brown, *Birth of the Messiah*, 168 – 70 (no choice); Hagner, *Matthew 1 – 13*, 27 (prefers Babylon). Davies and Allison, *Matthew*, 1:228; and T. T. Maalouf, "Were the Magi from Persia or Arabia?" *BSac* 156 (1999): 423 – 42, both prefer Arabia.

is virtually impossible to determine which one is correct, though the Persians were especially known for divination and astrology. The main thing is that they were well acquainted with Jewish messianic expectations, and all four areas had significant Jewish populations that went back centuries. They must not have known Mic 5:2, for they follow the natural surmise that a king would be born in the capital city and go to Jerusalem.

2:2 ... saying, "Where is the one born[9] King of the Jews? (λέγοντες, Ποῦ ἐστιν ὁ τεχθεὶς βασιλεὺς τῶν Ἰουδαίων;). When the Magi called Jesus "King of the Jews," it became a direct challenge to Herod, a sign to him that his rule may be nearing its end. A man who would murder wives and children because of a perceived threat would not hesitate to go after Jesus with a viciousness impossible to understand by sane people.

2:2 For we have seen his star when it rose (εἴδομεν γὰρ αὐτοῦ τὸν ἀστέρα ἐν τῇ ἀνατολῇ). The "star" has been variously explained with reference to natural phenomena,[10] but the most likely is a supernatural event, possibly similar to the pillar of fire in Exodus (that moved before the Israelites).[11] Actually both may be true; since the Magi were astrologers, they may well have been originally brought to Jerusalem by astrological phenomena and then were guided supernaturally to Bethlehem and the house.

Why call it "a star"? Two reasons: it looked like a bright star, and the language links it to messianic expectations, in particular Balaam's prophecy of Num 24:17, "a star will come out of Jacob." It is possible Matthew thought of the Magi as "Balaam's successors," who came to see Balaam's prophecy of a future world ruler from the Jews fulfilled.[12] The traditional "in the east" does not fit geographically, for Judea was west of Persia and Babylon. The word used here should be translated "at its rising" or "when it rose," thereby emphasizing the miraculous moment when God revealed the star to them. Jesus is called a rising sun/star in Luke 1:78; 2 Pet 1:19; Rev 22:16.

2:2 ... and have come to worship him (καὶ ἤλθομεν προσκυνῆσαι αὐτῷ). "Worship" (προσκυνέω) means to "pay homage" in the broad sense and to "worship" in the narrower sense. In the sense that kings were normally invested with divinity in the ancient world, the latter does fit here, and Matthew certainly wants the reader to think of worship.[13]

2:3 When King Herod heard this, he was deeply disturbed (ἀκούσας δὲ ὁ βασιλεὺς Ἡρῴδης ἐταράχθη). The temporal participle "when he heard" (ἀκούσας) and the main verb "he was

9. "The one born" (ὁ τεχθείς) constitutes a substantival participle used as subject, "the one born is ..."

10. It has been believed to be a supernova that suddenly appeared in the heavens (Kepler); a comet (e.g., Halley's comet appeared 12 – 11 BC); a conjunction of the planets Jupiter and Saturn with Mars in the constellation of Pisces, which occurred in 7 – 6 BC. These are all problematic, and the best option is that it was a supernatural event. See Brown, *Birth of the Messiah*, 171 – 73; Carson, "Matthew," 85 – 86. France, *Matthew* (TNTC), 82; and Blomberg, *Matthew*, 65, all of whom opt for the supernatural manifestation. For those who believe it was the conjunction of planets, see S. Parpola, "The Magi and the Star: Babylonian Astronomy Dates Jesus' Birth," *BRev* 17 (2001): 16 – 23.

11. Since this speaks of a star, it is also possible God revealed himself to them first in their astrological charts, then sent the star to guide them. Bruner, *Christbook*, 46, notes the embarrassment this could cause since it involves "*their idol* — the stars" but remarks that it was a sovereign act of God, who took the unusual in history (the four women in ch. 1) and the unusual in nature (ch. 2, the star) and used them for his glory. It would be similar to Acts 17:23, where Paul said the Athenians' idol to "an unknown god" was preparing them for the reality that Yahweh was that God.

12. Davies and Allison, *Matthew*, 1:231.They also point out that at that time there was widespread expectation of a ruler that was to come from the Jews (Tacitus, *Hist.* 13; Suetonius, *Vesp.* 4), though this is doubted by Carson, "Matthew," 86.

13. See Hagner, *Matthew 1 – 13*, 28.

deeply disturbed" (ἐταράχθη) are both aorist, referring to the incident of the mentally disturbed Herod as a complete whole. There is a deliberate contrast between Jesus as "King of the Jews" in v. 2 and "King Herod" here. This tension dominates this section, as the usurper (actually Herod) is filled with fear at the possibility that the true anointed "king" might arrive.

2:3 ... and all Jerusalem with him (καὶ πᾶσα Ἱεροσόλυμα μετ' αὐτοῦ). There are two possible reasons why Jerusalem would be disturbed as well: they are worried at how the insane Herod will react and fear the atrocities that may result (as indeed they did); or they join Herod in rejecting the idea of a coming Messiah and thereby prepare for the Jewish rejection in the rest of the gospel.[14] While the latter is possible, it doesn't really fit the context, and the fear of Herod is the more likely.

2:4 He called together all the chief priests and teachers of law for the people (καὶ συναγαγὼν πάντας τοὺς ἀρχιερεῖς καὶ γραμματεῖς τοῦ λαοῦ). The circumstantial participle "he called together" (συναγαγών) is best translated as another main verb (see on 4:20). This is not just the ruling body, the Sanhedrin, but "all" the religious leaders from Jerusalem and its environs. It is clear that while Herod thought of himself as king of the Jews, he was not conversant with the Jewish Scriptures, for he did not know Mic 5:2.

In the first century many Jews accepted astrology, and so Herod believes the Magi and consults the Jewish experts for the birthplace of the Messiah[15] (i.e., where the Magi will be going). The "chief priests" consisted of the high priests (Herod and Rome frequently changed the high priesthood) and their families as well as the heads of the priestly orders, the captain of the guard, and those in charge of finances.[16] The "teachers of law" (i.e., scribes) were the legal experts of Jesus' day, the lawyers as well as teachers of both biblical law and Jewish oral tradition. The chief priests were mostly Sadducees, while the teachers of the law were mostly Pharisees, though it is known that some priests were scribes.

2:4 ... and asked them where the Messiah was to be born (ἐπυνθάνετο παρ' αὐτῶν ποῦ ὁ Χριστὸς γεννᾶται). Herod obviously wanted all the data he could find in tracking down this upstart messianic king. There may well be a further contrast here (see 2:3) as the Magi but not the leaders act on the exciting possibility that Mic 5:2 may be fulfilled by the baby Jesus.[17]

2:5 And they said to him, "In Bethlehem of Judea, for this is how it has been written by the prophet" (οἱ δὲ εἶπαν αὐτῷ, Ἐν Βηθλέεμ τῆς Ἰουδαίας· οὕτως γὰρ γέγραπται διὰ τοῦ προφήτου). The experts (as would most Jews) answered that Bethlehem was the prophesied place. This became a problem later, since Jesus grew up in Nazareth, and the Jewish leaders stressed that as proof he could not be the Messiah (cf. Luke 4:22; John 1:46; 7:27, 41 – 42). So this section is in a sense apologetic, showing that Jesus was indeed born in Bethlehem and his birth did in fact fulfill Scripture. Technically, this is not one of the ten "fulfillment passages" in Matthew, for it does not have the same opening formula as 1:22; 2:15; and

14. So Ulrich Luz, *Matthew 1 – 7: A Commentary* (trans. W. C. Linss; Minneapolis: Augsburg, 1989), 113.

15. Savas Agourides, "The Birth of Jesus and the Herodian Dynasty: An Understanding of Matthew, Chapter 2," *Greek Orthodox Theological Review* 37 (1992): 135 – 46, believes that this reflects the messianic ambitions of Herod himself.

16. See Morris, *Matthew*, 37 – 38.

17. See Keener, *Matthew*, 103 – 4, who calls this "spiritual complacency."

others. But it is the same type of OT fulfillment[18] as those.

2:6 And you, Bethlehem in the land of Judah, are by no means least among the rulers of Judah (Καὶ σύ, Βηθλέεμ γῆ Ἰούδα, οὐδαμῶς ἐλαχίστη εἶ ἐν τοῖς ἡγεμόσιν Ἰούδα). This is a rabbinic style pearl-stringing combination of Mic 5:2 (first three lines) and 2 Sam 5:2 (last line in v. 6). The changes to the MT/LXX are interesting. First, "Bethlehem Ephrathah" is changed to "Bethlehem in the land of Judah," which fulfills the same purpose of specifying which Bethlehem is meant but also reflects the "Judah" of 1:2 – 3, the tribe from which the Davidic Messiah was to come. With the repetition of "Judah" in the second line there is added emphasis (to the fulfillment of Mic 5:2, commonly accepted in Judaism as a messianic prophecy) on the messianic nature of this child.

Matthew has also added "by no means" (οὐδαμῶς), which formally contradicts Mic 5:2 ("though small among the clans of Judah") but actually highlights the greatness that is the true meaning of the passage.[19] Matthew is interpreting the text to emphasize that the insignificant village of Bethlehem has become truly great because the Messiah was born there.[20]

2:6 ... because from you will come a ruler (ἐκ σοῦ γὰρ ἐξελεύσεται ἡγούμενος). Matthew has changed the MT "thousands" (= the clans of Israel) to "rulers" (ἡγέμοσιν) and then used the cognate "ruler" (ἡγούμενος) of the Messiah, probably to hint that the Christ child will "rule" over the rulers and that he, not those Rome whom has placed over the nation, will preside over God's people.

2:6 ... who will shepherd my people, Israel (ὅστις ποιμανεῖ τὸν λαόν μου τὸν Ἰσραήλ). This last line is taken from 2 Sam 5:2 (= 1 Chr 11:2) and points directly to David, the shepherd-king who led God's people. There is probably also an echo of Ezek 34:11 – 16, where God himself will become the shepherd of his people because the false shepherds, the leaders of the nation, have scattered his flock. So the Messiah has come to "shepherd" the nation back to God.

2:7 Then Herod secretly called the Magi and ascertained from them exactly the time the star had appeared (Τότε Ἡρῴδης λάθρᾳ καλέσας τοὺς μάγους ἠκρίβωσεν παρ' αὐτῶν τὸν χρόνον τοῦ φαινομένου ἀστέρος). Herod's cunning treachery is seen in his "secret" meeting with the Magi, probably so his intense interest and true intentions will not come out. He wants an exact determination ("to ascertain exactly" [ἀκριβόω] implies precise calculations) of the time the star appeared to them, undoubtedly as part of his plot to kill all the children in Bethlehem near that age (2:16).

2:8 So he sent them to Bethlehem and said, "Go and search very carefully for the infant" (καὶ πέμψας αὐτοὺς εἰς Βηθλέεμ εἶπεν, Πορευθέντες ἐξετάσατε ἀκριβῶς περὶ τοῦ παιδίου). With evil cunning Herod goes back to the Magi and enlists their help. He undoubtedly tells them what the religious experts have said and sends them on to Bethlehem, asking them to search "very carefully" ("carefully" [ἀκριβῶς], the adverbial cognate of "ascertain exactly" in v. 7, adding force to ἐκτάζω,

18. "It has been written" (γέγραπται) is perfect passive (a divine passive emphasizing inspiration) with stative force and emphasizing "completed action" with "existing results" (Wallace, 573 – 74).

19. See Carson, "Matthew," 87 – 88; Blomberg, *Matthew*, 64; France, *Gospel of Matthew*, 72. Hagner, *Matthew 1 – 13*, 29, notes that this reading may already have been circulating in Matthew's time.

20. R. T. France, "The Formula-Quotations of Matthew 2 and the Problem of Communication," *NTS* 27 (1981): 233 – 51, believes the differences between the MT and Matthew in 2:6, 15, 18, 23 are deliberate, apologetic, and intended to show the validity of Jesus as Messiah.

which already means "search diligently for") for the infant.[21]

2:8 "When[22] you have found him, report back to me so that I can also come and worship him" (ἐπὰν δὲ εὕρητε ἀπαγγείλατέ μοι, ὅπως κἀγὼ ἐλθὼν προσκυνήσω αὐτῷ). If the Magi had reported back to Herod, he probably would have sent soldiers to kill just that child. He appears to be with them in their quest to pay homage to the child, saying in effect, "I want to worship him as well." One wonders how the Magi could have been so gullible as to believe what seems a palpable attempt to deceive (Herod's character was well enough known in the court that Augustus is reported to have made a wordplay, saying, "I would rather be Herod's pig [ὗς] than his son [υἱός]"). Perhaps being from the east rather than Rome, they had not heard the reports.

2:9 After listening to the king, they departed. And look, the star they had seen when it rose, went before them until it came and stood before the place where the infant was (οἱ δὲ ἀκούσαντες τοῦ βασιλέως ἐπορεύθησαν, καὶ ἰδοὺ ὁ ἀστὴρ, ὃν εἶδον ἐν τῇ ἀνατολῇ, προῆγεν, αὐτοὺς ἕως ἐλθὼν ἐστάθη ἐπάνω οὗ ἦν τὸ παιδίον). We must remember that it is not a long way from Jerusalem to Bethlehem — only six miles. So it was a journey of a couple hours. For dramatic "look" (ἰδού), see 1:20, 23. Still, the "star" led the way, and this language fits none of the celestial phenomena suggested in 2:2b. It must have been a supernatural manifestation, for it not only "went before" them but also stopped and "stood" above the home in which Jesus was staying. The language is reminiscent of the pillar of fire and the cloud in the wilderness that "went ahead of" Israel to guide them along the way (Exod 13:21; 40:38).[23] God is still in control.

2:10 When they saw the star, they were filled with great joy (ἰδόντες δὲ τὸν ἀστέρα ἐχάρησαν χαρὰν μεγάλην σφόδρα). Matthew goes out of his way to emphasize the depth (or height!) of the Magi's joy. They not only "rejoiced" but did so with a "joy" that was both "great" and "extreme" (μεγάλην σφόδρα, a Hebraism for "very great" joy). The intensity of their joy in the divine guidance and in seeing the child Messiah is obvious.

2:11 When they came[24] into the house, they saw the infant with his mother Mary (καὶ ἐλθόντες εἰς τὴν οἰκίαν εἶδον τὸ παιδίον μετὰ Μαρίας τῆς μητρὸς αὐτοῦ). Some see a contradiction with Luke 2:7, which has Jesus born in a stable. But this event could well have taken place when the infant was older; since Herod killed all the children at the age of two and under (Matt 2:16), that could mean Jesus was one year old or more. The family would remain in the stable for only a short time. Moreover, the idea of a separate stable is wrongheaded. Palestinian homes at that time had mangers at the edge of the living area with the animals, kept either downstairs or (in a one-room home) in one end of the house. So this could be the same home in which Jesus was born.[25]

2:11 ... and they fell[26] on their knees and worshiped him (καὶ πεσόντες προσεκύνησαν αὐτῷ).

21. Matthew uses παιδίον nine times in ch. 2 (Luke uses it three times in Luke 2). The term refers to a small child, here the infant Jesus.

22. Probably for variety's sake, Matthew uses the rare particle ἐπάν ("when, as soon as") for the temporal idea rather than a temporal participle (his usual choice, as in 2:10).

23. Davies and Allison, *Matthew*, 1:246; Keener, *Matthew*, 104.

24. There are two consecutive temporal participles in vv. 10 – 11a.

25. See France, *The Gospel of Matthew*, 75.

26. After the two temporal participles in vv. 10 – 11a, Matthew in v. 11b uses two circumstantial participles ("they fell" [πεσόντες], "opening" [ἀνοίξαντες]), further defining the action of the main verbs (telling how it was accomplished).

This is the way eastern rulers were shown homage; people would prostrate themselves with their foreheads touching the ground. Still, in Matthew's mind this is in reality worship of the messianic King (with προσκυνέω having its basic force of "worship," cf. 2:2).[27]

2:11 And opening their treasure chests, they offered him gifts: gold, frankincense, and myrrh (καὶ ἀνοίξαντες τοὺς θησαυροὺς αὐτῶν προσήνεγκαν αὐτῷ δῶρα, χρυσὸν καὶ λίβανον καὶ σμύρναν). The "gifts" (θησαυρός refers to a "treasure chest" or box) are in keeping with homage shown to a ruler, and their lavish nature makes sense since this is a royal scene. Down through the centuries all kinds of imaginative metaphorical meanings have been read into the gifts (e.g., gold for his royalty, frankincense for his divinity, myrrh for his suffering and death), but that is unlikely. First, they are the type of expensive gifts given to a future king — gold was as highly prized then as today; frankincense and myrrh (both resinous gums taken from trees in Arabia) were fragrant spices used in the best perfumes.

Second, they reflect OT precedent; in fact, there is a fulfillment sense in these passages (see Ps 72:10 – 11, 15, in which "all kings" fall down in homage and give gifts [gold] to the king; Isa 60:3 – 6, where the nations rejoice and bring their riches [gold and frankincense]; and 1 Kgs 10:2, 10, where the Gentile Queen of Sheba gave gold, spices, and precious stones to Solomon, the son of David). The message is that when the nations are blessed and brought to Zion by the Messiah, they will bring gifts to the true and final King (Isa 60:3, 5, "Nations will come to your light ... the riches of the nations will come").[28]

2:12 After they were warned[29] in a dream not to return to Herod, they went back to their country another way (καὶ χρηματισθέντες κατ᾽ ὄναρ μὴ ἀνακάμψαι πρὸς Ἡρῴδην, δι᾽ ἄλλης ὁδοῦ ἀνεχώρησαν εἰς τὴν χώραν αὐτῶν). Matthew uses χρηματίζω for "warn," a term often chosen for divine revelation. The emphasis is on the supernatural nature of the warning; God continues to control the action. A major thrust of the first gospel is that when people try to thwart the divine will, God intervenes supernaturally to overcome all such hostile actions (cf. Job 42:2). The fact that this time no angel appears in the dream (cf. 1:20; 2:19) stresses even more the hand of God in the warning. So the Magi take another route home, and Herod's evil plan is thwarted.

27. The fact that only Jesus and his mother are present does not mean Joseph is removed from the scene, as if he has no relevance. Rather, the Christ child is emphasized, and Mary is in the scene only because no infant would be without his mother.

28. Davies and Allison, *Matthew*, 1:250, see a Jesus/Solomon typology since all three times gold and frankincense are found together in the OT they are linked to Solomon; gold and myrrh are brought to Solomon in association to the temple (1 Kgs 10:2, 25); such eschatological events as this are seen as a return to the days of Solomon (Hag 2:7 – 9).

29. Now we are back to a temporal participle (cf. vv. 10 – 11a) after the circumstantial participles (v. 11b).

Theology in Application

This wondrous story has been celebrated for centuries, though often for the wrong aspects — the belief that these were three kings who came in a royal caravan. The great likelihood that these were royal astrologers might be offensive to many, but we must remember that God accommodates himself to people where they are (consider it a "redemptive analogy") in order to "save some" (1 Cor 9:22). Moreover, on the basis of the view that the star was a supernatural manifestation, there would be no indication that God used astrology (though he could have).

1. Divine Providence at Work

This theme was essential to both parts of ch. 1 as well, but it must be mentioned here because it is the dominating theme. The prophetic fulfillment demonstrates that God prepared for this event in the distant past and that this is indeed the central moment in human history. God indeed superintends his creation and uses the nations to fulfill his will. Moreover, the dreams in chs. 1 – 2 mean that God will not allow his purpose to be thwarted (see Theology in Application section on 1:18 – 25).

2. Worship of the Christ-King

Worship permeates this story. These exalted personages represent the rest of the world, come to bow at the feet of the infant Jesus. Their great efforts to find the baby show their resolve. This is a real fulfillment of the Abrahamic promise that the Jewish people would be a source of blessing to the world (Gen 12:3; 15:5; 18:18; etc.).

3. Jesus as King of the Whole World, Not Just of the Jews

As in 1:1 – 17 the theme of universal mission is stressed. God has seen to it that the Gentiles come to worship the Christ child. In fact, here no representative of the Jewish people comes (though cf. Luke 2:8 – 18). While Jewish mission dominates the body of Matthew ("the lost sheep of the house of Israel," Matt 10:5 – 6; 15:24), that is framed in Matthew with Gentile mission (2:1 – 12; 28:19), and throughout Jesus keeps demonstrating for his disciples what the Gentile mission will be like (8:5 – 13, 28 – 34; 15:21 – 28). It is clear that Matthew wants his Jewish readers to understand God's plan for the mission to the world and their part in it.

4. Conflict and Presages of God's Victory over Evil

This conflict between Herod and Jesus, the Messiah-King, is at the heart of ch. 2 and typifies good vs. evil; Herod is the anti-king trying to preserve his usurped throne by taking the life of the true King. Herod's cunning, evil intentions, and lies are in keeping with the wicked world, and so he typifies the way the world opposes and plots against God,[30] as in Ps 2:1, "Why do the nations conspire and the peoples plot in vain?" But the reaction of God here is the same as in Ps 2:4, "The One enthroned in heaven laughs; the Lord scoffs at them." God, not Herod or the evil powers, is in control of his world, and all who rise against God are doomed. This is as important a message today as it was in Matthew's time.

5. Obedience for Those Seeking Christ

The Magi typify the "seekers" in our time, and it is important to realize that they obeyed everything that God sent them — first the star, then the prophecy, and finally the dream-vision. The heart of it is decision, and without the decision to follow God's leading, they would never have found the messianic King. Moreover, that led to worship of the Christ-King, not to further seeking! It is critical to realize that seekers, so long as they remain only seekers, continue to reject the Savior every service they attend. The task of the church is not just to be "seeker-sensitive" but far more to be "seeker-challenging," for until they *obey* and *worship* the Lord, they stand with Herod rather than the Magi. Of course, it is not too often that seekers are given stars and dream-visions to guide their way, but God is at work in their lives to the same extent he was the Magi's, and the Magi had to respond and accept what God told them. That is the same today.

30. Bruner, *Christbook*, 55 – 56, sees Herod as proof of original sin: "Herod is not dead; Herod lives on, in us.... The exaggerated ambitions, pretensions, greed for position, grudge against God, guile and finally human cruelty and insensitivity, which are all the fruit of our war with God — all these live still in us and must be contended with until the last judgment."

CHAPTER 4

Matthew 2:13 – 23

Literary Context

This episode concludes the infancy narratives on a note of treachery and the attempts of God's enemies to defeat his will. It also contains features from 2:1 – 12, such as the evil attempt of Herod to eliminate his rival and the divine intervention of God, who sends two more dream-revelations to Joseph, telling him when to leave and when to return. At the same time, this is all material unique to matthew.

- **I. Jesus' Origin and Preparation for Ministry (1:1 – 4:11)**
  - **A. The Birth and Infancy of Jesus (1:1 – 2:23)**
    1. The Genealogy of Jesus the Messiah (1:1 – 17)
    2. The Virginal Conception (1:18 – 25)
    3. The Visit of the Magi (2:1 – 12)
    4. **The Evil Actions of Herod and Flight to Egypt (2:13 – 23)**

Main Idea

There are two major, intertwined themes: the divine sovereignty in salvation history and the continual frustration of the forces of evil as they attempt to disrupt God's will. These are both primary themes in Matthew's gospel as a whole.

Translation

Matthew 2:13-23

13a Time — After they had left,
b Scene #1 (A) — **[A] behold the angel of the Lord appeared to Joseph in a dream,**
saying,
c Exhortation — *"Get up, take the infant and his mother, and escape to Egypt.*
d — *Stay there until I tell you,*
e Basis for 13c-d — *for Herod is going to search for the child in order to kill him."*
14a Result of 13c-e — **So he got up,**
took the infant and his mother during the night and
left for Egypt,
15a — **and he stayed there until the death of Herod**
b Fulfillment Formula for 14a-15a — so that the word spoken by the Lord through the prophet
might be fulfilled when he says:
c — *"Out of Egypt I called my son."* (Hos 11:1)

16a Scene #2 (B) — **[B] Then . . . he became very angry**
when Herod realized he had been deceived
by the Magi.
b Result of 16a — **And sending soldiers,**
he murdered all the children in Bethlehem and
its vicinity two years old and younger
c Accordance — on the basis of the time he had learned from the Magi.

17a Fulfillment Formula for 16b — **Then the word spoken by the prophet Jeremiah was fulfilled**
when it said:
18a — *"A voice was heard in Ramah,*
weeping and deep mourning,
Rachel weeping for her children,
b — *and she refused to be comforted,*
for they were no more." (Jer 31:15)

19a Time — After Herod died,
b Scene #3 (A') — **[A'] behold an angel of the Lord appeared**
in a dream
to Joseph in Egypt,
saying,
20a Exhortation — *"Get up,*
take the infant and his mother and
go to the land of Israel,
b Basis for 20a — *for those who were seeking the life of the infant are dead."*

21a Result of 20a — **So he got up,**
took the infant and his mother and
entered the land of Israel.
22a Problem — But after he heard that Archelaus was ruling in Judea
in place of his father
Herod,

Continued on next page.

Continued from previous page.

b		**he was afraid to return there.**
c	Resolution	So when he was warned in a dream,
d		**he moved back to the territory of Galilee.**
23a		And **he went and**
		settled in a town called Nazareth
b	Fulfillment Formula for 23a	in order to fulfill what was spoken through the prophets
c		that he will be called a Nazarene.

Structure and Literary Form

There are three sections in an ABA format, each ending with a fulfillment formula: Joseph is warned in a dream to flee to Egypt (vv. 13 – 15); Herod slaughters the innocent children (vv. 16 – 18); and a further dream leads the family to return, this time back to Nazareth (vv. 19 – 23). They are tightly interwoven, with all three scenes ending with a fulfillment formula (vv. 15, 18, 23) and the two Joseph scenes similar stylistically (genitive absolutes preceding an appearance of the "angel of the Lord" to Joseph [vv. 13, 19]). As stated above for both 1:18 – 25 and 2:1 – 12, this is haggadic midrash,[1] in which a historical scene (Herod's slaughter of the children in Bethlehem and the holy family's flight and return from Egypt) is interpreted as fulfilling OT prophecy.

Exegetical Outline

- ➡ **I. Flight to Egypt (2:13 – 15)**
  - A. Dream-warning by the angel (v. 13)
    - 1. Appearance to Joseph (v. 13a)
    - 2. Command to take the family to Egypt (v. 13b)
  - B. Obedience — flight and sojourn in Egypt until death of Herod (vv. 14 – 15a)
  - C. Fulfillment of Hos 11:1 (v. 15b)
- **II. Herod Slaughters the Innocent Children (2:16 – 18)**
  - A. Herod's anger (v. 16a)
  - B. The murder of all boys two and under (v. 16b)
  - C. Fulfillment of Jer 31:15 (vv. 17 – 18)

1. But not unhistorical; there is no reason to see this as fictive (see Blomberg, *Historical Reliability*, 43 – 53; Osborne, "Historical Narrative," 673 – 88).

III. The Holy Family Returns to Nazareth (2:19 – 23)
- A. The angel appears in a dream (vv. 19 – 20)
    - 1. Appearance to Joseph (v. 19)
    - 2. Command to bring the family back to Israel (v. 20)
- B. Obedience — return to Israel (v. 21)
- C. Second dream-warning and move to Nazareth (vv. 22 – 23a)
    - 1. Fear of Herod's son Archelaus (v. 22a)
    - 2. Dream-warning and withdrawal to Galilee (v. 22b)
    - 3. Settlement in Nazareth (v. 23a)
- D. Fulfillment of Isa 11:1 (v. 23b)

Explanation of the Text

The Magi are no longer the focus, just Herod and the holy family. The consequences are more horrible as well, the slaughter of the innocent children by a madman. Yet divine providence is more powerful than Herod; his plot is thwarted and the family is saved. In the process, more Scripture is fulfilled, showing that God was ready for Herod long before he was born.

Throughout the infancy narratives there have been parallels to the birth of Moses, including divine intervention, the attempts of the ruler of Egypt to stymie God's will by slaughtering innocent Hebrew children, and the flight of Moses as well as his return due to a divine revelation.[2] Jesus in one sense is a "new Moses," for he fulfills those events by reliving them. In the same way that God watched over Moses and kept him safe, so God watches over Jesus and protects his family from the evil plot. At the same time there may also be a parallel with Jacob: "The rescue of Israel's hopes by going to Egypt and the protective hand of a Joseph can recall the patriarchal saga of Jacob (later to be 'Israel') and his clans seeking refuge in Egypt during the time of famine and finding themselves saved by Joseph (Gen 42 – 48)."[3]

2:13 After they had left, behold the angel of the Lord[4] appeared to Joseph in a dream, saying (Ἀναχωρησάντων δὲ αὐτῶν ἰδοὺ ἄγγελος κυρίου φαίνεται κατ' ὄναρ τῷ Ἰωσὴφ λέγων). This is the second of three such angelic dream-warnings (1:20; 2:19 – 20; cf. 2:12; 27:19 where no angel is present), with the emphasis on God's revelation and Joseph's immediate obedience. Unlike 1:20, "appeared" (φαίνεται) is present tense, adding a dramatic "you are there" aura to the scene. Once more the emphasis is on divine providence as God intervenes in behalf of the holy family.

2:13 "Get up, take the infant and his mother" (Ἐγερθεὶς παράλαβε τὸ παιδίον καὶ τὴν μητέρα αὐτοῦ). There is a certain urgency in "get up, take," as the danger to the life of the Christ child is real. The phrase "the infant and his mother" repeats v. 11 and puts the emphasis on Jesus. It is clear that the infancy narrative as a whole centers

2. France, *Gospel of Matthew*, 63. See Hagner, *Matthew 1 – 13*, 34, for a more complete list of parallels; also John D. Crossan, "From Moses to Jesus: Parallel Themes," *BRev* 2 (1986): 18 – 27; and Allan Kensky, "Moses and Jesus: The Birth of the Savior," *Judaism* 42 (1993): 43 – 49.

3. Donald Senior, *Matthew* (ANTC; Nashville: Abingdon, 1998), 47.

4. For anarthrous "angel of the Lord" (ἄγγελος κυρίου) see 1:20.

on Jesus; all other characters (including Herod) are important only as they relate to him.

2:13 "... and escape to Egypt. Stay there until I tell you" (καὶ φεῦγε εἰς Αἴγυπτον, καὶ ἴσθι ἐκεῖ ἕως ἂν εἴπω σοι). Egypt was the perfect place for sanctuary. It had a large Jewish population (a million according to Philo), and it was the closest center of Diaspora Jews for the fleeing family.[5] Moreover, since the Ptolemaic period, Egypt had been friendly toward Jewish people.

2:13 "... for Herod is going to search for the child in order to kill him" (μέλλει γὰρ Ἡρῴδης ζητεῖν τὸ παιδίον τοῦ ἀπολέσαι αὐτό). "Is going" (μέλλει) here speaks of Herod's future "intended actions" (BAGD, 501). "Herod's evil intentions are a controlling factor in this chapter, and he is the archetypal anti-hero. Jesus brings life and freedom, he death and bondage. Jesus gives of himself completely; Herod lives for himself completely."[6] Several have noted here a Moses typology,[7] with the divine protection of the baby as Pharaoh/Herod slaughter the children; the LXX uses the verb "flee" (ἀναχωρέω, as used in Matt 2:14) for the first time when Moses flees Pharaoh in Egypt and becomes a refugee in Midian.

2:14 So he got up, took the infant and his mother (ὁ δὲ ἐγερθεὶς παρέλαβεν τὸ παιδίον καὶ τὴν μητέρα αὐτοῦ). As in 1:24, Joseph obeys the command immediately and flees with his family to Egypt. Egypt had often provided a haven for Jewish refugees (1 Kgs 11:40; 2 Kgs 25:26; Jer 26:21 – 23), and it does so once more. Like Jacob and his family at the start of the exodus events (Gen 46), Jesus, Mary, and Joseph flee Judea and live for a time in Egypt.

2:14 ... during the night and left for Egypt (νυκτὸς καὶ ἀνεχώρησεν εἰς Αἴγυπτον). Yet why go at night (the genitive of time in νυκτός relates the "kind" of time, i.e., time "during" which, cf. Wallace, 122 – 23)? Davies and Allison note three possibilities:[8] (1) to stress the parallel to Matt 26, when Jesus is overtaken by his enemies at night; (2) to avoid being seen, because of the danger of arrest by Herod (cover of darkness, cf. 28:13); (3) since the dream was at night, Joseph may have obeyed so quickly that he left that very night. The latter two stress the danger of the situation, and that is probably the message here.

2:15 And he stayed there until the death of Herod (καὶ ἦν ἐκεῖ ἕως τῆς τελευτῆς Ἡρῴδου). We do not know how long the family lived in Egypt.[9] It likely was not long, for Herod died in 4 BC, and the time from the birth to the slaughter of the boys to Herod's death must have been a fairly short time. They probably sold the gifts they received from the Magi to sustain themselves.

2:15 ... so that the word spoken by the Lord through the prophet might be fulfilled when he says: "Out of Egypt I called my son" (ἵνα πληρωθῇ τὸ ῥηθὲν ὑπὸ κυρίου διὰ τοῦ προφήτου λέγοντος, Ἐξ Αἰγύπτου ἐκάλεσα τὸν υἱόν μου). The use of Hos 11:1 (from the MT, not the LXX) is the second of ten fulfillment passages in Matthew (see on 1:22). This one is interesting, first because Hos 11 is not a messianic passage ("son" in Hos 11:1 refers to Israel: "When Israel was a child I loved

5. See Carson, "Matthew," 90.

6. Bruner, *Christbook*, 58.

7. Gundry, *Matthew*, 33; Bruner, *Christbook*, 58 – 59; Davies and Allison, *Matthew*, 1:259 – 60; Keener, *Matthew*, 107 – 8; Nolland, *Matthew*, 120; Hauerwas, *Matthew*, 40 – 41. See especially Daniel J. Harrington, *The Gospel of Matthew* (SP; Collegeville, MN: Liturgical Press, 1991), 47 – 49.

8. Davies and Allison, *Matthew*, 1:261.

9. Keener, *Matthew*, 112, thinks they remained in Egypt about a year. It could have been even less than that. Jesus was probably between two and three years old when he returned.

him, and out of Egypt I called my son"), and second because it seems to fit better with their return from Egypt ("out of") than with their move there.

As for the first, Matthew sees a typological correspondence between Israel's exodus experience and Jesus' sojourn in Egypt. Though not a direct messianic passage, this still constitutes fulfillment because Jesus as Messiah is corporately identified with Israel throughout its history (cf. the king and high priest, corporately identified with the nation at their time of office) and so fulfills its experiences.[10] Jesus as Son is reliving the experiences of God's children, Israel. Many see also a hint of Num 23:22; 24:8 here, where in Balaam's prophecy the exodus is recapitulated.

As for the second issue, Brown provides two reasons why the Hosea quote is here — the return is not so much a journey from Egypt as it is a journey to Nazareth, and Matthew wishes to place the reference to the exodus before the reference to the exile in 2:17 – 18.[11] Moreover, the emphasis here is not so much on the "*out of* Egypt" as it is on Jesus' reliving the exodus experience as a whole.

2:16 Then, when Herod realized[12] he had been deceived by the Magi, he became very angry (Τότε Ἡρῴδης ἰδὼν ὅτι ἐνεπαίχθη ὑπὸ τῶν μάγων ἐθυμώθη λίαν). The action returns to Herod and the Magi from 2:12. Because of the angel's warning, the Magi had slipped home another way and bypassed Jerusalem. Herod (this is said from his perspective) felt duped (ἐμπιάζω means to "trick, make a fool of" [BAGD]) by the Magi and so was outraged at what he thought was their duplicity.

2:16 ... and sending[13] soldiers, he murdered all the children in Bethlehem and its vicinity two years old and younger on the basis of the time he had learned from the Magi (καὶ ἀποστείλας ἀνεῖλεν πάντας τοὺς παῖδας τοὺς ἐν Βηθλέεμ καὶ ἐν πᾶσι τοῖς ὁρίοις αὐτῆς ἀπὸ διετοῦς καὶ κατωτέρω, κατὰ τὸν χρόνον ὃν ἠκρίβωσεν παρὰ τῶν μάγων). When the Magi failed to return and inform Herod regarding the whereabouts of the child-king, Herod blew his top, feeling he had been made a fool of, so he expanded his plan. Not knowing the exact location, he decided to slaughter all the boys in the whole region of Bethlehem. Apparently the Magi had informed him they had first seen the star two years earlier, so he told the soldiers to murder all boys that age or younger.[14] He may well have sent them from his fortress palace called Herodium just four miles southeast of Bethlehem.[15]

While there is no external documentation for this story, given the kind of person Herod was, it is plausible.[16] He was the type of leader who would murder his sons and even his beloved wife Mariamne because of suspected plots; he also ordered that two thousand Jewish leaders be crucified after his death just so the nation would mourn when he passed (it was not carried out, needless to say), so this Bethlehem tragedy was just another in a long line.

2:17 Then the word spoken by the prophet Jeremiah was fulfilled when it said (τότε ἐπληρώθη τὸ ῥηθὲν διὰ Ἰερεμίου τοῦ προφήτου λέγοντος).

10. See the excellent discussion in Carson, "Matthew," 91 – 92. On typology and the fulfillment formula, see on 1:22. Nolland, *Matthew*, 123, calls this "an Israel typology" that parallels the wilderness experience of Jesus in 4:1 – 11.

11. Brown, *Birth of the Messiah*, 220.

12. A further temporal participle (see vv. 10, 11a, 11b).

13. A circumstantial participle like v. 11b.

14. Carson, "Matthew," 94, estimates the age of Jesus as between six and twenty months old. It would have taken the Magi a few months to caravan from their country to Jerusalem, and Herod would err on the generous side in estimating the cutoff age for the boys to be killed.

15. Keener, *Matthew*, 110.

16. For the historicity of this episode see R. T. France, "Herod and the Children of Bethlehem," *NovT* 21 (1979): 98 – 120. There is no reason to doubt its actuality, for it is much in keeping with what terrible things he would do.

Here we have the third fulfillment passage in Matthew (with 1:22; 2:15). Jeremiah was the weeping prophet, and Matthew chose him for his scenes of tragedy (here and 27:9 – 10, on Judas' betrayal). Knowles argues that Matthew deliberately uses "then" (τότε) rather than "so that" (ἵνα) so as to avoid its purposive force, i.e., implying that God caused the evil intention of Herod in order to fulfill his divine plan. "Yet, paradoxically, even human opposition is part of messianic history and so must be accounted for within the providence of God."[17]

2:18 "A voice was heard in Ramah, weeping and deep mourning" (Φωνὴ ἐν Ῥαμὰ ἠκούσθη, κλαυθμὸς καὶ ὀδυρμὸς πολύς). It is debated whether Jeremiah refers to the Assyrian deportation of the northern tribes in 721 – 22 BC or the Babylonian deportation of the southern tribes in 587 – 86 BC;[18] it could be either or both (so Hagner).

2:18 "Rachel weeping for her children, and she refused to be comforted, for they were no more" (Ῥαχὴλ κλαίουσα τὰ τέκνα αὐτῆς, καὶ οὐκ ἤθελεν παρακληθῆναι, ὅτι οὐκ εἰσίν). The main image is Rachel in her grave (many believed her burial plot was in Ramah, cf. 1 Sam 10:2)[19] weeping in Ramah (in the area allotted to Benjamin about six miles north of Jerusalem) for her children carried off into exile. Ramah lay on the road the captives would have taken, so as Rachel was called the mother of the nation, she symbolizes the mourning of all the people of Israel standing alongside the road as the captives were taken off to oblivion.

Both verbs used here signify a loud wailing in the depths of grief. At the same time, however, there is an aura of hope behind the grief.[20] In Jeremiah the weeping is part of a larger section on the restoration of Israel by Yahweh. In Jer 31:2 the OT says, "The people who survive the sword will find favor in the wilderness; I will come to give rest to Israel"; and immediately following the quote (31:16 – 17) the prophet says, "Restrain your voice from weeping and your eyes from tears, for your work will be rewarded.... They will return from the land of the enemy. So there is hope for your descendants." In fact, 31:31 – 34 deals with the new covenant God will establish with his people (= Heb 8:8 – 12). Like Israel, the child will return from exile and bring a new hope with him.[21]

2:19 After Herod died, behold an angel of the Lord appeared in a dream to Joseph in Egypt (Τελευτήσαντος δὲ τοῦ Ἡρῴδου ἰδοὺ ἄγγελος κυρίου φαίνεται κατ' ὄναρ τῷ Ἰωσὴφ ἐν Αἰγύπτῳ). This verse begins with another temporal genitive absolute (another Matthean phrase, cf.1:18, 20; 2:1, 13), repeats 2:13, and shows the Lord continuing to guide Joseph and the holy family. This fourth dream scene (cf. 1:20; 2:12, 13) shows further that divine providence is still at work and the forces of evil are doomed to defeat. Herod died in 4 BC (probably soon after the massacre in Bethlehem), and the nation breathed a sigh of relief. More refugees than just Joseph's family returned. As stated above (see on 2:15), Joseph, Mary, and Jesus probably lived in Egypt a year or so.

17. Knowles, *Jeremiah in Matthew's Gospel*, 34 – 35.

18. See Brown, *Birth of the Messiah*, 205 – 6.

19. There were two rival traditions regarding the burial place of Rachel, the one near Ramah north of Jerusalem (1 Sam 10:2), and the other near Bethlehem (Gen 35:19; 48:7). Knowles, *Jeremiah in Matthew's Gospel*, 45 – 46, believes Matthew conflates the two, thereby associating Ramah with Bethlehem.

20. See Robert H. Gundry, *Use of the Old Testament*, 210, who says, "Just as the mourning of the Israelite mothers for the Babylonian exiles precluded a brighter future through divine preservation in a foreign land and restoration to Palestine, so the mourning by the mothers of the Bethlehem innocents is a prelude to the Messianic future through divine preservation of the infant Messiah in a foreign land and his later restoration to Palestine."

21. See also Brown, *Birth of the Messiah*, 206; Carson, "Matthew," 95; France, *Matthew* (TNTC), 87; Morris, *Matthew*, 46 – 47; Davies and Allison, *Matthew*, 1:269.

2:20 ... saying, "Get up, take the infant and his mother and go to the land of Israel" (λέγων, Ἐγερθεὶς παράλαβε τὸ παιδίον καὶ τὴν μητέρα αὐτοῦ καὶ πορεύου εἰς γῆν Ἰσραήλ). The circumstantial participle "get up" (ἐγερθείς) partakes of the force of the main verb (as also in v. 21) and should be translated as another imperative. The first part of the angel's message continues to reproduce 2:13 and establishes continuity between God's sending the family down to Egypt and bringing them back.

Again there is a parallel with Moses, as the language echoes Exod 4:19, where the Lord tells Moses in Midian, "Go back to Egypt, for all those who wanted to kill you are dead." At nearly every point of the plot in chs. 1 – 2, this Moses typology is evident.[22] Matthew bathes every aspect in typology and the fulfillment of Scripture. The point is the sovereign hand of God behind every detail of Jesus' birth and childhood.

2:20 "... for those who were seeking the life of the infant are dead" (τεθνήκασιν γὰρ οἱ ζητοῦντες τὴν ψυχὴν τοῦ παιδίου). Matthew's use of the plural "those who were seeking" (οἱ ζητοῦντες) is strange. It might be a generalizing plural standing for one person (Carson) or it might refer to Herod and those with him (Hagner — the soldiers; Brown — the chief priests and scribes of 2:4). In the context Herod and his soldiers make best sense. This does not mean all the soldiers were dead as well but that the hand guiding them was gone.

2:21 So he got up, took the infant and his mother and entered the land of Israel (ὁ δὲ ἐγερθεὶς παρέλαβεν τὸ παιδίον καὶ τὴν μητέρα αὐτοῦ καὶ εἰσῆλθεν εἰς γῆν Ἰσραήλ). The same instant obedience seen in 1:24; 2:14 occurs here. Joseph as a "righteous man" (1:19) was characterized by adherence to God's decrees, whether written in the Torah or delivered by an angel. The two "land of Israel" phrases that appear only here in the NT refer to all the land, both Judea and Galilee, and so prepare for the change of venue in 2:22b – 23.

2:22 But after he heard[23] that Archelaus was ruling[24] in Judea in place of his father Herod, he was afraid to return there (ἀκούσας δὲ ὅτι Ἀρχέλαος βασιλεύει τῆς Ἰουδαίας ἀντὶ τοῦ πατρὸς αὐτοῦ Ἡρῴδου ἐφοβήθη ἐκεῖ ἀπελθεῖν). Joseph probably wished to go back to Bethlehem, but he received word (this time not from divine revelation) that the wrong son of Herod was in charge of Judea. After Herod's death his kingdom was divided between three sons — Antipas was named tetrarch over Galilee and Perea; the half-brother Philip II tetrarch over Iturea and Traconitis, the territory north and east of the Sea of Galilee; and Archelaus ethnarch (the higher title) over Judea, Samaria, and Idumea.[25] Archelaus was much disliked because of his cruelty, and the Jews sent a delegation to Rome, complaining that Archelaus had massacred three thousand shortly before near the temple (Josephus, *Ant.* 17:200 – 18). Indeed he was deposed in AD 6 and exiled to Gaul.

2:22 So when he was warned in a dream, he moved back to the territory of Galilee (χρηματισθεὶς δὲ κατ' ὄναρ ἀνεχώρησεν εἰς τὰ μέρη τῆς Γαλιλαίας). This fourth dream-warning

22. Josephus, *Ant.* 2.205f, states that a scribe/astrologer told Pharaoh that a deliverer was to be born among the Hebrews, whereby Pharaoh in panic ordered all the male infants to be killed; but Moses' father was told in a dream that his son was to be the deliverer and so saved his son from the carnage. See France, *Matthew* (TNTC), 85; contra Luz, *Matthew 1 – 7*, 119, who says the parallels are primarily between Herod and Pharaoh.

23. A temporal participle (so also v. 22b), exactly as in 2:2.

24. The present tense "ruling" (βασιλεύει) after "that" (ὅτι) emphasizes Archelaus's ongoing rule in the past.

25. For the intrigue associated with this, see Harold W. Hoehner, "Herodian Dynasty," *DJG*, 320 – 22. Archelaus was actually named king in Herod's last will, but Augustus named him ethnarch with the promise he would be made king if he ruled well. He never did.

(2:12, 13, 19, fifth with 1:20 – 21) shows the extent to which God was watching over the child and protecting him. As Joseph was mulling over what to do as a result of his fear of Archelaus, God made it clear and took sovereign control.

2:23 And he went and settled in a town called Nazareth (καὶ ἐλθὼν κατῴκησεν εἰς πόλιν λεγομένην Ναζαρέτ). Joseph's choice of a town in Galilee was simplified by his past. Luke tells us that Nazareth was the former home of both him and Mary (Luke 1:26 – 27; 2:39). Nazareth was a fairly small village of fifty to sixty acres with about 480 population[26] and thus not significant in and of itself.[27]

2:23 ... in order to fulfill what was spoken through the prophets that he will be called a Nazarene (ὅπως πληρωθῇ τὸ ῥηθὲν διὰ τῶν προφητῶν ὅτι Ναζωραῖος κληθήσεται). The fulfillment formula Matthew uses is unique. He uses the plural "prophets" and replaces "saying" (λέγων) with "that" (ὅτι), thereby making the actual quote an indirect one[28] (the formulas usually employ λέγων for a quote, cf. 1:22; 2:17). The reason is that the statement ("He will be called a Nazarene") appears nowhere in the OT and must be a composite quote, i.e., a summary of several prophetic texts rather than a quotation from a particular passage.

Of the three options for its origin noted in the footnote,[29] the best seems to be a combination of one and three. First, "a Nazarene" (Ναζωραῖος) was a person from a small, backward town who could expect to be looked down as (in today's terms) a "hick from the sticks." This is what Nathaniel meant in John 1:46 (cf. 7:42, 52; Acts 24:5) when he asked, "Can anything good come from [Nazareth]?" So Jesus was despised and rejected like the prophets of old (Ps 22:6 – 13; 69:8; Isa 53:2 – 3). Second, and in contrast to the first, Matthew uses a midrashic word play of *nazōraios* with *nēzer* and sees Jesus as the "branch" of Isa 11:1.[30] He is the royal branch, the Davidic Messiah, but he arises from the "stump" of Jesse as the lowly, scorned one (cf. Jer 23:5; 33:15; Zech 3:8; 6:12).

26. James Strange, "Nazareth," *ABD*, 4:1050 – 51.

27. René Salm, "The Myth of Nazareth: The Invented Town of Jesus," *American Atheist* (March 2007): 12 – 13, says that after an eight-year research he has proven that Nazareth did not exist in the time of Jesus, having been destroyed about 730 BC by the Assyrian and not rebuilt until 70 – 130 AD between the two revolts. Moreover, when rebuilt it encircled a Roman graveyard, so it could hardly have been built by Jews. So, he argues, "Jesus of Nazareth" was unhistorical and invented by the evangelist. However, several points must be made in rejoinder. (1) Salm never took part in a dig, for he is not a professional archeologist. (2) The one who did oversee that dig, B. Baggati (*Excavations at Nazareth*, 2 vols. [Jerusalem, 1969]), as used by Jim Strange in "Nazareth," *ABD*, 4:1050 – 51, speaks of it as a village in the time of Jesus constructed in the 3rd century BC. Josephus lived in Yafia next to Nazareth and fortified it during the revolt (*Wars* 2.20.6 – 573; *Life* 52 – 270). Nazareth contained the type of *kokhim* tombs found from 200 BC — AD 70 and was known to be a small agricultural village containing silos, olive presses, and millstones in the first century. See also Jack Finegan, *Archaeology of the New Testament* (Princeton: Princeton Univ. Press, 1992), 27 – 33. Thanks are also due the advice of Barry Beitzel, a professional archeologist and mapmaker.

28. While "that" (ὅτι) can lead into a direct quote as well, that is not as likely in this context since this is a composite formula and the style differs from the other fulfillment formulas.

29. Brown, *Birth of the Messiah*, 209 – 13, surveys the possibilities: (1) derived from "Nazareth," such as Jesus belonging to a pre-Christian sect called *Nazōraioi* (no evidence of such until the church fathers) or Jesus as a resident of Nazareth (alluding to Judg 13:5; Soares-Prabhu, *The Formula Quotations*, 206 – 7); (2) derived from *nāzîr*, namely, one consecrated to God by a Nazirite vow (so Schweizer, Davies and Allison), such as Samson (Judg 13:2 – 7); (3) derived from *nēzar*, the "branch" of Isa 11:1 (so Filson, Brown, Hagner, Nolland, Witherington). E. Zuckschwerdt, "'Abermals' in Matt 2, 23," *TZ* 57 (2001): 422 – 25, believes the Nazirite tradition of the Samson narrative in Judg 13:1 – 25 is the primary background.

30. The primary problem of this is the fact that this only works in Hebrew, but writing for a Jewish Christian audience, Matthew could expect his readers to catch the wordplay (contra France, *Gospel of Matthew*, 92).

Theology in Application

This final section of Matthew's infancy narrative continues many of the themes in the other sections, and several are special to this part of the book (e.g., the fulfillment motif, God's protection of his Son). Others will be carried throughout the first gospel (e.g., conflict, Jesus' messianic status).

1. God Protects His Own

Absolutely nothing can happen that is outside God's larger plan, and his power cannot be turned aside (Job 42:2; Isa 14:27; Jer 32:27). When the infant Jesus is threatened by Herod's murderous intention, God intervenes and sends dream-warnings to Joseph (2:19, 23) to flee to Egypt, then to return. The same is true in our lives. God does not often send visions or angels, but he does superintend what happens to us. Paul was sent dreams, as at Troas (Acts 16:9; see also "Theology in Application" on 1:18 – 25). Also, Paul was "compelled by the Spirit" to go to Jerusalem (Acts 20:22) in spite of his companions telling him the Spirit said not to go (21:4, 12). Luke faithfully tells when there is a dream or angelic appearance, and the absence of that in these passages, I believe, means Paul felt led in those directions. God does intervene and guide our lives as he did Paul's, though most of us experience this divine providence in indirect ways. Nevertheless, we must realize that God is sovereign in our lives as well.

But how does this explain the hard times, when God seems to have disappeared and left us to our fates? How do we understand God's protection and superintending in times of crisis and disaster? There we have to realize the place of trials in our lives. God does not tempt us (Jas 1:13), but he does allow tests (Jas 1:2 – 4; 1 Pet 1:6 – 7), and the purpose is to make us more aware of our need to depend wholly on him. In times of serious trials, when many things are going wrong, we must turn and cry "Abba, Father" and join Jesus' Gethsemane prayer, "*Abba*, Father ... everything is possible for you. Take this cup from me. Yet not what I will, but what you will" (Mark 14:36). We must surrender to the divine providence, ask for deliverance, trust in God's wisdom, and know that "in all things God works for the good of those who love him" (Rom 8:28).

2. Evil Rampant in Our World

Matthew has a great deal to say about evil in his gospel, and this passage introduces the theme. The new kingdom will be in constant opposition to rampant wickedness of the kind exemplified in Herod. This is seen especially in Christ, who will be sent to the cross by such wicked people. The use of Jer 31:15 in Matt 2:18 to show that even the suffering of the innocents and of the infant Jesus was in accord with the divine plan; the mother of Israel laments for both as representative of the nation in the grip of evil and rejection.[31]

It is clear that the world is characterized by evil, and God's people can never expect the world to adopt their own set of ethical and moral criteria. This has ramifications for similar issues today. We should and must oppose such issues as abortion, homosexual practices,and drugs, but we should not allow these to dominate us, for in an evil world we must to some degree expect such things to happen. The best opposition is not picketing (though it does have its place) but the proclamation of the gospel. We cannot expect an unbeliever to change until they become children of God.

At the same time social injustice plagues our world and exists all around us. We must actively fight evil such as ghetto landlords or racial profiling or unfair business practices. This is a time for Christians to take a stand on the side of the poor and the marginalized; this is in fact part of the gospel message (as in the emphasis on social concern in the gospel of Luke), and we must be known for it! Yet evil triumphs only so long as God allows this wicked world to continue. It will be eradicated in the end when Christ becomes judge (13:24 – 30, 36 – 43, 47 – 52).

3. Opposition and Conflict as the World's Reaction to God's Children

Herod's reaction is in keeping with the natural man. When darkness faces light, it cannot react any other way than rejection and persecution. As John 3:18 – 20 says, darkness hates light because it does not want its evil deeds shown for what they are (cf. also John 15:18 – 16:4). While Herod fails to kill the Christ child at this time, the world of evil (Jews *and* Gentiles) will succeed in the end, but that is because Christ yields himself up to that rampant evil. The message is that Christ's followers must expect the same reception as Christ felt. There is more martyrdom today than ever before in history; it is just that it happens elsewhere for those of us in the west. But it can come at any time, and it is happening to our brothers and sisters around the world.

4. God's Salvation for This Evil World

In all the history of humanity, evil has never been allowed to triumph in the end. God brought the Israelites out of bondage at the exodus and brought his people back after both exiles. God used the nations to punish an apostate Israel, but then he judged them as well in due time. God is a God of salvation first and a God of judgment second. The Davidic "Branch," both Messiah and Savior, has arrived, and

31. Knowles, *Jeremiah in Matthew's Gospel*, 52.

as God saved him from Herod, so he will save us in the final analysis from all the evil that has turned against us. Jesus' return from Egypt is a promise to the church down through the ages that God ultimately delivers his people — thus the old adage, "The blood of the martyrs is the seed of the church." It was true with Jesus, it has been true throughout church history, and it is true now.

CHAPTER 5

Matthew 3:1 – 12

Literary Context

This section provides an introduction to the ministry of Jesus and functions as a primer for his messianic work: the Baptist prepares for Jesus' messianic ministry. Jesus is filled with the Spirit, and he defeats Satan in open combat, proving himself to be Son of God. The three events of this section flow together to describe how God readied Jesus and those around him for his incredible two- to three-year ministry.[1] First, the Baptist fulfills prophecy in becoming the forerunner to the Messiah; second, the baptism has the Spirit descending on and anointing Jesus for his ministry plus the Father identifying Jesus as his beloved Son (a critical christological identification); and third, Jesus proves himself to be the Son of God by defeating Satan in the wilderness. Thus, Jesus' ministry is launched on a note of power and victory.

I. Jesus' Origin and Preparation for Ministry (1:1 – 4:11)
- A. The Birth and Infancy of Jesus (1:1 – 2:23)
- **B. Inaugural Events in Jesus' Ministry (3:1 – 4:11)**
  - ➦ **1. John the Baptist (3:1 – 12)**
  - 2. The Baptism of Jesus (3:13 – 17)
  - 3. The Testing/Temptation of Jesus (4:1 – 11)

1. There are two considerations for dating the start of Jesus' ministry: (1) John 2:20 tells us he began in the forty-sixth year of rebuilding the temple (it was started in 19 BC = AD 27/28 for Jesus' mission); (2) Luke 3:1 says John began his ministry in "the fifteenth year of the reign of Tiberius Caesar." He began in August AD 14, which would make it AD 28 – 29. If Jesus was crucified in AD 30 (the majority view, though see Harold Hoehner, *Chronological Aspects of the Life of Christ* [Grand Rapids: Zondervan, 1977] who dates it in AD 32), his ministry lasted about two years. This is in keeping with the three Passovers of John, with the first and third coming at the beginning and end of Jesus' ministry.

Main Idea

The Baptist scene has a twofold purpose here: as the messianic forerunner, John announces that the kingdom is here and that the Messiah is about to announce himself; as the wilderness prophet, John brings an apocalyptic message of repentance and the coming of divine judgment. Now is the time to mourn for sin, for the divine warrior will come and judge the world, including especially the Jews. Moreover, repentance must produce fruit, that is, a new lifestyle in keeping with the arrival of God's kingdom.

Translation

Matthew 3:1-12

1a	Scene #1	**[1] In those days John the Baptist arrived,**
		preaching in the desert of Judea
2a		**and saying,**
b	Exhortation	*"Repent, for the kingdom of heaven has come near!"*
3a	Fulfillment Formula for 2a	For this is the one who was spoken about through the prophet Isaiah when he says,
b		*"The voice of one crying in the wilderness:*
c		*Prepare the way for the Lord;*
d		*make straight his paths!"* (Isa 40:3)
4a	Description	**John himself wore a garment of camel hair and**
		a leather belt around his waist.
b		**His food was locusts and wild honey.**
5a	Result of 2b-4b	**Then Jerusalem and**
		all Judea and
		the whole region of the Jordan began to come out to him,
6a		and **they were being baptized by him in the Jordan River,**
		confessing their sins.
7a	Scene #2	When he saw many of the Pharisees and Saddducees coming to the place he was baptizing,
b	Warning	**[2] he said to them,**
c		*"Offspring of vipers,*
		who warned you to flee from the wrath soon to come?
8a		*Produce fruit befitting repentance*
9a		*and do not presume to say among yourselves,*
		'We have Abraham as our father,'
b	Basis for 9a	*for I am telling you that God has the power to raise up children*
		for Abraham
		from these very stones.

Continued on next page.

Continued from previous page.

10a *The ax is already laid at the root of the trees.*
b *So every tree . . . is going to be cut down and thrown into the fire*
that does not produce good fruit
11a Comparison *I am baptizing you in water as associated with repentance*
but after me
one is coming
who is far greater than I
whose sandals I am not fit to carry.
b Description *He will baptize you in the Holy Spirit and fire*
12a *whose winnowing fork is in his hand;*
and he will clean his threshing floor.
b *He will gather his wheat into the barn but*
burn the chaff with unquenchable fire."

Structure and Literary Form

This section is made up of two parts (the first interacting with Mark 1:4 – 8 and the second with Q; cf. Luke 3:7 – 9), and each consists of two subsections. The first part is a *descriptive narrative* (3:1 – 6) dealing with (1) the significance of John's coming — his call for repentance and the fulfillment passage from Isa 40:3 on John as the "way" preparing for the coming of the "Lord" (Matt 3:1 – 3); and (2) John as the wilderness prophet leading the people to confess and be baptized (3:4 – 6).

The second part is a *proclamation narrative* (3:7 – 12), detailing the contours of his message itself, as he (1) warns the people of the imminent coming of apocalyptic judgment (vv. 7 – 10), and (2) points to the one who will "baptize . . . in the Holy Spirit and fire," namely, fiery judgment (vv. 11 – 12).

Exegetical Outline

➡ **I. The Ministry of the Baptist (3:1 – 6)**
  A. The Meaning of His Ministry (vv. 1 – 3)
    1. His desert ministry and message (vv. 1 – 2)
      a. Preaching in the desert (v. 1)
      b. Message of repentance (v. 2a)
      c. Reason: nearness of the kingdom (v. 2b)
    2. Isaianic fulfillment (v. 3)
      a. The voice in the desert (v. 3a)
      b. The way readied for the Lord (v. 3b)
  B. The Nature of His Ministry (vv. 4 – 6)
    1. His wilderness appearance (v. 4)
    2. His wilderness ministry (vv. 5 – 6)
      a. People come from everywhere (v. 5)

b. Confession and baptism (v. 6)

II. The Message of the Baptist (3:7 – 12)

A. Warning against Pharisees and Sadducees (vv. 7 – 10)

1. The coming wrath (v. 7)
2. Produce fruit proving repentance (v. 8)
3. No appeal to Abraham (v. 9)
4. Fiery judgment (v. 10)

B. Prophecy regarding the Coming One (vv. 11 – 12)

1. More powerful (v. 11a)
2. Baptize with Holy Spirit and fire (v. 11b)
3. Harvest of fiery judgment (v. 12)

Explanation of the Text

3:1 In those days John the Baptist arrived (Ἐν δὲ ταῖς ἡμέραις ἐκείναις παραγίνεται Ἰωάννης ὁ βαπτιστής). Matthew tells us nothing about Jesus' childhood. Indeed the only account of Jesus' childhood in the four gospels appears in Luke 2:41 – 52, the story about the young Jesus at the temple. "In those days" seems strange since the narrative skips the childhood of Jesus and goes straight to the beginning of his adult ministry (he would have been about thirty-three years old [6/5 BC – AD 28];[2] cf. Luke 3:23, "about thirty years old"). Its purpose is to link this closely with chs. 1 – 2 ("in the days of the Messiah"), namely, the days appointed for fulfilling God's plan. The historic present in "arrived" (παραγίνεται) pictures John "making his public appearance" (BAGD; cf. 3:13, where it is used of Jesus' first appearance as well). He is called "the Baptist" especially in Matthew, undoubtedly because of the significance of his ministry of baptism.

3:1 ... preaching in the desert of Judea (κηρύσσων ἐν τῇ ἐρήμῳ τῆς Ἰουδαίας). John considered himself primarily a street preacher (circumstantial participle[3] "preaching" [κηρύσσων]), proclaiming the message God had given him. "The desert of Judea" is between the Dead Sea and the lower Jordan River and south of Jerusalem; this is near the Qumran community, so some have thought him a former member of that community (his desert attire, his use of ceremonial washing, etc.).[4] But the differences are too great for such an association (he did not separate himself from the rest of the nation; his was a onetime baptism with little similarity to Qumran), and it is more likely that he saw himself as a wilderness prophet in the mold of Elijah.

As is the case with John, Jesus' actual childhood is not described apart from one event, Jesus at the temple as he prepares to leave his childhood (Luke 2:41 – 52).[5] Most likely he had a normal childhood without any unusual signs of his coming messianic ministry; he became an apprentice to his father and became the village carpenter after Joseph's death (he is called "the carpenter"

2. See the "Literary Context" on the reasons for this date.

3. On this see on 2:4, 20 – 21.

4. See W. F. Albright and C. S. Mann, *Matthew* (AB; Garden City, NY: Doubleday, 1971), 27, who say there is "no reason to doubt that John grew up in Qumran," due not only to his practice of baptism but also to his preaching the imminent arrival of the messianic kingdom.

5. For this reason the apocryphal gospels contain many incredible stories of his childhood. None of them is likely to be historical.

in Mark 6:3 = Matt 13:55). In all four gospels the Baptist's ministry as messianic forerunner inaugurates Jesus' ministry. This was an incredibly significant event, for God had been silent for four hundred years, as no prophet had come on the scene. The Jews believed the next prophet would have messianic significance.

3:2 ... and saying, "Repent" (καὶ λέγων, Μετανοεῖτε). John's message is revolutionary and apocalyptic. It must have been a shock to those who heard him. Here is no rabbi,[6] reasoning and giving options; here is no priest, leading ritual; here is no scribe, prescribing adherence to a set of rules. John speaks with a thunderous voice, demanding a new relationship with God. The present imperative "repent" (μετανοεῖτε) is striking (cf. Mark 1:4; Luke 3:3, "preaching a baptism of repentance") and calls for an ongoing and complete change of mind and action. While the Greek term could imply only an intellectual transformation, this draws from the OT and Jewish concept that demanded a lifestyle change as well (see on 3:8), giving an urgent message to "turn around" while there is time.[7] In the OT it meant a radical return to God of those who have broken the covenant with him.[8] The idea is that of turning from sin to God in every area of one's life, moral/ethical as well as mental.

3:2 "... for the kingdom of heaven has come near!" (ἤγγικεν γὰρ ἡ βασιλεία τῶν οὐρανῶν). The reason for this (γάρ) is the dawning of a new age, "the kingdom of heaven."[9] Mark 1:15 (= Matt 4:17) has Jesus say this, but Matthew here stresses that the Baptist said this as well. The idea of kingdom, it is now agreed, means "God is king" or better the verbal "God reigns." The Jewish expectation of a new world order developed throughout the OT, especially during the prophetic period. It was often called "the day of the Lord," connected especially with final judgment (Isa 13:6, 9; Joel 1:15; 2:31; Zech 14:1 – 21; cf. Ezek 7:7; Obad 15; Mal 3:2; 4:1, 5).

Five ideas emerge in the prophetic and intertestamental periods: the regathering of Israel (*4 Ezra* 13:39 – 41), the destruction of the nations (Dan 2:44; 7:26; *2 Bar.* 36 – 40), the reign of God's people (Dan 7:27; Wis 3:8; *T. Jud.* 25:1 – 2; Matt 19:28; 1 Cor 6:2; Rev 20:4), the harvest of judgment (Dan 12:2; *4 Ezra* 4:30; *2 Bar.* 72 – 74; Matt 3:12; 13:30, 40), and the transformation of this world into a new earth (Isa 65:17; 66:22; *1 En.* 45:3 – 5; *2 Bar.* 32:1 – 7; Matt 19:28; Rev 21:1).[10] By the time of Christ, virtually all the attention was given to the destruction of Rome, and this is why Jesus' twelve disciples never understood that he came to suffer and die — they

6. Here the term is used in its second-century rather than its first-century thrust. There were no ordained rabbis until the second century (post-AD 135). In Jesus' day it simply designated a "teacher" of Torah.

7. See J. Behm, "νοέω, etc.," *TDNT*, 4:999 – 1000; Carson, "Matthew," 99; Bruner, *Christbook*, 70; Harrington, *Matthew*, 51.

8. Hill, *Matthew*, 90.

9. Matthew uses "kingdom of heaven" nearly every time (except for 12:28; 19:24; 21:31, 43). Some see a distinction: older dispensationalists argued that "kingdom of God" was a spiritual reign in the lives of Jesus' true followers and "kingdom of heaven" the millennial reign (few follow that anymore), cf. M. Pamment, "The Kingdom of Heaven according to the First Gospel," *NTS* 27 (1981): 211 – 32, who argues that the kingdom of God is God's sovereignty in the present while the kingdom of heaven is the future reign. Likely neither are correct, for Matthew often replaces the kingdom of God sayings in Mark/Luke with kingdom of heaven. Matthew uses "kingdom of heaven" probably for two reasons: as a circumlocution for God so as not to offend pious Jews who objected to naming the name of God, and to emphasize that the new kingdom came from heaven and belonged to God.

10. See Wendell L. Willis, ed., *The Kingdom of God in Twentieth-Century Interpretation* (Peabody, MA: Hendrickson, 1987); Scot McKnight, "Kingdom of God/Heaven," *DJG*, 417 – 30. For a good survey see I. Howard Marshall, "The Hope of a New Age: The Kingdom of God in the New Testament," *Them* 11 (1985): 5 – 15.

had no basis for understanding this,[11] for they thought only of a conquering Messiah.

This cataclysmic event "has come near" (ἤγγικεν). It is debated whether the perfect tense used here (with stative force)[12] is synonymous with 12:28, "has come," or means it is imminent, "near at hand." The verb itself favors the latter; it is almost upon us. Yet it is disjunctive to set the one up against the other. Davies and Allison do an excellent job[13] of showing that Judaism as well as Christ viewed the coming of the kingdom as a series of events taking place over an extended period of time (e.g., *Jub.* 23; *1 En.* 91:12 – 17, 93). So the kingdom of God has come and is coming, and the people of God live between the ages, feeling the tension between the already and the not yet. In the Messiah the kingdom has arrived, yet the events have only been inaugurated, and the final stage is in the future.

3:3 For this is the one who was spoken about through the prophet Isaiah when he says (οὗτος γάρ ἐστιν ὁ ῥηθεὶς διὰ Ἠσαΐου τοῦ προφήτου λέγοντος). The reason for (γάρ) John's message in v. 2 is now stated; the call to repentance is necessary in light of the coming of the Messiah, for whom John is the divinely sent preparation. All four gospels quote Isa 40:3; in its context the Isaianic passage relates God's promise to bring the exiles home from Babylon on a divinely prepared highway, with the image of all obstacles being removed by God. The pesher-style[14] formula here ("this is that") points clearly to another fulfillment passage.

3:3 "The voice of one crying in the wilderness: Prepare the way for the Lord; make straight his paths!" (Φωνὴ βοῶντος ἐν τῇ ἐρήμῳ, Ἑτοιμάσατε τὴν ὁδὸν κυρίου, εὐθείας ποιεῖτε τὰς τρίβους αὐτοῦ). The task of the Baptist and of the church is to clear the path for the highway to Zion, that is, to be the means God uses to clear all obstacles for the coming of the Messiah. Matthew follows the LXX except in changing "the paths of our God" (LXX) to "his paths" in order to point clearly to Christ.[15] Therefore the Baptist is the messianic forerunner preparing the way for Christ.

This imagery is strong, for this was a primary theme verse for both Qumran (1QS 8:13 – 14) and Christianity. The early church even called itself "the Way" on the basis of this verse (Acts 9:2; 19:9, 23; 22:4; 24:14, 22). So it is fitting that Isa 40:3 inaugurates the Jesus story; the "straight paths" are the repentance of God's people. There is probably great emphasis on the switch from the aorist imperative "prepare" (ἑτοιμάσατε) to the present "make" (ποιεῖτε). At one level they are virtually synonymous, but the aorist "prepare" looks at the event as a whole, and the present "make" looks at the ongoing process by which it comes to pass.

3:4 John himself wore a garment of camel hair[16] and a leather belt around his waist. His food was locusts and wild honey (Αὐτὸς δὲ ὁ Ἰωάννης εἶχεν τὸ ἔνδυμα αὐτοῦ ἀπὸ τριχῶν καμήλου καὶ ζώνην δερματίνην περὶ τὴν ὀσφὺν αὐτοῦ, ἡ δὲ τροφὴ ἦν αὐτοῦ ἀκρίδες καὶ μέλι ἄγριον). John

11. They, like most Jews, probably understood the Suffering Servant of Isa 52 – 53 as referring to Israel, not the coming Messiah.

12. See Wallace, 573. Here the perfect verb does not connote completed action with existing results, for the emphasis is on the current state of the situation in salvation history, namely, the imminent coming of the kingdom.

13. Davies and Allison, *Matthew*, 1:389 – 92.

14. "Pesher" refers to the hermeneutical approach of Qumran, stemming from their belief that they directly fulfilled the mysteries, that is, every aspect of the message and history of the OT. Their interpretation was a "this is that" approach, namely, that every text pointed to them and was fulfilled in their community and experiences. See Osborne, *Hermeneutical Spiral*, 326 – 27.

15. Hagner, *Matthew 1 – 13*, 48.

16. This is a genitive of content, "made of camel's hair" (BDF §167).

is messianic forerunner in terms of Isaiah in v. 3, and now his dress is reminiscent of the wilderness prophet Elijah (forerunner in Mal 4:5; cf. Matt 17:10 – 13), both in terms of his coat (Zech 13:4) and his belt (2 Kgs 1:8). God is no longer silent, and the centuries of waiting are over. The Messiah is on his way, and the people of God are to ready themselves.

Locusts (including grasshoppers) and wild honey (probably taken by John himself from beehives) were the food of the poor, especially those living in the desert. Some have seen John as a Nazirite refusing meat and strong drink so as to serve God wholly. John clearly saw himself as a wilderness prophet, an austere man, and an ascetic, calling with a stern voice for the people to repent and turn to God.

3:5 Then Jerusalem and all Judea and the whole region of the Jordan began to come out to him (τότε ἐξεπορεύετο πρὸς αὐτὸν Ἱεροσόλυμα καὶ πᾶσα ἡ Ἰουδαία καὶ πᾶσα ἡ περίχωρος τοῦ Ἰορδάνου). The response to John's appearance and message is incredible. People "began to come" (ingressive imperfect, ἐξεπορεύετο) from everywhere around, not only Jerusalem but the whole of Judea and even the entire area of the Jordan (each one a wider area). The growth of John's popularity (cf. Josephus, *Ant.* 18.116 – 20) is reminiscent of Jesus in Mark 1:32 – 45 (= Matt 8:1 – 4, 14 – 17, though Matthew does not have the theme of Jesus' growing popularity there). The point is the great impact John made on the people.

3:6 ... and they were being baptized by him in the Jordan River (καὶ ἐβαπτίζοντο ἐν τῷ Ἰορδάνῃ ποταμῷ ὑπ' αὐτοῦ). The second consecutive imperfect "they were being baptized" (ἐβαπτίζοντο) shows the dynamic impact John made. It is a dramatic imperfect, picturing all the people flocking to him for baptism. The origins of John's baptism are disputed.[17] Some say Jewish ritual washings, others Qumran's daily lustrations, still others Jewish proselyte baptism. But Jewish washings were generally for ritual uncleanness, and John does not connect his baptism with that. Qumran's immersions were repeated daily, and John's was a onetime only event. Proselyte baptism is a possibility, though it was only for Gentiles, never Jews; the Baptist could be saying the nation has gone apostate and needs to repent. But there is no evidence for proselyte baptism before about AD 50 (though it may have gone back to John's time). For the most part, therefore, John's baptism appears a unique event,[18] probably linked to his point in v. 9 that the ancestry of the Jews is inadequate to make them right with God.

3:6 ... confessing their sins (ἐξομολογούμενοι τὰς ἁμαρτίας αὐτῶν). The circumstantial participle (cf. 2:4, 20, 21; 3:1) "confessing" (ἐξομολογούμενοι) records the necessary precursor to baptism, namely, confession. Confessing sin (cf. Mark 1:4, "for the forgiveness of sins") is remarkable in the context of baptism, following closely the thrust of proselyte baptism for Gentiles. Confession was mandated in the Torah (Lev 5:5; Num 5:6 – 7) and practiced in times of revival (Ezra 10:1; Neh 9:2). There is no hint here that confession was done at the time of baptism, but it is certainly connected (as in Mark 1:4). Most likely baptism[19] for John (as for the early church, cf. Acts 2:38; 22:16; Col 2:12; 1 Pet 3:21) meant the person had confessed and been

17. See G. R. Beasley-Murray, *Baptism in the New Testament* (Grand Rapids: Eerdmans, 1962), 1 – 44.

18. This is the conclusion of S. Benétreau, "Baptèmes et ablutions dans le Judaïsme: L'originalité de Jean-Baptiste," *FoiVie* 80 (1981): 96 – 108, who after an extensive discussion of Jewish ablutions among the Pharisees, Qumran, and proselyte baptism concludes that John's baptism was a unique event.

19. The imagery here in the Jordan River as well as the basic meaning of βαπτίζω (to "dip, immerse," *EDNT*, 1:192)

forgiven. It was an eschatological rite, meaning the repentant are now children of the kingdom.

3:7 When he saw many of the Pharisees and Sadducees coming to the place he was baptizing (Ἰδὼν δὲ πολλοὺς τῶν Φαρισαίων καὶ Σαδδουκαίων ἐρχομένους ἐπὶ τὸ βάπτισμα αὐτοῦ). We now turn from Markan parallels to Q (Luke 3:7 – 9). Again Matthew has added some of his own material to bring out specific nuances. The main thing Matthew edits is Luke 3:7, "the crowds," as Matthew emphasizes the Jewish leaders from within the crowds. It is possible that this was an official Sanhedrin delegation (the main ruling body of the Jews), for normally the two groups were opposed to each other.

The Pharisees (the name stemming from the Hebrew *perušîm*, "separatists") developed out of the Hasidim ("the pious ones") of the Maccabean period and were closely connected to the oral tradition or official interpretation of the Torah for that day. They were teachers of the law and advocated a scrupulous observance of purity and piety regulations. They saw themselves as "building a fence around the law" so as to help the common people keep its rules, and their influence grew throughout the NT period, though more from the respect of the people than from numbers (Josephus, *Ant.* 17:42 put their number at six thousand).[20]

If the Pharisees were the party of the common people, the Sadducees (the name probably stemming from the high priest Zadok [1 Kgs 1:8]) were the party of the aristocrats, consisting of many chief priests and the upper class. Many think they developed from the Hasmoneans, though no one knows for certain. They may have believed only the Torah was authoritative (though this is doubted by many) and so denied the resurrection/afterlife, angels, and a coming kingdom.[21] The two groups were usually opponents, and the fact they are together here (connected by a single article) may indicate that they were sent by the Sanhedrin.

3:7 ... he said to them, "Offspring of vipers, who warned you to flee from the wrath soon to come?" (εἶπεν αὐτοῖς, Γεννήματα ἐχιδνῶν, τίς ὑπέδειξεν ὑμῖν φυγεῖν ἀπὸ τῆς μελλούσης ὀργῆς;). When the Baptist calls them[22] "offspring of vipers,"[23] he means they are a spreading poison[24] (cf. Isa 14:29; Matt 12:34, 23:33) like the serpent in the garden (Gen 3). The rhetorical question ("who warned you?") emphasizes both the "who" (= "not I") and the "you" (= the hypocrisy of the leaders)[25] and should probably be seen as sarcasm: "Who warned you to flee from the coming wrath and come for baptism — when in fact you show no signs of repentance."[26] The presence of "soon to come" (μέλλω) underscores the imminence of the final judgment.

The wrath of God is not just anger but "the ineluctable condemnation by an all-holy and all-loving God of any sin which defiles his creation and which destroys the dignity of man as part of

best fits the practice of immersion, but the early church was probably not overly centered on the mode, and Christians should not fight over immersion/pouring/sprinkling; see Donald Bridge and David Phypers, *The Water That Divides: The Baptism Debate* (Downers Grove, IL: IVP, 1977).

20. See Keener, *Matthew*, 538 – 40.

21. See M. Stern, "Aspects of Jewish Society: The Priesthood and Other Classes," in *The Jewish People in the First Century*, ed. S. Safrai and M. Stern (two vols.; Philadelphia: Fortress, 1976), 609 – 12; Gary G. Porton, "Sadducees," *ABD*, 5:892 – 94.

22. John is not condemning those who have come to be baptized (contra Morris, *Matthew*, 57) but the leaders.

23. Another genitive of content (cf. v. 4), meaning their offspring "consisted of poisonous snakes."

24. Not their shrewdness, contra Blomberg, *Matthew*, 77.

25. Better than Davies and Allison, *Matthew*, 1:305, who prefer the first over the second (Francis W. Beare, *The Gospel according to Matthew: Translation, Introduction, and Commentary* [Philadelphia: Harper & Row, 1981], 93, prefers the second).

26. Carson, "Matthew," 103.

that creation."[27] The Jewish leaders have turned against God's plan by elevating their understanding of the Torah above God's will. They are about to reject God's prophet and his Messiah.

3:8 Produce[28] fruit befitting repentance (ποιήσατε οὖν καρπὸν ἄξιον τῆς μετανοίας). Both the leaders and the Jewish people as a whole believed they were right with God as long as they kept ritually pure. They were missing two things — repentance and the new lifestyle that resulted. This follows naturally from the command to repent, since that in itself connotes a changed life. Moreover, "fruit" refers not only to good works but to good character; as we will see in ch. 23, their external religion developed hypocrisy and poor character. The ethical demand to live a life that "corresponds to" (the meaning of ἄξιος here) conversion is a major Matthean theme. Most of the discourses that Matthew includes are ethical at heart.

3:9 And do not presume to say among yourselves, "We have Abraham as our father" (καὶ μὴ δόξητε λέγειν ἐν ἑαυτοῖς, Πατέρα ἔχομεν τὸν Ἀβραάμ). This follows the aorist command on v. 8 with an aorist prohibition, "do not presume" (μὴ δόξητε), with the infinitive completing it. Abraham was the father of the nation, and the Jewish people believed that their heritage was sufficient for them to be accepted by God.[29]

3:9 ... for I am telling you that God has the power to raise up children for Abraham from these very stones (λέγω γὰρ ὑμῖν ὅτι δύναται ὁ θεὸς ἐκ τῶν λίθων τούτων ἐγεῖραι τέκνα τῷ Ἀβραάμ). John tells the Pharisees and Sadducees that this is wholly inadequate, for God chose Abraham's descendants, and he can remove them as well (cf. Rom 9:14 – 23). It is God who is sovereign, not the nation, and his judgment is coming. John then makes a wordplay on "children" and "stones"; in the Aramaic that John used, these two words sound very much alike (*bĕnayyāʾ* and *ʿabnayyāʾ*, respectively). These were the rocks they could see lying about, and John is saying God could cause them to bear children/descendants of Abraham if he wanted.

The Jewish people are not automatically secure on the basis of their heritage.[30] There may be an echo of Isa 51:1 – 2, "Look to the rock from which you were cut and to the quarry from which you were hewn; look to Abraham, your father," interestingly in a context of comfort and promise. As Davies and Allison say, "From Abraham, a lifeless rock (cf. Gen 17:17; 18:10 – 14; Rom 4:17), God had miraculously caused to be born Isaac and descendants as numerous as the stars of heaven."[31] God could do so again, so the people dare not fail to obey him and develop lives in keeping with their covenant privileges.

3:10 The ax is already laid at the root of the trees (ἤδη δὲ ἡ ἀξίνη πρὸς τὴν ῥίζαν τῶν δένδρων κεῖται). This is a powerful OT metaphor (Isa 10:33 – 34; Jer 11:19; Ezek 17:1 – 4; 31:1 – 14),

27. Albright and Mann, *Matthew*, 26.

28. The aorist "produce" (ποιήσατε) depicts a life of fruitfulness as a complete whole (Wallace, 716 – 17).

29. Carson, "Matthew," 103, says this began in the intertestamental period with the emergence of a merit theology, as they believed that the merits of the patriarchs were sufficient to cover their descendants as well. See also Keener, *Matthew*, 125 – 26. On the issue of merit theology in Judaism, see *Justification and Variegated Nomism: A Fresh Appraisal of Paul and Second Temple Judaism* (ed. D. A. Carson, P. T. O'Brien, and M. A. Seifrid; Grand Rapids: Baker, 2001).

30. See C. R. Kazmierski, "The Stones of Abraham: John the Baptist and the End of Torah (Matt 3:7 – 10 par. Luke 3:7 – 9)," *Bib* 68 (1987): 22 – 40, who sees this as an independent pericope that stems from the honor-shame framework and is used to show the shame of Israel as they reject the kingdom message. He is wrong about the independence of this saying but correct about the honor-shame aspects.

31. Davies and Allison, *Matthew*, 1:308.

picturing the imminence ("already" [ἤδη] is first for emphasis) of judgment. Certainly final judgment is primarily in view (the present tenses are prophetic, emphasizing the certainty of it), though the destruction of Jerusalem should probably be included as well. The fact that the ax is ready to cut down the "root" is important; the goal is not pruning (John 15:2) but total destruction. When woodsmen cut down trees, they normally cut at the trunk, from which they want another tree to grow; but when the root is cut, the tree is gone forever.

3:10 So every tree that does not produce good fruit is going to be cut down and thrown into the fire (πᾶν οὖν δένδρον μὴ ποιοῦν καρπὸν καλὸν ἐκκόπτεται καὶ εἰς πῦρ βάλλεται). As in the vine and branches parable of John 15:1 – 6 (cf. Isa 5:1 – 7), the criterion is fruitfulness. When God's people become fruitless, divine judgment is imminent. This is as true today as it was in the first century. The idea of fiery judgment is prominent in Matthew (Matt 3:12; 5:22, 29 – 30; 10:28; 13:42, 50; 18:9; 23:15, 33; 25:41). The emphasis is that all people will be judged on the basis of their fruit/works (see also Prov 24:12; Jer 17:10; Matt 16:27; Rom 2:6; 14:12; 1 Cor 3:12 – 15; 1 Pet 1:17; Rev 2:23; 22:12).

3:11 I am baptizing you in water as associated with repentance (ἐγὼ μὲν ὑμᾶς βαπτίζω ἐν ὕδατι εἰς μετάνοιαν). John now contrasts himself with Jesus, both with respect to their baptism and their status. First, his is a water baptism linked with repentance. The use of "as associated with" (εἰς) is difficult, for it often connotes purpose ("I baptize so that you will repent"), but there is no indication whatsoever that repentance follows baptism (cf. Mark 1:4, "baptism of repentance," implicitly meaning repentance has already occurred). So it is common to see the εἰς as meaning association ("with reference to, in agreement with").[32]

3:11 But after me one is coming who is far greater than I, whose sandals I am not fit to carry (ὁ δὲ ὀπίσω μου ἐρχόμενος ἰσχυρότερός μού ἐστιν, οὗ οὐκ εἰμὶ ἱκανὸς τὰ ὑποδήματα βαστάσαι). John next contrasts his place in salvation history with that of the "Coming One" (ὁ ἐρχόμενος). This "Coming One" (a messianic title in 11:3; 21:9; 23:39), whom the Baptist precedes as forerunner, is infinitely "more powerful" (ἰσχύς; it may also have had a messianic connotation)[33] both in bringing the powerful kingdom and in the power of his ministry. In fact, John is actually unworthy of him. The metaphor chosen is found in all four gospels and stems from the rabbi/disciple relationship. The dirt on the feet was unclean, and only non-Hebrew slaves took off or "carried" the master's sandals. Disciples acted virtually as slaves in most aspects, but they were not required to take off the master's sandals (*b. Ketub.* 96a). Therefore, John is saying, "I'm not even worthy to be his slave."

3:11 He will baptize you in the Holy Spirit and fire (αὐτὸς ὑμᾶς βαπτίσει ἐν πνεύματι ἁγίῳ καὶ πυρί). The power of the Messiah (note emphatic "he" [αὐτός]) is particularly seen in the type of baptism he brings, not a water baptism like John but one in Spirit and fire. "Baptism in the Holy Spirit" looks back to Isa 11:2 ("The Spirit of the Lord will rest on him"); Ezek 36:25 – 27 ("I will put my Spirit in you"); 39:29 ("pour out my Spirit"); Joel 2:28 ("pour out my Spirit"). Most likely, this refers to the coming of the Holy Spirit to indwell

32. Carson, "Matthew," 104; Hagner, *Matthew 1 – 13*, 51; cf. Gundry, *Matthew*, 48, "baptism enabled people to actualize their repentance by carrying it out in symbolic action." Morris, *Matthew*, 61, takes it as causal, "baptize because of repentance," Bruner, *Christbook*, 78, as purpose, "I baptize with water to bring you into repentance."

33. Davies and Allison, *Matthew*, 1:315.

the believer at conversion (1 Cor 2:12; 12:13; Rom 8:14 – 17).

The mention of "and fire" has caused some controversy. Some think them antithetical, with the Spirit coming on the faithful and the fire of judgment on the unfaithful.[34] This would certainly fit the context of judgment. More and more, however, the two are being seen as a hendiadys ("spirit-fire" — note that one preposition introduces both, indicating they are a unity). Still, there is a question whether the "Spirit-fire" refers to judgment[35] or the refining fire of the Spirit.[36] But this disjunction is unnecessary. It is best to see both nuances: those who accept the message of the kingdom are purified by the Spirit while those who reject it face judgment.[37] Both nuances fit the OT background as well as the Judaism of Jesus' day (e.g., Qumran; cf. 1QS 4:20 – 21).

3:12 Whose winnowing fork is in his hand; and he will clean his threshing floor (οὗ τὸ πτύον ἐν τῇ χειρὶ αὐτοῦ, καὶ διακαθαριεῖ τὴν ἅλωνα αὐτοῦ). This is virtually a harvest parable, like the parable of the wheat and the weeds in 13:24 – 30, 36 – 43. It will take place at the final judgment when all humankind will be divided into the believers/wheat and the unbelievers/chaff and echoes OT passages like Isa 5:24; 34:10; Jer 7:20; Dan 2:35; Hos 13:3. A winnowing fork would scoop up the grain and throw it high in the air so that the wind could catch the lighter chaff and blow it away. The good wheat would be kept in the barn for later use while the useless chaff would be burned.[38]

3:12 He will gather his wheat into the barn but burn the chaff with unquenchable fire (καὶ συνάξει τὸν σῖτον αὐτοῦ εἰς τὴν ἀποθήκην αὐτοῦ, τὸ δὲ ἄχυρον κατακαύσει πυρὶ ἀσβέστῳ). The idea of "unquenchable fire" comes from Gehenna, the trash dump in the Kidron Valley outside Jerusalem, where fires burned day and night without stop (cf. Matt 5:22, 29, 30; 10:28; 18:9; 23:15).

Theology in Application

The story of the Christ and his coming demanded a messianic forerunner (Mal 4:5) who would "prepare the way" by inaugurating a prophetic style of preaching and bring back the wilderness prophet tradition. This was ably filled by John the Baptist, who called for repentance in light of a coming judgment and in so doing called the nation to a deeper awareness of its plight. John fulfilled not only Malachi but also Isa 40:3 as he boldly preached a devastating message and used a new form of baptism as the initiatory rite exemplifying the repentance he demanded.

34. Filson, *Matthew*, 66.

35. Gundry, "Matthew," 49; Davies and Allison, *Matthew*, 1:317 – 18; Beare, *Matthew*, 96.

36. Hill, *Matthew*, 94 – 95; France, *Matthew* (TNTC), 93; Carson, "Matthew," 105; Morris, *Matthew*, 62; Hagner, *Matthew 1 – 13*, 52.

37. Plummer, *Matthew*, 29; Blomberg, *Matthew*, 80.

38. Robert L. Webb, "The Activity of John the Baptist's Expected Figure at the Threshing Floor (Matthew 3.12 = Luke 3.17)," *JSNT* 43 (1991): 103 – 11, argues that since in this miniparable the winnowing is over, with the farmer ready to throw the wheat and chaff into the air, the imagery is indeed one of final judgment with the repentant to receive blessing (put in the granary) and the unrepentant judgment (the fire).

The Baptist's preaching was in itself a remarkable precursor to that of Christ with many parallels: "repent" (v. 2; cf. 4:17; 11:20 – 21; 12:41); "the kingdom of heaven has come near" (v. 2; cf. 4:17); "offspring of vipers" (v. 7; cf. 12:34; 23:33); "produce fruit" (vv. 8, 10; cf. 7:16 – 20; 12:33; 21:41, 43); children of Abraham (v. 9; cf. 8:11 – 12); fruitless trees "cut down and thrown into the fire" (v. 10; cf. 7:19); judgment by fire (vv. 11 – 12; cf. 5:22; 13:40 – 42; 18:8 – 9; 25:41); grain gathered in the granary (v. 12; cf. 13:30).[39]

1. The Coming of the Messiah Demands Repentance

Both the Baptist and Christ (cf. Luke 5:32; 15:7) preached repentance as the necessary prerequisite for entering the kingdom. Until the sinner turns from self and sin to God, there can be no forgiveness. Moreover, true repentance involves a total change that affects not just the mind but the heart and is shown in a new lifestyle and character (the "fruit" of v. 8). Today as well as in the first century there are too many halfhearted followers who talk the talk (make an external confession) but do not walk the walk (live for Christ in every area).

In that sense there are four categories of people attending the average church: (1) the unsaved who care little; (2) the unsaved who are "seekers"; (3) the quasi-Christians, who attend regularly and claim to be Christians but do little and have a basically secular outlook; (4) the true believers, who are at work for the Lord and growing. The third group is the focus here. Is their "repentance" real? We cannot know, for they demonstrate little "fruit" with their life. In that sense they have two final possibilities: some will be "saved — even though only as one escaping through the flames" (1 Cor 3:15), but many will be told by the Lord, "I never knew you. Depart from me, workers of evil!" (Matt 7:23). It is a major task of every pastor to challenge this group to quit playing games with their eternal destiny!

2. The Kingdom's Arrival and Its Destiny

This is stressed in each of the Synoptic Gospels and relates to Matthew's eschatology. On one level there is a distinct inaugurated eschatology, that with Christ the kingdom has come; yet on another level it is still future. God's people live in a state of tension between the already (the blessings we have in Christ) and the not yet (the final glory we will share at his second coming). Matthew has a great emphasis on the final aspect — the day of judgment is coming (see below).

3. The Task of the Church to Help Prepare for the Lord

The Baptist is the messianic forerunner, God's chosen one to clear the highway

39. See France, *Gospel of Matthew*, 98.

to Zion. But the early church believed this concept applied to them as well and called their movement "the Way" (Acts 9:2; 19:9, 23; 22:4; 24:14, 22). God's people are at all times to make a way for people to enter the kingdom. We are to be witnesses and to live a life that demonstrates to all that the only possible way to meaning and fulfillment in life is Christ. This is how the early church changed the world, and this is how God wants his people today to act as well. In vv. 4 – 6 John did this in the only way he knew how, by becoming the wilderness prophet and affecting all around him. Each of us must find our own God-led way to make a difference. Yet we are assured of one thing — God has made us as we are and placed us where we are to do just that!

4. Baptism for a Christian

The Baptist used baptism as an acted symbol of repentance, yet Christ also commanded that baptism be utilized by the church in much the same way. There is a great deal of debate today regarding the mode and meaning of baptism. But whether we sprinkle or immerse, whether we baptize infants in a covenant sense or believers after coming to Christ, 1 Pet 3:21 makes it clear that it is "the pledge of a clear conscience toward God"; in that sense it is an important experience in the life of every follower of Christ.

5. The Coming Final Judgment

Here John is addressing Jewish leaders, who have only an external religion and have not given themselves completely over to God. The Scriptures are abundantly clear that there will be a final judgment and that those who have rejected Christ will suffer eternal punishment. The book of Revelation tells us why: sin is a powerful, ongoing force, and every person will have rejected Christ again and again (Rev 9:20 – 21; 16:9, 11, 21). God will have no choice but to throw them into the lake of fire (Rev 20:11 – 15).[40] Universalists do not understand the power of sin; the truth is that after a billion years Hitler and Stalin will not repent — they will hate God more than they did the day they died!

However, there is another aspect of this final accounting that must also be stressed. Everyone (believer as well as unbeliever) will give account of their life to God. Even the leaders will do so (Heb 13:17). All will be "judged by works," a major theme of the OT (2 Chr 6:23; Job 34:11; Ps 28:4; 62:12; Prov 24:12) as well as of Jesus (Matt 3:8; 16:27) and the rest of the NT (2 Cor 5:10; 11:15; 2 Tim 4:14; 1 Pet 1:17). In Revelation both believers (Rev 2:23; 11:18; 14:13; 20:12; 22:12) and unbelievers (18:6;

40. See Grant R. Osborne, *Revelation* (BECNT; Grand Rapids: Baker, 2002), 38 – 40.

11:18; 20:13) will face this. In fact, every passage on the return of Christ in the NT (e.g., Matt 25; 1 Cor 15:58; 2 Cor 5:9 – 10; 1 Thess 5:11; 2 Thess 2:13 – 15) stresses the need for perseverance and readiness in light of the return of Christ.

6. Baptism in Spirit-Fire

There are two aspects of Spirit-baptism in the NT: the initial experience of receiving the Spirit at conversion (the primary thrust in Matt 3:12 for believers) and being "filled with the Spirit" (Eph 5:18). In the first sense, everyone will experience the "fire" of the Spirit, but for the unsaved it will be fiery judgment. The saved will have the refiner's fire, the purifying work of the Spirit (John 15:2). In the second sense believers must give themselves over to the Lord that they might experience the fullness of the Spirit in their lives. Thus, as in Ephesians, believers are "exhorted to allow the Spirit to have the fullest control that they are conscious of in their lives and to open themselves continually to the one who can enable them to walk wisely and to understand Christ's will and who can inspire their worship and thanksgiving."[41]

41. Andrew T. Lincoln, *Ephesians* (WBC 42; Dallas: Word, 1990), 345.

CHAPTER 6

Matthew 3:13 – 17

Literary Context

While John the Baptist introduced Jesus via his role as the forerunner, Jesus introduced his own ministry by submitting himself to John's baptism "to fulfill all righteousness." These two stages were necessary preparations for Jesus' messianic ministry. Jesus was the focus in chs. 1 – 2, and John the central character in 3:1 – 12. Now these two key figures in the salvation drama come together, and John fulfills his role by launching Jesus into his divine task via baptism. The feelings of inadequacy John shows in 3:14 are in keeping with 3:11b. He (like Peter in Luke 5:8) feels wholly unworthy in light of the supreme righteousness of Christ. This, then, prepares for the supreme victory of Jesus over Satan in 4:1 – 11, where Jesus takes on Satan in open combat and utterly defeats him, proving that he is indeed "the Son of God" (3:17; 4:3, 5).

B. Inaugural Events in Jesus' Ministry (3:1 – 4:11)

1. John the Baptist (3:1 – 12)
2. **The Baptism of Jesus (3:13 – 17)**
3. The Testing/Temptation of Jesus (4:1 – 11)

Main Idea

The main message is that in inaugurating his ministry via baptism, Jesus not only fulfills the OT (as in the first three chapters thus far) but also fulfills *all of God's righteous requirements* by identifying with us in our need to be reconciled to God.[1]

1. On Jesus' baptism as identification with us, see Bruner, *Christbook*, 83 – 84; Witherington, *Matthew*, 84 – 85.

Translation

Matthew 3:13-17

13a	Scene #1 Setting	**[1] Then Jesus went from Galilee to the Jordan to John**
b	Basis for 13a	in order to be baptized by him.
14a		But **John tried to stop him, saying,**
b	Objection	*"I need to be baptized by you, and you are coming to me?"*
15a	Answer	**Jesus answered him,**
b		*"Let it be so for now,*
c	Basis for 15b	*for it is fitting for us in order to fulfill all righteousness."*
d		**Then John let it happen.**
16a	Time	After Jesus was baptized,
b	Scene #2	**[2] he immediately got up from the water;**
c	Result of 16a	and **behold, the heavens were opened**
d	Epiphany	and **he saw the Spirit of God descending like a dove and resting upon him.**
17a		And **behold a voice sounded from heaven, saying,**
b		*"This is my Son whom I love;*
c		*I am well pleased with him."*

Structure and Literary Form

Matthew's rendition is distinct from that of Mark 1:9 – 11; Luke 3:21 – 22, and many think Matthew uses a special source here. However, the core (the baptism, the coming of the Spirit, the message of God) is in all three, so Matthew is simply adding details to the traditional form in order to give this a distinct tone. There are two sections here: a special Matthean section (3:13 – 15) that includes a dialogue between John and Jesus; and a section paralleling Mark that includes the baptism, the descent of the Spirit, and the message from God (3:16 – 17). The first is a question/answer passage and the second a pronouncement story,[2] as the action leads to God's heavenly declaration. Therefore, the two leading ideas are in v. 15 ("fulfill all righteousness") and v. 17 ("This is my Son whom I love").

2. Davies and Allison, *Matthew*, 1:320, for some strange reason call this a heavenly vision narrative interpreted by a voice, using the transfiguration narrative of 17:1 – 8 as a parallel. But there is no indication either here or in 17:1 – 8 that a vision is involved. The only possible evidence could come from Jesus "seeing" the Spirit descend in 3:16. But there is no visionary hint in that, and John (as well as others probably) is involved in the event as well. This is an apocalyptic event to be sure, but not a visionary one.

Exegetical Outline

- **I. Interaction between John and Jesus (3:13 – 15)**
  - A. Jesus comes to be baptized (v. 13)
  - B. John's humble question — unworthy (v. 14)
  - C. Jesus' response — fulfill all righteousness (v. 15)
- **II. The Events at the Baptism (3:16 – 17)**
  - A. The heavens opened (v. 16a)
  - B. The Spirit descends (v. 16b)
  - C. God testifies regarding his beloved Son (v. 17)

Explanation of the Text

There is tension in the fact that Jesus at one and the same time transcends John's baptism as the Messiah and yet submits to that baptism. "The baptism of Jesus, indeed, serves as a kind of transition between the work of preparation and the appearance on center stage of the one who brings fulfillment."[3] Moreover, there is also a Trinitarian thrust — both the Father and the Spirit participate in the anointing of the Son. There is an incredible aura of the power of God in this scene, and in fact the shaking of the heavens (a major apocalyptic image) occurs as Jesus comes up out of the water (v. 16), and God himself tells the onlookers who this Jesus really is, the very Son of God.

3:13 Then Jesus went from Galilee to the Jordan to John in order to be baptized by him (Τότε παραγίνεται ὁ Ἰησοῦς ἀπὸ τῆς Γαλιλαίας ἐπὶ τὸν Ἰορδάνην πρὸς τὸν Ἰωάννην τοῦ βαπτισθῆναι ὑπ' αὐτοῦ). The "then" (τότε) here shows that Jesus comes while John is conducting his ministry of baptism and preaching. Also, the same word is used to signify the arrival of Jesus, "went" (παραγίνεται, another historic present), as was used for John in 3:1; the two in a sense parallel each other.[4] Matthew has "to" (ἐπί) for "in" (εἰς) in Mark 1:9 and is used geographically for the trip from Nazareth "to" (BAGD, 288, δ) the Jordan. After this Jesus transcends his forerunner. In his baptism Jesus clearly takes the initiative.

3:14 But John tried to stop him (ὁ δὲ Ἰωάννης διεκώλυεν αὐτόν). When John sees Jesus, he tries to deter him from coming ("tried to stop" [διεκώλυεν], iterative imperfect to stress repeated attempts). John contrasts himself with Jesus (the emphatic pronouns *I* and *you* bring this out). There is a certain irony in John's difficulty baptizing the leaders because they were not worthy of baptism, while here he has difficulty allowing Jesus to be baptized because John is not worthy of him.[5]

3:14 ... saying, "I need to be baptized by you, and you are coming to me?" (λέγων, Ἐγὼ χρείαν ἔχω ὑπὸ σοῦ βαπτισθῆναι, καὶ σὺ ἔρχῃ πρός με;).

3. Hagner, *Matthew 1 – 13*, 34.

4. Beare, *Matthew*, 98, says this verb carries "a certain atmosphere of formality and solemnity (in the LXX), sometimes of an appearance of a king or a judge, sometimes of the coming of God or of his angel, or of the arrival of a prophet to speak for God (1 Sam 13:10)."

5. Carson, "Matthew," 107.

Since baptism signifies repentance, John realizes (note the emphatic "I" [ἐγώ]) that he is the one needing to repent, not Jesus. We do not know how John knew this; John 1:31 says John "did not know [Jesus]," though that may mean he did not know Jesus was the Messiah (they were cousins; cf. NLT, "I did not recognize him as Messiah"). How he realized Jesus' sinlessness here (implied) we do not know. He may have known Jesus as a supremely righteous man before, and at the least would have been told how he leaped in the womb for joy in the presence of the unborn baby Jesus (Luke 1:44). Since Mary and Elizabeth were cousins and met while they were carrying their babies (Luke 1:39 – 45), it is possible that as children John and Jesus spent some time together. Matthew does not tell us but simply relates the fact of John's humility.

3:15 Jesus answered[6] him, "Let it be so for now" (ἀποκριθεὶς δὲ ὁ Ἰησοῦς εἶπεν πρὸς αὐτόν, Ἄφες ἄρτι). Jesus replies to John with great force, saying, "Let it be done this way for now," with the emphasis on "for now" (ἄρτι), meaning that God's will for the present is for Jesus to begin his messianic ministry with baptism. The time is "now," not later. This is also seen in πρέπον, which in some contexts does not just mean "proper, fitting, morally right" but can approach divine necessity in terms of following God's will.[7]

3:15 "For it is fitting for us in order to fulfill all righteousness." Then John let it happen (οὕτως γὰρ πρέπον ἐστὶν ἡμῖν πληρῶσαι πᾶσαν δικαιοσύνην. τότε ἀφίησιν αὐτόν). The phrase "to fulfill all righteousness" has occasioned much discussion. "To fulfill" (πληρόω) thus far has meant accomplishing the predictions and experiences of the OT (1:22; 2:15, 17, 23), but it can also mean to "bring to completion" or "fill to the full" (BAGD, 670 – 71; cf. 13:48; 23:32 for this use). Here it probably has the latter sense. As connected with the will of God, it means to complete all that God has set out for him to do.

"Righteousness" (δικαιοσύνη) is a major concept in Matthew (3:15; 5:6, 10, 20; 6:1, 33; 21:32). While it appears only seven times, it is generally conceded to be the key term to Matthean ethics. The consensus view today is that it refers to "the demand of God on man to live according to a certain norm, the law" (as interpreted by Jesus)[8] and is "the all-embracing notion for the actions, behavior, and disposition for the disciples and followers of Jesus."[9] But there is an added salvation-historical sense here since Jesus is the one fulfilling this "righteousness." The best way to understand it[10] is to combine two nuances: (1) there is a salvation-historical thrust as Jesus identifies with his people (Isa 53:12) in preparing for the saving activity of God (his saving work is the will of

6. For "he answered" (ἀποκριθείς) as a circumstantial participle forming a single idea with the main verb, see on 4:4.

7. Hagner, *Matthew 1 – 13*, 56.

8. Benno Przybylski, *Righteousness in Matthew and His World of Thought* (Cambridge: Cambridge Univ. Press, 1980), 105.

9. J. Andrew Overman, *Matthew's Gospel and Formative Judaism: The Social World of the Matthean Community* (Philadelphia: Fortress, 1990), 92. He adds that the concept expresses "the demand placed upon humans and the response expected from members of the Matthean community" and that "the possession of *dikaiosynē* (is necessary) for entry into the kingdom," noting the connection of it with the judgment theme in Matthew.

10. Options are: (1) Obedience to God's will in satisfying every ordinance (Albright and Mann, *Matthew*, 31); but this gives it too much of a formal air; the reason is not cultic (that would be *dikaiōma*) but spiritual (*dikaiosynē here;* see Hill, *Matthew*, 96). (2) It anticipates Jesus' death as a baptism that secures the righteousness of man (Oscar Cullmann, *Baptism in the New Testament* [London: SCM, 1950], 18 – 19); this is too Pauline and is doubtful here. (3) Eschatological: Jesus announces that righteousness of life demanded by the act of baptism will be "fulfilled" by him in the kingdom (Hill, *Matthew*; G. Bornkamm, G. Barth, and H. J. Held, *Tradition and Interpretation in Matthew* [NTL; Philadelphia: Westminster, 1963]); this is closer but does not quite catch the thrust of the passage (see below).

God = "righteousness").[11] (2) Jesus obeys his Father's will (= all righteousness) by assuming the role of suffering Servant (Isa 53:11) and so endorses John's ministry.[12]

In this there is also a moral element, for Jesus' action is a moral conduct that obeys God's will, and so Jesus is fulfilling Scripture by doing it God's way.[13] In short, he "fills to the full" the "right" requirements of God in "the OT pattern and prediction about the Messiah."[14] He does not need to repent, but by submitting to baptism Jesus begins his messianic work by identifying with the human need and providing the means by which it can be accomplished.

3:16 After Jesus was baptized, he immediately got up from the water; and behold, the heavens were opened (βαπτισθεὶς δὲ ὁ Ἰησοῦς εὐθὺς ἀνέβη ἀπὸ τοῦ ὕδατος· καὶ ἰδοὺ ἠνεῴχθησαν [αὐτῷ] οἱ οὐρανοί). The following events transpire quickly one after another.[15] Jesus comes out of the water quickly, possibly signifying eagerness to begin his ministry, or perhaps it denotes the speed with which the scene progressed. The opening of the heavens (note the divine passive "were opened" [ἠνεῴχθησαν], indicating that God is acting) stems from OT apocalyptic language on the shaking of the heavens (cf. more explicitly Mark 1:10, "heaven being torn open"), which connotes divine intervention as in the coming of the eschaton or the giving of divine revelation (cf. Ezek 1:1 ["the heavens were opened and I saw"];[16] Isa 64:1; Hag 2:6; *Sib. Or.* 3.82; Matt 24:29). Here this connotes both the inauguration of the last days and the first time God has spoken directly in over three hundred years.[17]

3:16 And he saw the Spirit of God descending like a dove and resting upon him (καὶ εἶδεν τὸ πνεῦμα τοῦ θεοῦ καταβαῖνον ὡσεὶ περιστερὰν καὶ ἐρχόμενον ἐπ' αὐτόν). Jesus "sees" the Spirit descend on him. It is common today to label this a visionary experience since "the heavens opened" can be a formula for visions (Acts 7:56; 10:11), and the text says Jesus "saw" the Spirit descend,[18] but that is not necessary. Matthew renders this as a public event,[19] and Luke 3:22 has "in bodily form like a dove." It is possible that only Jesus saw this, but the fact that God says "This is my Son" means that the scene was intended for the onlookers as well.

There have been many suggestions for the imagery of the dove here, but the best is probably to see a combination of Gen 1:2 (the Spirit of God hovering over creation), thus signifying a new creation;[20] the Spirit as a symbol of Israel (Hos 7:11),

11. Filson, *Matthew*, 68; France, *Matthew* (TNTC), 95; Hagner, *Matthew 1 – 13*, 56; Morris, *Matthew*, 65. Nolland, *Matthew*, 154, says this involves the purpose of John and Jesus to bring about the kingdom in order to restore people to right relationship with God.

12. Carson, "Matthew," 108; Blomberg, *Matthew*, 81; France, *Gospel of Matthew*, 120.

13. Davies and Allison, *Matthew*, 1:326 – 27; Keener, *Matthew*, 132.

14. David L. Turner, "Matthew" (Cornerstone Biblical Commentary; Carol Stream, IL: Tyndale, 2006), 62.

15. This is seen in the temporal aorist participle "after he was baptized" (βαπτισθείς), emphasizing that the events took place just "after" the baptism was finished.

16. See Schweizer, *Matthew*, 53.

17. Jewish teachers believed the prophetic age had ended and God would no longer speak directly until the coming of the Messiah; they lived in the time of the *bath qol* ("daughter of the voice") and so gave expositions of Scripture rather than waiting for God to speak (thus with secondary authority).

18. M. M. B. Turner, "Holy Spirit," *DJG*, 345; Davies and Allison, *Matthew*, 1:330 – 31, 342.

19. Contra Blomberg, *Matthew*, 81, who maintains that Matthew does not describe the event but what ensues afterward.

20. Hill, *Matthew*, 96 – 97; France, *Matthew* (TNTC), 95; Davies and Allison, *Matthew*, 1:334; Hagner, *Matthew 1 – 13*, 58; Harrington, *Matthew*, 62. There is no dove mentioned but the symbolism is that of a bird hovering over land, and the rabbis likened this to a dove hovering over her young, cf. *b. Ḥag.* 15a.

with Jesus as the ideal, true Israelite;[21] the dove returning to Noah's ark (Gen 8:8 – 12) with the imagery of a new world being inaugurated;[22] and the dove as a messenger signifying to Jesus the divinely commissioned role set for him.[23] Putting them together, the descent of the Spirit signifies a new age being inaugurated in the coming of the Messiah, God's very Son.

3:17 And behold a voice sounded from heaven, saying, "This is my Son" (καὶ ἰδοὺ φωνὴ ἐκ τῶν οὐρανῶν λέγουσα, Οὗτός ἐστιν ὁ υἱός μου). The age of the *bath qol* (see footnote on 3:16) has now ended, and God speaks directly, affirming the significance of the baptism. Mark 1:11 and Luke 3:22 have "You are my Son" while Matthew has "This is my Son." So for Matthew the message is intended for the onlookers[24] (although only John the Baptist is mentioned in the story, this was likely a public event), especially for the Baptist, confirming his recognition of Jesus in 3:14. The message continues the fulfillment language of Matthew and echoes Ps 2:7 ("you are my Son"), a coronation psalm for the Davidic king, thereby showing that the anointing of Jesus by the Spirit was a messianic anointing of the King of kings (Rev 19:16).[25] The "Son of God" status is the key to this section, for in 4:3, 6 it becomes the keynote of the temptation narrative as well.[26]

3:17 "... whom I love; I am well pleased with him" (ὁ ἀγαπητός, ἐν ᾧ εὐδόκησα). As the Son Jesus is "beloved" of God, especially favored as the commissioned and enthroned royal Messiah. The second OT passage behind this is Isa 42:1, "Here is my servant, whom I uphold, my chosen one in whom I delight; I will put my Spirit on him." Jesus is being presented as the chosen Servant of Yahweh who brings pleasure to God (cf. Matt 12:18 – 20, which quotes the whole of Isa 42:1 – 4). So Jesus at one and the same time is the Spirit-filled Davidic Messiah, Son of God, and Servant.[27] This explains Jesus' self-understanding that he fulfills the Servant concept (cf. Matt 5:3 – 6; 11:2 – 6; 12:18 – 21; Luke 4:18 – 19) and the special Son.[28]

21. Morris, *Matthew*, 67.

22. Keener, *Matthew*, 132 – 33.

23. Nolland, *Matthew*, 156.

24. Keener, *Matthew*, 134, sees this as "an annunciation formula" like 27:37, calling this "a public theophany and testimony to Jesus." Strangely, Jack Dean Kingsbury, *Matthew as Story* (2nd ed.; Philadelphia: Fortress, 1988), 51, says only Jesus heard it, for otherwise the crowd (12:23; 16:13 – 14) and John (11:2 – 3) would have called him Son of God. Yet that fails to explain the "This is ..." introduction, and hearing something does not mean one completely understands it. "Son" language for the Jewish people would mean Jesus was an exceptional leader.

25. This can hardly be an adoption scene, as some have said. It is clearly a commissioning scene. Jesus was Son of God before this (cf. 1:23; 3:15).

26. Kingsbury, *Structure*, 50, goes so far as to say "Son of God" Christology dominates the whole, so that "I am well pleased" (εὐδόκησα) refers not to the Servant of Isa 42:1 but to God's pleased choice of Jesus as Son. However, that is unlikely because the verb does not come from Ps 2 but from the Isaiah passage. See Davies and Allison, *Matthew*, 1:341 – 42, for a detailed critique of Kingsbury. J. A. Gibbs, "Israel Standing with Israel: The Baptism of Jesus in Matthew's Gospel (Matt 3:13 – 17)," *CBQ* 64 (2002): 511 – 26, argues that the background is more Jer 38:20 LXX ("Ephraim is a beloved son to me") and that Jesus is seen as Servant and Israel rather than Son and King. This is interesting but not nearly as likely as Ps 2:7. Nolland, *Matthew*, 157, notes the possibility of an echo of Exod 4:22 – 23 ("Israel is my firstborn son") and says this fits the use of new exodus imagery in ch. 2.

27. Davies and Allison, *Matthew*, 1:339, follow Kingsbury in taking Son of God as the major title for Matthew and the others (Messiah, Son of David, Son of Man, Servant) as filling out its content.

28. Seen mainly in Jesus' use of "Father" for God (31x in Matthew, 100x in John); cf. *EDNT*, 53.

Theology in Application

Matthew wants his readers to understand the true significance of this one who was virgin-born and Magi-worshiped. Every line of this passage reverberates with exalted christological imagery. The Baptist's powerful ministry in 3:1 – 12 was in reality a preparation for the transcendent ministry of the one who followed.

1. Recognition of Our Unworthiness before Jesus

John the Baptist's humility reflects the necessary realization of the great heroes of the faith throughout biblical history. Moses (Exod 3:11 – 4:16), Gideon (Judg 3:15), Isaiah (Isa 6:5), Jeremiah (Jer 1:6 – 7), Ezekiel (Ezek 1:1 – 2:3), and Peter (Luke 5:8) all felt their inadequacy and unworthiness to serve the Lord. The fact is that we *are* unworthy of Christ and inadequate to do his work, but Paul answers that. He freely admitted that "in person he is unimpressive and his speaking amounts to nothing" (2 Cor 10:10), but he adds, "If I must boast, I will boast of the things that show my weakness" (11:30), and "I will boast all the more gladly of my weaknesses, so that Christ's power may rest on me" (12:9).

We all must come face to face with our sinfulness so that we will rest entirely on Christ. Then our inadequacies will be a means by which Christ's power will be all the more evident, for in him we will accomplish more than we ever could in our own strength and abilities. Our insufficiencies should force us to turn to Christ and his Spirit for the power to accomplish things for God. We all have seeds of greatness in us but must depend on the Spirit to unleash that power and maximize our potential for the glory of God.

2. Christ Aligned with Us So We Can Live Rightly before God

Jesus was baptized "to fulfill all righteousness," and in so doing was completely faithful to the will of his Father. To live rightly we too must combine faith with obedience, but it is possible only when we identify with Christ, who has shown us the right path. When Jesus submitted himself to John's baptism, the very ministry of John was also fulfilled. In actuality we are also fulfilled in it, for that act launched Jesus' ministry of redemption for us all. As we surrender to Christ and allow him to "fulfill" our potential, great things will begin to happen.

3. A Trinitarian Emphasis

For the first time the Trinity acts together on the pages of Scripture.[29] The Spirit comes on the Son, and the Father affirms him for all who were there. Of course this

29. See Bruner, *Christbook*, 88.

is not the full doctrinal statement of Chalcedon, but nevertheless it is true here. The Godhead is involved in human affairs, and salvation is triply guaranteed. In fact, this is the key to living the Christian life, completed when we allow the triune Godhead to work in us and through us (see 1 Pet 1:2; Rev 1:4 – 5).

4. Baptism Important in the Process of Salvation

By submitting to baptism as an anointing for his ministry at the same time as he identifies with human needs, Jesus authorizes the place of baptism in the process of salvation. It is true that Jesus himself never practiced baptism (John 4:2), but in his resurrection command (Matt 28:19) he instituted baptism as the initial Christian rite. In 1 Pet 3:20 – 21 baptism is part of the salvation experience; in itself it does not save, but it is still the "pledge" to follow the Lord made by the "good conscience." Although there are some who do not baptize, the first-century Christians would have been shocked, for it was a critical experience for them.

5. Jesus as the Embodiment of the Life of "Righteousness"

As noted above, "righteousness" is a major Matthean theme, and the seven occurrences center on the ethical side of obeying God and living under his commands. Jesus' submission to John's baptism is the supreme example of following God's will, and it gives us a model for doing the same. We are called to a life of discipleship and obedience, following God's will in every area of life.

6. The Spirit as an Empowering Presence in Jesus' Life

While the Spirit is not as central in Matthew as in Luke or John, he is still critical. In 12:28 Jesus says he drives out demons "through the Spirit of God," thus manifesting the kingdom's presence in this world. The kingdom is also behind healing miracles (10:7 – 8), and after Jesus healed the man with a shriveled hand (12:9 – 14), Matthew saw Jesus' activity fulfilling Isa 42:1 – 4 (Matt 12:18 – 21): "I will put my Spirit on him." Clearly, Jesus' ministry took place under the empowering presence of the Spirit, who manifests the presence of the kingdom in this world. This prepares for the rest of the NT (e.g., Rom 8) that defines the Christian life as "life in the Spirit."

7. The "Sons of God" Living so as to Please Him

Jesus as *the* Son of God was loved and brought pleasure to his Father. The believer is also a child of God, adopted and a co-heir with Christ (Rom 8:14 – 17). We too must therefore live in such a way as to please him (Rom 12:1 – 2; Eph 5:10; 1 Tim 2:3; 5:4).

CHAPTER 7

Matthew 4:1 – 11

Literary Context

The final event that launches Jesus' messianic ministry is the testing of Jesus. In the ancient world all sons of the king had to be tested and prove their right to the throne, and the heroes of the OT were put to the test before their ministries as well (e.g., Abraham with Isaac). Jesus passes the test and proves himself to be truly Son of God,[1] thus entering his ministry on a note of triumph. He is announced in 3:1 – 12, anointed and empowered in 3:13 – 17, and proven by combat here. There is wilderness typology and a deliberate contrast with Israel here: they failed the test in the wilderness, but Jesus is victorious.[2] In fact, the order of the temptations and Jesus' responses reverse the order of Israel's failures in Deut 6 – 8, as we will see.

I. Jesus' Origin and Preparation for Ministry (1:1 – 4:11)
- **B. Inaugural Events in Jesus' Ministry (3:1 – 4:11)**
  1. John the Baptist (3:1 – 12)
  2. The Baptism of Jesus (3:13 – 17)
  3. ➦ **The Testing/Temptation of Jesus (4:1 – 11)**

Main Idea

Jesus is obedient to the will of his Father in 3:13 – 17. His final obedience will be the cross, but prior to that Satan tests his "commitment to the will of his Father (the real criterion of true sonship)"[3] and the reality of Jesus as the Son of God. Jesus triumphs and shows himself to be "the true Israel, the 'Son of God' through whom God's redemptive purpose for his people is now at last to reach its fulfillment."[4]

1. Birger Gerhardsson, *The Testing of God's Son (Matt 4:11 & Par.): An Analysis of an Early Christian Midrash* (ConBNT 2.1; Lund: Gleerup, 1966), 19, calls this "the key term in the temptation narrative."

2. Turner, "Matthew," 65; see also Hauerwas, *Matthew*, 50 – 51.

3. Hagner, *Matthew 1 – 13*, 62. As Gerhardsson, *The Testing of God's Son*, 40 – 41, points out, the testing is carried out by Satan, but he is God's instrument in testing his own Son.

4. France, *Gospel of Matthew*, 128.

Translation

(See next page.)

Structure and Literary Form

This is a Q story, closely parallel to Luke 4:1 – 13 yet with a couple redactional changes, such as reversing the final two temptations (to end with a mountain scene, a major Matthean motif)[5] and removing Satan's claim in Luke 4:6 that he has the authority to "give" the kingdoms to Jesus. There is obviously a three-part structure in which Jesus is confronted by Satan three times (vv. 3 – 4, 5 – 7, 8 – 10) and fends him off by quoting Scripture. Davies and Allison correctly identify this as haggadic midrash on Deut 6 – 8 (the source of Jesus' three answers), citing the parallel in *b. Sanh.* 89b, in which Abraham and Satan debate by citing Scripture against each other.[6] It parallels the common rabbinic method of citing Scripture to prove a point and as such is clearly Jewish in background.

Exegetical Outline

➡ **Introduction (4:1 – 2)**

A. Led by the Spirit into the desert (v. 1)

B. Fasting for forty days (v. 2)

I. First Temptation — Turn Stones to Bread (4:3 – 4)

A. Satan challenges Jesus' Son of God status (v. 3a)

B. Temptation to turn stones to bread (v. 3b)

C. Jesus' response from Deut 8:3 – 4 (v. 4)

II. Second Temptation — Throw Himself from the Temple (4:5 – 7)

A. Setting: highest point of the temple (v. 5)

B. The temptation (v. 6)

1. Challenge and temptation (v. 6a)
2. Proof text from Ps 91:11 – 12 (v. 6b)

C. Jesus' response from Deut 6:16 (v. 7)

5. For a good discussion for the differences between Matthew and Luke here, see ibid., 126.

6. Davies and Allison, *Matthew*, 1:352 – 53. It is important to note that this does not obviate the historical veracity of this story, on which see Plummer, *Matthew*, 36 – 37; Morris, *Matthew*, 70 n.1; Hagner, *Matthew 1 – 13*, 63; Keener, *Matthew*, 136 – 37, contra Gerhardsson, *The Testing of God's Son*, 11. On the possibility that this was a visionary experience on Jesus' part, see Carson, "Matthew," 111. Pierre Grelot, "Les tentations de Jésus," *NRTh* 117 (1995): 501 – 16, argues that the historical temptation was entirely an internal experience on the part of Jesus.

Matthew 4:1-11

1a	Setting	**Then Jesus was led into the wilderness**
b	Purpose of 1a	by the Spirit to be tested by the devil.
2a	Result of 1a-b	After fasting forty days and forty nights,
b		**he became hungry afterwards.**
3a	Scene #1	**[1]** And **when the tempter came, he said to him,**
b	Test	*"If you are the Son of God,*
		speak so these stones become bread."
4a	Answer	But **Jesus answered . . .**
b		*"It is written:*
c		*'A person will not live by bread alone*
		but by every word
		that proceeds from the mouth of God.'" (Deut 8:3)
5a	Scene #2	**[2] Then the devil took him to the holy city and**
		had him stand on the highest point of the temple
6a	Test	and **said to him,**
b		*"If you are the Son of God, throw yourself down.*
c		*For it is written,*
d		*'He will command his angels concerning you,*
		and they will lift you up in their hands,
		lest you strike your foot
		against a stone.'"
		(Ps 91:11-12)
7a	Answer	**Jesus replied to him,**
b		*"It is written again,*
c		*'You dare not test the Lord your God.'"* (Deut 6:16)
8a	Scene #3	**[3] Again the devil took him on a very high mountain and**
		showed him all the kingdoms of the world and
		their glory.
9a	Test	And **he said to him,**
b		*"I will give you all these things,*
		if you fall down and worship me."
10a	Answer	**Then Jesus said to him,**
b		*"Go away, Satan, for it is written,*
c		*'You shall worship the Lord your God*
		and him alone shall you serve." (Deut 6:13)
11a	Conclusion	**Then the devil left him and behold,**
		angels came and were ministering to him.

III. Third Temptation — Worship Satan (vv. 8 – 10)

A. Setting: high mountain (v. 8)

B. The temptation: all kingdoms yours if you worship me (v. 9)

C. Jesus' response from Deut 6:13 (v. 10)

Conclusion: The Devil Leaves and Angels Come (v. 11)

Explanation of the Text

πειράζω has two meanings, "test" and "temptation." As in Jas 1:13, God does not tempt, but God does test. This test for Jesus becomes a temptation via Satan and the flesh.[7] So in this narrative, God is testing Jesus (note that the Spirit leads Jesus to the place of testing), and Satan is tempting him. As in the baptism narrative, Jesus aligns himself with the dilemma of humankind, this time in terms of temptation. However, unlike Adam and especially unlike Israel, Jesus emerges triumphant. The spiritual war between Jesus and Satan starts here, and Satan three times tries to deceive (cf. Rev 12:9; 20:3) Jesus into placing self-interest above obeying his Father's will.[8] But via three quotes from Deuteronomy, Jesus in effect tells him, "I know what you're doing. It worked with Israel, but it won't work with me."

In effect the three tests concern the Shema (Deut 6:5), which calls on Israel to "love the Lord your God with all your heart ... soul ... and strength."[9] The first temptation concerns the heart and how Israel's hunger was intended to test their heart for God (Deut 8:2). The second temptation tests Jesus' safety and his desire to save his soul/life and whether he will follow God even if it means his soul/life. The third tests his resolve to draw his strength from God alone rather than seek to rule the world by himself.[10]

4:1 Then Jesus was led into the wilderness by the Spirit (Τότε ὁ Ἰησοῦς ἀνήχθη εἰς τὴν ἔρημον ὑπὸ τοῦ πνεύματος). Note the use of passives here; Jesus was the focus of actions first by the Spirit (it is a *test*) and then by Satan (it is a *temptation)*. Matthew's "led ... by the Spirit" is not as forceful as Mark 1:12 (lit.), "the Spirit cast him out," but still it is a Spirit-led impetus that leads Jesus to head into the wilderness. The link with the baptism is clear; there the Spirit descends on Jesus, here he leads him to the confrontation with Satan. Divine sovereignty continues to control the story; this is not so much a temptation narrative (by Satan) as it is a testing narrative (by God).[11] "Wilderness" (ἔρημος, see on 3:1 for the place) in Scripture has three uses, all found here: it is the habitation of demons (Isa 13:21; 34:14 ["wild goats" = demons]; Matt 12:43; Rev 18:2); it is the place of testing, especially for Israel (Deut 6 – 8); and it is the place of divine comfort (1 Kgs 19:4 – 8; Rev 12:6, 14).

4:1 To be tested by the devil (πειρασθῆναι ὑπὸ τοῦ διαβόλου). The devil (the Greek) or Satan (the Hebrew, both meaning "accuser, slanderer") first appears in the OT as an accuser or prosecutor (Job 1:6 – 12; 2:1 – 7 [debated whether this is Satan or a prosecuting angel]) who attacks and tempts

7. See Gundry, *Matthew*, 54; Bruner, *Christbook*, 100.

8. As Wolfgang Stegemann, "Die Versuchung Jesu im Matthäusevangelium: Matt 4, 1 – 11," *EvT* 45 (1985): 29 – 44, says, the real temptation was for Jesus to take hold of his divine sonship and abandon the lowly path God had set before him.

9. See Jerome Murphy-O'Connor, "Was Jesus Tested?" *Priests & People* 14 (2000): 92 – 95, who takes the three temptations as exemplifying this threefold command.

10. See Gerhardsson, *The Testing of God's Son*, 76 – 78.

11. See Nolland, *Matthew*, 162.

God's people (1 Chr 21:1; Zech 3:1). In the intertestamental period this became far more frequent (*1 En.* 40:7; 54:6; *Jub.* 1:20; 10:1 – 14; 17:15 – 18; 4 Macc 18:8; *T. Abr.* 16a; CD 4:12 – 13), and permeates the NT (cf. esp. Rev 12:9; 20:3). πειρασθῆναι tells the purpose of Jesus being led into the wilderness "in order to be tested." So it is natural for Satan to be the one testing[12] Jesus. Since both are introduced with "by" (ὑπό) as the instrument of leading and tempting Jesus, the two are set in contrast to each other.[13] The comparison of Jesus' test with Israel's test has already begun. In Deut 8:2; 29:5; and Ps 136:16 it is God who leads Israel into the wilderness, while here it is the Spirit. Israel fails, while Jesus succeeds.

4:2 After fasting forty days and forty nights, he became hungry afterwards (καὶ νηστεύσας ἡμέρας τεσσαράκοντα καὶ νύκτας τεσσαράκοντα, ὕστερον ἐπείνασεν). The temporal aorist participle "after fasting" (νηστεύσας) tells how long the fasting lasted.[14] Forty days and nights of fasting (abstaining from food [probably not from water] to commune with God) reflects Israel's forty-year wandering (Deut 8:2) as well as the forty-day fasts of Moses (Exod 34:28; Deut 9:9) and Elijah (1 Kgs 19:8). Allusions to Moses and Israel are uppermost because they conform to the Jesus/Israel contrast. In fact, Israel became "hungry" in Deut 8:3. This is a natural lead-in to the first temptation, where Satan capitalizes on Jesus' hunger.

4:3 And when the tempter came, he said to him, "If you are the Son of God, speak so these stones become bread" (Καὶ προσελθὼν ὁ πειράζων εἶπεν αὐτῷ, Εἰ υἱὸς εἶ τοῦ θεοῦ, εἰπὲ ἵνα οἱ λίθοι οὗτοι ἄρτοι γένωνται). Matthew identifies Satan with his modus operandi by calling him "the tempter" (ὁ πειράζων), which gives a clue to what he is doing in the test. The condition of fact "if" (εἰ) shows that Satan is assuming the reality that Jesus is indeed the Son of God (on the title see 3:17). He is not challenging the truth of it but trying to tempt Jesus into using his sonship selfishly, to center on his elevated status rather than the humble path set by God. Since Jesus was obviously hungry (v. 2), it would hardly be wrong to use his messianic power to feed himself ("Why not?"). In effect Satan is also saying, "We know you are Son of God; now prove it by helping yourself." So the issue is whether Jesus will do it God's way or his own way.[15]

4:4 But Jesus answered,[16] "It is written, 'A person will not live by bread alone but by every word that proceeds from the mouth of God'" (ὁ δὲ ἀποκριθεὶς εἶπεν, Γέγραπται, Οὐκ ἐπ' ἄρτῳ μόνῳ ζήσεται ὁ ἄνθρωπος, ἀλλ' ἐπὶ παντὶ ῥήματι

12. Davies and Allison, *Matthew,* 1:355, point to three other "tests" (all using πειράζω) in Matthew, all centering on the Jewish leaders interrogating Jesus and Jesus answering by quoting Scripture (16:1; 19:3; 22:34 – 35). See also W. Wilkens, "Die Versuchung Jesus nach Matthäus," *NTS* 28 (1982): 481 – 83.

13. Blomberg, *Matthew,* 83, says, "By this phrasing, Matthew warns against two common errors — blaming God for temptation and crediting the devil with power to act independently of God. In the NT God is always so disassociated from evil that he is never directly responsible for tempting humans (Jas 1:13). Yet the devil is never portrayed as an enemy equal with but opposite to God; he always remains bound by what God permits" (e.g., Rev 13:5 – 8).

14. Wallace, 201. There is another temporal participle at the beginning of v. 3.

15. God's purpose in the test is different from Satan's. As Gerhardsson, *The Testing of God's Son,* 31, says, "God tempts his elect ones to test their character and inquire into their way of life." For Jesus, this was to show he is truly Son of God. In passing the test, Jesus shows his "proper filial relationship" to God, something also true of Israel (Wis 3:1 – 6; 11:9 – 10; 2 Macc 6:12 – 16, see Gerhardsson, *The Testing of God's Son,* 33).

16. The redundant use of the circumstantial participle "answering" (ἀποκριθείς) followed by the main verb "he said" (εἶπεν) occurs fifty-six times in Matthew and is best translated by a single verb, see M. Zerwick, *Biblical Greek* (Rome: Pontifical Biblical Institute, 1963), 127; Wallace, 649 – 50.

ἐκπορευομένῳ διὰ στόματος θεοῦ). Jesus' reply is taken from Deut 8:3, which comes from a passage in which God is challenging Israel to remember how he had taken care of them in the wilderness by giving them manna. Yet the greater gift is not manna but his commands and teaching. So Jesus is in effect saying, "Israel failed in this, but I will not."

There is also a sense in which Jesus is reliving (corporate identity) Israel's wilderness experience[17] but without yielding to the temptation. He recognizes the great importance of bread but says there is something far greater. The generic "a person" (ὁ ἄνθρωπος) applies this to every person, male or female. "Every word" proceeding from God stresses the "every," and while Jesus is mainly referring to direct commandments, he secondarily refers to Scripture for the Jews and his day. As Paul says (2 Tim 3:16), "All Scripture is God-breathed." There is no part of God's Word that is not essential for living right before God, and it is incredibly dangerous for churches to neglect the depths of that Word. A good parallel is John 4:34, "My food ... is to do the will of him who sent me and to finish his work" (cf. also 6:35).

4:5 Then the devil took him to the holy city and had him stand on the highest point of the temple (Τότε παραλαμβάνει αὐτὸν ὁ διάβολος εἰς τὴν ἁγίαν πόλιν, καὶ ἔστησεν αὐτὸν ἐπὶ τὸ πτερύγιον τοῦ ἱεροῦ).[18] The present tense "takes" (παραλαμβάνει) places this in the foreground of the action[19] and stresses the drama of the ongoing event (as in v. 8). Whether this is a vision or Satan actually transports Jesus to a mountain cannot be known for certain, though the fact that Satan shows Jesus "all the kingdoms of the world" in v. 8 makes the visionary form viable for these last two temptations. However, it is hard to see why Jesus would throw himself off the temple in a vision where nobody would see it. Either way, Satan takes Jesus to "the highest point" (πτερύγιον) of the temple, probably the flat corner on the southeast side that looks hundreds of feet down into the ravine of the Kidron Valley, a point so high it would make people dizzy (Josephus, *Ant.* 15.411 – 12).[20]

4:6 ... and said to him, "If you are the Son of God, throw yourself down" (καὶ λέγει αὐτῷ, Εἰ υἱὸς εἶ τοῦ θεοῦ, βάλε σεαυτὸν κάτω). Again Satan recognizes Jesus' special sonship and tries to use it against him. Satan first gives a seemingly ridiculous command ("throw yourself down"), with the aorist imperative "throw" (βάλε) looking at the action as a whole[21] and asking Jesus to do something that on the surface makes no sense.

4:6 "For it is written, 'He will command his angels concerning you, and they will lift you up in their hands, lest you strike your foot against a stone'" (γέγραπται γὰρ ὅτι Τοῖς ἀγγέλοις αὐτοῦ ἐντελεῖται περὶ σοῦ καὶ ἐπὶ χειρῶν ἀροῦσίν σε, μήποτε προσκόψῃς πρὸς λίθον τὸν πόδα σου). Satan anchors the command in Ps 91:11 – 12, a

17. Hagner, *Matthew 1 – 13*, 65; Davies and Allison, *Matthew*, 1:362 – 63.

18. Matthew reverses the order in Luke, which has this temptation last. Most scholars believe Matthew is original since he has the "Son of God" temptations together and there is a natural progression from the lesser to the most severe test, with the temptation to worship Satan last. Yet both also have theological reasons for their order, Luke ending with a temple scene (a major theme in Luke) and Matthew with a mountain scene (the place of revelation in Matthew). There is no way to be certain, and it does not matter, since the evangelists were not trying to be chronological (see Introduction).

19. Stanley E. Porter, *Idioms of the Greek New Testament* (Sheffield: Sheffield Academic Press, 1992), 23 – 25.

20. Πτερύγιον is the diminutive of the term for "wing," and many interpretations have been made, such as the roof of the temple, one of its towers, the wall surrounding the temple, or the top of the gate. Yet the best is probably the "highest point," which would be the portico overlooking the valley.

21. Wallace, 485.

psalm centering on God's protection of his people. Since God is "my refuge and my fortress" (91:2), I can trust him to shelter me from my troubles and rescue me from my dangers. In fact, he will send his angels to ensure I will not so much as dash my foot on a stone (vv. 11 – 12).

πρός is used here in an adversative sense, "against" (BAGD, 710 [4]). Satan has left out one clause ("to guard you in all your ways"), but he has not twisted the basic meaning as some have claimed. Rather, he has taken it out of context and used it literally for a selfish act, namely, for Jesus to throw himself down to prove to all[22] that he is indeed the Son of God (the psalm applies to the sons of God, namely, Israel). The implication is that if God would do this for Israel, the sons of God, how much more would he do so for *the* Son of God. As before, Satan takes a truth (God's protecting his own) and turns it into a self-centered act.

4:7 Jesus replied to him, "It is written again, 'You dare not test the Lord your God'" (ἔφη αὐτῷ ὁ Ἰησοῦς, Πάλιν γέγραπται, Οὐκ ἐκπειράσεις κύριον τὸν θεόν σου). Jesus does not respond to Satan's use of the psalm but instead uses another quote ("again" [πάλιν] refers to a further use of Scripture) from Deut 6:16. In Deuteronomy the test refers to Massah (meaning "testing," Exod 17:1 – 7). At Massah Israel "put the LORD your God to the test" (Deut 6:16 = Exod 17:2) by failing to trust him and demanding water, saying, "Is the LORD among us or not?" Massah and Meribah became symbols of putting God to the test and thereby bringing judgment down on the nation (Ps 95:7 – 9; cf. Heb 3:7 – 4:13). Jesus recognizes Satan's ruse for what it is; testing the Son of God is testing God.[23] Israel failed the test at Massah; Jesus relives that experience but emerges triumphant.

4:8 Again the devil took him on a very high mountain and showed him all the kingdoms of the world and their glory (Πάλιν παραλαμβάνει αὐτὸν ὁ διάβολος εἰς ὄρος ὑψηλὸν λίαν, καὶ δείκνυσιν αὐτῷ πάσας τὰς βασιλείας τοῦ κόσμου καὶ τὴν δόξαν αὐτῶν). As in v. 5 the main verbs are present tense, stressing the ongoing action of the test. Satan now proceeds to offer Jesus the greatest temptation of all, a shortcut to power and glory. "On a mountain" (εἰς ὄρος) is spatial but shades over to the function of "to" (πρός) or "in" (ἐν), "onto." The "very high mountain"[24] may recall Moses on Mount Nebo surveying the Promised Land (Deut 34:1 – 4, which has linguistic parallels with this passage); if so, it would mean Jesus is offered what Moses failed to receive and more.[25]

22. France, *Gospel of Matthew*, 127, doubts that this is addressed to Jesus' "messianic agenda," i.e., to Jesus proving to others that he is Messiah. He points out that no spectators are present for the temptations, thereby saying that they are addressed to Jesus' self-interest rather than to public acclamation. However, it seems more likely that both are involved. Jesus would hardly be tempted to throw himself off the temple just to prove to himself that God would rescue him.

23. Gerhardsson, *The Testing of God's Son*, 60, defines "tempting God" in this instance as "demand[ing] from God a token that he is going to keep his covenantal promises"; therefore, for Jesus it means "to endanger himself by his own act, so as to challenge God to save his life in accordance with the covenant promises."

24. This could be a vision (France, *Matthew* [TNTC], 99; Ridderbos, *Matthew*, 84 – 85; Blomberg, *Matthew*, 85) or an actual mountain from which Jesus could see surrounding kingdoms (see Keener, *Matthew*, 141 n202). Either way, the temptation is a real one.

25. Gerhardsson, *The Testing of God's Son*, 62; Hill, *Matthew*, 101 – 2; Hagner, *Matthew 1 – 13*, 68; Keener, *Matthew*, 41, contra Carson, "Matthew," 114; Gnilka, *Matthäusevangelium*, 90 (who sees it as an apocalyptic image similar to *2 Bar.* 76:3 – 4). Terence L. Donaldson, *Jesus on the Mountain: A Study in Matthean Theology* (JSNTSup 8; Sheffield: JSOT Press, 1985), 92 – 96, agrees that the Moses typology is present but believes the major motif is an eschatological Zion-typology drawn from Ps 2:6 – 8 (with its Son of God theology) and the intertestamental theme of the pilgrimage and testing of God's people (Bar 4:36 – 37; 5:1 – 9; *Pss. Sol.* 11:11 – 3). While this may be an aspect, in the Sinai imagery of the temptation narrative, Moses typology is predominant here.

Matthew likes mountain scenes (5:1; 8:1; 14:23; 15:29; 28:16) and so calls this a "very high" one (Luke 4:5 has "a high place"). Satan's offer at first glance is false, for God alone has true authority over the world, not him. Yet he is also called "prince of this world" (John 12:31; 14:30; 16:11) and "god of this age" (2 Cor 4:4), and demonic forces were said to control the nations (Dan 10:13, 20 – 21; *Jub.* 35:17; *T. Job* 8:1 – 3). In other words, God had allowed Satan certain authority in this world, and Satan is offering this to Jesus. The use of "all the kingdoms" along with "their glory" stresses the earthly aspect; Satan could only offer earthly glory, not lasting glory.

It is an actual temptation, not an unrealizable one. Jesus is to have dominion over the world as the Son of Man (Dan 7:13 – 14; cf. Ps 2:8; Rev 11:15), but that will be much later after he suffered as the atoning sacrifice for humankind. This temptation is to take it now, on his terms, not God's. Matthew may be developing a parallel to 28:16, 18, when Jesus will stand on a mountain and say, "All authority in heaven and on earth has been given to me."[26]

4:9 And he said to him, "I will give you all these things, if you fall down and worship me" (καὶ εἶπεν αὐτῷ, Ταῦτά σοι πάντα δώσω, ἐὰν πεσὼν προσκυνήσῃς μοι). This is given quite a different flavor than the first two temptations. There Satan used imperatives and the condition of fact "if" (εἰ). Here we have a future promise, "I will give to you" (σοι δώσω), with "all" (πάντα) referring only to the earthly glory, and the possible condition "if" (ἐάν). The promise is based on fulfilling the condition. Though Jesus will receive the kingdoms as his future inheritance (see above), Satan is offering them now without the difficulty of becoming the suffering Servant. But the price tag is incredibly high — idolatry, replacing Jesus' Father with Satan as an object of worship. The first two commandments read, "I am the Lord your God.... You shall have no other gods before me. You shall not make for yourself an image in the form of anything in heaven above or on the earth beneath or in the waters below" (Deut 5:6 – 8).

4:10 Then Jesus said to him, "Go away, Satan" (τότε λέγει αὐτῷ ὁ Ἰησοῦς, Ὕπαγε, Σατανᾶ). Now the impetus shifts to Jesus, for Satan[27] has to obey his command to leave (4:11). The use of the imperative and the brevity of the command are frequent in exorcisms (8:32; cf. Mark 1:25); Jesus takes charge, and the battle is over. The victory belongs to Jesus, and Satan can only skulk away.

4:10 "... for it is written, 'You shall[28] worship the Lord your God and him alone shall you serve'" (γέγραπται γάρ, Κύριον τὸν θεόν σου προσκυνήσεις καὶ αὐτῷ μόνῳ λατρεύσεις). For the third time Jesus quotes from Deut 6 – 8 (6:13), and it ends with "you will serve/worship him alone," in direct contrast to Satan's "worship me." Once more this echoes a place where Israel failed. In Deut 6:10 – 19 God warns Israel that he is a jealous God and will punish the nation severely if they commit idolatry (as they had done in Exod 32, the golden calf incident). For the final time, Jesus is victorious where Israel failed. This is a proleptic

26. See Davies and Allison, *Matthew*, 1:369.

27. "Satan" appears three times (4:10; 12:26; 16:23, though see also "Beelzebul" and "prince of demons" in 9:34; 10:25; 12:24) and is a Greek loanword from the Aramaic term for "Adversary." The name appears in 1 Chr 21:1; Job 1:6 – 12; 2:1 – 7; Zech 3:1 – 2, though it is debated whether those refer to the ruler of demons or an adversarial angel in God's council. Many think that the idea of demons and of Satan developed during the intertestamental period under Persian influence, but there are OT examples of such (see G. H. Twelftree, *DJG*, 163 – 64).

28. The use of the future tense for the imperative is used for "categorical injunctions ... in the legal language of the OT" (BDF §362), especially in OT quotes where it is a divine or eternal command.

anticipation of that final victory Jesus will attain at the cross (Rev 5:5 – 7; 12:11), yet also of the repeated victories in his many exorcisms (Matt 8:28 – 34; 12:25 – 28).

4:11 Then the devil left him (Τότε ἀφίησιν αὐτὸν ὁ διάβολος). The devil, completely defeated, slinks away and is replaced by angels. The present "to leave" (ἀφίησιν) may signify Satan leaves him but only for a while (cf. Luke 4:13, "until an opportune time").[29] Satan is often pictured by Christians as a superhuman so much more powerful than we are that we have no chance against him. That is not the picture in the NT. Satan was defeated once for all at the cross (Rev 5:6; 12:11) and "knows that his time is short" (12:12); Armageddon (19:17 – 21; cf. 20:7 – 10) is not his final defeat but is only the last act of defiance by an already defeated foe. Satan cannot overpower the believer but can only deceive (12:9, 20:3), and even that is controlled by God (1 Cor 10:13). The believer can always "resist" him by depending on God's strength (Jas 4:7). The "roaring lion" who looks for "someone to devour" (1 Pet 5:8) does so via a flood of temptation (Rev 12:15), from which God will deliver those who trust in him.

4:11 ... and behold, angels came and were ministering to him (καὶ ἰδοὺ ἄγγελοι προσῆλθον καὶ διηκόνουν αὐτῷ). Finally, angels minister to Christ (imperfect "were ministering" [διηκόνουν], stressing ongoing care). The one who refused to satisfy his hunger by misusing his miraculous powers and who refused angelic aid by jumping from the temple heights is now fed by those very angels. "To minister" (διακονέω) is often used for giving food,[30] yet it is also likely that "ministered" goes beyond food and encompasses every aspect of concerned aid.

Theology in Application

Keener notes the three categories for interpreting this story: (1) a salvation-historical approach, with Jesus' testing recalling that of Israel in the wilderness; (2) christological, affirming Jesus' messiahship against current political expectations; (3) paraenetic, with Jesus a model for believers when they are tested.[31] The best approach is to combine the first two, though I would alter the second to say Jesus proves himself to be Son of God by defeating Satan in the wilderness. The third is often misused in sermons, who take this story as showing that when we memorize Scripture we can defeat Satan every time. There is no hint in the context that Matthew is thinking of believers; it is christological from start to finish. The best one can say is that in the contrast between Jesus and Israel, the reader can identify with Israel and say that when we depend on Jesus, we can overcome Israel's failure. That is secondary but viable, and we will utilize this below.

Jesus exemplifies absolute surrender to the Father's will, and where Israel/we failed (in the areas of food, protection, and gaining kingdoms) Jesus succeeded by

29. Hill, *Matthew*, 102; Alan Hugh McNeile, *The Gospel according to Matthew* (Grand Rapids: Baker, 1980, originally 1915) 42; Davies and Allison, *Matthew*, 1:374; Morris, *Matthew*, 412.

30. Carson, "Matthew," 115.

31. Keener, *Matthew*, 137.

obeying God. Hagner says it well: "In this pericope we encounter a theme that is vital in the theology of the Gospels. The goal of obedience to the Father is accomplished, not by triumphant self-assertion, not by the exercise of power and authority, but paradoxically by the way of humility, service, and suffering. Therein lies true greatness (cf. 20:26 – 28)."[32]

One other possibility can be mentioned. Some have seen direct parallels between 1 John 2:16, the temptation of Eve, and this story. Again it must be said that this is not intended by Matthew and the parallels are theological rather than textual, but they are interesting:

1 John 2:16	Eve (Gen 3:6)	Christ
Cravings of sinful people	Good for food	First temptation
Lust of their eyes	Pleasing to the eye	Third temptation
Boasting	Desirable for gaining wisdom	Second temptation

1. A Model for Victory in the Time of Testing

The heroes of the faith go through testing throughout the Bible (Abraham, Joseph, Moses, David, Job, Elijah, Isaiah, Ezekiel; cf. Heb 11), and through it they learn the dependence on God that is necessary for a triumphant ministry. That is the same for believers today, and we need to look at our trials as a means of growing in faith (Heb 12:6 – 11; Jas 1:2 – 4; 1 Pet 1:6 – 7). As Keener observes,[33] "Disciples are destined for testing (6:13; 26:41), but Jesus their forerunner has gone before them and shown them how to overcome."

2. The True Son of God Is Not Self-Centered

Satan tempts Jesus first to be a self-centered magician.[34] Most of us succumb frequently in this area, and one could go so far as to say the average Christian in the Western world should probably have two prayers at every meal, thanksgiving before and asking forgiveness afterward. The heart of sin is placing self ahead of God, and that was the basic sin of Israel in the wilderness and also of the disciples in Mark (Mark 8:11 – 14, 32 – 33; 9:19, 28, 33 – 35; 10:33 – 45).

3. The True Son of God Is Not an Attention-Grabber

The second temptation was to prove to everyone his heavenly origin by forcing the angels to rescue him in spectacular fashion. Jesus did command the hosts of

32. Hagner, *Matthew 1 – 13*, 70.
33. Keener, *Matthew*, 139.
34. Ibid.

heaven, but he was not to use them for his own personal benefit. This is similar to the selfish prayer of Jas 4:3 that has only "your [own] pleasures" as a goal and so is not answered. Israel did this for forty years in the wilderness, always grumbling and complaining because God didn't acquiesce to their every whim, and they perished there. We are promised that Christ will give us what we want, but only if we pray "in [his] name" (John 14:13 – 14), but not that we can have our "pleasures" fed by praying that way. "In my name" means to pray in union with him; it was never intended to be only a formula that closes prayer (and too often almost a magical phrase to get God to say yes to our requests).

4. Jesus' Refusal to Do Anything to Gain His Own Kingdom

Christ was promised eternal dominion (Dan 7:14), but only after he had followed his Father's will by going to the cross as suffering Servant. We are promised that we are "co-heirs" with him (Rom 8:17) of a kingdom that cannot be taken from us (1 Pet 1:4 – 5), but only after we too have suffered with him (Phil 3:10; Col 1:24; 1 Pet 2:19 – 21; 3:13 – 17; 4:12 – 19). Israel failed in the wilderness, but we can be victorious by trusting in him completely and following the example of the one who paved the way to victory.

5. Satan a Defeated Foe

Davies and Allison observe that in Matthew whenever Satan and his legions appear (4:23; 8:16, 28; 9:32; 12:22; 13:39; 15:22; 17:18), they "wear the faces of defeat."[35] The theme is given in 12:29, the binding of Satan. Christ has now bound Satan in his house, and every exorcism is proof of that. Their powers "are strictly circumscribed, and they fail completely in the presence of the Son of God and those members of his community who are full of faith (cf. 17.14 – 21)." Christ has passed on his authority to the church (10:1), and so Satan has no true power over the believer (1 Cor 10:13; Rev 12:11) except through deception.

35. Davies and Allison, *Matthew*, 1:403.

CHAPTER 8

Matthew 4:12 – 17

Literary Context

The preliminary events are over, and it is time for Jesus to engage in his messianic mission. Like Mark 1:14, Matthew begins after John the Baptist is imprisoned; John 1 – 5 shows that Jesus' ministry actually began earlier, interspersing ministry in Judea and Galilee before moving to Capernaum. So the Synoptic Gospels actually begin later in Jesus' ministry.

Matthew begins his major organization here, interweaving five narrative and discourse sections (4:12 – 7:29; 8:1 – 11:1; 11:2 – 13:53; 13:54 – 18:54; 19:1 – 25:46)[1] between the infancy and passion narratives, and this outline will follow that plan. This first narrative section is the shortest of the five and summarizes the beginning ministry leading up to the Sermon on the Mount. Matthew here wants the reader to see the broad contours of that messianic ministry (preaching, discipling, healing).

I. Jesus' Origin and Preparation for Ministry (1:1 – 4:11)
II. The Kingdom Message Goes Out (4:12 – 7:29)
  A. Early Galilean Ministry (4:12 – 25)
    ➦ **1. Beginning the Capernaum Ministry (4:12 – 17)**
    2. The Call of the Disciples (4:18 – 22)

Main Idea

Primarily, this paragraph shows that Jesus' decision to resettle in Capernaum fulfills prophecy. The goal is to demonstrate again that God's plan is the Gentile mission, that is, the Gentile world in addition to the Jewish people. Also, it demonstrates Galilee as the place of "light" in contrast to the darkness settling over Judea.[2]

1. See also Carson, "Matthew," 51 – 57, for a similar outline.

2. France, *Gospel of Matthew*, 139.

Translation

Matthew 4:12-17

12a	Setting	After he heard that John had been arrested,
b	Action	**Jesus returned to Galilee.**
13a	Time	And after he left Nazareth,
b	Action	**he came and dwelt in Capernaum that was beside the sea,**
		in the regions of Zebulon and Naphtali,
14a	Fufillment Formula for 13b	so that what was spoken through Isaiah the prophet might be fulfilled, saying,
15a		*"Land of Zebulon and land of Naphtali,*
		the way of the sea, beyond the Jordan,
		Galilee of the Gentiles,
16a		*The people who sit in darkness have seen a great light;*
		and . . . a light has dawned
		on those who sit in the region and shadow of death." (Isa 9:2)
17a	Summary	**From that time Jesus began to preach and say,**
b	Exhortation	*"Repent, for the kingdom of heaven is near."*

Structure and Literary Form

This is largely M material from Matthew's special source. The facts of Jesus' move to Capernaum are found in the other gospels but not in this form. The fulfillment quotation is the center of the passage, and it demonstrates that God is behind and guiding Jesus' every decision. It was all foreseen and prepared for in Israel's past, so his messianic ministry is the culmination of the divine plan for the salvation of the world, as seen in his message of repentance (v. 17). In this aspect this passage can be subtitled "the geography of Jesus' mission," as it moves from Judea to Nazareth to Capernaum to the whole world ("Galilee of the Gentiles").

With the centrality of the fulfillment passage, this is a midrash (note discussion on this in the Introduction) on Isa 9:1 – 2, to show how God led Jesus from Judea to Nazareth to Capernaum in order to launch his ministry in fulfillment of God's prophetic will. Of the three parts, the first and last are historical summaries that explain the significance of the middle, OT passage.

Exegetical Outline

➡ **I. Jesus' Move to Galilee (4:12 – 13)**

A. The launching point — the Baptist's arrest (v. 12)

B. Move to Nazareth then Capernaum (v. 13)

II. Fulfillment of Isa 9:1 – 2 (4:14 – 16)

A. Galilee of the Gentiles (v. 15)

B. The dawning of the great light (v. 16)

III. Jesus' Message (4:17)

A. The need — repentance (v. 17)

B. The basis — arrival of the kingdom (v. 17)

Explanation of the Text

4:12 After he heard that John had been arrested[3] (Ἀκούσας δὲ ὅτι Ἰωάννης παρεδόθη). As stated above, the arrest of John was not immediate, and he had an extended ministry before he denounced the marriage of Herod Antipas and Herodias and got arrested (John 1:19 – 34; 3:22 – 30). His ministry undoubtedly lasted several months. During that time Jesus interspersed ministry in Judea and Galilee, even in Samaria (John 1 – 5).[4] The divine passive "had been arrested" (παρεδόθη) parallels Jesus' passion predictions ("delivered over to human hands," 17:22; 20:18) and signifies the Baptist's suffering is an anticipation of his Lord's suffering.

4:12 Jesus returned to Galilee (ἀνεχώρησεν εἰς τὴν Γαλιλαίαν). Jesus apparently takes John's arrest as a signal from God to shift his ministry to Galilee. Some think "withdraw" (ἀνεχώρησεν) indicates Jesus was fleeing a dangerous situation, as if John's arrest might herald his own.[5] However, that makes more of the scene than is there, and likely Jesus saw an opportunity to spread the gospel where it would be better received.[6] With fertile land and a large population broadened by trade and opportunity, Galilee was ripe for the harvest.

4:13 And after he left Nazareth, he came and dwelt in Capernaum that was beside the sea (καὶ καταλιπὼν τὴν Ναζαρὰ ἐλθὼν κατῴκησεν εἰς Καφαρναοὺμ τὴν παραθαλασσίαν). Another temporal aorist participle (see on 4:2) signals the move to Capernaum. It was natural for Jesus to return first home to Nazareth, but he quickly moved and

3. The aorist in a past tense setting (the point when Jesus heard the news) is best translated as a pluperfect, "had been arrested."

4. C. H. Dodd, *Historical Tradition in the Fourth Gospel* (Cambridge: Cambridge Univ. Press, 1965); France, *Gospel of Matthew*, 237 – 38, believes the trip in John 4:1 – 3 is the one mentioned here. That is certainly viable but impossible to prove. Carson, "Matthew," 116, gives three reasons why the Synoptists omitted the early Judean ministry: (1) They wished to indicate the end of the ministry of the forerunner before beginning Jesus' ministry. (2) John, writing later, may have wished to respond to groups of the Baptist's followers. (3) Galilee is significant for Matthew as the place of fulfilled prophecy in terms of the mission to "all nations" (28:19).

5. Rudolf Schnackenburg, *The Gospel of Matthew* (Grand Rapids: Eerdmans, 2002), 39; Davies and Allison, *Matthew*, 1:376; Senior, *Matthew*, 62.

6. Hill, *Matthew*, 103; Morris, *Matthew*, 80. Filson, *Matthew*, 72, says "he began his ministry with a challenge (to the same Herod Antipas who ruled both Judea and Galilee) rather than a retreat."

settled in Capernaum. It was far more central than Nazareth, on the northwest corner of the lake, and was a natural center from which to evangelize the region. Also, several of his disciples were from the Capernaum area (e.g., Peter [8:14, including Andrew, James, and John], Levi [9:9 – 13]).

Furthermore, it is possible that Nazareth was opposed to his message (13:54 – 57 = Luke 4:23 – 30 [where it comes before the Capernaum ministry]) and Capernaum was relatively open. However, as Bock notes, Luke has moved that Nazareth sermon on Isa 61:1 – 2 up, and Jesus had already ministered in Capernaum (Luke 4:23b).[7] So it does not really mean Nazareth opposed Jesus early in his ministry.

4:13 ... in the regions of Zebulon and Naphtali (ἐν ὁρίοις Ζαβουλὼν καὶ Νεφθαλίμ). Matthew stresses that it is where the ancient tribes of Zebulon (Nazareth) and Naphtali (Capernaum) took residence, to prepare for the prophecy of v. 15. The importance of the tribal names is seen in the chiasm in vv. 13b – 15:

A Galilee
  B by the sea
    C Zebulon and Naphtali
    C' Zebulon and Naphtali
  B' toward the sea
A' Galilee[8]

4:14 ... so that what was spoken through Isaiah the prophet might be fulfilled, saying (ἵνα πληρωθῇ τὸ ῥηθὲν διὰ Ἠσαΐου τοῦ προφήτου λέγοντος). This fifth of Matthew's ten fulfillment quotations (from Isa 9:1 – 2; see on 1:22) stresses once more divine providence, as God guides the life of his Son in keeping with prophetic expectation and so as to relive the experiences of the covenant people. Of course, Jesus' ministry in Galilee was at one and the same time God's will and a stumbling block in Jesus' ministry in Judea (John 1:46; 7:41, 52). In fact, many believe this fulfillment passage was intended partly to offset criticism of the Galilee-based ministry of Jesus.[9]

4:15 "Land of Zebulon and land of Naphtali, the way of the sea, beyond the Jordan, Galilee of the Gentiles" (Γῆ Ζαβουλὼν καὶ γῆ Νεφθαλίμ, ὁδὸν θαλάσσης, πέραν τοῦ Ἰορδάνου, Γαλιλαία τῶν ἐθνῶν).[10] The context of Isa 9:1 – 2 includes a prophecy of coming judgment (ch. 8) and a promise that in the future deliverance will come when "a child is born," who will be "Wonderful Counselor, Mighty God, Everlasting Father, Prince of Peace" (9:6 – 7). Matthew may have all this in mind as part of a theme centered on the Messiah who will return Israel from exile.[11]

Zebulon and Naphtali were together in the northern part of Galilee. They were allotted land (Josh 19:10 – 16, 32 – 39 respectively) surrounding the Sea of Galilee on the western side and north of the lake and then right next to that in the central portion of Galilee. Just as importantly, they were among the first tribes to be deported by Assyria (2 Kgs 15:29), an act that Isa 8 calls divine judgment. The "way of the sea" probably refers to the important road that in both Isaiah's day and

7. Bock, *Luke 1:1 – 9:50*, 397 – 98.

8. William G. Thompson, *Matthew's Advice to a Divided Community: Matt 17, 22 – 18,35* (AnBib 44; Rome: Pontifical Biblical Institute, 1970), 19, in Davies and Allison, *Matthew*, 1:379.

9. Keener, *Matthew*, 146.

10. This follows the LXX Isa 8:23 – 9:1 except for a couple of changes: Matthew has γῆ ("land") instead of χώρα ("region") and omits both "and others who inhabit the seacoast" and "the regions of Judea" (cf. Hagner, *Matthew 1 – 13*, 73). Many believe Matthew is following the MT rather than the LXX. The result is the centrality of Galilee for Matthew in the messianic tradition.

11. Carson, "Matthew," 118; cf. N. T. Wright, *Jesus and the Victory of God* (Christian Origins and the Question of God 2; Minneapolis: Fortress, 1996), where the theme is overstated but definitely shown to be a major motif for Jesus and the early church.

Jesus' time went from Damascus through Galilee to the Mediterranean (called the *via maris* by the Romans).[12]

"Beyond the Jordan" means the area east of the Jordan and may refer to the ministry of Jesus there but more likely provides a transition to "Galilee of the Gentiles." The Roman road brought Gentiles into the Transjordan territory (a large population lived there), and the Gentiles predominated east of ("beyond") the Jordan. One of the major themes here is the Gentile mission,[13] a perfect ministry for Jesus in Galilee and a key motif in Matthew's gospel. This is the message of the rest of the Isaianic quote.

4:16 "The people who sit in darkness have seen a great light" (ὁ λαὸς ὁ καθήμενος ἐν σκότει φῶς εἶδεν μέγα). In Isa 9:2 the people in darkness are undoubtedly the Jews living in pagan Galilee (there were far fewer Jews in Galilee in Isaiah's day, cf. Judg 18:7, 28) apart from the spiritual center in Jerusalem, while for Matthew they are mainly Jews living in spiritual darkness (λαός as the Jewish "people" of God in Matthew) but implying also the Gentiles dwelling in spiritual darkness. In Matthew Jesus begins ministering to the Jews (10:5–6; 15:24) but prepares for the Gentile mission (28:19). "In darkness" (ἐν σκότει) refers to the spiritual depravity into which the nation has descended, and the "great light" would be God's new revelation in Jesus.

4:16 "And on those who sit in the region and shadow of death, a light has dawned" (καὶ τοῖς καθημένοις ἐν χώρᾳ καὶ σκιᾷ θανάτου φῶς ἀνέτειλεν αὐτοῖς). It has "dawned" or shone brightly in this land, overcoming the "shadow of death" that hovered over all its inhabitants (note the movement from darkness to death). An epexegetical "and" (καί) links the two nouns, i.e., "the region of death, namely, its shadow." Death is both the home and the covering force hovering over the apostate nation. Moreover, by using "dawned" rather than the LXX "will shine," it means the light has come and originates in Jesus as he begins his messianic proclamation.

4:17 From that time Jesus began to preach and say (Ἀπὸ τότε ἤρξατο ὁ Ἰησοῦς κηρύσσειν καὶ λέγειν). "From that time" (ἀπὸ τότε) is a significant transition found three times in this gospel (4:17; 16:21; 26:16) and indicates a new start. Several believe that "from that time Jesus began to" (4:17; 16:21) indicates the major sections of Matthew's gospel and divide the book accordingly (1:1–4:16; 4:17–16:20; 16:21–28:20).[14] While this is viable, it probably reads too much into the phrase (see Introduction). More likely, it indicates a new phase to Jesus' ministry. The time of preparation is over, and Jesus begins to proclaim his kingdom message.

4:17 "Repent, for the kingdom of heaven is near" (Μετανοεῖτε, ἤγγικεν γὰρ ἡ βασιλεία τῶν

12. Beare, *Matthew*, 115; Hagner, *Matthew 1–13*, 73. France, *Gospel of Matthew*, 142, believes that Matthew refers to the Sea of Galilee here, but that may be reading more into the quote than is necessary (this became the Roman *via maris* ["Way of the Sea"], well-known in Matthew's day).

13. Hagner, *Matthew 1–13*, 73, and Nolland, *Matthew*, 173–74, do not see an intended reference to the Gentile mission, though they realize many of Matthew's readers may have done so. However, there is little reason to deny a Matthean emphasis given the importance of the universal mission in Matthew (see Introduction). Keener, *Matthew*, 146, calls it the most important theme of this paragraph. The critical place of "outsiders" in God's plan of salvation in Matthew is seen in the women of 1:3, 5, 6 and the Magi of 2:1–12 (so France, *Matthew* [TNTC], 101).

14. Kingsbury, *Structure*; France, *Matthew* (TNTC), 59; Blomberg, *Matthew*, 23. Others see this as marking a new section and place it with vv. 18–22. But it does not belong with that story and probably is meant as a transition verse concluding the section beginning the Capernaum ministry (4:12–17) and launching into the Galilean ministry following.

οὐρανῶν). In 3:2, the Baptist proclaimed, "Repent, for the kingdom of heaven has come near." Now his ministry has come to its end (4:12), and he has passed the baton to Jesus, who takes up the same message but with a new depth, for the "great light" has "dawned" (see v. 16) and the kingdom age is here. The meaning of "has come near"/"is near" (ἤγγικεν) as both already and not yet, as here and yet coming, continues in this context as well (see on 3:2). Jesus has inaugurated the kingdom events (for the kingdom as already present, see 12:28), but they will not be consummated until the eschaton. As Carson says, "with Jesus the kingdom has drawn so near that it has actually dawned."[15]

Theology in Application

Geography plays a large part in any ministry, and Jesus' messianic work is no exception. The main lesson about finding the Lord's will in such a situation is simple: surrender to his leading. That is also the message of the book of Acts, which was never intended to dictate the strategy for world evangelization but simply to say in terms of strategy, "The Holy Spirit guides the church." That is what happened with respect to Jesus.

1. God in Charge of Strategy

There are many possible explanations for Jesus' move to the north: the opposition of the religious leaders in Judea, the greater openness of the people in Galilee, even the desire to go back home. But the main issue was God's will. Jesus went where his sense of divine necessity took him. When the Baptist was arrested, Jesus knew that his time of preparation was over, and God was designating that the new time of kingdom proclamation had arrived.

2. God's Foreknowledge of Everything

The purpose of fulfillment passages is to assure the reader of divine providence and to show that all is part of a larger divine plan. Matthew signals this new beginning by showing that God had meant it to happen this way all along; the move to Galilee actually fulfills prophecy and so was divinely intended long before Jesus was born.

15. Carson, "Matthew,"117. Morris, *Matthew*, 83, says "the kingdom is here in his words and deeds" and yet "the best is yet to be."

3. God's Desire to Reach All the World

The move to "Galilee of the Gentiles" also prepares for the ultimate plan of God for the message to reach not only Israel but also the nations. The Gentiles had always been part of his plan (cf. Gen 12:3; 15:5; 18:18; et al.). So the message of repentance was the natural reaction to the coming of the kingdom age. Christ had his disciples minister only to the Jewish people (10:5, 6) but prepared them for the Gentile mission by himself ministering to Gentiles (8:5 – 13, 28 – 34; 15:21 – 28, 29 – 31) and announced that mission in two stages, prophesying that "many will come from the east and the west" to feast at the messianic banquet with Abraham (8:11) and then commanding the universal mission in 28:19.

4. Repentance as Proper Response to the Presence of the Kingdom

As stated in the discussion of 3:1 – 12, repentance is a total change of mind and heart that involves a new lifestyle as well as a new allegiance to God and Christ. It is the heart of the message of the NT as a whole, for without a mourning for sin and a complete turning from sin to God, there can be no new life in him. We enter the kingdom on our knees. The reason is that sin is antithetical to God; that is why Christ had to die on the cross as the atoning sacrifice for sin. Paul says that faith is the necessary response (eighteen times in Rom 3:19 – 4:25), and repentance is the first step of faith.

CHAPTER 9

Matthew 4:18 – 22

Literary Context

With the inauguration of the next phase of his ministry proper, Jesus begins by choosing his closest followers. It is time to include other heralds of the gospel. God had raised the forerunner, John, and then the Messiah himself had appeared. Now Jesus begins to gather together the messianic community, the church, and to deliver its marching orders. As in Mark 1:16 – 20, Jesus begins his ministry by choosing his closest followers and starts forming the Twelve (cf. Matt 10:1 – 4; cf. Luke 5:1 – 11, where Jesus calls them after his ministry has begun). In Matthew and Mark Jesus' ministry centers on the preparation of his disciples; they are part of his work from the beginning. His kingdom message is summarized (v. 17), then he chooses his assistants (they are already "apostles" in 10:2); finally he begins his ministry proper.

- **II. The Kingdom Message Goes Out (4:12 – 7:29)**
  - **A. Early Galilean Ministry (4:12 – 25)**
    1. Beginning the Capernaum Ministry (4:12 – 17)
    2. ➦ **The Call of the Disciples (4:18 – 22)**
    3. Summary of His Ministry (4:23 – 25)

Main Idea

Jesus calls his first followers and immediately gives them a new kind of ministry, fishing for people. There are three major points here: (1) The creative force in discipleship is Jesus, and the task of every follower is to surrender to his active presence. (2) The purpose of discipleship is evangelistic, to learn a whole new type of "fishing." (3) The demand is for radical surrender, to leave everything in order to follow Christ.

Translation

Matthew 4:18-22

18a	Setting	While Jesus was walking beside the Sea of Galilee,
b	Scene #1	**[1] he saw two brothers,**
		Simon called Peter and Andrew his brother,
		casting their nets into the lake,
		for they were fishermen.
19a	Exhortation	**Jesus said to them,**
b		*"Come after me, and I will make you fish for people,"*
20a	Result of 19a–b	and **immediately they left their nets and followed him.**
21a	Setting	Going a little further away
b	Scene #2	**[2] he saw two other brothers,**
		James the son of Zebedee and John his brother,
		in the boat with their father Zebedee,
		mending their nets,
c	Exhortation	and **he called them.**
22a	Result of 21c	And **immediately they left the boat and their father and followed him.**

Structure and Literary Form

This section closely parallels Mark 1:16 – 20, with only minor stylistic changes. It is a call narrative in two equal parts, with two sets of brothers called to become disciples. The structure of each is the same, with three parts: (1) Jesus sees two pairs of brothers fishing, then (2) calls them to be disciples, and finally (3) they immediately respond. There are slight differences, since the first pair is fishing while the second is getting ready to fish. The content of the call is found only in the first part, with the second presupposing the call. And in the second part the brothers leave their father as well as their fishing and embrace a whole new kind of fishing.

Exegetical Outline

➦ **I. Simon and Andrew Are Called (4:18 – 20)**

- A. Jesus sees them fishing (v. 18)
- B. Called to a new kind of fishing (v. 19)
- C. Immediate response — leaving their occupation (v. 20)

II. James and John Are Called (4:21 – 22)

- A. Jesus sees them fishing with their father (v. 21a)
- B. Jesus calls them (v. 21b)
- C. Immediate response — leaving their occupation and father (v. 22)

Explanation of the Text

With the message of v. 17 it is clear that Jesus' mission is uppermost, and he is marshaling his forces for missionary work, namely, the great catch he is anticipating. This is in keeping with the radical nature of his own messianic work. All other rabbi/disciple relations centered on the followers choosing the rabbi under which they wished to study, then memorizing the wise teaching of their master, and going out on their own only after the time of teaching was done. Jesus introduces a unique ingredient by first taking the initiative in choosing his disciples and then involving them in his ministry virtually from the start.

Moreover, Jesus not only teaches but acts in a whole new way, performing miracles and calling the people not to conformity with the oral tradition but to repentance and a new kind of relationship with God, then passing on his new authority to his disciples (10:1) and sending them out in exactly the type of mission he himself has engaged in (10:5 – 6). The emphasis is also on their radical response to the call. Simon and Andrew "immediately" (v. 20) leave both vocation and home. This introduces the theme of radical discipleship in Matthew; Jesus has absolute priority over occupation and family (see further below). This is also shown when we compare 1 Kgs 19:19 – 21 (the call of Elisha), where Elisha was plowing his field when Elijah called him. There he was allowed to kiss his parents good-bye, while here and in 8:21 – 22 there is no time to bid family farewell. The radical nature of Jesus' demand leaves no room for farewells.[1]

4:18 While Jesus was walking beside the Sea of Galilee (Περιπατῶν δὲ παρὰ τὴν θάλασσαν τῆς Γαλιλαίας).[2] The temporal present participle "while he was walking" (περιπατῶν) tells us Jesus' call came as he was walking by the lake. Simon and Andrew came from Bethsaida, a fishing village northeast of Capernaum on the lake, but they were living in Capernaum at this time (Mark 1:29). The Sea of Galilee is named such because it was the major lake of the district (thirteen miles long, nine at its widest point), and θάλασσα was often used for lakes. It was also called Lake Gennesaret (Luke 5:1, for the city southwest of Capernaum on the lake) and the Sea of Tiberias (John 6:1; 21:1, for the city built by Herod on the southwest part of the lake).

4:18 . . . he saw two brothers, Simon called Peter and Andrew his brother (εἶδεν δύο ἀδελφούς, Σίμωνα τὸν λεγόμενον Πέτρον καὶ Ἀνδρέαν τὸν ἀδελφὸν αὐτοῦ). It is clear the entire initiative is with Jesus, who sees the brothers and calls them. This was not the first time he met them, for they had already become followers shortly after Jesus was baptized by John; some or all of them were probably John's disciples and switched to follow Jesus (John 1:35 – 42). This prior relationship is not part of Matthew's story, since he wishes to emphasize Jesus' authoritative call and the disciples' immediate response. Still, this call is not out of the blue, for Jesus knew them beforehand. In John 1 we learn that Simon was his given name, and Jesus gave a prophecy that he would be called "Cephas" (the Jewish name = "Peter" [the "rock"], a Greek name, given first in John 1:42 and repeated in Matt 16:18).

1. Davies and Allison, *Matthew*, 1:393.

2. While Rudolf Bultmann, *The History of the Synoptic Tradition* (2nd ed,; trans. J. Marsh; Oxford: Blackwell, 1968), 28, doubts the historicity of this episode, calling it "a description of an ideal scene," few have followed him on this. See Hill, *Matthew*, 105; and especially Davies and Allison, *Matthew*, 1:394.

4:18 ... casting their nets into the lake, for they were fishermen (βάλλοντας ἀμφίβληστρον εἰς τὴν θάλασσαν· ἦσαν γὰρ ἁλιεῖς). The present participle "casting" (βάλλοντας) provides a dynamic picture, depicting the disciples in the act of fishing when the call came. The men were professional "fishermen" (ἁλιεῖς) and were throwing out a circular casting net, with lines going up to the men but weighted on the edges so that it sank to the bottom. It was then drawn back to the boat to catch any fish swimming by as it was taken up.[3] From Luke 5:3 – 7 the four were partners with two boats and hired hands (Mark 1:20) and so probably were in the lower-middle class economically.[4] Fishing was second only to agriculture as the economic staple of the region, so they were relatively well off in the Palestinian peasant culture (i.e., near the top of the lower classes).

4:19 Jesus said to them, "Come after me" (καὶ λέγει αὐτοῖς, Δεῦτε ὀπίσω μου). As stated above, Jesus departs from custom (disciples chose which rabbi they wanted to train under) by choosing his own followers. Hengel[5] points out the OT parallel in Yahweh, who called the prophets to their ministry; Jesus thus performs the work of his Father, and France says Jesus is acting more like a prophet here (e.g., Elijah calling Elisha in 1 Kgs 19:19 – 21).[6] Note that Jesus is the creative force and the disciples passive participants. Their part is to "come, follow" (cf. 1 Kgs 19:20) while Jesus is the active agent who "makes" or re-creates them. This is similar to the call of Israel to holy war (Judg 3:28; 1 Sam 11:6 – 7), involving total commitment. Discipleship is a life of obedience (this is not a suggestion but an absolute demand) and following the example of Jesus.

4:19 "... and I will make you fish for people" (καὶ ποιήσω ὑμᾶς ἁλιεῖς ἀνθρώπων). ἁλιεῖς ἀνθρώπων is a genitival construct (lit., "fishermen of people") with an objective genitive, "fish for people." Jesus' use of the fishing metaphor is brilliant. The purpose of fishing is to kill the fish and use it for food; in Jesus' new fishing the "prey" are caught and saved from destruction. This also reverses the OT metaphor, where the people netted are sent to divine judgment (Jer 16:16; Ezek 47:10; Amos 4:2; Hab 1:14 – 15), while here they are saved from that very judgment. Fishing kills, while Jesus' new fishing brings life! Both could be combined to say that in light of the certainty of the final judgment, Jesus is sending out his followers to save many from that terrible end. It is also likely (in light of v. 15) that ἀνθρώπων has a generic thrust to all "people" and not just the Jews.[7]

4:20 And immediately they left[8] their[9] nets and followed him (οἱ δὲ εὐθέως ἀφέντες τὰ δίκτυα ἠκολούθησαν αὐτῷ). Matthew stresses two things: the immediacy of their response and the radical nature of it. There is no hesitation (contra those in 8:19 – 21), and they rush to obey him. Leaving the nets brings out the radical sacrifice necessary to truly follow Jesus. In the scene they seemingly refuse even to take the time to haul in the fish and

3. Morris, *Matthew*, 85n.

4. See Carson, "Matthew," 119; Davies and Allison, *Matthew*, 1:397.

5. Martin Hengel, *The Charismatic Leader and His Followers* (trans. J. Greig; New York: Crossroad, 1981), 50 – 57. He argues for the authenticity of this scene on pp. 76 – 78.

6. France, *Gospel of Matthew*, 147.

7. As Davies and Allison, *Matthew*, 1:398 – 99, say, "Perhaps Matthew thought of the Gentiles as included in the 'people' (ἀνθρώπων, cf. 5:16; 10:22; 12:41)."

8. A circumstantial participle like "leaving" (ἀφέντες) is often best translated as another main verb. At first glance, with the article (οἱ) it seems to be a substantival participle ("those who left"), but it is better to see οἱ δέ as indicating the subject, "and *they*, leaving their nets, followed him" (for the participle following ὁ δέ, see BDF §251).

9. This is an example of the definite article standing in place of the possessive pronoun, see Wallace, 215 – 16.

take the boat to shore. The call of Jesus involves a complete break with the previous way of life (16:24–26; cf. Luke 9:62) and a voluntary surrender to a sacrificial lifestyle.

Keener[10] provides an excellent survey. Contrary to popular belief, the disciples probably did not quit their occupations; they kept their boats (John 21:1–3). However, following Jesus had absolute priority, and they were away a substantial amount of time sitting at Jesus' feet and going on itinerant missions with him. Moreover, when on one of their trips around Galilee (there were several) they would be gone for days at a time, with significant economic repercussions. So following Jesus meant a serious downturn in one's economic situation.

4:21 Going a little further away, he saw two other brothers, James the son of Zebedee and John his brother, in the boat with their father Zebedee, mending their nets (Καὶ προβὰς ἐκεῖθεν εἶδεν ἄλλους δύο ἀδελφούς, Ἰάκωβον τὸν τοῦ Ζεβεδαίου καὶ Ἰωάννην τὸν ἀδελφὸν αὐτοῦ, ἐν τῷ πλοίῳ μετὰ Ζεβεδαίου τοῦ πατρὸς αὐτῶν καταρτίζοντας τὰ δίκτυα αὐτῶν). This verse is framed with circumstantial participles, the first "going on" (προβάς), telling Jesus' action, the second "mending" (καταρτίζοντας), telling the brothers' action. The two other brothers and partners in the fishing business, James and John, were working on their nets after having finished (καταρτίζω is better "mending" after finishing[11] than "preparing" the nets prior to starting).[12] They would be scraping off the seaweed and fixing any tears in the net. Their father Zebedee is mentioned twice, obviously to prepare for their leaving him behind in v. 22.

4:22 ... and he called them. And immediately they left the boat and their father and followed him (καὶ ἐκάλεσεν αὐτούς. οἱ δὲ εὐθέως ἀφέντες τὸ πλοῖον καὶ τὸν πατέρα αὐτῶν ἠκολούθησαν αὐτῷ). As in v. 20. the reaction of James and John is immediate and radically severe (in Mark 1:20 Jesus calls them "without delay" but Matthew here transfers εὐθέως to their "immediate" response for emphasis). The disciples not only surrender their livelihood/boat (Simon and Andrew) but also their family/father (James and John). This does not mean Jesus denigrated the family, for he made it a great priority (5:27–32; 19:3–9, 19); rather, this teaches that Jesus is to have absolute allegiance even over family.[13]

Theology in Application

The core of this passage is mission: Jesus' desire to begin his work and his decision to involve disciples in his mission from the beginning. Davies and Allison call this "the birth of the Christian mission" as well as "the birth of the church,"[14] that moment when the kingdom community is formed to begin the mission task of reaching the world. Behind this is God's deep love for sinners and his desire to bring them to himself. So Jesus' first act after moving to Capernaum is to find that nucleus of followers to help him in that task. It is natural that Peter and Andrew, James and John will comprise that group, since they lived in Capernaum (Mark 1:29) and had already become followers of Jesus (John 1:35–42).

10. Keener, *Matthew*, 152–54.

11. So Carson, "Matthew," 120; Hagner, *Matthew 1–13*, 77.

12. As Morris, *Matthew*, 86.

13. See S. C. Barton, "Family," *DJG*, 226–29.

14. Davies and Allison, *Matthew*, 1: 404.

1. God Loves All People and Wants to Reach Them with His Salvation

It is critical to realize that Christ's first thought was not to establish himself in the religious hierarchy of Jerusalem or to become well known but to begin his mission. As John 1:9 says, he came "into this world" to "give light to everyone." And 2 Pet 3:9 tells us that God does not want "anyone to perish, but everyone to come to repentance." This is to be our priority as well. Jesus chose the meek and lowly, and we should make that a priority in our ministry. Too many churches neglect the downtrodden and minister only to their own kind, usually upper-middle class. We must follow Jesus in reflecting God's love to all regardless of social status, to seek those who are open to the kingdom truths. We too are called to "fish for people," to go wherever there is fishing to do. This does not mean wherever they are biting (as the church growth movement erroneously emphasizes), but wherever the fish are.

2. Jesus Wants Those He Can Mold into "Rescuers from Hell"

Jesus did not choose on the basis of status in society, religious hierarchy, or personality/charisma. He chose those on the marginal edges and not particularly outstanding (James and John were called the "sons of thunder," Mark 3:17, probably for their tempers). Yet they had potential, as proven by Jesus' telling Simon he would be known as "Peter" (the "rock," John 1:42). Jesus saw that they were not only believers but open to his life-changing power. So too he chooses us, not because we are so gifted that he cannot help but turn to us, but because he sees the same potential in us. The question is whether we are willing to surrender control of our life to him.

3. Jesus as the Creative Force in Discipleship

Too many think they know what is best for their lives and virtually tell God what they can do for him. Jesus wants those who will take the passive route and "follow" his guiding presence. He is the Creator not only of this world (John 1:3 – 4; 1 Cor 8:6; Col 1:16; Heb 1:2) but also of the kind of person who will accomplish great things for God. Many have talents but too few have spiritual gifts. A talent becomes a spiritual gift when it is given over to Christ to use for his glory.

But many of us are also given the kind of gift we do not have naturally, like Timothy at his ordination (1 Tim 4:14; 2 Tim 1:6 – 7). I believe this was the gift of leadership (or perhaps the gift of teaching so as to correct the false teachers);[15] Timothy was a loving person (Phil 2:20) but not a strong leader, exactly what he needed to be at Ephesus (1 – 2 Timothy). Jesus wanted to "make" him that person, but apparently he never developed the gift God had given him, and so far as we know he ended up

15. So I. H. Marshall, *The Pastoral Epistles* (ICC; Edinburgh: T&T Clark, 1999), 564.

a failure at Ephesus. We must allow Christ to shape us and to depend on him, not on our natural resources.

4. Discipleship: A Total, Radical Surrender to Christ

This is emphasized in all the gospels. Mark and Matthew say the first four disciples surrendered both occupation and family, and Luke 5:11 says they "left everything" to follow Christ. The problem today is so many want to give Christ virtually a "tithe" of their life, that is, one-tenth to him and 90 percent for themselves. Jesus makes it clear that such will not do. "No one who puts a hand to the plow and looks back is fit for service in the kingdom of God" (Luke 9:62). As Hagner says, "The call of God through Jesus is sovereign and absolute in its authority; the response of those who are called is to be both immediate and absolute, involving a complete break with old loyalties."[16] This will look different for each of us; but the truth is the same. Everything we hold back from God will hamper the quality of our life and keep us from realizing our true potential for him.

16. Hagner, *Matthew 1 – 13*, 78.

CHAPTER 10

Matthew 4:23 – 25

Literary Context

Christ has now fully prepared for his ministry proper. He has "fulfilled all righteousness" by being baptized (3:15), proven himself to be Son of God by passing the test against Satan, moved to Galilee in fulfillment of Scripture, and chosen a nucleus of his followers. Now he is ready to begin, and Matthew wants to tell of his actions as well as his teaching, i.e., his works and his words. So we begin with a summary of his early ministry in Galilee. Matthew centers on Jesus' message before an extended narration of his powerful ministry of healing, nature miracles, and exorcisms (chs. 8 – 9). In this sense 4:23 – 25 is transitional, concluding the preliminary stages of Jesus' ministry in chs. 3 – 4 and introducing the Sermon on the Mount in chs. 5 – 7.

II. The Kingdom Message Goes Out (4:12 – 7:29)
- **A. Early Galilean Ministry (4:12 – 25)**
  1. Beginning the Capernaum Ministry (4:12 – 17)
  2. The Call of the Disciples (4:18 – 22)
  3. ➦ **Summary of His Ministry (4:23 – 25)**

Main Idea

The three participles of v. 23 (teaching, preaching, healing) pretty much say it all; this is a favorite literary ploy of Matthew, for v. 23 is repeated nearly verbatim in 9:35 before the Mission Discourse of ch. 10. This section denotes two aspects: Jesus' powerful ministry (4:23) and his growing popularity (4:24 – 25). A third major theme can also be detected — the growing extent of his ministry that cannot be confined to Galilee but spreads to Syria, the Decapolis, and even back to Judea.

Translation

Matthew 4:23-25

23 Summary And he was going around all of Galilee,
teaching in their synagogues,
preaching the gospel of the kingdom, and
healing every disease and
every illness among the people.

24 News about him spread all over Syria, and
they brought him all their sick
who had various diseases and
were tormented
with severe pain as well as
demon-possession,
seizures, and
paralysis,
and he healed them.

25 Large crowds followed him
from Galilee,
the Decapolis,
Jerusalem,
Judea, and
the region across the Jordan.

Structure and Literary Form

Jesus' healing ministry and resultant popularity are the themes of the lengthy narrative in Mark 1:21 – 45. Matthew does not wish to tell all of that now (several of the incidents are in Matt 8 – 9) but wants to get to Jesus' first great teaching discourse and so provides a summary of his ministry here. This functions as an introduction to the following discourse.

Davies and Allison provide an excellent chart of the introductions to the five discourses showing the similarity of language:[1] the crowd (3x), mountain (2x), sitting (2x), his disciples coming to him (4x), disciples (5x), saying (6x, including 13:36 – 37), asking a question (3x), and change of scene (5x). This shows a remarkable unity in the introductions. There are two sections and three parts, with Jesus' ministry (v. 23) and his growing popularity (vv. 24 – 25), with the latter subdivided into the various illnesses he healed (v. 24) and the various places from which people came to follow him (v. 25).

1. Davies and Allison, *Matthew*, 1:411 (there is one error in that "sitting" occurs 2x, not 3x).

Exegetical Outline

- **I. Summary of Jesus' Ministry (4:23)**
  - A. Teaching
  - B. Preaching
  - C. Healing
- **II. Jesus' Growing Popularity (4:24 – 25)**
  - A. The diseases he healed (v. 24)
  - B. The places from which people came (v. 25)

Explanation of the Text

4:23 And he was going around all of Galilee (Καὶ περιῆγεν ἐν ὅλῃ τῇ Γαλιλαίᾳ). This is the first circuit of Galilee (for a second see 9:35). Here we see Jesus as an itinerant evangelist (with the imperfect "he was going" [περιῆγεν] highlighting his ongoing ministry) preparing for Paul and others to follow in his path. The three categories of his ministry are illuminating. While Galilee was small (seventy by forty miles), it had 204 cities/villages (see Josephus, *Life* 235), and it would take at least three months to traverse it (at the rate of two to three villages a day).[2]

4:23 ... teaching in their synagogues, preaching the gospel of the kingdom (διδάσκων ἐν ταῖς συναγωγαῖς αὐτῶν καὶ κηρύσσων τὸ εὐαγγέλιον τῆς βασιλείας). The three circumstantial participles (teaching, preaching, healing — present tenses to emphasize his continuous activity) neatly summarize Jesus' Galilean ministry. The synagogue "teaching" probably reflects his exposition of the OT (the gospel comes under his preaching); it was common to invite visiting rabbis/teachers to speak (cf. Luke 4:16 – 17; Acts 14:1; 17:2; et al.), and Jesus did so often.

The "gospel of the kingdom" refers to the kingdom content that was essential to Jesus' teaching; this is a key Matthean phrase and is found four times (4:23; 9:35; 24:14; 26:13), the only times "gospel" (εὐαγγέλιον) occurs in Matthew. All Jesus does here will also be done by the disciples in *imitatio Christi* in Matt 10. Teaching and preaching were the two aspects of every synagogue service[3] and defined the lectures Jesus gave outside the synagogues as well.

4:23 ... and healing every disease and every illness among the people (καὶ θεραπεύων πᾶσαν νόσον καὶ πᾶσαν μαλακίαν ἐν τῷ λαῷ). In addition to teaching and preaching, Jesus heals "every" disease and illness (the repetition of "every" [πᾶσαν] adds emphasis). This (and "all their sick" in v. 24) does not mean he healed every ill person in Galilee but rather everyone who was brought to him. This is an example of hyperbole, so favored in the first century. Moreover, this authority was passed to the disciples in 10:1. The church is to relive the life and authority of Jesus.

2. Carson, "Matthew," 120 – 21.

3. There is likely no real distinction intended here between teaching (*didachē*) and preaching (*kērygma*). While some have tried to do so, that better fits Paul than Matthew here. Both elements were in Jesus' synagogue sermons as well as his addresses to the crowds and disciples (see Luz, *Matthew 1 – 7*, 206 – 8).

4:24 News about him spread all over Syria (Καὶ ἀπῆλθεν ἡ ἀκοὴ αὐτοῦ εἰς ὅλην τὴν Συρίαν). The aorist "spread" (ἀπῆλθεν) looks at the widespread publicity as a single whole (see on 4:18). The mention of Syria[4] is unclear, because in one sense all of Palestine and the lands to the north were considered the Roman province of Syria, while in another sense it referred to the geographical area north of Galilee. Probably the latter is intended in light of "Galilee" in v. 23.

4:24 And they brought him all their[5] sick who had various diseases and were tormented with severe pain as well as demon-possession, seizures, and paralysis, and he healed them (καὶ προσήνεγκαν αὐτῷ πάντας τοὺς κακῶς ἔχοντας ποικίλαις νόσοις καὶ βασάνοις συνεχομένους καὶ δαιμονιζομένους καὶ σεληνιαζομένους καὶ παραλυτικούς, καὶ ἐθεράπευσεν αὐτούς). This rather complete list of illnesses is impressive; it moves from the comprehensive (the sick) to the general (disease and pain) to the specific (demon-possession [8:16, 28; 9:32; 12:22; 15:22], seizures [probably epilepsy, 17:15], and paralysis [8:6; 9:2, 6]).

"Sick" and "disease" (κακῶς and νόσος)[6] are virtual synonyms for illness and are used here for comprehensiveness. "Tormented" (βάσανος) is a strong word for the pain of many sicknesses and could even be translated "tortured." The Greek word translated here as "seizures" (from σεληνιάζομαι) literally means "moonstruck" and was used for what is called today epilepsy; many believe the term originated from the moon god *Selene* and thus may refer to demonization here. Christ healed everyone whatever their disease. This passage is in keeping with the Matthean emphasis on the universal healings of Jesus (see 8:16 – 17; 11:4 – 6 [where Jesus is the Isaianic Servant]; cf. also 14:35; 15:31).

4:25 Large[7] crowds followed him from Galilee, the Decapolis, Jerusalem, Judea, and the region across the Jordan (καὶ ἠκολούθησαν αὐτῷ ὄχλοι πολλοὶ ἀπὸ τῆς Γαλιλαίας καὶ Δεκαπόλεως καὶ Ἱεροσολύμων καὶ Ἰουδαίας καὶ πέραν τοῦ Ἰορδάνου). It is likely that when Matthew says large crowds "followed him," he meant many became true followers. The list is fairly comprehensive but omits the Samaritans, probably because Matthew is thinking of the Jewish people in all these regions (though see footnote 4 on Syria for possible Gentile connotations). The Decapolis was a confederation of ten Hellenistic cities in Syria from Damascus in the north to Philadelphia west of the lake. For "across the Jordan" see v. 15. As in v. 15 Jesus' fame had become so great that people from all over the region were drawn to him.

Theology in Application

The primary thrust is the incredible extent of Jesus' ministry. He impacted everyone he met and healed as many as came to him. His reputation exploded to the point that people were coming to him from everywhere. Yet it is not just the power

4. Syria in light of v. 25 probably is meant primarily of the Jewish people there (it had a large population) but secondarily could be part of Matthew's stress on the Gentiles. If so, it would continue the emphasis on Gentiles (the Magi, Syria) coming to Jesus (cf. also the women in the genealogy), so Gnilka, *Matthäusevangelium*, 1:108; Luz, *Matthew 1 – 7*, 206.

5. For this use of the article, see on v. 20.

6. For extensive discussion of its connection to sin and suffering see *TDNT*, 4:1091 – 98.

7. πολλοί means "many, numerous" and with "crowds" (ὄχλοι) means "large, great, extensive" (BAGD, 687).

of his ministry but also the compassion of his ministry that is so meaningful. We will see this "hermeneutic of love" again, as he was willing to break religious taboos and traditional demands (e.g., healing on a Sabbath) whenever there was a need. He healed everyone he could, each person who was brought to him. He cared deeply about them all.

1. An Itinerant Preacher and Minister

The only one who matched Jesus' extensive desire to reach out to the lost was Paul, whose ministry principle was: "It has always been my ambition to preach the gospel where Christ was not known, so that I would not be building on someone else's foundation" (Rom 15:20). Christ came "to seek and to save what was lost" (Luke 19:10), and that led not just to one mission trip (ch. 10) but to several. Today we talk about being "world Christians," i.e., believers whose vision encompasses the entire world. This is certainly one of Matthew's primary thrusts, to show how God's plan in Jesus from the start was worldwide in scope (the women in the genealogy, the Magi at Jesus' birth, the list of Syria and Decapolis here in v. 25). Each of us must participate in this vision.

2. Jesus' Incalculable Power

The list of illnesses moves from the broad to the narrow in v. 24, and its purpose is to show that the Son of God has authority over every kind of illness, including demon-possession. This will become even greater when Matthew adds nature miracles in ch. 8 and raising the dead in ch. 9. He wants his readers to understand the absolute authority Jesus has over everything in this world. This is summed up in 28:18, "All authority in heaven and on earth has been given to me," a direct allusion to Dan 7:13 – 14 to show that Jesus is the Son of Man from this prophecy and that he has universal dominion over everything.

3. Great Excitement

Every great revival in history has been accompanied by great excitement and innumerable converts, from the Josianic revival in 2 Chr 34:29 – 35:19, or the Wesley revival in England, or the two great awakenings in America. Jesus saw similar results, with people coming from everywhere to see him (even more, see Mark 1:21 – 45). This kind of "frenzy" is needed today. It is happening in China, and we desperately need to develop teachers there who can harness the energy and direct it to worldwide evangelism. Yet we also need that energy for the Lord in the Western world as well.

4. Jesus' Miraculous Works Transferred to the Disciples

In Matt 10:1 Jesus gives the disciples "authority" to cast out demons and to heal diseases; the question is whether this power is also transferred to the church and available today. This is debated in many circles, between the cessationist (that miraculous gifts ceased at the end of the apostolic age) and charismatic (that they are available today) views. We cannot discuss the debate at this time,[8] but I will present a "middle position" that says these gifts are available today but are only meant for those for whom the Spirits intends (1 Cor 12:11). This means that the church does have access to Christ's power, and miracles are available today.

Nevertheless, all agree about this, that God still heals today and that he is involved in our needs. There is supernatural power at work in this world, and we need to center on the sovereign God and his presence among us.

8. For a basic discussion of the sides see Wayne Grudem, *Systematic Theology* (Grand Rapids: Zondervan, 1995), 1031 – 46, and his bibliography on this issue on pp. 1085 – 87. For my middle position see my "Tongues, Speaking in," in *Evangelical Dictionary of Theology*, ed. Walter Elwell (Grand Rapids: Baker, 1984), 1100 – 1103.

Matthew 5:1 – 12

CHAPTER 11

Introduction to the Sermon on the Mount (Matthew 5 – 7)

One of the best-known and loved passages in Scripture, the Sermon on the Mount, has been considered Jesus' magnum opus. The amount of literature on it is incredible, and as many as thirty-six different interpretations have been made; there is general consensus for nine major interpretations:[1]

1. Since medieval times two levels of ethics have been seen, with the Sermon reflecting a higher moral code for clergy and monastic orders.
2. For Luther and his followers the sermon functions like the law in Paul, disclosing our depravity and bringing about repentance.
3. Many Anabaptists take the commands literally in terms of pacifism in the civil sphere.
4. Some liberals label it a paradigm for the social gospel as a call to produce the kingdom of heaven on earth.
5. Existentialists see it not as absolute but as a challenge to personal decision in light of human finitude.
6. Albert Schweitzer's interim ethic saw it as a temporary set of injunctions meant only for the short time before the kingdom arrived.
7. Similarly to Schweitzer, classical dispensationalists (e.g., the Scofield Bible) have limited its ethics to the millennial period.
8. The current tendency is to see the Sermon through the lens of inaugurated eschatology, that keeping the commands should be the goal of all believers but that they will be fully observed only after Christ has returned.
9. Some believe that this exemplifies Jesus as "a sage who expressed his eschatological convictions in Wisdom forms," so this is a set of wisdom teachings.[2]

1. The first eight are noted by Carson, "Matthew," 126 – 27; Blomberg, *Matthew*, 94 – 95; Keener, *Matthew*, 160. For a history of interpretation, see W. S. Kissinger, *The Sermon on the Mount: A History of Interpretation and Bibliography* (Metuchyen, NY: Scarecrow & ATLA, 1975); and Robert A. Guelich, *The Sermon on the Mount: A Foundation for Understanding* (Waco, TX: Word, 1982), 14 – 24.

2. Ben Witherington III, *Jesus the Sage: The Pilgrimage of Wisdom* (Minneapolis: Fortress, 1994), 183; idem, *Matthew*, 114 – 16. See also M. J. Suggs, *Wisdom, Christology, and Law in Matthew's Gospel* (Cambridge, MA: Harvard Univ. Press, 1970).

Probably a combination of the views 8 and 9 is best. There is a distinct wisdom flavor in the sermon, but primarily it is the new laws for the kingdom age, intended as an ethical model to be followed by the new citizens of the kingdom community.[3]

In Matthew's gospel the Sermon immediately follows the summary of Jesus' kingdom preaching (4:17, 23) and must be seen in that light. Therefore it establishes the ethical standards of righteousness for Jesus' followers. Overman says, "This section of the gospel has as its primary focus the ordering of relationships and behavior within the community."[4] France calls this "The Discourse on Discipleship," centering on the radically new lifestyle demanded of Jesus' followers who will become a "Christian counter-culture."[5] In that sense it is the law of the new covenant, the demands of discipleship in the eschatological community brought by Christ.[6] It is not a new messianic Torah but rather a transformation of the Torah of the OT into the Torah of the Messiah.[7]

Finally, the Sermon is not a set of impossible regulations so stringent that they cannot be obeyed but an ethical system that provides a goal for kingdom people, namely, God's perfection or completeness (5:48). Of course, none of us can attain the perfection of God, but we can strive to exemplify more of his mercy and love (5:45) as the guiding principles of our lives. The purpose of this Sermon is to provide guidance, to tell not just what to do but how to do it.

Furthermore, there is debate on the relation of the Sermon on the Mount to the Sermon on the Plain (Luke 6:20 – 49). Are they the same sermon (Origen, Chrysostom, Calvin, France, Carson, Hagner) or two different messages (Augustine, Morris)? The consensus has shifted recently toward identifying them as the same message — they have a similar format (all of Luke 6 is in Matt 5 – 7), the beginning and end are the same, and both are followed by Jesus' Capernaum ministry. Moreover, the term that Luke 6:17 uses for "plain/level place" can refer to a plateau on a

3. In contrast, Hauerwas, *Matthew*, 61 – 62, says it is not "a list of requirements" but is "the constitution of the people," describing the kind of life the kingdom community will lead. However, these two are not antithetical, for the regulations of conduct are indeed descriptive of the community. These two — laws and constitution — are not an either-or but a both-and.

4. Overman, *Matthew's Gospel and Formative Judaism*, 94. He assumes in too facile a way the common misperception that Matthew's gospel describes primarily the Matthean community. For the likelihood that the gospels were written for the whole church and not just a single community, see the excellent essay by Richard Bauckham, "For Whom Were Gospels Written?" 9 – 48. Still, Overman's comments fit the Christian community as a whole.

5. France, *Gospel of Matthew*, 153.

6. A further discussion is whether the sermon is a whole message delivered by Jesus on a single occasion (Carson, Morris, Blomberg) or whether Matthew combined many of Christ's sayings on discipleship ethics into a single whole (Calvin, Hagner, Betz, France). The fact that many of the sayings in Matthew are scattered elsewhere in Luke could point to a compilation in Matthew, but it can perhaps be better seen as a a single discourse on the grounds that it is a tightly united discourse and that Jesus was an itinerant preacher using material on more than one occasion (as in Luke), with this sermon an abbreviation of a longer message given on one occasion (cf. 7:28). So it is perhaps better to consider this a single message of Jesus.

7. Davies and Allison, *Matthew*, 1:565.

mountain. So it is best seen as the same sermon, with Matthew and Luke emphasizing different aspects of it.

The structure of the sermon can be seen many ways. Is the central part 5:17 – 20[8] or the Lord's Prayer in 6:9 – 13?[9] If there is a central portion, that would probably be 6:9 – 13 (which occurs in the center of the Sermon), but more likely there is no center as such. One could see a chiasm[10] or an exposition on higher righteousness.[11] The best structure is to see 5:3 – 16 as the introduction and 7:13 – 27 as the conclusion, with the central section comprised of three parts: the relationship of the law to the new covenant in Jesus (5:17 – 48), true versus false piety (6:1 – 18), and social ethics (6:19 – 7:12).[12]

Literary Context

The introduction to the Sermon on the Mount establishes the themes for the section. The beatitudes tell us the ethical substructure and help us to understand that God's rewards are connected to our own responsibility to live as children of the kingdom. As stated above, the Sermon on the Mount as a whole deals with the laws for the life of the new covenant community. Jesus has just summarized his message of repentance in light of the nearness of the kingdom (4:17), called his disciples to become followers in that kingdom (4:19), and conducted his first mission of healing and kingdom proclamation throughout Galilee (4:23 – 25). So the Sermon of chs. 5 – 7 is meant to tell the ethical requirements for those who are to become the new covenant community. The beatitudes begin that message with the eschatological rewards for those who follow those laws.

II. The Kingdom Message Goes Out (4:12 – 7:29)
- A. Early Galilean Ministry (4:12 – 25)
- **B. First Discourse: The Sermon on the Mount (5:1 – 7:29)**
  - ➦ **1. The Setting of the Sermon (5:1 – 2)**
  - **2. Introduction (5:3 – 16)**
    - **a. The Beatitudes (5:3 – 12)**
    - b. The Salt and Light Sayings (5:13 – 16)

8. Joachim Jeremias, *The Sermon on the Mount* (trans. N. Perrin; Philadelphia: Fortress, 1963), who argues that the rest contrasts the righteousness of the scribes/theologians (5:21 – 48) and the Pharisees/pious laity (6:1 – 18) with that of the disciples (6:19 – 7:27).

9. Gunther Bornkamm, "Der Aufbau der Bergpredigt," *NTS* 24 (1978): 419 – 32, who says 6:19 – 24 = the first three petitions; 6:25 – 34 = the fourth; 7:1 – 5 the fifth; 7:6 = the sixth and seventh. See also Guelich, *Sermon on the Mount*, 363 – 81, who takes a similar approach.

10. Daniel Patte, *The Gospel according to Matthew: A Structural Commentary on Matthew's Faith* (Philadelphia: Fortress, 1987), 65.

11. Beare, *Matthew*, 123.

12. For similar outlines see Dale C. Allison Jr., "The Structure of the Sermon on the Mount," *JBL* 106 (1987): 423 – 45; Gnilka, *Matthäusevangelium*, 112; Blomberg, *Matthew*, 95 – 96; Ulrich Luz, *The Theology of the Gospel of Matthew* (trans. J. Bradford Robinson; Cambridge: Cambridge Univ. Press, 1995), 48 – 49.

Main Idea

There are two primary themes in the beatitudes: (1) the centrality of the kingdom: the first eight beatitudes are framed by the present tense (the others have future tenses) and by "the kingdom of heaven belongs to them" (5:3, 10); the ninth (vv. 11 – 12) expands the eighth; and (2) the demand for ethical accountability (the central portion of each beatitude is the ethical responsibility, "poor in spirit," etc.). The Sermon centers on the ethical standards of righteousness for the community of the new covenant, so the beatitudes introduce that theme. (3) A subtheme of this section is the rewards and blessings for obedience (cf. 5:12, 19b, 45a; 6:4b, 6b, 14b, 18b, 22b, 30b, 33; 7:7 – 8, 11b, 25).[13]

Translation

(See next page.)

Structure and Literary Form

Four of the beatitudes are found in Luke 6:20 – 23 (the first, fourth, seventh, and ninth) and could be called Q material. Yet both Matthew's and Luke's are redacted (Matthew uses a third person form, Luke a second person form) and reflect different nuances of what Jesus originally said.[14] The beatitudes have been called "makarisms," from the Greek *makarios* ("blessed"). Such are found often in the OT (actually the LXX), as in Pss 1:1; 2:12d; 106:3; 119:1; 146:5; Prov 8:34; Isa 30:18, and were fairly common in Judaism[15] as well as the Hellenistic world. The Matthean form combines both: ethical mandate as well as eschatological blessing.[16]

13. See Lois K. Fuller, "The Concept of Reward in the Sermon on the Mount" (MA thesis, Trinity Evangelical Divinity School, 1982). Likewise, the opposite theme, judgment for those who do not obey, is also stressed (cf. 5:13b, 19a, 20b, 22, 26, 29b, 30b, 46; 6:1b, 2b, 5b, 15b, 16b, 23; 7:1 – 2, 19, 23, 27). In the same manner, God warns us as part of our motivation.

14. It is also common to argue that only three (see, e.g., Neil J. McEleney, "The Beatitudes of the Sermon on the Mount, Plain," *CBQ* 43 [1981]: 1 – 13 — the first, second, fourth) or four (Gundry, the first four) were uttered by Jesus, and the majority believe at least the eighth was created by Matthew. However, there is little reason to think of Matthew and the early church creating such sayings, and they all fit together logically (see Hagner, Carson). On the unity of the beatitudes as they stand, see George W. Buchanan, "Matthean Beatitudes and Traditional Problems," *Journal from the Radical Reformation* 3 (1993): 45 – 69.

15. Guelich, *Sermon on the Mount*, 64 – 65, says there are two types in intertestamental literature, one stemming from wisdom literature and centering on exhortation to proper conduct (Wis 3:13 – 14; Sir 14:1 – 2; *2 Bar.* 4:4) and the other from apocalyptic circles and centering on future-oriented promises or warnings (*1 En.* 99:10 – 15; 103:5; *2 Bar.* 10:6 – 7). For an excellent discussion of the background, see Walther Zimmerli, "Die Seligpreisungen der Bergpredigt und das Alte Testament," in *Donum Gentilicium* (ed. E. Bammel et al.; Oxford: Clarendon, 1978), 8 – 26.

16. Guelich, *Sermon on the Mount*, 109 – 11, sees the two as an either–or, debating whether the beatitudes are "entrance requirements" or "eschatological blessings," opting for the latter. Others take the ethical as stressed over the eschatological (Georg Strecker, *The Sermon on the Mount: An Exegetical Commentary* (trans. O. C. Dean Jr.; Nashville: Abingdon, 1988; German, 1985], 29 – 30). But surely these are too disjunctive, for the beatitudes are both moral mandate (the second aspect here) and promised reward (the third aspect).

Matthew 5:1-12

1a	Introduction	When Jesus saw the crowds,
b	Setting (Local)	**he ascended a mountain,**
c		and when he sat down,
d	Event	**his disciples came to him.**
2a		And **he opened his mouth and began to teach them, saying**
3a	Beatitude	*[1] "God blesses the poor in spirit,*
b	Promise	*for the kingdom of heaven belongs to them.*
4a	Beatitude	*[2] God blesses those who mourn,*
b	Promise	*for they will be comforted.*
5a	Beatitude	*[3] God blesses those who are meek,*
b	Promise	*for they will inherit the earth.*
6a	Beatitude	*[4] God blesses those who hunger and thirst after righteousness,*
b	Promise	*for they will be filled.*
7a	Beatitude	*[5] God blesses those who are merciful,*
b	Promise	*for they will receive mercy.*
8a	Beatitude	*[6] God blesses the pure in heart,*
b	Promise	*for they will see God.*
9a	Beatitude	*[7] God blesses those who make peace,*
b	Promise	*for they will be called children of God.*
10a	Beatitude	*[8] God blesses those who are persecuted*
		because of righteousness,
b	Promise	*for the kingdom of heaven belongs to them.*
11a	Beatitude	*[9] God blesses you*
		when people insult you,
		persecute you, and
		falsely say every kind of evil
		against you
		because of me.
12a		*Rejoice and*
		be glad,
b	Promise	*for your reward in heaven is great,*
c		*for in this way they persecuted the prophets before you."*

There are three aspects: the promise of blessing, the ethical requirement (beginning with "those who" rather than Luke's "are you," cf. Luke 6:20 – 22), and the proclamation of the blessing promised in the first part, introduced by "because, for" [ὅτι]). While in one sense we serve the Lord out of love, not for what we will get out of it, in another sense God wants us to know there will be reward for our service, so he tells us about that reward to motivate us.

Exegetical Outline

Organizing these beatitudes has proven difficult, and many simply refuse to outline them, considering them like the proverbs of the OT. But there is some pattern, and I will follow Hagner's approach,[17] grouping them in three categories: the needy (I prefer to call this "those who depend on God," vv. 3 – 6), those who live for God (vv. 7 – 9), and those who are persecuted (v. 10 and its expansion in vv. 11 – 12).[18]

- **I. The Setting of the Sermon (5:1 – 2)**
  - A. Jesus ascending a mountain (5:1a)
  - B. Disciples coming to Jesus (5:1b)
  - C. Jesus begins his teaching (5:2)
- **II. Those Who Depend on God (5:3 – 6)**
  - A. The poor in spirit (v. 3)
  - B. The mourners (v. 4)
  - C. The meek (v. 5)
  - D. The hungry and the thirsty (v. 6)
- **III. Those Who Live for God (5:7 – 9)**
  - A. The merciful (v. 7)
  - B. The pure in heart (v. 8)
  - C. The peacemakers (v. 9)
- **IV. Those Who Are Persecuted (5:10 – 12)**
  - A. The persecuted (v. 10)
  - B. The insulted and slandered (v. 11 – 12)

Explanation of the Text

5:1 When Jesus saw the crowds, he ascended a mountain (Ἰδὼν δὲ τοὺς ὄχλους ἀνέβη εἰς τὸ ὄρος). This begins with two oft-repeated forms, a temporal participle ("When he saw" [ἰδών], cf. 4:2 – 3) dealing with Jesus' "seeing," and a temporal genitive absolute ("when he sat down" [καθίσαντος αὐτοῦ], cf. 8:1, 5 — see below) dealing with Jesus' "sitting." The language of these verses seems to indicate a semirejection of the crowds on the part of Jesus (wanting to get away from them) and a desire to teach only the disciples. This does fit the message of the Sermon, but from 7:28 – 29 the crowds had come anyway, so the message was directed to both.[19] It is best not to see a rejection

17. Hagner, *Matthew 1 – 13*, 90 – 91. Three other patterns are worthy of discussion: (1) those who see two groups of four in vv. 3 – 10 (Walter Grundmann, *Das Evangelium nach Matthäus* [Berlin: Evangelische Verlagsanstalt, 1981]), 119; Jan Lambrecht, *The Sermon on the Mount: Proclamation and Exhortation* [Wilmington, DE: Michael Glazier, 1985], 61); (2) the chiastic structure of Neil J. McEleney, "The Beatitudes," 1 – 13, who argues for an A/A' (vv. 3, 10 with an inclusory formula), B/B' (vv. 4, 9 with divine passives), C/C' (vv. 5, 8 with futures + object), and D/D' (vv. 6, 7 with divine passives), but the content does not fit well; and (3) Davies and Allison, *Matthew*, 1:430 – 31, with three triads (vv. 3 – 5, 6 – 8, 9 – 12); but this is part of their tendency to see the whole of Matthew's gospel as a triadic arrangement, and again the content does not fit well.

18. Suggs, *Wisdom*, 121 – 27; and Turner, "Matthew," 79 – 80, argue that vv. 11 – 12 belong to vv. 13 – 16 because of the change to second person, the lengthened description of the persecution, and the two imperatives. This is viable, but the "blessed" (μακάριοι) at the start of v. 11 favors a continuation of the series; moreover, as Davies and Allison point out (*Matthew*, 1:430, from Daube), a lengthened form often closes such Jewish lists.

19. So Harrington, *Matthew*, 78, who maintains the crowds frame the sermon (5:1; 7:28 – 29) and so are also a distinct target for the message.

but rather a desire to address the disciples particularly, involving an inner circle (the disciples, active participants) and an outer circle (the crowds, passive participants).[20]

The mountain as elsewhere is the place of revelation (cf. 4:8; it does not have to be a mythical mountain, as many assert), but it is the first time the articular "the mountain"(τὸ ὄρος) appears (see also 8:1; 14:23; 15:29; 17:9, 20; 21:1; 24:3; 28:16). Donaldson, after a major study of OT and Second Temple background, finds the two major traditions behind this to be Sinai and especially Zion. In these there are four primary motifs: covenant, cosmic or heavenly reality, revelation, and eschatological (esp. messianic) events.[21] Here he sees a "mountain of teaching."

Many believe this section continues the Moses typology from the birth and temptation narratives. It recalls in some fashion the revelation Moses received on Sinai, with the centrality of law and righteousness in the sermon.[22] But others believe this must be carefully qualified as not a new Moses bringing a new Torah since Jesus is not merely a lawgiver but is providing a new set of kingdom ethics.[23]

Donaldson argues that the eschatological Zion tradition is predominant, with the image here of the great "gathering of the people of Israel around Jesus" at "the holy mountain of Yahweh."[24] While this is an aspect of the imagery here, the Moses tradition seems more central. The one superior to Moses and to those who "sit on Moses' seat" (23:3, the teachers) has begun his messianic ministry.[25] Moreover, as the Jewish people expected the Messiah to bring the final Torah, the Sermon is in a sense the "Torah of the Messiah," in which Jesus explicates the laws for the new kingdom community.

5:1 And when he sat down, his disciples came to him (καὶ καθίσαντος αὐτοῦ προσῆλθαν αὐτῷ οἱ μαθηταὶ αὐτοῦ). Jesus then "sits down" (the normal position for a "rabbi" teaching) with his "disciples." This is the first time "disciple" (μαθητής) appears in Matthew, and it naturally goes back to the calling of his first followers in 4:18 – 22. Yet the group here could hardly refer just to the four fishermen; it must be the wider group of followers also mentioned in 8:18. The Twelve came to Jesus gradually (Matthew joins in 9:9) and are not commissioned as such until 10:1 (= Mark 3:16 – 19).

5:2 And he opened his mouth and began to teach them, saying (καὶ ἀνοίξας τὸ στόμα αὐτοῦ ἐδίδασκεν αὐτοὺς λέγων). Now Jesus begins with a circumstantial participle "he opened" (ἀνοίξας) that is so much a part of the main clause that it is best translated as a main verb (see on 4:20). Rabbis normally taught while sitting down (v. 1) and stood to read Scripture (Luke 4:16). So Jesus is following precedent here and "begins to teach" (ingressive imperfect, see Wallace, 544 – 45). The disciples were those committed to following Jesus (4:18 – 22) and were closely involved in his ministry. They are the ones expected to live by the principles elucidated in the message that follows.

5:3 God blesses the poor in spirit (Μακάριοι οἱ πτωχοὶ τῷ πνεύματι). On the basis of OT parallels (Heb. *ʾašre*), it is common to translate "blessed" (μακάριος) as "fortunate, happy," in the sense that all will go well for those who live for God.[26] But that is to ignore the religious and

20. Davies and Allison, *Matthew*, 1:422.

21. Donaldson, *Jesus on the Mountain*, 81 – 83.

22. See Gundry, *Matthew*, 66; Luz, *Matthew 1 – 7*, 197 – 8; Nolland, *Matthew*, 192.

23. See Carson, "Matthew," 129; France, *Matthew* (TNTC), 107.

24. Donaldson, *Jesus on the Mountain*, 116 (cf. 114 – 18).

25. Keener, *Matthew*, 164.

26. Schweizer, *Matthew*, 80; France, *Matthew* (TNTC), 108; Keener, *Matthew*, 165 – 66; Blomberg, *Matthew*, 97; Witherington, *Matthew*, 120.

apocalyptic context. μακάριος is closely linked with the promise in the third part, which enumerates the blessing, and so it is best to translate "God blesses."[27] Those singularly blessed are "the poor in spirit" (οἱ πτωχοὶ τῷ πνεύματι, cf. Luke 6:20, "the poor"), with "in spirit" (τῷ πνεύματι) a dative of sphere, indicating the realm in which the person is "poor."[28]

This is not a spiritualized form of the Lukan original but closely connected, with both going back to Jesus' original saying. These are the economically destitute who are forced to rely entirely on God. Thus the best way to understand this is as a humility that leads God's people to depend wholly on him.[29] There is general agreement that the first three beatitudes reflect Isa 61:1 – 3, that famous passage quoted also in Luke 4:18 – 19. The Isaianic context is God's return to Zion to restore the glory of his people (chs. 60 – 62) after they have repented (ch. 59). So he has brought "good news" to the "poor" (61:1) that they will be set free and released. The poor are "lowly in spirit" (57:15) and have turned to God. Moreover, Jesus then becomes the Servant of Yahweh who fulfills OT promises and brings them to fruition.[30]

5:3 ... for the kingdom of heaven belongs to them (ὅτι αὐτῶν ἐστιν ἡ βασιλεία τῶν οὐρανῶν). The reason ("for," causal ὅτι) they are blessed as well as the content of that blessing is now spelled out. The promise is present ("belongs" [ἐστιν]) and not just future; in keeping with the Matthean emphasis on inaugurated eschatology, there is a tension between the already and the not yet (see "Theology in Application" on 1:1 – 17 [#2] and on 1:18 – 25 [#4]; and discussion of 3:2). The faithful disciple now belongs to the new kingdom Christ has inaugurated and at the final judgment will inherit it in full. There is both an authority and a privilege, as the powers of the kingdom are available to its citizens.

5:4 God blesses those who mourn (μακάριοι οἱ πενθοῦντες). Some interpret "those who mourn" (οἱ πενθοῦντες, a present tense substantival participle to stress the ongoing nature of it) as "mourn" in the midst of persecution or poverty, linking it with vv. 10 – 12;[31] others interpret it as "mourn" for sin.[32] Once again, however, it is best to see this as a both - and, namely, those who "groan under the burden of sorrow and guilt"[33] and thereby turn to God for forgiveness and help.

5:4 ... for they will be comforted (ὅτι αὐτοὶ παρακληθήσονται). In Isa 61:2 God promises to "comfort all who mourn," and in the context Isaiah refers to those who have been oppressed (60:15, 18) but have repented of their sins (59:9 – 15a) and center on God for both forgiveness and help. As

27. France, *Gospel of Matthew*, 160 – 61, protests that in that case it would demand *eulogētos*, but "blessed" (*makarios*) is the normal word used in such beatitudes (see the OT parallels mentioned above), and the eschatological promise demands God as the one who alone can give such blessings (cf. D. A. Carson, *The Sermon on the Mount: An Evangelical Exposition of Matthew 5 – 7* [Grand Rapids: Baker, 1978], 16; Bruner, *Christbook*, 136; Harrington, *Matthew*, 78; Morris, *Matthew*, 95. Gundry, *Matthew*, 68, says there is "more emphasis on divine approval than on human happiness," and Jan Lambrecht, *The Sermon on the Mount*, 46, says, "A blessing is actually accomplished by God: it comes from above."

28. Wallace, 155, says it is virtually equivalent to an adverb, "spiritually poor."

29. Carson, "Matthew," 131; Gundry, *Matthew*, 67; Beare, *Matthew*, 129.

30. Witherington, *Matthew*, 120.

31. See Guelich, *Sermon on the Mount*, 80 – 81; Hill, *Matthew*, 111; Bruner, *Christbook*, 139; Davies and Allison, *Matthew*, 1:448; Hagner, *Matthew 1 – 13*, 92; Nolland, *Matthew*, 201; Turner, "Matthew," 76; France, *Gospel of Matthew*, 165 – 66, seeing Isa 61:2 – 3 as background.

32. See Carson, "Matthew," 132 – 33; Bruner, *Christbook*, 138 – 39; Morris, *Matthew*, 97; M. Kehl, "'Selig die Trauernden, denn sie werden getröstet werden' (Matt 5.4)," *Geist und Leben* 73 (2000): 96 – 97.

33. Schnackenburg, *Matthew*, 47. See also Strecker, *Matthew*, 34 – 35; Blomberg, *Matthew*, 99.

in v. 3 they will be "comforted" (a divine passive = "by God") in the present but especially in the future (note the switch from present tense in v. 3 to future tense in v. 4). They are right with God and are the subject of his vindication and reward.

5:5 God blesses those who are meek (μακάριοι οἱ πραεῖς). The "meek" (οἱ πραεῖς) are not just those who are humble and unaggressive but stems from Ps 37:11, "The meek will inherit the land," where it translates the Hebrew *ʿanawim*, the "poor" of Isa 61:1 (the same Heb. term stands for both) who have been oppressed by wicked men (Ps 37:7, 11). As in v. 3 they were "meek" or humble because their circumstances drove them to God. At the same time, they are also "meek" or gentle toward others (see Matt 11:29; 21:5; three of the four NT occurrences are in Matthew). Broadus defines it as "freedom from pretension (1 Pet 3:14 – 15), gentleness (Matt 11:29; Jas 3:13), and patient endurance of injury — where it is proper to endure."[34] There are likely two ideas inherent in this: the spiritual quality of humility and gentleness as well as the need for social justice (seen in Isa 61) as we seek to alleviate the poverty and deprivation of those unfortunates who are forced into humble circumstances.

5:5 ... for they will inherit the earth (ὅτι αὐτοὶ κληρονομήσουσιν τὴν γῆν). In Ps 37:11 the "inheritance" (cf. Matt 19:29; 25:34) was the Promised Land, but here it is extended to mean the whole world. Those who are faithful will rule with Christ first for his reign on earth (Rev 20:4) and then for all eternity (Rev 22:5; cf. Matt 19:28). This is an apocalyptic promise meant for the future, not the present. Still, it is an encouragement in the present, for Jesus' followers know their present sacrifices will be worth it and they will be vindicated. Charette calls vv. 5, 12 the first reward passages in Matthew, built on the idea of a spiritual return from exile to the "land" and here a transcendent promise that relates to kingdom blessings.[35]

5:6 God blesses those who hunger and thirst after righteousness (μακάριοι οἱ πεινῶντες καὶ διψῶντες τὴν δικαιοσύνην). The key to this is the meaning of δικαιοσύνη; is it "righteousness" (the spiritual side) or "justice" (the socioeconomic side)? Many opt for the latter on the basis of the first three beatitudes, the Lukan parallel (Luke 6:21, "who hunger now"), and especially the connection with Isa 61:1 – 3; they hunger and thirst for justice from those who oppress them. This then becomes a prayer for God's intervention to deliver his suffering people.[36] Others take it in the same double-meaning sense observed above, as a desire for deliverance from oppression (cf. esp. Isa 61:3, "They will be called oaks of righteousness," NIV) and a desire to serve God.[37]

However, "righteousness" is a particularly important term for Matthew, especially in the Sermon on the Mount (5:6, 10, 20; 6:1, 33), and in each of those contexts it refers to right conduct in the eyes of God. So here it means hungering and thirsting for doing what is right before God. Note that one never truly attains it but at all times strives with all one's strength to obey God.[38]

5:6 ... for they will be filled (ὅτι αὐτοὶ χορτασθήσονται). The promise is the total

34. John A. Broadus, *Commentary on the Gospel of Matthew* (Philadelphia: American Baptist Publication Society, 1886), 90.

35. Blaine Charette, *The Theme of Recompense in Matthew's Gospel* (JSNTSup 79; Sheffield: JSOT Press, 1992), 84 – 88.

36. McNeile, *Matthew*, 51 – 52; Schweizer, *Matthew*, 91; Gundry, *Matthew*, 70.

37. Hagner, *Matthew 1 – 13*, 93; Blomberg, *Matthew*, 99 – 100; Keener, *Matthew*, 170; Nolland, *Matthew*, 203.

38. Davies and Allison, *Matthew*, 1:452 – 53. See also Filson, *Matthew*, 77 – 78; Guelich, *Sermon on the Mount*, 84 – 87; France, *Matthew* (TNTC), 110; Strecker, *Sermon on the Mount*, 37; Turner, "Matthew," 77.

satisfaction of their need. "To be filled" (χορτάζω, as in v. 4, a divine passive; God will satisfy their needs) when used of hunger refers to total satisfaction, a stomach completely full. So here it means the complete satisfaction of their spiritual needs by God, possibly also a sense of messianic "fulfillment" in Christ in an eschatological sense. This becomes real in Isa 61:3, where the nation will be "oaks of righteousness, a planting of the Lord for the display of his splendor." This will take place at the eschaton but is partly taking place now in the spiritual kingdom Jesus has inaugurated,[39] as God pours out his abundance in our lives (cf. Eph 1:7 – 8).

5:7 God blesses those who are merciful (μακάριοι οἱ ἐλεήμονες). While the first four beatitudes focus on an attitude or mindset centered on God, these next three center on the actions that follow, namely, living righteously (cf. "righteousness" above). A life that centers on "showing mercy" (ἐλεήμονες; a present participle emphasizing the continuous nature of it) to others, i.e., coming to the aid of the needy,[40] exemplifies the conduct God demands of his people. This is the same as in the Lord's Prayer (6:12, 14 – 15, where forgiveness is a similar attitude) and in Ps 18:25; Prov 14:21, 17:5; Hos 6:6; Matt 9:13; 12:7; 18:33; 23:23; Jas 2:13.

5:7 ... for they will receive mercy (ὅτι αὐτοὶ ἐλεηθήσονται). The reward here is both given by God and shown by God, and the mercy granted us by him is again inaugurated, i.e., shown in the near future as well as at the final judgment. Both Matt 6:14 – 15 ("if you refuse to forgive others, your Father will not forgive your sins either") and Jas 2:13 ("judgment without mercy will be shown to anyone who has not been merciful") state this same truth (for mercy at the final judgment, see 2 Tim 1:18; Jude 21). It is the principle of retribution: what we do to others God will do to us. Here the positive side is stressed. When we show mercy to others, we will receive mercy from God.

5:8 God blesses the pure in heart (μακάριοι οἱ καθαροὶ τῇ καρδίᾳ). This reflects Ps 24:3 – 4, where the pure ascend to the hill of God and stand in his holy place. There are two nuances — they are morally upright and not just ritually clean, and they are single-minded in their commitment toward God.[41] They love God with all their heart, soul, and mind (Deut 6:5; Matt 22:37) and serve him with all their strength (Mark 12:30). It is both an attitude of sincere loyalty to God and the action that results, namely, a wholehearted service of God.[42]

5:8 ... for they will see God (ὅτι αὐτοὶ τὸν θεὸν ὄψονται). It is these who "will see God," both now spiritually (Job 42:5; Heb 11:27) and in fullness after Christ returns (Heb 12:14; 1 Cor 13:12; 1 John 3:2 – 3; Rev 22:4)

5:9 God blesses those who make peace (μακάριοι οἱ εἰρηνοποιοί). Like the "merciful," this centers on relations with others. The term "peacemaker" only appears elsewhere in verb form in Col 1:20, where Jesus made peace by his blood on the cross, but the concept is found often (Ps 34:14; Isa 52:7; Rom 12:18; 14:19; Jas 3:18; Heb 12:14; cf. *1 En.* 52:11). This connotes both peace with God and peace between people — the latter flows out of the former. Jesus is the supreme peacemaker, who reconciles human beings with God through the cross (Col 1:20), so the supreme peacemaking is the proclamation of the gospel. As Guelich says, "It is the demonstration of God's love through Christ in all its profundity (John 3:16; Rom 5:1, 6 – 11). The peacemakers of 5:9 refer to those who,

39. See Gundry, *Matthew*, 70.

40. Augustine; cf. Bruner, *Christbook*, 147.

41. Carson, "Matthew," 134 – 35; France, *Matthew* (TNTC), 110; Blomberg, *Matthew*, 100.

42. Guelich, *Sermon on the Mount*, 90; Schnackenburg, *Matthew*, 48 – 49.

experiencing the *shalom* of God, become his agents establishing his peace in the world."[43]

However, Jesus has in mind here primarily the healing of divisions in the community,[44] so the primary thrust is reconciliation in the church (Jas 3:18) and then between the church and the world (Mark 9:50; Rom 12:18; 1 Pet 3:11). This was meaningful in Jesus' day and must have been difficult for Simon the Zealot, one of Jesus' disciples (Matt 10:4); the Zealots were a group of revolutionaries who fomented rebellion against Rome, became a Jewish sect in the 60s, and precipitated the war against Rome in AD 66 – 70.

5:9 ... for they will be called children of God (ὅτι αὐτοὶ υἱοὶ θεοῦ κληθήσονται). Faithful Israel was called "children of God" in the OT (Deut 14:1; Hos 1:10),[45] and now the new Israel becomes the special children and heirs of God as they become peacemakers in following Christ. "They will be called" (κληθήσονται) is again (as in vv. 4, 6) a divine passive, "God will call them his children," again both now (Rom 8:14 – 17) and at the eschaton (Luke 20:36; Rom 8:19, 23; Rev 21:7; *Pss. Sol.* 17:27).

5:10 God blesses those who are persecuted because of righteousness (μακάριοι οἱ δεδιωγμένοι ἕνεκεν δικαιοσύνης). The final set of beatitudes now centers on what the earth gives the believer, not what we give to others. "Persecuted" (δεδιωγμένοι) is a perfect passive participle, with the passive meaning here "by the world" and the perfect connoting the "state"[46] of being persecuted. Jesus makes it clear in the syllogism of John 15:18 – 16:4:

Major premise: I and my followers are one

Minor premise: the world hates and persecutes me

Conclusion: the world will hate and persecute you

So the peacemaker cannot expect a comfortable, easy life (cf. Acts 14:22; 2 Tim 3:12; 1 Pet 4:3 – 4, 12 – 16), and the merciful cannot expect mercy from a harsh world. As Jesus said in John 3:19 – 20, darkness hates light, because the children of light take away the world's pretension that it is light (note that the brightest lights in a city are found in the "red light" district, e.g., Las Vegas). Yet the text also says "because of righteousness." When we do good to the people of this world (Gal 6:10a), we cannot expect it back. When we follow the will of God and live as citizens of the kingdom, we will come into conflict with the world's ways.

5:10 ... for the kingdom of heaven belongs to them (ὅτι αὐτῶν ἐστιν ἡ βασιλεία τῶν οὐρανῶν). As stated in the first beatitude (5:3), the children of the new covenant community not only belong to that kingdom now but are guaranteed to inherit it (Rom 8:17; 1 Pet 1:5). The possessive genitive αὐτῶν with the verb "to be" is best translated "belongs to"; at one and the same time God's people are the downtrodden of earth and the possessors of the heavenly kingdom.

5:11 God blesses you when people insult you, persecute you, and falsely say every kind of evil against you because of me (μακάριοί ἐστε ὅταν ὀνειδίσωσιν ὑμᾶς καὶ διώξωσιν καὶ εἴπωσιν πᾶν πονηρὸν καθ' ὑμῶν ψευδόμενοι ἕνεκεν ἐμοῦ). Matthew switches from present (vv. 4, 6, 7) and perfect (v. 10) tense verbs to aorists here to

43. Guelich, *Sermon on the Mount*, 92.

44. This is the conclusion of L. J. White, "Peacemakers in Matthew's World," *TBT* 23 (1985): 29 – 34, who says that in the honor/shame culture of Matthew's day, this best fits the community life of the church.

45. Strecker, *Sermon on the Mount*, 41, points out that there the promise of divine sonship is connected to the reuniting of the northern and southern kingdoms. Here it is the reuniting of estranged members of the church.

46. See Porter, *Idioms*, 21 – 22.

envision the persecution as a single whole.[47] For rhetorical effect, Matthew changes the style in the ninth beatitude, having it addressed directly to the disciples in second person style ("you").[48] This adds verbal assault (insult, uttering evil things) to the persecution of v. 10. It is similar to Luke 6:22 ("insult you and reject your name as evil") and reflects the verbal onslaughts against Jesus made by his enemies. This is seen in "because of me" (ἕνεκεν ἐμοῦ), meaning that they suffer because they belong to the new kingdom community he has instituted and follow his teachings. In v. 10 it is "because of righteouness," here "because of me," for following Jesus is the path of righteousness.

5:12 Rejoice and be glad (χαίρετε καὶ ἀγαλλιᾶσθε). This expands the beatitude form of vv. 3 – 10. "Rejoice and be glad" paraphrases "blessed" (μακάριοί) and turns it into a virtual act of worship. The use of the progressive present tense (Luke 6:23 uses an aorist imperative) and the two nearly synonymous verbs makes the command emphatic. Believers should experience an ongoing exultant joy when privileged to suffer for the Lord; for the early church suffering was a joy because it meant a special "fellowship" with Christ (Acts 5:41; Phil 3:10; cf. Col 1:24), a new level of union with him.

5:12 ... for your reward in heaven is great (ὅτι ὁ μισθὸς ὑμῶν πολὺς ἐν τοῖς οὐρανοῖς). Jesus now places the "for" (ὅτι) here; the blessing is "great reward" (μισθός), a special Matthean term found ten times (six in this sermon) in his gospel and referring to the "wages" one has earned for following Christ. The reward is "in heaven" and refers to the eternal reward for remaining faithful to Christ. Charette says this is the only time in Matthew the reward is called "great" and that it here is transcendent and future, finalizing the promise in Gen 15:1 that Israel will inherit the "land" and here (with v. 5) extending that to the final heavenly kingdom.[49]

5:12 ... for in this way they persecuted the prophets before you (οὕτως γὰρ ἐδίωξαν τοὺς προφήτας τοὺς πρὸ ὑμῶν). A second reason for the joy (this time "for" [γάρ]) is the new connection with the prophets of the past who were persecuted for the same reasons (see Heb 11:32 – 40, whose reward was also not experienced in this life since "God had planned something better for us so that only together with us would they be made perfect").

Theology in Application

The beatitudes make a powerful sermon (or series of messages), and they get at the very heart of Matthean theology. Some speak of the Sermon on the Mount as "community-forming" in its scope, i.e., it tells the members of Matthew's church how God wants them to conduct their lives.[50] In this sense the beatitudes describe the attitudes and relationships that should typify believers as they live their lives in a world that has turned against them (5:10 – 12). Moreover, God guarantees their eternal reward for being faithful to this calling.

47. Wallace, 555, uses a good illustration: the present tense is like a motion picture, showing the action in progress, while the aorist is like a snapshot, picturing the action as a whole.

48. Nolland, *Matthew*, 196 – 97, believes the third person style in vv. 3 – 10 functions to restate 4:17 in terms of the imminent kingdom and its implications for the lives of the kingdom people, while the switch to second person highlights the implications this will have in terms of the world's reaction.

49. Charette, *Theme of Recompense*, 88 – 90.

50. Wayne A. Meeks, *The Moral World of the First Christians* (Philadelphia: Westminster, 1986), 136 – 37; Overman, *Matthew's Gospel and Formative Judaism*, 94 – 95.

1. Being a Part of God's Kingdom Community

Jesus has brought the kingdom into this world (4:17), and his followers are the citizens of this new covenant community. Citizenship (cf. Eph 2:19; Phil 3:20) contains both privilege and responsibilities. Both are spelled out in these beatitudes, responsibility in the qualities engendered and privilege in the rewards promised.

2. Sharing God's Concern for the Poor

Like the beatitudes and woes in Luke 6:20 – 26 (but not with the same emphasis), the first four beatitudes center on the poor. They are poverty-stricken, mourn in the midst of their oppression, are forced into a meek servility, and hunger and thirst after justice. Yet they are also fortunate, for they have come to the notice of God, and he has promised to vindicate them. Matthew does not quite have the same emphasis on the reversal of roles that Luke has (the poor will have everything, the rich will have nothing), but he comes close. Moreover, God's concerns are our concerns, and it is our task to bring mercy and peace to the downtrodden as well as to alleviate their suffering in any way we can.

3. Living in Dependence on God and Righteously for Him

The first four beatitudes deal primarily with a total reliance on God. Each provides an aspect of that sense of dependence. We begin with those who are humble before God, who have realized their absolute need to put their trust wholly in him. They seek their treasure in heaven, not on earth (Matt 6:19 – 21), and have placed all earthly concerns secondary to following him. Then there are those who "mourn" under both oppression and guilt for sin and who thereby turn to God for help and forgiveness. They grieve under both physical (mainly poverty) and spiritual (mainly sin) needs but turn to God rather than their own resources.

Too few Christians sincerely grieve for sin; we have become hardened not just to the sin around us but even more sadly to the sin within us. The "meek" are the ones who turn the other cheek and go the extra mile (5:39, 41) for the sake of others, who are so attuned to God that they do not react aggressively when hurt by others. Those who crave "righteousness" again seek justice when wronged (note how this fits into the "meek" who turn to God for justice rather than seek it for themselves) but also want to live rightly before God. As Keener says, "these humble people are also those who yearn for God above all else (cf. Zeph 2:3)."[51] This is exemplified in the three sections on almsgiving, prayer, and fasting in 6:1 – 18; they must be done entirely to please God, not to look pious to others.

51. Keener, *Matthew*, 169.

4. Directing Our Lives to Serve God and Others

The next three beatitudes center on how to live rightly before him. Attitude (the first four beatitudes) must lead to action (the next three). The first deals with human relationships, those who "show mercy" to the needy. A study of biblical texts shows that the main purpose of God's giving wealth to a person is not so that they can live luxuriously (though they can enjoy the blessing God has given them) but so that they can use that wealth to help the oppressed. The second deals with one's relationship to God, as the "pure in heart" are single-minded in their desire to live for him; their whole life is God-centered, and they seek to serve him above all else. Finally, the "peacemaker" serves in both directions, seeking to reconcile people to God and to one another. They are so important in the church and in the world, for they are the antithesis of those self-centered individuals who take peace from the earth in order to build their own kingdoms.

5. Vindication for Those Persecuted for Living for Him

The basic message of the whole NT is that Christ's followers should expect to face the same hatred and oppression he did. In fact, this is primary fellowship and oneness with him. There are three levels at which we should proclaim this in a society where persecution rarely happens. (1) In the world as a whole there is more oppression of Christians than ever before, and we should "mourn with those who mourn" (Rom 12:15; cf. 1 Cor 12:26). (2) As our society becomes increasingly secular, persecution could come soon, and we must be ready for it. (3) Many today are so afraid of being made fun of, let alone persecuted, that they compromise their walk.

6. Reward for All Who Sacrificially Live for God

God has given his kingdom, and we have become citizens of it. We no longer belong to this world. As the old adage says, we are a part of it, yet live apart from it. We are "foreigners and exiles" here (1 Pet 2:11; cf. 1:1, 17) and so live differently than the true members of this world. We do not live in order to gain reward, yet God has promised us just that. Each of the beatitudes ends in promise, and the promises must be understood as part of the already/not yet framework of the NT.

We already belong to the "kingdom of heaven" (5:3, 10), yet will receive it in fullness at the eschaton. We are already being comforted, filled to the full, and shown mercy, yet that will be finalized when Christ returns. We see God now, but will see him face to face in eternity. We have these blessings now to the extent that we are living completely for him, but we will experience them fully only in the final kingdom. Davies and Allison calls this a "practical theodicy" in the sense that it comforts and consoles Jesus' heavy-laden followers.[52]

52. Davies and Allison, *Matthew*, 1:467.

CHAPTER 12

Matthew 5:13 – 16

Literary Context

This continues the introduction to the Sermon on the Mount and as such helps the reader to understand the major themes of the message as a whole. Having introduced the blessings and rewards as well as the ethical responsibilities of those who form the citizens of the kingdom, Jesus now centers on the action side, using the metaphors of salt and light to tell what kind of people the citizens of the kingdom are supposed to be. Out of this will flow the Sermon proper. The first part, the relationship of the Torah to the new covenant of the kingdom, will elaborate this new ethical mandate via the Ten Commandments, now deepened to exemplify the new kingdom ethics.

II. The Kingdom Message Goes Out (4:12 – 7:29)
- **B. First Discourse: The Sermon on the Mount (5:1 – 7:29)**
  1. The Setting of the Sermon (5:1 – 2)
  2. **Introduction (5:3 – 16)**
     - a. The Beatitudes (5:3 – 12)
     - ➦ **b. The Salt and Light Sayings (5:13 – 16)**

Main Idea

The two metaphors used here are parallel to each other and form the basic point: the kingdom people must make a difference in this world. Since believers are salt and light, they must be visible and change the nature of the world around them. The concluding idea shows how this is to de done; "good deeds" will make a difference and draw the world to the light.

Translation

Matthew 5:13-16

13a	Assertion	*(A) "You are the salt of the earth.*
b	Condition/Result	*But if the salt loses its saltlike qualities,*
		by what can it be made salty again?
c		*It will have no value any longer*
d		*except to be thrown outside and trampled by people.*
14a	Assertion/Parallel 13a	*(B) You are the light of the world.*
b	Aphorism	*(1) A city sitting on a mountain cannot be hidden.*
15a	Aphorism	*(2) Neither do people light a lamp and*
		put it under a measuring bowl;
b		*rather, they put it on a stand,*
c		*and it shines on everyone in the house.*
16a	Exhortation	*In this way, let your light shine before others*
b	Purpose of 16a	*(1) so that they might see your good works and*
c	Purpose of 16a	*(2) give glory to your Father who is in heaven."*

Structure and Literary Form

Jesus presents these metaphors as parabolic maxims that designate the proper way of life for a disciple. The structure of each one is similar, with "salt of the earth" paralleling "light of the world" and "loses its saltlike qualities" paralleling "cannot be hidden" (though the latter flows out of a different metaphor, a city on a hill). But then they go on separate paths, with the salt saying stressing the negative (a useless disciple) and the light saying stressing the positive (shedding light on everyone). Together, they emphasize the fact that true discipleship is distinguished by the number of people who are affected by it.

Exegetical Outline

➡ **I. The Salt of the Earth (5:13)**

- A. Danger — losing its saltiness (v. 13a)
- B. Result 1 — no longer of value (v. 13b)
- C. Result 2 — thrown away and trampled (v. 13c)

II. The Light of the World (5:14 – 16)

- A. Key characteristic — cannot be hidden (v. 14b – 15)
- B. Example 1 — city on a hill (v. 14b)
- C. Example 2 — a lamp, not hidden but placed on a stand (v. 15)
- D. Conclusion — Light Shining before Others (v. 16)
  1. Purpose 1 — see your good deeds (v. 16a)
  2. Purpose 2 — Glorify God (v. 16b)

Explanation of the Text

5:13 You are the salt of the earth (Ὑμεῖς ἐστε τὸ ἅλας τῆς γῆς). The use of "you" (ὑμεῖς) ties this closely with the previous (vv. 11 – 12) as directed particularly to the disciples. The salt metaphor itself is broad. Davies and Allison list eleven possibilities;[1] and scholars differ as to which one is primary: preservative/prevent corruption (McNeile, Carson, Blomberg), fertilize (Gundry, Shillington),[2] adding flavor (Job 6:6; Schnackenburg, Harrington), or purify (2 Kgs 2:19 – 23; Hill, Luz). In addition, salt was often associated with wisdom and its use in the sacrificial system (Lev 2:13; Ezek 43:24).

Due to the breadth of the metaphor, it is impossible to single out any one, and it is best to allow it multiple aspects (Davies and Allison, Hagner). As such it means simply to make an impact on the world. It is also critical to note that Jesus says "of the earth"/"the world" rather than narrowing it to Israel. Thus together with "world" in v. 14 it refers to the Gentile mission as well as that to Israel (cf. 28:19).[3] The genitive (τῆς γῆς) may be a simple possessive genitive ("the earth's salt"), an objective genitive (the earth is "salted" by the believer), or a genitive of purpose (the salt that intends to fill the earth).[4] The second is most likely, for the follower of Christ is seen here as acting like salt (and light, v. 14).

5:13 But if the salt loses its saltlike qualities, by what can it be made salty again? (ἐὰν δὲ τὸ ἅλας μωρανθῇ, ἐν τίνι ἁλισθήσεται;). How can salt lose its effectiveness? Many have pointed out that salt does not lose its "salty" qualities; it is a stable compound. However, that is to take this too far. There are several explanations for Jesus' understanding in saying this, each of them part of the metaphor here: (1) ancient salt from salt marshes and the Dead Sea contained many impurities;[5] layers of salt have been discovered in the Dead Sea area, made insipid by the impurities of the soil. (2) If land is oversalted, it becomes infertile; salt cannot be restored once diluted. In the same way, salt blocks used in baking were thrown away after fifteen years as useless.[6] (3) Jesus' purpose was not scientific but ethical, making the point that his disciples must never allow themselves to become useless in their mission. The verb μωρανθῇ means to "become foolish" with the idea that such a disciple is a fool (cf. the "foolish" [μωραί] virgins in 25:2 – 3, 8).

5:13 It will have no value any longer except to be thrown outside and trampled by people (εἰς οὐδὲν ἰσχύει ἔτι εἰ μὴ βληθὲν ἔξω καταπατεῖσθαι ὑπὸ τῶν ἀνθρώπων). Salt that lost its saltlike character would have "no value" (a secondary meaning of ἰσχύω, BAGD, 384 [4]) for the home and could only be thrown away (in oriental metaphor, "thrown into the street"). Jesus is saying that his disciples dare not allow the world to dilute their effectiveness, or they belong on the garbage heap. Such Christians will indeed be "trampled" (implying judgment as in the parables of Matt 25) because they are ineffective and useless.[7]

5:14 You are the light of the world (Ὑμεῖς ἐστε τὸ φῶς τοῦ κόσμου). Light is one of Scripture's most common symbols. God is light (Ps 18:12; 104:2; 1 Tim 6:16; 1 John 1:5), Christ is light (Matt 4:16;

1. Davies and Allison, *Matthew*, 1:72 – 73.
2. V. G. Shillington, "Salt of the Earth? (Matt 5:13/Luke 14:34f)," *ExpTim* 112 (2001): 120 – 21.
3. See Gnilka, *Matthäusevangelium*, 1:135 – 36; Davies and Allison, *Matthew*, 1:472.
4. On the genitive of purpose, see Wallace, 100 – 101.
5. Carson, "Matthew," 138; Morris, *Matthew*, 104.
6. P. Fiedler, "μωρία et al.," *EDNT*, 449 – 50.
7. See Guelich, *Sermon on the Mount*, 122, who says this "connotes disdain and judgment (cf. Hos 5:11, LXX)."

John 1:7, 9; 8:12 ["light of the world"]; 9:5; 12:46), and God's people are light (Eph 5:8; 1 Thess 5:5), especially in terms of drawing the world to God through their light (Isa 42:6; 49:6 [both "a light for the Gentiles"]; 51:4; Phil 2:15). In the salt metaphor the world will taste the goodness of God; here they will see his goodness ("of the world" [τοῦ κόσμου] is an objective genitive; the believer "lights up the world"). In both cases they will be drawn to the kingdom truths and the relevance of these truths for their lives. The kingdom of God radiates through the lives of his children, and the light attracts the world as moths to a lamp.

5:14 A city sitting on a mountain cannot be hidden (οὐ δύναται πόλις κρυβῆναι ἐπάνω ὄρους κειμένη). To show the pervasiveness of this, Jesus uses a parallel metaphor, yet not a different one. The reason a city on a mountain cannot be hid is not only its visibility but also the fact that at night its light penetrates the darkness.[8] Bonhoeffer shows that any Israelite would immediately think of Jerusalem, but in this case the new Jerusalem constitutes Jesus' followers; like Jerusalem they must shine out to the world, for "discipleship is as visible as light in the night, as a mountain in the flatlands. To flee into invisibility is to deny the call. Any community of Jesus which wants to be invisible is no longer a community that follows him."[9]

5:15 Neither do people light a lamp and put it under a measuring bowl (οὐδὲ καίουσιν λύχνον καὶ τιθέασιν αὐτὸν ὑπὸ τὸν μόδιον). This anchors the meaning of v. 14. The lamp here is probably a small oil-burning portable one with a wick. It would be extremely foolish to light it and then hide it under a bowl ("measuring bowl" [μόδιος] is a common bowl used for measuring grain).[10] Jesus' point is that it is even more foolish for a disciple to hide the light of the gospel.

5:15 Rather, they put it on a stand, and it shines on everyone in the house (ἀλλ' ἐπὶ τὴν λυχνίαν, καὶ λάμπει πᾶσιν τοῖς ἐν τῇ οἰκίᾳ). Instead of hiding a lamp, one places it on a "lampstand"; this is not a "candlestick" (KJV) but a stand made of pottery or metal.[11] Is πᾶσιν neuter ("everything" in the house) or masculine ("everyone")? At first glance the neuter seems better since a lamp is to light up the house, not just its occupants; but in light of the emphasis on "people" (ἀνθρώπων) in vv. 13, 16 and the parallel in Luke 11:33 ("so that those who come in may see the light"), it is best to see this as masculine, "everyone in the house." This also lends it a missionary thrust: God's people must be taking God's light to the people of the world (v. 14). Discipleship must always be active; if it ceases to be at work, it is useless.

5:16 In this way, let your light shine before others so that they might see your good works and give glory to your Father who is in heaven (οὕτως λαμψάτω τὸ φῶς ὑμῶν ἔμπροσθεν τῶν ἀνθρώπων, ὅπως ἴδωσιν ὑμῶν τὰ καλὰ ἔργα καὶ δοξάσωσιν τὸν πατέρα ὑμῶν τὸν ἐν τοῖς οὐρανοῖς). This provides a conclusion not just to the light metaphor but also to vv. 13 – 16 as a whole. The evangelistic thrust of the passage now becomes apparent. The light of God must shine through the disciple's life, but note that this is not just witnessing but "good works" (= "righteousness," 5:6, 10, 20), that is, a lifestyle of goodness

8. Guelich, *Sermon on the Mount*, 127, and Carson, "Matthew," 139 – 40, also refer to OT prophecies on Jerusalem as the house on "the mountain of the Lord" (Isa 2:2 – 5; Mic 4:1 – 3), thus seeing the disciples fulfilling Israel's role to the nations (Isa 60:1 – 3). See also K. M. Campbell, "The New Jerusalem in Matthew 5.14," *SJT* 31 (1978): 335 – 63.

9. Dietrich Bonhoeffer, *Discipleship* (trans. B. Green and R. Krauss; Minneapolis: Fortress, 2001), 113, in Hauerwas, *Matthew*, 63.

10. It was a sizable bowl, as it measured about 8.75 liters or close to Luther's famous "hide it under a bushel."

11. Davies and Allison, *Matthew*, 1:477.

that is always helping others and demonstrating the love and concern of God for them.[12] The content of these "good works" will be explicated in the rest of the sermon.

This has also become a major NT teaching (cf. 2 Cor 4:6; Phil 2:15; Titus 2:8; 1 Pet 2:12, 15), called today "lifestyle evangelism." The idea of "glorifying God" in Revelation connotes repentance and conversion (Rev 14:6 – 7, 16:9) and likely does so here as well. The idea of "your Father in heaven" is a favorite phrase in Matthew (twenty times but only in Mark 11:25 elsewhere) and connotes the idea that in the kingdom a new intimacy (see on 6:9) has been made possible; the transcendent heavenly Father has reached down to humankind.

Theology in Application

The essence of the Sermon on the Mount is stated here. The citizens of the kingdom must be salt and light, and their goal is to reach the world with the light of the gospel. Strecker says vv. 16, 20 are the core of the Sermon,[13] showing that hearing must lead to doing, and that good deeds are the heart of discipleship. This is where Jesus surprised his disciples (and hearers) with his teaching. He never continued the status quo; he demanded that his followers go out and change the world. No passivity here; he demanded change, for God's righteousness to enter the world in such a way that it would never be the same.

The coming of God's kingdom is so much more than just being kind to others and performing good deeds. There is a demand to be different and to act differently, that is, to be right with God and to act the way God demands, by following Jesus in countercultural directions. Change is the name of the game, and it must occur at the ontological level (who we are) and at the functional level (how we live and act).

1. God's Calls to Discipleship — Mission to the World

In 4:19 Jesus defined discipleship from a mission perspective as "fishing for people" and as following Jesus in his task of bringing people into the kingdom. For Matthew (28:19) true discipleship is joining Jesus' mission to the world, and that is seen here in the parallel "salt *of the earth*" and "light *of the world*" metaphors. It is not just Judaism but the Gentiles who are also in view (as in the women named in the genealogies of 1:1 – 17 and the Magi in 2:1 – 11 as well as the Gentile areas mentioned in 4:23 – 25).

2. Discipleship as Active in the World

Both in the useless salt of v. 13 (the negative side) and the "good works" of v. 16 (the positive side), the child of the kingdom is meant to be dynamically involved in

12. Guelich, *Sermon on the Mount*, 124 – 25, rightly points out that this includes both words and deeds; discipleship is living the life of Christ in word and deed.

13. Strecker, *Sermon on the Mount*, 52.

this world. They are characterized as making a difference through "good works" in both word and deed. This is the heart of the Sermon — Jesus demands a new righteousness or living according to the will of God for his followers. Only they (emphatic "you yourselves") belong to this group, and only they have the privileges of kingdom citizenship.

But it also involves obligation — to live as salt and light in this world. The passive Christian is seen here as a "fool" (μωραίνω in v. 13) who no longer has any value. This will be developed further in Matthew, in that the one who lives for earthly treasure (6:19 – 21) and who is centered on earthly possessions (6:25 – 27) is to be pitied and is headed for judgment (5:13c; cf. 7:21 – 23). Like a burning lamp hidden under a bowl, the shallow disciples fail to live up to their whole purpose of being.

3. The Glory of God as the Goal of the Church

The new kingdom inaugurated in Christ involves an entirely new experience of Shekinah, the glorious dwelling of God among his people. This is brought out best in John 1:14, which says that in Jesus the Shekinah was encased in human flesh and walked this earth. The disciples basked in the presence of Shekinah and therefore in a glory they had never known possible. This glory is experienced especially in mission, through which God's light is made to shine on this world and his glory is made evident to this world.

CHAPTER 13

Matthew 5:17 – 20

Literary Context

The body of the sermon begins here. The central issue is the relationship of Jesus' kingdom teaching (in a sense, a new Torah) to the old Torah or law. When one realizes the radical nature of this new ethical teaching, it is understandable that Jesus begins with this issue.[1] He wants to make clear that he is unswerving in his adherence to the Torah. This supplements but does not replace Torah; rather, it is the true explication of Torah, the implications that have not previously been understood.

Moreover, Torah is caught up and fulfilled in this new kingdom teaching. It is clear that Jesus brings something entirely new to the table — a new righteousness; but that new righteouness is not opposed to the old but is the true implication of it. The six antitheses in 5:21 – 48 draw out and exemplify this fact.

- **II. The Kingdom Message Goes Out (4:12 – 7:29)**
  - **B. First Discourse: The Sermon on the Mount (5:1 – 7:29)**
    1. The Setting of the Sermon (5:1 – 2)
    2. Introduction (5:3 – 16)
    3. **The Relationship of the Law to the New Covenant in Jesus (5:17 – 48)**
       - ➦ **a. Jesus and the Law — Continuity (5:17 – 20)**
       - b. Examples — Six Antitheses on the New Righteousness (5:21 – 48)

Main Idea

The scribes and Pharisees had developed the oral tradition in order to explicate the law more clearly for the people; they wanted to make its meaning evident on the practical level of living it rightly. Jesus is saying in effect that they have failed to do so. Only he can "fulfill" it, that is, bring it to its intended end or goal.

1. The common misunderstanding that this reflects not the historical Jesus but conflicts in Matthew's church in unnecessary. These same issues were evident in Jesus' teaching.

Translation

Matthew 5:17-20

17a	Assertion	*"Do not think that I have come to destroy the law or the prophets.*
b	Contrast to 17a	*I have not come to destroy but*
c		*to fulfill it.*
18a	Basis #1	*[1] For I tell you the truth, until heaven and earth disappear,*
b		*not the smallest letter, not the least dot of a pen, will disappear from the law*
c		*until everything is accomplished.*
19a	Basis #2	*[2] Therefore, whoever breaks one of the least of these commandments and*
b		*teaches other people to do the same will be called least in the kingdom of heaven,*
c		*but whoever keeps and teaches them will be called great in the kingdom of heaven.*
20a	Result	*For I tell you that . . . you will never enter the kingdom of heaven*
b	Condition	*unless your righteousness is greater than that of the teachers of law and the Pharisees."*

Structure and Literary Form

Guelich calls these an "I have come" (ἦλθον) saying (v. 17), a legal saying (v. 18), a sentence of holy law (v. 19), and an entrance saying (v. 20).[2] Each fits into a pattern of sayings in Matthew and the other gospels by which Jesus challenges the legal assumptions of the Jewish leaders. The pattern of Jesus' logic is unmistakable. He begins by affirming the incredible value of Torah, stating that his mission is to bring it to its proper end, not to destroy or abolish it. The reason is that the law will last until the eschaton. It is meant to be followed as long as this world exists. Moreover, anyone who breaks even the smallest command will have no place in the kingdom.

Jesus' conclusion and the transition to his study of ethical righteousness in vv. 21–48 are the basis of his proclamation that his is a superior form of righteousness to that offered by the leaders. Paul says it succinctly when he claims: "Christ is

2. Guelich, *Sermon on the Mount*, 134–35.

the culmination of the law" (Rom 10:4); that is, he culminates the law in the sense that it points to him and is fulfilled in him.[3] While to many Jesus seemed to "destroy" the law by ignoring key elements like the Sabbath laws and by associating with the lower classes, Jesus wants them to realize that as Messiah, he is the true interpreter of Torah and so brings a higher righteousness. France says it well:

> If in the process it may appear that certain elements of the law are for all practical purposes "abolished," this will be attributable not to their loss of their status as the Word of God but to their changed role in the era of fulfillment, in which it is Jesus, the fulfiller, rather than the law which pointed forward to him, who is the ultimate authority.[4]

Exegetical Outline

→ **I. Jesus Fulfills the Law (5:17 – 19)**
  - A. Purpose of his coming — not to destroy, but to fulfill (v. 17)
  - B. Basis 1 — abiding value of Torah (v. 18)
    1. Limit 1 — heaven and earth's passing
    2. Extent — not the smallest part
    3. Limit 2 — all accomplished
  - C. Basis 2 — importance of Torah (v. 19)
    1. The least — breaking a commandment
    2. The greatest — obeying the commandments

II. The Greater Righteousness (5:20)
  - A. Condition — must exceed the scribes and Pharisees
  - B. Result — failure to enter the kingdom

Explanation of the Text

5:17 Do not think that I have come to destroy the law or the prophets (Μὴ νομίσητε ὅτι ἦλθον καταλῦσαι τὸν νόμον ἢ τοὺς προφήτας). The opening "do not think" (μὴ νομίσητε, the aorist here prohibits any such thinking at all)[5] is a common lead-in when disarming potential objections (cf. 10:34), so Jesus wants to be certain no one misunderstands what he is going to say in vv. 21 – 48. These must not be taken as attacks against the law; instead, Jesus' hearers should realize he is deepening the law. "The law or the prophets" means the whole of Scripture. There is to be no "abolishing" but rather a "fulfilling" of God's true intent in revealing these truths.

5:17 I have not come to destroy but to fulfill it (οὐκ ἦλθον καταλῦσαι ἀλλὰ πληρῶσαι). The meaning of "destroy/abolish" (cf. also v.17a) and

3. See Osborne, *Romans*, 265.
4. France, *Gospel of Matthew*, 183.
5. See Porter, *Idioms*, 225.

"fulfill" must be taken together, for they are antithetical. The key is the meaning of πληρόω, which has as its root meaning to "fill to the full." This term has been debated and has several options (Davies and Allison list nine):

1. Jesus fulfilled the law by obeying its commands; he actualized it by doing it.[6]
2. Jesus "established" or "validated" the law by realizing it completely in his teaching and deeds.[7]
3. Jesus completed or filled up the law's meaning in his own teaching and interpretation of Torah, thereby enabling the kingdom people to live the law more completely.[8]
4. Jesus fulfills the law by completing its "covenant-promise" in bringing about a new redemptive-historical relationship with God.[9]

Probably the best is to combine the last three: the meaning of the OT is completed by being fulfilled in Jesus; in both his deeds and his teaching he lifted the OT to a higher plane.[10] This is seen in the antitheses that follow; the law has a deeper meaning than ever before. Banks says it well: "The prophetic teachings point forward (principally) to the actions of Christ and have been revealed in them in an incomparably greater way. The Mosaic laws point forward (principally) to the teachings of Christ and have also been realized in them in a more profound manner."[11]

5:18 For I tell you the truth (ἀμὴν γὰρ λέγω ὑμῖν). In the OT the Hebrew *ʾāmēn* means to verify a key teaching, so Jesus uses this to highlight an important, solemn truth. He wants his disciples to listen carefully to an authoritative pronouncement. This important authority-formula occurs thirty-one times in Matthew at particularly critical points.

5:18 Until heaven and earth disappear, not the smallest letter, not the least dot of a pen, will disappear from the law (ἕως ἂν παρέλθῃ ὁ οὐρανὸς καὶ ἡ γῆ, ἰῶτα ἓν ἢ μία κεραία οὐ μὴ παρέλθῃ ἀπὸ τοῦ νόμου). The Greek ἰῶτα refers to the Hebrew letter *yôd*, the smallest letter of the alphabet; and κεραία refers to the small stroke that is used to distinguish letters (e.g., ב from כ) or an ornamental stroke added to a letter.[12] Together they mean that even the smallest part of the law will continue until the eschaton. The law is intact and as a whole will be preserved in the person and the authoritative teaching of the Messiah, Jesus. The disappearance of heaven and earth means the destruction of the original creation (2 Pet 3:10; Rev 20:11, 21:1). As long as the present world order continues, the OT is valid.

5:18 ... until everything is accomplished (ἕως ἂν πάντα γένηται). This moment of time is clarified by the second "until" (ἕως ἄν) clause, the fulfillment of all the prophecies inherent in Scripture, indeed the fulfillment of every passage, since the whole OT points forward to Christ. This is close to 24:34 ("I tell you the truth, this generation will not pass away until all these things take place"), where it refers to the prophecies of the Olivet Discourse.[13]

6. Adolf Schlatter, *Der Evangelist Matthäus* (Stuttgart: Calwer, 1929), 153; Keener, *Matthew*, 177; Bruner, *Christbook*, 167.

7. Hill, *Matthew*, 117.

8. Strecker, *Sermon on the Mount*, 54 – 55; Hagner, *Matthew 1 – 13*, 105 – 6; Davies and Allison, *Matthew*, 1:485 – 86; Nolland, *Matthew*, 218 – 19.

9. C. F. D. Moule, "Fulfillment-Words in the New Testament: Use and Abuse," *NTS* 14 (1967 – 68): 294; Guelich, *Sermon on the Mount*, 140; Turner, "Matthew," 85; Witherington, *Matthew*, 126.

10. Carson, "Matthew," 143 – 44; Morris, *Matthew*, 108.

11. Robert Banks, "Matthew's Understanding of the Law: Authenticity and Interpretation in Matthew 5:17 – 20," *JBL* 93 (1974): 231, also quoted in Morris, *Matthew*, 108.

12. See J. P. Meier, *Law and History in Matthew's Gospel: A Redactional Study of Mt. 5:17 – 48* (Rome: Biblical Institute Press, 1976), 51 – 52.

13. Meier, *Law and History*, 64 – 65, takes this as a reference to Jesus' death and resurrection, thus restricting the validity of the Torah to the period ending with the resurrection.

5:19 Therefore, whoever breaks one of the least of these commandments (ὃς ἐὰν οὖν λύσῃ μίαν τῶν ἐντολῶν τούτων τῶν ἐλαχίστων). "The least of these commandments" is sometimes taken to be Jesus' teaching[14] but in the context of v. 18 must refer to the commands of the OT.[15] However, as we saw in v. 17, these commands are valid as "fulfilled," i.e., as authoritatively and finally interpreted in Jesus' teaching. Thus, it is the law as experienced in Jesus' teaching.

5:19 ... and teaches other people[16] to do the same will be called least in the kingdom of heaven, but whoever keeps and teaches them will be called great in the kingdom of heaven (καὶ διδάξῃ οὕτως τοὺς ἀνθρώπους, ἐλάχιστος κληθήσεται ἐν τῇ βασιλείᾳ τῶν οὐρανῶν· ὃς δ' ἂν ποιήσῃ καὶ διδάξῃ, οὗτος μέγας κληθήσεται ἐν τῇ βασιλείᾳ τῶν οὐρανῶν). The emphasis on "teaching" as well as "keeping" the commands stems from the responsibility of the disciples to teach others. The Sermon on the Mount is not just preparing disciples but preparing the teachers of disciples. It is both deed and word that is at the heart of this passage, as we stated in v. 17.

The juxtaposition of "least" and "great" in the kingdom has occasioned debate since it implies a gradation of status in the kingdom. While some argue "the kingdom" is not the present kingdom,[17] most believe it is referring to just this in keeping with Jesus' teaching elsewhere (10:41 – 42; 18:4; 20:16, 23 and parallels). The Bible often states that every person, believer and unbeliever, will be "judged by works" (16:27; Rom 2:6; 14:12; 1 Cor 3:12 – 15; 2 Cor 5:10; 11:15; 2 Tim 4:14; 1 Pet 1:17), and so we take into eternity what we have done for the Lord here. Obedience ("keep" the commands) and disobedience ("break" the commands) will have their just reward.

5:20 For I tell you that unless your righteousness is greater than that of the teachers of law and the Pharisees (λέγω γὰρ ὑμῖν ὅτι ἐὰν μὴ περισσεύσῃ ὑμῶν ἡ δικαιοσύνη πλεῖον τῶν γραμματέων καὶ Φαρισαίων). Jesus begins with the same formula as in v. 18 (minus the ἀμήν), stressing the importance of the saying. As said in 3:15, "righteousness" here means living our lives in accordance with God's will. It is primarily ethical, related to "right" living before God. Here it must "exceed" or "surpass" (aorist περισσεύσῃ to depict one's life seen as a single whole) the legalistic righteousness of the scribes ("teachers of law," the legal experts)[18] and Pharisees (lay leaders of religious observance, see on 3:7); they are outside the kingdom.

The problem with this view is the earlier disappearance of earth and heaven (the two are parallel), which means the end of the age. Guelich, *Sermon on the Mount*, 148 – 49, sees a contrast: the law is valid (the first "until"), yet has been replaced by Jesus (the second "until"). But as Hagner says (*Matthew 1 – 13*, 107), it is better to see the two clauses as synonymous.

14. Schweizer, *Matthew*, 108; Robert Banks, *Jesus and the Law in the Synoptic Tradition* (SNTSMS 28; Cambridge: Cambridge Univ. Press, 1975), 222 – 23.

15. R. M. Johnston, "The Least of the Commandments: Deuteronomy 22:6 – 7 in Rabbinic Judaism and Early Christianity," *AUSS* 20 (1982): 205 – 15, says this refers especially to the "law of the bird's nest" in Deut 22, called the "least" of the laws in *y. Qidd.* 1:61b and *Dt. Rab.* 6:2.

16. Note the generic use of τοὺς ἀνθρώπους for "people." This is also the case for vv. 13, 16.

17. Blomberg, *Matthew*, 105, who says the present kingdom, not the final kingdom, is in view.

18. The "scribes" were originally official recorders of law and became an important group in Judaism, to some extent even supplanting the priests and Levites as interpreters of Torah (2 Chr 34:13; Ezra 7:12). They were the lawyers (legal experts in the Torah) of their day as well as the major teachers of Torah. In Jesus' day they banded together with the Pharisees (many *were* Pharisees) to stress the oral traditions for keeping the Torah. For extensive discussion, see David E. Orton, *The Understanding Scribe: Matthew and the Apocalyptic Ideal* (JSNTSup 25; Sheffield: JSOT Press, 1989), 39 – 133. He argues that Matthew gives a positive portrait overall on the scribes.

The problem is inherent in all legalistic movements: certain patterns are identified with holiness, but they are too easily external (acted out) rather than internal (truly believed and lived). The result is hypocrisy (see Matt 23). Therefore, a mere righteousness by fiat is insufficient. The lifestyle God demands is of the heart, lived out in daily actions.

5:20 ... you will never enter the kingdom of heaven (οὐ μὴ εἰσέλθητε εἰς τὴν βασιλείαν τῶν οὐρανῶν). The image of "entering the kingdom" as equivalent to both conversion and eternal life is found also in 7:21; 18:3, 8 – 9; 19:17, 23, 24; 23:14. As many have said, the present verse and v. 16 provide the basic theme for the whole Sermon.

Theology in Application

This seminal text is at the heart of the modern debate about the place of the OT in the NT. But it also has important ramifications for ethical systems today. How do we preach and teach the OT? How do we use it in our ethics? What was the actual relation of Jesus to the OT? Why is it important for the average believer to know that Jesus doesn't destroy the law, but fulfills it?

1. Jesus Fulfilled the OT in His Life and Teaching

All of the fulfillment passages in Matthew shows that the early church believed that Jesus fulfilled not just the direct prophecies but also the experiences of Israel such as the exodus from Egypt and the exile (2:15, 18). So the early church believed that the whole OT pointed to Jesus. Moreover, Jesus says here that his teaching sums up the meaning of the law and the prophets, meaning both that he is the official interpreter of Torah and that in his teaching the law is lifted to a higher plane, i.e., a deeper ethical standard. When the smallest part of the law is relevant until the end of time, that does not mean the sacrificial system will be necessary but that it is caught up in the once-for-all sacrifice of Jesus (see Heb 8 – 10).

Moreover, it is not just part of the law that is embodied in Jesus (e.g., in the separation of the moral from the ceremonial law in some Reformed theology) but the whole law that is fulfilled. Jesus uses the Ten Commandments as his examples in vv. 21 – 48. In v. 20 Jesus presents a deeper level of righteousness now mandated by the kingdom that has come. Jesus is indeed "the culmination of the law" (Rom 10:4); the law has not ceased but rather has had its true essence explicated in Jesus' life and teaching. Moreover, it is critical for believers today to realize that the OT and its ethics have not been "destroyed" or removed. The OT is not just types of Christ but contains a theology that is just as relevant today as it was two thousand years ago. We read it not as inferior or quasi-canon but as a Word of God for us today (see below).

2. The OT Is Still Part of the Canon and Should Be Preached Directly

There have been many attempts throughout history to negate the value of the OT for the church. Marcion removed everything Jewish from the NT in his canon. Bultmann said that the OT was merely the presupposition of the NT and should not be a part of a biblical theology. Many preachers in the popular church movement have used the OT only as "types of Christ" because of a misapplication of this passage and others. Yet it is clear that the OT is an essential part of the whole canon (in 2 Tim 3:16 it is the OT that Paul refers to as "God-breathed" Scripture) and should be preached as such. For instance, a message on the tabernacle should not consist entirely of an imaginative application of every splinter as a type of Christ but rather a study of themes such as the holiness of God or our complete dependence on and worship of God. A great message on the excuses we have for not serving God can come from Moses' example in Exod 3:11 – 4:17, and a terrific sermon on trials can be found in Isa 40:27 – 31. In other words, we need expository messages as much from Genesis or Ezekiel as we do from Matthew!

3. The Disciple Must Live Rightly with High Ethical Standards

One may well ask, "What problem is Jesus addressing in this passage? If the Pharisees were experts in keeping the law, yet failed, what is Jesus requiring of me?" The answer to this sums up the Sermon on the Mount itself. It is not enough to claim to be a follower of Christ; one must live like it. Works do not save us, but they are the necessary result of being saved. Without works/fruit there is no evidence that one is a believer at all (see below at 7:21 – 23).

Yet it works both ways. The Pharisees had external works but no heart of faith; that was their problem. Many so-called Christians claim faith but have no works (cf. Jas 2:14 – 26). The true disciple has a heart for Christ and the deeds that flow out of that heart attitude. This "greater righteousness" (v. 20) will be explicated in what follows in this chapter.

CHAPTER 14

Matthew 5:21 – 26

Introduction to Matthew 5:21 – 48

The six antitheses (on murder, adultery, divorce, oaths, retaliation, love of neighbor) function in two ways: they exemplify the "better righteousness" Jesus has just demanded, and they further explain how Jesus has fulfilled/deepened the law in the new ethics of the kingdom (introduced in 5:17 – 20). There is a deliberate contrast between the literal, legalistic teaching of the Pharisees and the high standards demanded here. The form is rabbinic: "You have heard that it was said" commonly introduced rabbinic discussion of a point of law,[1] but the second half ("but I am telling you") goes beyond Jewish teachers to give Jesus' authoritative interpretation of the true meaning of the commands.[2] It means in effect, "This is how you were taught, but I will now tell you what it really means."

It is common to discuss these in terms of authentic Jesus material vs. Matthean redaction[3] or of those sayings that develop the meaning of the command vs. those that contravene them.[4] We will consider these in a holistic manner, arguing that in each case Jesus is deepening the law and that even in those cases where he goes counter to the law, his purpose is not to contravene but to provide the true messianic understanding of the commands. Jesus is not contravening the law in essence but rather a shallow, external understanding of it. Davies and Allison calls this "not contradiction but transcendence," meaning that Jesus' "ideas surpass those of the Torah without contradicting the Torah."[5]

1. For examples see David Daube, *The New Testament and Rabbinic Judaism* (London: Univ. of London Press, 1956), 55 – 62.

2. Douglas J. Moo, "Law," *DJG*, 455, says they are not quite "antitheses" and points out the different nuances: "(1) 'you have heard, but I (in contrast to that) say to you'; (2) 'you have heard, but I (in addition to that) say to you'; (3) 'you have heard, and I (in agreement with that) say to you.'" On the whole, these are not contrasts but deepening of the legal ordinances.

3. For instance, Guelich, *Sermon on the Mount*, 265 – 71, and Strecker, *Sermon on the Mount*, 63 – 64, take antitheses 1, 2, 4 as authentic (from Q) and antitheses 3, 5, 6 as Matthean built along the lines of the others. However, there is no need to work so rigidly with the material, and every reason to see all six as part of the tradition going back to Jesus; cf. Carson, "Matthew," 148; Hagner, *Matthew 1 – 13*, 113; Keener, *Matthew*, 180 – 81.

4. Meier, *Law and History*, 135, says nos. 1, 2, 6 radicalize but do not revoke them while nos. 3, 4, 5 revoke at least the letter of the law. It is common for those who separate tradition from redaction to say that the traditional ones (1, 2, 4) deepen the law while the redactional ones (3, 5, 6) revoke the law.

5. Davies and Allison, *Matthew*, 1:507 – 8.

The six are broken in half with the lengthy formula, "You have heard that it was said to people long ago." Thus there are two triads here, probably centering on three injunctions mainly from Deuteronomy followed by three mainly from Leviticus.[6] The first two stem from the sixth and seventh commandments, while the last four are various ethical issues Jesus uses to demonstrate his messianic interpretation of Torah and to develop an ethical set of injunctions (in a sense, the "Torah of the Messiah") that will provide the ethics for the new covenant community. Moreover, the first two function at the level of thought life and the last four at the level of one's actions.

France denotes four ways of seeing these examples of "going beyond" the law and the tradition of the Pharisees:[7] (1) an "inward" concern with motive vs. an "outward" concern for a literal observance of regulations; (2) moving behind the rule itself to ascertain the greater principles for conduct as God's people; (3) centering not on the negative aspect of avoiding sin but on the positive purpose for "discovering and following what is really the will of God"; (4) substituting for what can be completely achieved (a distinct set of rules) a "totally open-ended ideal" of perfection (v. 48), which will not be ultimately achievable in this life.

Literary Context

In addition to being examples of the "better righteousness" Jesus demands of his followers, these six antitheses also provide examples of the way Jesus fulfills the Scriptures by deepening the ethical requirements. The key is that each shows the inner attitude behind the external act, thereby demonstrating the shallowness of pharisaic external requirements. Behind murder lies anger, so Jesus centers on the antidote to anger, namely, reconciliation.

II. The Kingdom Message Goes Out (4:12 – 7:29)
- **B. First Discourse: The Sermon on the Mount (5:1 – 7:29)**
  - **3. The Relationship of the Law to the New Covenant in Jesus (5:17 – 48)**
    - a. Jesus and the Law — Continuity (5:17 – 20)
    - **b. Examples — Six Antitheses on the New Righteousness (5:21 – 48)**
      - ➦ **(1) Murder = Anger (5:21 – 26)**
      - (2) Adultery = Lust (5:27 – 30)

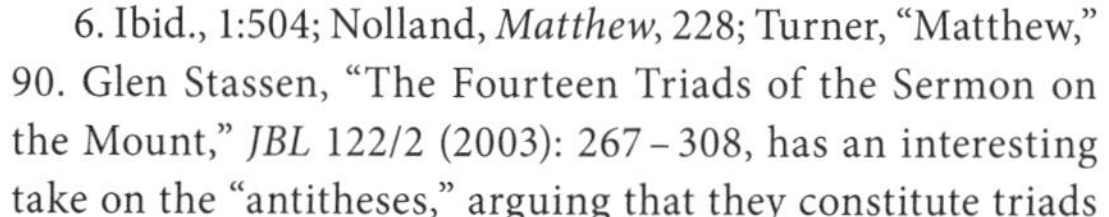
6. Ibid., 1:504; Nolland, *Matthew*, 228; Turner, "Matthew," 90. Glen Stassen, "The Fourteen Triads of the Sermon on the Mount," *JBL* 122/2 (2003): 267 – 308, has an interesting take on the "antitheses," arguing that they constitute triads instead of antitheses. He asserts that the illustrations are not illustrations, but rather the primary imperatives — a call to active peacemaking.

7. France, *Gospel of Matthew*, 197.

Main Idea

Jesus begins with murder as the most egregious of the sins, taking the life of another human being. The point is that anger is murder in the heart and so must be confronted as the basis of most murders. Jesus' purpose is to show that God's demands are deeper than the usual shallow understanding; murder in the heart is just as serious as murder in action.

Translation

Matthew 5:21-26

21a	Antithesis #1	*[1] "You have heard that it was said to people long ago:*
b		*'You shall not murder, and*
		whoever murders will be subject to judgment.'
		(Exod 20:13; Deut 5:17)
22a		*But I am telling you that everyone . . . faces judgment.*
		who is angry
		with his brother or sister
b		*Whoever calls his brother or sister 'raka' faces the Sanhedrin,*
c		*and whoever calls anyone "fool" faces fiery Gehenna.*
23a	Illustration #1	*Therefore,*
		if you are offering your gift at the altar and
b		*then remember that your brother or sister has something against you,*
24a	Exhortation	*leave your gift there at the altar.*
b		*First of all go to your brother or sister and be reconciled.*
c		*Only then can you go and offer your gift.*
25a	Illustration #2	*Make peace with your adversary quickly*
b		*while you are with him on the way to court,*
c	Basis #1 for 25a	*(i) lest your adversary hand you over to the judge, and*
d	Basis #2 for 25a	*(ii) the judge to the court official, and*
e	Basis #3 for 25a	*(iii) then you are thrown into prison.*
26a	Result of 26e	*I tell you the truth, you will never leave there*
b		*until you have paid the last penny."*

Structure and Literary Form

The form is typical. There is the antithesis proper, involving anger and contempt toward others (vv. 21 – 22). It is followed by two illustrations (some call them parables), one involving a "brother" to whom you need to be reconciled, and a second involving an "adversary" to whom you must be reconciled.[8] Throughout Jesus uses intensification, first in the name-calling of v. 22 and then in the two illustrations, which move from an internal situation in the community to an external situation involving a judicial sentence.

Exegetical Outline

➡ **I. The Antithesis (5:21 – 22)**

A. The tradition — murder (v. 21)

B. Jesus mandate — no anger (v. 22)

1. Anger leads to judgment (v. 22a)
2. Contempt leads to greater judgment (v. 22b)

II. Internal Illustration — Reconciliation with the Brother (5:23 – 24)

A. Setting — at the altar, realizing someone is angry (v. 23)

B. Action — reconciliation before worship (v. 24)

III. External Illustration — Reconciliation with an Adversary (5:25 – 26)

A. Setting — on the way to court (v. 25a)

B. Action — reconcile while you can (v. 25a)

1. Danger 1 — taken to the judge, then the officer, then the prison (v. 25b)
2. Danger 2 — pay the last penny (v. 26)

Explanation of the Text

5:21 You have heard that it was said to people long ago, "You shall not murder, and whoever murders will be subject to judgment" (Ἠκούσατε ὅτι ἐρρέθη τοῖς ἀρχαίοις, Οὐ φονεύσεις· ὃς δ᾽ ἂν φονεύσῃ, ἔνοχος ἔσται τῇ κρίσει). The "people long ago" could be the people of Israel (most interpreters) or the people in the synagogues who heard the Torah expounded. Either way, it means the traditional understanding of the sixth commandment (Exod 20:13; Deut 5:17), with the Hebraic use of the future "You shall not murder" (οὐ φονεύσεις) instead of the imperative for a divine command for all time (see also vv. 27, 33, 43). The penalty was not in the Torah but part of normal judicial process involving the local court that proclaimed judgment (ἔνοχος is a legal term, "subject to"). In the Jewish system a local court of twenty-three members adjudicated serious crimes like murder.

5:22 But I am telling you that everyone who is angry with his brother or sister faces judgment. Whoever calls his brother or sister "raka" faces the Sanhedrin, and whoever calls anyone "fool" faces fiery Gehenna (ἐγὼ δὲ λέγω ὑμῖν ὅτι πᾶς ὁ

8. This antithesis is unique to Matthew and stems from his own material (M). The only parallel is vv. 25 – 26 = Luke 12:57 – 59 (Q material). Most critical scholars believe Matthew has composed vv. 21 – 26 from his tradition, but the antithesis form is rabbinic (see Daube, *New Testament*, 55 – 56), and the style here, though certainly extreme, makes great sense (criterion of plausibility). This would explain why the crowds are so amazed at the authority of his teaching (7:28 – 29) and fits the historical Jesus very well.

ὀργιζόμενος τῷ ἀδελφῷ αὐτοῦ ἔνοχος ἔσται τῇ κρίσει· ὃς δ' ἂν εἴπῃ τῷ ἀδελφῷ αὐτοῦ, Ῥακά, ἔνοχος ἔσται τῷ συνεδρίῳ· ὃς δ' ἂν εἴπῃ, Μωρέ, ἔνοχος ἔσται εἰς τὴν γέενναν τοῦ πυρός). Jesus goes deeper than murder to the cause of murder, anger. Anger is murder in the mind (1 John 3:15), so Jesus shows that a similar fate awaits the angry person as awaits the murderer. Although "brother/sister" (ἀδελφός) seems to center mainly on the community of saints, Jesus certainly intends it more widely. The presence of ἀδελφός probably is meant to lead into the first illustration (the community), with the second (the secular adversary) also intended here.

The progression follows the process initiated in v. 21, the court system. Here it moves from the local court to the supreme court of the land, the Sanhedrin,[9] to the ultimate court, the judgment seat of God. Yet there is not a similar progression in the sin committed. The Aramaic loanword (ῥακά) was used to insult a person, roughly equivalent to "idiot" or "empty-headed fool" (*b. Ber.* 22a, 32a). "Fool" (μωρέ) was the Greek equivalent, also used as an insult, meaning "fool," though Jewish readers might think of the Hebrew *moreh*, referring to apostasy or wickedness. The two terms were fairly equivalent in thrust, referring to contempt for another (a type of anger), and so there is no escalation of the sin committed.

Jesus' point is that each of the three lead a person to judgment both on the earthly and the heavenly planes. Moreover, it is clear here that name-calling is at the core of showing angry contempt. This was even more true in ancient Judaism, where the name bespoke the essence of what a person was (e.g., "Jesus" = "Yahweh saves," 1:21).[10] "Gehenna" is a metaphor for hellfire, used seven times by Matthew, which refers to the Hinnon Valley, where in ancient times human sacrifices were offered to the pagan god Molech (2 Kgs 23:10) and where in Jesus' day garbage was burned day and night, making it a perfect metaphor for eternal fiery judgment.

5:23 Therefore, if you are offering your gift at the altar (ἐὰν οὖν προσφέρῃς τὸ δῶρόν σου ἐπὶ τὸ θυσιαστήριον). Jesus is recreating a serious scenario involving the sacrificial system, with the present tense "are offering" (προσφέρῃς) picturing the process of taking the sacrifice to the altar of the temple. We must remember that Jesus' disciples were from Galilee and rarely got to Jerusalem, so this only happened once or twice a year and was an important event (the "altar" is the sacrificial altar in the inner court of the temple). Also, there were probably long lines waiting, so the picture is of one who had been there some time and was finally able to perform his solemn duty.

5:23 ... and then remember that your brother or sister has something against you (κἀκεῖ μνησθῇς ὅτι ὁ ἀδελφός σου ἔχει τι κατὰ σοῦ). Jesus deliberately says it is the *other* person who is angry; you may be innocent![11] Still, the presence of anger in the church (note "brother/sister" [ἀδελφός]) is

9. While συνέδριον could refer to the local "council" (as in 10:17), it almost certainly refers to the supreme council of the land in Jerusalem (as in 26:59). It originated from the priestly aristocracy, which adjudicated in the days of Nehemiah (Neh 2:16; 5:7). In the time of Jesus it had seventy-one members with the high priest as head and the "chief priests" (the priestly nobility) as the most influential group, but important members were also drawn from the teachers of law (many of whom were Pharisees) and the elders (lay aristocracy). They dealt with the affairs of Judea (technically, Galilee and Perea were separate districts), as the Romans did not want to deal with local situations.

10. Hagner, *Matthew 1–13*, 116.

11. However, some (Hill, *Matthew*, 122; Blomberg, *Matthew*, 108) believe it is a "just claim." Plummer, *Matthew*, 79, goes so far as to say the person at the altar "has enmity in his heart," clearly an exaggeration. But as Guelich, *Sermon on the Mount*, 190, says, the question of fault is ambiguous and it is clearly the brother who holds the grudge.

a cancer that is so destructive that reconciliation is of uppermost importance, so much so that you must "leave your gift ... at the altar" and go to the person.

5:24 ... leave your gift there at the altar. First of all go to your brother or sister and be reconciled. Only then can you go and offer your gift (ἄφες ἐκεῖ τὸ δῶρόν σου ἔμπροσθεν τοῦ θυσιαστηρίου καὶ ὕπαγε πρῶτον διαλλάγηθι τῷ ἀδελφῷ σου, καὶ τότε ἐλθὼν πρόσφερε τὸ δῶρόν σου). Reconciliation in the kingdom community is so important that it has priority over worship. The imperative for "go" is present tense ("leave" and "be reconciled" are aorist), stressing the ongoing movement of the one who goes and seeks reconciliation. It is the core of the passage. The initiative is with the one who learns of the animosity, whether guilty or innocent. France points out that the disciples from Galilee would have to travel eighty miles back from Jerusalem to reconcile with the offended person, so this is deliberate exaggeration for effect.[12]

The church cannot allow animosity to take hold or it is doomed. Such was the situation at Philippi when Paul asked the leaders to get involved in the conflict between Euodias and Syntyche, which was splitting the church at Philippi (Phil 4:2 – 3). Jesus' point is that as long as there is sin in the church between members, worship is compromised. This is connected to Matthew's theme of forgiveness (see on 6:12, 14 – 15): to receive forgiveness from God, we must be forgiving to one another.

5:25 Make peace with your adversary quickly while you are with him on the way to court (ἴσθι εὐνοῶν τῷ ἀντιδίκῳ σου ταχὺ ἕως ὅτου εἶ μετ' αὐτοῦ ἐν τῇ ὁδῷ). The verb εὐνοέω (only here in the NT) means "to be well disposed/make friends with" another person, here an "adversary" (stated twice for emphasis) in a legal situation, probably a financial suit due to "pay the last penny."

5:25 ... lest your adversary hand you over to the judge, and the judge to the court official, and then you are thrown into prison (μήποτέ σε παραδῷ ὁ ἀντίδικος τῷ κριτῇ καὶ ὁ κριτὴς τῷ ὑπηρέτῃ καὶ εἰς φυλακὴν βληθήσῃ). Here the implicit reality is that you are guilty, for the sentence is clearly one of guilt. The command is to make peace with or settle matters with the person before it is too late. In fact, it is almost too late, for you are "on the way" to court with your adversary and there is little time. This brings out the urgency of reconciliation and may hint that judgment before God (v. 22) is imminent.

Luke 12:57 – 59 provides a good parallel, using this parable in a context of divine judgment. The main point is the urgency of reconciliation. The three steps of judgment are stated here for emphasis, saying you have no chance unless you make reconciliation. The court "servant" (ὑπηρέτης) is probably the same as the bailiff of Luke 12:58 (the Roman legal term), who puts the sentenced man in jail. So the process is virtually certain, and you must "sue for peace" to have any chance of going home.

5:26 I tell you the truth, you will never leave there until you have paid the last penny (ἀμὴν λέγω σοι, οὐ μὴ ἐξέλθῃς ἐκεῖθεν, ἕως ἂν ἀποδῷς τὸν ἔσχατον κοδράντην). If reconciliation does not occur, the full penalty will have to be paid. The emphasis on the emphatic future negative "never" (οὐ μή) means the full penalty is inevitable. κοδράντη is a Latin loanword ("quadrans") for one of the smallest coins in the Roman world, worth only one-fourth of an "as," which itself was one-sixteenth of a denarius. It was the second smallest coin, with the "lepton" (one-half of a

12. France, *Gospel of Matthew*, 203.

"quadrans," used in the parallel Luke 12:59) being the smallest. Think of it as the amount earned for one-sixty-fourth of a workday or = seven and a half minutes of work in an eight-hour day. The message is that you will receive the maximum penalty, so reconciliation is all the more urgent.

Theology in Application

At one level, this passage shows beyond doubt that Jesus is the transcendent interpreter of Torah, for he turns to the heart of the law, the Ten Commandments, for his first example, and it shows it must be understood in a deeper sense. At another level, Jesus establishes a key ethical standard for the kingdom people, showing that anger/hatred is tantamount to murder.

The community of the new covenant is clearly all about relationships. There can be no anger or contempt marring the life and worship of God's people, either inside (the first illustration) or outside (the second illustration) the community. Theology is not just about God and the spiritual life. Broader ethical issues are also theological because in Scripture the way we relate to others is the way we relate to God. To be angry or feel contempt for another is to disparage God's child and, therefore, God himself. We cannot separate relationships with others from our relationship with God.

1. Anger, an Insurmountable Obstacle to Community Life

Jesus absolutizes the issue of anger in the passage, introducing no exception such as righteous indignation. This does not mean that such does not exist (cf. Ps 4:4; Eph 4:26) but that Jesus wants to establish the basic principle that anger destroys community harmony. Moreover, it is not just anger but contempt and name-calling that do this, not only in the community proper but also in the home, which is the core of the community.

2. Contempt for Others, Human Pride, and God's Judgment

Self-centeredness is the core of sin, and it is total arrogance alone that can account for the human tendency to look down on others. When we look down on a small insect, they all look the same, and we do not disparage one more than another. When God looks down on us, the distance is far greater than that between us and an insect. How dare we consider ourselves better than another? We are all so inferior to God that we are equal to one another, and there is no basis for feeling superior. It is only our sinful desire to build ourselves up that enables us to feel contemptuous toward another. Our thought should be to help another in their area of weakness, knowing that we will need them to help us in our areas of weakness.

3. Maintaining Proper Relationships with the Unbeliever

This passage does not say that the "adversary" is not a believer, but the contrast with the previous two sections (where "brother" is mentioned) hints at this. It is a clear mandate throughout the NT that the believer is to maintain a good relationship with the unbeliever. This will be extended in 5:43 – 47, where Jesus says to "love your enemies" (cf. Rom 12:14 – 21), and in 19:19 and 22:39, where he says to "love your neighbor as yourself" (Lev 19:18; cf. Rom 13:9; Gal 5:14; Jas 2:8). The purpose of loving the enemy is to "heap burning coals on his head" (Rom 12:20 from Prov 25:22 = conviction) and to bring them to repentance via good works (1 Pet 2:12).

CHAPTER 15

Matthew 5:27 – 30

Literary Context

This second example is also taken from the Ten Commandments (the seventh, Exod 20:14; Deut 5:18) and further demonstrates Jesus' authoritative interpretation of Torah. In both instances (anger and lust), the inner thoughts become the basis of the outer actions (murder and adultery) and so constitute sin. At the same time, Jesus is also developing the ethical rules for the kingdom community. Each of the six examples centers on how God's people are to live among themselves as well as in a hostile world. In this case lust is at the core of adultery, which destroys God's purpose in marriage and displaces the life of the community.

II. The Kingdom Message Goes Out (4:12 – 7:29)
  B. First Discourse: The Sermon on the Mount (5:1 – 7:29)
    3. The Relationship of the Law to the New Covenant in Jesus (5:17 – 48)
      b. Examples — Six Antitheses on the New Righteousness (5:21 – 48)
        (1) Murder = Anger (5:21 – 26)
➦   **(2) Adultery = Lust (5:27 – 30)**
        (3) Divorce/Remarriage = Adultery (5:31 – 32)

Main Idea

There are two sections of this pericope. The first (vv. 27 – 28) shows that the person who lusts after another person sexually has already committed adultery in the heart and so has broken the seventh commandment. The second (vv. 29 – 30) states that all such sins must be forcibly cast out of our lives, for they will lead us to final judgment.

Translation

Matthew 5:27-30

27a	Antithesis #2	[2] "You have heard that it was said,
b		'You shall not commit adultery.' (Exod 20:14; Deut 5:18)
28a		But I am telling you that everyone who looks on a woman . . . has already committed adultery with her in his heart in order to lust after her.
29a	Solution #1 (A)	(i) Now if your right eye causes you to fall away from God,
b		gouge it out and throw it from you,
c	Basis for 29b (B)	for it is better that one of your body parts perish than that your whole body be thrown into Gehenna.
30a	Solution #2 (A)	(ii) And if your right hand causes you to fall away from God,
b		cut it off and throw it away from you,
c	Basis for 30b (B)	for it is better that one of your body parts perish than that your whole body be thrown into Gehenna."

Structure and Literary Form

The antithesis itself is followed by two hyperbolic statements that have contributed to the feeling that the Sermon transcends all normal paraenesis and makes astounding demands of all followers.[1] These two statements are formally parallel and are meant to be taken together rather than separately. They are also meant to be understood at the level of metaphor rather than of literal action.

Exegetical Outline

- **I. The Antithesis (5:27 – 28)**
  - A. The tradition — adultery (v. 27)
  - B. Jesus' mandate — no lust (v. 28)
- **II. The Solution — Forcibly Cast It Out (5:29 – 30)**
  - A. The actions needed
    1. Gouge out the eye (v. 29a)
    2. Cut off the hand (v. 30)
  - B. Reason — better to lose a little than to lose everything (vv. 29b, 30b)

1. Only vv. 28 – 29 have parallels elsewhere, repeated again in 18:8 – 9 and found in Mark 9:43, 45, 47. I believe it refers to individual sin in one's life here and corporately to false teachers in 18:8 – 9. As elsewhere, it is likely that this is authentic Jesus material used by Jesus on different occasions (see Hagner, *Matthew 1 – 13*, 119).

Explanation of the Text

5:27 You have heard that it was said, "You shall not commit adultery" (Ἠκούσατε ὅτι ἐρρέθη, Οὐ μοιχεύσεις). Adultery to the Jews meant sexual relations outside marriage, primarily by a married person. Jesus generalizes it to refer to all who have sexual relations outside marriage. In Judaism the sexual side was not stressed as much as the act of taking another man's wife, namely, theft.[2] Jesus stresses the moral side.

5:28 But I am telling you that everyone who looks on a woman in order to lust[3] after her has already committed adultery with her in his heart (ἐγὼ δὲ λέγω ὑμῖν ὅτι πᾶς ὁ βλέπων γυναῖκα πρὸς τὸ ἐπιθυμῆσαι αὐτὴν ἤδη ἐμοίχευσεν αὐτὴν ἐν τῇ καρδίᾳ αὐτοῦ). Jewish writing also equated lust with adultery in the heart, first in the tenth commandment against "coveting your neighbor's wife" (as well as house, servant, ox, donkey, or any possession, Exod 20:17; Deut 5:21) and then in other teaching (Job 31:1, 9; Sir 9:8; *Pss. Sol.* 4:4 – 6; *T. Iss.* 7:2). Jesus stresses that the purpose ("in order to" [πρὸς τό]) is to lust after her[4] and that the sin occurs "in the heart."

In our day this can occur any number of ways, with one of the more dangerous being internet pornography. In any sense, the present tense "looks" (βλέπων) indicates a studied looking with sexual intent. The culminative aorist "has committed adultery" (ἐμοίχευσεν) stresses the results, adultery of the heart.[5]

5:29 Now if your right eye causes you to fall away from God, gouge it out and throw it from you (εἰ δὲ ὁ ὀφθαλμός σου ὁ δεξιὸς σκανδαλίζει σε, ἔξελε αὐτὸν καὶ βάλε ἀπὸ σοῦ). As in vv. 21 – 26, Jesus offers two illustrations to demonstrate his point, but here the two parallel each other exactly and together tell how to avoid the sin. Jesus' choice of the eye and the hand makes great sense, for they are the primary elements in moving from lust (the eye) to adultery (the hand).[6] The "right" side was seen in antiquity as the more powerful side.

The idea of gouging out and cutting off, needless to say, demands a violent, decisive measure for removing the source of the temptation. The reason is seen in "to fall away" (σκανδαλίζει), a strong term that does not simply indicate temptation to general sin but that which leads one virtually into apostasy.[7] This would be moral apostasy or very serious sin.

5:29 . . . for it is better that one of your body parts perish than that your whole body be thrown into

2. Hill, *Matthew*, 123; Carson, "Matthew," 151.

3. The aorist "to lust" (ἐπιθυμῆσαι) after the present "looks" (βλέπων) places the looking in the foreground and the lusting in the background, cf. Porter, *Idioms*, 23 – 25.

4. It is generally agreed that there are two ways of understanding "her" (αὐτήν) here: either "lust after her" (αὐτήν as the object) or "get her to lust after him" (αὐτήν as the subject). Most agree that the former is more likely in the context. In Jewish society this teaching was always directed at a man.

5. "Heart" (καρδία) has often been misunderstood as the emotions, but in reality it denotes the whole inner person, especially the mind.

6. However, the hand plays a major role in lust as well through masturbation, cf. W. Deming, "Mark 9:42 – 10:2; Matthew 5:27 – 32 and B. Nid, 13b: A First-Century Discussion of Male Sexuality," *NTS* 36 (1990): 130 – 41. Carson, "Matthew," calls the right hand a euphemism for the sexual organ.

7. H. Giesen, "σκανδαλίζω," *EDNT*, 3:248, defines this as to "cause someone to fall away from (or reject) faith." However, Herbhert W. Basser, "The Meaning of '*Shtuth*', Gen. R. 11 in Reference to Matt 5.29 – 30 and 18.8 – 9," *NTS* 31 (1985): 148 – 51, argues this should be translated "offends you" due to the rabbinic discussion. However, its use in Matthew fits better the idea of "falling away." "Offends" fits the metaphor but not the situation in Jesus' day.

Gehenna (συμφέρει γάρ σοι ἵνα ἀπόληται ἓν τῶν μελῶν σου καὶ μὴ ὅλον τὸ σῶμά σου βληθῇ εἰς γέενναν). The seriousness of the sin is made even more so by the reference to "Gehenna" (γέεννα, see on v. 22), which implies the final judgment and eternal torment. Jesus wants to make certain that the disciples realize the importance of the issue. You do not take such lightly because it is far better to suffer in losing your most important appendage than to lose everything at the final judgment ("be thrown" [βληθῇ] is a divine passive pointing to God at the great white throne, Rev 20:11 – 15). It is all too common today for "Christians" to treat sexual lust, even sexual sin, lightly, and this again is an important message regarding how important the issues are and how strong the measures must be to defeat these terrible urges.

5:30 And if your right hand causes you to fall away from God, cut it off and throw it away from you, for it is better that one of your body parts perish than that your whole body be thrown into Gehenna (καὶ εἰ ἡ δεξιά σου χεὶρ σκανδαλίζει σε, ἔκκοψον αὐτὴν καὶ βάλε ἀπὸ σοῦ· συμφέρει γάρ σοι ἵνα ἀπόληται ἓν τῶν μελῶν σου καὶ μὴ ὅλον τὸ σῶμά σου εἰς γέενναν ἀπέλθῃ). This repeats the previous but centers on the hand that puts into action what the eye has stimulated. Again, Jesus is powerful in his imagery, for it too leads one to "fall away" from God, and the final result is the fires of Gehenna. The two parallel metaphors mean simply that one must violently throw away everything that causes the lust, lest their spiritual life and ultimately their eternal destiny be destroyed in the process

Theology in Application

In light of the number of Christian leaders and laypeople whose ministries are being destroyed by sexual sin of late, this is truly one of the critical passages to be preached and discussed. It has been estimated that better than one-half of men in the average congregation are caught up in internet pornography, and lust has become a way of life in our culture, caused by the dress codes of our day as well as the soft-porn movies that proliferate. Jesus' call for extreme measures must be heeded before it is too late. Adults as well as children should purchase the software to lock themselves out of X-rated sites, and accountability groups need to be set up in every church. All too many males (as well as many females) should be admitting, "I am a sexoholic," and should be getting help. This issue has become a pandemic, and every church and Christian group should be seeking solutions even more vigorously than in the past.

CHAPTER 16

Matthew 5:31 – 32

Literary Context

Jesus now departs from the thought life and turns to ethical actions; he also departs from the Decalogue and turns to general ethics. Yet this example is connected to the previous example via the issue of adultery. The commandment in view occurs in Deut 24:1 – 4, a passage that was debated among Jews. Moreover, Jesus now turns from thought (the first two antitheses) to action (the last four) to illustrate the "better righteousness" (v. 20) he demands from his followers.

II. The Kingdom Message Goes Out (4:12 – 7:29)
- **B. First Discourse: The Sermon on the Mount (5:1 – 7:29)**
  - **3. The Relationship of the Law to the New Covenant in Jesus (5:17 – 48)**
    - **b. Examples — Six Antitheses on the New Righteousness (5:21 – 48)**
      - (2) Adultery = Lust (5:27 – 30)
      - ➦ **(3) Divorce/Remarriage = Adultery (5:31 – 32)**
      - (4) Oaths Are Unnecessary (5:33 – 37)

Main Idea

Moses in the OT allowed divorce and remarriage, but Jesus sets a much higher standard, saying that divorce (remarriage implied) constitutes adultery. The basis of his assertion will be explained in 19:3 – 9, but the basic fact is stated here: in the eyes of God, marriage is a lifelong union and must not be broken. The exception clause is Jesus' interpretation of "something indecent" in Deut 24:1 and his interaction with the Jewish debate (see below).

Translation

Matthew 5:31-32

31a	Antithesis #3	*[3] "It was said,*
b		*'Whoever divorces his wife must give her official divorce papers.'* (Deut 24:1)
32a		*But I am telling you that anyone who divorces his wife . . . causes her to commit adultery*
b		*except by report of sexual immorality,*
c		*and whoever marries the divorced woman commits adultery."*

Structure and Literary Form

This is the shortest of the six, probably because Matthew knew he would develop it further in ch. 19. So it contains only the basic antithesis with no illustrative material.[1]

Exegetical Outline

- **I. Tradition: Divorce Needs a Certificate (5:31)**
- **II. Mandate: Divorce Causes Adultery (5:32)**
  - A. Divorce causes the wife to commit adultery
  - B. Divorce causes the one who marries the wife to commit adultery
  - C. Exception: Adultery

Explanation of the Text

5:31 It was said, "Whoever divorces his wife must give her official divorce papers" (Ἐρρέθη δέ, Ὃς ἂν ἀπολύσῃ τὴν γυναῖκα αὐτοῦ, δότω αὐτῇ ἀποστάσιον). This quotes Deut 24:1, the basic OT passage on divorce, and has two primary thrusts: the reason for legal divorce ("something indecent") and the demand for written papers that explain the reason and allow the spouse freedom to remarry. So the writ of divorce (see 1:19 for Joseph intending to give such to Mary) relinquished the husband's legal claim on the wife and gave her freedom to remarry. By Jewish law this

1. This passage is close to 19:7, 9, and 5:32 stems from the triple tradition (= Mark 10:11; Luke 16:18), but v. 31 parallels only 19:7. Still, there is no valid reason why this could not go back to Jesus, once the whole basis of tradition criticism is reworked as it is today (see Gerd Theissen and Annette Merz, *The Historical Jesus: A Comprehensive Guide* [Minneapolis, Fortress, 1997] for an excellent presentation of the new perspective).

could only be done by the husband, but the rabbis had developed ways an unhappy wife could apply pressure on the husband to grant her freedom.[2]

5:32 But I am telling you that anyone who divorces his wife (ἐγὼ δὲ λέγω ὑμῖν ὅτι πᾶς ὁ ἀπολύων τὴν γυναῖκα αὐτοῦ). The Jewish debate over Deut 24:1 ("indecency") centered on what could constitute grounds for divorce. The school of Shammai interpreted the *ʿerwat dābār* of Deut 24:1 (lit., "something that brings shame") conservatively, saying only sexual immorality and immodesty (e.g., going outside with hair unfastened) was valid. The school of Hillel broadened it all the way, saying any cause was sufficient, even burnt food or a more attractive woman.[3] Qumran did not allow divorce for any reason whatsoever (11QTemple 57:17 – 19).[4]

Jesus transcends the Jewish discussion by saying that divorce is not God's will and therefore that remarriage, with or without a certificate, constitutes adultery in God's eyes. Moreover, since the whole purpose of divorce in the ancient world (both Jews and Gentiles) was to permit remarriage, divorce here allows remarriage on the part of the innocent party.

5:32 ... except by report of sexual immorality, causes her to commit adultery, and whoever marries the divorced woman commits adultery (παρεκτὸς λόγου πορνείας ποιεῖ αὐτὴν μοιχευθῆναι, καὶ ὃς ἐὰν ἀπολελυμένην γαμήσῃ μοιχᾶται). The main question is the exception clause ("except by report of sexual immorality" [παρεκτὸς λόγου πορνείας]), which is close to Shammai in saying divorce and remarriage are allowed only for sexual immorality (though see under "Theology in Application" below). We must look at the two main terms closely.

There is general agreement that "adultery" (μοιχεία) always means adulterous affairs while married, but "sexual immorality" (πορνεία) is debated. It is a broad term meaning sexual immorality of any type, but a growing number have argued that it does not mean "adultery" here and that if Matthew had intended such he would have used μοιχεία. They contend that the term here refers to incestouous or illicit marriages along kinship lines, forbidden in Lev 18:6 – 18 but allowed in Gentile circles.[5] Other suggestions have been given,[6] but the problem is not in these possibilities but in restricting the term to only one of them. Again, πορνεία is broad and can fit most of them; it refers to sexual immorality in general.[7] In other words, Jesus is saying that in God's eyes marriage is a lifelong covenant and should not be sundered, but when sexual immorality of one kind or another occurs, this breaks the bond in God's eyes, and the innocent party can remarry.

2. See Guelich, *Sermon on the Mount*, 198.

3. See Meier, *Law and History*, 143; on the Jewish background in general, see David Instone-Brewer, *Divorce and Remarriage in the Bible: The Social and Literary Context* (Grand Rapids: Eerdmans, 2002).

4. See James R. Mueller, "The Temple Scroll and the Gospel Divorce Texts," *RevQ* 10 (1980): 247 – 56.

5. H. Baltensweiler, *Die Ehe im Neuen Testament* (Zurich: Zwingli, 1967), 93 (cf. 88 – 100); Meier, *Law and History*, 147 – 50; Joseph Fitzmyer, "The Matthean Divorce-Texts and Some New Palestinian Evidence," *TS* 37 (1976): 208 – 11 (cf. 197 – 226); Guelich, *Sermon on the Mount*, 204 – 9; Senior, *Matthew*, 78 – 79. Against this view see the excursus in Keener, *Matthew*, 467 – 69.

6. We can only list them: the Jewish engagement period, premarital unfaithfulness, polygamy, marriage to near kin, mixed marriage between a believer and an unbeliever. All have been suggested as the meaning of the exception clause here, but none give valid reasons for limiting its meaning to only a single option. In other words, they are all correct in part but too narrow, as they are all included in "sexual immorality" (πορνεία).

7. See David Janzen, "The Meaning of *Porneia* in Matthew 5:32 and 19:9: An Approach from the Study of Ancient Near Eastern Culture," *JSNT* 80 (2000): 66 – 80.

Theology in Application

Jesus now shows more deeply how relationships are to function in the kingdom age by addressing the deepest relationship of all, marriage. It is clear that he again has gone deeper than Jewish understandings by making marriage lifelong and restricting divorce even further than Shammai. While the exception clause is similar to Shammai, they allowed remarriage in a far broader set of circumstances (so Carson).

Yet Jesus is not providing the only exception, for Paul names at least one more (desertion by an unbelieving spouse, 1 Cor 7:15 – 16) and possibly two (divorce before one is a believer, 1 Cor 6:9 – 11). Moreover, the present tense "commits adultery" (μοιχᾶται) in no way means the couple will live in perpetual adultery.[8] It is not the unpardonable sin. It means that the present act and consummation of the remarriage is adulterous, and the couple should admit that and begin then to live by God's standards.[9]

8. See C. D. Osburn, "The Present Indicative of Matthew 19:9," *ResQ* 24 (1981): 193 – 203, who takes it as a gnomic present relating a general truth.

9. See Blomberg, *Matthew*, 111, as well as his "Marriage, Divorce, Remarriage and Celibacy: An Exegesis of Matt 19:3 – 12," *TJ* 11 n.s. (1990): 161 – 96.

CHAPTER 17

Matthew 5:33 – 37

Literary Context

The second half of the examples begins as Jesus moves from relationships to an issue of personal integrity. Here the "better righteousness" is developed in a new direction, namely, the truthfulness of one's character. The Jewish leaders had developed an incredible complexity of rules by which one could support the veracity of a statement by taking an oath (see below), but Jesus is saying that God's children don't need such external techniques but should stand on their own honesty and forthrightness.[1]

II. The Kingdom Message Goes Out (4:12 – 7:29)
- **B. First Discourse: The Sermon on the Mount (5:1 – 7:29)**
  - **3. The Relationship of the Law to the New Covenant in Jesus (5:17 – 48)**
    - **b. Examples — Six Antitheses on the New Righteousness (5:21 – 48)**
      - (3) Divorce/Remarriage = Adultery (5:31 – 32)
      - ➦ **(4) Oaths Are Unnecessary (5:33 – 37)**
      - (5) Retaliation Is Wrong (5:38 – 42)

Main Idea

The OT allows oaths for anchoring the truth value of a statement, but the Jewish people had taken this to incredible lengths with the variety of oaths accepted or rejected and the frequency of their use. To Jesus this was an issue of honesty and integrity, for any statement of a citizen of the kingdom should be self-authenticating and should be true at the core. There is no need to use oaths to support an assertion.

1. Don B. Garlington, "Oath-Taking in the Community of the New Age (Matthew 5:33 – 37)," *TJ* 16 (1995): 139 – 70, argues for both continuity (the OT also rejects the misuse of the divine name, Exod 20:7/Deut 5:11) and discontinuity (a total ban on oath-taking) that sets apart the new messianic community of Jesus.

Translation

Matthew 5:33-37

33a	Antithesis #4	[4] "Again you have heard that it was said to people long ago,
b		'You shall not break your oaths,
		but you will keep them before God.'
		(Exod 20:7; Lev 19:12; Num 30:2; Deut 23:21-23)
34a	Exhortation	But I am telling you, do not make any oath at all.
b	Example #1	(i) Not by heaven,
c	Basis for 34b	for it is the throne of God,
35a	Example #2	(ii) nor by earth,
b	Basis for 35a	for it is the footstool of his feet;
c	Example #3	(iii) nor toward Jerusalem,
d	Basis for 35c	for it is the city of the great king.
36a	Example #4	(iv) Nor swear by your head,
b	Basis for 36a	for you do not have the power to make a single hair white or black.
37a	Solution	But let your word stand on its own—a 'yes' is a yes and a 'no' is a no.
b	Basis for 37a	Anything beyond this stems from the evil one."

Structure and Literary Form

The form of the antithesis is basically the same, but Jesus' mandate is now elaborated with three examples (not illustrations like the first two).[2] It then concludes with a principial saying that provides the solution.

Exegetical Outline

- **I. Tradition: Keep Your Oaths (5:33)**
- **II. Mandate: Don't Make Oaths (5:34 – 36)**
  - A. Not by heaven — God's throne (v. 34)
  - B. Not by earth — God's footstool (v. 35a)
  - C. Not by Jerusalem — city of the great king (v. 35b)
  - D. Not by your head — you cannot change your hair color (v. 36)
- **III. Solution: Let Your Yes and No Stand on Their Own (5:37)**

2. The material here has no parallels in the other gospels but finds parallels in Matt 23:16 – 22 (only v. 22 has a verbal parallel, that heaven is God's throne) and Jas 5:12 (not to swear by heaven or earth, but let your yes be yes, etc.). So the material is traditional and better assigned to Jesus than Matthew (criterion of plausibility).

Explanation of the Text

5:33 Again you have heard that it was said to people long ago, "You shall not break your oaths, but you will keep them before God." (Πάλιν ἠκούσατε ὅτι ἐρρέθη τοῖς ἀρχαίοις, Οὐκ ἐπιορκήσεις, ἀποδώσεις δὲ τῷ κυρίῳ τοὺς ὅρκους σου). The lengthy introduction consists of "again" (πάλιν) plus a verbal repetition of 5:21, showing that Jesus breaks the antitheses into two halves, the first (vv. 21 – 32) centering on injunctions mainly from Deuteronomy and the second (vv. 33 – 48) on injunctions mainly from Leviticus (see introduction to 5:21 – 48). As Bruner says, Jesus here wants to protect speech in the same way he sought to protect sex in the previous two.[3]

Jesus' statement here is not a quote but summarizes material from several places, such as Exod 20:7; Lev 19:12; Num 30:2; Deut 23:21 – 23, with ἐπιορκήσεις meaning "break an oath" or "swear falsely." People in the ancient world would invoke one of the gods to affirm a statement, usually with the further, "may he strike me ill/dead if this is not true." For the Jews, God would thereby become a legal witness to the veracity of the claim. This was so pervasive that the Talmud devoted an entire tractate (*Šebuʿot*) to it, with all kinds of distinctions as to what was valid and what was not.

5:34 But I am telling you, do not make any oath at all (ἐγὼ δὲ λέγω ὑμῖν μὴ ὀμόσαι ὅλως). This is one the most stark of Jesus' pronouncements here, especially in light of the prevalence of oath-taking in his society. Yet it is important to realize that Jesus is not revoking all oaths, for God makes oaths (Heb 7:20 – 22, 28) as does Paul (Rom 1:9; 2 Cor 1:23; Gal 1:20). Rather, frivolous oaths on ordinary issues, some of which might even support patent falsehood, are prohibited. The call is for honesty and integrity in every area of life, as in the parallel Jas 5:12 ("Do not swear — not by heaven or by earth or by anything else. All you need to say is a simple 'Yes' or 'No' ").[4]

5:34 – 35 Not by heaven, for it is the throne of God, nor by earth, for it is the footstool of his feet; nor toward Jerusalem, for it is the city of the great king (μήτε ἐν τῷ οὐρανῷ, ὅτι θρόνος ἐστὶν τοῦ θεοῦ· μήτε ἐν τῇ γῇ, ὅτι ὑποπόδιόν ἐστιν τῶν ποδῶν αὐτοῦ· μήτε εἰς Ἱεροσόλυμα, ὅτι πόλις ἐστὶν τοῦ μεγάλου βασιλέως). The "not ... for" (μήτε ... ὅτι) format stresses three areas that are examples of common oaths. Guelich calls them "spurious oaths that had no binding power (cf. 23:16 – 22),"[5] and Meier says they are erroneous because they infringe on God's transcendent right to be God; that is, one tries to force God to affirm their own ideas.[6]

To swear by heaven is to invoke God's very throne (Ps 2:4; 11:4; Isa 66:1), and that is God's prerogative, not ours. To swear by earth also goes back to God, for he created it and it is his. It is God's right to use earth as his own footstool, not our right to use earth to bolster our own petty claims. To swear (facing) "toward" (εἰς) Jerusalem is to pretend that you can tell God what to do; it is his (the "great king," Ps 48:2) city, not yours to control.

5:36 Nor swear by your head, for you do not have the power to make a single hair white or black (μήτε ἐν τῇ κεφαλῇ σου ὀμόσῃς, ὅτι οὐ δύνασαι μίαν τρίχα λευκὴν ποιῆσαι ἢ μέλαιναν).

3. Bruner, *Christbook*, 198.

4. The common statement that Qumran also prohibited oaths is difficult. There is ambiguity, for while they turned away from oaths because such invoked God (who was not to be named), they still took an oath when joining the community (CD 15:1 – 3).

5. Guelich, *Sermon on the Mount*, 215.

6. Meier, *Law and History*, 155.

By the repetition of "to swear" (ὀμνύω), this example stands apart from the other three, probably because one's self becomes the basis of the oath. But Jesus reminds us that even this is inadequate because God ultimately has the power over us as well. We cannot turn our hair white (the wisdom of old age) or black (the strength of youth). God alone is sovereign, not us.

5:37 But let your word stand on its own — a "yes" is a yes and a "no" is a no (ἔστω δὲ ὁ λόγος ὑμῶν ναὶ ναί, οὒ οὔ). Literally this reads, "Let your word yes be yes and your no be no." On the basis of Semitic doubling, when duplicate wording adds emphasis (e.g., "very truly" in John), some translate, "Let your word be an emphatic yes or no."[7] That is a viable possibility but not as likely, for this principle means the same as Jas 5:12, "All you need to say is a simple 'Yes' or 'No.'" Either way, however, the call is for total honesty in one's speech.

5:37 Anything beyond this stems from the evil one (τὸ δὲ περισσὸν τούτων ἐκ τοῦ πονηροῦ ἐστιν). When Jesus concludes by saying that "anything more" (τὸ περισσόν) has its origin ("from" [ἐκ]) in Satan ("the evil one"), he means that anyone who centers on more and more oaths rather than personal integrity is following Satan.

Theology in Application

In 23:16–22 Jesus castigates the leaders for their casuistic debates over oath-taking, calling them "blind guides" (vv. 16, 19). The OT allowed oaths, and Judaism considered them essential; Jesus surprisingly says they are totally unnecessary. The message is clear: do not hide behind such "witnesses," for that keeps you from taking responsibility for what you say. Instead, live the truth of your words, and stand by everything you tell others. As many have said, this has been frequently misused in an absolutist sense to reject every kind of oath, as many throughout history who have rejected taking oaths in a court of law.

7. Strecker, *Sermon on the Mount*, 80; Guelich, *Sermon on the Mount*, 217–18. Others consider this an alternative oath formula, but that is unlikely since Jesus said emphatically, "Do not make any oath at all" (v. 34).

CHAPTER 18

Matthew 5:38 – 42

Literary Context

The final two antitheses are linked by a common thread — one's reaction to being wronged. Jesus apparently continues to contrast the surface understanding of OT ethical demands on the part of Jewish leaders with his own radical set of kingdom behaviors mandated by the new covenant perspective.

II. The Kingdom Message Goes Out (4:12 – 7:29)
- **B. First Discourse: The Sermon on the Mount (5:1 – 7:29)**
  - **3. The Relationship of the Law to the New Covenant in Jesus (5:17 – 48)**
    - **b. Examples — Six Antitheses on the New Righteousness (5:21 – 48)**
      - (4) Oaths Are Unnecessary (5:33 – 37)
      - ➦ **(5) Retaliation Is Wrong (5:38 – 42)**
      - (6) Love for Enemies (5:43 – 48)

Main Idea

The Jewish idea was that equal retaliation for evil action was valid, and the OT primarily tried to control it so justice was done. Jesus goes the other direction in two ways: (1) nonretaliation and submission to evil were to typify the kingdom people; and (2) not only should they refuse to seek vengeance, but they also should actively seek generosity, giving help to the very people who demanded things of them.

Translation

(See next page.)

Matthew 5:38-42

38a	Antithesis #5	*[5] "You have heard that it was said,*
b		*'An eye for an eye and a tooth for a tooth.'* (Exod 21:24; Lev 24:20; Deut 19:21)
39a		*But I am telling you not to resist an evil person at all.*
b	Illustration #1	*(i) Whoever slaps you on your right cheek, turn your other cheek to them as well.*
40a	Illustration #2	*(ii) And as for someone who wants to sue you and take your shirt, give that person your coat as well.*
41a	Illustration #3	*(iii) And whoever commandeers you to go one mile, go the second mile with him.*
42a	Illustration #4	*(iv) Give to the one who asks something from you, and*
b		*don't reject anyone who wants to borrow something from you."*

Structure and Literary Form

This is built exactly like the first two, with the antithetical form followed by a series of illustrations,[1] this time four of them in reverse order of severity, with an act of violence first followed by a legal situation, then conscription by a soldier, and finally a loan situation.[2] In all the principle is the same: to go the extra mile.

Exegetical Outline

→ **I. Antithesis (5:38 – 39a)**
- A. Tradition — eye for an eye (v. 38)
- B. Mandate — don't resist (v. 39a)

II. Illustrations (5:39b – 42)
- A. Turn the other cheek (v. 39b)
- B. Give away your cloak (v. 40)
- C. Go two miles (v. 41)
- D. Give the loan (v. 42)

1. The parallel passage in Luke 6:27 – 36 reverses these last two antitheses (retaliation and love of enemies) and centers on the latter theme. It is possible that both are utilizing Q (Carson, Senior, Harrington). The material here (vv. 39b – 40, 42) parallels Luke 6:29 – 30, so most believe Matthew added the antithetical form (Guelich, Strecker), but it is just as likely that this stems from a variant oral tradition (Hagner) that goes back to Jesus, an itinerant preacher who used similar material in different situations. Walter Wink, "Neither Passivity Nor Violence: Jesus' Third Way (Matt. 5:38 – 42/Luke 6:29 – 30)," *Forum* 7 (1991): 5 – 28, argues for the authenticity of vv. 38 – 42 on grounds of the criterion of dissimilarity, for Jesus was the first to present such a radical reaction to oppression.

2. Strecker, *Sermon on the Mount*, 83, speaks of "a downward sloping line from the greater evil to the lesser one: violent encounter, court trial, coercion, request."

Explanation of the Text

5:38 You have heard that it was said, "An eye for an eye and a tooth for a tooth" (Ἠκούσατε ὅτι ἐρρέθη, Ὀφθαλμὸν ἀντὶ ὀφθαλμοῦ καὶ ὀδόντα ἀντὶ ὀδόντος). This is a quotation of Exod 21:24; Lev 24:20; Deut 19:21 and is called *lex talionis* (Latin for "the law of retribution"), an ancient system found also in the Code of Hammurabi. In its OT context it is not so much encouraging retaliation as it is trying to control excesses by saying that the payment should exactly fit the crime and especially by making the punishment be part of the law court system rather than by individual vigilante actions. In other words, it gave the right to take a person to court rather than to seek revenge. In Jesus' day this was seldom applied literally; usually monetary retribution was utilized. The principle is found often in the NT (e.g., Mark 8:38; 1 Cor 3:17; Rev 16:5 – 7; 18:4 – 7; 19:2; 20:12 – 13).

5:39 But I am telling you not to resist an evil person[3] at all (ἐγὼ δὲ λέγω ὑμῖν μὴ ἀντιστῆναι τῷ πονηρῷ). This is similar to Jesus' prohibition of oaths (v. 34) in its shock value. On the surface it seems to reject the principle of justice, and many have rejected it throughout history (e.g., liberation theologians) for that reason. However, most agree that Jesus is speaking at the level of personal vengeance rather than legal rights. This principle of nonresistance or nonretaliation means in effect that the believer refuses to descend to the level of the aggressor and return evil for evil.[4] Keener adds that Jesus uses hyperbole throughout; it is not that one must never fight back but that the Christian must "value others above themselves in concrete and consistent ways."[5] They must renounce the right to confront a hostile person with violence but rather should depend on God for justice (cf. Rom 12:17 – 19; Rev 6:9 – 11).

Moreover, the thought of the whole is not to allow evil to occur unopposed but rather to answer evil with good. Bruner makes a good point when he says this involves evil done to you, not to your neighbor. Confrontation is mandated when we see mistreatment of the poor and other situations.[6] Robert Tannehill speaks of vv. 39 – 42 as "focal instance," calling the commands examples that form a pattern, extreme situations that demand the hearer imaginatively leap not to the specifics but to commensurate behavior in which retribution is replaced with forgiveness and generosity.[7] Witherington shows that while Moses limited revenge, Jesus taught the total abandonment of vengeance and its replacement with loving-kindness seen in action.[8]

5:39 Whoever slaps[9] you on your right cheek, turn your other cheek to them as well (ἀλλ' ὅστις σε ῥαπίζει εἰς τὴν δεξιὰν σιαγόνα σου, στρέψον αὐτῷ καὶ τὴν ἄλλην). In a culture where the right

3. Because of the presence of the article, Hagner, *Matthew 1 – 13*, 130 – 31, interprets this of an "evil deed" rather than a person. However, most take the Greek as short for "the evil person" (add "person" [ἀνθρώπῳ]). All agree this does not mean "the evil one," i.e., Satan.

4. Guelich, *Sermon on the Mount*, 219 – 20, restricts this to "oppose in court" (so also Gundry, *Matthew*, 220; Carson, "Matthew," 155; Davies and Allison, *Matthew*, 1:541, take this as a possibility). However, it is too narrow for this context. Only the second illustration (v. 40) is a legal situation.

5. Keener, *Matthew*, 195. So also Davies and Allison, *Matthew*, 1:541.

6. Bruner, *Christbook*, 205.

7. Robert Tannehill, *The Sword of His Mouth* (SNTSSup 1; Philadelphia: Fortress, 1975), 67 – 77, noted in Russel Pregeant, *Matthew* (Chalice Commentaries; St. Louis: Chalice, 2004), 48.

8. Witherington, *Matthew*, 136.

9. The present "slaps" (ῥαπίζει) looks at possible repeated acts of insult, and the aorist imperative "turn" (στρέψον) means that at each instance you must exemplify nonretaliation.

hand was the dominant one, this would involve a person striking you with a backhanded blow. In the first century that would be an intended insult.[10] "Turning the other cheek" would mean not only a refusal to retaliate but also placing one's self in a degrading and vulnerable situation. One takes the dishonor rather than the personally satisfying but morally wrong act of reprisal.

5:40 And as for someone who wants to sue you and take your shirt, give that person your coat as well (καὶ τῷ θέλοντί σοι κριθῆναι καὶ τὸν χιτῶνά σου λαβεῖν, ἄφες αὐτῷ καὶ τὸ ἱμάτιον). Here there is a legal situation involving a lawsuit ("to sue" [κριθῆναι]) demanding "the inner garment or tunic" (χιτῶνα). The "outer garment" (ἱμάτιον) was the more important, used not only as a cloak but also as bedding when sleeping in the open fields. The law said even the poor should have the right to keep their cloak (Exod 22:25 – 26; Deut 24:12 – 13). Therefore, the believer even relinquishes the more prized possession and is willing to appear naked before the court without either inner or outer garment.

5:41 And whoever commandeers you to go one mile, go the second mile with him (καὶ ὅστις σε ἀγγαρεύσει μίλιον ἕν, ὕπαγε μετ' αὐτοῦ δύο). Roman soldiers had the right to conscript civilians to carry burdens for them (e.g., Simon in Mark 15:21, who bore Jesus' cross), but the practice was despised by the Jewish people.[11] The actual term μίλιον refers to a thousand steps, which was almost a mile. Jesus' point fits the idiom "go the second mile" quite well. It pictures the believer offering to carry the load even further if the soldier so wishes.

5:42 Give to the one who asks something from you, and don't reject anyone who wants to borrow something from you (τῷ αἰτοῦντί σε δός, καὶ τὸν θέλοντα ἀπὸ σοῦ δανίσασθαι μὴ ἀποστραφῇς). This last illustration sums up the others. Jesus provides similar teaching said two ways, positively and then negatively. The first deals with general giving, the second with specific loans; neither expects repayment. The first would also include almsgiving, a key aspect of Jewish piety (see on 6:1 – 4). The main point is the type of generosity that never shrinks from helping needy people, what Paul calls the gift "of helping [others]" (1 Cor 12:28).

Theology in Application

Instead of demanding our rights and seeking justice over every wrong, perceived or otherwise, kingdom citizens expect little from this world and place their trust wholly in God. We defer to others and seek at all times to give rather than take. This is a radical departure from Jewish teaching and demands the type of new covenant outlook that is at the heart of Jesus' teaching. This in fact is impossible without the power of God. Hagner says it well: "It is the unworthy who have experienced the good things of the kingdom; and as they have experienced the surprise of unexpected grace, so they act in a similar manner toward the undeserving among them (cf. Luke 6:34 – 35)."[12] Christ has shown that type of mercy and grace toward his enemies and in so doing has provided the model for our actions (cf. 1 Pet 2:21 – 25).

10. France, *Gospel of Matthew*, 220, relates that the Code of Hammurabi, par. 202 – 5, has penalties for such insults, ranging from a small fine to the cutting off of an ear, depending on the social status of the individuals involved.

11. For specific examples see Keener, *Matthew*, 199.

12. Hagner, *Matthew 1 – 13*, 132.

CHAPTER 19

Matthew 5:43 – 48

Literary Context

This final antithesis acts as a summary of the others and concludes the series. The relationships involved are especially radical because they demand maintaining the same attitude toward outsiders that one has for insiders in the community.

II. The Kingdom Message Goes Out (4:12 – 7:29)
B. First Discourse: The Sermon on the Mount (5:1 – 7:29)
3. The Relationship of the Law to the New Covenant in Jesus (5:17 – 48)
b. Examples — Six Antitheses on the New Righteousness (5:21 – 48)
(5) Retaliation Is Wrong (5:38 – 42)
➦ **(6) Love for Enemies (5:43 – 48)**

Main Idea

If one loves only friends, they are no different than the pagans. To love one's enemies is to be truly a child of God and to have a heavenly rather than earthly perspective.

Translation

(See next page.)

Structure and Literary Form

Once again the antithetical form introduces the section (vv. 43 – 44), but it is followed by two motivations in v. 45, telling the reason for such behavior, and only then by two illustrations that take the form of rhetorical questions ("If you ... don't even?" vv. 46 – 47). It concludes with a climactic injunction (relating to all the antitheses, not just this one), calling for moral perfection (v. 48).[1]

Matthew 5:43-48

43a	Antithesis #6	[6] "You have heard that it was said,
b		'Love your neighbor and hate your enemy.' (Lev 19:18)
44a		But I am telling you, love your enemies and pray for those who persecute you
45a	Basis #1 for 44a	so that you might be children of the heavenly Father,
b	Basis #2 for 44a	because he makes his sun rise on the evil and the good alike
c		and sends rain on both the righteous and the unrighteous.
46a	Illustration #1	(i) For if you love those who love you, what credit is that of yours?
b		Don't even the tax collectors do the same thing?
47a	Illustration #2	(ii) And if you greet only your own kind of people, what more are you doing?
b		Don't even the pagans do the same thing?
48a	Exhortation	Therefore, you must be perfect as your heavenly Father is perfect."

Exegetical Outline

I. Antithesis (5:43 – 44)

A. Tradition — love neighbor and hate enemies (v. 43)

B. Mandate — love enemies and pray for them (v. 44)

II. Motivation or Reason (5:45))

A. To be God's children (v. 45a)

B. The forces of nature fall on both (v. 45b)

III. Illustrations (5:46 – 47)

A. Even tax collectors love their friends (v. 46)

B. Even pagans greet their friends (v. 47)

IV. Injunction: Like God, Be Perfect (5:48)

1. As stated on 5:38 – 42, this section also parallels Luke 6:27 – 36, with 5:38 – 42 = Luke 6:29 – 30 and 5:43 – 48 = Luke 6:27 – 28, 32 – 36.

Explanation of the Text

5:43 You have heard that it was said, "Love your neighbor and hate your enemy" (Ἠκούσατε ὅτι ἐρρέθη, Ἀγαπήσεις τὸν πλησίον σου καὶ μισήσεις τὸν ἐχθρόν σου). The first half stems from Lev 19:18 and with Deut 6:4 – 5 is used by Christ to sum up the Torah in Matt 22:34 – 40 (= Mark 12:28 – 34). Matthew most likely omits "as yourself" from "love your neighbor" in order to parallel the following "hate your enemy" (both are future tenses stressing the necessity of living this way for the rest of your life). The second half does not appear in the OT, but "it was said" can be either an inference from Deut 7:2; 23:3 – 7; 25:17 – 19; Ps 139:21 – 22 (drive out and destroy your enemies among the nations) or perhaps a popular understanding (see Sir 12) similar to Qumran (who taught hatred of the "sons of darkness" in 1QS 1:4; 2:4 – 9; 9:16, 21 – 23; 1QM 15:6). The imprecatory psalms also encouraged this attitude. In terms of Jewish contempt for Gentiles, this was a natural addendum.

5:44 But I am telling you, love your enemies (ἐγὼ δὲ λέγω ὑμῖν, ἀγαπᾶτε τοὺς ἐχθροὺς ὑμῶν). Two changes are important: (1) from the singular "enemy" to the plural "enemies," stressing the universal nature of the command, and (2) the use of the present imperative, stressing the ongoing need of such an attitude. This was revolutionary, and there is no evidence for such a command in Jewish literature.[2] Leviticus 19:33 – 34 commanded love for the resident alien, and Prov 25:21 speaks of acts of kindness for one's enemy (cf. also Exod 23:4 – 5; Job 31:29 – 30; Prov 17:5, 24:17), but nowhere is love commanded for one's enemy. Too much has been made of the differences between ἀγαπάω and φιλέω, as if the former is divine love and the latter human affection. The two verbs overlap considerably,[3] and the best definition of love here is probably "generous, warm, costly self-sacrifice for another's good."[4]

5:44 ... and pray for those who persecute you (καὶ προσεύχεσθε ὑπὲρ τῶν διωκόντων ὑμᾶς). This love is further defined by the command to "pray" even for your oppressors. It is common for critical scholars to think entirely of the persecution occurring in Matthew's day; while that would have been present in Matthew's mind, Jesus was speaking of the hatred he and his disciples were experiencing.[5] Many may think of the famous prayer in the musical *Fiddler on the Roof*, where the rabbi prays, "Bless and keep the Czar ... far away from us"!

In Luke 6:27 – 28 there are two other commands between the two here: "do good to those who hate you, bless those who curse you." The message is to return good for evil, to shower good deeds (prayer is one of them) down on those who malign you (cf. also Rom 12:14; 1 Cor 4:12). In Rom 12:20 this will "heap burning coals on [their] head" (coals of conviction and then judgment for those who reject the conviction) and in 1 Pet 2:12 will bring many to Christ (they will "glorify God on the day

2. Though see W. Wolpert, "Die Liebe zum Nächsten, zum Feind und zum Sünder," *TGl* 74 (1984): 262 – 82, who finds the idea undeveloped but present in Jewish and Greco-Roman literature and separates the category into love for personal enemies and love for sinners (enemies of God).

3. See Johannes P. Louw and Eugene A. Nida, *Greek-English Lexicon of the New Testament based on Semantic Domains* (2nd ed.; New York: United Bible Societies, 1989), 294. They believe that in some contexts the one distinction is that φιλέω speaks of "love and affection based upon interpersonal association," while ἀγαπάω connotes "love and affection based upon deep appreciation and high regard."

4. Carson, "Matthew," 158.

5. As Davies and Allison, *Matthew*, 1:552n, points out, the historical veracity of this is universally accepted, even in Bultmann, *History*, 105.

he visits us"). This probably defines the contents of the prayers.

5:45 ... so that you might be children of the heavenly Father (ὅπως γένησθε υἱοὶ τοῦ πατρὸς ὑμῶν τοῦ ἐν οὐρανοῖς). This clause and the next one are parallel and provide both the goal and the reason for loving your enemies. As McNeile says, "Sons are those who partake of their Father's character."[6] Plummer adds, "To return evil for good is devilish; to return good for good is human; to return good for evil is divine."[7] As the kingdom people show love and pray for those who are hostile toward them, they show the mark of God on their lives (cf. also 1 Pet 2:23 as basis for 3:9). The emphasis on "heavenly" may add a note of importance (see on Matt 6:9), showing that heaven is involved in the lives of the kingdom people (as in the emphasis on angels in 1 Cor 11:10; Heb 13:2, and in the letters to the seven churches in Rev 2 – 3).

5:45 ... because he makes his sun rise on the evil and the good alike and sends rain on both the righteous and the unrighteous (ὅτι τὸν ἥλιον αὐτοῦ ἀνατέλλει ἐπὶ πονηροὺς καὶ ἀγαθοὺς καὶ βρέχει ἐπὶ δικαίους καὶ ἀδίκους). The basis (ὅτι) of the action of Jesus' followers to love and pray for their enemies is God's own actions in bestowing blessings equally on his followers and his enemies.[8] The sunshine and rain are both natural blessings that form the basis of plant growth and therefore of life as a whole. God does not curse the wicked with all bad things and bless the good with all good things. Even those who reject God are made in his image and loved by him, so his people must reflect his goodness even toward their persecutors.

5:46 For if you love those who love[9] you, what credit is that of yours? Don't even the tax collectors do the same thing? (ἐὰν γὰρ ἀγαπήσητε τοὺς ἀγαπῶντας ὑμᾶς, τίνα μισθὸν ἔχετε; οὐχὶ καὶ οἱ τελῶναι τὸ αὐτὸ ποιοῦσιν;). This illustration and the next one take the form of rhetorical questions as Jesus challenges the disciples to go beyond the normal kind of relationships. Everyone, even the despised tax collectors, can reciprocate love to friends. Jesus is probably referring to the Jewish tax farmers, who purchased the rights to collect toll taxes. They were allowed to charge above the required amount and keep the extra. This led to widespread graft and cheating. So Jesus uses this most-despised group as his example. μισθός here is not used of a "reward" one earns but more "credit" that one receives for doing well.

5:47 And if you greet only your own kind of people, what more are you doing? Don't even the pagans do the same thing? (καὶ ἐὰν ἀσπάσησθε τοὺς ἀδελφοὺς ὑμῶν μόνον, τί περισσὸν ποιεῖτε; οὐχὶ καὶ οἱ ἐθνικοὶ τὸ αὐτὸ ποιοῦσιν;). The type of greeting a person received demonstrated their status in society, so the scribes and other elite loved effusive greetings (Matt 23:7). Jesus' point is that such greetings[10] should be given to strangers and even enemies, not just their fellow disciples (ἀδελφούς = same family or type of people). Even the despised "pagans" do that much, and the disciples should do much "better."

5:48 Therefore, you must be perfect as your heavenly Father is perfect (ἔσεσθε οὖν ὑμεῖς τέλειοι

6. McNeile, *Matthew*, 71.

7. Plummer, *Matthew*, 89.

8. The order of terms (evil/good, righteous/unrighteous) is chiastic, a stylistic ploy to add emphasis.

9. The aorist "you love" (ἀγαπήσητε) depicts your basic choice to love others, while the present "the ones loving" (ἀγαπῶντας) pictures the repeated acts of love others have bestowed on you.

10. Some read "impart a blessing" (Guelich, *Sermon on the Mount*, 232; Gundry, *Matthew*, 99) into the greeting here on the basis of its use in 10:12. That is possible in light of the greeting to fellow believers.

ὡς ὁ πατὴρ ὑμῶν ὁ οὐράνιος τέλειός ἐστιν). This first of all concludes 5:43 – 47, with "as your heavenly Father is" recapitulating v. 45 ("be children of [your] heavenly Father"). In this sense it means "have the same perfect love as your Father does." At the same time it provides the conclusion for all of 5:21 – 48, where it means ethical/moral perfection.

Jesus throughout the antitheses has absolutized the meaning of OT principles, and "perfection" is the best way to put together Jesus' teaching. This probably echoes Lev 19:2, "Be holy because I, the Lord your God, am holy," seen perhaps through Deut 18:13, "You must be blameless [LXX τέλειος] before the Lord your God." The future "you must be" (ἔσεσθε) is a Hebrew use of the future for a divine "You must," as in the Ten Commandments (see on v. 21).

"Perfect" (τέλειος) reflects the Hebrew *tāmîm*, used often of a "perfect" sacrifice ("without blemish," often in Leviticus) and of the ethical uprightness or "blamelessness" of God's people (Gen 6:9, 17:1; Deut 18:13; 2 Sam 22:24, 26), an absolute commitment and allegiance to God (Ps 15:2; 84:11). Qumran understood this in terms of perfect adherence to the law and wholeheartedly living[11] according to their teachings (CD 2:15; 1QS 1:8 – 9; 4:22 – 23; 1QM 7:5; 14:7).[12] It is impossible to know what Jesus originally said (in Aramaic), but "perfect" (τέλειος) here in this context stems from the above connotations and means wholehearted (many see "wholeness" here) obedience to *all* Jesus has said (cf. Matt 28:19, "keep everything I have commanded"), i.e., "complete" adherence to his teachings.

The key is "as your heavenly[13] Father," meaning that kingdom children are to emulate their Father in all they say and do. His perfection is the goal for our thoughts and action, for our relationships inside and outside the community. There is also a strong action sense, for the parallel in Luke 6:36 has "mercy" (οἰκτίρμονες) and shows that relationships with others is an essential aspect. We are to become like the Father, follow all that Jesus has said, and relate to all around us (believer and unbeliever) with mercy and love.

Theology in Application

Love for neighbor was the epitome of OT ethics (see Matt 22:39 – 40), but Jesus deepens that in a startling way. We are to love our neighbors even when they are hostile and do evil acts against us. Love for enemies, moreover, is not restricted to feelings of benevolence but meant to be shown in acts of kindness. The model for this difficult activity is nothing less than God himself, our Father. Like obedient children we must emulate our Father and act toward evil people as he does. If God can be merciful to wicked as well as good people, so must we. The perfect love of God will guide our reactions to their animosity.

11. See Brice L. Martin, "Matthew on Christ and the Law," *TS* 44 (1983): 68 – 69, who would translate this here as "wholehearted," meaning absolute adherence to its radical demands.

12. See G. Delling, *TDNT*, 8:73.

13. Seven of the eleven times "heavenly" (οὐράνιος) is found in the NT are in Matthew, always for the "heavenly Father" (5:48; 6:14, 26, 32; 15:13; 18:35; 23:9). This stresses the transcendence of God and helps the reader understand that heaven itself is involved with the lives of God's people on earth.

1. Responding to Acts of Aggression with Acts of Kindness

This is clear in Rom 12:14 – 21. We are called to leave vengeance to God and react with acts of love toward our enemies. In 1 Pet 2:11 – 12 this will demonstrate the error of their enemies' lives, convict them, and bring them to Christ. As Jesus refused to retaliate or make threats (1 Pet 2:23), so must we. We are called to perfect moral thinking as well as conduct, to exemplify a lifestyle far above those around us.

Obviously, few of us can approach such a standard in our lives. It is a goal for which to strive, not an absolute standard that must be lived at all times. Luz speaks of the "path of righteousness" (see 21:32), namely, seeking always a "better righteousness" (5:20) than before, such as growing daily in our conduct as we seek the will of God.[14] We are not all meant to be itinerant preachers like Jesus or Paul with "nowhere to lay" their heads. Many of us will be like Mary the mother of John Mark in Acts 12:12, living a regular life and using our home to serve the Lord. The key is growth in love and service, in every area of our lives striving to be more like God and Jesus.

2. Christ Followers Must Exemplify Jesus' Radical Love at a Corporate Level

This has led the Anabaptist tradition into what has been called "pacifism," that is, a life of nonresistance and a desire to respond to evil with love and forgiveness. Further, they believe this principle should be applied to civil as well as personal ethics and thus they oppose any violence whatsoever, including war. This desire to make "love of enemies" a fulcrum in church ethics and national policy provides a major challenge to every reader.

14. Luz, *Theology*, 55 – 58.

CHAPTER 20

Matthew 6:1 – 4

Introduction to Matthew 6:1 – 18

In one sense, this section,[1] like the previous one, exemplifies the authoritative teaching of Jesus on matters of OT law, for the three things mentioned in these verses are three basic aspects of Jewish piety[2] and summarize one's relationship with God.[3] France suggests that 5:20 – 48 centers on a positive righteousness that exceeds that of the scribes and Pharisees while this section centers on the wrong kind of righteous conduct done to impress others rather than God.[4] As with the antitheses, Jesus shows how the people of his day all too often understood these aspects, but he also tells how the people of the kingdom will perform them more deeply.

This is a very Jewish section and as such shows a situation in Jesus' day, not just Matthew's time. It demonstrates that our piety is part of our relationship with God and should never be done to impress others. Our motivation must always be God-oriented, never earth-centered (see also 6:19 – 21; Col 3:1 – 2). The section is composed of three admonitions (6:2 – 4, 5 – 6, 16 – 18), into which the Lord's Prayer is inserted. The parallelism between the three is striking:[5] a "when you" clause followed by "not like the hypocrites" and a report of their actions, concluding with an *amēn* statement about "fully receiving their reward." Then comes a positive command to give/pray/fast "in secret" and a promise of true reward.[6]

Literary Context

The "better righteousness" of 5:20 is seen in 5:21 – 48 of ethical relationships with others and in 6:1 – 18 of one's spiritual relationship with God. The problem

1. The material here is unique to Matthew, coming from the M source. The only parallel elsewhere is the Lord's Prayer (6:9 – 13 = Luke 11:2 – 4), which could be Q (so most) or teaching given on two separate occasions (so Carson, myself, see below).

2. For the importance of Jewish background to this section and especially to the prayer, see L. J. Prockter, "The Blind Spot: New Testament Scholarship's Ignorance of Rabbinic Judaism," *Scriptura* 48 (1994): 1 – 12.

3. Nolland, *Matthew*, 272, says, "whereas the focus in 5:21 – 48 has been on the neighbour, through chap. 6 it will be on how one relates to God."

4. France, *Gospel of Matthew*, 232.

5. See Guelich, *Sermon on the Mount*, 273 – 74; Strecker, *Sermon on the Mount*, 96 – 97; Hagner, *Matthew 1 – 13*, 137 – 38.

6. On the form here see further Hans-Dieter Betz, "A Jewish-Christian Cultic *Didache* in Matt. 6:11 – 18: Reflections and Questions on the Historical Jesus," in *Essays on the Sermon on the Mount* (Philadelphia: Fortress, 1985), 55 – 69.

with the "hypocrites" is that they used these pious acts externally to increase their status in the community rather than internally to serve God. Almsgiving is a perfect example because it is easy to let everyone know what a "good" person you are by advertising your largesse.

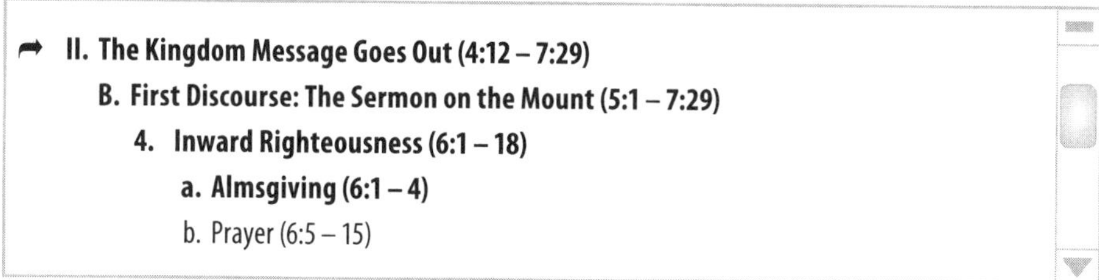

II. The Kingdom Message Goes Out (4:12 – 7:29)
B. First Discourse: The Sermon on the Mount (5:1 – 7:29)
4. Inward Righteousness (6:1 – 18)
a. Almsgiving (6:1 – 4)
b. Prayer (6:5 – 15)

Main Idea

When the believer gives, it must never be out in the open to be seen (and admired) by others but always secretly as an act of worship to God. Giving is a private affair done entirely to please the Father. Both have their reward, but the former yields an earthly reward (applause) and only the latter has an eternal reward.

Translation

Matthew 6:1-4

1a	Introductory Warning	*"Take care that you don't do your righteous deeds before others*
b		*in order to be seen by them.*
c	Result	*Otherwise, you have no reward from your Father in heaven.*
2a	Prohibition (A)	*Therefore,*
		when you give to the needy,
b		*don't announce it with trumpets*
c		*as the hypocrites do in the synagogues and*
		on the streets
d		*so they can receive glory*
		from others.
e	Result (B)	*I tell you the truth, they are fully receiving their reward.*
3a	Antithesis (C)	*But*
		when you give to the needy,
b		*do not let your left hand know what your right hand is doing*
4a	Purpose of 3b	*so that your giving may be in secret.*
b	Result (D)	*Then your Father who sees in secret will reward you."*

Structure and Literary Form

This passage comes from Matthew's special material (M) and begins with a *kelal* sentence — i.e., a formal introduction that provides the basic thesis for the whole unit. That means that v. 1 does not just introduce vv. 1 – 4 but the whole of vv. 1 – 18. The first admonition of the three (vv. 2 – 4) contains a prohibition, a positive command that provides the antithesis to the error of v. 2, and a promise of reward for those who are faithful.

Exegetical Outline

→ **I. Introduction to the Series (6:1)**
  A. Warning — not for attention (v. 1a)
  B. Result — no heavenly reward (v. 1b)

II. Prohibition against Ostentatious Giving (6:2)
  A. Command — don't give for the attention you receive (v. 2a)
  B. Promise — reward in full (v. 2b)

III. Positive Injunction to Give Secretly (6:3 – 4)
  A. Command — give secretly (vv. 3 – 4a)
  B. Promise — reward from the Father (v. 4b)

Explanation of the Text

6:1 Take care that you don't do your righteous deeds before others[7] **in order to be seen by them** (Προσέχετε δὲ τὴν δικαιοσύνην ὑμῶν μὴ ποιεῖν ἔμπροσθεν τῶν ἀνθρώπων πρὸς τὸ θεαθῆναι αὐτοῖς). This introduces the theme of 6:1 – 18, true "righteousness" (cf. 5:20), and Jesus is establishing a strong antithesis between the earthly and the heavenly in achieving this righteousness. There is a geometric progression: the more you have an earthly perspective, the fewer your rewards in heaven. We have stated throughout that "righteousness" (δικαιοσύνη) must be understood as action, that is, right conduct in doing the will of God (cf. 3:15; 5:6, 10, 20; 6:33), so "righteous deeds" is the proper way to understand it here. The righteous deeds here are almsgiving, prayer, and fasting. The will of God is not to perform these pious acts in order to get attention.[8]

6:1 Otherwise, you have no reward from your Father in heaven (εἰ δὲ μή γε, μισθὸν οὐκ ἔχετε παρὰ τῷ πατρὶ ὑμῶν τῷ ἐν τοῖς οὐρανοῖς). "Otherwise" (εἰ δὲ μή γε) is an idiom for drawing a contrast. Christ says that it is the intention of the heart rather than the respect of others that God sees (1 Sam 16:7; Rom 2:28 – 29). If the motive is wrong, the act has no value and will receive "no reward" in heaven ("in heaven" [τῷ ἐν τοῖς οὐρανοῖς]

7. The generic use of τῶν ἀνθρώπων for "people" is also found in 5:13, 16, 19.

8. As Carson says ("Matthew," 162), there is no contradiction with 5:14 – 16 (letting the light shine so people see our good deeds), for there the purpose is to glorify God while here the purpose is to glorify self.

modifies "Father" but also tells where the reward will be). The contrast is between earthly reward (v. 2b) and heavenly reward (v. 4b), between the temporal and eternal. This is also found in the other two sections (vv. 6, 18).

6:2 Therefore, when you give to the needy (Ὅταν οὖν ποιῇς ἐλεημοσύνην). The perfect example of the principle in v. 1 is giving (present "you give" [ποιῇς] for continuous repetition) to the poor. Almsgiving interestingly is not specifically commanded in the OT, but taking care of the poor and needy is given great attention, as in the tenth of all produce given to the Levites and the needy (Deut 14:28 – 29; cf. Exod 23:10 – 11; Lev 23:22). Social justice was strongly commanded (Isa 3:15; 10:1 – 2; Amos 2:6 – 8; 5:11; et al.). During the intertestamental period almsgiving became a critical aspect of true piety (Sir 3:30; Tob 4:10; 12:8 – 9). By the time of Jesus righteousness and almsgiving were virtually synonymous, and almsgiving was an important part of temple and synagogue services. Synagogues functioned as social agencies in the first century, providing relief for the poor who depended on contributions from people in the community.[9] Therefore, it was natural that ostentation became connected with giving; it was a perfect way to be seen as particularly pious.

6:2 . . . don't announce it with trumpets (μὴ σαλπίσῃς ἔμπροσθέν σου). The background for the idea of blowing trumpets (lit., "Don't trumpet before you") is debated. It used to be thought that trumpets were blown in the synagogue whenever large sums were given,[10] but evidence for such a practice is lacking. Still, there is evidence that large donors were recognized publicly. Similarly, some have thought these were the trumpet-like receptacles (built like a sophar-chest) in the temple for given gifts (cf. Mark 12:41 – 42),[11] but this too is a far stretch, unless Jesus is making a wordplay on these trumpet-shaped chests.[12] Perhaps it refers more generally to the blowing of trumpets at the beginning of fasts, connected with the giving of alms as part of the fasts.[13] While the latter two are possible, it is probably best just to take the trumpet as a metaphor for drawing attention to one's pious act of giving.[14]

6:2 ... as the hypocrites do in the synagogues and on the streets so they can receive glory from others (ὥσπερ οἱ ὑποκριταὶ ποιοῦσιν ἐν ταῖς συναγωγαῖς καὶ ἐν ταῖς ῥύμαις, ὅπως δοξασθῶσιν ὑπὸ τῶν ἀνθρώπων). A "hypocrite" originally was an actor who wore a mask in a Greek play, thereby pretending he was something he was not (they were always males). So it came to be used for a person who looked one way on the outside but was something else on the inside. Normally a hypocrite practices conscious deception, but Carson rightly notes that in this case the person is likely deceiving himself as well as others.[15] The mention of "synagogue" and "street" is that these are two major places where alms were given. To onlookers the gift was conspicuous and seemed pious, but

9. See France, *Gospel of Matthew*, 235.

10. Schlatter, *Matthäus*, 201 – 2; Pierre Bonnard, *L'évangile selon Saint Matthieu* (Neuchâtel: Delachaux & Niestlé, 1963), 78; Hill, *Matthew*, 133; Hagner, *Matthew 1 – 13*, considers it possible.

11. See G. Klein, "Matt 6.2," *ZNW* 6 (1905): 203 – 4; Neil J. McEleney, "Does the Trumpet Sound or Resound? An Interpretation of Matthew 6, 2," *ZNW* 76 (1985): 43 – 46.

12. So Davies and Allison, *Matthew*, 1:579; Blomberg, *Matthew*, 117, following McEleney.

13. A. Büchler, "St. Matthew 6 1 – 6 and Other Allied Passages," *JTS* 10 (1909): 266 – 70, followed by McNeile, *Matthew*, 74; Carson, "Matthew," 164.

14. Morris, *Matthew*, 136 – 37; Schnackenburg, *Matthew*, 64; Harrington, *Matthew*, 94; Keener, *Matthew*, 208.

15. Carson, "Matthew," 164, following D. A. Spieler, "Hypocrisy: An Exploration of a Third Type," *AUSS* 13 (1975): 273 – 79.

in reality it was ostentatious and for self-glory (to "receive glory from others"), i.e., for praise rather than from piety.

6:2 I tell you the truth, they are fully receiving their reward (ἀμὴν λέγω ὑμῖν, ἀπέχουσιν τὸν μισθὸν αὐτῶν). Jesus makes a solemn declaration ("I tell you the truth," cf. on 5:18, 26): such praise is all the reward they are ever going to get. The verb ἀπέχω is strong and stems from a commercial term meaning "receive a sum in full and get a receipt for it" (BAGD, 84); the present tense means "right now they are receiving" all the reward they will ever get. Plummer says it well: "They receive their pay then and there, and they receive it in full ... God owes them nothing. They were not giving but *buying*. They wanted the praise of men, they paid for it, and they have got it. The transaction is ended and they can claim nothing more."[16]

6:3 But when you give to the needy, do not let your left hand know what your right hand is doing (σοῦ δὲ ποιοῦντος ἐλεημοσύνην μὴ γνώτω ἡ ἀριστερά σου τί ποιεῖ ἡ δεξιά σου). One of Matthew's many genitive absolutes ("when you give" [σοῦ ποιοῦντος]) is used temporally here. In contrast to such hypocrites, all giving must be done in absolute secrecy. The left hand/right hand contrast is an idiom for total privacy, disregarding one's self entirely in the act of helping the poor.[17]

6:4 ... so that your giving may be in secret. Then your Father who sees in secret will reward you (ὅπως ᾖ σου ἡ ἐλεημοσύνη ἐν τῷ κρυπτῷ· καὶ ὁ πατήρ σου ὁ βλέπων ἐν τῷ κρυπτῷ ἀποδώσει σοι). This reinforces v. 3. All giving must be done with no desire for praise or notice from others. This verse provides the motive for such secret largesse: to receive a reward from God (rather than from others). The theme of reward is especially prominent in this Sermon and is more prevalent in Matthew than any other NT book (with Revelation second). The actual reward is not mentioned and has been variously speculated upon as God himself or the blessing of a good conscience and increased holiness.[18] It probably refers specifically to present reward (blessing from God) and generally to our reward in heaven (what we do for God and others on earth is banked in heaven and becomes our reward, Luke 16:9).

Of course, Jesus does not mean we give only because we want a heavenly reward. We give both because we love God and want to give back to him a portion of what he has given us and because we care about the plight of the needy. Still, God wants us to know, first, that he "sees" (present tense βλέπων means he is watching at all times)[19] what we are secretly doing (the meaning of "sees in secret") and second, that he will recompense us for all such sacrificial giving. "In secret" (ἐν τῷ κρυπτῷ) is found in both clauses for emphasis, and in the second it comes between "seeing" and "rewarding," probably modifying both. God sees what we do in secret and will reward us secretly.[20] "Your Father" appears only in 6:6, 16, 18 in the Synoptics and emphasizes the divine Father/son relationship.

16. Plummer, *Matthew*, 91.

17. So Hill, *Matthew*, 133; Plummer, *Matthew*, 97, calls it a current proverb. This is superior to Grundmann, *Matthäus*, 194, who says it is an Aramaic idiom for a dear friend, so that this means to hide it from all around you; or Gundry, *Matthew*, 102, that giving a gift with one hand is unobtrusive while using two calls attention to the act. Both are possible but extend the image too far.

18. See Morris, *Matthew*, 139.

19. The present tense also places the action in the foreground (Porter, *Idioms*, 23) and adds emphasis to God's watching us.

20. Nolland, *Matthew*, 276, calls this "a secret stockpile in heaven."

Theology in Application

Christian giving is a huge issue today. Many emphasize tithing even though it is an OT rather than NT demand. While the NT does not mandate tithing, it is clear that 10 percent is where we should start rather than a goal we should strive to attain. We have so much and give so little, while the people of God in both the OT and NT (and so many Christians worldwide today) have so little and give so much. This parallels 2 Cor 8:2, "In the midst of a very severe trial, their overflowing joy and their extreme poverty welled up in rich generosity." In 2 Cor 8 – 9 we see the center of a biblical theology of giving, stressing the joy and service behind generous stewardship. We give not out of necessity but out of privilege, both to tell ourselves that everything we have is from the Lord and to return to him some of the blessings he has given to us.

Sacrificial Giving

In our affluent society tithing is where we should begin! Statistics are an indictment to American giving. I saw a recent note that evangelicals gave 2.8 percent a decade ago, but now the average is 2.4 percent. I know of one church that discovered that nearly all their giving came from 15 percent of the members and another where 30 percent of their *members* had given nothing the previous year! Christian organizations are so desperate for funds that they actually encourage ostentatious giving by selling bricks with people's names on them or naming buildings or even whole seminaries after wealthy donors. The point is clear here — anyone who gives to be noticed and lauded has already received their reward; there is nothing in heaven waiting for them (cf. Luke 6:24).

Flowing out of Gratitude for God's Grace and Mercy

Giving is to be an act of worship and compassionate concern, not a statement of worth. The concept of reward is an important theme in the Sermon on the Mount (see also 19:29). The principle is that God will reward us on the basis of our spiritual priorities and deeds. If we live entirely for him and surrender earthly attachments and rewards, our reward will be heavenly and eternal.

CHAPTER 21

Matthew 6:5 – 15

Literary Context

This is the central one of the three pericopes presenting the deeper piety that the new "laws of the kingdom" mandate, and many believe it is the center of the Sermon because (1) it actually is at the center, and (2) the theme of total God-dependence is at the heart of the message of chs. 5 – 7.

- **II. The Kingdom Message Goes Out (4:12 – 7:29)**
  - **B. First Discourse: The Sermon on the Mount (5:1 – 7:29)**
    - **4. Inward Righteousness (6:1 – 18)**
      - a. Almsgiving (6:1 – 4)
      - ➦ **b. Prayer (6:5 – 15)**
      - c. Fasting (6:16 – 18)

Main Idea

There are two major messages. (1) Prayer, like giving, must be private rather than ostentatious (vv. 5 – 6) or filled with wordy jargon (vv. 7 – 8); the goal is to worship God and present your needs to him, not to gain notice for your piety. (2) The model for prayer (vv. 9 – 13) is also a model for Christian living, centering first on worship (v. 9a) and God's concerns (vv. 9b – 10) and only then on your own needs (vv. 11 – 13), and even then the primary needs are spiritual (the final two) and not just earthly (the first).

Translation

Matthew 6:5-15

5a	Prohibition (A)	*"When you pray,*
b		*you shall not be like the hypocrites,*
c		*for they love to pray*
d		*while standing*
		in the synagogues and
		on the street corners
e		*so that they can be seen by people.*
f	Result (B)	*I tell you the truth, they have received their reward.*
6a	Antithesis (C)	*But as for you,*
		when you pray,
b		*go into your closet,*
		shut the door, and
		pray to your Father who is unseen.
c	Result (D)	*Then your Father who sees in secret will reward you.*
7a	Prohibition (A)	*Now*
		when you pray
b		*do not babble as the Gentiles do,*
c	Explanation of 7b	*for they think they will be heard because of their many words.*
8a	Prohibition (A)	*Don't be like them,*
b	Basis of 8a	*for your Father knows what needs you have*
		before you can even ask him about them.
9a	Antithesis (C)	*Therefore, pray like this:*
b		*Our Father who is in heaven,*
c	Petition #1	*(i) may your name be kept sacred.*
10a	Petition #2	*(ii) May your kingdom come;*
b	Petition #3	*(iii) may your will be done on earth as it is in heaven.*
11a	Petition #4	*(iv) Give us today our daily needs.*
12a	Petition #5	*(v) And forgive us our sins*
b	Condition	*as we also forgive those*
		who sin against us.
13a	Petition #6	*(vi) And do not let us yield to temptation, but*
b		*deliver us from the evil one.*
14a	Addendum/Condition	*For if you forgive others*
		who sin against you,
b	Result	*your heavenly Father will forgive you,*
15a	Condition	*but if you refuse to forgive others,*
b	Result	*your Father will not forgive your sins either."*

Structure and Literary Form

Most believe that this is a Q passage and that Matthew has expanded an originally shorter form (in Luke 11:2 – 4). However, Lohmeyer has supported two different sources behind the Matthean and Lukan forms,[1] and Carson argues that in reality we need to recognize that Jesus gave this prayer on more than one occasion.[2] So this is M material.

The structure of the admonition (vv. 5 – 6) is exactly like that on almsgiving (see above) but is followed by a second admonition (vv. 7 – 8) with a slightly different form: the "whenever" clause here is followed by two prohibitions followed by "for" (γάρ) clauses that provide the reason for the prohibitions. Finally, the Lord's Prayer (vv. 9 – 13) contains a worshipful introduction followed by a series of requests that divide neatly into three "thou"-petitions (centering on concern for the things of God) followed by three "we"-petitions (centering on personal needs).[3]

Exegetical Outline

➡ **I. Problem of Ostentatious Prayer (6:5 – 6)**
- A. Prohibition — don't desire to be seen by men (no reward) (v. 5)
- B. Positive command — pray privately to the Father (reward) (v. 6)

II. Problem of Long-Winded Praying (6:7 – 8)
- A. Don't babble — only think they'll be heard (v. 7)
- B. Don't pray like this — your Father knows your needs (v. 8)

III. The Model Prayer (6:9 – 13)
- A. Introduction — worship (v. 9a)
- B. The thou-petitions (vv. 9b – 10)
- C. The we-petitions (vv. 11 – 13)

IV. Addendum (6:14 – 15)
- A. Forgive and be forgiven (v. 14)
- B. Don't forgive and be condemned (v. 15)

Explanation of the Text

6:5 When you pray, you shall not be like the hypocrites (Καὶ ὅταν προσεύχησθε, οὐκ ἔσεσθε ὡς οἱ ὑποκριταί). Jesus is not deriding any particular posture, for in Scripture people prayed in every position — standing (Luke 18:11, 13), sitting (2 Sam 7:18), kneeling (Luke 22:41), and prostrate on the ground (Matt 26:39). Standing with hands upraised was the normal form for prayer, and kneeling or

1. Ernst Lohmeyer, *The Lord's Prayer* (London: Collins, 1965), 293.

2. Carson, "Matthew," 168.

3. Keener, *Matthew*, 210, sees an ABAB pattern, with prohibitions in vv. 5, 7 and positive instructions how to pray properly in vv. 6, 9.

prostrating was done in time of serious need. Yet it is not the posture but the motive that matters.

The use of the future for a command ("you shall not be" [οὐκ ἔσεσθε]) is similar to the quotations from the OT in the antitheses (see 5:21, 27, 33, 43) and is a stronger form of command. The hypocrites (ὑποκριταί) care only about appearances (see v. 2 above) and so pray mainly in public places where they can impress people with their erudition and piety.

6:5 ... for they love to pray while standing in the synagogues and on the street corners so that they can be seen by people (ὅτι φιλοῦσιν ἐν ταῖς συναγωγαῖς καὶ ἐν ταῖς γωνίαις τῶν πλατειῶν ἑστῶτες προσεύχεσθαι, ὅπως φανῶσιν τοῖς ἀνθρώποις). The perfect tense "while standing" (ἑστῶτες) pictures the person taking a stance and continuing in it, obviously to be noticed by others. The synagogue was the center of Jewish life, not only of worship but of nearly every aspect of civic life. Like the temple, synagogues were called houses of prayer, and the ruler of the synagogue would regularly call on individuals to pray. Prayers were common in the synagogue, and the street corner was even more publicly visible. The people were expected to pray at the hour of the morning and evening sacrifices, the third and ninth hours (Ezra 9:5; Dan 9:21), and many would add a prayer at midday (Dan 6:10). The picture is of a person contriving to be at a busy street corner at the hour of prayer so everyone could observe such incredible piety.

6:5 I tell you the truth, they have received their reward (ἀμὴν λέγω ὑμῖν, ἀπέχουσιν τὸν μισθὸν αὐτῶν). Jesus uses another "amen" (ἀμήν) saying to highlight the importance of this truth (see on 5:18). His point is that they have received all the reward they will ever get, the plaudits of others (see on 6:2).

6:6 But as for you, when you pray, go into your closet, shut the door, and pray to your Father who is unseen (σὺ δὲ ὅταν προσεύχῃ, εἴσελθε εἰς τὸ ταμεῖόν σου καὶ κλείσας τὴν θύραν σου πρόσευξαι τῷ πατρί σου τῷ ἐν τῷ κρυπτῷ). The emphatic "you" (σύ) draws attention to the disciples' responsibility, "but as for you." The "closet" (ταμεῖον) is a small storage closet inside the otherwise single-room Palestinian home. It was the only room that could be locked, in one sense the least sanctified part of the home with food for animals, etc., but in another the most private part of the home.[4] The point is total privacy to commune with the Father apart from outside distractions.[5]

6:6 Then your Father who sees in secret will reward you (καὶ ὁ πατήρ σου ὁ βλέπων ἐν τῷ κρυπτῷ ἀποδώσει σοι). Prayer is seen as a private time of communion only with God "in secret" (ἐν τῷ κρυπτῷ), which means he dwells in the secret places where he is "unseen."[6] This of course does not disparage corporate prayer, but even that should be private in the sense of a time between God and his community. The major point is the complete absence of any desire to impress others. As in 6:4, 18 the reward[7]

4. Bruner, *Christbook*, 234.

5. There is a close similarity with Isa 26:20, "go ... enter your rooms and shut the doors behind you," although there the point is to hide from the wrath of God.

6. Note the development of "in secret" (ἐν τῷ κρυπτῷ). First the Father dwells "in the secret places" and then he sees what is done "in secret." This is a dominant motif and both repeats vv. 4, 6 and will be repeated in v. 18. For this idea, see Paul Ellingworth, "'In Secret'? (Matthew 6.4, 6, 18)," *BT* 40 (1989): 446 – 47.

7. There is a question whether "in secret" modifies God "seeing in secret" or rewarding "in secret." The phrase "in secret" (ἐν τῷ κρυπτῷ) is between the two verbs and could go either way. Nevertheless, the context favors the sense of God seeing what is done privately. The article (τῷ) shows that the prepositional phrase is adjectival, i.e., modifying "Father."

then will come from God and be both earthly blessing and heavenly, eternal joy.

6:7 Now when you pray[8] **do not babble as the Gentiles do** (Προσευχόμενοι δὲ μὴ βατταλογήσητε ὥσπερ οἱ ἐθνικοί). Jesus moves from ostentatious prayer to prattling prayers. The background of "babble" (βατταλογήσητε) is uncertain,[9] but all are agreed that it means the type of prayer that goes on and on with little or no content. Nolland says "it is likely to be a deprecatory way of speaking about the formulaic repetition of either intelligible (names of gods, petitionary formulas, etc.) or unintelligible ('words' of magical powers or the language of the gods) elements in order to multiply effectiveness with the gods."[10]

6:7 ... for they think they will be heard because of their many words (δοκοῦσιν γὰρ ὅτι ἐν τῇ πολυλογίᾳ αὐτῶν εἰσακουσθήσονται). The key is the "many words" (causal "because" [ἐν]) that characterize such prayers. This is not a diatribe against lengthy prayers per se (Jesus prayed all night, Luke 6:12, as well as lengthily in Mark 1:35; 6:46; 14:35 – 42) but rather the type of long prayer with endless repetition and virtually meaningless gibberish. The Gentiles who "think they will be heard" (a divine passive) because of such prayers may partly reflect the pagan practice of repeating an extensive list of the names of a god, thinking if they could get the correct name and pronounce it correctly, they could manipulate the god.[11] It was also common to utter nonsense syllables in magic incantations (similar to mantras in Eastern religions today).[12] The main thing is the utter emptiness of such a jingoistic prayer. These are not prayers of worship or intercession but self-centered prayers that try to control the gods.

6:8 Don't be like them, for your Father knows what needs you have before you can even ask him about them (μὴ οὖν ὁμοιωθῆτε αὐτοῖς, οἶδεν γὰρ ὁ πατὴρ ὑμῶν ὧν χρείαν ἔχετε πρὸ τοῦ ὑμᾶς αἰτῆσαι αὐτόν). God's knowledge of our needs will be stated again in 6:32 and is found in Isa 65:24, "Before they call I will answer." God's people do not need pagan-type length, for the pagans have no concept of a God who cares (1 Pet 5:7) and responds to his people. The idea of a loving Father who responds to the prayers of his people occurs throughout Scripture (Ps 55:22; Isa 30:19; Luke 11:9 – 13; 18:1 – 5; Rom 8:26 – 28; Rev 6:9 – 11). The kingdom citizen does not need to prattle on and on as if God is hard of hearing or has a short attention span. This is exemplified in the short, balanced, and profound prayer that follows.

Introduction to Jesus' model prayer. This prayer, as many have noted, would better be called "The Disciple's Prayer" (with the Lord's Prayer being John 17).[13]

8. "When you pray" (προσευχόμενοι) is another of Matthew's many temporal participles (see 1:18, 20; 2:3, 19, 22).

9. See Guelich, *Sermon on the Mount*, 282; Davies and Allison, *Matthew*, 1:587 – 88. There are three possibilities: (1) the Aramaic *bāṭēl*, meaning "thoughtless, ineffectual" speech or babbling; (2) from βάτος plus λέγειν, meaning futile exertion; (3) from βατταρίζω, meaning "stutter, stammer," thus onomatopoeia for "babble." It is difficult to know for certain.

10. Nolland, *Matthew*, 284.

11. See Gundry, *Matthew*, 104.

12. Blomberg, *Matthew*, 118.

13. Scholars debate whether this or the shorter form in Luke 11:2 – 4 (without the third petition [on God's will] and the sixth [on deliverance from the evil one]) is original, with most taking Luke as the more authentic. But it is better to see Jesus as praying both forms on different occasions (R. V. G. Tasker, *The Gospel according to St. Matthew* [TNTC; Grand Rapids: Eerdmans, 1961], 72; Carson, "Matthew," 167 – 68; Morris, *Matthew*, 143). Nearly everyone considers the prayer authentic, except for the Jesus Seminar, which considers it largely inauthentic (see J. D. Crossan, *The Historical Jesus: The Life of a Mediterranean Jewish Peasant* [San Francisco: Harper, 1991], 293 – 94; and R. W. Funk et al., *The Five Gospels: The Search for the Authentic Words of Jesus* [New York: Macmillan, 1993]). The only red-letter part of the prayer for them is "Father," as if Jesus started the prayer, lost his train of thought, and then went on to other things!!

It quickly became a liturgical prayer, prayed three times a day by mid-second century (*Did.* 8:3), and it was restricted to members of the church due to its holy contents. That certainly is one purpose, for liturgical prayers were common in Judaism.[14] But it is more than this. On the basis of "like this" (οὕτως, v. 9), it is also intended more as a model for prayer as well as a statement of Christian priorities and a guide to a philosophy for living the Christian life (i.e., it is meant to be lived as well as prayed).[15]

Finally, while some have considered this primarily an eschatological prayer (mainly for the final kingdom to arrive),[16] such a notion overstates the case. Certainly the thou-petitions have a definite eschatological tone (see below), but the we-petitions are mainly for present needs, and it is best to see an inaugurated thrust throughout (the tension between the now and the not yet). The first three are more eschatological and center on the coming of the kingdom, while the other three are more present in tone, centering on the physical and spiritual needs of God's people.[17] Moreover, the first three petitions echo the first table of the Decalogue (God-oriented) and the last three the second table of the Decalogue (personal needs).

6:9 Therefore, pray like this (Οὕτως οὖν προσεύχεσθε ὑμεῖς). The introduction is meaningful. The emphatic "you" (ὑμεῖς) and the present tense "pray" (προσεύχεσθε) make it intensely personal. This is only for true disciples, and each is to pray this way regularly. Moreover, "like this" (οὕτως) shows it provides the manner of praying more than the content of the prayer; it gives a model or outline of the type of prayer Jesus intends for the kingdom community.

6:9 Our Father (Πάτερ ἡμῶν). The address is highly theological. "Our Father" is Greek for the Aramaic *Abba* and does have parallels in Jewish prayers (*m. Soṭah* 9:15; *t. Ber.* 3:14),[18] with the "our" showing it is especially a community prayer, meant for the life of the church. The regular use of *Abba*, especially in its absolute form "Father," characterized Jesus' prayers[19] and was his great contribution to Jewish prayer theology, which tended to be more formal.[20] *Abba* brings in the centrality of relationship, the

14. Davies and Allison, *Matthew*, 1:595 – 7, shows the similarities of Jesus' prayer to the Jewish Kaddish, prayed in the synagogue at the end of the sermon, and to the Tefillah or Eighteen Benedictions (especially in its abbreviated form), also prayed three times each day. On this see also D. Baumgardt, "Kaddish and the Lord's Prayer," *JBQ* 19 (1991): 164 – 69.

15. For the ethical mandate inherent in the prayer, see David E. Garland, "The Lord's Prayer in the Gospel of Matthew," *RevExp* 89 (1992): 215 – 28.

16. Joachim Jeremias, *The Prayers of Jesus* (trans. J. Bowden et al.; Philadelphia: Fortress, 1964); Raymond E. Brown, "The Pater Noster as an Eschatological Prayer," *TS* 22 (1961): 175 – 208; Paul Trudinger, "The 'Our Father' in Matthew as Apocalyptic Eschatology," *DRev* 107 (1989): 49 – 54. They argue that the prayer for bread is mainly for the heavenly manna, the forgiveness of sins occurring at the last judgment, and that "don't let us be tested" is referring to the test at the end of this age.

17. J. B. Gibson, "Matthew 6:9 – 13/Luke 11:2 – 4: An Eschatological Prayer?" *BTB* 31 (2001): 96 – 105, considers the ethical/spiritual dimension the major thrust. Christ is calling on the disciples to reject "this generation" and live wholly for God.

18. Keener, *Matthew*, 217 – 18.

19. The only prayer in which he does not use "Father" is his cry of dereliction from the cross, "My God, my God, why have you abandoned me?"

20. Joachim Jeremias, *New Testament Theology: The Proclamation of Jesus* (trans. J. Bowden; New York: Scribner, 1971), 61 – 68, argues there were no Jewish parallels. This was challenged by James Barr, "*ʾAbbā Isn't Daddy*," *JTS* 39 (1988): 28 – 47, who pointed out several parallels and denied the uniqueness and meaning of Jeremias. Since then the consensus has been that Jeremias was still essentially correct, though overstating his case. J. D. G. Dunn, "Prayer," *DJG*, 618 – 9, points out that the use of *Abba* in Mark 14:36 and the creeds of Rom 8:15 and Gal 4:6 show the Aramaic form was used in the Greek-speaking churches, so it became central to liturgical worship. See Keener, *Matthew*, 217, for Hellenistic parallels in which Zeus, the head of the gods, was called "father."

intimacy between father and children; we share Jesus' sonship in his special filial relationship to his "Father." When we pray, we pray in the certainty that our "Father" is hearing us, the one who loves us so deeply and watches over us. There is a whole new intimacy and reverence in our prayer life.

6:9 ... who is in heaven (ὁ ἐν τοῖς οὐρανοῖς). The addition of "in heaven" tells of God's transcendence and sovereign power (it is found twenty times in Matthew with "Father" and only in Mark 11:25 elsewhere in the Synoptics), so "Father in heaven" means that Almighty God, the omnipotent One, who dwells in heavenly splendor and power, cares deeply for our needs.

6:9 May your name be kept sacred (ἁγιασθήτω τὸ ὄνομά σου). *The first God-oriented petition* is that the sacredness of God's name be magnified in every area of life. In the ancient world a person's name bespoke the very essence of the person (see on 1:21), so God's name tells who he is at the core of his being. Since holiness is at the heart of the divine character, that must be made evident in everything the disciple does.

There are two aspects of this: that God will make his holiness manifest throughout the world, and that we will honor his name in everything that we do (so the aorist passive "may it be kept sacred" [ἁγιασθήτω] has two implied subjects, God and us). This reflects the inaugurated thrust, for the sacredness of his name will not be truly triumphant until the eschaton arrives, and yet it must be visible to all in the lives of his people. For the Jews "one could ask with integrity for the future hallowing of God's name only if one lived in the present as if one valued it."[21]

6:10 May your kingdom come (ἐλθέτω ἡ βασιλεία σου). *The second God-oriented petition* is concerned mainly with the eschaton. The God-petitions are all tied together in the sense that they all reflect a desire for the coming of the final kingdom (cf. 1 Cor 16:22; Rev 22:20). God's name will never be finally honored until Christ's return.

Yet there is also an ABA pattern in the sense that the eschatological element is primarily in this second petition, surrounded by two that are perhaps primarily related to the present community. So while this second petition includes a desire that the kingdom come upon unbelievers (i.e., evangelism) and that God's people experience the kingdom in a new way (i.e., spiritual growth), it primarily centers on a desire for this world to end. The Jews said that any prayer that fails to ask for the kingdom is not a true prayer. So this prayer asks for the present kingdom to manifest itself in new ways, but especially asks that God end this present order and bring the kingdom in fullness.

6:10 May your will be done on earth as it is in heaven (γενηθήτω τὸ θέλημά σου, ὡς ἐν οὐρανῷ καὶ ἐπὶ γῆς). *The third God-oriented petition*[22] sums up the others, as God's will is that his name be honored and his kingdom arrive in fullness. Again, this is both present and future. God's will refers to his divine purposes first for his people and then for the world as a whole. This is a prayer that "his good, pleasing and perfect will" (Rom 12:2) be fully realized in the lives of his people.

At the same time, it is a prayer that the fullness of his will, known only in heaven at present, be fully consummated via the second coming. This

21. Keener, *Matthew*, 219.

22. All three verbs in the God-centered petitions are aorist, looking at the action as a single whole. Porter, *Idioms*, 228 – 29, points out that the aorist is the common imperative used in prayers. All of the prayers in Matthew are in the aorist, and in Luke 11:2 – 4 (the short form) only "give us our daily bread" employs a present tense, probably because the section following (Luke 11:5 – 13) centers on God's continual giving.

will come with the arrival of "a new heaven and a new earth" (Rev 21:1), when the old order passes away and the eternal order will begin. At present we cannot introduce his perfect will and lead the people of this world to embrace it. But we can proclaim his name and guide those around us to follow his will more fully. This will prepare for its finalization in the future, when God intervenes in world history to lead his creation to his completed will.

6:11 Give us today our daily needs (τὸν ἄρτον ἡμῶν τὸν ἐπιούσιον δὸς ἡμῖν σήμερον). *The first we-oriented petition* turns the attention from God to the pray-er, as seen in the switch from second person ("your") to first person ("our") as well as the two uses of "and" (καί) that links vv. 11–13 into a single unit (physical and spiritual needs). In general "bread" stands for food and then for all a person's needs. Its meaning is hotly debated, with many arguing it is the eschatological bread of the messianic banquet rather than the bread of today.[23] The majority, however, take it as a metaphor for a person's daily needs.

The most debated issue is the meaning of ἐπιούσιον. It rarely appears even in secular literature of the period and could have several meanings:[24] (1) necessary for existence (from ἐπί + οὐσία); (2) for the current day (from ἐπὶ τὴν οὖσαν [from εἰμί] ἡμέραν); (3) for the following day (from ἐπὶ τὴν ἐπιοῦσαν [from ἐπεῖναι] ἡμέραν); (4) for the coming day (from ἐπιέναι). Those who take it eschatologically tend to accept the fourth, and those who take it of current needs opt for the third. It is best in the context to combine the second and third and to translate it as, "give us our bread for today and tomorrow."

In terms of the Jewish prayers, the morning prayer is for today's bread, and the evening prayer for tomorrow's bread.[25] This is a prayer reflecting total God-dependence. When most pray it, they think, "Gimme, gimme, gimme." But this petition actually means, "I rely on you for my daily needs."[26] Moreover, it reflects an attitude that takes one day at a time, reflecting the first-century day laborer who was paid one day at a time.[27] The point is trusting God for each day's need, reflecting faith as "being sure of what we hope for and certain of what we do not see" (Heb 11:1). With God in charge, each day is taken care of.

6:12 And forgive us our sins (καὶ ἄφες ἡμῖν τὰ ὀφειλήματα ἡμῶν). *The second we-oriented petition* turns from physical needs to spiritual needs. This and the next petition show that while earthly needs are important, spiritual needs are paramount. The crucial term here is τὰ ὀφειλήματα, a commercial term meaning "debt"[28] but with a secondary metaphorical meaning (drawn from

23. Jeremias, *Prayers*, 100–102; Davies and Allison, *Matthew*, 1:609–10; Hagner, *Matthew 1–13*, 149. For a historical survey see David Hill, "'Our Daily Bread' (Matt 6.11) in the History of Exegesis," *IBS* 5 (1983): 2–10. Henri Bourgoin, "*Epiousios* expliqué par la notion de préfixe vide," *Bib* 60 (1979): 91–96, translates it "the essential bread" and interprets it as referring to the Eucharist.

24. From BAGD; Davies and Allison, *Matthew*, 1:607–8; Strecker, *Sermon on the Mount*, 117–8; Hagner, *Matthew 1–13*, 149–50; M. P. John, "Give Us This Day Our ... Bread (Matthew 6.11)," *TBT* 3 (1980): 245–47.

25. See Morris, *Matthew*, 146; Colin J. Hemer, "Epiousios," *JSNT* 22 (1984): 81–94.

26. Heinz Heinen, "Göttliche Sitomatrie: Beobachtungen zur Brotbitte des Vaterunsers," *TTZ* 99 (1990): 72–79, sees this reflecting the Roman practice of *sitomatrion*, the daily ration of grain, and therefore centers on our dependence on God.

27. Edward M. Yamauchi, "The 'Daily Bread' Motif in Antiquity," *WTJ* 28 (1966): 145–56; Carson, "Matthew," 171.

28. A few like S. T. Lachs, "On Matthew vi. 12," *NovT* 17 (1975): 6–8, take this literally of loans (especially in the year before they are forgiven at the Jubilee year), but that is unnecessary and does not fit the context.

Aramaic) of "sin," as a "debt" to God (Luke translates this and places "sin" in the text; cf. also 6:14 – 15 below). Matthew places great emphasis on forgiveness, as seen in the parable of 18:21 – 35 on the "unforgiving servant," which ends, "This is how my heavenly Father will treat each of you unless you forgive a brother or sister from the heart" (cf. 6:14 – 15). Ἀφίημι has a wide range of meanings: "let go, give up" as well as "cancel, remit," or "leave, abandon" or "let go, tolerate" (BAGD, 125 – 6). When used of sin it refers to remission of guilt and removal of the debt.

6:12 ... as we also forgive those who sin against us (ὡς καὶ ἡμεῖς ἀφήκαμεν τοῖς ὀφειλέταις ἡμῶν). The point here is that our experience of forgiveness must result in a change of heart on our part and a willingness to forgive those who have hurt us in a far less way than we have hurt God.[29] Forgiveness is a major theme in Matthew (see 9:5, 6; 12:31 – 32; 18:21, 35). A renewed fellowship with God means a renewed fellowship with others in the community. It is not that our forgiveness is the basis of God's forgiveness (yet see vv. 14 – 15 below), but rather that as we experience being pardoned by God, we must exercise in a greater willingness to pardon others. We are changed and strengthened by God's love, enabling us to have the enabling power to do it ourselves.

6:13 And do not let us yield to temptation (καὶ μὴ εἰσενέγκῃς ἡμᾶς εἰς πειρασμόν). *The third we-oriented petition* concerns the "tests" or "temptations" that we all undergo. πειρασμός can mean either a test/trial or a temptation (see on 4:1), and James moves from the test (Jas 1:2 – 5) to the temptation (1:13 – 15). At Jesus' test/temptation, he was tested by God and tempted by Satan (see on 4:1), and this makes "tempt" more likely since it is the "evil one" we are delivered from in the next line.[30] Yet whether a test or a temptation, the literal meaning ("don't lead us into temptation/test") is problematic, for Jas 1:13 says, "God cannot be tempted by evil, nor does he tempt anyone," and it is clear throughout Scripture that God tests all believers (see on 4:1 – 13). This cannot be a prayer asking God not to do what we already know he does not do.

It is increasingly common to see the eschatological interpretation here as well, i.e., a prayer that God will keep us from the final days of testing before the eschaton.[31] While that is certainly possible, it goes beyond the context, and one would expect a definite article before πειρασμός ("*the* test") in that case.[32] It is best seen as present temptation, probably with a permissive or causative sense, "don't let us succumb to temptation," meaning "give us strength" (cf. 1 Cor 10:13).[33]

6:13 ... but deliver us from the evil one (ἀλλὰ ῥῦσαι ἡμᾶς ἀπὸ τοῦ πονηροῦ). The second

29. Arland J. Hultgren, "Forgive Us, As We Forgive (Matthew 6:12)," *WW* 16 (1996): 284 – 90, calls this a "performative utterance," which brings reconciliation to the fractured relationships in the community.

30. For the view that it is a test and not a temptation, see Kenneth Grayston, "The Decline of Temptation — and the Lord's Prayer," *SJT* 46 (1993): 279 – 95. By contrast, W. M. Watt, "'Lead Us Not into Temptation,'" *ExpTim* 110 (1999): 80, interprets this of doubting God, thus as a prayer that God may keep us from situations when we question his presence in our lives. Such attempts are interesting and possible, but the context makes the experience of temptation the most viable.

31. In addition to those named in fns. 23, 28 above, see Keener, *Matthew*, 224 – 25; and Peter S. Cameron, "'Lead Us Not into Temptation,'" *ExpTim* 101 (1990): 299 – 301, who takes this of final judgment, "Do not judge us according to our deserts," because then the judgment would be inevitable.

32. Strecker, *Sermon on the Mount*, 122; Carson, "Matthew," 173.

33. Jeremias, *Prayers*, 202, saw this as an Aramaic permissive, "do not allow us to fall when tempted." See also Gundry, *Matthew*, 109; Davies and Allison, *Matthew*, 1:613; W. Ernest Moore, "Lead Us Not into Temptation," *ExpTim* 102 (1991): 171 – 72; Blomberg, *Matthew*, 120; R. J. Tournay, "Ne nous laisse pas entrer en tentation," *NRTh* 120 (1998): 440 – 43.

element of this petition (not a separate prayer) asks God for the flip side of "don't let us yield," namely, "deliver us from the evil one." The personalized form is better than the traditional "from evil"[34] because the articular "the evil one" (τοῦ πονηροῦ) favors the more personal concept, though of course "evil" and "the evil one" are virtually synonymous. In Matthew the "evil one" causes us to twist our words into lies (5:37), takes kingdom truths out of our heart (13:19), and sows evil in our lives (13:19)."Deliver" means "save us from" and connotes the idea of both protection and removal from his power. So the final petition asks God for strength and deliverance from the temptations wrought by Satan.

The traditional doxology ("for yours is the kingdom and the power and the glory forever. Amen") appears in only a few late manuscripts (L W Θ 0233 et al.), and several of the best manuscripts end here (ℵ B D Z et al.), with a variety of endings in others. This makes it almost certain that it is not original. It is possible that churches added their own doxology when praying this prayer, and this one emerged as the best summary of the contents of the prayer.[35] However, it (and the other endings) is based on 1 Chr 29:11 – 13 and is meaningful, so it is not wrong to utter the ending as a personal prayer.

6:14 For if you forgive others[36] who sin against you, your heavenly Father will forgive you (Ἐὰν γὰρ ἀφῆτε τοῖς ἀνθρώποις τὰ παραπτώματα αὐτῶν, ἀφήσει καὶ ὑμῖν ὁ πατὴρ ὑμῶν ὁ οὐράνιος). This is a remarkable addendum. We do not know the original scene, whether Jesus commented on more than just the fifth petition. However, this is the one that struck Matthew, and the early church obviously felt it was essential that community harmony precede worship. The positive part here virtually repeats the idea of v. 12 but reverses the two clauses and turns it into a conditional sentence, meaning that our experience of forgiveness is now predicated on our willingness to forgive others. The importance of right relationships among God's people cannot be overstated. It is at the heart of following God (cf. 1 Cor 13:13, "And now these three remain: faith, hope and love. But the greatest of these is love").

6:15 But if you refuse to forgive others, your Father will not forgive your sins either (ἐὰν δὲ μὴ ἀφῆτε τοῖς ἀνθρώποις, οὐδὲ ὁ πατὴρ ὑμῶν ἀφήσει τὰ παραπτώματα ὑμῶν). This is an incredibly serious warning. The child of the kingdom who has a fractured relationship with someone else in the community has also fractured his or her relationship with God. Obviously, this is not meant in an absolute sense. When we have been seriously hurt by another, it takes a great deal of time to come to the place where we can forgive the one who hurt us so much. Jesus here is speaking of a bitter person who refuses to forgive and wants to carry a grudge.

Nor does this verse mean that everyone who is angry is headed for eternal punishment. But it does mean that a split community has hurt its relationship with God (and the same with the individual). Davies and Allison points to the fact that a forgiveness logion is connected to a prayer saying not only here but also in Matt 18:15 – 35; Mark 11:20 – 25; Luke 17:3 – 6 and concludes, "The right of the eschatological community to utter the Lord's Prayer depends, as does the efficacy of the prayer, upon communal reconciliation."[37]

34. Though see E. Milton, "'Deliver Us from the Evil Imagination': Matt. 6:13b in Light of the Jewish Doctrine of the *Yêtzer Hārā'*," *RelStTh* 13 (1995): 52 – 67, who in light of the Jewish doctrine of the two *yetzers* ("impulses") interprets this of human imagination and its "inclination" to evil.

35. See Guelich, *Sermon on the Mount*, 297; Davies and Allison, *Matthew*, 1:615n.

36. As in 5:13, 16, 19; 6:1, 2, 5, 15, 16, 18, τοῖς ἀνθρώποις is used generically for "people."

37. Davies and Allison, *Matthew*, 1:617.

Theology in Application

Prayer is at the heart simple communion with our Father. It is an incredible gift, and perhaps no other religion has ever conceived of so loving a relationship with their god(s) as has the Judeo-Christian one. It must be said at the outset that God loves us far more than we love him, and so prayer is often misused by the Christian. At the heart prayer is simply returning to God the love he has shown us. It is a desire to share every aspect of life with the One who has done so much for us. Yet there are certain responsibilities that we have in prayer, and Jesus here reminds us of several.

1. Not Using Prayer to Get Attention

By definition prayer is a private communion with God, not a public manifestation of piety. To misuse the vertical love relationship with our Lord as a horizontal showcase to impress others is an abomination. There can be no worship where ostentation is in control (see the parable of the tax collector and the Pharisee; Luke 18:9 – 14).

2. Power of Prayer Based on Quality, not Quantity

The Gentiles acted as if their gods were hard of hearing and quite dense. They only heard requests after a great deal of imploring and wheedling. The Jews prayed the Eighteen Benedictions two or three times a day. Jesus does teach persistent prayer (Luke 11:9 – 13; 18:1 – 8) and Paul says to "pray continually" (1 Thess 5:17; cf. Rom 1:9 – 10; Eph 6:18; Col 1:3; 2 Tim 1:3), but these passages refer to regular prayers as much as to lengthy prayers.

This does not mean lengthy times of prayer are in and of themselves wrong. Martin Luther got up well before dawn to spend three hours in prayer. But length must not become a magic formula for getting God to hear, and the use of repetitive phrases and mantras will never be accepted by God. God desires a childlike attitude of loving communication. The deepest prayer is often uttered at work in the midst of pressure when one says simply, "Lord, I am in trouble. Give me wisdom, and thank you for being with me right now." That is a quality prayer! One wonders also whether some types of modern worship with the "7 – 11" style (seven words repeated eleven times) might fall into the error of needless repetition, which can produce emotional worship but seldom true worship.

3. The Heart of Prayer Is Worship

When we say, "Our Father who is in heaven," we are not uttering a formal address but celebrating a relationship. We are reminding ourselves of the deep intimacy and incomprehensible love of the One to whom we pray. Moreover, by uttering "our," we also celebrate the fact that we are "co-heirs with Christ" (Rom 8:17) and share his relationship with the Father. It is Christ's incredibly deep relationship with his Father that we share. We are part of the family of God and so corporately celebrate this new oneness with him and Christ in an "our" setting. That is the heart of worship — sharing this new intimacy first with Christ and then with "our" brothers and sisters.

4. Corporate, Not Just Individual, Prayer

The Lord's Prayer, with its plural pronouns and verbs, is meant to be uttered as a community. The NT is clear: every aspect of the Christian life is intended to be lived out together as the family of God. We pray together, grow spiritually together, and stimulate one another in each part of our spiritual growth. We were not made to be rugged individualists, and Christians who do not share with others live a life God never intended. Good examples of the power of corporate prayer are the prayers of Acts 4:24 – 26; 12:12; 13:1 – 3.

5. Concern with the Things of God before Our Own Needs

Jesus deliberately placed God-centered issues first, following both the Ten Commandments (Exod 20) and his own summary of the Torah (Matt 22:34 – 40). Primarily, the three God-centered petitions are concerned with the final coming of his kingdom. Only when his kingdom arrives in power and destroys evil will his name be truly honored and his will be truly done. Yet there are lifestyle issues as well. True prayer means that our greatest priority is to honor God in our lives and do his will. If we truly feel we are citizens of heaven (Phil 3:20) as well as "foreigners" and "exiles" on earth (1 Pet 1:1, 17; 2:11), we will live only to please our heavenly Father by doing his will.

6. Bringing All Our Personal Needs to God in Total Dependence on Him

The final three petitions summarize our earthly (the first petition) and spiritual (the other two) needs. They also show God's concern for the "little things" in our lives. This is also the message of 6:25 – 34; God will take care of our daily needs. But will we trust him or spend all our energy trusting only ourselves? There are two aspects of this: (1) there are the individual needs we have, but also (2) we must be corporately concerned for each other's needs. Still, it is prayer and thus demands that we are trusting God rather than self for our daily requirements.

7. God's Community Is All about Forgiveness and Reconciliation

We already saw this in 5:21 – 26, which was about seeking reconciliation when anger has broken the community apart. This tells how reconciliation is accomplished, namely, by the injured party being willing to forgive the hurts caused by others. In fact, Jesus goes further here: our own reconciliation with God is at stake. Bruner says "the unforgiving Christian becomes, *by that fact*, the unforgiven Christian. Consequently, this reading of the Lord's prayer teaches that there should be no praying of this prayer at all where there has not first been the attempt of its pray-ers, 'as far as in you lies' (Rom 12:18), to be on good speaking terms with everyone else in the community."[38]

38. Bruner, *Christbook*, 257.

CHAPTER 22

Matthew 6:16 – 18

Literary Context

The final of the three aspects of Jewish piety is now addressed, and again the topic of ostentatious religious activity is addressed. As with almsgiving and prayer, fasting too must be a private affair done for God alone and not to impress others with one's dedication to God.

- **II. The Kingdom Message Goes Out (4:12 – 7:29)**
  - **B. First Discourse: The Sermon on the Mount (5:1 – 7:29)**
    - **4. Inward Righteousness (6:1 – 18)**
      - b. Prayer (6:5 – 15)
      - ➦ **c. Fasting (6:16 – 18)**

Main Idea

The purpose of fasting is to remind oneself that God is uppermost in life, even over basic human drives. So it is a God-directed activity, and it is completely wrong to want others to see your piety and be impressed. Rather, only God should know that one is fasting.

Translation

(See next page.)

Matthew 6:16-18

16a	Prohibition (A)	*"When you fast,*
b		*don't look sad like the hypocrites do,*
c	Explanation	*for they distort their faces*
d		*in order to show others they are fasting.*
e	Result (B)	*I tell you the truth, they have fully received their reward.*
17a	Antithesis (C)	*But as for you,*
		when you fast,
b	Exhortation	*anoint your head with oil and wash your face*
18a	Purpose of 17b	*so that your fasting will not be seen by others but*
		by your Father
		who exists in the secret place.
b	Result (D)	*Then your Father . . . will reward you*
		who sees what is done in secret."

Structure and Literary Form

Like 6:1 – 4, 5 – 15, this passage takes the form of an admonition, with a prohibition of acting like the "hypocrites" and the promise of earthly reward only, then a positive command extolling proper behavior and a promise of eternal reward.[1]

Exegetical Outline

➡ **I. Prohibition of Ostentatious Fasting (6:16)**
   A. Command — don't look sad like the hypocrites do (v. 16a)
   B. Promise — reward in full (v. 16b)

II. Positive Injunction to Look Happy (6:17 – 18)
   A. Commands (vv. 17 – 18a)
      1. Keep your appearance joyful (v. 17)
      2. Only God should know you are fasting (v. 18a)
   B. Promise — eternal reward from God (v. 18b)

1. This is unique to Matthew, with no Synoptic parallels.

Explanation of the Text

6:16 When you fast, don't look sad like the hypocrites do (Ὅταν δὲ νηστεύητε, μὴ γίνεσθε ὡς οἱ ὑποκριταὶ σκυθρωποί). Fasting (present tense νηστεύητε for repeated activity) was a common activity in Judaism. There was required fasting on the Day of Atonement and the New Year, and the Pharisees fasted every Monday and Thursday. It was often coupled with the wearing of sackcloth and ashes or the tearing of clothes to heighten the feeling of mourning for sin.[2] The "hypocrites" went out of their way to make sure everyone knew they were fasting by being seen with long faces. "Sad" (σκυθρωποί) denotes a "solemn, gloomy, dismal, sad" look and signifies a deliberate attempt to be conspicuous by looking unhappy.

6:16 For they distort their faces in order to show others they are fasting. I tell you the truth, they have fully received their reward (ἀφανίζουσιν γὰρ τὰ πρόσωπα αὐτῶν ὅπως φανῶσιν τοῖς ἀνθρώποις νηστεύοντες· ἀμὴν λέγω ὑμῖν, ἀπέχουσιν τὸν μισθὸν αὐτῶν). Jesus calls it "distorting" or "disfiguring" their faces so as to be seen and lauded for their holiness. There is a deliberate wordplay here — they render themselves unrecognizable (ἀφανίζουσιν) in order to be recognized (φανῶσιν) by others.[3] As in vv. 2, 5, this admiration is all the "reward" they are ever going to get.

6:17 But as for you, when you fast, anoint your head with oil and wash your face (σὺ δὲ νηστεύων ἄλειψαί σου τὴν κεφαλὴν καὶ τὸ πρόσωπόν σου νίψαι). As in 6:6, the "you" (σύ) is emphatic; "your" fasting must be different. Greeks would oil their bodies after exercise and scrape off the sweat and oil with a curved instrument called a "strigil." Jews would put oil on their skin but would especially anoint their heads with oil, perhaps to "lubricate dry scalps."[4] Jesus' point is to clean yourself and look normal when fasting so no one will notice anything different. Note also that this assumes the disciples will fast. This does not contradict 9:14 – 15, which says the disciples weren't fasting, for Jesus says there that this would last only so long as "the bridegroom ... is with them." Afterward, the disciples would return to fasting.

6:18 ... so that your fasting will not be seen by others but by your Father who exists in the secret place. Then your Father who sees what is done in secret will reward you (ὅπως μὴ φανῇς τοῖς ἀνθρώποις νηστεύων ἀλλὰ τῷ πατρί σου τῷ ἐν τῷ κρυφαίῳ· καὶ ὁ πατήρ σου ὁ βλέπων ἐν τῷ κρυφαίῳ ἀποδώσει σοι). The message builds on v. 6 especially but also v. 4. Yet here it says the Father "who exists in the secret place" (τῷ ἐν τῷ κρυφαίῳ), probably meaning that his existence is in the secret realm, namely, heaven. The emphasis is on the development of "in secret" (ἐν τῷ κρυπτῷ): first, the Father dwells "in the secret places" and then he sees what is done "in secret."

Fasting, like almsgiving and prayer, must always be done not for the admiration of others but for the worship of God alone. Whenever fasting becomes a performance, it ceases to be righteous activity. Private communion with the Father is the true goal of fasting. Reward from God is predicated on the right attitude and motivation.

2. R. Banks, "Fasting," *DJG*, 233.

3. Plummer, *Matthew*, 105; Grundmann, *Matthäus*, 207; Gundry, *Matthew*, 111. Davies and Allison, *Matthew*, 1:618, calls this an oxymoron.

4. Keener, *Matthew*, 227 – 28. Guelich, *Sermon on the Mount*, 300, says that the emphasis is on looking normal. This is probably better than Behm, *TDNT*, 4:932, who says it is "eschatological joy" in preparation for a feast.

Theology in Application

Fasting is an intensely personal activity centering entirely on one's relationship with God, and it is an important Christian discipline for kingdom children in this interim age between the advents (Matt 9:15). Its purpose is to remind us that God is the most important aspect of our lives, far more important than major human drives like food or sex (1 Cor 7:5), and fasting places God first. To turn this into an attention-getting device and to prefer human admiration over the worship of God is blasphemous. One's entire devotion must be fixed on the Father.

Fasting is closely connected to prayer and therefore connotes an intense relationship and communion with God. But too many use it almost as magic to get God to answer their prayers, i.e., to so convince God of their sincerity that he will say "yes" to their request. It is good to fast during times of crisis but to center more on God — and not in the mistaken belief that this practice will be more efficacious even than prayer.

CHAPTER 23

Matthew 6:19 – 24

Introduction to Matthew 6:19 – 7:12

The final of the three central sections of the Sermon on the Mount concerns the community citizen's social responsibilities toward possessions (6:19 – 34) and others (7:1 – 12). In the former section, 6:19 – 21 establishes the theme (earthly vs. heavenly treasures), and 6:22 – 24 carries it further, centering on the choice between two masters. Then 6:25 – 34 contrasts worry with trusting God for one's needs. Thus 6:19 – 34 flows naturally out of 6:1 – 18 in the sense that it continues the emphasis on the centrality of God over earthly concerns. In 6:1 – 18 Jesus centered on the vertical aspect of piety; here he centers on the horizontal aspect of human needs, but the message is the same: center on God and his place in our lives, not on self and worldly concerns.

Turner shows how the passage is woven around three types of statements that repeat each other and reinforce the teaching: (1) prohibitions against materialistic concerns and anxiety (6:19, 25, 31, 34a); (2) exhortations demanding kingdom priorities in thought and action (6:20, 33); (3) motivation (via statements, proverbs, illustrations, rhetorical questions) toward obedience (6:21 – 24, 26 – 30, 32, 34b).[1]

Then in 7:1 – 12 Jesus turns to social relationships, centering on a prayer for help (7:7 – 8) along with an example on how God relates to his children (7:9 – 11) in the midst of the responsibilities. The three other sections center on ethical relationships, beginning with an admonition on judging others (7:1 – 5, community ethics), a saying on discernment and restraint in sharing the gospel (7:6, relationships with outsiders), teaching on prayer (7:7 – 11, relationship with God), and a concluding summary on the Golden Rule (7:12, summing up the section as a whole).

Literary Context

Jesus now turns from piety to possessions. Social values begin with choices regarding priorities. What is most important in one's life? Jesus narrows this down to the most critical tension — God or this world. Everyone seeks treasure and stores up

1. Turner, "Matthew," 108.

savings for the future. The question is which will be the master of one's life: God or earthly concerns. Every person will be a slave to something, and the choice centers on what one treasures most. The ultimate choice is between the things of God and the things of earth. What you see is what you will get. If it is the earthly that is in control, the result will be anxiety. If God is in control, the result will be trust. This is the subject of the second half of this section.

II. The Kingdom Message Goes Out (4:12 – 7:29)
B. First Discourse: The Sermon on the Mount (5:1 – 7:29)
5. Social Ethics (6:19 – 7:12)
a. God and Possessions (6:19 – 34)
➦ **(1) Kingdom Priorities and the Two Masters (6:19 – 24)**
(2) Anxiety and Trust (6:25 – 34)

Main Idea

This section centers on priority decisions: Will God or possessions rule in one's life? Which will be the master of one's life and therefore of one's ultimate destiny? Choose you this day whom/what you will serve!

Translation

(See next page.)

Structure and Literary Form

We have here three logia (or sayings) of Jesus (vv. 19 – 21, 22 – 23, 24) that combine to give a single message. The disciple must choose between pursuing wealth and pursuing God. There is an ABA structure, with the parable on the healthy/unhealthy eye separating the two discipleship sayings. All three stem from wisdom motifs[2] and have parallel structures, contrasting two alternatives and providing a concluding observation that establishes the consequences of making the wrong choice.

2. Hagner, *Matthew 1 - 13*, 156 – 7. He points out that all three are found in the *Gospel of Thomas* (logia 76, 24, 47 respectively), where they also have a wisdom setting. Moreover, there are parallels in Luke for the three, with vv. 19 – 21 = Luke 12:33 – 34; vv. 22 – 23 = Luke 11:34 – 36; and v. 24 = Luke 16:13. It is possible that both Matthew and Luke utilize Q here and are drawn from Q, yet the first shows significant differences and could stem from separate sources, and the other two could have their original order in Matthew while Luke has used them topically (so Carson, "Matthew," 176).

Matthew 6:19-24

19a	Prohibition (A)	*"Do not ever store up treasures*
		for yourselves
		on earth,
b		*where moth and corrosion destroy them*
		and thieves break in
		and steal them.
20a	Antithesis (A')	*Instead, store up treasures*
		for yourselves
		in heaven,
b		*where neither moth*
		nor corrosion can destroy them,
		and where thieves cannot break in and
		steal them.
21a	Basis for 19a-20b	*For where your treasure is, your heart will be there as well.*
22a	Assertion	*The eye is a lamp that provides light for the body.*
b	Inference A	*So if your eye is healthy, the whole body is filled with light.*
23a	Inference A'	*But if your eye is unhealthy, your whole body is full of darkness.*
b	Conclusion	*So if the light within you is dark,*
		how great that darkness really is.
24a	Assertion	*No one is able to serve two masters,*
b	Inference A	*for either he will hate the one and love the other or*
c	Inference A'	*be devoted to the one and despise the other.*
d	Conclusion	*You cannot serve God and wealth."*

Exegetical Outline

- **I. The Two Treasures (6:19 – 21)**
  - A. Treasures on earth (v. 19)
    - 1. Moth and rust corrode
    - 2. Thieves steal
  - B. Treasures in heaven (v. 20)
    - 1. Moth and rust do not corrode
    - 2. Thieves cannot steal
  - C. Conclusion — your heart determines your treasure (v. 21)
- **II. The Two Eyes (6:22 – 23)**
  - A. Thesis — the eye determines the body's light (vv. 22 – 23a)
    - 1. Good eye — plenty of light (v. 22)
    - 2. Bad eye — full of darkness (v. 23a)
  - B. Conclusion — dark eye = great darkness (v. 23b)

III. The Two Masters (6:24)
- A. The two options
  1. Hate one and love the other
  2. Devotion to one and contempt for the other
- B. Conclusion — cannot serve God and wealth

Explanation of the Text

6:19 Do not ever store up treasures for yourselves on earth (Μὴ θησαυρίζετε ὑμῖν θησαυροὺς ἐπὶ τῆς γῆς). The present prohibition "do not ever store up" (μὴ θησαυρίζετε) could be prohibiting an action going on ("stop storing up") or (better) stopping future actions ("don't at any time store up").[3] Either way it demands a complete break with such activity.

Originally meaning the box or hole in the ground where people "store up" or "deposit" their precious possessions, "treasure" (θησαυρός) came to mean what is precious or treasured by a person and by extension the great "treasure" one finds or is given. In the OT it came to mean heavenly gifts God gave his people from his heavenly storehouse (weapons of war in Jer 50:25, snow in Deut 28:12; Job 38:22). This later was extended to spiritual blessings and rewards (see on v. 20). Here it means temporary earthly rewards vs. eschatological rewards stored up in heaven (a major theme of the sermon, see "Main Idea" for 5:3 – 12).

6:19 ... where moth and corrosion destroy them and thieves break in and steal them (ὅπου σὴς καὶ βρῶσις ἀφανίζει, καὶ ὅπου κλέπται διορύσσουσιν καὶ κλέπτουσιν). Jesus' two examples were primary sources of wealth. Expensive cloth was everywhere a sign of wealth, and even the poor handed down garments as inheritance. Wealthy people would keep their clothes locked up for fear of their being ruined by moths. Precious metal has always been a source of wealth, and people would bury it under the floor or in the ground to hide it from potential thieves.[4]

ἀφανίζω is a strong term indicating the absolute "destruction, ruin" (BAGD, 124) of the source of wealth. βρῶσις is a problem in that it means "eating, food" and parallel with "moth" could mean another insect (as in Mal 3:1 LXX)[5] or "corrosion" (BAGD, 148), but probably not "rust" (possibly drawn from Jas 5:3). The idea of thieves "breaking in" could be a metaphor for digging through mud-brick walls or under the earthen floor of a house (διορύσσω means "dig through").

6:20 Instead, store up treasures for yourselves in heaven, where neither moth nor corrosion cannot destroy them, and where thieves cannot break in and steal them (θησαυρίζετε δὲ ὑμῖν θησαυροὺς ἐν οὐρανῷ, ὅπου οὔτε σὴς οὔτε βρῶσις ἀφανίζει, καὶ ὅπου κλέπται οὐ διορύσσουσιν οὐδὲ κλέπτουσιν). The idea of reward stored in heaven via good works, almsgiving, and acts of piety was frequent in Judaism (*Pss. Sol.* 9:5; Tob 4:8 – 9; *4 Ezra* 6:5; 7:77; 8:33; *2 Bar.* 24:1; Sir 29:10 – 13; *T. Levi* 13:5). In this context of wealth, this especially connotes using one's secular assets to help the needy or unfortunate financially (cf. Luke 16:9; 1 Tim 6:17 – 19). The message is that one

3. On this see Wallace, 714 – 17, who argues that "stop doing" is problematic, and the normal force is that of an "ongoing process."

4. Keener, *Matthew*, 230 – 31.

5. Guelich, *Sermon on the Mount*, 326 – 27, prefers an insect in the larva stage or "worm."

should not center on temporary rewards but work for eternal rewards (cf. 6:4, 6, 18).[6]

6:21 For where your treasure is, your heart will be there as well (ὅπου γάρ ἐστιν ὁ θησαυρός σου, ἐκεῖ ἔσται καὶ ἡ καρδία σου). Jesus concludes that what people "treasure" becomes the guiding principle for their whole life. "Heart" (καρδία) is the whole being, referring to "the inner person, the seat of understanding, knowledge, and will" (*EDNT*, 2:250). So it means we give total loyalty to that which is of ultimate significance. Jesus is asking whether worldly wealth or the things of God will rule our lives. As Plummer puts it, "We must store our wealth above, in order that our hearts may be drawn upwards. The two act and react upon one another."[7]

6:22 The eye is a lamp that provides light for the body (Ὁ λύχνος τοῦ σώματός ἐστιν ὁ ὀφθαλμός). The idea of the eye (last for emphasis) as a "lamp" producing light is a puzzling metaphor. Many have called this passage one of the most difficult in the gospels.[8] Betz believes that the eye metaphor is interpreted in vv. 22b – 23a and the lamp metaphor in v. 23b. Thus the lamp is the "light within you" and the image is moral rather than physiological.[9]

Another approach is to take the lamp as a metaphor only for v. 22 and all the rest as developing the idea of the eye. Does the body receive light from the eye (objective genitive) or see light through the eye (subjective genitive)? Most accept the former,[10] but it is closely linked to the meaning of the "healthy/unhealthy" (ἁπλοῦς/πονηρός) contrast in vv. 22 – 23.

6:22 So if your eye is healthy, the whole body is filled with light (ἐὰν οὖν ᾖ ὁ ὀφθαλμός σου ἁπλοῦς, ὅλον τὸ σῶμά σου φωτεινὸν ἔσται). Is the ἁπλοῦς/πονηρός contrast meant in a physiological sense ("healthy"/"sick") or a moral sense ("sincere, generous"/"wicked, miserly")? It is common to see this as a both-and rather than an either-or.[11] In short, the reader thinks of the physiological first and then is drawn by the context to the moral aspect.

So the idea is that the eye is the source of light for the body, and if that eye is sound, the entire body will be full of light. Then ἁπλοῦς, which is more an ethical term than a physiological term,[12] points especially to the meaning "singleness of purpose," "wholly dedicated" to God along with a "generosity" of heart.[13] In this context, all of this is probably intended. When the light of God is shining into one's life, a generous spirit is the result, and one will "lighten up" the lives of everyone around.

6:23 But if your eye is unhealthy, your whole body is full of darkness (ἐὰν δὲ ὁ ὀφθαλμός σου

6. Schlatter, *Matthäus*, 221 – 22, says that "in heaven" does not just mean eternal rewards but "with God" — i.e., God's blessings now that will become apparent in one's final reward.

7. Plummer, *Matthew*, 106. Strecker, *Sermon on the Mount*, 132, adds that when one's orientation is toward heaven, the will is not egotistically drawn to self.

8. See H. D. Betz, *Essays on the Sermon on the Mount* (Phildelphia: Fortress, 1985), 71.

9. Ibid., 74. However, Betz's further contention that Matthew is opposing a Platonic/Stoic anthropology is highly unlikely. This is a simple metaphor, not an anthropological statement. There is no evidence for a Neoplatonic basis here.

10. Though see Dale C. Allison, "The Eye Is the Lamp of the Body (Matthew 6:22 – 23 = Luke 11:34 – 36)," *NTS* 33 (1987): 61 – 83, for the other perspective, that ancients believed the eye contained the light and was a lamp itself.

11. Betz, *Essays on the Sermon on the Mount*, 85; Davies and Allison, *Matthew*, 1:638.

12. Guelich, *Sermon on the Mount*, 329; Betz, *Essays on the Sermon on the Mount*, 85.

13. Hagner, *Matthew 1 – 13*, 158. So also T. Zöckler, "Light within the Human Person: A Comparison of Matthew 6:22 – 23 and Gospel of Thomas 24," *JBL* 120 (2001): 487 – 99, after trying to find a Q source behind the Matthew and *Gospel of Thomas* readings.

πονηρὸς ᾖ, ὅλον τὸ σῶμά σου σκοτεινὸν ἔσται). The opposite is now presented. Again, "unhealthy" (πονηρός) is both physiological ("sick") and ethical ("evil, wicked"). The absence of light in a person's life produces great wickedness (cf. John 3:19 – 20), and in this context it means we keep all our wealth for ourselves and refuse to help others.

6:23 So if the light within you is dark, how great that darkness really is (εἰ οὖν τὸ φῶς τὸ ἐν σοὶ σκότος ἐστίν, τὸ σκότος πόσον). This means that moral "darkness" takes over our life. The idea of an "evil eye" will come up again in 20:15 and in Jewish circles spoke of an "evil intent," in this context self-centered, covetous attitudes.[14] Turner adds, "An evil and covetous eye will hoard earthly possessions only to see them decay. A good and generous eye will store up treasures in heaven that will never decay."[15]

6:24 No one is able to serve two masters (Οὐδεὶς δύναται δυσὶ κυρίοις δουλεύειν). The final saying in this context sums up the issues. The "two masters" are obviously God and wealth, a perfect contrast for the affluent Western world today. Technically, it was possible to serve two masters (e.g., Acts 16:16, the slave girl with several "owners"), but Jesus is speaking of ultimate issues. With two masters it would be impossible to give either total allegiance. In the case of God and wealth this is especially true because the two demand opposite things of the slave: possessions demand self-centered living, while God demands that we serve others. Moreover, God's demands are absolute; there is no room for serving wealth.

6:24 … for either he will hate the one and love the other (ἢ γὰρ τὸν ἕνα μισήσει καὶ τὸν ἕτερον ἀγαπήσει). The "he will hate/love" (μισήσει/ἀγαπήσει) dualism is often taken as a comparative (Luke 14:26; cf. Gen 29:30; Matt 5:43; John 12:25);[16] you will love the one more than the other, or in a weakened sense of "reject" the one and "prefer" the other. Yet the stark issues (God vs. wealth) makes it likely that Jesus intends the love/hate contrast.[17] To place possessions above God is idolatry (see "Theology in Application") and therefore constitutes "hate" in God's eyes.

6:24 … or be devoted to the one and despise the other (ἢ ἑνὸς ἀνθέξεται καὶ τοῦ ἑτέρου καταφρονήσει). The "love/hate" dichotomy is extended further in the ἀνθέξεται/καταφρονήσει contrast, with devotion set opposite to contempt. Contempt for God is an intense form of shame, and Jesus warned that those ashamed of God will receive shame (judgment) from God (Mark 8:38 = Luke 9:26).[18] The point of both is that anyone trying to please two masters will ultimately have to choose between them. Only one can receive true loyalty, and the other will inevitably face contempt and rejection, especially since the two are polar opposites (God vs. the world).

6:24 You cannot serve God and wealth (οὐ δύνασθε θεῷ δουλεύειν καὶ μαμωνᾷ). The thrust of the whole paragraph is stated here. Μαμωνᾶς is transliterated from the Aramaic *mammon*, meaning "wealth, property, possessions," and is pictured here as a slave owner. Implicit is the view of God as a benevolent master and wealth as

14. Davies and Allison, *Matthew*, 1:640. On the "evil eye" he notes Deut 15:9; Prov 23:6; 28:22; Tob 4:7; Sir 14:8; 26:11. The background for this is extensively surveyed in John H. Elliott, "The Evil Eye and the Sermon on the Mount: Contours of a Pervasive Belief in Social Scientific Perspective," *BibInt* 2 (1994): 51 – 84. He sees this as directed against envy and covetous desire.

15. Turner, "Matthew," 106.

16. Hill, *Matthew*, 143; Strecker, *Sermon on the Mount*, 134; Hagner, *Matthew 1 – 13*, 159.

17. So Luz, *Matthew 1 – 7*, 335.

18. Bock, *Luke 1:1–9:50*, 857, says, "Mark and Luke agree that being allied to Jesus prevents rejection by him at the judgment."

a malevolent owner (Paul and others consistently used the concept "slave" [δοῦλος] as a metaphor for one's relationship to God). The message is that we all are enslaved to something and must give our all to God as our loving Master, not to worldly wealth.

Theology in Application

The problem of wealth can hardly be overstated. Blomberg says, "It is arguable that materialism is the single biggest competitor with authentic Christianity for the hearts and souls of millions in our world today, including many in the visible church."[19] Materialism is in this sense a false religion, and wealth is idolatry (e.g., the rich fool [Luke 12:13 – 21] who is not "rich toward God"). Paul called "greed" idolatry (Col 3:5; Eph 5:5), meaning that it turns the pursuit of wealth into an idol.

Most of us in the First World are guilty of idolatry. In fact, when we read "the love of money is a root of all kinds of evil" (1 Tim 6:10), most of us rationalize and say, "Good, I'm okay because I don't really *love* it." We are fooling ourselves. Consider John the Baptist's diatribe against the "brood of vipers" in Luke 3:7 – 14, with every example centering on the accumulation of wealth. Luke's four beatitudes are paralleled by four "woes" in Luke 6:20 – 26, each with economic implications. Luke teaches a "reversal of roles" (those who seek wealth will have nothing in the final kingdom, those who have nothing now will have everything in eternity) as exemplified in the parable of the rich man and Lazarus (Luke 16:19 – 31).

Yet Hagner is also correct when he says, "The issue in these passages is not wealth primarily, but an absolute and unqualified discipleship."[20] The major point is undivided commitment to God; nothing should interrupt a complete centering on him. Anything that wrests control from God is our enemy, even if it be family (Luke 14:26, the one who "does not hate father and mother, wife and children, brothers and sisters — yes, even life itself" cannot be Jesus' disciple, meaning in comparison with their love of Jesus).

Yet the issue of wealth and possessions is the central one here. Neither Jesus nor the early church renounced wealth in and of itself. Zaccheus never relinquished all his possessions (Luke 19:1 – 10), and Mary, the mother of John Mark, used her home as one of the first house churches rather than selling it (Acts 12:12). Barnabas, the example of a giving Christian, sold only one field and not all his possessions (Acts 4:36 – 37). Hauerwas says it well:

> Possessed by possessions, we discover that we cannot will our way free of our possessions. But if we can be freed, our attention may be grasped by that which is so true, so beautiful: we discover we have been dispossessed. To seek first the

19. Craig Blomberg, *Neither Poverty nor Riches: A Biblical Theology of Material Possessions* (NSBT 7; Grand Rapids: Eerdmans, 1999), 132.

20. Hagner, *Matthew 1 – 13*, 160.

> righteousness of the kingdom of God is to discover that that for which we seek is given, not achieved.[21]

Let us consider a biblical philosophy of wealth. First, the creation principle says God gave us this world as a gift to enjoy, so it is not wrong to enjoy financial blessings he has bestowed. Yet that is the lesser principle. Mainly, when God bestows the world's riches on any person, he is giving such people a ministry of helps. He wants them to use their largesse to lift up the fallen, to alleviate the burdens of the downtrodden. There is no choice; God expects us to share with the needy, and the more we have, the more we must share (Luke 16:9 – 13; Acts 2:44 – 45; 4:32 – 35; Rom 12:8, 13; 2 Cor 9:5 – 13; Eph 4:28; 1 Tim 6:17 – 19).

21. Hauerwas, *Matthew*, 81.

CHAPTER 24

Matthew 6:25 – 34

Literary Context

This section continues the theme of possessions and wealth. The previous section (6:19 – 24) centered on the vertical aspect of one's relationship with God; this one concerns the horizontal aspect of one's personal life. Yet both engage divine concerns. In the first God is displaced by wealth, but in the second God's deep care for the individual removes anxiety. Also, 6:19 – 24 details the absolute demands God makes on his disciples, while 6:25 – 34, the absolute care God gives to his disciples. The two are alike in the sense that they relate to the presence of possessions in this life and encourage the disciple to place God above such earthly concerns.

II. The Kingdom Message Goes Out (4:12 – 7:29)
- **B. First Discourse: The Sermon on the Mount (5:1 – 7:29)**
  - **5. Social Ethics (6:19 – 7:12)**
    - **a. God and Possessions (6:19 – 34)**
      - (1) Kingdom Priorities and the Two Masters (6:19 – 24)
      - ➡ **(2) Anxiety and Trust (6:25 – 34)**

Main Idea

The demands of this world will produce deep anxiety in a person unless people learn to trust God. In this sense it flows out of the first we-petition in the Lord's Prayer, "Give us today our daily needs" (6:11, which means trusting God for our needs, not asking for more things), and the tendency will always be to "worry" (μεριμνάω occurs six times in these verses) about procuring such daily needs. The solution is to center on the God who cares and supplies those needs.

Translation

Matthew 6:25-34

25a	Introductory Exhortation	*"Because of this* *I am telling you, do not ever worry* *about your life, namely,*
b	Example of 25a	*what you should eat or drink,*
c	Example of 25a	*or about your body, namely,* *what you should wear.*
d	Rhetorical Question	*Doesn't your life consist of more than food and*
e		*your body consist of more than clothing?*
26a	Illustration #1	*[1] Consider closely the birds of the air:*
b		*They do not sow or harvest or store food in barns*
c		*and your heavenly Father feeds them.*
d	Rhetorical Question	*Aren't you worth much more than they are?*
27a	Rhetorical Question	*Moreover, who among you . . . can add even a single hour* *by worrying* *to your life?*
28a	Illustration #2	*[2] Also, why worry about clothing?*
b		*Learn a lesson* *from the way the lilies of the field grow* *without laboring or* *spinning.*
29a		*Yet I tell you, Solomon in all his splendor was never dressed so well as one of these.*
30a	Rhetorical Question	*So* *since God clothes the grass of the field,*
b		*which is alive one day and* *thrown into the oven* *the next day,*
c		*won't he even more clothe you,* *namely, you with so little faith?*
31a	Summary Exhortation	*So don't worry, saying,*
b		*(i) 'What do we eat?' or*
c		*(ii) 'What do we drink?' or*
d		*(iii) 'What do we wear?'*
32a	Basis #1 for 31a-d	*(a) For the pagans strive for all these things*
b	Basis #2 for 31a-d	*(b) and yet your heavenly Father knows that you need all these things.*
33a	Antithesis	*But seek first his kingdom and righteousness*
b	Promise	*and all these things will be given to you.*
34a	Summary Exhortation	*So don't worry about tomorrow,* *for tomorrow will worry about itself.*
b		*Each day has a sufficient supply of evil for itself."*

Structure and Literary Form

This passage, like 6:19 – 24, is another group of wisdom sayings (extolling proper virtues) that consists of an introductory command (v. 25) followed by two supporting illustrations (vv. 26 – 27, 28 – 30) and finishing with a pair of summary commands (vv. 31 – 33, 34).[1] This organization is similar to several of the antitheses in 5:21 – 48, with illustrative material following Jesus' commands.

Exegetical Outline

- **I. Command: Don't Worry About Life or Body (6:25)**
- **II. Illustrative Examples (6:26 – 30)**
  - A. Example of birds = life/food (vv. 26 – 27)
    1. God feeds the birds (v. 26a)
    2. You are more valuable, so don't worry (vv. 26b – 27)
  - B. Example of lilies = body/clothes (vv. 28 – 30)
    1. They don't labor yet are beautiful (vv. 28 – 29)
    2. God will clothe you too (v. 30)
- **III. Summary Commands (6:31 – 34)**
  - A. Don't worry about the needs of today (vv. 31 – 33)
    1. Don't be like pagans; trust God (vv. 31 – 32)
    2. Seek the kingdom and righteousness first (v. 33)
  - B. Don't worry about tomorrow (v. 34)

Explanation of the Text

6:25 Because of this I am telling you, do not ever[2] worry (Διὰ τοῦτο λέγω ὑμῖν, μὴ μεριμνᾶτε). "Because of this" (διὰ τοῦτο) refers to vv. 19 – 24, which commands total allegiance to God. The question that arises is, "How am I to take care of my basic needs if I am always serving God?"[3] Jesus' response is simple — because he is always serving you! The issue of anxiety for the material needs is the other side of the materialistic coin from the mind control of 6:19 – 24.

μεριμνάω, the dominant term in this paragraph (six times), is usually taken as a reference to mental anxiety or worry but can also mean "work hard, strive after" in an action sense.[4] While most take it in the former sense, there is a good likelihood it carries both meanings — strive after your

1. Verses 25 – 33 are closely paralleled by Luke 12:22 – 31 and stem from Q, while v. 34 is unique to Matthew and stems from his special source (M). For the general authenticity of this pericope, see Oda Wischmeyer, "Matthäus 6, 25 – 34 par: Die Spruchreihe vom Sorgen," *ZNW* 85 (1994): 1 – 22.

2. On this use of the present prohibition, see above on 6:19.

3. Davies and Allison, *Matthew*, 1:646. Strecker, *Sermon on the Mount*, 136 – 7; and Carson, "Matthew," 179, translate this "therefore" and see a more direct continuity between the sections: one must not only avoid materialism but the anxiety it causes. Both are possible, but the "because of this" makes a little more sense in the movement from 19 – 24 to 25 – 34.

4. Schlatter, *Matthäus*, 226 – 27; Joachim Jeremias, *The Parables of Jesus* (2nd ed.; New York: Scribner's, 1972), 214.

own needs and thus be filled with anxiety.[5] This fits the context of "seeking" (v. 33) and worry (vv. 31, 34). It is anxiety that drives the self-centered effort to supply your own needs (see also Josh 1:6 – 9; Ps 127:2; Isa 32:17; Phil 4:6 – 7; Heb 13:5; 1 Pet 5:7). Both constitute a failure to trust God.

6:25 ... about your life, namely, what you should eat or drink,[6] or about your body, namely, what you should wear (τῇ ψυχῇ ὑμῶν τί φάγητε ἢ τί πίητε, μηδὲ τῷ σώματι ὑμῶν τί ἐνδύσησθε). ψυχή here means "life" in the sense of physical existence in this world, and σῶμα refers to the physical body (both are datives of reference, "concerning, about"). The two parallel each other. Jesus then selects examples of each that will be expanded in the illustrations below. For sustaining life, he chooses food and drink, the basic need for existence. For the body, he chooses clothes, even more treasured in the ancient world than today (they were heirlooms passed from parent to child).

6:25 Doesn't your life consist of more than food and your body consist of more than[7] clothing? (οὐχὶ ἡ ψυχὴ πλεῖόν ἐστιν τῆς τροφῆς καὶ τὸ σῶμα τοῦ ἐνδύματος;). The expected answer is "yes" (οὐχί). Jesus uses an a fortiori argument (the rabbis called it *qal wahomer*, lit., "light and heavy," meaning "how much more"). Since God has given us life (more than just food) and a body (more than clothing), won't God take care of our food and clothing also?[8] If we center only on the lesser and fail to trust God for both, our life will be miserable. This provides the structure for the next few verses, with food the center of vv. 26 – 27 and clothing the center of vv. 28 – 30, then both summed up in v. 32.

6:26 Consider closely the birds of the air (ἐμβλέψατε εἰς τὰ πετεινὰ τοῦ οὐρανοῦ). The first illustration centers on food for life (the first listed in v. 25). Jesus calls for careful reflection ("consider closely" [ἐμβλέψατε εἰς]) on the birds (Luke 12:24 has "ravens," an unclean bird that brings out the contrast well). If God takes care of birds so well, won't he care for his children? Later rabbis considered prayers for birds too trivial to be worthwhile (*m. Ber.* 5:3),[9] yet Jesus says God cares for each and every one.

6:26 They do not sow or harvest or store food in barns (ὅτι οὐ σπείρουσιν οὐδὲ θερίζουσιν οὐδὲ συνάγουσιν εἰς ἀποθήκας). The first word (ὅτι) is not translated but is used to state the truth that they are to "consider." Jesus contrasts birds with human effort — they don't raise crops ("sow/harvest") or store them away for the future (in barns), yet they always have enough to live on. The point is that they instinctively trust God (his creation) for their needs, while we who have experienced so much more of him fail to do so. If God cares and provides for the "unimportant" birds, how much more will he care for us, his children?

6:26 ... and your heavenly Father feeds them. Aren't you worth much more than they are? (καὶ ὁ πατὴρ ὑμῶν ὁ οὐράνιος τρέφει αὐτά· οὐχ ὑμεῖς μᾶλλον διαφέρετε αὐτῶν;) Again Jesus uses *qal wahomer*, "how much more valuable are you than birds?" The birds have learned how to accept what God provides, and he watches over them. But the

5. Guelich, *Sermon on the Mount*, 335 – 36.

6. "What" (τί) with the subjunctive is deliberative question, which takes the subjunctive in both cases, picturing the individuals asking those very things. Note Wallace, 478.

7. The two genitives (τῆς τροφῆς and τοῦ ἐνδύματος) are genitives of comparison.

8. Carson, "Matthew," 179; Keener, *Matthew*, 234.

9. Keener, *Matthew*, 235. J. D. M. Derrett, "Birds of the Air and Lilies of the Field," *DRev* 105 (1987): 181 – 92, believes this a midrash by Jesus on Ps 104 (where the birds and the plants are cared for by God), teaching that priorities for this life must be predicated on the reality of the world to come.

apex of creation, those made in the image of God, have forgotten that lesson and continually fret over their basic needs.[10] As many have pointed out, Jesus is not disparaging the need to work for our needs. The birds are tireless in their pursuit of food. Jesus is asking for simple trust in God's provision (as indeed is implied in the Lord's Prayer, 6:11).

6:27 Moreover, who among you by worrying[11] can add even a single hour to your life? (τίς δὲ ἐξ ὑμῶν μεριμνῶν δύναται προσθεῖναι ἐπὶ τὴν ἡλικίαν αὐτοῦ πῆχυν ἕνα;) The terms ἡλικία and πῆχυς can mean either "height"/"cubit" or "age"/"hour." Both are viable, but the latter fits better in the context. Jesus could be using hyperbole in terms of adding eighteen inches to our height, but that would work better in our basketball-crazy society than in the first century. So the point is that worry cannot add even the smallest amount of time to one's life span. In fact, studies have shown that anxiety has the opposite effect of shortening one's life.

6:28 Also, why worry about clothing? (καὶ περὶ ἐνδύματος τί μεριμνᾶτε;). The second of Jesus' examples in v. 25 is now developed, clothing. Only the very wealthy could wear bright colors like purple or scarlet because of the expensive dyes needed. The average person would have an extra cloak to function as a blanket for sleeping in the fields (cf. 5:40 — the law protected the clothes of the poor) but little else. Yet as with food, God will provide for his people.

6:28 Learn a lesson from the way the lilies of the field grow without laboring or spinning (καταμάθετε τὰ κρίνα τοῦ ἀγροῦ πῶς αὐξάνουσιν· οὐ κοπιῶσιν οὐδὲ νήθουσιν). For his illustration Jesus turns to the beautiful wild lilies of Palestine (τὰ κρίνα), probably a reference to the wildflowers in general rather than a particular flower (perhaps an autumn crocus or anemone or gladiola but more likely spring flowers, cf. BAGD, 451). The gorgeous and varied colors would light up the fields.[12] Spinning (νήθουσιν) refers to the process of spinning cloth. The two together cover men's labor in the field and women's work of spinning at home.[13]

6:29 Yet I tell you, Solomon in all his splendor was never dressed so well as one of these (λέγω δὲ ὑμῖν ὅτι οὐδὲ Σολομὼν ἐν πάσῃ τῇ δόξῃ αὐτοῦ περιεβάλετο ὡς ἓν τούτων). Solomon's incredible wealth is described in 1 Kgs 10:14 – 29; 2 Chr 9:13 – 28. His splendid dress was proverbial in Jewish writings (e.g., Josephus, *Ant.* 8:35 – 41).[14] Yet it paled into drabness compared to the beauty of any one of the spring flowers, let alone a field of them. In other words, the beauty God creates is incomparably better than what even the wealthiest people can produce, so why not let God take care of your clothing? Again, this does not mean we do not work hard to provide for our family but rather that in doing so, we place our trust in and draw strength from God rather than trust in ourselves and our own profits (cf. Jas 4:13 – 17).

10. Blomberg, *Matthew*, 125n, adds, "We cannot help thinking of the perverse inversion of God's values among people who campaign more for animal rights than for human rights (including especially those of unborn humans)."

11. "By worrying" (μεριμνῶν) is a participle of means telling how the action is accomplished (see Wallace, 628 – 30).

12. J. N. Jones, "'Think of the Lilies' and Prov 6:6 – 11," *HTR* 88 (1995): 175 – 77, sees this as an inversion of Prov 6, where the industry of the ant leads to provision, while here the lily draws its beauty entirely from God, and that is infinitely superior to all that Solomon or anyone else could design. M. E. Irwin, "Considering the Lilies," *McMaster Journal of Theology* 2 (1991): 20 – 28, centers on the brevity of the life of the lily, thus on God's care for the brevity and beauty of the life he gives them.

13. Strecker, *Sermon on the Mount*, 138. Guelich, *Sermon on the Mount*, 339, sees the metaphor as laboring to collect fibers in the field and spinning them at home.

14. Warren Carter, "'Solomon in All His Glory': Intertextuality and Matthew 6.29," *JSNT* 65 (1997): 3 – 25, calls this a negative portrait of Solomon, as intertextual parallels show the anxious greed that drove Solomon.

6:30 So since God clothes the grass of the field, which is alive one day and thrown into the oven the next day, won't he even more clothe you, namely, you with so little faith? (εἰ δὲ τὸν χόρτον τοῦ ἀγροῦ σήμερον ὄντα καὶ αὔριον εἰς κλίβανον βαλλόμενον ὁ θεὸς οὕτως ἀμφιέννυσιν, οὐ πολλῷ μᾶλλον ὑμᾶς, ὀλιγόπιστοι;). The condition of fact εἰ is better translated "since, because" here. The "grass" has replaced the flowers because it was collected and used as fuel for the oven. Jesus' point is even stronger: if God cares enough even to "clothe" the grass, with its short life and bad ending (burnt in ovens), how much more will he take care of those made in his own image?

The last term ("you with so little faith" [ὀλιγόπιστοι]) is found frequently in Matthew (8:26; 14:31; 16:8; 17:20) and is used of the disciples elsewhere, so here too it probably has them in mind. "Little faith" does not connote a complete absence of faith but an inadequate, deficient faith. Those who struggle so hard for the things of this world lack a true faith in God.

6:31 So don't worry, saying, "What do we eat?" or "What do we drink?" or "What do we wear?" (μὴ οὖν μεριμνήσητε λέγοντες, Τί φάγωμεν; ἤ, Τί πίωμεν; ἤ, Τί περιβαλώμεθα;). There is an inclusio here, framing vv. 25 – 31 with commands not to worry over material concerns. The aorist prohibition "don't worry" (μεριμνήσητε) is global, characterizing a life as a whole that refuses to allow worry to dominate. Yet v. 32 adds material to it, showing that such concern for earthly needs is essentially pagan. So vv. 31 – 32 becomes the third illustration, and the repetition in v. 31 reemphasizes the point from v. 25. The three questions regarding food, drink, and clothing summarize the issues discussed in vv. 25 – 31 and highlight a person totally consumed with human concerns. God is ignored as the person thinks only of basic needs.

6:32 For the pagans strive for all these things, and yet your heavenly Father knows that you need all these things (πάντα γὰρ ταῦτα τὰ ἔθνη ἐπιζητοῦσιν· οἶδεν γὰρ ὁ πατὴρ ὑμῶν ὁ οὐράνιος ὅτι χρῄζετε τούτων ἁπάντων). The two "for" (γάρ) clauses in effect provide the reason why we do not need to be dominated by concerns for food, drink, or clothing. To allow such things to control our lives lowers us to the level of pagans, who have no faith in God and have nothing beyond this world. As Bruner puts it: "It is characteristic of the secular world to be obsessed with economic questions, to be almost entirely engrossed by consumer concerns, to be preoccupied with finding and getting better and better *things*" (italics his).[15]

So "all these things" (πάντα ταῦτα, twice for emphasis in this verse) must be put in their proper place, namely, under the heavenly[16] Father, who loves us and cares for us. The second "for" (γάρ) is in antithesis to the first: Pagans do such things, but we don't, for we have a Father who is aware of every need we have. Again, this does not mean we have no concern for personal needs but rather that we trust God in such areas. Finding the balance between the concern to eat healthy and exercise, etc., and the greater concern for the things of God (cf. 1 Tim 4:8) is a critical issue (yet see the next verse).

6:33 But seek first his kingdom and righteousness (ζητεῖτε δὲ πρῶτον τὴν βασιλείαν [τοῦ θεοῦ][17] καὶ τὴν δικαιοσύνην αὐτοῦ). In vv. 31 – 32 Jesus has commanded us to quit acting like pagans

15. Bruner, *Christbook*, 269.

16. "Heavenly" (οὐράνιος) reminds us that our true home is heaven (where our Father dwells), and all of heaven's powers are involved in meeting our needs. For this term in Matthew, see on 5:48.

17. "Of God" (τοῦ θεοῦ) is missing in א and B and was probably added to account for the "his" (αὐτοῦ) after "righteousness." Some recent versions (e.g., TNIV, NJB) do not contain "of God." For the opposite conclusion, see France, *Gospel of Matthew*, 264 – 65 n8.

and caring only for "all" our daily needs; here he turns to the positive side and commands us to put the things of God first. The whole theme of this section has been that God will take care of his people, so we should put our trust completely in him. Our Father is the supreme Giver, and it is tragic when we whom he loves care more for ourselves than him.

So Jesus says we must not just *refrain* from the things of the world but actively *replace* concern for earthly matters with an overriding concern for the things of God.[18] There is a wordplay from the "striving" (ἐπιζητέω, v. 32) of the world for earthly gain to the "seeking" (ζητέω, present tense to stress the ongoing nature of our search for God) of the believer for spiritual gain; the hyper-seeking (perfective ἐπί) of the world is for all the wrong things. France translates "seek first" as "make it your priority to find," with the higher purpose being kingdom values.[19]

First in our life must be "his kingdom and righteousness" ("his" [αὐτοῦ] governs both nouns). Concern for the kingdom[20] looks back to the God-petitions of 6:9b – 10; we must live and work as the kingdom community. While God's "righteousness" could be justification in a Pauline sense,[21] it almost certainly refers to God's demand that his people conduct their lives "rightly" according to his will (see 5:6, 10, 20; 6:1).[22] In other words, such a quest is seen in our lifestyle, as we live as citizens of the kingdom and put God first in "all these things."

6:33 ... and all these things will be given to you (καὶ ταῦτα πάντα προστεθήσεται ὑμῖν). "Will be given" (προστεθήσεται) is a divine passive and means "God will give" us our needs; yet as Blomberg says,[23] this seems contrary to the experience of many Christians who have faced deprivation and even starvation. The answer is not just to reserve the promise for eternity but better to follow Luke 12:33 and Mark 10:30a and see in this the Christian community as being God's instrument in sharing goods. God will take care of his people, but he often does so through others in the community.

6:34 So don't worry about tomorrow, for tomorrow will worry about itself (μὴ οὖν μεριμνήσητε εἰς τὴν αὔριον, ἡ γὰρ αὔριον μεριμνήσει ἑαυτῆς). The aorist prohibition "don't worry" (μὴ μεριμνήσητε), as in v. 31, looks at life as a single whole, characterized by an absence of worry. This too reflects the Lord's Prayer (6:11, "Give us today our daily needs"), as we live in our "today" and leave tomorrow entirely to God (cf. Jas 4:13 – 15). Since God has promised to take care of our every need (Matt 6:33b), we need not be anxious for what might happen.

6:34 Each day has a sufficient supply of evil for itself (ἀρκετὸν τῇ ἡμέρᾳ ἡ κακία αὐτῆς). Since all our "tomorrows" will have more than enough troubles of their own, we must let each day bear its own worries and not add to them with our own (cf. Prov 27:1). There is emphasis on "sufficient"

18. Carson, "Matthew," 181. See also Thomas E. Schmidt, "Burden, Barrier, Blasphemy: Wealth in Matt 6:33, Luke 14:33, and Luke 16:15," *TJ* 9 (1988): 171 – 89, who argues that this makes wealth and possessions a virtual abomination to God and a type of blasphemy.

19. France, *Gospel of Matthew*, 270.

20. Davies and Allison, *Matthew*, 1:660, note four options for understanding "seek his kingdom": purely eschatological as entrance requirements; prayer for the coming of the kingdom; bring in the kingdom through missionary work; and make the kingdom of first importance in the present. A combination of the last two is possible (so Guelich, *Sermon on the Mount*, 345), but the emphasis here is on present kingdom living.

21. So Filson, *Matthew*, 102. He calls it the vindicating action of God in a Deutero-Isaiah sense. Another possibility is to take "his" (αὐτοῦ) as a subjective genitive, meaning to seek God's righteous activity, but that is not as likely in a context emphasizing the believer's conduct.

22. Nolland, *Matthew*, 315, says this is "the righteousness that God requires of us, that he approves of, or something similar (cf. John 6:28 – 29; 2 Cor 1:12; Jas. 1:20)."

23. Blomberg, *Matthew*, 126. See also Schmidt, "Burden, Barrier, Blasphemy."

(ἀρκετόν), that is, on the "sufficiency" or "adequacy" of evil for each day. "Evil" is κακία, i.e., not just wickedness but also "trouble, misfortune" (BAGD, 397). There are sufficient disasters happening each day, so why add further "trouble" through a worried spirit?

Theology in Application

The basic message of the section is obvious — earthly concerns must always be superceded by heavenly priorities. That is the only solution for anxiety. There are four stages: realize you have a heavenly Father who loves you; "cast all your anxiety on him because he cares for you" (1 Pet 5:7); refuse to worry about material needs but leave them with him; put his concerns first in your life and live kingdom priorities. These are all related yet separate issues — a loving Father, a solid trust in him, a deliberate refusal to worry, a life centered on him.

1. God Must Be First in Our Lives

Matthew throughout emphasizes the total commitment demanded by Christ. The shallow believer is rejected as a disciple, for we must leave everything to follow him (4:20 – 22; 10:37 – 39; 16:24 – 25). It is a mistaken assumption to think that God is satisfied with halfhearted commitment. He does not want a "tithe" of our lives; he demands our all! Recall the rich fool of Luke 12:13 – 21, who was not "rich toward God." A great example is Phil 1:21; 3:7 – 11, where Paul values Christ above all things.

2. Our Earthly Needs Placed under His Providential Care

Matthew does not intend a totally passive approach to life. It is trust in the provision of God rather than an absence of working to meet our needs. It is trust in God to guide us and provide for us, not a lazy Christianity, that is in view. The emphasis is on the anxiety that a lack of dependence on God produces. Moreover, this promise that God will give "all these things" to us is no guarantee that hard times will never befall us. Rather, it means that in the hard times God will be guiding our steps and making sure that "in all things God works for the good of those who love him" (Rom 8:28).

3. Anxiety: Not a Sin but a Burden That Can Be Lifted

When John said "Do not let your hearts be troubled" (John 14:1), he did not mean a troubled heart was a sin, for Jesus himself had a troubled heart (John 11:33; 12:27; 13:21). Rather, he meant that real trust in God will enable us to overcome such anxiety (14:2). The troubled heart will only become a sin when it is allowed to dominate our lives, so that possessions become our god and constant anxiety is the result. As Paul says, "greed ... is idolatry" (Col 3:5; cf. Eph 5:5).

CHAPTER 25

Matthew 7:1 – 12

Literary Context

The first section on social ethics discussed the place of possessions in our life. This second section covers relationships with others and with God. The relationship with God (7:7 – 11) makes a new depth of social relationships possible. As throughout the Sermon on the Mount, these are the new relationships of the kingdom community, continuing the theme of the "better righteousness" of 5:20. After we have made God's "kingdom and righteousness" the priority of our lives, we must turn and consider the horizontal side, a "right" relationship with those inside and outside our community.

II. The Kingdom Message Goes Out (4:12 – 7:29)
- **B. First Discourse: The Sermon on the Mount (5:1 – 7:29)**
  - **5. Social Ethics (6:19 – 7:12)**
    - a. God and Possessions (6:19 – 34)
    - ➦ **b. Social Relationships (7:1 – 12)**
      - **(1) Prohibition against Judging Others (7:1 – 5)**
      - **(2) The Need for Discernment (7:6)**
      - **(3) A Prayer for Help (7:7 – 8)**
      - **(4) God Answers Prayer (7:9 – 11)**
      - **(5) The Golden Rule (7:12)**

Main Idea

In one sense this is a loosely connected series of admonitions, centering on the community first (vv. 1 – 5), then the outsider (v. 6), then God (vv. 7 – 11). Yet vv. 7 – 8 may well imply a plea for help in relating to others, with vv. 9 – 11 a promise of divine help in doing so; the final verse (v. 12) sums up the whole message on relationships. So the basic thrust is "right" relationships with everyone around us, fellow believers as well as unbelievers.

Translation

Matthew 7:1-12

1a	Prohibition	*"Don't ever judge another,*
b	Basis for 1a	*lest God judge you.*
2a	Basis for 1a	For *the way you judge others is the way God will judge you,*
b	Basis for 1a	and *the measure . . . is the measure you will receive*
		by which you measure others.
3a	Rhetorical Question #1	*Why do you see the speck of sawdust*
		in the eye of your brother or
		sister and yet
		ignore the large beam in your own eye?
4a	Rhetorical Question #2	*Or how can you say,*
b		*'Let me take the speck of sawdust from your eye' and*
		look, a large beam is in your eye?
5a	Accusation	*Hypocrite!*
b	Exhortation	*First remove the large beam from your eye,*
c	Result of 5b	and *then you will see clearly enough*
		to remove the speck of sawdust
		from the eye of your brother or sister.
6a	Prohibition (A)	*Do not give what is holy to dogs or*
b	Prohibition (A')	*throw your pearls in front of pigs.*
c	Result of 6a–b	*If you do,*
		the pigs will trample them under their feet and
		the dogs will turn and tear you apart.
7a	Exhortation/Promise (A)	*Ask and God will give it to you;*
b	Exhortation/Promise (A')	*seek and you will find it;*
c	Exhortation/Promise (A")	*knock and God will open the door for you.*
8a	Result (B)	*For everyone who asks receives,*
b	Result (B')	and *the one who seeks finds,*
c	Result (B")	and *for the one who knocks, God will open it.*
9a	Rhetorical Question #1	*Who is there among you, whose child asks for bread,*
		who would give him or her a stone?
10a	Rhetorical Question #2	Or *also when they ask for a fish,*
		would give him a snake?
11a	Comparison	So *if you . . . know how to give good gifts to your children,*
		though you are evil,
b		*how much more will your heavenly Father give good things*
		to those who ask him.
12a	Summary Exhortation	So *everything you would like people to do to you,*
b		*also do these things to them,*
c	Reason for 12a–b	for *this is the essence of the Law and the Prophets."*

Structure and Literary Form

This series of admonitions has a wisdom perspective centering on God's rules for relating to those within and without the community ("wisdom" is living life in God's world on the basis of God's rules). It has been common to see this as a miscellaneous hodgepodge of disconnected material,[1] but that is not the case. The whole centers on social relationships, and the progression moves from inside the community (vv. 1 – 5, not judging),[2] to outside the community (v. 6, restraint in sharing the gospel), to the prayer needed to make wise choices in both areas (vv. 7 – 11), and finally to the summation of the whole in the Golden Rule (v. 12).[3]

Exegetical Outline

I. Prohibition against Judging Others (7:1 – 5)
- A. God will judge you by the way you judge others (vv. 1 – 2)
- B. Deal with your bigger problem first (vv. 3 – 5)

II. Restraint in Sharing the Gospel (7:6)
- A. Sharing the good news with those who don't deserve it
- B. Result: they trample first your message and then tear you apart

III. Prayer for Help (7:7 – 11)
- A. The need to ask (vv. 7 – 8)
  1. The promise — God will give (v. 7)
  2. The promise — to everyone (v. 8)
- B. The certainty of God's response (vv. 9 – 11)
  1. An evil practical joke (vv. 9 – 10)
  2. The good gifts of God (v. 11)

IV. Conclusion: The Golden Rule (7:12)

Explanation of the Text

7:1 Don't ever judge another (Μὴ κρίνετε). Another present prohibition forbids judging others at any time. Yet we must carefully note the exact meaning of "judge" (κρίνετε); in this context it does not mean a court trial or admonition. It cannot refer to discerning or evaluating right and

1. See McNeile, *Matthew*, 90 – 91; Hill, *Matthew*, 146 – 48; France, *Gospel of Matthew*, 273.

2. Neil J. McEleney, "The Unity and Theme of Matthew 7:1 – 12," *CBQ* 56 (1994): 491 – 93, finds a chiasm in vv. 1 – 5 with an admonition against judging in vv. 1 – 5 and two sayings on retribution in v. 2 followed by two questions on guilt in vv. 3 – 4. There is definitely inclusion in vv. 1, 5 but probably not chiasm, for vv. 2, 3 – 4 are too different.

3. The material is found in various places in Luke (v. 1 = Luke 6:37; vv. 3 – 5 = Luke 6:41 – 42; vv. 7 – 11 = Luke 11:9 – 13; v. 12 = Luke 6:31), with v. 6 unique to Matthew and from his special source. The material apart from v. 6 stems from Q, but it is difficult to decide whether Matthew or Luke has more heavily "rearranged" the material (Carson, "Matthew," 183) and also if parts are due not to Q but to Jesus' delivering the material on more than one occasion. Of course, much of it probably was used by Jesus more than once.

wrong. All such are valid for believers (e.g., 1 Cor 5:5; Phil 3:2; Gal 6:1; Heb 3:13; 1 John 4:1).[4] So what does this judgmental attitude connote? It means looking down on a person with a superior attitude, criticizing or condemning them without a loving concern (the opposite of the second we-petition on forgiveness, 6:12).

The key component is the absence of love. Admonition has a humility that says, "I love you enough to want to help you, and tomorrow you will need to correct me." There is no sense of superiority, no desire to make yourself look good at the expense of another. Bruner says this prohibition is the flip side of the fifth beatitude (5:5, "God blesses those who are merciful") as well as of the fifth petition of the Lord's Prayer (6:12, "forgive us our sins") and recapitulates the commands in ch. 5 against anger, revenge, and hate.[5]

7:1 ... lest God judge you (ἵνα μὴ κριθῆτε). "Lest you be judged" (κριθῆτε) is a divine passive; God will judge the judgmental person. As throughout the Sermon, there is an inaugurated thrust. You will be under divine judgment now, but especially at the final judgment. This is an example of *lex talionis* (the law of retribution, see 5:38; cf. 5:7; 6:14 – 15; Jas 2:13): when we judge another, God will in turn judge us.

7:2 For the way you judge others is the way God will judge you (ἐν ᾧ γὰρ κρίματι κρίνετε κριθήσεσθε). The same principle of *lex talionis* is repeated here in two different ways. The absence of mercy and love in the way we treat others will result in unmerciful judgment from God at the final judgment (Jas 2:13, "judgment without mercy will be shown to anyone who has not been merciful").

7:2 ... and the measure by which you measure others is the measure you will receive (καὶ ἐν ᾧ μέτρῳ μετρεῖτε μετρηθήσεται ὑμῖν). This is a common Jewish proverb (cf. Mark 4:24) stemming from grain contracts,[6] and it restates the first half. A "measure" was the weight or scoop used to "measure" out goods purchased and came to signify the way one treats others. Here it means the "standard" by which we judge others. That will then become the standard by which God judges us.

7:3 Why do you see the speck of sawdust in the eye of your brother or sister and yet ignore the large beam in your own eye? (τί δὲ βλέπεις τὸ κάρφος τὸ ἐν τῷ ὀφθαλμῷ τοῦ ἀδελφοῦ σου, τὴν δὲ ἐν τῷ σῷ ὀφθαλμῷ δοκὸν οὐ κατανοεῖς;). By the use of "brother or sister" (ἀδελφός), Jesus has in mind primarily the kingdom community itself. Such judgmentalism is especially dangerous among God's people. The κάρφος is a small piece of wood or chaff that has lodged in a person's eye. There is rabbinic hyperbole in the contrast between the speck and the log (a δοκός or large beam used in a building). We censor a tiny flaw in another person and conveniently forget the great shortcomings in ourselves.

7:4 Or how can you say, "Let me take the speck of sawdust from your eye" and look, a large beam is in your eye? (ἢ πῶς ἐρεῖς τῷ ἀδελφῷ σου, Ἄφες ἐκβάλω τὸ κάρφος ἐκ τοῦ ὀφθαλμοῦ σου, καὶ ἰδοὺ ἡ δοκὸς ἐν τῷ ὀφθαλμῷ σοῦ;). This virtually repeats v. 2 for emphasis (with "look" [ἰδού]

4. On the other hand, Bernd Kollmann, "Jesu Verbot des Richtens und die Gemeindedisziplin," *ZNW* 88 (1997): 170 – 86, believes this was a radical command and that the later NT writers softened it in light of the needs of church discipline. However, this is not necessary when we see what Jesus was really saying.

5. Bruner, *Christbook*, 272. G. S. Hendry, "Judge Not: A Critical Test of Faith," *ThTo* 40 (1983): 113 – 29, says the issue is whether we have the faith to trust God's judgment or have to take that judgment on ourselves.

6. The rule was that the purchaser's instrument of measure would be used for both the delivery and the payment for the grain to ensure fairness, see Nolland, *Matthew*, 318.

added for dramatic effect). There you notice the small flaw, and here you self-righteously confront the person and offer to remove it from them. The hubris involved is incredible. As Bruner says, "The tragicomic feature in this story is a log-eyed reformer saving a speck-eyed sinner, a Redwood teaching a shrub to be low-profile."[7] We must first take care of our great problems before we can correct another's small difficulty.

7:5 Hypocrite! First remove the large beam from your eye, and then you will see clearly enough to remove the speck of sawdust from the eye of your brother or sister (ὑποκριτά, ἔκβαλε πρῶτον ἐκ τοῦ ὀφθαλμοῦ σοῦ τὴν δοκόν, καὶ τότε διαβλέψεις ἐκβαλεῖν τὸ κάρφος ἐκ τοῦ ὀφθαλμοῦ τοῦ ἀδελφοῦ σου). On "hypocrite" see 6:2, 5, 16. The hypocrisy is pretending you have no faults as you look down on someone else and criticize them.[8] While many have interpreted this to mean you should not judge at any time,[9] that clearly does not fit the context, for v. 6 in many ways is a judgment as to whether an individual is worthy of the gospel (see also on v. 1). It is obvious here that once you have dealt with your problems, you will have "clear" sight to help others with their difficulties.

7:6 Do not give what is holy to dogs or throw your pearls in front of pigs (Μὴ δῶτε τὸ ἅγιον τοῖς κυσίν μηδὲ βάλητε τοὺς μαργαρίτας ὑμῶν ἔμπροσθεν τῶν χοίρων). Jesus turns to the reverse situation from 7:1 – 5. There one should not criticize a member of the community for their small faults. Here one should not give to the outsider what is sacred.[10] The problem moves from severe censoring to lax sharing.[11] The consensus understanding of this[12] is that the "holy ... pearls" are the gospel truths and that this is a mission setting.

The image moves from the holy to the luxurious. Pearls were considered more precious even than diamonds and were the epitome of luxury. The "dogs"/"pigs" are not all unbelievers but those adamantly opposed to the gospel. While Gentiles were called "dogs" by the Jews, Paul turns this upon the Judaizers (Phil 3:2), and Matthew has a clear sense of mission to the Gentiles (Matt 28:19); although 10:5; 15:24 commands an exclusive Jewish mission for the disciples, Jesus prepares throughout for the future Gentile mission. Moreover, this closely parallels shaking the dust off the feet as a sign of rejection (10:14), and everywhere this occurs in the gospels and Acts (Mark 6:11; Luke 9:5; 10:11; Acts 13:51; 18:6) it is the Jews who are the instigators. So

7. Bruner, *Christbook*, 274.

8. For background on the imagery here, see P. T. Crocker, "Nets, Styli, and Ophthalmology — A Mystery Solved," *BurH* 27 (1991): 59 – 63, who says that a bone stylus rather than a metal one was used to remove specks from a person's eye.

9. Schweizer, *Matthew*, 169; Hill, *Matthew*, 147; Strecker, *Sermon on the Mount*, 143; Guelich, *Sermon on the Mount*, 352 – 53.

10. P. G. Maxwell-Stuart, "'Do Not Give What Is Holy to the Dogs' (Matt 7:6)," *ExpTim* 90 (1979): 341, argues for a scribal error in changing "valuable" (τίμιον) to "holy" (ἅγιον) on the grounds that they misunderstood the original economic metaphor. But this is hardly mandated, and there is no evidence for such an original reading. Stephen Llewelyn, "Matt 7:6a: Mistranslation or Interpretation," *NovT* 31 (1989): 97 – 103, shows that "holy" is the correct reading (though he wrongly sees it as Eucharistic in thrust).

11. Morris, *Matthew*, 167; Davies and Allison, *Matthew*, 1:674.

12. Some have understood "what is holy" as the elements of the Eucharist and the dogs/swine as unbelievers participating in it; others see a mistranslated Aramaic "ring" and therefore a gold ring in a pig's snout (Prov 11:22). Neither interpretation, however, fits the basic metaphor of a dog and pig turning on the disciple and tearing him apart. Thomas J. Bennett, "Matthew 7:6 — A New Interpretation," *WTJ* 49 (1987): 371 – 86, tries to link this verse with 7:1 – 5 by taking not giving to dogs as a further injunction against judging and the warning of being trampled as "or you will be judged." This is an interesting attempt to place v. 6 more closely into the context, but it does not really fit the background of v. 6 as well as the more traditional understanding.

this refers to anyone who has rejected the gospel "with vicious scorn and hardened contempt,"[13] but especially to the Jewish people, who should know better and who have the prophetic background to realize Jesus is indeed the Messiah.

7:6 If you do, the pigs will trample them under their feet and the dogs will turn and tear you apart (μήποτε καταπατήσουσιν αὐτοὺς ἐν τοῖς ποσὶν αὐτῶν καὶ στραφέντες ῥήξωσιν ὑμᾶς). There is a chiasm (ABBA) in the verse, as the pigs "trample" the disciples, and the dogs "turn and tear [them] apart." It must be realized that the dogs were not pets but wild scavengers who often traveled in packs like wolves, and the pigs were not really barnyard animals but more like wild boars. So the metaphor adds persecution to rejection. The unbelievers will not just fail to respond but will actually oppress the saints (cf. Prov 9:8; Matt 10:17 – 31).[14]

7:7 Ask and God will give it to you; seek and you will find it; knock and God will open the door for you (Αἰτεῖτε καὶ δοθήσεται ὑμῖν, ζητεῖτε, καὶ εὑρήσετε, κρούετε καὶ ἀνοιγήσεται ὑμῖν). The two prohibitions not to judge each other and not to share with the unworthy show that the disciples desperately need wisdom from God,[15] so Jesus turns to the subject once more of prayer. But this is different from 6:5 – 13, for it deals not with the problems of proper prayer but with the power of prayer to accomplish results. The three imperatives are in the present tense and signify "habitual prayer."

The idea of persistent prayer is more emphasized in Luke (Luke 18:1 – 8 as well as 11:9 – 13), but Matthew still stresses this (the verbs for prayer in Matt 6:5, 6, 7, 9 are also present tense). The importance of faithful asking is also stressed in John 14:12 – 14 and Jas 4:2 – 3, where it is expected that the basis of true prayer is union with Christ and his purposes rather than selfish craving. For OT parallels, see Deut 4:29; Prov 1:28; 8:17; Jer 29:13. The stress is on the simplicity of prayer; one need only "ask/seek/knock" to gain God's full attention! There is no need for fancy, repetitive prayers (6:5, 7), just basic requests offered to a loving Father. In this there is an echo of the prayer for daily needs in 6:11 as well as to the teaching of 6:25 – 34.

Still, the main thrust is not just the need for prayer but the certainty of God's response.[16] The first and third response verbs ("give" [δοθήσεται], "open" [ἀνοιγήσεται]) are divine passives, centering on the God who answers. Marshall sees three options for understanding this:[17] (1) beggars' wisdom,[18] with the beggar knowing that perseverance will accomplish the purpose; (2) universal experience (i.e., a proverbial truth); (3) apodictic assertion, a truth centering on the authority of

13. Carson, "Matthew," 185. Guelich, *Sermon on the Mount*, 354; Meier, *Matthew*, 69 – 70 connect this with apostates, but while it is close to the true meaning, it is too restrictive in this context.

14. For another interpretation, see Hermann von Lips, "Schweine füttert man, Hunde nicht — ein Versuch, das Rätsel von Matthäus 7:6 zu lösen," *ZNW* 79 (1988): 165 – 86, who sees this as a Hellenistic metaphor for acting wrongly to others and thus receiving reparation as a result. This fits but not as well as the interpretation herein.

15. So Schweizer, *Matthew*, 172; contra Gundry, *Matthew*, 123, who says the emphasis is not on our asking but on God's giving; the message is both — we ask, God gives.

16. This is explored by M. J. Murray and K. Meyers, "Ask and It Will Be Given to You," *RelS* 30 (1994): 311 – 30, who say that God demands dependence and asking before he gives so that his people can know him better and learn to rely on him. However, while the issue of dependence is part of this, D. Basinger, "Petitionary Prayer: A Response to Murray and Meyers," *RelS* 31 (1995): 475 – 84, shows the inadequacy of this overall. They are asking the wrong question, and the answer presented above is more satisfactory.

17. I. Howard Marshall, *Commentary on Luke* (NIGTC; Grand Rapids: Eerdmans, 1978), 467 – 68. See also Davies and Allison, *Matthew*, 1:679 – 80, who accepts Marshall's conclusion.

18. Jeremias, *Parables*, 159 – 60.

the speaker (Marshall's choice). A fourth option may be best: it pictures a dependent child asking "Father" for something needed;[19] this fits the emphasis on *Abba* in the Lord's Prayer (see on 6:9). A child expects a loving response and will get one. There was a Jewish tradition that celebrated men of God with "holy *chutzbah*, or boldness," who had the power to receive great things from God.[20] Jesus boldly promises this power to his disciples.

7:8 For everyone who asks receives, and the one who seeks finds, and for the one who knocks, God will open it (πᾶς γὰρ ὁ αἰτῶν λαμβάνει καὶ ὁ ζητῶν εὑρίσκει καὶ τῷ κρούοντι ἀνοιγήσεται). This does more than simply restate v. 7; with the "for" (γάρ) it grounds the commands in further promise and extends it to the present. God's response is guaranteed. Jesus switches to the present tense (from the futures in v. 7) in the second half of the first two clauses to emphasize the divine response in the present situation. God's faithfulness in responding to prayer is distinctly highlighted. Yet "everyone" (πᾶς ὁ) does not mean any person whatsoever; in the context of the Sermon it refers to the citizens of the kingdom, and even then to the qualifications noted in v. 7 (union with Christ and his purposes).

7:9 Who is there among you, whose child asks for bread, who would give him or her a stone? (ἢ τίς ἐστιν ἐξ ὑμῶν ἄνθρωπος, ὃν αἰτήσει ὁ υἱὸς αὐτοῦ ἄρτον, μὴ λίθον ἐπιδώσει αὐτῷ;). The illustration chosen by Jesus concerns a terrible practical joke played by a parent on a child who sits down for lunch, expecting a loving parent to take care of them. The type of loaf baked would resemble the shape of a smooth round stone, so the child would end up hungrily grabbing a stone instead. Satan tempted Jesus to turn a stone into bread (4:3), and here the parent reverses that, substituting a stone for bread. The form of the question with the negative particle μή expects the answer, "Of course not!" No parent would ever do such a capricious and cruel thing.

7:10 Or also when they ask for a fish, would give him a snake? (ἢ καὶ ἰχθὺν αἰτήσει – μὴ ὄφιν ἐπιδώσει αὐτῷ;). The second illustration is an even more horrible joke, for while a stone is a silly thing, a snake is actually dangerous. This was probably an eel-like fish, which resembles a snake. So as the child went to bite down on the fish, he or she was bitten in turn by the snake (or if it is assumed the snake is dead, that the child is revolted, so Nolland). Again, no parent would be so cruel. Luke 11:12 adds an even worse example, a scorpion substituted for an egg (a scorpion rolled up resembles an egg).

7:11 So if you, though you are evil, know how to give good gifts to your children (εἰ οὖν ὑμεῖς πονηροὶ ὄντες οἴδατε δόματα ἀγαθὰ διδόναι τοῖς τέκνοις ὑμῶν). The heart of every person is "deceitful above all things and beyond cure" (Jer 17:9 — by using "you" [ὑμεῖς], Jesus separates himself from sinful humanity), yet parents still have common grace (Calvin) to love their children and give them "good gifts." The concessive participle "though you are" (ὄντες) stresses the fact that such goodness is contrary to their character.

7:11 ... how much more will your heavenly Father give good things to those who ask him (πόσῳ μᾶλλον ὁ πατὴρ ὑμῶν ὁ ἐν τοῖς οὐρανοῖς δώσει ἀγαθὰ τοῖς αἰτοῦσιν αὐτόν). If this is true, "how much more" (argument from the lesser to the greater) can we realize that God has only "good things" in mind for his children who come to him in prayer. The "heavenly Father" looks back directly to the Lord's Prayer (6:9), and the "ask/

19. Keener, *Matthew*, 244.

20. Ibid, 245.

give" is in inclusio with "ask and God will give it to you" in 7:7. There is an interesting parallel in Luke 11:13, where the "good thing" the Father gives is specified as the "Holy Spirit," in keeping with Luke's emphasis on the Spirit.

7:12 So everything you would like people to do to you, also do these things to them (Πάντα οὖν ὅσα ἐὰν θέλητε ἵνα ποιῶσιν ὑμῖν οἱ ἄνθρωποι, οὕτως καὶ ὑμεῖς ποιεῖτε αὐτοῖς). The so-called "Golden Rule" especially sums up the implications of the social ethics in 7:1 – 11 but in a way concludes all of 5:17 – 7:11, since there is inclusio between this verse and 5:17 – 20 ("Do not think that I have come to destroy the law or the prophets").[21] There is general agreement that Jesus was developing Lev 19:18, "Love your neighbor as yourself" (cf. Matt 22:39 – 40, where this verse sums up the second table of the Decalogue).[22] This is another form of *lex talionis* (law of retribution), here meaning that we should treat others as we wish to be treated.[23]

Three things make this a particularly strong statement: the present tenses, meaning this must be an ongoing principle; "everything" (πάντα ὅσα ἐάν), making it a universal demand; and "in this way also you" (lit. trans. of οὕτως καὶ ὑμεῖς), stressing the obligation of every disciple to live accordingly. This is closely connected to the "love your enemies" command of 5:44 (the two are together in Luke 6:31, 35). Here we go beyond the rule of reciprocity, as all other people are treated as we wish to be treated. In 5:44 we go beyond the rule of forgiveness and reinstatement and love those who have made themselves our enemies.[24]

7:12 ... for this is the essence of the Law and the Prophets (οὗτος γάρ ἐστιν ὁ νόμος καὶ οἱ προφῆται). Many translate ἐστιν as "sums up," but it is slightly better to translate "the essence of the Law and Prophets" in terms of elucidating its true meaning. This was a frequent debate among teachers of the law. In fact, this is not new with Jesus; it was well-known in many cultures,[25] and the negative form was given by Hillel when asked to summarize the law, "What is hateful to yourself, do to no other; that is the whole law and the rest is commentary" (*b. Šabb.* 31a; cf. also Tob 4:15; Sir 31:15).[26]

With this emphasis in 5:17 – 20 and 7:12, Jesus undoubtedly intends the whole Sermon to be an

21. Carson, "Matthew," 188. Luke 6:31 uses this in a different context, preceded by the prohibition of retaliation (Luke 6:29 – 30 = Matt 5:39 – 42) and followed by an exhortation to love your enemies (Luke 6:32 – 36 = Matt 5:43 – 47). Most believe Luke is closer to Q and that Matthew has redactionally inserted it here, but it is just as likely that Jesus used this saying in both contexts.

22. Building on that connection, Hauerwas, *Matthew*, 89, says, "Jesus (in 22:37 – 40) makes explicit what is implicit in the statement of the Golden Rule in the sermon, namely, that love of neighbor and love of God are interdependent. If we are to know how to love our neighbor we must love God as God has loved us. This is the presumption that animates the law and the prophets."

23. For the prevalence of this in the ancient world, see Keener, *Matthew*, 248, especially the negative form found in Jewish ethics, e.g., Tob 4:15 and Philo ("what you hate, do not do to anyone"). J. Topel, "The Tarnished Golden Rule (Luke 6:31): The Inescapable Radicalness of Christian Ethics," *ThSt* 59 (1998): 475 – 85, calls these the Golden Rule and the Silver Rule, arguing that in this Jesus has radicalized the ethics of his day.

24. See the explanation of this in Paul Ricoeur, "The Golden Rule: Exegetical and Theological Perplexities," *NTS* 36 (1990): 392 – 97, who notes the tension between the reciprocity here and the overabundant love of 5:44. See also C. Theobald, "La règle d'or chez Paul Ricoeur: une interrogation théologique," *RSR* 83 (1995): 43 – 59, who sees loving enemies not so much as a tension but a virtual reapplication of the Golden Rule in human affairs. Theobald is correct.

25. See A. Dihle, *Die goldene Regel* (Göttingen: Vandenhoeck und Ruprecht, 1962), 8 – 12, 80 – 109, as in Hagner, *Matthew 1 – 13*, 176.

26. It is common to contrast the negative form with the positive, as if Jesus developed a superior moral code. However, this overstates the differences, and as Keener notes (*Matthew*, 248) the two forms mean basically the same thing.

exposition of the true meaning of the whole law as the Torah of the Messiah. In this way 7:12 especially catches the "essence" of the section on social relationships in 6:19 – 7:11. Like 22:35 – 40, one could say that 6:1 – 18 fulfills the first table of the Decalogue (relationship with God), and 6:19 – 7:11 fulfills the second table (relationships with others).

Theology in Application

This is a particularly rich section on social relationships, and it shows how important it is for the citizens of the kingdom to maintain their relationships both inside and outside the community as part of their walk with God. We cannot pretend that the only thing that matters is our vertical walk with God. As a result of our rugged individualism (certainly one of the most anti-Christian aspects of our society!), too many believers think they do not need church but can relate to God at home. The early Christians would have been shocked at such hubris, for virtually every NT command is plural and is meant to be worked out in community, i.e., with the help of each other. The problem of judgmentalism could not occur without a community in which believers are meant to interact.

1. Avoiding Criticism of Others and Attending to Our Own Walk with God

There is general agreement that the basis of this is the love commandment. Where there is love, there can only be concern, not a censorious spirit. Moreover, it is sheer hypocrisy to center on someone else's fault rather than our own many faults. To use another's failure to condemn and look down on them is a greater sin than theirs! Only when we have a spirit of meekness and carefully consider our own greater sins will we have a right to restore a brother or sister (Gal 6:1). Yet at the same time, we must watch out for each other, and at times we will need to admonish another *in love* (cf. Eph 4:15; Heb 3:13). In a true community/family the members care enough for each other to be vigilant. So at times exposure must be practiced, but only in order to bring them back fully to the Lord. The next week it will probably be we who need to be restored.

2. Not Wasting the Lord's Truths on the Unworthy

This 7:6 is a difficult passage to apply. If we go far in this, we may leave every seeker too early. The best way to understand the command is to see the way the early church used it in the "shake the dust off your feet" passages (Matt 10:14; Mark 6:11; Luke 9:5; 10:11; Acts 13:51; 18:6). It was used sparingly and only when people who should know better (God's chosen, the Jews) rejected their Messiah strongly. Should Samuel Zwemer have left the Muslims long before his seventy-year ministry was over (with only seven converts)? Should the Auca martyrs' wives have left the tribe who murdered their husbands? These are difficult questions. However, the pattern in Acts says otherwise. Only when the people know what they are doing is it valid to reject them. Thus this is best practiced with cult groups who have split off from the church and deliberately rejected the gospel (but even then only when it is clear that they are closed to the truth).

3. When Making Decisions about Admonishing, Ask the Lord

Again, this is a general truth first. God wants us to ask. It is clear that the emphasis is on the simple act of bringing our needs to God. The three terms — "ask, seek, knock" — are a single word (in the Greek as well as English) in order to stress the ease of prayer emphatically. As the hymn puts it, "O, what peace we often forfeit, O what needless pain we bear, all because we do not carry everything to God in prayer."[27] At the same time, Jesus wants us to apply this prayer especially in times of helping a fellow Christian deal with sin in his or her life and when deciding when to break off contact with an unbeliever who may no longer deserve the gospel. Such decisions cannot be made by mere human reasoning; they must be made from our knees. We need God's wisdom in making such choices.

4. God Will Respond to Our Prayers

As our loving Father, God will always respond. Yet the text also says he "will ... give good things." That limits our prayer requests to those that are in line with God's purposes, and it limits his giving to what is good for us. This is a critical aspect of a prayer theology. Some have taken passages such as this (cf. Mark 11:22 – 24; John 14:12 – 14; 15:16; 16:23 – 24; 1 John 3:22; 5:14 – 15) and developed a "name it and claim it" theology, which says God will give us whatever we want. This "materialism made spiritual" is incredibly dangerous, indeed heretical, because it says we control God.

Nothing can be further from the truth. God is sovereign, not we. The promise is that God will respond with "good things," not anything we like. Think of yourselves as parents. When your child asks for more money, more candy, more free time, what do you say? If you truly love them, you will often say "No!" because you know it will not be *good* for them to have it. If God is our loving Father, he will give only what he *knows* is best (Heb 12:6 – 10). In this sense God's "no" is actually a "yes" because it stems from his love for us.

27. Bruner, *Christbook*, 278.

5. Do Only to Others What You Wish to Receive from Them

This simple principle would by itself revitalize human relationships if people everywhere were to begin to live by it. It not only summarizes the OT law but also provides a capstone for Jesus' new covenant principles, setting the standard for the "greater righteousness" of 5:20, i.e., righteousness in action in human relationships. It builds on the "good gifts" we receive from God (v. 11), so that we in turn do only good to one another as well.

Note that the whole emphasis is on what we do for others; there is no expectation of getting something back in return (it is "do to others *what*," not "do to others *so that*"). So the kingdom comes both in the advent of the Messiah, the Son of God, and in a new level of ethical commitment on the part of the new covenant people. This is not a radical humanism (as some have said), for it is completely dependent on the relationship with God implied in vv. 7 – 11. We can only be good to our neighbor if we have truly experienced God's goodness to us. Then we have a proper model to follow and a proper source of strength.

CHAPTER 26

Matthew 7:13 – 29

Literary Context

Jesus has now finished giving his new kingdom principles, and he draws his Sermon to a close by removing any possibility of neutrality and demanding a response. The Sermon on the Mount has been all about the ethical obligation to live a superior righteousness. This involves the thought life as the key to relationships in the new community (5:17 – 48), the priority of God in every aspect of our religious life (6:1 – 18) as well as in our relation to material possessions (6:19 – 34), and in our social relationships inside and outside the community (7:1 – 12). Now is the time of decision, and Jesus wants us to realize the seriousness of our choices. The path to God is narrow and hazardous, but it is the only path to take.

- **II. The Kingdom Message Goes Out (4:12 – 7:29)**
  - **B. First Discourse: The Sermon on the Mount (5:1 – 7:29)**
    - 5. Social Ethics (6:19 – 7:12)
    - ➦ **6. Conclusion — The Two Paths (7:13 – 27)**
      - **a. The Two Ways (7:13 – 14)**
      - **b. False Prophets (7:15 – 23)**
      - **c. The Two Builders (7:24 – 27)**
    - **7. Conclusion to the Sermon — Jesus' Authority (7:28 – 29)**

Main Idea

There are only two paths in responding to the kingdom demands in the Sermon — unquestioning obedience/commitment to God or going the way of the world — and Jesus illustrates this by using a common Jewish metaphor on "the two ways" (Deut 30:15 – 19; Ps 1:6; Prov 28:6, 18; Jer 21:8; *4 Ezra* 7:3 – 9; *Did.* 1 – 6; *Barn.* 18 – 20) and illustrating it in three separate warnings. All three warn about the terrible danger of playing games with our eternal destiny. There is only one path to eternal salvation, and all other attempts will travel the broad road to ruin.

Translation

Matthew 7:13-27

13a	Exhortation	"Enter through the narrow gate,
b	Basis for 13a	for wide is the gate and
		broad is the road that leads to destruction, and
		there are many who enter through it.
14a	Basis for 13a	But how narrow is the gate and
		confined the road that leads to life, and
		there are few who enter it.
15a	Warning	Watch out for false prophets,
b		who come to you in sheep's clothing but
		inwardly are rapacious wolves.
16a	Assertion	You will recognize them on the basis of their fruits.
b	Illustration/ Rhetorical Question	Grapes cannot be picked from thorn bushes, or
		figs from thistles, can they?
17a		(A) So every good tree produces good fruit,
b		(B) but a rotten tree produces bad fruit.
18a		(A') A good tree cannot produce bad fruit,
b		(B') nor a rotten tree produce good fruit.
19a	Warning	Every tree . . . is going to be cut down and
		that fails to produce good fruit
		thrown into the fire.
20a	Restatement of 16a	So then, you will recognize them on the basis of their fruits.
21a	Warning	Not everyone . . . will enter the kingdom of heaven
		who says to me, 'Lord, Lord,'
b		but only those who do the will of my Father in heaven.
22a	Illustration of 21a and b/ Assertion	Many will say to me on that day,
b	Question #1	'Lord, Lord, we prophesied in your name, didn't we?
c	Question #2	And we cast out demons in your name and
		performed many miracles ⇨
		in your name, didn't we?'
23a	Counter-Assertion	And then I will confess to them,
b		'I never knew you.
c		Depart from me, workers of evil.'
24a	Illustration/ Comparison (A)	Therefore, everyone
		who hears these words of mine and
		puts them into practice
		will be like a wise person who built a house on a rock.

Continued on next page.

Continued from previous page.

25a	Result of 24a (B)	*Then the rain descended and*
		the floods rose,
		the winds blew and beat against that house
b		and *it did not fall,*
c	Basis for 25b	for *it was grounded on the rock.*
26a	Comparison (A′)	*Everyone*
		who hears these words of mine and
		does not put them into practice
		will be like a foolish person who builds a house on sand.
27a	Result of 26a (B′)	*The rain descended and*
		the floods rose,
		the winds blew and struck that house.
b		*It fell and its destruction was great."*

Matthew 7:28-29

28a	Conclusion	It happened that	
			when Jesus had finished saying these things,
b	Reaction	**the crowds were amazed at his teaching**	
29a	Basis for 28b	for he was teaching	as one who had great authority,
b	Basis for 28b		not like their teachers of law.

Structure and Literary Form

This is typical Jewish dualism also stemming from wisdom motifs, contrasting the way of the wise with that of the fool.[1] The only debate is whether there are three or four sections (separating vv. 15 – 20 [false prophets] from vv. 21 – 23 [false believers]), but the charismatic gifts claimed in v. 22 (prophecy, exorcism, miracles) links vv. 21 – 23 closely with vv. 15 – 20. So the three warnings progress from the narrow and wide gates (vv. 13 – 14) to false and true prophets (vv. 15 – 23) and finally to the wise and foolish builders (vv. 24 – 27). The section closes with a statement on Jesus' authority with the crowds (vv. 28 – 29).

1. Again this material is widely scattered in Luke, with Matt 7:13 – 14 = Luke 13:23 – 24; 7:16 – 17 = Luke 6:43 – 45; 7:21 loosely resembling Luke 6:46; 7:22 – 23 = Luke 13:25 – 27; 7:24 – 27 = Luke 6:47 – 49. It is widely assumed that the Q sermon ends with the fruit saying (7:16 – 17) and the two builders (7:24 – 27), for that is where Matthew parallels Luke, and that Matthew has added the other material from various sources. That is certainly viable, and the question of source criticism in the Sermon is complex and worthy of a book in itself. However, it is equally possible that Luke decided to omit much of the material and include it elsewhere and that Jesus used this material often in various contexts. This commentary will continue to affirm the hypothesis that Jesus preached this particular Sermon on one occasion (see introduction to 5:1 – 7:27).

Exegetical Outline

- **I. The Two Gates (7:13 – 14)**
  - A. Command: enter the narrow gate (v. 13a)
  - B. The wide gate to destruction for many (v. 13b)
  - C. The narrow gate to life for only a few (v. 14)
- **II. False Prophets (7:15 – 23)**
  - A. Command watch out for false prophets (v. 15a)
  - B. Characteristics of false prophets (vv. 15b – 20)
    - 1. Look like sheep but are wolves (v. 15b)
    - 2. Recognized by their fruit (vv. 16 – 20)
      - a. Good fruit will not come from bad trees (v. 16)
      - b. Good fruit comes from good trees, and bad from bad trees (vv. 17 – 18)
      - c. Necessity of destruction (v. 19)
      - d. Thesis restated, recognize by their fruit (v. 20)
  - C. False prophets on judgment day (vv. 21 – 23)
    - 1. Key criterion: do God's will (v. 21)
      - a. Claiming "Lord, Lord" not enough
      - b. Only good works will suffice
    - 2. Their claim: charismatic works (v. 22)
    - 3. Jesus' claim: "I never knew you evildoers" (v. 23)
- **III. The Wise and Foolish Builders (7:24 – 27)**
  - A. The wise builder (vv. 24 – 25)
    - 1. Builds house on the rock (v. 24)
    - 2. Result: storms cannot dislodge it (v. 25)
  - B. The foolish builder (vv. 26 – 27)
    - 1. Builds house on sand (v. 26)
    - 2. Result: storms destroy it (v. 27)
- **IV. Conclusion (7:28 – 29)**

Explanation of the Text

7:13 Enter through the narrow gate (Εἰσέλθατε διὰ τῆς στενῆς πύλης). Jesus uses the Jewish doctrine of "the two ways" (see above) in a powerful warning against taking the easier road. Those in Jesus' audience who agree with his teaching yet do nothing about it are in great danger. The Christian life was never meant to be easy, and true followers are expected to work hard at aligning their lives with these exhortations.

While there is a present aspect to the command to "enter (now),"[2] the larger context is eschatological, and the final judgment is in view. The way

2. The aorist "enter" (εἰσέλθατε) could refer to conversion but is better seen globally as a complete act; our life will at all times be moving toward the narrow gate.

we conduct our lives now will determine the verdict at the Great Assize. This is not a works righteousness emphasis but rather in keeping with Jas 2:14 – 26 (= Eph 2:10), that true faith will be seen in the works it produces. No good works means there was never faith in the first place. The "narrow gate" does not so much mean that only a small minority will enter it (the emphasis in Luke 13:24, which uses the image of a "door" rather than a "gate") as that the entrance will entail great difficulty, restricting admission on those things Jesus has prohibited.[3]

7:13 For wide is the gate and broad is the road that leads to destruction, and there are many who enter through it (ὅτι πλατεῖα ἡ πύλη καὶ εὐρύχωρος ἡ ὁδὸς ἡ ἀπάγουσα εἰς τὴν ἀπώλειαν καὶ πολλοί εἰσιν οἱ εἰσερχόμενοι δι᾽ αὐτῆς). Jesus expands his gate metaphor to the more familiar "way/road" metaphor. Some have thought this means one enters the gate (when rejecting Jesus or at conversion) and then walks the road of death/life (so Luz, Beare), but most agree the two parts of the verse are synonymous, with Jesus using both for emphasis. The broad road is the way of the world, which accepts any pattern of life. People can carry anything they wish along it, so "many" will travel this road. The problem is that the final destination[4] of such a road is eternal "destruction."

7:14 But how[5] narrow is the gate and confined the road that leads to life, and there are few who enter it (τί στενὴ ἡ πύλη καὶ τεθλιμμένη ἡ ὁδὸς ἡ ἀπάγουσα εἰς τὴν ζωήν καὶ ὀλίγοι εἰσὶν οἱ εὑρίσκοντες αὐτήν). In a reversal of image Jesus now intones the proper path to follow. The true gate to salvation (articular τὴν ζωήν, "*the* [eternal] life") is quite narrow, and the road is as well.[6] "Confined" is a good translation[7] for τεθλιμμένη, from the cognate θλῖψις, "trouble, persecution."[8] There well may be the idea of hardship and persecution, as in Acts 14:22, "We must go through many hardships to enter the kingdom of God." The persecution of the saints is a major Matthean motif (5:10 – 11, 44; 10:16 – 23, 35 – 36; 13:21; 23:34 – 35; 24:9 – 13, 16 – 21) and is likely implied here.[9]

There is also the difficult ethical path demanded in 5:17 – 7:12; such a life in this evil world will be nigh impossible without the power of the Spirit and the love of God in the life of the believer. Only a "few" will be willing to travel that difficult road, but the final result will be eternal "life." Jesus has made the options crystal clear: take the easy

3. So Plummer, *Matthew*, 115; Guelich, *Sermon on the Mount*, 386; Carson, "Matthew," 188.

4. The present participle "leads" (ἀπάγουσα) again looks at the ongoing life of a person, and εἰς ("to") here is equivalent to πρός ("to"), as the two prepositions were sliding together in meaning (see Zerwick, *Biblical Greek*, §97).

5. Two major codices (א B) have "because" (ὅτι) rather than "how" (τί), and it is difficult to know whether the omicron was misplaced or added due to the difficulty of the interrogative "what, why" here. It is more likely that the reading should remain τί, with a meaning similar to the Aramaic *mah*, "how" (David A. Black, "Remarks on the Translation of Matthew 7:14," *FiloNT* 2 [1989]: 193 – 95); contra G. H. R. Horsley, "Tί at Matthew 7:14: 'Because' not 'How,'" *FiloNT* 3 (1990): 141 – 43, who argues for the causal force. In this context "how" has a better fit.

6. J. D. M. Derrett, "The Merits of the Narrow Gate (Matt 7:13 – 14; Luke 13:24)," *JSNT* 15 (1982): 20 – 29, sees a commercial metaphor referring to the narrow city gate, where tax collectors would not be congregating, with Isa 59:14 as possible background.

7. So Hagner, *Matthew 1 – 13*, 179.

8. Andrew J. Mattill, "The Way of Tribulation," *JBL* 98 (1979): 531 – 46, takes this eschatologically to be the final tribulations of the end time on the basis of the connection between "troubles" and "life" and the implications of the "narrow gate" as leading to the final judgment. But this overstates the influence of this language elsewhere, and this context is more general of choices now rather than at the end time.

9. In contrast, εὐρύχωρος can mean not only "broad" but also a "comfortable" life free of trouble (Davies and Allison, *Matthew*, 1:700). So the "many" seek a life of relative ease and only the "few" choose the troublesome way of Christ.

way and find destruction, or walk the difficult path and attain true life.

7:15 Watch out for false prophets (Προσέχετε ἀπὸ τῶν ψευδοπροφητῶν). False prophets lead those in God's flock to abandon the narrow road for the broad one and thereby lead them to destruction. There is much debate as to the reference behind "false prophets" here, and many assume it refers to the situation of Matthew's day rather than Jesus' time.[10] Yet this is a false dichotomy, for it is likely that Jesus was referring to Jewish opponents of his day, utilizing OT language regarding false prophets (cf. 1 Kgs 22:19 – 23; Jer 6:13 – 14; 8:10 – 11; 14:14; 23:10 – 22; Lam 2:14; 4:13; Ezek 13:1 – 23), and Matthew was applying this to false teachers of his own time.

Charette says the identification of these "false prophets" is kept deliberately vague so that vv. 15 – 23 could have "wide and continuing application."[11] These two levels are the basis for understanding any gospel. So Jesus calls for constant vigilance (present "watching" [προσέχετε]) against the ongoing danger. Moreover, this could also be a prophecy against future developments similar to that in 24:11, "many false prophets will rise up and deceive many" (cf. 24:24; Acts 20:29). On NT prophets in Jesus' teaching, see also Matt 10:41; 13:57; 23:34; John the Baptist (11:9; 21:26) and Jesus himself (13:57; 21:11, 46) were considered prophets.

7:15 ... who come to you in sheep's clothing but inwardly are rapacious wolves (οἵτινες ἔρχονται πρὸς ὑμᾶς ἐν ἐνδύμασιν προβάτων, ἔσωθεν δέ εἰσιν λύκοι ἅρπαγες). These are like the "hypocrites" of 6:2, 5, 16, who pretend to be one thing but inside are quite another. The "sheep" are the citizens of the new covenant community, the congregation of God, and the false prophets/teachers counterfeit themselves in the "clothing" of leaders of the community. The use of the "wolf" metaphor to designate false teachers who "snatch away, plunder" (ἅρπαγες) God's people is found often (Isa 11:6; Jer 5:6; Ezek 22:27; Sir 13:17; *1 En.* 89:10 – 27; Matt 10:16; John 10:12; Acts 20:29; *Did.* 16:13), and the idea of false prophets/teachers as part of the last days is developed in 24:4 – 12, 23 – 28; 2 Thess 2:3 – 8; 1 Tim 4:1; 2 Tim 3:1; 2 Pet 3:3; 1 John 2:18). So these appear as genuine believers but hide their true intentions, which is to tear apart ("rapacious") the flock.

7:16 You will recognize them on the basis of their fruits (ἀπὸ τῶν καρπῶν αὐτῶν ἐπιγνώσεσθε αὐτούς). "On the basis of [by][12] their fruits" frames this section (cf. v. 20) and is the main idea. Full knowledge, of course, must await the eschaton, but Jesus tells his followers they will be able to "recognize" (future tense ἐπιγνώσεσθε is probably gnomic here, referring to any time in the present or future)[13] false teachers on the basis of their "fruits" (καρπῶν).

"Fruit" in the NT is more than just the deeds of people but everything they are (e.g., the "fruit of the Spirit" in Gal 5:22 – 23), including what they say as well as how they act. A preacher can wow a congregation with rhetorical skill yet fail to live a life of obedience or exemplify the lifestyle of a true follower. It is as true today as then that people can

10. Davies and Allison, *Matthew*, 1:701, notes the three options generally propounded for "false prophets": (1) Jewish opponents, possibly the Pharisees (Hill) or zealots (Schlatter, Grundmann); (2) Christian opponents, possibly enthusiasts like at Corinth (Kingsbury) or legalistic Jewish Christians (Guelich, Gundry, Pregeant); (3) a general eschatological warning of heretics to come in the last days (Strecker). For a detailed analysis, see also David Hill, "False Prophets and Charismatics: Structure and Interpretation in Matthew 7:15 – 23," *Bib* 57 (1976): 327 – 48; Nolland, *Matthew*, 335; Guelich, *Sermon on the Mount*, 391.

11. Charette, *Theme of Recompense*, 125.

12. Zerwick (*Biblical Greek*, §90) shows how in the Koine period ἀπό ("by") was beginning to be used for ὑπό ("by") on occasion.

13. See Hagner, *Matthew 1 – 13*, 183.

get caught up with the charisma of gifted speakers and fail to look at their lives. Superstars among Christian leaders can get away virtually with anything today!

7:16 Grapes cannot be picked from thorn bushes, or figs from thistles, can they? (μήτι συλλέγουσιν[14] ἀπὸ ἀκανθῶν σταφυλὰς ἢ ἀπὸ τριβόλων σῦκα;). The interrogative particle μήτι expects the answer "of course not"; evil can never produce good fruit. Jesus uses the idea of bad trees and good fruit. The bad trees are the false prophets. From a distance the small blackberries on a buckthorn can be mistaken for grapes, and the small flowers on some thistles can make one think a fig is growing, but closer inspection will always reveal the truth.[15] All believers should be "Berean Christians," who "examined the Scriptures every day to see if what [their preachers] said was true" (Acts 17:11).

Perhaps an even better example (the Bereans were non-Christians) might be 1 John 4:1, where we are told to "test the spirits to see whether they are from God." The life and teachings of every leader must at all times exemplify scriptural demands, for they will give an account to God (Heb 13:17; Jas 3:1). It is one thing to perform miracles (v. 22) and quite another to do God's will (v. 21).

7:17 So every good tree produces good fruit, but a rotten tree produces bad fruit (οὕτως πᾶν δένδρον ἀγαθὸν καρποὺς καλοὺς ποιεῖ τὸ δὲ σαπρὸν δένδρον καρποὺς πονηροὺς ποιεῖ). σαπρόν is a strong term, indicating a "rotten" or "decayed" tree (BAGD, 742). Such a tree will produce bad fruit, if any at all (cf. Jas 3:12). So it is with a false prophet. Since God is not a part of their lives, they cannot in any sense produce ultimate good; sooner or later their basically evil (πονηρός, note the double meaning) nature will surface and be seen in their lives and their teaching.

7:18 A good tree cannot produce bad fruit, nor a rotten tree produce good fruit (οὐ δύναται δένδρον ἀγαθὸν καρποὺς πονηροὺς ποιεῖν, οὐδὲ δένδρον σαπρὸν καρποὺς καλοὺς ποιεῖν). For emphasis Jesus restates the same truth of v. 17 the other way. Since God is involved with true prophets, their lives will show his presence. But the false prophet will never be able to consistently perform good deeds or teach truth. Sooner or later their true nature will surface.

The point of the whole section is that the saints must at all times be watchful to make certain their leaders fulfill their calling. This does not mean a critical attitude (so 7:1 – 5) but it does entail loving concern and spiritual vigilance. Too many charlatans have appeared throughout church history for us to be complacent. Without the ethics and morality of this Sermon, any so-called Christian message is false. As Bruner says,

> the test of their reality is not how they come on but how they come off; not how they appear but what they produce; not how they seem but the theological and moral influence of their teaching and life in the community. Thus the prayer at the end of the Lord's Prayer, "deliver us from evil," also means "deliver us from false prophets and their amoral, immoral, or supermoral messages."[16]

7:19 Every tree that fails to produce good fruit is going to be cut down and thrown into the fire (πᾶν δένδρον μὴ ποιοῦν καρπὸν καλὸν ἐκκόπτεται καὶ εἰς πῦρ βάλλεται). Jesus now gives a prophecy regarding the final destination of false prophets (see also v. 23). The prophetic present "is going to be cut down" (ἐκκόπτεται) refers to the inevitability of judgment for such charlatans; it is

14. This is an impersonal plural with passive force, cf. BDF §130.2; Davies and Allison, *Matthew*, 1:709.

15. So Carson, "Matthew," 191.

16. Bruner, *Christbook*, 285.

"going to" (or "must") happen. This imagery is similar to John 15:2, 6, where fruitless branches are first "cut off," then "picked up, thrown into the fire and burned." In 3:10 the Baptist says the same thing to the Pharisees and Sadducees (with the image of the "ax … at the root of the trees" to stress imminent judgment), so this was a standard prophecy of judgment. Without fruit there is no hope, for fruit is the necessary proof that one has truly believed in Jesus (Gal 2:8 – 10; Jas 2:14 – 26). Jesus elsewhere uses "Gehenna" as his metaphor for the fiery judgment to come (Matt 5:22, 29, 30; 10:28; 18:9; 23:15, 33).

7:20 So then, you will recognize them on the basis of their fruits (ἄρα γε ἀπὸ τῶν καρπῶν αὐτῶν ἐπιγνώσεσθε αὐτούς). The strong connective "so then" (ἄρα γε) draws an important inference from vv. 16b – 19 and "you will recognize them on the basis of their fruits" establishes an inclusion with v. 16a. The whole purpose of the constant vigilance (v. 15a) is to consider the fruits of every Christian leader so as to recognize and separate the good from the bad, the wolves from the true shepherds (cf. also John 10:1 – 2, 8 – 10, 12 – 13; 1 John 4:1).

7:21 Not everyone who says to me, "Lord, Lord," will enter the kingdom of heaven (Οὐ πᾶς ὁ λέγων μοι, Κύριε κύριε, εἰσελεύσεται εἰς τὴν βασιλείαν τῶν οὐρανῶν). These could well be the false prophets and their followers, for they are engaged in charismatic activity in the name of Christ. Entrance into the kingdom is at the heart of the Sermon, for it is all about the kingdom ethics demanded of God's people in the new community. The future "will enter" (εἰσελεύσεται) most likely emphasizes especially the final judgment and entrance into the eternal kingdom. Without adherence to these ethical mandates, entrance will not be allowed.

Luke 6:46 parallels this ("Why do you call me, 'Lord, Lord,' and do not do what I say?") and places the saying between the passage on the tree with good and bad fruit and the story of the wise and foolish builders at the end of the Sermon on the Plateau. In Jesus' time, "Lord, Lord" would have been a title of immense respect (= "revered teacher"); but Jesus infused it with more meaning, and for Matthew and his church this would be a major christological confession (Acts 10:36; Rom 10:9; 1 Cor 12:3; Phil 2:11; Col 2:6).[17] To repeat something twice (e.g., John's double *amēn*) gives it great emphasis. So Jesus presents himself here as Lord of the final harvest, the eschatological Judge of the end time.

7:21 … but only those who do the will of my Father in heaven (ἀλλ' ὁ ποιῶν τὸ θέλημα τοῦ πατρός μου τοῦ ἐν τοῖς οὐρανοῖς). The message here is that mere confession is useless unless accompanied by action. One can make a profession, but without a changed life, such an affirmation is without merit. So living under obedience to "the will of [the] Father" (this is especially God's will as unfolded in the Sermon itself = the love commandments of 22:37 – 40) is not an option but a necessity for entering the kingdom. A life of obedience (present tense "do" [ποιῶν] for continuous action) to his will is, in fact, the definition of the "greater righteousness" of 5:20 (cf. also 3:15; 5:6, 10; 6:1, 33).

7:22 Many will say to me on that day (πολλοὶ ἐροῦσίν μοι ἐν ἐκείνῃ τῇ ἡμέρᾳ). "On that day" means the Day of the Lord, when all will stand before God in final judgment (Isa 10:20; Joel 1:15; 3:18; Amos 8:9; 9:11; Zeph 1:10, 14; Zech 14:4; Mal 3:17 – 18; Matt 13:24 – 30, 36 – 43, 47 – 52; 24:30, 51; 25:12, 30, 46; *1 En.* 45:3). So the picture is that of a

17. Strecker, *Sermon on the Mount*, 166, says, "This Semitically shaped double naming reflects the *Kyrios* Christology that leads back to the Aramaic liturgical acclamation *marana tha* (1 Cor 16:22, 'O Lord, come!'), and in the Pauline communities corresponds to the cry 'Jesus is Lord' (1 Cor 12:3)."

defendant standing before the Judge and explaining his or her actions.[18]

7:22 "Lord, Lord, we prophesied in your name, didn't we? And we cast out demons in your name and performed many miracles in your name, didn't we?" (Κύριε κύριε, οὐ τῷ σῷ ὀνόματι ἐπροφητεύσαμεν, καὶ τῷ σῷ ὀνόματι δαιμόνια ἐξεβάλομεν, καὶ τῷ σῷ ὀνόματι δυνάμεις πολλὰς ἐποιήσαμεν;). The confessional cry of these defendants parallels that of the false prophets. The three claims (prophecy, exorcism, miracles) were all performed by Jesus and his disciples. While prophecy was forthtelling (proclaiming God's message) as well as foretelling, in this context the latter is undoubtedly meant. There is no reason to doubt that they actually did so, for Satan and his followers certainly can perform miracles (24:24; 2 Thess 2:9; Rev 13:13 – 15, 16:14; 19:20), though there is no evidence Satan ever cast out his own fallen angels (cf. Matt 12:26 and parallels). Yet the point is clear: such deeds are insufficient in themselves; what matters is not acts of power but the fruit of the Spirit (cf. 1 Cor 12 – 14).

In 1 Cor 13:2 Paul says that a person who prophesies and performs great miracles but has no love is "nothing." God wants a life of righteous obedience, not just spectacular deeds. The false prophets and their followers even claim to have done this "in Jesus' name," i.e., claiming his authority behind their deeds (not magical incantations using his name but claiming to be his representatives, cf. Mark 9:38 – 41); the locatival dative "in your name" (τῷ σῷ ὀνόματι) means "in union with you" (cf. 10:22; 18:5, 20). By stating it three times in succession, they underscore their claim to be legitimate followers. Yet a claim is not enough if lives do not reflect that claim.

7:23 And then I will confess to them, "I never knew you" (καὶ τότε ὁμολογήσω αὐτοῖς ὅτι Οὐδέποτε ἔγνων ὑμᾶς). Their false confession is met by Jesus' own confession (called "judicial language" that is solemn and public and connotes irreversibility)[19] that he never knew them as true disciples. The future "I will confess" (ὁμολογήσω) again speaks of the final judgment, when Jesus will "plainly speak" (another meaning of the verb) the truth. "I never knew you" is a renunciation formula[20] that hardly means Christ knew nothing about them but rather that they were never at any time his true followers.

In other words, these people like Judas pretended to be disciples and probably even acted like disciples (indeed, possibly thought they were disciples) but were never actually committed to him. They were committed to the power Jesus represented and to the status they thought they had, but they never allowed the will of God to control their actions. This is not an anti-charismatic saying but rather means that such actions will never suffice in and of themselves apart from a life committed to doing God's will.

7:23 "Depart from me, workers of evil" (ἀποχωρεῖτε ἀπ' ἐμοῦ οἱ ἐργαζόμενοι τὴν ἀνομίαν). The rejection is complete. They must "depart" (present imperative dramatically picturing them departing) from Jesus, for they have no place in the final kingdom. Jesus draws this from Ps 6:8, where David repudiates his enemies ("evildoers") from the standpoint that God has heard his plea. This retains the LXX "evil" (ἀνομία), perfect for this context because it defines sin as

18. Betz, *Essays on the Sermon on the Mount*, 127, says that the atmosphere presupposes that the negative verdict has already been passed and that these counterfeit Christians now give a "frightened appeal, indeed a protest against the words of condemnation already pronounced by Jesus." However, Betz is wrong to call Jesus the prosecuting attorney in the story. He is the eschatological Judge here (cf. 3:11 – 12; 16:27; 19:28; 25:31 – 46), so Keener, *Matthew*, 254.

19. BAGD, 568; Davies and Allison, *Matthew*, 1:717.

20. Davies and Allison, *Matthew*, 1:717. Strecker, *Sermon on the Mount*, 167, calls it a "banishment formula," and France, *Gospel of Matthew*, 295, a "formula of repudiation."

a transgression of the divine "law"; throughout Matthew (13:41; 23:28; 24:12) this has a double meaning as both "wickedness" and "lawlessness." Gnilka says that "lawlessness" (ἀνομία) refers to anyone who fails to do the will of the Father, i.e., fails to keep the higher "righteousness" demanded in 5:20.[21] These "workers of evil" are allowed by God to participate in the "powers of the coming age" (Heb 6:5) but fail to live for God and so are denied entrance into "life."

7:24 Therefore, everyone who hears these words of mine and puts them into practice (Πᾶς οὖν ὅστις ἀκούει μου τοὺς λόγους τούτους καὶ ποιεῖ αὐτούς). This effectively sums up the theme of 5:17 – 7:23. It is inadequate to speak without doing (7:21 – 23) and also inadequate to hear without doing (7:24 – 27). Obedience as the necessary result of true hearing was emphasized in the OT (Deut 28:15, 31:12; Josh 1:7 – 8; Ezek 33:31 – 32), Judaism (*m.* ʾ*Abot* 3:18; *b. Sanh.* 106b), and the NT (Matt 12:50; Rom 2:13; Jas 1:22 – 25; 2:14 – 20). Both the Hebrew and the Greek connote the message that one has not truly "heard" (ἀκούω) until one has "obeyed" (ὑπακούω). "To do" (ποιέω) occurs nine times in 7:17 – 26, where the emphasis is on putting Jesus' teaching into practice via a lifestyle centered on the will of the Father. Here both verbs are present tense to stress the ongoing nature of obedience; it is lifelong. What we do determines who we are!

"These words of mine" refer to the teachings of the Sermon as fulfilling the Torah and producing the laws for the community of the new covenant. The necessity of adding works to faith is given ultimate significance here, for one's eternal destiny depends on it.[22]

7:24 ... will be like a wise person who built a house on a rock (ὁμοιωθήσεται ἀνδρὶ φρονίμῳ, ὅστις ᾠκοδόμησεν αὐτοῦ τὴν οἰκίαν ἐπὶ τὴν πέτραν). The parable of the two builders contrasts the doer with the hearer and is a parable of judgment that provides a natural conclusion to the Sermon in terms of the ultimate significance of obeying Jesus' principles in it. Those who obey and live out Jesus' teachings are wise (φρόνιμος, "prudent, thoughtful, discerning"), a term found seven times in Matthew in its wisdom sense of one who comprehends the situation and does what Jesus commands (*EDNT*, 3:440). Those who merely listen without practicing these truths are fools. These latter are clearly the false Christians of vv. 15 – 23. This wisdom contrast between the wise and foolish is also central to the parable of the bridesmaids in 25:1 – 13. Luke 6:48 has more detail (building, digging deep, laying a foundation in rock), but Matthew has more symmetry in the two halves (vv. 24 – 25, 26 – 27).

7:25 Then the rain descended and the floods rose, the winds blew and beat against that house (καὶ κατέβη ἡ βροχὴ καὶ ἦλθον οἱ ποταμοὶ καὶ ἔπνευσαν οἱ ἄνεμοι καὶ προσέπεσαν τῇ οἰκίᾳ ἐκείνῃ). Unlike Luke 6:47 – 49 that pictures just a flood, Matthew has "a multiple assault: a storm bringing battering winds along with heavy autumnal rains and associated flooding."[23] The torrential rains especially in the fall would turn the dry wadis into raging torrents,[24] and this will prove the quality of the workmanship. It has been common to interpret the storm as the troubles of life (e.g., Augustine) or the end-time storm of divine judgment (most commentators today on the basis of passages like Isa 28:2, 17 – 19; Ezek 13:10 – 15),

21. Gnilka, *Matthäusevangelium*, 1:461.

22. As stated above (on 7:13), this is not works righteousness, for as in Eph 2:8 – 10 and Jas 2:14 – 26, works do not produce faith but rather are the necessary evidence that faith has occurred.

23. Nolland, *Matthew*, 343.

24. Guelich, *Sermon on the Mount*, 404; Carson, "Matthew," 194.

but this is probably simply local color and part of the story. The whole parable describes divine judgment in the present as well as the final judgment of one's works, but the details need not be allegorized.

7:25 ... and it did not fall, for it was grounded on the rock (καὶ οὐκ ἔπεσεν, τεθεμελίωτο γὰρ ἐπὶ τὴν πέτραν). The wordplay between "beat against" (προσέπεσαν) and "fall" (ἔπεσεν) emphasizes the durability of the house built wisely. It was "beaten against" by the winds but it did not "fall" down. As above, there is no allegorizing of "rock" meaning Jesus. The message is that the house built wisely will stand, and the life built on obedience will stand now and at the final judgment.

7:26 Everyone who hears these words of mine and does not put them into practice will be like a foolish person who builds a house on sand (καὶ πᾶς ὁ ἀκούων μου τοὺς λόγους τούτους καὶ μὴ ποιῶν αὐτοὺς ὁμοιωθήσεται ἀνδρὶ μωρῷ, ὅστις ᾠκοδόμησεν αὐτοῦ τὴν οἰκίαν ἐπὶ τὴν ἄμμον). The "fool" (transliterated *moron*) is defined as the obverse, namely, the one who hears but fails to practice Jesus' teaching. No one in Palestine would build a home on sand, for the sudden flash floods that came frequently would carry any such building away almost before the people could begin living in it. In Psalms and Proverbs "fools" are those who leave God out of their life (Ps 14:1; 53:1; Prov 12:15 – 16; 14:33; etc.).

7:27 The rain descended and the floods rose, the winds blew and struck that house. It fell and its destruction was great (καὶ κατέβη ἡ βροχὴ καὶ ἦλθον οἱ ποταμοὶ καὶ ἔπνευσαν οἱ ἄνεμοι καὶ προσέκοψαν τῇ οἰκίᾳ ἐκείνῃ καὶ ἔπεσεν, καὶ ἦν ἡ πτῶσις αὐτῆς μεγάλη). Here the torrential rains and floods (note the progression of clauses that dramatically spell out the disaster) destroy the foolish house and it falls into total ruin. The emphasis is on the "great" destruction as a picture of the great judgment to come. In v. 13 destruction is promised to those who choose the wide gate and the broad path, and that final destruction is pictured in the burning of the rotten trees in v. 19 and the destruction of the house built on sand here. Jesus concludes his Sermon by making it clear that the truths taught therein are not merely to be heard but must be heeded. Unless the life is changed, no salvation has occurred, and at the final judgment ultimate destruction will be the verdict.

7:28 It happened that when Jesus had finished saying these things (Καὶ ἐγένετο ὅτε ἐτέλεσεν ὁ Ἰησοῦς τοὺς λόγους τούτους). All five of Matthew's discourses end with some form of "It happened that when Jesus had finished ..." (7:28; 11:1; 13:53; 19:1; 26:1), but this is the only one that continues with the crowd's reaction and stands in inclusion with 4:23 – 5:2 with both its emphasis on the crowds following, going up/down the mountain (cf. 8:1), and the emphasis on his teaching. Matthew wants us to know the effect that Jesus' teaching had on the bystanders, and it stands not just as the first discourse but as the quintessential discourse that sets the scene for everything else.

7:28 The crowds were amazed at his teaching (ἐξεπλήσσοντο οἱ ὄχλοι ἐπὶ τῇ διδαχῇ αὐτοῦ). This is close in wording to Mark 1:22 (= Luke 4:32), though in Mark it is a general reference to his teaching while here it refers to the whole block of his Sermon. The amazement of the crowds is frequent in Matthew after Jesus teaches (13:54; 19:25; 22:33), emphasizing the power and authority of his teaching. The crowds must have followed Jesus and his disciples up the mountain (he seems to want to escape the crowds in 5:1) and are reacting with astonishment at his message. The imperfect "were amazed" (ἐξεπλήσσοντο) depicts an ongoing feeling of wonder as they went home.

7:29 For he was teaching as one who had authority, not like their teachers of law (ἦν γὰρ διδάσκων αὐτοὺς ὡς ἐξουσίαν ἔχων καὶ οὐχ ὡς οἱ γραμματεῖς αὐτῶν). This parallels Mark 1:22, and the durative force continues with both the imperfect periphrastic "he was teaching" (ἦν διδάσκων) and the present participle "one who has" (ἔχων). These verses seem to reach beyond this occasion and embrace the ongoing power of Jesus' message. ἐξουσία has a double meaning, embracing the "power" as well as the "authority" of Jesus' teaching.

The scribes were the legal experts of Jesus' time, the lawyers as well as teachers of law (see on 2:4; 5:20). The style of the scribes is found in the Talmud; they tended to repeat earlier teaching and interact at a secondary level (the *bath qol* or "daughter of the voice" of God). The fact that the text says "their scribes" separates them from Jesus and his disciples. Jesus spoke with the authority of the Son of God and simply told the truth with power. As one can see in the Sermon on the Mount, Jesus never interacted with previous teaching and did not even depend on Torah. His was an authority never seen before (or since!). His teaching "fulfilled" Torah and lifted it to a higher plane (cf. 5:17 – 20).

Theology in Application

In the average church we might delineate six groups (half unbelievers and half "believers"): (1) those who want little to do with Christianity but are there due to parental pressure and the like; (2) those who are neutral and somewhat open but have different priorities; (3) seekers who are interested and searching but not yet ready to convert; (4) quasi-Christians who attend regularly and seem to be believers but have not entered into an authentic relationship with Jesus Christ and have not yet become active in the church; (5) young Christians who are open and starting to grow; and (6) mature Christians who earnestly seek to follow the Lord. This section is addressed to the latter three, especially groups four and five. Jesus concludes his Sermon on the Mount the way he began it, with both promise and challenge. To him there are not really six categories but only two — the path of obedience and the path of disobedience. Only the former has any hope for eternity.

1. The Path You Take Determines Your Destiny

The middle two categories above (the seeker and the quasi-Christian) have the mistaken idea that it is all right to be neutral, to want to get to heaven but yet hold on to the things of this world. Jesus makes it clear that such will not in the end suffice. As Senior points out,[25] there are two themes in this conclusion: there are only two kinds of people, and they will have to face judgment before God. The so-called "neutral" followers are not followers at all. Without taking the narrow path through the narrow gate there is nothing to look forward to except destruction. There is no real "life" now, but especially no eternal life to come. Yes, the narrow path is one of sacrifice and suffering, but the end result will be more than worth it. Those who choose the easy way reject the life of discipleship Jesus demands.

25. Senior, *Matthew*, 109.

2. Maintaining the Purity of the Church

False prophets/teachers are a great danger to God's people, and that is precisely because they present themselves as genuine sheep, yet are actually ravening wolves whose purpose is to destroy the church. A perusal of the rest of the NT makes this clear: John normally emphasizes the unity of the church (John 10:16; 17:11, 20 – 26) but in 10:1 – 13 Jesus warns of the false shepherds/hired hands who will steal the flock and abandon them when the wolf/Satan comes. Paul in Acts 20:29 – 30 warns the Ephesian church of "savage wolves" who "will not spare the flock," and he does so again in Eph 4:14. The problem of false teachers dominates Colossians, Phil 3:1 – 4:1, the Pastorals, 2 Peter/Jude, 1 John and Revelation (especially the churches of Ephesus, Pergamum, and Thyatira).

We must at all times be on the watch for deviations from orthodoxy. Yet we must do so carefully, separating the cardinal doctrines (e.g., the Trinity, deity of Christ, substitutionary atonement, the return of Christ) from those on which we should agree to disagree and maintain a larger unity (e.g., spiritual gifts, the millennium or rapture, mode of baptism, the Calvinism/Arminianism debate, gender roles). Too often we are fighting the wrong battles while true heretics steal our sheep.

3. The Insufficiency of Church Activity without Obedience

Jesus uses the example of charismatic activity stemming from false prophets and their followers. They have duplicated the powerful ministry of Jesus and his disciples — prophecy, exorcism, and miraculous acts of power — but their lives show that they have never put into practice what Jesus demands of true followers, namely, the lifestyle demanded in this Sermon. So when they stand before the eschatological Judge at the great white throne (Rev 20:11 – 15), they will discover that their stance before God has been nothing but pretense. Jesus by no means is opposed to such acts of power, for he frequently performed such works himself. But such deeds must flow out of a life characterized by a superior righteousness (5:20), and without that such deeds are worthless.

This applies closely to many quasi-Christians. They attend faithfully and have some involvement in the church, but they have never actually given themselves over to Jesus, and their lives/fruits show this. In the final analysis, they are "rotten" trees that produce no true fruit. Quasi-Christians have only two possibilities: some will be saved "only as one escaping through the flames" (1 Cor 3:15); that is, they will get to heaven but have virtually no rewards to show for what they have done with their lives in the church.[26] But all too many will face a Matt 7:23 destiny: "I never

26. See 1 Cor 3:10 – 15, which is a strongly debated passage, and it is important to be as clear as possible. (1) The concern is the "building" of the church, not the general works of the believer. (2) The passage is dominated by indefinite pronouns such as "someone," "each one," "anyone" and shifts the focus from Paul and Apollos to the leaders of the

knew you. Depart from me, workers of evil." This is too high a price to pay; shallow so-called "Christians" are playing games with their eternal destiny and must be warned. I believe a major purpose of every pastor must be to wake up the slumbering "Christians" (Rev 3:2 – 3; 16:15) and get them on the path of following the will of the Father (cf. Rom 12:2; 1 Pet 4:2)!

4. Building Lives on the Solid Rock of Obedience to Christ

Jesus alone provides the teaching that leads to eternal life. So the one who listens must choose between the temporary satisfaction of worldly ways and the final reality of Christ. Everything built on this temporary world is doomed, both now (new cars last but a few years; the palaces of previous centuries lie in ruins) and especially in eternity. So we dare not be unprepared like the five bridesmaids (25:1 – 13) or hide the talents God has given us (25:14 – 30). Rather, we must be disciples who act and follow the ethical guidelines of our Master.

The emphasis is on obedience, not just adherence to Christ. As 5:19 says, "whoever keeps and teaches them [Jesus' commandments] will be called great in the kingdom of heaven." We must put feet to our claims and live our beliefs, remembering that those "who endure to the end will be saved" (10:22; 24:13).

5. Jesus' Incredible Authority

The Sermon has presented the laws of the kingdom and demanded a superior righteousness (5:20) for the citizens of the new covenant community. The conclusion (vv. 28 – 29) cements that with the realization of Jesus' incredible authority on the part of the crowds. The Sermon is powerful both in content and form, and the foundation behind it is neither rabbinic tradition nor even the Torah itself. The authority comes from within, from the messianic authority of his Person. In Jesus, God has spoken in an entirely new way. The crowds could be linked with the "seekers" above, for they are interested in Jesus and his authority; yet they fail to respond as he demands. They form the audience and correspond to many readers of Matthew's gospel. They are being called to repentance and to participation in the gospel message.

Corinthian church who were building out of their so-called "wisdom" a church made of perishable material (wood, etc. = worldly wisdom) rather than imperishable material (gold = the cross of Christ). So the "fire" of the final judgment that "tests [and reveals] the quality of each person's work" (v. 13) will demonstrate whether one's work in the church survives into eternity (= "reward") or is "burnt up" (= "loss"). Paul does not define what the "reward" is; in fact, Scripture as a whole fails to do so. But it is clear that it refers to what we take into eternity as opposed to what is only a temporary, earthly benefit. This is frequently called "saved by the skin of one's teeth," Anthony C. Thiselton, *The First Epistle to the Corinthians* (NIGTC; Grand Rapids: Eerdmans, 2000), 315 (cf. 307 – 15); cf. also Gordon D. Fee, *The First Epistle to the Corinthians* (NICNT; Grand Rapids: Eerdmans, 1987), 136 – 45.

CHAPTER 27

Matthew 8:1 – 4

Introduction to Jesus' Miracle Stories (Matthew 8:1 – 9:34)

As chs. 5 – 7 detailed Jesus' authoritative words, this section details his authoritative deeds.[1] This section is perfect proof of Matthew's editorial skill. He has taken several parts of Mark[2] and woven into it Q material[3] to fashion his own literary masterpiece. Mark 1:21 – 45 centers on Jesus' growing popularity with the scribes and 2:1 – 3:6 his growing rejection on the part of the leaders. That is not the case here. This section is primarily christological and details Jesus' miraculous power and authority together with his demands for discipleship.

Scholars differ on the structure of this section. Since there are ten miracles here, some see a link with the ten Egyptian plagues and a new Moses typology,[4] but there are actually nine miracle stories (the healing of the woman with the hemorrhage and the raising of the ruler's daughter are together in 9:18 – 26), and there is no true new Moses motif here (though there is some Moses typology). The more natural way is to see three blocks of three miracles each (8:1 – 17; 8:23 – 9:8; 9:18 – 34), broken by discipleship sections (8:18 – 22; 9:9 – 13, 14 – 17).[5]

The first triad concerns authority over illness, the second set over nature, demons, and paralysis, and the third set over disabilities and death.[6] The primary

1. Nolland, *Matthew*, 351n, notes the places where Matthew has removed Markan mention of Jesus in a synagogue, presumably teaching (8:14 = Mark 1:29; 8:18 = Mark 4:36; 9:1 = Mark 2:2; 9:9 = Mark 2:13; 9:18 = Mark 5:21). There is incidental teaching especially in the two discipleship sections, but the emphasis is on action.

2. In order, 8:1 – 4 = Mark 1:40 – 45; 8:14 – 15 = Mark 1:29 – 31; 8:16 – 17 = Mark 1:32 – 34; 8:23 – 27 = Mark 4:35 – 41; 8:28 – 34 = Mark 5:1 – 20; 9:1 – 8 = Mark 2:1 – 12; 9:9 – 13 = Mark 2:13 – 17; 9:14 – 17 = Mark 2:18 – 22; 9:18 – 26 = Mark 5:21 – 43; 9:27 – 31 = Mark 10:46 – 52; 9:32 – 34 = Mark 3:22.

3. In order, 8:5 – 10 = Luke 7:1 – 10; 8:11 – 12 = Luke 13:28 – 29; 8:18 – 22 = Luke 9:57 – 60.

4. Grundmann, *Matthäus*, 245 – 46. Gundry, *Matthew*, 37 – 38, considers it possible. Witherington, *Matthew*, 175 – 77, sees this as a wisdom motif.

5. See Davies and Allison, *Matthew*, 2:2, 3 – 4; Hagner, *Matthew 1 – 13*, 195 – 96; Turner, "Matthew," 126 – 27; France, *Gospel of Matthew*, 300. Schnackenburg, *Matthew*, 81, sees a geographical movement here from Capernaum (8:1, 5, 14) to the east bank (8:18, 28) to "his own town" (9:1). While true, this is not a structural indicator. Jack D. Kingsbury, "Observations on the 'Miracle Chapters' of Matthew 8 – 9," *CBQ* 40 (1978): 559 – 73, divides this into four sections on Christology (8:1 – 17), discipleship (8:18 – 34), the separation of Jesus and his followers from Israel (9:1 – 17), and faith (9:18 – 34). Such topical arrangements, however, are too reductionistic.

6. Keener, *Matthew*, 258. Blomberg, *Matthew*, 137, sees the first set as pointing to Jesus' ministry to social outcasts, the second set to Jesus' sovereignty over Satan's realm, and the third set to the growing polarization of the Jewish responses to Jesus. But there are outcasts elsewhere (the demon-possessed, another woman), and the rejection of Jesus begins in 9:3. Still, these themes are present in the section.

thrust is Jesus' all-embracing "power and authority" (ἐξουσία); of the nine verses where "authority" (ἐξουσία) is found in Matthew, five are connected to this section (7:29, introducing it; then 8:9; 9:6, 8 and 10:1 immediately following). Every aspect of life is subject to him. The Sermon on the Mount provided Jesus' authoritative words, and now we see his authoritative deeds.

As we will see, a second theme is the place of faith in the process, seen in the leper, the centurion, the woman with the hemorrhage, and the two blind men. Twelftree sees three primary themes — Jesus' authority, faith, and discipleship as he becomes the new Moses responding to the sick, struggling out of mercy, and bringing them to himself to become disciples.[7]

Literary Context

This first of the series of nine miracle stories adds the sense of Jesus' powerful deeds to those of his powerful words in chs. 5 – 7. Also, together with the next miracle it features Jesus' mission strategy — first to the Jews (vv. 1 – 4 = 10:5 – 6; 15:24) and then later to the Gentiles (vv. 5 – 13 = 28:19). Finally, as Harrington shows,[8] this section provides a bridge from the Sermon on the Mount to the miracle cycle by stressing the statement that Jesus fulfills the law (5:17 – 20) and Lev 14 in terms of the injunctions on leprosy.

II. The Kingdom Message Goes Out (4:12 – 7:29)
III. The Kingdom Comes with Authority (8:1 – 11:1)
A. Authority and Discipleship in Jesus' Ministry (8:1 – 9:34)
1. Three Healing Miracles (8:1 – 17)
➦ **a. Healing the Leper (8:1 – 4)**
b. Healing the Centurion's Servant (8:5 – 13)

Main Idea

The primary emphasis is certainly on Jesus' authority; he is center stage throughout. As said above, this miracle is probably first to highlight his keeping the law (cf. 5:17 – 20). At the same time, it also underscores Jesus' special ministry to outcasts (seen in this section, vv. 1 – 17),[9] specifically the leper here, as well as highlighting this man's faith.[10]

7. Graham Twelftree, *Jesus the Miracle Worker* (Downers Grovce, IL: IVP, 1999), 121 – 24.

8. Harrington, *Matthew*, 115.

9. Blomberg, *Matthew*, 137; Hagner, *Matthew 1 – 13*, 200; Pregeant, *Matthew*, 62.

10. Plummer, *Matthew*, 121, considers this the reason Matthew placed this miracle first.

Translation

Matthew 8:1-4

1a	Transition	After he descended from the mountain,
b	Setting (Social)	**large crowds followed him.**
2a	Action (A)	**And look, a leper came and knelt before him, saying,**
b	Entreaty	*"Lord, if you want, you have the power to heal me."*
3a		Reaching out his hand,
b	Response (B)	**Jesus touched him, saying,**
c		*"I do desire this. Be healed!"*
d	Result of 3a-c (C)	And **his leprosy was immediately cured.**
4a		**Jesus said to him,**
b	Exhortation	*"Tell this to no one.*
c		*Instead, go show yourself to the priest and offer the gift Moses commanded as a witness to them."*

Structure and Literary Form

Matthew has chosen the healing of a leper as the first in his series. Since no other gospel does that, it must be deliberate. Moreover, as will be shown, Matthew also shortens the story greatly, omitting Mark 1:41a (Jesus' compassion), 44 ("strong warning"), and 45 (the man's disobedience).[11] This miracle story contains three main parts (after the transitional v. 1), each with an action followed by dialogue. The first centers on the leper and the latter two on Jesus. The brevity is striking, as no description of the man is present, and no onlookers are mentioned, surprising after the mention of the "large crowds" in v. 1. All attention is on Jesus.

Exegetical Outline

→ **I. Transition (8:1)**
- A. Descent from the mountain (v. 1a)
- B. Large crowds following (v. 1b)

II. The Leper Comes to Jesus (8:2)
- A. The leper kneels before Jesus (v. 2a)
- B. Complete trust in Jesus' healing power (v. 2b)

III. The Healing (8:3)
- A. Jesus touches the man (v. 3a)
- B. The power of his healing word (v. 3b)

11. Schweizer, *Matthew*, 210; Carson, "Matthew," 197, point out that Matthew condenses stories on Jesus as Messiah by 10 percent, controversy stories by 20 percent, and miracle stories 50 – 55 percent.

IV. Jesus' Commands to the Healed Man (8:4)

A. Say nothing to anyone (v. 4a)

B. Show the priests you are healed (v. 4b)

Explanation of the Text

8:1 After he descended from the mountain, large crowds followed him (Καταβάντος δὲ αὐτοῦ ἀπὸ τοῦ ὄρους ἠκολούθησαν αὐτῷ ὄχλοι πολλοί). Matthew likes genitive absolutes and frequently uses them temporally[12] to carry along the action at the beginning of a scene (cf. 8:5, 16, 28; 9:32, 33; 17:14, 22, 24; et al.). Some (see above) take the descent from the mountain as paralleling Moses' descent from Sinai (Exod 34:29) and so see this as a new Moses motif, but it is likely that this frames the Sermon on the Mount with a trip up (5:1) and then down the mountain. Still, the Greek is nearly verbatim with the LXX account, so there may well be a Moses typology[13] (see "Main Idea" on 2:13 – 23 as well as 2:13, 20; 4:8), though not a new Moses motif. Jesus has just given the Torah of the Messiah in fulfillment of the Mosaic law. The "large crowds followed" (here "followed" [ἀκολουθέω] does not connote discipleship but interest in Jesus) repeats 4:25 and 7:28, showing the Sermon had relevance not just for the disciples but even for the uncommitted crowds.

8:2 And look, a leper came[14] and knelt before him, saying (καὶ ἰδοὺ λεπρὸς προσελθὼν προσεκύνει αὐτῷ λέγων). Matthew's characteristic "and look" (καὶ ἰδού) draws the reader's attention to the vividness of the story (see 7:4; 8:24, 29, 32, 34; 9:3, 10, 18, 20, 32; etc.). Leprosy in the ancient world included Hansen's disease (if it existed then) but also referred to a number of skin diseases that were more than skin deep with the hair on it turning white (Lev 13:3, 20), like psoriasis or ringworm. This was in some ways the most serious illness for cultic regulations (see Lev 13 – 14) and became a symbol for sin's pollution.

Leprosy was an unclean disease (those who touched a leper had to be ritually cleansed before sacrificing), and lepers were ostracized from family/community (often forming their own community) and forced to isolate themselves from contact with others. They had to wear torn clothes and unkempt hair and to shout out to people, "Unclean!" (Lev 13:46); they were considered the living dead. An entire Jewish tractate (*Negaʿim*) is dedicated to the issue. The healing of lepers was considered a messianic act (Matt 11:5); Moses (Num 12) and Elisha (2 Kgs 5) were the only ones who healed lepers in the OT. The leper here is bold and breaks the law by approaching Jesus[15] and kneeling before him — an act of submission and deep respect.

8:2 "Lord, if you want, you have the power to heal me" (Κύριε, ἐὰν θέλῃς δύνασαί με καθαρίσαι). When the man calls Jesus "Lord" (from Q; cf. Luke 5:12), he is affirming Jesus' healing authority.[16] Most likely the man intends great respect, while Matthew wants the reader to see more. The man's

12. Wallace, 655, says they are temporal about 90 percent of the time.

13. So Davies and Allison, *Matthew*, 2:9. Hagner, *Matthew 1 – 13*, 198, considers it possible.

14. A circumstantial participle that becomes virtually a main verb (cf. 4:20).

15. James R. Edwards, "The Use of Προσέρχεσθαι in the Gospel of Matthew," *JBL* 106 (1987): 65 – 74, and Grundmann, *Matthäus*, 248, believe the act of "coming to Jesus" and "kneeling" means worship. However, that is probably reading too much into this context.

16. Carson, "Matthew," 198, states that "this leper spoke and acted better than he knew."

humility and faith are remarkable at this early date and are particularly emphasized. To him Jesus has the power (δύνασαι) to heal him; the only question is whether Jesus "wants" to do so ("if" [ἐάν] is a possible condition and shows the man's hesitancy). He throws himself at Jesus' feet and depends on his grace. There is double meaning in "to heal" (καθαρίσαι): he wants to be "healed" and then "cleansed" (the major meaning) of the disease. Only after being cleansed can he return to his family.

8:3 Reaching out his hand, Jesus touched him, saying, "I do desire this. Be healed!" And his leprosy was immediately cured (καὶ ἐκτείνας τὴν χεῖρα ἥψατο αὐτοῦ λέγων, Θέλω, καθαρίσθητι· καὶ εὐθέως ἐκαθαρίσθη αὐτοῦ ἡ λέπρα). People in the first century did not touch lepers. For one thing, they were considered contagious, and for another it would render the person unclean. That is why lepers were ostracized. Many also think that Jesus, living normally in this world, would from time to time contract ritual uncleanness, and like everyone else go through ritual purification. So Jesus' incredible compassion is evident as he "stretches out" (another circumstantial participle, see 2:4, 20 – 21) his hand to touch the man. He didn't have to; he could have healed him with a word. The touch conveyed empathy and sensitivity with the poor man's tragic state.

Did Jesus become unclean? Certainly not! In Jesus' touch it was not uncleanness that was communicated but rather the healing power of the supreme Holy Man (as was believed then). To the healing touch is added the powerful command, "Be healed!" The effect is immediate. As stated above, the word translated here as "healed" (καθαρίζω) means both "cured" and "cleansed" of ceremonial uncleanness.

8:4 Jesus said to him, "Tell this to no one" (καὶ λέγει αὐτῷ ὁ Ἰησοῦς, Ὅρα μηδενὶ εἴπῃς). Jesus' first response seems strange. Mark turns this into a major theme called the "messianic secret." Matthew follows Mark on this, without as much emphasis but still with a fair amount of material (cf. 9:30; 12:16; 16:20; 17:9). It is generally agreed that Jesus did so to avoid the Jewish misunderstanding that the Messiah would be a conquering king rather than a suffering Servant. At the same time, there is evidence that some Jews believed the Messiah would not become such until he had finished his work (for Jesus, the cross).[17] Jesus is indeed Messiah, the Son of God, but his "true significance could only be grasped in the light of the cross."[18]

8:4 "Instead, go show yourself to the priest and offer the gift Moses commanded as a witness to them" (ἀλλὰ ὕπαγε σεαυτὸν δεῖξον τῷ ἱερεῖ καὶ προσένεγκον τὸ δῶρον ὃ προσέταξεν Μωϋσῆς, εἰς μαρτύριον αὐτοῖς). Three imperatives (go, show, offer) dominate this sentence and look at the action as a whole.[19] Leviticus 13 – 14 provides instructions for certifying that a former leper is indeed clean and free to return home. They were to be examined by the priests to certify there were no more skin eruptions, then to present a sacrificial "gift" to God in thanksgiving for being cured.

17. Richard N. Longenecker, *The Christology of Early Jewish Christianity* (Grand Rapids: Baker, 1981), 68 – 73. The "messianic secret" was first developed by Wilhelm Wrede, *The Messianic Secret* (trans. J. C. G. Greig; Cambridge: James Clarke & Company, 1971), who said the early church invented it to explain why they had never realized Jesus was Messiah during his lifetime. This has been widely rejected because it does not fit the data.

18. Robert A. Guelich, "Mark, Gospel of," *DJG*, 522.

19. Wallace, 500, uses the image of a parade. The present tense ("go") looks at it from the perspective of an observer in the stands as it passes by ("internal perspective"), while the aorist ("show," "offer") views it from a blimp, not as a progressive series of events but as a single whole parade ("external perspective").

The εἰς phrase shows purpose, "in order to testify,"[20] but there is some question as to whether αὐτοῖς means a witness "against" (dative of disadvantage) the priests and people that Jesus is indeed the Messiah,[21] a witness "to" (indirect object) the priests and people that Jesus upholds the demands of Torah,[22] a witness "for" (purpose) the viability of the cure,[23] or a witness to them that he has indeed been healed by Jesus.[24] The first is unlikely, since there is no sense of antipathy toward the priests in this story, and Jesus' command for silence means he does not want his messianic nature promoted. Probably a combination of the other three is best. The purpose of the presentation to the priests is that the man may reenter society, and certainly there is a witness that Jesus indeed healed him. Moreover, the connection between 8:1 and 5:17–20 shows that here Jesus is fulfilling but not destroying the law.

Theology in Application

While in the story Jesus wants to keep his messianic office from the people, Matthew certainly expects his readers to recognize the reality of his messianic authority. This theme was already established in 4:12–25, where Jesus began his preaching and miraculous ministry in Galilee, but here it becomes a major theme after the Sermon when the compendium of miracles is introduced. Jesus is indeed Lord of all, and every aspect of creation follows his command.

1. Jesus Filled with Compassion for the Unfortunate

Though Matthew has omitted the "compassion" of Mark 1:41, his actions clearly show his concern and care for the man. This has often been called the "love hermeneutic"; that is, Jesus' concern for people so outweighed legal prescriptions (such as touching a leper rendering one unclean) that he ignored them in order to meet the need. This, as we will see, is a hallmark of Jesus' ministry. God will right all barriers between peoples and vindicate the downtrodden.

2. True Faith

True faith does not *demand* that Jesus fulfill the request but rather surrenders to the knowledge that Jesus *can do so* if he wishes. The leper is an example of true faith and prepares for the centurion in the next story. From 6:5–13 the centrality

20. Prepositions like εἰς ("in," "to") with verbal nouns (like "witness") often have the same force as εἰς τό plus an infinitive, in this case forming a purpose clause.

21. So France, *Matthew* (TNTC), 153.

22. Broadus, *Matthew*, 176; Plummer, *Matthew*, 125; Albright and Mann, *Matthew*, 92; Beare, *Matthew*, 205; Keener, *Matthew*, 263.

23. Hagner, *Matthew 1–13*, 200; Morris, *Matthew*, 190.

24. Blomberg, *Matthew*, 140.

of prayer is surrender to the will of God and not just an unending series of self-centered demands. Note the total confidence as well as the complete surrender to his will in "if you want."

3. Jesus Fulfills the Law

This is a complex issue. In one sense Jesus is faithful to the Torah, having the leper fulfill its demands. At the same time, Jesus ignores the injunction about touching a leper and is not rendered unclean. Carson says it well: "In one sense Jesus does submit to the law. He puts himself under its ordinances. But the result is startling: the law achieves new relevance by pointing to Jesus."[25] So here too Jesus has authority, this time as the final interpreter of Torah.

25. Carson, "Matthew," 199.

CHAPTER 28

Matthew 8:5 – 13

Literary Context

The order here is interesting, for it moves from a Jewish to a Gentile context. Yet the two have one thing in common — both the leper and the Gentile were removed from respected Jewish society; both were outcasts. This affirms Jesus' concern for the marginalized but goes one step further in that it is proleptic of 28:19, in which the mission of the church is to encompass both Jew and Gentile. Jesus at the outset exemplifies his salvation-historical shift from Jew to Gentile. From now on it will be "faith," not ancestral pedigree, that determines God's people.

- **III. The Kingdom Comes with Authority (8:1 – 11:1)**
  - **A. Authority and Discipleship in Jesus' Ministry (8:1 – 9:34)**
    - **1. Three Healing Miracles (8:1 – 17)**
      - a. Healing the Leper (8:1 – 4)
      - ➦ **b. Healing the Centurion's Servant (8:5 – 13)**
      - c. Healing Peter's Mother-in-Law (8:14 – 17)

Main Idea

The emphasis is not so much on the miracle as on the centurion's "great faith" in humbly placing himself under Jesus' authority. He thereby becomes an example of the place of faithful Gentiles in the kingdom[1] and a contrast to unfaithful Israel that will be outside God's mercy. Still, Jesus' power is present, for in the first miracle he healed with a touch while now he heals at a distance.

1. France, *Gospel of Matthew*, 309, shows how this parallels the story of the Canaanite woman in 15:21 – 28. Both exemplify the Gentiles coming to the Jewish Messiah, both show Jesus' initial reluctance overcome by their faith, both have Jesus lauding them for that faith, and these are the only two miracles in Matthew that have healing at a distance.

Translation

Matthew 8:5-13

5a	Setting (Temporal)	After Jesus entered Capernaum,
b	Action (A)	**a centurion came to him begging for help, saying,**
6a	Entreaty	*"Lord, my servant lies paralyzed at home, suffering horribly."*
7a	Response (B)	And **Jesus said to him,**
b		*"I will come and heal him."*
8a	Counter-Response	**The centurion responded,**
b		*"Lord, I am not worthy that you should come under my roof,*
c	Entreaty	*but merely say the word, and my servant will be healed.*
9a	Illustration	*For I am also a man possessing authority,*
b		*having soldiers under me,*
c		*and I tell one,*
d		*'Go,'*
e		*and he goes,*
f		*and another,*
g		*'Come,'*
h		*and he comes;*
i		*or I tell my slave,*
j		*'Do this,'*
k		*and he does it."*
10a	Counter-Response	When Jesus heard this,
b		**he was astounded and said to those following him,**
c	Assertion	*"I tell you the truth, I have found no one in Israel with such great faith.*
11a	Prophecy	*I tell you, many from the east and the west will come and sit down at the feast with Abraham and Isaac and Jacob in the kingdom of heaven.*
12a		*But the children of the kingdom will be thrown into outermost darkness,*
b		*where there will be weeping and grinding of teeth."*
13a	Pronouncement (B)	**Jesus told the centurion,**
b		*"Go, let it be done for you just as you have believed."*
c	Result (C)	And **the servant was healed that very hour.**

Structure and Literary Form

This is a Q story (= Luke 7:1 – 10), but goes its own direction in vv. 11 – 13. While many viably believe Matthew inserted Jesus' pronouncement in vv. 11 – 12 from Q (it is in a different place in Luke 13:28 – 29),[2] that is not necessary, for this passage is entirely consistent with the surrounding material.[3] This begins and ends as a miracle story (vv. 5 – 9, 13), but in between there is a pronouncement story centering on Jesus' startling proclamation contrasting the Jews and the Gentiles vis-à-vis entrance into the kingdom (vv. 10 – 12).[4] By combining these two forms Matthew has constructed a powerful literary device for teaching that God's salvific intention is universal in scope and that participation is to be on the basis of faith, not pedigree. There are four aspects to the story: the request and Jesus' willingness to intercede (vv. 5 – 7), the centurion's humble demurral (vv. 8 – 9), Jesus' proclamation of his great faith in contrast with Israel (vv. 10 – 12), and the healing (v. 13).

Exegetical Outline

→ **I. The Centurion's Request Granted (8:5 – 7)**
- A. The request for help (v. 5 – 6)
- B. Jesus' promise to heal (v. 7)

II. The Centurion's Humble Demurral (8:8 – 9)
- A. His unworthiness (v. 8a)
- B. His faith that Jesus can heal (v. 8b)
- C. His recognition of Jesus' authority (v. 9)

III. Jesus' Twofold Reply (8:10 – 12)
- A. Jesus astonished at the great faith exhibited (v. 10)
- B. Contrast between the Gentiles and the Jews (v. 11 – 12)
- C. Gentiles at the messianic feast (v. 11)
- D. Israel outside in darkness (v. 12)

IV. The Healing of the Servant (8:13)

2. E.g., R. T. France, "Exegesis in Practice: Two Examples," in *New Testament Interpretation: Principles and Methods*, ed. I. H. Marshall (Grand Rapids: Eerdmans, 1977), 260; Hagner, *Matthew 1 – 13*, 202; Keener, *Matthew*, 269; Harrington, *Matthew*, 117.

3. Carson, "Matthew," 202, adds that there are significant differences in wording and that Jesus as an itinerant preacher would certainly have used material like vv. 10 – 12 more than once.

4. This may well be the only miracle story that is found in Q, as it is paralleled in Luke 7:1 – 10, where Matthew omits the intermediaries who attest to the piety of the centurion and Luke omits the statement about participating in the messianic feast, so Keener, *Matthew*, 264; contra Robert A. J. Gagnon, "The Shape of Matthew's Q Text of the Centurion at Capernaum: Did It Mention Delegations?" *NTS* 40 (1994): 133 – 42, who argues that Q did not have delegations. It is common to think that the delegation is a nonhistorical addition, but Matthew often abbreviates stories from Mark or Q, and such messengers were common in that day (see Marshall, *Luke*, 278). A similar story in John 4:46 – 53 about the healing of the son of a royal official in Capernaum shows striking similarities (a Gentile official asks Jesus to heal his servant/son, whom Jesus heals from a distance at "the exact time"), but the differences outweigh the similarities, cf. Leon Morris, *The Gospel according to John* (Grand Rapids: Eerdmans, 1971), 288.

Explanation of the Text

8:5 After Jesus entered Capernaum,[5] **a centurion came to him begging for help** (Εἰσελθόντος δὲ αὐτοῦ εἰς Καφαρναοὺμ προσῆλθεν αὐτῷ ἑκατόνταρχος παρακαλῶν αὐτὸν). Capernaum (cf. 4:13) was an important fishing village and commercial center Jesus used as his residence at this time. As a major city on the trade route, it had a Roman battalion,[6] and one of the centurions approached Jesus. As a non-Jew (either Roman or Syrian) he commanded a "century" of a hundred soldiers (eighty total, made up of ten *contubernia* or basic units of eight soldiers in a tent) and was an important leader.[7] For this man to approach Jesus would be unusual because of the contempt both sides showed the other.[8] From Luke 7:3 – 5 we know he was a God-fearer who had helped build (so was a patron of) a synagogue. His "begging" (another circumstantial participle, see vv. 2 – 3) is also unusual, for normally centurions gave orders. This shows his desperate state as well as his basic recognition of Jesus' greater authority (see below).

8:6 … saying, "Lord, my servant lies paralyzed at home, suffering horribly" (καὶ λέγων, Κύριε, ὁ παῖς μου βέβληται ἐν τῇ οἰκίᾳ παραλυτικός, δεινῶς βασανιζόμενος). The "Lord" of the leper's plea in 8:2 is repeated, emphasizing further the authority of Jesus as Lord of creation (though, of course, the centurion hardly realizes this). The meaning of "servant" (παῖς) is difficult for it stands between Luke's "servant" (δοῦλος, 7:2) and John's "son" (υἱός, 4:46) and can stand for either. Here, however, it almost certainly is a "servant" in keeping with Luke (see footnote above).[9] His piety is seen in his humble respect for Jesus as well as his great concern for the suffering of his servant.[10]

8:7 And Jesus said to him, "I will come and heal him" (καὶ λέγει αὐτῷ, Ἐγὼ ἐλθὼν θεραπεύσω αὐτόν). It is possible that this is a question rather than a promise, "Should I come [another circumstantial participle like v. 2] and heal him?"[11] Those who argue this say it makes best sense of the emphatic "I" as well as of the humble reply by the centurion.[12] If this is the case, Jesus could be showing a reluctance to come, perhaps because he is a Gentile. Yet direct statement makes perfect sense, with the "I" pointing to Jesus as completely willing

5. For the genitive absolute, see on 8:1; as an aoristic temporal, it is best translated "after."

6. Schnackenburg, *Matthew*, 82, thinks these are Syrian mercenaries under Herod Antipas, ruler of Galilee. Nolland, *Matthew*, 354, points out that Herod Antipas followed his father in utilizing non-Jewish soldiers (Josephus, *Ant.* 17:198; 18:113 – 14).

7. See Everett Ferguson, *Backgrounds of Early Christianity* (Grand Rapids: Eerdmans, 1987), 38 – 39; Keener, *Matthew*, 264; G. L. Thompson, "Roman Military,' *DNTB*, 991 – 95. They arose from the rank-and-file soldiers who had to be Roman citizens and signed up for twenty years. Upon retirement they were elevated to the equestrian or knight class just below the aristocrats. The major military unit was the "legion" (there were about twenty-five total) consisting of sixty centuries and totaling about 5280 in each.

8. Yet Witherington, *Matthew*, 183, shows that Roman anti-Semitism was mitigated by their veneration of people from the East, particularly from Egypt and Israel, for their magical powers. So this centurion would to an extent be drawn to a Jewish holy man like Jesus, who was reputed to be both a sage and a miracle worker.

9. Carson, "Matthew," 200, thinks it may be the earlier healing of the royal official's son in John 4:46 – 53 that has led to the centurion's faith in this instance.

10. Keener, *Matthew*, 266, points out that this slave would be the entire family of the centurion's household since military were not allowed to have legal families with them during their two decades of military service (most took concubines).

11. So TNIV; Gnilka, *Matthäusevangelium*, 1:301; Carson, "Matthew," 201; Davies and Allison, *Matthew*, 2:22; Harrington, *Matthew*, 113; France, *Gospel of Matthew*, 313.

12. McNeile, *Matthew*, 104, says that if this is a statement, "the humble answer, with its profound faith, is called forth by no apparent cause." See also Morris, *Matthew*, 193.

once more.[13] Moreover, the humble response also fits; he is surprised at Jesus' willingness and realizes his inadequacy. The emphasis once more is on the compassion of Christ, now willing to help even a despised Roman.

8:8 The centurion responded, "Lord, I am not worthy that you should come under my roof" (καὶ ἀποκριθεὶς ὁ ἑκατόνταρχος ἔφη, Κύριε, οὐκ εἰμὶ ἱκανὸς ἵνα μου ὑπὸ τὴν στέγην εἰσέλθῃς). He uses the respectful "Lord" a second time (8:6) and acknowledges his inferior status as well as Jesus' authority.[14] "I am not worthy" (οὐκ εἰμὶ ἱκανός) could reflect Jewish prohibitions against entering the homes of Gentiles,[15] which thus recognizes he has no right to ask Jesus into his home. But he probably also realizes how little he deserves Jesus' healing presence. This sense of unworthiness happens throughout Scripture (Gen 18:27; Job 42:6; Isa 6:5; Luke 5:8) when people come face to face with their own fallenness. The centurion is not a follower at this point but might recognize the presence of God in Jesus and thus realize how little he deserves his help. The first is definitely present, and there may be a hint of the latter.

8:8 "... but merely say the word, and my servant will be healed" (ἀλλὰ μόνον εἰπὲ λόγῳ, καὶ ἰαθήσεται ὁ παῖς μου). Jesus has not healed at a distance in Matthew before this time, so this is an astounding leap of faith, especially on the lips of a Roman. Such healings were extremely rare and considered evidence of special powers.[16] It is clear that the centurion realizes the extent of Jesus' miraculous power and so knows Jesus can do whatever he wants.

8:9 "For I am also a man possessing authority, having soldiers under me" (καὶ γὰρ ἐγὼ ἄνθρωπός εἰμι ὑπὸ ἐξουσίαν, ἔχων ὑπ' ἐμαυτὸν στρατιώτας). The centurion reasons from his own position of authority to Jesus. The phrase "possessing authority" (ὑπὸ ἐξουσίαν) does not just mean he himself is "under" others but rather that he has received great authority from his superiors. Only Caesar had ultimate authority, but he delegated it to the governor and then to the legate, tribune, and centurion. The centurion was, in fact, the key leader in a legion (see above) and had autonomous authority to direct his men in battle. His commands came with the authority of the emperor himself.

8:9 "... and I tell one, 'Go,' and he goes, and another, 'Come,' and he comes; or I tell my slave, 'Do this,' and he does it" (καὶ λέγω τούτῳ, Πορεύθητι, καὶ πορεύεται, καὶ ἄλλῳ, Ἔρχου, καὶ ἔρχεται, καὶ τῷ δούλῳ μου, Ποίησον τοῦτο, καὶ ποιεῖ). Enumerating the extent of his own authority over people, the centurion reasons that Jesus has the same kind of authority over disease. The progression in the three commands is stylistic to show his absolute authority over his men (the same triad appears in Luke 7:8). God is behind Jesus, so he has unlimited power not just over people (the extent of a Roman's authority) but over nature as well. A centurion not only could make his troops obey his every whim but also had the power to coerce anyone to do what he wished (cf. 27:32; Luke 3:14). Moreover, like any owner of slaves (δοῦλος always means "slave" in the NT),[17] he had supreme authority to make the slave do whatever he wished. Therefore, the word of Jesus, stemming from a far greater authority, could accomplish anything.

13. So NRSV; NLT; Hagner, *Matthew 1 – 13*, 204; Blomberg, *Matthew*, 141; Beare, *Matthew*, 207.

14. See France, "Exegesis," 255.

15. Hagner, *Matthew 1 – 13*, 204. Hill, *Matthew*, 158, calls it "an attitude of respect," Harrington, *Matthew*, 114, a "model of politeness."

16. See Keener, *Matthew*, 267.

17. See Murray J. Harris, *Slave of Christ: A New Testament Metaphor for Total Devotion to Christ* (NSBT 8; Downers Grove, IL: IVP, 2001).

8:10 When Jesus heard this, he was astounded and said to those following him (ἀκούσας δὲ ὁ Ἰησοῦς ἐθαύμασεν καὶ εἶπεν τοῖς ἀκολουθοῦσιν). Like Mark, Matthew normally uses terms of amazement for the reaction of the crowds to Jesus. In fact, this is the only time in Matthew Jesus marvels at anything. "Those following" are not Jesus' followers but the crowds who accompany Jesus (cf. Luke 7:9, specifically referring to "the crowd following").

8:10 "I tell you the truth, I have found no one in Israel with such great faith" (Ἀμὴν λέγω ὑμῖν, παρ' οὐδενὶ τοσαύτην πίστιν ἐν τῷ Ἰσραὴλ εὗρον). The "amen" (ἀμήν) saying, as in 5:18, 26, etc., points to a particularly important truth. "No one in Israel" is emphasized, preparing for the major theme beginning in ch. 11 on the unbelief of Israel. "Faith" is also a major theme in Matthew (cf. 9:2, 22, 28 – 29; 15:28; 17:20; 18:6; 21:21 – 22; 23:23) and here is appropriating faith that moves from the miraculous to participation in the new age of salvation (more in vv. 11 – 12).[18]

The emphasis on the "great faith" highlights the uniqueness of the centurion's belief in Jesus in contrast to Israel; "so great" (τοσαύτην) can express quantity or quality and here means that there is no "faith as strong as this" (BAGD, 823). Matthew is much stronger than Luke here.[19] Luke 7:9 has no such faith "even" in Israel, while Matthew makes it much more stark and then adds the incredible material in vv. 11 – 12.[20] The faith of this military man is indeed remarkable. Such men were normally the ones who most mistreated the Jews and looked down on them with contempt. That one of the very people most mistrusted by the Jewish people would be the one who showed them what faith really was is astounding.

8:11 "I tell you, many from the east and the west will come sit down at the feast with Abraham and Isaac and Jacob in the kingdom of heaven" (λέγω δὲ ὑμῖν ὅτι πολλοὶ ἀπὸ ἀνατολῶν καὶ δυσμῶν ἥξουσιν καὶ ἀνακλιθήσονται μετὰ Ἀβραὰμ καὶ Ἰσαὰκ καὶ Ἰακὼβ ἐν τῇ βασιλείᾳ τῶν οὐρανῶν). Now faith in the miraculous power of Jesus becomes the faith that enables the Gentiles to have a part in the final kingdom. "I tell you" is half the "amen" (ἀμήν) formula (v. 10) and continues the solemn atmosphere. The people from "east and west" (Luke 13:29 adds "north and south" — all four points of the compass) stems from Ps 107:3 (cf. Isa 43:5 – 6; 49:12) and could be the Gentiles,[21] with "east" referring perhaps to the "Magi from the East" in 2:1 and "west" to Rome and then the Gentile mission as a whole.[22]

18. Davies and Allison, *Matthew*, 2:25, speak of three uses of faith/believe in Matthew: intellectual assent (24:23, 26), acceptance and loyalty to Jesus and his message (18:6; 21:25; 27:42), and belief in the power of Jesus to perform great wonders (the miracle stories). This third is found here, though there may be overtones of the second in light of vv. 11 – 12.

19. At the same time, as noted in Nolland, *Matthew*, 356, Jesus does not say there is no faith in Israel, just that it is not as "great" as the centurion's. Nevertheless, Israel is the place where faith would be expected, so this saying is still an indictment of the nation.

20. See France, "Exegesis," 259.

21. Davies and Allison, *Matthew*, 2:27 – 28, doubt this and take the procession to be those Jewish people who are open to Jesus. This is in keeping with the OT passages (Ps 107:3, etc.) that picture the remnant returning to Zion. France, *Matthew: Evangelist*, 212, agrees that this is "the scattered people of Israel" regathered to Zion and sees this as further evidence for the church as "true Israel." Morris, *Matthew*, 195; and France, *Gospel of Matthew*, 317 – 18 (note he has changed his mind), are probably right in saying that people from everywhere are meant, including many Gentiles, The point here is that the Gentiles join the regathered Jewish people in the church, with the emphasis on the Gentiles in this context.

22. Carson, "Matthew," 203, notes three groups of OT passages: (1) Israel gathered from all corners of the earth (Ps 107:3; Isa 43:5 – 6; 49:12); (2) Gentiles worshiping God in all parts of the earth (Isa 45:6; 59:19; Mal 1:11); and (3) Gentiles coming to Jerusalem (Isa 2:2 – 3; 60:3 – 4; Mic 4:1 – 2; Zech 8:20 – 23). He sees this fitting best the first type and follows France ("Exegesis," 261 – 63) in seeing here a typology in which the Gentiles are gathered from the four corners of the earth as the "new Israel." I believe the third category is also part of the imagery.

The catalogue of nations at Pentecost (Acts 2:9 – 11) swept from the east to the south and west, signifying the procession of the nations to Zion in Isa 2:2 – 5; 49:22 – 23; 55:5; 60:3, 5, 11; Jer 3:17; Mic 4:1 – 5; Zech 8:20 – 23. The nations all gather for the messianic banquet, also prophesied in Isaiah (Isa 25:6 – 8) and developed in Joel 2:24 – 28; *1 En.* 62:12 – 14; *2 Bar.* 29:8; Matt 22:1 – 14; 25:10; Luke 22:30; Rev 19:9. The Jewish people reclined in their festal banquets in a Hellenistic manner. The idea of sharing the banquet with the patriarchs was the highest honor imaginable (cf. "Abraham's side" in Luke 16:22). The universal mission is a major theme in Matthew (see 1:5 – 6; 2:1 – 12; 3:9; 4:14 – 16, 25; 8:5 – 13, 28 – 34; 10:18; 12:21, 42; 13:38; 15:21 – 28, 29 – 31; 24:14, 31; 25:31 – 46; 28:19).

8:12 "But the children of the kingdom will be thrown into outermost darkness" (οἱ δὲ υἱοὶ τῆς βασιλείας ἐκβληθήσονται εἰς τὸ σκότος τὸ ἐξώτερον). The "children of the kingdom" are those who should inherit it, namely, Israel (called "sons of the covenant" at Qumran, 1QM 17:8). "Children of" in Scripture is a metaphor for those who are characterized by a thing, here "kingdom children"; this is ironic. Israel should have belonged to the kingdom but has rejected their Messiah. "Outermost darkness" (τὸ σκότος τὸ ἐξώτερον) is that darkness that is completely "outside" the light of God, namely, the place of final punishment. It is in complete contrast with the light and joy of the banquet scene.

8:12 "... where there will be weeping and grinding of teeth" (ἐκεῖ ἔσται ὁ κλαυθμὸς καὶ ὁ βρυγμὸς τῶν ὀδόντων). The weeping and grinding of teeth (objective genitive — they "grind their teeth") are due to the sorrow and anguish of absolute separation from God.[23] This type of wailing normally occurred at funerals and with the grinding of teeth conveys utter despair; the grinding adds the idea of terrible pain (see on 13:42; in Rev 16:10 the darkness of the fifth bowl produces this type of agony). Charette calls this a "frenzy of misery," including remorse and self-loathing as a result of realizing what they have lost ("outermost darkness" = the complete absence of the light and presence of God) and what they have yet to endure.[24] Jesus used two metaphors for final damnation: Gehenna (5:29) and this one (primarily in Matthew, cf. 13:42, 50; 22:13; 24:51; 25:30, but also in Luke 13:28). "Gehenna" emphasizes the punishment and "outermost darkness" the absolute separation from God.

The eschatological contrast between Jews and Gentiles at the final judgment is startling, especially since Matthew will be emphasizing Jesus' commands to restrict the mission just to Israel (10:6; 15:24). Obviously Matthew is preparing for the later mission to the Gentiles (28:19). Schnabel sums up the implications well: "Jesus separates the kingdom of God from the conditions stipulated in the Old Testament and in Second Temple Judaism: he challenges the privileged position of Israel; he revokes membership in Israel as *condition sine qua non* for salvation; he teaches the future integration of Gentiles (as Gentiles) in the kingdom of God."[25]

8:13 Jesus told the centurion, "Go, let it be done for you just as you have believed" (καὶ εἶπεν ὁ Ἰησοῦς τῷ ἑκατοντάρχῃ, Ὕπαγε, ὡς ἐπίστευσας γενηθήτω σοι). Jesus sends the centurion home. The healing is not described, for Jesus heals the

23. The articles before each are emphatic, "the weeping" and "the grinding," thus stressing the anguish of those facing final judgment. This imagery was often used in Judaism (cf. *1 En.* 63:10; 108:3; *4 Ezra* 7:93; *Pss. Sol.* 14:9, 15:10). Davies and Allison, *Matthew,* 2:31, say "grinding" (ὁ βρυγμός) also connotes anger (the verb form is used of rage, cf. BAGD, 148).

24. Charette, *Theme of Recompense,* 140 – 41.

25. Eckhard J. Schnabel, *Early Christian Mission* (2 vols.; Downers Grove, IL: IVP, 2004), 1:335.

servant from a distance (cf. 15:28, another Gentile scene). In fact, in context the healing occurs at "that very hour" (see below), with the emphasis on Jesus' power. The "just as" (ὡς) cannot mean Jesus healed the servant "because of" the centurion's faith or "in proportion to" his faith but rather occurred "just as" he had hoped.[26] His faith did not control the miracle but allowed him to participate in it.

8:13 And the servant was healed that very hour (καὶ ἰάθη ὁ παῖς αὐτοῦ ἐν τῇ ὥρᾳ ἐκείνῃ). Burchard believes that the miracle happened as much for the centurion as for his slave, and that in this, salvation has come not just to Israel but for the nations, so that the universal mission is found here in embryo.[27] Twelftree speaks of Matthew's "rewriting of the ending" in order to highlight the centurion's faith. "The importance of this theme to Matthew is obvious in that only twice is Jesus portrayed as granting the request of a Gentile, both times in response to faith (cf. Matt 15:21 – 28). Thus Jesus' call to the Jews is overcome, and the barrier between Jew and Gentile is shattered by faith."[28]

Theology in Application

This is a remarkable story in many ways, not only for the great healing power of Jesus Messiah but also for the incredible faith of a pagan military commander who puts the Jewish people to shame.

1. Concern for the Despised and Rejected

This continues the theme in the first episode. The people ignored by mainstream society constituted Jesus' special mission (the Samaritan woman, John 4:4 – 38; the leper, Matt 8:1 – 4; Matthew the tax collector, Matt 9:9 – 13; the widow's son, Luke 7:11 – 16; the sinful woman, Luke 7:36 – 50; and many others). He wanted to show God's love for them. Here is another reversal of the world's mores that the coming of the kingdom mandates. The priorities of depraved humanity are reversed by God. The downtrodden are lifted up; those shown injustice are vindicated by God. The despised Gentiles will become the target group of the new mission soon to be inaugurated. Jesus is preparing for that day.

2. The Role of Faith

Faith does not control God's healing presence but allows the individual to experience it in a special way. It is mistaken to take the "just as" (ὡς) of v. 13 as meaning the man's faith was the causative agent in the healing of his slave. But it does mean that Jesus honored the man's faith. Our faith does not bring about the miracle but

26. Carson, "Matthew," 203.

27. Christoph Burchard, "Zu Matthäus 8, 5 – 13," *ZNW* 84 (1993): 278 – 88 (esp. 285 – 86).

28. Twelftree, *Jesus the Miracle Worker*, 110.

does channel the presence of God into a situation. The centuries-old debate as to whether prayer changes things will never be ultimately resolved this side of heaven, but a close examination of the effects of prayer throughout Scripture has convinced me that prayer brings God's presence in a new way. So in that sense prayer does change things; it matters when more and more pray and when we pray more intensely. More than that we cannot say, for Scripture never truly resolves the tension.

3. Anticipating the Gentile Mission

The universal mission is not launched here, but Jesus prepares for it in a startling way. Matthew has given other glimpses of God's concern to reach the world, as in the genealogy at 1:3, 5, 6 and the coming of the Magi in 2:1 – 12. Here the theological basis is given; God's people have no faith and are rejecting the Messiah. Certainly at the same time God's plan from the Abrahamic covenant was for his chosen people to bring "blessing" to the nations (Gen 12:3; etc.). Since his own people have rejected this, he will now fulfill this through the new Israel, the church. This theme will come into full fruition in the Great Commission (28:18 – 20), which will summarize the primary themes of Matthew's gospel.

CHAPTER 29

Matthew 8:14 – 17

Literary Context

This is the third healing miracle in which Jesus centers on social outcasts (here a woman), and now it is one of his own followers, Peter's mother-in-law. This is the shortest story and is followed by a summary episode demonstrating Jesus' growing fame as well as the extent of his power — he cast out demons as well. With this is found another of Matthew's fulfillment passages (v. 17) to show that his healing authority is messianic in nature.

III. The Kingdom Comes with Authority (8:1 – 11:1)
- **A. Authority and Discipleship in Jesus' Ministry (8:1 – 9:34)**
  - **1. Three Healing Miracles (8:1 – 17)**
    - a. Healing the Leper (8:1 – 4)
    - b. Healing the Centurion's Servant (8:5 – 13)
    - ➦ **c. Healing Peter's Mother-in-Law (8:14 – 17)**

Main Idea

Once more this passage is primarily christological in essence, centering on the universal authority of Jesus to heal everyone brought to him, so that this fulfills Scripture.

Translation

(See next page.)

Matthew 8:14-17

14a	Setting (Temporal/Spatial) (A)	When Jesus entered Peter's house,
b	Problem (B)	**he saw Peter's mother-in-law lying in bed with a fever.**
15a	Action/Solution (C)	**He touched her hand,**
b	Result (B')	and **the fever left her.**
c	Result of 15b (A')	**Then she rose up and began serving him.**
16a	Scene: Summary Setting	When evening arrived,
b	Problem	**they brought many demon-possessed people to Jesus**
c	Solution	and **he cast out the spirits with a word and** **healed all who were ill.**
17a	Result/ Fulfillment Formula	**As a result, what was spoken through Isaiah the prophet was ↵** **fulfilled saying,**
b		*"He took on himself our weaknesses and* *bore our diseases."* (Isa 53:4)

Structure and Literary Form

As elsewhere, Matthew's parallelism is noteworthy. The miracle story (vv. 14 – 15) is carefully shortened from Mark 1:29 – 31 and given in chiastic form with two triads:[1] (a) Jesus sees Peter's mother-in-law (b) lying sick (c) with a fever (d) and touches her hand so that (c') the fever leaves her and (b') she rises and (a') serves Jesus. The simplicity and directness of the narrative provides a vivid touch with Jesus center stage in the first half and the woman center stage in the second half. The summary passage (vv. 16 – 17) abbreviates Mark 1:32 – 34, again with much parallelism in the three clauses — they brought, he cast out demons, he healed the sick.

Exegetical Outline

➡ **I. The Healing of Peter's Mother-in-Law (8:14 – 15)**

- A. Jesus' action (vv. 14 – 15a)
  - 1. Sees her sick (v. 14)
  - 2. Touches her hand (v. 15a)
- B. The results: she rises and serves him (v. 15b)

1. Hagner, *Matthew 1 - 13*, 208 – 9.

II. Summary: Miracles That Evening (8:16 – 17)

A. They bring the demon-possessed to him (v. 16)

1. Drove out the spirits
2. Healed the sick

B. Fulfillment of Isa 53:4 (v. 17)

Explanation of the Text

8:14 When Jesus entered Peter's house, he saw Peter's mother-in-law lying in bed with a fever (Καὶ ἐλθὼν ὁ Ἰησοῦς εἰς τὴν οἰκίαν Πέτρου εἶδεν τὴν πενθερὰν αὐτοῦ βεβλημένην καὶ πυρέσσουσαν). Another temporal participle ("when he entered" [ἐλθών], cf. 6:3, 7; 8:1) begins the action. Peter has obviously done well in his fishing business, because he has his own home, large enough for his mother-in-law to live with his family. The extended family aspect of ancient society would make this natural. In Matthew's story, there is no one but Jesus and the woman (Mark has the four present — Peter, Andrew, James, and John — and Luke has them ask Jesus to heal her). Matthew wants the attention only on Jesus. In fact, this is the only time in Matthew that Jesus heals without a request.

There is a chance that this very home may have been discovered. A fifth-century octagonal church (octagons showed veneration) has been unearthed in Capernaum, built over a first-century home that had become a house church, and there are records in the fourth and sixth centuries of pilgrims visiting a house church that had been Peter's home. Moreover, it is also possible that Jesus stayed there when in Capernaum.[2] While there, he sees her lying in bed ill with a fever.[3]

8:15 He touched her hand, and the fever left her. Then she rose up and began serving him (καὶ ἥψατο τῆς χειρὸς αὐτῆς, καὶ ἀφῆκεν αὐτὴν ὁ πυρετός· καὶ ἠγέρθη καὶ διηκόνει αὐτῷ). Touching as a means of healing occurs also in 8:3; 9:29; 20:34. Here, however, he touches a woman. The Pharisees frowned on this as well as touching someone with a fever. Once more Jesus ignores such legalities in time of need. At his healing touch she is instantly cured and gets up to serve Jesus. The imperfect "began serving" (διηκόνει) may be inceptive ("began to") or durative ("continued to"), and the verb itself may have a double meaning, not just taking care of Jesus' needs but beginning a life of discipleship at this point.[4]

8:16 When evening arrived (Ὀψίας δὲ γενομένης). Matthew presents 5:1 – 8:17 as a single day's activity (8:1, "After he descended from the mountain"; 8:5, "after [he] entered Capernaum"; 8:14, "when Jesus entered Peter's house"; 8:16, "when evening arrived"),[5] similar to Mark 1:21 – 34. The day thus begins and ends with summary statements

2. James F. Strange and Herschel Shanks, "Has the House Where Jesus Stayed in Capernaum Been Found?" *BAR* 8 (1982): 26 – 37. See also Davies and Allison, *Matthew*, 2:33 – 34. Davies and Allison conclude, "There is a good chance, then, that sometime during the first century A.D. Peter's residence in Capernaum was turned into a Christian centre and that this church was eventually converted into the octagonal structure whose ruins now lie midway between the Jewish synagogue and the Sea of Galilee."

3. The two final participles, "lying in bed with a fever" (βεβλημένην καὶ πυρέσσουσαν), are circumstantial, telling how Jesus "saw" the state of the woman. The first is perfect, meaning her "state-of-being" was fevered; the second is present, meaning it was a raging fever.

4. So Blomberg, *Matthew*, 143.

5. Another temporal genitive absolute, see 1:18, 20; 2:1, 13, etc.

(4:23 – 25; 8:16 – 17) showing Jesus as authoritative in word and deed.

8:16 . . . they brought many demon-possessed people to Jesus (προσήνεγκαν αὐτῷ δαιμονιζομένους πολλούς). News of Jesus' miracles traveled fast, and now many are brought to Jesus. Matthew centers on the "demon-possessed" here and mentions such in three summaries (4:24; 7:22; 8:17) and five exorcism stories (8:28 – 34; 9:32 – 34; 12:22 – 24; 15:22 – 28; 17:14 – 20). Jesus' authority extended not only to nature and physical illness but to the spirit world as well. This is the second occurrence of "demon-possessed" (δαιμονιζομένους) in Matthew, and it will become a major theme in terms of Jesus' authority and victory over the cosmic powers (of nature as well as of the satanic realm; see 4:24; 8:28 – 34; 9:32 – 34; 10:8; 11:18; 12:22 – 29; 15:21 – 28; 17:14 – 23 for demons; and 8:23 – 27; 14:22 – 33 for storms).

8:16 And he cast out the spirits with a word and healed all who were ill (καὶ ἐξέβαλεν τὰ πνεύματα λόγῳ καὶ πάντας τοὺς κακῶς ἔχοντας ἐθεράπευσεν). The evil spirits are not overpowering beings. John tells us that Satan works through deception (Rev 12:9; 20:3) more than power. Jesus has complete authority over them and so "casts them out" (ἐκβάλλω is almost a technical term in the gospels for exorcism) "with a word." As in 8:8 (cf. 8:3, 26, 32) the authority of his "word" is more than sufficient, unlike other ancient exorcists, who prattled on and on with incantations and oaths. Only Matthew uses the absolute "the spirits" (τὰ πνεύματα) here (Mark and Luke have "demons," and elsewhere in the gospels they are called "unclean" or "evil spirits"), probably to keep the emphasis on Jesus' power over them. Also, he heals "all" who are ill, stressing the universal mercy of God and the extent of Jesus' authority.

8:17 As a result, what was spoken through Isaiah the prophet was fulfilled (ὅπως πληρωθῇ τὸ ῥηθὲν διὰ Ἠσαΐου τοῦ προφήτου). Matthew considers Jesus' healing ministry a fulfillment of prophecy (cf. 1:22; 2:15, 17, 23; 4:14), in this case Isa 53:4. Interestingly, Matthew is closer to the MT ("he took up our illnesses and bore our sorrows") than the LXX ("he bears our sins and suffers pain for us," clearly a spiritual interpretation of the MT). This is probably Matthew's own translation of the MT[6] and sees Jesus' healing ministry as the work of the *Ebed Yahweh* ("Servant of Yahweh") of Isaiah. The context of Isa 53 centers on the vicarious suffering of the Servant who is "pierced for our transgressions" and "crushed for our iniquities."

8:17 . . . saying, "He took on himself our weaknesses and bore our diseases" (λέγοντος, Αὐτὸς τὰς ἀσθενείας ἡμῶν ἔλαβεν καὶ τὰς νόσους ἐβάστασεν). The question is whether Isa 53:4 is literal (diseases) or spiritual (a euphemism for sin, as in the LXX). Yet as Gundry points out, "Along with forgiveness of sins . . . physical well-being was thought to characterize the messianic age (cf. Isa 29:18; 32:3 – 4; 35:5 – 6)."[7] So Matthew is justified in seeing Jesus' healing ministry as the work of the suffering Servant.

At the same time, there is likely another nuance, seen in Dodd's observation that an isolated quote often implies the OT context as well.[8] Matthew uses Isa 53 often (20:28; 26:28; 27:12, 57)

6. Contra M. J. J. Menken, "The Source of the Quotation from Isaiah 53:4 in Matthew 8:17," *NovT* 39 (1997): 313 – 27, who thinks Matthew used a revised LXX.

7. Gundry, *Matthew*, 150. See also John Oswalt, *The Book of Isaiah, Chapters 40 – 66* (NICOT; Grand Rapids: Eerdmans, 1998), 386, who notes that this picks up the theme of Isa 53:3, the very servant who was "despised" because he "knows illness" has actually "carried our sickness" in himself.

8. C. H. Dodd, *According to the Scriptures* (London: Nisbet, 1952), in Carson, "Matthew," 205.

and likely intends a further nuance here, in which the healing of physical illnesses is a harbinger of the greater healing of spiritual illnesses at the cross. "The healings anticipate the passion in that they begin to roll back the effects of the sins for which Jesus came to die."[9]

Theology in Application

1. Jesus as Lord of All

The authority and power of Jesus come full circle here as he heals Peter's mother-in-law with a touch and casts out demons with a word. The contrast with first-century magicians and exorcists is stark. Jesus needs no elaborate incantations or lengthy oaths imploring half the angels in heaven for help. Jesus' power is internal, inherent in his very being, and he is able to cure everyone brought to him and to defeat the powers of evil (see Col 2:15; 1 Cor 15:24; cf. Isa 35:5 – 6; 53:4).

2. Looking Ahead to Jesus' Greater Healing Work

As Hagner says, "Disease is not the true enemy to be overcome: that enemy is sin, for the fallen world produced by sin lies ultimately behind the suffering and sickness of this age."[10] So Jesus' miracles are symbols of the greater victory to be won by the suffering Servant on the cross. They are also proleptic of the final removal of both sin and disease at the end of the age.

3. The Power of Jesus

The center point is not the availability of healing but the power of Jesus. In many charismatic circles it is thought that Isa 53:4 means that healing is part of the atonement,[11] i.e., that healing is available to everyone today as well. In one sense that is partly correct (cf. Jas 5:13 – 18), for God's healing presence is indeed for all. But that does not mean everyone will be healed, for God is sovereign over all and decides what is best in each instance.[12]

While faith is central in the first two healings here, it is not in every healing, and definitely faith does not create the healing. Paul was not healed of his "thorn in [the] flesh" (2 Cor 12:7 – 10), and he stated in Rom 8:26 – 28 that we do not know how to pray in accordance with the will of God; only the Spirit does. It is due to the Spirit's

9. Gundry, *Matthew*, 150. See also Carson's extensive discussion, "Matthew," 205 – 6. For the argument that many different readings of v. 17 can be equally valid, see Daniel Patte, "Textual Constraints, Ordinary Readings, and Critical Exegesis: An Androcritical Perspective," *Semeia* 62 (1993): 59 – 79.

10. Hagner, *Matthew 1 – 13*, 211.

11. For an argument against healing as part of the atonement, see R. L. Mayhue, "For What Did Christ Atone in Isa 53:4 – 5?" *MSJ* 6 (1995): 121 – 41, who argues that in vv. 14 – 17 atonement is for spiritual, not physical, healing.

12. See Douglas J. Moo, "Divine Healing in the Health and Wealth Gospel," *TJ* n.s. 9 (1988), 191 – 209.

intercession that "in all things God works for the good of those who love him," and in this instance that means whether we are healed or not. God alone is sovereign, not our faith. When we are not healed physically, God is doing what is best for us, and his very refusal to heal us physically becomes the means of healing us spiritually, so that God's healing presence is always involved.

CHAPTER 30

Matthew 8:18 – 22

Literary Context

"Matthew inserts these discipleship stories into his nexus of miracles to teach that faith in Jesus must always be united with obedience."[1] The second theme of the larger section of chapters 8 and 9 (after the lordly authority of Jesus) is the call for radical discipleship. We have already seen the basis of such in the radical faith of the leper and the centurion in the first two miracles of this section.[2] Here two other would-be disciples come to Jesus and want to go the second step after faith, becoming followers.

III. The Kingdom Comes with Authority (8:1 – 11:1)

A. Authority and Discipleship in Jesus' Ministry (8:1 – 9:34)

1. Three Healing Miracles (8:1 – 17)
2. **The Demands of Discipleship (8:18 – 22)**
3. Three Miracles Showing His Authority (8:23 – 9:8)

Main Idea

Discipleship is not a casual thing, like joining a club or a sports team; it cannot be an occasional activity, one of many to which we give a bit of allegiance. To follow Jesus is costly, demanding the surrender of other allegiances and the absolute priority of Jesus in our lives. As Jesus makes clear to the two who would follow him, the kingdom has now come, and to become citizens of that kingdom means to renounce other citizenships, to become "foreigners and strangers" (Heb 11:13; 1 Pet 1:1, 17; 2:11) to this world.

1. Bruner, *Christbook*, 313, from Grundmann, *Matthäus*, 257.

2. Nolland, *Matthew*, 363, speaks of a "discipleship frame" around the second triad of miracles (8:18 – 22 and 9:9 – 13 framing 8:23 – 9:8).

Translation

Matthew 8:18-22

18a	Setting	When Jesus saw the crowd around him,
b	Exhortation	**he ordered his disciples to go across to the other side of the lake.**
19a	Request (A)	And **a scribe came to him and said,**
b		*"Teacher, I want to follow you wherever you go."*
20a	Response/Aphorism (B)	**Jesus said to him,**
b		*"Foxes have their dens and the birds of the air their nests,*
		but the Son of Man has nowhere to lay his head."
21a	Request (A)	**Then another of his disciples said to him,**
b		*"Lord, let me first go and bury my Father."*
22a	Response/Aphorism (B)	But **Jesus replied,**
b		*"Follow me, and let the dead bury their own dead."*

Structure and Literary Form

This paradigm story[3] is put together by Matthew to give an important discipleship direction to the miracle section. This is seen in the fact that Matthew has sandwiched a Q episode (vv. 19 – 22 = Luke 9:57 – 60) into a Markan story (v. 18 = Mark 4:35; vv. 23 – 27 = Mark 4:36 – 41) to yield a two-part emphasis on what it means to follow Jesus. The parabolic use of the stilling of the storm as a discipleship story becomes a proper denouement for the twofold interaction here.

The parallelism is obvious: would-be disciples seek advice on following Jesus, and Jesus makes startling replies on the demands of discipleship. As Hengel says, "Jesus plunges the disciples into total lack of security … and requires a break even with the strongest of human links, the family."[4]

Exegetical Outline

➡ **I. Command to Cross the Lake (8:18)**

II. Two Discipleship Interactions (8:19 – 22)

A. A scribe wants to follow (vv. 19 – 20)

B. A disciple wants to bury his father (vv. 21 – 22)

3. On this form see Martin Dibelius, *From Tradition to Gospel* (trans. B. L. Woolf; Cambridge: James Clarke, 1971), 37 – 69.

4. Hengel, *Charismatic Leader*, 5.

Explanation of the Text

8:18 When Jesus saw the crowd around him, he ordered his disciples to go across to the other side of the lake (Ἰδὼν δὲ ὁ Ἰησοῦς ὄχλον περὶ αὐτὸν ἐκέλευσεν ἀπελθεῖν εἰς τὸ πέραν). Another temporal participle ("when he saw" [ἰδών]) begins a mini-travel narrative (a discipleship journey) as Jesus orders the disciples across the lake, then stills the storm during the trip and casts demons out of two demoniacs on the other side. Here Jesus replicates 5:1 in his apparent desire to get away from the crowds. His interest is in discipleship rather than evangelism at this point. He wants his disciples to leave the Jewish side (Galilee) and cross to the Gentile side. The command to go further demonstrates his authority.[5]

8:19 And a scribe came[6] to him and said, "Teacher, I want to follow you wherever you go" (καὶ προσελθὼν εἷς γραμματεὺς εἶπεν αὐτῷ, Διδάσκαλε, ἀκολουθήσω σοι ὅπου ἐὰν ἀπέρχῃ). Before they can get in the boat, Jesus is interrupted by a person from the crowd who wants to be a disciple. Surprisingly, the request comes from "a[7] scribe," usually an opponent in Matthew (5:20; 7:29; 9:3). In Luke 9:57 it is (lit.) "a certain person," so Matthew is emphasizing that this is indeed a scribe. As a result, many believe this element is negative, with the scribe being an opponent who is rejected by Jesus.[8] But this does not fit the context.

It is thus better to see this scribe as a potential disciple,[9] with Jesus stating what true discipleship must entail. His desire is to learn from the words and deeds of the master "teacher."[10] "Follow" is the key term for discipleship in all the gospels and entails both personal commitment and cost,[11] but he does not seem to understand this on the basis of Jesus' response. "Wherever you go" probably means this scribe would like to get in the boat and accompany Jesus and his disciples to the other side of the lake, thereby continuing to sit at Jesus' feet and watch his actions.

In Jewish practice, a disciple chose which rabbi he wished to follow, and that is what the man is doing. He may have already examined several others and selected Jesus as the one he wished to study under.[12] Still, the central figure in his request is

5. Hans-Joachim Held, "Matthew as Interpreter of the Miracle Stories," in *Tradition and Interpretation in Matthew*, ed. G. Bornkamm, G. Barth, and H. J. Held (NTL; Philadelphia: Westminster, 1963), 202, believes that "to order" (κελεύειν) connotes a call to discipleship as Jesus calls for the crowds to follow him. However, this reads too much into the scene, which centers on the difficulties and cost of discipleship more than on a universal call.

6. "Came" (προσελθών) is another circumstantial participle like vv. 2, 7.

7. "One" (εἷς) here may function as an indefinite article, cf. BDF §247.2; Davies and Allison, *Matthew*, 2:41. It could also be equivalent to "a certain one" (τις), "a certain scribe," also BDF §247.2; Morris, *Matthew*, 200.

8. So Gnilka, *Matthäusevangelium*, 1:310; Jack D. Kingsbury, "On Following Jesus: The 'Eager' Scribe and the 'Reluctant' Disciple (Matthew 8:18 – 22)," *NTS* 34 (1988): 45 – 59 (48 – 49); France, *Gospel of Matthew*, 325 – 26. Blomberg, *Matthew*, 146, calls this "inadequate discipleship."

9. V. 21 calls the second "another of his disciples," and the scribe offers to "follow you wherever you go," likely showing a desire to become a disciple. In fact, the second would-be "disciple" shows more reluctance than the first. See Hill, *Matthew*, 161; Carson, "Matthew," 207 – 8. France, *Matthew* (TNTC), 159, says, "While the scribes as a class are normally mentioned as in opposition to Jesus, as individuals they were potential disciples." Some believe he is already a disciple; see M.-J. Lagrange, *Évangile selon Saint Matthieu* (Paris: Lecoffre, 1948), 171; Hill, *Matthew*, 162 (possible); Gundry, *Matthew*, 151 – 52.

10. Grundmann, *Matthäus*, 152. "Teacher" in Matthew is never used by disciples but by those either in opposition (9:11; 12:38; 22:16, 24, 36) or with an inadequate understanding (here, 17:24; 19:16).

11. Jack D. Kingsbury, "The Verb AKOLOUTHEIN ('To Follow') as an Index of Matthew's View of His Community," *JBL* 97 (1978): 56 – 73 (58); and "Following Jesus," 46.

12. Wilkins, *Matthew*, 347.

Jesus himself. Bruner writes, "The subject of the sentence, not only grammatically, is the Bible teacher himself.... And when listened to carefully his remark has overtones of 'Jesus, this is your lucky day: I have decided to be your disciple.'"[13]

8:20 Jesus said to him, "Foxes have their dens and the birds of the air their nests" (καὶ λέγει αὐτῷ ὁ Ἰησοῦς, Αἱ ἀλώπεκες φωλεοὺς ἔχουσιν καὶ τὰ πετεινὰ τοῦ οὐρανοῦ κατασκηνώσεις). Jesus obviously sees a halfhearted commitment in the man, for he cuts to the heart of the matter, the extent one is willing to go to follow Jesus. With a vivid metaphor (perhaps even a proverb), Jesus points out that God's creatures have homes; foxes have their lairs, holes in the ground, and birds have their nests in the trees, but Jesus the Son of Man (see excursus below) has no such home.

8:20 "... but the Son of Man has nowhere to lay his head" (ὁ δὲ υἱὸς τοῦ ἀνθρώπου οὐκ ἔχει ποῦ τὴν κεφαλὴν κλίνῃ). There is a certain hyperbole in the response, for Jesus made his home in Capernaum (4:13) and may even have had his own house (9:28; 13:1, 36; 17:25),[14] though most say he likely stayed in the homes of his disciples (8:14; 9:10).[15] Rather, he speaks of his itinerant ministry and lifestyle (cf. 2:13 – 14; 12:15; 15:21; 16:1 – 5),[16] as does Paul when he notes the "homeless" nature of the apostolic ministry (1 Cor 4:11, cf. Heb 11:13 – 16). There will be no comfortable, settled life for one who truly follows Jesus. To the man's "wherever you go" Jesus adds, "OK, will you go this far?" Jesus does not want shallow commitments but demands that the one who truly "follows" him count the cost (cf. Luke 14:25 – 35) and make a radical commitment.

8:21 Then another of his disciples said to him, "Lord, let me first go and bury my Father" (ἕτερος δὲ τῶν μαθητῶν [αὐτοῦ] εἶπεν αὐτῷ, Κύριε, ἐπίτρεψόν μοι πρῶτον ἀπελθεῖν καὶ θάψαι τὸν πατέρα μου). It is best to see this as another would-be disciple,[17] perhaps a member of the larger circle of Jesus' followers, and that he has what to any Jew would seem a viable situation. We do not know whether the father is near death or has already died. If the latter, the request could be for just a few hours. But the text does not answer that.

Since the Torah commanded one to "honor" one's parents (Exod 20:12 = Deut 5:16), burial duties were a sacred responsibility (Gen 25:9; 35:29; 50:5 – 6, 13; Tob 4:3; 6:14 – 16; *b. Ber.* 31a), and the only exceptions were a high priest or someone who had taken a Nazirite vow[18] (Lev 21:10 – 11; Num 6:6 – 7); even priests had to place burial duties first (Lev 21:2). Elisha asked Elijah's permission to say good-bye to his parents, and it was granted (1 Kgs 19:19 – 21). So the request at first glance seems completely valid.[19] Still, there is a distinct development in the two who come to Jesus: the first promises too much (what he cannot deliver) while

13. Bruner, *Christbook*, 314.

14. So Kingsbury, "Following Jesus," 50.

15. E.g., France, *Matthew* (TNTC), 161. This is only the second time "disciple" (μαθητής) is found in Matthew (see 5:1).

16. So Maurice Casey, "The Jackals and the Son of Man (Matt 8.20/Luke 9.58)," *JSNT* 23 (1985): 3 – 22, who emphasizes the parallels between the migratory habits of the jackals and birds and the migratory ministry of Jesus.

17. It is interesting to see the conclusions of those who take ἕτερος as "one of a different kind." Kingsbury, "Following Jesus," 47 – 48, says the first is a would-be disciple and the second a true disciple, while Gundry, *Matthew*, 151, 153 (and later in his "On True and False Disciples in Matthew 8:18 – 22," *NTS* 40 [1994]: 433 – 41), says the first is a true disciple and the second a false disciple. However, it is better to see ἕτερος as "another of the same kind" and both as potential disciples rather than actual disciples.

18. See Markus Bockmuehl, "'Let the Dead Bury Their Dead' (Matt 8:22/Luke 9:60): Jesus and the Halakhah," *JTS* 49 (1998): 553 – 81, who thinks this reflects a Nazirite situation.

19. France, *Gospel of Matthew*, 329, follows Kenneth E. Bailey, *Through Peasant Eyes: More Lucan Parables, Their Culture and Style* (Grand Rapids: Eerdmans, 1980), 25 – 27,

the second promises too little (what he does not want to sacrifice).

8:22 But Jesus replied, "Follow me, and let the dead bury their own dead" (ὁ δὲ Ἰησοῦς λέγει αὐτῷ, Ἀκολούθει μοι, καὶ ἄφες τοὺς νεκροὺς θάψαι τοὺς ἑαυτῶν νεκρούς). The present tense imperative "follow" (ἀκολούθει) demands lifelong commitment. Jesus' curt response here is even more shocking than his first one. Scholars have attempted to explain its startling nature.

1. It mistranslates the Aramaic *m*ᵉ*tinîym* ("undecided, waverers") for *mîtîn* ("dead"), so it would read, "Let those who waver bury their own dead."[20]
2. It is an Aramaic proverb, "Let the dead past bury its dead," and so means to leave your former life behind.[21]
3. The Aramaic original actually should read, "Let the gravediggers bury the dead."[22]
4. It refers not to burial duties but to taking care of a parent until they die.[23]
5. This man is returning to fulfill the second stage of burial duties by placing his father's bones in an ossuary a year later.[24]
6. Jesus intends this to be the last stage of the pre-messianic period (cf. Ezek 39:11 – 16).[25]
7. Let the spiritually dead bury the physically dead.[26]
8. It is meant to be harsh like 10:37 and means even the greatest obligation dare not deter one from following Jesus.[27]

The best option is probably a combination of the latter two; the others are viable (not the first, as it is far too conjectural) but tend to water down the force of the statement. Jesus often used aphorisms for their shock value and here wants to demonstrate the extent of a total commitment to himself, which took absolute priority even over the greatest of obligations such as one's parents (cf. Luke 14:26, "hate father and mother"). This was not meant to be a general rule on the priority of Jesus and was not to be followed in all instances (cf. Matt 5:29 – 30; 19:21). Still, it is a shocking statement intended to demand radical commitment in light of the overriding importance of kingdom duties.[28]

in taking this instead as an idiom for fulfilling a son's duties for the rest of the father's life, so it then asks for "an indefinite postponement of discipleship." Yet that seems to read too much into this simple request and out of keeping with the introduction of the person as "another of his disciples."

20. Matthew Black, "Let the Dead Bury Their Dead," *ExpTim* 61 (1949 – 50): 219 – 20.

21. McNeile, *Matthew*, 109 – 10.

22. Günther Schwartz, *"Aphes tous nekrous thapsai tous heautōn nekrous,"* *ZNW* 72 (1981): 272 – 76.

23. Bailey, *Through Peasant Eyes*, 26 – 27.

24. Byron R. McCane, "'Let the Dead Bury Their Own Dead': Secondary Burial and Matt 8:211 – 22," *HTR* 83 (1990): 31 – 43; Keener, *Matthew*, 276.

25. J. D. M. Derrett, "Two 'Harsh' Sayings of Christ Explained," *DRev* 103 (1985): 218 – 29.

26. Schlatter, *Matthäus*, 289; Hengel, *Charismatic Leader*, 8; Davies and Allison, *Matthew*, 2:56; Morris, *Matthew*, 203; France, *Gospel of Matthew*, 330.

27. Kingsbury, "Following Jesus," 56.

28. See Hengel, *Charismatic Leader*, 14 – 15, who believes it was Jesus' view of the imminent coming of the kingdom that meant "there was no time to be lost" and led to "the abandonment of all human considerations and ties." This fails to reckon with the fact that Jesus also expected some time before the final kingdom came, but the urgency of kingdom work is still a critical feature.

"Son of Man" as a Christological Title

There may be no aspect of Jesus studies that has garnered more ink than this one. This is the first time "Son of Man" appears in Matthew, but it is found eighty-one times in the gospels (thirty in Matthew) and is the primary term Jesus uses of himself. There are several possible background sources: (1) the Ezekiel "son of man," used by God for Ezekiel ninety-three times to indicate he is a mortal human being[29] (cf. also Ps 8:4); (2) the "one like a son of man" in Dan 7:13, an eschatological figure[30] who has dominion over the whole earth; (3) there is evidence that *bar nāšā* in Judaism was a circumlocution for "I";[31] (4) Jewish apocalyptic (e.g., the *Similitudes of Enoch* [*1 En.* 37 – 71][32] and *4 Ezra* 13) uses the title. What, then, is the background for Jesus' use? Some (e.g., Vermes and Casey above) believe only the generic use for "I" was used by Jesus, but that is not widely accepted. In fact, all the above[33] were probably influential in Jesus' use of the title.[34]

There are three major types of Son of Man sayings (with the thirty occurrences in Matthew categorized in each): (1) the earthly work of the Son of Man (8:20; 9:6; 11:19; 12:32; 13:37; 16:13); (2) the suffering Son of Man (12:40; 17:9, 12, 22; 20:18, 28; 26:2, 24, 45); and (3) the apocalyptic Son of Man (10:23; 12:8; 13:41; 16:13, 27, 28; 19:28; 24:27, 30, 37, 39, 44; 25:31; 26:64). Note that the earthly side predominates in the earlier passages and the other two in later passages as Jesus moves toward the cross. Hengel sums it up well:

> The earthly and suffering Son of Man are a cipher with which Jesus, in certain situations, expresses both his authority (indeed, we may say as *Messias designatus*), and his humility and tribulation, which ultimately lead him to suffering

29. Dan Block, *The Book of Ezekiel, Chapters 1 – 24* (NICOT; Grand Rapids: Eerdmans, 1997), 30 – 31.

30. The actual meaning of "one like a son of man" in Daniel is debated. Some believe it to be quasi-divine, others an angelic figure, still others a messianic figure, and some a purely human image, "one like a human being." The general consensus is that it connotes an individual ("one like a man") who is a corporate figure symbolizing the "holy people" of Dan 7:18, 22, 25, 27, either angels or (perhaps more likely) the Jewish people. See Tremper Longman III, *Daniel* (NIVAC; Grand Rapids: Zondervan, 1999), 186 – 88; I. H. Marshall, "Son of Man," *DJG*, 780 – 81.

31. See Geza Vermes, "The Present State of the 'Son of Man' Debate," *JJS* 29 (1978): 123 – 34; Maurice Casey, "General, Generic, and Indefinite: The Use of the Term 'Son of Man' in Jewish Sources and the Teaching of Jesus," *JSNT* 29 (1987): 21 – 56.

32. This was highly doubted as a source for Jesus' use of the title on the grounds that it was post-Christian, but recently there has been a growing feeling that it is pre-Christian but that it refers to Enoch himself (see Carson, "Matthew," 210). The title was known in the time of Christ, though probably not widely used.

33. On the authenticity of Jesus' use of Dan 7 in his Son of Man sayings, see the excellent discussions of Carson, "Matthew," 211 – 13; Marshall, "Son of Man," 779 – 80; Davies and Allison, *Matthew*, 2:47 – 52.

34. Bultmann, *Theology of the New Testament*, 1:29 – 31, proposed that Jesus was not speaking of himself but a later apocalyptic figure based on the *Similitudes of Enoch*. But even a casual perusal of the Son of Man sayings must demonstrate that Jesus was describing himself (e.g., the earthly sayings) and prophesying the events that concerned himself.

and death ... (including) the coming Son of Man, who appears as a mysterious heavenly figure."[35]

It is generally agreed that Jesus chose this title for its ambiguity. It could at one and the same time connote his human nature and his divine mission. That is the case here. Jesus is providing a supreme irony that the one whose suffering will bring about the apocalyptic solution to sin has no home. As Davies and Allison say, "The one without a home is the majestic judge of mankind."[36] M. H. Smith adds, "in the aphorism about foxholes and bird nests, by being called emphatically 'the son of man,' he who is declared to have 'no place to lay his head' is suddenly seen as one who is usually believed to have 'all things under his feet' (Ps 8.6b)."[37]

Theology in Application

Discipleship is at the heart of Matthew's gospel. The Sermon on the Mount is primarily interested in teaching disciples how to be citizens of the kingdom. So here the "faith" of the leper (8:2) and the centurion (8:10) lead naturally to a discussion of true discipleship.

1. Reaching the Whole Person

Jesus is at all times concerned with the person as a whole, healing not just one's body but one's spirit as well. The primary term in miracles is "to save" (σῴζειν), which connotes both spiritual healing and spiritual salvation, inner healing as well as outward. So in the midst of his healing, Jesus provides lessons on discipleship. Healing must be experienced inwardly as well as outwardly, but it demands more than just a casual interest. One must put Jesus above everything, even family (cf. 4:22), and be willing to undergo hardship for the sake of Christ.

2. Disciples and Leaders

The church should not be too quick to accept disciples or appoint leaders. Jesus establishes an important principle, that followers must be scrutinized to make certain they are serious in following Jesus. Paul says that leaders should "not be a recent

35. Martin Hengel, "Jesus the Messiah of Israel: The Debate about the 'Messianic Mission' of Jesus," in *Authenticating the Activities of Jesus* (ed. Bruce Chilton and Craig A. Evans; Leiden: Brill, 2002), 343. On the "coming Son of Man," see also Carsten Colpe, *TDNT*, 8:433 – 41.

36. Davies and Allison, *Matthew*, 2:52.

37. M. H. Smith, "No Place for a Son of Man," *Forum* 4/4 (1988): 83 – 107, noted in Davies and Allison.

convert" (1 Tim 3:6); that is, they should be mature in their walk with Christ. The level of one's commitment and spiritual maturity must be ascertained before they are given responsibilities. For instance, sports stars and entertainers are too quickly used as speakers when they should actually be discipled first.

3. Counting the Cost

Shallow Christians are not accepted by Jesus as disciples until they have counted the cost and deepened their commitment. Both of these men are more sincere than many who attend church regularly but are unwilling to get involved. Yet Jesus still sends them away with a curt, startling demand for a deeper surrender to him. Too many think they can get into heaven on the basis of a basic "faith" while clinging to the world. Yet James says clearly that "faith without deeds is dead" (Jas 2:26); unless we show by the way we live our lives that Christ is first, we are not disciples. We are saved by grace apart from works (Eph 2:8 – 9), but our good works are a necessary proof that we have found faith.

CHAPTER 31

Matthew 8:23–27

Literary Context

There are two emphases here, as this continues the discipleship emphasis of the previous pericope[1] and also reintroduces the authority theme of the first set of miracles (8:1–17). This is Jesus' first nature miracle and begins a topical series containing his three major types of miracles—nature, exorcism, and healing.

III. The Kingdom Comes with Authority (8:1–11:1)
- **A. Authority and Discipleship in Jesus' Ministry (8:1–9:34)**
  1. Three Healing Miracles (8:1–17)
  2. The Demands of Discipleship (8:18–22)
  3. **Three Miracles Showing His Authority (8:23–9:8)**
     - **a. Calming of the Storm (8:23–27)**
     - b. Exorcism of Two Demon-Possessed Men (8:28–34)
     - c. Healing of the Paralytic (9:1–8)

Main Idea

There are two primary thrusts here: the all-embracing authority of Jesus, who not only has power to heal diseases and cast out demons but who also has power over nature itself;[2] and the testing of the disciples' faith, as they are not certain that Jesus has this authority over nature.

1. Jesus' crossing with his disciples to "the other side of the lake" in 8:18 brings together 8:18–22 and 8:23–27 as discipleship stories (so Bornkamm, Barth, and Held, *Tradition and Interpretation*, 53–54; Turner, "Matthew," 129).

2. See Paul F. Feiler, "The Stilling of the Storm in Matthew: A Response to Günther Bornkamm," *JETS* 26 (1983): 399–406, who argues that Christology is the main focus, not discipleship.

Translation

Matthew 8:23-27

23a	Setting	When he got into the boat,
b	Action	**his disciples followed him.**
24a	Problem	And **look, a fierce storm arose in the lake,**
b	Result of 24a	with the result that the boat was being swamped by the waves,
c	Reaction	but **Jesus was sleeping.**
25a	Request	So **they came and woke him up, saying,**
b		*"Lord, save us, we're about to die!"*
26a	Response	And **he said to them,**
b		*"Why are you so afraid, you of so little faith?"*
c	Resolution	**Then he arose,**
		rebuked the winds and the sea, and
		there came a great calm.
27a	Result of 26c	**The men were filled with wonder and said,**
		"What kind of person is this that even the winds and the waves obey him?"

Structure and Literary Form

This is a miracle story, and both Matthew and Luke (Luke 8:22 – 25) build on Mark 4:36 – 41 and shorten his version significantly. Mark has the disciples in the forefront as they "took [Jesus] ... in the boat," while Matthew has Jesus in the forefront as "his disciples followed him." Also, Mark centers on the disciples' rude challenge, "Don't you care if we drown?" Matthew has them cry, "Lord, save us, we're going to drown!" and transposes "Why are you so afraid?" to the point just after their cry to be saved rather than after Jesus stills the storm (as in Mark). Finally, Matthew softens Mark's "Do you still have no faith?" to "you of so little faith." In short, Matthew centers equally on Jesus' authority and the centrality of faith for discipleship.[3]

There is in general a four-part development: the appearance of the storm (vv. 23 – 24), the interaction between Jesus and the disciples (vv. 25 – 26a), the stilling of

3. Scholars as so often are divided on these two emphases. Bornkamm's magisterial article ("The Stilling of the Storm in Matthew," *Tradition and Interpretation*, 52 – 57) calls this "a kerygmatic paradigm of the danger and glory of discipleship" (57) and says little about Christology. On the other hand, J. P. Heil, *Jesus Walking on the Sea* (AnBib 87; Rome: Pontifical Biblical Institute, 1981), calls this a "sea-rescue epiphany" (84) intended to show the disciples Jesus has the power to save them. The best is to see a balance of both in the story.

the storm (v. 26b), and the shocked reaction of the disciples (v. 27). Still, the chiastic outline of Davies and Allison[4] has merit:

Jesus boards (v. 23a)
- The disciples follow (v. 23b)
  - A storm arises (v. 24a-b)
    - Jesus is sleeping (v. 24c)
      - The disciples address Jesus (v. 25)
      - Jesus addresses the disciples (v. 26a)
    - Jesus arises and rebukes the storm (v. 26b)
  - The storm calms (v. 26c)
- The disciples are amazed (v. 27)

Jesus disembarks (v. 28)

Exegetical Outline

➡ I. The Appearance of the Storm (8:23 – 24)
- A. They enter the boat (v. 23)
- B. The fierce storm arises (v. 24)
  1. The unexpected storm (v. 24a)
  2. The waves enter the boat (v. 24b)
  3. Jesus is sleeping (v. 24c)

II. The Interaction (8:25 – 26a)
- A. The disciples' fear (v. 25)
- B. Plea for rescue (v. 25a)
- C. Cry of despair (v. 25b)
- D. Jesus' reply (v. 26a-b)
- E. Challenges their fear (v. 26a)
- F. Challenges their little faith (v. 26b)

III. Jesus Stills the Storm (8:26c)
- A. Rebukes the wind and waves (v. 26c)
- B. Complete calm results (v. 26d)

IV. The Shocked Reaction of the Disciples (8:27)
- A. His personhood (v. 27a)
- B. His authority (v. 27b)

Explanation of the Text

8:23 When he got into[5] the boat, his disciples followed him (Καὶ ἐμβάντι αὐτῷ εἰς τὸ πλοῖον ἠκολούθησαν αὐτῷ οἱ μαθηταὶ αὐτοῦ). There is a distinct discipleship air here. The distinctive "the

4. Davies and Allison, *Matthew*, 2:68. So also Nolland, *Matthew*, 369; Turner, "Matthew," 131.

5. "When he got into" (ἐμβάντι) is a temporal participle, common in Matthew (cf. vv. 1, 5, 16, 18).

disciples followed" is closely connected with the centrality of "follow" in the previous episode (8:19, 22) and hints that this is the proper act of discipleship in contrast to the inadequate hyperpromise of the first would-be disciple and insufficient commitment of the second one in 8:18 – 22. Discipleship demands submission, and the disciples obey Jesus.

8:24 And look, a fierce storm arose in the lake, with the result that the boat was being swamped by the waves (καὶ ἰδοὺ σεισμὸς μέγας ἐγένετο ἐν τῇ θαλάσσῃ, ὥστε τὸ πλοῖον καλύπτεσθαι ὑπὸ τῶν κυμάτων). Matthew introduces this with his typical "look" (ἰδού), pointing to an important development. Hagner takes "storm" (σεισμός) literally as an earthquake,[6] but this word is commonly used of a violent storm on the sea with huge waves (BAGD, 746). This occurred regularly on that lake, since it was six hundred feet below sea level and ringed with mountains to the east, so that the air would surge through the mountains and kick up huge waves sometimes eight to nine feet high. The waves were large enough that they begin to fill the boat with water, threatening to swamp it.

8:24 But Jesus was sleeping (αὐτὸς δὲ ἐκάθευδεν). The dramatic imperfect "was sleeping" (ἐκάθευδεν) pictures Jesus fast asleep as the storm rages. Some believe this is an allusion to Jonah,[7] who slept as the storm raged (Jonah 1:5), but the situations are too different (Jonah was in rebellion against God) and the parallels too far-fetched. In the OT sleep in difficult situations symbolized a deep trust in God (Job 11:18 – 19; Ps 3:5 – 6; Prov 3:24 – 26); that is the likely message here, as the calm of Jesus is in absolute contrast with the deep anxiety of the disciples. Bornkamm allegorizes this, with the boat symbolizing the church and the storm the difficult situations discipleship entails.[8] While there is some plausibility in applying this miracle to "the storms of life," it goes too far to allegorize every detail. The major purpose is to tell the story.

8:25 So they came[9] and woke him up, saying, "Lord, save us, we're about to die!" (καὶ προσελθόντες ἤγειραν αὐτὸν λέγοντες, Κύριε, σῶσον, ἀπολλύμεθα). The use of "Lord" (κύριε) here replaces Mark's "teacher" and points to the authority of Jesus as Lord of all. Of course, the disciples didn't mean all this, but in the theology of the first gospel it is significant (eighty times in Matthew vs. eighteen in Mark). Yet one must be careful not to read too much into the language. Many see every word as liturgical, as if the message dealt with spiritual "salvation" (σῶσον) in light of spiritual "death" (ἀπολλύμεθα), with the solution being to acknowledge Jesus as "Lord" (κύριε).[10] This interpretation, like the discipleship interpretation above (the ship as the church), reads more into the language than is there. "Save us, we're about to die"[11] reflects their fear that death is near, not a soteriological message.

8:26 And he said to them, "Why are you so afraid, you of so little faith?" (καὶ λέγει αὐτοῖς,

6. Hagner, *Matthew 1 – 13*, 221.

7. O. Lamar Cope, *Matthew: A Scribe Trained for the Kingdom of Heaven* (New York: Ktav, 1977), 96 – 98; Davies and Allison, *Matthew*, 2:72. They see Jonah as the major background motif, but the most that can be said is that Jesus' stilling the storm may echo God's stilling the storm in Jonah 1:15 – 16.

8. Bornkamm, "Stilling of the Storm," 56 – 57. See also Senior, *Matthew*, 101 – 2.

9. The circumstantial participle "they came" (προσελθόντες) is essentially the same as in v. 19.

10. See Bonnard, *Matthieu*, 120; Hagner, *Matthew 1 – 13*, 222; Bruner, *Christbook*, 318; Beare, *Matthew*, 215; Blomberg, *Matthew*, 149.

11. The aorist imperative "save us" (σῶσον) is virtually a prayer, with the aorist the basic tense in prayers (Porter, *Idioms*, 228 – 29). The present "we're about to die" (ἀπολλύμεθα) is a futuristic use of the present, stating an event (from their perspective) that is definitely "going to" happen in the near future.

Τί δειλοί ἐστε, ὀλιγόπιστοι;). The fear/faith dichotomy is frequent in Scripture (e.g., Matt 6:25 – 34; John 14:1 – 2; Phil 4:6) and portrays the basic premise that when the believer depends entirely on the covenant God, the machinations of the world hold no fear. Jesus, who so trusted God that he slept through the storm, is aghast at the low level of faith on the part of the disciples. Matthew uses "you of so little faith" (ὀλιγόπιστοι) often (6:30; 14:31; 16:8) to describe the inadequate God-centeredness of the disciples.[12] It is always the result of a basic self-interest and an earth-centered perspective, thus producing fear. It must be remembered that they cry out to Jesus for help and so at the deepest level do have a basic trust, but they also feel they are about to perish, and so it is terror rather than faith that drives them.

8:26 Then he arose, rebuked the winds and the sea, and there came a great calm (τότε ἐγερθεὶς ἐπετίμησεν τοῖς ἀνέμοις καὶ τῇ θαλάσσῃ, καὶ ἐγένετο γαλήνη μεγάλη). The circumstantial participle (cf. vv. 2, 7, 19, 25) "he arose" (ἐγερθείς) can have double meaning, considering this a harbinger of Jesus' resurrection and exaltation to authority (28:18). It is common to see this as spiritual warfare, with demonic forces behind the storm. Jesus is then casting out the cosmic powers behind the heaving sea.[13] There are OT parallels for God's controlling the dark powers of chaos behind the waters (Job 38:8 – 11; Ps 77:16 – 18; 104:7; *1 En.* 60; *2 En.* 19; cf. the defeat of Leviathan [the dragon of the deep] in Ps 74:13 – 14; 89:9 – 10; Isa 27:1); and Jesus' "rebuke" of the storm parallels the exorcism in 17:18 (but "rebuke" [ἐπιτιμάω] is used more frequently for exorcisms in Mark and Luke).

It is best to say there may be an echo of cosmic conflict here, but the main thrust is Jesus' power over nature. Jesus was the agent of creation behind this world (John 1:3; 1 Cor 8:6; Col 1:16; Heb 1:2) and so controls the forces of nature. Twelftree points out that Matthew omits the words of command (unlike Mark 4:39), similarly to the exorcism in 8:32, concluding that he "did not want it thought that Jesus' ability to control demonic and stormy situations was in what was said rather than in who said them."[14]

8:27 The men were filled with wonder and said, "What kind of person is this that even the winds and the waves obey him?" (οἱ δὲ ἄνθρωποι ἐθαύμασαν λέγοντες, Ποταπός ἐστιν οὗτος ὅτι καὶ οἱ ἄνεμοι καὶ ἡ θάλασσα αὐτῷ ὑπακούουσιν;). This is the second time amazement has occurred (in v. 10 Jesus is amazed); usually it is the crowds, but in ch. 8 it is Jesus, then the disciples. Matthew may be using "men" (ἄνθρωποι) to indicate a wider group than just the disciples (i.e., all who heard of it),[15] but probably he is contrasting the disciples' human frailty with the "divine majesty" of Jesus,[16] namely, "what sort of man" he is. This is a message to the reader as well (who should feel the same wonder); what do we conclude about the kind of person whom the sea must obey? As with Yahweh in the OT (2 Sam 22:16; Ps 65:7 – 8; 89:8 – 9; 107:29; Isa 50:2), this "rebuke" of the sea shows Jesus' absolute sovereignty over creation.

12. Many critical scholars believe that here Matthew softens Mark's harsh, "Do you still have no faith?" Yet this overstates the case, for Matthew certainly emphasizes their lack of true faith in much the same way.

13. Hill, *Matthew*, 166; Filson, *Matthew*, 115; Davies and Allison, *Matthew*, 2:74; Blomberg, *Matthew*, 149 – 50; Harrington, *Matthew*, 123; contra France, *Gospel of Matthew*, 337n.

14. Twelftree, *Jesus the Miracle Worker*, 113.

15. France, *Matthew* (TNTC), 162.

16. Gundry, *Matthew*, 157. Cf. also Morris, *Matthew*, 206.

Theology in Application

This is the perfect miracle for this part of Matthew, as it blends Christology with discipleship. There are three levels at which this must be taken.

1. Master of Nature and Lord of All

This is the theme throughout the miracle stories and should not be overpressed here, but it is still a major motif, perhaps *the* major theme. For all believers who are tied as much to this world as they are to Jesus, the message is all-important. This world will always let us down; only Christ is worthy of our allegiance and will "*never* leave or forsake" us (Josh 1:5; cf. Gen 28:15; Deut 31:6, 8; Ps 9:10).

2. A Living Faith in God's Sovereignty

Every time the disciples turn from dependence on Christ to their own situation, they fail utterly. As in Mark, this is a prelude to a major theme in the rest of Matthew's gospel. The "little faith ones" will struggle with this throughout, as do all of us!

3. Discipleship and Risk and "Rough Seas"

While it is wrong to allegorize the boat as the church, this miracle story does in a general sense teach that disciples will undergo difficult times, the "storms" of life. Life will never be easy, and we must at all times remain aware that God has never promised to keep us from such difficulties.[17] We must remember Jesus said that when we sacrifice home and family, we "will ... receive a hundred times as much in this present age ... along with persecutions" (Mark 10:29).

4. Facing Our fears in Christ

As Wilkins states, the answer to fear is faith.[18] In the midst of the terrible storm, these experienced commercial fishermen turned to the carpenter for help. Even though they had only "little faith," it was sufficient to enlist the power of Jesus on their behalf. Yet it was not enough to allay their fear. Thus when they had experienced his sufficiency, they said, "What kind of person is this?" We know what kind of God-man he is, so we can find solace and the strength to handle life's boundless surprises (Phil 4:13, 19).

17. For this as a "missionary" story presaging the later mission of the disciples, see D. Bryce, "Sailors, Seismologists, and Missionaries (Matthew 8:23 – 27)," *LTJ* 36 (2002): 2 – 11.

18. Wilkins, *Matthew*, 359.

CHAPTER 32

Matthew 8:28 – 34

Literary Context

This middle of the three miracles for this section of Matthew involves the second type of miracle, an exorcism, and again demonstrates the authority of Jesus. The one who rebukes the storm also rebukes the evil forces. He is Lord of all, and the demons have no power over him.

III. The Kingdom Comes with Authority (8:1 – 11:1)
- **A. Authority and Discipleship in Jesus' Ministry (8:1 – 9:34)**
  - **3. Three Miracles Showing His Authority (8:23 – 9:8)**
    - a. Calming of the Storm (8:23 – 27)
    - ➦ **b. Exorcism of Two Demon-Possessed Men (8:28 – 34)**
    - c. Healing of the Paralytic (9:1 – 8)

Main Idea

Unlike Mark, where this miracle story follows several confrontations over demons (see Mark 5:1 – 20, following 1:23 – 28, 34; 3:11 – 12, 22 – 30), this is the first full description of such an incident in Matthew (brief mentions in 4:24; 8:16). There are two important aspects of the message: demons always torture the people they possess, and they are entirely under Jesus' control. There is a spiritual battle here, but it is one-sided.

Translation

Matthew 8:28-34

28a	Setting (Temporal/Spatial)	After he arrived at the other side in the region of the Gadarenes,
b	Action (A)	**two demoniacs . . . met him** **who had come out of the tombs.**
c	Description	**They were very violent,**
d	Result of 28c	with the result that no one could pass that way on the road.
29a		And look, they cried out, saying,
b	Question #1	*"What do we have in common, Son of God?*
c	Question #2	*Have you come here to torment us before the appointed time?"*
30a	Setting	**Some distance from them a large herd of pigs was feeding.**
31a	Wish	But **the demons begged him, saying,**
b		*"If you are going to drive us out, send us into the herd of pigs."*
32a	Action	And **he said to them,**
b	Command (B)	*"Go!"*
c	Result #1 (C)	**So they came out and entered the pigs,**
d		and **look, the whole herd rushed down the steep bank into the lake** **and drowned in the water.**
33a	Result #2	**Those tending the herd fled,** **went into the town, and** **reported everything,** **even the exorcism of the demoniacs.**
34a		And **look, the whole town went out to meet Jesus.**
b		When they saw him,
c	Result #3	**they begged him to leave their region.**

Structure and Literary Form

This miracle story, like the stilling of the storm, is greatly reduced from Mark (seven verses vs. twenty), and several differences are noticeable. (1) Most obviously, Matthew has two demoniacs rather than one. (2) The Christology is even more at center stage. (3) The effects of the possession are not as elaborate, noting only their violent strength. (4) The exorcism is more simplified, with the elements that could sound like magic removed.[1] (5) The great brevity of Jesus' dialogue — in the whole story, all he says is "Go!" — further emphasizes the power of his word. (6) The ending is truncated compared to Mark, with the healed man and his desire to become a disciple removed from the story.

1. Hagner, *Matthew 1 – 13*, 225; Keener, *Matthew*, 281.

The result is a complete emphasis on the power of Jesus over the cosmic forces. The structure is: (1) two violent demoniacs appear (v. 28); (2) their confrontation with Jesus (v. 29); (3) Jesus casts them out and allows them to enter a herd of pigs (vv. 30 – 32); (4) the whole city begs Jesus to leave (vv. 33 – 34).

Exegetical Outline

➡ **I. The Two Demoniacs Appear (8:28)**
- A. Departure from the tombs
- B. Their fierce violence

II. Confrontation with Jesus (8:29)
- A. Nothing in common
- B. Affirmation of his true nature
- C. Torment before the appointed time

III. Exorcism and Entering a Herd of Pigs (8:30 – 32)
- A. Their request to enter the pigs (vv. 30 – 31)
- B. Jesus casts them out and lets them enter the pigs (v. 32a)
- C. The herd drowns (v. 32b)

IV. The Whole City Begs Jesus to Leave (8:33 – 34)

Explanation of the Text

8:28 After he arrived at the other side in the region of the Gadarenes (Καὶ ἐλθόντος αὐτοῦ εἰς τὸ πέραν εἰς τὴν χώραν τῶν Γαδαρηνῶν). Matthew's typical temporal genitive absolute again begins the episode (cf. 8:1, 5) and carries on the action from the previous scene. Jesus gave orders to cross the lake in v. 18, entered the boat in v. 23, and now arrives on the "other side" of the lake.

One of the well-known discrepancies in the gospels is the place where he disembarks. Mark 5:1 and Luke 8:26 say he arrives in the region of the "Gerasenes," and Matthew here states it was the region of the "Gadarenes."[2] Both Gadara and Gerasa were cities of the Decapolis, a league of ten Hellenistic cities east of the Jordan and going north into Syria. Gerasa was thirty miles to the southeast of the lake; and Gedara was five miles southeast of the lake, but it had territory that reached to the lake and included a city named Khersa on the shore. Khersa could easily be the "Gerasa" of Mark/Luke. Thus the discrepancy would only be on the surface.[3]

2. All three passages have text-critical difficulties, as scribes tried to reconcile the differences. For Matthew "Gadarenes" (Γαδαρηνῶν) is read in (ℵ *) B C^{txt} (Δ) Θ etc., "Gerasenes" (Γερασηνῶν) in it vg cop^{sa} syr$^{h\ mg\ 2}$, and Gergesenes (Γεργεσηνῶν) in ℵ ^{c} C^{mg} K L W etc. The manuscript evidence is stronger for the first, and most believe the second reading is an assimilation to harmonize with Mark and Luke, the third a later correction, perhaps proposed by Origen. See Metzger, *Textual Commentary on the Greek New Testament* (2nd ed.; Stuttgart: Deutsche Bibelgesellschaft, 2002), 23 – 24.

3. See Blomberg, *Historical Reliability*, 149 – 50.

8:28 ... two demoniacs who had come out[4] of the tombs met him (ὑπήντησαν αὐτῷ δύο δαιμονιζόμενοι ἐκ τῶν μνημείων ἐξερχόμενοι). Jesus encounters two demoniacs, another discrepancy since Mark and Luke have just one. Matthew does this often — two demoniacs, two blind men (9:27 – 31; 20:29 – 34), two donkeys (21:2); two in the field and at the mill (24:40 – 41), two servants (24:45 – 51). It is common for critical scholars to think this unhistorical, with the number expanded due to the need for two or more witnesses in Deut 19:15.[5] Matthew may have stressed the detail for this reason, but that does not mean he made it up. He could have been compensating for having omitted earlier accounts of such miracles from Mark (the demoniac of Mark 1:23 – 28, the blind man of Mark 8:22 – 26),[6] or Mark and Luke could have simply stressed the prominent one of the two for dramatic purposes.[7]

The tombs were a natural home for the demon-possessed, lepers, and others driven from their homes because of being in a constant state of uncleanness. The wealthy utilized caves and had several compartments for the dead down through the generations, so the front sections were clear and provided shelter from the elements. This detail adds a note of death and the powers of evil (cf. Rom 5:14; Rev 6:8; 20:13, 14 for death personified as a malignant power).

8:28 They were very violent, with the result that no one could pass that way on the road (χαλεποὶ λίαν, ὥστε μὴ ἰσχύειν τινὰ παρελθεῖν διὰ τῆς ὁδοῦ ἐκείνης). Mark spends much more time describing their superhuman strength (broke the chains that bound him), self-torture (bruising himself), and ritual suicide (cutting himself with stones); Matthew, by contrast, simply emphasizes the extreme violence of the two men. They apparently saw the road as their territory (like animals) and opposed anyone who came that way. The use of "to be strong" (ἰσχύειν) means no one had sufficient "strength" to oppose them and many were overpowered by the demoniacs.

8:29 And look, they cried out, saying, "What do we have in common, Son of God?" (καὶ ἰδοὺ ἔκραξαν λέγοντες, Τί ἡμῖν καὶ σοί, υἱὲ τοῦ θεοῦ;). Matthew's characteristic "and look" (see on 8:2, 24) points to a critical section. When the demons see Jesus, they know their time of freedom is over. τί ἡμῖν καὶ σοί is literally, "What is it to us and to you," an idiom meaning "We have nothing in common" and "leave us alone" (cf. Judg 11:12; 2 Sam 16:10; Mark 1:24; John 2:4). The battle is joined.

When the demons add the title "Son of God" (Mark/Luke — "Son of the Most High God"), they are not acting as Jesus' PR team, telling everyone who he is. In the ancient world it was believed that everyone had a hidden name that expressed their true essence. To discover that name was to gain a certain power over a person.[8] Twelftree notes that "the demons attempted to disarm Jesus by exposing his allegiance and special relationship with God (Ps 106:16; Sir 45:6; *b. Pesaḥ.* 112b)."[9] At

4. "Coming out" (ἐξερχόμενοι) could be circumstantial but is just as likely an adjectival participle modifying "two demoniacs." The present tense dramatically pictures them exiting the tombs.

5. W. R. G. Loader, "Son of David, Blindness, Possession, and Duality in Matthew," *CBQ* 44 (1982): 580 – 82; Hagner, *Matthew 1 – 13*, 225; Tweltree, *Jesus the Miracle Worker*, 114 – 15.

6. Gundry, *Matthew*, 158; Keener, *Matthew*, 282.

7. McNeile, *Matthew*, 112; Carson, "Matthew," 217; Wilkins, *Matthew*, 353. France, *Gospel of Matthew*, 339 – 40, says it cannot be adequately explained and prefers to leave it a mystery.

8. James R. Edwards, *The Gospel according to Mark* (PNTC; Grand Rapids: Eerdmans, 2002), 57 – 58.

9. Graham Twelftree, "Demon, Devil, Satan," *DJG*, 166. He also notes Mark 5:7, when the demon says, "In God's name don't torture me," the phrase suggests to bind or compel a person to do something.

the same time, they knew his absolute lordship as God's Son and had to acknowledge his superiority.[10] Throughout the gospels the highest Christology occurs in the mouth of demons; they *know* who Jesus is! Realizing the absolute authority of Jesus as Son of God, the demons realize they have already lost.

8:29 "Have you come here to torment us before the appointed time?" (ἦλθες ὧδε πρὸ καιροῦ βασανίσαι ἡμᾶς;). The culminative aorist "have you come" (ἦλθες, Wallace, 559 – 61) stresses the results of Jesus' arrival. Revelation 12:12 says that Satan is "filled with fury, because he knows that his time is short." In both cases the "time" is the final judgment when Satan and his minions are thrown into the lake of fire (*1 En.* 15 – 16; 55:4; *Jub.* 10:8 – 9; *T. Levi* 18:12; Rev 19:20; 20:10, 14). The "torture" will be horrific and involve "the smoke of their torment [arising] for ever and ever" (Rev 14:11).

The demons are well aware of their coming destiny (καιρός meaning their appointed "time"). The Son of God has arrived before the appointed hour of their destruction, and they want him to leave them alone. The arrival of the kingdom is unexpected, and they do not understand the inaugurated aspect of it; like the Jewish people, they apparently think that when the Messiah came, he would immediately initiate the final battle.

8:30 Some distance from them a large herd of pigs was feeding (ἦν δὲ μακρὰν ἀπ' αὐτῶν ἀγέλη χοίρων πολλῶν βοσκομένη). The imperfect periphrastic "was feeding" (ἦν ... βοσκομένη) pictures the herd gently grazing on the hillside. The presence of pig farms tells us definitely that we are in Gentile territory. Pigs were unclean[11] animals (Lev 11:7; Deut 14:8), so Jesus has come deliberately to a place where he might minister to Gentiles (cf. also 8:5 – 13; 15:21 – 28). Transjordan had a mixed population (Josephus, *J.W.* 3:51 – 58) but was predominantly Gentile, and Gedara was a major Gentile city in the region.

Does this conflict with Jesus' restriction of his and the disciples' mission to the Jews (10:5 – 6; 15:24)? No, for this was another harbinger of the later Gentile mission that Matthew has been anticipating all along (e.g., the Gentile women in Jesus' royal genealogy, 1:3, 5, 6; the Magi, 2:1 – 12; the centurion's faith, 8:5 – 13) and will finalize in the Great Commission of 28:19. Jesus wants to give his followers a glimpse of the mission they will be sent to accomplish at Pentecost (Acts 2). The fact that the herd was "some distance" away replaces Mark's "on the nearby hillside" and stresses the distance between Jesus and the unclean pigs. They are proper for demons but not for Jesus.

8:31 But the demons begged him, saying, "If you are going to drive us out, send us into the herd of pigs" (οἱ δὲ δαίμονες παρεκάλουν αὐτὸν λέγοντες, Εἰ ἐκβάλλεις ἡμᾶς, ἀπόστειλον ἡμᾶς εἰς τὴν ἀγέλην τῶν χοίρων). The condition of fact εἰ ἐκβάλλεις could well be read, "Since you are going to cast us out" but should probably retain the "if" because they are hoping their riposte in v. 29 succeeds and Jesus will leave them alone. In Mark 5:12 they give a command, "Send us among the pigs," while here they recognize the superiority of Jesus and ask him to do so (the imperfect "begged" [παρεκάλουν] depicts their persistent pleading).

10. Robert A. Guelich, *Mark 1 – 8:26* (WBC 34A; Dallas: Word, 1989), 57, says it is more the inferior recognizing a superior. The demon wants to force Jesus to leave him alone but recognizes the deity of Christ and that the battle is over.

11. This has no connection with pigs as filthy animals, wallowing in the mud. Pigs were unclean because they had split hooves and did not chew the cud (Lev 11:7; Deut 14:8). For the Jews, uncleanness was a defiling presence in opposition to God.

Rather than being sent away (to the desert areas of 12:43, the abyss of Luke 8:31, or the dungeons of 2 Pet 2:4, all three synonymous for the traditional habitats of demons), the demons plead to be allowed to enter a herd of pigs and to make their home there (the image of 12:43 – 45). The home in unclean pigs fits the depiction of demons as "evil spirits" (10:1; 12:43, often in Mark) and highlights their true nature. Mark 5:9, 13 tells us that their name was "Legion" (many spirits — a Roman legion contained six thousand soldiers) and that the herd numbered two thousand, probably the combined herds of an entire village.

8:32 And he said to them, "Go!" (καὶ εἶπεν αὐτοῖς, Ὑπάγετε). Jesus speaks for the first and only time in this story. It was normal for exorcists to prattle on and on, finding out the name of the demon and its territory of operation, and using various incantations to try to get it to leave. Jesus' great authority is forcefully presented, for he needs only one word, "Go" or "Be gone" (BAGD), and the demons must instantly obey.

8:32 So they came out and entered[12] the pigs, and look, the whole herd rushed down the steep bank into the lake and drowned in the water (οἱ δὲ ἐξελθόντες ἀπῆλθον εἰς τοὺς χοίρους· καὶ ἰδοὺ ὥρμησεν πᾶσα ἡ ἀγέλη κατὰ τοῦ κρημνοῦ εἰς τὴν θάλασσαν καὶ ἀπέθανον ἐν τοῖς ὕδασιν). The moment the demons enter the pigs, the unfortunate animals stampede down the hillside and drown. We are not told whether the demons killed the pigs or they panicked and made a suicidal plunge into the water. Both may well be the case.[13]

We know that the basic purpose of demon-possession is to torture and kill those whom God created, animals or people (cf. Mark 5:3 – 5; 9:18, 20, 22, 26; Rev 9:1 – 19). At any rate, the result is the destruction of the herd, the normal conclusion of demonic activity. The SPCA would picket Jesus today, but no one would have faulted him in the ancient world. The choice was the destruction of the men or the pigs, and Jesus allowed the lesser evil.[14] In doing so he proved to everyone the true nature of the demons — both their uncleanness and their destructive character.

8:33 Those tending the herd fled, went into the town, and reported everything, even the exorcism of the demoniacs (οἱ δὲ βόσκοντες ἔφυγον, καὶ ἀπελθόντες εἰς τὴν πόλιν ἀπήγγειλαν πάντα καὶ τὰ τῶν δαιμονιζομένων). Mark 5:15, 18 – 20 tells of the results for the man, who was in his right mind and wanted to become a follower. Jesus instead sent him home to become the first missionary to the Gentiles. Matthew centers on the townspeople and their reaction to the news about their herd and the demon-possessed men (from their own town?). The use of ascensive "even" (καί) places special emphasis on their report about Jesus' exorcisms.

12. There is an interesting use of three spatial prepositions here, with the circumstantial participle "they came out" (ἐξελθόντες) followed by the verbal idea "they departed into" (ἀπῆλθον εἰς). Considering the three in turn, the demons went "out of the men" and "away" from them, then entered "into" the pigs. The two prepositional prefixes here, as often, retain their spatial thrust.

13. Davies and Allison, *Matthew*, 2:84, says Jesus sends the herd into the water in order to send the demons back to the "watery chaos" from which they came. This seems much less likely, for the stampede into the water is caused by the demons entering the pigs rather than by a command of Jesus. Several others (Grundmann, Bonnard, Gundry, Luz) note the shift from the singular "rushed" to the plural "they died" and believe it is the demons who die and go to the torments of hell. However, that is unnecessary, for the switch to the plural "they" would better fit the "pigs" (with the singular from "the herd rushed"); see Carson, "Matthew," 219; Hagner, *Matthew 1 – 13*, 228.

14. France, *Matthew* (TNTC), 164, "for Jesus the liberation of two men took precedence over such considerations." So also Robert Mounce, *Matthew* (Good News Commentary; New York: Harper & Row, 1985), 80.

8:34 And look, the whole town went out to meet[15] Jesus (καὶ ἰδοὺ πᾶσα ἡ πόλις ἐξῆλθεν εἰς ὑπάντησιν τῷ Ἰησοῦ). Jesus is the central focus throughout this story, so Mark's extensive conclusion is simplified by Matthew to their request that Jesus leave. Luke 8:37 provides the reason (they are afraid), but Matthew leaves it open.

8:34 When they saw him, they begged him to leave their region (καὶ ἰδόντες αὐτὸν παρεκάλεσαν ὅπως μεταβῇ ἀπὸ τῶν ὁρίων αὐτῶν). The temporal participle "when they saw" (ἰδόντες) shows that the moment they saw Jesus, they began to beg him to leave. Their livelihood has been taken from them in a violent act, and they are certainly in shock as they see all those carcasses floating in the water. To them Jesus was a terrible sorcerer, and they may have feared for their lives too.

It may be that Matthew wants to expose as well the true values of the townspeople: they prefer swine to the Savior.[16] There is a sense in which this is correct, for the story ends with a rejection of Jesus in contrast with the surrounding episodes (8:27; 9:8), where the onlookers are filled with awe. Yet this is implicit rather than explicit; the historical reason is their fear of Jesus (Luke 8:37), and Matthew may be hinting at the rejection that Jesus would be facing more and more. Still, this reaction is caused by the threat that the authority of Jesus poses,[17] and that is the major thrust.

Theology in Application

As stated throughout, the primary theme is the absolute authority of Christ in word and deed. In every area of trouble — nature, illness, and demon-possession — he has total control and he alone can calm the seas, cure illness, and drive out demons. The demons may try everything they can think of (as here) to gain some control and get Jesus to leave them alone, but he casts them out with a single word! Yet there are several subthemes as well:

1. The Demonic Realm Is Real

In C. S. Lewis's *The Screwtape Letters*, senior demon Screwtape tells his nephew Wormwood that if he gets his human to think he is not there, he can control everything the person does. That is the case with too many Christians. A friend of mine calls this pragmatic atheism; that is, we intellectually believe in Satan but act as if he doesn't exist.

Spiritual warfare is very real, and anyone from a third-world country will attest to the reality of demon-possession. At the same time, the battle is over. Jesus has conquered Satan once for all on the cross (see "Theology in Application" on 4:1 – 11), and his authority to bind Satan is given to his followers (10:1). Yet we can still be

15. "In" (εἰς) with a verbal noun "coming to meet" (ὑπάντησιν) forms a verbal clause, here indicating purpose ("in order to meet").

16. So Plummer, *Matthew*, 134; Carson, "Matthew," 219; Morris, *Matthew*, 212.

17. See Wilkins, *Matthew*, 358.

"devoured" by Satan (1 Pet 5:8), and our victory is dependent on the degree to which we are centered on Christ.[18]

2. The Demons and their Own Followers

Demons want only to torment (Rev 9:1 – 11) and kill (Rev 9:13 – 19) even their own followers. There is no sense in which demons actually help any person achieve success, not in the long term. They do not possess people so they can have bodies; they possess because they know their time is short (Matt 8:29 = Rev 12:12), and the only way they can get back at God is to torture his creatures (animals as well as people) until the final day of judgment.

3. The Church's Authority over the Demonic World

Unlike some today, God's people do not have to multiply words and use invocations to drive out demons. We do not have to find out the name of the demon or the territory in which it operates. Jesus provides the model, and all we need is the name of Jesus (cf. Acts 3:6, 16; 16:18) to have authority over the demons (Matt 10:1 = Mark 3:15; 6:7). Inability comes not because we have failed to use the right formula but because we center on ourselves rather than on Jesus (Matt 17:17, 20).

4. The Gentile Mission

The Abrahamic covenant stated that God chose Abraham and his progeny to be a "blessing to the nations" (Gen 12:3; 15:5; 18:18; 22:18; et al.), but at first glance it seems that Jesus agrees with Jewish particularism against a Gentile mission (10:5, 6; 15:24). But this passage and others in Matthew (see on v. 30) show that Jesus made frequent trips to Gentile areas to give his disciples a glimpse of the later universal mission that would be launched in the resurrection command of 28:19.

18. For an excellent brief article on the implications of this exorcism for today, see Clinton E. Arnold, "Exorcism 101: What Can We Learn from the Way Jesus Cast Out Demons?" *ChrTo* 45/11 (2001): 58.

CHAPTER 33

Matthew 9:1 – 8

Literary Context

This third of the set of authoritative miracles centers on Jesus' power over not only illness but over sin itself.[1] Matthew greatly abbreviates Mark 2:1 – 12 and centers on Jesus' authority in contrast to the negative reaction of the leaders. So in the context of chs. 8 – 9 this continues the emphasis on Jesus' authority, has a small discipleship aspect (the forgiveness of sins), and begins the theme of conflict with the Jewish authorities that will continue through the rest of Matthew's portrayal.[2] In shortening the story and removing many of the vivid details, Matthew has simplified the narrative in order to center on the forgiveness of sins.

III. The Kingdom Comes with Authority (8:1 – 11:1)
- **A. Authority and Discipleship in Jesus' Ministry (8:1 – 9:34)**
  - **3. Three Miracles Showing His Authority (8:23 – 9:8)**
    - a. Calming of the Storm (8:23 – 27)
    - b. Exorcism of Two Demon-Possessed Men (8:28 – 34)
    - ➦ **c. Healing of the Paralytic (9:1 – 8)**

Main Idea

All the action revolves around the central aspect, the forgiveness of sins, showing that spiritual healing has precedence over physical healing and that the two are indissoluble. Behind it all, of course, is the authority of Jesus to provide both spiritual and physical healing. The conflict is part of the rejection of God's new work by the leaders.

1. Wilkins, *Matthew*, 354, says Jesus is "demonstrating his authority over Satan's domain of disease, illness, and, surprisingly, sin."

2. In Mark and Luke, this episode precedes the stilling of the storm and the exorcism of the demoniacs (8:23 – 34). For a viable harmonization of the Synoptic accounts, see Carson, "Matthew," 220 – 21. All three Synoptics probably have a topical arrangement here. For the issue of chronology and historicity, see the Introduction to this commentary.

Translation

Matthew 9:1-8

1a	Action/Setting	**Jesus got into the boat,**
		crossed to the other side of the lake, and
		went to his own town.
2a	Event/Action	And **look, some men brought a paralytic to him, lying on a mat.**
b		When Jesus saw their faith,
c	Action	**he said to the paralytic,**
d		*"Take courage, son, your sins are forgiven."*
3a	Objection	And **look, some of the teachers of law said among themselves,**
b		*"This man is blaspheming."*
4a		Discerning their thoughts,
b	Response/Accusation	**Jesus said,**
c		*"Why are you thinking evil thoughts in your hearts?*
5a		*For which is easier, to say,*
b		*'Your sins are forgiven,'*
c		*or to say,*
d		*'Rise up and walk'?*
6a	Purpose of 6b	*But so that you can know that the Son of Man has authority*
		on the earth to forgive sins,"
b	Action	**then he said to the paralytic,**
c		*"Rise up, take your mat, and go to your house."*
7a	Result #1 Healing	**So he rose up and went to his house.**
8a	Result #2 Response	**When the crowds saw this,**
		they were filled with awe and
		glorified God,
b	Description	who had given such authority to human beings.

Structure and Literary Form

The setting of Jesus' teaching and the friends' lowering the paralytic through the roof in Mark 2:1 – 4 are omitted, and the story itself is greatly abbreviated. Some have called this a controversy story, but vv. 3 – 5 are not the central element. It is still primarily a miracle story, with a pronouncement (v. 2) as well as conflict (vv. 3 – 5).

There are three main parts: the opening (vv. 1 – 2) provides a transition in terms of the boat scenes of 8:23 – 9:8, as Jesus crosses back to Capernaum, there encounters the paralytic, and responds to the faith of the group (the man himself as well as those who brought him) by forgiving the man's sins. In the central section (vv. 3 – 5) the Jewish leaders accuse Jesus of blasphemy, and he answers that the authority to forgive is intimately connected with authority to heal. In the twofold conclusion (vv. 6 – 7) the healed man walks and the crowd is filled with awe.

Exegetical Outline

- ➦ **I. Setting (9:1 – 2)**
  - A. Crossing the lake to Capernaum (v. 1)
  - B. A paralytic brought on a mat (v. 2a)
  - C. Jesus sees their faith and forgives the man's sins (v. 2b)
- **II. Conflict and Resolution (9:3 – 6)**
  - A. The charge of blasphemy (v. 3)
  - B. The countercharge (vv. 4 – 5)
    1. Charge one: their evil thoughts (v. 4)
    2. Charge two: is healing or forgiveness easier? (v. 5)
  - C. The command to go home healed (v. 6)
    1. Purpose: know the authority of the Son of Man (v. 6a)
    2. Proof: command to go home healed (v. 6b)
- **III. Twofold Result (9:7 – 8)**
  - A. The man goes home (v. 7)
  - B. The crowd marvels and praises God (v. 8)

Explanation of the Text

9:1 Jesus got[3] into the boat, crossed to the other side of the lake, and went to his own town (Καὶ ἐμβὰς εἰς πλοῖον διεπέρασεν καὶ ἦλθεν εἰς τὴν ἰδίαν πόλιν). This concludes the journey motif started in 8:23, where Jesus crossed the lake the first time, calming a terrible storm, and then cast out the demons in the Gentile Gadarenes. Now he returns to Galilee and goes back to Capernaum, which he has made "his own" hometown since 4:13. Matthew tells us nothing of his immediate activities, omitting Mark 2:1 – 2 about the crowd gathering at Jesus' door and his teaching them.

9:2 And look, some men brought a paralytic[4] to him, lying on a mat (καὶ ἰδοὺ προσέφερον αὐτῷ παραλυτικὸν ἐπὶ κλίνης βεβλημένον). Matthew moves straight to the main event, skipping Mark's details (Mark 2:4) about lowering the man through the flatbed roof, with "look" (ἰδού) pointing to a dramatic turn in the action. Jesus has already healed paralyzed people (4:24), so a group of men feel he can do the same for their friend. The man cannot move, so they have to bring him on a mat or stretcher, probably something like a modern bedroll.

3. "Getting in" (ἐμβάς) is a circumstantial participle, partaking of the force of the main verb, and is best translated as another main verb.

4. Dwight N. Peterson, "Translating παραλυτικός in Mark 2:1 – 12," *BBR* 16/2 (2006): 261 – 72, points out that the term in the first century referred simply to a person who could not walk for any number of reasons (injury, stroke, etc.) and so is better translated "cripple" or "lame person," though "paralytic" can still be used so long as it is clarified.

9:2 When Jesus saw their faith, he said to the paralytic, "Take courage, son, your sins are forgiven" (καὶ ἰδὼν ὁ Ἰησοῦς τὴν πίστιν αὐτῶν εἶπεν τῷ παραλυτικῷ, Θάρσει, τέκνον· ἀφίενταί σου αἱ ἁμαρτίαι). It is interesting that it was "their faith" (πίστιν αὐτῶν), namely, that of the paralytic and those who brought him, that leads to forgiveness.[5] We cannot know how much faith was involved; at the least, they believed Jesus could heal the man, as he had healed paralytics earlier (4:24). Sickness and sin were closely linked in antiquity. Romans 5:12 tells us that when sin entered the world, death accompanied it, and all sickness is in one sense related to sin (cf. also Lev 26:16; Deut 28:22, 35; 2 Chr 21:15 – 19). In other words, sin was the generating force for sickness and death.

This does not mean individual illnesses are caused by specific sins. Several passages make it clear sickness is not always the result of sin (Job; John 9:2 – 3). The relation of sickness to sin is hinted at in the quote of Isa 53:4 in Matt 8:17 and seen throughout Jesus' healing ministry in his use of "save" (σῴζω) for healing (combining spiritual and physical healing, cf. Matt 9:21 – 22; Mark 3:4; 5:23, 28, 34; 6:56; 10:52; et al.). Paul develops this in the relation between sin and death in Rom 5 – 6.

The message here is that Jesus is Lord over the world of sin as well as sickness.[6] The kingdom of God has broken into the world, and every aspect of the realm of evil — sin as well as sickness — must be removed. It is important to note that Jesus uses the divine passive "are forgiven" (ἀφίενται),[7] which means "God has forgiven your sins." Yet Jesus is clearly more than the divine agent proclaiming forgiveness, for in v. 6 he claims for himself the authority to forgive. Probably he includes himself as Son of God in the divine passive.

9:3 And look, some of the teachers of law said among themselves, "This man is blaspheming" (καὶ ἰδού τινες τῶν γραμματέων εἶπαν ἐν ἑαυτοῖς, Οὗτος βλασφημεῖ). With his second consecutive "look" (ἰδού), Matthew stresses the dramatic development of the story. The scribes (see 2:4; 5:20; 7:29) considered themselves the official interpreters of Torah and so watched every nuance of Jesus' teaching and actions, having already rejected his validity as a teacher, let alone as Messiah. To them Jesus was usurping God's role as forgiver of sins and so by definition was "blaspheming" or reviling the name of God.

The verb used here means "to slander," and Jewish law said the concept stemmed from Lev 24:15 – 16, "anyone who blasphemes the name of the Lord is to be put to death." The later Mishnah demanded the actual pronouncing and profaning of God's name itself (*m. Sanh.* 7:5), and it is clear Jesus has not done that. But by extension Jesus has taken on himself the prerogatives of God; as Mark 2:7 adds, "Who can forgive sins but God alone?"[8] So for the leaders Jesus has assumed the divine function and has thus blasphemed. From their perspective they are correct;[9] their mistake is in rejecting Jesus as Messiah and Son of God. This is

5. Contra Blomberg, *Matthew*, 153, who restricts the faith to those bringing the paralytic.

6. This does not mean the man's sins had to be forgiven before he could be healed, contra Davies and Allison, *Matthew*, 2:89. In most of the miracle stories forgiveness does not occur (the only other one is Luke 7:48), so it is not a precondition for healing.

7. Some manuscripts (C L W Θ) have the perfect "have been forgiven" (ἀφέωνται), but there is better manuscript evidence for the present "are forgiven" (ἀφίενται), (א B lat et al.), and the emphasis is on the present experience of forgiveness.

8. One Qumran document (4QNab 1:4 [see Keener, *Matthew*, 289]) has an exorcist "forgiving sins," but it is the exception that proves the rule.

9. As Morris, *Matthew*, 216, says, "They viewed Jesus as no more than another Galilean, and thus as someone to be understood within ordinary human limits. For such a person to claim to bestow forgiveness was for them nothing less than blasphemy."

Matthew's first conflict story, but it will become a dominant theme in the rest of the book.

9:4 Discerning their thoughts, Jesus said, "Why are you thinking evil thoughts in your hearts?" (καὶ ἰδὼν ὁ Ἰησοῦς τὰς ἐνθυμήσεις αὐτῶν εἶπεν, Ἱνατί ἐνθυμεῖσθε πονηρὰ ἐν ταῖς καρδίαις ὑμῶν;). The scribes were mulling the issue over only "among themselves" (ἐν ἑαυτοῖς, v. 3) and had not yet gone public. Jesus supernaturally knows what they are thinking (evidence of his omniscience, cf. 12:25; 22:18; Luke 6:8; 11:17; John 2:25; 6:61, 64) and immediately challenges their evil intent. Their hearts are guilty of "evil thoughts" (πονηρά), which connotes an attitude of malice toward Jesus.[10] It was important to test teachers/leaders to see if they were truly from God (1 Thess 5:21; 1 Cor 14:29; 1 John 4:1), but the scribes were not concerned to find out the truth. They had already rejected Jesus[11] and so wanted only to condemn him; that is where the malicious "evil" lay. In turning against Jesus, they were turning against God.

9:5 "For which is easier, to say 'Your sins are forgiven,' or to say, 'Rise up and walk'?" (τί γάρ ἐστιν εὐκοπώτερον, εἰπεῖν, Ἀφίενταί σου αἱ ἁμαρτίαι, ἢ εἰπεῖν, Ἔγειρε καὶ περιπάτει;). The verbs here in quotation marks are present tense, meaning that both the forgiving and the healing are perceived as ongoing in effect. In reality, of course, forgiving sins is much more difficult than healing the sick, for only God can do it. But from an earthly perspective, it is easier to pronounce forgiveness, the effects of which can neither be seen nor authenticated. So Jesus is speaking from the human perspective of the scribes.

9:6 "But so that you can know that[12] the Son of Man has authority on the earth to forgive sins" (ἵνα δὲ εἰδῆτε ὅτι ἐξουσίαν ἔχει ὁ υἱὸς τοῦ ἀνθρώπου ἐπὶ τῆς γῆς ἀφιέναι ἁμαρτίας). So Jesus offers apologetic proof of his power and authority, something that can be empirically confirmed, something they can "know" has happened. The purpose ("so that" [ἵνα]) of the healing now becomes proof (NLT, "So I will prove to you"; JB, "But to prove to you") of his divine right to pronounce forgiveness. This kind of "authority" can only come from God, and thus the one with this power can be trusted in his other claim of authority. Once again (see on 8:20) Jesus uses the "Son of Man" title for himself, here in the glorified Danielic sense of his eschatological power to forgive sins.[13] In Dan 7:13 – 14 the Ancient of Days gives the "one like a son of man" dominion over the earth,[14] and here Jesus is exercising it.

10. So Hagner, *Matthew 1 - 13*, 233.

11. Wilkins, *Matthew*, 355 – 56, shows five ways Jesus threatened the leaders in Matthew: (1) he challenged their interpretation and application of Torah (5:17 – 48); (2) he challenged their understanding of the way God worked, in both healing on the Sabbath (12:1 – 14) and forgiving sins (9:1 – 8); (3) he threatened their claim to be guardians of the law when he contrasted his righteousness with theirs (5:20); (4) he threatened their popularity in attracting the crowds to himself (21:15); and (5) he threatened their national security because of the excitement caused by his radical ministry (21:12 – 13).

12. BAGD, 556e, says "we know that" (οἴδαμεν ὅτι) is often used as a formula for a well-known fact; here the idiom is an absolute truth that they need to realize.

13. Hill, *Matthew*, 172, says it means, "the Son of Man whom you expect as Judge only in the last days is active now *on earth*, acting with authority, even to the extent of forgiving sins" (italics his).

14. Davies and Allison, *Matthew*, 2:93, show the options for "on the earth" (ἐπὶ τῆς γῆς): the Son of Man has already appeared on the earth; Jesus can forgive sins even during his earthly ministry; God forgives in heaven, and Jesus forgives on the earth; Jesus is the only one on earth who can forgive sins (their preference). Of these the Danielic connection favors a fifth option — the earthly dominion of the Danielic Son of Man. As Hagner, *Matthew 1 - 13*, 234, says, the person of Dan 7:13 – 14 has brought with him the blessings of the eschaton, one of which is the authority to forgive sins on earth.

9:6 Then he said to the paralytic, "Rise up, take your mat, and go to your house" (τότε λέγει τῷ παραλυτικῷ, Ἐγερθεὶς ἆρόν σου τὴν κλίνην καὶ ὕπαγε εἰς τὸν οἶκόν σου). Jesus is comprehensive here for effect. He heals the man (understood) and then tells him to rise up,[15] take his sleeping mat, and go home, completely normal for the first time. You can picture the man bounding off in absolute joy. The charge of blasphemy has been totally disproven and Jesus' divine authority doubly established, power over both sickness and sin!

9:7 So he rose up and went to his house (καὶ ἐγερθεὶς ἀπῆλθεν εἰς τὸν οἶκον αὐτοῦ). The obedience of the man is ironic, so simple and yet so profound in its implications. The wording of the response closely matches Jesus' command, further emphasizing his authority. The man who was so infirm that he had to be carried to Jesus on a stretcher now has the physical strength to walk home without help.

9:8 When the crowds saw this, they were filled with awe and glorified God, who had given such authority to human beings (ἰδόντες δὲ οἱ ὄχλοι ἐφοβήθησαν καὶ ἐδόξασαν τὸν θεὸν τὸν δόντα ἐξουσίαν τοιαύτην τοῖς ἀνθρώποις). Instead of telling how the scribes reacted to the miracle, Matthew contrasts their reaction in v. 3 with that of the crowds here. The crowds are "awestruck" when they "see" (temporal participle) Jesus' authority in word and deed. While "fear" is a common feature of theophanies, it is more likely that the feeling they experience is more one of awe, as seen in their "glorifying" God in the next phrase. φοβέω and cognates cover a range of feelings from "terror" to "reverence," and "awe" seems to be the concept that catches all aspects best. The crowds recognize the divinely given authority Christ possesses and are filled with awe, thus glorifying the God who "had given such authority."

They recognize that the miracle indeed proved Jesus as the God-sent agent he claimed to be and so give praise to God for him. Yet their ignorance is also shown, for Matthew carefully has them say "had given such authority to *human beings* [τοῖς ἀνθρώποις]," which shows they do not recognize him as Messiah or Son of Man.[16] Some believe that the reference to "human beings" means that the authority is given to all or to ecclesiastical authorities (cf. 16:19; 18:18),[17] but that is unlikely. It goes beyond the context; the passage is christological, not ecclesiastical.[18]

Theology in Application

This continues the message of ch. 8 on the authority of Jesus, the primary theme of the whole section; but now a new element is added, his authority to forgive sin. There are several important themes in this passage:

15. ἐγερθείς in both vv. 6 and 7 is another circumstantial participle that borrows the force of the verb it modifies.

16. Gundry, *Matthew*, 165, claims Matthew's point is that "Jesus is the God whom the crowds glorify." It is difficult to know whether deity is the point here, but it is possible.

17. So France, *Matthew* (TNTC), 166; Davies and Allison, *Matthew*, 2:96; Schnackenburg, *Matthew*, 88; Harrington, *Matthew*, 122; Hagner, *Matthew 1 – 13*, 234; Senior, *Matthew*, 104.

18. See Carson, "Matthew," 218. Morris, *Matthew*, 218, quotes Calvin: "This power is quite different from that which was entrusted to the Apostles, and which today the pastors of the Church exercise, for they do not so much remit, as testify that they are remitted, in declaring the mission that they are enjoined to fulfill."

1. The Primary Human Dilemma: Not Sickness but Sin

Sin is the origin of all sickness and suffering. Here we are at the heart of the human equation and the basic question in all God-talk: How can a loving, all-powerful God allow the innocent to suffer? In an ultimate sense, there are no innocents. It is clear in Scripture that we are all conceived and born in sin (Ps 51:5). We have inherited our sin condition from Adam (Rom 5:12 – 21), and we therefore live in a sin-sick world. In fact, all creation "groans" with us, longing to be released from what we have brought upon God's creation (Rom 8:19 – 22). Thus, when tsunamis, mudslides, avalanches, plane crashes, and the like happen, we cannot help but ask, "Where is God?"

Yet we must also realize that we have brought such things on ourselves. Through our trespass sickness and death have entered this world, and we must live with the consequences. It is not God; we have brought it on ourselves! Yet at the same time, the kingdom of God has entered this world through Christ, and the solution is in process of being realized. God is sovereign over these tragedies, and through the Spirit's intercession "in all things God works for the good" of God's people, even in tragedies (Rom 8:26 – 28).

2. The Cross as the Final Solution

It is common in many circles to highlight the individual aspects of what Christ has done, as in his many miracles for individuals. For many the presence of miracles is the highest good in our day as well. Yet it is clear here that forgiveness precedes healing, and the cross is the greatest miracle of all! There is a corporate dimension to the Christian experience, and in the cross we are all brought together in Christ. This does not denigrate the value of supernatural miracles, for God is still at work today. But spiritual healing is the greatest miracle of all.

3. Expecting Opposition When Proclaiming Truth

Jesus cites a syllogism in John 15:18 – 16:4:

You and I are one.
The world hates me.
The world will hate you.

Throughout the NT suffering and persecution are seen as a privilege, a sharing, or fellowship in the suffering of Christ (Acts 5:41; Rom 8:17; 2 Cor 1:5; 4:10; Gal 6:17; Phil 3:10; Col 1:24; 1 Pet 4:13). John 3:19 – 20 says it well: "This is the verdict: Light has come into the world, but people loved darkness instead of light because their deeds were evil. All those who do evil hate the light, and will not come into the light for fear that their deeds will be exposed." The message is clear. We are children of light and our mission is to shine the light of the gospel on the children of darkness. Why should we be surprised when those children turn on us in anger and reprisal for exposing their myth that they live in light? It is a given that the brightest places in every major city are the red-light districts and the gambling halls. Their pretense is exposed for what it is by the light of Christ, and so they hate the light-bearers and turn on them.

CHAPTER 34

Matthew 9:9 – 13

Literary Context

As stated in the introduction to this section, Matthew has organized chs. 8 – 9 with sets of three miracles separated by discipleship sections. The first discipleship segment centered on the radical demands of Jesus (8:18 – 22). This one centers on the reality and meaning of that new kingdom presence. (1) It means a new social paradigm, as Jesus has come not for the elite or the superficially pious but for the true sinners, the downtrodden, and the despised (9:9 – 13). The forgiveness of sins in the previous pericope (9:1 – 8) now leads to Jesus' ministry to sinners. Here Jesus goes beyond just reaching out to these despised people. He invites one of them to join his apostolic band!

(2) It means many spiritual disciplines, such as fasting, are temporarily suspended for joy that the kingdom has arrived (9:14 – 17).

(3) Blomberg brings out a further nuance. In 8:18 – 22 Matthew centered on inadequate responses to Jesus' call; here he highlights the proper response in light of strong criticism from the leaders and even from the disciples of the Baptist.[1]

III. The Kingdom Comes with Authority (8:1 – 11:1)
- **A. Authority and Discipleship in Jesus' Ministry (8:1 – 9:34)**
  - 3. Three Miracles Showing His Authority (8:23 – 9:8)
  - **4. Discipleship and the Reality of the New Kingdom (9:9 – 17)**
    - ➦ **a. The Call of Matthew (9:9 – 13)**
    - b. Fasting and the Reality of the New Kingdom (9:14 – 17)

Main Idea

One of the major themes of Jesus' ministry is here introduced — his scandalous (to the leaders) preoccupation with reaching out to sinners. This leads to a major

1. Blomberg, *Matthew*, 154; so also France, *Gospel of Matthew*, 350.

confrontation with the leaders, leading to the key pronouncement of Jesus regarding a major mission principle — namely, that the ministry of the church is not so much to those who believe they are right with God but to those who know they are sinners. This is the joy of God's salvation, that it embraces us in the midst of our sin (Rom 5:8).

Translation

Matthew 9:9-13

9a	Setting (Temporal)	As Jesus was leaving that place,
b	Setting (Social)	**he saw a man named Matthew sitting at the tax collection booth and**
c	Exhortation	**said to him,**
d		*"Follow me."*
e	Result/Response	**Then he got up and followed him.**
10a	Setting (Spatial)	It happened that while Jesus was at a banquet in Matthew's house,
b	Action	and **look, many tax collectors and sinners came and shared the banquet with Jesus and his disciples.**
11a		When the Pharisees saw this,
b	Objection	**they asked his disciples,**
c		*"Why does your teacher eat with tax collectors and sinners?"*
12a	Response	When Jesus heard this,
b		**he said,**
c	Proverb	*"It is not the healthy who need a doctor, but those who are sick.*
13a	Aphorism	*Now go learn what this means,*
b		*'I desire mercy, not sacrifice.' (Hos 6:6)*
c	Pronouncement	*For I have not come to call the righteous but sinners."*

Structure and Literary Form

The narration follows Mark 2:13 – 17 fairly closely, with the use of "Matthew" instead of "Levi son of Alphaeus" and the insertion of v. 12a (see below). As in Mark there is a call narrative (Matt 9:9), in which Jesus calls a tax collector to become a disciple, followed by an instantaneous response, and then a pronouncement story (a short narrative concluding with a definitive pronouncement by Jesus, 9:10 – 13) in which the Pharisees challenge his sharing the table with such outcasts. This short story prepares for the authoritative saying, which has three parts: a proverbial saying that only the sick need medical help; a divine OT truth that God wants action (mercy), not just external worship (sacrifice); and the concluding proclamation that Jesus' ministry is to sinners, not to the self-proclaimed righteous.

Exegetical Outline

➡ **I. The Call of Matthew to Become a Disciple (9:9)**
   A. The setting — Matthew at his toll booth
   B. The call to follow Jesus
   C. Matthew's acceptance and response

II. Table Fellowship with Sinners (9:10 – 13)
   A. The setting — dining with tax collectors and sinners (v. 10)
   B. The complaint of the Pharisees (v. 11)
   C. Jesus' response (vv. 12 – 13)
      1. The proverb on who needs a doctor (v. 12)
      2. The challenge to mercy (v. 13a)
      3. The pronouncement regarding ministry to sinners (v. 13b)

Explanation of the Text

9:9 As Jesus was leaving that place, he saw a man named Matthew (Καὶ παράγων ὁ Ἰησοῦς ἐκεῖθεν εἶδεν ἄνθρωπον … Μαθθαῖον λεγόμενον). Jesus apparently "leaves" (temporal participle) Capernaum and is walking outside the city when he comes across Matthew's tax collection booth. In Mark 2:14 he is named "Levi son of Alphaeus," and it is debated why he is named "Matthew" here,[2] a name that in Hebrew means either "gift of Yahweh" (*Mattatyâ*) or "faithful" (if from *ʿemet*). It was common for people to have two or even three names (a Hebrew, Greek, or Latin name or even two Hebrew names, as here) as with Saul/Paul or Simon/Peter. That is undoubtedly the case with Levi/Matthew. Why Matthew uses this name is unknown; perhaps like Peter he later became known more by this name.

9:9 … sitting[3] at the tax collection booth (καθήμενον ἐπὶ τὸ τελώνιον). The Jewish people had an especially onerous situation because they had to pay in effect three taxes: Jewish males over the age of twenty had to pay the annual half-shekel (one day's wage) temple tax; non-Roman citizens had to pay the tribute or "direct tax," including the land tax (for those who owned property) and head tax (one denarius or day's wage per year); and everyone had to pay "indirect taxes," such as sales tax, customs duty, tolls, etc. Tax collectors like Matthew sat in booths at the gates of the city to

2. Gnilka, *Matthäusevangelium*, 1:330 – 31; and Davies and Allison, *Matthew*, 2:98 – 99, list several theories: (1) Levi and Matthew are the same person; (2) the author knew Levi was not in the list of 10:2 – 5 and so chose "Matthew" out of the list; (3) the author knew Matthew was a toll collector from the tradition behind 10:3 and so linked him with the Levi in Mark; (4) the name "Matthew" was chosen by assonance, i.e., the similar sound with *mathētēs* ("disciple"); (5) the name was chosen to connect with the fictitious author said to be behind the gospel; (6) there was a Matthew connected to the community and tradition behind the gospel. Of these the first makes the most sense.

3. "Sitting" (καθήμενον) is an adjectival participle modifying "a man" (ἄνθρωπον).

collect tolls and customs duties on goods coming from Herod Philip's territory into that of Herod Antipas. They were part of organizations to which Rome farmed out (to the highest bidder) the responsibility. For customs duties they did not pay Rome but the municipal government, yet still they could charge extra for "commissions" on the taxes, which became their pay.

Needless to say, dishonesty was rampant, and they were among the most despised workers in the ancient world. Matthew would have collected taxes under Herod Antipas either at the lake where ships brought trade goods (if they were collecting taxes from fishermen)[4] or more likely along the Via Maris, the major trade route from the north that passed by Capernaum.[5] The taxes would have been paid on trade goods as well as on fish caught by the commercial fishermen in the lake (two different groups of tax collectors).

9:9 ... and said to him, "Follow me" (καὶ λέγει αὐτῷ, Ἀκολούθει μοι). That Jesus would call such a person to join his team would be startling at the very least. We know of no prior contact between them, but apart from John 1:35 – 51 we would not have known about a prior relationship with Simon and Andrew either. At any rate, Jesus commands Matthew, "Follow me" (ἀκολούθει; cf. 4:20; 8:19, 22), a present imperative that calls for a lifetime of discipleship. Matthew's immediate obedience is just as startling.

9:9 Then he got up[6] and followed him (καὶ ἀναστὰς ἠκολούθησεν αὐτῷ). Luke 5:28 adds that he "left everything" to follow Jesus. Matthew probably left more than perhaps any other of the disciples. As a tax collector he would have been fairly wealthy, and while the fishermen in the group kept their boats (John 21:3) and probably went back to their fishing from time to time, Matthew could hardly return to his former occupation. In fact, he likely did not want to do so, for the Jews looked on tax collectors both as collaborators with the Romans and as unclean because of their graft and because they continually handled pagan coins and came into contact with Gentiles.[7]

9:10 It happened that while Jesus was at a banquet in Matthew's house (Καὶ ἐγένετο αὐτοῦ ἀνακειμένου ἐν τῇ οἰκίᾳ). Matthew and Mark relate the setting generally, but Luke 5:29 tells us "Levi held a great banquet for Jesus at his house." This tells us that Matthew was wealthy, for his house was large enough for such a banquet. The temporal genitive absolute (see on 1:18) ἀνακειμένου also shows this, for Jewish people only "reclined at table" (ἀνάκειμαι) for such banquets or festive meals.[8] This was a Roman custom with the guests reclining on couches facing the food on a central table, with the Jews following this custom at religious festivals and banquets. Meals were important social occasions in the first century, defining peer groups and social status. As the saying went, "To share a meal is to share a life," for it was a kind of alliance, a declaration that a person was accepted into the group.[9]

9:10 And look, many tax collectors and sinners came and shared the banquet with Jesus and his disciples (καὶ ἰδοὺ πολλοὶ τελῶναι καὶ

4. McNeile, *Matthew*, 117.

5. Wilkins, *Matthew*, 364.

6. Here and in v. 10 are circumstantial participles that virtually become another main verb (see 2:4; 4:20).

7. Keener, *Matthew*, 292 – 93, says that taxes could have been as high as 30 – 40 percent when all were paid. They would often search a travelers belongings as well as their person looking for undeclared goods. Tolls were normally 3 percent and the proceeds went to the municipal treasuries rather than to Rome. Still, Jewish texts considered tax collectors the worst of sinners and as unclean as a leper.

8. So Joachim Jeremias, *Eucharistic Words of Jesus* (Philadelphia: Fortress, 1966), 48 – 49.

9. See S. S. Bartchy, "Table Fellowship," *DJG*, 796 – 800.

ἁμαρτωλοὶ ἐλθόντες συνανέκειντο τῷ Ἰησοῦ καὶ τοῖς μαθηταῖς αὐτοῦ). Matthew did not invite the local elite (who probably shunned him) but his own kind (on "look" [ἰδού], see 9:2 – 3). This was a celebratory meal meant to introduce Jesus to his friends and to explain his change of allegiance/ occupation.

The "sinners" (ἁμαρτωλοί) here are closely aligned with the tax collectors as those despised by the Pharisees. They could be the *ʿam hāʾāreṣ* ("the people of the land"), the common people who did not live by the strict rules of the Pharisees. But the Pharisees could hardly have refused contact with the vast majority of Jews; that would have turned them into Essenes. More likely, these "sinners" were the more blatant offenders of the *halakōt* ("rules of conduct"), wicked people such as pimps and prostitutes (used in 21:31), thieves, gamblers, etc.[10] Jesus is accompanied by his "disciples," probably his close followers (not the general group of 5:1; 8:21), commissioned as the Twelve in 10:1.

9:11 When the Pharisees saw this, they asked his disciples, "Why does your teacher eat with tax collectors and sinners?"[11] (καὶ ἰδόντες οἱ Φαρισαῖοι ἔλεγον τοῖς μαθηταῖς αὐτοῦ, Διὰ τί μετὰ τῶν τελωνῶν καὶ ἁμαρτωλῶν ἐσθίει ὁ διδάσκαλος ὑμῶν;). Jesus and his disciples are sharing table fellowship (present tense "eats" [ἐσθίει] to dramatize the ongoing meal) with these disreputable people. The Pharisees (see on 3:7), who are probably not at the banquet but notice what is happening, were scrupulous in their eating habits, not just in terms of the food laws but with whom they shared their meals.

For Jesus and his disciples to eat with such people was scandalous; it meant they were accepting these tax collectors and identifying with them and sinners. Yet this characterized Jesus' ministry. He was called "a glutton and a drunkard" (Matt 11:19 = Luke 7:34) because he regularly shared meals with such people and was their "friend" (Matt 11:19). So the criticism was natural, as they were rendering themselves unclean and violators of Torah by their association with such people.[12]

9:12 When Jesus heard this, he said, "It is not the healthy who need a doctor, but those who are sick"[13] (ὁ δὲ ἀκούσας εἶπεν, Οὐ χρείαν ἔχουσιν οἱ ἰσχύοντες ἰατροῦ ἀλλ' οἱ κακῶς ἔχοντες). This saying was a common proverb in the ancient world,[14] built on the obvious fact that doctors are needed for the sick rather than for people in good health. Jesus, of course, means it allegorically of spiritual sickness. Here the strong/healthy are the Pharisees and the weak/sick are the tax collectors and sinners. He is not saying the leaders are actually "healthy." Rather, he says, "I have not come for those who *believe* they are healthy but for those who *know* they are sick" (see also v. 13). This has led to one of the great depictions of Jesus down through history as the Great Physician.

10. See E. P. Sanders, "Jesus and the Sinners," *JSNT* 19 (1983): 5 – 36; Michael J. Wilkins, "Sinner," *DJG*, 757 – 60; Keener, *Matthew*, 294 – 96.

11. The single article governing "tax collectors and sinners" (τελωνῶν καὶ ἁμαρτωλῶν) shows they are considered a single entity; see Wallace, 257 on this use of Colwell's rule. On p. 280 he states that in this case the first group (tax collectors) are considered part of the second group (sinners), so we could translate, "tax collectors and other sinners."

12. The Pharisees would not be opposed to bringing such people to repentance; rather, it was the radical association with such people that was the issue. The Pharisees would have dealt with them at a distance (through teaching, etc.) rather than associating intimately with them at table.

13. In the cases of both "the healthy" and "the sick," Matthew uses present tense substantival participles to emphasize the continuous nature of their spiritual condition.

14. For examples, Davies and Allison, *Matthew*, 2:103, lists Menander, fragment 591K ("For the one whose body is ill needs a physician"); Plutarch, *Apophthegmata laconica* 230F ("Physicians are not among the healthy but spend their time among the sick"); Diogenes Laertius 6.1.1 ("Physicians are commonly with the sick but they do not catch the fever").

9:13 "Now go learn what this means, 'I desire mercy, not sacrifice' " (πορευθέντες δὲ μάθετε τί ἐστιν, Ἔλεος θέλω καὶ οὐ θυσίαν). "Go [for this circumstantial participle, see on v. 9] and learn" was a rabbinic expression for Torah study,[15] and in the context of the Pharisees who prided themselves on their knowledge of Scripture, it is a particularly powerful comeback. Since they call Jesus "teacher" (9:11), he will give them a "learning" assignment! Jesus takes his text from Hos 6:6 (quoted again in 12:7). In Hosea the apostate nation still followed the letter of the law (sacrifice) but had forgotten the heart of the law (mercy and love). Jesus is saying the Pharisees are recapitulating the same terrible error.

"Mercy" (ἔλεος, first for emphasis) in Hosea translates the Hebrew *ḥesed* or "steadfast love,"[16] the very thing the Pharisees lack (see Matt 23). They are assiduous in their covenant observance, even making up new "oral laws" so the common people will not inadvertently break the Torah. But they have no feelings of mercy toward the outcasts of society.[17] A major NT ethic is that the way we treat others shows our true relation to God. By failing to have a heart of mercy toward sinners, the Pharisees show they are not right with God.

9:13 "For I have not come to call the righteous but sinners" (οὐ γὰρ ἦλθον καλέσαι δικαίους ἀλλὰ ἁμαρτωλούς). As in v. 12, this means, "I have not come to call those who claim they are righteous but those who know they are sinners." It is closely connected to the forgiveness of the sins of the paralytic in 9:2 and shows that personal salvation is a major theme here. The "call" is a call to salvation and discipleship; Luke 5:32 adds "to repentance," the basis for discipleship.

This does not mean that Jesus is not interested in the salvation of the Pharisees. We can see the challenge and progress to salvation of one of them, Nicodemus, in John 3:1 – 15; 7:50 – 51; 19:39 – 42. Rather, it means Jesus' ministry is one of salvation, and therefore the sinners are his focus; yet the necessary goal of salvation in this life is discipleship. There is a sardonic challenge to the self-righteousness of the Pharisees, but it is muted.[18]

Theology in Application

This is an important passage on the universal nature of God's salvation as well as the necessity of God's people espousing the same divine love for all peoples, even notorious sinners.

1. God's Offer of Salvation to All

The gospel is meant for all, and this is nowhere better exemplified than in Jesus' choice of a tax collector to be one of the Twelve. It was a deliberate choice on his

15. See Schlatter, *Matthäus*, 307; Gnilka, *Matthäusevangelium*, 1:332.

16. See France, *Matthew*, 168.

17. As Carson, "Matthew," 225, explains, this is not an absolute negation of "sacrifice." It is cast in Semitic antithesis, where "not A but B" means "B is of more basic importance than A."

18. Davies and Allison, *Matthew*, 2:106 – 7, note four possibilities to the meaning of "not come to call the righteous": (1) It was presumed that they were already saved; (2) Jesus realized it would do no good because they were too stubborn to respond (see 13:14 – 15); (3) the whole emphasis is on "sinners," so one cannot know anything about the "righteous"; (4) it is presupposed that everyone is a sinner, so the "righteous" are those who will not see that they are no different than others. They say they cannot judge between the last three; all are possible. Still, in this context the Pharisees are clearly looking down on the others and consider themselves superior.

part, and it was certainly intended to tell all that anyone may come to Jesus and find salvation. There are many today who believe that they have sinned too much, that God cannot love anyone like them. This is clearly wrong. Salvation is a gift of grace, and God's mercy is infinite, as shown by the entire OT with God again and again forgiving his wayward people and accepting them back.

The metanarrative of the Bible as a whole is God's overcoming Adam's sin and bringing people to himself who have continually rejected his mercy (cf. Rom 5:12 – 21). At the same time, Jesus turns their lives around and does great things through them. If he could use a despised tax collector in this way, he can use each of us to do great things.

2. Jesus Aligned with Society's Downtrodden

Too many suburban churches minister only to their own kind and do little to help the inner-city poor. If a homeless person were to enter the doors of the church, many would be mortified. The "sinners" today are, if anything, even worse than in Jesus' day — murderers, rapists, pedophiles. Do we reach out to such with the love that Jesus showed? If Jesus were to appear today, where would he be ministering? I think we all know the answer. He would shock our comfortable Christians just as much as he did the religious establishment in his own day.

3. God Desires Mercy More Than Sacrifice

Too many of us are Pharisees at heart, hypocrites who talk the talk but do not walk the walk. It is easy to become "churchified," i.e., to perform all the external rituals but fail to have a heart for God and others. The Pharisees loved only their own kind but had no mercy or love for the despised in society. A true biblical church will have a community-wide ministry that shows God's love to all around. This is true for ministry both outside and inside the church.

For instance, the church of Ephesus in Rev 2:1 – 7 was a model of orthodoxy but had "forsaken the love [it] had at first," primarily brotherly love (note "do the things you did at first" [v. 5], i.e., good deeds toward each other) but also a love for God that must result in that community love. It is shocking how many believers go through hard times with no one offering a helping hand in the church. In the early church "there were no needy persons among them" (Acts 4:34), for the members did whatever they had to (even selling property or homes!) to meet the financial crisis. Can *any* church in the West come close to that biblical ideal?

Matthew 9:14 – 17

35 CHAPTER

Literary Context

We saw the kingdom in action in the previous episode, dealing with the effects of the kingdom in reaching the despised and rejected with the gospel. Now we turn to the meaning of the kingdom and its relationship to the traditions that accompanied the demands of the old ways. It is not only the Pharisees but even the disciples of John the Baptist who question the new reality that Jesus is introducing.

- **III. The Kingdom Comes with Authority (8:1 – 11:1)**
  - **A. Authority and Discipleship in Jesus' Ministry (8:1 – 9:34)**
    - **4. Discipleship and the Reality of the New Kingdom (9:9 – 17)**
      - a. The Call of Matthew (9:9 – 13)
      - ➦ **b. Fasting and the Reality of the New Kingdom (9:14 – 17)**

Main Idea

Jesus continues to challenge the old traditions. He not only freely associates with sinners, but also he and his disciples do not even observe a key religious practice like fasting (see on 6:16 – 18). The reason is that Christ is bringing with him a new era, a kingdom reality that cannot be simply immersed into the old ways of Judaism.

Translation

Matthew 9:14-17

14a	Setting	**Then John's disciples came to him, saying,**
b	Question	*"Why do we and the Pharisees fast*
		but *your disciples do not fast?"*
15a		**Jesus answered,**
b	Answer	*The guests of the bridegroom cannot mourn*
		while he is with them, can they?
c		But *the time will come*
		when the bridegroom is taken away
		from them,
d		and *then they will fast.*
16a	Illustration #1	*[1] No one sows a patch of unshrunk cloth on an old garment,*
b	Result	for *the patch will rip away from the garment and*
		the tear will become worse.
17a	Illustration #2	*[2]* Nor *do people pour new wine into old wineskins.*
b	Result	Otherwise, *the wineskins tear apart,*
		the wine pours out, and
		the skins are destroyed.
c	Solution	Instead, *they pour new wine into new wineskins, and*
		both are preserved."

Structure and Literary Form

This section follows Mark 2:18 – 22 but with a few changes (see below) and is a controversy story (Matt 9:14 – 15) containing a parable (v. 15) and followed by two extended metaphors (vv. 16 – 17). Many have argued for an artificial connection, as if Matthew has loosely attached two different traditions. However, that is unnecessary, for all three Synoptists combine the two parts, and the two latter sayings fit well with the story itself, explaining why Jesus did not have his disciples practice fasting. If one tries to mix the new way of Jesus with the old way of Judaism, both will be destroyed. In 5:17 – 20 Matthew stresses Jesus' continuity with the past; here he expresses the discontinuity.

Exegetical Outline

➡ **I. The Controversy over Fasting (9:14 – 15)**

A. The question from the Baptist's disciples (v. 14)

1. They and the Pharisees fast
2. Jesus' disciples do not fast

B. Jesus' response (v. 15)
   1. The wedding guests do not mourn
   2. They will mourn when the bridegroom is gone

II. The Two Metaphors regarding the Kingdom (9:16 – 17)

A. A patch of cloth on a garment (v. 16)
   1. A new patch on an old garment
   2. The patch pulls away
   3. The garment is even worse

B. Wine in wineskins (v. 17)
   1. New wine in an old wineskin
   2. The wine expands and the skin bursts
   3. Both the wine and the skin are ruined
   4. Solution: new wine into new wineskins

Explanation of the Text

9:14 Then John's disciples came to him (Τότε προσέρχονται αὐτῷ οἱ μαθηταὶ Ἰωάννου). It is interesting that in Mark 2:18 people ask the question, and in Luke 5:33 it is the same Pharisees from the banquet scene who ask. Why does Matthew have John's disciples asking? In a larger sense the question likely came from the whole crowd, including disciples of both the Pharisees and John.[1] Matthew may center on the disciples of the Baptist to show the difference between the asceticism of John and Jesus' joyous celebration of the coming of the kingdom (see also 11:18 – 19).[2]

9:14 ... saying, "Why do we and the Pharisees fast but your disciples do not fast?" (λέγοντες, Διὰ τί ἡμεῖς καὶ οἱ Φαρισαῖοι νηστεύομεν πολλά, οἱ δὲ μαθηταί σου οὐ νηστεύουσιν;). διὰ τί literally means "on account of what" or "for what reason?" The connection with the previous story is clear. There we saw Jesus feasting in celebration of the kingdom's new openness to sinners, while here we see that he and his disciples do not fast because of the joy of the kingdom's arrival.

As stated in 6:16, the Pharisees (and probably the Baptist's followers) fasted not only for the required times of Day of Atonement and New Year but also every Monday and Thursday. Thus they are surprised at the absence of such an important observance (one of the primary religious expectations) on the part of Jesus' followers (most likely referring to the weekly fasts; Jesus and his followers probably observed the Day of Atonement fast, commanded by Lev 16:29 – 34).[3] In fact, Jesus had taught his disciples to fast privately in 6:16 – 18, so he intended for them to do so later.

9:15 Jesus answered, "The guests of the bridegroom cannot mourn while[4] he is with them, can

1. Bock, *Luke 1:1–9:50*, 515, comments on the "they" in Luke 5:33 and believes it was the whole crowd asking the question.

2. Davies and Allison, *Matthew*, 2:108, bring out another possibility, that this is "the third story in a row in which a different religious group has shown itself to be at cross-purposes with Jesus — the scribes in 9:3 – 8, the Pharisees in 9:9 – 13, the disciples of John the Baptist in 9:14 – 17."

3. France, *Matthew* (TNTC), 169, says Jesus "presumably observed the Day of Atonement at least, but not the Pharisaic routine."

4. ἐφ' ὅσον means "as long as."

they? (καὶ εἶπεν αὐτοῖς ὁ Ἰησοῦς, Μὴ δύνανται οἱ υἱοὶ τοῦ νυμφῶνος πενθεῖν ἐφ᾽ ὅσον μετ᾽ αὐτῶν ἐστιν ὁ νυμφίος;). The interrogative particle (μή) in a question expects the answer, "No." The "sons of the bridal chamber" (lit. trans. of οἱ υἱοὶ τοῦ νυμφῶνος) could be just the groomsmen but are more likely all the invited guests since Jesus is making a blanket statement of his followers as a whole, using the joy of a wedding as a metaphor for the appearance of the messianic kingdom.

Weddings were a special time of joy, and the guests were free from other religious duties during the celebration time (*b. Sukk.* 25b; *m. Ber.* 2:5). The celebrations lasted seven days (Tob 11:19; *JosAsen* 21:8; *t. Ber.* 2:10) and were proverbial for intense joy, with wine and food in abundance (see John 2:1 – 11). In contrast, fasting symbolized mourning for sin to the Jews (see 6:16). In the OT Yahweh is the bridegroom of Israel (Isa 54:5 – 6; 62:5; Jer 3:14; Hos 2:16 – 20), while Jesus is the groom of the church at the messianic wedding banquet (Matt 22:2; 25:10 – 13; Eph 5: 25 – 27; Rev 19:7 – 9).

9:15 But the time will come when the bridegroom is taken away from them (ἐλεύσονται δὲ ἡμέραι ὅταν ἀπαρθῇ ἀπ᾽ αὐτῶν ὁ νυμφίος). France notes that this is the first time in Matthew that Jesus speaks of being "taken away," with the verb connoting "a violent and unwelcome removal."[5] Feuillet sees a reference to the Isaianic suffering Servant here (cf. Isa 53:8, "By oppression and judgment he was taken away").[6] All recognize this as a prophecy of his coming death. At that time grief-stricken fasting will be appropriate. Indeed, it became mandatory; in *Did.* 8:1 Christians were told to fast on Wednesday and Friday in contradistinction to the Monday and Thursday Jewish fasting.

9:15 ... and then they will fast (καὶ τότε νηστεύσουσιν). It is common to believe that the first half of this verse may be authentic but that the second half appears too early in Jesus' ministry to be authentic.[7] Yet as Albright and Mann assert, this is unnecessary. "Jesus can hardly be unaware of the well-nigh inevitable consequences of his proclamation of the reign of God. A violent end could safely be predicted for one making such a proclamation."[8]

9:16 No one sows a patch of unshrunk cloth on an old garment, for the patch will rip away from the garment and the tear will become worse (οὐδεὶς δὲ ἐπιβάλλει ἐπίβλημα ῥάκους ἀγνάφου ἐπὶ ἱματίῳ παλαιῷ· αἴρει γὰρ τὸ πλήρωμα αὐτοῦ ἀπὸ τοῦ ἱματίου καὶ χεῖρον σχίσμα γίνεται). The next two analogies (Luke 5:36 calls them "parables") expand on Jesus' point regarding the appearance of the new covenant reality and its incompatibility with the old covenant. Just as the joy of the new covenant cannot cohere with the mourning of the old ways, so the new kingdom as a whole cannot be forced into the old one, lest both be destroyed. This first analogy is clear. The old garment has long ago shrunk, but the new cloth has not. To sew a new piece of cloth[9] onto an old robe to repair it is foolish, for as soon as the new patch is washed it too will shrink, pulling the threads from the old robe and ripping it anew.[10]

5. France, *Gospel of Matthew*, 356.

6. André Feuillet, "La controverse sur le jeûne (Mc 2,18 – 20; Matt 9,14 – 15; Lc 5,33 – 35)," *NRTh* 90 (1968): 252 – 56; see also Hagner, *Matthew 1 – 13*, 243, who follows him.

7. E.g., Davies and Allison, *Matthew*, 2:11; Beare, *Matthew*, 231.

8. Albright and Mann, *Matthew*, 107.

9. "Unshrunk cloth" (ῥάκους ἀγνάφου) is a genitive of content (BDF §167).

10. See Michael G. Steinhauser, "The Patch of Unshrunk Cloth (Matt 9:16)," *ExpTim* 87 (1976): 312 – 13, who explains the grammatical difficulties by positing that "the patch" (τὸ πλήρωμα) be understood as the "fill" or thread and material by which the new cloth is sown onto the old cloak. The sense is that the shrinking patch draws the thread and material it is sown onto away from the cloak and causes a new tear in both the old cloak and the new patch.

9:17 Nor do people pour new wine into old wineskins. Otherwise, the wineskins tear apart, the wine pours out, and the skins are destroyed (οὐδὲ βάλλουσιν οἶνον νέον εἰς ἀσκοὺς παλαιούς· εἰ δὲ μή γε, ῥήγνυνται οἱ ἀσκοί καὶ ὁ οἶνος ἐκχεῖται καὶ οἱ ἀσκοὶ ἀπόλλυνται). The skins of goats (oxen or camels for large casks), tanned and toughened, were used to transport liquid; but as they became old the skins would get hard and brittle. New wine probably refers to wine that has just begun the process of fermentation; it kept expanding through the process, so the brittle skin would break as the new wine expanded beyond the space allowed. The point ("otherwise" [εἰ δὲ μή γε] is an intensive conjunction that shows unexpected results, cf. BAGD, 153, β) is that both are ruined, the skin through ripping apart and the wine by running onto the ground. The message is the unsuitability of the old covenant as a vessel for the new covenant.

9:17 Instead, they pour new wine into new wineskins, and both are preserved (ἀλλὰ βάλλουσιν οἶνον νέον εἰς ἀσκοὺς καινούς, καὶ ἀμφότεροι συντηροῦνται). The last comment is found only in Matthew and is in complete accordance with Matthew's emphasis on continuity with Judaism; the Torah was not annulled but fulfilled in Christ (5:17 – 20). Yet at the same time, this goes beyond the normal understanding of the equation of Jewish Torah and Jesus' new kingdom truths. It is critical to notice that "both" (ἀμφότεροι) refers not to the new wine and old wineskins (Judaism) but to the "new wineskins" of the previous clause, namely, the new forms of Jesus' kingdom teaching as found in the Sermon on the Mount.

Gospel and law are brought together only in Jesus.[11] Jesus has not come to amalgamate Judaism with Christianity. New forms are needed. The OT has not been annulled but fulfilled, and this requires the Torah of the Messiah, a new set of ethical norms and gospel practices established by Jesus. The early Palestinian church did not realize the fullness of what Jesus meant and considered themselves the new messianic sect of Judaism. It was not until the Gentile movement had begun that they gradually understood the enormity of this truth.

Theology in Application

The new kingdom reality Jesus inaugurated in his ministry has important ramifications for the church today, and several issues need to be explored. The question is whether the tenor of this passage is being lived out in what the church has become in the twenty-first century.

1. A Time of Joy but Also a Time of Serious Reflection

The NT commands "joy" even in the midst of serious trials (Jas 1:2 – 4; 1 Pet 1:6 – 7) because God will sovereignly work everything out for our good (Rom 8:26 – 28). We don't need a troubled heart (John 14:1) and can place our hope firmly

11. See Carson, "Matthew," 227; Hagner, *Matthew 1 – 13*, 244. See also the discussion in Carson of the discontinuity seen by dispensationalists here.

on the God who promised, giving us a whole new level of access to God and worship (Heb 10:20, 22 – 25). So joy characterizes the new community in Christ.

At the same time, evil is rampant in our world, and the same cosmic forces that led Christ to the cross are at work to destroy his work in the church (Eph 6:10 – 18; 1 Pet 5:8; Rev 13:7). In this interim period between the advents, there is a mixture of joy and grief among God's people. More believers are being martyred than ever before, and most believe the final end times are near (on fasting see "Theology in Application" on 6:16 – 18).

2. Reflecting the Newness of the Gospel Christ Proclaimed

The old forms of the Jewish religion are often reflected in the sort of traditions of worship we demand. People down through the ages have sought a comfort zone in every area of life, and that is normally determined by the traditions they inherit. The debate today between hymns and praise songs reflects the debate when the hymns first were introduced over a century ago and people called them "secular" or "carnal" because they reflected the song styles of their day. Jesus demanded openness to new ways of worship and Christian living, and the church must at all times be fresh and contemporary.[12] This does not mean for us a rejection of the traditional patterns, but it does require an openness to fresh ideas and style.

3. Jesus Determines the Pattern for Christian Living

In our age of rugged individualism many Christians think nothing of living part of their life Christ's way (often restricted to church attendance) while maintaining a secular lifestyle and set of priorities. The studies by Gallup and Barna of the way the average evangelical Christian believes, thinks, and lives should frighten us all! This is similar to the Judaizers in Paul's day, who wanted to be half Jewish, half Christian. In both cases the result is syncretism, and God will not accept that. Christ has set the rules for the Christian life (e.g., in the Sermon on the Mount), and they are not optional. The "new" way of Christ is the only way the kingdom community can live, and in each case "if you know the good you ought to do and don't do it, you sin" (Jas 4:17).

12. See Blomberg, *Matthew*, 159, who mentions in this regard H. Snyder, *The Problem of Wineskins: Church Structure in a Technological Age* (Downers Grove, IL: IVP, 1975).

CHAPTER 36

Matthew 9:18 – 26

Literary Context

This final set of three miracles continues the emphases in the others on Jesus' authority and compassion for the marginalized in society (8:16 – 17; 9:2, 22) as well as on the faith of those healed (8:10, 13; 9:2, 22, 28 – 29). The contrast between Jesus' popularity with the crowds (8:1; 9:8, 26, 31, 33) and the opposition of the leaders is again noted (9:3, 11, 34), who for the first time attribute his exorcisms to Satan (9:34; cf. 12:22 – 32). The contrast between the simple faith of the ruler of the synagogue in 9:18 and the radical rejection of the Pharisees in 9:34 is stark.

III. The Kingdom Comes with Authority (8:1 – 11:1)
- **A. Authority and Discipleship in Jesus' Ministry (8:1 – 9:34)**
  - 4. Discipleship and the Reality of the New Kingdom (9:9 – 17)
  - **5. Three Healing Miracles Showing Compassion (9:18 – 34)**
    - ➦ **a. Healing a Woman and Raising a Young Girl (9:18 – 26)**
    - b. Healing Two Blind Men (9:27 – 31)
    - c. Exorcizing a Young Man (9:32 – 34)

Main Idea

The joy of the presence of the new kingdom continues in this double healing narrative. In each aspect both the faith of the participants[1] and the compassionate healing presence of Jesus are highlighted, and the result is the growing fame of Jesus (9:26, 31).

1. Held, *Tradition and Interpretation*, 180, goes so far as to call this a teaching episode on faith rather than a miracle story. That goes too far but does demonstrate the importance of faith here.

Translation

Matthew 9:18-26

18a	Setting	While he was telling them this,
b	Action (A)	**look, a ruler came and knelt in front of him saying,**
c	Problem	*"My daughter has just died;*
d	Entreaty	but *come,*
		put your hand on her, and
		she will live."
19a	Response	**Then Jesus got up and along with his disciples followed him.**
20a	Action (B)	And **look, a woman . . .** **came behind him and**
		who had suffered a bleeding disorder
		for twelve years
		touched the hem of his robe,
21a	Basis for 20a	for she was saying
		to herself,
b		*"If only I can touch his robe, I will be healed."*
22a	Action/ Pronouncement	Now **Jesus turned and seeing her, said,**
b		*"Take courage, daughter, your faith has healed you."*
c	Result of 22a-b/ Healing	And **the woman was healed from that very hour.**
23a	Setting	When Jesus came to the house of the ruler and
		saw the flute players and
		the crowd in an uproar,
24a	Command/ Pronouncement (A')	**he said,**
b		*"Go away, for the girl is not dead but asleep."*
c	Result of 24b	And **they laughed at him.**
25a	Setting	Now when the crowd was driven out,
b	Action	**he came and took her by the hand,**
c	Result of 25b	and **the girl rose up.**
26a	Reaction to 25b	And **the news about this spread throughout the whole region.**

Structure and Literary Form

Matthew has characteristically greatly reduced the story, being a third the length of Mark 5:21 – 43 and half the length of Luke 8:40 – 56. However, the essential details are present, and the gist of the story is much the same.[2] The primary

2. On the trustworthiness of this account, see Blomberg, *Historical Reliability*, 134 – 36.

structural feature is the intercalation or sandwiching of the story of the hemorrhaging woman into the raising of the young girl. The result of this feature (Mark has several sandwiching stories while Matthew has just this one) is that the two stories interpret and intensify each other in an ABA pattern (A = raising of the girl, B = hemorrhaging woman).

One interesting difference is that in Mark 5:23 the ruler says his daughter is near death while in Matt 9:18 he says she has just died. So in Matthew the raising of the dead is more prominent, and the healing of the hemorrhaging woman prepares for the greater miracle at the same time that her faith is a model for the ruler (though this is stressed more in Mark).

Exegetical Outline

➦ **I. The Request of the Ruler (9:18 – 19)**
- A. The coming of the ruler (v. 18a)
- B. The request in faith (v. 18b)
- C. Jesus and his disciples come (v. 19)

II. The Healing of the Hemorrhaging Woman (9:20 – 22)
- A. The coming of the woman (vv. 20 – 21)
  1. Her sad plight (v. 20)
  2. Her faith (v. 21)
- B. Jesus lauds her faith and heals her (v. 22)

III. Jesus Raises the Child from Death (9:23 – 26)
- A. Jesus sends away the mourners (v. 23 – 24)
  1. The flute players and the weeping crowds (v. 23)
  2. His message — the girl is sleeping (v. 24a)
  3. Their reaction — laughter (v. 24b)
- B. Jesus raises her from the dead (v. 25)
- C. Result — the report went everywhere (v. 26)

Explanation of the Text

9:18 While he was telling them this, look, a ruler came and knelt in front of him (Ταῦτα αὐτοῦ λαλοῦντος αὐτοῖς ἰδοὺ ἄρχων εἷς ἐλθὼν προσεκύνει αὐτῷ). Matthew's introductory "while he was telling them this" (another temporal genitive absolute, see 1:18; 9:10) is used to connect this with Jesus' teaching on the new kingdom presence.[3] Thus the miracles are part of the new reality and provoke joy. The "ruler" (εἷς is used here as an indefinite article, see BAGD, 231, 3b) is Jairus, the synagogue ruler of Mark 5:22.

3. On the discrepancy with Mark 5:21, "When Jesus had again crossed over by boat," and Luke 8:40, "when Jesus returned (from healing the Gerasene demoniac)," see Carson, "Matthew," 229.

Normally an ἄρχων was a civil community leader (there were seven of them) and the ἀρχισυνάγωγος was the president of the synagogue (one of three officers), but often the same person held both offices. He would be a wealthy patron and member of the synagogue board who was responsible for the order and progress of worship. He apportioned tasks in it like the reading of Scripture or giving of the homily and was in charge of finances as well as of maintaining the building. He may have been elected to a term of office, though at times the office remained in a family for generations.[4] For a highly respected community leader like this to fall down at the feet of Jesus was unusual and shows both his desperate plight and the incredible esteem he has for Jesus.

9:18 ... saying,[5] "My daughter has just died; but come,[6] put your hand on her, and she will live" (λέγων ὅτι Ἡ θυγάτηρ μου ἄρτι ἐτελεύτησεν· ἀλλὰ ἐλθὼν ἐπίθες τὴν χεῖρά σου ἐπ' αὐτήν, καὶ ζήσεται). There are stories of the raising of the dead in the OT (Elijah in 1 Kgs 17:17–24 and Elisha in 2 Kgs 4:32–37), and if the man somehow believed Jesus was Messiah (or even a great prophet), he could extrapolate from the great healing stories he had heard about and think Jesus might be able to raise his daughter.[7] His simple yet profound faith in Jesus parallels that of the centurion in 8:8–9 and is a highlight of the story. He sincerely believes that a mere touch from Jesus will suffice to bring his daughter to life.[8]

9:19 Then Jesus got up and along with his disciples followed him (καὶ ἐγερθεὶς ὁ Ἰησοῦς ἠκολούθησεν αὐτῷ καὶ οἱ μαθηταὶ αὐτοῦ). The compassionate response of Jesus is immediate. The idea of Jesus "getting up" (ἐγερθείς) may well be prophetic of the soon "raising" of the little girl (cf. 9:25). The reference to the disciples (Mark has the crowds) may be to emphasize them as official witnesses of the event.

9:20 And look, a woman who had suffered a bleeding disorder for twelve years (Καὶ ἰδοὺ γυνὴ αἱμορροοῦσα δώδεκα ἔτη). Matthew's characteristic "look" (ἰδού) opens this episode as well as the one in 9:18. This unfortunate woman has been suffering what was probably vaginal bleeding, a menstrual flow that had not stopped for twelve years. Mark tells us she had spent all the money she had on physicians, with no result. We must understand that it was not just the physical danger from so much loss of blood but also the fact that Lev 15:25–30 said she was ritually unclean for that entire time. In other words, she was a virtual leper who would have had to leave family and village, lest contact with her render everyone unclean. It is impossible for us to imagine the agony of heart and soul this poor woman had been through all that time.

9:20 ... came behind him and touched the hem of his robe (προσελθοῦσα ὄπισθεν ἥψατο τοῦ κρασπέδου τοῦ ἱματίου αὐτοῦ). There is a progression of faith from the synagogue ruler (implicit in v. 18) to the woman (explicit in v. 21 and the center of the episode). The courage it took to steal into the town and sneak behind Jesus is also

4. See Wolfgang Schrage in *TDNT*, 7:844–47; and Safrai and Stern, ed., *Jewish People in the First Century*, 933–37. Under him the synagogue "attendant" (Luke 4:20) was a paid official who actually ran the synagogue and was master of ceremonies for the service. The third official may have been the schoolmaster.

5. ὅτι in a context like this is used to introduce direct discourse.

6. The circumstantial participle ἐλθών becomes virtually another main verb (see 9:1, 9, 13). This occurs again in vv. 19, 20, 22, 25, 27b, 31.

7. Mark tells us he came while his daughter was still alive. Matthew abbreviates that fact both in the interest of length and to zero in on the key point.

8. The use of the indicative "she will live" rather than the "so that" (ἵνα) clause of Mark 5:23 stresses even more his faith. He is certain she will come back to life.

astounding, for if detected she would have been thrown out of the area as unclean. She reasons that with Jesus as a powerful healing prophet (perhaps Messiah), she did not have to have direct contact. Just a touch would be enough.

Healing experienced through touch was not unheard of (Mark 3:10), as was the healing power of the clothing of a holy man (cf. Matt 14:36; Acts 19:12). Most likely the "hem of his robe" refers to the four corners at the bottom of the robe where the "tassels" required by Num 15:38 – 41; Deut 22:12 were found (they were to remind the people to obey the divine commands).

9:21 For she was saying to herself, "If only I can touch his robe, I will be healed" (ἔλεγεν γὰρ ἐν ἑαυτῇ, Ἐὰν μόνον ἅψωμαι τοῦ ἱματίου αὐτοῦ σωθήσομαι). The imperfect "she was saying" (ἔλεγεν) pictures the woman saying this to herself as she approaches Jesus. This is a step forward from the ruler. He believed that Jesus' touch was sufficient; she believes that even an indirect touch by her (apparently without the direct knowledge of Jesus) will suffice. After twelve years of shunning crowds (and being shunned by them), her reticence is understandable. Yet her faith is clearly uppermost. Davies and Allison develop an interesting syllogism here:

Major premise: An act of faith allows a person to experience healing.
Minor premise: Touching Jesus' garment is an act of faith.
Conclusion: Therefore the woman is made well.[9]

9:22 Now Jesus turned and seeing her, said, "Take courage, daughter, your faith has healed you" (ὁ δὲ Ἰησοῦς στραφεὶς καὶ ἰδὼν αὐτὴν εἶπεν, Θάρσει, θύγατερ· ἡ πίστις σου σέσωκέν σε). Matthew omits Mark's extensive narration (5:30 – 34) about Jesus' perception that power had gone out and his interaction first with the crowd and then with the woman. The result is even greater stress on Jesus' supernatural knowledge and the centrality of the woman's great faith. The "take courage, daughter" (the only place in Matthew Jesus calls a woman "daughter," showing great affection) repeats the statement in 9:2 to the paralyzed man and calms her fears. The use of "healed" (σῴζω) for healing in v. 21 and here probably stresses the combined physical and spiritual effects of the healing/salvation experience (the word means spiritual salvation in 1:21; 10:22; 19:25).[10]

9:22 And the woman was healed from that very hour (καὶ ἐσώθη ἡ γυνὴ ἀπὸ τῆς ὥρας ἐκείνης). Finally, Matthew emphasizes the finality of the healing by relating that she was saved "from that very hour." This is not a temporary healing with a future relapse (like many in our day!).[11]

9:23 When Jesus came to the house of the ruler and saw the flute players and the crowd in an uproar (Καὶ ἐλθὼν ὁ Ἰησοῦς εἰς τὴν οἰκίαν τοῦ ἄρχοντος καὶ ἰδὼν τοὺς αὐλητὰς καὶ τὸν ὄχλον θορυβούμενον). This verse is dominated by two temporal participles ("came" [ἐλθών], "saw" [ἰδών]) that carry the action forward. The scene returns to the situation of the ruler whose daughter has just died. Jesus now arrives at his house and looks over the scene.

9. Davies and Allison, *Matthew*, 2:128. See also Manfred Hutter, "Ein altorientalischer Bittgestus in Matt 9:20 – 22," *ZNW* 75 (1984): 133 – 35, who shows that touching a hem was an ancient symbol for deep trust and prayer, thus highlighting her faith.

10. As elsewhere, "save" (σῴζω) means that physical healing has also become spiritual healing.

11. Vernon K. Robbins, "The Woman Who Touched Jesus' Garment: Socio-Rhetorical Analysis of the Synoptic Accounts," *NTS* 33 (1987): 502 – 15, provides an interesting study of the three accounts and their different rhetorical purposes. He finds Matthew to center on the dialogue and the theology of healing.

The emphasis in Jewish funerals was on loud mourning, and families would hire professional mourners (cf. 2 Chr 35:25, where Jeremiah composes a lament to Josiah, one of the tasks of professional mourners; Jer 9:17 – 20) as well as "flute players," professional musicians hired for many public occasions, including funerals. The Jewish people did not embalm corpses and so had to bury them within twenty-four hours. The scene is quite tumultuous.

9:24 ... he said, "Go away, for the girl is not dead but asleep" (ἔλεγεν, Ἀναχωρεῖτε, οὐ γὰρ ἀπέθανεν τὸ κοράσιον ἀλλὰ καθεύδει). Jesus, knowing that he is about to raise the "girl" (τὸ κοράσιον, a diminutive of κόρη, "girl"; but in Jewish terms, at twelve years old [Mark 5:42] she is almost ready for marriage) to life, tells the mourners to leave; they will no longer be needed. As in the case of fasting above, there is no more need for grief but only for joy. "She sleeps" (καθεύδει) is a euphemism for death (Acts 13:36; 1 Thess 4:14, 5:10; Eph 5:14), but Jesus uses it metaphorically to say her death is merely temporary, just a short "sleep."[12]

9:24 And they laughed at him (καὶ κατεγέλων αὐτοῦ). The ridicule (the imperfect is dramatic for effect) is certainly occasioned by Jesus' statement that she is only sleeping (they interpret him literally), and Matthew uses it to underscore not their mockery but the reality of the miracle. The little girl is truly dead.

9:25 Now when the crowd was driven out, he came and took her by the hand, and the girl rose up (ὅτε δὲ ἐξεβλήθη ὁ ὄχλος, εἰσελθὼν ἐκράτησεν τῆς χειρὸς αὐτῆς, καὶ ἠγέρθη τὸ κοράσιον). The picture is of Jesus forcefully "casting out" (ἐκβάλλω, a strong verb used elsewhere for casting out demons) the mourners.[13] As with the hemorrhaging woman, she is healed by touch. This is a tender scene, as he almost gallantly takes her by the hand[14] and raises her up, except this is a resurrection from the dead! As promised in 9:19, she "rises" (ἠγέρθη) not just from her bed but from death. This is the first of three such raisings from the dead (cf. the widow's son in Luke 7:11 – 17 and Lazarus in John 11; cf. Matt 11:5, where this is a sign that Messiah has come).[15]

9:26 And the news about this spread throughout the whole region (καὶ ἐξῆλθεν ἡ φήμη αὕτη εἰς ὅλην τὴν γῆν ἐκείνην). This is a major theme of this section, as Jesus' fame continues to grow (9:8, 26, 31, 33). In Mark 5:43 Jesus tells the family to say nothing, but they are unable to keep quiet. Matthew centers only on the spreading report. The region might be that surrounding Capernaum but more likely is all of Galilee.

12. Some have inferred that she actually was only in a coma (primarily the rationalists of the past, like Schleiermacher), but this can hardly be the case in the presence of professional mourners.

13. See Gerd Theissen, *The Miracle Stories of the Early Christian Tradition* (Edinburgh: T&T Clark, 1983), 61, as noted in Davies and Allison, *Matthew*, 2:132.

14. Wallace, 132, notes that κρατέω with the genitive (as here) stresses a gentle, tender touch, while with the accusative it connotes seizing the hand forcefully.

15. E. R. Kalin, "Matthew 9:18 – 26: An Exercise in Redaction Criticism," *CurTM* 15 (1988): 39 – 47, makes a good point that Matthew has redacted the story from Mark to emphasize the fulfillment of Jesus' declaration to the Baptist in 11:5, "the dead are raised."

Theology in Application

Most of the themes in this passage have already been explored elsewhere and so will have a shorter discussion at this point.

1. The Authority of Jesus at a Climax

This is the primary theme of the whole unit of 8:1–9:34. Yet it reaches a high point here as Jesus progresses from healing a serious illness to raising the dead. Every kind of supernatural miracle has occurred in this section — nature miracle, exorcism, healing miracle, and now the ultimate occurs as a harbinger of the climax that becomes the center point of history, the resurrection of Christ himself. The one who has the power to raise a little girl has the power also to conquer death himself.

2. Compassion for the Unfortunate

This was a major theme in the first set of miracles as well as in 9:9–13. Here this theme too climaxes, for Jesus in both cases makes himself ritually unclean first by being touched by a woman with menstrual bleeding and second by touching a corpse. This is often called the "hermeneutic of love," i.e., a willingness to break Jewish taboos in order to help the suffering. Here too is a lesson for us that challenges our unwillingness to do the same for the needy. Mercy for the hurting and suffering around us should be the hallmark of the church, but it is all too rare.

3. Faith and the Individual

Faith allows a person to participate in the work of God. Both the woman and the father of the girl are characterized by humility and a total dependence on Christ. It is true that Jesus does not depend on the faith of the participants to work his healing power, but it is faith that turns healing into σῴζω, i.e., a salvific experience. God is sovereign over this world, and through faith, namely a God-dependent lifestyle, we experience his sovereignty at the depths of our being.

4. Being Raised Physically as Well as Spiritually

This miracle is not only proleptic of Jesus' resurrection but of the greatest miracle of all — the raising of a soul to eternal life. John 14:12 says it best: "All who have faith in me will do the works I have been doing, and they will do even greater things than these, because I am going to the Father." What is the "greater" miracle? Bringing eternal life to the lost. Then those who have found life in him will experience the final raising of the dead at the eschaton (1 Cor 15:22–23, 51–53; 1 Thess 4:16–17).

CHAPTER 37

Matthew 9:27 – 31

Literary Context

This section follows naturally the raising of the dead miracle, as both are signs of the messianic age in 11:5. Also, this continues the climaxing of Jesus' authority in his miracles, as this too is a miracle par excellence. No blind man had ever been healed before (John 9:32); the only story close is the opening of the servant's eyes in 2 Kgs 6:17, who sees the heavenly host. For the Jews the healing of the blind would be proof positive that the Messiah had indeed arrived (Isa 35:5, "Then will the eyes of the blind be opened").

III. The Kingdom Comes with Authority (8:1 – 11:1)
- **A. Authority and Discipleship in Jesus' Ministry (8:1 – 9:34)**
  - **5. Three Healing Miracles Showing Compassion (9:18 – 34)**
    - a. Healing a Woman and Raising a Young Girl (9:18 – 26)
    - ➦ **b. Healing Two Blind Men (9:27 – 31)**
    - c. Exorcizing a Young Man (9:32 – 34)

Main Idea

The themes here are similar to the previous miracle stories — the authority of Jesus, the faith of the participants, and the publicity that ensued. The third of these is highlighted because of the reappearance of the "messianic secret" (see 8:4), as the two men are unable to keep quiet after experiencing the healing power of Jesus.

Translation

Matthew 9:27-31

27a	Setting	As Jesus was leaving there,
b	Action	**two blind men followed him,**
c	Entreaty	crying out and saying,
d		*"Son of David, have mercy on us."*
28a	Setting	After he had entered the house,
b	Action	**the blind men came to him,**
c	Question	and **Jesus asked them,**
d		*"Do you believe that I am able to do this?"*
e	Answer	**They answered him,**
f		*"Yes, Lord."*
29a	Action	**Then he touched their eyes, saying,**
b	Pronouncement	*"According to your faith let it be done to you."*
30a	Result/Healing	And **their eyes were opened.**
b	Warning	**Then Jesus warned them sternly,**
c		*"See that no one knows of this,"*
31a	Result/Response	but **they went out and spread the news about him throughout the whole region.**

Structure and Literary Form

This miracle story is a doublet with the similar healing of two blind men in 20:29 – 34, itself a triple tradition story (= the Bartimaeus episode of Mark 10:46 – 52; Luke 18:35 – 43). It is common to call this a fabrication built on the triple tradition story of ch. 20.[1] There are striking similarities with 20:29 – 34: two blind men; "Have mercy on us, Son of David"; Jesus' touching their eyes; and the healing. However, there are equally striking differences: Galilee vs. Jericho; following Jesus vs. sitting by the road; a house scene vs. a road scene; the persistence of the blind men in the face of rebuke in 20:31; the question about their faith here; and the spreading of the news in this story vs. following him there.

In other words, these are separate stories[2] used by Matthew to highlight Jesus' authority over blindness. The structure follows many of the miracle stories, with the problem identified, a plea for help, Jesus' compassionate touch, and the resultant proclamation of Jesus' miraculous power.

1. So Held, "Matthew as Interpreter," 219 – 20; Grundmann, *Matthäus*, 276; Gnilka, *Matthäusevangelium*, 1:344; Schnackenburg, *Matthew*, 91 – 92; Gundry, *Matthew*, 176.

2. See Carson, "Matthew," 232; Hagner, *Matthew 1 – 13*, 252; Blomberg, *Matthew*, 162; Morris, *Matthew*, 233.

Exegetical Outline

- **I. The Coming of the Blind Men (9:27)**
  - A. Following Jesus (v. 27a)
  - B. The cry for mercy from the Son of David (v. 27b)
- **II. The Interrogation in the House (9:28)**
  - A. They seek audience with the Davidic Messiah (v. 28a)
  - B. Jesus questions them about faith (v. 28b)
- **III. The Miracle and Its Aftermath (9:29 – 31)**
  - A. Jesus touches and heals them (vv. 29 – 30a)
  - B. Jesus warns them to tell no one (v. 30b)
  - C. They spread the news everywhere (v. 31)

Explanation of the Text

9:27 As Jesus was leaving[3] there, two blind men followed him (Καὶ παράγοντι ἐκεῖθεν τῷ Ἰησοῦ ἠκολούθησαν αὐτῷ δύο τυφλοί). Matthew ties this with the previous miracle by emphasizing Jesus' departure "from there" (ἐκεῖθεν), possibly from the ruler's home or from the vicinity of the previous miracles, namely, the vicinity around Capernaum (9:1, 9). Either way he goes to "the house" (9:28), either his own home or the one where he is staying (we do not really know whether he had a home of his own, cf. 8:20). As he proceeds, he is "followed" by two blind men (on Matthew's tendency to have two, see on 8:28).

Eye trouble is common in Palestine, with the bright sun and the constant dust.[4] Moreover, there were religious repercussions, as blindness was often regarded as punishment for sin (Gen 19:11; 2 Kgs 6:18; John 9:1 – 3; *b. Šabb.* 108b – 9a) and could keep a man from joining the priesthood (Lev 21:20).[5] So these men were doubly tragic figures.

9:27 ... crying out and saying, "Son of David, have mercy on us" (κράζοντες καὶ λέγοντες, Ἐλέησον ἡμᾶς, υἱὸς Δαυίδ). Matthew stresses the seriousness of their cry to show their desperate plight. Their cry for "mercy" fits the theme of the compassionate Christ we have already seen and is taken from the psalms (Ps 4:1; 6:2; 9:13; 26:11; 30:10; et al.). He will respond. Matthew has already stressed the Davidic nature of Jesus' messianic office in the genealogy of 1:1 – 17 (see esp. on 1:1). The cry is rather remarkable on their lips, for no one as yet has come close to understanding this aspect of Jesus (except for the demons).

Many have noted that the Son of David title is often associated with the needy and with Jesus' healing (9:27; 12:23; 15:22; 20:30 – 31 [= Mark 10:47 – 48; Luke 18:38 – 39]) ministry, perhaps to link Jesus with David's son, Solomon, possibly known as a healer;[6] but more likely it is affirming Jesus as the true Messiah of Israel who heals the

3. Again a temporal participle as in vv. 8, 9, 18, 23, 28.

4. See Morris, *Matthew*, 233.

5. See Davies and Allison, *Matthew*, 2:135.

6. Klaus Berger, "Die königlichen Messiastraditionen des Neuen Testaments," *NTS* 20 (1973 – 74): 3 – 9; Dennis C. Duling, "Solomon, Exorcism, and the Son of David, " *HTR* 68 (1975): 235 – 52; idem, "The Therapeutic Son of David: An Element in Matthew's Christological Apologetic," *NTS* 24 (1978): 392 – 410; Davies and Allison, *Matthew*, 135 – 36; contra Ulrich Luz, *Matthew 8 – 20* (trans. N. C. Linns; Minneapolis: Augsburg, 2002), 47 – 48; France, *Gospel of Matthew*, 366 – 67, who say there is little Jewish evidence for Solomon as a healer.

nation's sick. In this sense the two blind men represent true Israel responding properly to the call of God in contrast to the leaders (12:22 – 24).[7] They believe the messianic promises of Isa 35:5, "Then will the eyes of the blind be opened." The healing of the blind was viewed as the messianic miracle par excellence, and these two men view Jesus as the Messiah, the heir of David.

9:28 After he had entered the house, the blind men came to him, and Jesus asked them, "Do you believe that I am able to do this?" (ἐλθόντι δὲ εἰς τὴν οἰκίαν προσῆλθον αὐτῷ οἱ τυφλοί, καὶ λέγει αὐτοῖς ὁ Ἰησοῦς, Πιστεύετε ὅτι δύναμαι τοῦτο ποιῆσαι;). The "house" (note the articular τὴν οἰκίαν) could be Peter's or the one Jesus was staying in (see above). Jesus does not respond immediately to their plea, probably to question them about their faith and possibly to avoid making the miracle public (9:30). Matthew more than any other gospel writer wants to develop the importance of faith (present tense "you believe" [πιστεύετε] is dramatic here) in Jesus' healing ministry (cf. 8:2, 10, 13; 9:2, 18, 22, 28 – 29). δύναμαι here means "have the power to"; Jesus is testing their faith in his wonder-working power as Messiah.

As stated several times above, this is not because faith is essential to Jesus' power to heal. But it is critical to the spiritual experience of the one being healed. Through faith, healing becomes more than a physical experience (see on 8:10); it becomes "salvation" (σῴζω; see on 9:21, 22). Here alone does Jesus ask if the men have faith. He is well aware of the answer, for their faith has already been shown in "Son of David, have mercy on us." So Jesus is doing this to draw the men into the experience, to ascertain the level of their faith.

9:28 They answered him, "Yes, Lord" (λέγουσιν αὐτῷ, Ναί, κύριε). The response of the two blind men is immediate and decisive. It is difficult to know how much to read into "Lord" (κύριε). Since the men have already affirmed him as "Son of David," it should not be weakened to "Yes, sir." At the same time, they can hardly understand him as the cosmic Lord. Probably it is messianic. The emphasis is on the depth and certainty of their faith. Marshall summarizes "Lord" well, calling it

> the normal address by sympathetic, committed people to Jesus, sometimes corresponding to the use of "Rabbi" in Mark. Although this term need be no more than a basic title of respect, the frequency of usage and the contextual indicators suggest that there is a rather high degree of reverence in its use.[8]

9:29 – 30 Then he touched their eyes, saying, "According to your faith let it be done to you." And their eyes were opened. (τότε ἥψατο τῶν ὀφθαλμῶν αὐτῶν λέγων, Κατὰ τὴν πίστιν ὑμῶν γενηθήτω ὑμῖν. καὶ ἠνεῴχθησαν αὐτῶν οἱ ὀφθαλμοί). Healing via touch is a frequent method of Jesus in Matthew (8:3, 15; 9:25; 14:36; 20:34) and represents the compassionate touch of the Son of David. The phrase "according to faith" (κατὰ τὴν πίστιν) does not mean faith was the basis of their healing — Jesus' sovereign authority is the sole basis — but rather that Jesus is responding to the fact of their faith. Bruner translates it well: "You believe; you have it."[9] There is no meritorious aspect to faith; rather, it allows one to participate in the God-given blessing (cf. the eighteen uses of "faith" [πίστις] in Rom 3:21 – 4:20), to be touched spiritually as well as physically.

7. So Luz, *Matthew 8 – 20*, 48.

8. I. Howard Marshall, *New Testament Theology: Many Witnesses, One Gospel* (Downers Grove, IL: IVP, 2004), 112.

9. Bruner, *Christbook*, 349.

9:30 Then Jesus warned them sternly, "See that no one knows of this" (καὶ ἐνεβριμήθη αὐτοῖς ὁ Ἰησοῦς λέγων, Ὁρᾶτε μηδεὶς γινωσκέτω). The "messianic secret" is better known in Mark than in Matthew but appears here often as well (see on 8:4, cf. also 12:16; 16:20; 17:9). Jesus did not want his messianic nature bandied about because the Jewish people expected only a messianic king but not a suffering Servant (Jesus' disciples made the same mistake). The language here is particularly strong, with ἐνεβριμήθη (meaning "filled with anger"[10] in John 11:33, 38) a stern admonition here, almost a rebuke. Jesus could not be more direct; he wanted no one to know.

9:31 But they went out and spread the news about him throughout the whole region (οἱ δὲ ἐξελθόντες διεφήμισαν αὐτὸν ἐν ὅλῃ τῇ γῇ ἐκείνῃ). Scholars are divided as to whether this is active disobedience[11] or whether the message is that when Jesus touches your life you cannot be silent.[12] There are probably aspects of both here. The men are so overwhelmed with the incredible miracle they have experienced that no amount of warning can keep them silent, so they disobey Jesus. Yet it is doubtful that Matthew is emphasizing their disobedience. The emphasis is on Jesus' desire to avoid publicity and the impossibility of remaining silent when touched by Jesus. So as in 9:26, the news spreads throughout Galilee.

Theology in Application

Again, the themes here repeat earlier stories, especially the absolute authority of Jesus as "Lord" (9:28). The new aspect is the healing of the blind, and as in the raising of the dead in the previous miracle, this is the greatest of miracles. These two culminate the power and authority of Jesus as Lord of all.

1. All Can Come to Jesus and Be Healed

The two blind men had no historical reason to suppose they could be healed; it had never happened before. Yet their belief that Jesus was the Davidic Messiah led them to believe that Isa 35:5 could finally come true, and they came to him. The healing presence of Christ — physical and spiritual — is still available today. It is not based on any merit of our own but on the gracious compassion and mercy of God.

2. Faith as Participation in God's Merciful Work

As stated above, faith is an appropriating force, not a meritorious deed. The blind men were healed not on the basis of the quality of their faith but because they threw themselves on the mercy of Jesus. By faith we enter into God's sovereign deeds and experience them spiritually; faith turns an event into a relationship, as we experience God as well as his work.

10. See George R. Beasley-Murray, *John* (WBC 36; Waco, TX: Word, 1987), 192 – 93, who lists the commentaries on John by Westcott, Hoskyns, Barrett, Brown (to which can be added Schnackenburg, Carson, Whitaker, Osborne).

11. Davies and Allison, *Matthew*, 2:138, who say that the tendency to "mute" the clear meaning of the language began as early as Chrysostom; Morris, *Matthew*, 235.

12. Hagner, *Matthew 1 – 13*, 254.

Matthew 9:32 – 34

CHAPTER 38

Literary Context

This final miracle of this section repeats the exorcism of 8:28 – 34. It is connected to the previous healing of the blind in the sense that this man has a speech impediment. Many consider 9:27 – 34 a unit and label this the healing of the physical senses (seeing, speaking, hearing). That is true, but still 9:18 – 34 certainly forms the final triad of miracles and completes the picture of Jesus' great authority. It provides a natural conclusion for the ten miracles of 8:1 – 9:34.

III. The Kingdom Comes with Authority (8:1 – 11:1)
- **A. Authority and Discipleship in Jesus' Ministry (8:1 – 9:34)**
  - **5. Three Healing Miracles Showing Compassion (9:18 – 34)**
    - a. Healing a Woman and Raising a Young Girl (9:18 – 26)
    - b. Healing Two Blind Men (9:27 – 31)
    - ➦ **c. Exorcizing a Young Man (9:32 – 34)**

Main Idea

Most likely the deafness is emphasized more than the demon-possession so that it can stand with the healing of the blind men (9:27 – 31) and conclude the wondrous display of the authority of Jesus Messiah, Son of David, over all physical impairments. Also, this is a further fulfillment of the messianic prophecy of Isa 35:5 – 6, "Then will the eyes of the blind be opened . . . and the mute tongue shout for joy" (cf. also 11:5), thereby preparing for the list in 11:5, "The blind receive their sight and the lame walk, the lepers are cleansed and the deaf hear." Finally, the contrast in the reactions of the crowds and Pharisees sums up the twin themes of Jesus' popularity and opposition.

Translation

Matthew 9:32-34

32a	Setting	As the blind men were going out,
b	Action	**look, a demon-possessed man who could not speak was brought to Jesus.**
33a	Action	After the demon had been cast out,
b	Result/Healing	**the man . . . spoke who had been unable to talk.**
c	Reaction #1	**The crowds were astonished and said,**
d		*"Nothing like this has ever been seen in Israel."*
34a	Reaction #2 (Contrast 33c)	But **the Pharisees said,**
b		*"He is casting out demons by the prince of demons."*

Literary Form and Structure

This is another doublet (like 9:27 – 31) with a similar healing of the deaf in 12:22 – 24, and again many critical scholars believe this to be a Matthean fabrication to emphasize Jesus' healing power. However, once more that is unnecessary, for there are critical differences between the stories, with the demon-possessed man in ch. 12 not only mute but blind as well, and there Jesus "heals" him rather than exorcizes him, with the people asking, "Could this be the Son of David?" It is more likely that Matthew simply adds another of the many miracle stories rather than making it up. The structure here reflects others of the same ilk, with Jesus casting out the demon, the crowd marveling, and the Pharisees rejecting Jesus by attributing his power to Satan.

Exegetical Outline

➦ **I. The Miracle (9:32 – 33a)**
- A. A demon-possessed mute brought to Jesus (v. 32)
- B. Jesus casts out the demon (v. 33a)

II. The Two Reactions (9:33b – 34)
- A. The crowd is astonished (v. 33b)
- B. The leaders accuse Jesus of demon-possession (v. 34)

Explanation of the Text

9:32 As the blind men were going out, look, a demon-possessed man who could not speak was brought to Jesus (Αὐτῶν δὲ ἐξερχομένων ἰδοὺ προσήνεγκαν αὐτῷ ἄνθρωπον κωφὸν δαιμονιζόμενον). The temporal genitive absolute (see vv. 10, 18, 33) "they were going out" (αὐτῶν ἐξερχομένων) could refer to Jesus and his disciples leaving, but the connection with v. 31 and the two healed men "going out" makes it almost certain that it refers to their departure. Matthew thus provides a strong link between the two miracle stories.

The term translated here as "could not speak" (κωφός) can refer to a deaf or a dumb man, but the fact that the man talks after being healed in v. 33 means he is unable to speak (he could have been a deaf-mute, for they are often connected). Demons often used illness to torture people, as in 12:22 (blind and mute), 15:22, 28 (suffering), and 17:14 – 18 (epilepsy).

9:33 After the demon had been cast out, the man who had been unable to talk spoke (καὶ ἐκβληθέντος τοῦ δαιμονίου ἐλάλησεν ὁ κωφός). The request to heal the man is presupposed, as is the actual event. Matthew centers on the results. The term "cast out" (ἐκβάλλω) is the normal word used for casting out demons, describing a violent act in which the demon is expelled from the person. With the exorcism, the man is healed and able to speak.

9:33 The crowds were astonished and said, "Nothing like this has ever been seen in Israel" (καὶ ἐθαύμασαν οἱ ὄχλοι λέγοντες, Οὐδέποτε ἐφάνη οὕτως ἐν τῷ Ἰσραήλ). The incredulous wonder of the onlookers is a frequent theme (8:27; 15:31; 21:20), though not nearly as dominant here as in Mark 1:21 – 45. Still, their comment sums up all the miracles Jesus has performed, especially the last triad (raising the dead, healing the blind and mute, casting out a demon). The broad statement "nothing ... ever been seen" provides a climax, almost as if even Elijah could not match such deeds. Jesus is the great healing prophet like nothing ever before seen. The Messiah has arrived, and God's promises are about to be consummated!

9:34 But the Pharisees said, "He is casting out demons by the prince of demons" (οἱ δὲ Φαρισαῖοι ἔλεγον, Ἐν τῷ ἄρχοντι τῶν δαιμονίων ἐκβάλλει τὰ δαιμόνια).[1] The imperfect "said" (ἔλεγον) after the aorist of v. 33 places this charge in the foreground of the action[2] and stresses the ongoing spread of this false premise. The contrast between the response of the crowds and the Pharisees could hardly be more stark. The former are filled with wonder, but the Pharisees make the opposite conclusion and accuse Jesus himself with being demon-possessed. Since he is the great teacher and wonder worker, it must be Satan, "the prince of demons" who has given him such great power.

Notice again that the Pharisees have already rejected Jesus completely. They cannot deny his great power; it has been demonstrated again and again. Thus, they can only conclude that since such authority could not have come from God, it must have come from Satan. Again, Mark 2:1 – 3:6, 3:20 – 35 is more dynamic in tracing the

1. Some manuscripts from the Western textual tradition (D it$^{a, d, k}$ syr^{s}) omit this verse, and some like Theodore Zahn consider it added due to influence from 12:24 or perhaps Luke 11:15. However, the overwhelming manuscript evidence from its inclusion in the other traditions, including both Alexandrian and Byzantine, makes it very likely that it is authentic.

2. See Porter, *Idioms*, 23 – 25.

developing opposition to Jesus, but Matthew still contains the motif, and this sums up the theme thus far (cf. 2:7 – 10; 8:10 – 12; 9:3 – 4, 11, 14) and at the same time prepares for the rejection theme that follows (10:17, 21 – 23, 25; 11:2, 20 – 24; 12:14, 22 – 24). Here they are obviously countering the awe of the crowds and trying to convince them of the error of their reaction to Jesus.

Theology in Application

This miracle closes the important section of 8:1 – 9:34, and it is time to provide a general summary of the themes covered in it. This final triad of miracles functions as a conclusion to the section and contains all of the themes:

1. Jesus Has Authority as the Healing Royal Messiah

The primary motif throughout is the authority of the Lord Messiah. Every type of miracle is found here — power over nature, healing, exorcism, raising the dead. Never before had anything like this been seen, both in the quantity and the quality of the miracles. Jesus cast out demons with just a word, and he healed with a touch. Gone are the lengthy incantations and the elaborate ritual. He is indeed the Son of David, the Messiah who heals the ills of the nation. As in John 5:36; 10:25; 14:11, Jesus' miracles are witnesses to the reality that he is indeed "God with us" (Matt 1:23).

2. Jesus Calls for Faith in Those He Heals

Faith is not a necessary ingredient in Jesus' healing, but it turns "healing" (θεραπεύω) into "salvation" (σῴζω) and brings the person into the process. Faith that in the OT was in Yahweh is now in Jesus as the divine agent of God. God has now decisively intervened in salvation history and brought salvation and spiritual (as well as physical) healing to the world.

3. In Jesus the OT Promises Have Been Decisively Fulfilled

In the last two miracles of this section Isa 35:5 – 6 has come to fruition (preparing for 11:5) and further demonstrates Matthew's theme of OT fulfillment (see 1:1 – 17; 22 – 23; 2:15, 17 – 18, 23; 4:14 – 16; 8:17). Christ is the Messiah who completes the OT promises and relives the experiences of Israel. For Matthew the OT looked forward to Christ and prepared the way for him. As Davies and Allison write:

> So while the OT gives meaning to Matthew's story of Jesus, it is not less true that Matthew's story of Jesus gives meaning to the OT. The Matthean perspective can be illustrated and put this way: when reading 9:27 – 34 one should think of Isa 35:5 – 6, and when reading Isa 35:5 – 6 one should think of Matt 9:27 – 34.[3]

3. Davies and Allison, *Matthew*, 2:140.

4. No Neutrality When Encountering Christ

The crowds increasingly hold Jesus in awe, while the leaders increasingly reject and oppose him. It is common to think that "seekers" are neutral, interested yet not ready to make a commitment. This is somewhat true, but we must remember that every service or Christian activity they attend, they leave having rejected Christ again. As such they grow increasingly hardened to the gospel, gradually shifting from a crowdlike attitude to a leaderlike attitude. Neutrality is not an option!

5. Miracles Are Deeds as Well as Transparent Parables of Jesus' Relationship with Humanity

Luz speaks of two ways this transparency works out. (1) These stories are indirectly transparent as the "church's foundation story," since the events relate to the way God has established the kingdom community as the new Israel. (2) They are directly transparent as "the basis of personal experience," since the church is also given authority to perform miracles (10:1, 8).[4] So the work of Jesus in these chapters is constitutive of the church's new walk with God and power to perform great works for God.

4. Luz, *Matthew 8 – 20*, 52 – 53.

CHAPTER 39

Matthew 9:35 – 38

Introduction to the Mission Discourse (Matthew 9:35 – 11:1)

Matthew's editorial brilliance continues in this section. The opening verse (9:35) parallels 4:23 and frames chs. 5 – 9 with a summary of Jesus' missionary activity and healing power. It also parallels 11:1 and establishes a two-step process that draws the section together around Jesus' authority and compassion in his mission.

In this immediate section Matthew collapses Mark's commission (Mark 3:13 – 19 = Matt 10:1 – 4) and his mission discourse (Mark 6:7 – 13 = Matt 10:9 – 13) into a single episode in order to stress the disciple's involvement in Jesus' mission. In addition, Matthew has used Q material[1] (9:37 – 38 = Luke 10:2; 10:9 – 10 = Luke 9:3 and 10:4; 10:18 – 20 = Luke 12:11 – 12; 10:24 = Luke 6:40; 10:26 – 33 = Luke 12:2 – 9; 10:34 – 36 = Luke 12:51 – 53; 10:37 – 38 = Luke 14:25 – 27; 10:39 = Luke 17:33) and of course his own special material, most likely his own reminiscence. It is possible that this is constructed along the lines of God's commissioning of Moses in Exod 3:1 – 4:17,[2] with the disciples sent out on a new exodus in their mission.

The result is a powerful section in which Jesus goes way beyond the pedagogy of his day (disciples of rabbis did little but memorize the teachings of their master) by involving the disciples in his ministry and passing on to them his own authority *at the very beginning of their training*! Moreover, he uses the material as a preview of what is to come in the ensuing chapters,[3] so that it functions as an anticipation of the later missionary activity. Finally, the discourse itself widens the perspective from the immediate mission of the Twelve (10:5 – 15) to the subsequent mission of the church (10:16 – 42), and from the Jewish mission (10:1 – 15) to the coming

1. H. Weder, "Die Suche nach den Söhnen und Töchtern des Friedens: Auslegung der Botenrede der Logienquelle (Matt 10 und Luke 10)," *Zeichen der Zeit* 44 (1991): 54 – 59, argues that the two mission discourses of Matt 10 and Luke 10 derived in their main contours from Q.

2. See Robert E. Morosco, "Matthew's Formation of a Commissioning Type-Scene out of the Story of Jesus' Commissioning of the Twelve," *JBL* 103 (1984): 539 – 56. It is probably better to see this as a commissioning based on OT commissionings in general, but certainly Exod 3 – 4 is a precursor.

3. Luz, *Matthew 8 – 20*, 60, gives several examples: 10:6 (cf. 15:24; 28:18 – 20); 10:15 (cf. 11:20 – 24); 10:17 – 22 (cf. 24:9 – 14); 10:25 (cf. 12:22 – 30); 10:38 – 39 (cf. 16:16 – 21; 27:31 – 56); 10:40 – 42 (cf. 18:1 – 14; 25:31 – 46).

Gentile mission (10:16 – 42). The latter especially centers on the certainty of rejection, persecution, and even death as they follow Jesus on his mission.

There is general agreement on a basic breakdown into 9:35 – 38; 10:1 – 4, 5 – 15, 16 – 23, 24 – 25, 26 – 31, 32 – 33, 34 – 36, 37 – 39, 40 – 42. Most also accept 9:35 – 10:4 as the introduction. I will follow Weaver in breaking the discourse proper into three major sections, each one ending with an *amēn* saying: 10:5 – 15, 16 – 23, 24 – 42.[4]

Literary Context

Matthew 9:35 – 38 functions as a theological primer to the Mission Discourse. Jesus begins by telling his disciples that the mission is a part of his ministry (9:35) and a result of his compassion (v. 36). His teaching and deeds were the focus of chs. 5 – 9, and they are framed by the summaries of 4:23 and 9:35. Moreover, the call to the disciples to pray for workers is continued in 10:1 – 4, where Jesus commissions them to be the very workers for whom they have prayed.

III. The Kingdom Comes with Authority (8:1 – 11:1)
B. Second Discourse: Mission and Opposition (9:35 – 11:1)
1. Introduction (9:35 – 10:4)
➦ **a. The Call for Workers (9:35 – 38)**
b. The Commissioning of the Twelve (10:1 – 4)

Main Idea

The disciples' mission continues Jesus "teaching" and "preaching" the gospel (9:35); moreover, by repeating the themes of 4:23, it shows that this mission is the very one Jesus has been doing all along. Through his teaching (chs. 5 – 7) and miraculous deeds (chs. 8 – 9), the harvest has been readied, and it is time to get to work. So the disciples are called on to intercede with God for more workers and then commissioned to become those very workers.

4. Dorothy J. Weaver, *Matthew's Missionary Discourse: A Literary Critical Analysis* (JSNTSup 38; Sheffield: JSOT Press, 1990), 74. Davies and Allison, *Matthew*, 2:160 – 62, have developed a chiastic outline that is interesting and viable but not ultimately compelling:

Narrative introduction (9:35 – 10:4)
A Introductions to missionaries and their reception (10:5 – 15)
B Tribulation and familial division (10:16 – 23)
C Jesus and his disciples are called Beelzebul (10:24 – 25)
D Consolation and encouragement (10:26 – 31)
C' Jesus and his disciples confess/deny each other (10:32 – 33)
B' Tribulation and familial division (10:34 – 39)
A' Reception of missionaries and its reward (10:40 – 42)
Narrative conclusion (11:1)

Translation

Matthew 9:35-38

35a	Summary	**Jesus went throughout all the towns and villages**
b	Action	teaching in their synagogues,
c	Action	preaching the gospel of the kingdom, and
d	Action	healing every disease and illness.
36a	Setting	When he saw the crowds,
b	Response	**he had compassion on them**
c	Basis for 35b	because they were harassed and helpless,
d	Comparison	like sheep without a shepherd.
37a		**Then he told his disciples,**
b	Assertion/Aphorism	*"The harvest is huge, but the laborers are few,*
38a	Command/Exhortation	so *pray to the Lord of the harvest that he send out workers into his harvest."*

Structure and Literary Form

This combines a summary passage with a pronouncement story centering on the metaphor of a ripe harvest for the mission Jesus is sharing with his disciples. It is common to see three parts: the summary (v. 35), the description of Jesus' compassion for the people (v. 36), and the call to the disciples to pray (vv. 37 – 38). However, it may be better to see two groups of two, with the description of Jesus' mission (summary and compassion, vv. 35 – 36), and Jesus' challenge to the disciples (the harvest need and the call for prayer, vv. 37 – 38).

Exegetical Outline

➦ **I. Description of Jesus' Mission (9:35 – 36)**
   A. Teaching, preaching, and miracles in all the towns (v. 35)
   B. Compassion for the crowds (v. 36)

II. The Call for Prayer (9:37 – 38)
   A. The need for workers (v. 37)
   B. Call to pray for workers (v. 38)

Explanation of the Text

9:35 Jesus went throughout all the towns and villages (Καὶ περιῆγεν ὁ Ἰησοῦς τὰς πόλεις πάσας καὶ τὰς κώμας). In 4:23 Jesus ministered "around all of Galilee"; here he makes a second mission trip through the entire region. The central theme in this verse is πάς, found three times in v. 35 (cf. 28:18 – 20). Jesus' ministry is completely comprehensive; he has come for every person and ministers to everyone with whom he comes in contact. Matthew may also be hinting here of a ministry beyond Galilee (as exemplified in his ministry in Gentile lands in 8:18, 23, 28 – 34). There is a universal aura here.

9:35 ... teaching in their synagogues, preaching the gospel of the kingdom, and healing every disease and illness (διδάσκων ἐν ταῖς συναγωγαῖς αὐτῶν καὶ κηρύσσων τὸ εὐαγγέλιον τῆς βασιλείας καὶ θεραπεύων πᾶσαν νόσον καὶ πᾶσαν μαλακίαν). This repeats 4:23 almost verbatim and summarizes his ministry as teaching, preaching, and healing (all circumstantial participles, see on v. 18), undoubtedly referring especially to the material in chs. 5 – 9. Heretofore Jesus has conducted his mission virtually singlehandedly, and his disciples have remained in the background.[5] That is about to change, as the passive disciples are to be commissioned as active agents in the divine mission, reenacting each aspect of Jesus' work. In that sense, this is the end of an era. The phrase "gospel of the kingdom" is important in Matthew (4:23; 9:35; 24:14) and means Jesus' joyful news concerns the inbreaking kingdom, that is, the new reign of God in him.

9:36 When he saw[6] the crowds, he had compassion on them because they were harassed and helpless, like sheep without a shepherd (Ἰδὼν δὲ τοὺς ὄχλους ἐσπλαγχνίσθη περὶ αὐτῶν, ὅτι ἦσαν ἐσκυλμένοι καὶ ἐρριμμένοι ὡσεὶ πρόβατα μὴ ἔχοντα ποιμένα). As Jesus ministered to the "crowds," he "had compassion" (ἐσπλαγχνίσθη), a strong verb that literally refers to "visceral emotions" and here connotes "filled with compassion" for a person's plight. The reason for Jesus' great pity is that the people were essentially rudderless because their "shepherds," the leaders of Israel, had failed them. Two verbs describe their position: ἐσκυλμένοι, meaning to be "harassed, weary, beaten, troubled," and ἐρριμμένοι, meaning to be "thrown down, helpless, confused."

The idea of "sheep without a shepherd"[7] is frequent in the OT (esp. Ezek 34:5 – 6, but also Num 27:17; 1 Kgs 22:17; 2 Chr 18:16; Zech 10:2; cf. Jdt 11:19), always concerning the failure of Israel's leaders. In Ezek 34 God had to rescue the nation because the false shepherds, the leaders, had failed them. So the people here have no one to guide them and are "the lost sheep of the house of Israel" (10:6; 15:24),[8] so that Jesus feels great pity for their helpless state. This picture fits the crowds closely, for they flock after Jesus but have no purpose or direction. They are enamored with him but unwilling to make a commitment. They have been "beaten up" by the leaders but are helpless to do anything about it. The answer is found in 2:6, in the prophecy of Mic 5:2 that from Bethlehem would come "a ruler who will shepherd ... Israel." That answer is standing before them, but they do not realize it.

9:37 Then he told his disciples, "The harvest is huge, but the laborers are few" (τότε λέγει τοῖς μαθηταῖς αὐτοῦ, Ὁ μὲν θερισμὸς πολύς, οἱ δὲ ἐργάται ὀλίγοι). Harvest imagery in the OT was generally used for future judgment (Isa 24:13, 27:12; Hos 6:11; Joel 3:13), and Matthew uses it this way in 3:12; 13:30, 39. Here, however, it functions positively for a harvest of souls.[9] The harvesters

5. Weaver, *Missionary Discourse*, 76.

6. This is a temporal participle like vv. 8, 9, 23.

7. Davies and Allison, *Matthew*, 2:148, see in this an implicit reference to Jesus as the messianic shepherd and then see Moses typology (a shepherd in Exod 3:1) in Jesus as the final Moses-type redeemer. This is certainly to read much more into the text than is warranted, for there is no real emphasis on Jesus as the true shepherd, let alone on a Moses typology (surely David would be a better model if the imagery were here, cf. Ezek 34:23).

8. See Hagner, *Matthew 1 – 13*, 260.

9. On this positive rather than negative use of "harvest," see Hengel, *Charismatic Leader*, 75; Schnackenburg, *Matthew*, 94; France, *Gospel of Matthew*, 373.

are not to be the angels (13:39) but the disciples; this is not final judgment but mission.[10] At that time, there are not many of them. In his ministry Jesus has proven just how large the harvest really is, so the need is great.

9:38 "... so pray to the Lord of the harvest that he send out workers into his harvest" (δεήθητε οὖν τοῦ κυρίου τοῦ θερισμοῦ ὅπως ἐκβάλῃ ἐργάτας εἰς τὸν θερισμὸν αὐτοῦ). The solution is concerted prayer. When the going gets tough, the tough get on their knees! God, not Jesus, is "Lord of the harvest," and he alone has the sovereign authority to govern the harvest. Albright and Mann call this one "the chief harvester," the one who hires and fires workers,[11] so it is he who will authorize the workers for the eschatological harvest to come.

Many believe the "workers" are mainly those of Matthew's church, but there is little reason for this, as if Matthew has put these words on Jesus' lips (though see below). Jesus would more likely then ask the disciples to pray that others might join their band of followers and become harvesters. Yet in the context there is an even better interpretation. In 4:19 Jesus promised the disciples he would "make [them] fish for people," but up to this time he has performed the mission by himself. He now begins to fulfill the promise of 4:19 and involves the disciples in his mission in two stages: first by having them pray for workers (here) and second by commissioning them to become the very workers they have been praying for (10:1 – 4). Weaver draws two conclusions: (1) Jesus is telling his disciples he will not complete God's mission by himself; (2) for the first time he calls "his disciple to take specific and crucial action in regard to his ministry," a major shift in which they are now an essential part of Jesus' mission.[12]

Theology in Application

This is a turning point in Matthew's story of Jesus, as he switches to a new kind on rabbi-disciple relationship — not just teaching the disciples but also involving them in his ministry and mission. The significance of this is far-reaching for us as well.

1. Serving the Lord in Church

It is not enough just to attend church; we must begin serving the Lord in and through the church. Too many people in our ruggedly individualistic society are content simply to sit in the service and listen. Jesus does not allow that; he demands we get to work and use our gifts to enhance the body (cf. Rom 12:3 – 8; 1 Cor 12:12 – 27; Eph 4:15 – 16). For too many "Christians," Jesus is little more than the last line item on their portfolio — medical insurance, accident insurance, mortgage insurance, life insurance, and now eternal life insurance, paid for by church

10. However, Blaine Charette, "A Harvest for the People? An Interpretation of Matthew 98.37f," *JSNT* 38 (1990): 29 – 35, believes this is not a call to mission, since there is no OT background for such. Rather, the harvest image centers on the blessings to come in the new age of salvation (Hos 6:11; Joel 3:18; Amos 9:13 – 15). The mission aspect is found in vv. 35 – 36.

11. Albright and Mann, *Matthew*, 114.

12. Weaver, *Missionary Discourse*, 79 – 80.

attendance. They are playing games with their eternal destiny, and they must wake up to the demands of discipleship — they *must* get involved!

2. A Universal Mission

The importance of "all" in 9:35 must be recognized. The model Jesus gives us portrays a ministry to everyone with need, physical or spiritual. For instance, there used to be debates in mission circles between evangelism and social concern. That is the disjunctive fallacy, turning a both-and into an either-or. Mission is incomplete without a balance between the two. In Third World situations, social concern is the best evangelistic tool. In our churches too, we have too easily bought into the homogeneous principle and ministered only to our own kind. It should be called the homogeneous fallacy! It has limited value for evangelism, but not for church growth, at least not according to Scripture (Acts 6:1 – 6; Eph 2:11 – 18). It will work but is a secular tool, built on market analysis rather than biblical principles.

3. The Compassionate Heart of Christ

Bruner says, "Mission is not motivated by Jesus' disgust for people because they are such sinners ... (but) by the simpler fact of Jesus' compassion for lost people."[13] Too often missionaries have a patriarchal air about them and bring Western civilization as much as the gospel. We need to love the people and their cultures when we go and to treasure the opportunity to show God's love for them. Jesus saw their helplessness, and his heart went out to them. The same love and compassion must motivate our ministry today.

4. The Work of God's Harvest Demands Workers

As stated above, the historical meaning of v. 37 is that Jesus was involving the disciples in his mission for the first time. Yet the contextualization does involve Matthew's church and indeed our church as well. God's harvest is every bit as ripe today as it was in Jesus' day, and every Christian is called to follow the mission parameters of Acts 1:8, "first to (our) Jerusalem, then to (our) Judea, and then to the uttermost parts of the earth."

5. Relationship of Mission and Prayer

The mission is God's work, and our primary task is prayer. Accoridng to Bruner, "it is in Matthew's interest that the church learn that mission is a divine matter, that mission is *missio dei*, and that the closest we can get to the proper allocation of resources and to the recruitment of personnel is prayer."[14] Too often ministry is

13. Bruner, *Christbook*, 363.

14. Ibid., 365.

human-centered and market-driven, with the Lord effectively left out of it. Such ministry may be successful, but it will be like the church of Sardis in Rev 3:1: "you have a reputation of being alive, but you are dead." The church moves forward on its knees, and as Paul stated, "I planted the seed, Apollos watered it, but God has been making it grow" (1 Cor 3:6). Prayer is faith in action and provides the power that alone makes for a successful ministry.

CHAPTER 40

Matthew 10:1 – 4

Literary Context

This second part of the introduction to the Mission Discourse provides the answer to the prayer for workers in 9:37. The workers are to be the disciples themselves. The great salvation-historical switch to the disciples as agents in the divine mission began with that prayer and now culminates in their own commissioning to service in Jesus' work.

III. The Kingdom Comes with Authority (8:1 – 11:1)

B. Second Discourse: Mission and Opposition (9:35 – 11:1)

1. Introduction (9:35 – 10:4)

a. The Call for Workers (9:35 – 38)

➦ **b. The Commissioning of the Twelve (10:1 – 4)**

Main Idea

The mission movement anticipated in 4:19 and 9:38 now comes to fruition as Jesus commissions his followers as "apostles" (agents "sent" from God) and gives them authority over demons and illness. They now become "the Twelve" (the first time this term is used in Matthew), the righteous remnant who represent the twelve tribes in the new Israel, the church.

Translation

Matthew 10:1-4

1a	Setting/Action	**Jesus called his twelve disciples to him, and**
b	Action	**gave them authority to drive out unclean spirits and**
		to heal every disease and illness.
2a	List	Now **the names of the twelve apostles are as follows:**
b		First, Simon who is called Peter and his brother Andrew,
c		as well as James son of Zebedee and his brother John,
3a		Philip and Bartholomew,
b	Description	Thomas and Matthew the tax collector,
c		James the son of Alphaeus and Thaddaeus,
4a		Simon the Cananaean and Judas Iscariot,
b	Description	who also betrayed him.

Structure and Literary Form

This, of course, is a commissioning narrative[1] (although I like Hagner's term "empowering" better because of the centrality of "authority" [ἐξουσία]) and consists of two parts, the commissioning (v. 1) and the names of the twelve disciples (vv. 2 – 4). Davies and Allison tell us the function of the names: "Unlike a genealogy, in which the names outline a pre-history, a list of students indicates a post-history. In our gospel the genealogy in 1:2 – 17 shows Jesus' pre-history to lie in Israel, in Abraham's descendents, while the list of disciples in chapter 10 shows his post-history to be in the church."[2]

Exegetical Outline

➡ **I. The Commissioning service (10:1)**
- A. The call (v. 1a)
- B. The empowering (v. 1b)

II. The List of the Twelve (10:2 – 4)

Explanation of the Text

10:1 Jesus called[3] his twelve disciples to him (Καὶ προσκαλεσάμενος τοὺς δώδεκα μαθητάς αὐτοῦ). The disciples were already with him (9:35 – 38), so this is probably a semitechnical phrase to emphasize an official commissioning ceremony called at Jesus' initiative. The disciples have prayed for God

1. It is a triple tradition passage (v. 1 = Mark 6:7; Luke 9:1; vv. 2 – 4 = Mark 3:16 – 19; Luke 6:13b – 16).

2. Davies and Allison, *Matthew*, 2:150.

3. Here we have another of Matthew's many circumstantial participles that functions virtually as a main verb (see on 4:20).

to act (9:38), and now in Jesus he does. The disciples become the very laborers they have prayed for God to send.

We learn for the first time that the disciples whom Jesus has been gathering (4:18 – 22; 9:9) were to constitute "twelve" (three times in vv. 1, 2, 5).[4] Unlike Mark (Mark 3:13 – 19), Matthew has not involved the disciples earlier. Jesus establishes his ministry fully (4:23 – 9:34) and then calls his followers to follow his model. They have been passive observers but now are to be active participants. The choice of the number twelve is, of course, highly symbolic. The Twelve represent the twelve patriarchs and the twelve tribes as the initiators of the new kingdom community, the new Israel (cf. 19:28 – 30).

10:1 . . . and gave them authority to drive out unclean spirits and to heal every disease and illness (ἔδωκεν αὐτοῖς ἐξουσίαν πνευμάτων ἀκαθάρτων ὥστε ἐκβάλλειν αὐτὰ καὶ θεραπεύειν πᾶσαν νόσον καὶ πᾶσαν μαλακίαν). The primary theme in chs. 8 – 9 was Jesus' "authority" (ἐξουσία) over every infirmity and calamity (see esp. 8:9; 9:6, 8), and he now passes that on to the Twelve. This is another remarkable aspect; they are not just sent out (to fail or succeed on their own) but are given the very authority God and Jesus share! Jesus is the "stronger" power who has bound Satan in his own fortress (Mark 3:27 = Matt 12:29), and he now gives that very power to his disciples.

Every exorcism is a binding of Satan (see 12:29), and the Twelve now have the authority "to drive out unclean spirits."[5] Moreover, "every disease and illness" (note the stress on "all" [πᾶς]; they are given Jesus' power over "all" infirmities!) here is exactly the same Greek phrase found in 4:23; 9:35 and demonstrates even more that the very authority/power Jesus possesses has now been transferred to his followers. They will continue the work of God in Jesus and are empowered for that very task.

10:2 Now the names of the twelve apostles are as follows (Τῶν δὲ δώδεκα ἀποστόλων τὰ ὀνόματά ἐστιν ταῦτα). Matthew provides an official list of the names of those who will launch the new kingdom community, the church. For the only time in his gospel, he calls them "apostles," a term debated[6] but likely derived from the Hebrew *šāliaḥ* and reflecting the rabbinic idea of the *šāliaḥ* as an agent "sent" to represent a person. This is critical in the "sent one" motif in the gospel of John[7] and in the use of "apostle" (ἀπόστολος) in Acts (28x) and Paul (33x). Here the emphasis is that they are already authoritative agents of Jesus and of God.

10:2 First, Simon who is called Peter and his brother Andrew, as well as James son of[8] Zebedee and his brother John (πρῶτος Σίμων ὁ λεγόμενος Πέτρος καὶ Ἀνδρέας ὁ ἀδελφὸς αὐτοῦ, καὶ Ἰάκωβος ὁ τοῦ Ζεβεδαίου καὶ Ἰωάννης

4. In the past, several (e.g., Bultmann, *Theology of the New Testament*, 1:37; Beare, *Matthew*, 239 – 40) have doubted the historicity of choosing twelve disciples on the grounds that it was a later eschatological creation of the early church. However, the band of twelve is pervasive not only in the gospels but in Acts and Paul (1 Cor 15:5, the earliest creed) and undoubtedly was the act of the historical Jesus. For arguments, see Scot McKnight, "Jesus and the Twelve," *BBR* 11 (2001): 203 – 31 (esp. 205 – 10); Schnabel, *Early Christian Mission*, 1:294 – 95.

5. "Unclean spirit" occurs only here and in 12:43 in Matthew but is common in Mark to emphasize how abhorrent and evil they are.

6. See F. H. Agnew, "The Origin of the New Testament Apostle-Concept: A Review of Research," *JBL* 105 (1986): 75 – 96. Since the rabbinic evidence stems from the second century, many doubt that the concept was present in NT times. However, its use in John as well as in 2 Cor 8:23; Phil 2:25 favors this idea in the NT (cf. also Davies and Allison, *Matthew*, 2:154; Witherington, *Matthew*, 315).

7. See Andreas Köstenberger, *The Missions of Jesus and the Disciples according to the Fourth Gospel* (Grand Rapids: Eerdmans, 1998), 96 – 121, 180 – 98.

8. This is a Greek idiom in which the article stands for "son of."

ὁ ἀδελφὸς αὐτοῦ). The list is given in six pairs, probably to stress the Deuteronomic demand for two witnesses (Deut 17:6, 19:15, also reflected in the Jewish practice of sending officials in pairs, *b. Sanh.* 26b) and possibly a reflection of Mark 6:7 ("he began to send them out two by two"). There are three other lists: Mark 3:16 – 19; Luke 6:13 – 16; Acts 1:13. The order is different in them, and some of the names change. Each will be dealt with as they come up.

Matthew begins with the first four Jesus called in 4:18 – 22 and lists them in the order found there: Simon and Andrew, James and John. Simon is labeled "first" (πρῶτος, most define this as "first among equals"), and we are told he was later "called Peter." Both labels reflect the fact that he became "the rock" (prophesied by Jesus when he first met Simon in John 1:42), the first leader of the apostolic band after Jesus' death (see also Matt 16:18 – 19). Andrew is prominent in John 1:35 – 51 but was not included for some reason in Jesus' inner circle (Peter, James, and John), who were privileged to be invited to the raising of Jairus's daughter, the transfiguration, and Gethsemane. James and John are called "the sons of thunder" in Mark 3:17, perhaps due to their loudness or tempers but also perhaps with a positive eschatological nuance, that they will share the "eschatological thunderstorm" with Jesus.[9]

10:3 Philip and Bartholomew, Thomas and Matthew the tax collector (Φίλιππος καὶ Βαρθολομαῖος, Θωμᾶς καὶ Μαθθαῖος ὁ τελώνης). Carson and Wilkins surmise that the disciples may have been divided into smaller groups of four, each with a leader, since in all four passages Peter, Philip, and James the son of Alphaeus head up a list of four disciples (with the order varying only within the lists of four).[10] This cannot be proven but is viable. Philip is not the same as the Philip of Acts 7 – 8; he does not appear anywhere else in the Synoptics but does play a role in John 1:43 – 51; 6:5; 12:21 – 22; 14:8 – 14. Bartholomew is not mentioned anywhere else but may be the Nathanael of John 1:44 – 50, mainly on the basis of his association with Philip both in John 1 and in all three Synoptic lists.

Thomas is called "Didymus" ("Twin," also the meaning of "Thomas" in Aramaic) in John 11:16, 21:2 and is often known as "doubting Thomas" because of John 20:24 – 29. There is a good likelihood that church tradition correctly notes that later he evangelized in India.[11] Matthew identifies himself as a "tax collector," reflecting his story in 9:9 – 13.

10:3 James the son of Alphaeus and Thaddaeus (Ἰάκωβος ὁ τοῦ Ἁλφαίου καὶ Θαδδαῖος). James son of Alphaeus could be Levi's brother (also a "son of Alphaeus" in Mark 2:14). Others link him with Clopeas (Luke 24:18) or with James the younger, son of Mary in Mark 15:40; Matt 27:56; Luke 24:10, but that is uncertain.[12] Thaddeus[13] is probably the same person as "Judas son of James" in Luke 6:16 and Acts 1:13. It was common in the ancient world to have more than one name (e.g., Saul/Paul), and he may have taken the name Thaddaeus (perhaps a nickname meaning "beloved") in order not to be identified with Judas Iscariot.

10:4 Simon the Cananaean and Judas Iscariot, who also betrayed him (Σίμων ὁ Καναναῖος καὶ Ἰούδας ὁ Ἰσκαριώτης ὁ καὶ παραδοὺς αὐτόν).

9. See Marcus, *Mark 1 – 8*, 264.

10. Carson, "Matthew," 237; Wilkins, *Matthew*, 386 – 87.

11. See the evidence presented in Schnabel, *Early Christian Mission*, 1:880 – 95.

12. See Michael J. Wilkins, "Disciples," *DJG*, 180.

13. Many manuscripts have expanded this to "Thaddaeus called Lebbaios" or even "Lebbaeus, whose surname was Thaddaeus" (KJV), but the Alexandrian, Western, Caesarean, and Egyptian readings agree on the simpler "Thaddaeus," and this is to be preferred. See Metzger, *Textual Commentary*, 26.

Simon the Cananaean is the same as "Simon the Zealot" in Luke 6:15 and Acts 1:13 (καναναῖος is Aramaic for "zealot"). Zealots were nationalists and insurrectionists who fought against the Romans and in the 60s (when they became an official Jewish group like the Pharisees or Sadducees) were the principal cause of the great war that lead to the destruction of the temple. Simon would have been one of the nationalists who became a follower of Jesus.[14]

Judas Iscariot[15] is mentioned more in Matthew than any other disciple except Peter. In fact, these are the only two whose future is told — one the rock of the church and the other the betrayer of the Savior. Why did Jesus select such a one? It is doubtful that he was unaware of the type of person he was; some think Jesus chose Judas to fulfill prophecy. John 12:6 says that as treasurer of the group, he was a thief and often stole from it.

Theology in Application

1. Successful Mission because of Authority Stemming from Jesus

There is only one authentic mission, the one assigned by God to Jesus, and the disciples are called to carry on that mission, not one they establish on their own. Moreover, in order to conduct that mission Jesus passes on his own authority to them. This is an astounding promise, for Jesus has demonstrated that authority first in the teaching of the Sermon on the Mount and then in the wondrous deeds of chs. 8 – 9. The disciples are given this for their mission, and through them that is passed on to the church (John 14:12; 2 Tim 2:2).

2. Choosing the Weak of This World to Demonstrate the Greatness of the Kingdom

The highest level of society represented among the Twelve was the four professional fishermen. Others included a tax collector, an insurrectionist, and a traitor. Of course, there were many leaders of society who followed him, like the centurion of 8:5 – 13, Jairus the ruler of the synagogue, and Joseph of Arimathea and Nicodemus, who together buried him. But for his closest associates and the leaders of the emerging church, Jesus deliberately selected the dregs of society (see also 1 Cor 1:26 – 29 for this point). He continues to do so with you and me. As Paul said on more than one occasion, we should rejoice in our weakness, because in our insufficiency God's strength becomes all the more manifest.

14. Several scholars (e.g., Davies and Allison, Keener — many leave it an open question) doubt that Jesus would have included an insurrectionist and believe this means Simon was "zealous for the law." However, one who would choose a tax collector would also be disposed to choose his opposite, a revolutionary. How the two got along is a real question, yet the same Jesus who brought both to God could also heal their natural animosity toward one another.

15. There is significant debate over the meaning of "Iscariot." The best option is still "man of Kerioth" (Aramaic *ʾîš qerîyôt*), though many are attracted to a Greek origin for *sikarios*, "assassin." Witherington, *Matthew*, 478, believes from this that Judas was a zealot who partly betrayed Jesus out of disillusionment with his passive messianic style of ministry. Others suggested are "false one," "man of Jericho," "redhead" or "(red) dyer" (Aramaic *sāqor*), "man from Sychar," and "bag carrier." We can never know for certain.

CHAPTER 41

Matthew 10:5 – 15

Literary Context

The disciples have been passive participants in Jesus' ministry, but now their perspective completely changes as Jesus commands active involvement in God's mission to the world. They were told to pray in 9:38; now they are told to go. This second of Matthew's discourses centers on Jesus' instructions for accomplishing the missionary task God has set for the disciples and the church (vv. 5 – 15) as well as the reception they can expect to receive from the people to whom they go (vv. 16 – 42). They have prayed, been given authority, and been divided into pairs; now it is time to engage in their active mission.

III. The Kingdom Comes with Authority (8:1 – 11:1)

B. Second Discourse: Mission and Opposition (9:35 – 11:1)

1. Introduction (9:35 – 10:4)
2. ➦ **Instructions for the Jewish Mission (10:5 – 15)**
3. Persecution in the Mission (10:16 – 23)

Main Idea

Primarily, Jesus is including the disciples in the very activities in which he has engaged, e.g., caring for the sheep of Israel (10:6 = 9:36), proclaiming the gospel of the kingdom even further (10:7 = 4:17), performing his deeds (10:8 = chs. 8 – 9),[1] going without the world's goods (10:9 – 10 = 8:20), and experiencing opposition (10:14 = 9:34).

1. Luz, *Matthew 8 – 20*, 70.

Translation

Matthew 10:5-15

Verse	Function	Text
5a	Action/Summary	**Jesus sent these twelve and instructed them, saying:**
b	Prohibition	*"Do not take the road to the Gentiles or*
c		*enter a town of the Samaritans,*
6a	Exhortation	*but go only to the lost sheep of the house of Israel.*
7a		*As you go,*
b	Exhortation	*proclaim this message:*
c		*'The kingdom of heaven has come near.'*
8a	Exhortation	*Heal the sick,*
b	Exhortation	*raise the dead,*
c	Exhortation	*cleanse lepers,*
d	Exhortation	*cast out demons.*
e	Exhortation	*Freely you have received,*
f		*so freely give.*
9a	Prohibition	*Do not acquire gold or silver or copper for your money belt.*
10a	Prohibition	*Do not take a bag for the journey, nor*
b	Prohibition	*two shirts or sandals or staff,*
c	Basis for 9a–10b	*for workers are worthy of their pay.*
11a	Exhortation	*Whatever town or village you enter,*
b		*search for some worthy person in it,*
c		*and stay there until you leave.*
12a	Exhortation	*When you enter a household,*
b		*greet it,*
13a	Circumstance #1	*and if that household is worthy,*
b	Result/Exhortation	*let your peace rest on it,*
c	Circumstance #2	*but if they are not worthy,*
d	Result/Exhortation	*let your peace return to you.*
14a	Exhortation	*Whoever does not receive you or listen to your message shake the dust off your feet*
b		*when you go outside that home or that city.*
15a	Warning/ Pronouncement	*I tell you the truth, it will be easier for the land of Sodom and Gomorrah on the day of judgment than for that town."*

Structure and Literary Form

Matthew combines Mark (Mark 6:8 – 10) and Q (Luke 9:3 – 4, 10:7) in 10:9 – 11, Q (Luke 10:6) in 10:13, and Mark (Mark 6:11) in 10:14, then uses his own special material in 10:5 – 6, 12, 15. This is an exhortation passage, with a total of sixteen imperatives falling into three subsections that describe the whole scope of their responsibilities: where they are to minister (vv. 5 – 6), what type of ministry they are to do and how they are to do it (vv. 7 – 10), and how to handle the responses/reception they receive (vv. 11 – 15).[2]

Exegetical Outline

➡ **I. Their Sphere of Ministry (10:5 – 6)**
- A. Negative: not to Gentiles or the Samaritans (v. 5)
- B. Positive: to the lost sheep of Israel (v. 6)

II. How to Conduct Their Ministry (10:7 – 10)
- A. The message: the kingdom is near (v. 7)
- B. Their deeds: healing, raising, cleansing, exorcizing (v. 8a)
- C. Ministry without charge (v. 8b – 10)
  1. Thesis 1: freely give (v. 8b)
  2. Total reliance on God rather than one's own resources (vv. 9 – 10a)
  3. Thesis 2: worthy of hire by "the Lord of the harvest" (9:38) (v. 10b)

III. Handling the Reception from the Community (10:11 – 15)
- A. Finding lodging (v. 11)
- B. Giving or withholding peace from a home (vv. 12 – 13)
- C. Rejection and judgment of the unworthy (vv. 14 – 15)

Explanation of the Text

10:5 Jesus sent these twelve and instructed[3] them (Τούτους τοὺς δώδεκα ἀπέστειλεν ὁ Ἰησοῦς παραγγείλας αὐτοῖς). As "apostles" (ἀπόστολοι, 10:2) it is natural that they be "sent" (ἀποστέλλω) by Jesus on their mission. They are the divine "agents" who take "the gospel of the kingdom" (9:35) to the Jewish people. The "instructions" are the directions by which they are to conduct their mission.[4]

10:5 ... saying: "Do not take the road to the Gentiles or enter a town of the Samaritans" (λέγων, Εἰς ὁδὸν ἐθνῶν μὴ ἀπέλθητε καὶ εἰς πόλιν

2. Weaver, *Missionary Discourse*, 83 – 84. France, *Gospel of Matthew*, 380, has a slightly different outline — to whom they are to go (vv. 5 – 6), the nature of their mission (vv. 7 – 8), and how they are to be taken care of (vv. 9 – 15).

3. Unlike v. 1 and most other places in Matthew, the circumstantial participle here is the second verb.

4. The historicity of the Mission Discourse is called into question by scholars who believe it is the creation of the later church to fit their situation (e.g., Beare, *Matthew*, 241, and his "The Mission of the Twelve and the Mission Charge: Matthew 10 and Parallels," *JBL* 89 [1970]: 1 – 13), but it is found in both the Markan and Q traditions (criterion

Σαμαριτῶν μὴ εἰσέλθητε). The use of "road" (ὁδός) with the genitive in a geographical context means "to take a road or a path to" a place.[5] The sent disciples are not to follow the road north or east to the Gentile areas, nor are they to go south to the land of the Samaritans.[6] So on this mission they are restricted to Galilee and to the Jewish people there.[7]

10:6 "... but go only to the lost sheep of the house of Israel" (πορεύεσθε δὲ μᾶλλον πρὸς τὰ πρόβατα τὰ ἀπολωλότα οἴκου Ἰσραήλ). After the aorist commands on v. 5, this verse uses the present imperative πορεύεσθε to emphasize the ongoing nature of the mission.[8] On the surface this seems to contradict the Great Commission of 28:19, which commands the disciples to "go and make disciples from all the nations." Why restrict their ministry to the Jewish people?[9] Yet this follows Jesus' own pattern, for he stayed in Galilee for the most part and in 15:24 he states that he was sent only "to the lost sheep of the house of Israel" (an epexegetical genitive — the lost sheep are all of Israel). The "lost sheep" were all the Jewish people (not a portion who are "lost," like tax collectors and sinners or the common people) and refers back to 9:36, where Jesus saw them as "harassed ... sheep without a shepherd."

At the same time, however, Jesus was willing to minister to Gentiles (8:5 – 13) and even to go to Gentile areas (8:28 – 34) and Samaritan towns (Luke 9:51 – 56; 17:11 – 19; John 4:1 – 42) to minister. He strongly includes the nations in God's salvation (Matt 8:11 – 12; 21:43; 25:32) and stresses "the significance of Jesus for the Gentiles (2:1 – 12; 4:14 – 16, 24 – 25)."[10] In fact, when Jesus said he came only for Israel (15:24), he had traveled all the way to Tyre and Sidon (two days' journey out of Galilee) and was ministering to a Canaanite woman (15:21 – 28).

The best answer to this seeming anomaly is salvation-historical, that Jesus restricted his and the disciples' ministries to the Jewish people but deliberately went to Gentile regions on occasion to prepare his disciples for their later universal mission.[11] So this command fits only the time of Jesus' ministry to his own people. Schnabel sees a twofold perspective: this short-term missionary tour is a paradigm for the permanent mission of the future, and it provides training for that later missionary activity.[12] In one sense, Paul followed

of multiple attestation) and fits closely the situation of Jesus' ministry (criterion of plausibility). For further arguments, see Carson, "Matthew," 240 – 43; Schnabel, *Early Christian Mission*, 1:290 – 93.

5. So most commentators (e.g., Carson, Gundry, Davies and Allison, Luz, Morris). BAGD, 554, says it is an objective genitive connoting "direction toward" a thing.

6. The Samaritans lived in the region between Judea and Galilee and were the result of the Assyrian practice of forced intermarriage with pagans after the fall of the northern kingdom in 722 BC. When the Jews returned from exile, they refused to accept these "half-breeds," and centuries of animosity resulted, made absolute when the Hasmonean ruler John Hyrcanus destroyed the Samaritan temple on Mount Gerizim in 128 BC. In Jesus' day the tensions were considerable.

7. Morris, *Matthew*, 245.

8. Moreover, the aorists form the background and this present the foreground of Jesus' mission command, see Porter, *Idioms*, 23 – 25.

9. Schuyler Brown, "The Twofold Representation of the Mission in Matthew's Gospel," *ST* 31 (1977): 21 – 32 (esp. 30 – 32), represents many critical scholars when he posits a situation in Matthew's community between those who wanted to restrict the mission to Israel and others who want to go to the Gentiles. This is unnecessary, for it fits Jesus' day far more closely.

10. France, *Matthew* (TNTC), 178.

11. Julius J. Scott, "Gentiles and the Ministry of Jesus: Further Observations on Matt 10:5 – 6," *JETS* 33 (1990): 161 – 69, believes that Jesus' restriction here stems from his desire to establish a remnant from the Jewish people as the new Israel as the basis for the Gentile mission.

12. Schnabel, *Early Christian Mission*, 1:293. Hagner, *Matthew 1 – 13*, 271, says Matthew also preserved this tradition as a message to his readers that God was still faithful to his covenant promises and purposes.

this pattern in his missionary journeys and in his "first to the Jew, then to the Gentile" of Rom 1:16.

10:7 As you go, proclaim this message, "The kingdom of heaven has come near" (πορευόμενοι δὲ κηρύσσετε λέγοντες ὅτι Ἤγγικεν ἡ βασιλεία τῶν οὐρανῶν). They are to continue the message of the Baptist (3:2) and Jesus (4:17). As stated in those passages, this meant that the longed-for final kingdom of God (for "kingdom of heaven," see on 3:2) is both imminent and has indeed arrived in Jesus. In Jesus, God's future kingdom is already active and present in this world.[13] Gnilka says it well: their preaching concerned "the universal, worldwide liberating and saving reign that comes from God to us, a rule that is in its essence and in its completion a reality of the future, indeed the future itself, but a reign that can already be experienced in the present as it is proclaimed and pronounced."[14]

10:8 Heal the sick, raise the dead, cleanse lepers, cast out demons (ἀσθενοῦντας θεραπεύετε, νεκροὺς ἐγείρετε, λεπροὺς καθαρίζετε, δαιμόνια ἐκβάλλετε). In 10:1 the disciples were given authority to perform the first and fourth miracles; now two more are added, and all four were performed by Jesus in chs. 8 – 9. This also prepares for 11:5, where Jesus uses these to prove to John and his messengers that he is indeed the expected Messiah. So the Twelve are to participate in Jesus' divine mission and are given his authority both in word (10:7) and in deed (10:8).

10:8 Freely you have received, so freely give (δωρεὰν ἐλάβετε, δωρεὰν δότε). The poetic balance of this aphoristic piece is impressive; the centerpiece is "freely" (δωρεάν) — the free gift of grace one has received from God must produce a life of giving. This introduces 10:9 – 10. Jesus reminds them that they received the kingdom and the gifts of the kingdom without charge. Moreover, they have received the authority to heal, raise the dead, and cast out demons as a free gift from God. Therefore, Jesus expects them to give these things to others without charge (the aorist tenses are global: this is to characterize their life as a whole). The disciples were not to profit from their ministry but use it the same way Jesus did — to help others.[15] Salvation is a free gift of grace; ministry should reflect the same selfless concerns. This is a principle that deserves more discussion among Christian leaders today. Perhaps it is so convicting that the only alternative is to act as if Jesus never said it (see "Theology in Application" below)!

10:9 Do not acquire gold or silver or copper for your money belt (Μὴ κτήσησθε χρυσὸν μηδὲ ἄργυρον μηδὲ χαλκὸν εἰς τὰς ζώνας ὑμῶν). This could mean either, "don't take money with you" or "don't charge for your services." In Mark 6:8 the former is intended, perhaps here the latter (cf. 10:8b). Missionaries are not to receive compensation for their ministry. Belts were wider than they are today, and people would tuck their tunics into their belt as well as carry coins in them.

10:10 Do not take a bag for the journey, nor two shirts (μὴ πήραν εἰς ὁδὸν μηδὲ δύο χιτῶνας). As Weaver points out,[16] the list is representative of all those items a person will need for a journey, in other words, an open-ended series. The "bag" is a

13. Keener, *Matthew*, 316. Schlatter, *Matthäus*, 330, explains well the reason why Matthew has omitted "repent"; on the basis of the other two passages, he expects the reader to know that repentance is part of the message.

14. Gnilka, *Matthäusevangelium*, 1:364, translated in Schnabel, *Early Christian Mission*, 1:295.

15. France, *Gospel of Matthew*, 383 – 84, says that like Paul (2 Cor 11:7), the disciples were not to charge for their services in contrast to pagan philosophers and teachers, who expected not only room and board but fees for their services.

16. Weaver, *Missionary Discourse*, 193 – 94.

traveler's knapsack that would carry food and provisions for the journey. The extra tunic or shirt[17] was a change of clothes as well as a pillow or cover when sleeping in the fields.

10:10 ... or sandals or staff (μηδὲ ὑποδήματα μηδὲ ῥάβδον). The prohibition of sandals (walking shoes) and staff (a walking stick often used as a weapon when endangered) is a well-known conundrum, because while Luke follows Matthew (Luke 9:3; 10:4), Mark 6:8 – 9 says to take nothing *except* staff and sandals. There have been several attempts to explain the contradiction: (1) Mark has the shepherd's crook for travel and Matthew/Luke have the shepherd's club for protection and danger (but the terms do not fit this); (2) they are different ways of saying the same truth, namely, dependence on God (doesn't solve the inconsistency); (3) Mark allows them to take a staff and sandals, while Matthew does not allow them to procure an extra (yet the other items are the same in the three accounts, so why not these?); (4) Matthew and Luke follow Q, a different set of instructions given on another occasion. This latter best explains the discrepancy.[18]

Jesus and his disciples took several mission trips, and each was a short-term experience, with Jesus stressing different theological aspects of the mission each time. Many have connected Mark's allowing staff and sandals with Exod 12:11, where the Israelites on the eve of the exodus are told to eat the Passover in haste, with staff in hand and sandals on the feet. In this way the mission may be seen as a new exodus. In Matthew/Luke it may be following a tradition similar to *m. Ber.* 9:5, "one may not enter the holy mount with his staff or with his shoes or with his money belt" (cf. also Exod 3:5 at the burning bush). This would stress the holiness of the mission.

The major point is that the mission is for serving God, not for self-aggrandizement. The purpose is to remove all material encumbrances and incentives so as to focus entirely on God's work.[19] As Witherington says, "probably what is in view is not going out and acquiring more than what one already has. 'Go as you are' is the motto."[20] At the same time, the basic principle is twofold: do not use ministry for profit, and depend on God rather than self.

10:10 For workers are worthy of their pay[21] (ἄξιος γὰρ ὁ ἐργάτης τῆς τροφῆς αὐτοῦ). At first glance this seems to contradict Jesus' prohibition against compensation. Yet its meaning stems from 9:38 and "the Lord of the harvest." The actual meaning is that missionaries should not receive pay from the people to whom they minister but accept it from "the Lord of the harvest," namely, God himself, with "worthy" (ἄξιος, first for emphasis) meaning the "appropriate pay" or reward for the laborer (*EDNT*, 1, 113). In fact, "pay" (τῆς τροφῆς) literally means, "worthy *of their food*"; the point seems to be that they are to depend on God through the hospitality of others. Rather than earning a wage, they accept hospitality and so express full dependence on God. Their trust must be in God, and their purpose must not be worldly profit but heavenly reward (6:19 – 21).

10:11 Whatever town or village you enter, search for some worthy person in it (εἰς ἣν δ' ἂν πόλιν

17. Some have thought of this as the beggar's bag, such as used by wandering cynics, but the word is quite general and hardly fits that. There is little evidence that cynic philosophers ever went to Palestine.

18. See Grant R. Osborne, "The Evangelical and Redaction Criticism: Critique and Methodology," *JETS* 22 (1979): 315 (cf. 305 – 22); Carson, "Matthew," 245; Blomberg, *Historical Reliability*, 145 – 46.

19. See Schnabel, *Early Christian Mission*, 1:297 – 98.

20. Witherington, *Matthew*, 220.

21. The genitive "of pay" (τῆς τροφῆς) may well be objective: they "deserve their pay."

ἢ κώμην εἰσέλθητε, ἐξετάσατε τίς ἐν αὐτῇ ἄξιός ἐστιν). Like Jesus (9:35) they will go to the "towns and villages" of Galilee. They are not to depend on themselves or on the success of their work (in terms of earning money) to meet their needs. Instead, they must depend on God and on those people to whom they go for their daily upkeep. The "worthy" person is probably someone willing to house the itinerant missionary for the length of the stay and so is "deserving" of the reward (BAGD, 78).

They must carefully scrutinize (the meaning of ἐξετάσατε) the inhabitants for the right place to stay, yet not for the luxurious nature of the place but for the "worthiness" of the owner. The implication is that the person is open to the message as well as the messenger (the sheep and the goats analogy of 25:31 – 46 addresses the reward and punishment for those who respond).

10:11 ... and stay there until you leave (κἀκεῖ μείνατε ἕως ἂν ἐξέλθητε). They are to "remain" there until the mission is finished. This means they should not be thinking of their selfish comfort and continue to look for a better place to stay but be satsified with their lodgings.

10:12 When you enter a household,[22] greet it (εἰσερχόμενοι δὲ εἰς τὴν οἰκίαν ἀσπάσασθε αὐτήν). Luke spells the greeting out, "When you enter a house, first say, 'Peace to this house.'" The Hebrew greeting was "*shalom*," and here it likely refers to the gospel greeting, that is, the offer of God's peace through the "gospel of the kingdom." As Keener points out, greetings were a requirement of Near Eastern social etiquette, and for the Jewish people these were also "wish-prayers" of well-being for others.[23] Jesus takes the greeting to the next level, where the wish-prayer becomes an offer of salvation, of attaining the true "peace of God."

10:13 ... and if that household is worthy, let your peace rest on it (καὶ ἐὰν μὲν ᾖ ἡ οἰκία ἀξία, ἐλθάτω ἡ εἰρήνη ὑμῶν ἐπ' αὐτήν). As stated above, the "worthiness" of the household means their receptivity to the gospel "peace." If they respond and accept the gospel, then God's peace "rests" or remains on that home (note that this peace resides in the missionary who has the authority to dispense it). Probably this goes beyond just the home in which they are lodging to the homes they visit in their evangelization of the town.

10:13 But if they are not worthy, let your peace return to you (ἐὰν δὲ μὴ ᾖ ἀξία, ἡ εἰρήνη ὑμῶν πρὸς ὑμᾶς ἐπιστραφήτω). Obviously, there is a charismatic power in the greeting, for the "peace" is virtually personified as an active force that either "rests" on a home or "returns" to the missionary. The idea here of rejection and opposition will become the dominant theme in vv. 16 – 42. Since the reception of the agent is the reception of the sender (10:40), their welcome or refusal to the missionary was tantamount to accepting or rejecting the gospel. If the peace of God were to leave a house and return to the missionary, that house would be under God's judgment.

10:14 Whoever does not receive you or listen to your message ... when you go outside that home or that city (καὶ ὃς ἂν μὴ δέξηται ὑμᾶς μηδὲ ἀκούσῃ τοὺς λόγους ὑμῶν, ἐξερχόμενοι ἔξω τῆς οἰκίας ἢ τῆς πόλεως ἐκείνης). The movement of

22. The term οἰκία means not only the house itself but the people who dwell in it. Some (e.g., Davies and Allison, *Matthew*, 2:175 – 76; Gnilka, *Matthäusevangelium*, 1:368) believe this reflects the house-church situation of Matthew's day, but that reads too much into the text. It would be natural for Jesus himself to put it this way, for Jews avoided inns as dens of iniquity (which they were), and Jesus would naturally have emphasized staying in private homes.

23. Keener, *Matthew*, 320.

the message now comes full circle. At first the emphasis was positive; the disciples were to search for a "worthy" family and stay with them (v. 11). Then it was mixed; some would receive them, others reject them (vv. 12 – 13). Now it turns completely negative; they can expect mainly rejection (vv. 14 – 15). This prepares the way for the prophecy of vv. 16 – 23 to follow.

Note that the response is twofold: rejection and refusal to listen. There is the welcome into the home and there is the openness to the message; it is these that define the "worthy" individual. The response of the rejected missionary is also twofold: leave that place and shake the dust off the feet. Both are prophetic parables of rejection in turn. When Jesus "withdrew" from a place, it often was a sign that God had rejected them (15:21; 19:1).

10:14 ... shake the dust off your feet (ἐκτινάξατε τὸν κονιορτὸν τῶν ποδῶν ὑμῶν). When Jewish people had been in Gentile areas, they would shake the unclean dust from their feet as an act of repudiation[24] (for this in the early church, see Acts 13:51; cf. 18:6). This means that God has declared the place unclean, virtually pagan, and unworthy of the "gospel of the kingdom." To continue preaching there is to cast "pearls in front of pigs" (7:6).

10:15 I tell you the truth, it will be easier for the land of Sodom and Gomorrah on the day of judgment than for that town (ἀμὴν λέγω ὑμῖν, ἀνεκτότερον ἔσται γῇ Σοδόμων καὶ Γομόρρων ἐν ἡμέρᾳ κρίσεως ἢ τῇ πόλει ἐκείνῃ). For an "amen" (ἀμήν) saying, see on 5:18, 26; this is the seventh of thirty-two in Matthew, always affirming an especially important saying as coming straight from God. Sodom and Gomorrah were the paradigm of wicked cities, their sin so great that God destroyed them completely (Gen 18 – 19), and they forever after became a euphemism for God's wrath against sin (Isa 1:9; 13:19; Jer 50:40; Amos 4:11; 2 Pet 2:6). The "day of judgment" is the final great white throne judgment of Rev 20:11 – 15, emphasized often in Matthew (Matt 11:22, 24; 12:36; cf. 5:22, 29 – 30; 8:12; 13:42, 50; 18:9; 22:13; 23:15, 33; 24:51; 25:30). The reason it will be worse is because now they have rejected God's Messiah, that "so great a salvation" that God has provided in these last days (Heb 2:3; 10:29; 12:25).

Theology in Application

This passage is incredibly rich in its significance for modern ministry. At the same time, we must be careful to delineate properly how literally we should contextualize it. Did the disciples go barefoot through their ministry, and should we? Should all ministers of the gospel go without pay? These and other issues must be carefully considered.

1. Jewish People Having a Place of Preeminence in Christian Mission

It is debated whether Rom 1:16 ("to the Jew first") is the paradigm for our day or whether it should be restricted to the first-century mission.[25] However, there is no

24. See Gundry, *Matthew*, 190; Keener, *Matthew*, 320; Morris, *Matthew*, 250; Harrington, *Matthew*, 141.

25. See Moo, *Romans*, 68 – 69, who lists Barrett and Hendrickson as holding a restricted view, adding that such attempts are "without success."

hermeneutical reason for such a restriction, especially in light of Rom 11:25 – 32 ("all Israel will be saved"). There should be a certain priority given to Jewish mission. This does not mean that every believer and every mission has to engage in such a ministry. But we must make certain that such is taking place and should support such ministries with our prayers.

2. Authority over Illness and Demons Given to the Church

The promise of 10:1, 8 still remains. Naturally, there is vociferous debate on this from the cessationist (the charismatic gifts were sign gifts meant only for the apostolic age) and Pentecostal (every believer should "seek the higher gifts" and exemplify them) sides. Yet the middle position as expressed in the Christian and Missionary Alliance ("seek not, forbid not") catches the biblical teaching best (see also "Theology in Application" on 4:23 – 25). In 1 Cor 12:11 Paul says the Spirit chooses who will receive which gift, and 1 Cor 12:29 – 30 says of each gift, "All do not practice it, do they?" (the μή expects the answer "no" to each question). Finally, "eagerly desire the greater gifts" in 1 Cor 12:31 is a plural command and refers to the church as a whole, not the individual believer.

The point is that we as the kingdom community have authority over the spirits. We do not have to follow the latest gossip coming from the popular church (e.g., that we have to ascertain the names of the demons or the territories they inhabit). The instruction is actually simple: "Heal the sick, raise the dead, cleanse lepers, cast out demons." This does not mean we control God and do whatever we wish; rather, under his sovereignty the church has been given authority, and miracles do happen (most clearly in China but actually around the world).

3. Avoiding the Profit Motive

These are difficult days when all too many well-known Christian leaders are charging huge amounts for ministry and justifying it via the secular supply-and-demand principle. Many have fee structures (always a large fee), and some own several homes and fly in their own jets. I would not want to face the Lord after such a "ministry." Jesus is absolutely clear: "Freely you have received, so freely give" (v. 8). We must remember that the first "woe" in Luke 6:24 was given to the disciples, not the crowds, "But woe to you who are rich, for you have already received your comfort." Whenever we minister for gain — whether money, fame, or power — there will be no reward in heaven but rather judgment (the meaning of "woe").

This does not mean a minister should not be paid. Paul quotes Deut 25:4 ("Do not muzzle the ox while it is treading out the grain") and Luke 10:7 ("Workers deserve their wages") to support his statement, "The elders who direct the affairs of the church well are worthy of double honor [I prefer 'pay' here]" (1 Tim 5:17 – 18; cf. 1 Cor 9:9). The balance is that the Christian leader accepts remuneration but does not demand a certain amount. Carson aptly states, "The church does not pay its ministers; rather, it provides them with resources so that they are able to serve freely.... In practice, this means that the ideal situation occurs when the church is as generous as possible, the ministers do not concern themselves with material matters and are above selfish material interest."[26] Those resources are to be sufficient but not extravagant.

In many places (e.g., America and Korea) such things have gotten out of hand. It is not wrong to accept gifts, but it is wrong to expect or even demand gifts. In the early church they did not take all of Jesus' detailed commands literally. They certainly went on mission with sandals and walking stick, and Paul and Barnabas were supported by Antioch on their missions. While Paul often supported himself on mission, he did not demand it of others yet was willing to accept gifts (e.g., 2 Cor 11:7 – 9; Phil 4:10 – 19). But they never failed to observe the theological charge behind this: depend entirely on the Lord, and never minister for profit.

4. Charismatic Authority for Special Agents of God

These "apostles" were "sent ones" and as such partook of the authority of the quintessential agent of God not only in deed but also in word. Their "greeting" was the offer of the *shalom* or "peace of God," which was an active force for salvation. It had the power to bless or curse and was a new covenant proclamation. This is developed further in John 20:21 – 23, here Jesus says, "As the Father has sent me, I am sending you," and in that passage the Godhead is the sender, and the authority is seen in 20:23, "If you forgive the sins of anyone, their sins are forgiven; if you do not forgive them, they are not forgiven." Since the Godhead speaks through the "sent ones," they have a charismatic authority in their very proclamation.

5. Expecting Opposition

This will be the theme in the rest of the Mission Discourse. Yet how do we preach this in a context where so few of us are being persecuted? I see three levels at which this is relevant for us. (1) There are more martyrs now than ever before, and the church in much of the rest of the world is suffering greatly; "remember those in prison as if you were together with them in prison" (Heb 13:3). (2) We may not be suffering opposition now, but if this nation continues to become more and more pagan (and it is), suffering may be in the near future, and we must be ready. (3) Many of us may not be mocked and made fun of because we go out of our way not to be known as committed Christians. Compromise and secularity define all too many so-called "Christians."

26. D. A. Carson, *When Jesus Confronts the World* (Grand Rapids: Baker, 1987), 125.

CHAPTER 42

Matthew 10:16 – 23

Literary Context

From the Jewish context of 10:5 – 15, Jesus now expands the horizon to the universal mission. The mission to both Jew and Gentile (preparing for 28:19) will be the perspective of the rest of the Mission Discourse. The rejection theme from vv. 13 – 15 is now expanded into a prophetic warning of the severity of the opposition the disciples will experience. As "sheep in the midst of wolves," even their families will turn against them. Also, in vv. 5 – 15 the apostles are the actors, taking the initiative with authoritative proclamation, but here they are the recipients, and other people take the initiative with active opposition, with the disciples responding in vv. 16b, 17a, 19 – 20, 23.[1]

III. The Kingdom Comes with Authority (8:1 – 11:1)

B. Second Discourse: Mission and Opposition (9:35 – 11:1)

1. Introduction (9:35 – 10:4)
2. Instructions for the Jewish Mission (10:5 – 15)
3. **Persecution in the Mission (10:16 – 23)**

Main Idea

On their mission, which will begin with Israel but extend to the Gentile lands, the disciples should expect arrest, persecution, and even death. Yet their response must not be in kind; they are to be shrewdly "innocent" and trust the Lord to give them the proper response when hauled before the courts. Moreover, the entire mission of the church, from the Jewish mission of the disciples (v. 17) to the later Gentile mission of the church (v. 18), stems from the commissioning and sending of Jesus.

1. Weaver, *Missionary Discourse*, 90.

Translation

Matthew 10:16-23

16a	Assertion	*"Look, I am sending you as sheep in the midst of wolves.*
b	Command	*Be as shrewd as serpents and as innocent as doves.*
17a	Warning	*Be on guard around people;*
b	Basis #1 for 17a	*(i) for they will deliver you to councils*
c	Basis #2 for 17a	*(ii) and beat you in their synagogues,*
18a	Basis #3 for 17a	*(iii) and you will be led before governors and kings*
b	Purpose	*for my sake as a witness*
		to them and
		the Gentiles.
19a	Setting	*Now when they deliver you up,*
b	Exhortation	*do not worry how or what you will respond,*
c	Promise/Basis for 19b	*for what you should say will be given you at that time.*
20a		*For it will not be you who speaks,*
b	Contrast	*but the Spirit of your Father who speaks through you.*
21a	Warning	*So brother will deliver brother to his death and*
		a father his child,
b		*and children will rebel against their parents and*
		have them put to death.
22a		*You will be hated by all for my name's sake,*
b	Promise	*but the one who endures to the end will be saved.*
23a	Setting	*When they persecute you in this city,*
b	Exhortation	*flee to the next.*
c	Assertion	*For I tell you the truth,*
		you will never complete your mission to the cities of Israel
d		*before the Son of Man returns."*

Structure and Literary Form

The Synoptic parallels for this are found in Mark's Olivet Discourse (vv. 17 – 22 = Mark 13:9 – 13) as well as Q (v. 16 = Luke 10:3; v. 19 = Luke 12:11 – 12). Many believe Matthew has transposed a passage from the eschatological discourse and placed it in this setting.[2] But while the great similarity in wording makes this viable, it is not totally necessary, as Jesus the itinerant teacher would have used the material in more than one setting.[3] Moreover, the switch to the universal mission does

2. Robert E. Morosco, "Redaction Criticism and the Evangelical: Matthew 10 a Test Case," *JETS* 22 (1979): 323 – 31; Grundmann, *Matthäus*, 292; Gundry, *Matthew*, 191; Hagner, *Matthew 1 – 13*, 275; Harrington, *Matthew*, 146.

3. See Carson, "Matthew," 240 – 43.

not contradict the "to Israel only" command of 10:5 – 6, for this includes Israel and Jesus has been preparing the disciples for the Gentile mission in the future (see on 8:10 – 12, 28 – 34; cf. 15:21 – 28).

This passage contains a series of prophetic warnings of future opposition and hatred that the missionary can expect when taking the kingdom truths worldwide. The passage contains a thesis statement (v. 16) followed by two sets of warning and promise statements:[4] warning of arrests and beatings (vv. 17 – 18) followed by a promise of guidance by the Spirit (vv. 19 – 20); and warning of rejection and hatred by families (vv. 21 – 22) followed by a promise of the coming of the Son of Man (v. 23).

Exegetical Outline

➦ **I. Thesis: Handling Conflict (10:16)**
- A. Model: sheep among wolves (v. 16a)
- B. Method: shrewd innocence (v. 16b)

II. Persecution and Promise in the Worldwide Mission (10:17 – 20)
- A. Persecution (vv. 17 – 18)
  1. Jewish: in the councils and synagogues (v. 17)
  2. Gentiles: before governors and kings (v. 18)
- B. Promise: the Spirit's presence (vv. 19 – 20)
  1. God will give you the words (v. 19)
  2. The Spirit will speak through you (v. 20)

III. Persecution and Promise from Family and Everyone (10:21 – 23)
- A. Betrayed to death by family (v. 21)
- B. Hated by everyone (v. 22a)
- C. Twofold promise (vv. 22b – 23)
  1. Those who remain firm will be saved (v. 22b)
  2. The coming of the Son of Man (v. 23)

Explanation of the Text

10:16 Look, I am sending you as sheep in the midst of wolves (Ἰδοὺ ἐγὼ ἀποστέλλω ὑμᾶς ὡς πρόβατα ἐν μέσῳ λύκων). This is a transition verse and as such can be seen as the final verse of 10:5 – 16 (Hill, Carson, France, Schnackenburg, Blomberg, Schnabel) or the first verse of 10:16 – 23 (Davies and Allison, Hagner, Weaver, Luz, Keener, Wilkins, Senior, France). As it introduces the strong rejection motif of vv. 17 – 23, I prefer the latter.

4. So Schnabel, *Early Christian Mission*, 1:301. He places v. 16 with the preceding paragraph (see below) but catches the arrangement of vv. 17 – 23 well.

Again, Jesus addresses them as "sent ones" (10:2, 5), with the present tense "I am sending" (ἀποστέλλω) emphasizing the ongoing nature of their mission, and he now tells what they will face. They are "sheep"[5] (building on the Jewish people as "sheep" in 9:36) placed "in the midst of wolves." Gundry observes, "The figure of sheep, which has recently represented the lost and shepherdless people of Israel (9:36; 10:6), now represents Jesus' missionaries, who are threatened by the wolflike leaders of the people. Thus a certain solidarity exists between the persecuted missionaries and the harried people; both suffer from the same source."[6] The image of a "wolf" echoes 7:15, where Jesus calls false prophets "rapacious wolves" and goes back to the use of sheep among wolves to depict Israel among the nations.[7]

10:16 Be as shrewd as serpents and as innocent as doves (γίνεσθε οὖν φρόνιμοι ὡς οἱ ὄφεις καὶ ἀκέραιοι ὡς αἱ περιστεραί). With what well may have been a proverbial saying (cf. Rom 16:19),[8] Jesus calls on his followers to be "shrewd" (φρόνιμοι) like serpents and at the same time "innocent" (ἀκέραιοι) like doves toward unbelievers while on mission as they face the snarling "wolves." The first is probably an echo of Gen 3:1, where the serpent was described as "more crafty" (φρονιμώτατος LXX) than the other animals. Here it means a shrewd, carefully calculated awareness of others, calling for a behavior that is circumspect and careful to represent the gospel in such a way as to bring people to God without provoking them.[9]

At the same time their "innocence" must be evident to all, with the demeanor of a gentle dove in relationship to others. As Wilkins says, "Without innocence the keenness of the snake is crafty, a devious menace; without keenness the innocence of a dove is naïve, helpless gullibility."[10] So the Christian is to interact with outsiders with a practical wisdom and a behavioral innocence so the kingdom truths go out with divine power without hindrance. If persecution comes, it must be unearned. Yet come it will, as we will see.

10:17 Be on guard[11] around people (προσέχετε δὲ ἀπὸ τῶν ἀνθρώπων). The Greek in the rest of this verse is chiastic: "(a) they will deliver you (b) to councils, and (b') in synagogues (a') they will beat you." Jesus first speaks of Jewish persecution in this verse and then Gentile persecution in v. 18. But the opening warning applies to both; they must be wary of those to whom they go, for arrest and physical persecution are inevitable.

10:17 ... for they will deliver you to councils and beat you in their synagogues (παραδώσουσιν γὰρ ὑμᾶς εἰς συνέδρια, καὶ ἐν ταῖς συναγωγαῖς αὐτῶν μαστιγώσουσιν ὑμᾶς). Most local "sanhedrins" or councils had a court of three judges that tried cases, and the law said that for a first offense the person was to be warned and released, but at the

5. It is difficult to know if the idea of defenseless passivity (see Keener, *Matthew*, 322) is part of the metaphor, but that is indeed emphasized in Rev 13:9 – 10.

6. Gundry, *Matthew*, 191. Yet it is clear that while the leaders are part of the wolves, the image goes beyond them to all the people to whom they go; cf. Weaver, *Missionary Discourse*, 198 n106.

7. Luz, *Matthew 8 – 20*, 87, who lists *1 En*. 89:55; *4 Ezra* 5:18; *Esther Rabbah* 10:11 on 9:2.

8. *Midr. Cant.* 2:4 calls on the Jewish people to be "sincere as doves" toward God but "as serpents" toward the Gentiles, but that is from a later time. Turner, "Matthew," 151, says, "This command inculcates wisdom accompanied by integrity, a combination of intellectual and ethical characteristics."

9. Schnabel, *Early Christian Mission*, 1:301, says it means to "behave circumspectly, prudently, carefully considering the dangers, so that their reliance on God's protection becomes evident." Witherington, *Matthew*, 218, believes this sends the disciples out as "sages," but that reads too much into the passage.

10. Wilkins, *Matthew*, 392.

11. The present "be on guard" (προσέχετε) demands ceaseless vigilance.

second offense they should be beaten (see Acts 4:18 – 21; 5:40).[12] That is the situation Jesus is envisaging. Paul says in 2 Cor 11:25 that he had been beaten with rods three times (cf. Acts 16:22); while μαστιγόω often means a "scourging" like Jesus suffered, the beating here likely refers to the flogging decreed in Deut 25:1 – 3.

10:18 And you will be led before governors and kings for my sake as a witness to them and the Gentiles (καὶ ἐπὶ ἡγεμόνας δὲ καὶ βασιλεῖς ἀχθήσεσθε ἕνεκεν ἐμοῦ εἰς μαρτύριον αὐτοῖς καὶ τοῖς ἔθνεσιν). Jesus appeared before the Roman governor Pilate, and Paul appeared before Sergius Paulus (Acts 13), Felix (Acts 24), Festus (Acts 25), and the emperor Nero himself. This was a reality, not just a mere possibility. But this will be done "for my sake" (ἕνεκεν ἐμοῦ), and the authority of Christ will be evident throughout, as seen in the fact that this dangerous situation will be "as a witness to them" (εἰς μαρτύριον αὐτοῖς), which means that Christ will turn the situation around as an opportunity for the gospel (cf. esp. Acts 24:124 – 16; 26:19 – 23, 28 – 29). This does not mean "a witness against them" (dative of disadvantage) but a positive "witness to them" (dative of advantage). In fact, not only the rulers but also all "the Gentiles" would receive the witness of such events, as exemplified in Paul's reflections on his own Roman trial in Phil 1:12 – 14. This is part of the "Gentile mission" theme in Matthew (cf. 1:5 – 6; 2:1 – 12; 4:14 – 16, 25; 8:5 – 13).

10:19 Now when they deliver you up, do not worry how or what you will respond (ὅταν δὲ παραδῶσιν ὑμᾶς, μὴ μεριμνήσητε πῶς ἢ τί λαλήσητε). It is one thing to stand before the synagogue council where you grew up, but quite another to stand before the highest officials of the Roman conquerors! The "deliver ... up" (παραδῶσιν)[13] repeats the verb of v. 17, and the forceful arrest (the same verb is used in the passion predictions [17:22; 20:18, 19] for Jesus' arrest) is presented as an inevitable event (not "if" but "when"). If you go out on mission, you *will* face opposition.

Note that the response of the missionary when arrested is not to fight back but only to proclaim the gospel (cf. Rev 13:10). Their first response to the dangerous situation is to be an absence of anxiety ("do not worry" [μὴ μεριμνήσητε], on which see 6:25), especially concerning the manner of their defense, for God will give them the Holy Spirit to turn the trial into an opportunity for witness. Whether standing before synagogue councils or kings, they are not to worry. The use of "how or what" (πῶς ἢ τί) is meant to be comprehensive — neither the manner nor the content is a problem.

10:19 For what you should say will be given you at that time (δοθήσεται γὰρ ὑμῖν ἐν ἐκείνῃ τῇ ὥρᾳ τί λαλήσητε). "Will be given" (δοθήσεται) is a divine passive, meaning "God will give" the words to say. Moreover, the disciples will be given the proper defense "at that time," when they need it. This does not mean they should not prepare their defense,[14] as if it will be a spur-of-the-moment revelation. Rather, it means that "every time" they need to defend themselves or the gospel,

12. See Douglas R. A. Hare, *The Theme of Jewish Persecution of Christians in the Gospel according to St. Matthew* (Cambridge: Cambridge Univ. Press, 1967), 43. He points out that the Mishnah stipulates thirty-nine (forty minus one) stripes.

13. Luz, *Matthew 8 – 20*, 84, calls this "the determinative catchword of the section."

14. This passage among others has been used in some traditions to mean preachers will be given their message as they walk up to the pulpit, and thus it is wrong to prepare messages beforehand. This is a clear misinterpretation of the message. Rather, Jesus means that the Spirit will inspire the believer when defending the gospel. It is in a context of the law court, not the pulpit.

God will guide them. For OT parallels, see Exod 4:12 (Moses); Ps 119:41 – 46 (when taunted, even by kings); Isa 50:4 (the Servant); Jer 1:9 (Jeremiah).

10:20 For it will not be you who speaks, but the Spirit of your Father who speaks through you (οὐ γὰρ ὑμεῖς ἐστε οἱ λαλοῦντες ἀλλὰ τὸ πνεῦμα τοῦ πατρὸς ὑμῶν τὸ λαλοῦν ἐν ὑμῖν). Davies and Allison thinks the choice of λαλέω ("speaks") rather than λέγω ("speaks") may be due to an early tendency to use λαλέω for "inspired or ecstatic utterance."[15] As the Spirit came down on Jesus at his baptism (3:16), so the Spirit alights on the missionary in time of need. France says that "this is the only passage which gives practical substance to the promise of 3:11 that Jesus would baptize his people with the Holy Spirit, in that only here is a particular gift or ability said to come to the disciples through the Spirit 'in you.'"[16]

The "speaking" (present tense to stress the repeated nature of this) is virtual prophetic utterance as the Spirit fills the captive with the same gospel power (10:12 – 13) that is exercised in his or her mission (cf. the Paraclete in John 15:26 – 27). This Spirit-inspired response highlighted the early trials before the Jews (Matt 26:64; Acts 4:8 – 12, 19 – 20; 5:29 – 32; 7:1 – 53; 21:37 – 22:21; 23:1 – 7; 28:17 – 28) and the Romans (esp. John 18:28 – 19:16; Acts 16:22 – 34; 23:10 – 26; 26:1 – 29).

10:21 So brother will deliver brother to his death and a father his child, and children will rebel against their parents and have them put to death (παραδώσει δὲ ἀδελφὸς ἀδελφὸν εἰς θάνατον καὶ πατὴρ τέκνον, καὶ ἐπαναστήσονται τέκνα ἐπὶ γονεῖς καὶ θανατώσουσιν αὐτούς). Weaver points to a twofold escalation here — from general rejection to that by actual family members, and from basic persecution to its ultimate form, death.[17] Not only will the disciple be persecuted by synagogue and government officials; they will be rejected and even sent to their deaths by their own family members (see also 10:34 – 36, where the OT parallel, Mic 7:6, is quoted). This would have been even more devastating in the first century, when the nuclear family was so much tighter than it is today. As Carson notes, conversion will bring shame on the family, and in a shame-based culture this would be deemed betrayal.[18]

I know of an instance in a Muslim land when a recent convert's wife placed ground glass in his meal, killing him; she became a hero in the region. In a similar vein, I have had students who have experienced family rejection after following Christ. Some have even had funerals conducted by their families, signifying that to them the new believer was dead! Yet this is worse, for this entails betraying one's own relatives, the missionaries, to their actual deaths. This is not hyperbole; there were many martyrs — the Baptist, Jesus, James, Peter, Paul, Antipas (Rev 2:13).

10:22 You will be hated by all for my name's sake (καὶ ἔσεσθε μισούμενοι ὑπὸ πάντων διὰ τὸ ὄνομά μου). The future periphrastic "you will be hated" (ἔσεσθε μισούμενοι) makes this all the more dynamic. These verses, with the betrayal by family members and the "hated by all" (ὑπὸ πάντων means "every group," for Jesus did not mean fellow believers or converts would hate them) tone, stem from the Jewish doctrine of the "messianic woes," a belief that surrounding the coming of the Messiah a great deal of eschatological suffering would be experienced by not only the Messiah but also his followers (Dan 9:20 – 27, 12:1 – 4; *1 En.* 80:2 – 8, 98:4 – 9; *4 Ezra* 5:11 – 13, 7:10 – 35; *Sib. Or.* 3.538 – 44; *2 Bar.* 25 – 27; cf. Matt 24:22 – 23a; Col 1:24; 1 Pet 4:12 – 19; Rev 6:11). The reason the

15. Davies and Allison, *Matthew*, 2:185.

16. France, *Gospel of Matthew*, 393.

17. Weaver, *Missionary Discourse*, 97.

18. Carson, *When Jesus Confronts the World*, 140.

world hates them is that they come in the "name" (ὄνομα) of Jesus (see on 7:22; 18:5, 20). They are hated not because of who they are but because of whom they represent.

10:22 But the one who endures to the end will be saved (ὁ δὲ ὑπομείνας εἰς τέλος οὗτος σωθήσεται). As already stated, this "enduring" does not imply active resistance but rather passive endurance (the aorist "endures" [ὑπομείνας] looks at one's life as a whole). There are two connotations: enduring the trial and standing firm for the Lord through it all.

The meaning of "to the end" (εἰς τέλος) is debated. Is it the end of the persecution (Hill, France, Morris), the end of life (Carson, Blomberg [who combine this option and the next one]), or to the end of the age (Davies and Allison, Luz, Harrington)? It is repeated in 24:13, where it could refer to the destruction of Jerusalem (the main theme of 24:3 – 28) or to the parousia (the following verse says, "then the end will come").

In this context all three may well be included. In the context of suffering in the midst of mission the end of persecution could well be in mind (the meaning of v. 23 to the disciples) — the one who remains firm throughout will partake of Christ's salvific blessings. Yet also in the context of the messianic woes the endurance refers to the end of life and indeed to the final end of all persecution at the eschaton. "Saved" here does not mean they will be rescued from death but rather that they will experience fully the blessings of salvation, both now and in eternity.

10:23 When they persecute you in this city, flee to the next (ὅταν δὲ διώκωσιν ὑμᾶς ἐν τῇ πόλει ταύτῃ, φεύγετε εἰς τὴν ἑτέραν). The persecution "in this city"[19] sums up the mission thus far, namely in "this place" and "the next place." They can expect active opposition in "this city," and when that happens they will continue to the next stage of the universal mission in "the next city." The basic point is one of realism: do not risk your life unnecessarily but continue in your mission.[20] In other words, the very fact of persecution ensures the ongoing mission from one city to the next. This provides the context for the controversial rest of the verse. In fact, the emphasis is not on fleeing persecution but on the continuance of the mission in light of v. 23b.[21]

10:23 For I tell you the truth, you will never complete your mission[22] to the cities of Israel before the Son of Man returns (ἀμὴν γὰρ λέγω ὑμῖν, οὐ μὴ τελέσητε τὰς πόλεις τοῦ Ἰσραὴλ ἕως ἂν ἔλθῃ ὁ υἱὸς τοῦ ἀνθρώπου). This "amen" (ἀμήν) saying points to a particularly significant point (see on 5:18). The meaning of this is debated. Luz sees three different meanings depending on the setting in the life of Jesus: imminent expectation, the pre-Matthean stage (with the comfort intensified), and Matthew's understanding (a hated church resting its hope on the parousia).[23] The basic problem is whether Jesus was mistaken in his belief that the

19. J. M. McDermott, "Mt. 10, 23 in Context," *BZ* 28 (1984): 230 – 40, believes v. 23a is pre-Matthean but v. 23b a redactional addition. Scot McKnight, "Jesus and the End-Time: Matthew 10:23," *SBLSP* 25 1986), 501 – 20, believes Matthew has reworked a pre-Matthean saying. More likely, both parts go back to Jesus, see Davies and Allison, *Matthew*, 2:189; Carson, "Matthew," 250 – 53.

20. See Plummer, *Matthew*, 152; Blomberg, *Matthew*, 176, who says, "Jesus calls his followers to bravery but not foolishness." Believers must not seek out persecution.

21. See Gundry, *Matthew*, 194; Weaver, *Missionary Discourse*, 100. Roman Bartnicki, "Das Trostwort an die Jünger in Matt 10,23," *TZ* 43 (1987): 564 – 67, says the purpose is entirely consolation (the mission will be successful and ongoing in spite of persecution) rather than apocalyptic expectation.

22. The wording of Hagner, *Matthew 1 – 13*, 275.

23. Luz, *Matthew 8 – 20*, 91, 94.

eschaton was imminent. Several interpretations have been given.[24]

1. This refers to Jesus' reunion with them at the end of this particular mission of the Twelve (Chrysostom).
2. It is the resurrection of Jesus (Barth).
3. It is fulfilled in Pentecost and the coming of the Spirit (Calvin).
4. It refers to Jesus' coming in judgment against Israel at the destruction of Jerusalem in AD 66 – 70 (France, Carson, Hagner, Schnabel).
5. Jesus expected the end to arrive before the disciples completed their mission but was wrong (Schweitzer).
6. Jesus expected the eschaton within a generation or so and was wrong (Hill).
7. Jesus expected a lengthy period before the end (13:24 – 33; 18:15 – 18; 19:28; 21:43; 23:32; 28:19) and so is saying that the mission to Israel is ongoing and will not conclude until the parousia (Gnilka, Davies and Allison, Blomberg, Wilkins, Turner).

This last makes the best sense. Probably "the cities of Israel" goes beyond Galilee and Judea (which would have been the disciples' understanding) to the diaspora as well (in light of the presence of the worldwide mission in vv. 18 – 22). Does the idea of completing the mission refer to continual flight or ongoing mission? The two cannot be separated, as we noted above. The sense is that even when the universal mission will be the focus of the church, the mission to Israel still must have some priority (see on 10:5 – 6).

Theology in Application

This passage is rich in mission themes, and its implications for the church today are immense. Jesus in sending his disciples out on the Jewish mission was preparing them for the later mission to the world.

1. Ready for Opponents

The church must be ready for the wolves, that is, for opponents who will not only reject but also physically abuse believers. The book of Acts testifies to the extent this can take, with the deaths of Stephen and James. Opposition stalked Paul everywhere he went. In light of this, the "sent ones" must be wise in their preparations and shrewd in their assessment of situations, yet maintaining a basic innocence that makes certain that when persecution comes, it is not deserved.

The latter has two connotations: proper behavior that does not invite reprisal, and a gentleness of demeanor that remains open to people. Bruner says it well, "His portrait of sheep among wolves was to impress upon disciple-missionaries that they are vulnerable; his portrait of snakes is to teach them not to be stupidly vulnerable."[25] Still, they must expect to be "hated by all" to whom they go, not every person but every group. Rejection is certain; the disciples will not be universally loved and

24. Combining the options in Carson, "Matthew," 250 – 53; McKnight, "Matt 10:23," 509 – 20; Davies and Allison, *Matthew*, 2:189 – 92; Morris, *Matthew*, 257 – 58. For the history of interpretation of this difficult passage, see U. Luz and M. Künzi, *Das Naherwartungslogion Matthäus 10.23: Geshichte seiner Auslegung* (Tübingen: Mohr, 1970).

25. Bruner, *Christbook*, 381.

appreciated. The reason is found in John 3:19, namely, that darkness hates the light, for the light of Christ in us removes the facade of the dark things that they are light (note the brightness of gambling halls and red-light districts) and forces them to confront their true nature. Thus the world has to be in complete opposition to the church.

2. Our Own Families

Again, that our own families can be against us is not universally experienced, but many Christians have suffered rejection from their closest relatives. In Mark 10:29 – 30 Jesus says those who have lost home and family will "receive a hundred times as much in this present age: homes, brothers, sisters, mothers, children and fields — along with persecutions." This, of course, means that in the church one will find a new family, but persecution will not cease. Jesus identifies that "new family" in Matt 12:49 – 50 as being his followers who do "the will of my Father in heaven."

3. The Spirit Will Use Every Crisis Situation to Enhance the Gospel

This is proven in the summary passages of Acts (Acts 2:47; 6:7; 9:31; 12:24; 19:20). Every crisis situation is an opportunity to watch the Spirit work, and he turns the situation around and gives increased strength to the church and to the gospel. When arrested, the Spirit will inspire the believers in their response. Our task is to both endure the opposition and remain firm for the gospel in the midst of it. The Spirit will take over from there.

4. Danger Mitigated by Promise

As the exegetical outline above suggests, this passage is organized to show that God's promises are especially with his people in their dangerous mission. Even the fact of ongoing persecution will enhance the gospel, for it will enable and guide the missionaries to keep moving from place to place (10:23a). Moreover, the opposition is framed by the presence of the Holy Spirit and the promise of vindication at the eschaton. Even in the midst of persecution God is still sovereign (the basic theme of Revelation).

5. The Theme of Imitatio Christi[26]

Everything the disciples will do in 10:5 – 23 (go to Israel, preach the kingdom truths, perform miracles, give of themselves freely, face persecution, pass from town to town, become arrested and tried) parallels what Jesus has been doing in his mission. They are sent by Jesus and emulate him in their ministry.

26. See especially Davies and Allison, *Matthew*, 2:197; Pregeant, *Matthew*, 75.

CHAPTER 43

Matthew 10:24 – 31

Literary Context

Imitatio Christi introduces the first section (10:24 – 25), then three prohibitions against fear dominate the rest (10:26, 28, 31). This latter provides a break from the heavy predictions of persecution that come before and after this passage. Disciples imitate Christ not only in persecution but also in fearless proclamation.

III. The Kingdom Comes with Authority (8:1 – 11:1)
B. Second Discourse: Mission and Opposition (9:35 – 11:1)
4. Sharing in Jesus' Mission (10:24 – 42)
➦ **a. No Need to Fear (10:24 – 31)**
b. Confession and Conflict in Discipleship (10:32 – 42)

Main Idea

There are four reasons why one need not fear in the face of universal persecution.

1. As disciples, they are to be like their Master and so should expect persecution and not be surprised by it (vv. 24 – 25).
2. The time is coming when everything will be disclosed, so God's servants must boldly proclaim what Jesus has taught them (vv. 26 – 27).
3. Those who can only kill the body are not worth fear; that must be reserved for the one who is Judge at the final judgment (v. 28).
4. God knows every part of his creation, and human beings are at the apex of that creation, so he will watch out for us (vv. 29 – 31).

Translation

Matthew 10:24-31

24a	Comparison	*[A] "Disciples are not above their teacher*
b		*[B] nor are slaves above their master.*
25a	Inference	*[A′] It is sufficient for disciples to be like their teacher and*
b		*[B′] for slaves to be like their master.*
c	Example	*If they call the master of the house 'Beelzebul,'*
d		*how much more will they vilify the members of the household.*
26a	Prohibition	*So do not be afraid of them,*
b	Basis #1 of 26a	*[C] for there is nothing hidden that will not be revealed or*
c	Parallel 26b	*[C′] secret that will not be made known.*
27a	Command	*[D] What I tell you in the darkness, proclaim in the light,*
b	Parallel 27a	*[D′] and what is whispered in your ear, shout from the rooftops.*
28a	Restatement of 26a	*And do not ever be afraid of those*
b	Basis #2 of 26a	*who put the body to death but cannot kill the soul,*
c	Antithesis of 26a	*but continue to fear the one who has the power to destroy both soul and body in Gehenna.*
29a	Question (Rhetorical)	*Are not two sparrows sold for a penny?*
b	Aphorism	*Yet not one of them will fall to the ground without the knowledge and consent of your Father.*
30a	Aphorism	*Indeed, even the very hairs of your head are all numbered.*
31a	Restatement of 26a	*So do not ever be afraid.*
b	Basis #3 of 26a	*You are worth more than many sparrows."*

Structure and Literary Form

This is a Q passage (vv. 24 – 25a = Luke 6:40; vv. 26 – 31 = Luke 12:2 – 7) with v. 25b a M passage (a doublet of 12:24). The paragraph consists of a proverbial saying (vv. 24 – 25) and three imperative/indicative combinations (vv. 26 – 27, 28, 29 – 31) that comfort the beleaguered missionary with the knowledge that God is sovereign over all their suffering and oppression.

Exegetical Outline

➦ I. The Relationship of Teacher and Disciple (10:24 – 25)

A. Disciples not above the teacher (v. 24)

B. Disciples emulate the teacher (v. 25a)

C. Disciples vilified like their teacher (v. 25b)

II. Commands Not to Fear (10:26 – 31)
- A. First reason: the time of disclosure (vv. 26 – 27)
  1. The hidden truths made public (v. 26)
  2. The open proclamation of the kingdom truths (v. 27)
- B. Second reason: whom you should fear (v. 28)
  1. Negative: don't fear your persecutors (v. 28a)
  2. Positive: fear only God (v. 28b)
- C. Third reason: the care of a loving Father (vv. 29 – 31)
  1. His care for insignificant sparrows (v. 29)
  2. He knows all about you (v. 30)
  3. Your greater worth (v. 31)

Explanation of the Text

10:24 Disciples are not above their[1] teacher (Οὐκ ἔστιν μαθητὴς ὑπὲρ τὸν διδάσκαλον). This is almost a tautology, for in the Jewish world a disciple was considered a virtual slave of his rabbi, as seen in the next clause. So naturally no disciple could ever be "greater than" his teacher. The point here is that if the teacher is maligned, why should the student expect to be accepted? I tell my students regularly to read 2 Cor 11:16 – 33 every six months and ask, "Am I better than Paul? Should I expect everything always to go well in my ministry?" Christian leaders today do not know how to handle adversity!

10:24 ... nor are slaves above their master (οὐδὲ δοῦλος ὑπὲρ τὸν κύριον αὐτοῦ). This states the first maxim another way. Disciples were the slaves of their rabbi, and the rabbi was "lord" over his followers (see also on 3:11). Paul frequently called himself the "slave" (δοῦλος) of Christ (Rom 1:1; 1 Cor 7:22; Gal 1:10; Phil 1:1; et al.), and the sealing of the saints in Rev 7:3 – 4 meant they were God's slaves, connoting ownership, allegiance, and protection.[2] This is true here as well. Philo said it well (*De cherubim* 107), "To be the slave of God is the highest boast of man, a treasure more precious not only than freedom, but than wealth and power and all that mortals most cherish."[3]

10:25 It is sufficient for disciples to be[4] like their teacher and for slaves to be like their master (ἀρκετὸν τῷ μαθητῇ ἵνα γένηται ὡς ὁ διδάσκαλος αὐτοῦ καὶ ὁ δοῦλος ὡς ὁ κύριος αὐτοῦ). Not only are disciples/slaves not greater than their teacher/master, but it is also their goal and privilege to act like and perhaps to attain a status like their rabbi/lord. This is at the heart of discipleship, seen in the frequent use of μιμητής ("imitate") for the discipleship process (1 Cor 4:16, 11:1; Eph 5:1; 1 Thess 1:6; cf. Phil 3:17). Jesus' disciples have been included in his ministry (Matt 4:18 – 22) and been given authority over the demonic realm (10:1) and over human illness (10:8). Christ had indeed made them "like their master."

10:25 If they call the master of the house "Beelzebul," how much more will they vilify the

1. This is an example of the article standing for the possessive pronoun, see Wallace, 215 – 16. Note the presence of the pronoun in the second half of the verse

2. See Osborne, *Revelation*, 310.

3. Quoted in Davies and Allison, *Matthew*, 2:193.

4. The Greek "that" (ἵνα) clause functions very much like the infinitive (both in Greek and in English).

members of the household (εἰ τὸν οἰκοδεσπότην Βεελζεβοὺλ ἐπεκάλεσαν, πόσῳ μᾶλλον τοὺς οἰκιακοὺς αὐτοῦ). "If" (εἰ) introduces a condition of fact, for they have already accused Jesus of this. The subject of "they call" (ἐπεκάλεσαν) is certainly the Jewish leaders, for it is they who make this charge in 9:34; 12:24. The third set of terms is now used for Jesus' relationship with the disciples — disciple/rabbi and slave/lord in vv. 24 – 25a and now master/members of the household. The patriarch of the household was sacrosanct, so if they malign him, they will naturally feel free to do much more to the mere members.

"Beelzebul" has not appeared yet in Matthew, although in 9:34 he was called "the prince of demons," the same phrase used to define "Beelzebul" in 12:24. The meaning has been disputed. It has been common (even in the NIV, but corrected in TNIV) to label this "Beelzebub" ("lord of the flies"), an ancient insult to the Canaanite deity; but the Greek has "Beelzebul," which could mean "lord of the dung" (*bāᶜēl zibbûl*), but is better "lord of the heights" — in fact a play on words with the "lord of the house" in v. 25a.[5] He was the chief God of Ekron (2 Kgs 1:2) but here is the "prince of demons," Satan (9:34; 12:24), a being who had several other names in Jewish circles — Azazel, Belial, Beliar, the Dragon, Mastema. The leaders are accusing Jesus of gaining control over demons by allying himself with Satan. The disciples should expect at least as much.

12:26 So do not be afraid of them (Μὴ οὖν φοβηθῆτε αὐτούς). There is no need to fear such adversaries ("them" [αὐτούς] refers to the leaders, as in v. 25). The aorist "be afraid" (φοβηθῆτε) is global, meaning a lack of fear is to characterize their lives. This imperative introduces and dominates the passage (see also vv. 28, 31). Christ's purpose is to encourage them that in the midst of the opposition and hatred, there is no need to fear. The sovereign God, not they, is in charge.

10:26 For there is nothing hidden that will not be revealed or secret that will not be made known (οὐδὲν γάρ ἐστιν κεκαλυμμένον ὃ οὐκ ἀποκαλυφθήσεται καὶ κρυπτὸν ὃ οὐ γνωσθήσεται). The perfect passive (divine passive — hidden by God) periphrastic "it is hidden" (ἐστιν κεκαλυμμένον) has a stative thrust; these mysteries have at all times been hidden by God. Some have interpreted this apocalyptically as the judgment day, when God will disclose all the secrets of humankind and reveal the final realities, thereby vindicating the saints and punishing their persecutors.[6] Yet while that may be the thrust in Luke 12:2 – 3, it is unlikely here. Up to this point the "gospel of the kingdom" (4:23; 9:35; 24:14; 26:13) was "hidden" and "secret" in that few had heard it. It was secret because Jesus heretofore had taught it primarily to the disciples (the Sermon on the Mount was given mainly to the disciples [5:1 – 2], and the ministry of chs. 8 – 9 consisted mainly of miracles). But now it is time on this mission to proclaim it publicly, to "reveal" these truths to all and "make them known." The passive voices mean that God will be speaking through the disciples.[7]

Yet at the same time, it is too disjunctive to make a radical separation between these two

5. E. C. B. MacLaurin, "Beelzeboul," *NovT* 20 (1978): 156 – 60; Nolland, *Matthew*, 435; Turner, "Matthew," 153.

6. So Davies and Allison, *Matthew*, 2:203; Luz, *Matthew 8 – 20*, 100 – 101 (who mentions Jerome, Hilary, Theodore of Mopsuestia, Cyril of Alexandria as holding this view); Blomberg, *Matthew*, 177.

7. This view is supported by Schlatter, *Matthäus*, 344; France, *Matthew* (TNTC), 186; Hagner, *Matthew 1 – 13*, 285; Harrington, *Matthew*, 150.

views. Although the primary thrust is present mission, there is an emphasis in the later context on final judgment as well (cf. 10:28b, 32, 33), and an inaugurated thrust is probably best — i.e., present disclosure in missionary proclamation and final vindication at the eschaton.

10:27 What I tell you in the darkness, proclaim in the light, and what is whispered in your ear, shout from the rooftops (ὃ λέγω ὑμῖν ἐν τῇ σκοτίᾳ εἴπατε ἐν τῷ φωτί, καὶ ὃ εἰς τὸ οὖς ἀκούετε κηρύξατε ἐπὶ τῶν δωμάτων). This states the same thing as v. 26, but with different metaphors. The time of "darkness" when Jesus' teaching was "whispered in your ears" refers to his private instruction of the disciples. But they in a sense have graduated, with 10:1 – 4 being their ordination service, so now they must proclaim these truths "in the light ... from the rooftops." In the first century important public announcements were given from the flat rooftops. So Jesus is saying this mission is to be one of fearless proclamation, public and powerful in its intensity.[8]

10:28 And do not ever be afraid of those who put the body to death but cannot kill the soul (καὶ μὴ φοβεῖσθε ἀπὸ τῶν ἀποκτεννόντων τὸ σῶμα, τὴν δὲ ψυχὴν μὴ δυναμένων ἀποκτεῖναι). After the aorist in v. 26a, the present prohibition μὴ φοβεῖσθε means "do not at any time be afraid" (in both clauses of v. 28). The emphasis on martyrdom echoes 10:21, where family members turn their own loved ones in to be put to death. This is the most any persecutor can do to them.

Jesus is not drawing an absolute distinction between the two parts of a human being, body and soul, as if we are a dualistic being rather than a whole person. Still, he is saying that if all a person can do is destroy your mortal body, that is nothing to fear. The most important part of a person, the soul, will live on. Moreover, we all look forward to a new "spiritual body" (1 Cor 15:44) anyway, to be received at the parousia.

10:28 ... but continue to fear the one who has the power to destroy both soul and body in Gehenna (φοβεῖσθε δὲ μᾶλλον τὸν δυνάμενον καὶ ψυχὴν καὶ σῶμα ἀπολέσαι ἐν γεέννῃ). God alone is sovereign over both the temporal body and the eternal soul. Thus he alone deserves to be feared, for he can destroy not only the body but cast the whole person into everlasting torment.[9] On "Gehenna" see 5:22; it is one of two metaphors for eternal punishment found in Matthew (for the other, see Matt 8:12). Here the final judgment noted in 10:26 is found.

10:29 Are not two sparrows sold for a penny? (οὐχὶ δύο στρουθία ἀσσαρίου πωλεῖται;). Sparrows were by far the cheapest food (considered food for the poor), as a "penny" (ἀσσαρίου, genitive of price, cf. BDF §179) was the smallest coin in the Roman world, worth one-sixteenth of a denarius, so less than an hour's wage.

10:29 Yet not one of them will fall to the ground without the knowledge and consent of[10] your Father (καὶ ἓν ἐξ αὐτῶν οὐ πεσεῖται ἐπὶ τὴν γῆν

8. It is fairly common (Davies and Allison, Hagner) to see the time of darkness as the pre-Easter period and the time of light as the post-Easter period. This is unnecessary and depends on the Sitz im Leben approaches that characterized the old redaction-critical period. In this narrative context the darkness refers to the time before the mission of ch. 10, and the mission itself is the time of light.

9. This is not a statement on the annihilation of the soul. It is clear that torment in the lake of fire is seen to be eternal punishment, not annihilation (see Matt 18:8; 25:41, 46; cf. also Rev 14:11, 19:3, 20; 20:10). As Luz says (*Matthew 8 – 20*, 102n), the orthodox view understands "the suffering of the soul in hell metaphorically as its 'death.'"

10. BAGD, 65 (ἄνευ). On this construction see T. Hirunuma, "ἄνευ τοῦ πατρός, 'Without (of) the Father,'" *FiloNT* 3 (1990): 53 – 62, who surveys this construction in ancient Greek literature and believes it speaks of divine providence, the "intention" or "will" of the Father.

ἄνευ τοῦ πατρὸς ὑμῶν). In Luke 12:6, we read about "five sparrows sold for two pennies," slightly less than here. As in 6:25 – 26 Jesus uses an a fortiori argument (the rabbis called it *qal wahomer*, "how much more") to contrast the lesser (the least important food source) with the greater (humanity, the apex of God's creation). God registers and cares for the smallest sparrow; how much more will he care for us. Note the deliberate use of "your Father," with all the force of the "Abba" theme behind it (see on 6:9).[11]

10:30 Indeed, even the very hairs of your head are all numbered (ὑμῶν δὲ καὶ αἱ τρίχες τῆς κεφαλῆς πᾶσαι ἠριθμημέναι εἰσίν). With another a fortiori point, Jesus shows that even the smallest part of the human body, the innumerable hairs of one's head, are controlled and known to God. The idea of God caring for the very hairs of the head was a frequent emphasis (1 Sam 14:45; 2 Sam 14:11; 1 Kgs 1:52; Luke 21:18; Acts 27:34). The theme is God's loving providence over his people. He knows and watches over every detail of our lives. The God who is sovereign over history is in control of every aspect of the life and ministry of his "sent ones."[12]

10:31 So do not ever be afraid. You are worth more than many sparrows (μὴ οὖν φοβεῖσθε· πολλῶν στρουθίων διαφέρετε ὑμεῖς). The present prohibition (echoing v. 28) refers to any time in the future. Here is the conclusion to the a fortiori argument of 10:29 – 31; since humankind is worth much more than sparrows and since God cares for each sparrow, how much more will he care for his people. There will never be a need to fear, for the infinite worth of every individual before God, especially those sent on mission, means he will be monitoring everything that happens.

Theology in Application

This is a remarkable passage and shows two things: God is sovereign over all human affairs, and the believer need never worry. Regarding whatever happens we can "cast all [our] anxiety on him because he cares for [us]" (1 Pet 5:7). Within this framework, there are several issues worth discussing further:

1. The Believer to Emulate Christ in Every Area

The goal of all spiritual growth is Christlikeness, as seen in Eph 4:13 ("become mature, attaining to the whole measure of the fullness of Christ") and 4:15 ("in all things grow up into him who is the head"). Part of this growing maturity is to experience the messianic woes, i.e., "participation in his sufferings" (Phil 3:10),

11. J. D. M. Derrett, "Light on Sparrows and Hairs (Matt 10, 29 – 31," *EstBib* 55 (1997), 341 – 53, believes there is an added message, that as birds have the natural ability of birds to escape traps and people control their hair, so the believer under persecution can trust God for the wisdom to anticipate the evil intentions of their enemies. This is an interesting possibility but goes beyond the clear meaning of the text.

12. Davies and Allison, *Matthew*, 2:209, contrast this passage with the others since they center on deliverance from danger and ask, "One thus wonders how 10:30 can have the same import as a proverb which promises rescue from tribulation." See also Dale C. Allison, "The Hairs of Your Head Are All Numbered," *ExpTim* 101 (1990): 334 – 36, who says this does not provide promise of divine help so much as consolation that God is aware of suffering. Yet the context of this verse concerns persecution and suffering, and the promise of God's providential care is closely related here to those other texts.

and like the apostles "rejoice because [we have] been counted worthy of suffering disgrace for the Name" (Acts 5:41). To be maligned or even put to death is to share in the sufferings of our Lord and becomes a time of intense partnership with him. As Paul says in 2 Tim 3:12, "everyone who wants to live a godly life in Christ Jesus will be persecuted."

2. The Time of Intense Disclosure of Eternal Truths

When Jesus said these words to his disciples, they knew nothing of what was to come or of the true glory of Christ that was to be revealed. As Peter later said, the prophets and the angels were intensely interested in the time of fulfillment that we now inhabit (1 Pet 1:9 – 11), so we should be rejoicing in who we are and in what we experience (1 Pet 2:4 – 10). This is a time for bold proclamation, for these are the last days, and the future is secure in God's sovereign control.

3. A Deep Faith in God's Providential Care

These troubled times call for a deep faith in God's providential care, for the blood of the martyrs is indeed the seed of the church. Each decade in the last fifty years has seen an unbelievable escalation of anti-Christian opposition and persecution. Many groups have surveyed the world situation and chronicled this outpouring of hatred. Yet these decades have also signaled an unprecedented explosion of the gospel. The truth of 10:23 has come true in our day: the more the persecution, the greater the triumph of the gospel.

This is nowhere more true than in China. When the terrible persecution started, the church was small, one to three million total. After more than thirty years of affliction, the church now numbers seventy to a hundred million! Leaders there say that it is all attributable to suffering. Through the hard times in China, the church has triumphed.

4. God's Care for His Own

This section of Matt 10 is primarily one of encouragement in the midst of trouble and affliction. In it Jesus wants to tell us that God is not only in control but cares deeply for us. Suffering is allowed, yes, but only what will strengthen believers and enable them to proclaim the gospel fearlessly. This is proven even more strongly in Rev 13:7 in the context of 12:11, one of the great ironic portions of Scripture. In 13:7 God allows the beast to "make war against God's [holy] people and to conquer them," namely, through martyrdom. At the same time, however, the saints are conquering Satan by that very same martyrdom (12:11). In other words, when Satan takes the life of a saint, he reproduces his action at the cross (filling Judas [John 13:27] and leading Christ to his death) and participates in his own defeat!

CHAPTER 44

Matthew 10:32 – 11:1

Literary Context

Jesus finalizes his Mission Discourse by demanding fearless confession in the midst of conflict. As such it acts as a concluding summary of the themes in the rest of this passage.

- **III. The Kingdom Comes with Authority (8:1 – 11:1)**
  - **B. Second Discourse: Mission and Opposition (9:35 – 11:1)**
    - **4. Sharing in Jesus' Mission (10:24 – 42)**
      - a. No Need to Fear (10:24 – 31)
      - ➦ **b. Confession and Conflict in Discipleship (10:32 – 42)**
        - **(1) Fearless Confession (10:32 – 33)**
        - **(2) Conflicts Produced (10:34 – 36)**
        - **(3) Counting the Cost (10:37 – 39)**
        - **(4) Results — Oneness (10:40 – 42)**
    - **5. Conclusion (11:1)**

Main Idea

Confessing Jesus is not an option; every believer who refuses to acknowledge Jesus before the world will be disowned by Christ, with judgment the result (vv. 32 – 33). Since the presence of the final kingdom in Christ will drive a sword even between family relationships (vv. 34 – 36), the only solution is to place Christ even above family in your life and to lose all for him (vv. 37 – 39). But at the same time, you are now identified completely with Christ, and whatever people do to you they are doing to Christ (vv. 40 – 42).

Translation

Matthew 10:32-42

32a	Condition	"Therefore, everyone who publicly confesses me before people,
b	Consequence/Promise	I will acknowledge before my Father in heaven,
33a	Condition	but whoever denies me before people,
b	Consequence/Warning	I will also deny before my Father in heaven.
34a	Assertion	Do not think that I have come to bring peace upon the earth.
b	Restatement of 34a	I have come not to bring peace but a sword.
35a	Basis for 34a	For I have come to divide:
b		'a man against his father, and
c		a daughter against her mother and
d		a daughter-in-law against her mother-in-law, and
36a		your enemies will be those of your own household.' (Mic 7:6)
37a	Assertion	Anyone who loves a father or mother more than me is not worthy of me,
b	Parallel 37a	and anyone who loves a son or daughter more than me is not worthy of me.
38a	Expansion of 37a	And whoever does not take up their cross and follow after me is not worthy of me.
39a	Basis	Whoever finds their life will lose it,
b		and whoever loses their life for my sake will find it.
40a	Assertion	Whoever receives you receives me,
b		and whoever receives me receives the one who sent me.
41a	Expansion #1/Promise	Whoever receives a prophet who is known as a prophet will receive a prophet's reward,
b	Expansion #2/Promise	and whoever receives a righteous person who is known as righteous will receive a righteous person's reward.
42a	Expansion #3	Whoever gives even a cup of cold water to one of these little ones who is known as my disciple,
b	Promise	I tell you the truth, they will not in any way lose their reward."

Matthew 11:1

1a	Conclusion/Transition	And it happened that
		when Jesus had finished giving orders to his twelve disciples,
b	Summary	**he went on from there to teach and preach in the other towns.**

Structure and Literary Form

This is a disparate collection of sayings held together by a twofold common thread of proclaiming Jesus' name before a hostile world and the meaning of discipleship. There are no imperatives, and each section flows into the next by continuing these two interdependent motifs. As stated above, there are four sections moving from fearless confession (vv. 32 – 33)[1] to the divisions produced by that confession (vv. 34 – 36) to the necessity of counting the cost (vv. 37 – 39) to the resultant oneness between Jesus and his followers (vv. 40 – 42).

Exegetical Outline

➡ **I. Fearless Confession (10:32 – 33)**
- A. Those who acknowledge (v. 32)
- B. Those who deny (v. 33)

II. Divisions Produced (10:34 – 36)
- A. Result: not peace but a sword (v. 34)
- B. Division in households (Mic 7:6) (vv. 35 – 36)

III. Counting the Cost (10:37 – 39)
- A. The what — Christ first over family (v. 37)
- B. The how — take up the cross and follow (v. 38)
- C. The basis — finding and losing (v. 39)

IV. Oneness between Jesus and His Followers (10:40 – 42)
- A. Oneness expressed: receiving the message (v. 40)
- B. The reward received (v. 41)
- C. The reward for those who help (v. 42)

V. Conclusion (11:1)

Explanation of the Text

10:32 Therefore, everyone who publicly confesses me before people (Πᾶς οὖν ὅστις ὁμολογήσει ἐν ἐμοὶ ἔμπροσθεν τῶν ἀνθρώπων). The emphasis on the public nature of the witness ("before people" [ἔμπροσθεν τῶν ἀνθρώπων]) is part of the teaching in the sermon on "for my sake" (10:18) and "for my name's sake" (10:22) as well as the oneness between Jesus and his followers in 10:24 – 25. Jesus is the focus of the mission. He has sent his disciples, and they are proclaiming his name. In fact, this also sums up their witness both in mission (10:5 – 15) and in the courtroom (10:18 – 21).[2] The

1. This passage is a transition that can function both as the conclusion to vv. 24 – 31 (so France, *Gospel of Matthew*, 405) or as an introduction to the final section (as here).

2. Strangely, this is another area scholars debate as an either-or, as if a difference exists in the context between witnessing before the crowds and in the courtroom (see Weaver, *Missionary Discourse*, 207 n181). It is clearly both that are in mind.

recipients in both situations are those persecuting the messengers. So this is witness in the midst of serious conflict. The term "confesses" (ὁμολογέω) is used of confessing Jesus as Messiah (John 9:22) or Lord (Rom 10:9)[3] and here has the idea of public proclamation of allegiance to Jesus.

10:32 ... I will acknowledge before my Father in heaven (ὁμολογήσω κἀγὼ ἐν αὐτῷ ἔμπροσθεν τοῦ πατρός μου τοῦ ἐν τοῖς οὐρανοῖς). The verbs are the same tense (future) in both clauses; for Jesus' followers it entails future open witness, and for Jesus it becomes acknowledgment before the Father and the heavenly court (16:27; 25:31), undoubtedly on the day of judgment. Luz points out that it is more than the disciples' witness in court and more than Jesus' intercession before God on their behalf; his "'confessing' before the court is an irrevocable statement of judgment (cf. 7:23)."[4] Davies and Allison see the background in Dan 7, with the Great Assize and the Ancient of Days on his throne before the heavenly court (7:9 – 10) and "the one like a son of man" coming before the throne (7:13 – 14) and defeating the beast (7:26 – 27).

Here the Son of Man on the throne confesses or denies people before the heavenly court.[5] God is seen here as the "Father" of both Jesus and us. We share in Jesus' relationship with the Father (see on 10:29), but in our case there is both reward (here) and judgment (10:33), depending on how we carry out our responsibility to proclaim Jesus to the world. The passage here is not just meant for professional missionaries and preachers but also for everyday Christians as light bearers to the world.

10:33 But whoever denies me before people, I will also deny before my Father in heaven[6] (ὅστις δ' ἂν ἀρνήσηταί με ἔμπροσθεν τῶν ἀνθρώπων, ἀρνήσομαι κἀγὼ αὐτὸν ἔμπροσθεν τοῦ πατρός μου τοῦ ἐν τοῖς οὐρανοῖς). There is an exact parallelism between vv. 32 and 33, with the obvious contrast being between acknowledging or denying Christ and the destiny that each brings about. This is a strong warning, for "to deny" (ἀρνέομαι) here means to renounce Christ and is language of apostasy.[7] In this persecution passage, it means that people cave in to pressure and renounce Christ to avoid beating or death.

It is clear that our status before God is completely tied to our relationship with Christ. Our eternal destiny depends on our acceptance or renunciation of Christ. Further, he along with God will be the Judge at the final judgment (cf. 7:21 – 23), and his witness about us will be the determining factor in where we spend eternity. At the same time, this is not just speaking of the apostate but also of the weak Christian who tries to remain anonymous, i.e., refuses to stand up for Christ at school or in the workplace. Such a one is, in effect, "ashamed" of Christ, and in another saying of Jesus on this same topic, he will be "ashamed" of that person (Mark 8:38) on the day of judgment.

10:34 Do not think that I have come to bring peace upon the earth (Μὴ νομίσητε ὅτι ἦλθον βαλεῖν εἰρήνην ἐπὶ τὴν γῆν). The introductory

3. BAGD, 568, calls the use of "in me" (ἐν ἐμοί) here an Aramaism and points out that *2 Clem.* 3:2 uses the accusative when quoting this.

4. Luz, *Matthew 8 – 20*, 104.

5. Davies and Allison, *Matthew*, 2:214 – 15.

6. In Mark 8:38 a saying similar to this one is a Son of Man saying. See Carson, "Matthew," 255 – 56, for a strong argument from this against Bultmann's claim that when Jesus used "Son of Man" he was speaking of another being. This passage demonstrates that in the Synoptic tradition Jesus used "Son of Man" for himself.

7. Weaver, *Missionary Discourse*, 207 n183, says this "points not to the mere failure to witness, but rather to the straightforward rejection of one's relationship to Jesus, that is, to open apostasy." According to W. Schenk (*EDNT*, 1:153), "to deny" (ἀρνέομαι) is a neutral term for opposition or renunciation, so in a positive context can connote repentance and in a negative context apostasy. This is a negative context.

"do not think" (μὴ νομίσητε) sounds a note of extreme caution as it warns Christ's followers that things are not as they seem and the traditional answers do not fit the situation. The threefold repetition of "I have come" (ἦλθον, culminative aorists centering on the results of his coming) in vv. 34 – 35 shows Jesus is centering on the purpose of his mission here. The Jews (and Jesus' disciples) believed the messianic age would be typified by peace (Isa 9:6; 26:3, 53:5). In fact, Jesus said in 5:9, "God blesses those who make peace," and in 10:12 – 13 the missionary is to give the peace greeting upon entering a home. So it was natural for the disciples to believe Jesus had come to bring peace. In the Farewell Discourse (John 14:27) Jesus said, "Peace I leave with you," and in the resurrection narrative he thrice said, "Peace be with you" (John 20:19, 21, 26).

So why is Jesus reversing that message here? Peace is the result of the salvation he is bringing, but the mission to the lost world will not result in peace for those who take the gospel to the world. In other words, peace will not be experienced by the missionaries, but it will come to those who respond to their message. Also, peace is absent in the mission "upon the earth" (ἐπὶ τὴν γῆν), but a heavenly peace is present for those converted. Here it would be helpful to note that classic expression of the conquering Messiah found in *Pss. Sol.* 17 – 18 (a first-century work), where also there would be no peace until the Messiah was established.

10:34 I have come not to bring peace[8] but a sword (οὐκ ἦλθον βαλεῖν εἰρήνην ἀλλὰ μάχαιραν). The idea of a "sword" in the OT normally symbolized judgment by God (Isa 27:1; 66:16; Jer 12:12; 25:29; Ezek 38:21) or destruction by enemies (Judg 3:21; 2 Sam 2:16; 20:10; Job 5:20; Jer 2:30). Jesus is obviously referring to the latter (the last two OT passages describe the apostate nation killing the prophets), and Jesus tells his followers to expect severe hostility, even martyrdom. There is a critical tension here, as the believer finds peace with God but opposition from the world.[9] By entering new life in the Spirit, we may lose our lives in this world (see 10:39 below), but God will be with us in a new way.

10:35 For I have come to divide "a man against his father, and a daughter against her mother and a daughter-in-law against her mother-in-law" (ἦλθον γὰρ διχάσαι ἄνθρωπον κατὰ τοῦ πατρὸς αὐτοῦ καὶ θυγατέρα κατὰ τῆς μητρὸς αὐτῆς καὶ νύμφην κατὰ τῆς πενθερᾶς αὐτῆς). This was far more radical in the time of Jesus, when society centered on the nuclear family and family ties were central. In addressing the situation, Jesus quotes Mic 7:6 (LXX),[10] which describes the terrible state of affairs under Ahaz, in which "the faithful have been swept from the land" (7:2) and everyone has turned against their neighbors, even within families. Jesus believes this is typologically fulfilled in the church's mission.[11] The sword of Matt 10:34 will penetrate even families

8. "Bring peace" (lit., "throw peace") is widely recognized as a Semitism, cf. Str-B, 1:586; Schlatter, *Matthäus*, 349 – 50.

9. S. G. F. Brandon, *Jesus and the Zealots* (New York: Scribner's, 1967), 320 – 21, among others, believes this shows Jesus to be an insurrectionist who wants to overthrow Rome. Yet this seriously misunderstands the "sword" image here. In the context he is definitely centering on what will be done *to* his followers, not what will be done *by* them.

10. There are a few small differences, like "against" (κατά) for "against" (ἐπί) and "man" (ἄνθπωπος) for "son" (υἱός), but none that change the meaning. For the use of Mic 7:6 eschatologically in pre-Christian targums and *m. Sot.* 9:15, see D. L. Büchner, "Micah 7:6 in the Ancient Old Testament Versions," *JNSL* 19 (1993): 159 – 68.

11. Again, it is common to assign this verse to the situation in the Matthean church, but we must recall Jesus was divided from his own family (Matt 12:46 – 50), and Luz, *Matthew 8 – 20*, 111, shows it could be linked with Luke 12:49; 14:26 in the *logia Jesu*. This was a frequent apocalyptic theme (cf. *1 En.* 56:7; *Jub.* 23:16; *4 Ezra* 6:24), and there is no reason Jesus could not have spoken these words.

and violently cause the closest relationships to be severed.[12] When the kingdom truths enter society, choices will be made, resulting even in family members turning against those who choose Christ, betraying them to their deaths (10:21). Beare provides first-century background:

> This came about in Gentile families perhaps even more acutely than in Jewish; for all the members of the family had a part to play in the domestic cult which was carried on every day, as well as in the ceremonies of the public cults. A son or a daughter converted to Christianity could not so much as pour a libation to the household gods, or walk in procession to the temple, or to Eleusias. Such an attitude could not fail to infuriate the parents.[13]

10:36 "And your[14] enemies will be those of your own household" (καὶ ἐχθροὶ τοῦ ἀνθρώπου οἱ οἰκιακοὶ αὐτοῦ). Also taken from Mic 7:6, this draws the ultimate conclusion, that your closest family will become your enemies. After the relationship is severed (v. 35), the enmity between former family members ensues (v. 36). Davies and Allison write, "As chaos and darkness came before the first creation (Gen 1:2), so division and strife must come before the second creation; the last things are as the first."[15]

10:37 Anyone who loves a father or mother more than me is not worthy of me, and anyone who loves a son or daughter more than me is not worthy of me (Ὁ φιλῶν πατέρα ἢ μητέρα ὑπὲρ ἐμὲ οὐκ ἔστιν μου ἄξιος, καὶ ὁ φιλῶν υἱὸν ἢ θυγατέρα ὑπὲρ ἐμὲ οὐκ ἔστιν μου ἄξιος). The movement in this section has been from fearless witness (vv. 32 – 33) to the negative reaction of the world to that witness (vv. 34 – 36) and now to how the disciples are to react in light of that violent rejection (vv. 37 – 39). Here we are at the heart of discipleship, counting the cost and placing Christ above everything in our lives.

The movement is noteworthy in another way. In one sense the family disowns the believer (vv. 35 – 36) and in another sense the believer sets aside allegiance to the family (v. 37). The key term is "worthy" (ἄξιος, discussed in 10:10 – 11); one is "worthy" or "deserving" of Jesus only if he is placed ahead of all earthly attachments, even family ties. The use of "loves" (φιλῶν) points to both affection and loyalty.[16] Jesus, of course, recognizes the deep love between parents and children (15:4 – 6; 19:19), but he demands the deeper commitment. This is the core of discipleship; if Jesus is not first, we do not "deserve" to be his disciple.

10:38 And whoever does not take up their cross and follow after me is not worthy of me (καὶ ὃς οὐ λαμβάνει τὸν σταυρὸν αὐτοῦ καὶ ἀκολουθεῖ ὀπίσω μου, οὐκ ἔστιν μου ἄξιος). It has been common to call this anachronistic because Jesus has not yet given his passion prediction (16:21, 24),[17] but this is surely unnecessary, since the practice of bearing the cross to one's crucifixion was

12. B. J. Malina, *The New Testament World: Insights from Cultural Anthropology* (Atlanta: John Knox, 1981), 101 (in Keener, *Matthew*, 330) explains that the daughter-in-law is named because it is she who moves into the husband's house, while the daughter here is probably the unmarried daughter who is still around to reject her mother. Keener says, "Jesus' mission separates disciples from the values of their society, and society responds with persecution."

13. Beare, *Matthew*, 249.

14. τοῦ ἀνθρώπου is used generically, "a person's enemies."

15. Davies and Allison, *Matthew*, 2:220.

16. Schweizer, *Matthew*, 251, believes "loves" (φιλέω) is especially chosen to speak of family ties, but Morris, *Matthew*, 267n, correctly notes that there is little difference between φιλέω and "loves" (ἀγαπάω) in the NT (see also *EDNT*, 3:425).

17. E.g., Hagner, *Matthew 1 – 13*, 292. It is also common to see this as a formulation of the church rather than a *logia Jesu*, cf. the list of options in Davies and Allison, *Matthew*, 2:222 – 23; and esp. Luz, *Matthew 8 – 20*, 113 – 15, who concludes it most likely goes back to Jesus.

commonly known. When the condemned prisoner bore his crossbeam to the execution site (the pole remained there), it meant he was already dead. So the metaphor signified a death to self,[18] or self-denial. At the same time, there is likely an *imitatio Christi* motif, as Jesus challenges his disciples that they must be willing to die (as he would) if they are to be his followers (a possibility already stated in 10:21, 28).[19] In other words, true discipleship involves both a death to self and a willingness to die for Jesus (cf. also Mark 8:34; Luke 9:23, 14:27; John 12:26).

10:39 Whoever finds their life will lose it, and whoever loses their life for my sake will find it (ὁ εὑρὼν τὴν ψυχὴν αὐτοῦ ἀπολέσει αὐτήν, καὶ ὁ ἀπολέσας τὴν ψυχὴν αὐτοῦ ἕνεκεν ἐμοῦ εὑρήσει αὐτήν). This summarizes the themes in the section thus far. Jesus has demanded that his followers sacrifice family and embrace being hated by all in order to follow him and carry his kingdom message to the world. Now he puts it together under the rubric of "losing their life," certainly a definition of "taking up their cross." In opposition to this, "finding their life" (with the aorist participle "finding" [εὑρών]) means to live selfishly, to seek the rewards of this world, while "losing their life" means to forsake the rewards of this world and live for God (cf. Matt 6:19 – 21; Col 3:1 – 2).

Here again we are at the heart of discipleship (see further 16:24 – 26). As Plummer says, "In general, those whose sole aim is to win material prosperity, lose the only life which is worth living; and those who sacrifice material prosperity in Christ's service, secure the higher life."[20] There is a distinct movement from physical life to eternal life; to live for the present is to lose the future!

10:40 Whoever receives you receives me, and whoever receives me receives the one who sent me (Ὁ δεχόμενος ὑμᾶς ἐμὲ δέχεται, καὶ ὁ ἐμὲ δεχόμενος δέχεται τὸν ἀποστείλαντά με). The mission is still uppermost (the present tenses throughout these next three verses continue the theme of lifelong ministry). After the demands of discipleship and the warning of intense suffering this will entail, Jesus encourages his disciples with the basic fact of this whole discourse: as they go with Jesus' kingdom message, they have his authority and are completely identified not only with him but with God himself.[21]

In a two-step saying, Jesus says the way the outsider acts[22] toward the agent is the way they treat both him and the Sender; the idea of Jesus and the disciple as "sent" from God is dominant in John (cf. John 20:21 – 23) and is at the heart of missionary theology. "It is this awesome fact [union with Jesus], both in its positive and its negative formulations, which gives ultimate significance to everything which the disciples do in their role as 'apostles,' those 'sent out' by Jesus."[23] It is true that throughout history (and also today), this authority has been often restricted to the apostles themselves as symbolizing the pope or the bishops or

18. The present tense "take up" (λαμβάνει) signifies that this will be a continuous act of self-sacrifice.

19. See Albright and Mann, *Matthew*, 132; Luz, *Matthew 8 – 20*, 115. Weaver, *Missionary Discourse*, 115, says: "A solidarity of suffering thus exists between Jesus and his disciples: the disciples must suffer that which Jesus has suffered before them, if they wish to remain his disciples."

20. Plummer, *Matthew*, 157.

21. Luz, *Matthew 8 – 20*, 120, calls this "emissary law," that an agent goes out with the full authority of the one who commissions him or her (cf. *b. Ber.* 63b; *b. Ketub.* 11b; *Numbers Rabbah* 22 (192d); *b. Sanh.* 110a).

22. "Receives" (δέχομαι, six times in vv. 40 – 41) has a double meaning here. At one level it connotes the way the people treat Jesus' emissaries, but at another level it returns to the theme of 10:12 – 14, where the reception of the messenger implies the reception of the gospel (see Broadus, *Matthew*, 232 – 33).

23. Weaver, *Missionary Discourse*, 117.

official ministers in their preaching,[24] but clearly in Matt 10 it depicts the authority of every believer as "sent out" on mission, an authority based on our mystical union with Christ.

10:41 Whoever receives a prophet who is known as a prophet will receive a prophet's reward (ὁ δεχόμενος προφήτην εἰς ὄνομα προφήτου μισθὸν προφήτου λήμψεται). Verses 41 – 42 provide a threefold example of the reception of Jesus' emissaries — the prophets, the righteous, the little ones. The phrase εἰς ὄνομα προφήτου is a rabbinic idiom often translated "because he or she is a prophet," with ὄνομα meaning they are known ("named") or recognized by people as a prophet (undoubtedly a Christian prophet,[25] not an OT prophet). Those who accept, show hospitality to, and respond to a prophet in even the smallest way (the "cup of cold water" in v. 42) will be rewarded by God for their kindness and openness to the gospel. A "prophet's reward" could be a reward from the prophet, the same reward a prophet receives, or (best) a reward in keeping with helping God's prophets (cf. Elijah and Elisha in 1 Kgs 17:8 – 24; 2 Kgs 4:8 – 37).[26]

10:41 And whoever receives a righteous person who is known as righteous will receive a righteous person's reward (καὶ ὁ δεχόμενος δίκαιον εἰς ὄνομα δικαίου μισθὸν δικαίου λήμψεται). In Matthew a "righteous person" is one who lives life in accordance with the will of God (see on 5:6, 10, 20; 6:33; 13:43, 49).[27] This is not a special category of Christian like a prophet but a description of the true believer, parallel with the "little ones" of v. 42. This is not a separate office in the church but a depiction of the disciple in mission as one living life God's way. εἰς ὄνομα is a Semitic idiom meaning "because he is named/known as" (see on v. 41a). God will reward this act of kindness and acceptance as well. The μισθός is not just the "wages" earned but a gracious reward from God in all three cases in vv. 41 – 42. It is an eschatological reward, given at the Great Assize when Jesus will reward the pious and judge the wicked.

10:42 Whoever gives even a cup of cold water to one of these little ones who is known as my disciple, I tell you the truth, they will not in any way lose their reward (καὶ ὃς ἂν ποτίσῃ ἕνα τῶν μικρῶν τούτων ποτήριον ψυχροῦ μόνον εἰς ὄνομα μαθητοῦ, ἀμὴν λέγω ὑμῖν, οὐ μὴ ἀπολέσῃ τὸν μισθὸν αὐτοῦ). In the hot climate of Palestine, giving cold water[28] to a weary traveler was an expected aspect of basic hospitality. Yet even this basic act will be rewarded by God. The disciples are called "little ones" because they are insignificant, without status, and powerless in society,[29] a term perhaps derived from apocalyptic circles (cf. Zech 13:7; *1 En.* 62:11; *2 Bar.* 48:19).[30] Yet the marginalized in the world are showcases for the power of God. So Jesus is speaking of the

24. Carson, "Matthew," 258, believes there is a downward spiral with v. 40 = the apostles, then from the "prophets" and "righteous men" to the "little ones" or general believers. There may be some truth in this for Jesus' day (the "righteous" would be more mature believers and the "little ones" general followers), but it is clear that all the categories in 10:40 – 42 apply to every Christian on mission.

25. Some take the "prophet" generally as a missionary who "speaks for God" (Plummer, *Matthew*, 147) or any Christian who speaks God's word (Bruner, *Christbook*, 401), or as itinerant teachers (Davies and Allison, *Matthew*, 2:226), but more likely it is an actual prophet like Agabus (Acts 11:28; 21:10).

26. See France, *Matthew* (TNTC), 190.

27. Hill, *Matthew*, 196, strangely thinks "the righteous" are only the itinerant teachers in the church. This is unlikely.

28. μόνον is emphatic, "*merely* a cup of cold water."

29. Some have suggested that "little ones" (μικρός) refers to "(little) children" (mainly due to the parallel in Mark 9:37, "Whoever welcomes one of these little children in my name welcomes me"), but that is unlikely in this context of the disciple's mission.

30. So Davies and Allison, *Matthew*, 2:229.

smallest of services to the weakest of people, yet an act noticed and rewarded by God. The language is strong ("not in any way lose") and indicates a great reward (emphasized also by the introductory "amen" [ἀμήν] saying, cf. 10:15, 23).[31]

11:1 And it happened that when Jesus had finished giving orders to his twelve disciples, he went on from there to teach and preach in the other towns (Καὶ ἐγένετο ὅτε ἐτέλεσεν ὁ Ἰησοῦς διατάσσων τοῖς δώδεκα μαθηταῖς αὐτοῦ, μετέβη ἐκεῖθεν τοῦ διδάσκειν καὶ κηρύσσειν ἐν ταῖς πόλεσιν αὐτῶν). This verse concludes the Mission Discourse. Like the previous discourse, it ends with "it happened that when Jesus had finished" (see on 7:28; cf. 13:53; 19:1; 26:1), which provides a transition to the action narrative that follows in chs. 11 – 12. It is significant that Matthew chooses διατάσσω, thus emphasizing the command function of the instructions. It is even more significant that he does not speak of the successful completion of the disciples' mission (contra Mark 6:12 – 13), probably so as to reemphasize the message of v. 23, that the mission to Israel would never finish until the parousia.[32]

Jesus' mission throughout Galilee[33] repeats 4:23; 9:35 and frames the disciples' mission with Jesus' own, showing again that the mission of the church is but an extension of Jesus' mission and must be carried out entirely under his authority. Jesus' mission here centers on "teaching and preaching" (healing is omitted), probably because the ensuing narrative centers on Jesus' teaching ministry, with the only miracle being in 12:22 – 23 (and even there it leads into teaching).

31. It is interesting that the three ἀμήν sayings here (10:15, 23, 42) come at the end of sections and highlight a summary truth centering on the eschaton.

32. See Davies and Allison, *Matthew*, 2:239; Hagner, *Matthew 1 – 13*, 296 – 97. Others offer other reasons: (1) this feature makes the focus on Christology and so returns to the narrative thread of 9:35 (Gundry, *Matthew*, 203; Luz, *Matthew 8 – 20*, 123); (2) the mission still lies in the future (Weaver, *Missionary Discourse*, 126); or (3) this emphasizes that the Mission Discourse has ongoing value for the church (Harrington, *Matthew*, 155).

33. The use of αὐτῶν ("their cities") has led many to assume it is anachronistic, stated from the standpoint of the later separation between synagogue and church, but Carson shows ("Matthew," 260) that it could easily be an instance of "pronominal sense-construction" to stress the growing separation between Jesus and the Jews. At the same time, it could also be used to emphasize the crowds as the focus of Jesus' ministry (see Grundmann, *Matthäus*, 303). This phrase is found often in Matthew (4:23; 7:29; 9:35; 10:17; 11:1; 12:9 – 10; 13:54), with much the same meaning.

Theology in Application

As the concluding paragraph to the Mission Discourse, 10:32 – 42 recapitulates many of the themes developed earlier. Nevertheless, we will look at them anew through the eyes of the text here. One major issue is the opinion of some that the Mission Discourse applies only to those engaged in missionary work, but this is answered in 10:40 – 42, where the disciples are further described not just as prophets but as the "righteous" and the "little ones." All believers are included in the discourse, because all of God's people are meant to be part of his mission. Some are missionaries to the "the ends of the earth," others to their "Jerusalem" (Acts 1:8). But whether at home/work/school or overseas, we are all to be engaged in mission.

1. Wholehearted Adherence to Jesus Resulting in Bold Witness

All followers of Jesus must stand up and be counted. Closet Christians are indeed "ashamed" of Christ (a form of rejection), and Christ will be "ashamed" of them at the final judgment (Mark 8:38 = Luke 9:26), which also means rejection. Here 10:32 – 33 states this more starkly, with "acknowledge"/"deny" language, but the truth is the same. Whether denying Jesus before an earthly tribunal or refusing to take a stand for Jesus in daily life, one is still refusing to "acknowledge" him and thus will face divine judgment. This does not mean that every Christian must be a bold, aggressive witness; rather, when opportunities come, we should seize the initiative. Most of all, we should make our allegiance known. The judgment does not mean that all such will face eternal torment, but it does mean they will give account to God in some fashion (unspecified in Scripture).

2. Rejection

Following Jesus is costly and may mean rejection by those closest to the disciple. Shallow preachers make it sound as if conversion to Christ means the cessation of all problems in this world, as if we are "the king's kids" and are supposed to lead lives of royalty. That is heresy, for Scripture could not be clearer that Jesus has brought a sword, not a checkbook, to earth. We are to be royalty, but not until the final kingdom has arrived (Rev 20:4; 22:5). Now sacrifice and at times death awaits us, and we must be aware of the price we pay in *imitatio Christi*. I have heard of Christians whose own families have killed them or turned them over to the authorities to be killed. In such cases there is the paradox of internal peace with God but external chaos and tragedy in this life. Yet we are called to this, to "lose our life" for Christ, and that means a willingness to suffer (cf. 16:24 – 25; 20:22 – 23a).

3. Total Allegiance

The true child of God belongs to a new family and has a new citizenship (Phil 3:20). We are "foreigners" and "exiles" in this world (1 Pet 1:1, 17; 2:11). Jesus is everything. Even the strong ties and love of family recede into the background. In fact, even self is set aside as we "take up the cross," entailing both self-denial and a willingness to die for Jesus if necessary. This is far from understood by Western Christians, but believers in the rest of the world do not merely understand it but live it daily.

4. In Union with Christ our Lord

When we face terrible odds and the hostility of the world against us, we are not alone. According in Phil 3:10, we share Jesus' sufferings, and whether the world around us is kind or filled with animosity, what they do to us is being done both to Christ and to God, for we are one with them. The union between Christ and God is extended to us, and we go out not just with Christ's authority but with Christ in us (cf. John 6:56; 15:4 – 7; 17:21, 23; 1 John 2:24; 3:24; 4:15). We are his "righteous ones" (when we live out what we believe), and though we are "little" or insignificant in the eyes of the world, we have incredible significance in God and for God. The way people treat us is the way they treat God, and God will turn their actions back upon their own heads as either reward or judgment.

Matthew 11:2 – 6

CHAPTER 45

Introduction to Preaching and Teaching in the Midst of Opposition (Matthew 11:2 – 13:53)

Matthew 11:2 indicates a turning point in Matthew. There has been sporadic opposition (mainly 9:3 – 4, 11, 14, 34), but primarily a positive atmosphere as Jesus showed his authority and called for faith. The success of his ministry caused astonishment (7:28; 8:27; 9:8, 33), and the news went everywhere (4:24 – 25; 8:34; 9:26, 31). In the Mission Discourse he prophesied great trouble for future missions (10:14, 17 – 22, 25, 28, 35 – 36), and that begins here as the opposition intensifies in chs. 11 – 12. Of the nine pericopae in 11:1 – 12:50, six deal with rejection and judgment (11:2 – 19, 20 – 24; 12:1 – 8, 9 – 14, 22 – 37, 38 – 42), and the section begins with the doubt even of John the Baptist (11:3). Then Matthew adds to the parables of Mark 4 the parables of the weeds (13:24 – 30, 36 – 43) and of the net (13:47 – 52), both centering on the harvest that leads to final judgment. The section ends with Jesus rejected even in his own hometown (13:53 – 58).

At the same time, this is a christological section, as Jesus is the coming Messiah (11:2 – 6), eschatological Judge (11:20 – 24; 12:39 – 42; 13:12 – 15, 30, 41 – 43), one with the Father (11:25 – 27), Wisdom drawing the weary to herself (11:28 – 30), Lord of the Sabbath (12:1 – 8), suffering Servant (12:15 – 21), the strong binder of Satan who brings the kingdom (12:28 – 29), and the revealer of heavenly mysteries (13:11, 35). So the two themes of rejection and christological glory develop side by side.

Regarding the section on the deeds of Jesus (11:2 – 12:50), the key is to structure the nine pericopae. We arrive at nine by deciding that the two Sabbath miracles of 12:1 – 8, 9 – 14 are separate rather than a single episode, and then deciding that Jesus' saying about the return of the evil spirit (12:43 – 45) goes with 12:38 – 42 rather than being a separate pericope (actually, there are three separate parts of that episode: 12:38 – 40, 41 – 42, 43 – 45). In the nine episodes, there is a clear two-plus-one structure in each triad, with the first two being rejection stories and the third a christological saying in which Jesus brings salvation and hope to his followers (11:25 – 30; 12:15 – 21, 46 – 50).[1] So just as chs. 8 – 9 featured three triads of miracle stories, so also this section contains three triads (11:2 – 30; 12:1 – 21, 22 – 50) that contrast opposition to Jesus with Jesus as the one sent to provide healing and salvation.

Literary Context

Matthew 11:2 – 6 begins the third narrative-discourse section (after 4:12 – 7:29 and 8:1 – 11:1), and it turns from initial success to growing rejection. From the doubts of John the Baptist (11:2 – 6) to the rejection of both the Baptist and Jesus (11:18 – 19) to the refusal of the Galilean towns to repent (11:20 – 24), the theme of Jewish obduracy begins to develop, following the pattern of Israel in the OT. Yet at the same time the salvific love of the Godhead stands in stark contrast, as the Father has revealed his truths through Jesus, who now offers rest to those who come to him (11:25 – 30). Further, the Baptist's doubts give Jesus the chance to recapitulate his wondrous deeds (11:4 – 5), providing a summary of the three triads of miracles in chs. 8 – 9.

III. The Kingdom Comes with Authority (8:1 – 11:1)
IV. Preaching and Teaching in the Midst of Opposition (11:2 – 13:53)
A. Jesus' Deeds: Revelation and Rejection (11:2 – 12:50)
1. Revelation and Rejection Begun (11:2 – 30)
a. Jesus and John the Baptist (11:2 – 19)
➡ **(1) John's Doubts and Jesus' Response (11:2 – 6)**

Main Idea

Jesus' ministry was not corresponding to the Jewish messianic expectations; even John the Baptist had perceived this and wonders if Jesus is indeed the promised Messiah. His query allows Jesus to summarize his ministry thus far and show that his miracles are evidence that the time of salvation has indeed arrived. Then he demands that decisions must be made about him.

1. See also Davies and Allison, *Matthew*, 2:233 – 34; Luz, *Matthew 8 – 20*, 178, 197. On this Paul S. Minear, "On Seeing the Good News," *ThTo* 55 (1998): 163 – 74, sees as central Jesus the humble servant who takes on himself the burdens of all who come (11:29 – 30).

Translation

Matthew 11:2-6

2a	Setting	But when John was in prison,
b	Action/Response	**he heard about the deeds of the Messiah and**
		sent his disciples to ask him,
3a	Question	*"Are you the One who was to come,*
b		*or should we look for someone else?"*
4a	Answer	**Jesus answered them,**
b		*"Go and report to John what you have heard and seen:*
5a		*The blind receive their sight and the lame walk,*
b		*the lepers are cleansed and the deaf hear,*
c		*the dead are raised and*
		the poor are given the good news.
6a	Promise	*And blessed is anyone who does not fall away because of me."*

Structure and Literary Form

Matthew uses a Q passage (= Luke 7:18 – 23) with a few differences noted below.[2] This is a pronouncement story in which the question of the Baptist leads to Jesus' powerful response. As such there are two parts, John's question (vv. 2 – 3) and Jesus' answer (vv. 4 – 6). The response is carefully structured. The command is in typical Matthean style with the circumstantial participle "going" (πορευθέντες) followed by an aorist imperative (cf. 2:8; 9:13; 10:7 [present tenses]; 17:27; 28:19), and the miracles are carefully arranged in pairs, concluding with a beatitude calling for decision.

Exegetical Outline

- **I. The Baptist's Doubtful Questions (11:2 – 3)**
  - A. The setting (v. 2)
  - B. The query (v. 3)
    1. Is Jesus the expected Messiah? (v. 3a)
    2. Should John seek someone else? (v. 3b)
- **II. Jesus' Authoritative Response (11:4 – 6)**
  - A. Report this answer to John (v. 4)
  - B. The summary of Jesus' miracles (v. 5)
  - C. The beatitude demanding response (v. 6)

2. On the authenticity of this passage, see Keener, *Matthew*, 333 – 34.

Explanation of the Text

11:2 But when John was in prison, he heard about the deeds of the Messiah and sent[3] his disciples (Ὁ δὲ Ἰωάννης ἀκούσας ἐν τῷ δεσμωτηρίῳ τὰ ἔργα τοῦ Χριστοῦ πέμψας διὰ τῶν μαθητῶν αὐτοῦ). Mark places the flashback to the death of John the Baptist here after his Mission Discourse (6:14–29), but Matthew saves that scene for 14:11–12 and instead places a scene from John's imprisonment here. John's imprisonment is recounted in 4:12 at the beginning of Jesus' Galilean ministry. Josephus tells us that Herod Antipas imprisoned the Baptist in his fortress at Machaerus east of the Dead Sea (*Ant.* 18.5.2), and he was there for about a year before his death. John had heard reports of "the deeds of the Messiah" (τὰ ἔργα τοῦ Χριστοῦ), probably referring (cf. "what you have heard and seen" in v. 4) both to Jesus' preaching and teaching (chs. 5–7; 10) and to his miraculous works (chs. 8–9) and their messianic origin ("of the Messiah" [τοῦ Χριστοῦ], a subjective genitive and titular = "performed by the Messiah").[4] Since he could not ask Jesus in person, he did so "through [διά] his disciples" (Luke 7:18 tells us there were two of them).

11:3 ... to ask him, "Are you the One who was to come, or should we look for someone else?" (εἶπεν αὐτῷ, Σὺ εἶ ὁ ἐρχόμενος ἢ ἕτερον προσδοκῶμεν;). In 3:11 the Baptist called Jesus "[after me] one is coming" (see also 21:9; 23:39), a title not common in Judaism and possibly stemming from Ps 118:26; Isa 59:20; Dan 7:13, 9:25; Hab 2:3. The question of John's doubts has produced many solutions, such as the view of the early church fathers that John was asking for the sake of his followers, not himself, or the view that John wanted to force Jesus into a public declaration, or that he was discouraged in prison and simply needed reassurance.[5]

The key is probably John's radical call to repentance (3:2, 11) and his proclamation of judgment on the nation (3:7–10), concluding with his prophecy that the Messiah would bring the final harvest of sinners to "unquenchable fire" (3:12).[6] Jesus did not center on such a message (though he did include that emphasis, see 5:22, 29, 30; 10:28) but rather proclaimed the age of salvation and healed the sick. So John's doubts are real and he wonders if he "should look for someone else,"[7] with προσδοκάω meaning to "wait for, look for, expect" (BAGD, 712). In this context of active searching, "look for" is probably the best translation.

11:4 Jesus answered them, "Go and report to John what you have heard and seen" (καὶ ἀποκριθεὶς ὁ Ἰησοῦς εἶπεν αὐτοῖς, Πορευθέντες ἀπαγγείλατε Ἰωάννῃ ἃ ἀκούετε καὶ βλέπετε). The circumstantial participle "go" (πορευθέντες, see on v. 2) followed by an imperative anticipates 28:19 ("Go and make disciples"), and as there the participle has imperative force as well. This

3. "Hearing" (ἀκούσας) and "sending" (πέμψας) are two of Matthew's many circumstantial participles and partake of the emphasis of "to ask" (εἶπεν), virtually becoming main verbs (see 4:20; 10:1, 5 etc.).

4. Blomberg, *Matthew*, says "Messiah" is from Matthew's perspective, not John's, "otherwise the question would be meaningless." While the reports John received could have interpreted the miracles as messianic (with John doubting anyway), there is not a lot of evidence that Jesus was called Messiah this early (though see John 1:41, 44). Matthew uses "Messiah" (τοῦ Χριστοῦ) here (it has not appeared since 2:4) to tell his readers the true identity of the one John is doubting.

5. See Don Verseput, *The Rejection of the Humble Messianic King: A Study of the Composition of Matthew 11–12* (Frankfurt: Peter Lang, 1986), 61–62; Davies and Allison, *Matthew*, 2:241; Morris, *Matthew*, 274–75.

6. See Bruner, *Christbook*, 408.

7. Gundry, *Matthew*, 205, points out that "another" (ἕτερος) is in the emphatic position and means "a different kind of Coming One."

does not mean John's disciples had been with Jesus some time and had personally seen all these events. Rather, the "what you" refers to the reports of those deeds and teachings reported to John's disciples by Jesus' followers. Jesus does not answer the questions directly but simply points to the messianic words and deeds that are proof of his messianic office.

11:5 The blind receive their sight and the lame walk, the lepers are cleansed and the deaf hear, the dead are raised and the poor are given the good news (τυφλοὶ ἀναβλέπουσιν καὶ χωλοὶ περιπατοῦσιν, λεπροὶ καθαρίζονται καὶ κωφοὶ ἀκούουσιν, καὶ νεκροὶ ἐγείρονται καὶ πτωχοὶ εὐαγγελίζονται). This list[8] at one and the same time sums up the miracles of chs. 8–9 and is built on several passages in Isaiah on the coming messianic age, specifically Isa 26:19; 29:18; 35:5–6; 42:18; 61:1. Jesus interprets his miracles as fulfilling the Isaianic vision of the expected age of salvation; it has now arrived in Jesus. Also, the Isaianic passages have judgment in their contexts (e.g., 35:4, "with vengeance, with divine retribution"; 61:2, "the day of vengeance of our God"), meaning the judgments are delayed but will inevitably come.[9]

So the Baptist's implicit question is answered. The healing of the blind (Isa 29:18; 35:5; 42:18) alludes to Matt 9:27–31, the healing of the lame man (Isa 35:6) is found in 9:1–8; the cleansing of the leper is found in 8:1–4; the healing of the deaf (Isa 29:18; 35:5; 42:18) is found in 9:32–34; the raising of the dead (Isa 26:19) is found in 9:18–19, 23–26. The preaching of good news to the poor (Isa 61:1) may stem from 5:3 or 9:35–36 but also may allude straight to Isaiah.[10] The first five are "what you have seen" and the last "what you have heard" from v. 4—thus the deeds and words of Jesus. Moreover, all the verbs are present tense, emphasizing the continued effects of Jesus' miraculous Isaianic ministry.

11:6 And blessed is anyone who does not fall away because of me (καὶ μακάριός ἐστιν ὃς ἐὰν μὴ σκανδαλισθῇ ἐν ἐμοί). As in 5:3–12, "blessed" (μακάριος) means "God blesses those who...." On σκανδαλίζω see 5:29; it literally means to "trip and fall down" and in Matthew is often a strong term for "falling away," with aspects of apostasy (see also 13:21; 24:10; 26:31, 33).[11] In other Matthean contexts it can have overtones of taking offense, leading to anger, revulsion, and rejection (13:57; 15:12; 17:27). Here the idea is rejection, and it can be either a refusal to accept Jesus' offer of salvation or a turning back on the part of followers.[12]

Just as v. 5 summarized the deeds of Jesus, this summarizes the Mission Discourse, especially that part demanding decision and warning of the danger of rejecting/denying him (10:14–15, 32–33, 39). It means that God's blessing rests on those who make a decision for Christ and stick with it. So this is a warning first to John and his followers that their discouragement because Jesus does not fit their parameters dare not lead to abandoning him, but it is also a warning to all readers that they must decide whom they are to follow.[13] As Luz states, "These experiences of salvation make a claim; they require a decision for or against Jesus."[14]

8. Jeremias, *Theology*, 20–21; and Witherington, *Matthew*, 231, point to the poetic form of the list, centering on Jesus fulfilling the OT hopes.

9. So Carson, Matthew," 262; Turner, "Matthew," 159.

10. See Hagner, *Matthew 1–13*, 301; France, *Gospel of Matthew*, 424.

11. Bruner, *Christbook*, 413, paraphrases this well, "And God bless you, John, if you do not throw the whole thing over because I am different."

12. With "fall away" (σκανδαλίζω) the phrase ἐν ἐμοί is causal, "because of me."

13. Verseput, *Humble Messianic King*, 75, takes the saying as gnomic, not referring to John but to all who read this. That does not fit the context. It is most natural as a warning both to John and all who hear.

14. Luz, *Matthew 8–20*, 135.

Theology in Application

This is another transition passage, which both sums up what has gone before and leads into what is to come. The Baptist speaks for all readers who are addressed and challenged by Jesus and who have to accept God's Messiah for who he is and not for who they think he should be.

1. Not the Messiah Everyone Is Expecting

John expected an apocalyptic prophet with the same kind of message of judgment he espoused. Jesus did teach about judgment and the coming kingdom (5:22, 29 – 30; 6:10, 23; 7:1 – 2, 13, 19; 8:12; 10:14 – 15, 23, 28, 33, 39). However, that was part of a larger picture of the Isaianic age of salvation Christ had brought to humankind. Jesus had come to be the suffering Servant who conquered sin, not the conquering King who came to destroy the enemies of God's people. Neither John nor Jesus' followers were ready for this type of Messiah. But things are different today. Everyone wants to make Jesus in their own image, to create a comfortable Christ who makes life easier and simpler. Sadly, that is the kind of Christ too often preached from modern pulpits. Jesus is not the comfortable Christ; God demands we come to him on his terms, not ours!

2. A Demand for Decision and a Call to Faithfulness

Throughout the Mission Discourse, Jesus demanded that his followers join his mission to bring the good news of salvation to the lost world and challenge people to "receive" (10:12 – 14, 40 – 41) the message and believe. Here is the demand of the gospel stated as a beatitude and yet in negative terms to emphasize the danger of rejection. This is meant for believers (John) as well as unbelievers (John's disciples) and is a serious warning against "falling away," however we define it. John was discouraged because Jesus had not brought about the eschaton and did not fit his categories. Many today have the same doubts; they want Jesus to bring about reward and victory, yet Jesus continues to call us to a life of commitment and suffering in the midst of evil.

CHAPTER 46

Matthew 11:7 – 15

Literary Context

This is the second part of a triad (three sections within 11:2 – 19) within a triad (three parts of 11:2 – 30) and moves into the major themes of rejection and Christology that dominate chs. 11 – 12. The movement is from John's place in salvation history (vv. 7 – 10) to the violent reaction of many regarding the coming of the kingdom inaugurated by John and Jesus (vv. 11 – 15) to Israel's rejection of this new kingdom reality (vv. 16 – 19).

- **IV. Preaching and Teaching in the Midst of Opposition (11:2 – 13:53)**
  - **A. Jesus' Deeds: Revelation and Rejection (11:2 – 12:50)**
    - **1. Revelation and Rejection Begun (11:2 – 30)**
      - **a. Jesus and John the Baptist (11:2 – 19)**
        - (1) John's Doubts and Jesus' Response (11:2 – 6)
        - ➦ **(2) Jesus' Testimony about John (11:7 – 15)**
        - (3) Rejection by Israel (11:16 – 19)

Main Idea

Jesus sums up the significance of John for salvation history. Primarily, John is the forerunner like Elijah preparing the way for Jesus and the coming of the kingdom; since John is Elijah, Jesus is the Messiah who brings the age of salvation.[1] From this Jesus also addresses the violent reactions to the kingdom as the forces of evil turn against it, yet the kingdom is the dawning of the age of salvation, and everyone must heed it.

1. See Verseput, *Humble Messianic King*, 56, who entitles this section, "The Presence of Salvation."

Translation

Matthew 11:7-15

7a	Setting	As John's disciples were leaving,
b	Action	**Jesus began to tell the crowds about John:**
c	Rhetorical Question #1	*[1] "What did you go out into the wilderness to see,* *a reed blowing in the wind?*
8a	Rhetorical Question #2	*[2] If not, what did you go out to see,* *a man wearing expensive clothes?*
b		*Look, those wearing fine clothes are found in king's palaces.*
9a	Rhetorical Question #3	*[3] So what did you go out to see?*
b		*A prophet?*
c	Answer	*Yes, I tell you, even more than a prophet!*
10a	Identification #1/ Fulfillment	*This is the one about whom it was written,*
b	OT Quotation	*'Behold, I am sending my messenger* *ahead of you,*
c		*who will prepare your way* *ahead of you.'* (Mal 3:1)
11a	Assertion	*I tell you the truth, among those born from women there has not arisen anyone greater than John the Baptist,*
b		*yet the one who is least in the kingdom of heaven is greater than he is!*
12a	Setting	*But from the days of John the Baptist* *until the present,*
b	Assertion	*the kingdom of heaven is subject to violence,* *and violent people attack it.*
13a	Explanation	*For all the prophets and the law prophesied until John.*
14a	Condition of 14b	*And if you are willing to accept it,*
b	Identification #2/ Fulfillment	*he himself is Elijah, the one about to come.*
15a	Exhortation	*Whoever has ears, let them listen!"*

Structure and Literary Form

This is another Q passage with vv. 7 – 11 = Luke 7:24 – 28, v. 12 similar to Luke 16:16, and vv. 13 – 15 coming from M. The first half (vv. 7 – 10) centers on three rhetorical questions, with each followed by another question and then a response by Jesus (the latter two). This is then followed by Jesus' own evaluation of John's significance in a series of indicative declarations (vv. 11 – 14) followed by a challenge to listen (v. 15). So there are two major sections (vv. 7 – 10, 11 – 15), each composed of a series of affirmations.

Exegetical Outline

➦ **I. John's Identity (11:7 – 10)**
    A. Weak and unstable? (v. 7)
    B. Living in luxury? (v. 8)
    C. A prophet, yet more, the messianic forerunner, Mal 3:1 (vv. 9 – 10)
II. Jesus' Evaluation (11:11 – 14)
    A. The greatness of John (v. 11)
        1. None greater (v. 11a)
        2. The least in the kingdom is greater (v. 11b)
    B. The violent attack on the kingdom (v. 12)
    C. John's identity further defined (vv. 13 – 14)
        1. The turning point of the ages (v. 13)
        2. Elijah has come (v. 14)
III. A Challenge to Listen Carefully (11:15)

Explanation of the Text

11:7 As John's disciples were leaving, Jesus began to tell the crowds about John, "What did you go out into the wilderness to see, a reed blowing in the wind?" (Τούτων δὲ πορευομένων ἤρξατο ὁ Ἰησοῦς λέγειν τοῖς ὄχλοις περὶ Ἰωάννου, Τί ἐξήλθατε εἰς τὴν ἔρημον θεάσασθαι; κάλαμον ὑπὸ ἀνέμου σαλευόμενον;). Another of Matthew's many genitive absolutes (temporal) begins this section. With their question asked, John's followers are about to return to the prison when Jesus suddenly addresses the crowds about John and his significance. This was probably the popular topic of the day. John was justly famous throughout the land as the first prophet in four hundred years, and his arrest had caused a sensation. Everyone had been talking about it.

As in John 1:19 – 28, everyone wanted to know what kind of prophet he was and why he ministered as he did. Jesus now challenges the crowds with their own perception of John, but with quite different images, using a thrice-repeated rhetorical question, "What did you go into the wilderness to see?" τί could be "What" (pointing back to vv. 2 – 6) or "why" (pointing ahead to following material) and could even mean, "Could it be that you went out in the wilderness to see...?" The meaning is much the same either way, and nearly all use "What."[2]

First, Christ asks if they expected a weak, unstable person. A reed could be a bamboo-like cane used for surveying (Ezek 40:3; Rev 11:1) but here is undoubtedly the tall grass or papyrus reeds by the side of the lake easily swayed by any breeze. John would then be fickle and vacillating, easily moved by public opinion.[3] But John was a bold prophet, not a politician.

2. See Nolland, *Matthew*, 454, who says there is little difference between them.

3. Other options are: a reference to Exod 14 – 15 and God sending a wind to drive back the Sea of Reeds, thus signifying John as a miraculous prophet repeating the exodus events (Davies and Allison, *Matthew*, 2:247); or an allusion to Herod Antipas (Gerd Theissen, *The Gospels in Context: Social and Political History in*

11:8 If not, what did you go out to see, a man wearing expensive clothes? Look, those wearing fine clothes are found in king's palaces (ἀλλὰ τί ἐξήλθατε ἰδεῖν; ἄνθρωπον ἐν μαλακοῖς ἠμφιεσμένον; ἰδοὺ οἱ τὰ μαλακὰ φοροῦντες ἐν τοῖς οἴκοις τῶν βασιλέων εἰσίν). John was an austere prophet wearing a garment of camel's hair and a leather belt (3:4), not a court prophet like Elymas in Acts 13:6–12, who would dress in luxurious raiment and live in the palace. Certainly Herod Antipas would come to mind, in whose fortress John was imprisoned.[4] John was not a fancy sycophant who sided with the rulers but a bold prophet whose pronunciations got him arrested.

11:9 So what did you go out to see? A prophet? Yes, I tell you, even more than a prophet (ἀλλὰ τί ἐξήλθατε ἰδεῖν; προφήτην; ναί λέγω ὑμῖν, καὶ περισσότερον προφήτου). The conclusion, of course, was expected. John was a prophet, as everyone knew. Yet he was far more than a prophet, for he was privileged to prepare the way for the Messiah. He performed no miracles as Elijah did, but he did have the same hard-hitting message, i.e., that of calling an apostate nation back to God. He transcended the prophetic office not through either of these but through his relationship to the Christ as the messianic forerunner.

11:10 This is the one about whom it was written, "Behold, I am sending my messenger ahead of you, who will prepare your way ahead of you" (οὗτός ἐστιν περὶ οὗ γέγραπται, Ἰδοὺ ἐγὼ ἀποστέλλω τὸν ἄγγελόν μου πρὸ προσώπου σου, ὃς κατασκευάσει τὴν ὁδόν σου ἔμπροσθέν σου). To understand the true significance of the Baptist, Jesus quotes Mal 3:1. John thus is not only a prophet but fulfills prophecy. The use of "this" (οὗτός) centers squarely on John,[5] and Jesus views John as the one for whom the prophecy "was written." This is a paraphrase of Mal 3:1, though many believe the first line, "I am sending my messenger ahead of you" conflates Mal 3:1 with Exod 23:20 (where God sent an angel before Israel as they headed toward the Promised Land), made possible by the fact that the two were quoted together in synagogue readings.[6] If so, there is a further parallel: as God sent the angel to guide his people into Canaan, so Jesus sends John to prepare the entrance into the promised kingdom.[7]

However, the main emphasis is clearly on Malachi. The equation between God in the OT and Jesus here as the "Senders" is important; Jesus at the least is the divine Agent of Yahweh and likely is equated with Yahweh.[8] This is further seen in "ahead of you" (twice) and "your way." In Malachi it is "before me" (Yahweh) while here the "you" is obviously Jesus. So John is the turning point of salvation history, preparing for the final fulfillment of God's plan of salvation in Jesus. In Mal 4:5 the one whom God is preparing is explicitly identified with Elijah, so John is the Elijianic forerunner. John is smoothing the way, removing obstacles for the highway to Zion.

11:11 I tell you the truth, among those born from women there has not arisen anyone greater than John the Baptist (ἀμὴν λέγω ὑμῖν,

the Synoptic Tradition [trans. L. M. Maloney; Minneapolis: Fortress, 1991], 28–41). Neither is likely in light of the much clearer interpretation given here.

4. Theissen, *Gospels in Context*, 34–35.

5. Several (e.g., Davies and Allison, *Matthew*, 2:249) see this as Qumran pesher-style exegesis, but that is not necessary (see Joseph A. Fitzmyer, "The Use of Explicit Old Testament Quotations in Qumran Literature and in the New Testament," *NTS* 7 (1960–61): 362–63) and there are also parallels in rabbinic literature (Schlatter, *Matthäus*, 363, lists *t. Soṭah* 6, 6.7; Isa 11:2).

6. Stendahl, *School of St. Matthew*, 50; Gundry, *Matthew*, 207–8.

7. Davies and Allison, *Matthew*, 2:249.

8. So France, *Matthew* (TNTC), 194; Morris, *Matthew*, 279–80.

οὐκ ἐγήγερται ἐν γεννητοῖς γυναικῶν μείζων Ἰωάννου τοῦ βαπτιστοῦ). This ἀμήν-saying (see on 5:18) restates v. 9 another way. No one ever born has been more important than John. He is not just "more than a prophet" but is "more than" anyone — prophet, priest, or king. He is the culmination of the old covenant and the launching pad for the new covenant. As the climax of the old, he is the greatest; as the beginning of the new he is the greatest.

11:11 Yet the one who is least in the kingdom of heaven is greater than he is! (ὁ δὲ μικρότερος ἐν τῇ βασιλείᾳ τῶν οὐρανῶν μείζων αὐτοῦ ἐστιν). This turns on the interaction between "the one who is least" (μικρότερος) and "greater" (μείζων). There are three possible ways of understanding this. (1) Some believe μικρότερος means "younger" and refers to Jesus, who is younger than John but greater than he.[9] Yet that is obscure and not the more likely interpretation. (2) Others take an eschatological approach, saying the kingdom is future for Matthew, so the contrast is between the greatest in the present age (John) and the least in the coming age of the kingdom's reality.[10] (3) The majority view states that while John was the herald and initiator of the new covenant, he was not fully a part of "the kingdom of heaven." He consummated the old, and therefore even the "least"[11] of the citizens in the kingdom Christ is establishing is greater because they are part of the new order.[12]

The latter two are both viable, and both take a salvation-historical view of the kingdom. However, the inaugurated eschatology of Matthew with his already/not yet view of the kingdom makes the third view more probable. John was the greatest of the prophets in climaxing the old aeon and launching the new. Jesus was in process of establishing the new, so John was not a full part of the new kingdom. Those who would reap the benefits of the "kingdom of heaven" Jesus was establishing experienced the greater blessings that John made possible.

11:12 But from the days of John the Baptist until the present, the kingdom of heaven is subject to violence, and violent people attack it (ἀπὸ δὲ τῶν ἡμερῶν Ἰωάννου τοῦ βαπτιστοῦ ἕως ἄρτι ἡ βασιλεία τῶν οὐρανῶν βιάζεται, καὶ βιασταὶ ἁρπάζουσιν αὐτήν). There is no way to make this verse simple.[13] The problem lies in the cognates "is subject to violence" (βιάζεται) and "violent people" (βιασταί). They occur side by side and can be understood positively ("forceful advance") or negatively ("suffering violence"). Thus there are four combinations here: (1) totally positive ("the kingdom forcefully advances [through God], and forceful people [the disciples] seize it");[14] (2) totally negative ("the kingdom suffers violence [persecution], and violent people [the leaders] plunder it");[15] (3) negative/positive (the kingdom suffers violence, but forceful people

9. So Chrysostom, Augustine, Oscar Cullmann, *The Christology of the New Testament* (Philadelphia: Westminster, 1959), 32; Grundmann, *TDNT*, 4:534 – 35; idem, *Matthäus*, 307, argues this on the grounds that John would be excluded from the kingdom in the other views.

10. McNeile, *Matthew*, 154; Verseput, *Humble Messianic King*, 87 – 90; Davies and Allison, *Matthew*, 2:251 – 52.

11. The comparative "greater" (μείζων) has superlative force here, cf. BDF §61/2; Porter, *Idioms*, 123.

12. So Plummer, *Matthew*, 162; Schweizer, *Matthew*, 262; Hill, *Matthew*, 200; France, *Gospel of Matthew*, 428 – 29. Schnackenburg, *Matthew*, 106, says, "The Baptist is not thereby excluded from the coming Reign of God but only relativized in his meaning for salvation history."

13. An entire monograph has been written on it: Peter S. Cameron, *Violence and the Kingdom: The Interpretation of Matthew 11:12* (Frankfurt: Peter Lang, 1984).

14. NIV, Ridderbos, *Matthew*, 217; Verseput, *Humble Messianic King*, 94 – 99; Keener, *Matthew*, 339 – 40. See Luke 16:16, which says "the good news of the kingdom of God is being preached, and people are forcing their way into it."

15. TNIV, NRSV; Hill, *Matthew*, 200 – 201; Gundry, *Matthew*, 209 – 10; France, *Matthew*, 195; Hagner, *Matthew 1 – 13*, 306 – 7; Bruner, *Christbook*, 417; Mounce, *Matthew*, 104.

lay hold of it");[16] (4) positive/negative ("the kingdom is forcefully advancing, but violent people plunder it").[17]

In assessing these options, it is best to see βιάζεται as passive rather than middle (= "forcefully advancing"),[18] and thus as negative ("suffers violence") and to see βιασταί in its common negative use as "violent people." So the saying is most likely totally negative. As Stenger says, βιασταί comes from a family of words meaning "violent" and with "attack" (ἁρπάζω) must mean "violent people attack it"; so the two clauses must be synonymous.[19] Therefore Jesus' statement here goes back to ch. 10 and refers to the persecution that characterizes the age of mission. John the Baptist is a prime example, imprisoned and soon to be killed at the hands of Herod Antipas. "From the days of John the Baptist until the present" thus refers to the arrest of John and the opposition Jesus and his disciples have already experienced. Blomberg summarizes it well: "Despite the many blessings of the arriving kingdom ... John has been arrested by Herod. The Jewish teachers are increasingly opposing Jesus, and people are growing more and more discontent with Jesus' refusal to promote revolution."[20]

11:13 For all the prophets and the law prophesied until John (πάντες γὰρ οἱ προφῆται καὶ ὁ νόμος ἕως Ἰωάννου ἐπροφήτευσαν). Jesus now sums up the points he has been making. The age of the prophets has ended, and the law has been fulfilled (5:17 – 20). The normal order ("law and prophets") has been reversed because the stress is on the prophetic function of the whole canon, with πάντες emphatic, "all" the prophetic canon pointing to Jesus. The prophets as well as the law "prophesied" about John but especially about Jesus the Messiah. So again John is the turning point between the ages.[21] All before pointed to this moment, the arrival of Jesus the Messiah and the kingdom, and John was privileged to prepare the way.

11:14 And if you are willing to accept it, he himself is Elijah, the one about to come (καὶ εἰ θέλετε δέξασθαι, αὐτός ἐστιν Ἠλίας ὁ μέλλων ἔρχεσθαι). The "if" (εἰ) clause is a condition of fact; Jesus speaks to the people positively as being open to the truth. He now makes explicit what was implicit in the Malachi quote of v. 10; John is indeed the expected Elijah, the forerunner to the Messiah. This hardly means John was Elijah *redivivus* ("revived" or brought back from the dead; John himself denied this in John 1:21), but rather that John comes "in the spirit and power of Elijah" (Luke 1:17). "The one about to come" (with μέλλω emphasizing an imminent event) is a messianic title and reflects the common Jewish expectation that Mal 4:5 predicted the appearance of Elijah as preparation for the Messiah (e.g., Sir 48:10).

11:15 Whoever has ears, let them listen! (ὁ ἔχων ὦτα ἀκουέτω). This call to both willingness to hear and the importance of listening carefully is frequent in Jesus' teaching and the rest of Scripture (Matt 13:9, 43; Mark 4:9, 23; Luke 14:35; Rev 2:7, 11; et al.). It always points to a particularly critical truth and the importance of paying close heed to it, with the present tenses stressing the ongoing response that Jesus demands. Jesus is calling for both a willingness to hear his teaching and an appropriate response to it, best paraphrased, "you had better listen." Jesus' teaching not only about

16. Schlatter, *Matthäus*, 367 – 69.

17. NLT; Carson, "Matthew," 265 – 67; Nolland, *Matthew*, 457 – 58; Turner, "Matthew," 161.

18. G. Schrenk, "βιάζομαι," *TDNT*, 2:609 – 14.

19. W. Stenger, "βιάζομαι," *EDNT*, 1:216.

20. Blomberg, *Matthew*, 188.

21. It is frequently debated whether John is pictured in vv. 11 – 13 as outside or inside the kingdom. This is an unnecessary debate, for John provides the transition from the old era to the new and so belongs to both.

John but also about himself is in mind. This is a time of violent opposition, and the disciples must realize its seriousness as well as the exciting truths that surround the new age that has dawned.

Theology in Application

John the Baptist is a central figure in the Bible, as Jesus says — the turning point from the old to the new era of salvation history. That is the time of fulfillment, when the promises of "all the prophets and the law" (v. 13) come to fruition in the coming of the kingdom under Jesus. And John was the prophesied forerunner who prepared the way for Jesus.

1. The Time of Fulfillment

We are living in the time of fulfillment. This is also the message of 1 Pet 1:3 – 12, where those suffering persecution are told to endure by realizing what special people they were. The prophets and even the angels (1:10 – 12) longed to see the time of fulfillment worked out in the persecuted saints. Peter's theme is about suffering as the path to glory (1:11b), exactly the message here and in ch. 10. The OT saints longed to see the day we now live in, and Jesus is telling the crowds this truth by relating John's place in bringing it to pass.

2. Roles of John and Us

John was the greatest person of his time, but every citizen of the kingdom is greater. Jesus is saying it is better to experience the blessings of the kingdom than to be the one who inaugurates it. John's greatness lay in his being the transition to the new age, but he was never able to experience the benefits of it. Christians today need to realize what we have: the new access to God, the power of prayer, the experience of the fullness of the Spirit. It is too easy to take these privileges for granted and to complain about what we do not have. Matthew wants his readers to "hear" and understand this key truth — we live in the kingdom reality and have all the blessings of the new age before us.

3. Violent Oppression

This is also a time of violent opposition to the new kingdom reality. A major theme of chs. 11 – 12 (stemming from the Mission Discourse of ch. 10) is the reality of violent opposition. "Violent people attack" the new kingdom, even one's own family (10:21, 35 – 36), and so the followers must expect to go through the same hatred and persecution as did John and Jesus.

CHAPTER 47

Matthew 11:16 – 19

Literary Context

This final part of the section on Jesus and John builds on the violent reaction of v. 12 and details the rejection of John and Jesus by the people. As such it leads directly into God's condemnation of the nation in 11:20 – 24. The intertwining of John and Jesus continues. They were connected in inaugurating the new kingdom reality in vv. 7 – 15 and now are also linked in experiencing the nation's rejection.[1] Jesus has told them the significance of John; now he tells them how they will respond.

IV. Preaching and Teaching in the Midst of Opposition (11:2 – 13:53)
- **A. Jesus' Deeds: Revelation and Rejection (11:2 – 12:50)**
  - **1. Revelation and Rejection Begun (11:2 – 30)**
    - **a. Jesus and John the Baptist (11:2 – 19)**
      - (1) John's Doubts and Jesus' Response (11:2 – 6)
      - (2) Jesus' Testimony about John (11:7 – 15)
      - ➦ **(3) Rejection by Israel (11:16 – 19)**
    - b. Woes on Unrepentant Towns (11:20 – 24)

Main Idea

The response of the people is negative. Israel has rejected the gospel in 10:13b – 14, 17, 21 – 22, 35 – 36; 11:12. Now Jesus extends his description of their rejection first via a proverb on complaining children and second by detailing how the people have rejected first John and now himself.

1. Pregeant, *Matthew*, 79, says, "the reader is clear that Jesus and John are united not only by a common message but also by their rejection from a majority of the people. Crowds still follow Jesus, but there is no general movement toward repentance."

Translation

Matthew 11:16-19

16a	Question	*"T o what can I compare this generation?*
b	Comparison/Illustration	*It is like children who sit in the marketplace and call to others:*
17a	A	*'We played the flute for you,*
b	Result	and *you did not dance;*
c	B (Parallel 17a)	*we sang a dirge for you,*
d	Result (Parallel 17b)	and *you did not mourn.'*
18a	B' Assertion	For *John came neither eating nor drinking,*
b	Result	and *they say,*
c		*'He has a demon.'*
19a	A' Assertion (Parallel 18a)	*The Son of Man came eating and drinking,*
b	Result (Parallel 18b)	and *they say,*
c		*'Look, a man who is a glutton and a drunkard, a friend of tax collectors and sinners.'*
d	Question	And *wisdom is vindicated by her deeds."*

Structure and Literary Form

Again, this follows Q (= Luke 7:31 – 35)[2] and has an artfully constructed literary structure, beginning (vv. 17 – 18) with an extended simile on complaining children (= Israel), with the first couplet on Jesus (playing the flute) and the second on John (singing a funeral dirge). This is followed by a chiastic application first to John and then Jesus (vv. 18 – 19a), concluding with an aphorism on Wisdom.

Exegetical Outline

➡ **I. What This Generation Is Like: Complaining Children (11:16 – 17)**

   A. Refuse to dance to Jesus' music (v. 16)

   B. Refuse to mourn John's prophetic dirge (v. 17)

II. Application: Reject John and Jesus (11:18 – 19a)

   A. Call John demon-possessed (v. 18)

   B. Call Jesus a glutton and a drunkard (v. 19a)

III. Conclusion: Wisdom Is Justified (11:19b)

2. On the authenticity of the passage, see Davies and Allison, *Matthew*, 2:259 – 60.

Explanation of the Text

11:16 To what can I compare this generation? It is like children who sit in the marketplace and call to the others (Τίνι δὲ ὁμοιώσω τὴν γενεὰν ταύτην; ὁμοία ἐστὶν παιδίοις καθημένοις ἐν ταῖς ἀγοραῖς ἃ προσφωνοῦντα τοῖς ἑτέροις). Whenever Jesus uses "generation" (γενεά), it is always describing his contemporaries (the nation, not just the leaders) in a context of wickedness, unbelief, and rejection (cf. also 12:39, 41 – 42, 45; 16:4; 17:17; 23:36; 24:34). He uses an analogy of children playing in a marketplace, a common occurrence. But this time the children are dissatisfied and complaining, unhappy with whatever game is played. "The others" (τοῖς ἑτέροις) would be another group of children playing the games with them.

11:17 "We played the flute for you, and you did not dance; we sang a dirge for you, and you did not mourn" (λέγουσιν, Ηὐλήσαμεν ὑμῖν καὶ οὐκ ὠρχήσασθε· ἐθρηνήσαμεν καὶ οὐκ ἐκόψασθε). There seem to be two groups of children — the one calling out and inviting the other to a game, the other refusing to join no matter what the game. There are obviously two opposite games, one a celebration with dance (likely a wedding game, as flutes were common in weddings), the other a funeral game with mourning. There are also two differing interpretations, one in which the wedding game is linked to Jesus and the funeral game to John,[3] the other in which the two games are not separate but simply manifestations of Israel's refusal to play God's "game."[4]

In the proverb, there are two groups, one calling and the other responding. The question is, are the cries that of Jesus and John, with the generation being those refusing to play, or are those crying the Jewish people, upset that Jesus and John refuse to play by their rules? If we posit a deliberate chiasm in the order of vv. 17 – 19a, a lot of the difficulties to the first more allegorical interpretation disappear:

A Jesus inviting to a wedding (v. 17a)
  B John preaching a message of judgment (funeral, v. 17b)
  B' the people rejecting John's ascetic ministry (v. 18)
A' the people rejecting Jesus' joyous kingdom ministry (v. 19).

So the Jewish people are like children refusing to respond to Jesus' wedding game and also refusing to respond to John's funerary proclamation of judgment. Nolland develops this similarly, with the children being John and Jesus calling the people to a "mock judgment scene" (the "marketplace" [ἀγορά] denoting the place where the court sat) and the people refusing to play.[5] It is impossible to be dogmatic; both are viable. However we take it, the message is essentially the same: John and Jesus are both rejected by their contemporaries.

11:18 For John came neither eating nor drinking, and they say, "He has a demon" (ἦλθεν γὰρ Ἰωάννης μήτε ἐσθίων μήτε πίνων, καὶ λέγουσιν, Δαιμόνιον ἔχει). The use of "came" (ἦλθεν) in both halves for John and Jesus goes back to the use of ἦλθον language in 9:1, 13; 10:34, 35 for the

3. McNeile, *Matthew*, 157 – 58; Bonnard, *Matthieu*, 164; Hill, *Matthew*, 201 – 2; Schweizer, *Matthew*, 263 – 4; France, *Gospel of Matthew*, 433 – 34; Verseput, *Humble Messianic King*, 112 – 15; Bruner, *Christbook*, 422; Blomberg, *Matthew*, 189 – 90.

4. Grundmann, *Matthäus*, 311; Davies and Allison, *Matthew*, 2:262; Hagner, *Matthew 1 – 13*, 310; Keener, *Matthew*, 341; Wilkins, *Matthew*, 418.

5. Nolland, *Matthew*, 462 – 63, building on W. J. Cotter, "The Parable of the Children in the Marketplace, Q (Lk) 7:31 – 35: An Examination of the Parable's Images and Significance," *NovT* 29 (1987): 289 – 304.

mission. John's ascetic ministry as a wilderness prophet meant he refused luxury and ate "locusts and wild honey" (3:4b). His was a proclamation of judgment, suited for the funeral dirge of v. 17b. Yet he was rejected and even thought to be demon-possessed. There is no record of such a charge (though there was for Jesus, cf. 9:34, 12:24), but it is likely to have happened.

11:19 The Son of Man came eating and drinking (ἦλθεν ὁ υἱὸς τοῦ ἀνθρώπου ἐσθίων καὶ πίνων). Jesus' joyous ministry suited a wedding game (v. 17a), a fitting analogy in light of Jesus' use of wedding imagery in 9:15 to depict his ministry as well as the Baptist's depiction of himself as "the friend of the bridegroom" (= best man) in John 3:29. Here "Son of Man" is a circumlocution for Jesus himself, with little of the glorified figure of Dan 7:13 – 14 in this context (see excursus after 8:22).

11:19 And they say, "Look, a man who is a glutton and a drunkard, a friend of tax collectors and sinners" (καὶ λέγουσιν, Ἰδοὺ ἄνθρωπος φάγος καὶ οἰνοπότης, τελωνῶν φίλος καὶ ἁμαρτωλῶν). This begins with Matthew's characteristic "look" (ἰδού, see on 8:2, 24; 19:16) and consists of a series of appositives in which Jesus is described in two pairs of related characteristics. Jesus often shared table fellowship with disreputable people, and clearly 9:10 – 13 is in mind, when Matthew gave a banquet in Jesus' honor and the Pharisees objected to Jesus' presence among "tax collectors and sinners" (cf. also Luke 15:1 – 2).

The principle here was, "To share a meal is to share a life," and meals meant fellowship, acceptance, and identity between "friends." Social values and hierarchical boundaries controlled such occasions. "Anyone who challenged these rankings and boundaries would be judged to have acted dishonorably, a serious charge in cultures based on the values of honor and shame. Transgressing these customs consistently would make a person an enemy of social stability."[6] There was a close link between purity in terms of food laws and purity in terms of companions at meals. "Pharisees regarded their tables at home as surrogates for the Lord's altar in the temple in Jerusalem and therefore strove to maintain in their households and among their eating companions the state of ritual purity required of priests in Temple service."[7] Jesus challenges such exclusivity and used meals as evangelistic opportunities, showing "tax collectors and sinners" that he accepted them and wanted to help them.

11:19 And wisdom is vindicated (καὶ ἐδικαιώθη ἡ σοφία). Jesus' wondrous deeds will inevitably "justify" or vindicate his claims. This (= Luke 7:35) is the only place in the Synoptics where personified Wisdom appears directly, and it is thus at the heart of so-called Wisdom Christology in Matthew and the gospels. Bultmann believed the background was an ancient "wisdom myth," in which a preexistent Wisdom lay hidden in heaven and sent out emissaries to take her message to earth.[8] Building on this M. Jack Suggs argued that Matthew saw Jesus not as Wisdom's emissary but as Wisdom Incarnate, and his deeds are Wisdom's deeds.[9] While most agree with Sugg's thesis of a central wisdom motif, few posit a full-blown Wisdom Christology.

Marshall Johnson and Frances Gench both take a detailed look at the primary passages for such a Sophia approach (11:19, 25 – 30; 23:34 – 36, 37 – 39) and conclude that Matthew uses wisdom themes but not a Wisdom Christology. There is not a lot of evidence for such a "myth" with "envoys of Sophia," and it is more likely that Matthew uses wisdom motifs not to present Jesus as Wisdom herself

6. Bartchy, "Table Fellowship," *DJG*, 796.
7. Ibid.
8. Bultmann, *Synoptic Tradition*, 115 (cf. 69 – 108).
9. See Suggs, *Wisdom*.

but as the Son of God who speaks with divine authority and "mediates God's revelation."[10] France says personified Wisdom in Proverbs is essentially practical in guiding lives to exemplify God's goodness, so this says in effect that John and Jesus have displayed such lives that are "justified" against the criticism of the leaders.[11]

11:19 ... by her deeds (ἀπὸ τῶν ἔργων αὐτῆς). Luke 7:35 has "by all her children," but the two mean virtually the same thing. As Verseput points out, this proverbial aphorism turns the two statements on John and Jesus into more than mere descriptions of "this generation": "they are a scathing indictment of the chosen people who align themselves against the clearly evident plan of God."[12] There is no evidence that this was a current proverb in Jesus' day, but it has the quality of one, with personified Wisdom (cf. Prov 8; Sir 24, 51; Wisd 7 – 8) and a gnomic aorist.[13]

It seems clear that Jesus identifies himself with the work of Wisdom, so that Wisdom's deeds are Jesus' deeds (and those of his followers).[14] So this means that Jesus himself is ἐδικαιώθη, "justified" or "vindicated" on the basis of[15] the deeds named in 11:1, 5.[16] In other words, Jesus is proven right by his works (both word and deed) as well as the works of John the Baptist and his disciples in ch. 10,[17] so that the indifference and outright rejection of Jesus' contemporaries will simply bring divine judgment on them (see the next section).

Theology in Application

The theme of rejection now takes top spot. As before, John and Jesus are intertwined, and here it is on the reaction of the people to their quite different ministries.

1. People Will Find a Way

If people want to reject, they will find a way. John and Jesus had ministries that were in some ways the polar opposite of one another. Those who wanted a solemn, serious presentation of truth centering on judgment should have preferred John. Those who wanted an upbeat, joyous celebration of God's kingdom presence should have been drawn to Jesus. But the Jewish people did not want truth; they wanted

10. Frances Taylor Gench, *Wisdom in the Christology of Matthew* (New York: Univ. Press of America, 1997), 209. See also Marshall D. Johnson, "Reflections on a Wisdom Approach to Matthew's Christology," *CBQ* 36 (1974): 44 – 64.

11. France, *Gospel of Matthew*, 435.

12. Verseput, *Humble Messianic King*, 115.

13. See BDF §333; Hagner, *Matthew 1 – 13*, 311.

14. Ben Witherington, *The Christology of Jesus* (Minneapolis: Augsburg/Fortress, 1990), 51 – 52; and his *Matthew*, 235, and Keener, *Matthew*, 343, see Jesus as Wisdom, contra Carson, "Matthew," 271; Simon Gathercole, "The Justification of Wisdom (Matt 11:19b/Luke 7:35)," *NTS* 49 (2003): 476 – 88, and Wilkins, *Matthew*, 419, see this as God's wisdom manifested in the "deeds" or lifestyle of John and Jesus in vv. 17 – 18a. This is likely another instance of both-and. God's "wise" work is personified in Jesus.

15. For ἀπό with a passive verb meaning "by," see Zerwick, 90; Gench, *Wisdom*, 141.

16. Morris, *Matthew*, 286 – 87, takes this of the works Jesus' followers do in keeping with the parallel "children" in Luke 7:35. This is possible but not as likely in this context of Jesus' "deeds."

17. Gench, *Wisdom*, 181, says that because the "deeds" are not just "Jesus' works but also those of John and the disciples, one cannot posit a full-blown identification of Jesus with Sophia." Rather, there is "a theological construal of *sophia*," in which God's wise purposes come to pass in Jesus.

conformity to their preconceived religious norms. So they rejected both John and Jesus.

So it is today. The problem is the human condition, and total depravity reigns in our day in the same way it did in Jesus' day. Churches that are market-driven and try to appeal to the "itching ears" (2 Tim 4:3) of popular demands will never in the end truly reach the lost. Only by proclaiming God's deep truths and letting the Spirit take over can depravity be overcome.

2. God's Vindication of Truth

God's messengers should never seek popularity and acceptance. We need the boldness of John and Jesus and must allow God to justify our ministry; we must refuse to play the numbers game of worldly popularity. John and Jesus did not worry about what people thought or even how people reacted. They proclaimed truth the way God led them, and so must we. Will our vindication come from the world (even from members of our church) or from God? We need more fearless proclaimers and fewer shallow popularizers!

CHAPTER 48

Matthew 11:20 – 24

Literary Context

There has been a steady movement in ch. 11 from reaction to rejection and now to judgment on the nation for its consistent refusal to respond properly to John or to Jesus. In spite of their different styles, both preached a message of repentance (John in 3:1, 8, 11; Jesus in 4:17; 11:20, 21; 12:41), and yet the nation has refused to repent. So divine judgment is their reward.

- **IV. Preaching and Teaching in the Midst of Opposition (11:2 – 13:53)**
  - **A. Jesus' Deeds: Revelation and Rejection (11:2 – 12:50)**
    - **1. Revelation and Rejection Begun (11:2 – 30)**
      - a. Jesus and John the Baptist (11:2 – 19)
      - ➦ **b. Woes on Unrepentant Towns (11:20 – 24)**

Main Idea

God has brought the age of salvation through Jesus to the nation. The kingdom has been inaugurated. Yet entire towns have not only failed to recognize it but have refused to repent and accept the salvation Jesus has brought before them and proved via his miracles and preaching (11:5). As a result, God's judgment is upon them.

Translation

(See next page.)

Structure and Literary Form

Another Q passage (= Luke 10:12 – 15), this paragraph falls naturally into two woe oracles, first against Chorazin and Bethsaida (vv. 21 – 22) and then against

Matthew 11:20-24

20a	Action	**Then he began**
		to denounce the towns
		in which he had done most of his miracles
b	Basis for 20a	because they refused to repent.
21a	Exclamation (A)	*"Woe to you, Chorazin.*
b	Exclamation (A′)	*Woe to you, Bethsaida.*
c	Basis for 21a-b (B)	*Because if the miracles that occurred in you had been done in Tyre and Sidon,*
d		*they would have repented long ago in sackcloth and ashes.*
22a	Assertion (C)	*Nevertheless I tell you, God will be more tolerant*
		toward Tyre and Sidon
		on the day of judgment
		than to you.
23a	Question	*And as for you, Capernaum, will you be exalted*
		up to the heavens?
b	Exclamation (A)	*No, you will descend down to Hades,*
c	Basis for 23a-b (B)	*because*
		if the miracles . . . had been done in Sodom,
		that occurred in you
d		*it would have remained until this day.*
24a	Assertion (C)	*Nevertheless I tell you,*
		God will be more tolerant
		toward the land of Sodom
		on the day of judgment
		than to you."

Capernaum (vv. 23 – 24). Each follows the same pattern: a statement of judgment (v. 23a differs in form) followed by identical ὅτι εἰ clauses contrasting the cities to Tyre and Sidon/Sodom, who would have repented if they had seen such miracles. Each section then concludes with a "more tolerant" statement that prophesies the severe judgment the towns will face.

Exegetical Outline

➡ **I. Setting: Denunciation of the Towns (11:20)**

II. Judgment on Chorazin and Bethsaida (11:21 – 22)

A. Pronouncement of judgment (v. 21a)

B. Reason: contrast with Tyre and Sidon (v. 21b)

C. Proclamation of severe judgment (v. 22)

III. Judgment on Capernaum (11:23 – 24)

A. Pronouncement of judgment (v. 23a)

B. Reason: contrast with Sodom (v. 23b)

C. Proclamation of severe judgment (v. 24)

Explanation of the Text

11:20 Then he began to denounce the towns in which he had done most of his miracles because they refused to repent (Τότε ἤρξατο ὀνειδίζειν τὰς πόλεις ἐν αἷς ἐγένοντο αἱ πλεῖσται δυνάμεις αὐτοῦ, ὅτι οὐ μετενόησαν). The rejection is now an accomplished fact, so Jesus begins (cf. "he began" [ἤρξατο], followed by a present infinitive denoting the inauguration of a continuing activity) to rebuke the people of Israel for their unbelief and rejection. Here the negative results of the mission of 9:35 – 10:42 are stated directly. Jesus had performed "most" of his "miracles" (δυνάμεις) right there and thereby proved that the age of salvation had begun (see on 11:5), but the people had refused to respond to the import of these miracles and did not "repent." Note that Jesus never sought fame or attention but only repentance (4:17). He wanted the people to get right with God. When they would not change their ways, he had to denounce them, with ὀνειδίζω meaning "insult" in an adversarial context and "reproach" in a proclamation context (here).

11:21 Woe to you, Chorazin. Woe to you, Bethsaida (Οὐαί σοι, Χοραζίν, οὐαί σοι, Βηθσαϊδά). It is fairly common to see in the "woes" (οὐαί) pity and compassionate regret[1] or a mixture of doom and pity,[2] yet this term is always used in the OT for judgment oracles (e.g., Isa 5:8, 11, 18 – 22; Ezek 16:23, 24:6; Amos 5:18; 6:1, 4; Hab 2:6 – 19), and both the Hebrew *hôy* or *ʾôy* and the Greek οὐαί are onomatopoetic and signify intense anger or grief. In the OT there is rarely any idea of pity or compassion, and the literary device has links with funerary lamentations and prophetic curses.[3] While some do see aspects of pity in the NT usage, many others agree that in eschatological contexts such as this one, judgment or condemnation is the major thrust.[4] This seems better here, for the day of judgment is certainly in mind, and it is unbelief that is condemned.

There is no mention of either Chorazin or Bethsaida anywhere else in Matthew. Chorazin was a medium-sized town noted for its wheat production and identified with modern Khirbet Karazeh about two miles north of Capernaum.[5] Bethsaida was on the northern tip of the lake just on the western side of the Jordan River in Gaulanitis (but geographically part of Galilee)[6] and was the original home of Simon and Andrew as well as Philip (John 1:44, 12:21). Jesus had two mission trips through Galilee in Matthew (4:23; 9:35), walked on the water on the way there in Mark 6:45, and healed a blind man there in Mark 8:22 and many others in Luke 9:10.

11:21 Because if the miracles that occurred in you had been done in Tyre and Sidon, they would have repented long ago in sackcloth and ashes

1. Morris, *Matthew*, 288.

2. Carson, "Matthew," 273; Blomberg, *Matthew*, 191.

3. See Ronald E. Clements, "Woe," *ABD*, 6:945 – 46.

4. Norman Hillyer, "Woe," *NIDNTT*, 3:1052. David Garland, *The Intention of Matthew 23* (NovTSup 52; Leiden: Brill, 1979), 70 – 72, separates the eschatological woes of 11:21 and ch. 23 from the personal woes of 18:7; 24:19; 26:24, which he believes are more laments. Verseput, *Humble Messianic King*, 123 – 24, demurs and qualifies Garland by saying it deals with the *expectation* of judgment rather than the pronouncement of judgment. This is probably correct, but still it is a cry of judgment and not of pity.

5. R. W. Smith, "Chorazin," *ABD*, 1:911 – 12.

6. Cf. James F. Strange, "Bethsaida," *ABD*, 1:692.

(ὅτι εἰ ἐν Τύρῳ καὶ Σιδῶνι ἐγένοντο αἱ δυνάμεις αἱ γενόμεναι ἐν ὑμῖν, πάλαι ἂν ἐν σάκκῳ καὶ σποδῷ μετενόησαν) This is a contrary-to-fact condition, meaning the miracles had not occurred in Tyre and Sidon as they had in Galilee. The mention of Tyre and Sidon goes back to the judgment prophecies in Isa 23 and Ezek 26 – 28, where they were condemned for their luxurious living and arrogance. Those prophecies were fulfilled when Alexander the Great had his army build a causeway a half mile long and two to three hundred yards wide to the island of Tyre and sacked the city in 332 BC.[7]

Jesus' point is based on the note in 11:5 that his miracles demonstrated that the age of salvation had come. If totally pagan Tyre and Sidon had seen the same miracles done in Galilee, they would have realized their need of salvation and "repented." Sackcloth was an abrasive cloth of camel hair worn in times of mourning, and ashes were placed on the head to signify grief in times of death/disaster or sorrow for sin (Esth 4:1 – 3; Isa 58:5; Dan 9:3; Jonah 3:6 – 9). Galilee had seen those miracles but reacted in unbelief and refused to repent.

11:22 Nevertheless I tell you, God will be more tolerant toward Tyre and Sidon on the day of judgment than to you (πλὴν λέγω ὑμῖν, Τύρῳ καὶ Σιδῶνι ἀνεκτότερον ἔσται ἐν ἡμέρᾳ κρίσεως ἢ ὑμῖν). Jesus' conclusion: at the last judgment (cf. 10:15; 12:36; 13:30, 42 – 43, 50) "God will be more tolerant toward"[8] those arrogant pagan cities than toward Galilee, which had rejected the import of Jesus' miracles. Carson draws three conclusions: (1) the Judge has "contingent knowledge" and "knows what Tyre and Sidon would have done"; (2) God owes revelation to no one; (3) final judgment depends on opportunity, so there will be "degrees of torment in hell" (Matt 12:41; 23:13; cf. Luke 12:47 – 48; Rom 1:20 – 2:16).[9] "From everyone who has been given much, much will be demanded" (Luke 12:48); Galilee had received the greatest ministry humankind would ever know, so their judgment would be correspondingly more severe.

11:23 And as for you, Capernaum, will you be exalted up to the heavens? No, you will descend down to Hades (καὶ σύ, Καφαρναούμ, μὴ ἕως οὐρανοῦ ὑψωθήσῃ; ἕως ᾅδου καταβήσῃ). Capernaum was Jesus' hometown and the central headquarters for the Galilean mission (4:13, 8:5; 9:1). Several of his miracles had been performed there (8:5 – 17; 9:2 – 13, 18 – 34); in fact, in Mark 1:21 – 37, the entire area had been galvanized, so much so that "the whole town gathered" (Mark 1:33) and "everyone [was] looking for" Jesus (1:37). "Exalted up to the heavens ... descend down to Hades" alludes to Isa 14:13, 15, the condemnation of the king of Babylon and of Babylon itself ("morning star, son of the dawn," Isa 14:12) for its proud boasting and self-exaltation.

Capernaum, a town of about 1,500 population, was the leading city in the area, well-situated geographically and economically. Jesus condemns its pride[10] and prophesies that like Babylon, it will be brought to ruin, using the powerful "lifted up ... brought down" image of Isaiah. μή is emphatic — "you will not!"[11] "Hades" (cf. 16:18) is

7. D. R. Edwards, "Tyre," *ABD*, 6:690.

8. This structure (an unexpressed subject of ἔσται) functions similarly to a divine passive, with God the implicit actor in the judgment scene.

9. Carson, "Matthew," 273.

10. So Hill, *Matthew* , 203; Albright and Mann, *Matthew*, 143; Keener, *Matthew*, 344. Others (Grundmann, *Matthäus*, 314; Schweizer, 267; Bruner, *Christbook*, 434 – 35) say Capernaum was too small to have that kind of pride and believe it to be pride based on the fact that Jesus called it home. Yet that does not fit the fact that their reaction to Jesus was one of unbelief. This was pride in local importance.

11. This word μή introduces a question expecting a "no" answer ("You will not be exalted to the heavens, will you?"); but I like the translation of the TNIV, which uses the word to introduce the following statement, "No."

the place of the dead, often the grave, but it is also linked conceptually to "Gehenna" (cf. 5:22, 29 – 30; 10:28), and here it probably has the latter connotation of eternal punishment. So the "descent down to Hades" is not the physical destruction of the city but the eternal judgment it was facing.

11:23 ... because if the miracles that occurred in you had been done in Sodom, it would have remained until this day (ὅτι εἰ ἐν Σοδόμοις ἐγενήθησαν αἱ δυνάμεις αἱ γενόμεναι ἐν σοί, ἔμεινεν ἂν μέχρι τῆς σήμερον). The contrary-to-fact condition construction (εἰ . . . ἄν) means this was not the case; they had not seen such miracles. Sodom and Gomorrah were destroyed by God for their terrible wickedness (Gen 18 – 19), and their name became proverbial for evil and destruction (Isa 1:9; Matt 10:15; Rom 9:29; 2 Pet 2:6 = Jude 7). Yet here Jesus says even Sodom would have repented and been spared destruction ("remained until this day") if they had witnessed the same miracles mentioned in 11:5, 21); even that paradigm of wicked cities would have understood the import of the miracles. So Capernaum is doubly condemned.

11:24 Nevertheless I tell you, God will be more tolerant toward the land of Sodom on the day of judgment than to you (πλὴν λέγω ὑμῖν ὅτι γῇ Σοδόμων ἀνεκτότερον ἔσται ἐν ἡμέρᾳ κρίσεως ἢ σοί). As in v. 22 God the Judge will show more mercy for Sodom than for Capernaum, for in his omniscience he knows that they would have repented if they had experienced the miracles Capernaum had seen. So Capernaum can expect a more severe condemnation than Sodom at the last judgment.

Theology in Application

There are many judgment passages in Matthew (e.g., 3:7 – 12; 7:21 – 23; 8:10 – 12; 11:2 – 19, 20 – 24; 12:1 – 8, 9 – 14, 22 – 37, 38 – 42; 13:24 – 30, 36 – 43, 47 – 52; 19:28 – 29; 21:33 – 22:14; chs. 24 – 25), so we will be visiting this issue several more times. There is a place for fear in this life, and Jesus was not afraid to let people know the implications of unbelief. As Hauerwas says,

> Jesus' pronouncement of judgment on the cities in which he performed deeds of power makes us, contemporary Christians, profoundly uncomfortable. We want a gospel of love that insures when everything is said and done that everyone and everything is going to be okay.... But the gospel is judgment because otherwise it would not be good news.[12]

1. God's Omniscience

God is omniscient, and everyone will get exactly what they deserve. The principle of law in Roman jurisprudence was called *lex talionis*, the law of retribution. It meant that the criminal would pay the exact penalty that was fitting for their crime.

12. Hauerwas, *Matthew*, 115 – 16.

That is God's law as well, and no one will get away with anything. God knows not only what did happen but what would have happened in different circumstances. There is no use pretending we can hide anything from God. We will all be judged by our works (Matt 16:27; Rom 2:6; 1 Cor 3:12 – 15; Rev 22:12).

2. Degrees of Punishment

As there are degrees of reward, there will probably also be degrees of punishment. This is debated, but it is likely that Dante's *Inferno* had it right in principle. In Rev 20:12 – 13 it says the dead are judged "according to what they have done," which could signify that each person will receive exactly the penalty that is in keeping with their deeds (cf. Luke 12:47 – 48).[13] In that sense, the Galilean towns will receive a more severe penalty because they had been given more. Bruner makes a powerful observation:

> *Christian* communities are in special trouble on judgment day, not because Jesus has not really been in the communities, but because he has.... Every member of a church has Jesus, for Jesus is present in his Word, fellowship, and sacraments. But Jesus does not *have* every member of his church; he has only those who, under the impact of his miraculous grace, are actually changing.[14]

13. Of course, the issue of degrees of rewards is also debated. Craig Blomberg, "Degrees of Reward in the Kingdom of Heaven," *JETS* 35 (1992): 159 – 172, denies that there will be such and believes that everyone will receive the same reward, the crown of life (1 Cor 9:25; 2 Tim 4:8; Jas 1:12). This will be discussed again at the parable of the workers in the vineyard (20:1 – 16), but let me simply state that I disagree and believe that every person receives as her reward everything done in this life for God and for others.

14. Bruner, *Christbook*, 425.

CHAPTER 49

Matthew 11:25 – 30

Literary Context

The revelation of the true significance of John the Baptist (11:7 – 10) has led Jesus into an extended meditation on the unbelief and rejection of the Jewish people (11:11 – 19) and the consequent judgment they will experience (11:20 – 24). Jesus now continues his discussion of the state of the nation but concludes this section on a positive note by showing God's wisdom in producing salvation through revealing his Son in spite of the rebellion of his people. God's chosen people have rejected the revelation of God in Jesus, so God is turning to the "infants" (v. 25), those whom Jesus invites into his "rest" (v. 28).

IV. Preaching and Teaching in the Midst of Opposition (11:2 – 13:53)
- **A. Jesus' Deeds: Revelation and Rejection (11:2 – 12:50)**
  - **1. Revelation and Rejection Begun (11:2 – 30)**
    - a. Jesus and John the Baptist (11:2 – 19)
    - b. Woes on Unrepentant Towns (11:20 – 24)
    - ➦ **c. The Father Reveals the Son (11:25 – 30)**

Main Idea

Jesus traces several themes here. (1) God's own elect sovereignty is made known in revealing the kingdom truths not to the so-called "wise" but to "infants," i.e., the "little ones" (10:42), Jesus' followers (11:25 – 26). (2) The intimate union of Father and Son is demonstrated in their unique knowledge of each other and in the revelation Jesus has provided (v. 27). (3) Jesus invites all who will to become followers and find rest in him by taking his easy "yoke" upon themselves (vv. 28 – 30).

Translation

Matthew 11:25-30

25a	Praise	**At that time Jesus replied,**
b		*"I thank you, Father, Lord of heaven and earth,*
c	Basis for 25b	*that you have hidden these things from the wise and learned and*
d	Basis for 25b	*revealed them to infants.*
26a	Basis for 25c-d	*Yes, Father, for this was your good pleasure.*
27a	Assertion	*All things have been given to me by my Father.*
b	Assertion	*No one knows the Son except the Father,*
c	Parallel 27b	*and no one knows the Father except the Son and*
d	Expansion of 27c	*anyone to whom the Son wishes to reveal him.*
28a	Exhortation (A)	*Come to me, all you weary and burdened people,*
b	Result of 28a (B)	*and I will give you rest.*
29a	Exhortation (A')	*Take my yoke upon you and learn from me,*
b	Basis for 29a	*for I am meek and humble in heart,*
c	Result of 29a (B')	*and you will find rest for your souls.*
30a	Basis for 29c	*For my yoke is easy and my burden is light."*

Structure and Literary Form

The first half (vv. 25 – 27) is a Q passage (= Luke 10:21 – 22), but vv. 28 – 30 is M material. In Luke the context is that of the success of the mission of the seventy (10:1 – 17) and the authority of the disciples over the cosmic powers (10:18 – 20), while in Matthew it is opposition and rejection. It is widely recognized that there are three parts to this section. (1) Verses 25 – 26 are a prayer of thanksgiving for God's elect will in revealing the kingdom to the "infants." (2) Verse 27 is a christological affirmation showing that the divine revelation resides in Jesus because of the intimate mutual knowledge of Father and Son. (3) Verses 28 – 30 are an invitation to the "infants" to come and find rest in the humble king; it is a wisdom saying and looks to Jesus as the presence of God in this world.

The progression of thought is this: Jesus thanks God for his sovereign will in revealing salvation, then takes on himself that authority as the Son, and finally uses that authority to invite the weary to enjoy salvation and rest in him. In all of this Jesus is God's Wisdom,[1] the voice and presence of God in this world and the true

1. Eduard Norden, *Agnostos Theos: Untersuchungen zur Formgeschichte religiöser Reden* (Berlin: Teubner, 1913), 276 – 308, believed that 11:25 – 30 was form-critically similar to Sir 51 as Hellenistic mysticism presenting Jesus as Wisdom proclaiming union with God. Following him, critical scholars have agreed that this is a wisdom passage but disagreed both with the Hellenistic background (many posit Jewish sources) and the unity of the passage (many believe Matthew put the passage together).

authoritative interpreter of God's truth. Betz calls vv. 28 – 30 "theologically identical with the makarisms of the Sermon on the Mount."[2]

Exegetical Outline

- ➡ **I. Prayer of Thanksgiving (11:25 – 26)**
  - A. Recipient: Lord of heaven and earth (v. 25a)
  - B. Content: God's revelation (v. 25b)
    - 1. Hidden from the wise
    - 2. Revealed to the infants
  - C. The basis: God's pleasure (v. 26)
- **II. Jesus as the True Revelation (11:27)**
  - A. All committed to Jesus
  - B. Mutual knowledge of Father and Son
  - C. Revelation from the Son to the followers
- **III. Invitation to Come (11:28 – 30)**
  - A. Come and find rest (v. 28)
    - 1. The offer
    - 2. The recipients: the weary and burdened
  - B. Take my yoke and find rest (v. 29)
    - 1. The offer
    - 2. The reason: the gentle and humble Savior
  - C. Conclusion — easy yoke/light burden (v. 30)

Explanation of the Text

11:25 At that time Jesus replied,[3] "I thank you, Father, Lord of heaven and earth" (Ἐν ἐκείνῳ τῷ καιρῷ ἀποκριθεὶς ὁ Ἰησοῦς εἶπεν, Ἐξομολογοῦμαί σοι, πάτερ, κύριε τοῦ οὐρανοῦ καὶ τῆς γῆς). Matthew will use "at that time" (ἐν ἐκείνῳ τῷ καιρῷ) twice (11:25; 12:1), and in both places it provides a bridge from one event to the other. It does not mean the events were simultaneous but should be translated, "at nearly the same time."[4] Jesus' prayer flows out of the condemnation of the Galilean cities and prepares for another rejection scene in 12:1 – 8. Thus the "answering" probably means Jesus is responding to the Jews' refusal to accept his message.[5]

However, Andres Feuillet, "Jésus at la sagesse divine d'après les Évangiles Synoptiques," *RB* 62 (1955): 161 – 96, argues that the saying was an authentic wisdom logion of Jesus.

2. Hans-Dieter Betz, "The Logion of the Easy Yoke and Rest," *JBL* 86 (1967): 10 – 24 (esp. 24).

3. The expression ἀποκριθεὶς εἶπεν is called by Wallace, 650, a "redundant (a.k.a. pleonastic) participle." It occurs frequently in Matthew (12:39; 13:11, 37; 19:27; et al.). This idiom emphasizes what is said and is normally translated with a single verb.

4. See Yong-Eui Yang, *Jesus and the Sabbath in Matthew's Gospel* (JSNTSup 138; Sheffield: Sheffield Academic Press, 1997), 166.

5. So Hagner, *Matthew 1 – 13*, 318, contra Davies and Allison, *Matthew*, 2:273, who say Jesus is not "answering" anything and the phrase is just an "enlarged equivalent for 'said'" (following Plummer). While that is often true, in this context Hagner is more correct.

In "I thank" (ἐξομολογοῦμαι, the present tense shows this is Jesus' constant cry) there is the idea of both thanksgiving (used in many thanksgiving psalms) and praise. The term can also connote confession, but when addressed to God denotes praise for his mighty deeds (Ps 6:5; 9:1; 35:18; Sir 51:1; et al.). Jesus praises God for his elect wisdom. The Father – Son[6] relationship dominates (twice in vv. 25 – 26, preparing for v. 27), for the sovereign authority of the Father (see on 6:9) is passed on to the Son. "Lord of heaven and earth" looks to God as the creator and sustainer of the universe, the basis for God as the revealer of heavenly truths. It is the sovereign God with authority over all things who has acted in this way.

11:25 "... that you have hidden these things from the wise and learned" (ὅτι ἔκρυψας ταῦτα ἀπὸ σοφῶν καὶ συνετῶν). The "hidden ... revealed"[7] dichotomy has overtones of divine election. God has chosen to reject one group and turn to the other. The ambiguous "these things" (ταῦτα) probably refers to the words and deeds of Jesus, the disclosure of the kingdom reality in Jesus as well as in John (11:1 – 24).[8] There is a realized eschatology at work here, for in Jesus the last days have begun, and this is the age of revelation. This prepares for the similar motif of concealing/revealing in 13:11, also using the apocalyptic idea of the "mysteries of the kingdom" revealed.[9]

The language is similar to 9:13, where "I have not come to call the righteous but sinners" should be paraphrased, "I have not come to call those who think they are righteous but those who know they are sinners" — repeated here in "those who think they are wise" vs. "those who know they are infants." Who are "the wise and learned"? It is common to identify them with the leaders, in particular the scribes and Pharisees, who were the experts in law.[10] Certainly this is viable, for they are mentioned frequently (12:2, 14, 24, 38); yet the larger context of Matt 10 – 12 is broader. In ch. 11 it is all of unbelieving Israel that is the focus, and that fits well here; Israel was the recipient of the Torah and looked upon itself as the wisdom of God among the nations. So it is best to see a deliberate ambiguity with the Pharisees and scribes in a narrower sense and the unbelieving nation in a broader sense as the focus.[11] This echoes Isa 29:14, "the wisdom of the wise will perish, the intelligence of the intelligent will vanish."

11:25 "... and revealed them to infants" (καὶ ἀπεκάλυψας αὐτὰ νηπίοις). The "infants" (νηπίοις), then, are the opposite, the simple (Ps 19:7; 119:130) and unlearned who have become Jesus' followers.[12] Jesus often calls his followers the "little ones" or "the least" (10:42; 11:11; 18:6, 10, 14; 25:40, 45), and he used the image of children to depict true disciples as those who are insignificant in the eyes of the world, yet completely open to God's truths (18:2 – 5; 19:14; 21:16).[13] The Jewish people

6. France, *Gospel of Matthew*, 444, says Jesus here "breaks new ground" in addressing God as "Father" rather than "our Father" (elsewhere). This "unprecedented" form establishes a new prayer relationship of intimacy with God the "Father."

7. Both are aorists, looking at the divine action as a single whole.

8. So Verseput, *Humble Messianic King*, 138.

9. See Yang, *Jesus and the Sabbath*, 154 – 55.

10. Hill, *Matthew*, 205; Bonnard, *Matthieu*, 167 – 68; Beare, *Matthew*, 265

11. So Celia Deutsch, *Hidden Wisdom and the Easy Yoke: Wisdom, Torah and Discipleship in Matthew 11.25 – 30* (JSNTSup 18; Sheffield: JSOT Press, 1987), 30 – 31; Carson, "Matthew," 275; Verseput, *Humble Messianic King*, 137.

12. Some have argued that these are the *ʿam hāʾāreṣ*, the common people among the Jews as opposed to the learned scribes and Pharisees (Grundmann, *Matthäus*, 316; Luz, *Matthew 8 – 20*, 162 – 64). But this does not really fit the context of Jewish rejection.

13. See Jacques Dupont, "Les 'simples' (*petâyim*) dans la Bible et à Qumrân: A propos des νήπιοι de Mt. 11,25; Lc.

were the "people of the book" and yet rejected the one to whom the book pointed. God reveals his truths only to those who open themselves up to him with a childlike simplicity and receptivity, not to those who in their pride and self-sufficiency feel no need for it.

11:26 "Yes, Father, for this was your good pleasure" (ναί ὁ πατήρ, ὅτι οὕτως εὐδοκία ἐγένετο ἔμπροσθέν σου). The reason (ὅτι) for Jesus' praise is the Father's "pleasure," a concept strongly related to the predestinarian thrust of the whole (Schweizer calls this God's "gracious elective will").[14] The "this" (οὕτως) refers back to the thanksgiving of v. 25. God in his providence and wisdom has concealed his truths from the rebellious nation and revealed them to the receptive children he has chosen.

11:27 All things have been given to me by my Father (Πάντα μοι παρεδόθη ὑπὸ τοῦ πατρός μου). This verse has been called the "Johannine thunderbolt" because it so closely resembles the emphases of John on the Father – Son relationship and the deity of Christ.[15] The emphatic position of "all things" (πάντα) must be recognized at the outset. The one "sovereign over heaven and earth" has given "all" authority over to the Son (see also 28:18). Here it is closely related to the sonship of Jesus and to the "passing on" of authority from the Father.[16]

παραδίδωμι is often used for the "passing on"[17] of tradition from rabbi/teacher to disciple (Mark 7:13; Luke 1:2; 1 Cor 11:2, 23; 15:3), so here it is the giving or passing on of revelatory authority from the Father to the Son.[18] Yet this is even broader; Jesus has dominion over "all things" and therefore is sovereign over heaven and earth (cf. Rom 11:36; Col 1:16 – 17; Eph 1:21 – 22; Heb 1:3).

11:27 No one knows the Son except the Father, and no one knows the Father except the Son (καὶ οὐδεὶς ἐπιγινώσκει τὸν υἱὸν εἰ μὴ ὁ πατήρ, οὐδὲ τὸν πατέρα τις ἐπιγινώσκει εἰ μὴ ὁ υἱός). The intimate mutual knowledge shared by the Father and the Son is an astonishing statement by Jesus (cf. John 3:35; 5:19 – 30; 6:46; 7:16, 28 – 29; 8:27 – 29, 54 – 55). Matthew's use of "know" (ἐπιγινώσκω, the present tenses are gnomic, knowledge shared in eternal past, present, and eternal future) here is critical (Luke 10:22 has "know" [γινώσκω]). While the two could be synonymous,[19] it is likely that there is perfective force in the prefix ἐπι – with the meaning "know exactly, completely, through and through" (BAGD, 291), with the added idea of recognizing and acknowledging.[20] Both have exclusive knowledge of the other, and so the only one who can reveal the Son is the Father, and the only one who can reveal the Father is the Son (cf. John 1:18).

10,21," in *Studi sull' Oriente e la Bibbia* (Genoa: Editrice Studio e Vita, 1967), 329 – 36.

14. Schweizer, *Matthew*, 269.

15. On the authenticity of this verse and its Semitic cast, see Carson, "Matthew," 276. Gench, *Wisdom*, 92, shows that the recent movement has been away from the skepticism and gnostic background assumed earlier and toward "Jewish derivation and at least the possibility of dominical authenticity."

16. Deutsch, *Hidden Wisdom*, 29 – 30; and Yang, *Jesus and the Sabbath*, 156. France, *Matthew* (TNTC), says it is "the knowledge they share."

17. Here the aorist is culminative, stressing the results of the action (see Wallace, 559 – 61).

18. Some in the context relate it only to the revelation discussed in vv. 25 – 26 (see A. M. Hunter, "Crux Criticorum — Matt. XI.25 – 30 — A Reappraisal," *NTS* 8 [1962]: 241 – 49 [esp. 246]), but it is surely much broader than that. It is closely related to the "them" (ταῦτα) of v. 25 and as such certainly refers to the revelatory work of Christ, but it is also all-inclusive of the cosmic authority wielded by the Son as seen in 28:18 (both stemming from Dan 7:13 – 14).

19. Bultmann, *TDNT*, 1:703; Deutsch, *Hidden Wisdom*, 35; Nolland, *Matthew*, 472.

20. See Hagner, *Matthew 1 – 13*, 320; Gundry, *Matthew*, 216 – 17. Verseput, *Humble Messianic King*, 142 – 43, shows the background is not a Hellenistic-gnostic motif (as Bultmann and others have said) but stems from Jewish thought. Moreover, it is not synonymous with election but reflects personal knowledge.

There is only one other place in the Synoptics the absolute "the Son" (ὁ υἱός) is used (Mark 13:32 = Matt 24:36), and the concept is closely related to Matthew's Son of God Christology (3:17; 8:29; 14:33; 16:16; 17:5; 27:54)[21] rather than Son of Man.[22] The main idea is that God has shared his authority and his wisdom with his unique Son,[23] and Jesus alone can truly reveal his Father (cf. John 1:18).

11:27 ... and anyone[24] to whom the Son wishes to reveal him (καὶ ᾧ ἐὰν βούληται ὁ υἱὸς ἀποκαλύψαι). This combines the two major themes of 11:25–27, election and revelation. The hidden apocalyptic secrets have been hidden by God's elect will (vv. 25–26) and made known only to the Son (v. 27a), who reveals them only to the chosen (v. 27b).[25] Neither the recipients nor the content of the revelation is explicitly stated, though the context makes both readily apparent. The recipients are the "infants" of v. 25, and the content is both the "these things" revealed in v. 25 and the Father himself in v. 27a.[26] The revelation of the heavenly secrets comes from the Father in v. 25 first to the Son (v. 27a), and then from the Son to the receptive followers in v. 27b. This is tantamount to a declaration of the deity of Christ. He is more than Agent; he is the Revealer!

11:28 Come to me, all you weary and burdened people (Δεῦτε πρός με πάντες οἱ κοπιῶντες καὶ πεφορτισμένοι). Jesus has chosen to reveal his kingdom truths, but to the weary children rather than to the learned. This is one of Scripture's beautiful passages on the meaning of the gospel. The language here is similar to 4:19, "Come after (ὀπίσω) me," and as in that passage this too is a call to discipleship.[27] The all-inclusive "all" (πάντες) must encompass recalcitrant Israel as well as the world, yet only to those among the "wise" who cease to center on their man-made wisdom and learning and become like children.

The two participles[28] refer to the troubled and beaten-down of this world. The verb translated "weary" (κοπιάω) refers to those who "labor hard" and are "weary," and "burdened" (φορτίζω) means to "carry a burden" or "be burdened." At one level it speaks to those forced to carry the burden or "yoke" of the law with all its regulations (here

21. Hagner, *Matthew 1–13*, 320; Hill, *Matthew*, 207; France, *Matthew* (TNTC), 199; Senior, *Matthew*, 133.

22. So Schnackenburg, *Matthew*, 110.

23. Gundry, *Matthew*, 217–18; Keener, *Matthew*, 347.

24. This use of ἐάν after a relative pronoun means "anyone" or "to whomever," see BAGD, 211 (II).

25. Most have taken this as a wisdom passage paralleled in Sir 51, but Davies and Allison, *Matthew*, 2:283–86, have argued strongly for a Moses typology from Exod 33:12–14 in terms of reciprocal communication between Moses and God (in keeping with the new Moses motif they trace through Matthew). While interesting, this does not seem as close as the Wisdom motif here, cf. Hagner, *Matthew 1–13*, 321. Graham N. Stanton, "Salvation Proclaimed: X. Matthew 11:28–30: Comfortable Words?" *ExpTim* 94 (1982): 3–9, also rejects the wisdom and Sir 51 connection; he sees it rather as a call to discipleship. It is hard to see why the passage cannot be both.

26. Deutsch, *Hidden Wisdom*, 28.

27. There are several parallels with Sir 24:19–22; 51:23–27 ("come to me," "yoke," toil," "find rest [serenity]"), and so it is common to see in this a wisdom motif with Jesus as the personified Wisdom of God. However, Verseput, *Humble Messianic King*, 145, and Carson, "Matthew," 278, believe the parallels too sparse and the idea of deliberate wisdom theology in Matthew too speculative. Verseput argues that the Christology is a messianic, Son of God emphasis rather than wisdom. Yet this is too disjunctive, and there is no reason why a wisdom motif cannot be joined to the messianic thrust. There are at least echoes of and perhaps an allusion to Sirach here. Deutsch, *Hidden Wisdom*, 130–39; Gench, *Wisdom*, 120–22; and France, *Gospel of Matthew*, 447, see too many parallels to be mere chance but also see the parallels within a larger Son Christology.

28. The first participle is present tense and the second perfect tense, yet the tenses function together to depict the people who are in a continual state of weariness and burden.

Jesus contrasts himself with the Pharisees; cf. 23:4 on the "heavy burdens [φορτία]" the scribes and Pharisees place on the people); on another level it is all who are burdened with life's afflictions.[29] These are not yet disciples[30] but those among the crowds who are searching (called "seekers" today).

So these people are experiencing not only the weariness of trying to maintain all the scribal requirements but also fighting the struggles and anxieties of daily life (Isa 40:30; Sir 11:11), their oppression as the poor (*1 En.* 103:9 – 13) or as captives (Jer 31:25; Lam 5:5), and the weariness of idolatrous living (Isa 57:10); thus, they are waiting for God's deliverance (Ps 6:7; 69:4). Since the new exodus has not yet occurred, they long to be restored, but right now they are suffering from religious demands, the burden of daily life, and oppression both from the Romans and from their own leaders.[31]

11:28 ... and I will give you rest (κἀγὼ ἀναπαύσω ὑμᾶς). This is not just rest from the oral tradition (though it includes that) but rest from all the labors of life. It is the eschatological rest promised for the kingdom age (*4 Ezra* 7:36; 8:52) and is closely aligned with the "rest" theme of Heb 3:7 – 4:16, especially the "Sabbath-rest" of 4:3 – 11. In the Hebrews passage as here, the rest is both present and future, both the present relationship with God and the eternal rest in heaven. In coming to Jesus, the disciple enters the rest of God (Heb 4:3, "we who have believed enter that rest").

11:29 Take my yoke upon you (ἄρατε τὸν ζυγόν μου ἐφ' ὑμᾶς). As Deutsch points out, "the note of obligation and responsibility in v. 29a represents a shift in mood in 11:25 – 30. The revelation of vv. 25 – 27 has an essentially passive quality — it is *given*. Here, however, with the image of the yoke implying responsibility, there is introduced an active note."[32] This invitation repeats that of v. 28 ("Come to me") but with a slightly different image. Nowhere in Jewish writing does anyone say such a thing. Judaism always said to accept the yoke of the law and obey it, but never to "take" it.

The "yoke" (ζυγός) was originally a balance or pair of scales and was then used to designate the harness placed on oxen to join them for farming or pulling carts. Later it was used for a harness placed on captives or slaves and became a metaphor for subjection to a conquering nation or king, with the idea of a master-slave relationship.[33] This subjection can come from a foreign conqueror (Isa 14:29; 47:6) or from their own king (1 Kgs 12:4 = 2 Chr 10:4). As such it signified subjection and servitude, positively in worshiping God or obeying Torah or wisdom (Sir 6:23 – 31; 51:26 – 27; Bar 3:37 – 4:1), or negatively for subjection to a conquering force.

The positive side is intended in this passage, with the negative side, the heavy burden of the law, an implicit contrast here and in 23:4 (cf. "yoke of slavery" in Gal 5:1; 1 Tim 6:1). So what is the "yoke" of Christ? Some have made it obedience to God's will[34] or to Jesus himself.[35] This latter is certainly

29. It is common to make these competing theories, but that is unnecessary. The inclusive "all" (πάντες) would surely make this applicable to all who are burdened, cf. Davies and Allison, *Matthew*, 2:288; Nolland, *Matthew*, 475 – 76.

30. Nearly all scholars, but Stanton, "Matthew 11:28 – 30," 4 – 6, believe Jesus is addressing disciples suffering under the heavy demands of discipleship. This is unlikely in this context of mission.

31. Emily Wang, "The Humbleness Motif in the Gospel of Matthew" (PhD diss., Trinity Evangelical Divinity School, 2005), 61.

32. Deutsch, *Hidden Wisdom*, 42 – 43.

33. Charles L. Tyer, "Yoke," *ABD*, 6:1026 – 27.

34. Filson, *Matthew*, 144.

35. Michael Maher, "Take My Yoke upon You (Matt XI.29)," *NTS* 22 (1975): 97 – 103; Bonnard, *Matthieu*, 170; Wang, *Humbleness Motif*, 78 – 79. The idea of loyalty to the person of Jesus is stressed by Samuele Bacchiocchi, "Matthew 11:28 – 30: Jesus' Rest and the Sabbath," *AUSS* 22 (1984): 289 – 316.

part of it, but there is more. The key is the connection of "yoke" to wisdom and Torah. Jesus is the Wisdom of God and the final interpreter of Torah (see on 5:17 – 20). So the "yoke" is not just following Jesus in discipleship but loyalty and obedience to his definitive teaching, the Torah of the Messiah.[36] It prepares for the emphasis in the NT letters on our being "slaves" of God and Christ (Rom 1:1; Gal 1:10; et al.).[37]

In addition, "yoke" implies a personal relationship with Christ as the disciple relinquishes control over to Jesus.[38] Nolland speaks of "the unusual imagery of an animal placing the yoke on itself" and stresses the "emphasis on (willing) obedience to instruction."[39] There may be a further image that Jesus is in the yoke with us carrying most of the load. Since a yoke connected two oxen in tandem, the idea of taking Jesus' yoke means joining him in God's work.

11:29 ... and learn from me (καὶ μάθετε ἀπ' ἐμοῦ). "Learn" (μάθετε, the aorist tenses in v. 29 look at the action as "complete and undifferentiated,"[40] i.e., as a whole-life process) is the cognate of "disciple" (μαθητής) and connotes discipleship (see also 9:13; 24:32). This further enhances the interpretation above that Jesus' teaching is the "yoke." The emphasis here is on the person of the teacher rather than the content of the teaching. On the basis of 11:25 – 30 the content would be "these things" of v. 25 and "all" of v. 27, namely, the revelation of God's kingdom truths in Jesus. Bruner says, "The personal 'learn from me' existentializes Jesus' instrumental 'take my yoke'" and paraphrases, "Take my Word upon you and let me be your personal teacher through it."[41]

The essence of true discipleship is hearing and doing all that Jesus teaches (cf. 28:19, "teaching them to keep everything I have commanded you"). This in fact is the meaning of "righteousness" in Matthew, living life by God's (and Jesus') rules (see on 3:15; 5:6, 10, 20; 6:1, 33). For Jesus (indeed, for the NT as a whole) to "hear" is to "obey," to "learn" is to "do."

11:29 ... for I am meek and humble in heart (ὅτι πραΰς εἰμι καὶ ταπεινὸς τῇ καρδίᾳ). This is an important Christological statement on the humility of Jesus. While some have taken "for" (ὅτι) as explicative, "learn from me *that* I am meek,"[42] it is better to see it as causal, providing the reason for learning and obeying Jesus.[43] Jesus can identify with and teach the "weary and burdened" because like them he is "meek and humble." Matthew has a fair amount on the humble gentleness of Jesus as the basis for humility in discipleship (5:5; 18:1 – 4; 19:13 – 15; 21:5; 23:12).[44] Note the emphasis throughout vv. 25 – 30 on Jesus: "come to me," "I will give," "take my yoke," "I am meek," "my yoke," "my burden." Jesus is the sole authoritative revealer and the archetype for true living.

"Meek" (πραΰς) as in 5:5 (where it stems from Ps 37:7, 11) means "freedom from pretension (1 Pet 3:14 – 15), gentleness (11:29; Jas 3:13), and patient endurance of injury — where it is proper to endure."[45] So it speaks of Jesus' gentle nature and meekness toward God and others (for wisdom background see Sir 6:24 – 31; 24:3 – 22; 51:23 – 30).

36. See Yang, *Jesus and the Sabbath*, 158 – 59; Hagner, *Matthew 1 – 13*, 324; Davies and Allison, *Matthew*, 2:289 – 90; Keener, *Matthew*, 349.

37. See Harris, *Slave of Christ*, for the meaning of this metaphor.

38. Betz, "Easy Yoke," 23.

39. Nolland, *Matthew*, 476 – 77.

40. Porter, *Idioms*, 35.

41. Bruner, *Christbook*, 439.

42. Plummer, *Matthew*, 170n.

43. Gench, *Wisdom*, 94, believes both ideas may be present, with "meek and humble" describing both the content of the learning and the ground of Jesus' invitation.

44. See Wang, *Humbleness Motif*, passim.

45. Broadus, *Matthew*, 90.

"Humble" (ταπεινός) is closely related and refers to a submission to God and a willingness to take a low position in relation to others. The Greeks considered it to be the least of the virtues because it connoted servility, but Jesus elevated it to the greatest of the virtues because it is a voluntary giving of one's self to others. The best definition is in Phil 2:3 – 4: "in humility value others above yourselves, not looking to your own interests but each of you to the interests of others." The dative of sphere "in heart" (τῇ καρδίᾳ) modifies both qualities and shows they are internal qualities at the core of Jesus' character.

11:29 . . . and you will find rest for your souls (καὶ εὑρήσετε ἀνάπαυσιν ταῖς ψυχαῖς ὑμῶν). Note how in v. 28 Jesus is the actor ("I will give you rest") while here the follower is the actor, finding rest through taking Jesus' yoke in discipleship. The promise here quotes Jer 6:16 (changing the LXX "purification" [ἁγνισμός] to "rest" [ἀνάπαυσις] so as to link it with "rest" in v. 28), where Jerusalem is under siege because they have rejected God's promise of rest for those who "walk in the good way." Jesus' followers who take his yoke will find the rest the Israelites of Jeremiah's time forfeited. As elsewhere this rest is inaugurated, present in the sense that the believer has peace in the midst of life's troubles, and future because final vindication is promised for Jesus' lowly followers (Rev 7:13 – 15; 21:3 – 4).

11:30 For my yoke is easy and my burden is light (ὁ γὰρ ζυγός μου χρηστὸς καὶ τὸ φορτίον μου ἐλαφρόν ἐστιν). Jesus' followers will find rest because (γάρ), in contrast to the yoke of the Pharisees (see on the "burdened" of v. 28), discipleship in him is "easy" and "light." χρηστός means "kind" when applied to people, but here means "good, pleasant, kindly, easy to wear" (BAGD, 886). ἐλαφρός means "light, easy to bear." Following Jesus will not be easy in terms of the good life (secularly defined) because it demands radical surrender and involves the world's hostility (7:14, "narrow is the gate and confined the road that leads to life," cf. also ch. 10), but it is easy and light because it involves union with the gentle, lowly King and produces a new dimension of "rest" in him.[46] France concludes that the "lightness of Jesus' yoke" is due not just to his "personal character" (v. 29) but even more to his "new interpretation of the Torah, which, in contrast to the scribal concern for detailed regulation, enables a person to see beyond the surface level of dos and don'ts to the true underlying purpose of God."[47]

Theology in Application

This is one of the truly magnificent passages of Scripture. There is a richness of depth, a beauty of texture that sets it apart. So much is contained here — the sovereignty of God, his elective love, and at the same time, his justice and judgment. Then there is the deep Christology, the challenge for discipleship, and the contrast between Jesus and the religious leaders of his day.

1. Those Whom God Wants

God wants the simple and receptive, not the proud know-it-alls who remain closed to the transforming power of the kingdom. This functions at two levels. As

46. Deutsch, *Hidden Wisdom*, 46.

47. France, *Gospel of Matthew*, 451.

stated so well in 1 Cor 1 – 3, the rationalizing power of the intelligentsia in the world is incredible, and too often church leaders exemplify that false "wisdom." They have developed "political correctness" and have created a mechanism for justifying the most heinous acts on the basis of societal needs and mores. In our postmodern world truth will always be sacrificed on the altar of pragmatism.

Basically depraved humanity does not *want* to believe the ways of God, for darkness hates light and wants nothing to do with it (John 3:19 – 20). The "wise" want everything on their terms and by their definitions, and it is the same today as it was in Jesus' day. The kingdom was countercultural and did not fit into human categories but into God's. So today as well God turns to those with a childlike openness to the kingdom reality. One caveat needs to be made. This is not an anti-intellectual passage, as if Jesus says serious study of the Word of God is wrong and theologians should be regarded as the enemy. Carson says it well: "The contrast is between those who are self-sufficient and deem themselves wise and those who are dependent and love to be taught."[48]

2. God's Sovereignty

God is sovereign and works out his salvation his way rather than the way we want. The issue here is similar to that in Romans 9: God chooses or rejects whomever he wishes. Whether we see his predestinarian will as absolute or based on foreknowledge, the fact of divine choice is real. At the same time, human responsibility is equally taught here (as in 11:20 – 24 and 12:1 – 14 surrounding this passage). Theological systems have debated this for centuries, and each side believes they alone are right. What is interesting is the total absence of debate in the early church on this issue. They simply allowed the tension to stand, and Jesus refused to overemphasize either side. We should definitely follow his example and refuse to allow ourselves to be divided on this issue. There is mystery in the kingdom, and God has not yet given us all the truth there is.[49] We need humility and less arrogance, to be more the receptive children and less the proud learned on this!

3. Jesus as the Son and God's Final Revelation

I like what Luther said: "Stop speculating about the Godhead and climbing into heaven to see who or what or how God is; hold onto this man Jesus, he is the only God we've got!"[50] He is presented as Yahweh incarnate with "all" divine authority

48. Carson, "Matthew," 275.

49. This does not mean we should not take a side, but that we should hold our position with humility and be heuristic on all such issues.

50. *Luther's Works*, 26:28 – 29 on Gal 1:3, as quoted in Bruner, *Christbook*, 432.

on earth. The "Christian" life by definition is Christ-centered in every area, and all truth stems from him as he "exegetes" the Father (John 1:18). The mutual knowledge of Father – Son is passed onto the believer in the mutual union we have with Christ (John 6:56; 15:4 – 7; 1 John 2:24; 3:24; 4:15; Phil 3:10).

4. Rest Offered to the Burdened

Apart from Christ, perhaps the most correct bumper sticker ever written said, "Life's a bummer, and then you die!" Watching the lives of the rich and famous proves that. No one has an easy road through this world. Yet for every person there is an alternative. Everyone has a "yoke," but we can choose whether we will wear the world's yoke or Christ's yoke. If we choose the way of the world (or of organized religion, for that matter), we will, like the Jews, be weighted down by practices and regulations that provide no solace for the weary soul. The people who get drunk and besotted one Saturday will have to do it again and again every Saturday. There is no rest or consolation in this.

Jesus' yoke is more than a way of life or of thinking. It is a relationship, a following, a commitment. It is choosing to walk the walk of Jesus, to approach life his way, to attain "the whole measure of the fullness of Christ" (Eph 4:13c). Therefore rest is not just a sense of peace and tranquility in the chaos of life. It too is a relationship, a rest in him and in dependence on him. It is like a small boy with a big brother; he knows there are all sorts of things he cannot do but believes that with big brother's help there is nothing he cannot do. So it is with Christ; we approach life's vicissitudes and obstacles with a sense almost of omnipotence. Every crisis becomes an opportunity to watch Christ work.

6. Choosing between the Heavy Burden of the World and the Light Burden of Jesus

There is no ultimate satisfaction from choosing the secular way — whether it be escapist movies, the pleasure scene, expensive vacations, or ultimate wealth and success. You never have enough, and the thrill lasts only a moment and must be endlessly repeated. Jesus' way is easy and light not because it takes little effort and involves little sacrifice. In fact, following Jesus is exactly the opposite and demands everything we have. It is light because it is the only way that works, the only lifestyle that actually produces ongoing satisfaction and well-being.

Certainly there are many times each of us would dispute this, when God's way seems insuperably more difficult and less satisfying. That's why Jesus called it the "narrow gate" and the "confined road" (Matt 7:14). But in the end there will be no lasting joy or even well-being in the world's way. The rules of the Pharisees never stopped burdening the Jews with endless regulations over every area of life. The so-called "freedom" of the libertine world of our time functions in the opposite direction, yet burdens even more terribly. Note the summary of Doug Webster:[51]

> ... for those who live under the yoke there is absolutely no other way to live. Who in their right mind would go back to the gods of Self, Money, Lust and Power? Who would return on bended knee to the shrines of pious performance and judgmentalism? Is not love better than hate, purity better than lust, reconciliation better than retaliation? And is not "better" really "easier" when measured in character rather than convenience, rest for the soul rather than selfish pride?

51. Doug Webster, *The Easy Yoke* (Colorado Springs: NavPress, 1995), 201, in Wilkins, *Matthew*, 434.

CHAPTER 50

Matthew 12:1–8

Literary Context

The second triad of stories in this section continues the two-plus-one format of ch. 11, with two controversy narratives ending in rejection (vv. 1–8, 9–14) followed by a christological passage on God's offer of salvation through Jesus the humble servant (vv. 15–21). The immediately preceding context dealt with the easy yoke of Christ.[1] Now we turn to the heavy yoke of the Pharisees and the demands of the oral tradition vs. the way of Christ. As Nolland says, "conflict with the Pharisees will be the unifying motif of chap. 12."[2]

IV. Preaching and Teaching in the Midst of Opposition (11:2–13:53)
- **A. Jesus' Deeds: Revelation and Rejection (11:2–12:50)**
  1. Revelation and Rejection Begun (11:2–30)
  2. **Rejection of the Humble Servant (12:1–21)**
     - ➦ **a. Harvesting Grain on the Sabbath (12:1–8)**
     - b. Healing the Man with the Withered Hand (12:9–14)

Main Idea

The issue here is not just the Sabbath laws but also the oral tradition vs. the kingdom reality of Christ. The way of the Pharisees centered on the heavy burden (cf. 11:30; 23:4) of legal righteousness, while Jesus gave a freedom of action not seen before, a righteous conduct that centered on following God rather than a set of laws. The section ends with Jesus, not the law, as "Lord of the Sabbath."

1. As Pregeant, *Matthew*, 82, says, "Jesus' 'easy' yoke stands in explicit contrast to the rigid and burdensome teachings of the Pharisees (see also 23:4)."

2. Nolland, *Matthew*, 480.

Translation

Matthew 12:1-8

1a	Setting (Temporal)	At that time
b	Setting (Spatial)	**Jesus on the Sabbath went through the grain fields.**
c	Action	**His disciples became hungry and**
		began to pluck some heads of grain to eat.
2a	Objection	But **the Pharisees saw this and said,**
b		*"Look, your disciples are doing what is illegal on the Sabbath."*
3a	Response #1	**He replied,**
b	Rhetorical Question #1	*"Haven't you read what David did*
c		*when he and his companions became hungry?*
4a	Rhetorical Question #2	*How he entered the house of God,*
b		and *they ate the bread of the Presence,*
c		*which was illegal to do but*
		was only allowed for the priests?
5a	Rhetorical Question #3	Or *haven't you read in the law that on the Sabbath the priests in the temple desecrate the Sabbath and are innocent?*
6a	Response #2	But *I tell you that there is something here*
		even greater than the temple.
7a	Condition	But *if you had known what this means:*
b		*'I desire mercy and not sacrifice,'* (Hos 6:6)
c	Result	*you would never have condemned these innocent men.*
8a	Conclusion/ Pronouncement	For *the Son of Man is Lord of the Sabbath."*

Structure and Literary Form

This is a triple tradition story (= Mark 2:23 – 28; Luke 6:1 – 5), but Matthew adds M material on "something … greater than the temple" (vv. 5 – 7). This is a combination of a conflict narrative[3] and a pronouncement story and has three main

3. For the authenticity of this and other conflict narratives, see Keener, *Matthew*, 351 – 53.

parts: an accusation (vv. 1 – 2), a two-part response by Jesus (vv. 3 – 5) consisting of three questions that contain a haggadic illustration regarding David (vv. 3 – 4) and a halachic illustration of priests working on the Sabbath (v. 5), and three statements by Jesus (vv. 6 – 8) that he is greater than the temple and is the Lord of the Sabbath.[4] The disciples are "guiltless" (v. 7) because they are following Jesus rather than Torah or tradition. At the same time, the opposition and rejection that characterized ch. 11 actually increases in intensity here.

Exegetical Outline

➦ I. The Accusation by the Pharisees (12:1 – 2)

- A. Setting: plucking grain on the Sabbath (v. 1)
- B. The charge: breaking the Sabbath laws (v. 2)

II. Jesus' First Response (12:3 – 5)

- A. Illustration of David eating the showbread, intended for the priests (vv. 3 – 4)
- B. Illustration of priests working on the Sabbath (v. 5)

III. Jesus' Second Response (12:6 – 8)

- A. Jesus greater than the temple (v. 6)
- B. God's demand for mercy rather than sacrifice (v. 7)
- C. Jesus, Lord of the Sabbath (v. 8)

Explanation of the Text

12:1 At that time Jesus on the Sabbath went through the grain fields (Ἐν ἐκείνῳ τῷ καιρῷ ἐπορεύθη ὁ Ἰησοῦς τοῖς σάββασιν διὰ τῶν σπορίμων). As in 11:25, "at that time" (ἐν ἐκείνῳ τῷ καιρῷ) provides a transition from one event to the other. In addition to the triadic organization noted above, there is also an ABA pattern in 11:20 – 12:8, with Jesus' invitation to the weary to find salvation sandwiched between Galilean rejection scenes. Galilee had particularly fertile land and contained many farms, with wealthy people buying large tracts of land and breaking it up into tenant farms (see also the parables of the sower [13:3 – 23] and the wicked tenants [21:33 – 46]). The σπορίμων were the "grain fields" and στάχυας the heads of wheat,[5] which came ripe in March/April. Unlike today, when roads go around properties, in the ancient world roads went right through the fields, so that grain was growing right up to the walkway on both sides.

12:1 His disciples became hungry and began to pluck some heads of grain to eat (οἱ δὲ μαθηταὶ αὐτοῦ ἐπείνασαν καὶ ἤρξαντο τίλλειν στάχυας καὶ ἐσθίειν). Only Matthew tells us that the disciples plucked some of the heads of grain because they were "hungry" (Matthew adds "to eat," probably to emphasize the parallel with David in

4. See Gnilka, *Matthäusevangelium*, 1:443; Hagner, *Matthew 1 – 13*, 327 – 28.

5. See Louw and Nida, *Greek-English Lexicon*, 33, who describe it as "the dense spiky cluster in which the seeds of grain" grew at the top of the plant. This made a nice snack for travelers.

vv. 3 – 4).[6] Travelers were allowed to do so (Lev 19:9 – 10; Deut 23:24 – 25), but this was the Sabbath. Complex Sabbath laws were in place. The OT only stipulated that the Sabbath was to be holy and a day of rest from work (Exod 20:8 – 11 = Deut 5:12 – 15), but the Jewish people needed directions on what constituted work on the Sabbath, so the Mishnah developed thirty-nine rules on what could or could not be done then (*m. Šabb.* 7:2).[7] They were strict enough that a mishnaic tract said, "The rules for the Sabbath are like mountains hanging by a hair, for Scripture is scanty and the rules many (*m. Ḥag.* 1:8)."[8]

Traveling and carrying loads was excluded in Isa 58:13 – 14; Jer 17:21 – 22, but people were allowed to travel "a Sabbath day's walk" (Acts 1:12) or 2,000 cubits (= 1,100 meters; cf. *m. Soṭah* 5:3; *y. Ber.* 5.9a). Jesus and his disciples were probably following this restriction, for he is not criticized regarding this. Keeping the Sabbath was one of the central tenets of the Jewish religion. In the Maccabean revolt several groups were slaughtered because they would not fight on the Sabbath (1 Macc 2:31 – 41) until the rebels formulated a new rule allowing defensive warfare on the Sabbath; and breaking Sabbath rules was considered a capital crime (Exod 31:14 – 15; 35:2; *m. Sanh.* 7.4).

12:2 But the Pharisees saw[9] this and said, "Look, your disciples are doing what is illegal on the Sabbath" (οἱ δὲ Φαρισαῖοι ἰδόντες εἶπαν αὐτῷ, Ἰδοὺ οἱ μαθηταί σου ποιοῦσιν ὃ οὐκ ἔξεστιν ποιεῖν ἐν σαββάτῳ). Exceptions to the rules were allowed for temple service or when a life was in danger, but that was not the case here. By the strict rules of the Pharisees, many of the regulations were being broken:

> Plucking the grain was reaping, rubbing it to separate the grain from the husks (Luke tells us that they did this) was threshing, blowing away the husks may well have been interpreted as winnowing, and for good measure they may have seen the whole as preparation of food, which they also regarded as prohibited (all food eaten on the Sabbath had to be prepared on the previous day).[10]

Harvesting was not allowed on the Sabbath even at harvest time (Exod 34:21; *Jub.* 50:12; *m. Šabb.* 7.2). Everything that could be accomplished on Friday was supposed to be done then (e.g., food preparation, the setting of fires, the drawing of water), so the Sabbath could be a day of rest (so Nolland). The Pharisees probably were watching (there were not many Pharisees in Galilee, so this was not accidental)[11] and so brought their formal accusation to Rabbi Jesus (a rabbi was culpable for the actions of his disciples).[12] By making this a legal charge, Matthew heightens the contrast between the heavy yoke of the Pharisees and the merciful yoke of Jesus (cf. 11:28 – 30).[13]

6. Overman, *Matthew's Gospel and Formative Judaism*, 80.

7. See similar lists in *Jub.* 2:29 – 30; 50:6 – 13; CD 10:14 – 11:18.

8. S. Safrai, "The Sabbath," *The Jewish People in the First Century*, 2:804 – 7. See also Yang, *Jesus and the Sabbath*, 53 – 99; E. Lohse, "σάββατον," *TDNT*, 7:11 – 18.

9. For this use of a circumstantial participle as virtually a main verb, see 4:20; 11:2.

10. Morris, *Matthew*, 300.

11. Keener, *Matthew*, 351. Many have used this as a reason to doubt the historicity of the scene (e.g., Schweizer, Sanders). But as Yang explains (*Jesus and the Sabbath*, 168 – 69), the common *Erub* practice of placing stones every 2,000 meters would have guided Jesus, and Pharisees would either have seen them or actually been tailing them to find grounds for accusation. There is little reason to doubt the story.

12. There were no ordained rabbis in Jesus' day, and the later practice did not develop until after AD 135. Still, the title was used for teachers of Torah, and Jesus was called "rabbi" (Mark 9:5; 10:51; cf. Matt 23:7 – 8). Moreover, he had disciples like Hillel or Gamaliel (but not rabbinic "schools" such as developed over a century later). So the term is valid so long as we do not read the later practice into Jesus' ministry.

13. Verseput, *Humble Messianic King*, 159.

12:3 He replied, "Haven't you read what David did when he and his companions became hungry?" (ὁ δὲ εἶπεν αὐτοῖς, Οὐκ ἀνέγνωτε τί ἐποίησεν Δαυὶδ ὅτε ἐπείνασεν καὶ οἱ μετ' αὐτοῦ;). "Have you read" (ἀνέγνωτε) is a culminative aorist that emphasizes what should have been the results, namely, their knowledge of the Torah.[14] The presence of "not" (οὐκ) here and in v. 5 expects the answer "yes": "You have read this, haven't you?" In Jewish writing the story Jesus alludes to forms a haggadic argument because it is by analogy from historical data and is told via rhetorical questions. The story comes from 1 Sam 21:1 – 6, when David was fleeing from Saul and was hungry.[15] This occurred at Nob just a couple miles south of Jerusalem.

12:4 How he entered the house of God, and they ate the bread of the presence, which was illegal to do but was only allowed for the priests? (πῶς εἰσῆλθεν εἰς τὸν οἶκον τοῦ θεοῦ καὶ τοὺς ἄρτους τῆς προθέσεως ἔφαγον, ὃ οὐκ ἐξὸν ἦν αὐτῷ φαγεῖν οὐδὲ τοῖς μετ' αὐτοῦ, εἰ μὴ τοῖς ἱερεῦσιν μόνοις;). David went into the tabernacle and asked for five loaves but seemingly took all twelve loaves of the consecrated bread meant only[16] for the priests. So David was allowed to disobey the law for the sake of his "hunger" (he "became hungry" [ἐπείνασεν] in v. 3 deliberately repeats the disciples' "hunger" in v. 1). Jesus is making another *qal wahomer* argument (from the lesser to the greater; see those at 6:25 – 26 and 10:29 – 30): If David and his men could break the Torah for the sake of hunger, how much more could Jesus and his disciples?[17]

David was not condemned for his actions, and neither should Jesus' disciples be accused.[18] Verseput calls this a haggadic example of divine compassion: God in his mercy had allowed the boldness of David, and Jesus likewise allows his disciples to still their hunger on the Sabbath.[19] So the Pharisees have misunderstood the true place of the law, and indeed other Jewish groups did not take such a narrow view.[20]

12:5 Or haven't you read in the law that on the Sabbath the priests in the temple desecrate the Sabbath and are innocent? (ἢ οὐκ ἀνέγνωτε ἐν τῷ νόμῳ ὅτι τοῖς σάββασιν οἱ ἱερεῖς ἐν τῷ ἱερῷ τὸ σάββατον βεβηλοῦσιν καὶ ἀναίτιοί εἰσιν;). This is a halachic argument (precept of law) and centers on a point of Torah.[21] By the fact that the priests engage in temple duties on the Sabbath (preparing the consecrated bread, presenting offerings,

14. Davies and Allison, *Matthew*, 2:314, make an interesting observation: when addressing the crowds, Jesus normally says, "Have you not heard?" but when addressing the leaders, he says, "Have you not read?" They were supposed to be the legal experts and should have known better.

15. Later rabbis speculated that this happened on the Sabbath (*b. Menaḥ* 95b), but Jesus makes no point of this.

16. μόνοις is last for emphasis; it was *only* for the priests.

17. D. M. Cohn-Sherbok, "An Analysis of Jesus' Arguments concerning the Plucking of Grain on the Sabbath," *JSNT* 2 (1979): 31 – 41, argues that Jesus' analogy here is weak and would not have been accepted by the Pharisees because the link between eating showbread and working on the Sabbath is weak, and while David was involved in the event, Jesus was not. This is probably correct regarding the strict rabbinic rules regarding analogies, nevertheless, the very purpose of analogy is to bring together similar events (one desecrating the temple, the other the Sabbath). Moreover, there is evidence many ancient rabbis interpreted the 1 Samuel incident as a Sabbath story (see Carson, "Matthew," 280).

18. Banks, *Jesus and the Law*, 114 – 18; and Davies and Allison, *Matthew*, 2:310 – 11, provide good surveys of the various theories as to precisely how Matthew uses 1 Sam 21 here, such as the urgency of the eschatological mission (Borg), Jesus attacking only the oral tradition and not the Torah itself (Cranfield), Jesus following a greater good, namely, the love commandment (Davies and Allison), and the greater authority of Jesus as Messiah (Banks).

19. Verseput, *Humble Messianic King*, 162.

20. Yang, *Jesus and the Sabbath*, 170, names the Sadducees, Essenes, and Josephus (*Ant.* 13.297) as differing.

21. For "haven't you read in the law," see the parallel in Neh 8:3. In each case it means they have not fully understood what they have read. David Hill, "On the Use and Meaning

cf. Num 28:9 – 10), they too are guilty of Sabbath violations, yet the rabbis considered their temple service an exception (*b. Šabb.* 132b). Since they are doing God's work, they are "guiltless" (ἀναίτιοι) even though technically they "profane/desecrate" (βεβηλόω, a very strong term) the Sabbath.[22]

12:6 But I tell you that there is something here even greater than the temple (λέγω δὲ ὑμῖν ὅτι τοῦ ἱεροῦ μεῖζόν ἐστιν ὧδε). Using a similar *qal wahomer* argument as in vv. 3 – 4 (see also 6:25 – 26; 10:29 – 30), Jesus points to himself as not just "greater" than the priests but even "greater" than the temple (note the emphatic position of "the temple" [τοῦ ἱεροῦ])! The neuter (rather than masculine) "greater" (μεῖζον) is significant, pointing to the kingdom ministry and messianic office of Jesus and not just his person.[23] The point is that if the temple service took precedence over the Sabbath, then Jesus and his ministry have even greater authority over the Sabbath, for he supercedes the temple.

Moreover, if the priests who serve the temple are innocent, how much more the disciples who serve the one greater than the temple. The disciples are even more guiltless than the priests because they serve the greater one. This point goes back to 5:17 – 20, where Jesus pointed to himself as "fulfilling" the Torah (see on that passage). He therefore provides the authoritative interpretation of the law. The Pharisees have made two fatal errors: they have misinterpreted the law, and they have refused to accept the reality of Christ as Messiah and Son of God. This, then, is the heart of the passage (along with v. 8): Jesus is the final authority for Torah.

12:7 But if you had known what this means: "I desire mercy and not sacrifice," you would never have condemned these innocent men (εἰ δὲ ἐγνώκειτε τί ἐστιν, Ἔλεος θέλω καὶ οὐ θυσίαν, οὐκ ἂν κατεδικάσατε τοὺς ἀναιτίους). This is a contrary-to-fact condition (εἰ ... ἄν) that assumes the Pharisees in fact do not understand the mercy of God. It pursues the implications of "something greater than the temple." If neither Sabbath nor temple have ultimate authority, what about the accusation of v. 2? Jesus approaches this first by accusing the Pharisees of a lack of understanding, then quoting Hos 6:6, a passage Jesus had already quoted in 9:13, where he concluded, "I have not come to call the righteous but sinners" (see on that verse for background). The Pharisees are still making the same mistake, being assiduous about legal observance but neglecting the weighty matter of *ḥesed* (the term in Hosea), "loving-kindness, mercy."

Verseput surveys the various understandings of the Hosea passage here.[24] (1) It is a criticism of the Pharisees, who ignore the love commandment for strict adherence to the letter of the law (Zahn, Grundmann, Hare, Beare). (2) Its purpose is to justify the disciples by advocating the supremacy of the moral law over the cultic law (Allen, Strecker). (3) It is a statement about God's merciful kindness (G. Barth). (4) It is about Jesus, who has acted according to the will of God in his deeds and has shown compassion to his disciples (Verseput, Hagner, Yang). The best is probably

of Hosea VI. 6 in Matthew's Gospel," *NTS* 24 (1978): 114 – 15; and Davies and Allison, *Matthew*, 2:313, believe vv. 5 – 6 are added because Matthew viewed the David analogy insufficient due to its haggadic basis; but Yang, *Jesus and the Sabbath*, 178, shows that Jesus hardly depended on rabbinic hermeneutics but rather on his own authority and so added this to strengthen the force of the christological claim in vv. 3 – 4.

22. E. Levine, "The Sabbath Controversy according to Matthew," *NTS* 22 (1976): 480 – 83, narrows down the reference to the *ʿōmer* (reaping of the first sheaves) offering. This is unnecessary and unconvincing.

23. So Gundry, *Matthew*, 223; Hagner, *Matthew 1 – 13*, 330. Carson, "Matthew," 281 – 82, notes other suggestions, such as the service/worship of God, the love command, or Jesus himself.

24. Verseput, *Humble Messianic King*, 166 – 68.

a combination of (1) and (4). Jesus is saying that mercy rather than legal observance is the heart of God's will and that he has correctly exemplified this with respect to his disciples, who are thereby "guiltless" before God.[25]

> By quoting Hos 6:6 in v. 7, Jesus shows what God's original intention for the sabbath was — that is, the sabbath was instituted for the benefit of the people and was presented not as a burden but as an expression of mercy; that intention is now fulfilled by Jesus himself, the merciful one, under whose authority the disciples are guiltless because they rightly understood and behaved according to the true meaning and intention of the sabbath.[26]

12:8 For the Son of Man is Lord of the Sabbath (κύριος γάρ ἐστιν τοῦ σαββάτου ὁ υἱὸς τοῦ ἀνθρώπου). Everything said thus far has moved to this point.[27] The "for" (γάρ) establishes both the reason for vv. 7 – 8 and the conclusion to all that has happened. The "Lord" (κύριος) is in the emphatic position and stresses the fact that Jesus[28] has absolute authority over the Sabbath as cosmic Lord and the final interpreter of Torah (see on v. 6). "The Sabbath" (τοῦ σαββάτου) is an objective genitive, meaning that Jesus exhibits supreme lordship/authority over the Sabbath and its regulations. The use of the title "Son of Man" (see the excursus after 8:22) centers on the "one like a son of man" who is the glorified Lord of the universe in Dan 7:13 – 14.[29]

In the OT God is master of the Sabbath, and here Jesus has that authority, continuing the high Christology of Matthew. Jesus is greater than the temple (that had precedence over the Sabbath) and thus is also Lord over the Sabbath. The Sabbath rest is embodied in Jesus, who offers "rest for your souls" in 11:28 – 30. As in 5:17 – 20 Jesus has not abolished the Sabbath but has fulfilled it and now provides the true parameters for the people of God to experience the Sabbath rest.

25. Overman, *Matthew's Gospel and Formative Judaism*, 82, follows Eduard Schweizer ("Matthew's Church," in *The Interpretation of Matthew* [ed. G. Stanton; Philadelphia: Fortress, 1983], 129) in concluding that Matthew's community still observed Torah and practiced Sabbath observance. Yet this is unwarranted, for Jesus stands above the law, and his followers in Matthew "complete" the law in following Jesus. The Palestinian church probably did worship in synagogues on the Sabbath and had their own worship on "the first day of the week," and in Rom 14 Jewish Christians still followed Torah, but they were the "weak."

26. Yang, *Jesus and the Sabbath*, 188.

27. Turner, "Matthew," 168, points out that this is the third statement teaching Jesus' superiority to Jewish ways, after his being greater than David (v. 3, cf. 22:41 – 45) and than the temple (v. 6).

28. Matthew has omitted Mark 2:27a, "The Sabbath was made for people, not people for the Sabbath," most likely to center entirely on the christological significance of Jesus' authority here and to make absolutely certain the reader understands "Son of Man" as Jesus, not humankind.

29. See France, *Gospel of Matthew*, 462, against the view of some that "Son of Man" should be taken here not as a title but in a generic way, meaning "human beings are in control of the Sabbath."

Theology in Application

Many issues coalesce on this passage: primarily Christology, with a new appreciation for the extent of the authority of Jesus, Son of Man and Son of God, but also Jesus' relation to the law, here Sabbath observance. Jesus' authority in this passage refers to Jesus as our reference point as well as our example for understanding how obedience to God's law looks (i.e., internal change) vs. the Pharisees, who mastered how to behave externally but missed the heart of the matter.

1. Jesus Having the Authority of Yahweh

Matthew never explicitly asserts the deity of Christ, but he implicitly does so with passages like this one, where Jesus does in the new covenant what Yahweh did in the Old (cf. "God with us," 1:23; ruler, 28:18; omnipresent, 18:20, 28:20; Trinitarian, 28:19; authority to forgive sins, 9:1 – 8). The message here is that Jesus is Lord of all and sovereign over not just the Sabbath but over all religious law and conduct. As Bruner notes, "With a sovereign freedom Jesus exalts himself above all those realities that the people of God held dearest: the Sabbath day, the sanctuary temple, and the Scripture law."[30]

2. Mercy Triumphs over Legalistic Observance

Many today have still not learned this lesson and turn Sabbath observance into casuistry rather than rest. When there is a series of demands placed on the Christian, with more "don'ts" than "dos," we have legalism. Yet there is another extreme to avoid. For too many Christians, Sabbath is related only to the hour in church, and the rest of the day is lived just like Friday or Saturday. It is still to be a "day of rest," and while Mark's observation, "The Sabbath is made for people, not people for the Sabbath," is correct, we should not turn this into just another day. I often ask, "Is God more pleased with Eric Liddell (the movie *Chariots of Fire*) and his refusal to play soccer or run races on the Sabbath or with us and our turning Sunday into just another shopping day?" We are free to enjoy the Sabbath, but enjoy it we must.

30. Bruner, *Christbook*, 446.

CHAPTER 51

Matthew 12:9 – 14

Literary Context

This second controversy continues the Sabbath debate but this time is a healing miracle. The Pharisees are still watching to see if Jesus disobeys their regulations (v. 10b, probably also the reason they saw Jesus' disciples in the fields in 12:1 – 2) and again accuse him of unlawful activities.

IV. Preaching and Teaching in the Midst of Opposition (11:2 – 13:53)
A. Jesus' Deeds: Revelation and Rejection (11:2 – 12:50)
2. Rejection of the Humble Servant (12:1 – 21)
a. Harvesting Grain on the Sabbath (12:1 – 8)
➦ **b. Healing the Man with the Withered Hand (12:9 – 14)**

Main Idea

The issue here is the real meaning and purpose of the Sabbath. The Pharisees had removed the joy and rest from the Sabbath by their detailed regulations; Jesus wants to return its true essence by doing good on it. The Sabbath is a time for healing and saving, not for hating and plotting.

Translation

(See next page.)

Structure and Literary Form

This is a triple tradition story, and Mark in Mark 3:1 – 6 (= Luke 6:6 – 11) concludes his major section on the growing opposition from the leaders (2:1 – 3:6) by detailing the plot to kill Jesus early in his ministry. Matthew typically shortens Mark

Matthew 12:9-14

9a	Setting	**Jesus went from there and entered their synagogue,**
10a	Action/Setting	and **look, a man with a shriveled hand was there.**
b	Question/Accusation	And **they questioned Jesus to find a reason to accuse him, saying,**
c		*"Is it lawful to heal on the Sabbath?"*
11a	Response/Illustration	**Then he asked them,**
b		*"What person among you,*
		if you have one sheep fallen into a pit on the Sabbath,
		would fail to grab it and pull it out?
12a	Pronouncement	*How much more valuable is a human being than a sheep!*
b	Pronouncement/ Conclusion	*So then, it is lawful to do good on the Sabbath."*
13a	Command	**Then he told the man,**
b		*"Stretch out your hand."*
c		So **he stretched it out**
d	Result of 13b/Healing	and **it was completely restored,**
e		as healthy as the other hand.
14a	Conclusion/ Result of 11a-13e	But **the Pharisees went out and took counsel against Jesus,**
b		plotting how they might kill him.

(omits Mark 3:3 and much of vv. 4 – 5a) while adding the illustration of the sheep fallen in the pit (vv. 11 – 12a).[1] It is often called a pronouncement story,[2] though the pronouncement comes in v. 12b rather than at the end (yet it is still uppermost); the miracle is secondary, so this is not a miracle story per se. It may be best to call it a combination of a pronouncement story with a controversy narrative since the conflict is at the heart of the pericope.

The story is not as central as it is in Mark but still deepens the opposition from the previous story. There are three parts: (1) the synagogue setting (vv. 9 – 10a); (2) the challenge with Jesus' response (vv. 10b – 12); and (3) the ending with its absolute contrast between the healing and the plot to kill Jesus (vv. 13 – 14).

Exegetical Outline

→ **I. Setting in the Synagogue (12:9 – 10a)**

A. Entering the synagogue (v. 9)

B. The man with a shriveled hand (v. 10a)

II. Sabbath Controversy with the Pharisees (12:10b – 12)

1. Some posit a Q source behind v. 11 = Luke 14:5 (a child or an ox pulled from a well in a similar story about a healing), but the details and the story are sufficiently different that it is more likely that Jesus as an itinerant teacher used similar metaphors to challenge the leaders on two occasions.

2. See Yang, *Jesus and the Sabbath*, 197, who names Taylor, Dibelius, Bultmann, and Theissen.

A. Their accusation (v. 10b)
B. Jesus' response (vv. 11 – 12)
1. Saving an endangered sheep on the Sabbath (v. 11)
2. The greater value of a person (v. 12a)
3. Pronouncement: lawful to do good (v. 12b)

III. The Contrasting Conclusion (12:13 – 14)
A. Jesus heals the man (v. 13)
B. The Pharisees plot to kill Jesus (v. 14)

Explanation of the Text

12:9 Jesus went from there and entered their synagogue (Καὶ μεταβὰς ἐκεῖθεν ἦλθεν εἰς τὴν συναγωγὴν αὐτῶν). The introductory "went from there" (another of Matthew's many circumstantial participles, see v. 2) shows the relationship between the two stories. The two events in Matthew seemingly occur on the same Sabbath, with the trip through the fields on the way to the synagogue. However, Luke 6:6 tells us the two occurred on different Sabbaths, so "went from there" is a literary (rather than chronological) link to bring the stories together. As in 4:23; 9:35; 10:17; 13:54 Matthew calls it "*their* synagogue" to stress the conflict with the leaders.[3]

12:10 And look, a man with a shriveled hand was there (ἰδοὺ ἄνθρωπος χεῖρα ἔχων ξηράν). For "look" (ἰδού) used dramatically (a stylistic trait of Matthew), see on 1:20. Luke 6:6 tells us it was the right hand, emphasizing the seriousness of the situation. ξηράν means "dried up" and could be either shriveled or paralyzed. The main thing is the sad condition of the man; since in that world everyone worked with their hands, he would have been especially handicapped.

12:10 And they questioned Jesus to find a reason to accuse him, saying, "Is it lawful to heal on the Sabbath?" (καὶ ἐπηρώτησαν αὐτὸν λέγοντες, Εἰ ἔξεστιν τοῖς σάββασιν θεραπεῦσαι; ἵνα κατηγορήσωσιν αὐτοῦ). Here the same Pharisees ("they") who made the accusation in 12:2 look for still another excuse to charge Jesus with wrongdoing. By now the leaders have already made up their minds that Jesus is a false prophet who is dangerous to their cause. So they are not testing him but rather gathering evidence to be used against ("accuse") him in a court of law[4] (note how unconcerned they are with the situation of the man, in contrast to Jesus in vv. 12 – 13).

The centrality of "is it lawful" (ἔξεστιν) here (it occurs later in Mark and Luke) brings the legal question to the foreground. The question[5] itself is valid. The law was specific: one could heal on the Sabbath if it was a life-threatening situation (*m. Yoma* 8:6).[6] If it was not such, one should wait

3. So France, *Matthew* (TNTC), 204; Davies and Allison, *Matthew*, 2:317; contra Hagner, *Matthew 1 – 13*, 333, who says it is a general reference to a Jewish synagogue. It is also common to see "their" (αὐτῶν) as reflecting Matthew's community in its conflict with the Jewish synagogue, but that is not necessary, for it has a literary function in this context.

4. Verseput, *Humble Messianic King*, 178, shows that "to accuse" (καταγορέω) presupposes a court setting.

5. For the interrogative particle εἰ introducing a direct question (normally an indirect question), see BDF §440.3. In Luke 6:7 Jesus perceives their thoughts, but here they speak the question out loud. This brings out their culpability more directly.

6. On the question whether this halachic principle reflects Jesus' time, see Yang, *Jesus and the Sabbath*, 199 – 200, who points out that the Pharisees assume such a position here.

until the next day. This is not life-threatening, so in their mind Jesus is contemplating an illegal act.

12:11 Then he asked them, "What person among you, if you have one sheep fallen into a pit on the Sabbath, would fail to grab it and pull it out?" (ὁ δὲ εἶπεν αὐτοῖς, Τίς ἔσται ἐξ ὑμῶν ἄνθρωπος ὃς ἕξει πρόβατον ἕν, καὶ ἐὰν ἐμπέσῃ τοῦτο τοῖς σάββασιν εἰς βόθυνον, οὐχὶ κρατήσει αὐτὸ καὶ ἐγερεῖ;). The miracle is more central in Mark 3:3 and Luke 6:8, where Jesus places the man in the middle of the action. Here Jesus' reply itself is the central element. The introductory "what person among you" (τίς ἐξ ὑμῶν ἄνθρωπος, used generically for any "person") provides a challenge, asking in effect, "What sort of people are you?"

The example cited envisages a poor man who owns only a single sheep,[7] so its loss would be a great hardship. Jewish writings differ on this. Qumran did not allow such an animal to be rescued on the Sabbath (CD 11:13 – 14), but the rabbis differed, some allowing only food to be thrown to the animal to keep it alive, others allowing bedding and the like to be lowered so the animal might climb out (*b. Šabb.* 1:28b). Note that none of the rabbis allowed the owner to go in and rescue the animal, only to place something in the pit so the animal could climb out on its own. For this reason many believe (probably rightly) that Jesus is not alluding to a legal ruling but to common practice.[8]

12:12 "How much more valuable is a human being than a sheep!" (πόσῳ οὖν διαφέρει ἄνθρωπος προβάτου). This is another *qal wahomer* (from lesser to greater) argument by Jesus (with "sheep" [προβάτου] a genitive of comparison). If rescuing a sheep is important enough to contravene the Sabbath laws, how much greater would be rescuing a suffering person. Since people are more valuable than sheep, common sense requires that the laws allow healing on the Sabbath.

12:12 "So then, it is lawful to do good on the Sabbath" (ὥστε ἔξεστιν τοῖς σάββασιν καλῶς ποιεῖν). Jesus gives his conclusion (ὥστε, "therefore"). As seen often in this commentary, Jesus is the final interpreter of Torah (5:17 – 20; 10:40 – 41; 11:10; 12:8). Now he makes another pronouncement of the Torah of the Messiah, catching the true essence of the Sabbath and its basic purpose — "to do good" (καλῶς ποιεῖν).[9] If true for an animal, how much more for the apex of God's creation, a human being. Jesus' point is that the "good" must benefit people, not the religious establishment and its legal structure. It is the individual *person* that is of supreme value to God, so when a law allows an afflicted situation to continue, it is an inadequate law. As Mark 2:27 says, "The Sabbath was made for people, not people for the Sabbath." So Jesus was not breaking the law but fulfilling it (Matt 5:17) and allowing it to be an expression of God's love rather than legalistic requirements.

12:13 Then he told the man, "Stretch out your hand." So he stretched it out and it was completely restored, as healthy as the other hand (τότε λέγει τῷ ἀνθρώπῳ, Ἔκτεινόν σου τὴν χεῖρα. καὶ ἐξέτεινεν καὶ ἀπεκατεστάθη ὑγιὴς ὡς ἡ ἄλλη). The healing anchors the meaning of the principle: since the Sabbath is for good, Jesus does the good deed. Yet the act of healing is not described; rather, its result — the restored wholeness — is emphasized. Matthew goes to great length to emphasize the completeness of the healing, for each term ("restored," "healthy,"[10] "as the other hand") would have been sufficient in itself. In stretching out his hand (aorist

7. Luz, *Matthew 8 – 20*, 192, contra Carson, "Matthew," 284, who believes "one" (ἕν) is a Semitism for "a sheep."

8. See Yang, *Jesus and the Sabbath*, 202 – 3.

9. We must remember that this is dealing with oral tradition more than with Torah regulations, although the Pharisees equated the two.

10. "Healthy" (ὑγιής) refers to physical health or wholeness.

imperative for an emphatic command — Do it!), the man shows the type of faith emphasized in 8:10; 9:2, 18, 22, 28 – 29.[11] Again Jesus proves his lordship over the Sabbath (12:8) and shows its true purpose is to bring rest to the distressed (11:28 – 29), to be an instrument of mercy (12:7) rather than guided by halachic rules.[12]

12:14 But the Pharisees went out[13] and took counsel against Jesus, plotting how they might kill him (ἐξελθόντες δὲ οἱ Φαρισαῖοι συμβούλιον ἔλαβον κατ᾽ αὐτοῦ ὅπως αὐτὸν ἀπολέσωσιν). This is a shocking conclusion after the miracle and is meant to climax the growing theme of rejection (cf. 8:10 – 12; 9:3 – 4, 11, 14, 34; 10:17 – 19, 21 – 22, 28, 34 – 36; 11:11 – 12, 18 – 19, 20 – 24, 25; 12:2, 10) — a terrible reaction that will increase to the passion itself (12:24; 15:2; 21:23; 22:15; 26:4).

"Took counsel" (συμβούλιον ἔλαβον) is a Semitic expression for a plot, but one would expect this to lead to a synagogue trial rather than a death sentence. The sequence from warning to flogging seen with respect to the Twelve in Acts 4:1 – 22, 5:17 – 42 should have been the goal. Jesus had never been brought before the authorities, though they had sent numerous delegations. There hardly seems to have been any attempt to seek the truth. The Jewish leaders were threatened by his popularity and repulsed by his messianic authority.[14] It is not that there was little basis for their conclusion; rather, their hardness of heart is the emphasis. Jesus' mercy is in complete contrast with their lack of it. So the plot to "kill"[15] or destroy Jesus begins here in Galilee and will culminate in the Sanhedrin trial in Jerusalem.

Theology in Application

The vehemence with which the Sabbath laws were debated and enforced seems strange to many modern readers. It must be understood that the Sabbath was a socio-religious rite that was at the heart of Jewish self-identity. Yet those of us who have grown up with strict Sabbath rules (e.g., no eating out or no sports on Sunday) can understand (see discussion at the end of 12:1 – 8). However, the issue is not just the Sabbath but larger issues of praxis and Christology.

11. See Filson, 147; France, *Matthew* (TNTC), 205.

12. Yang, *Jesus and the Sabbath*, 208 – 9, makes an interesting point. Jesus does not break the OT Sabbath law or even the rabbinic restrictions. He does not stretch forth his hand (to work) or either touch or hold the man; he simply speaks. This shows the falseness of the Pharisaic reaction even more.

13. Another circumstantial participle, as in v. 9.

14. Hare, *Persecution*, 135 – 36, and Carson, "Matthew," 284 – 85, show this is the real reason for the plot. Sabbath disputes would never lead to such a penalty. It is Jesus' messianic claims that are the issue.

15. France, *Gospel of Matthew*, 454, 466, interprets this as to "get rid of" Jesus, believing it is not clear if the plot went as far as death at this point.

1. The Law of Love and Mercy to Take Priority

Too often today legal precedent has priority over individual needs. I have seen this at every level — home, church, seminary, mission field. Christian organizations (like secular ones) protect themselves by making rules so they do not have to deal with individual situations. As a result people's needs are not met, and justice once again is sacrificed on the altar of convenience or rote policy. Jesus established the basis here: every rule must result in "doing good" at the individual level (the one whose sheep is in the pit) if it is to be valid.

2. Confronting Jesus' Claims to Messianic Authority

The leaders could not accept Jesus' absolute claims and so plotted to take his life. There is no neutrality. Jesus confronts every person with the light of God (John 1:4, 9) and forces decision. He is Lord of the Sabbath (Matt 12:8), God incarnate (John 1:14), the only path to salvation (John 14:6; Acts 4:12). We can accept or reject it, but we must confront it.

CHAPTER 52

Matthew 12:15 – 21

Literary Context

In the two-plus-one framework of the three triads in chs. 11 – 12 (see the intro to 11:2 – 12:50), this is the second "one" detailing the purpose and person of Christ (cf. 11:25 – 30). As in 11:2 – 30, the first two sections have centered on conflict and rejection of Jesus by the Jews. Now this third details his redemptive plan. Here Jesus' servanthood contrasts absolutely with the Pharisees' murderous intent.

IV. Preaching and Teaching in the Midst of Opposition (11:2 – 13:53)
- **A. Jesus' Deeds: Revelation and Rejection (11:2 – 12:50)**
  - **2. Rejection of the Humble Servant (12:1 – 21)**
    - a. Harvesting Grain on the Sabbath (12:1 – 8)
    - b. Healing the Man with the Withered Hand (12:9 – 14)
    - ➦ **c. The Humble Servant (12:15 – 21)**

Main Idea

In the midst of opposition, Jesus is still engaged in his miraculous redemptive ministry (vv. 15 – 16) as the suffering Servant of Yahweh (vv. 17 – 21). As the Servant, he fulfills Isa 42:1 – 4 (continuing Matthew's fulfillment theme) and in connection with 11:29 is the gentle, humble Servant who does not retaliate but returns good for evil. As the Pharisees plot violence against the Son of God, Jesus takes the lowly path, serving both God and humankind.

Translation

(See next page.)

Matthew 12:15-21

15a Response and Summary — Knowing this,
b **Jesus withdrew from that place**
c and **a large group followed him**
d and **he healed them all.**
16a And **he warned them not to reveal who he was,**
17a Purpose/ Fulfillment Formula — **so that what was spoken through the prophet Isaiah might be fulfilled:**
18a OT Quotation — *"Look, my servant*
b *whom I have chosen,*
c *my beloved*
d *in whom I delight.*

e *I will place my Spirit on him,*
f *and he will proclaim justice to the nations.*
19a *He will neither quarrel nor cry out;*
b *no one will hear his voice in the streets.*
20a *A bruised reed he will not break,*
b *and a smoldering wick he will not put out*

c *until he brings justice to victory.*

21a *And the Gentiles will put their hope in his name."*
(Isa 42:1-4)

Structure and Literary Form

The first part (vv. 15 – 16) is a summary of Mark 3:7 – 12 (Matthew follows Mark's order here with 12:1 – 14 = Mark 2:23 – 3:6), but he greatly abbreviates Mark (removing the geographical references and the exorcisms with the Son of God emphasis) and so has a strong Matthean flow. The fulfillment quotation (vv. 18 – 21) is M material. The passage thus combines another summary passage (with 4:23 – 25; 9:35 – 36) and a fulfillment passage. The two parts first examine the Messiah's work (vv. 15 – 16) and then the Messiah's task (vv. 17 – 21) in the face of implacable opposition.

Exegetical Outline

➡ **I. The Messiah's Work (12:15 – 16)**

A. The setting: withdrawal and popularity (v. 15a)

B. Messianic healing (v. 15b)

C. Messianic secret (v. 16)

II. The Messiah's Task (12:17 – 21)
- A. Fulfillment of Isa 42:1 – 4 (v. 17)
- B. The servant (v. 18)
  1. Chosen and loved by God
  2. Endowed with the Spirit
  3. Message of justice
- C. His demeanor (vv. 19 – 20a)
  1. No retaliation
  2. Little response
  3. Gentleness
- D. Justice for the nations (vv. 20b – 21)

Explanation of the Text

12:15 Knowing this, Jesus withdrew from that place (Ὁ δὲ Ἰησοῦς γνοὺς ἀνεχώρησεν ἐκεῖθεν). Jesus "knew" (a circumstantial participle [cf. vv. 9, 14] hinting at omniscience)[1] the murderous intent of his enemies and so "withdrew." It was not yet time to give himself over to his destiny. There may be a further hint of Jesus' demeanor in 12:19; rather than fight back, the gentle Messiah withdraws.[2] Yet there is often a sense of judgment when Jesus withdraws. His enemies have rejected him, so he now turns his back on them, in effect leaving them to their fate. Putting both ideas together, we can say Jesus retreats from the belligerent leaders and leaves judgment up to God. As stated in 10:23, being forced to flee was used by God to spread the gospel from town to town.

12:15 And a large group[3] followed him (καὶ ἠκολούθησαν αὐτῷ [ὄχλοι] πολλοί). There is a further contrast here between the opposition by the Pharisees and the continued interest shown by the crowds. Every time Jesus goes somewhere, the people enthusiastically follow (esp. 4:25; 8:1 with similar language). There is no hint of discipleship in "followed" (unless one sees here potential disciples).

12:15 And he healed them all (καὶ ἐθεράπευσεν αὐτοὺς πάντας). The use of "all" (πάς) is frequent in Matthew and stresses the universal compassion of Jesus. The hostility of the leaders is further contrasted to the mercy of Jesus. This does not mean everyone who came to him was sick[4] but that he healed every sick person who came. Here and in 8:16 Matthew heals "all" the sick, while the Markan parallels (Mark 1:34; 3:10) have he "healed many." Jesus' power in Matthew is limitless.

12:16 And he warned them not to reveal[5] who he was (καὶ ἐπετίμησεν αὐτοῖς ἵνα μὴ φανερὸν

1. Though McNeile, *Matthew*, 171, theorizes Jesus had friends who warned him of the plot.

2. See Verseput, *Humble Messianic King*, 190 – 91, "[Matthew] desires to show a humble Jesus, retiring from confrontation to show mercy to those who come unto him." He lists 2:14, 22; 4:12; 14:13; 15:21 among passages where Jesus "retreats in the face of hostility."

3. While "group" (ὄχλοι) is present in C D L W TR et al., it is missing in ℵ B. It is likely that later scribes added it in conformity to other passages like 4:25; 8:1; 12:23; 15:30; 19:2 and so was not originally part of Matthew.

4. So Filson, *Matthew*, 148.

5. This is either ἵνα for indirect discourse or an example of a ἵνα clause used substantivally and virtually equivalent to an infinitive (see BDF §388 for the ἵνα encroaching on the infinitive esp. in Mark, Matthew, John).

αὐτὸν ποιήσωσιν). While the messianic secret is better known in Mark, it is still present in Matthew. Jesus' purpose is clear: the Jewish people (and Jesus' disciples) were looking for a conquering king, not a suffering Messiah. Jesus' messianic work would not be finished until the cross, and only then could it be understood (see further on 8:4; 9:30). Here this strongly prepares for the true purpose of Jesus as the Isaianic Servant in the quote that follows. France adds that "it provides a link with the assertion of Isa 42:2 that the servant will not make a lot of noise, and 'no one will hear his voice in the streets.'"[6]

12:17 ... so that[7] what was spoken through the prophet Isaiah might be fulfilled (ἵνα πληρωθῇ τὸ ῥηθὲν διὰ Ἠσαΐου τοῦ προφήτου λέγοντος). Matthew sees both Jesus' command for silence and his withdrawal fulfilled in his servant ministry as prophesied by Isaiah. As Bruner says, both silence and withdrawal seem strange, for messiahs normally move forward and make themselves known. Yet Jesus is the humble Servant.[8] The fulfillment formula[9] is unique to Matthew and found ten times (1:22 – 23; 2:15, 17 – 18, 23; 4:14 – 16; 8:17; 12:17 – 21; 13:35; 21:4 – 5; 27:9 – 10) to indicate Jesus' fulfillment of OT messianic expectations. The emphasis is on God's sovereign control[10] of salvation history in such a way that Jesus is the culmination of his plan.

The servant songs of Isaiah were already used in 8:17, where Jesus fulfilled Isa 53:4. Matthew clearly emphasizes Jesus as the *ʿebed yhwh* ("servant of Yahweh," see also 8:17). The suffering Servant is a frequent theme in Matthew and points to Isa 42, 52 – 53 and the messianic image of the Servant. Here vv. 17 – 18 are linked closely with Jesus as the humble, gentle messianic King of 11:28 – 30. There are indications that Isa 42 was used messianically in Judaism,[11] and Matthew considers this a direct fulfillment. This use of Isa 42:1 – 4 is the longest OT quotation in Matthew, but its form differs from both the LXX and the MT and may reflect some Targumic readings but is likely Matthew's own translation.[12] Many of the details point specifically to themes in this section.[13]

12:18 Look, my servant whom I have chosen, my beloved in whom I[14] delight (ἰδοὺ ὁ παῖς μου ὃν ᾑρέτισα, ὁ ἀγαπητός μου εἰς ὃν εὐδόκησεν ἡ ψυχή μου). The choice of "servant/son" (παῖς) rather than "servant" (δοῦλος) may be deliberate to give a double meaning of "servant" and "son," pointing directly to Jesus as the Son who is the Servant of Yahweh (so Nolland). Since the affirmation by God at Jesus' baptism (3:17) and transfiguration (17:5) alludes to Isa 42:1 (see on those passages), there is a direct connection between Son and Servant in Matthew.

In the MT the Servant is called "the one whom I uphold, my chosen," while here it is "whom I have chosen, my beloved" (with ὁ ἀγαπητός μου probably chosen to strengthen the connection with 3:17). Jesus is the chosen Son who is loved and who

6. France, *Gospel of Matthew*, 469. I disagree with his further assertion that Matthew is relatively uninterested in the Markan messianic secret and its appearance here is "perfunctory."

7. Here "so that" (ἵνα) is used in its normal fashion for a purpose clause (cf. v. 16).

8. Bruner, *Christbook*, 453.

9. On the formula see especially Soares-Prabhu, *The Formula Quotations*, 46 – 63.

10. The passive participle "was spoken" (ῥηθέν) is likely a divine passive, making God the one who spoke through Isaiah, cf. Verseput, *Humble Messianic King*, 193.

11. Jeremias, *TDNT*, 5:681 – 82, notes *Tg. Isa.* 42:1; 43:10; 52:13; *Tg. Zech.* 3:8 as using "servant" messianically.

12. See Gundry, *Use of the Old Testament*, 110 – 16; Hagner, *Matthew 1 – 13*, 336 – 37.

13. See Cope, *Matthew*, 44.

14. "My soul" (ἡ ψυχή μου) does not refer to "soul" here but is often a Semitism reflecting selfhood (BDF §283 (4); BAGD, 894 [f]) and so is translated "I."

brings "delight" to his Father. Note the progression: Jesus is Son and Servant, the gentle Messiah who fulfills Isa 42 and 53. He is the elect one,[15] chosen to fulfill the Father's will. He is deeply loved by the Father, the unique filial relationship reminiscent of John 1:14, 18, the "one and only Son." As loved, he also brings deep pleasure to his Father. Note also the contrast with the Pharisees, who have rejected Jesus and plan to kill him, while the Father loves and delights in him.[16]

12:18 I will place my Spirit on him (θήσω τὸ πνεῦμά μου ἐπ᾿ αὐτόν). There are eight consecutive future tense main verbs in vv. 18 – 21, and Matthew's intention is to show that all were Isaianic prophecies fulfilled in Jesus. The Spirit dwelling on Jesus is also linked with Jesus' baptism when the Holy Spirit descended on Jesus like a dove (3:16b). The endowment with the Spirit is closely related to Jesus' task of proclaiming the kingdom truths[17] and also points ahead to the teaching on the Spirit in 12:31 – 32, in which the Pharisees lack the Spirit and are guilty of the unpardonable sin.[18]

12:18 ... and he will proclaim justice to the nations (καὶ κρίσιν τοῖς ἔθνεσιν ἀπαγγελεῖ). The Spirit's endowment is especially related to Jesus' proclamation of justice. κρίσις for many means more "justice" than "judgment" (cf. vv. 20c – 21, where God's Servant turns "justice to victory," leading to the conversion of the Gentiles). Carson calls this "righteousness broadly conceived as the self-revelation of God's character for the good of the nations (cf. Isa 51:4), yet at the same time calling them to account."[19] Thus, some aspects of "judgment" are still connoted, as Jesus proclaims that the kingdom has arrived and the judgment has come, leading to God's "justice" on the nations.[20]

The Gentile mission is once again in view (cf. 1:5, 6; 2:1 – 12; 4:15 – 16, 24; 8:5 – 13, 28 – 34; 10:18) and prepares for the commission to the Gentiles in 28:18 – 20. The judgment on the Jewish people for their obduracy (11:20 – 24; 12:39 – 42) will lead to the inclusion of the Gentiles. Still, this does not mean the total rejection of the Jewish people; rather, they become part of the "nations" for whom salvation has come (28:19).[21]

12:19 He will neither quarrel nor cry out; no one will hear his voice in the streets (οὐκ ἐρίσει οὐδὲ κραυγάσει, οὐδὲ ἀκούσει τις ἐν ταῖς πλατείαις τὴν φωνὴν αὐτοῦ). The Isaianic Servant will not "open his mouth" (Isa 53:7). Jesus' reaction to the loud, insistent opposition of the Pharisees will not be to retaliate verbally. As the humble messianic Servant, Jesus refuses to "retaliate" or "make threats" but rather "entrusts himself to him who judges justly" (1 Pet 2:23). This hardly means Jesus will not speak at all. He will "proclaim justice," but he will not respond to his opponents. The public proclamation will be positive, not negative, related to the good news rather than defending himself against the leaders (the "hypocrites" who in Matt 6:5 pray loudly "on the street corners [to] be seen by others"). This closely fits Jesus' withdrawal and command for silence in vv. 15 – 16, which Matthew saw

15. As Verseput, *Humble Messianic King*, 195 – 96, brings out, the choice of "I choose" (αἱρετίζω) is deliberate and a departure from Isaiah, bringing out the idea of election rather than protection and connoting "God's choice of a person for a particular task."

16. Yang, *Jesus and the Sabbath*, 218.

17. Verseput, *Humble Messianic King*, 197.

18. See Jerome H. Neyrey, "The Thematic Use of Isaiah 42:1 – 4 in Matthew 12," *Bib* 63 (1982): 459 – 60; Yang, *Jesus and the Sabbath*, 218.

19. Carson, "Matthew," 286.

20. Verseput, *Humble Messianic King*, 197 – 98, goes further. This is Jesus' cry for repentance in light of the imminent judgment of God on the world.

21. See the excellent discussion of this in Yang, *Jesus and the Sabbath*, 219, who points to this theme subsequently in Matt 12:30 – 50; 15:1 – 12, 21 – 28; 21:28 – 22:11; 23; 24:14; 28:18 – 19.

fulfilled in the Isaiah quote here. The Servant neither went to "the streets" nor allowed those healed to do so. He proclaimed only God, not himself.

12:20 A bruised reed he will not break, and a smoldering wick he will not put out (κάλαμον συντετριμμένον οὐ κατεάξει καὶ λίνον τυφόμενον οὐ σβέσει). Who are the "bruised reed" and the "smoldering wick" (both stand first for emphasis)? There is general agreement that the two are metaphors for the weak and helpless, the "harassed and helpless" of 9:36, the "weary and burdened" of 11:28.[22] Reeds were proverbially noted for their frailty, and the flame of the wick was weak and about to go out. The gentle Servant would handle them delicately and make certain they were not lost or destroyed. He would not increase their burden but would instead give them rest.

12:20 ... until he brings justice to victory (ἕως ἂν ἐκβάλῃ εἰς νῖκος τὴν κρίσιν). This seems to combine Isa 42:3c ("in faithfulness he will bring forth justice") and 4b ("till he establishes justice on earth")[23] to proclaim the future eschatological victory of Christ and the kingdom. It is generally agreed that "to victory" (εἰς νῖκος) means "successfully" and that ἐκβάλῃ is a strong verb meaning to forcefully bring something about (it is used in 12:24, 26, 27, 28 for "casting out" demons). The gentle ministry of Jesus will continue through him and his disciples until the end of the age.[24]

12:21 And the Gentiles will put their hope in his name (καὶ τῷ ὀνόματι αὐτοῦ ἔθνη ἐλπιοῦσιν). Matthew has omitted the first half of Isa 42:4 to center on this aspect.[25] He is emphasizing, as he did in 8:5 – 13, that the Gentiles (referring not just to "the nations" but to "the Gentiles" who live in them) are part of God's plan in fulfillment not only of the Abrahamic covenant but also of the Isaianic prophecies of the procession of the nations to Zion. Jesus the gentle Messiah is the hope of the Gentiles as well as the Jews.

It is important to realize that in the very section where Jesus restricts his and the disciples' ministries to the Jewish people (10:5 – 6; 15:24), Matthew shows that Jesus' ultimate intention is to reach the Gentiles as well (see also 1:5 – 6; 2:1 – 12; 4:14 – 16, 25; 8:5 – 13; 10:18). These are not contradictory but supplementary, as indicated long before in the prophecies of Isaiah. The "name" (ὄνομα) in biblical circles means the "person" of Jesus[26] and replaces "the law" in the MT, demonstrating again that the law points to Jesus.[27]

Theology in Application

We have just seen the heart of Matt 11 – 12. The humility of the one who calls the burdened to find rest in him (11:25 – 30) is anchored in the Isaianic prophecy of the gentle Servant of Yahweh. This is also closely aligned with the baptism scene of 3:13 – 17 and recalls the emphases there — servanthood, beloved, bringing God pleasure, endowed with the Spirit (see on that passage).

22. Hill, *Matthew*, 214; Carson, "Matthew," 286 – 87; Grundmann, *Matthäus*, 326; Davies and Allison, *Matthew*, 2:326 (who mention other options like the apostles, Gentiles, Christians, or the poor). Schnackenburg, *Matthew*, 113, sees these as "sinners" in general.

23. Gundry, *Use of the Old Testament*, 114 – 15 (who adds Hab 1:4); Davies and Allison, *Matthew*, 2:326.

24. Verseput, *Humble Messianic King*, 201.

25. Gundry, *Use of the Old Testament*, 115 – 16, notes how this agrees with the LXX against the MT and theorizes that this and the LXX may represent a lost text form that is more original than the MT. That is indeed possible.

26. Morris, *Matthew*, 312.

27. Carson, "Matthew," 287.

1. Jesus the Gentle Servant

Thus far we have seen Jesus in the power and boldness of his miraculous ministry and prophetic preaching. Now we see the other side of Jesus, stated first in 11:28–30. He is the meek and humble Messiah who is here to serve God and humankind. This is exemplified especially in the cross, when he becomes the atoning sacrifice for Jew and Gentile alike.

2. God's People to Exemplify the Humility of Servanthood

Jesus, then, is the archetype of ethical "righteousness" in Matthew, i.e., living life according to God's will (see 3:15; 5:6, 10, 20; 6:1, 33). God's people are to be servants like Jesus. As Davies and Allison say, "Matthew's emphasis on the love commandment (7:12; 19:19; 22:39) goes hand in hand with his desire to interpret Jesus with the christological category of servant."[28]

3. Servants in Ministry

Servants do not fight back but trust God and minister as well as mediate the kingdom to the needy. Jesus' gentle, sensitive ministry never needed to retaliate for the indignities he suffered at the hands of his opponents. He trusted God to vindicate him and centered on those who needed him, healing their "bruises" and strengthening their "flickering flames." This is a true servant ministry every Christian should emulate, alleviating the suffering of the afflicted and lifting up the downtrodden rather than just spending time with the strong, who do not realize their need for God.

4. Guaranteeing Justice and Judgment

Jesus' ministry was a foretaste of the final judgment, when the oppressed will find justice and those who have opposed God's work will experience divine judgment. It began with his ministry to the harassed and burdened (11:28–30) and his conflict with the leaders, both metaphors for God's *bēma*, or judgment seat. Bruner sums it up well: "The Servant is quiet but not quietistic; nonviolent but not noninvolved; gentle but passionate for justice — a justice, we are promised, that he shall one day successfully bring to victory."[29]

28. Davies and Allison, *Matthew*, 2:328–29.

29. Bruner, *Christbook*, 454.

CHAPTER 53

Matthew 12:22 – 37

Literary Context

This begins the final triad of the three in 11:2 – 12:50 (see discussion at 11:2). As with the other two triads, this one also has the same two-plus-one format, with the first two centering on conflict scenes and the final one dealing with the community of Jesus' followers. Davies and Allison label these "an extended objection story ... an extended testing story ... and a succinct correction story. Whereas the objection story and the testing story serve primarily to register Israel's unbelief, the correction story is about the family of God and holds forth the possibility of faith."[1]

IV. Preaching and Teaching in the Midst of Opposition (11:2 – 13:53)

A. Jesus' Deeds: Revelation and Rejection (11:2 – 12:50)

2. Rejection of the Humble Servant (12:1 – 21)

3. Controversy and Community (12:22 – 50)

➦ **a. Confrontation over Beelzebul (12:22 – 37)**

(1) The Healing of the Demon-Possessed Man (12:22 – 23)

(2) The Conflict with the Pharisees (12:24 – 30)

(3) The Unforgivable Sin (12:31 – 32)

(4) Good and Evil Speech (12:33 – 37)

Main Idea

The intense opposition to Jesus moves into a second critical phase, from the decision that he must die (12:14) to the attribution of his power over the demonic realm to Satan. This gives Jesus the opportunity to give significant teaching about (1) the conflict between the two realms of God and Satan/good and evil, including (2) an absolute statement that the kingdom has already arrived (v. 28) and Satan has been bound, his house plundered (v. 29). (3) Jesus then accuses the leaders of

1. Davies and Allison, *Matthew*, 2:332.

committing the unpardonable sin (vv. 30 – 32) and (4) shows that people's words reveal their character (33 – 37), thereby detailing the source of the leader's blasphemy.

Translation

Matthew 12:22-37

22a	Action	**Then a demon-possessed blind and mute man was brought to Jesus,**
b	Action/Healing	and **Jesus healed him,**
c	Result of 22b	with the result that the mute man could both speak and see.
23a	Reaction #1	[1] And **the whole crowd was astonished and said,**
b		*"Could this be the Son of David?"*
24a	Reaction #2	[2] But **the Pharisees heard this and exclaimed,**
b		*"This man does not cast out demons* *except through Beelzebul,* *the prince of demons."*
25a		Knowing their thoughts,
b	Response #1/Aphorism	**Jesus responded,**
c		*"Every kingdom divided against itself will be made desolate,*
d	Parallel 25c/Aphorism	and *every city or household divided against itself cannot stand.*
26a	Inference from 25c-d	So *if Satan casts out Satan, he is thereby divided against himself.*
b	Rhetorical Question	*How can his kingdom stand?*
27a	Response #2/ Condition/Result	And *if I cast out demons through Beelzebul,* *by whom do your followers cast them out?*
b		So then *they will be your judges.*
28a	Condition/Result	But *if I . . . cast out demons* *through the Spirit of God,* *then the kingdom of God has come upon you.*
29a	Response #3/Illustration	Or *how can someone enter the house of a strong man and* *steal his goods*
b		*except he first bind the strong man?*
c		And *then he can plunder his house.*
30a	Conclusion/Aphorism	*The one not with me is against me,*
b		and *the one not gathering with me is scattering.*
31a	Assertion	*Because of this I tell you, people will be forgiven every sin* *and blasphemy,*
b	Warning	but *blasphemy of the Spirit will not be forgiven.*
32a		And *whoever speaks a word against the Son of Man will be* *forgiven,*
b	Parallel 31b	but *whoever speaks against the Holy Spirit will not be* *forgiven*
c	Clarification	*either in this age or in the age to come.*

33a	Condition/Result #1 (A)	*If you consider a tree to be good, then its fruit will be good.*
b	Condition/Result #2 (B)	*If you consider a tree bad, then its fruit will be bad.*
c	Thesis/Aphorism	*For a tree is known by its fruit.*
34a	Rhetorical Question	*Offspring of vipers, how can you speak good when you are evil?*
b	Basis of 34a	*For it is from the abundance of the heart that the mouth speaks.*
35a	Restatement of 33a (A)	*Good people produce good things from their treasure house,*
b	Restatement of 33b (B)	*and evil people produce evil things from their treasure house*
36a	Warning	*For I tell you that people will give account on the day of judgment for every careless word they speak.*
37a	Basis for 36a	*For by your words you will be justified,*
b		*and by your words you will be condemned."*

Structure and Literary Form

The Synoptic connections are complex, as this stems from Mark 3:22 – 30 (Matt 12:24 – 26, 29, 30 – 32 is triple tradition material), Q (vv. 22 – 23 = Luke 11:14; vv. 27 – 28 = Luke 11:19 – 20; vv. 30 = Luke 11:23; vv. 33 – 35 = Luke 6:43 – 45), and M material (vv. 36 – 37). This is also a doublet with 9:32 – 34 (= 12:22 – 24). As for form, there is a healing narrative (vv. 22 – 23) followed by a conflict narrative (vv. 24 – 32) and then a paraenetic challenge (vv. 33 – 37). The whole unit is called by Davies and Allison an objection story (see above). There are four parts to this unit.

1. The exorcism and healing (vv. 22 – 23) consist of bringing the man to Jesus, the healing, and the astonishment that resulted.
2. The controversy (vv. 24 – 30) consists of the charge of the Pharisees (v. 24) and Jesus' fivefold response (vv. 25 – 26, 27, 28, 29, 30).
3. The charge of blasphemy (vv. 31 – 32) has an ABAB pattern between what can be forgiven and what cannot.
4. The paraenetic material (vv. 33 – 37) consists of an introduction on a tree producing fruit (v. 33), followed by teaching on good and bad speech (vv. 34 – 35) as well as judgment for careless words (v. 36), and a conclusion on judgment for one's speech (v. 37).

Exegetical Outline

➡ I. The Healing of the Demon-Possessed Man (12:22 – 23)

A. The healing and exorcism (v. 22)

B. The astonishment of the people (v. 23)

II. The Conflict with the Pharisees (12:24 – 30)
- A. The charge of demon-possession (v. 24)
- B. Jesus' response (vv. 25 – 30)
  1. The division of Satan's kingdom (vv. 25 – 26)
  2. Jesus vs. Beelzebub (vv. 27 – 28)
     - a. The example of exorcism by the Pharisees (v. 27)
     - b. The arrival of the kingdom (v. 28)
  3. The binding of Satan (v. 29)
  4. Warning about those not with Jesus (v. 30)

III. The Unforgivable Sin (12:31 – 32)
- A. Forgiveness and blasphemy of the Spirit (v. 31)
- B. Speaking against Jesus and the Spirit (v. 32)

IV. Good and Evil Speech (12:33 – 37)
- A. Introduction: trees producing good or evil fruit (v. 33)
- B. Teaching on good and bad speech (vv. 34 – 35)
- C. Judgment for careless words (v. 36)
- D. Conclusion: justification or judgment on one's speech (v. 37)

Explanation of the Text

12:22 Then a demon-possessed blind and mute man was brought to Jesus (Τότε προσηνέχθη αὐτῷ δαιμονιζόμενος τυφλὸς καὶ κωφός). Matthew's typical "then" (τότε) provides a loose connection with the previous events. The miracle is told in the briefest possible way, for its purpose is to prepare for the controversy that follows. The withdrawal (v. 15) is over and a new period of conflict takes place. This is the only place a "blind[2] and mute" person is healed, and it is clear that his double malady is caused by demonic possession (the present tense participle stresses the "demonized blind and mute man"). The doublet of 9:32 – 34 is similar, with a demon cast out, the crowd amazed, and the Pharisees accusing Jesus of drawing his power from Satan. However, there it was a dumb person, and the language is different enough that these are probably separate incidents.

12:22 And Jesus healed him with the result that the mute man could both speak and see (καὶ ἐθεράπευσεν αὐτόν, ὥστε τὸν κωφὸν λαλεῖν καὶ βλέπειν). The healing is also succinct, though the fact that the man could then both see and talk is emphasized ("with the result" [ὥστε] stresses the effects of the healing). Here Jesus' love and compassion (cf. 9:35 – 36) are central, and his mercy to the downtrodden (11:5, 28; 12:15) is demonstrated.[3]

12:23 And the whole crowd was astonished and said, "Could this be the Son of David?" (καὶ ἐξίσταντο πάντες οἱ ὄχλοι καὶ ἔλεγον, Μήτι οὗτός ἐστιν ὁ υἱὸς Δαυίδ;). Amazement is a

2. Some have thought the blindness a metaphor for Israel's spiritual blindness (e.g., Loader, "Son of David," 570 – 85 [esp. 577 – 78]), but this does not fit. There is no hint of Israel's inability to speak, so why blindness?

3. Verseput, *Humble Messianic King*, 213 – 14, sees in this a metaphor for Israel in the control of the evil one, with Jesus offering healing but, unlike the man here, being rejected. In light of vv. 43 – 45 (the parable of the returning spirit), this is possible but is too allegorical for this passage. That message needs to await vv. 43 – 45.

significant feature of miracle stories throughout the gospels (Matt 8:27; 9:8, 33; Mark has a great deal more). ἐξίσταντο is strong and could be translated, "They were beside themselves."[4]

The question is debated. Some see the interrogative particle μήτι as negative, translating, "This man isn't the Son of David, is he?" and seeing this as a further example of rejection.[5] But with the strong astonishment the crowd feels, rejection is unlikely, and μήτι can also be used of a question expressing doubt, as in the Samaritan woman of John 4:29 (see BAGD, 520; BDF §427, 2, 3), hence the translation, "Could this be...?" The "Son of David" title is a favorite of Matthew (see on 1:1; 9:27), especially in healing stories, and points to Jesus as the royal Messiah who has compassion and heals. The people are filled with wonder, feeling that they may have encountered the Messiah.

12:24 But the Pharisees heard this and exclaimed, "This man does not cast out demons except through[6] Beelzebul, the prince of demons" (οἱ δὲ Φαρισαῖοι ἀκούσαντες εἶπον, Οὗτος οὐκ ἐκβάλλει τὰ δαιμόνια εἰ μὴ ἐν τῷ Βεελζεβοὺλ ἄρχοντι τῶν δαιμονίων). The contrast (adversative "but" [δέ]) between the crowds and Pharisees is made explicit. Rather than the wonder the crowds felt and their hesitant affirmation of Jesus' messianic status, the leaders are resolute, filled with animosity and attributing his power to satanic influence. The crowds believe God may be behind Jesus, while the Pharisees see only Satan (on Beelzebul, see 10:25; and on "the prince of demons," 9:34). This is Satan himself. Their logic is impeccable — they cannot deny that Jesus can heal the sick and cast out demons, and at the same time they cannot admit that God might be behind him. There is only one recourse: it is black magic. By making this charge, they have taken away the last possibility of reconciliation. They are now beyond the pale of redemption, as vv. 31 – 32 will make clear.

12:25 Knowing[7] their thoughts, Jesus responded (εἰδὼς δὲ τὰς ἐνθυμήσεις αὐτῶν εἶπεν αὐτοῖς). Jesus begins his countercharge. Matthew is even longer than Mark in vv. 25 – 30 (which is unusual) and adds material from Q and his own material (see above), so he considers this an important section. He begins once more with Jesus' supernatural knowledge (cf. 9:4; 22:18), in Matthew always knowledge of evil intent (in this case not just what they said publicly in v. 24 but also the hostility that lay behind it). "Thoughts" (ἐνθυμήσεις) connote one's opinions and thoughts and has a verbal thrust, "what they were thinking."[8]

12:25 "Every kingdom divided against itself will be made desolate, and every city or household divided against itself cannot stand" (Πᾶσα βασιλεία μερισθεῖσα καθ' ἑαυτῆς ἐρημοῦται, καὶ πᾶσα πόλις ἢ οἰκία μερισθεῖσα καθ' ἑαυτῆς οὐ σταθήσεται). Jesus uses the metaphors of a kingdom, a city, and a household (probably an extended household like Abraham's [Gen 14:14] that was virtually a fortress). If any of them is "divided against itself," signifying internal dissension, its doom is certain. ἐρημόω means "to lay waste, make desolate," with its cognate noun meaning "desert." Rome was afraid of no one, for they knew their army was virtually invincible. But they were terrified of civil war, which had several times

4. Luz, *Matthew 8 – 20*, 202; France, *Matthew* (TNTC), 207.

5. NASB; Blomberg, *Matthew*, 20.

6. For "through" (ἐν) used instrumentally, see BAGD, 261 (c).

7. This could be a causal participle, "because he knew," but with Matthew's proclivity for temporal participles, this is closely linked with the main verb, "Jesus knew their thoughts and replied."

8. Louw and Nida, *Greek-English Lexicon*, 1:30.15.

threatened their extinction (and would once again in AD 68 – 69 after the suicide of Nero).

12:26 So if Satan casts out Satan, he is thereby divided against himself. How can his kingdom stand? (καὶ εἰ ὁ Σατανᾶς τὸν Σατανᾶν ἐκβάλλει, ἐφ᾿ ἑαυτὸν ἐμερίσθη· πῶς οὖν σταθήσεται ἡ βασιλεία αὐτοῦ;). Satan (see on 4:10) and Beelzebul are one and the same, and Jesus' point is that if[9] Satan is casting out himself (i.e., the demons under his control), then his kingdom too would be characterized by internal discord and would self-destruct in a civil war. That dominion is no different than any other kingdom and cannot survive internal strife.

12:27 And if I cast out demons through Beelzebul, by whom do your followers cast them out? So then they will be your judges (καὶ εἰ ἐγὼ ἐν Βεελζεβοὺλ ἐκβάλλω τὰ δαιμόνια, οἱ υἱοὶ ὑμῶν ἐν τίνι ἐκβάλλουσιν; διὰ τοῦτο αὐτοὶ κριταὶ ἔσονται ὑμῶν). Jesus' logic is irrefutable. He takes the opposite tack: "Let's say you are correct and my power over demons comes from Satan himself. Then what does that say about your own followers?" The phrase "your sons" (οἱ υἱοὶ ὑμῶν) could mean either Jewish exorcists in general or, more likely, the Pharisees' own followers. Rabbi/disciple relations were often spoken of as "father/son."

Exorcism in the first century was a thriving business, both in pagan and Jewish societies. Those performing it would employ complex incantations (which they said came from Solomon), magical charms, and even visual effects (cf. Josephus, *Ant.* 8:45 – 48; Tob 8:2 – 3), so Jesus is saying that their practices would be endangered as well. There is an implicit contrast between Jesus ("I") and the "sons" of the Pharisees, for Jesus needed only an authoritative word. Jesus' deeds are superior to theirs, as seen in 9:33 when the crowd said, "Nothing like this has ever been seen in Israel."[10] If Jesus' superior power comes from Satan, how much more their inferior authority?

"They will be your judges" means that the practices of the Pharisees prove them wrong about Jesus. "They would 'judge' them for ascribing to Satan what they, the exorcists, knew came from God."[11] The future "they will be" (ἔσονται) may point to the final judgment, but there is a realized aspect as well. The very presence of such exorcisms in their own ranks proves them wrong.

12:28 But if I through the Spirit of God cast out demons, then the kingdom of God has come upon you (εἰ δὲ ἐν πνεύματι θεοῦ ἐγὼ ἐκβάλλω τὰ δαιμόνια, ἄρα ἔφθασεν ἐφ᾿ ὑμᾶς ἡ βασιλεία τοῦ θεοῦ). Now "if" (εἰ) returns to its normal use as a condition of fact. In v. 27 Jesus argued from the charge that his power came "through Beelzebul." Now[12] he points out the true source of his ministry, saying that his power actually comes "through [instrumental ἐν in both cases] the Spirit."[13] It is not demonic power but divine presence that has led to the authoritative demonstrations.

Luke 11:20 has virtually the same wording as Matthew in this verse except that Luke has "finger of God" (δακτύλῳ θεοῦ) rather than "Spirit of God" (πνεύματι θεοῦ). It does not matter which is original in Q,[14] but Matthew emphasizes the Spirit in 10:20 as well as in 12:31 – 32 in contrast

9. "If" (εἰ) here and in v. 27 are not conditions of fact but encroach on "if" (ἐάν). Jesus assumes the "if clause" is true for the sake of argument.

10. Verseput, *Humble Messianic King*, 223.

11. Morris, *Matthew*, 316.

12. The adversative "but" (δέ) establishes an antithesis between the premise of v. 27 and that of v. 28.

13. Hagner, *Matthew 1 – 13*, 343. Note that in both verses the "through" (ἐν) phrase is at the beginning for emphasis.

14. Most take Luke as the original, but R. G. Hammerton-Kelly, "A Note on Matthew xii.28 par. Luke xi.20," *NTS* 11 (1964 – 65): 167 – 69; and J. D. G. Dunn, *Jesus and the Spirit: A Study of the Religious and Charismatic Experience of Jesus and the First Christians as Reflected in the New Testament*

to "unclean spirits" in 12:43 – 45. The presence of the Spirit is proof positive that the kingdom is here. Elsewhere the authority belongs to Jesus for conquering the cosmic powers, but here it is the Spirit who fills him (see 3:16; 4:1; 12:18). It is both the Spirit in him and his internal authority as Son of God (note the Trinitarian implications) that are behind Jesus' power over demonic forces.

This is an important verse in Matthew's kingdom theology,[15] for while in 4:17 the kingdom was imminent ("it is near" [ἤγγικεν], see on that verse), here the kingdom has already "arrived" (ἔφθασεν, an aorist emphasizing what has already taken place, possibly with a culminative force on the results[16] of the arrival), thus an already/not yet format.[17] Moreover, the presence of the Spirit is a direct claim by Jesus regarding his messianic status, for it was prophesied that God would endow the Messiah with the Spirit (Isa 11:2, 61:1 – 2; *Pss. Sol.* 17:37; 18:7; *1 En.* 49:2 – 4; *T. Levi* 18:7).[18]

12:29 Or how can someone enter the house of a strong man and steal his goods except he first bind the strong man? (ἢ πῶς δύναταί τις εἰσελθεῖν εἰς τὴν οἰκίαν τοῦ ἰσχυροῦ καὶ τὰ σκεύη αὐτοῦ ἁρπάσαι, ἐὰν μὴ πρῶτον δήσῃ τὸν ἰσχυρόν;). Now Jesus uses a *mashal* or extended metaphor probably built on Isa 49:24 – 25[19] to demonstrate the significance of his ministry. This is in a sense the thesis statement of Jesus' ministry of exorcism. Every time he casts out a demon it demonstrates the "binding of Satan" motif (δύναμαι here has its full meaning, "have the power to") found often in Jewish writings (Tob 3:17; *Jub.* 10:7, 48:15; *1 En.* 10:4 – 5; *T. Levi* 18:12).[20]

Satan's realm is under assault and in the process of being taken down. He pictures Satan's kingdom as an extended household/fortress (see above on v. 25) controlled by a powerful individual (like Abraham in Gen 14:14) who feels impregnable. The thief must calculate the man's strength and be ready for it before he can plunder his possessions. Clearly, Jesus is stronger than Satan and enters his cosmic household whenever he wants, binds the devil, enters his kingdom at will, and takes his possessions by casting out demons.[21] τὰ

(London: SCM, 1975), 44 – 46, argue for Matthew's originality. See Carson, "Matthew," 289, for a rejoinder to Dunn's view that the Spirit rather than Jesus has brought the kingdom here.

15. This is perhaps the second time Matthew has "kingdom of God" rather than "of heaven" (it is a text critical possibility in 6:33; cf. also 19:24; 21:31, 43). Here "God" is used in antithesis to "Satan/Beelzebul" in vv. 26 – 27, and "kingdom of God" is opposed to "his kingdom" in v. 27. France, *Gospel of Matthew*, 480, believes it occurs where the context demands "a more 'personal' reference to God himself than the more oblique language of his heavenly authority."

16. Turner, *Grammar*, 72, calls this a "perfective" aorist, which he defines also as an "effective or resultative" use, stemming normally from the meaning of the verb (in this case the results of the "arrival" of the kingdom). Proponents of aspect theory say this stems not from the tense but from the verb, but in either case the emphasis is present in situations like this.

17. See R. F. Berkey, "ΕΓΓΙΖΕΙΝ, ΦΘΑΝΕΙΝ, and Realized Eschatology," *JBL* 82 (1963): 177 – 87. Chrys C. Caragounis, "Kingdom of God, Son of Man, and Jesus' Self-Understanding, Part I," *TynBul* 40 (1989): 3 – 23, argues that this is a futuristic aorist, but Nolland, *Matthew*, 501, shows that this (while indeed possible) does not fit the context, since Jesus says in effect, "What you can see here is God's rule come into effect."

18. Verseput, *Humble Messianic King*, 226 – 27; Davies and Allison, *Matthew*, 2:339.

19. The Isaiah passage details God freeing Israel from her enemies as "plunder taken from warriors." See Gnilka, *Matthäusevangelium*, 1:459; Luz, *Matthew 8 – 20*, 204.

20. Nolland, *Matthew*, 502, says, "Jesus' effortless exorcisms point to a bound Satan, that is, to the reality of a new state of power realities, the coming of the kingdom of God."

21. Many scholars have noted the discrepancy between the parables of the divided kingdom (vv. 25 – 27) that assume Satan's realm is intact and powerful, and vv. 29 – 30 that assume that Satan's realm is invaded and defeated (for a survey of interpretations, see Joel Marcus, "The Beelzebul Controversy and the Eschatologies of Jesus," in *Authenticating the Activities of Jesus* (ed. Bruce Chilton and Craig A. Evans; [Leiden: Brill, 2002], 247 – 77). The answer is that the first passage looks at Satan's realm as it appears to people, intact and thriving, and the second to Satan's realm as it actually is with the coming of Christ and the kingdom.

σκεύη would be the demon-possessed people who belong to Satan and are liberated by Jesus. This binding here is already taking place in Jesus' ministry, but in John 12:31; 14:30; 16:11; Col 2:13 – 15; 1 Pet 3:19 it occurs at the cross/resurrection; and in Rev 12:12; 20:10 it occurs at the end of history.[22]

12:29 And then he can plunder his house (καὶ τότε τὴν οἰκίαν αὐτοῦ διαρπάσει). The "plundering" is the total defeat of Satan and rendering him powerless. Implicit here but explicit in Luke 11:22 is the sharing of the "plunder" with Jesus' followers, namely, the blessings of salvation and especially the power over Satan (see 10:1). France interprets this in light of Isa 49:24 – 25 as a releasing of Satan's captives.

12:30 The one not with me is against me, and the one not gathering with me is scattering (ὁ μὴ ὢν μετ' ἐμοῦ κατ' ἐμοῦ ἐστιν, καὶ ὁ μὴ συνάγων μετ' ἐμοῦ σκορπίζει).[23] This Q passage (= Luke 11:23) is a critical warning. In the cosmic war against Satan no one can be neutral — there are no Switzerlands! Most agree that those who are "not with" (μὴ … μετά) Jesus are not the Pharisees. Some think they are the Jewish exorcists of v. 29,[24] but it is better to see the saying as addressed to the crowds, thus a challenge to make a commitment for Jesus.[25]

With the verbs "to be" and the present tenses, Jesus emphasizes a direct encounter with his claims. The opposite idea comes in Mark 9:40, when Jesus told his disciples (about the unidentified man casting out demons in Jesus' name), "whoever is not against us is for us."[26] The image of "gather/scatter" stems from the OT (Isa 40:11, 49:6a; Jer 23:2 – 3; Ezek 34:12 – 13, 16; Zech 13:7 – 9) and intertestamental (Tob 13:5; Bar 4:37; *Pss. Sol.* 11:2) images of God the shepherd gathering back to himself those from Israel scattered in the exile.[27] Jesus is the shepherd of the last days, and everyone must choose either to join him in gathering his sheep or to oppose him and scatter his flock. There is no middle ground.

12:31 Because of this I tell you, people will be forgiven every sin and blasphemy (Διὰ τοῦτο λέγω ὑμῖν, πᾶσα ἁμαρτία καὶ βλασφημία ἀφεθήσεται τοῖς ἀνθρώποις).[28] In 12:24 the Pharisees made a charge against Jesus, and in his response of vv. 25 – 30 he has defended himself. Now he takes the offensive and makes a charge against the Pharisees based on their very accusation. Typical of Matthew, there is a strong parallelism in an ABAB pattern between vv. 31 and 32: every sin and blasphemy forgiven/but not blasphemy against the Spirit; a word against the Son of Man forgiven/but not speaking against the Holy Spirit. The result is a strong emphasis on the horror of blaspheming the Spirit.

The introductory "because of this" (διὰ τοῦτο) links this not just with v. 30[29] but with all of vv. 24 – 30, i.e., the conflict between Jesus and the Pharisees.[30] This first part builds on the OT

22. See Davies and Allison, *Matthew*, 2:342.

23. Some (e.g., TNIV, Carson, Blomberg) take v. 30 with vv. 31 – 32 rather than with vv. 25 – 29, believing that it introduces the teaching about blasphemy against the Holy Spirit. As often with a transition passage, it both concludes the preceding and leads into the following. However, it fits better with the conflict over Satan, telling those listening that they must make a decision.

24. Hagner, *Matthew 1 – 13*, 344.

25. Luz, *Matthew 8 – 20*, 205.

26. As McNeile, *Matthew*, 177, says, "they are not contradictory, if the one was spoken to the indifferent about themselves, and the other to the disciples about someone else."

27. Verseput, *Humble Messianic King*, 411 n96, shows that while "gathering" could be a harvest image, with "scattering" it is best seen as a shepherd metaphor in terms of gathering the scattered sheep.

28. Although in a sense this is a triple tradition saying, Matthew appears to build on Mark 3:28 in v. 31 and on Q (Luke 12:10) in v. 32.

29. So Carson, "Matthew," 290 – 91.

30. McNeile, *Matthew*, 177 – 78; Gundry, *Matthew*, 237; Hagner, *Matthew 1 – 13*, 346 – 47.

emphasis on the depth of God's mercy and forgiveness (Ps 25:11; 65:3; 78:38; Isa 1:18, 43:25; Mic 7:19), with emphasis on "every" (πᾶς, *every* sin and blasphemy). It is possible that "sins" are offenses against people and "blasphemies" offenses against God,[31] but more likely sins are deeds and blasphemies words against both people and God. This is remarkable, for Jewish teaching had long discussions on what constituted blasphemy, with some linking it to speaking against Torah and others to participating in idolatry but most linking it to the utterance of the divine name. When Jesus says here "every blasphemy," it must include the above, even blaspheming God.[32]

12:31 But blasphemy of the Spirit will not be forgiven (ἡ δὲ τοῦ πνεύματος βλασφημία οὐκ ἀφεθήσεται). The unpardonable sin is found not just here but in Heb 6:4 – 6; 10:26 – 31; 1 John 5:16, building on the "sin with a high hand" of Num 15:30 – 31, defiant blasphemy of Yahweh that was punished by being cut off from the covenant people (probably meaning execution). In what way can all other blasphemies be forgivable but not that against the Spirit?[33] The key is the Spirit as the active force of God in this world. To slander God or Jesus is one thing, but to slander his work in this world through the Spirit is another. Since the Spirit is the instrument through which God's eschatological salvation has entered the world, blaspheming that divine tool of salvation behind Jesus cannot be forgiven[34] (see further on v. 32).

12:32 And whoever speaks a word against the Son of Man will be forgiven (καὶ ὃς ἐὰν εἴπῃ λόγον κατὰ τοῦ υἱοῦ τοῦ ἀνθρώπου, ἀφεθήσεται αὐτῷ). The switch from "blaspheme" to "speak against" is stylistic; the two are synonymous and refer to the scurrilous accusations of the Pharisees. The two parallel "whoever" (ὃς (ἐ)άν) clauses stress the idea of "any person at any time," including all three groups — leaders, crowds, disciples.

12:32 But whoever speaks against the Holy Spirit will not be forgiven (ὃς δ' ἂν εἴπῃ κατὰ τοῦ πνεύματος τοῦ ἁγίου, οὐκ ἀφεθήσεται αὐτῷ). The question of distinction between Jesus and the Spirit as well as the apparent unforgivable nature of apostasy from Jesus in Heb 6:4 – 6 has occasioned many different interpretations, such as:[35] (1) a post-Easter saying contrasting the earthly Jesus with the post-Easter Spirit; (2) sayings against the hidden Son of Man, namely, the earthly Jesus vs. the work of the Spirit (Athanasius); (3) rejection of those not in the church vs. rejection of those who have become part of the church (Augustine). None of these are satisfactory.

The answer was discussed in v. 31. By taking the work of the Spirit in Jesus' exorcisms and attributing it to Satan, the Pharisees have blasphemed God's work via the Holy Spirit. France says, "It is thus a complete perversion of religious values, revealing a decisive choice on the wrong side in the battle between good and evil, between God and Satan."[36] They can slander Jesus but not the Holy Spirit who works through him. In this sense both Peter's denials and Paul's persecution of Christians were forgivable.

In terms of Heb 6:4 – 6 and 1 John 5:16 a couple of other points could be made. There is a salvation-historical dimension, for during his ministry the glory of the Son of Man was incarnate and to

31. So Davies and Allison, *Matthew*, 2:345.

32. See Verseput, *Humble Messianic King*, 236 – 37.

33. "Of the Spirit" (τοῦ πνεύματος) is an objective genitive, "blaspheming the Spirit." By being placed within the article and noun, this is emphasized.

34. Verseput, *Humble Messianic King*, 237.

35. Combining Verseput, Davies and Allison, Luz. Both Davies and Allison and Luz say no answer is satisfactory.

36. France, *Gospel of Matthew*, 482.

an extent hidden, but after his resurrection he was exalted to the "name … above every name" (Phil 2:9 – 11). Thus, what constituted blasphemy of the Spirit here is extended to blasphemy of Jesus the Lord in Heb 6 and 1 John 5.

12:32 … either in this age or in the age to come (οὔτε ἐν τούτῳ τῷ αἰῶνι οὔτε ἐν τῷ μέλλοντι). This solidifies the effects. This is indeed the unpardonable sin. Forgiveness is not possible either now or in eternity. Jesus is speaking of the final judgment. They are under indictment now, and there is no chance that they will receive forgiveness when they stand before the *bēma* of God (Rev 20:11 – 15).

12:33 If you consider a tree to be good, then its fruit will be good. If you consider a tree bad, then its fruit will be bad. For a tree is known by its fruit (Ἢ ποιήσατε τὸ δένδρον καλὸν καὶ τὸν καρπὸν αὐτοῦ καλόν, ἢ ποιήσατε τὸ δένδρον σαπρὸν καὶ τὸν καρπὸν αὐτοῦ σαπρόν· ἐκ γὰρ τοῦ καρποῦ τὸ δένδρον γινώσκεται). The configuration of "if you consider … if you consider" (ἢ ποιήσατε … ἢ ποιήσατε) constitutes imperatives that in effect become "if"-clauses,[37] and the verb (ποιέω) in this context means to "consider" or "suppose," asking for judgment from the hearers.[38] At the same time, there is a double meaning, for the image comes from the practice of cultivating trees so that they will become fruitful, so the verb (ποιέω) also means "make" a tree good or bad.

If we put these two meanings together, it means what you "consider" to do/make, you will do. This parallels 7:17, "every good tree produces good fruit" (7:15 – 20 is on false prophets), and challenges the crowd to judge carefully between the Pharisees and Jesus. The "good tree" is Jesus, who proclaims God's truths, and the "bad tree" is the leader who opposes God in Jesus and speaks against him. "A tree is known by its fruit" (cf. 7:20) challenges the hearers to differentiate between the evil talk/blasphemy of the Pharisees and the kingdom truths of Jesus. The point is that the Pharisees have "made" (double meaning) themselves evil, and so their proclamations have become evil.

12:34 Offspring of vipers, how can you speak good when you are evil? (γεννήματα ἐχιδνῶν, πῶς δύνασθε ἀγαθὰ λαλεῖν πονηροὶ ὄντες;). "Offspring of vipers" (γεννήματα ἐχιδνῶν) has already been used in 3:7 and appears again in 23:33, always of the leaders, meaning they are a spreading poison. Jesus draws the conclusion from the previous verse. Since they have shown themselves to be bad trees producing evil fruit, how dare they pretend to speak good things? Evil cannot produce good (on the "evil" of the Pharisees, see also 12:39; 16:4; 22:18).

12:34 For it is from the abundance of the heart that the mouth speaks (ἐκ γὰρ τοῦ περισσεύματος τῆς καρδίας τὸ στόμα λαλεῖ). The "abundance" (περίσσευμα) here is related to the "treasure house" of v. 35 and speaks of what fills and controls a person's life, i.e., what they treasure. In other words, what we are determines what we say. So the Pharisees cannot speak good because their heart is overrun with evil.

12:35 Good people[39] produce good things from their treasure house, and evil people produce evil things from their treasure house (ὁ ἀγαθὸς ἄνθρωπος ἐκ τοῦ ἀγαθοῦ θησαυροῦ ἐκβάλλει ἀγαθά, καὶ ὁ πονηρὸς ἄνθρωπος ἐκ τοῦ πονηροῦ θησαυροῦ ἐκβάλλει πονηρά). Jesus now moves from speaking to the more general idea of actions and uses the metaphor of a "treasure house."[40]

37. Hagner, *Matthew 1 – 13*, 349 – 50, cf. John 14:1b, "If you believe God, you will also believe me."

38. So Hill, 218; Grundmann, *Matthäus*, 331; Verseput, *Humble Messianic King*, 244.

39. Generic "person" (ἄνθρωπος) appears often in Matthew (4:4, 19; 5:13, 16; et al.).

40. θησαυρός can refer both to the storehouse where treasure is kept and the treasure itself. Here both ideas are

The verb "produce" (ἐκβάλλω) has double meaning and is deliberately chosen to echo the "casting out" of demons in 12:24, 26, 27, 28. Jesus has "produced" or brought about good (for this use see on v. 20) in "casting out" demons while the Pharisees can only "produce evil" when they oppose God and his agent, Jesus. They have "treasured" evil, and now they produce it.

12:36 For I tell you that people will give account on the day of judgment for every careless word they speak (λέγω δὲ ὑμῖν ὅτι πᾶν ῥῆμα ἀργὸν ὃ λαλήσουσιν οἱ ἄνθρωποι ἀποδώσουσιν περὶ αὐτοῦ λόγον ἐν ἡμέρᾳ κρίσεως). The judgment that is implicit in vv. 33 – 35 now becomes explicit and echoes v. 32c. The introductory "for I tell you" (λέγω δὲ ὑμῖν) points to the importance of the saying (cf. 3:9; 5:20, 22, 28, 32, 34, 39, 44 [the antitheses]; 6:25, 29; 8:11; 11:22, 24; 12:6, 31). They had better listen. The verb "will give account" (ἀποδώσουσιν) is used in Matt 5:26, 18:25 – 30 for paying back a debt and in 6:4, 6, 18 of God rendering a reward, either good or bad. It connotes final judgment in these and other passages (Heb 13:17; Rev 18:6, 22:12).

Here this verb especially centers on final judgment (note the future tense) with the added "on the day of judgment" (ἐν ἡμέρᾳ κρίσεως). Stress is especially placed on the basis for the judgment (first for emphasis), "every careless word" (πᾶν ῥῆμα ἀργόν). When used of people, ἀργός means "idle, useless, lazy," and when used of words it means "empty, idle, careless." BAGD (104) interprets it here as "*a careless word* which, because of its worthlessness, had better been left unspoken."

Verseput speaks of two possible connotations for this phrase, both of which may be correct: words that accomplish nothing good and are therefore bad, or words that have no effect and accomplish nothing, i.e., "unimportant, meaningless talk of the incidental or casual variety."[41] Paul addresses this in Eph 4:29 when he prohibits "unwholesome talk" and calls for words that "build others up" and "benefit" them (cf. Jas 3:1, 13 – 18; Jude 15). With the Pharisees the first connotation, evil speech, is in mind, but Jesus generalizes it for all speech that fails to edify others. The point is that we (non-Christian and Christian alike) will give account to God for everything we say, and the principle is *lex talionis*, the "law of retribution."

12:37 For by your words you will be justified, and by your words you will be condemned (ἐκ γὰρ τῶν λόγων σου δικαιωθήσῃ, καὶ ἐκ τῶν λόγων σου καταδικασθήσῃ). This is Matthean parallelism at its best, producing a proverbial saying[42] on divine judgment that makes the "give account" of v. 36 far more specific. If our speech is good and useful, we will be "justified" or acquitted (the legal connotation of δικαιωθήσῃ, with the future tense pointing to the last judgment in light of v. 36); but if it is bad (as in the good and bad trees of v. 33), we will be "condemned." Our words reflect the true essence of who we are (vv. 34 – 35) and will provide irrefutable evidence on judgment day.

present, for it refers to the heart from which what is of supreme value (their "treasure") is produced.

41. Verseput, *Humble Messianic King*, 249.

42. McNeile, *Matthew*, 181; Hill, *Matthew*, 219; and Harrington, *Matthew*, 185, believe Jesus may be using an actual proverb.

Theology in Application

This is a key passage in Matthew, the high point so to speak of opposition in the book. At the same time, the authority of Jesus is never more clear, and we see here that Satan is already defeated and bound by Jesus. Further, there is a stress not only on the Pharisees but also on the accountability of all of us before God for the words we speak.

1. No Assumptions

We must never assume that religious leaders are good just because they claim to be so. The Pharisees sounded good. They had developed the oral tradition and were self-appointed guardians of Torah. On the surface their diatribe against Jesus was in keeping with the OT demand to test the prophets. Yet, as Jesus points out, their hearts were far from God and they had rejected his Son without warrant. In judging religious figures, we must look beyond their words to their hearts and test whether they are genuinely serving God or themselves. Most founders of cults come from evangelical churches and are unmasked too late. Our churches must teach theology and create Berean Christians who examine "the Scriptures every day to see if what [teachers/preachers say are] true" (Acts 17:11).

2. Conqueror over Satan

Jesus has once for all conquered Satan. Let me rephrase J. B. Phillips' classic *Your God Is Too Small* and say, "Your Satan is too big." We make the error of comedian Flip Wilson and too often say, "The devil made me do it," when in reality we did it ourselves. Satan is not an overpowering figure; he has been bound by Jesus, and every exorcism is an invasion of Satan's realm literally at will. Moreover, Jesus' authority over Satan has been passed on to the church, and every believer can bind Satan (Matt 10:1; cf. Mark 3:15; 6:7; Luke 4:36; 9:1). The long-awaited kingdom of God has already arrived (12:28), and the citizens of the kingdom have kingdom authority. Satan has control over his followers but not over believers. With them he can only deceive (Rev 12:9; 20:3; cf. 1 Cor 10:13); in this sense he is the greatest con man who ever lived.

3. The Unforgivable Sin

There is an unforgivable sin, and Christians must be aware of the danger. It is common on passages like 12:31 – 32; Heb 6:4 – 6; 1 John 5:16 for people to fall back on eternal security and say, "It cannot happen to us." That is a serious error, for Calvinists as well as Arminians recognize that the people described in Heb 3:1; 6:4 are members of the church who for all intents and purposes seem to be Christians. Therefore, whatever our theological persuasion, this is a real warning for our churches and should be preached as such. People in our churches do commit this final sin, and it is supremely sad because anyone who has done so has no future but "only a fearful expectation of judgment and of raging fire that will consume the enemies of God" (Heb 10:27).

4. Speech and Action

What we say shows the kind of person we are. Jesus in vv. 33 – 35 shows how the mouth reflects the heart, i.e., the true person within us. James 1:19 states this well: "Everyone should be quick to listen, slow to speak and slow to become angry." In other words, "watch your mouth," for as in Jas 3:5 the tongue is a small spark that sets a great forest ablaze. We must weigh our words carefully, avoid rudeness, and make certain that we edify rather than tear down others. James 3:1 – 4:12 especially concerns slander, but we must realize that gossip is passive slander and in some ways worse than slander, for slander at least is honest, wanting to hurt another person (cf. 2 Cor 12:20). Gossip doesn't care enough to worry who is hurt but turns slander into entertainment!

5. Judgment Coming

Many think only the unsaved will be judged and Christians rewarded at the final judgment. But there are many passages that indicate leaders will "give account" to God (Heb 13:17), and teachers will be "judged more strictly" (Jas 3:1). All Christian leaders will have their deeds pass through the fire, where they will be judged by God (1 Cor 3:12 – 15).[43] The key idea is judgment according to works (Matt 16:27; Rom 2:6; 14:12; 1 Cor 3:12 – 15; 2 Cor 5:10; 11:15; 2 Tim 4:14; 1 Pet 1:17), and in Revelation the author speaks of both believers (Rev 2:23; 11:18; 14:13; 20:12; 22:12) and unbelievers (18:6; 20:13).

6. Answering to God for Every Careless Word

There is much in the NT on the sin of the tongue, beginning with the major section of Jas 3:1 – 4:12 and including Eph 4:29; 5:4; Col 3:8. The basic principle is given in Jas 1:19 (quoted above). We must weigh our words carefully and make sure they help others rather than tear them down, that they glorify God rather than self, and that they have worth rather than being worthless.

43. For the discussion of this passage see "Theology in Application" on 7:13 – 27.

CHAPTER 54

Matthew 12:38 – 45

Literary Context

This final controversy passage of chs. 11 – 12 shows further the absolute rejection of Jesus by the leaders. Their demand for a sign demonstrates their rejection of all the previous miracles and ministry of Jesus. His deeds and words were more than enough to prove to anyone who was open that he was the Messiah sent from God. Jesus points to this rejection with his powerful parable of the return of the demons (vv. 43 – 45).

- **IV. Preaching and Teaching in the Midst of Opposition (11:2 – 13:53)**
  - **A. Jesus' Deeds: Revelation and Rejection (11:2 – 12:50)**
    - **3. Controversy and Community (12:22 – 50)**
      - a. Confrontation over Beelzebul (12:22 – 37)
      - ➦ **b. Controversy over the Sign of Jonah (12:38 – 45)**
      - c. Family and Community (12:46 – 50)

Main Idea

Rejection governs every aspect of this passage. First Jesus' enemies reject him in their demand for a sign; then Jesus rejects them in his proclamation of their future judgment by Nineveh and the Queen of the South. At the same time, Jesus is also proclaiming his exalted status by saying he is "greater than Jonah" and "greater than Solomon." Finally the parable of the return of the demons shows the true nature of "this evil generation" as under the control of Satan (a reversal of their charge in 12:24).

Translation

Matthew 12:38-45

38a	Setting	**Then some of the teachers of law and Pharisees answered him, saying,**
b	Request	*"Teacher, we want to see a sign from you."*
39a	Response	But **Jesus responded,**
b	Assertion	*"An evil and adulterous generation seeks a sign,*
c	Pronouncement	and *no sign will be given them*
d		*except the sign of Jonah the prophet.*
40a	Illustration/ Comparison	For *just as Jonah was in the belly of the great fish for three days and three nights,*
b	Prophecy	so *also will the Son of Man be in the heart of the earth for three days and three nights.*
41a	Warning #1 (A)	*[1] The people of Nineveh will rise up at the judgment against this generation and condemn it,*
b	Basis for 41a (B)	*because they repented at the preaching of Jonah;*
c	Comparison (C)	and *look, one greater than Jonah is here.*
42a	Warning #2 (A)	*[2] The Queen of the South will rise up at the judgment against this generation and condemn it,*
b	Basis for 42a (B)	*because she came from the ends of the earth to hear the wisdom of Solomon;*
c	Comparison (C)	and *look, one greater than Solomon is here.*
43a	Illustration	*When an unclean spirit comes out of a person,*
b		*it goes through waterless places seeking rest and does not find it.*
44a		*Then he says,*
b		*'I will return to my house that I left.'*
c		*When it arrives, it finds the house unoccupied, swept clean, and put in order.*
45a		*Then it goes and brings with it seven other spirits more wicked than itself.*
b		And *they enter and make their home there.*
c	Result of 45b	And *the final condition of that person is worse than the first.*
d	Conclusion/Warning	*This is how it will also be for this evil generation."*

Structure and Literary Form

This is another triple tradition passage, with Matthew drawing on both Mark 8:11 – 12 and Luke 11:16, 29 – 32 in 12:38 – 42 and Q material for 12:43 – 45 (= Luke 11:24 – 26), with some M material (the "three days and three nights" of v. 40). This is also another doublet (with 16:1 – 4). Davies and Allison call this a testing story, Luz a riddle with explanation.[1] There are three parts: the sign of Jonah (vv. 38 – 40), the examples of Nineveh and the Queen of the South (vv. 41 – 42), and the parable of the return of the demons (vv. 43 – 45).

Exegetical Outline

➡ **I. The Sign of Jonah (12:38 – 40)**
- A. The demand for a sign (v. 38)
- B. Jesus' response (vv. 39 – 40)
  1. His charge against them (v. 39a)
  2. His refusal to give a sign (v. 39b)
  3. The example: Jonah and the three days (v. 40)

II. The Examples of Judgment (12:41 – 42)
- A. The people of Nineveh (v. 41)
  1. Their repentance
  2. The one greater than Jonah
- B. The Queen of the South (v. 42)
  1. She listened to Solomon
  2. The one greater than Solomon

III. The Parable of the Return of the Demons (12:43 – 45)
- A. Departing the person and wandering (v. 43)
- B. Returns to an empty house (v. 44)
- C. Returns with seven more spirits (v. 45a)
  1. Possess the person
  2. Result — worse than before
- D. Application to "this evil generation" (v. 45b)

Explanation of the Text

12:38 Then some of the teachers of law and Pharisees answered him, saying (Τότε ἀπεκρίθησαν αὐτῷ τινες τῶν γραμματέων καὶ Φαρισαίων λέγοντες). The use of "answered" (ἀπεκρίθησαν) links this closely with the Beelzebul interaction of vv. 22 – 37 and has the leaders responding to

1. Davies and Allison, *Matthew*, 2:351; Luz, *Matthew 8 – 20*, 213.

Jesus' claims there (not to his charges). The scribes ("teachers of the law") have not been seen since 9:3 and are here probably to add to the legal charges implicit in the scene; the single article linking the scribes and Pharisees shows they are working together.

12:38 "Teacher, we want to see a sign from you" (Διδάσκαλε, θέλομεν ἀπὸ σοῦ σημεῖον ἰδεῖν). In Matthew "teacher" (διδάσκαλε) is usually used by Jesus' opponents (8:19; 9:11; 17:24; 22:16, 24, 36; though cf.26:18), and while respectful (= "rabbi"), it shows they refuse to accept his claim to be Messiah.[2] They have rejected the validity of Jesus' miracles and so demand (the significance of "we want" [θέλομεν], with the present tense putting this in the foreground and stressing their ongoing demands) a "sign" (σημεῖον), a special divine proof (as in John, the term refers to a symbolic wonder that points to the reality of the person performing it).[3] They seek a heaven-sent spectacle (cf. 16:1, "sign from heaven"), like the exodus "signs" that forced the Hebrews to believe (Exod 4:8, 30 – 31; cf. Judg 6:17; 1 Kgs 13:3; Isa 7:14; Jer 44:29). Jesus, of course, will never produce a wondrous event just to draw attention to himself (see the temptation narrative of 4:1 – 11), especially when the demand comes from a position of rejection. Their insolence is obvious.

12:39 But Jesus responded, "An evil and adulterous generation seeks a sign" (ὁ δὲ ἀποκριθεὶς εἶπεν αὐτοῖς, Γενεὰ πονηρὰ καὶ μοιχαλὶς σημεῖον ἐπιζητεῖ). The "evil and adulterous generation" alludes to the wilderness generation of Deut 1:35; 32:5, 20,[4] with the image of adultery having its frequent OT connotation of spiritual unfaithfulness to God (Isa 1:21; 57:3 – 9; Jer 3:10; Ezek 23:1 – 49; Hos 1:2; 2:2, 5; 3:1). Here Jesus generalizes the leaders as representing the whole "generation" of the Jewish people in rejecting him. The intensified "seeks" (ἐπιζητεῖ) means they "continually strive for, demand" the sign from God, part of their insolent hostility.

12:39 "... and no sign will be given them except the sign of Jonah the prophet" (καὶ σημεῖον οὐ δοθήσεται αὐτῇ εἰ μὴ τὸ σημεῖον Ἰωνᾶ τοῦ προφήτου). The divine passive "will be given" (δοθήσεται) shows that Jesus is speaking for God, who refuses to answer their demand. Yet it is a relative refusal, for God does provide a sign, though it is rooted in the past rather than the present. The use of Jonah[5] controls the following in terms of both the resurrection typology of v. 40 and the example of Nineveh's repentance in v. 41.

12:40 For just as Jonah was in the belly of the great fish for three days and three nights (ὥσπερ γὰρ ἦν Ἰωνᾶς ἐν τῇ κοιλίᾳ τοῦ κήτους τρεῖς ἡμέρας καὶ τρεῖς νύκτας). The correlative conjunctions "just as ... so also" (ὥσπερ ... οὕτως) lead into a typological correspondence, with Jonah in the fish a type of Christ's burial and resurrection. The Jonah material is taken verbatim from Jonah 2:1 LXX (= 1:17). It is common to state that the original logion had Jesus' preaching as the sign of Jonah (as in Luke 11:30), and that the later church added this verse to apply it

2. Hagner, *Matthew 1 – 13*, 353.

3. Olof Linton, "The Demand for a Sign from Heaven (Mark 8, 11 – 12 and Parallels)," *ST* 19 (1965): 112 – 29, shows that signs did not have to be miracles, though they often were.

4. Verseput, *Humble Messianic King*, 259.

5. "Of Jonah the prophet" Ἰωνᾶ τοῦ προφήτου) is an epexegetical genitive, "the sign that is Jonah the prophet." In defense of the authenticity of the Jonah reference in vv. 39b – 40 against those who think this is added by the later church, see Carson, "Matthew," 295, who holds that Luke "veils the specificity of an original Matthew 12:40" rather than Matthew expanding an original Luke 11:30.

to the resurrection.[6] However, Jewish interest in the Jonah story centered on his deliverance from the belly of the fish (chs. 1 – 2) more than on his preaching to Nineveh (chs. 3 – 4), and so the sign here makes perfect sense.[7]

12:40 ... so also will the Son of Man be in the heart of the earth for three days and three nights (οὕτως ἔσται ὁ υἱὸς τοῦ ἀνθρώπου ἐν τῇ καρδίᾳ τῆς γῆς τρεῖς ἡμέρας καὶ τρεῖς νύκτας). Many have trouble with "so also" (οὕτως) because it means Jesus had supernatural awareness of his coming death and resurrection, yet that is seen also in his passion predictions (as well as the "lifted up" sayings in John 3:14; 8:28; 12:32). The resurrection is God's great sign to Israel, as also seen in the speeches of Acts (2:24, 32, 36; 3:15; 13:30, 33, 34, 37; 17:31).[8]

The "three days and three nights" Jesus was "in the heart of the earth" is a reference to his burial rather than to his descent into Hades, which many have seen in 1 Pet 3:19 – 20. The "heart of the earth" is Sheol, but that is the grave, the place of the dead, rather than a compartmentalized Hades as in the parable of Luke 16:19 – 31.[9]

Finally, there is a discrepancy in the fact that Jesus was in the grave only thirty-six hours, from dusk on Friday until dawn on Sunday. However, Jewish reckoning considered a partial day to be a full day (cf. Gen 42:17 – 18; 1 Sam 30:12 – 13; Esth 4:16; 5:1), so Jesus was in the grave Friday, Saturday, and Sunday; and the terminology fits.

12:41 The people[10] of Nineveh will rise up at the judgment against this generation and condemn it, because they repented at the preaching of Jonah (ἄνδρες Νινευῖται ἀναστήσονται ἐν τῇ κρίσει μετὰ τῆς γενεᾶς ταύτης καὶ κατακρινοῦσιν αὐτήν, ὅτι μετενόησαν εἰς τὸ κήρυγμα Ἰωνᾶ). This is similar to the argument of 11:20 – 24, where Jesus said God would be "more tolerant" to Tyre and Sidon and to Sodom and Gomorrah at the last judgment than to the crowd he is addressing.

The imagery of "rise up" and "judgment" builds on the resurrection of Jesus in v. 40 to depict the final resurrection at the last judgment. The future "will rise up" (ἀναστήσονται) depicts a new type of resurrection, with the Ninevites raised to stand as hostile witnesses at God's *bēma*, or judgment seat, against the unbelief of the Jews. The people of Nineveh repented after Jonah preached judgment to them (Jonah 3:5). They will condemn (i.e., be a legal witness against) the Jewish generation of Jesus' day, which has refused to repent after Jesus has proclaimed both salvation and judgment to them.

12:41 ... and look, one greater than Jonah is here (καὶ ἰδοὺ πλεῖον Ἰωνᾶ ὧδε). Matthew's characteristic "look" (ἰδού) makes the scene more dramatic here and in v. 42 (see on 1:20). Moreover, Jesus[11] is as "greater than Jonah" as the Messiah is greater than a prophet and as the Son of God is greater than one of God's children. Let us also note a theme similar in 8:5 – 13, for both the Ninevites

6. See R. A. Edwards, *The Sign of Jonah in the Theology of the Evangelists and Q* (London: SCM, 1971), 25 – 26; Luz, *Matthew 8 – 20*, 218 – 19; Hagner, *Matthew 1 – 13*, 354.

7. See France, *Matthew*, 213, as well as his *Jesus and the Old Testament* (Grand Rapids: Baker, 1982), 80 – 82.

8. See Davies and Allison, *Matthew*, 2:355.

9. The best article on 1 Pet 3:19 – 20 is still France, "Exegesis," 252 – 81.

10. ἄνδρες, like ἄνθρωπος (v. 11), can also be generic for "person, someone" see BAGD, 67 (6).

11. The neuter πλεῖον, as in v. 6, can be translated "something greater" and refer to Jesus' kingdom preaching or something similar. But as Davies and Allison say (*Matthew*, 2:358), neither kingdom nor preaching can be distinguished from Jesus and the neuter likely points to the "Christ-event" and thus to Jesus himself. In 12:6 we translate "something greater" because the contrast is with the temple, while here we translate "one greater" because Jesus is contrasted with people.

and the Queen of the South are Gentiles who responded to God's messenger, while the Jews have rejected God's Son. Thus the path is further prepared for 28:19 and the mission to the "nations."

12:42 The Queen of the South will rise up at the judgment against this generation and condemn it, because she came from the ends of the earth to hear the wisdom of Solomon (βασίλισσα νότου ἐγερθήσεται ἐν τῇ κρίσει μετὰ τῆς γενεᾶς ταύτης καὶ κατακρινεῖ αὐτήν, ὅτι ἦλθεν ἐκ τῶν περάτων τῆς γῆς ἀκοῦσαι τὴν σοφίαν Σολομῶνος). This is "the queen of Sheba," who in 1 Kgs 10:1 – 13 (= 2 Chr 9:1 – 12) came "to test Solomon with hard questions" (1 Kgs 10:1), much like the Jewish leaders have been doing. The difference is that she sought truth and was willing to accept Solomon's "wisdom." So at the final judgment she too will "rise up" (a different future verb, ἐγερθήσεται, with the same function as the one in v. 42 for emphasis) to bear witness against the generation of Jesus' day, which was not open to Jesus' greater wisdom.

12:42 And look, one greater than Solomon is here (καὶ ἰδοὺ πλεῖον Σολομῶνος ὧδε). France points to 12:6, where Jesus is "greater than the temple" (and its priesthood); he then observes, "taking the three verses together (12:6, 41, 42) we see Jesus as greater than temple (priesthood), prophet and king (wise man), a comprehensive list of those through whom God's message came in the Old Testament."[12]

12:43 When an unclean spirit comes out of a person, it goes through waterless places seeking rest and does not find it (Ὅταν δὲ τὸ ἀκάθαρτον πνεῦμα ἐξέλθῃ ἀπὸ τοῦ ἀνθρώπου, διέρχεται δι' ἀνύδρων τόπων ζητοῦν ἀνάπαυσιν, καὶ οὐχ εὑρίσκει). This is a mini-travel narrative dominated by two "go" (ἔρχομαι) verbs that picture the movement of the demon as it "goes out" (ἐξ-) and then "passes through" (δι'-) on its way "seeking but not finding" a place to rest. The unrest and frustration is obvious.

The previous section (vv. 22 – 37) centered on Jesus' exorcisms, so he turns to a parable on exorcism to sum up his argument. This parable tells the results of the Jewish rejection of their Messiah. The person freed of the demon represents the Jewish people (once again especially the leaders but including all of "this generation") on behalf of whom their Messiah has bound Satan (12:29).[13] The conjunction δέ contrasts the present generation with the Ninevites and the Queen of the South. Wherever Jesus went, through all the towns of Galilee and surrounding areas (cf. 4:23; 9:35), demons "went out" (with ἐξέλθῃ ἀπό stressing both "going out" and "away from") and evil was defeated. God's salvation was present. In the story itself the demon (on "unclean spirit," see 10:1), once cast out, wanders aimlessly through wilderness areas devoid of water, the common habitation of demons (Deut. 32:10 – 18; Isa 13:21; 34:14 ["wild goats or satyrs"]; Tob 8:3). The demon seeks respite from the arid lands but cannot find it.

12:44 Then he says, "I will return to my house that I left" (τότε λέγει, Εἰς τὸν οἶκόν μου ἐπιστρέψω ὅθεν ἐξῆλθον). Jesus has virtually turned the demon into a homeless traveler. The action stops with his frustrated exclamation.

12. France, *Matthew* (TNTC), 214; cf. also Wilkins, *Matthew*, 452.

13. This makes more sense than interpreting it of other exorcists whose power is inferior to that of Jesus. That would involve going back to 12:27 and overemphasizing the place of Jewish exorcists there. The immediate context does not allow this. Darrell Bock, *Luke 9:51 – 24:53* (BECNT; Grand Rapids: Baker, 1996), 1091 – 92, notes two other possibilities: it is a figurative reference to those who do not respond to Jesus, or Jesus is picturing the danger of those who experience exorcism but do not follow up with faith. The latter is a possible secondary interpretation.

Finding no rest in the desert places, the demon makes a decision to go back (ὅθεν, "from which") to his old "home," namely, the person from whom he had been cast out. Apparently the person has no power to stop the demon from returning.

12:44 When it arrives,[14] **it finds the house unoccupied, swept clean, and put in order** (καὶ ἐλθὸν εὑρίσκει σχολάζοντα σεσαρωμένον καὶ κεκοσμημένον). The present tenses continue. This is a story with uninterrupted action. The demon finds two things upon "arrival." (1) The house/person is even better than before — clean, orderly, and ready for occupancy; the exorcism has "cleaned house." (2) It is empty and ready for the taking. In other words, the person has been freed but left spiritually empty. The attractive new dwelling cries out for an inhabitant, and the implied situation is "First come, first served."

Jesus could be addressing especially the crowds here, who have taken a strict neutrality toward him, excited at his obvious authority but not willing to commit (see 12:30, "the one not with me is against me"). Yet Israel as a whole is certainly intended because of "this generation" in 12:45d,[15] and the point is that in rejecting their Messiah, they are left empty and unprotected (primary thrust, with the crowds a secondary emphasis). Jesus' ministry had cast out the uncleaness and readied "this generation" for a new, unprecedented time of plenty, but the people have rejected him and so are left devoid of content.

12:45 Then it goes and brings with it seven other spirits more wicked than itself (τότε πορεύεται καὶ παραλαμβάνει μεθ' ἑαυτοῦ ἑπτὰ ἕτερα πνεύματα πονηρότερα ἑαυτοῦ). The house/person has more room because it has been empty so long, so the demon goes back to invite his friends, even more unsavory than he is. It's like a biker gang returning to the scene of the crime because it feels safe to continue its crime spree.

We shouldn't read too much demonology into this scene. It is a story, and many of the details, like degrees of evil in the demonic realm, are probably local color rather than theology. The number seven stresses completeness. This is a full contingent of demons.

12:45 And they enter and make their home there. And the final condition of that person is worse than the first (καὶ εἰσελθόντα κατοικεῖ ἐκεῖ· καὶ γίνεται τὰ ἔσχατα τοῦ ἀνθρώπου ἐκείνου χείρονα τῶν πρώτων). Since the house is empty and helpless, the eight demons easily take over and have the house to themselves. Moreover, the use of present tense κατοικεῖ suggests a permanent occupation. The demons are there to stay. Before the exorcism the person had been possessed by one demon; now there are eight even more evil spirits! No wonder "the final condition" is "worse," a perfect picture of Israel after rejecting their Messiah and allowing Satan to have full sway!

12:45 This is how it will also be for this evil generation (οὕτως ἔσται καὶ τῇ γενεᾷ ταύτῃ τῇ πονηρᾷ). The point is that Israel had experienced a great cleansing when God sent his Son and Messiah to them. But they had refused to repent and had rejected Jesus. So "this generation" is filled with "evil" and is an empty house, with even greater evil to come. In the future tense "it will be" (ἔσται), some see the destruction of

14. Many have seen "arrives" (ἐλθόν) as conditional, "if it comes and finds" (e.g., France, *Matthew* [TNTC], 214; Morris, *Matthew*, 329), but in the developing story a temporal is better, for the demon has already determined to return. There is no need to read this as if Jesus' own exorcisms are now open to such disasters. This is a parabolic story about Israel and not a theological statement about the exorcisms of Jesus and the church.

15. So Nolland, *Matthew*, 515. Turner, "Matthew," 177, sees it as Israel as a whole but the Pharisees in particular.

Jerusalem or the final judgment.[16] That would be possible in light of "the final condition … is worse than the first," but it is too allegorical, [17] for it seems clear that "the final condition" here relates to "evil" rather than future judgment (cf. 23:38, "your house is left to you desolate"). "They had been confronted with divine power, and if they tried to live empty lives, lives that did not replace evil by the presence of the Holy Spirit, there was nothing before them but the grimmest of prospects."[18] It is possible that the "worse" condition was committing the unforgivable sin (12:31 – 32), but more likely it is that evil will control "this generation."

Theology in Application

Chapters 11 – 12 have been developing the sad story of the Jewish rejection of their Messiah, and it has reached a crescendo in the two pericopae of the Beelzebul incident (12:22 – 37) and the sign of Jonah (12:38 – 42), concluding with Jesus' parable on the sorry condition of "this evil generation" (12:43 – 45).

1. Never Close Your Mind to Clear Evidence

The Pharisees had seen the miracles Jesus had performed and the truths Jesus taught. Yet they refused all that evidence and demanded a heavenly sign from Jesus. No wonder all they received was a future sign plus the promise of judgment from Jesus. Even the Gentile Ninevites and the Queen of the South were open to truthful proclamations. A closed mind always leads one to false conclusions. This functions at the theological level as well as at the ministry level — the old "my mind is made up, don't confuse me with facts" syndrome.

2. The Centrality of Jesus' Resurrection

Not only Jesus but all those who preached in Acts (Acts 2:24, 32, 36; 3:15; 13:30, 33, 34, 37), including Paul (Acts 17:31; 1 Cor 15:3 – 8), centered on the resurrection in their preaching. Whenever I have doubts (as do we all), I always ask, What is the likelihood that the resurrection happened as an historical event?[19] The arguments are convincing and bolster our faith.

16. So Cope, *Matthew*, 44; Hagner, *Matthew 1 – 13*, 357; Luz, *Matthew 8 – 20*, 221.

17. See Verseput, *Humble Messianic King*, 275, "By all appearances, then, we are confronted with a story whose point — for Matthew, at least — lies in the exchange of one demon for eight, a new tyrannization by spirits yet more evil, so that the final state becomes worse than the first. All else besides the threat of this consignment to a greater evil is limited in significance to the picture-half of the parable."

18. Morris, *Matthew*, 330.

19. See my *Three Crucial Questions about the Bible* (Grand Rapids: Baker, 1995), 32 – 43.

3. Evangelism and Discipleship

As stated above, there are two aspects to the meaning of the parable in vv. 43 – 45: the primary meaning, the greater evil awaiting Israel for rejecting her Messiah; and the secondary thrust, the danger to the crowds of remaining neutral (and thus empty) to the kingdom proclamation. Here we might add those who seemingly come to Jesus but without commitment. Many mission groups and even whole denominations are guilty of fostering what we might call "quasi-Christians" by centering only on evangelism and ignoring discipleship. I know of one large denomination whose mission board has pulled people away from teaching to center on evangelism. Mission boards have often been guilty of a lack of vision for training leaders and publishing good material. This has fostered syncretism and cults worldwide.

Yet this is a fundamental misinterpretation of the Great Commission (28:19), which commands us to "make disciple from all nations," not just "evangelize" them. In other words, evangelism without discipleship is unbiblical! We initially cast out the demons but fail to fill the house with the Spirit of God. I am convinced that failure to challenge the quasi-Christians is one of the great sins of the modern church. Our market-driven, seeker-friendly approaches allow shallow half-believers to remain comfortable in the hope that they will at least reach heaven while they grow farther and farther away from the Lord. As Bruner says, "Merely influenced by Jesus but, with rare exceptions, not really gathered by him or gathering for him; tidied up but not taken in by him, this Christian world will be virgin territory for an invasion of spirits." The only answer is to "be [constantly] filled with the Spirit" (Eph 5:18), "perhaps the best one-verse commentary on the meaning of the Gospel story of the return of the unclean spirit."[20]

20. Bruner, *Christbook*, 470.

CHAPTER 55

Matthew 12:46 – 50

Literary Context

In the introduction to 11:1 – 12:50 we noted that there were three triads (11:1 – 30; 12:1 – 21, 22 – 50), with the first two of each centering on opposition and the third consisting of a christological saying or story in which Jesus brings salvation and hope to his followers (11:25 – 30; 12:15 – 21, 46 – 50). In this final section of chs. 11 – 12, Matthew turns from Jesus' implacable foes to his true family of followers. The theme returns to Jesus' offer of rest to the "weary and burdened" in 11:28 – 30, if they will come to him and do "the will of my Father" (12:50).

- **IV. Preaching and Teaching in the Midst of Opposition (11:2 – 13:53)**
  - **A. Jesus' Deeds: Revelation and Rejection (11:2 – 12:50)**
    - **3. Controversy and Community (12:22 – 50)**
      - a. Confrontation over Beelzebul (12:22 – 37)
      - b. Controversy over the Sign of Jonah (12:38 – 45)
      - ➡ **c. Family and Community (12:46 – 50)**

Main Idea

This is not a confrontation story between Jesus and his family (as it is in Mark 3:31 – 35) but a discipleship story, in which Jesus says his true family is the circle of devoted followers who sincerely seek to do "the will of my Father." In other words, spiritual roots are even deeper than genealogical roots, an incredible point in the society of that day that treasured genealogical lines. The primary thrust is v. 50, summarizing Jesus' ethical teaching in the Sermon on the Mount and its centrality of "righteousness" (5:6, 10, 20; 6:1, 33) to define discipleship as doing God's will.

Translation

Matthew 12:46-50

46a	Setting	While he was still speaking to the crowds,
b	Action	**look, his mother and brothers stood outside, wanting to talk to him.**
47a	Request	**So someone said to him,**
b		*"Look, your mother and brothers are standing outside, wanting to speak to you."*
48a	Response/Question	But **Jesus replied to him,**
b		*"Who is my mother,*
c		and *who are my brothers?"*
49a	Answer to 48b-c	And **he stretched his hand over his disciples and said,**
b		*"Behold my mother and my brothers.*
50a	Basis of 49b and Conclusion	For *whoever does the will of my Father in heaven is my brother and sister and mother."*

Structure and Literary Form

This is a triple tradition story (Mark 3:31 – 35 = Luke 8:19 – 21), with Matthew omitting the conflict part of Mark's story in order to turn this into a pronouncement story, in which Jesus uses his family as an opportunity to speak of his new family. There are two parts to the structure: Jesus' mother and brothers want to talk to him (vv. 46 – 47), and Jesus uses the occasion to say his followers are also his family (he never rejects his actual family, vv. 48 – 49), concluding with a statement on doing God's will as the defining mark of his new family (v. 50).

Exegetical Outline

➡ **I. The Arrival of Jesus' Family (12:46 – 47)**
- A. The arrival of his family (v. 46)
- B. The report of their arrival (v. 47)

II. Jesus' Response (12:48 – 50)
- A. His question (v. 48)
- B. His gesture to his new family (v. 49)
- C. The requirement for his new family (v. 50)

Explanation of the Text

12:46 While he was still speaking to the crowds, look, his mother and brothers stood outside, wanting to talk to him (Ἔτι αὐτοῦ λαλοῦντος τοῖς ὄχλοις ἰδοὺ ἡ μήτηρ καὶ οἱ ἀδελφοὶ αὐτοῦ εἱστήκεισαν ἔξω ζητοῦντες αὐτῷ λαλῆσαι). Matthew links this closely to the preceding controversy by saying Jesus was "still (ἔτι) talking to the crowds" (another temporal genitive absolute, see 1:18, 20; 2:1) when his mother and brothers arrived. Out of the wreckage of the nation's rejection of him, Jesus has forged a new kingdom community. The use of "look" (ἰδού) three times in this pericope stresses the dynamic nature of the story.

Mark 3:20 – 21 tells us that his family thought he had lost his mind and came to take him home, but Matthew omits that. He does not want to link Jesus' family with his opponents but with his true followers. The fact that the text here says Jesus has "brothers" (see the list of names in 13:55) causes conflict with Roman Catholic dogma concerning Mary's perpetual virginity, so Catholic scholars have often suggested that they were either Jesus' cousins (Jerome, Augustine) or children of Joseph by a previous marriage (Clement of Alexandria, Origen, Eusebius). Yet while ἀδελφοί can refer to relatives, its more natural sense in a context like this is blood brothers.[1] Since Joseph is not mentioned here or anywhere else as present during Jesus' miracles, the most natural conclusion is that he had died some time earlier.

12:47 So someone said to him, "Look, your mother and brothers are standing outside, wanting[2] to speak to you" (εἶπεν δέ τις αὐτῷ, Ἰδοὺ ἡ μήτηρ σου καὶ οἱ ἀδελφοί σου ἔξω ἑστήκασιν ζητοῦντές σοι λαλῆσαι).[3] The imagery of Jesus' family outside and someone else bringing the news to him shows Jesus was inside a house addressing a group composed of his disciples and some from the crowd. The wording of the message is virtually identical to v. 46 and is used to emphasize the scene. The family is outside, Jesus inside with his new family.

There is no mention here of the fact that Jesus' brothers were unbelievers at this stage (see John 7:5 for this), but the implicit outside/inside (with emphasis in vv. 46 – 47 on their situation "outside" [ἔξω] Jesus' orbit and ministry) setting would fit this. As Bruner says, "The word 'outside' says that Jesus' family was deliberately outside the orbit of Jesus' actual, 'churchly,' intimate teaching ministry. They are outsiders, near to, but not insiders (within). (This position is exactly the dangerous situation of emptiness warned of in the preceding story)."[4]

12:48 But Jesus replied to him, "Who is my mother, and who are my brothers?" (ὁ δὲ ἀποκριθεὶς εἶπεν τῷ λέγοντι αὐτῷ, Τίς ἐστιν ἡ μήτηρ μου καὶ τίνες εἰσὶν οἱ ἀδελφοί μου;). The rhetorical double question powerfully sets the scene for the proclamation of v. 50. Jesus gives his mother and his brothers separate emphasis to drive the point home more powerfully. This is made all the more poignant in the fact that they are standing right outside the house. Riddles were

1. For the Roman Catholic view, see John McHugh, *The Mother of Jesus in the New Testament* (Garden City, NY: Doubleday, 1975), 200 – 254. For a response, see Carson, "Matthew," 299.

2. "Wanting" (ζητοῦντες) is a present circumstantial participle defining further why they are standing outside.

3. This verse seems redundant and is missing from some key manuscripts (א * B L Γ ff[1] k et al.); it is included by several (א [(1),2] C [D] W Z TR lat et al.) and could well have been omitted due to homoioteleuton ("to speak" [λαλῆσαι] closes vv. 46, 47). So most cautiously accept the verse as authentic.

4. Bruner, *Christbook*, 472.

an important teaching tool in the ancient world, and Jesus gives this a riddle-like air.[5]

12:49 And he stretched his hand over his disciples and said, "Behold my mother and my brothers" (καὶ ἐκτείνας τὴν χεῖρα αὐτοῦ ἐπὶ τοὺς μαθητὰς αὐτοῦ εἶπεν, Ἰδοὺ ἡ μήτηρ μου καὶ οἱ ἀδελφοί μου). The idea of "stretching out his hand" (a circumstantial participle describing antecedent action) is a strong gesture and should not be minimized as just "pointing to his disciples." While sometimes used as a gesture (Acts 26:1), with "over" (ἐπί) it connotes protection by a higher power and here may indicate they stand under the care of the one who will be with them until the end of the age (Matt 28:20).[6] They are his new family, the messianic community.

In Matthew "brothers" (ἀδελφοί, five times in this pericope) is often used in an ecclesiastical sense as a metaphor for discipleship (18:15, 21, 35; 19:29; 23:8; 25:40; 28:10),[7] and this passage introduces that critical motif. The family metaphor for the new messianic community is an important motif and hints at a level of caring and sharing often missing in the "busy-with-too-many-things" lifestyle of our times.

12:50 "For whoever does the will of my Father in heaven is my brother and sister and mother" (ὅστις γὰρ ἂν ποιήσῃ τὸ θέλημα τοῦ πατρός μου τοῦ ἐν οὐρανοῖς αὐτός μου ἀδελφὸς καὶ ἀδελφὴ καὶ μήτηρ ἐστίν). ὅστις ἄν stresses the universal thrust of this — "anyone whoever." The new kingdom community established by Jesus is now given a new relationship with him: they are also his family. It is significant that Jesus includes "sister" (ἀδελφή) with the "mother and brothers" of vv. 46 – 49. He wants to be all-inclusive of the relationships in the new family of God established by him. Hagner brings out how this "stands in considerable tension with the contemporary Jewish perspective," where women had few equal rights but "is consonant with the progressiveness of Jesus on the issue of women seen elsewhere in the Gospels."[8] It also shows that Jesus has in mind more than just the Twelve but all who follow him.

The major emphasis is on the criterion for discipleship, "whoever does the will." Jesus already stressed in 7:21 that the only ones who will enter the kingdom are "those who do the will of my Father in heaven": (1) God is "my Father in heaven," which stresses the unique intimacy between Jesus and the Father. (2) God is the "heavenly Father," a frequent Matthean theme (5:16, 45, 48; 6:1, 9, 14, 26, 32; 7:11, 21; 10:32, 33; 15:13; 16:17; 18:14, 19, 35) highlighting the transcendence of God and his sovereign power exercised for his people, thus especially renewing the Lord's Prayer of 6:9, "Our Father who is in heaven."[9]

The ethical mandate is to "do the will of the Father," i.e., to obey his commands and live according to his precepts, which renews another element of the Lord's Prayer, "may your will be done on earth as it is in heaven" (6:10). This, in fact, is the definition of the key theme of "righteousness" in Matthew (see "Main Idea" above), and God's will is stressed also in 6:10; 7:21; 21:31; 26:42. The only way to be a true disciple is to live "rightly" before God, to follow his mandates.

Jesus alone knows the mind of the Father (11:27), so those rules for conduct are found in Jesus' teaching. We are at the heart of Matthew's gospel, where a life of faithfulness to God's will is the core

5. Verseput, *Humble Messianic King*, 285.

6. Luz, *Matthew 8 – 20*, 225.

7. Verseput, *Humble Messianic King*, 285 – 86.

8. Hagner, *Matthew 1 – 13*, 360; see also Grant R. Osborne, "Women in Jesus' Ministry," *WTJ* 51 (1989): 159 – 91.

9. See the excellent study in Verseput, *Humble Messianic King*, 288 – 93, where he notes a strong covenantal aspect of obedience resulting in God's favor in Jewish writings, while in Jesus' teaching a new aspect is found, namely, that in Jesus a new allegiance is mandated.

responsibility of the kingdom people. The idea of God's guiding will is dynamic and especially related to Jesus' kingdom teaching in Matthew's gospel. Those who follow and keep these precepts are the family of God, Jesus' "brother and sister and mother."

Theology in Application

This is a rich passage like the other two in this section (11:25 – 30; 12:15 – 21), and it typifies the offer of salvation made available to the nation by Jesus. It is set in absolute contrast to the rigorous demands of the Pharisees, and here Jesus offers a new relationship to the promise of rest in 11:28 – 30 and of hope in 12:21, namely, becoming part of the family of God's Messiah and Son.

1. A New Family

For those who lose their earthly family in following Jesus, God will give a new family in his messianic community. There is a great deal in Matthew's gospel on losing family — some metaphorical, as when James and John leave their father after being called to fish for people (4:21 – 22), and when Jesus tells a would-be follower to "let the dead bury their own dead" after he asked permission to first bury his father (8:22). Other times it is prophetic, as when Jesus tells of the extent of opposition in mission by forecasting betrayal by one's own family members (10:21 – 22, 35 – 36) and warns his followers against loving father or mother more than Jesus (10:37), or when he tells Peter that everyone who loses their family for his sake will have a hundred times as many (= the church as a family) in the present (19:29 – 30). The present passage is the theological kingpin of this theme. Leaving his family outside the house as a metaphor, Jesus says his deeper family is his band of disciples.[10]

2. The Church as Family

There is a succession of metaphors in ecclesiology, each more intense than the other. We are first an assembly (ἐκκλησία), then a community, and finally a family. Each level involves deeper intimacy, more sharing, and greater caring — indeed, more time spent together. This should be a major strategy of every local church or Christian group. See the metaphor of the church as the household of God (Eph 2:19; 1 Tim 3:15) and Paul's frequent use of "brothers and sisters" to refer to fellow believers (e.g., Rom 1:13; 7:1; 1 Cor 1:10, 2:1). In 1 Tim 5:1 – 2 and 1 John 2:12 – 14 family imagery is used to challenge the various groups in the church.

10. Hauerwas, *Matthew*, 125, says, "To be a disciple of Jesus is to be made part of a new community in which the family is reconstituted.... (Jesus') singleness ... is a sign that God's kingdom will not grow by biological ascription ... but by witness and conversion. Through such growth Christians will discover brothers and sisters we did not know we had. Such is the wonder and the threat of the kingdom brought in Christ."

3. Discipleship and a Lifestyle of Obedience

As stated above, this is at the heart of Jesus' teaching in Matthew, beginning with the Sermon on the Mount. The deepening of Torah in the antitheses of 5:21 – 48 centers on thinking and doing, and it is clear that a disciple is identified as one who lives out what Jesus teaches. The disciples inside the home are sitting at Jesus' feet, both learning and submitting to his will (cf. Mary in Luke 10:38 – 42). So discipleship is learning the precepts of Jesus and then obediently practicing them in daily life. The shallow quasi-Christian who attends but never obeys is not a disciple and must realize he or she is in danger of Matt 7:23, "I never knew you. Depart from me, workers of evil."

CHAPTER 56

Matthew 13:1 – 23

Introduction to Jesus' Kingdom Parable Discourse (13:1 – 53)

Jesus now interprets the significance of 11:2 – 12:50 in a series of seven parables, with three of them explained by Jesus; the material is drawn from Mark, Q, and M sources. These are parables centering on "the kingdom of heaven" (in virtually every parable), and they develop the implications of its arrival — about kingdom conflict, judgment, and decision, reflecting the implications of the preceding material, especially the controversy over Jesus.[1] The format of the Parable Discourse differs widely from the other discourses, with regular lead-ins to the various parables and sections: vv. 10 – 11, 18, 31, 33, 34 – 35, 36 – 37, 51.

The structure of the passage is debated. Most see the key at 13:36, when Jesus leaves the crowd to teach only his disciples and so see two parts in the chapter (vv. 1 – 35, 36 – 52).[2] However, other structural outlines have been suggested. Gerhardsson has an interesting thesis, that the whole section flows out of the parable of the sower, with the parable of the wheat and tares explicating the meaning of the seed by the wayside, the parables of the mustard seed and leaven developing the seed on rocky ground, the parables of the hidden treasure and pearl explaining the seed on thorny ground, and the parable of the net developing the seed on fruitful soil.[3] As intriguing as this is, it does not fit the details of the text. Wenham provides the standard chiastic approach by turning the scribe trained for the kingdom into a parable and seeing it in inclusion with the parable of the sower,[4] but that stretches the connections, since the explanations of the three parables do not coincide well with this outline.[5]

1. France, *Matthew* (TNTC), 215, says, "Chapters 11 – 12 have illustrated the growing divisions among men in their attitude to Jesus, culminating in the sharp contrast between true disciples and all others in 12:46 – 50. Division, and the problem of how some could reject Jesus' message while others responded, are the underlying themes of this chapter too; the parables thus provide some explanation of the attitudes revealed in the preceding narrative."

2. So Carson, Kingsbury, Gnilka, Luz, Hagner, Turner.

3. Birger Gerhardsson, "The Seven Parables in Matthew XIII," *NTS* 19 (1972 – 73): 16 – 37.

4. David Wenham, "The Structure of Matthew XIII," *NTS* 25 (1978 – 79): 516 – 22; also Rainer Riesner, "Der Afbau der Reden im Matthäus-Evangelium," *TBei* 9 (1978): 177 – 78; Blomberg, *Matthew*, 213.

5. See Ivor H. Jones, *The Matthean Parables: A Literary and Historical Commentary* (SNT 80; New York: Brill, 1995), 291 – 92, who points out that chiasmus is found more in Luke

Perhaps best is the triadic structure of Davies and Allison (vv. 1 – 23, 24 – 43, 44 – 52).[6] This fits the triadic construction of chs. 11 – 12 but more importantly has a symmetry of its own, with the first two sections ending in effect with Jesus' discussion of parables and interpretation of a parable (vv. 10 – 23, 34 – 43) and the third with Jesus' interpretation followed by a concluding discussion (vv. 49 – 52). The most important question is the significance of Jesus leaving the crowd in 13:36, which many take as demanding a two-part structure. Yet there is a real parallelism between vv. 10 and 36, in both of which the disciples come and ask about parables. So there are two insider (disciples) / outsider (crowds) sections (vv. 10 – 17, 36 – 43), not one, and this fits the triadic organization quite well.

Literary Context

The narrative of chs. 11 – 12 centered on the hostility and rejection of Jesus' opponents in contrast to Jesus' offering himself to the "weary and burdened" (11:28) as well as his identity as the Isaianic "chosen servant" who will bring "justice" (12:18). The parable of the soils brings together all three groups Jesus has impacted — the hardened leaders (the first soil), the excited yet uncommitted crowds (the second and third soils), and the disciples (the fourth soil).[7]

IV. Preaching and Teaching in the Midst of Opposition (11:2 – 13:53)
- A. Jesus' Deeds: Revelation and Rejection (11:2 – 12:50)
- **B. Third Discourse: Kingdom Parables (13:1 – 53)**
  - ➦ **1. Parable of the Soils (13:1 – 23)**
    - **a. The Parable Presented (13:1 – 9)**
    - **b. The Purpose of Parables (13:10 – 17)**
    - **c. Interpretation of the Soils (13:18 – 23)**

Main Idea

This story centers not on the sower or the seed but on the four kinds of soil. It is clear that everyone reacts to the kingdom teaching (the seed) presented by Jesus (the sower); the soils represent the receptivity of the differing groups to Jesus'

than in Mark or Matthew and that even 13:13 – 18, where chiasmus has often been found, lacks the pattern.

6. Davies and Allison, *Matthew*, 2:370 – 72, accepted by Nolland, *Matthew*, 522.

7. Witherington, *Matthew*, 258, calls this parable "a helpful commentary on the varied responses Jesus and his disciples were getting to the Dominion message."

proclamation. They do react in different ways, but there is no neutrality; no one can remain outside the convicting power of God's truth.

Translation

Matthew 13:1-23

1a	Setting (Temporal and Spatial)	**On that day Jesus went out of the house and sat by the lake.**
2a	Action	**Then such great crowds gathered around him**
b	Action	**that he got into a boat and sat there,**
c		and **the whole crowd stood on the shore.**
3a	Summary	**[A] He spoke many things to them in parables, saying:**
b	Action	*"Look, a sower went out to sow.*
4a		*As he sowed,*
b	Circumstance #1	*[1] some seeds fell on the path,*
c	Result of 4b	*and the birds came and ate them.*
5a	Circumstance #2	*[2] But other seed fell on rocky ground,*
b	Description	*where there was not much soil.*
c	Result of 5a	*It immediately sprang up*
d	Basis of 5c	*because the soil was shallow.*
6a	Basis of 6b and d	*But when the sun arose,*
b	Result of 6a and c	*the plants were scorched;*
c	Basis of 6b and d	*and because they had no roots,*
d	Result of 6a and c	*they withered.*
7a	Circumstance #3	*[3] But other seed fell among thorn bushes,*
b	Result of 7a	*and the bushes grew up and choked them.*
8a	Circumstance #4	*[4] Yet other seed fell on good soil and*
b	Result of 8a	*began to bear fruit,*
c		*some a hundredfold, some sixtyfold, and some thirtyfold.*
9a	Warning/Exhortation	*Whoever has ears, let them listen!"*
10a		**[B] Then his disciples came and asked him,**
b	Question	*"Why are you speaking to them in parables?"*
11a	Answer #1	**He replied to them,**
b	Assertion	*[1] "It is because knowledge . . . has been given to you of the mysteries of the kingdom of heaven,*

Continued on next page.

Continued from previous page.

c		*but it has not been given to them.*
12a	Assertion	*For whoever has, more will be given,*
b		*and there will be abundance,*
c		*but whoever does not have,*
		even what they have will be taken away.
13a	Answer #2/Assertion	*[2] For this reason I am speaking to them in parables,*
b	Basis for 13a	*(a) because seeing, they do not see,*
c	Basis for 13a	*(b) and hearing, they neither hear nor understand.*
14a	Purpose/Fulfillment	*The prophecy of Isaiah is fulfilled in them, saying,*
b	OT Quotation	*(b') 'With hearing you will hear and*
		never understand,
c		*(a') and seeing you will see and*
		never perceive.
15a		*For the heart of this people has become calloused,*
b		*they barely hear with their ears,*
c		*and they have closed their eyes,*
d		*lest they should see with their eyes and*
e		*hear with their ears and*
f		*understand with their heart,*
g		*and they repent*
h		*and I have to heal them.'* (Isa 6:9-10)
16a	Blessing	*But blessed are your eyes*
b	Basis for 16a	*because they see and*
c	Blessing	*your ears*
d	Basis for 16c	*because they hear.*
17a	Assertion	*For I tell you the truth,*
		many prophets and righteous people desired to see what you see
		but did not see it, and
b		*to hear what you hear*
		but did not hear it.
18a	Exhortation/Explanation	*[A'] Therefore, you must listen to the parable of the sower:*
19a	Identification of 4b	*[1] When anyone hears the message of the kingdom*
		and does not understand,
b		*the evil one comes and*
		snatches away what was sown in their heart.
c		*This is the one who hears what was sown*
		along the path.
20a	Identification of 5a	*[2] Now as for the seed sown on rocky ground,*
b		*this is the one who . . . immediately receives it with joy*
		upon hearing the message.
21a		*Yet it has no root but is short-lived.*

b When trouble or persecution comes
on account
of the message,
c they immediately fall away.
22a Identification of 7a [3] And as for the seed sown among the thorn bushes,
b this is the one who hears the message,
but the anxiety of this age and
the deceitfulness of wealth choke the message
c so that it becomes unfruitful.
23a Identification of 8a [4] But as for the seed sown in good soil,
b this is the one who hears the message and
understands it,
c who indeed bears fruit and
produces,
one a hundredfold,
another sixtyfold, and
another thirtyfold."

Structure and Literary Form

Most of the material here is taken from Mark, but 13:10 – 17 draws material from Mark 4:25 (= v. 12) and Q (vv. 16 – 17 = Luke 10:23 – 24). This pericope introduces the seven parables and so functions as a conclusion for what precedes (note especially "the same day") and a thematic control for what follows. All the parables relate to the sowing of the kingdom truths. The parable genre is discussed in the excursus (below), but here Jesus adds another nuance by providing a negative purpose for them.[8] Thus there are three sections — the parable proper, the purpose statement for parables, and the interpretation of the parable.

Jones sees four aspects — an ambiguous parabolic picture, incomprehension, Jesus' critical rejoinder, and his explanation, with the "mystery" being especially the ongoing revelation of Jesus' identity as "the one who makes clear the Father's will," truths that carry with them great responsibilities on the part of the followers.[9] As John 1:5 says, darkness cannot overcome light; wherever the light of divine truth penetrates, darkness must recede. Still, there are some who totally reject the gospel, others who are excited for a time and then fall way, and others who embrace it and grow.

Within this Jesus tells why he uses the elusive parable form — he wants to solidify the rejection of those who oppose him (13:10 – 17). So this is indeed a "turning-point"

8. See Kenneth E. Bailey, *Poet and Peasant* (Grand Rapids: Eerdmans, 1976), 61 – 62, and Carson, "Matthew," 306, for a possible chiastic arrangement of 13:13 – 18. Jones, *Matthean Parables*, 292, doubts that there is a chiastic structure there.

9. Jones, *Matthean Parables*, 302.

in Matthew's gospel,[10] as Jesus reacts to the Jews' radical rejection of him by turning to a form of speech (parable) that anchors their rejection (esp. vv. 13 – 15). Jones adds, "The strength of Matthew's narration of *The Sower* is this: that disappointment and failure are possible."[11] This approach sees not so much reception of the gospel as the natural rejection of it by large segments of the population. This is likely an aspect of the meaning, although the theme of receptivity is, I believe, paramount in 13:3 – 9, 18 – 23.

Exegetical Outline

➡ **I. The Parable of the Soils (13:1 – 9)**
- A. The setting (vv. 1 – 2)
- B. The parable (vv. 3 – 9)
  1. The sower begins to sow (v. 3)
  2. The seeds on the path eaten by birds (v. 4)
  3. The seeds on the stony ground (vv. 5 – 6)
     - a. Rapid growth due to shallow soil (v. 5)
     - b. Equally rapid wilting when the sun took the moisture (v. 6)
  4. The seeds among thorns that choke them (v. 7)
  5. The seeds that grow and grow on good soil (v. 8)
- C. The warning to listen carefully (v. 9)

II. The Purpose of Parables (13:10 – 17)
- A. The question about parables (v. 10)
- B. Answer 1: The difference between insiders and outsiders (vv. 11 – 12)
  1. The mysteries given only to you (v. 11)
  2. More given only to the one who has (v. 12)
- C. Answer 2: God's punishment for their guilt (vv. 13 – 17)
  1. Their guilt (v. 13)
  2. Their punishment, Isa 6:9 – 10 (vv. 14 – 15)
  3. The blessedness of the disciples (vv. 16 – 17)
     - a. They see and hear (v. 16)
     - b. The prophets longed to see and hear what they do (v. 17)

III. The Interpretation of the Parable (13:18 – 23)
- A. Meaning of the seed on the path (v. 19)
- B. Meaning of the seed sown on stony soil (vv. 20 – 21)
- C. Meaning of the seed sown on thorny soil (v. 22)
- D. Meaning of the seed sown on good soil (v. 23)

10. J. D. Kingsbury, *The Parables of Jesus in Matthew 13: A Study in Redaction Criticism* (London: SPCK, 1969), 31.

11. Jones, *Matthean Parables*, 299.

The Interpretation of Parables

From the days of Origen and the Alexandrian School in the third century, allegorizing has dominated the understanding of parables. For instance, in the Good Samaritan parable (Luke 10:25 – 37) according to Augustine, the injured man is Adam, headed for paradise (Jericho), but is waylaid by temptation and life's pleasures (the robbers) that led to sin (the wounds). But Christ (the Samaritan) healed him (oil = compassion, wine = Jesus' blood) and brought him to the church (the inn).[12] Luther followed this method, but Calvin refused to spiritualize parables. His was a lone voice until Adolf Jülicher's *Die Gleichnisreden Jesu* (1888), which went to the opposite pole and argued every parable has only a single picture with a single point.

Throughout the twentieth century, this radical anti-allegorizing polemic dominated as a result, in part, to the magisterial works on parables by C. H. Dodd (1935), who added the idea of realized eschatology to the picture, and Joachim Jeremias (1947), who argued the parables must be situated within the life and times of Jesus and argued that any allegorical elements in parables must be attributed to the later church, not Jesus. The single-point approach is still influential today, but its weaknesses are more and more realized:[13]

1. Parables do have more than one point, as seen also in both Jewish and rabbinic parables.
2. One cannot insist on a rigid distinction between parable and allegory, and many of Jesus' parables do indeed have allegorical details.
3. Recognizing allegorical elements in a parable does not constitute imposing a modern allegorical meaning on it.
4. Jülicher imposed Hellenistic categories on Jewish parables; parables by nature are analogies comparing details in the story with spiritual truths.

Recently, however, a reader-oriented approach has developed in which parables are seen as autonomous and polyvalent, intended to be interpreted differently on the basis of the reading strategy employed by every reader. Some scholars argue that the original meaning is not available to the modern reader and that each parable must be an existential experience or "language event" calling for decision in the present.[14] This, however, is completely dependent on a postmodern perspective that says the author's intended meaning (or

12. See Osborne, *Hermeneutical Spiral*, 308.

13. See Robert H. Stein, *An Introduction to the Parables of Jesus* (Philadelphia: Westminster, 1981), 54 – 56; Craig L. Blomberg, *Interpreting the Parables* (Downers Grove, IL: IVP, 1990), 36 – 47.

14. See Susan Wittig, "A Theory of Multiple Meanings," *Semeia* 9 (1977): 75 – 103 (esp. 80 – 82); John Dominic Crossan, *Cliffs of Fall: Paradox and Polyvalence in the Parables of Jesus* (New York: Seabury, 1980).

even subsequent meanings) is not available today, a position shown often as untenable.[15]

The consensus today is that there are allegorical elements in the parables, and the task of the interpreter is to ascertain those intended by Jesus (allegory) rather than those read into the text by the modern reader (allegorizing). The key is the historical meaning communicated by Jesus in each gospel context. The goal of parable interpretation is to see both what Jesus intended them to say (historical context) and how the evangelists embedded them in their respective gospels (literary context).

This, of course, does not mean the reader plays no part, as if objective exegesis is possible. As Hagner says, parables were at all times meant to be "performative (or a 'language event') as well as informative."[16] Rather, readers are to align themselves with Jesus' use of the parable and allow it to challenge them accordingly. They are a "speech-event," an illocutionary challenge and a perlocutionary[17] encounter that never allows us to remain neutral; they grasp our attention and force us to interact with the presence of the kingdom in Jesus, either positively (those "around" Jesus in Mark 4:10 – 12) or negatively (those "outside").

Scholars are beginning to agree that Matt 16:19 and especially John 20:23 ("If you forgive the sins of anyone, their sins are forgiven; if you do not forgive them, they are not forgiven") relate primarily to the proclamation of divine truths; the hearer must respond, and this response leads to salvation or judgment. This is applicable to the parable. For those who reject the presence of God in Jesus (as do the leaders of the Jews), the parable becomes a sign of sovereign judgment, further hardening their hearts. For those who are open (e.g., the crowds), the parable encounters and draws them to decision. For those who believe (i.e., the disciples), the parable teaches them further kingdom truths.[18]

When interpreting parables, several factors must be kept in mind. Obviously, background information is invaluable in recreating the picture Jesus develops. The earthy details make a parable come alive. The more difficult issue is deciding between local color (those points that are merely part of the story) and theology-laden details (those parts that carry symbolic meaning). The decision is made on the basis of the literary context/emphases. Is compartmentalized Hades in the parable of the rich man and Lazarus (Luke 16:19 – 31), for example, part of the story (local color) or a theological description of the intermediate

15. See Osborne, *Hermeneutical Spiral*, 500 – 521; Kevin J. Vanhoozer, *Is There a Meaning in This Text? The Bible, the Reader, and the Morality of Literary Knowledge* (Grand Rapids: Zondervan, 1998).

16. Hagner, *Matthew 1 - 13*, 365.

17. For these "speech act" categories, see the discussion in the Introduction on "Implied Reader."

18. See Osborne, *Hermeneutical Spiral*, 295 – 96. On illocution and perlocution, see ibid., 119 – 20, 502 – 3.

state? Most say the former because of the lack of any such doctrine elsewhere and the fact that this adds little to the context.

Blomberg posits that a parable has as many points as it has characters, yielding one point per character.[19] This works most of the time, but it does not fit the parable of the sower/soils, since there is not just a sower, seed, and soil (yielding three points) but four kinds of soil that dominate Jesus' parable and interpretation. So it is best not to seek a general formula but allow each parable in its context to guide the interpreter.

One other aspect must be noted. Many of Jesus' parables do not simply follow common experience but actually reverse common experience and present a story that actually shocks the reader. This is because the kingdom reality is the reverse of this world. For instance, the parable of the shrewd manager in Luke 16:1 – 13 (the parable proper is 16:1 – 8a) has mystified interpreters for centuries, and elaborate theories have been constructed to explain why the owner (= God?) would "commend" the dishonest steward for cheating him of his profits. The key is to realize the owner is not God but simply part of the story, and the parable describes the way the secular world does business, i.e., uses its resources to get ahead. The surprising ending is explained in 16:8b, where the manager is seen as one of "the people of this world" who deals with "their own kind" (as also the tenant farmers who owe crops to the owner) shrewdly. This, then, is contrasted to "the people of the light," who are to be shrewd by giving their resources away (the opposite of the manager) to help others.

Explanation of the Text

13:1 On that day Jesus went out[20] of the house and sat by the lake (Ἐν τῇ ἡμέρᾳ ἐκείνῃ ἐξελθὼν ὁ Ἰησοῦς τῆς οἰκίας ἐκάθητο παρὰ τὴν θάλασσαν). The time note that the parables were delivered "on that day" links the parable section closely with the events of ch. 12 and especially with the rejection Jesus has encountered. These are parables of conflict and relate to the opposition Jesus has just met. This is undoubtedly the same house where Jesus encountered the Pharisees and where his family waited to speak with him in the previous episodes. It could well be Peter's house in Capernaum, where he earlier healed Peter's mother-in-law (8:14 – 15).

Jesus "goes out" of that house, apparently to teach; he will return to this house again in v. 36 to address his disciples (another outside/inside perspective; cf. 12:47). As he sits on the shore by the lake, he takes the position of a rabbi teaching his students (cf. 5:1; 15:29; 23:2; 24:3; rabbis sat when teaching and stood when preaching; see on 12:2).

19. Blomberg, *Parables*, 163.

20. "Went out" (ἐξελθών) is another circumstantial participle that should be translated as another main verb (so also in vv. 4, 10), see 2:4; 4:20.

13:2 Then such great crowds gathered around him that he got into a boat and sat there, and the whole crowd stood on the shore (καὶ συνήχθησαν πρὸς αὐτὸν ὄχλοι πολλοί, ὥστε αὐτὸν εἰς πλοῖον ἐμβάντα καθῆσθαι, καὶ πᾶς ὁ ὄχλος ἐπὶ τὸν αἰγιαλὸν εἱστήκει). This alone of the Matthean discourses is addressed primarily to the crowds. The crowds are the focus in vv. 1 – 9, 24 – 35, with the disciples the focus in vv. 10 – 23, 36 – 52. His popularity continues to grow, and quickly there are too many to be addressed sitting by the lake. He has to get in a boat so that[21] they all can see and hear him (needed on more than one occasion, cf. Luke 5:1 – 3). Jesus is now able to address the large crowd. Wilkins says local tradition locates this at an inlet called "The Cove of the Parables," a horseshoe-shaped inlet that would provide a natural amphitheater with acoustics perfect for such an address.[22]

13:3 He spoke many things to them in parables (καὶ ἐλάλησεν αὐτοῖς πολλὰ ἐν παραβολαῖς). The "many things" (πολλά) refers to all the teaching in parables in this chapter. Verse 34 says, "he refused to say anything to them except via parables." Mark 4:2 says Jesus "taught" here, but Matthew prefers the more apt "spoke" for the process of telling parables.[23] "Parable" (παραβολή) builds on the Hebrew *māšāl* and can refer to stories, illustrations, similitudes, proverbs, or even riddles. The basic meaning of the term is "comparison," so it is a literary device drawing an analogy or comparison from everyday experience to deepen one's understanding of a concept. This is the first time the term appears in Matthew, and it will be used twelve times in this chapter.

13:3 ... saying, "Look, a sower[24] went out to sow" (λέγων, Ἰδοὺ ἐξῆλθεν ὁ σπείρων τοῦ σπείρειν). For dramatic "look" (ἰδού) see on 1:20. Galilee was well known for the quality of its soil, and farmers proliferated in the countryside, some with small individual farms but most as tenant farmers on land belonging to an absentee wealthy landlord. They would sow the seed by hand, pulling it out of a seed bag and scattering it on the ground. It has been debated whether in first-century Palestine they plowed the ground before or after seeding it, and there is evidence for both. In fact, it is possible that they often plowed before and after sowing the seed in order to break the ground and then cover the seeds with dirt.[25]

It has been common to center on the sower (= Jesus, imparting a primarily christological meaning) or on the seed (= the kingdom message, thus centering on gospel proclamation). While both emphases are true, the rest of the parable centers on the soils, and the primary thrust is the receptivity of people to the kingdom message Jesus has been bringing.

13:4 As he sowed,[26] some seeds fell on the path (καὶ ἐν τῷ σπείρειν αὐτὸν ἃ μὲν ἔπεσεν παρὰ τὴν ὁδόν). In the ancient world roads (probably a footpath) did not skirt property but went right

21. In this context "that" (ὥστε) connotes result — the crowds were huge, with the result that he had to get in a boat.

22. Wilkins, *Matthew*, 473.

23. Kingsbury, *Parables*, 28 – 31, follows Bornkamm in asserting that Matthew restricts "teaching" (διδάσκω) to the explication and interpretation of the law and adds his view that Matthew here is presenting Jesus as delivering an apology to outsiders, an enigmatic form of speech intended to affirm their rejection. As such, he calls this a "turning-point" in Matthew's gospel.

24. The substantival participle "a sower" (ὁ σπείρων) is, as often, best translated as a noun.

25. See Philip B. Payne, "The Order of Sowing and Ploughing in the Parable of the Sower," *NTS* 25 (1978): 123 – 29; idem, "The Authenticity of the Parable of the Sower and Its Interpretation," in *Gospel Perspectives* (ed. R. T. France and David Wenham; Sheffield, JSOT Press, 1980), 1:163 – 207.

26. Wallace, 495, calls this an adverbial infinitive of contemporaneous time. Its force is synonymous with a present temporal participle "while."

through the fields, so most likely the farmer did not intend seed to fall on the hard-packed path, but the wind carried a few seeds there as he scattered it "alongside" (παρά) the road.

13:4 ... and the birds came and ate them (καὶ ἐλθόντα τὰ πετεινὰ κατέφαγεν αὐτά). Because the seed could not be hidden in the dirt, birds would naturally pluck them off the path. At the time for sowing, the sky would be filled with hungry birds ready to devour every exposed seed.

13:5 But other seed fell on rocky ground, where there was not much soil (ἄλλα δὲ ἔπεσεν ἐπὶ τὰ πετρώδη ὅπου οὐκ εἶχεν γῆν πολλήν). The imperfect "they have" (lit., εἶχεν) places the absence of soil in the foreground of the action[27] and stresses the ongoing problem. In places there is a limestone layer inches under the soil. The stony underlay traps the moisture and keeps it close to the surface. Palestine is dominated by an "early" (autumn) and a "later" (spring) rain in the harvest season (Deut 11:14; Jer 5:24), and this could picture the end of the autumn rainy season (with the moisture trapped and unable to sink deep in the soil) followed by a time of heavy sun.

13:5 It immediately sprang up because the soil was shallow (καὶ εὐθέως ἐξανέτειλεν διὰ τὸ μὴ ἔχειν βάθος γῆς). Since[28] there was little depth of soil above the limestone layer, the seedlings in that shallow soil are immersed in moisture and sprout up rapidly. So at first the farmer is excited by the quick success of the plants.

13:6 But when the sun arose, the plants were scorched; and because they had no roots, they withered (ἡλίου δὲ ἀνατείλαντος ἐκαυματίσθη καὶ διὰ τὸ μὴ ἔχειν ῥίζαν ἐξηράνθη). Another of Matthew's temporal genitive absolutes ("when the sun arose" [ἡλίου ἀνατείλαντος], see 1:18, 20) begins this verse. The stony layer keeps the plant from being able to sink roots deep into the ground, and the hot sun quickly sucks the moisture right out of the shallow soil. As a result, the exciting growth is short-lived, and the plant is first burnt by the sun and then shriveled by the parched soil. In Palestine even today one can see a fully ripe flower shrivel in seconds when hit by the hot sun and hot wind from the desert.

13:7 But other seed fell among thorn bushes, and the bushes grew up and choked them (ἄλλα δὲ ἔπεσεν ἐπὶ τὰς ἀκάνθας, καὶ ἀνέβησαν αἱ ἄκανθαι καὶ ἔπνιξαν αὐτά). The "thorn bushes" (ἄκανθαι) are wild hedges of thorns, a type of weed with strong roots that steal all the moisture from the soil, thereby "choking" the good plant. This plant lasts longer than the others, and note how the lifetime of the plants grows increasingly greater as the parable progresses.

13:8 Yet other seed fell on good soil and began to bear fruit, some a hundredfold, some sixtyfold, and some thirtyfold (ἄλλα δὲ ἔπεσεν ἐπὶ τὴν γῆν τὴν καλὴν καὶ ἐδίδου καρπόν, ὃ μὲν ἑκατόν, ὃ δὲ ἑξήκοντα, ὃ δὲ τριάκοντα). Galilee was well known for the general quality of its soil, and such yields as expressed here—even a hundredfold (meaning each plant produces a hundred plants)—are not unknown. The ingressive imperfect "began to bear" (ἐδίδου, Wallace, 544) emphasizes the beginning of the harvest.

Jeremias saw these yields as too high and believed Jesus did so deliberately in order to signify the overabundant blessings of the messianic age.[29] Many have seen the parable this way, interpreting

27. See Porter, *Idioms*, 23–25.

28. "Because" (διὰ τό) plus an infinitive forms a causal clause.

29. Jeremias, *Parables*, 150, argues that the normal yield was tenfold.

it as a parable of seedtime and harvest, as the proclamation of Jesus' day regarding the final harvest of the eschaton.[30] This is unnecessary, for examples of such in Jewish or Christian literature are much higher (e.g., Papias, who called for a ten thousand to one yield [Irenaeus, *Adv. Haer.* 5.33.3 – 4] or *b. Ketub.* 111b – 112a [one grape will fill a ship]).[31] Moreover, Gen 26:12 reports Isaac as having a hundredfold yield in his crop. In other words, it is a great crop but not a miraculous one.

More difficult is to explain why Matthew has reversed Mark 4:8 (thirtyfold, sixtyfold, hundredfold). Most believe that in both Mark and Matthew the threefold success of fruitfulness on the part of the disciples parallels the threefold failure in the first three types of soil. Some suggest it may have been to emphasize failure rather than success in light of Israel's cool response to Jesus;[32] but that does not fit the fact that these are the disciples, not the Jews. It may well be little more than Matthew's way of showing variety among the disciples, from the greatest to the least. In both the negative and the positive sense responses will differ.

13:9 Whoever has ears, let them listen! (ὁ ἔχων ὦτα ἀκουέτω). As in 11:15 (cf. 13:43) Jesus calls for both a willingness to listen (present tense for an ongoing response) and a motivation to respond properly to the message (used also in the letters to the seven churches in Rev 2–3). Jesus is demanding a serious examination of its meaning on the part of his hearers. Many have called this a prophetic warning to the hearers/readers to open their minds and hearts to the spiritual truths being conveyed.

13:10 Then his disciples came and asked him, "Why are you speaking to them in parables?" (Καὶ προσελθόντες οἱ μαθηταὶ εἶπαν αὐτῷ, Διὰ τί ἐν παραβολαῖς λαλεῖς αὐτοῖς;). The disciples have apparently been listening while Jesus addressed the crowds. Apparently some time later they "come to"[33] him, for Jesus' reply is meant only for them. It seems clear that they are confused and do not understand the parable.[34] So they ask him why he is using such an enigmatic form of teaching;[35] it is hard enough for them, but the crowds could hardly catch the meaning. Jesus has used the parable form before (7:24 – 27; 9:15 – 17; 11:16 – 19), but he now has increased their number and made them even more difficult to comprehend.[36]

13:11 He replied[37] to them, "It is because knowledge of the mysteries of the kingdom of heaven has been given to you, but it has not been given to them" (ὁ δὲ ἀποκριθεὶς εἶπεν αὐτοῖς, ὅτι ὑμῖν δέδοται γνῶναι τὰ μυστήρια τῆς βασιλείας τῶν οὐρανῶν, ἐκείνοις δὲ οὐ δέδοται). Jesus "answers" (for the grammar here see on 11:25) with one of the more important theological proclamations of Matthew. The opening "because" (ὅτι) does not introduce the quotation but is causal, answering the disciples' question "why." There is a strong emphasis on divine election here,[38] as "it has been given" (δέδοται) is a divine passive. God has

30. See the discussion in Kingsbury, *Parables*, 35 – 36.

31. See Davies and Allison, *Matthew*, 2:385.

32. Davies and Allison, *Matthew*, 2:402; Jones, *Matthean Parables*, 297 – 98.

33. Kingsbury, *Parables*, 40 – 41, believes that "come to" (προσελθόντες) carries cultic overtones of coming before deity and thus ascribes to Jesus a "lordly dignity" that demands reverence.

34. See Carson, "Matthew," 307, who answers those (Bornkamm, Kingsbury, Grundmann) who see the disciples positively as understanding the parable and as idealized figures. But Jesus has to explain it in vv. 18 – 23, and they ask about the meaning of a later parable in v. 36. It seems clear that they do not understand.

35. Present tense "speaking" (λαλεῖς) dramatically pictures Jesus' teaching here.

36. Hagner, *Matthew 1 – 13*, 372.

37. For "replied" (ἀποκριθείς) as a circumstantial participle and translating the two verbs as a single idea, see on 4:4.

38. See the excursus on divine sovereignty and human responsibility in Turner, "Matthew," 185.

chosen to reveal his "mysteries" to only a select few, namely, Jesus' followers.

At the same time, human responsibility is distinctly present. The disciples have accepted Jesus' teaching and followed him, while those to whom God has not revealed these truths have clearly rejected Jesus. Knowledge (substantival infinitive "to know" [γνῶναι]) is here seen as a grace-gift from God, revealed to those whom he selects (11:25; 16:17) and to be kept from those unworthy (7:6). The "mysteries" (μυστήρια) correspond to the Jewish *rāz*, used in Dan 2:27 – 28, Qumran (1QS 9:17; 1QH 1:21), and apocalyptic writing (*1 En.* 68:5; *4 Ezra* 10:38, 12:36 – 37; *2 Bar.* 81:4; et al.).[39] The mysteries stem from the appearance of the kingdom in Jesus and are heavenly secrets previously hidden but now made known to the citizens of the kingdom, often centering on the eschatological events of the last days.[40] In a sense "apocalyptic" refers to the process of revealing these truths and the "mystery" to the content of these truths.

The content of the "mystery" concerns "the kingdom of heaven," especially the arrival of the kingdom and the kingdom teaching of Jesus, truths that can only be comprehended by his followers. The Jews expected the kingdom, but only at the final end of history, while in Jesus it has arrived now and is at work through Jesus and his followers. God has "given" this knowledge to the disciples (the insiders), not to the crowds or their leaders (the outsiders). This "insider"/"outsider" distinction[41] is a critical theological point in Matthew (as in Mark).

13:12 For whoever has, more will be given, and there will be abundance (ὅστις γὰρ ἔχει, δοθήσεται αὐτῷ καὶ περισσευθήσεται). Luz calls this "an early Christian wandering logion" or proverb originally dealing with wealth (Prov 9:9; 11:24; 15:6; *4 Ezra* 7:25) but used by Jesus of discipleship (cf. 25:29).[42] While v. 11 has stressed sovereignty, this one stresses responsibility. The issue is the one who "has" vs. the one who "has not." The "for" (γάρ) that introduces the verse makes it the reason for God's grace-gift (divine passive "will be given" [δοθήσεται]) only to the insiders. The disciples already "have" knowledge of the kingdom, for they have believed and followed Jesus. The question is to what the "more" that will be in "abundance" refers. Kingsbury takes it eschatologically of the gift of the kingdom in abundance,[43] but few agree, preferring to see this as the gift of even greater insight into the kingdom truths. The "abundance," then, will be the full revelation Jesus has for them.

13:12 But whoever does not have, even[44] what they have will be taken away (ὅστις δὲ οὐκ ἔχει, καὶ ὃ ἔχει ἀρθήσεται ἀπ' αὐτοῦ). Those who have rejected Jesus will be kept from any such knowledge, indeed will be removed from the kingdom reality itself (here Kingsbury's point makes sense). Matthew 21:43 also employs the passives "taken away" and "given" and refers to the Jewish people themselves ("Therefore I tell you that the kingdom of God will be taken away from you and given to a people who will produce its fruit"). There the Jewish people have rejected knowledge of Jesus, so "even what they have," i.e., being God's kingdom people, will be "taken away" by God. In the present passage it is more

39. On the Semitic origin and background see Raymond E. Brown, *The Semitic Background of the Term "Mystery" in the New Testament* (Philadelphia: Fortress, 1968).

40. Some read a great deal into Matthew's plural (cf. Mark 4:11 with the singular) as referring to all that Jesus taught, not just the parables of ch. 13 (Kingsbury, Luz, Schnackenburg), but it could also refer to the number of parables here (Gundry) or perhaps the multiple elements of Jesus' kingdom teaching (Carson). This last seems the best interpretation since the kingdom is so central here.

41. See the discussion of this in France, *Gospel of Matthew*, 508 – 10.

42. Luz, *Matthew 8 – 20*, 246.

43. Kingsbury, *Parables*, 46.

44. This is ascensive καί for a "point of focus" as "even" (Wallace, 670 – 71).

general — those who do not perceive and respond to Jesus' kingdom message will lose what kingdom blessings they do have.

13:13 For this reason I am speaking to them in parables, because seeing they do not see, and hearing they neither hear nor understand (διὰ τοῦτο ἐν παραβολαῖς αὐτοῖς λαλῶ, ὅτι βλέποντες οὐ βλέπουσιν καὶ ἀκούοντες οὐκ ἀκούουσιν οὐδὲ συνίουσιν). This is a further answer after vv. 11 – 12 to the question "why" in v. 10. There are two causal indicators here, "for this reason" (διὰ τοῦτο) and "because" (ὅτι), both meaning that the obduracy that the people of Israel have shown in chs. 11 – 12 is the reason Jesus is speaking to the crowds in parables. The use of present tenses throughout the verse emphasizes the ongoing nature of this.

While vv. 11 – 12 have centered on divine sovereignty, this elucidates human responsibility. As Luz says, "Israel's failure to see and hear is for Matthew an established fact. It is not caused by Jesus' parables; it is more the case that Jesus speaks in parables in 'response' to this lack of understanding."[45] Many see a contradiction between Matthew's "because" (ὅτι) and the "so that" (ἵνα) in Mark 4:12, with Matthew saying Israel's hardness is the reason for parables and Mark saying Jesus speaks in parables for the purpose of causing Israel's hardness.[46]

This seeming contradiction is similar to the so-called contradiction between Paul and James over faith and works. Paul says works cannot produce salvation while James says works are the necessary proof of salvation. They are two sides of the same coin. The same is true here. Matthew looks at Israel's rejection as the reason and Mark as the result of Jesus' use of enigmatic parables. Another illustration might help. Who caused Pharaoh's hardness in Exodus, God or Pharaoh himself? In reality, Pharaoh hardened his heart, and God hardened it further in judgment. This is the case here. Jesus responds to Israel's rejection by using parables to confirm and anchor that rejection.[47]

Here Jesus introduces Isa 6:9 – 10, and Matthew strengthens Mark by summarizing the Isaianic material in v. 13 and then quoting it at length in vv. 14 – 15. Isaiah 6 is Isaiah's commissioning service, as he sees the holy God lifted up on his throne and surrounded by the seraphim. The prophet is told by God to take to the people a message that will cause rejection by the obstinate and apostate nation. Jesus sees the same in the current generation: like ancient Israel, the people still see God's work in Jesus but fail to perceive it. They hear the words of Jesus but fail to understand them. Thus, the parables are "stones of stumbling deliberately placed in Israel's path, much like what Isaiah was instructed to do in Isaiah 6."[48]

This passage became a major apologetic passage in the early church for explaining the hardness of unbelieving Israel (cf. Mark 4:12 = Luke

45. Luz, *Matthew 8 – 20*, 246. He adds, "In the parables discourse the people's lack of understanding is condensed in narrative form."

46. Carson, "Matthew," 308 – 9, lists four possible approaches: (1) Matthew editorially changed it to provide a moral basis for Jesus rejecting the Jews (Kingsbury, Dupont); (2) harmonizing — "because" they refused to hear, Jesus used parables "in order to" keep them from hearing; (3) softening Mark's *hina* to a consecutive, "with the result that," so that it is similar to Matthew's causal; (4) vv. 11 – 12 center on divine predestination, while v. 13 centers on human responsibility, namely, Israel's guilt and "spiritual dullness." Carson prefers the last, while I would combine 2 and 4.

47. Kingsbury, *Parables*, 49 – 51, asks if this contains Matthew's "theory of parables," i.e., parables were only for disciples and were meant to be a "riddle" to the unbelieving Jews. Yet this cannot be, for elsewhere Jesus uses parables to speak to the Jews, e.g., the parable of 7:24 – 27 directed to the crowds (5:1; 7:28 – 29) as well as the disciples (cf. also 21:28 – 32, 33 – 46). Here the emphasis is on Jewish hardness, but they are still the focus of Christ's salvific ministry.

48. Witherington, *Matthew*, 264.

8:10; John 12:39 – 40; Acts 28:26 – 27). "Understand" (συνίημι) is a major discipleship term in Matthew. While Mark centers on the disciples' inability to understand, Matthew shows that due to the presence of Jesus they can do so (cf. 13:51; 15:15 – 20; 16:9 – 12; 17:10 – 13).[49] This is in contradistinction to the Jewish people, who are both unwilling (their guilt) and unable (divine judgment) to understand.

13:14 The prophecy of Isaiah is fulfilled in them (καὶ ἀναπληροῦται αὐτοῖς ἡ προφητεία Ἠσαΐου). This is a modified form of the normal fulfillment formula (omitting the "so that" [ἵνα] and using an intensified "fulfilled" [ἀναπληροῦται] for the fulfillment) and is the only fulfillment passage personally spoken by Jesus.[50] Like the others, it is typological and says the situation behind Isa 6 is being reenacted in the current generation. The hardness of the nation in Isaiah's day is "fulfilled" or "comes to completion" in the hardness of the people in Jesus' day.

13:14 … saying, "With hearing you will hear and never understand, and seeing you will see and never perceive" (ἡ λέγουσα, Ἀκοῇ ἀκούσετε καὶ οὐ μὴ συνῆτε, καὶ βλέποντες βλέψετε καὶ οὐ μὴ ἴδητε). Now the full quote is given, building on the preliminary partial quote in v. 13. The redundancy is for emphasis; it switches from third to second person to make the effect more pronounced. In v. 13 there were two present tense participles for "seeing" and "hearing" (probably concessive ["although"] but possibly temporal ["while"]), while here there is an adverbial dative and a participle, but the effect is the same. Israel was seeing and hearing the most important message humankind would ever receive, but because of their hardness they "never" (note the emphatic "never" [οὐ μή] in both clauses) were able truly to see or hear. Their spiritual perception and understanding are negated by their rejection of their Messiah.

13:15 For the heart of this people has become calloused, they barely hear with their ears, and they have closed their eyes (ἐπαχύνθη γὰρ ἡ καρδία τοῦ λαοῦ τούτου, καὶ τοῖς ὠσὶν βαρέως ἤκουσαν καὶ τοὺς ὀφθαλμοὺς αὐτῶν ἐκάμμυσαν). The second "for" (γάρ) of the context (v. 12) again provides the reason for divine judgment.[51] The completeness of their obduracy is shown as having invaded their hearts, their ears, and their eyes. One could say they have experienced a spiritual heart attack, deafness, and blindness, only this time they have inflicted it upon themselves. παχύνω means to be "fat" or "well-nourished literally but in its metaphorical sense refers to one who is 'dull' or 'impervious' to truth" (BAGD). This is close to the "hardness of your heart" of 19:8 (cf. Mark 3:5; 10:5), which describes why God allowed divorce in the Torah. They see Jesus' messianic work and the power of his life, and they hear his teaching as the final interpreter of Torah, but their hearts are not

49. Held, in *Tradition and Interpretation*, 106 – 12; Davies and Allison, *Matthew*, 2:392 – 3. This is disputed by Andrew H. Trotter, "Understanding and Stumbling: A Study of the Disciples' Understanding of Jesus and His Teaching in the Gospel of Matthew" (PhD diss., Cambridge University, 1986), who argues the disciples continue to misunderstand in Matthew. Yet passages like 16:12 ("Then they understood …") seems to support the above thesis. Still, Held and Davies and Allison et al. are wrong when they say Matthew "idealizes" the disciples. His is a realistic approach, noting their failures but showing how Jesus gives them strength to overcome.

50. Kingsbury, *Parables*, 39; Soares-Prabhu, *Formula Quotations*, 31 – 35; Davies and Allison, 2:394, say this is a later interpolation in Matthew because of the redundancy with v. 13 and its non-Matthean flavor, but there is no evidence for such a conjecture.

51. In the MT and LXX these are imperatives, so that these are judgment commands telling Isaiah to "go and make their hearts calloused." Here they are indictments, describing what the people have already done.

open to these truths; their hardened hearts both blind them and shut their ears to the truth.

13:15 ... lest they should see with their eyes and hear with their ears and understand with their heart, and they repent and I have to heal them (μήποτε ἴδωσιν τοῖς ὀφθαλμοῖς καὶ τοῖς ὠσὶν ἀκούσωσιν καὶ τῇ καρδίᾳ συνῶσιν καὶ ἐπιστρέψωσιν καὶ ἰάσομαι αὐτούς). Now the judgment comes. "Lest" (μήποτε) is debated; does it refer to the culpability of Israel that does not want to turn to God (Luz, Hagner) or to the sovereign judgment of God who does not want them to turn to him (Carson, Blomberg, Wilkins)?

In light of the context of judgment in vv. 11 – 12 and the first person ἰάσομαι (lit., "I will heal") in this clause, the latter is better. So in essence it means, "I want them to remain this way lest...." Their guilt has produced a sovereign judgment, and Jesus' use of parables is part of that judgment. The parables as riddles will stymie any possibility of "turning" back to God.[52] They have committed in effect an "unpardonable sin" (explicit in the parallel Mark 3:28 – 29; 4:12), and God has turned his back on them! The parables will shut their eyes and close their ears. Once more human responsibility and sovereign decision are intertwined.

13:16 But blessed are your eyes because they see and your ears because they hear (ὑμῶν δὲ μακάριοι οἱ ὀφθαλμοὶ ὅτι βλέπουσιν καὶ τὰ ὦτα ὑμῶν ὅτι ἀκούουσιν). The emphatic position of "your" (ὑμῶν, "But as for you") produces a strong contrast with the crowds. The disciples have experienced the blessing of God and are fortunate[53] because unlike the people, they have opened their eyes and ears to Jesus. Jesus concluded the parable by commanding that his listeners open their ears (13:9), but only the disciples have done so. Thus they are the fortunate ones.

13:17 For I tell you the truth, many prophets and righteous people desired to see what you see but did not see it, and to hear what you hear but did not hear it (ἀμὴν γὰρ λέγω ὑμῖν ὅτι πολλοὶ προφῆται καὶ δίκαιοι ἐπεθύμησαν ἰδεῖν ἃ βλέπετε καὶ οὐκ εἶδαν, καὶ ἀκοῦσαι ἃ ἀκούετε καὶ οὐκ ἤκουσαν). For "amen" (ἀμήν) sayings, see on 5:18. It is often mentioned that the early Christians were the privileged generation, the fulfillment of all the messianic longing of the past (cf. John 8:56; Heb 11:13, 39 – 40; 1 Pet 1:10 – 12). Jesus wants the disciples to realize how fortunate they are. The OT saints (the "righteous," i.e., all those who waited for the Messiah and remained faithful to Yahweh, cf. also 23:29) and especially the prophets longed to see the kingdom of God arrive and to hear the Messiah present the final Torah teaching. The disciples have seen the day dawn and heard the kingdom truths (cf. 11:4 – 5), and they need to realize how truly blessed they are.

13:18 Therefore, you must listen to the parable of the sower (Ὑμεῖς οὖν ἀκούσατε τὴν παραβολὴν τοῦ σπείραντος). Since the "mysteries" are intended for the disciples (v. 11) and they have open ears (v. 16), Jesus concludes ("therefore" [οὖν]) that they must "listen" (v. 9) as he explains the meaning of the parable. The second emphatic "you" (ὑμεῖς, cf. v. 16) plus the aorist imperative "listen" (ἀκούσατε, looking at their attentive listening as a complete whole) commands the disciples, since they are the privileged insiders (v. 17), to listen carefully.

52. ἐπιστρέφω means to "turn" or "turn back" and in a religious sense is repentance or conversion language.

53. Possibly both aspects of "blessed" (μακάριος) are intended here, the vertical divine blessing and the horizontal happiness experienced by those who are blessed. For the term see on 5:3.

13:19 When anyone hears the message[54] of the kingdom and does not understand (παντὸς ἀκούοντος τὸν λόγον τῆς βασιλείας καὶ μὴ συνιέντος).[55] Jesus begins with a temporal genitive absolute referring to "every person" who listens to his teaching[56] (it is clear that Jesus is the sower) about the kingdom.[57] The clause "and does not understand" brings in all the imagery from the Isaiah quote in vv. 13 – 16. They have hardened their hearts and stopped their ears from hearing and heeding the message; they do not wish to understand. This is not inadvertent ignorance but studied rejection, a "sin with a high hand" (Num 15:30 – 31, "sins defiantly" in TNIV) that must be punished.

13:19 ... the evil one comes and snatches away what was sown in their heart. This is the one who hears what was sown along the path (ἔρχεται ὁ πονηρὸς καὶ ἁρπάζει τὸ ἐσπαρμένον ἐν τῇ καρδίᾳ αὐτοῦ, οὗτός ἐστιν ὁ παρὰ τὴν ὁδὸν σπαρείς). It is clear that Satan (called "the evil one" because that defines his character, cf. 5:37; 6:13) is in control of them (the present tenses stress his ongoing power over them). Birds are often identified with the demonic forces in Jewish literature (*Jub.* 11:11 – 12; *Apoc. Abr.* 13:3 – 7), and here Satan like a bird swoops down and takes the sowed word out of the hardened hearts of those who have rejected Christ in chs. 11 – 12.[58] These people have both rejected the message of Christ and opened themselves to Satan's control. Satan is portrayed throughout the gospels as the enemy of all who come in contact with the proclaimed word.[59]

The ending of this first type of soil is enigmatic, for Jesus uses the masculine "this" (οὗτος) rather than the neuter, so it seems to refer not to the seed but the one who receives the seed. This is in keeping with the beginning "when anyone hears," so the emphasis in this first explanation centers on the hardened hearts (note that the seed was sown "in their heart," the place of conviction). In the other three, Jesus begins with the seed sown, but here the change in order emphasizes the guilt of the Jewish people for rejecting the kingdom message.

13:20 Now as for the seed sown on rocky ground, this is the one who, upon hearing[60] the message, immediately receives it with joy (ὁ δὲ ἐπὶ τὰ πετρώδη σπαρείς, οὗτός ἐστιν ὁ τὸν λόγον ἀκούων καὶ εὐθὺς μετὰ χαρᾶς λαμβάνων αὐτόν). There is emphasis on the "immediate" results (with "immediately" [εὐθύς] essentially repeating v. 5). This soil is different from the first, as the refusal to understand is replaced by "receives it with joy." These people have not only "heard" but "accepted" the kingdom news, and it filled them

54. Wallace, 133, discusses the use of the genitive after "hear" (ἀκούω) for those who understand and the accusative for those who do not understand (as here).

55. On the authenticity of the explanation here, see Luz, *Matthew 8 – 20*, 242 – 44. He finds arguments against it to be unconvincing. For a stronger presentation see Payne, "Authenticity of the Parable of the Sower," 163 – 207.

56. λόγος refers not just to a "word" here but to the whole "message" of Jesus. This is a common use of the term.

57. τῆς βασιλείας is an objective genitive referring to the message "about the kingdom."

58. Interestingly, in Mark 4:10 – 12, 15, it is the leaders who committed the unpardonable sin in 3:28 – 30 that are especially in view.

59. Jones, *Matthean Parables*, 307, follows those who see this primarily as a description of the dangers facing the life of the Christian community, and so the powers of evil are threatening the disciples here. Yet if we are correct in taking this as describing the three groups addressed in Jesus' ministry thus far — the leaders, the crowds, and the disciples — this does not really apply to the disciples. The one who "does not understand" could refer to all three groups, of course, but as the first type of soil it especially has the leaders in mind.

60. ἀκούων and λαμβάνων are substantival participles, the "hearer" and "receiver."

with "joy." The first indications are good, especially since "receive" (λαμβάνω) often refers to a conversion experience (John 1:12; cf. 1 Thess 1:6, "welcomed the message ... with the joy given by the Holy Spirit"). But here it falls short of such an experience. These are probably those among the crowd who are amazed and enthralled with Jesus but have not yet become true followers.

13:21 Yet it has no root but is short-lived. When trouble or persecution comes on account of the message, they immediately fall away (οὐκ ἔχει δὲ ῥίζαν ἐν ἑαυτῷ ἀλλὰ πρόσκαιρός ἐστιν, γενομένης δὲ θλίψεως ἢ διωγμοῦ διὰ τὸν λόγον εὐθὺς σκανδαλίζεται). They follow Jesus not out of true belief or commitment, but for the excitement of following the great wonder-worker and rabbi. The image of a "root" is a common ancient metaphor for commitment. Maurer explains, "Since the flora of Palestine is often threatened by heat or drought, special attention is directed to the root as the part of the plant which guarantees the existence of the whole [and] ... gives purchase and stability."[61] Here that stability is missing.

The response of these hearers is temporary, what Luz calls "living in the here and now" ("short-lived" [πρόσκαιρος] in contrast to "eternal" [αἰώνιος]).[62] When asked to suffer (another temporal genitive absolute like in v. 6) the same type of opposition Jesus faced on behalf of the kingdom "message" (τὸν λόγον, as in vv. 19, 20), they will stop following him. Jesus has spoken of persecution frequently (5:10 – 12; 10:17 – 25, 28, 34 – 36; 11:18 – 19) and will call his followers to persevere in the face of it (23:34 – 36; 24:9 – 13).[63] As in 5:29 (also 24:10) "fall away" (σκανδαλίζω) means apostasy, in this case a rejection of Christ by a quasi-follower.

13:22 And as for the seed sown among the thorn bushes, this is the one who hears the message, but the anxiety of this age and the deceitfulness of wealth choke the message, so that it becomes unfruitful (ὁ δὲ εἰς τὰς ἀκάνθας σπαρείς, οὗτός ἐστιν ὁ τὸν λόγον ἀκούων, καὶ ἡ μέριμνα τοῦ αἰῶνος τούτου καὶ ἡ ἀπάτη τοῦ πλούτου συμπνίγει τὸν λόγον καὶ ἄκαρπος γίνεται). Now it is not persecution but worldly anxiety and wealth that choke the life out of the hearer. Jesus has taught about the worries of life in the Sermon on the Mount (6:25 – 34) and will be teaching on the problem of wealth in 19:16 – 24. These issues become a major motif in Luke (Luke 1:51 – 53; 3:10 – 14; 4:18; 6:20 – 26; 12:13 – 21, 22 – 34; 14:25 – 35; 16:1 – 13, 19 – 31; 18:18 – 30), but the issue is still important to Matthew. The true disciple does not allow the concerns of life to have precedence over following Jesus.

There may be double meaning in ἀπάτη, since it can mean "deceitfulness" or "delight," so the emphasis may be that riches are "a deceptive pleasure."[64] The two genitives ("of this age" [τοῦ αἰῶνος τούτου], "of wealth" [τοῦ πλούτου]) are probably subjective, "this age" producing "anxiety" and "wealth" producing "deceit." The riches of this life are seductive and can choke the spiritual life out of a follower. The result[65] of such worry and wealth is an "unfruitful" life, which in the metaphor means the plant is choked before it can bear fruit. In John 15:1 – 8 bearing fruit is the obligatory sign of discipleship. God demands "much fruit," and those who bear no fruit face everlasting punishment. Works cannot save (Eph 2:8 – 9), but they are the necessary result of salvation (Jas 2:14 – 26).

13:23 But as for the seed sown in good soil, this is the one who hears the message and understands

61. Christian Maurer, "ῥίζα," *TDNT*, 6:985.

62. Luz, *Matthew 8 – 20*, 249.

63. See Hagner, *Matthew 1 – 13*, 380.

64. Wilkins, *Matthew*, 481.

65. In BAGD, 392 – 93, καί can introduce result, "and so, so that." This makes good sense here.

it (ὁ δὲ ἐπὶ τὴν καλὴν γῆν σπαρείς, οὗτός ἐστιν ὁ τὸν λόγον ἀκούων καὶ συνιείς). Clearly this category contrasts directly with the hardened soil of v. 19 and the message of Isa 6:9 – 10 in vv. 13 – 15. Understanding (again, the present tenses emphasize the continual nature of the receptivity) is a critical aspect of discipleship in Matthew. While Mark emphasizes the disciples' lack of understanding (6:52; 8:17, 21), Matthew shows how the presence of Jesus turns their misunderstanding into understanding (13:23, 51; 16:12; 17:13).[66] This is a central theme, and Luz goes so far as to call this "virtually the fundamental text of Matthean hermeneutics" because it combines understanding with bearing fruit and action — thus obedience and ethical practice.[67] Discipleship is defined by ethical conduct, as seen throughout the Sermon on the Mount, especially "righteousness" in 5:6, 10, 20; 6:1, 33.

13:23 ... who indeed bears fruit and produces, one a hundredfold, another sixtyfold, and another thirtyfold (ὃς δὴ καρποφορεῖ καὶ ποιεῖ ὃ μὲν ἑκατόν, ὃ δὲ ἑξήκοντα, ὃ δὲ τριάκοντα). The present tense "bears fruit" (καρποφορεῖ) continues the stress on fruitfulness as the ongoing characteristic of the true disciple. The fruit is not specified but in Matthew must mean ethical living, conduct that reflects the kingdom obligations specified in Jesus' discourses of chs. 5 – 7, 10 thus far. While the first three soils reflect the conflict of chs. 10 – 12, this final soil is positive paraenesis, calling the disciples to right living.

This continues the definition of true Christianity in Matthew: it is more than mere profession but is shown in righteous conduct and obedience to Jesus' teaching. As stated on v. 8, the remarkable yield shows the power of God in the lives of his followers and proceeds from the greatest to the least to stress the diversity of responses disciples make. Yet even thirtyfold is a great result, and the kingdom reality makes a great difference in the lives of Jesus' followers.

Theology in Application

Davies and Allison say this parable is not meant for exhortation but rather for explanation, to verify why Jesus failed to bring about the repentance of Israel.[68] This is not correct, for both explanation and exhortation are involved. It does sum up the conflict and rejection theme from chs. 10 – 12, but it also warns all four types of soil about the repercussions of failing to accept Jesus' "seed" message and allowing it to take root in their lives.

This is especially true of 13:10 – 17, where the danger is that God will reject those who reject Christ. Wilkins speaks of the type of discipleship envisaged as "clandestine kingdom disciples," i.e., a kingdom that had not yet come in a "display of political and militaristic might" but was to be lived out in lives of faith

66. It is common among critical scholars to assume Mark is more original (misunderstanding) and this is a Matthean addition and not historical, cf. Barth, "Understanding," in *Tradition and Interpretation*, 107; Hill, *Matthew*, 228; Kingsbury, *Parables*, 61. However, this is unnecessary, for Matthew stresses their (limited but still very real) understanding while Mark centers on what they did not perceive (in keeping with his theme of discipleship failure. See Carson, "Matthew," 314; Keener, *Matthew*, 381 – 82.

67. Luz, *Matthew 8 – 20*, 250.

68. Davies and Allison, *Matthew*, 2:402 – 3.

and commitment. It is an "undercover kingdom," proclaimed via changed lives and persevering faith.[69] I am going to contextualize the four types of soil for today and place the middle portion (vv. 10 – 17) with the first type of soil. I will also combine the parable with its interpretation. That is how I teach/preach this parable.

1. Rejection for Those Hardened

Those who have hardened themselves to the gospel must realize that God will reject them as well. The hard-packed road typified the leaders and others in Israel who had committed the unpardonable sin (12:31 – 32); as a result, God no longer wanted them to repent. Jesus' teaching on the purpose of parables (vv. 10 – 17) centered on this group, using Isa 6:9 – 10 to show how parables reenacted Isaiah's message to apostate Israel in confirming the rejection of those who had turned their hearts against God's Messiah. For them Jesus used his parables to further confuse and darken their already hardened hearts. The division in Israel was now widened, for the parables extended the gulf between those who opened themselves to the message and those who closed their hearts from it.

2. Interest and Excitement Insufficient

Seekers must realize that their interest and excitement are not enough unless they truly come to Jesus. The stony-ground followers project amazement and even wonder but without the depth of commitment that will persevere through hard times or persecution. When people remain seekers while coming week after week, they are hardening themselves Sunday after Sunday as they fail to find Jesus as their Savior. Until one is "rooted in Christ," it is impossible to endure through the difficult times of life or through the type of opposition described in ch. 10.

3. The Danger for Quasi-Christians

The quasi-Christian[70] will fail to withstand the anxieties of life or the lure of materialism and will eventually fall away to spiritual ruin. The thorny-ground followers also have no strong roots in Christ and are easily choked off by the pressures of life. Without a deep-seated trust in God, the worries of everyday life stifle what little spiritual life they have. Their true priorities are their bank account and status in the community, and so the pleasures of life will ultimately seduce them away from God. This is an area too often ignored in churches, and I believe the major strategy of every church must be to wake up these people and to help them to realize how they are wasting their lives on what ultimately will not matter.

69. Wilkins, *Matthew*, 492 – 93.

70. I would define a "quasi-Christian" as a person who attends regularly and seems to show some interest but never gets involved in the life of the church or uses their gifts to enhance the church. They are often called "Sunday Christians" or "nominal Christians."

4. Committed Followers

The committed followers of Christ are urged to live fruitful lives and to multiply their effectiveness for Christ. The sky is the limit for the fruitful-soil followers. By surrendering every area of their lives to Christ and using all their gifts to glorify him, they will have an effect unimaginable. Most of us look at ourselves and wonder whether God made a mistake when he made us. We have so little to offer, so few gifts. We could not be more wrong. Paul was laughed at by his opponents in Corinth, yet he said he rejoiced in his weakness because it just made the power of God at work in him all the more evident (2 Cor 11:30). God made us to glorify him and placed within each of us seeds of greatness that will multiply a hundredfold or sixtyfold or thirtyfold (God decides how much it grows) when we surrender to his power at work in us.

CHAPTER 57

Matthew 13:24 – 30

Literary Context

This second parable of the seven builds on the parable of the sower in two ways. (1) Both are parables of seed that produces plants. (2) In the parable of the sower we saw both those who have rejected Jesus' kingdom proclamation and those who have accepted it. In the parable of the wheat and the weeds, these two categories are now explained further in terms of judgment. The wheat is clearly the fruitful soil and the weeds the other three categories. Moreover, the "enemy" in this parable parallels "the evil one" in the parable of the sower. So the first two parables explain the difficult situation of the gospel sown in an evil world, resulting in unbelief mingled with belief.

The explanation of this second parable is given later in order to frame the section (inclusio) of 13:24 – 43 with this theme of future judgment and vindication. Several (e.g., Hagner, Jones) have noted that Matthew seemingly replaces the parable of the seed growing secretly in Mark 4:26 – 29, also about a sower falling asleep but with a positive message regarding the power of God in making the kingdom grow. If this is so, Matthew wants to center both on the negative element of the enemy (Satan) trying to sabotage the harvest and on the judgment and vindication at the harvest itself.

IV. Preaching and Teaching in the Midst of Opposition (11:2 – 13:53)
- **B. Third Discourse: Kingdom Parables (13:1 – 53)**
  1. Parable of the Soils (13:1 – 23)
  2. **Parables of the Kingdom Growing (13:24 – 43)**
     - ➦ **a. Parable of the Weeds (13:24 – 30)**

Main Idea

Many listening to Jesus' teaching would be wondering why God allows evil to flourish right alongside the good; when will he finally end the presence of evil in this world?[1] Christ is saying that this is not the time for the final victory over evil, but this is the time for sowing the kingdom seed. As the kingdom message is sown in the hearts of humankind, Satan will cause many to reject and oppose it; yet the kingdom will flourish in the hearts of others, and God will exercise judgment at the end of the age.

Translation

Matthew 13:24-30

24a	Introduction	**He placed another parable before them, saying,**
b	Comparison	*"The kingdom of heaven is like a man*
		who sowed good seed
		in his field
25a		*but while people were sleeping,*
b	Action	*his enemy came and*
		sowed weeds in the midst of the wheat,
		then departed.
26a		*So when the wheat sprouted and produced fruit,*
b	Result of 25b	*then the weeds also appeared.*
27a	Question	*Then the slaves came to the landowner and said,*
b		*'Sir, you sowed good seed in your field, didn't you?*
c		*So where did the weeds come from?'*
28a	Answer	*And he said to them,*
b		*'A person who is an enemy did this.'*
c	Question	*Then his slaves asked again,*
d		*'So do you want us to go and gather them together?'*
29a	Answer	*But he responded,*
b		*'No, lest . . . you uproot the wheat along with them*
c		*when you gather the weeds.*
30a		*Let both grow together until the harvest.*
b		*And at the time of the harvest*
c		*I will tell the reapers,*
d		*'First gather the weeds together and*
		tie them in bundles to be burned.
e		*Then gather the wheat into my barn.'"*

1. Many commentators have seen this addressing the Matthean church and a discipline situation there with some members causing problems (= the weeds), e.g., G. Barth, "Auseinandersetzung um die Kirchenzucht im Umkreis des Matthäusevangelium," *ZNW* 69 (1978): 158 – 77; Gundry, *Matthew*, 262 – 63. However, that makes little sense here, and the field is undoubtedly the world where the gospel is sown, cf. Carson, "Matthew," 316 – 17; Davies and Allison, *Matthew*, 2:408 – 9; Morris, *Matthew*, 351.

Structure and Literary Form

This parable comes from Matthew's special source (M) and has no parallel elsewhere in the gospels. Matthew apparently replaces Mark's parable of the seed growing by itself (4:26 – 29) with this one, probably a result of his desire to include teaching on the last judgment (cf. also 13:47 – 50).[2] There are two major parts to the story: the setting (vv. 24 – 26) and the dialogue between the owner and his servants (vv. 27 – 30). However, the dialogue can be split into two parts, with the first calling on the workers to do nothing about the weeds (vv. 27 – 30a) and the second announcing the future harvest when the weeds are to be gathered and burnt (v. 30b). So this is "a drama with three acts in which the last act is simply announced."[3] Jesus' followers are not to separate the wheat from the weeds (cf. Rev 22:11), for God will do so at the final harvest of this age. Thus this parable also answers how and when that judgment will occur.

Exegetical Outline

➦ **I. The Setting: a Wealthy Farm (13:24 – 26)**
- A. The owner sows good seed (v. 24)
- B. The enemy sows weeds among the wheat (v. 25)
- C. The weeds grow along with the wheat (v. 26)

II. The Dialogue between the Owner and the Workers (13:27 – 30a)
- A. First interchange (vv. 27 – 28a)
  1. Question: how did the weeds get there? (v. 27)
  2. Answer: the enemy did it (v. 28a)
- B. Second interchange (vv. 28b – 30a)
  1. Question: should we take out the weeds? (v. 28b)
  2. Twofold answer (vv. 29 – 30a)
     - a. No, lest you destroy some of the wheat in the process (v. 29)
     - b. Let them grow together until the harvest (v. 30a)

III. Wait for the final harvest (13:30b)
- A. The weeds will be gathered
- B. They will be tied into bundles
- C. They will be burnt

2. For redactional theories, see David Catchpole, "John the Baptist, Jesus, and the Parable of the Tares," *SJT* 31 (1978): 557 – 70; Jones, *Matthean Parables*, 312 – 21.

3. Luz, *Matthew 8 – 20*, 252.

Explanation of the Text

13:24 He placed another parable before[4] them, saying, "The kingdom of heaven is like a man who sowed good seed in his field" (Ἄλλην παραβολὴν παρέθηκεν αὐτοῖς λέγων, Ὡμοιώθη ἡ βασιλεία τῶν οὐρανῶν ἀνθρώπῳ σπείραντι καλὸν σπέρμα ἐν τῷ ἀγρῷ αὐτοῦ). Jesus' introduction ("The kingdom of heaven is like ...")[5] will introduce all six remaining parables in this chapter (13:24, 31, 33, 44, 45, 47). These are kingdom parables, teaching various truths regarding the inbreaking and future of God's final kingdom in Jesus. These are the "mysteries" Jesus spoke of in 13:11. While the first parable seemed to concern a peasant, probably a tenant farmer, this concerns a wealthy landowner with many day laborers helping care for the farm. The "good seed" is said to be "wheat" in v. 25, a crop for which Galilee was well known and the staple food product of the Roman empire.

13:25 "But while people[6] were sleeping, his enemy came and sowed weeds in the midst of the wheat, then departed" (ἐν δὲ τῷ καθεύδειν τοὺς ἀνθρώπους ἦλθεν αὐτοῦ ὁ ἐχθρὸς καὶ ἐπέσπειρεν ζιζάνια ἀνὰ μέσον τοῦ σίτου καὶ ἀπῆλθεν). The "enemy" is probably a rival farmer, and it was not unknown for such antagonists to sow (at night) dangerous "weeds" in a rival's field. It occurred with sufficient frequency that Rome even had a law against doing such things.[7] The weed was "darnel," a poisonous weed that carried a fungus that could attack the wheat as well. This plant was hard to distinguish from wheat at the earliest stages, though as soon as leaves appeared a person could identify the narrow leaves of darnel.[8]

13:26 So when the wheat sprouted and produced fruit, then the weeds also appeared (ὅτε δὲ ἐβλάστησεν ὁ χόρτος καὶ καρπὸν ἐποίησεν, τότε ἐφάνη καὶ τὰ ζιζάνια). As soon as the heads of grain with leaves appear, the darnel also becomes evident. Then the workers know something is amiss, for they see the weeds distributed all over field.

13:27 Then the slaves came[9] to the landowner and said, "Sir, you sowed good seed in your field, didn't you? So where did the weeds come from?" (προσελθόντες δὲ οἱ δοῦλοι τοῦ οἰκοδεσπότου εἶπον αὐτῷ, Κύριε, οὐχὶ καλὸν σπέρμα ἔσπειρας ἐν τῷ σῷ ἀγρῷ; πόθεν οὖν ἔχει ζιζάνια;). The slaves who worked the farm are mystified by the great amount of weeds throughout the wheat fields and so ask the landowner (lit., "master of the house," cf. 10:25), using the respectful "sir," whether he had made a mistake in planting the seed. They want to know the source of the poisonous weeds. It is a mystery to them.

13:28 And he said to them, "A person who is an enemy did this" (ὁ δὲ ἔφη αὐτοῖς, Ἐχθρὸς ἄνθρωπος τοῦτο ἐποίησεν). The use of "person"

4. παρατίθημι with the dative (here and in v. 31) generally means to "set before" and in teaching means to "put, place" an idea "before" others (BAGD, 623).

5. It is commonly recognized that "it is like" (ὡμοιώθη) should not be translated to say "the kingdom is like a man" but rather is an Aramaic idom meaning, "it is the case with the kingdom as with this story...." See Zerwick, *Biblical Greek*, §65; Kingsbury, *Parables*, 67; Davies and Allison, *Matthew*, 2:411.

6. As Davies and Allison, *Matthew*, 2:412, point out, this probably refers to "people sleeping" (= "at night") rather than to "servants sleeping" (as NIV). "While" (ἐν τῷ with the infinitive) is a temporal clause, virtually synonymous with the "when" (ὅτε) clause in the next verse.

7. Keener, *Matthew*, 386 – 87. There is no reason for the conclusion of Schweizer, *Matthew*, 303, that the detail of the enemy sowing weeds is unlikely and secondary. Rome would hardly have a law against something that never happened.

8. Luz, *Matthew 8 – 20*, 254; Nolland, *Matthew*, 545.

9. This (and in v. 28b) is another circumstantial participle translated as a main verb (see 2:4; 4:20; 13:1, 11).

(ἄνθρωπος) makes it emphatic (lit., "enemy person").[10] Possibly also it is used to say the incident was not supernatural but the work of a single hostile person.[11] The owner knows it is the work of a rival farmer.

13:28 Then his slaves asked again, "So do you want us to go and gather them together?" (οἱ δὲ δοῦλοι λέγουσιν αὐτῷ, Θέλεις οὖν ἀπελθόντες συλλέξωμεν αὐτά;). It would be natural to want to rip out the offensive weeds, and the slaves are ready to do just that.

13:29 But he responded, "No, lest when you gather[12] the weeds, you uproot the wheat along with them" (ὁ δέ φησιν, Οὔ, μήποτε συλλέγοντες τὰ ζιζάνια ἐκριζώσητε ἅμα αὐτοῖς τὸν σῖτον). The problem with tearing out the weeds is that their roots are intertwined with the good wheat. The roots of the darnel are bigger and stronger than the roots of the wheat, so the good crop will be destroyed as well.

13:30 "Let both grow together until the harvest" (ἄφετε συναυξάνεσθαι ἀμφότερα ἕως τοῦ θερισμοῦ). The owner tells the slaves to wait until the final harvest. Scholars are divided on this. Some like Luz take this to be unusual, but others consider this normal. I agree with the latter group, for in light of the problem of pulling up wheat with the weeds it makes good sense to wait until the harvest when wheat that is pulled up along with the weeds can be separated into the pile to be harvested. This is an important point, for it shows Jesus is not teaching an imminent coming of the kingdom but is getting his disciples ready for a lengthy period before the harvest is to come. Evil will exist alongside the good until the eschaton.

13:30 "And at the time of the harvest I will tell the reapers, 'First gather the weeds together and tie them in bundles to be burned. Then gather the wheat into my barn'" (καὶ ἐν καιρῷ τοῦ θερισμοῦ ἐρῶ τοῖς θερισταῖς, Συλλέξατε πρῶτον τὰ ζιζάνια καὶ δήσατε αὐτὰ εἰς δέσμας πρὸς τὸ κατακαῦσαι αὐτά, τὸν δὲ σῖτον συναγάγετε εἰς τὴν ἀποθήκην μου). When the crop has become ripe, the harvest will occur. At that time the reapers (which many think a separate group from the slaves of vv. 27 – 28 since in v. 41 the reapers are angels) will separate the weeds from the wheat. The weeds will be tied in bundles to be burned[13] (many farmers used it for animal food, but Jesus is developing a different image),[14] an obvious symbol of divine judgment. The weeds are separated out first, an order that fits the book of Revelation, where the last judgment (20:11 – 15) precedes eternal reward (21:1 – 22:5). Evil must be destroyed before good can predominate. At that time the good wheat crop is taken to the granary.

Theology in Application

Since Jesus explains this parable in vv. 36 – 43, its application will be explained there.

10. "Enemy" (ἐχθρός) could also be in apposition and adjectival, "a hostile person."

11. Morris, *Matthew*, 350.

12. This participle is used temporally.

13. "For the purpose of" (πρὸς τό plus the infinitive) emphasizes purpose, namely, God's intention for fiery judgment.

14. Gundry, *Matthew*, 265, calls this "a piece of unrealism" since the normal practice was to cut off the tops of the wheat stalks and then burn the field. However, this custom is mentioned just as often, and neither predominated (see Davies and Allison, *Matthew*, 2:415). Witherington, *Matthew*, 267, says, "In wood-poor Israel, weeds would be dried and used for fuel."

58 CHAPTER

Matthew 13:31 – 35

Literary Context

These two parables add a further nuance to the others, namely, the seeming insignificance of the kingdom and its incredible future. The mustard seed parable shares with the first two the presence of sowing the seed in the field and the growth of the plant. The tree also signifies the universal mission of the church, with the Gentiles joining God's people in fulfillment of the procession of the nations to Zion in the OT. The parable of the yeast shares the idea of growth. Also, the stupendous growth parallels the hundredfold, sixtyfold, and thirtyfold growth of the plant in 13:8. But there it is the growth of the individual disciple, while here it is the corporate growth of the kingdom and its community.

IV. Preaching and Teaching in the Midst of Opposition (11:2 – 13:53)
- **B. Third Discourse: Kingdom Parables (13:1 – 53)**
  - **2. Parables of the Kingdom Growing (13:24 – 43)**
    - a. Parable of the Weeds (13:24 – 30)
    - ➦ **b. Parable of the Mustard Seed (13:31 – 32)**
    - **c. Parable of the Yeast (13:33)**
    - **d. Parables Fulfilling Prophecy (13:34 – 35)**

Main Idea

The kingdom now seems small and insignificant among the other religions, but its future is unlimited and will far surpass the other religions of the Greco-Roman world. As Davies and Allison say, these are parables of contrast between the present experience of Jesus and his followers (the reality of the insignificant seed) and the expected future (the hope of the great tree), with the end finding its origin in the beginning.[1] The yeast parable is similar: the kingdom for the present seems unimpressive, but it will spread throughout the world.

Translation

Matthew 13:31-35

31a	Introduction	Now **he set before them another parable, saying,**
b	Comparison	*"The kingdom of heaven is like a mustard seed*
		that a person took and sowed in his field.
32a		*It is the smallest of all the seeds,*
b		but *when it is full grown,*
c		*it is the largest of plants and*
d		*becomes a tree,*
e		*with the result that the birds of the air come and nest in its branches."*
33a	Introduction	**He spoke another parable to them:**
b	Comparison	*"The kingdom of heaven is like yeast*
		that a woman took and mixed into three measures of wheat flour
c		*until it permeated the dough."*
34a	Summary	**Jesus spoke all these things in parables to the crowds;**
b		**in fact, he continually refused to say anything to them except via parables,**
35a	Purpose/ Fulfillment Formula	**so that what was spoken through the prophet might be fulfilled:**
b	OT Quotation	*"I will open my mouth in parables;*
c		*I will utter things hidden since the creation of this world."* (Ps 78:2)

Structure and Literary Form

This third parable, from the triple tradition (= Mark 4:30 – 32; Luke 13:18 – 19), has two parts, the sowing of the seed (v. 31) and the contrast between its miniscule size now and how it will become the "largest of plants" in the future (v. 32). The

1. Davies and Allison, *Matthew*, 2:415 – 16.

fourth parable is from Q (= Luke 13:20 – 21). Finally, the discourse on parables is drawn from Mark 4:33 – 34 and has two parts, the first narrating Jesus' decision to use only parables in addressing the crowds (v. 34) and the second showing that Jesus' use of parables fulfills prophecy (v. 35).

Exegetical Outline

→ **I. The Parable of the Mustard Seed (13:31 – 32)**
- A. Introductory formula (v. 31a)
- B. The sowing of the seed (v. 31b)
- C. The contrast (v. 32)
  1. The smallest of seeds
  2. The largest of plants
  3. The birds nesting in its branches

II. The Parable of the Yeast (13:33)
- A. Introductory formula (v. 33a)
- B. The story (v. 33b)

III. Discourse on Parables (13:34 – 35)
- A. Jesus using only parables to the crowds (v. 34)
- B. Parables fulfilling Ps 78:2 (v. 35)

Explanation of the Text

13:31 Now he set before them another parable, saying, "The kingdom of heaven is like a mustard seed that a person took[2] and sowed in his field" (Ἄλλην παραβολὴν παρέθηκεν αὐτοῖς λέγων, Ὁμοία ἐστὶν ἡ βασιλεία τῶν οὐρανῶν κόκκῳ σινάπεως, ὃν λαβὼν ἄνθρωπος ἔσπειρεν ἐν τῷ ἀγρῷ αὐτοῦ). This is closely associated with the previous two parables by the hook words "person," "sowed," and "field." Also, it is labeled as another kingdom parable and so is intended to add a further nuance to the unveiling of the meaning of the kingdom in this world.

13:32 It is the smallest of all the seeds, but[3] when it is full grown, it is the largest of plants (ὃ μικρότερον μέν ἐστιν πάντων τῶν σπερμάτων, ὅταν δὲ αὐξηθῇ μεῖζον τῶν λαχάνων ἐστίν). The mustard seed was one of the smallest seeds (though not the smallest). This is not an error on Jesus' part, through some have claimed it as such. Jesus is using rabbinic hyperbole to stress the great difference between its miniscule size (it can barely be seen in the palm of a hand) and the great tree it produces (nine to ten feet high), and at the same time this was the smallest seed known to his Palestinian audience.

This was such a startling fact (a plant growing so much in one season from such a small seed) that it became proverbial for rapid growth; in fact, it was often said not to plant such in a garden

2. Here and in v. 33 we have another circumstantial participle, as in vv. 1, 11, 27.

3. μέν ... δέ connotes "on the one hand ... on the other hand" and emphasizes the contrast.

because it took up so much space (see Nolland, Witherington). That is Jesus' point, namely, the contrast between the kingdom's insignificant beginning and the greatness of its future.[4] As Kingsbury points out, the Jews expected a spectacular entrance of the kingdom, but Jesus declares that it has an insignificant beginning in the person of Jesus and the church he establishes in his disciples. The "Kingdom of God has already appeared, but contrary to Jewish expectation, in lowliness."[5]

13:32 ... and becomes a tree, with the result that the birds of the air come and nest in its branches (καὶ γίνεται δένδρον, ὥστε ἐλθεῖν τὰ πετεινὰ τοῦ οὐρανοῦ καὶ κατασκηνοῦν ἐν τοῖς κλάδοις αὐτοῦ). In the process of "growth," its greatness is assured. It becomes a tree (another rabbinic hyperbole, since it is a bush or shrub rather than a tree) large enough for birds to build nests in its branches. It is debated whether we should see allegorical significance in the coming of the birds. Some say there is no such figurative meaning (Filson, Hagner), but since several OT passages identify the birds with the Gentiles coming in procession to Israel (Ezek 17:23, 31:6; Dan 4:9–12, 20–22), many scholars believe this signifies the Gentile mission (Hill, Gundry, Luz, Davies and Allison, Morris, Nolland). In light of the strong emphasis on the Gentile mission in Matthew, the allegorical meaning seems intended here.

Crossan provides an interesting interpretation in which Jesus is intentionally being provocative by choosing a "bush" instead of a tree.[6] Since a bush was considered dangerous and invasive in people's garden, Jesus might be speaking about the subversive and dangerous nature of the kingdom for the secular world. This is a provocative possibility, but the emphasis here is more on the growth of the kingdom than its subversive nature. Still, both ideas might cohere together — the kingdom will grow and triumph by subverting the present evil world.

13:33 He spoke another parable to them: "The kingdom of heaven is like yeast that a woman took and mixed into three measures of wheat flour until it permeated the dough" (Ἄλλην παραβολὴν ἐλάλησεν αὐτοῖς· Ὁμοία ἐστὶν ἡ βασιλεία τῶν οὐρανῶν ζύμῃ, ἣν λαβοῦσα γυνὴ ἐνέκρυψεν εἰς ἀλεύρου σάτα τρία ἕως οὗ ἐζυμώθη ὅλον). Yeast was similar to the mustard seed in its smallness and the great effect it had on the dough. So the message is similar to the previous parable — the insignificant thing growing into greatness. In the Palestinian kitchen the wife would take old dough, already filled with yeast, and mix it into new dough, thus causing the yeast to penetrate all the new dough. ἐνέκρυψεν could mean "hid" and introduce imagery of the "hidden" truths of the gospel, thus pointing to 13:35, 44; but more likely it means simply to "put something into something."[7]

The amount is highly unusual. Three measures (an "ephah" in the OT) equals 39.4 liters or 14.75

4. Luz, *Matthew 8–20*, 258–61, notes four main interpretations down through history: (1) ecclesiological, the church miraculously growing into a worldwide religion; (2) individual, Christ, with the mustard seed symbolizing the proclaimed word, the church, or the gospel; (3) cosmopolitical, with the church permeating the world as its members penetrate the world; and (4) eschatological, the final victory of the kingdom in this world. Jeremias, *Parables*, 148–49, adds a fifth, seeing this as depicting the resurrection cycle instituted by Jesus, the miracle of life coming out of death. While interesting, these tend to go too far in seeing symbolic meaning. The third is the closest, with the insignificant band of Jesus and his disciples beginning a movement that would change the world.

5. Kingsbury, *Parables*, 80, 87.

6. See John Dominic Crossan, "The Seed Parables of Jesus," *JBL* 92 (1973): 244–66.

7. Carson, "Matthew," 319. Yet there could be a double meaning in this context in which the earthly task of "mixing" the dough also signified the "hidden" truths of the gospel permeating the world.

gallons, about fifty pounds of flour. Thus this is not a daily event but a banquet; that much would feed 100 – 150 people.[8] So Jesus is saying that an insignificant amount of yeast-dough could permeate an entire village. Often yeast occurs as a negative image, describing the spreading power of evil (Matt 16:6 par; Luke 12:1; 1 Cor 5:6 – 7; Gal 5:9), but here it is positive, speaking of the spread of the kingdom in history, more eschatological success than the messianic banquet. Scott, however, says the yeast metaphor is always negative, in keeping with the properties of yeast and the difference between leavened and unleavened bread in Judaism, so this parable was unconventional and shocking.[9] Yet he overstates the negative elements (such as the "hidden" nature of the yeast) and fails to recognize the positive use of the metaphor in the OT and Judaism (e.g., at Pentecost, Lev 23:17).

13:34 Jesus spoke all these things in parables to the crowds; in fact, he continually refused to say anything to them except via parables (ταῦτα πάντα ἐλάλησεν ὁ Ἰησοῦς ἐν παραβολαῖς τοῖς ὄχλοις καὶ χωρὶς παραβολῆς οὐδὲν ἐλάλει αὐτοῖς). Matthew tells us the same truth positively in the first clause and negatively in the second clause. There is an interesting switch from the global aorist "spoke" (ἐλάλησεν) in the first phrase to the imperfect "was saying" (ἐλάλει) in the second. The first looks at his dialogue with the crowds as a single whole and the second as an ongoing speech-event. The speaking in parables has already been stated in 13:3, 13, but here we learn that Jesus apparently refused to use any other form of teaching with them.[10]

On the basis of 13:10 – 17 this means that Jesus considered the crowds to be outsiders (cf. 13:11 – 12). This is a turning point in Jesus' ministry as he turns from the crowds and in the rest of ch. 13 addresses only the disciples. Jesus is rejecting those who are not willing to open their ears to "hear" (cf. 11:15, 13:9) and is implicitly applying 13:10 – 17, where the parables are meant to confirm the rejection of those who are not open to Jesus' kingdom message. In other words, Jesus considers the crowds to be outsiders (cf. 13:11 – 12).

13:35 … so that what was spoken through the prophet[11] might be fulfilled (ὅπως πληρωθῇ τὸ ῥηθὲν διὰ τοῦ προφήτου λέγοντος). The formula quotation (see on 1:22) portrays Jesus' parables as a fulfillment of prophecy. The quotation is from Ps 78:2, yet that psalm is attributed to Asaph. In what way was Asaph a "prophet"? (1) Since Ps 78:2 introduces a prophetic fulfillment, its author could rightly be called a prophet. (2) Asaph is said to have "prophesied" in 1 Chr 25:2 and is called a "seer" in 2 Chr 29:30.[12]

8. So Gundry, Luz, Davies and Allison, Keener. Carson, "Matthew," 319, provides an alternate amount that agrees with the TNIV and equates three seahs with the OT "ephah" or "bath" or about 22 liters total. Since ancient measurements were imprecise, it is impossible to be certain which is correct. The main point is the large amount noted by Jesus, an amount Gundry, *Matthew*, 268, says was "the largest amount of dough a woman could knead."

9. Bernard B. Scott, *Hear Then the Parable: A Commentary on the Parables of Jesus* (Minneapolis: Fortress, 1989), 324 – 29. He builds on what he sees as negative elements (the leaven, the hiding of it in the dough, the permeation by the leaven) to say the parable pictures the marginal, the corrupt, and the pagan coming into the kingdom.

10. This becomes difficult in light of the fact that Jesus taught directly in following material (e.g., 15:3 – 10; 17:17, 25; 19:4 – 12, 17 – 21). Blomberg, *Matthew*, 221, says that this refers only to this occasion. Carson, "Matthew," 320, interprets it as meaning "parables were an essential part of his spoken ministry" (so also Morris, *Matthew*, 354).

11. There is a text-critical difficulty here, for a number of witnesses (א * H f[1] f[13] 33 et al.) read "through Isaiah the prophet." Some call this minority reading authentic because it is the "more difficult reading" (Isaiah clearly did not write the psalm). However, it was a common practice among scribes to add the name of a prophet when none was included, and that is what probably occurred here.

12. Hagner, *Matthew 1 – 13*, 390; Morris, *Matthew*, 354.

13:35 "I will open my mouth in parables" (ἀνοίξω ἐν παραβολαῖς τὸ στόμα μου). The wording of this first line is taken from the LXX, but the second line seems to be an independent translation of the MT. Psalm 78 presents the history of Israel intended to show God's gracious mercy and mighty deeds in spite of the nation's many failures. The second verse states that history would be presented to them as a "parable" and a "riddle," i.e., giving new hidden truths in the process. The first line repeats the message of 13:12 – 13, where Jesus said he would use parables when addressing outsiders, because their nature as riddles would stymie the crowds and confirm their rejection.

13:35 "... I will utter things hidden since the creation of this world"[13] (ἐρεύξομαι κεκρυμμένα ἀπὸ καταβολῆς κόσμου). This second line turns to the nature of the kingdom message, showing it has been "hidden" but is now in process of being revealed by Jesus. "Since the creation of this world" links this with God's plan of salvation in redemptive history and shows that a new kind of teaching can be found in Jesus, revealing hidden truths never heard before (the "mysteries" of v. 11). "Since the creation" (ἀπὸ καταβολῆς, "foundation") became a technical NT expression for the beginning of God's creation (cf. John 17:24; Eph 1:4; Heb 4:3, 9:26; 1 Pet 1:20; Rev 13:8, 17:8). It sounds as if the two aspects contradict each other, but in reality they supplement each other. For those in the crowds who have turned against Jesus, parables confirm their rejection; but for those open to Jesus' truths, they reveal hidden secrets regarding the reality of the kingdom. Parables are kingdom-centered and as such reveal new truths and are proof that the final kingdom has arrived.

Theology in Application

The two parables of this section build on each other and clarify further the reality of the kingdom of heaven and its arrival in human history.

1. The Kingdom Present in Jesus

Like a mustard seed, the kingdom was present in Jesus, and his unimpressive disciples did not seem to amount to much. As the crowds followed, they were amazed at the miracles but were not drawn to the group as a whole. There is little evidence that many were converted at that time. The leaders went further, actively opposing Jesus and his little band because in their eyes this teacher/rabbi and his disciples constituted blasphemy in the land of Israel.

But looks are deceiving, for God had his hand on this small group, and his Son, the expected Messiah, would make it possible for people in every nation to find salvation. So today the power of the cross seems hidden to the world as a whole. In

13. A diversified number of manuscripts ($\aleph^1$ B f^1 e k et al) omit "world"(κόσμου), and since it is a stereotypical phrase in the NT, this more difficult reading may well be better (so Carson, "Matthew," 323, who takes it as "the foundation of the nation"). Still, an impressive number support the longer reading ($\aleph^*$ C D L W Θ et al.), so we can cautiously accept the longer reading as viable (see Metzger, *Textual Commentary*, 33 – 34).

fact, in the pluralism of our postmodern culture, we have become the new enemies of society because we dare to say there is only one way to God. Yet those who mock the truths of the kingdom will inevitably lose, and God with his people will triumph. In each of us there are seeds of greatness, and God wants to use each of us in establishing his kingdom reality on earth.

2. Continued Growth

Like yeast the kingdom will continue to grow until it permeates the world. The parable of the yeast builds on one aspect of the mustard seed parable, that of growth. Jesus promises that growth will signify the kingdom community, the church. As Kingsbury says, "God, through the vehicle of the Church, is even now at work in power to spread out his kingly rule, and this will terminate only with the setting up of his latter-day Realm."[14]

I wonder if Paul ever conceived of the possibility that within four hundred years the church would conquer Rome and displace the Greco-Roman gods. The same thing has happened in our day. Who would have ever thought that one-third of the population of Korea would be Christian, or that in spite of (actually *because of*) terrible persecution by the communist government, there would be a hundred million Christians in China. The same phenomenal growth is occurring in Latin America and Africa. We must recognize that God is still in control, and even though evil will increase, the kingdom will continue to grow in each succeeding generation until the eschaton.

3. Jesus' Ongoing Ministry

Jesus continues to speak in an enigmatic fashion today, and seekers had better beware of playing games with their eternal destiny. The crowds in the gospels are like seekers in our day, amazed and interested in this Jesus but unwilling to take the final step of belief. Jesus does not intend to make it easy to enter the kingdom (in spite of some shallow preachers in our day who try to water down the gospel). He demands full commitment, a radical discipleship that does not leave room for wishy-washy "Christians."

Being a devoted follower of Christ has never been easy, nor will it ever be. You cannot "have your cake and eat it too" in following Christ. His truths, like parables, take time and effort to unlock. There are hidden realities that can only be known by serious Bible study and absolute commitment to Christ. This is the problem with the popular church movement of our time: it demands microwave Christianity that can be warmed up with little effort. Such an approach produces weak quasi-Christians who do not know how to "walk the walk" or "talk the talk."

14. Kingsbury, *Parables*, 87.

CHAPTER 59

Matthew 13:36–43

Literary Context

This second section of the Parable Discourse ends with Jesus' interpretation of the parable of the wheat and weeds. It also marks the end of Jesus' public ministry, as he teaches only his disciples for the rest of the chapter. The reason Jesus has not done so earlier is because he did not find time alone with his disciples until this point. The parables were for outsiders as well as insiders, but the explanation was only for insiders (see 13:11–12). Since the parables unlock the "mysteries" of the kingdom, they are only for the true followers.

IV. Preaching and Teaching in the Midst of Opposition (11:2–13:53)
- **B. Third Discourse: Kingdom Parables (13:1–53)**
  - **2. Parables of the Kingdom Growing (13:24–43)**
    - a. Parable of the Weeds (13:24–30)
    - b. Parable of the Mustard Seed (13:31–32)
    - c. Parable of the Yeast (13:33)
    - d. Parables Fulfilling Prophecy (13:34–35)
    - ➦ **e. Parable of the Weeds Explained (13:36–43)**

Main Idea

As in the parable itself in 13:24–30, the main idea is that the righteous and the wicked coexist in this world, and no one can separate them until the final harvest at the end of the age. What is added to the parable is the work of the "enemy," the "evil one" of 13:19, 38–39, who controls the unrepentant and sows them among the believers. Although church leaders often cannot truly distinguish the true believer and the unbeliever, God will do so when he sends his angels to gather the wicked and throw them into the fiery furnace, while the saints will glow with the glory of the sun.

Translation

Matthew 13:36-43

36a	Setting	**Then he left the crowd and went into his house.**
b	Question	**His disciples came to him and asked,**
c		*"Explain to us the parable of the weeds in the field."*
37a	Answer	**So he answered them,**
b	Identification of 24b	*"The one who sows the good seed is the Son of Man.*
38a		*The field is the world.*
b		*The good seed is the children of the kingdom,*
c	Identification of 25b	but *the weeds are the children of the evil one.*
39a		And *the enemy who sows them is the devil.*
b	Identification of 30a-e	*The harvest is the end of the age,*
c		and *the harvesters are the angels.*
40a	Comparison	*So just as the weeds are gathered together and*
		burned in the fire,
		so it will be at the end of the age.
41a		*The Son of Man will send his angels,*
b		and *they will gather out of his kingdom everyone*
		who causes sin and
		does evil.
42a		*Then they will cast them into the fiery furnace,*
b		*where there will be weeping and grinding of teeth.*
43a	Conclusion	*Then the righteous will shine like the sun*
		in the kingdom of their Father.
b	Exhortation	*Whoever has ears, let them listen!"*

Structure and Literary Form

This is a didactic section intended to explain the meaning of the parable of the weeds. Like the parable itself, it is derived from Matthew's special source. It consists of (1) the setting and a request for an explanation (v. 36); (2) the explanation itself (vv. 37 – 43a); and (3) a concluding exhortation to listen (v. 43b). The explanation is made up of (a) the identification of the various parts of the story (vv. 37 – 39); (b) the explanation of the basic metaphor (v. 40); (c) and the harvest of the wicked to fiery punishment (vv. 41 – 42) and the righteous to glory in God's kingdom (v. 43a). It is an allegorical parable but should not be allegorized; that is, no elements except those explained by Jesus should be given allegorical meaning (e.g., the people sleeping, the servants, the wheat producing fruit, etc.). Those are part of the story and have no theological significance.

Exegetical Outline

➡ **I. The Setting (13:36)**
- A. Spatial setting: a home
- B. Rhetorical setting: the request

II. Explanation of the Parable (13:37 – 43a)
- A. The parts of the story explained (vv. 37 – 39)
  1. The sower — the Son of Man
  2. The field — the world
  3. The good seed — the kingdom people
  4. The weeds — Satan's followers
  5. The enemy — the devil
  6. The harvest — the eschaton
  7. The harvesters — the angels
- B. The basic metaphor (v. 40)
- C. The harvest at the eschaton (vv. 41 – 43a)
  1. The sending of the angels (v. 41a)
  2. The gathering of the wicked (vv. 41b – 42)
  3. The gathering of the righteous (v. 43a)

III. Concluding Exhortation (13:43b)

Explanation of the Text

13:36 Then he left[1] the crowd and went into his[2] house (Τότε ἀφεὶς τοὺς ὄχλους ἦλθεν εἰς τὴν οἰκίαν). This is the turning point. Jesus leaves the crowd (and his time of ministry to them) and goes into the house for a private tutorial with his disciples. The rest of the chapter describes this private teaching time. It is deliberate and in a sense a rejection of the crowds by Jesus. In 13:1 Jesus left his house (the scene of his conflicts in ch. 12, possibly Peter's house in Capernaum). Now he returns to that home.

13:36 His disciples came to him and asked, "Explain to us the parable of the weeds in the field" (καὶ προσῆλθον αὐτῷ οἱ μαθηταὶ αὐτοῦ λέγοντες, Διασάφησον ἡμῖν τὴν παραβολὴν τῶν ζιζανίων τοῦ ἀγροῦ). The disciples do not understand any better than the crowds, but they are distinguished in their trust in Jesus and their desire for an explanation. Jesus will explain it to them because they are insiders, the children of the kingdom (see 13:11 – 12). He will not explain it to the crowds because there is no faith stance by which they can assimilate these truths.

13:37 So he answered them, "The one who sows the good seed is the Son of Man" (ὁ δὲ ἀποκριθεὶς εἶπεν, Ὁ σπείρων τὸ καλὸν σπέρμα ἐστὶν ὁ υἱὸς τοῦ ἀνθρώπου). As in the parable of the sower, Jesus the Son of Man proclaims kingdom truths.

1. For this use of a circumstantial participle, see on v. 1.

2. This is an example of the article standing for the possessive pronoun, see Wallace, 216.

This is the Danielic glorified Son of Man, for he is sowing the seed that will result in his dominion over the world (cf. Dan 7:13 – 14).

13:38 The field is the world (ὁ δὲ ἀγρός ἐστιν ὁ κόσμος). While some throughout church history have interpreted this as the church,[3] the meaning is clear and makes sense in light of the universal mission in Matthew (see 1:5 – 6; 2:1 – 12; 4:14 – 16, 25; 8:5 – 13; 10:18; 12:21, 42). Matthew has in mind the worldwide mission of the church, to Gentiles as well as Jews. Note that there is no emphasis in this parable on the church as the force by which the kingdom reaches the world. God is the power behind the spreading power of the kingdom.

13:38 The good seed is the children of the kingdom, but the weeds are the children of the evil one (τὸ δὲ καλὸν σπέρμα οὗτοί εἰσιν οἱ υἱοὶ τῆς βασιλείας· τὰ δὲ ζιζάνιά εἰσιν οἱ υἱοὶ τοῦ πονηροῦ). The antagonists are spelled out (adversative "but" [δέ]). The worldwide mission of proclaiming the gospel will produce a world in which the saints rub shoulders with sinners. "The children" (οἱ υἱοί) with a genitive is an idiom describing the chief characteristic of a group, so the battle is between the kingdom and the cosmic forces of evil for the souls of humankind, and some belong to God's kingdom and others to Satan.

13:39 And the enemy who sows them is the devil (ὁ δὲ ἐχθρὸς ὁ σπείρας αὐτά ἐστιν ὁ διάβολος). The two terms for the ruler of the cosmic powers, "evil one" and "devil," are interchangeable in Matthew (the first in 5:37; 6:13; 13:19; the second in 4:1, 5, 8, 11; 25:41). By interspersing the titles here, Christ wants hearers to know who the antagonist is. In this world the war between good and evil cannot be avoided, and there is no middle ground. One either belongs to the kingdom or the powers of evil, and the two forces exist side by side in this world.[4]

13:39 The harvest is the end of the age, and the harvesters are the angels[5] (ὁ δὲ θερισμὸς συντέλεια αἰῶνός ἐστιν, οἱ δὲ θερισταὶ ἄγγελοί εἰσιν). The image of a harvest, so important to ancient Mediterranean life, was a natural metaphor for the eschatological consummation (Isa 17:5; Jer 51:33; Joel 3:13; *4 Ezra* 4:30 – 32; Rev 14:14 – 20). Likewise, "the end of the age" was a common concept to describe the destruction of evil and the beginning of eternity (cf. Matt 13:40, 49; 24:3; 28:20; Heb 9:26). The picture of the angels as harvesters makes sense since angels are often associated with the eschaton (*1 En.* 46:5, 54:6, 63:1; Matt 16:27, 24:31, 25:31; Rev 14:15, 17 – 19).

13:40 So just as the weeds are gathered together and burned in the fire, so it will be at the end of the age (ὥσπερ οὖν συλλέγεται τὰ ζιζάνια καὶ πυρὶ καίεται, οὕτως ἔσται ἐν τῇ συντελείᾳ τοῦ αἰῶνος). "Just as ... so" (ὥσπερ ... οὕτως) makes the comparison emphatic. Here begins the true thrust of the parable, and Jesus spells out the major point, in startling fashion ignoring the present sowing of the seed and centering only on the final harvest. The previous verses (vv. 37 – 39) formed a dictionary of sorts identifying the characters in

3. See Carson, "Matthew," 325, who lists the early church fathers, Augustine (who made this the official position of the church), Calvin and most of the Reformers, as well as recent redaction critics who see this as describing the Matthean church.

4. Jones, *Matthean Parables*, 341 – 42, provides an interesting possibility, that in the church as well the wicked must be allowed to be present in order to give time for those who are open to become believers (cf. also Keener, *Matthew*, 389). While this is possible, the true thrust of this is the world, not the church (see below), and so it is at best secondary.

5. Both "end of the age" (συντέλεια τοῦ αἰῶνος) and "angels" (ἄγγελοι) are anarthrous on the basis of Colwell's rule, in which a predicate nominative coming before the verb "to be" lacks the article in order to distinguish it from the subject.

the story, and now (vv. 40 – 43) Jesus weaves them together into a narrative, though he skips over the first half and centers only on the harvest itself. He also reverses the order of the parable, first telling the final harvest of the weeds (the majority of the story) and then the harvest of the wheat. Fiery judgment will be the lot of those who have chosen to follow "the evil one," and though they seem to flourish now, at "the end of the age" the truth will win out.

13:41 The Son of Man will send his angels, and they will gather out of his kingdom (ἀποστελεῖ ὁ υἱὸς τοῦ ἀνθρώπου τοὺς ἀγγέλους αὐτοῦ, καὶ συλλέξουσιν ἐκ τῆς βασιλείας αὐτοῦ). This is the glorified Danielic Son of Man who will have dominion over the world (Dan 7:13 – 14) and bring world history to a close.[6] Jesus joins Yahweh as Judge at the final judgment seat. The imagery of the Son of Man sending his angels to gather people to the final harvest comes full circle in Matthew. In 24:30 – 31 he gathers the elect to himself, while here he gathers the sinners to final judgment. Then in 16:27 and 25:31 – 33 he gathers both the righteous and the wicked to the final accounting with God.[7]

The presence of angels at the end of history is common in Matthew (16:27; 24:30 – 31; 25:31 – 33) but also frequent in the rest of Scripture (Dan 7:10; 12:1; 1 Thess 4:16; Rev 14:15, 17 – 19). The fact that they are gathered from "his kingdom" has caused many again to surmise that Jesus is talking about the church,[8] but that is hardly the case since Jesus has already defined the "field" as the "world."[9] So this means that all over the world where the kingdom seed has been sown, people are gathered to final judgment.

13:41 ... everyone who causes sin and does evil (πάντα τὰ σκάνδαλα καὶ τοὺς ποιοῦντας τὴν ἀνομίαν). The angels gather (the neuter) "everything that causes sin" and (the masculine) "all who do evil." Most likely this means sinners and the evil that they do (present tense for repeated acts of sin).[10] σκάνδαλον is a major concept in Matthew. It means "those who cause others to fall away" and in 18:6 – 7 those who lead Christ's "little ones" astray. The verb form occurs thirteen times. In 5:29 – 30 it speaks of sins that cause one to fall away and must be cut out of one's life, and in 13:21 it describes the person with "no root," who falls away when persecution occurs. So Christ removes all evildoers and destroys their deeds that have led people into sin and caused them to fall away from God.

Several believe this alludes to Zeph 1:3 (*hammakšēlôt ʾet-hārᵉšāʿîm*, "the idols that cause the wicked to stumble"),[11] a passage on the day of the Lord when God will sweep away all that causes sin from the face of the earth. The sinners are described here as "evil" or "lawless" (ἀνομίαν), i.e., those who have no regard for God's laws and freely transgress them. As Kingsbury points out, it is the antithesis of "righteousness" in the sense that it suggests moral chaos and offenses against the will of God.[12]

13:42 Then they will cast them into the fiery[13] furnace, where there will be weeping and

6. Luz, *Matthew 8 – 20*, 268, says, "In Matthew the Son of Man is the Lord of judgment who accompanies the church on its entire way through lowliness, suffering, and resurrection."

7. See Hagner, *Matthew 1 – 13*, 393 – 94.

8. E.g., Bornkamm, Barth, and Held, *Tradition and Interpretation*, 44; Hill, *Matthew*, 237.

9. See Schweizer, *Matthew*, 311; Schnackenburg, *Matthew*, 133.

10. See Kingsbury, *Parables*, 102, for the argument that this should designate people rather than things. Blomberg, *Matthew*, 223, argues correctly that these are not two categories but one.

11. Hill, *Matthew*, 236 – 37; Carson, "Matthew," 326; Davies and Allison, *Matthew*, 2:430

12. Kingsbury, *Parables*, 104 – 5.

13. "Of fire" (τοῦ πυρός) is an adjectival genitive.

grinding of teeth (καὶ βαλοῦσιν αὐτοὺς εἰς τὴν κάμινον τοῦ πυρός· ἐκεῖ ἔσται ὁ κλαυθμὸς καὶ ὁ βρυγμὸς τῶν ὀδόντων). This may allude to Dan 3:6, where those who refused to worship Nebuchadnezzar were told they would be "thrown into a blazing furnace." If so, this would be the reverse of that incident, for instead of the righteous being wrongly cast in, the wicked will be justly cast into fiery punishment.

Matthew uses two metaphors for eternal punishment: utter darkness with weeping and grinding of teeth (8:12; 22:13; 24:51; 25:30) and the fires of Gehenna (5:22, 29, 30; 10:28; 18:9; 23:15, 33; cf. *4 Ezra* 7:36). The two are combined here and in 13:50. "Weeping" notes the sorrow of those being punished, and "grinding of teeth" (objective genitive) could refer to the torment they will suffer (Luz), utter despair (McNeile), or intense anger (Davies and Allison). All could well be connoted in this image, though terrible pain is the most likely in light of the imagery of the fiery furnace.

13:43 Then the righteous will shine like the sun in the kingdom of their Father (τότε οἱ δίκαιοι ἐκλάμψουσιν ὡς ὁ ἥλιος ἐν τῇ βασιλείᾳ τοῦ πατρὸς αὐτῶν). For Matthew, the "righteous" are those who live their lives according to God's will (see on 3:15; 5:6). The description of them "shining like the sun" is similar to 17:2, where Jesus is transfigured and "his face shone like the sun." So the saints will share Christ's glory in eternity.

There is also an allusion to Dan 12:3, "Those who are wise will shine like the brightness of the heavens, and those who lead many to righteousness, like the stars for ever and ever." In that final chapter, Daniel writes of the eschaton and God's children who are delivered to eternal bliss. Some see a difference between "the kingdom of the Son of Man" (v. 41) and "the kingdom of their Father" (here),[14] but that is unlikely here. Throughout the NT the Father and the Son share the reigns of authority. This phrase "the Father's kingdom" is found only here and in 26:29 (though it is found in *Gospel of Thomas* 57, 76, etc.). The emphasis here is probably on the relationship between God and his children in eternity. We will share the glory and splendor of God as his children.

13:43 Whoever has ears, let them listen! (ὁ ἔχων ὦτα ἀκουέτω). As in 11:15; 13:9, the charge to listen carefully shows the importance of Jesus' teaching in this section. Those who ignore these truths do so at their own peril!

Theology in Application

The parable of the weeds has several implications and a rich theological heritage. The context is critical. This parable is part of the seven parables of conflict in ch. 13 and with the others is interpreting the kingdom reality behind the unbelief and rejection in chs. 11 – 12. As such it is portraying the true spiritual reality of the unbelieving Jews of those chapters but at the same time expanding the horizon to the world of humankind as a whole, Gentile as well as Jew.

14. Luz, *Matthew 8 – 20*, 270, takes the first to be the kingdom now and the second to be the kingdom in eternity, when the Son hands over dominion to the Father (1 Cor 15:24 – 28).

15. Davies and Allison, *Matthew*, 2:431.

1. Living as Part of, yet Apart from, the World

One of the major points of the parable is that wheat and weeds must live together. Both inside and outside the local church, it is not always easy to tell who is a believer and who is not. Moreover, Christians must shine their light within the darkness of the world and must never be cloistered by themselves. This does not mean that communities or conclaves of believers should not exist. But when they do, they should open themselves up to nonbelievers. So the present situation is one of mutual coexistence between the children of light and the children of darkness.

2. Evil to Flourish until the Eschaton

Christians should not be surprised when proabortion and progay laws are established. After all, we are living in a fallen world, and throughout history evil seems to prosper. It is right to fight such laws but wrong to expect to turn America or any nation into a purely Christian nation (cf. Rev 22:11). Jesus himself said the majority would take the broad path and only a few the narrow path to salvation. In the parable of the soils only one of the four was fruit-bearing.

3. Satan at Work in This World

This is the age of cosmic conflict, and the enemy in the parable is the devil, while the weeds are the "children of the evil one." As Davies and Allison say, "human failure is part of a wider problem, namely, the cosmic struggle between God and Satan."[15] Too many Christians in the First World are hardly aware of the battle and live as if there is no demonic presence around. This is a serious mistake, for we are up against "a roaring lion looking for someone to devour" (1 Pet 5:8).

4. Evil to be Destroyed Only at the End of the Age

We brought sin into this world (Rom 5:12), and God will allow it to remain until this age is finished. The "messianic woes" (Col 1:24; 1 Pet 4; Rev 6:9 – 11) tell us that God has set a certain amount of suffering and a certain number of martyrs, and then he will remove evil once and for all. Until that time, the children of the kingdom and the children of the evil one will exist side by side, and indeed in the church it is difficult to distinguish true from false believers. Some will enter eternity with little to show for their life on earth (1 Cor 3:15), and others will be told, "I never knew you; depart from me" (Matt 7:23). The one thing we can be certain of is the absolute justice of God's every decision (Rev 15:3; 16:5 – 7; 19:1 – 2) and the certainty of these final events that will end the reign of evil and death on earth.

CHAPTER 60

Matthew 13:44 – 53

Literary Context

The Parable Discourse has interpreted the meaning of the rejection of Jesus in chs. 11 – 12 by centering on conflict, the presence of evil in the world, and the certain growth and triumph of the kingdom. The next two parables (13:44, 45 – 46) center on the supreme value of the kingdom, worth giving up everything to obtain. As such they build on the parables of the mustard seed and leaven; in light of the greatness of the kingdom, one should do anything needed to obtain it.

The dragnet parable sums up the message and repeats that of the weeds — judgment day is coming. One should embrace the kingdom not only because of its supreme worth but also because the only alternative is terrible beyond belief. In light of this, the final parable (v. 52) looks at the disciples as scribes trained to both understand and transmit these new kingdom truths. Crossan in his work on these parables[1] sees them as a key to Jesus' kingdom parables, arguing that they in turn reveal the advent of the kingdom, its reversal or undoing of the world's values, and the action of God in his new kingdom with the new possibilities this presents.

- **IV. Preaching and Teaching in the Midst of Opposition (11:2 – 13:53)**
  - **B. Third Discourse: Kingdom Parables (13:1 – 53)**
    - 2. Parables of the Kingdom Growing (13:24 – 43)
    - ➦ **3. Final Parables for the Disciples (13:44 – 52)**
      - **a. The Hidden Treasure (13:44)**
      - **b. The Costly Pearl (13:45 – 46)**
      - **c. The Dragnet (13:47 – 50)**
      - **d. The Scribe Trained for the Kingdom (13:51 – 52)**
    - **4. Conclusion (13:53)**

1. John Dominic Crossan, *Finding Is the First Act: Trove Folktales and Jesus' Treasure Parable* (Philadelphia: Fortress, 1979), 26 – 36, as noted in Davies and Allison, *Matthew*, 2:437 – 38.

Main Idea

Several ideas are intertwined in this collection of parables. (1) The kingdom has overwhelming value,[2] worth everything a person has (vv. 44 – 46). (2) Certain judgment is reserved for those who reject the kingdom (vv. 47 – 50). (3) Finally, the disciples have attained an understanding that makes them responsible to teach others the new truths of the kingdom as well as the old truths of the Torah (vv. 51 – 52).

Translation

(See next page.)

Structure and Literary Form

All this material is peculiar to Matthew and comes from his special source. The three parables all begin the same way, "The kingdom of heaven is like" followed by the dative.[3] The first two have the same basic structure, beginning with the discovery of a precious find, the sale of everything one has, and the purchase of the treasured thing. The third parable is similar to the parable of the weeds, with the casting of the dragnet, the gathering of good and bad fish, the separation and throwing away of the bad, and then the interpretation of the parable, detailing the final judgment and punishment awaiting the wicked. Finally, the disciples acknowledge their understanding of the parables and are told by Jesus in effect that they are scribes of the kingdom who add the new kingdom truths to the old teaching of Torah.

Exegetical Outline

➦ **I. Two Parables on the Value of the Kingdom (13:44 – 46)**
- A. Parable of the hidden treasure (v. 44)
  - 1. Discovering the hidden treasure (v. 44a)
  - 2. Selling everything and purchasing the field (v. 44b)
- B. Parable of the costly pearl (vv. 45 – 46)
  - 1. Discovering the valuable pearl (vv. 45 – 46a)
  - 2. Selling everything and purchasing the pearl (v. 46b)

II. Parable on Judgment — the Dragnet (13:47 – 50)
- A. The parable told (vv. 47 – 48)
  - 1. Fish caught in the net (v. 47)

2. Among others, Roger Winterhalter and George W. Fisk, *Jesus' Parables: Finding Our God Within* (New York: Paulist, 1993), 13, posits that the treasureis the indwelling Christ, but the centrality of the kingdom throughout ch. 13 makes this unlikely.

3. For the meaning of this formula, see on 13:24.

Matthew 13:44-53

44a Comparison *[A] "The kingdom of heaven is like a treasure hidden in a field,*
b *[B] which a man found and hid again.*
c *[C] Out of joy he went and sold all he had and then*
d *[D] bought that field.*

45a Comparison *[A] Once more, the kingdom of heaven is like a merchant*
looking for beautiful pearls.

46a *[B] When he found a pearl of great value,*
b *[C] he went and sold everything he had and*
c *[D] purchased it.*

47a Comparison *Once more, the kingdom of heaven is like a dragnet*
that was thrown into the sea and
gathered every kind of fish.

48a *When the net was full,*
b *they brought it onto the shore and sat down.*
c *Then they separated the good fish into baskets and*
d *threw away the bad ones.*

49a Identification of 47a-48d *So it will be at the end of the age.*
b *The angels will come and separate the wicked*
from the righteous.
50a *Then they will cast them into the fiery furnace,*
b *where there will be weeping and gnashing of teeth.*

51a Question *Have you understood all these things?"*
b Answer **They replied,**
c *"Yes."*
52a Comparison **Jesus responded,**
b *"For this reason every teacher of the law*
who becomes trained as a disciple in the kingdom of heaven
c *is like a master of a household*
d *who brings out of his storehouse things*
new and old."

53a Conclusion And it happened that
when Jesus had finished these parables,
b **he moved on from there.**

2. Bad fish thrown away (v. 48)
B. The parable interpreted (vv. 49 – 50)
1. Angels separate the wicked from the righteous (v. 49)
2. The wicked thrown into the fiery furnace (v. 50)

III. The End: Disciples as Scribes (13:51 – 52)
A. The disciples understand (v. 51)
B. Jesus calls them scribes (v. 52)
1. Trained in the kingdom (v. 52a)
2. Bringing forth treasures new and old (v. 52b)

IV. Conclusion (13:53)

Explanation of the Text

13:44 The kingdom of heaven is like a treasure hidden in a field (Ὁμοία ἐστὶν ἡ βασιλεία τῶν οὐρανῶν θησαυρῷ κεκρυμμένῳ ἐν τῷ ἀγρῷ). As with the parables of the mustard seed and yeast, the kingdom is seen as enigmatic and "hidden" from the world. It is disputed whether there should be any emphasis on hiddenness, and several commentators fail to discern any such nuance (e.g., Luz, Beare, Blomberg, Morris). Still, the enigmatic, hidden nature of the kingdom is a theme in this chapter (see 13:35), so it should be seen here as well.

At the same time, it is part of the background to the parable. In a society that had no banks or safety-deposit boxes, all one could do with valuables was hide them underground. Archaeologists have often found jars of gold coins or even precious jewels and pearls buried in a field. This parable would be such a case, as the original owners were either killed on a journey or died suddenly and the treasure remained hidden. It is a story that captures the imagination in every culture and time, for buried treasure is a universal symbol of personal fortune.

The major discussion centers on the legality of a person finding such a treasure and keeping it for himself. Should the treasure belong to the owner of the field or to the tenant farmer who has discovered it while tending the field?[4] Luz notes similar trials, where King Kazia married the son of the finder to the daughter of the seller, and Apollonius of Tyana determined which was the better person and gave the treasure to that one. Both in Roman and Jewish law the treasure would belong to the one who buys the field, so long as the original owner was not aware of the hidden treasure.[5] At the same time, as Derrett shows, if a laborer "lifted" the treasure out of the ground, it would belong to the owner.[6] Still, this is not a central point of the story, and Jesus does not intend such questions. Neither legal nor moral issues are part of the story.

4. Since there are so many agricultural parables in the context, this is the more likely scenario. However, Jesus does not stipulate either figure in the story, so this should not overly constrain us.

5. Luz, *Matthew 8 – 20*, 276 – 77; Witherington, *Matthew*, 272. For the many stories in antiquity on finding treasure, see Crossan, *Finding*, 11 – 71. *Gospel of Thomas* 109 contains a similar parable but has the treasure used for money-lending in a section against such practices (108 – 10). The Matthean version is obviously the more original; *Thomas* 109 adapts the parable to a different and later issue.

6. J. D. M. Derrett, *Law in the New Testament* (London: Dartman, Longman, & Todd, 1970), 1 – 16.

13:44 ... which a man found[7] and hid again. Out of joy he went and sold all he had and then bought that field (ὃν εὑρὼν ἄνθρωπος ἔκρυψεν, καὶ ἀπὸ τῆς χαρᾶς αὐτοῦ ὑπάγει καὶ πωλεῖ πάντα ὅσα ἔχει καὶ ἀγοράζει τὸν ἀγρὸν ἐκεῖνον). The tenant farmer put the treasure back in the ground because he knew that the owner would keep it for himself. Morris points out that the owner could have said the man was his agent and therefore take the treasure for himself. The only way the farmer could ensure that it would be his was to purchase the field for himself. However, being poor, it took everything he owned to afford it. Still, he sold all his possessions "out of joy" (the odds of such a find were as infinitesimal then as now) because he knew it would be more than worth it.

The point is obviously the absolute value of the kingdom, worth surrendering everything to attain.[8] No other aspect is highlighted in this short parable, so clearly this is a call for radical discipleship (and especially of financial sacrifices needed)[9] in light of the overwhelming value of the kingdom. Only a few know its worth, and they should surrender everything to obtain it.

13:45 Once more, the kingdom of heaven is like a merchant looking for beautiful pearls (Πάλιν ὁμοία ἐστὶν ἡ βασιλεία τῶν οὐρανῶν ἀνθρώπῳ ἐμπόρῳ ζητοῦντι καλοὺς μαργαρίτας). The use of "once more" (πάλιν) shows that this parable repeats the message of the previous one. This time the central figure is a jewel merchant (the opposite of the poor peasant in the previous story) looking for a first-class pearl.[10] The ἔμποροι (only in Rev 18:3, 11, 15, 23 elsewhere in the NT; for this use of ἄνθρωπος see v. 28) were wholesale dealers who traveled the world selling huge quantities of merchandise (*EDNT*, 1:446). Many believe they, even more than the military, conquered the world for Rome.

Davies and Allison take "looking" (ζητοῦντι, an adjectival participle) to be a key term in the story—the kingdom is not open to all but only to those who seek it (Matt 6:33).[11] However, this should not be overstressed, for the treasure parable has the person accidentally "finding," while this one has a merchant deliberately "seeking." In other words, they build on each other, and the key is not so much the mode of discovery as it is the total surrender that accompanies it.

13:46 When he found a pearl of great value, he went and sold everything he had and purchased it (εὑρὼν δὲ ἕνα πολύτιμον μαργαρίτην ἀπελθὼν πέπρακεν πάντα ὅσα εἶχεν καὶ ἠγόρασεν αὐτόν). Pearls were considered the most luxurious[12] of jewels and came from the Red Sea (common pearls), the Persian Gulf (the most expensive), and India. They were worth at times the equivalent of millions of dollars (so Jeremias). Note nothing is said about reselling it for profit. It could be this is simply assumed and omitted, but it is more likely that the omission has theological relevance.

Collectors throughout history have purchased a priceless heirloom or artwork simply for the

7. Another of the many circumstantial participles, see vv. 1, 11, 27, 31, 36.

8. Jones, *Matthean Parables*, 348, sees two features: the incredible value of the treasure and the enormous difficulty in attaining it, involving moral and ethical risk as all worldly goods and values are sacrificed.

9. See Blomberg, *Parables*, 280; Turner, "Matthew," 194.

10. The parallel in *Gospel of Thomas* 76 is capable of several interpretations but seems to differ in that a small-time merchant discovers a pearl among some goods. He shrewdly evaluates its worth as a business venture and uses financial acumen to make his purchase. See Jones, *Matthean Parables*, 352–53.

11. Davies and Allison, *Matthew*, 2:439.

12. πολύτιμος, often translated "of great price," occurs three times in the NT (Matt 13:46; John 12:3; 1 Pet 1:7) and means "very precious, valuable" (BAGD).

enjoyment of it with no thought of profit. The message is that the kingdom is priceless, and no sacrifice is too great for attaining it. It demands the surrender of all earthly value but is more than worth it. Beare points to Luke 14:33 ("those of you who do not give up everything you have cannot be my disciples") and concludes, "Anyone who counts the cost of discipleship has completely failed to grasp the greatness of the reward."[13]

13:47 Once more, the kingdom of heaven is like a dragnet that was thrown into the sea and gathered[14] every kind of fish (Πάλιν ὁμοία ἐστὶν ἡ βασιλεία τῶν οὐρανῶν σαγήνῃ βληθείσῃ εἰς τὴν θάλασσαν καὶ ἐκ παντὸς γένους συναγαγούσῃ). In 4:19 the disciples are called by Jesus and told, "I will make you to fish for people." It is obvious there and here that this embraces all of humanity ("every kind of fish") and thus refers to the universal mission of the church. Still, some interpret this of the church, with faithful and unfaithful members (the invisible and visible church).[15] However, this does not fit the imagery of harvest either here or in 13:24–30.

The dragnet[16] had floats (cork or a light wood) on top and weights underneath and was either put between two boats or anchored on shore and then drawn in a semi-circle by a boat. It would trap "every kind of" fish swimming near the surface, both those edible and those not.[17]

13:48 When the net was full, they brought it onto the shore and sat down. Then they separated the good fish into baskets and threw away the bad ones (ἣν ὅτε ἐπληρώθη ἀναβιβάσαντες ἐπὶ τὸν αἰγιαλὸν καὶ καθίσαντες συνέλεξαν τὰ καλὰ εἰς ἄγγη, τὰ δὲ σαπρὰ ἔξω ἔβαλον). This too was the common experience of fishermen. After they had pulled the net filled with fish onto shore, they weeded out the bad ones. These would already have died after being pulled from the seas, so they could only be thrown away. The basis of the separation of good from bad fish was probably ceremonial, i.e., clean and unclean (Lev 11:9–12, all without fins and scales, e.g., shellfish), but it could also apply to edible and inedible fish. Fishermen in the Sea of Galilee would separate at least twenty-four species of fish in the lake on the basis of both categories.[18]

It is common to picture the sitting down as symbolic of the Son of Man sitting on his *bēma* (judgment seat) in judgment (cf. Rom 14:10; 2 Cor 5:10),[19] which would fit the interpretation in vv. 49–50. "Outside" (ἔξω) is emphatic, picturing the loss of covenant privileges of those "outside" the kingdom (cf. 5:13; 10:14).

13:49 So it will be at the end of the age. The angels will come and separate the wicked from the righteous (οὕτως ἔσται ἐν τῇ συντελείᾳ τοῦ αἰῶνος· ἐξελεύσονται οἱ ἄγγελοι καὶ ἀφοριοῦσιν

13. Beare, *Matthew*, 315. Crossan, *Finding*, 93–98, sees an existential meaning here, that one must embrace not only the abandonment of worldly things but even of morals and indeed the paradox of abandoning even this parable of abandonment, i.e., accepting the negation that the kingdom brings to life. Carson, *Matthew*, 328–29, shows the weakness of this theory, saying it is "so anachronistic as to make a historian wince" and does not do justice to the parable in its context.

14. These two participles ("thrown" and "gathered") are adjectival.

15. This is similar to the debates over the parable of the weeds (see introduction to 13:24–30). For those who take this of the church, see Kingsbury, *Parables*, 118; Gundry, *Matthew*, 279; Hagner, *Matthew 1–13*, 399; Scott, *Parable*, 314. Contra Davies and Allison, *Matthew*, 2:440; Blomberg, *Matthew*, 224; Keener, *Matthew*, 393.

16. Luz, *Matthew 8–20*, 283, says the dragnet was 250–450 meters long and about two meters wide with a rope at each end.

17. The parallel in the *Gospel of Thomas* 8 is clearly secondary and concerns a fisherman catching a horde of small fish in his net along with one great fish. He threw all the small ones back and kept the large one, probably symbolic of Jesus' words as divine wisdom.

18. Keener, *Matthew*, 392.

19. So Luz, *Matthew 8–20*, 283.

τοὺς πονηροὺς ἐκ μέσου τῶν δικαίων). Unlike the parable of the weeds (13:24 – 30), the fate of the righteous is not spelled out, only that of the wicked. It is clear that the separation is not now in the present but at the eschaton or last judgment (see 13:39 on "end of the age").[20] The point is similar to v. 41, with the angels harvesting the world to separate the wheat from the weeds. Here the final judgment is again the focus, as the righteous are separated from the wicked. In Matthew the "righteous" are those who persevere in right living according to God's will (see on 5:6, 10, 20; 6:1, 33).

13:50 Then they will cast them into the fiery furnace, where there will be weeping and gnashing of teeth (καὶ βαλοῦσιν αὐτοὺς εἰς τὴν κάμινον τοῦ πυρός· ἐκεῖ ἔσται ὁ κλαυθμὸς καὶ ὁ βρυγμὸς τῶν ὀδόντων). This is a verbatim repetition of 13:42 (see that verse for details), which again describes the terrible fate of the wicked in eternal punishment. This is not about the present time but has relevance for the present. At this time we cannot separate the good fish from the bad. Our task is fishing for souls, and we must leave it up to God to separate the good from the bad at the final judgment. However, we must also warn the wicked of the future eternal punishment that awaits as a result of their evil deeds.

13:51 "Have you understood all these things?" They replied, "Yes" (Συνήκατε ταῦτα πάντα; λέγουσιν αὐτῷ, Ναί). Jesus has already said that he has given them "knowledge of the mysteries of the kingdom" (13:11), that they will be given even more (13:12a), and that they have an "abundance" of the kingdom truths (13:12b). The result will be divine blessings in what they see and hear (13:16), an abundance that even the prophets themselves longed for (13:17). As a result they will hear the Word and "understand" it (13:23a), producing an ever-increasing crop of fruitfulness (13:23b).

With this in mind, this is probably not a passage detailing the hubris of the disciples in thinking they understand when they do not. This does not mean they understood fully; in fact, in 15:16 they are reproved for being so dull. But they are beginning to perceive the reality of what Jesus has been teaching them. "All these things" (ταῦτα πάντα) refers back to v. 34, with Jesus speaking "all these things" in parables, followed in v. 36 with the disciples asking Jesus to explain the parable of the weeds to them. So the thrust here is that the disciples basically caught what Jesus was saying and began to assimilate the reality of the kingdom.

13:52 Jesus responded, "For this reason every teacher of the law who becomes trained as a disciple in the kingdom of heaven" (ὁ δὲ εἶπεν αὐτοῖς, Διὰ τοῦτο πᾶς γραμματεὺς μαθητευθεὶς τῇ βασιλείᾳ τῶν οὐρανῶν). This "parable"[21] concludes the parable chapter, since v. 53 contains the formula ("when Jesus had finished ...") that concludes every discourse unit (7:28; 11:1; 19:1; 26:1). "For this reason" (διὰ τοῦτο) draws a conclusion from the progress of understanding seen in 13:11 – 12, 16 – 17, 23, and concluding in 13:51, where the disciples claim to have understanding. Thus it sums up the whole chapter and not just this section. Jesus seemingly accepts this (he will later demur in 14:31; 15:16; 16:9) and labels the apostolic band in their newfound understanding of the new Torah of the kingdom (see on 5:17 – 20) a group of Christian scribes ("teacher[s] of the law").

20. It is common to take vv. 49 – 50 as a later redaction on the grounds that it is artificial and builds only on v. 48b (so Hill, *Matthew*, 238 – 39; Jones, *Matthean Parables*, 357), but the inconsistencies can actually support authenticity, since later redaction would try to clear them up (see Grundmann, *Matthäus*, 355 – 56; Carson, "Matthew," 330; Blomberg, *Parables*, 201 – 2).

21. It is almost universally believed that this verse is a Matthean construction, and the only question for most is whether it is a Matthean invention (Hill, Gnilka, Gundry,

As stated in 5:20, a scribe was both an official interpreter of Torah and a teacher of it. Matthew as a former tax collector was a scribe, and so he is building on his own memories here.

Orton brings out that scribes also had an eschatological function in apocalyptic writings (e.g., Ezra as scribe in *4 Ezra*) interpreting the mysteries of divine revelation and in prophetic inspiration (cf. 13:11).[22] Following Freyne, he believes the disciples in Matthew (as in Mark) should be seen in light of *maśkîlîm* of Dan 11–12, whose role was to "understand" in the last days (12:10) and had a mission to cause many to understand (12:3).[23] So this means the disciples are now the official interpreters of the new laws of the kingdom, and Jesus has prepared them for that role.[24]

Since Matthew writes "every teacher of the law" (πᾶς γραμματεύς), it is commonly believed that he is describing his own role as well.[25] This does not mean the disciples are seen as replacing the Jewish teachers of law but more that they have the same function in the new "kingdom of heaven" Jesus has established. Through the parables and teaching of the mysteries (13:11), the apostolic band has been "discipled" or "trained" (μαθητευθείς)[26] and so can both understand the meaning of the mysteries and teach others the new kingdom laws.

Here we have another passage that demonstrates the centrality of the teaching office in the early church. As Orton says, "They stand in direct contrast to the so-called 'wise and understanding' (11.25) from whom 'these things' (ταῦτα, cf. πάντα, v. 27) have been 'hidden' (cf. 13:35) and stand in the apocalyptic tradition as those—typically *scribes*—to whom the divine mysteries are revealed."[27]

13:52 "... is like a master of a household who brings out of his storehouse things new and old" (ὅμοιός ἐστιν ἀνθρώπῳ οἰκοδεσπότῃ ὅστις ἐκβάλλει ἐκ τοῦ θησαυροῦ αὐτοῦ καινὰ καὶ παλαιά). The parable proper likens the disciples as kingdom scribes to a homeowner with a storeroom (lit., "treasure"). The οἰκοδεσπότης ("homeowner") is featured often in Matthean parables and can refer to a landowner (13:27; 20:1, 11) as well as "master of a household" (10:25; 21:33; 24:43; and here). The aspect of "treasure" in θησαυρός comes to the fore when we think of God's truths as a treasure-house of wisdom.

The picture, of course, is that of the householder going into his storehouse on a daily basis and carrying out food, clothes, and other necessities as they are needed. In the parable the "treasured" storehouse relates to the heart/mind (12:34b–35, "Good people bring [as there, ἐκβάλλει here is a strong verb connoting a forceful "casting out" of the good treasure] good things out of the good stored up in them").

Davies and Allison) or stems from a source he has reworked (Manson, Held, Orton, Jones, Luz, Hagner). There is no question that a great amount of Matthean language is utilized—*for this reason, scribe, become a disciple, kingdom of heaven, householder, treasure, brings out* (see statistics in Orton, *The Understanding Scribe*, 230–31). However, there is too little reason for this to be a *de novo* saying and every reason for supposing that the source is Jesus himself (Carson, Blomberg).

22. Orton, *The Understanding Scribe*, 65–75.

23. Ibid, 148–51; Sean Freyne, "The Disciples in Mark and the Maskilim in Daniel," *JSNT* 16 (1983): 7–23.

24. Contra the many who see these as a class of Christian scribes in Matthew's community (so Hill, Strecker, Davies and Allison). There is no evidence of such a group in the early church. Others (e.g., Origen, McNeile) have thought these to be scribes who were converted and became Jesus' disciples, but that is to miss the metaphor and take it too literally.

25. France, *Matthew* (TNTC), 230.

26. Some like McNeile, *Matthew*, 205, see the two possibilities as competing and argue that the verb is better translated "instructed in the kingdom" than "become a disciple." Yet the two flow together both linguistically and theologically, for disciples are naturally trained in the new kingdom reality. In other words, the dative connotes they are both disciples *of* the kingdom (Carson) and are instructed *in* the kingdom (Hagner).

27. Orton, *The Understanding Scribe*, 144.

Yet what are the "things new and old," and is there any emphasis in the order? First, these are not "the new in place of the old" (= replacement, so Marcion et al.); nor are they the Jesus tradition (the old) given new meaning in new situations (Schlatter, Schnackenburg). Rather, this refers to the new reality of Jesus fulfilling that of the old covenant reality.

The items that come out of the storehouse, which God has placed in the disciples, relate to the kingdom truths that are central throughout ch. 13. This is why the "new" is first. The new "mysteries" must first be understood by the disciples (and the later church) and then transmitted to the believing community. In other words, the disciples will understand and teach both the truths of the old covenant (cf. 5:17 – 20) and the new covenant teachings of Jesus.

13:53 And it happened that when Jesus had finished these parables, he moved on from there (Καὶ ἐγένετο ὅτε ἐτέλεσεν ὁ Ἰησοῦς τὰς παραβολὰς ταύτας, μετῆρεν ἐκεῖθεν). Scholars differ in making these transition verses (7:28; 11:1; 13:53; 19:1; 26:1) the closing verse of the Parable Discourse or the first verse of the following narrative. However, since each such verse effectively closes the discourse unit, I prefer to link them with that section (see on 7:28; 11:1). This verse also follows the others in having Jesus move on to a new ministry territory after finishing his discourse (8:1, he descends to the valley; 11:1, he moves on to other towns and preaches; cf. 19:1; 26:6). Here Jesus leaves the area around Capernaum and returns to his hometown of Nazareth, about fifteen miles west of the southern tip of the lake.

Theology in Application

This concluding section of the parable chapter sums up many of the issues. The central focus, of course, is the arrival of the kingdom and its implications for all humanity, but especially for the children of the kingdom. As the fulfillment of OT expectations and God's great gift to humanity, it demands first every person's decision and then our all-consuming passion.

1. God's Kingdom Veiled Yet Great

This is a paraenetic section. The kingdom is hidden in this world, known only to those who belong to it. Yet it is the most precious, valuable reality this world has. Therefore, the two parables of 13:44 – 46 present a four-stage scenario: seek, discover, surrender, and purchase. In this sense these parables sum up not just ch. 13 but the entire gospel thus far. Christ has brought with him the consummated kingdom that the OT was waiting for, but neither the world as a whole nor the Jewish people have recognized or accepted it. Yet it is the fulfilled promise of God and the sum of everything humankind has wanted. In light of this, there is only one possible reaction, the radical surrender of one's whole life in order to have it. It is the greatest prize this world will ever see, but to have it one must throw off all worldly values.

2. God and the Future

God knows where everyone stands vis-à-vis Christ, and terrible judgment awaits those who reject him and do evil. The parable of the dragnet (vv. 47 – 50) is similar to that of the weeds (vv. 36 – 43) and has an identical ending (v. 50 = v. 42), emphasizing the horror of turning away from Christ and God's goodness. In this world, even in the church, the good and the bad live side by side, and we cannot finally separate them. But at the eschaton, God will do so unerringly, and justice will prevail.

This is the final answer to the age-old question of why the wicked flourish while the righteous so often have nothing. That scenario is only true in this world. But in the final kingdom eschatological separation and judgment will occur, and those who are playing games with God as well as those who flaunt their evil will pay eternal consequences.

3. Kingdom Scribes

True disciples are kingdom scribes who both understand the revealed mysteries and teach them in the church. Matthew, unlike Mark, has the disciples regularly coming to understanding (cf. Matt 14:28 – 33 vs. Mark 6:52; Matt 16:12 vs. Mark 8:21), teaching that the presence of Christ makes the difference.[28] This is the high point of that theological emphasis. With the understanding Jesus gave them, they would become the scribes of the church: first comprehending the eschatological mysteries of the newly revealed kingdom and then being sent on a mission to teach other believers these truths.

Moreover, they would preach this both in terms of the old covenant reality (teaching the OT) and the new Torah that Messiah Jesus brought (the new covenant reality). It is important to realize this was not a message only for the disciples or for professional teachers in the church but for the church as a whole. We are all commissioned here to share these truths with others. Throughout Matthew the disciples are corporately identified not just with the future clergy but with the church as a whole. These teachings are meant for us all! Each of us in our own way must pass on the traditions of the church.

28. This is not contradictory but a redactional emphasis. Mark teaches the same thing but through the "little people" (i.e., the woman with the hemorrhage, the Syrophoenician woman, the father of the demon-possessed child, blind Bartimaeus) and the tension between Mark 16:7 and 16:8 (the disciples would find the faith to overcome their failure only when they met the Risen Lord in Galilee).

CHAPTER 61

Matthew 13:54 – 58

Introduction to Growing Withdrawal and Discipleship (Matthew 13:54 – 18:35)

This section follows the Matthean format of narrative (Jesus' deeds, 13:54 – 17:27) and discourse (Jesus' words, 18:1 – 18:35). The difficult part is determining the outline of the narrative section. Is it ongoing (so Carson) or does it consist of two parts, a movement upward to the confession of Peter at Caesarea Philippi (13:54 – 16:20) and then downward toward the cross via the passion predictions (16:21 – 17:27, so Luz)? It depends on how one looks at it. The events at Caesarea (16:13 – 28) are a unity and belong together, yet at the same time the confession is a turning point in all three Synoptic Gospels, and the passion predictions dominate the second half of the narrative. Thus I will adopt the twofold outline.[1]

Moreover, Matthew largely follows Mark here, with only a few Matthean additions (Peter walking on the water, 14:28 – 33; the blessings on Simon, 16:17 – 20; the temple tax, 17:24 – 27) and omissions (the hardening of the disciple's hearts, Mark 6:52, 8:17; the healing of the deaf-mute and blind man, Mark 7:32 – 36, 8:22 – 26; the effects of the demons on the epileptic child, Mark 9:18, 20, 22, 26). Thus the movement of the action is the same in Matthew as in Mark, upward to the confession[2] and downward toward the cross, with discipleship gradually replacing ministry to the multitudes. This is marked by the two rejection stories that begin the section in 13:54 – 14:12, continue in the debate over the cleansing rituals in 15:1 – 20 and in the

1. Here I disagree with Luz, *Matthew 8 – 20*, who divides 13:53 – 16:20 into three parts (13:53 – 14:33; 14:34 – 15:39; 16:1 – 20) based on three "withdrawals from the leaders of Israel" in 13:53; 14:34; 15:39. Yet it is difficult to call these "withdrawals" because they are part of general geographical movement rather than rejection of the leaders. In fact, in 13:53 – 54 Jesus moves toward his hometown (and rejection by them) rather than away from the leaders. See also Jerome Murphy-O'Connor, "The Structure of Matthew XIV-XVII," *RB* 82 (1975): 360 – 84; and D. W. Gooding, "Structur littéraire de Matthieu, XIII, 53 a XVIII, 35," *RB* 85 (1978): 227 – 52.

2. Nolland, *Matthew*, 578 – 79, sees a different structure. While acknowledging that 13:54 – 58 is both a conclusion to the previous and an introduction to 14:1 – 16:20, he sees a "slightly rough chiasm" with 14:1 – 2 (3 – 12 appended) = 16:13 – 20 (prefaced with 1 – 12) — Herod's and Peter's opinions; 14:13 – 21 = 15:29 – 39 — the feeding miracles; 14:34 – 36 = 15:21 – 28 — healings; and 15:1 – 20 in the center — Jesus and tradition. Several of the correspondences are present, but it is difficult to see why the debate over tradition is the center of the section. I prefer to see a linear movement contrasting opposition with developing discipleship, culminating in Peter's confession.

demand for a sign in 16:1 – 12, and are finalized in the temple tax. Thus the rejection of Jesus by the nation is a counterpoint to his centering on his disciples.

Literary Context

This sums up several themes from chs. 11 – 13, primarily the unbelief and rejection of Jesus by the Jewish people. The parable section has contrasted the greatness of the kingdom with the unbelievers who have done evil and will face judgment. These themes coalesce here in the first two stories (13:54 – 14:12), and in the rest of the section rejection by the Jewish people will intersperse with pericopae where Jesus disciples the Twelve.

IV. Preaching and Teaching in the Midst of Opposition (11:2 – 13:53)

V. Rejection, Suffering, and Glory (13:54 – 18:35)

A. Jesus' Deeds: Rejection, Discipleship, and Glory (13:54 – 17:27)

1. Rejection and Discipleship (13:54 – 16:20)

➦ **a. Teaching and Rejection at Nazareth (13:54 – 58)**

Main Idea

The major motif here, of course, is unbelief and rejection, and this builds on 10:21, 35 – 36 in narrowing the rejection to "members of [one's] family" (and hometown). The message is that like Christ (10:24 – 25), a follower of him must expect opposition from those closest.

Translation

(See next page.)

Structure and Literary Form

In one sense this is a pronouncement story leading to the "prophet without honor" saying of v. 57, but on the whole it is a controversy story showing the antagonism of Jesus' own hometown.[3] It is organized in chiastic fashion:[4]

3. It is difficult to know if this is the same event as Luke 4:16 – 31, Jesus' inaugural address. It too featured the rejection of the townspeople and the saying on the rejection of a prophet but added the prophetic speech from Isa 61:1 – 2 and the people's determination to kill Jesus. Most evangelical scholars (e.g., Blomberg, Hagner, Keener — Carson and Morris are uncertain) conclude these two incidents are built on the same story.

4. See Fraans van Segbroek, "Jésus rejeté par sa patrie

Matthew 13:54-58

54a	Setting (A)	**He came into his hometown** and
b	Action	**began teaching them in their synagogue.**
c	Result/Reaction	**As a result, the people were amazed and said,**
d	Question #1 (B)	*"Where did he get such wisdom and miraculous powers?*
55a	Question #2 (C)	*Isn't he the carpenter's son?*
b	Question #3 (D)	*Isn't his mother Mary and his brothers*
		James and
		Joseph and
		Simon and
		Judas?
56a	Question #4 (C')	*Aren't all of his sisters with us?*
b	Question #5 (B')	*So where did this man get all these things?"*
57a	Result	And **they were scandalized by him.**
b	Response #1	**So Jesus said to them,**
c	Proverb	*"Nowhere is a prophet without honor*
		except in his own hometown and among his family."
58a	Response #2 (A')/ Result	And **he did not do many miracles there because of their unbelief.**

A Jesus' arrival at Nazareth (v. 54a)

B "Where" (πόθεν) saying on the origin of Jesus' wisdom and deeds (v. 54b)

C "Not" (οὐχ) saying about Jesus (v. 55a)

C' "Not" (οὐχ/οὐχί) sayings about Jesus' family (vv. 55b – 56a)

B' "Where" (πόθεν) saying on the origin of Jesus' teaching and deeds (v. 56b)

A' Jesus' rejection at Nazareth (vv. 57 – 58)

At the center of the arrangement lie the questions about his family, and they are also mentioned in Jesus' climactic statement that even a prophet's family refuse him honor.

Exegetical Outline

➡ **I. Jesus' Return to Nazareth (13:54b)**

A. His purpose: to teach

B. Their reaction: astonishment

II. The Response of the People (13:54c – 57a)

A. Their questions (vv. 54c – 56)

(Matt 13, 54 – 58,)" *Bib* 448 (1968): 167 – 98; Davies and Allison, *Matthew*, 2:451.

1. Two "where" questions on the source of his wisdom and deeds
2. Three "is not" questions regarding his family

B. Result — scandalized (v. 57a)

III. The Response of Jesus (13:57b – 58)

A. In word — a prophet without honor (v. 57b)

B. In deed — few miracles (v. 58)

Explanation of the Text

13:54 He came into his hometown and began teaching them in their synagogue (καὶ ἐλθὼν εἰς τὴν πατρίδα αὐτοῦ ἐδίδασκεν αὐτοὺς ἐν τῇ συναγωγῇ αὐτῶν). Jesus' "hometown" (πατρίς) is certainly Nazareth, though only Luke 4:16 names it. As was Jesus' usual practice (4:23; 9:35; 12:9), he begins to teach in the local synagogue, undoubtedly the very one in which he worshiped growing up. What is certainly a beautiful occasion for Jesus (local boy makes good and returns home to share his learning) quickly turns sour. The imperfect ἐδίδασκεν could refer to an ongoing practice but is probably ingressive, "began teaching" on this occasion (as in v. 8).

13:54 As a result, the people were amazed and said, "Where did he get such wisdom and miraculous powers?" (ὥστε ἐκπλήσσεσθαι αὐτοὺς καὶ λέγειν, Πόθεν τούτῳ ἡ σοφία αὕτη καὶ αἱ δυνάμεις;). "As a result" (ὥστε) shows that Jesus' teaching in Nazareth led to these questions. The crowds and even the leaders often show wonder (7:28; 8:27; 9:33; 15:31; 22:22, 33; 27:14); and though some scholars believe this is a skeptical shock (so Luz), there is no reason to suppose this was the immediate reaction, though it quickly turns negative. They question both his teaching ("wisdom" [ἡ σοφία]) and his miraculous deeds (αἱ δυνάμεις).

Matthew has conflated three separate ideas in Mark 6:2b — the origin of his power and the meaning of both his wisdom and miracles. Obviously, the people of Nazareth wonder if they are good or evil, whether they stem from God or demonic powers. They cannot believe that "this one" (τούτῳ) whom they knew as a simple village citizen has such power. Jesus received no rabbinic training, and it was inconceivable that a mere commoner like themselves could say and do such things.

13:55 "Isn't he the carpenter's son?" (οὐχ οὗτός ἐστιν ὁ τοῦ τέκτονος υἱός;). The use of "not" (οὐχ) in all three questions in vv. 55 – 56 expects the answer "yes": "He is, isn't he?" This is an important passage showing that the apocryphal infancy gospels that attributed miraculous powers to the infant Jesus (e.g., making clay pigeons that come to life) are not true. Jesus was never known as a miracle worker but first as the son of the carpenter Joseph and later, after Joseph died, as the village carpenter.

Since Jesus began his ministry when he was about thirty-four years old (from his birth around 6 BC [Herod died in 4 BC and Jesus had been in Egypt awhile] until he began his ministry in AD 28 [cf. Luke 3:1; John 2:20]), he had been the village carpenter (part of it with his father) for at least twenty-one years (sons began their adult livelihood at about thirteen years of age). In that time he had done little to show what he was to become. A "carpenter" (τέκτων) would work in either wood or stone (often both); there was not much wood in Palestine, but from the start the early church fathers considered him a carpenter. Perhaps he worked with both.

13:55 "Isn't his mother Mary and his brothers James and Joseph and Simon and Judas?" (οὐχ ἡ μήτηρ αὐτοῦ λέγεται Μαριὰμ καὶ οἱ ἀδελφοὶ αὐτοῦ Ἰάκωβος καὶ Ἰωσὴφ καὶ Σίμων καὶ Ἰούδας;). Joseph was mentioned earlier, so Mary is now named. In 12:46 – 49 (for the Roman Catholic view, see on that passage) these were the ones who came to speak with Jesus (cf. John 2:12; 6:42; Acts 1:14). James became the head elder of the Jerusalem church (Acts 12:17; 15:13) and wrote a NT letter, as did Judas (Jude). They were not believers during Jesus' lifetime and possibly were converted through resurrection appearances (though the NT mentions this only for James, 1 Cor 15:7). The order could be from the oldest to the youngest (normal procedure), but Mark 6:3 reverses the last two, so it is impossible to know for certain.

13:56 "Aren't all of his sisters with us?" (καὶ αἱ ἀδελφαὶ αὐτοῦ οὐχὶ πᾶσαι πρὸς ἡμᾶς εἰσιν;). Jesus' sisters are mentioned here and in Mark 6:3. They are never named. The presence of "with us" (πρὸς ἡμᾶς) means the sisters still resided in Nazareth and were probably at the synagogue listening to Jesus. The people in Nazareth know Jesus' family and his occupation and cannot accept that he is now the great rabbi (see on 12:2) and miracle worker all Galilee is talking about. That goes against over thirty years of watching him in a very small town.[5]

13:56 "So where did this man get all these things?"(πόθεν οὖν τούτῳ ταῦτα πάντα;). This is the conclusion. Again, the people of Nazareth wonder about the source — is God or Satan behind Jesus' authority in word and deed? They apparently decide that Satan is behind Jesus. "All these things" (ταῦτα πάντα) refers to all the miracles and teaching/parables in preceding chapters.

13:57 And they were scandalized by him (καὶ ἐσκανδαλίζοντο ἐν αὐτῷ). Amazement turns to skepticism and then opposition. As in 5:29 – 30; 11:6; 13:21, "they were scandalized" (σκανδαλίζομαι) means a lot more than just personal offense. It connotes deep sin and has connotations of apostasy. Here it denotes total rejection (in Luke 4:29 they try to throw him off a cliff, a common type of execution). Clearly they consider him a false prophet and false teacher.

13:57 So Jesus said to them, "Nowhere is a prophet without honor except in his own hometown and among his family" (ὁ δὲ Ἰησοῦς εἶπεν αὐτοῖς, Οὐκ ἔστιν προφήτης ἄτιμος εἰ μὴ ἐν τῇ πατρίδι καὶ ἐν τῇ οἰκίᾳ αὐτοῦ). This proverb applied to the biblical prophets (e.g., Jeremiah) as well as to Jesus. The presence of "family" (οἰκία) here is probably due to 12:46 – 50 and to the mention of his brothers and sisters above in vv. 55 – 56a.[6] This saying is peculiar to Jesus and does not occur outside the NT (cf. Mark 6:4; Luke 4:24; John 4:44).[7]

13:58 And he did not do many miracles there because of their unbelief (καὶ οὐκ ἐποίησεν ἐκεῖ δυνάμεις πολλὰς διὰ τὴν ἀπιστίαν αὐτῶν). "Unbelief" (ἀπιστία) sums up the rejection theme of chs. 11 – 12 (though the term itself appears only here in Matthew, cf. "unbelieving" [ἄπιστος] in 17:17). Mark 6:5 has that "he *could not* do any

5. Archaeology has shown Nazareth consisted of about sixty acres and thus would have had a maximum population of about 480, cf. James F. Strange, "Nazareth," *ABD*, 4:1050; and Richard A. Horsley, *Galilee: History, Politics, People* (Valley Forge, PA: Trinity Press International, 1995), 193.

6. Davies and Allison, *Matthew*, 2:459, point out that οἰκία may mean "city" and be in synonymous parallelism with "hometown" (πατρίς) and thus not a reference to Jesus' family. However, that is not as likely as the traditional interpretation of "family."

7. There are similar sayings regarding philosophers in Dio Chrysostom 47.6; Epictetus, *Diss* 3.16.11, see Luz, *Matthew 8 – 20*, 303n.

miracles there," and it is common to say that Matthew softens Mark in order to maintain Jesus as in charge of the situation (Segbroek, Gnilka, Davies and Allison, Luz, Schnackenburg, Nolland).

But this overstates the case. Matthew does stress Jesus' control and the guilt of the people of Nazareth, but the purpose is not to water down Mark's presentation. As Carson says, Matthew likely centers on (1) the paucity of the miracles and (2) the meaning of his mission rather than on Jesus' reluctance to perform miracles.[8] There is no real difference, for in both gospels Jesus still does a few miracles but not many because of their unbelief. The emphasis in both is not on Jesus' inability but on their unbelief and God's judgment on the people for it. As Keener concludes, Jesus demands faith and "*would* not act because of their unbelief" (italics his).[9]

Theology in Application

This story begins a new section that takes the themes of the last section further. Jesus continues to address the crowds, but the polarization between Jesus and the Jewish people continues, and now those who knew him best turn against him. Thus we will see Jesus turning more and more to the disciples and preparing them for the time when they take over his mission.

1. Familiarity Breeds Contempt

The people among whom Jesus grew up expected him to remain the village carpenter. In that society there was virtually zero socioeconomic mobility, and everyone spent their lives in the occupation their fathers and grandfathers handed down to them. While it is true that many prophets came from similar peasant backgrounds, they too were rejected by their former friends.

The Jewish people in general also tried to force Jesus into their narrow expectations of what a Messiah should be (i.e., both a faithful practitioner of the written and oral Torah and a political conqueror). When Jesus refused to fit their preconceptions, they also turned on him. In fact, this prepares for the next section, where John's death at the hands of Herod foreshadows Jesus' death at the hands of the Jewish leaders. As Hagner says, "Familiarity with Jesus became a liability, since he was thereby forced into a preconceived framework."[10] As we take the message of Christ to a lost world, we may also have family who rejects or opposes our call from God. We may have to choose between family and friends and serving Christ.

8. Carson, "Matthew," 336. See also Blomberg, *Matthew*, 228; Morris, *Matthew*, 367.

9. Keener, *Matthew*, 397; so also Witherington, *Matthew*, 280; Turner, "Matthew," 157.

10. Hagner, *Matthew 1 – 13*, 406.

2. Our Greatest Opposition

We must always be ready to find our greatest opposition from those who know us best. Jesus already said in 10:21, 35 – 37 that we must be prepared for our own family to take the lead in opposing our mission. This is the flip side of the first theological point. Jesus said often, "It is sufficient for disciples to be like their teacher, and slaves to be like their master" (10:25; cf. John 15:18 – 16:4). Since Jesus' fellow Jews and those in his own hometown turned against him, why should we be surprised and shaken when that happens to us? Davies and Allison conclude, "Thus there is no safe haven, no sacred space uncontaminated by hostility; there is no one group of people that will, as a unit, embrace Jesus. Opposition is truly pandemic."[11]

3. Faith and Power

Jesus demands faith if we are to experience his power. As in v. 58, the Jewish refusal to believe led to a diminution of the power of God in their midst. This does not mean that our faith is necessary to unleash divine power, as if we control God (the error of the prosperity gospel). That is the Pelagian heresy intensified, since by this we don't just save ourselves but tell God what to do. But when we trust self instead of God, judgment will come on us as it did on the people of Nazareth. I have often thought this is why we see fewer miracles than those in the Third World. Our approach to God is tainted by our materialistic culture, and we have too little God-centeredness as we try to put our trust in him. As in Col 3:1 – 2 we must set our hearts "on things above, not on earthly things."

11. Davies and Allison, *Matthew*, 2:461.

CHAPTER 62

Matthew 14:1 – 12

Literary Context

This is the second of the rejection stories that begin this unit. The story of the end of John the Baptist shows the extent of the opposition to Jesus and those who are part of his kingdom ministry. As such this foreshadows the end of Jesus; he too will die at the hands of the leaders.

V. Rejection, Suffering, and Glory (13:54 – 18:35)

A. Jesus' Deeds: Rejection, Discipleship, and Glory (13:54 – 17:27)

1. Rejection and Discipleship (13:54 – 16:20)

a. Teaching and Rejection at Nazareth (13:54 – 58)

➦ **b. Herod, Jesus, and the Baptist (14:1 – 12)**

c. Feeding of the 5,000 (14:13 – 21)

Main Idea

Herod represents the leaders of Israel both in his false understanding of Jesus and in his persecution and murder of God's messengers — in this case, John the Baptist. At the same time, John represents Jesus in his bold proclamation and willingness to suffer the consequences and also in his arrest and martyrdom at the hand of God's enemies.[1] So this intensifies the rejection of 13:54 – 58 and demonstrates how far that rejection will go, namely, to death.

1. As France, *Gospel of Matthew*, 552, says, "this pericope is not just a flashback but also a foreshadowing of what is to happen to the 'second John.'"

Translation

Matthew 14:1-12

1a	Introduction/Setting	**At that time Herod the tetrarch heard the reports about Jesus,**
2a	Identification	**he said to his servants,**
		"This is John the Baptist risen from the dead
		and because of this
b	Basis for 2a	*the powers are at work in him."*
3a	Action	For **Herod had arrested John, bound him, and imprisoned him**
b	Basis for 3a	because of Herodias, the wife of his brother Philip.
4a	Basis for 3a	For **John had told him,** *"It is not lawful for you to have her."*
5a	Desire	**Herod wanted to kill him but**
b		**was afraid of the people**
c	Basis for 5b	because they considered him a prophet.
6a	Setting	When Herod's birthday came,
b	Action	**the daughter of Herodias danced in the midst of the guests and pleased Herod.**
7a	Result of 6b	**For this reason he made an oath to give her whatever she asked.**
8a		Directed by her mother,
b	Request	**she said,**
c		*"Give me here on a platter the head of John the Baptist."*
9a	Response to 8b-c	**The king was grieved,**
b		but because of his oath and his dinner guests
c	Response to 8b-c	**he ordered that it be given her.**
10a	Response to 8b-c	**So he sent people and had John beheaded in the prison.**
11a		**His head was brought on a platter and given to the girl,**
b		and **she took it to her mother.**
12a	Conclusion	**John's disciples came, took the corpse, and buried it.**
b		Then **they went and reported it to Jesus.**

Structure and Literary Form

This story abbreviates Mark 6:14 – 29 and is another controversy narrative, this time using the martyrdom of John to illustrate the extent of the opposition to Jesus and the kingdom heralds God has sent.[2] There are significant similarities to several

2. It is common to doubt the historicity of this story (Beare, Luz) because of differences of detail with Josephus, *Ant.* 18.240 – 56, and Bultmann classifies it as a legend. However, Josephus is hardly known for his accuracy, and it seems likely that Mark/Matthew and Josephus are drawing from two different traditions of the same event, one Herodian (Josephus) and the other Christian (Mark). See Harold Hoehner, *Herod Antipas* (SNTSSup 17; Cambridge: Cambridge Univ. Press, 1972), 124 – 49; Keener, *Matthew*, 397.

OT stories regarding conflict between a king and a prophet, especially Ahab and Jezebel vs. Elijah in 1 Kgs 17 – 18 (see also the book of Esther with Mordecai vs. Haman, though they are not prophet and king respectively). There are two parts to the story, Herod's false opinion of Jesus (vv. 1 – 2) and the flashback to the arrest and death of John the Baptist (vv. 3 – 12). The latter has three parts — the arrest and imprisonment of John (vv. 3 – 5), the dance of Herodias's daughter and her terrible request (vv. 6 – 8), and the death and burial of John (vv. 9 – 12).[3]

Exegetical Outline

➡ **I. Herod's False Opinion of Jesus (14:1 – 2)**
- A. The Baptist raised from the dead (vv. 1 – 2a)
- B. The powers at work in Jesus (v. 2b)

II. Flashback: Arrest and Death of John (14:3 – 12)
- A. Arrest and imprisonment (vv. 3 – 5)
  - 1. The reason for his arrest (vv. 3 – 4)
    - a. Herod's liason with his brother's wife (v. 3)
    - b. Bold denunciation of his unlawful marriage (v. 4)
  - 2. Herod's intention thwarted by his fear (v. 5)
- B. The dance and its aftermath (vv. 6 – 8)
  - 1. Setting: Herod's birthday (v. 6a)
  - 2. The dance of Herodias' daughter (v. 6b)
  - 3. The terrible aftermath (vv. 7 – 8)
    - a. Herod's promise (v. 7)
    - b. Her request: the head of John (v. 8)
- C. The death and burial of John (vv. 9 – 12)
  - 1. Sadly, Herod grants the request (v. 9)
  - 2. John beheaded (v. 10)
  - 3. Head brought to the daughter, then to the mother (v. 11)
  - 4. John buried (v. 12)

Explanation of the Text

14:1 At that time Herod the tetrarch heard the reports about Jesus (Ἐν ἐκείνῳ τῷ καιρῷ ἤκουσεν Ἡρῴδης ὁ τετραάρχης τὴν ἀκοὴν Ἰησοῦ). "At that time" is a loose connective that ties the two episodes together. Mark has the mission of the Twelve between the two (6:7 – 13), but Matthew has already related that story in 10:5 – 15. The "report"[4] is likely connected to both Jesus' deeds and his words. He

3. On the historicity of the story, see Davies and Allison, *Matthew*, 2:465 – 66; Keener, *Matthew*, 397 – 98.

4. This is an example of "hear" (ἀκούω) with the accusative where no actual understanding takes place (see Wallace, 133). Note also the emphatic use of the cognates, "hear ... reports" (ἀκούω ... ἀκοήν).

has supplanted the Baptist as the great prophet of his day. This is the only place in Matthew that Herod Antipas is mentioned, son of Herod the Great (2:1) and brother of Archelaus (see on 2:22). He was "tetrarch," ruling one fourth of the province, namely, Galilee and Perea from AD 4 – 39. So Herod has been on his throne about twenty-five years.

14:2 He said to his servants, "This is John the Baptist risen from the dead" (καὶ εἶπεν τοῖς παισὶν αὐτοῦ, Οὗτός ἐστιν Ἰωάννης ὁ βαπτιστής· αὐτὸς ἠγέρθη ἀπὸ τῶν νεκρῶν). Clearly Herod's conscience has been troubling him, and he thinks Jesus is the resurrected John possibly come back to get even. He must have believed the Jewish idea of physical resurrection but superstitiously interpreted it from a Hellenistic perspective of spirits seeking revenge. The Herods demonstrated an amalgamation of Jewish and Hellenistic views. There were a number of such shallow speculations of Jesus (16:14), and Herod may have gotten this from one such rumor.

14:2 "... and because of this the powers are at work in him" (καὶ διὰ τοῦτο αἱ δυνάμεις ἐνεργοῦσιν ἐν αὐτῷ). The miraculous "powers" of Jesus went beyond the Baptist, who never performed miracles. So Herod assumes that the miracle of coming back from the dead has now given John the authority to perform such deeds. This would mean that the powers of the age to come have entered human history, though it is difficult to know how much of this was in Antipas's mind.

14:3 For Herod had arrested[5] John, bound him, and imprisoned him because of Herodias, the wife of his brother Philip (Ὁ γὰρ Ἡρῴδης κρατήσας τὸν Ἰωάννην ἔδησεν αὐτὸν καὶ ἐν φυλακῇ ἀπέθετο διὰ Ἡρῳδιάδα τὴν γυναῖκα Φιλίππου τοῦ ἀδελφοῦ αὐτοῦ). The two "for" (γάρ) clauses in vv. 3 – 4 give a series of reasons for the action of the paragraph. Herod arrested John, and that was caused by John's condemnation of the ruler. The arrest is mentioned in 4:12 (the historical timing) as the event that occurred just before Jesus launched his Galilean ministry. Matthew follows Mark in reserving the details for this flashback.

The arrest was partly political, partly moral, for John had decried Herod's marriage to Herodias, his niece. He had been married to the daughter of Aretas, king of Nabatea south of Perea. In fact, Aretas as a result of the divorce went to war and defeated Antipas, but he was saved when the Romans intervened. Herodias, however, had been married to Herod Philip I (who had not been given a kingdom to rule).[6] When John condemned this moral and legal sin (see v. 4), Herod decided to make John an example to others who also decried the new marriage; and he arrested John (Josephus, *Ant.* 18.118 – 19, says it was for "sedition," which to Herod it certainly was), imprisoning him in the fortress of Machaerus (*Ant.* 18.109 – 15), a large palace rebuilt by Herod the Great east of the Dead Sea.

14:4 For John had told[7] him, "It is not lawful for you to have her" (ἔλεγεν γὰρ ὁ Ἰωάννης αὐτῷ, Οὐκ ἔξεστίν σοι ἔχειν αὐτήν). The affair of Herod Antipas and Herodias and subsequent divorce of their spouses in order to marry each other was a

5. This first of the three verbs is another of Matthew's many circumstantial participles that virtually become a main verb; see on 4:20. This is true also of vv. 5, 9, 10, 12 (2x), 15b, 24, 25, 29, 30 (3x!), 31.

6. There is a discrepancy, for Josephus calls Herodias's first husband "Herod." Yet as Hoehner, *Herod Antipas*, 133 – 36, shows, Herod liked the name Philip and would at times call sons by different marriages by the same name. The one Philip (I), son of Mariamne, is the one in this story. The other Philip (II), son of Cleopatra, was tetrarch of Iteria and Traconitis and is the one named in Luke 3:1.

7. Wallace calls this a pluperfect use of the imperfect "had told" (ἔλεγεν).

huge scandal among the Jews. In Lev 18:16; 20:21 sexual relations and marriage to one's brother's wife is prohibited — thus John's "it is not lawful." So on many levels the behavior of Antipas and Herodias was wrong, and John's condemnation was indicative of a national scandal (Josephus, *Ant.* 18.109 – 25).

14:5 Herod wanted to kill him but was afraid of the people because they considered him a prophet (καὶ θέλων αὐτὸν ἀποκτεῖναι ἐφοβήθη τὸν ὄχλον, ὅτι ὡς προφήτην αὐτὸν εἶχον). Here John once more foreshadows Jesus, for the Jewish leaders later wish to kill Jesus but are afraid of the people, who consider Jesus a prophet (21:46; 26:5);[8] the progressive imperfect (εἶχον) stresses the ongoing nature of John's popularity (in the same way the present tense participle "wanted" [θέλων] shows Herod's ongoing desire to kill John).

There is a small discrepancy with Mark 6:19 – 20, which says Herod was protecting John from the wrath of Herodias, and it was she who wanted him dead. However, in v. 9 Herod is deeply distressed at having to order John's death, and v. 5 probably reflects Matthew's abbreviation of the events, as Herod vacillated back and forth between his admiration of John and his desire to appease his wife.[9] Luz points to the OT tradition of murdered prophets, a frequent emphasis in Matthew (Matt 5:12; 17:12; 21:33 – 41; 22:3 – 6; 23:29 – 36)[10] and possibly a typological fulfillment as John and Jesus relive the fate of the prophets.

14:6 When Herod's birthday came, the daughter of Herodias danced in the midst of the guests and pleased Herod (γενεσίοις δὲ γενομένοις τοῦ Ἡρῴδου ὠρχήσατο ἡ θυγάτηρ τῆς Ἡρῳδιάδος ἐν τῷ μέσῳ καὶ ἤρεσεν τῷ Ἡρῴδῃ). Mark 6:21 tells us the attendees were "high officials and military commanders and the leading men of Galilee." This dance is unusual, for such an undoubtedly lascivious dance was normally done by courtesans. The fact that it was the princess (named Salome in Josephus, *Ant.* 18.136 – 37[11] and probably between twelve and fourteen years old [so Hoehner]) who performed it would at first have shocked everyone and then been regarded as a high honor to Herod. The low morals of Herod's court were well known, and he is greatly pleased with the girl and her dance.

14:7 For this reason he made an oath to give her whatever she asked (ὅθεν μεθ' ὅρκου ὡμολόγησεν αὐτῇ δοῦναι ὃ ἐὰν αἰτήσηται). Mark 6:23 adds "up to half my kingdom." This is reminiscent of Esth 5:2 – 3, when King Xerxes was pleased with Esther and promises to grant her request "up to half the kingdom." There it has a positive result while here it is tragically negative. It is strange that Herod would "make an oath," but that was likely due to his drunken state.

14:8 Directed by her mother, she said, "Give me here on a platter the head of John the Baptist" (ἡ δὲ προβιβασθεῖσα ὑπὸ τῆς μητρὸς αὐτῆς, Δός μοι, φησίν, ὧδε ἐπὶ πίνακι τὴν κεφαλὴν Ἰωάννου τοῦ βαπτιστοῦ). Mark 6:19 tells how Herodias had "nursed a grudge" against John and wanted his death. προβιβάζω means "to cause to come forward" and in this type of context denotes "instruct, prompt, urge." Salome faithfully followed her mother's directions and asked for the head of

8. This is the reverse of 10:41, where Jesus said the one who "receives a prophet" will receive "a prophet's reward." It is also closely connected to 13:57, where Jesus proclaimed that a prophet will often be dishonored among his own people.

9. For a lengthy discussion harmonizing the two accounts, see Hoehner, *Herod Antipas*, 149 – 64.

10. Luz, *Matthew 8 – 20*, 307.

11. See David Flusser, "A New Portrait of Salome," *Jerusalem Perspective* 55 (1999): 18 – 23, who on the basis of her portrait here and in Josephus argues that she was not an immoral young girl but a proper princess with even a coin minted with her portrait on it in AD 56 – 57.

the one righteous man in the fortress. ὧδε ("here") means much the same as Mark's "at once"; she wanted the Baptist's head delivered in that very banquet hall right then.

Herodias obviously did not want to give Herod any time to think about it. It was common for victorious conquerors to have the heads of their enemies put on public display (it was a Roman rather than Jewish practice), but at a banquet to have John's head served up as if it were a delectable dish on a "platter" is hideous beyond belief. No better proof of the absolute depravity of Herod's court could be given.

14:9 The king was grieved, but because of his oath and his dinner guests he ordered that it be given her (καὶ λυπηθεὶς ὁ βασιλεὺς διὰ τοὺς ὅρκους καὶ τοὺς συνανακειμένους ἐκέλευσεν δοθῆναι). Herod clearly did not want to acquiesce to the request, and λυπηθείς means to be "filled with grief" or "distress" at something you would avoid if possible. For two reasons[12] he had to give in: his "oath" (the plural is probably to emphasize the serious nature of it) could not easily be rescinded; and his "dinner guests" (συνανακειμένους = "recline at table") had heard the oath, so his reputation was at stake. So Herod gave the order, foreshadowing Pilate, who would also be the reluctant executioner of Jesus.[13]

14:10 So he sent people and had John beheaded in the prison (καὶ πέμψας ἀπεκεφάλισεν τὸν Ἰωάννην ἐν τῇ φυλακῇ). The article τῇ is demonstrative, "in that prison." The soldiers carry out the sentence immediately, and John's short but powerful ministry as prophet and forerunner to the Messiah was at an end. Like most despots Herod was not worried that Jewish as well as Roman law said a person should not be executed without a trial (cf. Jesus and Paul).

14:11 His head was brought on a platter and given to the girl, and she took it to her mother (καὶ ἠνέχθη ἡ κεφαλὴ αὐτοῦ ἐπὶ πίνακι καὶ ἐδόθη τῷ κορασίῳ, καὶ ἤνεγκεν τῇ μητρὶ αὐτῆς). Such a grisly scene was not uncommon in the ancient world. Alexander Janneus had eight hundred rebels crucified and their families slaughtered before them while he feasted with his concubines, and Fulvia (Marc Antony's wife) had the head of Cicero brought to her and pierced its tongue with a pin for opposing her husband.[14] Greco-Roman banquets would have separate dining halls for men and women, so Salome had to take it to her mother.[15]

14:12 John's disciples came, took the corpse, and buried it. Then they went and reported it to Jesus (καὶ προσελθόντες οἱ μαθηταὶ αὐτοῦ ἦραν τὸ πτῶμα καὶ ἔθαψαν αὐτό, καὶ ἐλθόντες ἀπήγγειλαν τῷ Ἰησοῦ). We do not know what happened to John's head. Perhaps his disciples (11:2) were allowed to take it with his body and give it an honorable burial. There is a contrast between them and Jesus' disciples, who deserted Jesus at his arrest (Matt 26:56b), apparently with none of the Twelve assisting in Jesus' burial [27:57 – 61]). We are not told why John's disciples immediately went to inform Jesus of the tragedy, but from 3:11 – 15; 11:1 – 6 many of them would know of John's witness to Jesus. The baton has been passed from the great prophet to the greater Prophet!

12. The phrase could modify Herod's grief or the reason he ordered John's death. In fact, a variant reading arose to clear up the discrepancy — "the king was grieved; but ..." (ἐλυπήθη ὁ βασιλεὺς· διὰ δέ), supported by ℵ C K W X Byz et al. However, the reading in the text is supported by B D Θ f^1 f^{13} et al. and is preferred because it is the less likely reading.

13. So Davies and Allison, *Matthew*, 2:474.

14. So Carson, "Matthew," 339. He points out that Jerome records Herodias as doing the same as Fulvia with John's head.

15. Keener, *Matthew*, 400.

Theology in Application

The death of the Baptist continues the tradition of a nation that murders its own prophets (Matt 5:12; 23:31 – 35) and foreshadows the death of Jesus himself at the hands of the nation. As such, it also provides a theological underpinning for the fact that all God's people can expect persecution and opposition even unto death (10:17 – 31), a point even more central for Mark, who inserts the mission of the Twelve between the rejection at Nazareth and the death of the Baptist (Mark 6:1 – 6, 7 – 13, 14 – 29).

A major theme in this unit is the striking parallels between the death of John and that of Jesus (cf. 17:11 – 13). Davies and Allison calls it a "christological parable."[16] John was the messianic forerunner, and that means that he was also the forerunner of messianic suffering and death. Hagner sums it up well:[17] "those who murdered John are far more pitiable than is John himself. In this instance, to be 'dead' is more blessed than to be 'alive'; for the one murdered truly lives, while those who murdered him are in reality the dead." As Jesus himself said in 10:28: "Do not ever be afraid of those who put the body to death but cannot kill the soul, but continue to fear the one who has the power to destroy both soul and body in Gehenna."

16. Davies and Allison, *Matthew*, 2:476. They summarize these parallels as (1) Herod = Pilate; (2) both John and Jesus are seized and bound (14:3 = 21:46; 27:2); (3) fearing the crowds (14:5 = 21:46); (4) both rulers were asked by others to kill John and Jesus (14:6 – 11 = 27:11 – 26); (5) both buried by disciples (14:12 = 27:57 – 61).

17. Hagner, *Matthew 14 – 28*, 413.

CHAPTER 63

Matthew 14:13 – 21

Literary Context

The two stories of rejection and death that have recapitulated the conflict of chs. 11 – 13 are now finished, and we enter a section on Jesus' miraculous power (note "the powers" in 13:54) and discipleship. That carries through ch. 14 until we arrive at the next conflict narrative of 15:1 – 20. This juxtaposition of four themes — Christology,[1] conflict, discipleship, and miracles — will carry through this section.

- **V. Rejection, Suffering, and Glory (13:54 – 18:35)**
  - **A. Jesus' Deeds: Rejection, Discipleship, and Glory (13:54 – 17:27)**
    - **1. Rejection and Discipleship (13:54 – 16:20)**
      - a. Teaching and Rejection at Nazareth (13:54 – 58)
      - b. Herod, Jesus, and the Baptist (14:1 – 12)
      - ➦ **c. Feeding of the 5,000 (14:13 – 21)**
      - d. Walking on the Water (14:22 – 33)

Main Idea

The primary theological theme is that "God will provide," along with its concomitant motif, faith. Jesus' compassion is demonstrated as he feeds the needy crowd, and he involves the disciples at a deeper level in this miracle than at any other time, asking them to realize that he will take care of them. This theme carries over to the walking on the water pericope, where the disciples are tested and fail to show they have learned the lesson.[2]

1. Nolland, *Matthew*, 587, says this section is to be read "primarily in terms of its contribution to Christology. The Emmanuel perspective of Mt. 1:23 is evident; here in the ministry of Jesus God is with us."

2. Many have tried to dismiss the historicity of this miracle, beginning with the rationalistic explanation by Schleiermacher and others that this was actually a miracle of sharing. When a little boy (or Jesus himself) shared his meager meal, everyone

Translation

Matthew 14:13-21

13a	Response	When Jesus heard what had happened,
b	Action	**he withdrew from there in a boat privately to a solitary place.**
c	Response	Yet when the crowds heard of this,
d	Action	**they followed him by foot from the towns.**
14a	Setting	When Jesus landed,
b		**he saw a huge crowd.**
c	Response/Action	**He had compassion on them and healed their sick.**
15a	Setting (Temporal)	When evening arrived,
b	Action	**the disciples came to him and said,**
c	Problem	*"This is an isolated place and the hour is already late.*
d		*So send the crowds away*
e		*so that they go into the villages and*
		buy food for themselves."
16a	Response/Command	But **Jesus replied,**
b		*"There is no need for them to leave.*
c		*You give them something to eat."*
17a	Objection	**So they then responded,**
b		*"We have nothing here*
		except five loaves of bread and two fish."
18a	Response	**He answered,**
b	Command	*"Bring them here to me."*
19a		**Then he ordered the crowds to sit down on the grass.**
b	Action	Taking the five loaves and two fish,
c		**he looked up to heaven and gave thanks.**
d	Action	Breaking the loaves,
e		**he gave them to the disciples,**
f		and **the disciples distributed them to the crowds.**
20a	Resolution of 15c	**They all ate and were full,**
b		and **they gathered twelve full baskets of scraps left over.**
21a	Conclusion	**The number of those who ate was about five thousand men**
		along with women and children.

was touched and shared theirs as well. Others like D. F. Strauss or R. Bultmann have simply called it a mythical legend. Yet this meets the criterion of multiple attestation (occurs in every tradition) and can only be dismissed through antisupernatural bias. See France, Hagner, Blomberg, Keener.

Structure and Literary Form

This is often called a "gift miracle" story, meaning the miracle occurs as a gift from God.[3] Like many stories in Matthew, this one is abbreviated from Mark (Matthew omits about a third of Mark's story).[4] The story has three parts — an introductory scene with the crowds following Jesus and Jesus' compassion on them (vv. 13 – 14), a dialogue with the disciples in which Jesus challenges them to care for the crowds (vv. 15 – 18), and the miracle itself (vv. 19 – 21).

Exegetical Outline

➦ **I. The Scene (14:13 – 14)**
- A. Jesus withdraws and the crowds follow (v. 13)
- B. Jesus' compassion and healing ministry (v. 14)

II. Dialogue with the Disciples (14:15 – 18)
- A. First interaction (vv. 15 – 16)
  1. Disciples' request: send the crowds home (v. 15)
  2. Jesus' response: you feed them (v. 16)
- B. Second interaction (vv. 17 – 18)
  1. Disciple's complaint: insufficient food (v. 17)
  2. Jesus' response: bring them to me (v. 18)

III. The Feeding Miracle (14:19 – 21)
- A. The series of actions (v. 19)
  1. The crowd sat down
  2. Jesus gave thanks over the bread and fish
  3. The breaking of the loaves
  4. The disciples distribute the bread and fish to the people
- B. The people filled, with twelve baskets of pieces left over (v. 20)
- C. The number — 5,000 men with added women and children (v. 21)

Explanation of the Text

"We move from Antipas's lavish but degenerate feast to one with a simpler menu but a more wholesome atmosphere."[5] This is the only miracle found in all four gospels, and in Matthew and Mark it is also connected to the feeding of the four thousand (Mark 8:1 – 13 = Matt

3. Theissen, *Miracle Stories*, 104.

4. This is also well known for the so-called "minor agreements of Matthew and Luke," used by some to support Matthean priority. Both omit Mark 6:31, 37b – 38a, 39c – 40, 41c. Both add "the disciples following" (v. 13 = Luke 9:13), Jesus' healing the crowds (v. 14 = Luke 9:11), "food" (βρώματα, v. 15 = Luke 9:13), "about" (ὡσεί, v. 21 = Luke 9:14). It may be that Matthew and Luke used an independent tradition as well as Mark, but that is only speculation.

5. France, *Gospel of Matthew*, 558.

15:32–39). This indicates the vast importance it had for the church because of the depth of its theology. It reproduces both the manna in the wilderness and Elisha's multiplication of loaves in 2 Kgs 4:38–44. In the Exod 16 story God gave the manna to the people, and here Jesus does the same, becoming the giver of manna that satisfies the multitudes. In 2 Kgs 4 Elisha fed one hundred with twenty loaves of bread. Notice that Elisha multiplied the bread fivefold (a loaf was enough for one person) while Jesus multiplied it a thousand times (a fact that would have been noticed by the early church).

This was truly a messianic miracle pointing forward to the messianic banquet,[6] an eschatological meal often emphasized by Jesus (Matt 8:11; Luke 14:15; 22:30) and also a common theme in Judaism, building on Isa 25:6, "On this mountain the Lord Almighty will prepare a feast of rich food for all peoples, a banquet of aged wine — the best of meats and the finest of wines" and developed further during the intertestamental period (*1 En.* 62:14; *2 Bar.* 29:8; 2 Esd 2:38). Thus it can be said that Jesus here is depicted both as the prophet Elisha and the new Moses.[7] Finally, from the meaning of table fellowship in the ancient world, there is a theology of community here; Jesus is establishing a new community, with himself as the head of the family (v. 19).[8]

14:13 When Jesus heard what had happened, he withdrew from there in a boat privately to a solitary place (Ἀκούσας δὲ ὁ Ἰησοῦς ἀνεχώρησεν ἐκεῖθεν ἐν πλοίῳ εἰς ἔρημον τόπον κατ᾽ ἰδίαν). There is some debate on the referent to "when he heard" (ἀκούσας, a temporal participle, as also in vv. 13b, 14), some connecting it to the report of Herod's musings in vv. 1–2 (Carson, Blomberg, Morris), others to the news about John the Baptist's death reported in v. 12 (McNeile, Hill, Hagner). Certainly the more natural is to have Jesus "hearing" (v. 13) the report of the Baptist's death (v. 12). Yet the story of his death is presented as a flashback, and Cope in an illuminating article considers "for" (γάρ) in v. 3 to be a common conjunction for introducing an excursus and "but" (δὲ) in v. 13 to be resumptive, thus going back to v. 2.[9]

Jesus wishes to remove himself from a politically tricky situation, the second time he has done so (cf. 12:15). Luke 9:10 tells us the "solitary place" was at Bethsaida on the northeast part of the lake, an area outside the area Antipas controlled.[10] The addition of "privately" (κατ᾽ ἰδίαν) means Jesus wishes to spend time alone with the disciples and prepare them for the terrible events soon to come.

6. Twelftree, *Jesus the Miracle Worker*, 129, calls this "the most significant aspect," noting that fish and bread appear in Jewish texts on the eschatological banquet (*2 Bar.* 29:1–8; *4 Ezra* 6:52); at Qumran the shared meals correspond to the final banquet (1QSa, and the parallels with the Elisha miracle point this direction).

7. Some believe this depicts Israel as "still lost and wandering in the wilderness," with Jesus thus returning them from exile, cf. Witherington, *Matthew*, 286.

8. So France, *Matthew* (TNTC), 235. It is more difficult to see here eucharistic connotations (so Gnilka, Gundry, France, Luz, Davies and Allison). This has often been opposed by Protestant exegetes because it was interpreted of the mass in Catholic circles, but it must be admitted that there are several similarities (taking of bread, blessing, breaking, distributing, eating). There is no evidence Jesus intended it as such, though Matthew's wording may indicate he saw such symbolism here (see Blomberg, *Matthew*, 232–33).

9. O. Lamar Cope, "The Death of John the Baptist in the Gospel of Matthew," *CBQ* 38 (1976): 515–19. In Mark 6:30–31 Jesus withdraws to give his disciples a rest after returning from their mission, but Matthew has placed the mission earlier in ch. 10. The two reasons in Mark and Matthew are not contradictory but supplemental.

10. Mendel Nun, "The 'Desert' of Bethsaida," *Jerusalem Perspective* 53 (1997): 16–17, 37, says this "desert place" was actually pastureland. Schnackenburg, *Matthew*, 142, tells other sites traditionally associated with the feeding miracle: Some take it to be the west bank a few miles south of Capernaum, others the east bank toward the north, a less populated place.

14:13 Yet when the crowds heard of this, they followed him by foot from the towns (καὶ ἀκούσαντες οἱ ὄχλοι ἠκολούθησαν αὐτῷ πεζῇ ἀπὸ τῶν πόλεων). Jesus might escape Antipas, but he could not escape his popularity with the crowds. For them to follow πεζῇ (an instrumental dative, "by foot") means they had to travel several miles around the lake and across the upper Jordan, possibly having seen the direction Jesus and his disciples were rowing or hearing his plans. They arrive at the spot ahead of Jesus, a remarkable feat. This shows how anxious they are to be with him.

14:14 When Jesus landed, he saw a huge crowd. He had compassion on them and healed their sick (καὶ ἐξελθὼν εἶδεν πολὺν ὄχλον καὶ ἐσπλαγχνίσθη ἐπ' αὐτοῖς καὶ ἐθεράπευσεν τοὺς ἀρρώστους αὐτῶν). We see here Jesus' adaptability and love. He wants to be alone with his followers, yet when he disembarks he sees this great horde of people. Most of us would be annoyed, but not Jesus. He has the same compassion for them now that he had in 9:36 and will again in 15:32. So instead of being irritated, he "healed" apparently everyone who was ill. "The mercy of Israel's Messiah for his people is important for Matthew; it can be seen almost always in his healings."[11]

14:15 When evening arrived,[12] the disciples came to him and said, "This is an isolated place and the hour is already late. So send the crowds away so that they go into the villages and buy food for themselves" (ὀψίας δὲ γενομένης προσῆλθον αὐτῷ οἱ μαθηταὶ λέγοντες, Ἔρημός ἐστιν ὁ τόπος καὶ ἡ ὥρα ἤδη παρῆλθεν· ἀπόλυσον τοὺς ὄχλους, ἵνα ἀπελθόντες εἰς τὰς κώμας ἀγοράσωσιν ἑαυτοῖς βρώματα). Jesus apparently arrived around midday, and late that evening he is still ministering to the people, perhaps unaware that the sun has almost set. The disciples are concerned, for it is past dinnertime and something has to be done (perhaps thinking of their own hunger). So they make the logical suggestion that the people be dismissed in order to purchase food in the surrounding villages. It is obvious that in the haste to get to Jesus, no one of the crowd had thought to get food for the evening meal.

Some have thought that the disciples lack faith in Jesus' miracle-working power, but that is not really intimated here. The emphasis is neither on their faith nor the lack of it; it is on Jesus' involving them in the event to come. They make the request we all would make in that situation.[13] Keener points out that wherever the place was, it was isolated, and the largest towns — Capernaum and Bethsaida, had only two to three thousand inhabitants; the presence of "grass" (v. 19) means it was spring when the grain stores would be low.[14] So the disciples are thinking of the best of difficult options.

14:16 But Jesus replied, "There is no need for them to leave. You give them something to eat" (ὁ δὲ Ἰησοῦς εἶπεν αὐτοῖς, Οὐ χρείαν ἔχουσιν ἀπελθεῖν· δότε αὐτοῖς ὑμεῖς φαγεῖν). The present tense ἔχουσιν sandwiched between the aorist imperatives of vv. 15 and 16b places the needs of the crowd in the foreground for emphasis.[15] Jesus does not want to end his ministry to the people. "The shepherd cares for his flock."[16] Jesus turns

11. Luz, *Matthew 8 – 20*, 314, pointing to the use of "mercy" in 9:27; 15:22; 17:15; 20:31 and to "compassion" in 9:36 (after 9:35); 15:32 (after 15:29 – 31); 20:34.

12. This is a temporal genitive absolute construction.

13. We shouldn't read too much into the imperative "send" (ἀπόλυσον), as if the disciples were telling Jesus what to do. This was a suggestion, perhaps even more a request. On the issue of the disciples' faith, see Carson, "Matthew," 341 – 42, who points out that the issue of the disciples' faith/understanding is not raised in this story, and there is no hint whatsoever that Jesus wants them to perform the miracle for him.

14. Keener, *Matthew*, 404.

15. Porter, *Idioms*, 23 – 25.

16. Schnackenburg, *Matthew*, 142.

their command around, telling the disciples to get the food (the redundant "you" [ὑμεῖς] puts the emphasis on the disciples' responsibility).

This is a key to the miracle, because at every level Jesus will involve the disciples in what is to transpire. He wants the disciples to learn that God's agents must care for God's flock. This is probably supposed to echo Elisha at the feeding miracle in 2 Kgs 4:43, "Give it to the people to eat, For this is what the LORD says, 'They will eat and have some left over,'" which is also echoed here in "they all ate and were full" (v. 20).

14:17 So they then responded, "We have nothing here except five loaves of bread and two fish" (οἱ δὲ λέγουσιν αὐτῷ, Οὐκ ἔχομεν ὧδε εἰ μὴ πέντε ἄρτους καὶ δύο ἰχθύας). The disciples are aghast. How can they provide for five thousand men and their families (cf. v. 21)? Mark 6:37 = John 6:7 notes they said it would take two hundred denarii or two-thirds of a year's wages to purchase enough food. All the food they had found in the crowd was that of one small boy (John 6:9) who had five (barley, the grain for the poor [John 6:9]) loaves and two fish, probably pieces of dried or pickled fish used to give the bread flavor. Barley bread and fish were the basic Galilean peasant diet.

In vv. 16 – 17 there is a strong allusion to 2 Kgs 4:42 – 44, where Elisha told the man who brought twenty barley loaves, "Give it to the people [a hundred of them] to eat" (4:42). In both cases we must realize that these were not modern loaves that could be sliced up for many people but smaller loaves about the size of a bun, so that the amount the boy had was meant for him alone,[17] at best for a couple children. Jesus is about to turn the food of the poor into a messianic banquet!

14:18 He answered, "Bring them here to me" (ὁ δὲ εἶπεν, Φέρετέ μοι ὧδε αὐτούς). The disciples have exhausted their meager ideas and resources. It is now time for Jesus to act, so he demands the small meal be given him (the present φέρετε is dramatic, picturing the act of bringing the food to him).[18] The disciples are involved but passive. The message is clear: none of us can accomplish anything of consequence in our own strength. Matthew (who alone has this) makes abundantly clear the sovereignty of Jesus alone over the situation.

14:19 Then he ordered the crowds to sit down on the grass (καὶ κελεύσας τοὺς ὄχλους ἀνακλιθῆναι ἐπὶ τοῦ χόρτου). Verse 19 consists of three successive circumstantial participles (ordering, taking, looking), all modifying the final verb ("he gave thanks" [εὐλόγησεν]) and giving the action that defines the primary idea of thanking God for the miracle about to happen. Jesus takes control; "order" (κελεύω) is a strong verb for giving a command.[19] The infinitive "to sit down" (ἀνακλιθῆναι) is used for "reclining" at banquets and is probably deliberate here. This simple repast will be turned into a sumptuous feast.

14:19 Taking the five loaves and two fish, he looked up to heaven and gave thanks (λαβὼν τοὺς πέντε ἄρτους καὶ τοὺς δύο ἰχθύας, ἀναβλέψας εἰς τὸν οὐρανὸν εὐλόγησεν). Jesus takes the position of head of the new family he is instigating. The sequence of verbs — take, bless, break, give — is found both in the Last Supper scene (26:26 – 27) and in the regular meal of Acts 27:35.[20] Primary

17. Morris, *Matthew*, 378. There is no symbolism in the numbers five and two — that is undoubtedly historical reminiscence.

18. Wallace, 502, pictures the aorist as a complete snapshot and the present as a motion picture.

19. Louw and Nida, *Greek-English Lexicon*, 425, say it connotes "to state with force and/or authority what others must do."

20. Donald A. Hagner, *Matthew 14 – 28* (WBC 33B; Dallas: Word, 1993), 418.

here is the table fellowship of the family, though eucharistic connotations may also be present (see the introduction to this section). "He gave thanks" (εὐλόγησεν) refers not to blessing the food but to blessing or (better) thanking God for the food. The normal prayer was "Blessed are you, O Lord our God, King of the Universe, who brings forth bread from the earth" (*m. Ber.* 6:1).

14:19 Breaking the loaves, he gave them to the disciples, and the disciples distributed them to the crowds (καὶ κλάσας ἔδωκεν τοῖς μαθηταῖς τοὺς ἄρτους, οἱ δὲ μαθηταὶ τοῖς ὄχλοις). The breaking of the bread again connotes mainly family celebration of the meal but perhaps secondarily the Eucharist. At this second level (after v. 16) Jesus again involves the disciples in the miracle, with the result that they mediate the miracle to the people.[21] In the Greek the second verb is missing and borrows the first, so that the order is, Jesus *gives* the broken bread to the disciples, and they *give* it to the people.

14:20 They all ate and were full, and they gathered twelve full baskets of scraps left over (καὶ ἔφαγον πάντες καὶ ἐχορτάσθησαν, καὶ ἦραν τὸ περισσεῦον τῶν κλασμάτων δώδεκα κοφίνους πλήρεις). This verse is filled with the symbolism of completeness — *all* were *full*, *twelve full* baskets. Yet note that the miracle is never described, just the results of it. Between Jesus' blessing it and the disciples' distributing it, a miracle of epic proportions has occurred! The fact that everyone was "stuffed" (χορτάζω means to "eat to the full, be satisfied") fits the idea of the messianic banquet in which all the hungry are to be completely satisfied (cf. Matt 5:6; Luke 6:21).

The incredible bounty is demonstrated when Jesus tells the disciples to gather up the scraps, a Jewish custom that was not so much cleaning up the environment as making sure nothing was wasted. Twelve baskets are gathered, presumably one for each of the disciples, who now complete their involvement in the miracle at every level — the beginning (vv. 15 – 18), the middle (v. 19b), and the end (v. 20b). The κόφινος was a small wicker basket used for carrying provisions when traveling. This makes the point that there is far more left after everyone has been filled than before they started.

The fact that there are twelve baskets left after the feeding of the five thousand (= the twelve tribes or the twelve disciples?) and seven left after the feeding of the four thousand (= God's perfect work?) may be significant, for these are certainly the two most important numbers for the early church. The people are completely satisfied. But rather than any particular symbol, the numbers probably show simply that God is in perfect control, giving graciously to his people.

14:21 The number of those who ate[22] was about five thousand men along with women and children (οἱ δὲ ἐσθίοντες ἦσαν ἄνδρες ὡσεὶ πεντακισχίλιοι χωρὶς γυναικῶν καὶ παιδίων). Matthew wants the reader to know this is not an exact number but an approximate count (ὡσεί; how could one begin to count that size of crowd in the ancient world?). This is an astounding number and also points to the multitudes to be present at the messianic banquet. Matthew follows Jewish practice by giving the number of adult males, but then adds that women and children were also present. This means the total there would likely be at least double that.

21. However, this does not symbolize the future mediators of the Eucharist, namely, the clergy. That is a type of allegorical symbolism that goes beyond the text.

22. The present tense "the ones eating" (οἱ ἐσθίοντες) likely emphasizes the dramatic ongoing banquet.

Theology in Application

This is one of the richest of Jesus' miracles theologically, as seen in the fact that it is the only miracle story found in every Jesus tradition. It reaches to the past (the manna, the Elisha miracle of 2 Kgs 4), the present (God's provision for his people), and the future (the messianic wedding feast). It is difficult to overstate its importance.

1. Jesus Christ Is Sovereign

The entire NT attests to the deity of Christ and his oneness with the Father (esp. emphasized in John and Revelation). As a member of the Godhead Jesus created this world (John 1:3 – 4; 1 Cor 8:6; Col 1:16; Heb 1:2), and he both sustains and controls it. Therefore he asks the disciples here to realize this reality and to depend wholly on him. He is Alpha and Omega (Rev 1:17; 2:8; 22:13), meaning he is Lord over history; and God's people must entrust themselves to his omnipotent and omnipresent (Matt 1:23; 18:20; 28:20) presence in their lives. The disciples needed to experience not only the power and provision of Jesus in their lives, but also how they can participate in that power and see it flow through them.

2. Mercy and Compassion

Through his mercy and compassion, Jesus will provide for our needs. Most take messianic provision to be the single major theme of the story. It took a long time for the disciples to learn this — indeed, until after Pentecost. This is perhaps one of the reasons why Jesus repeated it again (15:29 – 39). This is the distinguishing mark of true follower; our minds must focus on the things of God rather than merely human concerns (Mark 8:33b); we must seek and think heavenly rather than earthly pursuits (Col 3:1 – 2); and we must search after heavenly rather than earthly treasures (Matt 6:19 – 21). One of the most difficult aspects of the Christian walk is to learn contentment whatever the circumstances so that it does not matter whether we are in need or have plenty, for we know the Lord is in charge (cf. Paul's testimony in Phil 4:11 – 12).

3. Prophet and Messiah

Jesus is the great prophet and Messiah who will bring history to a close. Here three major symbols intertwine: Jesus the new Moses who will give us the hidden manna (Rev 2:17), the Elisha prophet who multiplies the bread, and the Messiah who will enable us to participate in the messianic banquet. Jesus has controlled the past, will control the future, and already controls the present. This is the meaning of the title of God in Rev 1:4 — "who is, and who was, and who is to come" (cf. Rev

4:8; 11:17; 16:5) — slightly out of order with "who is" (i.e., the present) first. The readers of Revelation know God is in control (the entire OT tells that) and will control history. Their discouragement comes because he does not seem to be in control of the present. The message is that God is sovereign over the present even though it doesn't seem like it.

4. Involvement in Christ's Powerful Work

This is a discipleship story as well as a miracle story. More than in any miracle, the disciples are central in every aspect. Jesus wants them first to realize he will take care of them and to understand that they can mediate his power to the world. This is seen in the miracles of Acts. Luke has chosen miracles that reproduce those of Jesus to show that "in the name of Jesus" the church reenacts the life and ministry of Jesus (e.g., Acts 9:32 – 34 = Luke 5:18 – 26; Acts 9:36 – 42 = Luke 8:49 – 56). God's power is available to the church.

5. Jesus Is Establishing a New Community

The meaning of table fellowship is unity and community. Meals symbolized "friendship, intimacy, and unity," involving reconciliation and making a person part of one's extended family, i.e., "social, religious, and economic equals."[23] So in providing this meal for the crowds, Jesus is inviting them to become part of his new family of kingdom people and promising those who respond that he will provide for their needs.

23. Bartchy, "Table Fellowship," 796.

CHAPTER 64

Matthew 14:22 – 33

Literary Context

In Mark and John the two nature miracles of the feeding of the five thousand and the storm on the Sea of Galilee are also clustered together and obviously build on each other both christologically and in terms of discipleship. The themes begun here will reverberate throughout the rest of this narrative section, building to a climax in Peter's confession and the blessing Jesus pronounces over him.

V. Rejection, Suffering, and Glory (13:54 – 18:35)
- **A. Jesus' Deeds: Rejection, Discipleship, and Glory (13:54 – 17:27)**
  - **1. Rejection and Discipleship (13:54 – 16:20)**
    - c. Feeding of the 5,000 (14:13 – 21)
    - ➦ **d. Walking on the Water (14:22 – 33)**
    - e. Healings at Gennesaret (14:34 – 36)

Main Idea

Christologically, Jesus shows further that he is Lord of creation, who commands wind and wave to do his will, climaxing in the acclamation of v. 33. In discipleship the disciples still have not truly learned that God will provide for their needs. In the moment of testing they are overwhelmed by the danger of the storm; they have only a "little faith" but are growing.

Translation

Matthew 14:22-33

22a	Introduction/Command	**Immediately Jesus impelled the disciples to get into the boat and go ahead of him to the other side**
b		until he dismissed the crowds.
23a		After he dismissed the crowds,
b	Event	**he ascended a mountain by himself to pray.**
c	Setting	When evening arrived,
d		**he was there alone,**
24a	Problem	but **the boat was already a great distance from land,**
b		battered by the waves
c		because the wind was against it.
25a	Setting	But in the fourth watch of the night
b	Action	**Jesus came to them, walking on the lake.**
26a		But when the disciples saw him walking on the lake,
b	Result of 25b	**they were terrified, saying,**
c		*"It's a ghost!"*
d		And **they cried out with fear.**
27a	Response	**Immediately Jesus spoke to them, saying,**
b		*"Have courage.*
c		*It is I.*
d		*Don't be afraid!"*
28a	Condition	**Peter answered,**
b		*"Lord if it's you, order me to come to you on the water."*
29a	Response	**So Jesus said,**
b		*"Come."*
c	Result of 29b	And **Peter got down out of the boat, walked on the water, and came to Jesus.**
30a		But seeing how strong the wind was,
b		**he was filled with fear.**
c	Problem	**He began to sink and cried out, saying,**
d		*"Lord, save me!"*
31a	Resolution of 30c	But **immediately Jesus reached out his hand, grabbed Peter, and**
b	Rebuke	**said to him,**
c		*"You of little faith!*
d		*Why did you doubt?"*
32a	Action	After they got back in the boat,
b	Resolution of 24a-c	**the wind ceased.**
33a	Result of 32a	**Then those who were in the boat worshiped Jesus, saying,**
b		*"Truly you are the Son of God!"*

Structure and Literary Form

Matthew again builds on Mark (Mark 6:45 – 52) but with little of his characteristic abbreviation, and he adds his own special material in vv. 32 – 36. His primary alteration reflects his emphasis on Jesus and on discipleship, for he omits Mark's "they had not understood about the loaves; their hearts were hardened" (6:52) and instead concludes with "they worshiped Jesus, saying, 'Surely you are the Son of God!' " Matthew is faithful to Mark (the disciples do fail) but clearly wants to portray a more positive picture in the final analysis. There are four parts: (1) the setting, as Jesus sends the disciples and crowds away to be alone in prayer (vv. 22 – 23a); (2) the storm and Jesus' intervention (vv. 23b – 27), (3) Peter's attempt to walk on the water (vv. 28 – 31), and (4) the twofold conclusion (vv. 32 – 33).

Exegetical Outline

➡ **I. Setting (14:22 – 23a)**
- A. Jesus dismisses the disciples and crowd (v. 22)
- B. Jesus goes up a mountain to pray (v. 23a)

II. The Storm and Jesus' Intervention (14:23b – 27)
- A. The differing situations that evening (vv. 23b – 24)
  1. Jesus alone in prayer (v. 23b)
  2. The boat buffeted by wind and wave (v. 24)
- B. Jesus comes to them (vv. 25 – 27)
  1. Jesus walks on the water to them (v. 25)
  2. The disciples' terror (v. 26)
  3. Jesus calls for courage (v. 27)

III. Peter Attempts to Walk on the Water (14:28 – 31)
- A. Peter starts to walk on the water (vv. 28 – 29)
  1. His trusting request (v. 28)
  2. His initial success (v. 29)
- B. His fearful failure (vv. 30 – 31)
  1. He begins to sink and cries for help (v. 30)
  2. Jesus' rebuke for lack of faith (v. 31)

IV. The Twofold Conclusion (14:32 – 33)
- A. The waves cease (v. 32)
- B. The disciples worship (v. 33)

Explanation of the Text

14:22 Immediately Jesus impelled the disciples to get into the boat and go ahead of him to the other side until he dismissed the crowds (Καὶ εὐθέως ἠνάγκασεν τοὺς μαθητὰς ἐμβῆναι εἰς τὸ πλοῖον καὶ προάγειν αὐτὸν εἰς τὸ πέραν, ἕως οὗ ἀπολύσῃ τοὺς ὄχλους). "Immediately" (εὐθέως) links this closely with the previous episode, and Jesus' command to his disciples to depart is in fact the final aspect of that story. Jesus again takes sovereign control, and ἀναγκάζω is a strong verb meaning to "compel" or "force" someone to do a thing.[1] He wants the disciples at this stage to be tested in terms of the lesson of the feeding miracle and so sends them to the other side of the lake in a boat.[2] Will they entrust themselves entirely to God's provision?

Another reason for Jesus to be by himself is given in John 6:14 – 15; the people conclude that Jesus is a prophet and are going to try to force him to become messianic king. So Jesus withdraws from them and (as here) sends them home. He will have nothing to do with their plan, so similar to the devil's in Matt 4:8 – 10.[3]

14:23 After he dismissed the crowds, he ascended a mountain by himself to pray. When evening arrived,[4] he was there alone (καὶ ἀπολύσας τοὺς ὄχλους ἀνέβη εἰς τὸ ὄρος κατ' ἰδίαν προσεύξασθαι. ὀψίας δὲ γενομένης μόνος ἦν ἐκεῖ). Jesus is quintessentially a man of prayer, and at this stage in his ministry it is all the more important to commune with his Father (the infinitive has purposive force, "in order to pray"). He needed private time with God, and this is probably the major reason he has dismissed the disciples and the crowds. For the "mountain" motif in Matthew, see 4:8. Some have taken Jesus "ascending the mountain" as a theophany scene, but this reads too much into the text here. More likely this follows the OT theme of prayer to the God of the mountains (e.g., Exod 32:31 – 34; Ps 121:1).

14:24 But the boat was already a great distance from land, battered by the waves because the wind was against it (τὸ δὲ πλοῖον ἤδη σταδίους πολλοὺς ἀπὸ τῆς γῆς ἀπεῖχεν βασανιζόμενον ὑπὸ τῶν κυμάτων, ἦν γὰρ ἐναντίος ὁ ἄνεμος). Matthew says they had rowed "many stadia" (a "stadion" = two hundred yards); John 6:19 specifies that they had gone twenty-five to thirty stadia or three to three and a half miles across the northern tip of the lake (about four to five miles wide here). A severe storm hit (see on 8:24 for the topography of the lake that caused storms), and the boat was under severe distress (βασανίζω is a strong verb meaning to "torture" or "cause great distress," often used of illness or even demonic oppression). Some scholars go so far as to see cosmic powers at work. There

1. Louw and Nida, *Greek-English Lexicon*, 476.

2. Whether Jesus supernaturally knew the storm was coming cannot be known. Since Bornkamm's essay in *Tradition and Interpretation*, scholars have tended to assume the boat symbolizes the church. Yet as we said in 9:23 – 24, this is too allegorical (i.e., not endemic to Matthean themes) and not likely.

3. There is a Synoptic problem here. Matthew says they were to go "to the other side," and Mark specifies this as "to Bethsaida," namely, Bethsaida Julius, just up a short way from where they were on the east side of the lake. Yet John 6:17 says they started across toward Capernaum, and due to the wind they landed at Gennesaret (see v. 34 below), a small plain on the northwest shore between Capernaum and Tiberias. How do we reconcile this data? Carson, "Matthew," 343, has the best solution. Jesus sent them across but had told them to wait at Bethsaida "until" (ἕως οὗ) he dismissed the crowds and spent some time alone with God. If he was late, they were to leave. This probably occurred and explains why they were still on the sea after 3:00 a.m.

4. There are two temporal participles here, the first a regular participle ("after dismissing") and the second a genitive absolute duplicating v. 15 ("after evening arrived").

was a strong headwind (ἐναντίος, "against it"), and huge waves threatened the lives of the disciples.

14:25 But in the fourth watch of the night Jesus came to them, walking on the lake (τετάρτῃ δὲ φυλακῇ τῆς νυκτὸς ἦλθεν πρὸς αὐτοὺς περιπατῶν ἐπὶ τὴν θάλασσαν). After a great deal of time in prayer (from dusk to 3:00 a.m) Jesus becomes aware of their plight. The "night" was sunset to sunrise, and while the Jews divided it into three "watches" (Judg 7:19, from φυλακή, a guard watching at his post), the Romans had four, and this was used in the first century. So this was the last period of nighttime, 3 – 6 a.m. The disciples have been rowing for their lives for several hours and are about at the end of their strength and resolve. Luz calls this "at the same time the biblical time of God's helpful intervention" (Exod 14:24; Ps 46:5; Isa 17:13 – 14),[5] and France adds that this evokes "the OT imagery of God walking on or through the sea (Job 9:8; Ps 77:19; Isa 43:16)."[6] While the old rationalist explanation had Jesus walking on the shore, the text makes it clear that he was indeed walking on the water.

Actually, there are a series of miracles here. (1) Jesus sees their plight, three miles away through a raging storm. We must realize they had left about dusk, six to nine hours earlier. We would have thought they had long ago reached the other side (how long does it take to row four-plus miles?). (2) Jesus walks (present tense stresses the dramatic picture of Jesus "walking" from wave to wave) right to them (we wouldn't be able to do that even with a GPS system!). Just picture Jesus calmly strolling from one eight-foot wave to the next with the wind and rain whipping around him! (3) Finally, of course, he again calms the storm (as in 8:26).

14:26 But when the disciples saw him walking on the lake (οἱ δὲ μαθηταὶ ἰδόντες αὐτὸν ἐπὶ τῆς θαλάσσης περιπατοῦντα). Matthew centers on the disciples' fear and terror as a sign of lack of faith "when they saw" (temporal participle) Jesus on the water. Christ had shown them in the previous miracle that he would provide for their needs, and he would expect that his appearance would comfort them. Mark 6:48 tells us he "was about to pass by them," not because he didn't care but because he expected them to remember the earlier lesson. The OT has a great deal of imagery of God treading on the waters (Job 9:8; 38:16; Ps 77:19), and Jesus is fulfilling that motif; he is Yahweh clearing the path through the sea for his people to pass through.

14:26 ... they were terrified, saying, "It's a ghost!" And they cried out with fear (ἐταράχθησαν λέγοντες ὅτι Φάντασμά ἐστιν, καὶ ἀπὸ τοῦ φόβου ἔκραξαν). Many have thought that Matthew waters down Mark's message of discipleship failure here, but it is just as clear in Matthew's account. Instead of faith the disciples feel only fear and terror, and Matthew makes that even more explicit than in Mark. Their cry that he is a "ghost" (only here and in Mark 6:49 in the NT) is a natural result of their fear and lack of faith.

The sea was seen as the home of evil spirits. When a person drowned in the Hellenistic world, they had no hope of crossing the River Styx, for there could be no proper burial without a coin in the mouth to pay the fare for that crossing. Thus they would be doomed to wander for eternity. This was not the Jewish belief, but still the idea of the "abyss" or home of demons (Rev 9:1, 2, 11; cf. 13:1)[7] was the unfathomable depths of the sea. In a sense,

5. Luz, *Matthew 8 – 20*, 319. See also his excellent section on the background of Hellenistic gods and heroes who walked on water. It was generally seen as impossible for human beings and reserved for the gods.

6. France, *Gospel of Matthew*, 566.

7. On water symbolizing chaos and evil, see Davies and Allison, *Matthew*, 2:84.

they are saying, "What this is constitutes what we will be soon!"

14:27 Immediately Jesus spoke to them, saying, "Have courage. It is I. Don't be afraid!" (εὐθὺς δὲ ἐλάλησεν ὁ Ἰησοῦς αὐτοῖς λέγων, Θαρσεῖτε, ἐγώ εἰμι· μὴ φοβεῖσθε). As in many supernatural appearances and theophanies (28:5 par.), Jesus first calms fears and gives his followers courage (cf. 9:2; Acts 23:11).[8] The emphasis is on ἐγώ εἰμι, which has two levels of meaning. The first is that of the disciples, who are assured that it is not an evil spirit but that "It is I, Jesus," who is walking beside their boat. The second is the deeper theological ramification, for this translates the assurance of Yahweh to the patriarchs in Gen 15:1; 26:1 – 4; 28:13; 46:3 ("I am Yahweh, do not be afraid").

ἐγώ εἰμι is, in fact, the sacred tetragrammeton, *yhwh*, meaning "I am (that I am)"[9] in Exod 3:14 as well as in Isa 41:4, 13; 43:10; 51:12. So it is meant to function as a divine self-authentication formula. As Hauerwas says, "This is the 'I am' of Ps. 77:19, the 'I am' who provides a way through the sea, a path through the mighty waters, leaving footprints unseen."[10] As Yahweh treads the waters, so does Jesus.

14:28 Peter answered,[11] "Lord if it's you, order me to come to you on the water" (ἀποκριθεὶς δὲ αὐτῷ ὁ Πέτρος εἶπεν, Κύριε, εἰ σὺ εἶ, κέλευσόν με ἐλθεῖν πρὸς σὲ ἐπὶ τὰ ὕδατα). Matthew now turns to an aspect of the story found only in his special material, probably the product of his own memory. Peter has a small amount of faith (v. 31) but not much understanding. After this, it is nearly always Peter who responds to Jesus (15:15; 16:16, 22; 17:4, 24; et al.), usually with only a modicum of understanding. Peter has a great deal of bravado but not a lot of wisdom, yet! His potential is obvious, and probably for this reason Jesus responds. He will become the "rock" on which Jesus "will build [his] church" (16:18), so he is naturally at center stage.

The "if it's you" (εἰ σὺ εἶ) is a condition of fact, elaborating the preceding "Lord" (κύριε): "Since you are Lord over creation,[12] tell me to participate in your miraculous power." We cannot know why Peter asks Jesus to "order" (the same strong verb as in vv. 9, 19) him to come to him on the water, but at least his priorities are right. He knows only Jesus has the power to enable him to do so. Jesus is the Lord of the wind and the waves, and so Peter has now learned the lesson of the feeding miracle — Jesus can provide the power for his followers to perform miracles! This is an important first step in Simon becoming "Peter the rock" and fulfilling Jesus' prophecy regarding him (two stages: John 1:42; Matt 16:18).

14:29 So Jesus said, "Come." And Peter got down out of the boat, walked on the water, and came to Jesus (ὁ δὲ εἶπεν, Ἐλθέ. καὶ καταβὰς ἀπὸ τοῦ πλοίου ὁ Πέτρος περιεπάτησεν ἐπὶ τὰ ὕδατα καὶ ἦλθεν πρὸς τὸν Ἰησοῦν). It is interesting that Jesus "walked on the lake" (vv. 25, 26) while Peter "walked on the water," possibly to separate Peter's act and recognize the short distance he walked. Still, it was a great act of faith, albeit a brief one. We should not center just on the failure but also recognize the initial faith that led him to attempt the impossible under his Master's tutelage.

14:30 But seeing how strong[13] the wind was, he was filled with fear. He began to sink and cried out, saying, "Lord, save me!" (βλέπων δὲ τὸν

8. Theissen, *Miracle Stories*, 58 – 59, calls this a word of assurance.

9. See D. W. Baker, "God, Names of," *DOTP*, 362 – 65.

10. Hauerwas, *Matthew*, 140.

11. On this idiom in Matthew, see 3:15; 4:4.

12. Peter hardly understood the full significance of this, but Matthew shows he had caught a glimmer of the truth.

13. ἰσχυρόν is present in B C D K L P Byz et al. but missing in ℵ B* 073 33 et al. Still, it is present in both Alexandrian and Western readings, and many believe it is necessary to explain why Peter's faith faltered, cf. Metzger, *Textual Commentary*, 38.

ἄνεμον ἐφοβήθη, καὶ ἀρξάμενος καταποντίζεσθαι ἔκραξεν λέγων, Κύριε, σῶσόν με). Peter's brief encounter with faith ended once he felt the fury of the storm. He starts thinking about his perilous situation rather than the enabling power of Jesus and so begins to sink into the water. He has walked some distance and is almost all the way to Jesus (v. 31), but he cannot go the final step. The cry "Lord, save me" is similar to the cry at the storm of 8:25 ("Lord save us; we're about to die"), and a connection is made between the two similar episodes. Luz believes Matthew crafts this deliberately after Ps 69:2 – 3, 15 – 16 ("I sink in … the deep waters.… Do not let the floodwaters engulf me.… Answer me, LORD") and thus intends the reader to pray with the psalmist in the words of Peter's cry.[14]

14:31 But immediately Jesus reached out his hand, grabbed Peter, and said to him, "You of little faith! Why did you doubt?" (εὐθέως δὲ ὁ Ἰησοῦς ἐκτείνας τὴν χεῖρα ἐπελάβετο αὐτοῦ καὶ λέγει αὐτῷ, Ὀλιγόπιστε, εἰς τί ἐδίστασας;). Jesus' power is not dependent on the level of Peter's faith. He grabs Peter's hand and rescues him from the watery grave. This too may well build on OT imagery of Yahweh's "reaching down [his] hand" to rescue his people "from the mighty waters" (Ps 144:7; cf. 2 Sam 22:17). Then Jesus chastises[15] Peter's "little faith" (cf. 6:30; 8:26; 16:8: 17:20).

As elsewhere, there is some question whether this refers to unbelief (France) or a faith that proved inadequate (i.e., there was some faith at first, so Carson, Blomberg, Morris). The latter is almost certainly correct. Peter did have enough faith to cry out to Jesus. But he did not have enough to overcome his fear. Instead he "doubted" (ἐδίστασας), or "had a divided mind or loyalty"[16] split between God and this world. As long as his trust was in Jesus, he walked on water, but when the centrality of the world situation intervened, his faith disappeared.[17]

14:32 After they got back in the boat, the wind ceased (καὶ ἀναβάντων αὐτῶν εἰς τὸ πλοῖον ἐκόπασεν ὁ ἄνεμος). Now Matthew introduces the end of the story in Mark 6:51, the stilling of the storm and the disciples' astonishment. "After they got back" (ἀναβάντων αὐτῶν) is another temporal genitive absolute (v. 15; cf. 1:18, 20), picturing Jesus holding onto Peter as they climb into the boat. Again, the language is reminiscent of 8:26, where in spite of the "little faith" of the disciples Jesus causes a "great calm" to replace the storm.

14:33 Then those who were in the boat worshiped Jesus, saying, "Truly you are the Son of God!"[18] (οἱ δὲ ἐν τῷ πλοίῳ προσεκύνησαν αὐτῷ λέγοντες, Ἀληθῶς θεοῦ υἱὸς εἶ). Matthew omits Mark 6:52 (the "hardened hearts" of the disciples) in order to give the polar opposite of an ending.[19] The astonishment in Mark is intensified as the

14. Luz, *Matthew 8 – 20*, 321.

15. After two aorist verbs ("reached out" [ἐκτείνας], "grabbed" [ἐπελάβετο]), the present tense "says" (λέγει) is in the foreground of the action (Porter, *Idioms*, 23 – 25) and the attention is on Jesus' rebuke.

16. David DeGraaf, "Some Doubts about Doubt: The New Testament Use of ΔΙΑΚΡΙΝΩ," *JETS* 48 (2005): 733 – 55, argues that "doubt" (διακρίνω) connotes division and contention more than doubt. As Nida and Louw, *Greek-English Lexicon*, 370 – 71, show, "doubt" (διστάζω) is a virtual synonym, and the same argument came be made here. Peter was not controlled totally by his doubt but vacillated between Jesus and this world (cf. Jas 1:6 – 8).

17. See C. R. Carlisle, "Jesus' Walking on the Water: A Note on Matthew 14.22 – 33," *NTS* 31 (1985): 151 – 55, who asserts that one of Matthew's major purposes was to present Peter as a model for discipleship.

18. θεοῦ υἱός is anarthrous not because it refers to "a son of god" in a Hellenistic sense but because of Colwell's rule, in which a predicate nominative coming before the verb "to be" lacks the article in order to distinguish it from the subject (see also 13:39). On this see Harris, *Jesus as God*, 310 – 11; Wallace, 256 – 63.

19. This does not mean Matthew and Mark contradict one another. Mark redactionally chose to stop the story two-thirds

disciples[20] fall at Jesus' feet in worship (connoted by "worshiped" [προσκυνέω] but not meant literally in the boat). The confession goes beyond Mark, where only the demons (Mark 3:11; 5:7) and the centurion (Mark 15:39) call Jesus "Son of God" (on the title, see 4:3). Here the title is at its highest, for Jesus is virtually seen as Yahweh treading on the waters and stilling the storm.

Matthew presents the gradual process by which the disciples come to understanding and overcome their failures as a result of Jesus' presence with them (see on 13:11 – 12, 16 – 17, 23, 51 – 52; 16:12). Of course, this hardly means full understanding, for Jesus will castigate their ignorance in 15:16; 16:9. The disciples have no concept of deity until John 20:28 and later. They use the title in a vaguely messianic sense, but understanding is dawning, and Matthew expects the reader to see all the title portends.

Theology in Application

This pericope is so intimately tied with the preceding feeding of the five thousand that most of the themes there are continued and deepened, especially the sovereignty of Christ and discipleship understanding.

1. Jesus as Son of God

Jesus as God's Son has the authority of Yahweh over the wind and the waves. Twelftree says, "Of all Matthew's miracle stories, it is this one that portrays the highest Christology," with Jesus the new Moses who does not just act for God, but rather God acts in him to conquer the storm and rescue his people.[21] Still, Jesus is not just the agent of God but himself contains the authority and power of God.

This passage comes the closest in Matthew to establishing the deity of Christ. As in John (John 1:1, 18; 10:30; and the "I Am" sayings, esp. the absolute form in 8:24, 28, 58; 13:19), the "I am" used here establishes Jesus as God of very God, and so the Son of God title is given an incredibly rich texture. The one who can multiply the loaves also treads on the water and calms the storms, things in the OT that only Yahweh as God of the storms can do (Ps 65:7, 89:9; 93:4; 107:29). He is Lord of the whole of creation.

2. The Role of Faith

Faith is especially needed and demonstrated in times of trial and trouble. Jesus taught his disciples to rely on his merciful provision in the feeding scene, but here he leads them into a time of testing that will prove their mettle. As Jesus himself

of the way through, at the point of failure (in keeping with his theme in the rest of his gospel). Matthew, like Paul Harvey, "told the rest of the story"! They supplement each other.

20. There is a strange tendency to make "those in the boat" refer to all but Peter who watched him walk on the water (e.g., Davies and Allison, Morris). But Peter has climbed back in the boat and surely would be worshiping with the others!

21. Twelftree, *Jesus the Miracle Worker*, 132.

was led by the Spirit into the time of testing by Satan (4:1 – 11), so he leads the disciples into the time of their testing. Unlike Jesus (and like Israel in the wilderness), however, they ultimately fail the test, though with partial success shown in their "*little* faith." While the boat does not signify the church, the storm does signify the difficulties of life (as was the case in the stilling miracle of 8:23 – 27).

3. Victory through Depending Totally on Christ

In the feeding miracle Jesus wanted to involve the disciples in his authoritative act, and this continues here. When Peter asked to walk on the water, that was the response Jesus wished. As long as Peter focused on Jesus, he was able to take step after step on the water. However, when he turned to consider the earthly situation, he failed and began to sink into the depths. The entire NT builds on this, as victory over sin and temptation is completely related to the degree to which we are centered wholly on Christ. Peter is the model disciple even in his failure. He is an all-too-human figure, struggling with his growing awareness of Christ, as do we all.

4. Calming Our Fears and Giving Us Understanding

When overwhelmed by external struggles and at wit's end, Jesus is the one who soothes our anxious hearts, who can truly remove our worries and turns our fears to joy and our defeats to victory (Phil 4:6 – 7; Jas 1:2 – 4; 1 Pet 1:6 – 7). Moreover, out of the struggle comes a deeper understanding of the reality of Christ. Out of the disciples' initial defeat they were guided by Jesus into a new awareness of him as "the Son of God," and they are beginning to grow in their understanding of that reality.

CHAPTER 65

Matthew 14:34 – 36

Literary Context

This is a transition that adds healing miracles to the nature miracles of 14:13 – 33. Matthew uses such summary transitions throughout his gospel (4:23 – 25; 8:16 – 17; 9:35) to lead into a new section, in this case a controversy story (15:1 – 20) followed by further healings (15:21 – 31). The three themes — opposition, miraculous power, and discipleship — continue to flow through this narrative.

V. Rejection, Suffering, and Glory (13:54 – 18:35)

A. Jesus' Deeds: Rejection, Discipleship, and Glory (13:54 – 17:27)

1. Rejection and Discipleship (13:54 – 16:20)

c. Feeding of the 5,000 (14:13 – 21)

d. Walking on the Water (14:22 – 33)

➦ **e. Healings at Gennesaret (14:34 – 36)**

Main Idea

The authority of Jesus over nature now extends even to those who touch his garment. Before Jesus usually had to touch a person in an active way and command the disease to leave. Now one could be healed by touching not just his person but even his robe.

Translation

Matthew 14:34-36

34a	Setting (Temporal)	After they crossed over,
b	Setting (Spatial)	**they came to the land of Gennesaret.**
35a		When the people of that place recognized him,
b	Summary	**they sent a message throughout the whole of that region and**
c		**brought to him all who were sick.**
36a		And **they begged him just to be allowed to touch the hem of his robe.**
b		**And as many as touched it were healed.**

Structure and Literary Form

Matthew continues to abbreviate Mark (this time Mark 6:53 – 56). This healing summary centers on miracles rather than on Jesus' itinerant ministry (Matthew omits Mark 6:56a). There are three parts to the summary: the arrival at Gennesaret (v. 34), the bringing of all the sick to him (v. 35), and healing merely by touching his garment (v. 36).

Exegetical Outline

➦ **I. Arrival at Gennesaret (14:34)**

II. Extensive Healing Ministry (14:35)

A. The word goes out

B. All the sick brought to Jesus

III. The Extent of His Healing Power (14:36)

A. Seeking to touch his garment

B. Healing power flows from his garment

Explanation of the Text

14:34 After they crossed over,[1] **they came to the land of Gennesaret** (Καὶ διαπεράσαντες ἦλθον ἐπὶ τὴν γῆν εἰς Γεννησαρέτ). The storm had blown the disciples off course for Capernaum (see on 14:22), so they land at Gennesaret, a small fertile plain a few miles south of Capernaum and north of Magdala. An alternate name for the Sea of Galilee was Lake Gennesaret.

1. This is a temporal aorist participle, i.e., "after crossing over" (so also v. 35).

14:35 When the people[2] of that place recognized him, they sent a message throughout the whole of that region and brought to him all who were sick (καὶ ἐπιγνόντες αὐτὸν οἱ ἄνδρες τοῦ τόπου ἐκείνου ἀπέστειλαν εἰς ὅλην τὴν περίχωρον ἐκείνην καὶ προσήνεγκαν αὐτῷ πάντας τοὺς κακῶς ἔχοντας). Jesus' fame has preceded him, and as soon as people recognize him (another temporal participle), word goes throughout the surrounding villages, and people begin to gather. His fame as a healer made people bring all their sick to him. The picture is of Jesus' compassion for the common people. He plays no favorites and cares deeply for every person he encounters.

14:36 And they begged him just to be allowed to touch the hem of his robe. And as many as touched it were healed (καὶ παρεκάλουν αὐτὸν ἵνα μόνον ἅψωνται τοῦ κρασπέδου τοῦ ἱματίου αὐτοῦ· καὶ ὅσοι ἥψαντο διεσώθησαν). Apparently the story of the hemorrhaging woman who was healed simply by touching the edge of his robe in 9:20 has become well known. Also, there may have been so many sick that they despaired of getting an audience with Jesus. So they continue "pleading" (progressive imperfect παρεκάλουν) just to be allowed to touch the hem of his garment (as in 9:20 this probably refers to the four corners at the bottom of the robe where the "tassels" required by Num 15:38–41; Deut 22:12 were found). The power of Jesus is so great that anyone who does so is healed.

As in the use of "save" (σῴζω) in 9:21–22, "healed" (διεσώθησαν) here also stresses the combined physical and spiritual effects of the healing/salvation experience (σῴζω means spiritual salvation in 1:21; 10:22; 19:25). Physical healing becomes spiritual healing.

Theology in Application

Several issues flow into and out of these three verses. (1) They summarize the broad theme of Jesus as Lord of creation with authority over every aspect of nature — food, storm, and illness. In fact, his power is so great that people do not have to be touched by him physically; all they need do is touch a piece of his clothing (this too will be passed on to Jesus' followers in Acts 19:11–12). (2) Jesus' acceptance of and concern for all people is evident. Unlike the leaders, Jesus did not restrict himself to his own kind but aligned himself with the common people and cared for them all. (3) Jesus ignores issues of religious purity, willingly allowing himself to be touched by the diseased and unclean (thus preparing for the debates of the next episode, so Carson).

2. It is frequently said that ἄνδρες here must mean only "men" (e.g., TNIV, Luz) because of its use in v. 21 for "five thousand men" apart from women. But that does not mandate that Matthew intended just "men" here. It is the immediate context that determines word usage rather than use in a previous section. There is no contextual reason for restricting this just to the men of the region, and ἄνδρες is well known as having also an inclusive sense for men and women in Luke 5:8; John 6:10; Acts 4:4 (see *EDNT*, 1:99).

CHAPTER 66

Matthew 15:1 – 20

Literary Context

Following the order of Mark, Matthew returns to the theme of controversy and conflict, centering on the debate with the Pharisees and scribes over the washing of hands. The themes of this section — Christology, discipleship, and confrontation — continue to be interspersed throughout, with opposition in 13:54 – 14:12; 15:1 – 20; 16:1 – 12, and Christology and discipleship in 14:13 – 36; 15:32 – 39; and 16:13 – 20.

V. Rejection, Suffering, and Glory (13:54 – 18:35)
A. Jesus' Deeds: Rejection, Discipleship, and Glory (13:54 – 17:27)
1. Rejection and Discipleship (13:54 – 16:20)
d. Walking on the Water (14:22 – 33)
e. Healings at Gennesaret (14:34 – 36)
➦ **f. Jesus and Tradition (15:1 – 20)**
(1) The Leaders — The Tradition of the Elders (15:1 – 9)
(2) The Crowd Called to Understanding (15:10 – 11)
(3) The Message Explained to the Disciples (15:12 – 20)
g. Further Healings (15:21 – 31)

Main Idea

Two ideas are intertwined in this section — external tradition and internal purity. The first is central to vv. 1 – 9, the second central to vv. 10 – 20. Yet both combine in the theme that the life of the follower of Jesus must be controlled not so much by external codes of conduct forced from without but by the inner person of the heart that proceeds from within.

Translation

Matthew 15:1-20

1a	Action	**Then Pharisees and scribes from Jerusalem came to Jesus, saying,**
2a	Accusation	*"Why do your disciples transgress the tradition of the elders?*
b	Basis for 2a	*For they do not wash their hands when they eat bread."*
3a	Counter-Accusation #1	**But Jesus answered,**
b		*[1] "And why do you transgress the commandment of God*
		because of your tradition?
4a	Basis for 3b	*For God said,*
b	OT Quotation	*'Honor your father and mother,'* (Exod 20:12),
c	OT Quotation	*and 'Let the one . . . be put to death*
		who speaks evil of father or mother.'
		(Exod 21:17)
5a		*But you say,*
b		*'Whoever says to his father or mother,*
c		*"Whatever you would have benefited from me*
		is now a gift devoted to God,"
6a		*will never honor their father or mother.'*
b	Result of 5a-6a	*So because of your tradition you nullify the word of God.*
7a	Counter-Accusation #2	*[2] Hypocrites!*
b		*Isaiah was right when he prophesied about you:*
8a	OT Quotation	*'This people honors me with their lips,*
b		*but their heart is far from me.*
9a		*They worship me in vain,*
b		*teaching mere human commandments*
		as doctrine.'" (Isa 29:13)
10a	Exhortation	**Then Jesus called the crowd together and told them,**
b		*"Listen and understand!*
11a	Assertion	*It is not what goes into the mouth that defiles a person but*
b	Contrast 11a	*what comes out of the mouth that defiles a person."*
12a	Question	**Then his disciples came and asked,**
b		*"Do you know that the Pharisees were scandalized*
		when they heard your message?"
13a	Explanation #1	**[1] Jesus replied,**
b	Analogy	*"Every plant . . . will be uprooted*
		that my heavenly Father has not planted.
14a	Command	*Leave them;*
b		*they are blind guides.*
c	Analogy	*Now if the blind guide the blind, both will fall into the pit."*
15a	Question	**Then Peter asked,**
b		*"Explain this analogy to us."*
16a	Explanation #2	**[2] But Jesus replied,**

Continued on next page.

Continued from previous page.

b		*"Are you yourselves also still so dull?*
17a	Restatement of 11a-b	*Can't you perceive that everything which goes into the mouth proceeds into the stomach and passes into the toilet?*
18a		But *the things that proceed from the mouth come from the heart,*
b		and *they do defile a person.*
19a	Basis for 18a-b	For *from the heart proceed evil thoughts, murder, adultery, sexual immorality, theft, false witness, blasphemies.*
20a	Conclusion	*These are the things that defile a person,*
b		but *eating with unwashed hands does not defile a person."*

Structure and Literary Form

In this controversy narrative Matthew characteristically adapts Mark 7:11 – 23 but omits Mark 7:2 – 4 (explaining the ceremony) as well as 7:19 (explaining that Jesus made all foods clean), transposes Mark 7:8 – 13 on the practice of "Corban" to an earlier spot at Matt 15:4 – 6 (without naming the practice), and then adds a parable followed by a condemnation of the leaders as "blind guides" in 15:12 – 14 and a concluding note on the washing of hands in 15:20b. The narrative breaks down into three parts: Jesus interacts with the Pharisees and scribes (vv. 1 – 9), the crowd (vv. 10 – 11), and the disciples (vv. 12 – 20). In all three sections, the issue of outer and inner purity is central.

Exegetical Outline

➡ **I. The Leaders — the Tradition of the Elders (15:1 – 9)**
- A. The challenge of the Pharisees and scribes (vv. 1 – 2)
  - 1. The charge: transgress the tradition (v. 2a)
  - 2. The reason: don't wash at meals (v. 2b)
- B. Jesus' countercharge (vv. 3 – 6)
  - 1. The charge stated: transgress God's command via tradition (v. 3)
  - 2. The charge explained (vv. 4 – 6)
    - a. The Scriptural teaching (v. 4)
    - b. Their practice (vv. 5 – 6a)
    - c. Result: they annul the word of God (v. 6b)
- C. Second charge: Isaiah prophesies against them (vv. 7 – 9)
  - 1. Lip-worship but distant hearts (v. 8)
  - 2. Empty worship through human doctrines (v. 9)

II. The Crowd Called to Understanding (15:10 – 11)
- A. Defilement not from what goes into the mouth (v. 11a)
- B. Defilement by what comes out of the mouth (v. 11b)

III. The Message Explained to the Disciples (15:12 – 20)
- A. First explanation (vv. 12 – 14)
  1. Parable: plants not planted by the Father (v. 13)
  2. Problem: the blind leading the blind (v. 14)
- B. Second explanation (vv. 15 – 19)
  1. Peter's request and Jesus' charge (vv. 15 – 16)
  2. What goes into the mouth doesn't defile (v. 17)
  3. What goes out of the mouth truly defiles (v. 18)
  4. The sin that comes from the heart (v. 19)
- C. Conclusion: the heart defiles, not eating with unwashed hands (v. 20)

Explanation of the Text

15:1 Then Pharisees and scribes from Jerusalem came to Jesus, saying (Τότε προσέρχονται τῷ Ἰησοῦ ἀπὸ Ἱεροσολύμων Φαρισαῖοι καὶ γραμματεῖς λέγοντες). The historic present "came" (προσέρχονται) makes the coming more vivid (Wallace, 526). This is probably a semi-official delegation from Jerusalem sent to test Jesus' knowledge and faithfulness to Torah (both written and oral). This is the only time in Matthew the Pharisees are named first (probably following Mark 7:1). The mention of Jerusalem stresses the hostility of the leaders and moves the action toward the climactic scene at the passion. It was unusual for such a lofty group to visit this backwater area of Galilee. France says this provides "a foretaste of the confrontation to come."[1]

15:2 "Why do your disciples transgress the tradition of the elders?" (Διὰ τί οἱ μαθηταί σου παραβαίνουσιν τὴν παράδοσιν τῶν πρεσβυτέρων;). The leaders of the Jews center not on Jesus but on his disciples (cf. 9:14) as representative of his teaching. The present tense of the three verbs in v. 2 picture the many violations the disciples have made to their tradition.[2] The Pharisees called their oral Torah "the tradition of the elders" (Josephus, *Ant.* 13.297; cf. Gal 1:14, "the traditions of [the] fathers").

In Jesus' time these rules for the conduct of daily lives were transmitted orally but later were written in the Mishnah, with an entire tractate, *Yadayim*, filled with minute details on the washing of hands.[3] They originally had a good purpose, to enable a people living in a culture far removed from the seminomadic culture that existed at the time of the giving of the law to understand and keep the law. They called it "building a fence around the law," i.e., keeping the common people from inadvertently breaking the law. But the number of details quickly turned it into a burdensome set of pedantic rules.

15:2 "For they do not wash their hands when they eat bread" (οὐ γὰρ νίπτονται τὰς χεῖρας αὐτῶν ὅταν ἄρτον ἐσθίωσιν). This particular rule does not come from the written Torah but apparently originated in the Pharisaic desire to extend the ritual required for priests at the laver (to prepare them for the temple ceremonies) to the ordinary family at meals (cf. Exod 30:17 – 21).

1. France, *Gospel of Matthew*, 575.
2. Wallace, 502, depicts the aorist tense as a "snapshot" looking at the action as a whole and the present tense as a "motion picture" centering on the ongoing action.
3. See Carson, "Matthew," 348.

The Pharisees scrupulously applied these rules to themselves. There is some agreement that in the first century such a practice was generally demanded only by Pharisaic "pietists" and was not widely observed until the second century.[4] Booth argues that such purity could only be attained by complete immersion and that this was a narrow group of Pharisees trying to convince Jesus and his disciples to join their movement.[5]

15:3 But Jesus answered,[6] "And why do you transgress the commandment of God because of your tradition?" (ὁ δὲ ἀποκριθεὶς εἶπεν αὐτοῖς, Διὰ τί καὶ ὑμεῖς παραβαίνετε τὴν ἐντολὴν τοῦ θεοῦ διὰ τὴν παράδοσιν ὑμῶν;). Jesus refuses to defend his teaching but instead goes on the offense against the Pharisaic tradition. Theirs is the far more serious transgression (this continues the present tenses from v. 2). Jesus disregarded the man-made teaching of the elders, for they set aside the very Word of God,[7] and their tradition was the very cause ("because" [διά]) of that grievous disobedience.

15:4 For God said,[8] "Honor your father and mother," and, "Let the one who speaks evil of father or mother be put to death" (ὁ γὰρ θεὸς εἶπεν, Τίμα τὸν πατέρα καὶ τὴν μητέρα, καί, Ὁ κακολογῶν πατέρα ἢ μητέρα θανάτῳ τελευτάτω). Jesus stresses not only the fifth commandment but also the fact that the two quotes (from Exod 20:12; 21:17, respectively) were divine in origin ("God said"). The Decalogue had special importance as the summation of the Torah. "Honor" (τίμα, an emphatic present meaning "at all times") meant not just to hold one's parents in high esteem but to care for them financially and in every way; it was incumbent not just on the young but adult children as well (cf. 1 Tim 5:8, "worse than an unbeliever").

Jesus then adds the commandment against reviling or "speaking evil" of a parent, part of a paragraph detailing capital death penalty cases (Exod 21:12 – 21) and was interpreted not only of cursing a parent but also of insubordination against parents. Jesus wants to show how serious the responsibilities to parents were.

15:5 But you say, "Whoever says to his father or mother, 'Whatever you would have benefited from me is now a gift devoted to God'" (ὑμεῖς δὲ λέγετε, Ὃς ἂν εἴπῃ τῷ πατρὶ ἢ τῇ μητρί, Δῶρον ὃ ἐὰν ἐξ ἐμοῦ ὠφεληθῇς). The emphatic "you" (ὑμεῖς) highlights their serious error. Mark 7:11 names this practice as "Corban" (transliterated Aramaic for a "[temple] gift"), i.e., a "gift" devoted to God (Lev 27:9, 16). This was property or money pledged to the temple, to be given after a person died. That money could no longer be used for outside things like caring for parents, but it was available for one's own use until death. "Benefited from me" refers to the parental right to receive support from their children. This tradition allowed children to escape their biblical obligation of taking care of their parents by dedicating their money as a gift to God upon their death.[9]

15:6 "... will never honor their father or mother." So because of your tradition you nullify the

4. See Luz, *Matthew 8 – 20*, 330; Turner, "Matthew," 207. See also Safrai and Stern, *Jewish People*, 802.

5. R. P. Booth, *Jesus and the Laws of Purity: Tradition History and Legal History in Mark 7* (JSNTSup 13; Sheffield: JSOT Press, 1986), 189 – 203.

6. For the translation of this idiom see on v. 15.

7. "Of God" (τοῦ θεοῦ) is a subjective genitive, "what God commands," though it could also be possessive, "God's commandments."

8. Some manuscripts (א * C K L W Byz etc.) have "commanded" instead of "said," probably due to "the commandment of God" in v. 3.

9. See J. Bailey, "Vowing Away the Fifth Commandment: Matthew 15:3 – 6/Mark 7:9 – 13," *ResQ* 42 (2000): 193 – 209, for a study of Jewish backgrounds to this misuse of Corban, including the growing opposition of rabbis to this practice.

word[10] **of God** (οὐ μὴ τιμήσει τὸν πατέρα αὐτοῦ· καὶ ἠκυρώσατε τὸν λόγον τοῦ θεοῦ διὰ τὴν παράδοσιν ὑμῶν). By using the emphatic negative "never" (οὐ μή), Jesus emphasizes the negative results when tradition is placed over Scripture. To refuse to support one's parents is to dishonor them in the deepest way possible. J. D. M. Derrett states that first-century writings interpret the "honor" of the commandment to include financial support of parents.[11] "Nullify" (ἀκυρόω) has a strong juridical force and here means to legally invalidate or revoke the very Word of God.

15:7 Hypocrites! Isaiah was right when he prophesied about you (ὑποκριταί, καλῶς ἐπροφήτευσεν περὶ ὑμῶν Ἠσαΐας λέγων). Gundry says that by delaying the Isaiah quotation until now, Matthew "makes it the climax of Jesus' counter-accusation."[12] For "hypocrite" (ὑποκριτής) see on 6:2. The Pharisees are people who claim to be one thing but whose actions prove them to be something else (used also of the Pharisees in 22:18; 23:13, 14, 15). Isaiah 29:13 is from an OT passage frequently used in the NT (Matt 11:5; Rom 9:20; 1 Cor 1:19; Col 2:22).[13] What does Jesus mean when he says Isaiah actually "prophesied" about them, especially since he was speaking of the people of his own time? Jesus uses typology here; that is, the Pharisees and scribes fit the pattern perfectly and are a typological fulfillment of that passage.

15:8 "This people honors me with their lips, but their heart is far from me" (Ὁ λαὸς οὗτος τοῖς χείλεσίν με τιμᾷ, ἡ δὲ καρδία αὐτῶν πόρρω ἀπέχει ἀπ' ἐμοῦ). The people of Isaiah's time as well honored God in temple worship and performed the sacrifices and sang the Hallel psalms, but in reality in their heart of hearts they were not serving him (progressive present "honor" [τιμᾷ]). They said the right things but did not think the right thoughts. A detailed Torah tradition without heart commitment is irrelevant before God.

15:9 "They worship me in vain, teaching mere human commandments as doctrine" (μάτην δὲ σέβονταί με, διδάσκοντες διδασκαλίας ἐντάλματα ἀνθρώπων). Such worship is folly, an empty, worthless thing. The last line is the key to this first section. The Pharisees claim to be developing doctrine when they are giving no more than man-made rules, and such things are purposeless and have no value before God. Moreover, it is God who says this through the words of Isaiah. There can be no greater contrast between God's law and the Pharisaic code. The alliteration of διδάσκοντες διδασκαλίας powerfully presents the importance of "teaching doctrine" and making certain it is based on God's truth, not on mere "human"[14] ideas.

This is a warning for our day and not just for Jesus' day. Again, we are at the heart of what it means to be a true follower of Christ: to think the things of God rather than of humankind (Mark 8:33b), to seek and think the things above rather than the things on earth (Col 3:1 – 2), to seek treasure in heaven rather than treasure on earth (Matt 6:19 – 21).

15:10 Then Jesus called[15] **the crowd together and told them, "Listen and understand!"** (Καὶ προσκαλεσάμενος τὸν ὄχλον εἶπεν αὐτοῖς, Ἀκούετε καὶ συνίετε). Now Jesus turns from the

10. Because of the specific fulfillment passage here, some copyists switch to either "law" (νόμος) or "commandment" (ἐντολή). But the manuscript evidence for "word" (λόγος) is too strong (ℵ B D 700 892 et al.).

11. J. D. M. Derrett, *Studies in the New Testament* (Leiden: Brill, 1977), 1:112 – 17.

12. Gundry, *Matthew*, 305.

13. For the authenticity of this as a logion of the historical Jesus, see Thomas R. Hatina, "Did Jesus Quote Isaiah 29:13 against the Pharisees? An Unpopular Proposal," *BBR* 16 (2006): 79 – 94.

14. Taking "human" (ἀνθρώπων) as an adjectival genitive.

15. This is another circumstantial participle that takes the force of the main verb, see on 4:20. See also vv. 12, 22, 25, 29, 32.

leaders to address the crowd. He has made his point to the Pharisees and wants to make certain the crowd understands the issues as well. They have stayed in the background and listened, probably out of respect for the famous experts. No more; Jesus brings them to the forefront, for they are the true goal of his teaching.

Also, so far the attention has been on the external tradition and its authority. Here Jesus turns to the deeper issue of inner purity and defilement. He wants the crowd not just to "hear" but to "understand" these truths (again, note the present tenses for ongoing "hearing" and "understanding"). If all they do is listen, they will remain the crowd, but when they understand and respond, they will become disciples.[16] As France notes, "understand" has become "the distinctive response of true disciples" (cf. 13:13 – 15, 19, 23, 51).[17]

15:11 "It is not what goes into the mouth that defiles a person but what comes out of the mouth that defiles a person" (οὐ τὸ εἰσερχόμενον εἰς τὸ στόμα κοινοῖ τὸν ἄνθρωπον, ἀλλὰ τὸ ἐκπορευόμενον ἐκ τοῦ στόματος τοῦτο κοινοῖ τὸν ἄνθρωπον). It is common to take this as a crux interpretum for the understanding of the law in Matthew. This passage states the theme that is then expanded as Jesus explains it to the disciples. Mark 7:19 takes this as meaning Jesus "declared all foods clean," but Matthew fails to make this comment.

How far does Matthew wish to take Jesus' statement here? In spite of the fact that many (e.g., Luz, Davies and Allison, Hagner) believe Matthew is not overthrowing the food laws, it is doubtful if Matthew is in disagreement with Mark. It is certainly true that the main point here has to do with the oral tradition rather than the Torah, but in omitting Mark's statement Matthew may even wish to broaden Jesus' teaching here to cover all the purity laws. France seems more correct in saying that Jesus "states a principle of inward religion which was destined in time to undercut for the Christian church the whole elaborate system of ceremonial purification of the Old Testament and of later Judaism."[18]

The crowds and disciples hardly caught all this, but Jesus certainly intended it. The key contrast is between "into" (εἰς) and "out of" (ἐκ). It is not external things like food coming "into" the mouth that produce impurity[19] but those thoughts and words from the heart that proceed "out of"[20] the mouth that make a person impure. The rabbis should not disagree with this second point, but the whole import hits too close to home. Jesus already said this in 12:34 of the Pharisees, "For it is from the abundance of the heart that the mouth speaks." One's words reflect the heart, and that is the true source of defilement. Words and actions, not external piety, are the true measure of a person.

15:12 Then his disciples came and asked, "Do you know that the Pharisees were scandalized when they heard[21] your message?" (Τότε

16. Davies and Allison, *Matthew*, 2:526, make a good point here. Vv. 10 – 11 show that we cannot expand the image of the Pharisees to say Jesus is castigating all of Judaism, for Jesus still has a positive attitude toward the crowds. The leaders and the rest of the nation are still distinct.

17. France, *Gospel of Matthew*, 582.

18. France, *Matthew* (TNTC), 243 – 44 (see also his *Gospel of Matthew*, 583 – 84). See also Plummer, *Matthew*, 483 – 84; McNeille, *Matthew*, 226; Gundry, *Matthew*, 305 – 6.

19. κοινόω stems from the term for "common, ordinary" but in a religious context means that which is "profane" and therefore renders one ceremonially defiled or "impure." This is also another instance when "a person" (τὸν ἄνθρωπον) is used generically for "someone" (τίς), see BDF §301 (2).

20. The two participles ("what goes in" [τὸ εἰσερχόμενον], "what comes out" [τὸ ἐκπορευόμενον]) are substantival and function as the subjects of the two clauses. The present tenses connote what is their common practice.

21. Aorist temporal participle "when they heard" (ἀκούσαντες), looking at their investigation as a whole (see Porter, *Idioms*, 35).

προσελθόντες οἱ μαθηταὶ λέγουσιν αὐτῷ, Οἶδας ὅτι οἱ Φαρισαῖοι ἀκούσαντες τὸν λόγον ἐσκανδαλίσθησαν;). Now the disciples, who have also been quiescent, come into the picture. They have been watching the interaction and noticing how upset the Pharisees have become. As in 5:29; 11:6, "scandalized" (σκανδαλίζω) has a double meaning; the Jewish leaders have been "offended" or angered, but even more there are connotations of falling into sin and apostasy, here connected with a rejection of God's Messiah. They realize Jesus was speaking of their overly extensive purity laws and are angry.

15:13 Jesus replied, "Every plant that my heavenly Father has not planted will be uprooted" (ὁ δὲ ἀποκριθεὶς εἶπεν, Πᾶσα φυτεία ἣν οὐκ ἐφύτευσεν ὁ πατήρ μου ὁ οὐράνιος ἐκριζωθήσεται). Jesus' "reply" (see on v. 15 for the grammar) is a strong denunciation, a thinly veiled diatribe against the Pharisees as "plants" that have not originated with God. All in Israel is not of God. To be "planted" by God[22] means to be part of his garden, to be his chosen people, the elect community. Several Jewish texts use this image: e.g., Ps 44:2 ("planted our ancestors"), 80:8 – 11 (planting the vine from Egypt); Isa 60:21 ("the shoot I have planted"). So this verse says unequivocally that the Pharisees are not of God, not true Israel.

A passage that comes close to this is Jer 45:4, where God told a discouraged Baruch of his judgment against the apostate nation: "I will ... uproot what I have planted, throughout the earth" (cf. also Isa 5:1 – 7). The idea here, then, is that judgment will come as a result of apostasy, which fits "scandalized" (σκανδαλίζω) in v. 12.[23] "Will be uprooted" (ἐκριζωθήσεται) is a divine passive that means at the last judgment God will reject and destroy them, a reference back to the parables of the weeds (13:24 – 30 [this verb is used in v. 29 of "uprooting" plants], 36 – 43) and the net (13:47 – 52). The use of "heavenly Father" (see on 5:48) means the judgment is a heavenly one and has eternal ramifications.

15:14 Leave them; they are blind guides. Now if the blind guide the blind, both will fall into the pit (ἄφετε αὐτούς· τυφλοί εἰσιν ὁδηγοί [τυφλῶν].[24] τυφλὸς δὲ τυφλὸν ἐὰν ὁδηγῇ, ἀμφότεροι εἰς βόθυνον πεσοῦνται). Since the Pharisees are not of God and are headed toward judgment, Jesus tells the disciples to have nothing to do with them. Yet another viable translation is "Let them be," and there are nuances of that as well. There is no use debating with those who are intractable. You expect them to oppose whatever you say, so leave them alone.

Romans 2:19 shows that the Jewish people considered themselves to be "a guide for the blind, a light for those who are in the dark." Isaiah 42:6 – 7 called Israel to be "a light for the Gentiles, to open eyes that are blind" (cf. 49:6; Wis 18:4). In a play on words Jesus says here they think of themselves as "guides *for* the blind" ("blind" [τυφλῶν] as objective genitive) but are actually "guides *that* are blind" ("blind" [τυφλῶν] as epexegetical genitive); they are only "the blind guiding the blind," meaning they are more blind to God than the people they try to bring to him! When the blind take the

22. ἐφύτευσεν is a culminative aorist emphasizing the results of the action, see Wallace, 559.

23. See S. von Dobbeler, "Auf der Grenze. Ethos und Identität der matthäischen Gemeinde nach Matt 15, 1 – 20," *BZ* 45 (2001): 55 – 78, for an attempt to see this as a rebuke of some Pharisees but not of Israel as a whole. He believes Matthew wants his church to remain within Judaism as a messianic sect. On this see the Introduction to this book.

24. B D 0237 omit "blind" (τυφλῶν), but the UBS committee felt its presence best explained the variants and so placed it in brackets. See Metzger, *Textual Commentary*, 39.

blind by hand, both end up "falling into the pit" (cf. Luke 6:39).

The Jewish leaders considered themselves teachers of the law, but Jesus says that is not true. They are blind to God's true law, for they have no heart for him and in fact have rejected God's Son and Messiah. Therefore they are blind to God's truths, and even worse they will only increase the blindness of the people they influence. It may be that "pit" (βόθυνον) here also contains an allusion to Sheol, at times called "a pit" (*šāḥat*, so Davies and Allison).

15:15 Then Peter asked,[25] **"Explain this**[26] **analogy to us"** (Ἀποκριθεὶς δὲ ὁ Πέτρος εἶπεν αὐτῷ, Φράσον ἡμῖν τὴν παραβολὴν [ταύτην]). Peter once again speaks for the whole group of disciples (cf. 10:2; 16:16; 17:4; 18:21). "Analogy" (παραβολή) does not refer to a "parable" here. On the surface it connotes the analogy of God's planting in v. 13, but Jesus' response includes all the material from vv. 11 – 14, so the idea of what goes into and comes out of the mouth is also (mainly) intended. As in 13:36, 49 Jesus needs to explain the analogy, but as he said in 13:11, 16 – 17, such "parables" are meant for the true followers.

15:16 But Jesus replied, "Are you yourselves also still so dull?" (ὁ δὲ εἶπεν, Ἀκμὴν καὶ ὑμεῖς ἀσύνετοί ἐστε;). "But" (δέ) here is a strong adversative contrasting Jesus to the disciples. The disciples have been growing in their understanding. In 13:51 – 52 they said they understood the parables and Jesus called them "teachers of the law." In 14:33 they partially overcame their "little faith" and realized Jesus was "truly ... the Son of God." But now they show their true colors and how far they have yet to go by failing to comprehend Jesus' teaching on the failure of the Pharisees. This is stressed by the emphatic "yourselves also" (καὶ ὑμεῖς) with ἀκμήν ("even yet"). Jesus is incredulous that the disciples, after all that has transpired and all the teaching they have received at his feet, can still be so "dull" (ἀσύνετος), uncomprehending, senseless, and foolish. Jesus told the crowds to "listen and understand" (v. 10), and now his very disciples have failed to do so. They should have understood immediately what Jesus said.

15:17 "Can't you perceive that everything which goes into the mouth proceeds into the stomach and then passes into the toilet?"(οὐ νοεῖτε ὅτι πᾶν τὸ εἰσπορευόμενον εἰς τὸ στόμα εἰς τὴν κοιλίαν χωρεῖ καὶ εἰς ἀφεδρῶνα ἐκβάλλεται;). They should have "preceived" (present tense νοέω for ongoing mental perception) what Jesus had meant. This explains the first half of v. 11 that the food that goes into the mouth does not defile a person. Jesus' point is that the natural processes of the body take care of food so that it simply passes through the system without affecting one's stand with God. All foods that could possibly defile one have no effect and simply disappear. This is in essence what Mark 7:19 says and fits Mark's conclusion, "In saying this, Jesus declared all foods clean."

15:18 "But the things that proceed from the mouth come from the heart, and they do defile a person" (τὰ δὲ ἐκπορευόμενα ἐκ τοῦ στόματος ἐκ τῆς καρδίας ἐξέρχεται, κἀκεῖνα κοινοῖ τὸν ἄνθρωπον). This now explains the second half of v. 11, the words that come from[27] the mouth. The

25. For the redundant use of the circumstantial participle, see Zerwick, *Biblical Greek*, 127; Wallace, 649 – 50. It is common to translate "answering, he said" as a single verb. See also vv. 3, 13, 24, 26, 28 in this chapter alone! Matthew uses this construction fifty-six times.

26. "This" (ταύτην) is omitted in ℵ B f[1] 700 892 et al,. but could have been left out because the actual "parable" is somewhat removed (Metzger, *Textual Commentary*, 39).

27. As in v. 11, "the things that proceed" (τὰ ἐκπορευόμενα) is a substantival participle that functions as the subject of the clause; see also v. 20.

καρδία refers to the whole person — the thoughts, the feelings, and all that makes people what they are.[28] Jesus' point centers on the two prepositions, on the difference between what goes "into" (εἰς) and what comes "out of" (ἐκ) the mouth. It is not external things like food but the inner thoughts of the heart that truly define one and tell what kind of person they are. So, as in v. 11, this is the actual source of defilement. This is the true characteristic of the "hypocrite" (v. 7), a person who works hard at looking good and centers on all the external things but ignores the true source of the defilement, the inner reality of the heart.

15:19 For from the heart proceed evil thoughts, murder, adultery, sexual immorality, theft, false witness, blasphemies (ἐκ γὰρ τῆς καρδίας ἐξέρχονται διαλογισμοὶ πονηροί, φόνοι, μοιχεῖαι, πορνεῖαι, κλοπαί, ψευδομαρτυρίαι, βλασφημίαι). Mark 7:21 records thirteen sins that proceed from the heart (with "from" [ἐκ] denoting origin), Matthew seven. The first, "evil thoughts," might be the general aspect defined further in the rest, i.e., thoughts of murder, of adultery, etc. Luz sees two accents here: Matthew centers on sins of the tongue and of the thought life, and he shortens Mark's vice catalogue[29] to concentrate on sins from the second table of the Decalogue.[30] These are murder (sixth), adultery (seventh), stealing (eighth), and false witness (ninth and not in Mark's list).

However, it is strange that Matthew does not include coveting from Mark's list, the tenth commandment. He may expect the reader to add it mentally from the list. "Blasphemies" (βλασφημίαι) most likely has a double meaning, referring to slander and blasphemy, but in light of their attacks on Jesus Messiah, religious blasphemy might be uppermost for Matthew.

15:20 These are the things that defile a person, but eating with unwashed hands does not defile a person (ταῦτά ἐστιν τὰ κοινοῦντα τὸν ἄνθρωπον, τὸ δὲ ἀνίπτοις χερσὶν φαγεῖν οὐ κοινοῖ τὸν ἄνθρωπον). Jesus now goes back to the issue of v. 2 and gives his legal verdict. He applies the general principle of v. 11 to the specific case of hand-washing and concludes that no external act like the ritual washing of hands has anything to do with true purity. Therefore, the fact that the disciples eat with unwashed hands cannot render them unclean. As many have noted, the discussion in Matthew centers primarily on the Pharisaic tradition rather than the ceremonial laws of the Torah; but the larger issue of the ceremonial law is still implicit,[31] and Matthew is not in disagreement with Mark.

28. See Hans Walter Wolff, *Anthropology of the Old Testament* (London: SCM, 1974), 46, for the heart as the seat of the rational as well as the emotional side of a person.

29. Vice lists as in Matthew and Mark are common in the NT (Rom 1:29 – 31; 1 Cor 6:9 – 10; Gal 5:19 – 21; Eph 5:3 – 5). Such vice (and virtue) catalogues were common in the Hellenistic world as well as in Second Temple Judaism, including Qumran. Most likely, the OT/Jewish background is the primary source. See Colin G. Kruse, "Virtues and Vices," *DPL*, 962 – 63.

30. Luz, *Matthew 8 – 20*, 334. See also Grundmann, *Matthäus*, 374.

31. Luz, *Matthew 8 – 20*, 335 (along with Davies and Allison, *Matthew*, 2:537 – 38), makes far too detailed a conclusion on the basis of 15:1 – 20, namely, that Matthew affirms the binding nature of the Torah laws of purity and did not even reject the tradition of the elders but only "where the tradition of the elders is in conflict with God's command itself." When the words of this passage are examined without reading too much into redactional differences (which many scholars seem to do), it is hard to see how Matthew is not in general agreement with Mark that the food laws (among other aspects of ritual purity) are no longer binding.

Theology in Application

There are three levels at which we must understand this passage: the historical level of the Pharisaic traditions, the later level of Matthew and his Christian readers, and the level of the reader today. For Jesus' day this has relevance for the whole picture of Jesus as the final interpreter of Torah and for the implications of the coming of the kingdom for Jewish religious practices (see on 5:17 – 20). Jesus has gotten at the very heart of the issue of the oral tradition and indeed at the Torah as a whole. It is the heart that matters more than the outward manifestation.

The prophets often said the same, such as, "I desire mercy, not sacrifice" (Hos 6:6; cf. 1 Sam 15:22 – 23; Isa 1:11 – 20; Jer 7:21 – 22; Amos 5:21 – 24). For Matthew's readers in the later church, it spoke to issues of a Jewish-Christian lifestyle and their relationship with tradition as well as Torah; it is at this level that the larger implications would be evident and what Mark said explicitly about the food laws would be realized. For the contemporary church the issue has to do with external vs. internal piety as well as church traditions in our time.

1. Judging Human Teaching

Human teachings must always be judged on the basis of their adherence to the truths of God found in his Word. In every Jewish and Christian movement certain historical hobbyhorses are raised to the level of dogma, both in the areas of theory and praxis. I grew up in a fundamentalist tradition where it was essential not to go to movies, play cards, dance, or drink wine. In and of themselves those are not necessarily bad things to avoid, but they became the external signs of a true Christian.

Moreover, many of those who assiduously kept those rules failed to observe the weightier matters of God's Word, like love, compassion, and mercy. I saw many of their children rebel against Christianity because they observed the hypocrisy of their parents. Our lifestyle as well as our doctrinal system must at all times flow out of the demands of God's revealed truths, not just out of church tradition. Colossians 2:8 (cf. vv. 6 – 19) talks about the danger of "deceptive philosophy" emerging from the imposition of "human tradition" on God's truths.

2. Purity in the Eyes of God

Closely linked with the first principle is this next one. People are often far more concerned with looking good than with actually being good. We can sing in the choir, take the offering, attend the right meetings with a smile on our face, but until we live the life at home that we pretend to live at church, we are hypocrites. Moreover, Jesus' point here as well as in the parables of the weeds and the net in ch. 13 is that God knows and will judge us by the true reality of our heart, not by the pretension of our external appearances. We may discover that our Armani suits and our Dior dresses are in the eyes of God nothing but the emperor's new clothes (cf. Rev 3:18b)! The importance of inward righteousness is also found in Rom 2:28 – 29 ("circumcision of the heart") and 1 Pet 3:3 – 4 ("your inner self, the unfading beauty of a gentle and quiet spirit").

3. Make Certain God Is in Your Life

Few in history have worked harder at maintaining their religious life than did the Pharisees. Perfectly good intentions lay behind their detailed oral Torah and the practices they enjoined. The problem was not in their desires but in the fact that the externals took precedence over the internal reality of the truths of God. When they rejected God's Messiah, they rejected the God of the Bible, and that led them to depend even more on the externals. When the inner reality is gone, the external appearance is all one has, and it becomes idolatry.

The problem was not in the washed hands or in the kosher food but in the fact that God was no longer behind it. When Messianic Jewish Christians follow kosher today, that is fine, because they are using the practice as part of their ethnic worship of the true Messiah. Paul himself did that when in Jewish circles (1 Cor 9:20, 22). External acts of piety are appropriate in and of themselves as long as they exhibit the true reality of the inner life of the Spirit.

4. Heart and Life

Consider the sins of your heart before you consider the actions of your life. The problem with the Pharisees was the false order of their priorities, and that is our difficulty as well. Until the heart is changed, actions will never suffice. When evil thoughts predominate, we never dare think our actions are viable. That is what happens with internet pornography. When we are immersed in such pernicious thoughts, how can we pretend to be serving God elsewhere? We are negating the so-called "good" we pretend to do. We must get our house in order before we start thinking our actions are good.

CHAPTER 67

Matthew 15:21 – 31

Literary Context

There are several connections with this story and what precedes. We return to the miracle genre, but this goes once more into the arena of discipleship, as a Gentile woman becomes a model to the disciples of understanding and faith.[1] Since she is a Gentile, this relates to the idea of the "blind guides" (used by the Jews in Gentile conversion) and of the Gentile mission in Matthew (e.g., 1:5 – 6; 2:1 – 12; 4:14 – 16, 25; 8:10 – 12, 28 – 34; 10:18; 12:21, 42; 13:38).

V. Rejection, Suffering, and Glory (13:54 – 18:35)
- **A. Jesus' Deeds: Rejection, Discipleship, and Glory (13:54 – 17:27)**
  - **1. Rejection and Discipleship (13:54 – 16:20)**
    - f. Jesus and Tradition (15:1 – 20)
    - ➦ **g. Further Healings (15:21 – 31)**
      - **(1) The Faith of the Canaanite Woman (15:21 – 28)**
      - **(2) Summary Healings (15:29 – 31)**
    - h. Feeding of the 4,000 (15:32 – 39)

Main Idea

This is a story of persistent faith and humility, the heart of discipleship; and the fact that it is shown by a Gentile woman is startling indeed and parallels the faith of the Gentile centurion in 8:5 – 13. Thus the second theme is the universal mission, specifically the place of Israel and the Gentiles in salvation history.[2] Then the third

1. In a clever article, James M. Scott, "Matthew 15.21 – 28: A Test-Case for Jesus' Manners," *JSNT* 63 (1996): 21 – 44, shows how this story utilizes the parabolic method of reversal of expectation to have the woman, an outsider, "convert" Jesus and demonstrate a new level of discipleship.

2. On this see especially Judith Gundry-Volf, "Spirit, Mercy, and the Other," *ThTo* 51 (1995): 508 – 23, who sees this as a major exemplar of crossing ethnic boundaries and overcoming exclusion to produce the new community of faith.

theme is that of Jesus' authority as Lord of creation, especially over illness (stressed in the summary passage of vv. 29 – 31).

Translation

Matthew 15:21-31

Verse	Function	Text
21a	Setting (Temporal)	After Jesus left that place,
b	Setting (Spatial)	**he withdrew to the region of Tyre and Sidon.**
22a	Action	And **look, a Canaanite woman from that area came to him and cried out,**
b	Request #1	*"Have mercy on me, Lord, Son of David.*
c		*My daughter is terribly ill, possessed by a demon."*
23a	Response #1	But **Jesus did not answer her with even a single word.**
b	Request #2	And **his disciples came and requested,**
c		*"Send her away because she keeps crying out at us."*
24a	Response #2	So **Jesus responded,**
b		*"I was not sent to anyone except to the lost sheep of the house of Israel."*
25a	Request #2	**Then she came and fell down before him, saying,**
b		*"Lord, help me!"*
26a	Response #3/Analogy	But **Jesus responded,**
b		*"It is not good to take the children's bread and throw it to the dogs."*
27a	Request #3	But **she replied,**
b		*"Yes Lord.*
c	Analogy	*Yet indeed their dogs eat the crumbs that fall from the table of their masters."*
28a	Response #4	**Then Jesus responded,**
b		*"Woman, your faith is great.*
c		*Let it happen for you as you want."*
d	Result/Healing	And **her daughter was healed from that very hour.**
29a		Moving on from there,
b	Setting (Spatial)	**Jesus passed along the Sea of Galilee.**
c	Setting (Spatial)	**Then he ascended a mountain and sat down.**
30a	Action	**Large crowds came to him,**
b		bringing with them the lame, the blind, the crippled, the mute, and many others.
c		**They laid them at his feet,**
d	Result of 30a-c/Healing	and **he healed them.**
31a	Reaction #1 of 30d	**As a result, the crowd marveled**
b		when they saw the mute speaking, the crippled whole, the lame walking, and the blind seeing.
c	Reaction #2 of 30d	And **they glorified the God of Israel.**

Structure and Literary Form

At the heart, this section consists of a series of healing miracle stories, but at the same time vv. 21 – 28 is also a discipleship story with an extended dialogue between Jesus and the Gentile woman. Davies and Allison rightly point to the mixed form behind this passage, concluding it is "a miracle story which contains elements characteristic of both pronouncement stories and controversy dialogues."[3] This first passage is drawn from Mark 7:24 – 30 but not so much abbreviated as transformed with some material added from Matthew's special source (vv. 23 – 24) that parallels 10:5 – 6. The summary miracle story of vv. 29 – 31 is also Matthean and parallels other summary passages like 4:23 – 25; 8:16; 9:35 – 36; 14:13 – 14, 34 – 36.

The story of the Canaanite woman revolves around three dialogue sequences (vv. 21 – 24, 25 – 26, 27 – 28) leading up to the concluding remark regarding her "great faith," followed by the healing/exorcism of her daughter. The summary story centers on Jesus healing four types of illnesses and the crowds wondering at his authority.

Exegetical Outline

→ **I. The Faith of the Canaanite Woman (15:21 – 28)**
- A. First encounter (vv. 21 – 24)
  1. Setting: Tyre and Sidon (v. 21)
  2. The woman's request to help her demon-possessed daughter (v. 22)
  3. Jesus' silence and the disciples' response (v. 23)
  4. Jesus' response: I was sent only to Israel (v. 24)
- B. Second encounter (vv. 25 – 26)
  1. Her second plea for help (v. 25)
  2. Jesus' response: the bread not for dogs (v. 26)
- C. Third encounter (vv. 27 – 28)
  1. Her plea: let the dogs have the crumbs (v. 27)
  2. Jesus' response: her great faith (v. 28a)
  3. The result: the daughter healed (v. 28b)

II. Summary Healings (15:29 – 31)
- A. Setting: on the mountain (v. 29)
- B. Healing four types of diseases (v. 30)
- C. The wonder of the crowds at the four types of healing miracles (v. 31)

3. Davies and Allison, *Matthew*, 2:544.

Explanation of the Text

15:21 After Jesus left[4] that place, he withdrew to the region of Tyre and Sidon (Καὶ ἐξελθὼν ἐκεῖθεν ὁ Ἰησοῦς ἀνεχώρησεν εἰς τὰ μέρη Τύρου καὶ Σιδῶνος). The idea of leaving and withdrawing occurs also in 12:15; 14:13. In those settings there was a negative context of opposition and death; and the setting of opposition is still somewhat present, so that Jesus is once more "withdrawing" from his enemies as well as symbolically rejecting them and turning his back on them.

At the same time, both here and in v. 29 there is also geographical movement in a travel setting. Jesus is on his way to his destiny at Jerusalem. Tyre and Sidon were major Hellenistic cities thirty and fifty miles from the northern edge of Galilee. Many scholars believe Jesus never left Jewish areas and therefore went to the borders of the regions that extended far eastward, with the woman coming out to meet him. But there is no reason to doubt the Markan note (Mark 7:24, 31) that Jesus went through the regions, and it is likely that he wanted to get away from the leaders as well as prepare the disciples for the next stage of salvation history, namely, their future ministry to Gentiles.

15:22 And look, a Canaanite woman from that area came to him and cried out (καὶ ἰδοὺ γυνὴ Χαναναία ἀπὸ τῶν ὁρίων ἐκείνων ἐξελθοῦσα ἔκραζεν λέγουσα). As in 8:5 – 13 this is a startling development in the Jewish setting of chs. 11 – 15, especially regarding the controversy with the Pharisees over purity laws in the last story. This is especially seen in the choice of "Canaanite" (Χαναναία, only here in the NT),[5] a term not only for Gentiles but also for the Phoenician people themselves[6] but used probably due to its OT associations with the enemies of Israel. Together with "Tyre and Sidon" (Mark has only "Tyre") it highlights the negative connotations behind the woman's ethnic origins.

In this sense Matthew is highlighting the startling nature of the whole story, for women or Gentiles would not normally "come" (a circumstantial participle, see on v. 12) to Jesus. Jesus' first reaction is in keeping with what the people would expect (rejection of the repugnant unclean Gentile), but her incredible retort and Jesus' concluding positive response jars with the opening of the story and is the real purpose of Matthew's rendition. This is a technique (reversal of expectation) used in Jesus' parables (see introduction to ch. 13) and is effective here.

15:22 "Have mercy on me, Lord, Son of David. My daughter is terribly ill, possessed by a demon" (Ἐλέησόν με, κύριε υἱὸς Δαυίδ· ἡ θυγάτηρ μου κακῶς δαιμονίζεται). The fact that this woman calls Jesus "Lord" and "Son of David" is startling. She may have been a God-fearer or proselyte to use such language; at the very least she is well acquainted with Jewish beliefs. "Son of David" recalls the healing of the two blind men in 9:27 – 31, who also called out for mercy from

4. ἐξελθών is a temporal aorist participle and as such is best translated "after he left."

5. Günther Schwarz, "Syrophoinikissa-Chananaia (Markus 7.26/Matthäus 15.22)," *NTS* 30 (1984): 626 – 28, shows that Mark's "Syrophoenician" and Matthew's "Canaanaite" are both based on the Aramaic *kena'anîtā*.

6. So Luz. Schnabel, *Early Christian Mission*, 1:338, follows Theissen, *Gospels in Context*, 61 – 80, in positing that she was probably a wealthy Hellenistic woman from a city that was an agricultural center in the area. This is possible though ultimately unprovable.

the "Son of David" (see also 12:23). There it was noted that this title is often used in healing contexts (9:27; 12:23; 15:22; 20:30 – 31), probably to emphasize that the Davidic Messiah is caring for his flock.

"Lord" (κύριε) was hardly used with full understanding by the woman, but Matthew and his readers would have seen an allusion to Jesus as the Lord of creation who controlled illness and the cosmic forces of evil (see 14:28, 30). The little girl is in a dire situation, "terribly ill" (κακῶς for suffering in illness, cf. 4:24) and demon-possessed (like the boy in 17:14 – 21, with κακῶς used in 17:15). The demon, as elsewhere (cf. 17:14 – 19), used the illness to further torture the child.

15:23 But Jesus did not answer her with even a single word (ὁ δὲ οὐκ ἀπεκρίθη αὐτῇ λόγον). Jesus' silence is to some extent understandable, for she represents everything reprehensible about Gentiles to the Jews. On the surface he seems to be rejecting her request, but in the larger context it is more likely that he is testing her, waiting for further response.

15:23 And his disciples came and requested, "Send her away because she keeps crying out at us" (καὶ προσελθόντες οἱ μαθηταὶ αὐτοῦ ἠρώτουν αὐτὸν λέγοντες, Ἀπόλυσον αὐτήν, ὅτι κράζει ὄπισθεν ἡμῶν). The use of imperfect "requested" (ἠρώτουν) and present tense "crying out" (κράζει) shows the woman's great persistence. She will not take no for an answer and keeps shouting for mercy, exactly the response Jesus may have been looking for. The disciples are growing irritated by her continual "hounding" (Hagner's translation) of them and want Jesus to dismiss her. Many believe in "send her away" that they mean "set her free" or heal her so she will go away.[7] The latter is not as likely, for this is a negative context, and it is better to see this as "make her go away."

15:24 So Jesus responded, "I was not sent to anyone except to[8] the lost sheep of the house of Israel" (ὁ δὲ ἀποκριθεὶς εἶπεν, Οὐκ ἀπεστάλην εἰ μὴ εἰς τὰ πρόβατα τὰ ἀπολωλότα οἴκου Ἰσραήλ). At first glance Jesus seems to acquiesce with the disciples' request. He responds with the very words he used in instructing the disciples on their mission in 10:5 – 6. This is another crux interpretum for Matthew's view of mission and the place of the Gentiles in it, and "the lost sheep of the house of Israel" is taken from 10:6 (see discussion there). The Jewish people are hopeless, like "sheep without a shepherd" (the failure of its leadership, cf. 9:36) and "lost" both in a national sense and especially in their stance before God.

This passage is the turning point from a Jewish-based mission (10:5 – 6) to the universal mission to all the nations, Jews and Gentiles, hinted at in 8:16 – 17; 10:18 (in the context of 10:5 – 6) and made explicit in 28:19. Here Jesus is at first agreeing with the disciples to leave the woman and her daughter.[9] This fits the context well at this point and shows an initial reluctance to extend his ministry to the Gentiles in the church's mission.

Here Jesus continues the salvation-historical centrality of Israel in God's plan of salvation, his special grace to his chosen people. But in the ensuing narrative Jesus extends that grace to the Gentile woman as "a signal of this coming, unheard-of grace of God,"[10] yet an extension that

7. So McNeile, Carson, France, Hagner, Morris; contra Gundry, Davies and Allison, Luz.

8. Here "into" (εἰς) is used with the force of "to" (πρός), see Zerwick, *Biblical Greek*, 97 – 98.

9. If the view that the disciples want to heal her and send her on her way is correct (see above), Jesus would be rejecting that suggestion and saying he does not want to do so. That does not make sense, since the disciples, not Jesus, would be on her side, which hardly fits Jewish sensitivities on that issue.

10. Luz, *Matthew 8 – 20*, 340.

has been hinted at in the place of the Gentiles throughout Matthew's gospel (cf. 1:5 – 6; 2:1 – 12; 8:10 – 12, 28 – 34; 10:18). Blomberg calls this "a test or prompt of some kind designed to draw out the woman into further discussion ... to see what kind of belief this woman has."[11]

15:25 Then she came[12] and fell down before him, saying, "Lord, help me!" (ἡ δὲ ἐλθοῦσα προσεκύνει αὐτῷ λέγουσα, Κύριε, βοήθει μοι). Jesus rightly saw in her a persistent faith in his grace and mercy.[13] While often προσκυνέω means to "worship" (cf. 4:9 – 10; 14:33), it has the force of submission and pleading (cf. 8:2; 9:18), and that is the likely thrust here (with the imperfect tense dramatically pushing her act to the foreground).[14] She appeals once more to Jesus as "lord"[15] over illness (v. 22) and begs for him to help her daughter.

15:26 But Jesus responded, "It is not good[16] to take the children's bread and throw[17] it to the dogs" (ὁ δὲ ἀποκριθεὶς εἶπεν, Οὐκ ἔστιν καλὸν λαβεῖν τὸν ἄρτον τῶν τέκνων καὶ βαλεῖν τοῖς κυναρίοις). This startling parabolic retort on the part of Jesus at first glance seems rude and antagonistic. In fact, Beare calls it "brutal" and a "violent rebuff": "These words exhibit the worst kind of chauvinism."[18] Matthew omits Mark 7:27b, "First let the children eat all they want," thus making Jesus' reply all the more stark.[19] The "bread" is certainly the kingdom blessings, here specifically God's healing presence. The "children" are the Jews and the "dogs" Gentiles. The latter was a common Jewish epithet, building on the fact that dogs were unclean animals and in Palestine were scavengers and homeless mongrels.

The major debate centers on "dog" (κυνάριον), specifically whether the force of the ι – diminutive renders this a "little dog," perhaps even a household pet.[20] The problem is that diminutives had lost their force by the first century, so this is difficult to prove; but the diminutive in the "*small* fish" of 15:34b does retain its force, so it is at the least possible here. It is likely that Jesus is using the term in the Jewish sense, for this fits his refusal to include the Gentiles in his mission, while the Canaanite woman changes the metaphor in the next verse.

15:27 But she replied, "Yes Lord. Yet indeed their[21] dogs eat the crumbs that fall from the table of their masters" (ἡ δὲ εἶπεν, Ναί κύριε, καὶ γὰρ τὰ κυνάρια ἐσθίει ἀπὸ τῶν ψιχίων τῶν πιπτόντων ἀπὸ τῆς τραπέζης τῶν κυρίων αὐτῶν). Her reply is brilliantly put. This amazing

11. Blomberg, *Matthew*, 243.

12. Another circumstantial participle as in vv. 10, 12, 22.

13. It is possible that "she came" (ἐλθοῦσα) means she was out of earshot and did not hear the interchange between Jesus and his disciples (see Davies and Allison, Morris), but that is unnecessary. The tenor of the story centers more on her tenacious plea for mercy, and ἐλθοῦσα often in Matthew simply carries the action forward (12:44; 13:4, 54; 14:12).

14. See Porter, *Idioms*, 23.

15. In Matthew "Lord" (κύριος) often has force as a virtual title pointing the reader to Jesus' cosmic "lordship." The woman hardly understands all of this.

16. Some Western texts (D it syr[c,a]) have the stronger "it is necessary" (ἔξεστιν) rather than "it is good" (ἔστιν καλόν).

17. The aorist tense of the two infinitives looks at the action as a whole, as a "snapshot" rather than a "motion picture," see Wallace, 554 – 55.

18. Beare, *Matthew*, 342.

19. Keener, *Matthew*, 417, and Schnabel, *Early Christian Mission*, 1:338, build on Theissen, *Gospels in Context*, 66 – 80, that Jesus here reverses the socioeconomic reality of power then, in which she as a member of the privileged class in Tyre took the bread from the Jewish peasants. Jesus says the "bread" belongs to the Jews first.

20. Many Gentiles had dogs as pets — so Davies and Allison, Hagner, Blomberg, Keener; contra Carson, France.

21. An example of the article used for the possessive pronoun, see on 13:36.

story is the only time anyone "beats" Jesus in a debate. He concedes her point — and she is a woman and a Gentile! I agree with Dufton that here the woman switches to the household pet.[22] There is no linguistic evidence to support this, but the switch to the image of dogs eating the crumbs from the master's table[23] supports this image of a pet. The woman's humility is striking. She willingly admits to and accepts her secondary status to the Jews and shows a perfect willingness to partake of the "crumbs"[24] left over from Jewish preeminence in the kingdom. This woman is certain that Jesus has more than enough authority and power to care for her daughter with what is left over.

There is some debate as to whether the plural κυρίων refers to the Jews (Keener) or to Jesus himself (in kind of a plural of majesty). Either is possible, since the one would stress the superiority of the Jews in salvation history, the other would follow the fact that she calls Jesus "Lord" (κύριος) in vv. 22, 25. The more natural is the former, with the Gentiles eating from the Jewish table, an image much in keeping with Rom 11.

15:28 Then Jesus responded,[25] "Woman, your faith is great" (τότε ἀποκριθεὶς ὁ Ἰησοῦς εἶπεν αὐτῇ, Ὦ γύναι, μεγάλη σου ἡ πίστις). The capstone of the story is Jesus' remark regarding her "great faith" (with "great" [μεγάλη] first for emphasis), reminiscent of a similar remark to the Gentile centurion in 8:10, "I have found no one in Israel with such great faith." These two stories are tied together as glimpses of the later faith the Gentiles would demonstrate in the universal mission.[26]

There are four levels of faith in Matthew: the "un-faith" of the Jewish people (13:58), the faith of those whose faith turns healing into "salvation" (σῴζω, 9:2, 22, 28 – 29; 15:28; 21:21 – 22), the "little faith" of Peter and the disciples (see on 14:31), and the persistent faith of the centurion and the woman here (8:10; 15:28), the model for true discipleship. This latter must be defined as a total dependence and trust in Jesus. In this sense too (as even more so in Mark) this Gentile woman is a model of discipleship for the Twelve, who have had only "little faith" thus far. Rhoades and Michie call her one of "the little people" in Mark, i.e., one of the group of characters who appear only once (the hemorrhaging woman, the father of the demon-possessed child, blind Bartimaeus) but who show the faith that the disciples still lack.[27] While not as prominent in Matthew, this still applies here.

15:28 "Let it happen for you[28] as you want" (γενηθήτω σοι ὡς θέλεις). It is important to realize that Jesus has not departed from his mission only "to the lost sheep of the house of Israel." Rather, because of her "great faith," he has granted her request as an exception to his God-sent mission. This is why it is a salvation-historical transition to the full switch to the universal mission in the resurrection command of 28:19.

22. F. Dufton, "The Syrophoenician Woman and Her Dogs," *ExpTim* 100 (1989): 417. See also Davies and Allison, Morris, Keener.

23. The idea that the "Lord's table" (cf. "the Lord's table" in 1 Cor 10:21) is a metaphor for the eucharistic celebration is intriguing but not a propos to the context. It is too allegorical, with no contextual marker.

24. The "crumbs" are probably the scraps that fall off the table while the children are eating, though Jeremias, *Parables*, 184, thinks they are the scrap pieces of bread used to wipe the hands at the end of the meal and then tossed to the floor.

25. For this grammatical construction see on v. 15.

26. For this see Jerome H. Neyrey, "Decision-Making in the Early Church: The Case of the Canaanite Woman (Matthew 15:21 – 28)," *Science et esprit* 33 (1981): 373 – 78, who says that her faith connotes a switch from the Jewish to the Gentile mission.

27. David Rhoads and Donald Michie, *Mark as Story: An Introduction to the Narrative of a Gospel* (Philadelphia: Fortress, 1982), 131 – 32.

28. A dative of advantage, see BDF §188.

15:28 And her daughter was healed from that very hour (καὶ ἰάθη ἡ θυγάτηρ αὐτῆς ἀπὸ τῆς ὥρας ἐκείνης). The exorcism is presented once more as a healing (cf. 4:24; 9:33; 17:14 – 18). The mother's persistent faith draws her into the healing power of Jesus, and her daughter is completely whole from that very moment (Mark is more dramatic, with the woman returning home to find her daughter in bed but free of the demon). Jesus again heals at a distance (a near verbatim parallel to the centurion in 8:13).

15:29 Moving on from there, Jesus passed along the Sea of Galilee. Then he ascended a mountain and sat down (Καὶ μεταβὰς ἐκεῖθεν ὁ Ἰησοῦς ἦλθεν παρὰ τὴν θάλασσαν τῆς Γαλιλαίας, καὶ ἀναβὰς εἰς τὸ ὄρος ἐκάθητο ἐκεῖ). This is a transition summary of Jesus' ministry like 4:23 – 25; 8:16; 9:35 – 36; 14:13 – 14, 34 – 36. Some believe it fits better with the following section since the mountain scene permeates both vv. 29 – 31 and vv. 32 – 39, and the two stories flow together. Still, the passage centers on healing miracles and draws out the implications of the miracle in v. 28.

In reality, as a transition it belongs with both passages. Jesus leaves[29] the region of Tyre and apparently travels east toward Decapolis (cf. Mark 7:31) and climbs a hill "beside" (παρά) the shore of the lake, meaning he is still in Gentile territory. There he "sits down," the normal posture for rabbinic teaching (cf. 5:1; John 6:3). This means Jesus begins teaching there and the healing miracles come later. Since he is there three days (v. 32), he certainly teaches during that time.

Donaldson sees similar theology to the other mountain scenes in Matthew, believing "mountain" (ὄρος) here utilizes a Mount Zion typology and points to an eschatological image of the messianic banquet in this scene.[30] In light of the imagery present and the connection with the feeding of the five thousand in 14:13 – 21, this is likely. The remarkable thing is that this takes place in Gentile territory, a further harbinger and preparation for the universal mission.[31]

15:30 Large crowds came to him (καὶ προσῆλθον αὐτῷ ὄχλοι πολλοί). Jesus' popularity with the crowds never waned, and once more they swarm to him. For some reason Matthew decides not to relate his teaching and centers on his deeds, perhaps to build on the "healing" of v. 28.

15:30 ... bringing with them the lame, the blind, the crippled, the mute, and many others. They laid them at his feet, and he healed them (ἔχοντες μεθ' ἑαυτῶν χωλούς, τυφλούς, κυλλούς, κωφούς, καὶ ἑτέρους πολλούς, καὶ ἔρριψαν αὐτοὺς παρὰ τοὺς πόδας αὐτοῦ, καὶ ἐθεράπευσεν αὐτούς). Just as the woman "knelt down" before Jesus in v. 25, so the people here place (the present circumstantial participle ἔχοντες pictures the entire period as they "kept bringing" their sick to him) the sick "at his feet" in humble submission.

Of the four categories of sick mentioned, Mark 7:31 – 37 centers on the healing of a deaf and mute person. Matthew prefers to tell the types of illness healed, probably to build on the idea of Jesus as Lord of creation and sovereign over all earthly

29. With "moving on" (μεταβάς) as a circumstantial participle telling how Jesus proceeds along through Syria just north of Galilee.

30. Donaldson, *Jesus on the Mountain*, 130 – 31, followed by Davies and Allison, Hagner.

31. France, *Gospel of Matthew*, 597, says that he is "unmoved by the current fashion ... to deny any Gentile element in vv. 29 – 38" because of the similarity of these healings to previous Jewish healings. He argues that Matthew records Gentile healings precisely to show the extension of Jesus' Jewish ministry to the Gentiles.

forces and maladies as central to the whole of 14:13 – 15:39. "Lame" (χωλούς) speaks of crippled or lame limbs and occurs also in 11:5; 18:8; 21:14. Jesus heals the "blind" (τυφλούς) in 9:27 – 28; 11:5; 12:22, 20:30 – 34; 21:14. The "crippled" (κυλλούς) are mentioned only here (cf. also 18:8) and refers to being maimed or crippled.[32] The "mute" (κωφούς) are either deaf or mute (in light of v. 31, the mute) and are healed in 9:32 – 33; 11:5; 12:22.

15:31 As a result,[33] the crowd marveled when they saw the mute speaking, the crippled whole,[34] the lame walking, and the blind seeing (ὥστε τὸν ὄχλον θαυμάσαι βλέποντας κωφοὺς λαλοῦντας, κυλλοὺς ὑγιεῖς καὶ χωλοὺς περιπατοῦντας καὶ τυφλοὺς βλέποντας). The wonder of the crowd and of Jesus' disciples is another frequent feature as they experience Jesus' authority in word (7:28; 13:54; 19:25; 22:22, 33; 27:14) and deed (8:27; 9:33; 21:20). Matthew dramatically and powerfully reflects the healing of these people by having the mute "speak" and the lame "walk." The list here is in a different order from v. 30 and reflects 11:5, so that Matthew is probably alluding to Isa 35:5 – 6 and the list of miracles that will typify the joy of the redeemed when the eschatological highway to Zion is erected by God. This is a further sign of the fulfillment of that prophecy.

15:31 And they glorified the God of Israel (καὶ ἐδόξασαν τὸν θεὸν Ἰσραήλ). The natural reaction is to praise and glorify God (as in 5:16; 9:8). The title "the God of Israel" (τὸν θεὸν Ἰσραήλ) occurs only here in Matthew but is frequent in the OT (e.g., Exod 5:1; 1 Chr 16:36; Isa 29:23) and in Second Temple Judaism (e.g., 1QM 13:2; *T. Sol.* 1:13). Some say it could be used only by Gentiles, others that it is used mainly in a Jewish context.[35] Most likely it was used in both contexts.

Theology in Application

The close parallels to the healing of the centurion's servant in 8:5 – 13 means that the themes begun there continue here. This intensifies those themes, for now this episode is placed in direct contrast to Jesus' mission only to the Jews. The two together are central to the Matthean theme of the universal mission as part of a salvation-historical shift Jesus is preparing for; that is, it signals the future inclusion of the Gentiles in God's plan of salvation. At the same time both stories make clear two points: entrance into the kingdom is solely predicated on the basis of faith, and the Gentiles do not become Jewish proselytes but enter into the blessings as Gentiles.

32. Louw and Nida, *Greek-English Lexicon*, 273, differentiates χωλός as "a disability that involves the imperfect function of the lower limbs" and κυλλός as "a disability in one or more limbs, especially the leg or foot, often as the result of some deformity." They are similar in meaning.

33. "As a result" (ὥστε) here implies result.

34. "The crippled whole" (κυλλοὺς ὑγιεῖς) is omitted in ℵ f[1] 700* 892 lat) but present in a wide variety of others (see Metzger, *Textual Commentary*, 40).

35. Used by Gentiles, see Gundry, Carson, France; used in a Jewish context, see Davies and Allison; also J. R. C. Cousland, "The Feeding of the Four Thousand *Gentiles* in Matthew? Matthew 15:29 – 39 as a Test Case," *NovT* 41 (1999): 1 – 23.

1. The Worldwide Mission of the Church

There is general agreement that the primary theme here is salvation-historical. Luz puts it well: "the power of God's love that bursts the borders of Israel."[36] For our day this means that all peoples of the world, including the despised and the marginalized, are special objects of redemptive grace — Palestinians as well as Israelis, Sunnis and well as Shi'ites. The love and grace of God mean the demise of tribalism and a new love between groups that have been characterized by ethnic hatred for generations.

We also must keep in mind the dictum of Rom 1:16, "first to the Jew, then to the Gentile." This story, indeed Matthew as a whole, does not envisage a "replacement theology" in which Gentile mission replaces Jewish mission. There is still a central place for Jewish evangelism in the worldwide mission; they are still the elect people of God, and it is God's mercy that the Gentiles have been allowed to join them as objects of divine grace (cf. Rom 11:11 – 16).

2. True Faith

True faith persists in total humility and dependence on Christ. The paraenetic dimension of the story centers on the Canaanite woman's complete submission to Jesus, a humility that gave her a new boldness to accept her unworthiness and throw herself entirely on the abundance of Jesus' mercy, large enough to encompass the despised and unworthy Gentiles as well as God's true sheep, the Jews. All true disciples will embrace her attitude and her totally focused attention on Jesus rather than on herself. If she truly was one of the wealthy elite of the region (possible), this is an even better example that the people of status, power, and prestige must reverse the world's standards and become beggars at the feet of Jesus. It is a faith that surrenders and makes Jesus central rather than physical descent or economic status that is the true basis of salvation and discipleship.

3. Sovereignty over the Created Order

Matthew has a particular emphasis on Jesus as the sovereign Lord who heals "all the sick" (see on 4:23 – 24; 8:16; 12:15). The exorcism here is a healing miracle, and this is then expanded in the double list of those healed that extends his healing power to cover every type of malady. Hagner brings out a further christological nuance: in these miracles the God of Israel is at work, further proving Jesus' identity as the messianic King who has inaugurated the kingdom and shown further his faithfulness to his covenant people Israel.[37] God and Jesus are still reaching out to "the lost sheep of the house of Israel."

36. Luz, *Matthew 8 – 20*, 341.

37. Hagner, *Matthew 14 – 28*, 446.

James 5:15 says that "the prayer offered in faith will make [the sick] well." Does this mandate the "health and wealth" gospel and its teaching that we should all be healthy and healed? That is to deny the sovereignty of God. As with Paul's "thorn in [the] flesh" in 2 Cor 12:7 – 10, we rely on God's sovereign choice, not our own demands. Remember Jesus' Gethsemane prayer, "Yet not as I will, but as you will" (Matt 26:39), which must be our prayer as well. We will be healed, but that healing may be spiritual more than physical.

CHAPTER 68

Matthew 15:32 – 39

Literary Context

This doublet[1] of the feeding of the five thousand (14:13 – 21) serves as a culmination and climax to the upward movement of Jesus' ministry that leads to Peter's confession at Caesarea Philippi. It demonstrates God's provision for his people and the messianic power over nature on behalf of God's people. Furthermore, as addressed to the crowd even more than to Jesus' followers (who again help to distribute the blessing), it is a message to the "lost sheep" that they will find their needs met in God's Messiah, Jesus.

V. Rejection, Suffering, and Glory (13:54 – 18:35)
- **A. Jesus' Deeds: Rejection, Discipleship, and Glory (13:54 – 17:27)**
  - **1. Rejection and Discipleship (13:54 – 16:20)**
    - f. Jesus and Tradition (15:1 – 20)
    - g. Further Healings (15:21 – 31)
    - ➦ **h. Feeding of the 4,000 (15:32 – 39)**
    - i. Demand for a Sign (16:1 – 4)

Main Idea

The primary thrust is the same here as in 14:13 – 21, namely, that Jesus' compassion and provision are demonstrated in his feeding the needy crowd. Again he involves the disciples at a deeper level in this miracle than at any other time, allowing

1. The great debate is whether as doublets these are versions of the same story (so Bultmann, Hill, Beare, R. M. Fowler, *Loaves and Fishes: The Function of the Feeding Stories in the Gospel of Mark* [Chico, CA: Scholars Press, 1981]). There is no doubt that Matthew has deliberately told the two stories the same way, but does that mean they are one and the same event? Yet there is no doubt that both Mark 8:19 – 20 and Matt 16:9 – 10 consider them separate events, and the differences in detail are sufficient to warrant this being a separate incident. See Carson, Hagner, Morris, and Blomberg, *Historical Reliability*, 146 – 47, for arguments regarding the historical reliability of the two accounts.

them to share in his messianic ministry. This event is therefore a call to recognize the reality of who Jesus is, on the part of both the crowds and the disciples. Finally, by taking place on the eastern shore of the lake, it includes the Gentiles, so this continues the emphasis in the Canaanite woman story of Gentile inclusion in the kingdom provisions.

Translation

Matthew 15:32-39

32a	Action/Assertion	**Then Jesus called his disciples to him and said,**
b		*[1] "I have compassion for the crowd.*
c	Basis for 32b	*For they have already remained with me for three days and*
d	Problem	*have nothing to eat.*
e		*[2] I do not want to send them away hungry,*
f		*lest they faint on the road."*
33a	Objection	**His disciples asked,**
b		*"Where in this wilderness can we get sufficient bread to feed such a crowd?"*
34a	Question	**Jesus asked them,**
b		*"How many loaves do you have?"*
c	Answer	And **they replied,**
d		*"Seven, and a few small fish."*
35a	Action/Command	**He commanded the crowd to sit down on the ground.**
36a	Action	**Then he took the seven loaves and the fish.**
b		After giving thanks,
c	Action	**he broke them and gave them to the disciples,**
d	Action	and **they distributed the food to the crowds.**
37a	Resolution of 32c	**They all ate and were full,**
b		and **there were more than seven baskets full of fragments left over.**
38a	Conclusion	**The number of those who ate was four thousand men along with women and children.**
39a		After Jesus dismissed the crowds,
b	Transition/Setting	**he got into the boat and came into the region of Magadan.**

Structure and Literary Form

Once again Matthew abbreviates Mark's feeding story (Mark 8:1 – 10), but not by much, omitting mainly Mark 8:1a, 7. This second "gift miracle" again has three main parts (though this time the departure is part of this scene): an introductory scene with Jesus speaking of his compassion on the crowds (Matt 15:32), a shorter dialogue with the disciples in which Jesus challenges them but takes the initiative (vv. 33 – 34), the miracle itself (vv. 35 – 38), and Jesus' departure (v. 39).

Exegetical Outline

➡ **I. Jesus' Compassion on the Crowds (15:32)**
   A. Compassion for their plight (v. 32a)
   B. The dilemma: no food (v. 32b)

II. Challenging the Disciples (15:33 – 34)
   A. The inadequate supply of food (v. 33)
   B. The amount gathered: seven loaves and a few fish (v. 34)

III. The Second Feeding Miracle (15:35 – 38)
   A. The crowd reclines on the ground (v. 35)
   B. The actions of table fellowship (v. 36)
   C. The miracle: an overabundant supply (v. 37)
   D. The number of the crowd (v. 38)

IV. The Departure to the Region of Magadan (15:39)

Explanation of the Text

15:32 Then Jesus called[2] his disciples to him and said, "I have compassion for the crowd" (Ὁ δὲ Ἰησοῦς προσκαλεσάμενος τοὺς μαθητὰς αὐτοῦ εἶπεν, Σπλαγχνίζομαι ἐπὶ τὸν ὄχλον). Since the crowd has already assembled in vv. 29 – 31, there is no emphasis here on the crowd coming. The scene shifts straight to Jesus' remarks to the disciples, paralleling Mark 8:1b – 2. His compassion repeats that of Matt 9:36 (leading to mission), and of 14:14; 15:32 (leading to miracles). The crowd is so filled with amazement that they do not want to leave and so stay with Jesus until it is getting dangerously late, and Jesus is aware of their predicament.

15:32 "For they have already remained with me for three days and have nothing to eat. I do not want to send them away hungry, lest they faint on the road" (ὅτι ἤδη ἡμέραι τρεῖς προσμένουσίν μοι καὶ οὐκ ἔχουσιν τί φάγωσιν· καὶ ἀπολῦσαι αὐτοὺς νήστεις οὐ θέλω, μήποτε ἐκλυθῶσιν ἐν τῇ ὁδῷ). Since it is late in the day and the people have exhausted their food supply because of the three days they have remained with Jesus (with present tenses emphasizing the long time in the wilderness), there is significant danger should they now begin the long trek home. In a weakened condition as a result of insufficient food, they could collapse on the way back (note that this detail is different from 14:14 – 15 and suggests a separate event). Moreover, the dialogue setting of 14:15 – 18 has changed. Jesus now takes charge and tells them what he "intends" (θέλω) to do, namely, to feed them rather than sending them home.

15:33 His disciples asked, "Where in this wilderness can we get sufficient bread to[3] feed such a crowd?" (καὶ λέγουσιν αὐτῷ οἱ μαθηταί, Πόθεν ἡμῖν ἐν ἐρημίᾳ ἄρτοι τοσοῦτοι ὥστε χορτάσαι ὄχλον τοσοῦτον;). The disciples have forgotten[4] all about the previous miracle. Those who take the two

2. "Called" (προσκαλεσάμενος), a circumstantial participle that functions as a main verb; see on v. 10.

3. ὥστε shows result, "so that we can feed"; see BAGD, 900.

4. Note the emphatic "we" (ἡμῖν). The disciples are caught up in themselves and perhaps remember that in 14:16 Jesus told them to get food, though they have strangely forgotten the rest.

as a single story always ask how anyone could have forgotten such a stupendous miracle in so short a time. Carson makes three points:[5] (1) If they realized the first miracle anticipated the messianic banquet, they might not want to extend that privilege to the Gentiles in the crowd. (2) In John 6:26 Jesus has rebuked the crowds for just wanting food, so the disciples may be reluctant to bring up the subject. (3) Most of all, we all struggle with unbelief, and the disciples could easily have never expected such a miracle to happen again. Their major concern is the complete lack of resources in a wilderness area to find enough food for the vast crowd. They are unable to comply with any such implied request.

15:34 Jesus asked them, "How many loaves do you have?" And they replied, "Seven, and a few small fish" (καὶ λέγει αὐτοῖς ὁ Ἰησοῦς, Πόσους ἄρτους ἔχετε; οἱ δὲ εἶπαν, Ἑπτά καὶ ὀλίγα ἰχθύδια). Again, note the difference in detail from 14:17. Now there are seven loaves available and a small amount of fish (as in 15:26, 27 the ι – diminutive in ἰχθύδια here retains its force, "*small* fish"). As before, there is no possibility of feeding the crowd with so little food (for "seven," see on v. 37).

15:35 He commanded the crowd to sit down on the ground (καὶ παραγγείλας τῷ ὄχλῳ ἀναπεσεῖν ἐπὶ τὴν γῆν). Jesus again shows his authority and orders the crowd to sit down. ἀναπίπτω is close in meaning to ἀνακλίνω in 14:19, both meaning to "recline" and giving the impression of a banquet setting.

15:36 Then he took the seven loaves and the fish.[6] After giving thanks, he broke them and gave[7] them to the disciples, and they distributed the food to the crowds (ἔλαβεν τοὺς ἑπτὰ ἄρτους καὶ τοὺς ἰχθύας καὶ εὐχαριστήσας ἔκλασεν καὶ ἐδίδου τοῖς μαθηταῖς, οἱ δὲ μαθηταὶ τοῖς ὄχλοις). This repeats Mark 8:6 somewhat closely and echoes the liturgical flavor. The repast becomes a sacred meal and anticipates the messianic banquet. Any eucharistic emphasis is again secondary, though some say that "after giving thanks" (a temporal participle from εὐχαριστέω, replacing the "bless" [εὐλογέω] of 14:19) reflects the Eucharist more directly here,[8] since "give thanks" (εὐχαριστέω) is used in the tradition in Luke 22:19; 1 Cor 11:24. But "bless" (εὐλογέω) is used in the words of institution in Matt 26:26 = Mark 14:22, so both have any eucharistic thrust as secondary.

15:37 They all ate and were full, and there were more than seven baskets full of fragments left over (καὶ ἔφαγον πάντες καὶ ἐχορτάσθησαν. καὶ τὸ περισσεῦον τῶν κλασμάτων ἦραν ἑπτὰ σπυρίδας πλήρεις). Again, this is close to 14:20, except that now there are seven baskets of scraps left over. It is likely that like the "twelve" in the earlier story, this number is symbolic of the perfect provision of God for his people. It is more of a stretch to say with some that the "twelve" connotes provision for the Jews (twelve tribes) and the "seven" connotes provision for the Gentiles, for there is not enough linguistic evidence in the story to support restricting this event to the Gentiles. Matthew's term for "baskets" here (σπυρίδας) refers to a slightly larger basket woven from rushes, while 14:20 has a different word (κοφίνους) that speaks of small wicker baskets for carrying provisions.[9]

5. Carson, "Matthew," 358.

6. Now Matthew returns to the more common "fish" (ἰχθύς), showing he was not dwelling on the size of the fish.

7. The use of the imperfect "gave" (ἐδίδου) after the aorists probably places the act of distributing the bread and fish in the foreground of the story (see Porter, *Idioms*, 23) and dramatically pictures the process of distribution.

8. So Davies and Allison, Luz, Hagner; contra Schnackenburg.

9. Carson thinks it possible that this points to Gentiles because "basket" (κοφίνους) was normally used by Jews to carry kosher food; but that could be reading too much into the terms used, and the evidence comes from Rome (Juvenal) rather than Palestine.

15:38 The number of those who ate was four thousand men along with women and children[10] (οἱ δὲ ἐσθίοντες ἦσαν τετρακισχίλιοι ἄνδρες χωρὶς γυναικῶν καὶ παιδίων). This is another near verbatim reflection of the earlier feeding (14:21), but now with four thousand rather than five thousand men present. As before, the great size of the crowd, possibly looking forward to the messianic banquet, is stressed.

15:39 After Jesus dismissed the crowds, he got into the boat and came into the region of Magadan (Καὶ ἀπολύσας τοὺς ὄχλους ἐνέβη εἰς τὸ πλοῖον καὶ ἦλθεν εἰς τὰ ὅρια Μαγαδάν). As in 14:22, Jesus "dismisses" the crowd (temporal aorist participle ἀπολύσας), but in the earlier passage he sent the disciples off in the boat while he went up a mountain to pray. Now he enters the boat and goes away. We do not really know where "Magadan" (Μαγαδάν) was, nor where "Dalmanutha" of Mark 8:10 was located. The most common surmise links it with Magdala on the west coast of the lake not too far from Tiberias.[11]

Theology in Application

The very same themes as in the feeding of the five thousand (14:13 – 21) are here. The sovereign authority of Christ is even more strongly presented here, as he takes charge rather than asking the disciples a series of questions. Also, the merciful provision of God and Christ for the needs of the people is evident. Discipleship failure on the part of the "little-faith ones" is somewhat present and will become more evident in 16:5 – 11. Finally, Jesus as the great messianic prophet who is establishing a new community is evident in the banquet scene.

The important implicit addition is the extension of these blessings to the Gentiles, not explicit in the text but implicit in the setting and possibly in some details (like the term for "baskets"; see on v. 37). A further addition could be the eschatological Zion typology that looks forward to the coming of the final kingdom (see on v. 29). Also, by deliberately telling the story in such a way that the parallelism with the other feeding miracle is obvious, the themes are extended further and given even greater stress.

10. Some major witnesses (א D vg syr[1] et al.) reverse the order to "children and women." Though this is a less likely reading, the manuscripts favoring the normal order are too diverse and strong.

11. This problem led several later scribes to substitute "Magdala," a known village. They were wrong in their textual change but possibly inadvertently correct in their choice.

CHAPTER 69

Matthew 16:1–4

Literary Context

We return to the theme of Jewish opposition (13:58–14:12; 15:1–20), and this scene echoes the demand for a sign in 12:38–42. The same irony permeates this one, for again this is a major miracle section, and the leaders are unwilling to accept the God-given "signs" and demand that Jesus act on their own terms. Moreover, Jesus has just returned to Galilee after leaving because of opposition (15:21) and is immediately greeted with more rejection. This will prompt two further withdrawals (symbolizing God's rejection of the people), first to the other side of the lake (vv. 4b–5) and then north to Caesarea Philippi (v. 13).

V. Rejection, Suffering, and Glory (13:54–18:35)
- **A. Jesus' Deeds: Rejection, Discipleship, and Glory (13:54–17:27)**
  - **1. Rejection and Discipleship (13:54–16:20)**
    - g. Further Healings (15:21–31)
    - h. Feeding of the 4,000 (15:32–39)
    - ➦ **i. Demand for a Sign (16:1–4)**

Main Idea

As in 12:38–40, rejection governs this passage, first the Jewish leaders' rejection of Jesus in their demand for a sign and then Jesus' rejection of them in the sign of Jonah. Verses 2b–3 adds the idea of "the signs of the times," meaning that any alert child of God should see that the kingdom age has indeed dawned. Since the leaders have refused to observe and read these signs, they are rejected by Jesus and by God.[1]

1. See J. Swetnam, "Some Sign of Jonah," *Bib* 68 (1987): 74–79, who says the sign for Matthew is the destruction of Jerusalem.

Translation

Matthew 16:1-4

1a	Action	**Pharisees and Sadducees**	**came to Jesus and**
b			testing him,
c	Request		**asked him to show them a sign from heaven.**
2a	Response	But **Jesus responded,**	
b	Analogy	*"When evening arrives,*	
c		*you say,*	
d		*'It will be nice weather,*	
e		*for the sky is red';*	
3a		*and early in the morning,*	
		'Today it will be stormy,	
		for the sky is red and dark.'	
3b	Question	*How can you know how to read the face of the sky, yet cannot read the signs of the times?*	
4a	Answer to 1c	*An evil and adulterous generation demands a sign,*	
b		*but no sign will be given it*	
c		*except the sign of Jonah."*	
d	Conclusion	And **Jesus left them and went away.**	

Structure and Literary Form

Tannehill calls this an inquiry type of pronouncement story,[2] as the Pharisees' request leads to Jesus' proclamation of judgment. The source of the story is probably a combination of Mark 8:11 – 13 (= Matt 16:1 – 2a, 4) and a Q saying (Luke 12:54 – 56 = Matt 16:2b – 3). The episode has four parts: the demand for a sign (v. 1), Jesus' response on the signs of the times (vv. 2 – 3), his rejection of their request (v. 4a-b), and his withdrawal from them (v. 4c).

2. Robert C. Tannehill, "Varieties of Synoptic Pronouncement Stories," *Semeia* 20 (1981): 114 – 16, from Davies and Allison, *Matthew*, 2:578.

Exegetical Outline

- → **I. The Pharisees and Sadducees Demand a Sign (16:1)**
- **II. Jesus Tells Them to Read the Signs of the Times (16:2 – 3)**
  - A. The analogy of the weather (vv. 2 – 3a)
  - B. Their need to discern the times (v. 3b)
- **III. Jesus Rejects Their Request (16:4a-b)**
  - A. They are an evil and adulterous generation (v. 4a)
  - B. No sign but the sign of Jonah (v. 4b)
- **IV. Jesus Withdraws from Them (16:4c)**

Explanation of the Text

16:1 Pharisees and Sadducees came to Jesus (Καὶ προσελθόντες οἱ Φαρισαῖοι καὶ Σαδδουκαῖοι). As in 3:7 (the last time the Sadducees have appeared), these two opposing parties[3] in the Sanhedrin (they differed in both outlook and doctrine) now join together again (note the single article governing both, which by Sharp's rule means they function as a single entity here) to oppose a common foe, the (to them) pretender Jesus Messiah.

16:1 . . . and testing him, asked him to show them a sign from heaven (πειράζοντες ἐπηρώτησαν αὐτὸν σημεῖον ἐκ τοῦ οὐρανοῦ ἐπιδεῖξαι αὐτοῖς). Jesus was "tested"[4] first by Satan (4:1, 3, 7) and will continue to be "tested" by Satan's emissaries in the ensuing narratives (19:3; 22:18, 35).[5] This is not a test to discern the truth as to whether he is from God or is a false prophet, for these groups have already judged him and sought his life (12:14). They do not want a sign (the anarthrous σημεῖον connotes the qualitative aspect, something of "divine significance") and have rejected the validity of all his miracles. They are only looking for reasons to turn the crowds against him. So theirs is a test like Israel's "testing" God in the wilderness (Exod 17:2; Deut 6:16; Ps 78:18; 95:9) that brought divine wrath down on themselves. As in 12:38 they demand a heaven-sent spectacle like the exodus "signs" that forced the Hebrews to believe (Exod 4:8, 30 – 31), though in reality the Jewish leaders want Jesus to be unable to deliver such a sign.

16:2 – 3a But Jesus responded,[6] "When evening arrives, you say, 'It will be nice weather, for the

3. The Sadducees do not appear in Matt 12:38 or Mark 8:11 – 13, and many believe Matthew adds them on the basis of 16:16 and the situation of his community in AD 85, after the Sadducees had been annihilated in the great war of AD 66 – 70. However, as Carson, "Matthew," 360, points out, there is little reason to suppose such an artificial reference, for these were the two major groups of the Sanhedrin and were an official delegation. As Witherington, *Matthew*, 305, says, "Sometimes the enemy of one's enemy turns out to be a friend," and this shows the authorities are taking heed of the Pharisees' warnings and sending an official delegation.

4. This verse begins with two circumstantial participles ("coming," "testing") that detail the circumstances surrounding their question.

5. Nolland, *Matthew*, 647, shows how as in 4:1 πειράζω moves between "test" and "tempt" here, with testing primary in this instance.

6. This is controversial, for vv. 2b – 3 are missing in some important manuscripts (ℵ B f^{13} 157 *al* $syr^{c,a}$ et al.). Jerome said that most manuscripts he found omitted it, though he added it to the Vulgate in the end. It is common to regard it as an interpolation assimilated from Luke 12:54 – 56 or as a separate gloss (so Hill, Beare, Gnilka, Luz, T. Hirunama, "Matthew 16:2b – 3," in *New Testament Textual Criticism* (ed.

sky is red'; and early in the morning, 'Today it will be stormy, for the sky is red and dark' " (ὁ δὲ ἀποκριθεὶς εἶπεν αὐτοῖς, [Ὀψίας γενομένης λέγετε, Εὐδία, πυρράζει γὰρ ὁ οὐρανός· καὶ πρωΐ, Σήμερον χειμών, πυρράζει γὰρ στυγνάζων ὁ οὐρανός). Jesus' response[7] uses an analogy from weather observation to correct the false assumptions of the leaders. Blomberg captures the analogy well:

> As clouds move from west to east, the dawn sunlight will tint them in the west, portending rain as the day progresses. In the evening the same phenomenon suggests that the clouds have almost disappeared, bringing good weather instead. We preserve this proverb today with the rhyme: "Red sky in morning, sailors take warning; red sky at night, sailors delight.[8]

16:3 "How can you know how to read the face of the sky, yet cannot read the signs of the times?" (τὸ μὲν πρόσωπον τοῦ οὐρανοῦ γινώσκετε διακρίνειν, τὰ δὲ σημεῖα τῶν καιρῶν οὐ δύνασθε;]). The point is that the Jewish leaders can read the less important weather signs; but because they are closed to God's new work in Jesus, they are "unable" (οὐ δύνασθε, last for emphasis) to read the divinely given signs that the kingdom of heaven has dawned[9] (not the final day of the Lord, as some have taken it). In Jesus' words and deeds, those signs have been given, and the leaders are "totally lacking in spiritual discernment"[10] so that they will be held accountable by God for their failure. The use of "the sky" (τοῦ οὐρανοῦ) is probably a deliberate pun on their demand for a "sign from heaven" in v. 1 (so Hagner).

16:4 "An evil and adulterous generation demands a sign, but no sign will be given it except the sign of Jonah" (Γενεὰ πονηρὰ καὶ μοιχαλὶς σημεῖον ἐπιζητεῖ, καὶ σημεῖον οὐ δοθήσεται αὐτῇ εἰ μὴ τὸ σημεῖον Ἰωνᾶ). This is a nearly verbatim repetition of 12:39. As there, the "evil and adulterous generation" reenacts the wilderness generation of Deut 1:35; 32:5, 20, and the image of adultery has the OT connotation of spiritual unfaithfulness to God (Isa 1:21; 57:3 – 9; Jer 3:10). The leaders, then, embody the whole "generation" of the Jewish people in rejecting Christ.

The "sign of Jonah" is not explained here, but its meaning is clear from 12:40 – 41. It represents first the resurrection of Jesus (cf. 12:40; the Sadducees rejected any idea of the afterlife, see 22:23 – 33) and second the repentance of Nineveh (cf. 12:41), a repentance the "wicked generation" of Jesus' day is unwilling to embrace. Therefore they will receive no other sign, for they are under indictment by God and will face judgment.

16:4 And Jesus left[11] them and went away (καὶ καταλιπὼν αὐτοὺς ἀπῆλθεν). Jesus' withdrawal repeats the frequent image in Matthew (4:12; 12:15, 14:13; 15:21) and with 16:13 implies a rejection of the leaders. He will not encounter them again until 19:3.

E. Epp and G. D. Fee; Oxford: Clarendon, 1981], 35 – 45). But these verses could have been omitted in assimilation to Mark or because in the Egyptian climate (Alexandrian tradition) a red sky did not preclude fair weather. So it is best to include them cautiously (see Metzger, Gundry, Davies and Allison, Carson, Hagner, Blomberg, France).

7. For this construction see on 3:15; 4:4.

8. Blomberg, *Matthew*, 247 – 48.

9. Turner, "Matthew," 217, adds "the significance of Jesus' epiphany as the Son of God on earth."

10. Morris, *Matthew*, 414. διακρίνω means to "discern, judge, differentiate" between competing truths.

11. It is often best to translate a circumstantial participle as another main verb. They tell accompanying action and are often equal in force to the main verb. BDF §419 calls this an "idiomatic (pleonastic)" use.

Theology in Application

As would be expected, this repeats the theological message of 12:38 – 42, and as in the case of 15:32 – 39 it further enhances those themes. Davies and Allison say it well: "Seeing is not believing. If the Sadducees and Pharisees of our story were not persuaded by Jesus, neither would they have been won over by a spectacular sign from heaven (cf. Luke 16:31). The truth is that one does not see until one believes."[12] The theme of opposition and rejection is uppermost, and the warning to those in Matthew's day and in our day against refusing to watch and respond to God's clear signs could not be more clear. To fail to repent in light of the dawning of the kingdom in Jesus can mean only one thing — judgment.

Moreover, the resurrection is implicit and points forward to the passion events when God's plan of salvation will be enacted in human history. That is clearly the primary "sign" that God has performed in human history, and it demands response. Hauerwas applies this to us: "To see the truth, to recognize the signs of the Kingdom, requires that we be rightly formed by the virtues acquired by following Jesus. To know the truth requires the acquisition of the habits of truthfulness. Knowledge and virtue are inseparable."[13]

12. Davies and Allison, *Matthew*, 2:582.

13. Hauerwas, *Matthew*, 147.

CHAPTER 70

Matthew 16:5 – 12

Literary Context

As in Mark 8:14 – 21, this contains a scene of discipleship failure that parallels Matt 14:22 – 33 (= Mark 6:45 – 52). But in Matthew (unlike Mark) the failure is turned around by the presence of Christ, and understanding ensues (v. 12). This new level of understanding prepares for the important confession in 16:13 – 20. Throughout Matthew the disciples' growing understanding is mitigated by bouts of ignorance and doubt (15:16) — they are the "little-faith ones" (8:26; 14:31; 16:8).

V. Rejection, Suffering, and Glory (13:54 – 18:35)
- **A. Jesus' Deeds: Rejection, Discipleship, and Glory (13:54 – 17:27)**
  - **1. Rejection and Discipleship (13:54 – 16:20)**
    - h. Feeding of the 4,000 (15:32 – 39)
    - i. Demand for a Sign (16:1 – 4)
    - ➦ **j. Warning about the Leaders (16:5 – 12)**
    - k. Peter's Confession and Jesus' Blessing (16:13 – 20)

Main Idea

This passage combines opposition and discipleship. The first part (vv. 5 – 6) is a warning about the spreading evil of the Pharisees and Sadducees, the second part concerns the "little-faith" obtuseness of the disciples that is turned around by the presence of Jesus into understanding. As the final interpreter of Torah, Jesus once more instructs the disciples, so this continues the emphases we have already seen dominating this section of Matthew.

Translation

Matthew 16:5-12

5a	Setting	When the disciples came to the other side,
b	Circumstance	**they had forgotten to bring bread.**
6a	Warning	But **Jesus told them,**
b		*"Be watchful and beware of the yeast*
		of the Pharisees
		and Sadducees."
7a	Response	But **they began discussing this among themselves and said,**
b		*"It's because we didn't bring any bread."*
8a		But knowing their thoughts,
b		**Jesus said,**
c	Indictment or Rebuke	*"You of little faith,*
d	Rhetorical Question #1	*[1] why are you discussing among yourselves that you have no bread?*
9a	Rhetorical Question #2	*[2] Can't you yet understand?*
b	Rhetorical Question #3	*[3] Don't you remember the five loaves for the 5,000 and how many baskets you took up?* Or
10a	Rhetorical Question #4	*[4] the seven loaves for the 4,000 and how many baskets you took up?*
11a	Rhetorical Question #5	*[5] How is it that you don't understand that I was not talking to you about bread?*
b	Restatement of 6b	But *at all times beware of the yeast*
		of the Pharisees
		and Sadducees."
12a	Conclusion	**Then they understood**
b		that he had not told them to beware of yeast in bread but of the teaching of the Pharisees and Sadducees.

Structure and Literary Form

This is a controversy story on two levels: first in Jesus' indictment of the leaders for their evil teaching, and second in Jesus' indictment of the disciples for their lack of understanding. It abbreviates and reworks Mark 8:14 – 21, replacing Mark's "the yeast of ... Herod" with the Sadducees in v. 6 and removing the harsh indictment of the hardened hearts, blindness, and deafness of Mark 8:17b – 18 (with allusions to Jer 5:21; Ezek 12:2), and it removes the disciples' responses to Jesus' challenges regarding the two feeding miracles (Mark 8:19 – 20). The main addition is the dawning of understanding in v. 12, which replaces Mark's "Do you still not understand"? There are three parts of the narrative:[1] the warning about the leaders (vv. 5 – 6), the challenge to the disciples about their lack of perception (vv. 7 – 11), and the final understanding of the disciples (v. 12). The two main parts are framed by the warning about the leaders' spreading evil (vv. 6b, 11b).

Exegetical Outline

➡ **I. Indictment of the Pharisees and Sadducees (16:5 – 6)**
   A. The setting: the disciples arrive but without bread (v. 5)
   B. Jesus warns them of the spreading evil of the leaders (v. 6)

II. Indictment of the Disciples (16:7 – 11)
   A. Their misunderstanding (v. 7)
   B. Jesus' challenge to them (vv. 8 – 11)
      1. Their little faith (vv. 8 – 9a)
      2. Challenge to remember the two feeding miracles (vv. 9b – 10)
      3. Challenge to perceive the warning (v. 11)

III. The Disciples Finally Understand (16:12)

Explanation of the Text

16:5 When the disciples came[2] to the other side, they had forgotten to bring bread (Καὶ ἐλθόντες οἱ μαθηταὶ εἰς τὸ πέραν ἐπελάθοντο ἄρτους λαβεῖν). On the basis of this verse, one could surmise that Jesus had apparently crossed over the lake ahead of the disciples (16:4b), and they now join him on "the other side," probably the sparsely populated eastern shore. Yet Mark 8:14 – 15 has the conversation take place between Jesus and the disciples in the boat. How do we reconcile this? Most likely Matthew is simply abbreviating Mark (as he does elsewhere), and as a result his narrative is indistinct on this. There is nothing in Matthew to preclude Jesus' being with them in the boat.

The main thing here is the note that the disciples have somehow forgotten to bring food with them on the journey. This sets the scene for Jesus' comment about yeast in the next verse and for their strange surmise that his "yeast" meant actual bread. They are consumed by their mistake (the absence of food) and so are not listening carefully.

16:6 But Jesus told them, "Be watchful and beware of the yeast of the Pharisees and Sadducees" (ὁ δὲ Ἰησοῦς εἶπεν αὐτοῖς, Ὁρᾶτε καὶ προσέχετε ἀπὸ τῆς ζύμης τῶν Φαρισαίων καὶ Σαδδουκαίων). Taking his cue from the absence of bread, Jesus turns it into an analogy of yeast (see on 13:33) for the spreading evil of the "teaching" (v. 12) of the leaders. The best background is found in 1 Cor 5:6; Gal 5:9: "A little yeast leavens the whole batch of dough." As only a small amount of yeast spreads into the dough and virtually takes it over, so the false teaching of the leaders[3] spreads into

1. Due to the complexity of the story, nearly everyone has a different outline — France (vv. 5 – 7, 8 – 10, 11 – 12); Luz (vv. 5 – 6, 7 – 10, 11 – 12); Carson (vv. 5 – 7, 8 – 12); Davies and Allison (vv. 5, 6 – 11, 12); Hagner (vv. 5, 6, 7, 8 – 11a, 11b, 12).

2. ἐλθόντες is a temporal participle, "when they came."

3. Davies and Allison, *Matthew*, 2:588, say the leaven here is a metaphor for their false teaching and its "corrupting influence, an evil tendency which, although insignificant to start with, quickly multiplies to corrupt the whole."

the nation and turns them against their Messiah. Nolland calls it "the negative counterpart to the kingdom as leaven in 13:33."[4] We must remember that the bread of Passover was unleavened (Exod 12:14 – 20), so yeast became a natural image for the pervasive power of wickedness. The two warnings are similar and build to a crescendo; the disciples must *always* be wary and vigilant (present tense imperatives) in the face of such pernicious doctrine.[5]

16:7 But they began discussing this among themselves and said, "It's because[6] we didn't bring any bread" (οἱ δὲ διελογίζοντο ἐν ἑαυτοῖς λέγοντες ὅτι ἄρτους οὐκ ἐλάβομεν). Scholars have long debated this puzzling reaction from the disciples. How could they have so misread what Jesus said? Yet it seems clear: their minds are on their hunger, so they catch only the part about the yeast. Matthew tells us they "began discussing" (inceptive imperfect διελογίζοντο) Jesus' saying, a term that has negative connotations in Matthew (15:19; 21:25, so Hagner) and probably points to their ignorance at this point. The next verse shows that the discussion was more on their predicament than on Jesus' analogy.

16:8 But knowing[7] their thoughts, Jesus said, "You of little faith, why are you discussing among yourselves that you have no bread?" (γνοὺς δὲ ὁ Ἰησοῦς εἶπεν, Τί διαλογίζεσθε ἐν ἑαυτοῖς, ὀλιγόπιστοι, ὅτι ἄρτους οὐκ ἔχετε;). The present tenses in vv. 8 – 11 show that these questions are in the foreground of the action[8] and form the heart of the passage. Again the central focus is on Jesus' description of them as "little-faith ones" (cf. 6:30; 8:26; 14:31). The debate is always whether "little" means a modicum of faith (namely, doubt, see on 6:30) or no faith at all. The latter seems unlikely in Matthew, for the emphasis is almost always on the overcoming of that slight faith and the process of coming to understanding.

Jesus is clearly upset at the disciples' lack of comprehension and their total concern with the mundane (who wouldn't be!), and he cries out against their vapid dialogue. So here the lack of faith is connected to their failure to trust God's provision for their physical needs. As Brown says, there are two areas where their misunderstanding and "little faith" overlapped: Jesus' enigmatic saying, but even more the truth that Jesus had the ability to provide for their needs. So the reminder in vv. 9 – 10 of his previous displays of power to provide was to help them "understand the extent of Jesus' authority."[9]

16:9 – 10 Can't you yet understand? Don't you remember the five loaves for the 5,000 and how many baskets you took up? Or the seven loaves for the 4,000 and how many baskets you took up? (οὔπω νοεῖτε, οὐδὲ μνημονεύετε τοὺς πέντε ἄρτους τῶν πεντακισχιλίων καὶ πόσους κοφίνους ἐλάβετε; οὐδὲ τοὺς ἑπτὰ ἄρτους τῶν τετρακισχιλίων καὶ πόσας σπυρίδας ἐλάβετε;). As France says, "Not only have [the disciples] failed to grasp Jesus' metaphorical teaching because of their

4. Nolland, *Matthew*, 652. See also R. C. Newman, "Breadmaking with Jesus," *JETS* 40 (1997): 1 – 11, who separates the danger into two — the desire for a narrow rigidity by the Pharisees and a desire for power and wealth by the Sadducees.

5. It is interesting that Luke 12:1 in a different context has Jesus say, "Be on your guard against the yeast of the Pharisees, which is hypocrisy," a quite different use of the metaphor. It is common to take Matt 16:6 = Luke 12:1 as a Q saying found also in Mark (Grundmann, Davies and Allison, Bock), but it is equally viable to see Jesus as an itinerant teacher who uses such pithy sayings on more than one occasion.

6. The "because" (ὅτι) here could be recitative ("they said *that* they brought no bread," so NRSV, NASB) or an idiom for a question ("Why didn't we bring bread?" so Turner) but is best causal as here (so Carson, Morris)

7. γνούς could be a causal participle ("because he knew") or circumstantial ("knowing"). Due to Matthew's proclivity for circumstantial participles, the latter is more likely.

8. Porter, *Idioms*, 23 – 25.

9. Brown, *Disciples*, 105 – 6.

preoccupation with their material problem, but even at the material level they have failed to learn the lesson of the miracles of feeding."[10] "You remember" (μνημονεύετε, present tense to stress the need for sustained activity) is a strong verb that means much more than just thinking about a past activity. It means to pay close attention to what you recall, gain insight, and "renew and strengthen faith."[11]

So Jesus reminds his disciples of the two feeding miracles when God met their material needs. How could they have forgotten those powerful reminders? Matthew probably omits the positive response of the disciples in Mark 8:19 – 20 for the sake of dramatic flow. He wants the challenge to come strictly from Jesus without interruption, and so he defers their response until the end, where, in keeping with 14:33, they finally discover, through Jesus' instruction, the faith and understanding they lack.

16:11 How is it that you don't understand that I was not talking[12] to you about bread? (πῶς οὐ νοεῖτε ὅτι οὐ περὶ ἄρτων εἶπον ὑμῖν;). This final challenge prepares for their insight in v. 12. With the reminders that Jesus had given them and at this stage the look of incomprehension on their faces, Jesus is incredulous at their lack of insight.

16:11 But at all times beware of the yeast of the Pharisees and Sadducees (προσέχετε δὲ ἀπὸ τῆς ζύμης τῶν Φαρισαίων καὶ Σαδδουκαίων). Jesus returns to the warning of v. 6b, the main point of the instruction, repeating it verbatim except for the omission of "be watchful" (ὁρᾶτε). It is this restatement (with the final present imperative of vv. 8 – 11 demanding ongoing vigilance) that finally sinks through their fog and brings in a dawning comprehension. Obviously the disciples had not really heard it the first time, so like any elementary teacher addressing learning-challenged children, Jesus has to repeat it a second time so that they finally catch that "1 + 1 = 2."

16:12 Then they understood that he had not told them to beware of[13] yeast in bread but of the teaching of the Pharisees and Sadducees (τότε συνῆκαν ὅτι οὐκ εἶπεν προσέχειν ἀπὸ τῆς ζύμης τῶν ἄρτων ἀλλὰ ἀπὸ τῆς διδαχῆς τῶν Φαρισαίων καὶ Σαδδουκαίων). The two issues in this pericope are encapsulated in this lengthy summary. Matthew could have simply said, "Then they understood," but he wants to make certain that the reader catches the two issues — the disciple's misunderstanding/lack of faith and the dangerous teaching of the leaders[14] (subjective genitives — what they teach the people).

As in 13:11 – 12, 16, 23, 43, 44 – 45, 52, the goal is the great joy of "the knowledge of the mysteries" (13:11), realized in part in 14:33 and here. Of course it is not full realization, for clearly in Matthew it is a gradual development of dawning perception, but this is another step forward. For this reason, those who say the "little faith" of v. 8 is unbelief must be wrong, for there is a continual process of discipleship; understanding and faith do take place in chs. 13 – 16. The ebb and flow from understanding to incomprehension and back involves a growth process.

10. France, *Matthew* (TNTC), 251.

11. See *EDNT*, 2:435.

12. A past tense clause after a present tense main clause is always translated as an imperfect, see Wallace, 457 – 58.

13. προσέχω normally means to "pay attention to something" (followed by the dative), but with ἀπό it connotes "beware of" or "be on your guard against" something (BAGD, 714).

14. France, *Matthew: Evangelist and Teacher*, 106 – 8, notes the redactional emphasis of Matthew on the "Pharisees and Sadducees" (vv. 6, 11, 12, the latter two only in Matthew) and admits this is the strongest argument for a Gentile author of the first gospel, for it seems to wrongly equate the "teaching" of these two dissimilar groups. Yet as France admits, this is surely an oversimplification, for likely the equation of the two designates the leaders as a whole since they were the two major parties that made up the Sanhedrin.

Theology in Application

It is interesting to note how some take the dangerous teaching of the leaders as the nearly the sole issue (Luz, Davies and Allison) while others center only on the discipleship failure (Hagner, Wilkins). In reality, both constitute the theological purpose of the pericope and must be taken together.

1. Being Vigilant regarding False Teaching

Matthew almost certainly intended the Pharisees and Sadducees to picture false teachers in his own day. The pages of the New Testament are rife with them: the Judaizers of Acts, Galatians, and Philippians; the secularists of Corinth; the Jewish-Hellenistic mix of Colossians; the proto-Gnostics of 1 John; the Nicolaitans of Rev 2. The warning of Jesus here is a warning to all of us to be watchful and guard against false teachers in our time. I have heard statistics regarding 10,000 different cults around the world, half of them in the United States!

Yet there are two issues in this, for the NT (especially John and Paul) combines two aspects, unity and purity. The church must be one and learn to work around disagreements (John 10:16b; 17:21 – 26) and at the same time must fight false teaching (John 10:1, 5, 8, 12 – 13). We must identify what constitutes false teaching — such as the return of Christ but not rapture or millennial debates, the Holy Spirit but not debates over spiritual gifts, substitutionary atonement but not predestination or eternal security. It is sad that churches today split over all the minor issues and allow true heretics (like Jim Jones and David Koresh) to flourish.

2. Mundane Things

We dare not allow the mundane things of life to obscure our faith and understanding. The disciples were "little-faith ones" not because they had no faith but because their faith was obscured by self-interest and the priority of personal needs and wants, in this case, food. That characterizes all of us most of the time. We do not "have in mind the concerns of God, but merely human concerns" (Mark 8:33b). We have not learned to "set your minds on things above, not on earthly things" (Col 3:1 – 2). Our treasures are on earth rather than in heaven (Matt 6:19 – 21). Faith is not just the act of trusting God to do things for us. It is an attitude, a lifestyle of absolute God-dependence and reliance on Christ.

The disciples failed until they learned this lesson. The understanding they gathered here was actually another step in a lifelong process of learning to let go and let God. But they were learning, as we will see as we continue through Matthew. The question is: Are we learning?

3. Growing through Listening

We must keep growing in our walk, but we can only do so when we listen only to Jesus. The great thing about discipleship in Matthew is the step-by-step process by which Jesus led his disciples one leap forward at a time. But this is the key. Jesus was the instructor who guided the process, and whenever the disciples lost sight of that, they slipped back, as in vv. 5 – 7 of this story. Faith and understanding are explicitly related in Matthew. Because the disciples failed to understand, they failed to "grasp and rely on Jesus' inexhaustible power."[15]

The problem we all have is listening to the wrong advice, either from our basic self or from the ways of the world. We are too often secularists in pious guise. The growing biblical illiteracy in the midst of the growing popularity of Bible studies is mystifying but partly due to an absence of asking what God really said through the inspired authors. Many churches hardly open the Word, and (probably) the majority of pastors rarely dig deeply into biblical truth. If this doesn't change, the evangelical movement will continue to slide into secularity. We must start to care about God's truth and make certain it, not just our market-driven research and the latest ideas, guides our steps.

15. Donald J. Verseput, "The Faith of the Reader and the Narrative of Matthew 13:53 – 16:20," *JSNT* 46 (1992): 3 – 24 (see 23), quoted in Brown, *Disciples*, 111 – 12.

CHAPTER 71

Matthew 16:13 – 20

Literary Context

The entire narrative thus far has prepared for this climactic moment. Most outlines of the Synoptics call the Caesarea Philippi episode the center of the story, so that Jesus' ministry moves up to this episode and the recognition of the messianic nature of Jesus, then down to the cross. At the same time, this echoes vv. 5 – 12 in the sense that Peter moves from misunderstanding to blessing. So the discipleship aspect of the previous pericope is developed further here. "Thus the theme of identity, woven into the preceding narrative in various ways, comes to a head."[1]

- **V. Rejection, Suffering, and Glory (13:54 – 18:35)**
  - **A. Jesus' Deeds: Rejection, Discipleship, and Glory (13:54 – 17:27)**
    - **1. Rejection and Discipleship (13:54 – 16:20)**
      - i. Demand for a Sign (16:1 – 4)
      - j. Warning about the Leaders (16:5 – 12)
      - ➦ **k. Peter's Confession and Jesus' Blessing (16:13 – 20)**

Main Idea

The single central idea is Christology, the messiahship of Jesus; Matthew contains by far the longest confession, as Peter links Jesus as "Messiah" with Jesus as "the Son of the living God." The second idea is discipleship, as Peter struggles with what that means. The third is blessing, as Jesus confers on Peter (and the church with which he is corporately identified) the authority of the kingdom power in Jesus.

1. Pregeant, *Matthew*, 111.

Translation

Matthew 16:13-20

13a	Setting (Temporal and Spatial)	After Jesus arrived in the region of Caesarea Philippi,
b	Question	**he asked his disciples,**
c		*"Who do people say the Son of Man is?"*
14a		**They replied,**
b	Answer #1	*[1] "Some say John the Baptist,*
c	Answer #2	*[2] others Elijah,*
d	Answer #3	*[3] still others Jeremiah or one of the prophets."*
15a	Question	**Jesus asked,**
b		*"But who do you say that I am?"*
16a	Answer	**Simon Peter answered,**
b		*"You are the Messiah, the Son of the living God!"*
17a	Response/Blessing	**Jesus responded,**
b		*"Blessed are you, Simon son of Jonah!*
c	Basis for 17b	*Because flesh and blood did not reveal this to you,*
d		*but my Father who is in heaven.*
18a	Assertion #1/ Prophecy	*[1] So I am telling you,*
b		*You are Peter,*
c		*and on this rock I will build my church.*
d	Assertion #2/ Prophecy	*[2] And the gates of Hades will not overpower it.*
19a	Assertion #3/ Prophecy	*[3] And I will give you the keys of the kingdom of heaven.*
b	Assertion #4/ Prophecy	*[4] Whatever you bind on earth will have been bound in heaven,*
c		*and whatever you loose on earth will have been loosed in heaven."*
20a	Exhortation/Command	**Then he ordered the disciples to tell no one that he was the Messiah.**

Structure and Literary Form

This is a combination of a paradigm event and a pronouncement story. It is paradigm in terms of Christology and discipleship, pronouncement in terms of the beatitude. Matthew builds on Mark and adds his own special material (vv. 17 – 19), omitting the healing of the blind man from Mark 8:22 – 26, probably to link the discipleship aspects of vv. 5 – 12 and vv. 13 – 20 more clearly and to provide a better development of his themes.

The structure is well-rounded. Dialogue dominates the first two parts (vv. 13 – 16), consisting of two questions: first about the public conception regarding

Jesus' identity (vv. 13 – 14), second about the disciples' perception (vv. 15 – 16). After Peter's confession, the beatitude occurs (vv. 17 – 19),[2] consisting of the source of Peter's revelation (v. 17) and the new authority granted to Peter/the church (vv. 18 – 19), with its four parts: Peter the rock, authority over the power of death, the keys of the kingdom, and the authority to bind and loose. Finally, Jesus gives an injunction to silence (v. 20).

Exegetical Outline

➦ **I. The Dialogue about Jesus' Identity (16:13 – 16)**
- A. The setting: area of Caesarea Philippi (v. 13a)
- B. First dialogue: public perception (vv. 13b – 14)
  1. Jesus' question (v. 13b)
  2. Disciple's response: eschatological prophet (v. 14)
- C. Second dialogue: the disciple's perception (vv. 15 – 16)
  1. Jesus' question (v. 15)
  2. Peter's response: Messiah, Son of God (v. 16)

II. The Beatitude Given Peter (16:17 – 19)
- A. The beatitude pronounced (v. 17a)
- B. The source of Peter's revelation (v. 17b)
- C. The new authority granted (vv. 18 – 19)
  1. Peter the rock (v. 18a)
  2. Authority over the power of death (v. 18b)
  3. The keys of the kingdom (v. 19a)
  4. Authority to bind and loose (v. 19b)

III. The Injunction to Silence (16:20)

Explanation of the Text

16:13 After Jesus arrived[3] in the region of Caesarea Philippi (Ἐλθὼν δὲ ὁ Ἰησοῦς εἰς τὰ μέρη Καισαρείας τῆς Φιλίππου). The withdrawal of Jesus begun in 16:4 is now completed as he and his disciples go about twenty-plus miles north of Galilee in a mainly Gentile area in the foothills of Mount Hermon and near the source of the Jordan. Caesarea Philippi had been rebuilt by Herod Philip and renamed in honor of the emperor Caesar Augustus (who ceded it to Herod the Great in 20 BC) and himself. This name also distinguished it from Caesarea Maritima on the coast. It is a rather remarkable choice for this event both because of its Gentile setting but even more because the previous town (Panacea) contained a famous pagan shrine, a grotto to the god Pan. While this

2. For the view that Matthew is inserting traditional material rather than creating it de novo, see Davies and Allison, *Matthew*, 2:602 – 15; France, *Gospel of Matthew*, 614n.

3. The temporal aorist participle ἐλθών is translated "after he arrived."

was mainly for retreating from the opposition, it also continued the movement toward the Gentile mission, although that is minimal in this section.

16:13 ... he asked his disciples, "Who do people say the Son of Man[4] is?"[5] (ἠρώτα τοὺς μαθητὰς αὐτοῦ λέγων, Τίνα λέγουσιν οἱ ἄνθρωποι εἶναι τὸν υἱὸν τοῦ ἀνθρώπου;). Matthew substitutes "Son of Man" (see on 8:20) to Mark's "I," making this a section of incredibly high Christology. As we will see in the first passion prediction (v. 21), the emphasis is on the suffering Son of Man.[6] Luz points out that the disciples had begun to understand the title (10:23; 13:37, 41), but the outsiders did not (11:19; 12:40; cf. 8:20). So this contrasts the two understandings, thus "distinguishing the 'knowing' disciples from the people."[7]

16:14 They[8] replied, "Some say John the Baptist, others Elijah, still others Jeremiah or one of the prophets" (οἱ δὲ εἶπαν, Οἱ μὲν Ἰωάννην τὸν βαπτιστήν, ἄλλοι δὲ Ἠλίαν, ἕτεροι δὲ Ἰερεμίαν ἢ ἕνα τῶν προφητῶν). Herod Antipas considered Jesus as the Baptist returned from the dead (14:2), and apparently this was a popular rumor among those who had never seen the two together. Those who thought Jesus to be Elijah were referring to the Elijah messianic forerunner prophesied in Mal 3:1; 4:5 – 6. This was ironic, because the first perception was the answer for the second perception; that is, John was the messianic forerunner (11:9 – 10, 14; 27:47, 49).

The reference to Jeremiah (added to Mark) does not seem so evident. Knowles explores the five options:[9] (1) as a "typical prophet," but one would expect Isaiah or Zechariah first; (2) as a "representative prophet," since his name is first on some lists (e.g. *b. B. Bat.* 14b), but that too is somewhat weak; (3) a "Jeremiah typology" in terms of parallels between Jeremiah's call, authority, and struggle, but there is not enough to verify such a typology; (4) Jeremiah a "messianic forerunner" from certain expectations of Jeremiah as an eschatological prophet in Jewish literature (2 Macc 2:1 – 12; 15:11 – 16, possibly 2 Esd 2:18, though it seems to be a second-century work of a Christian author), but there is not a lot of evidence; (5) as a "Jeremiah identified with Jesus" — this is best, stemming from the fact that Jeremiah was the "weeping prophet," the prophet of doom, and Jesus often proclaimed similar judgment over the nation and would face a similar death (tradition said Jeremiah was stoned). "One of the prophets" shows how inextricably the coming Messiah was linked to the prophetic age. One not explicitly named is the "prophet like [Moses]" of Deut 18:15 – 18, probably included in this final designation.

16:15 Jesus asked, "But who do you say that I am?" (λέγει αὐτοῖς, Ὑμεῖς δὲ τίνα με λέγετε εἶναι;). The adversative "but" (δέ) with emphatic "you" (ὑμεῖς) shows Jesus' intention to contrast the common expectations with the developing understanding of the disciples. He is also preparing them for the movement from now on to his messianic destiny in Jerusalem. So this is the critical node of the narrative thus far, and Jesus wants them to verbalize their commitment.

16:16 Simon Peter answered,[10] "You are the Messiah, the Son of the living God!"(ἀποκριθεὶς δὲ

4. Several ancient manuscripts (D L Θ et al.) add με (= "I, the Son of Man"), but in several different positions, and this was probably added on the basis of the parallel texts in Mark 8:27; Luke 9:18, which contain "I" but not "Son of Man."

5. "To be" (εἶναι) here is an infinitive used for an indirect question, see BDF §368.

6. The title here could be a circumlocution for "I," see Hagner; contra Davies and Allison.

7. Luz, *Matthew 8 – 20*, 360.

8. οἱ is an example of the article used for the pronominal subject, "they" (see BDF §249).

9. Knowles, *Jeremiah* in *Matthew's Gospel*, 82 – 95.

10. See v. 2 for this frequent Matthean idiom; it occurs again in v. 17.

Σίμων Πέτρος εἶπεν, Σὺ εἶ ὁ Χριστὸς ὁ υἱὸς τοῦ θεοῦ τοῦ ζῶντος). Jesus has been labeled "Christ" often (1:1, 16 – 18 in editorial contexts; 2:4 by Herod; 11:2 implied by the Baptist), but never by his followers until now. In addition, he has been called Son of God by demons (4:3; 8:29) and even by the disciples themselves (14:33). But this is a confessional setting, a creedal cry that Jesus wants to wrest from them. He wants to settle once and for all where they stand.

"Simon Peter" (see 4:18; 10:2) once again emerges as leader and speaks for the whole group. As Hagner says, "This was something they undoubtedly discussed again and again, and they had come to their conclusion.... He is their leader and their spokesman (*primus inter pares*), but he is also *their* representative, indeed the representative of the whole church."[11] It is doubtful that Peter saw the christological depth that is intended by Matthew, but he probably did perceive the unique relationship Jesus had to his heavenly Father.

The extended title that Jesus is Son of "the living God" (Deut 5:26; Josh 3:10; Ps 42:2) is Jewish.[12] Note the radical difference with the rumors of the people, who have linked Jesus with various eschatological prophets. For Simon and the Twelve, he is more than a forerunner but the expected Messiah himself. It is common (Davies and Allison, Luz, Hagner, Nolland) to see here the Davidic expectations fulfilled (1 Sam 7:4 – 16), and indeed the base of the messianic expectation through the prophets was the covenant promise of an eternal throne to the house of David. That could only be fulfilled with the coming Davidic Messiah (see on 1:1; cf. 9:27; 12:23; 15:22). Soon Jesus will qualify this in a way Peter and the others cannot handle (vv. 21 – 23).

16:17 Jesus responded, "Blessed are you, Simon son of Jonah!" (ἀποκριθεὶς δὲ ὁ Ἰησοῦς εἶπεν αὐτῷ, Μακάριος εἶ, Σίμων Βαριωνᾶ). Matthew departs from Mark to add his own special material and thereby modify the harshness of Peter's failure in Mark by showing how Jesus first lauded and blessed Peter's important confession. This adds emphasis to the importance and divine source for that insight. In light of the insight God has granted to Simon, Jesus pronounces a beatitude (see on 5:3), i.e., God's blessing, on him. As already noted in 5:3 – 12, μακάριος is not human happiness but divine favor, though the joy and fortunate status of the individual is a by-product. It combines religious ecstasy and human joy.

The full name "Simon son of Jonah" (Σίμων Βαριωνᾶ) [13] occurs only here, though in John 1:42; 21:15 – 17 it is "son of John" (Ἰωάννου). Most think the name here is a shortened form of the one in John, but others see symbolic meaning attached, linking Simon with the prophet Jonah, perhaps to add a prophetic nuance to Peter's insight here. This latter is interesting but not provable.

16:17 "Because flesh and blood did not reveal this to you, but my Father who is in heaven" (ὅτι σὰρξ καὶ αἷμα οὐκ ἀπεκάλυψέν σοι ἀλλ᾽ ὁ πατήρ μου ὁ ἐν τοῖς οὐρανοῖς). The stress on the revelatory source of Peter's confession turns it into an eschatological proclamation. This is not a merely human ("flesh and blood" [σὰρξ καὶ αἷμα)]) supposition (cf. the "traditions/merely human commandments" of the Pharisees in 15:2 – 9 or the "human things" of Peter in 16:23). God has

11. Hagner, *Matthew 14 – 28*, 468.

12. J. Galot, "La première profession de foi chrétienne," *Esprit et vie* 97 (1987): 593 – 99, concludes a series of articles in which he argues that Peter's confession took place on the Day of Atonement. That is difficult to prove, but the imagery is definitely present, since on the Day of Atonement the high priest uttered the divine name, and here Jesus is standing as it were in Yahweh's place.

13. Βαριωνᾶ is Aramaic and means "son of (Βαρ) Jonah (-ιωνᾶ)."

given Peter this insight. Nolland sees an echo of 11:25 – 27 in the juxtaposition of "revealed," "Father," and "Son": as the Son reveals the Father to the infants in 11:25 – 27, so now the Father reveals the Son to those who open up to him.[14]

16:18 So I am telling you, "You are Peter" (κἀγὼ δέ σοι λέγω ὅτι σὺ εἶ Πέτρος). The switch from the aorist "he said" (εἶπεν) in vv. 16 – 17 to the present "I am telling you" (λέγω) here places this in the foreground (see on 16:8) or emphatic position. Jesus had already prophesied to Simon that he would become *Cephas* (Aramaic), *Peter* (Greek),[15] "the rock," in John 1:40 – 42, the first time Jesus met Simon after his brother Andrew (a disciple of the Baptist) had brought Simon to him. This bestowal of a new name parallels that of Abram/Abraham (Gen 17:5) and Jacob/Israel (Gen 32:28) and signifies a new status and ministry (see Davies and Allison). Here Jesus reiterates that earlier prophetic promise and links it to Simon's creedal affirmation. Simon has made his stand for Jesus; now Jesus makes his stand for him!

16:18 "... and on this rock I will build my church" (καὶ ἐπὶ ταύτῃ τῇ πέτρᾳ οἰκοδομήσω μου τὴν ἐκκλησίαν). "This rock" (ταύτῃ τῇ πέτρᾳ, first for emphasis) has become a minefield through the centuries. The play on words from "Peter" (πέτρος) in the first part of Jesus' affirmation to "rock" (πέτρα) in the second has led many to say "this rock" is not Simon but either Christ (Origen, Augustine) or Simon's confession.[16] Since the Reformation this has been argued repeatedly because Peter as the rock was an essential piece in the Roman Catholic view of apostolic succession and the papacy.

However, this is an inadequate reason for denying the most obvious understanding, and the majority today recognize that Peter is the rock here, though in the context it is certainly the Peter who confesses Christ. Behind the rock metaphor are images that relate first to the temple (the foundation stone, Ps 118:22) in terms of its stability and permanence[17] and then to the netherworld, and second to the rock/temple as the gate to Hades (see Carson, Davies and Allison, Hagner, Nolland).

Thus Peter as the rock prepares for the two promises that follow. Jesus is the builder (οἰκοδομέω) and cornerstone, but Peter is the first leader/rock/foundation on whom Jesus erects the superstructure.[18] This is the first of three times "church" (ἐκκλησία) appears in Matthew (twice in 18:17). While some have taken the two components (ἐκ and καλέω) to interpret it as "called-out" believers, the term meant simply an "assembly" of people meeting for a common purpose. Thus it refers to the Christian assembly, in Paul usually the local church. Jesus is establishing the new Israel,

14. Nolland, *Matthew*, 666.

15. It has often been argued that Cephas/Peter was not a proper name in the first century, but its use as a name has been proven by Joseph A. Fitzmyer, "Aramaic *Kepha*ʾ and Peter's Name in the New Testament," in *To Advance the Gospel* (New York: Crossroad, 1981), 112 – 24. See also Chrys C. Caragounis, *Peter the Rock* (BZNW 58; Berlin: de Gruyter, 1990), 23 – 25.

16. This latter has been argued at length by Caragounis, *Peter the Rock*, and accepted by Garland, *Reading Matthew*, 170 – 71; and Pregeant, *Matthew*, 111 – 12.

17. J. D. M. Derrett, "'Thou Art the Stone, and upon this Stone ...' *DRev* 106 (1988): 276 – 85, sees this wordplay as built on Isaianic stone texts (Isa 28:16; 54:11 – 12), thus calling Peter the masonry stone and the bedrock on which God would build his messianic congregation.

18. Max-Alain Chevallier, "'Tu es Pierre, tu es nouvel Abraham' (Matt 16/18)," *ETR* 57 (1982): 375 – 87, represents some who believe Peter is presented as a new Abraham, founder of Christianity, on the grounds that the wording reflects Isa 51:1 – 2, "look to the rock from which you were cut ... look to Abraham, your father," with Abraham the rock of Israel as found in the Jewish tractate *Yalqut Shimeoni* 1:766 and many medieval commentators. This is possible, but the wording is inexact, the tract late, and God is more likely the rock in Isaiah.

the new community of God, and Peter will be its first foundation.

16:18 "... and the gates of Hades will not overpower it" (καὶ πύλαι ᾅδου οὐ κατισχύσουσιν αὐτῆς). Sheol/Hades was often pictured as having stone portals at the entrance to the underworld, the realm of the dead (cf. Job 17:16; Ps 9:13; Isa 38:10; Wis 16:13; *Pss. Sol.* 16:2; 1QH 6:24–26). However, the exact meaning is difficult. Does it mean the evil powers of the cosmic world are nullified, or that the power of death cannot overcome the church ("it" [αὐτῆς] refers to "church" [ἐκκλησία])?[19]

The consensus view today, probably the correct one, is best stated in Paul's use of Isa 25:8 and Hos 13:14, "Death has been swallowed up in victory. 'Where, O death, is your victory? Where, O death is your sting?' " (1 Cor 15:54b–55). With Jesus' death and resurrection as the firstfruit and then in the eschatological promise to the people of God, death can not "overpower" the believer ("gates" here are fortifications), and the church will never be extinguished.[20] Moreover, there is likely an aspect of Jesus' principle in 12:29 and 10:1, 8; the church has been given authority to bind the powers of evil and death. The powers are not nullified, but they have been made subject to the citizens of the kingdom.

16:19 And I will give you the keys of the kingdom of heaven (δώσω σοι τὰς κλεῖδας τῆς βασιλείας τῶν οὐρανῶν). From the gates Jesus moves to the keys that open the gates. Also, the image moves from the underworld to the heavenly realm. "Keys" (κλεῖδας) in the ancient world symbolized access to power and the ability to open the doors to the heavenly realms. So to possess keys means considerable authority. In Isa 22:20–22 Eliakim became the chief steward of Hezekiah's household and was given "the key to the house of David; what he opens no one can shut, and what he shuts no one can open," repeated in Rev 3:7 of Christ (also Rev 1:18). In this sense Peter here becomes the "chief steward" of the new kingdom community.

One question is whether the keys open the present kingdom reality or the final future kingdom. As Nolland says, "It is unlikely to suppose that we should be asked to choose between the two ... engagement with the kingdom as present will be the prelude for entry into the kingdom as future."[21] In this context there is an inaugurated perspective with the emphasis on the already. With Christ the kingdom has entered this world in a new way (see on 3:2), and Peter (corporately identified with the church) wields its authority. As Wilkins says, "Peter, the representative disciple ... is the one in the book of Acts who opens the door of the kingdom to the Jews on Pentecost (Acts 2), to the Samaritans (Acts 8), and finally to the Gentiles (Acts 10)."[22] Yet this promise is also given to the church, the main focus in v. 18b and intended here as well.

16:19 Whatever you bind on earth will have been bound in heaven, and whatever you loose on earth will have been loosed in heaven (καὶ ὃ ἐὰν δήσῃς ἐπὶ τῆς γῆς ἔσται δεδεμένον ἐν τοῖς οὐρανοῖς, καὶ ὃ ἐὰν λύσῃς ἐπὶ τῆς γῆς ἔσται λελυμένον ἐν τοῖς οὐρανοῖς). The first issue here is the force of the future perfect passive periphrastic "will have been bound" (ἔσται δεδεμένον); should the two expressions in each clause retain their perfect force ("will have been bound/loosed") or be translated as futures ("will be bound/loosed")? It has been common to stress a past aspect of the

19. Davies and Allison, *Matthew*, 2:630–32, list some twelve options that have been suggested.

20. For a history of interpretation of this, see Luz, also J. P. Lewis, " 'The Gates of Hell Shall Not Prevail against It' (Matt 16:18): A Study of the History of Interpretation," *JETS* 38 (1995): 349–67.

21. Nolland, *Matthew*, 676.

22. Wilkins, *Matthew*, 566.

perfect to say that the decisions on earth "have already been made" in heaven,[23] so that the church moves as guided by divine inspiration.

While this makes good sense, the more recent appraisal of the perfect tense shows that it often does not have past time sense but rather is stative in force, thus emphasizing the present and future aspect ("will be bound/loosed").[24] So some make God's decision subsequent, thus ratifying Peter's/the church's decision.[25] Surely this cannot be correct, as if God is bound to accept the church's decisions. The best is probably to see Peter and the church inspired by God as he works in their midst while they discover and live his will and way. Now and in the future God will be present guiding his people.

Yet we still have to understand the binding and loosing image. There was an incredible diversity of uses of this metaphor in the ancient world. In Job 38:31 God binds and looses the starry host, referring to his creation of the universe. In Jewish works like *b. Šabb.* 4a the terms refer to acceptable behavior, in *b. Šabb.* 81b they are used for magic spells, and in *b. Moʾed Qaṭ.* 16a they are used of the ban, namely, exclusion from the community. In Judaism and the NT it is used for binding Satan (Mark 3:27 par.) and loosing people from demonic possession (Tob 3:17, 8:3; *T. Levi* 18:12).[26] The concept can also refer to forgiving and retaining sins (*Tg. Neof.* Gen 4:7; cf. Matt 18:18; John 20:23), for keeping or absolving vows (*b. Ḥag.* 10a), or parallels with the rabbinic *šᵉrāʾ* and *ʾāsar* for the halakhic conduct required by a proper interpretation of Torah.[27]

How do we choose between the options here? Some believe it is the power to defeat the cosmic forces of evil,[28] others to open doors to the kingdom in the mission of the church, thereby bringing into the church only those who confess their sins as Peter did,[29] or still others to determine what is sin and what is not in the community,[30] or perhaps to accept or forbid members to remain in the church.[31] Probably the best interpretation is to bring together this image of evangelism with that of discipleship, i.e., the authority of Peter and the church to declare the kingdom truths as they interpret and proclaim Jesus' teaching, guiding the new community regarding what is forbidden and what is permitted in both doctrine and conduct (thus including discipline in the church, cf. 18:18).[32]

Along with this is the authority of their teaching to bring people to decision and lead them to either forgiveness or judgment (the meaning of John 20:23). A key is the "on earth/in heaven" contrast.

23. J. R. Mantey, "Distorted Translations in John 20:23; Matthew 16:18 – 19," *RevExp* 78 (1981): 409 – 16; see also Albright and Mann, Carson, Gundry, France, Morris.

24. Porter, *Idioms*, 20 – 23; and his "Vague Verbs, Periphrastics, and Matt 16:19," *FiloNT* 1 (1988): 158 – 61; A. del Coro, "To Put or Not to Put a Footnote: Matthew 16:19," *BT* 53 (2002): 226 – 33 (also Hagner, Blomberg, Nolland).

25. Henry J. Cadbury, "The Meaning of John 20:23, Matthew 16:19, and Matthew 18:18," *JBL* 58 (1939): 251 – 54; also Davies and Allison.

26. Nolland, *Matthew*, 678.

27. See Davies and Allison, *Matthew*, 2:635 – 38; Luz, *Matthew 8 – 20*, 365.

28. Joel Marcus, "The Gates of Hades and the Keys of the Kingdom (Matt 16:18 – 19)," *CBQ* 50 (1988): 443 – 55, who sees a contrast between the gates of Hades in 16:18 and the keys of the kingdom (implying heaven's gates) in 16:19, so the cosmic forces are bound and the kingdom's forces released in the binding and loosing. See also Richard H. Hiers, "'Binding' and 'Loosing': The Matthean Authorization," *JBL* 104 (1985): 233 – 50.

29. Georg Korting, "Binden oder lösen: Zu Verstockungs- und Befreiungstheologie in Matt 16, 19; 18,18,21 – 35 und Joh 15, 1 – 17; 20,23," *SNTSU* 14 (1989): 39 – 91; Blomberg, *Matthew*, 254; Keener, *Matthew*, 430; Wilkins, *Matthew*, 567.

30. J. D. M. Derrett, "Binding and Loosing (Matt 16:19, 18:18; John 20:23)," *JBL* 102 (1983): 112 – 17.

31. Herbert W. Basser, "Derrett's 'Binding' Reopened," *JBL* 104 (1985): 297 – 300.

32. So Carson, "Matthew," 372 – 73; Hagner, *Matthew 14 – 28*, 473; Morris, *Matthew*, 426; Turner, "Matthew," 222 – 23.

The church exists on earth but with a heavenly authority behind it. As the church takes the teaching of Jesus and lives it in this world both in terms of opening the doors of the kingdom to converts and opening the truths of the kingdom to the new messianic community, it does so with the authority and guidance of God.

16:20 Then he ordered the disciples to tell no one that he was the Messiah (τότε διεστείλατο τοῖς μαθηταῖς ἵνα μηδενὶ εἴπωσιν ὅτι αὐτός ἐστιν ὁ Χριστός). This passage is framed (vv. 16. 20) with the messianic nature of Jesus, making it the christological high point thus far. While Mark is better known for the "messianic secret" motif (see on 8:4), Matthew does contain references to it. Here it makes perfect sense. The Jewish people had nothing but erroneous speculations regarding Jesus' identity (vv. 13 – 14), and Jesus had come to be not a prophet but the Messiah, yet a messiah entirely different than any of them thought, including Jesus' disciples (as will be seen in vv. 21 – 23 below). The Jews expected a political conqueror, not a suffering servant. They awaited the messianic destruction of the Romans (cf. John 6:15), and Peter proved this when he drew his sword at Jesus' arrest (cf. 26:51; John 18:10).

Theology in Application

This is one of the richest and best-known passages in Matthew, and the theological implications are immense.

1. The Messiah and His Kingdom

The central truth of history is the coming of Jesus Messiah and his establishment of the kingdom. In the first century, messianic fervor was in the air, but confusion reigned as to what that meant, and for most it was the desire for liberation from oppression. The same was true of kingdom expectations. Here the Messiah is connected to the new messianic community, the kingdom people, the church, which he is "erecting" on his own foundation and then that of Peter (v. 18b).

2. Peter Is the Foundation and Representative Disciple

These promises are all addressed to Simon Peter as the "rock," who will be the first foundation/leader of the church. This is true of all four gospels. In this sense he is the archetypal disciple for all of us, the one who is given authority on our behalf and passes that authority down to us. Further evidence of Peter's representative role (rather than one of papal succession) is the fact that binding and loosing language is repeated with reference to all the apostles in 18:18. We will see that both in his success here and in his failure in the next section.

So Peter is the model for discipleship patterns as he is the first to recognize the true significance of Jesus, yet at the same time he struggles with his faith and understanding. Matthew chronicles that process in Peter as an example for all disciples.

As Hauerwas says, "It is not Peter's task to make the church safe and secure or to insure its existence. Rather, it is Peter's task to keep the church true to its mission, which is to witness to the Messiah."[33]

3. The Church as a New Eschatological Authority

The authority of the church is twofold. (1) It has power over the realm of death both in terms of the eternal life that is guaranteed through resurrection and in terms of its ongoing presence in this world. The powers of death cannot prevail over it. (2) It has authority to take the truths of Christ and live them, authenticating right living and disciplining those who fail to live according to Christ's teaching (cf. 28:20a, "teaching them to keep everything I have commanded you"). Matthew centers on ethics (see the introduction to chs. 5 – 7), the "righteous" living that must characterize the citizens of the kingdom. Here the teaching office of the church is given authority by Christ to understand and apply his kingdom ethics. Finally, it has authority to spread the gospel to the world, opening the doors of the kingdom to Jew and Gentile alike.

33. Hauerwas, *Matthew*, 150.

CHAPTER 72

Matthew 16:21 – 28

Literary Context

With "from that time on" (v. 21) we begin the second half of this narrative section (13:54 – 17:27), indeed, the second half of Matthew's gospel. Immediately after Peter's confession of Jesus as Messiah, Jesus starts to prepare the disciples for the true meaning of that confession.[1] The announcement of the passion had to await the realization on the part of the disciples that he is the Messiah, for the passion defines his messianic office. So now the movement of the narrative is downward, and the discipleship sayings that follow (vv. 24 – 28) flow out of the announcement, defining the true followers as those who "take up their cross" in imitation of the Messiah.

V. Rejection, Suffering, and Glory (13:54 – 18:35)
- **A. Jesus' Deeds: Rejection, Discipleship, and Glory (13:54 – 17:27)**
  - 1. Rejection and Discipleship (13:54 – 16:20)
  - **2. The Movement to the Cross (16:21 – 17:27)**
    - ➦ **a. First Passion Prediction and Discipleship (16:21 – 28)**
      - **(1) Jesus Predicts His Death (16:21)**
      - **(2) Peter and Jesus Rebuke One Another (16:22 – 23)**
      - **(3) The Path of Discipleship (16:24 – 28)**
    - b. Transfiguration (17:1 – 13)

Main Idea

The road to Jerusalem and the cross now begins, and it involves three things — Jesus' passion prediction, the failure of the disciples to understand the meaning of

1. This is another example of the extent to which outlines are somewhat artificial, for 16:13 – 23 is also a unified whole with three parts — the people's misidentification of Jesus, Peter's confession of the truth about Jesus, and Jesus' clarification of the true meaning of that confession.

that for his messianic office, and Jesus' teaching on the path of discipleship that flows out of his passion prediction. As Jesus gave himself totally to his coming death, so the disciples must give themselves up to God and die to life centered in this world. All previous categories the disciples have known are radically reversed, and the requirements as well as the perspective of the messianic kingdom have been redefined in a way they can hardly comprehend.

Translation

Matthew 16:21-28

21a	Transition	**From that time on Jesus began to show his disciples:**
b	Assertion/Prophecy	[1] that he must go to Jerusalem and
c		[2] suffer many things at the hands of the elders, the chief priests, and the teachers of law and
d		[3] be put to death and
e		[4] be raised on the third day.
22a	Objection/Rebuke	**Peter took him aside and began to rebuke him, saying,**
b		*"Far be it from you, Lord!*
c		*This will never happen to you!"*
23a	Response/Rebuke	But **Jesus turned to Peter and said,**
b		*"Get behind me, Satan!*
c		*You are a stumbling block to me,*
d	Basis for 23c	*because you are not setting your mind on the things of God* but
e		*on human things."*
24a	Expansion on 21	**Then Jesus told his disciples,**
b	Action	*"If anyone wants to come after me,*
c	Condition #1	*[1] let them deny themselves,*
d	Condition #2	*[2] take up their cross, and*
e	Condition #3	*[3] continue to follow me.*
25a	Clarification #1	*(i)* For *whoever wants to save their life will forfeit it,*
b	Contrast 25a	and *whoever forfeits their life for my sake will find it.*
26a	Clarification #2	*(ii)* For *what good will it be for a person to gain the whole world and lose their very soul in the process?*
b		Or *what should a person give in exchange for their soul?*
27a	Promise #1	*(a)* For *the Son of Man is going to come in the glory of his Father with his angels,*
b	Promise #2	*(b)* and *then I will reward each one on the basis of their deed.*
28a	Promise #3	*(c) I tell you the truth, there are some standing here who will not experience death*
b	Time	*until they see the Son of Man coming in his kingdom."*

Structure and Literary Form

This could be called an "objection story" (vv. 21 – 23, Davies and Allison) followed by a discipleship discourse (vv. 24 – 28). It follows Mark 8:31 – 9:1 fairly closely, with the most important addition the phrase "from that time on" (v. 21), which inaugurates the movement to the cross. There are three parts: the first of the three passion predictions (v. 21), the two rebukes between Peter and Jesus (vv. 22 – 23), and the sayings on discipleship (vv. 24 – 28).

Exegetical Outline

➡ **I. Jesus Predicts His Death (16:21)**
   A. Suffer in Jerusalem
   B. Suffer at the hands of the leaders
   C. Death and resurrection

II. Peter and Jesus Rebuke Each Another (16:22 – 23)
   A. Peter's rebuke and rejection of the passion (v. 22)
   B. Jesus' rebuke (v. 23)
      1. Peter an instrument of Satan
      2. Peter a stumbling block
      3. Peter thinking humanly instead of the things of God

III. The Path of Discipleship (16:24 – 28)
   A. The definition of a disciple (v. 24)
   B. Two clarifications (vv. 25 – 26)
      1. Saving and losing your life (v. 25)
      2. Gaining and forfeiting your life (v. 26)
   C. Eschatological promises (vv. 27 – 28)
      1. The coming of the parousia and its reward (v. 27)
      2. The imminence of the parousia (v. 28)

Explanation of the Text

16:21 From that time on Jesus began to show his disciples (Ἀπὸ τότε ἤρξατο ὁ Ἰησοῦς δεικνύειν τοῖς μαθηταῖς αὐτοῦ). "From that time on he began" (ἀπὸ τότε ἤρξατο) also began 4:17 at the start of Jesus' Galilean ministry, so this introductory formula frames the two parts of Matthew's narrative, the movement upward to the Caesarea Philippi confession, and the movement downward to the cross. The use of "to show" (δεικνύειν, present tense here for the ongoing nature of the demonstration) is also strong (Mark 8:31 has "teach"), connoting a visualization of the message and meaning he wants to make things crystal clear to the disciples.[2]

2. See *EDNT*, 1:280.

16:21 ... that he must go to Jerusalem and suffer many things at the hands of the elders, the chief priests, and the teachers of law (ὅτι δεῖ αὐτὸν εἰς Ἱεροσόλυμα ἀπελθεῖν καὶ πολλὰ παθεῖν ἀπὸ τῶν πρεσβυτέρων καὶ ἀρχιερέων καὶ γραμματέων). We do not know at what point in his life Jesus realized that he had come to give his life as a sacrifice for sin, but it must have been early. He is aware of his impending death in 9:15, hints at it in 10:38, and must know of the plot against his life in 12:14. But now he is explicit and explains that his movement to Jerusalem is divine necessity ("must" [δεῖ]), the very will of God.

"Must" (δεῖ) is followed by four aorist infinitives that form the passion prediction and stress the fact of these events.[3] First, Jesus' destiny is Jerusalem, where both the temple sacrifices and the hostile authorities await him.[4] Second, there he will "suffer many things," a general summary of all the indignities and torment at the hands of the authorities. These are spelled out in more detail in the third prediction (20:19) and encompass all of the events from the arrest to the crucifixion. The three groups mentioned here are governed by a single article and so together constitute the Jewish leadership. The teachers of law (scribes) and the chief priests have been discussed at 2:4. The "elders" were originally the heads of the families and clans but in the intertestamental period were the heads of the aristocratic families, gradually joining with the other two groups here (the Pharisees are included in the scribes here) to form the Sanhedrin, the ruling council of Jewry. In Jewish communities generally a council of seven elders oversaw daily life. So Jesus is saying the national leaders will conspire against him in Jerusalem.

16:21 ... and be put to death and be raised on the third day (καὶ ἀποκτανθῆναι καὶ τῇ τρίτῃ ἡμέρᾳ ἐγερθῆναι). Jesus' death and resurrection form the third and fourth infinitives that detail the divine necessity (δεῖ earlier in this verse) for Jesus' destiny. The idea of the suffering and dying Messiah from Isa 53 (for the theme of suffering, also Ps 16; 22; 31; 41; 69) was not understood by Judaism, who generally interpreted the *ʿebed yhwh* as the nation rather than the Messiah. So Jesus is explaining something beyond the disciple's ability to comprehend.

Yet death will be swallowed up in victory (1 Cor 15:54, from Isa 25:8). The divine passive "be raised" (ἐγερθῆναι) stresses the vindication of Jesus' death by God. The "third day" theme is connected to the "three days and three nights" of 12:40 and will be found again at 17:23; 20:19; 27:63. It became a major creedal affirmation in the early church, and 1 Cor 15:4 (cf. John 2:19) records that Jesus was "raised on the third day according to the Scriptures"; this is often linked with Hos 6:2 ("on the third day he will restore us," cf. also 2 Kgs 20:5; Jonah 1:17) but is probably even broader, to the whole OT tradition of a third-day deliverance.[5] Jesus was placed in the grave Friday afternoon and raised Sunday morning and by Jewish reckoning was in the grave "three days and three nights" inclusively.

16:22 Peter took him aside[6] and began to rebuke him, saying, "Far be it from you, Lord! This will never[7] happen to you!" (καὶ προσλαβόμενος αὐτὸν ὁ Πέτρος ἤρξατο ἐπιτιμᾶν αὐτῷ λέγων,

3. Wallace, 502, shows that the aorist turns the action into a "snapshot" and the present turns it into a motion picture.

4. Donald J. Verseput, "Jesus' Pilgrimage to Jerusalem and Encounter in the Temple: A Geographical Motif in Matthew's Gospel," *NovT* 36 (1994): 105 – 21, sees this as part of a four-stage travel narrative in Matthew (with 17:22 – 27; 19:1; 21:1 – 23:39) as Jesus becomes the exiled king going to confront the holy city.

5. See Fee, *1 Corinthians*, 726 – 27.

6. Another of Matthew's many circumstantial participles that becomes virtually a main verb, see 4:20. See also v. 23 ("turned").

7. It is debated whether "never" (οὐ μή) has retained its emphatic force; but though it is primarily in quotes from the LXX and sayings of Jesus, it is generally recognized that it does (see Porter, *Idioms*, 283; Wallace, 468).

Ἵλεώς σοι, κύριε· οὐ μὴ ἔσται σοι τοῦτο). As one would expect, Peter cannot handle this new revelation, so polar opposite from everything the disciples intended when they affirmed Jesus as Messiah. The use of "began (ἤρξατο) to rebuke" pictures Peter as just beginning his forceful objection (yet given dramatic force with the present tense infinitive following). Matthew calls it a "rebuke" to stress the total turnaround by Peter from confessing adherent to critical opponent, but also to parallel him with Jesus' more powerful rebuke in the next verse.

The phrase ἵλεώς σοι has led to two different possible understandings. It occurs frequently in the LXX in the sense, "May God be merciful/gracious/kind to you," so some think it may be a mild prayer that God not allow this to occur. But more likely it reflects the Hebrew *ḥālîlâ*, "far be it from me," and is a confrontational form of "Never!"[8] This is confirmed when Peter adds the very strong, "This will never [οὐ μή] happen."

16:23 But Jesus turned to Peter and said, "Get behind me, Satan!" (ὁ δὲ στραφεὶς εἶπεν τῷ Πέτρῳ, Ὕπαγε ὀπίσω μου, Σατανᾶ). The dramatic "turn" by Jesus heightens the power of the scene. In opposing the divine destiny set before Jesus, Peter has become a tool of Satan to thwart God's plan. Obviously, Jesus is not saying Peter is demon-possessed or part of the cosmic forces. ὕπαγε ... Σατανᾶ reflects the temptation story at 4:10, "Go away, Satan," and means Peter's Satan-inspired attitude must disappear.[9]

16:23 "You are a stumbling block to me"[10] (σκάνδαλον εἶ ἐμοῦ). Hagner says it well: "Peter, 'the rock' (v. 18), had become in effect a stone of offense or a 'rock of stumbling' (Isa 8:14) to Jesus (as Jesus himself would become to others [cf. Rom 9:33; 1 Pet 2:6 – 8]), a σκάνδαλον, a 'stumbling block' (cf. the cognate verb in 11:6), in the path of the accomplishment of God's will," perhaps with the imagery of clearing away an obstacle/stone from that path.[11] Peter was standing in the way of God's will.

16:23 "... because you are not setting your mind on the things of God but on human things" (ὅτι οὐ φρονεῖς τὰ τοῦ θεοῦ ἀλλὰ τὰ τῶν ἀνθρώπων). "Are ... setting your mind" (φρονεῖς, present tense to emphasize Peter's ongoing mental state) connotes intentions, attitudes, disposition — in other words, the mind-set of a person. Peter's mind-set is not framed by God's perspective but by the purely human expectations of Israel's messianic hopes.

The two sources of spiritual failure (Satan and self) are both emphasized here. Jesus' statement here has long been recognized as the heart of true discipleship in the sense of focusing on heavenly rather than earthly concerns and is closely linked in thrust with 6:19 – 21, which teaches us to seek treasure in heaven rather than treasure on earth.

16:24 Then Jesus told his disciples, "If anyone wants to come after me" (Τότε ὁ Ἰησοῦς εἶπεν τοῖς μαθηταῖς αὐτοῦ, Εἴ τις θέλει ὀπίσω μου ἐλθεῖν). Flowing out of Peter's discipleship failure and lack of comprehension, Jesus now makes clear what discipleship must be and expands this to apply to "anyone [who] wants" (with εἰ as a condition of fact, which assumes they do want to be disciples). Clearly the impetus is on individual decision. "To come after me" (ὀπίσω μου ἐλθεῖν) means "to become a disciple" and is synonymous

8. See Carson, "Matthew," 378.

9. Others have interpreted this in a positive sense as "Follow after me," see D. C. Stoutenberg, " 'Out of My Sight!', 'Get Behind Me!', or 'Follow After Me!': There Is No Choice in God's Kingdom," *JETS* 36 (1993): 173 – 78. He takes all three as aspects of the scene here.

10. "To me" (ἐμοῦ) is an emphatic possessive adjective, stressing that Peter had become an obstacle to Jesus.

11. Hagner, *Matthew 14 – 28*, 480.

with "follow me" in the next part, thereby framing the definition with the desire to follow (an echo of 4:19; 9:9) the path of Christ.

16:24 "Let them deny themselves, take up their cross, and continue to follow me" (ἀπαρνησάσθω ἑαυτὸν καὶ ἀράτω τὸν σταυρὸν αὐτοῦ καὶ ἀκολουθείτω μοι). The key to discipleship is self-denial, with Jesus the archetype, who will surrender himself up to death, and Peter the antithesis, who demands that Jesus conduct his messianic office according to the human perspective. To follow as God demands is to renounce the centrality of self.

"Take up their cross" (ἀράτω τὸν σταυρὸν αὐτοῦ, see also on 10:38) is an incredibly powerful metaphor in a world where rebels and malcontents could regularly be seen dying on crosses. The disciples had to know, with all the opposition to Jesus by the officials, that this was a real possibility for them. In the Roman world it was common for the condemned criminal to carry his own cross to the place of execution, so this is an apt analogy. It is likely that there is a twofold thrust: cross-bearing as a symbol of the total denial of self, and a willingness to die for Christ if necessary. Again Jesus is the supreme model who has done both.

Finally, this reality alone makes it possible to fulfill the command "continue to follow me" (ἀκολουθείτω μοι, this present tense after a series of aorists places the third command in the foreground and stresses a life of continuous discipleship). Until the kingdom reality outweighs every consideration, even one's own life, one is not a true follower.

16:25 For whoever wants to save their life will forfeit it, and whoever forfeits their life for my sake will find it (ὃς γὰρ ἐὰν θέλῃ τὴν ψυχὴν αὐτοῦ σῶσαι ἀπολέσει αὐτήν· ὃς δ᾽ ἂν ἀπολέσῃ τὴν ψυχὴν αὐτοῦ ἕνεκεν ἐμοῦ εὑρήσει αὐτήν). The double "for" (γάρ) in vv. 25 – 26 shows that Jesus is providing a clarification of the meaning of self-denial. The key is your own priorities. Jesus uses the language of personal desire or volition ("wants" [θέλω]) to make his point; there are choices that have to be made.

The contrast is clear: earthly pursuits vs. eternal life. The entire tone is eschatological, and the play on words between "save" (σῴζω) and "forfeit" (ἀπόλλυμι) yields the contrast between seeking to "preserve" the earthly heritage yet in fact actually "destroying" that life and losing it forever. The gain/loss antithesis reaches full crescendo, for the more kingdom values descend into gaining the things of this life, the more the loss comes at the other end. This is not kingdom living! There is further emphasis on "for my sake" (ἕνεκεν ἐμοῦ); to be a child of God and follower of Christ means to live not for ourselves but to forfeit willingly all these things "for [his] sake."

16:26 For what good will it be for a person[12] to gain the whole world and lose their very soul in the process? (τί γὰρ ὠφεληθήσεται ἄνθρωπος ἐὰν τὸν κόσμον ὅλον κερδήσῃ τὴν δὲ ψυχὴν αὐτοῦ ζημιωθῇ;). The proverbial nature of this saying has long been recognized. Jesus alters his approach from v. 25 with a pair of rhetorical questions regarding what has value or worth ("benefit, profit," cf. 15:5) for the long haul. He moves out of the realm of theory, providing a specific example, earthly gain and possessions. In light of the overwhelming importance of the eternal realm, making the temporary "gains" of life to be one's goal must stand as the most foolish choice of all. The image of "gaining the whole world" is the ultimate dream of the ages (Satan offers this to Jesus in 4:8), yet in

12. Here and in v. 27 is another generic use of ἄνθρωπος for "person" (BDF §301 2.).

the final analysis it is an empty pit devoid of lasting content or pleasure.

History is replete with such characters, slaughtering millions or cheating thousands out of their livelihood, only to die exactly as they have lived. Accumulation without "soul" is one definition of the "meaninglessness" of Ecclesiastes. Luxury and wealth provide the death knell to discipleship. The exact nuance of "soul" (ψυχή) here is difficult to define. Its basic thrust is the principle of life, the whole person, and at times it can stand for the reflexive pronoun "one's self." So in this sense it can have the same meaning it has in v. 25, one's "life." Yet at the same time it can confer "the seat and center of life that transcends the earthly," that part of the person that knows God and relates to the spiritual realm (BAGD, 893). This is likely the case here, the self in its God-relationship.

16:26 Or what should a person give in exchange for their soul? (ἢ τί δώσει ἄνθρωπος ἀντάλλαγμα τῆς ψυχῆς αὐτοῦ;). "Give in exchange" (δώσει ... ἀντάλλαγμα) is a commercial metaphor for traded transactions, giving up one thing to gain another. To trade the temporary for the eternal is folly. Several (Davies and Allison, Luz, Nolland) believe Ps 49:8 – 9 is behind this, "the ransom for a life is costly, no payment is ever enough — so that someone should live on forever and not see decay." Both there and here, one cannot purchase salvation or true life with earthly resources. Nothing in this world can suffice, so the purchase can only be made by God.

16:27 For the Son of Man is going to come in the glory of his Father with his angels (μέλλει γὰρ ὁ υἱὸς τοῦ ἀνθρώπου ἔρχεσθαι ἐν τῇ δόξῃ τοῦ πατρὸς αὐτοῦ μετὰ τῶν ἀγγέλων αὐτοῦ). The third "for" (γάρ) in a row links this closely with the previous clarification of vv. 25 – 26. There the point was choice of temporal earthly or eternal heavenly priorities. Now the attention is entirely on the latter. Matthew takes a different approach than Mark 8:38, omitting the saying on being ashamed of Jesus, moving the parousia portion to the front, and linking it with the motif of eschatological reward. μέλλει stresses the imminent coming ("about to, on the point of," BAGD) presented in the next verse.

The idea of the "Son of Man" (see excursus after 8:22) returning "in the glory of his Father" reflects Dan 7:13 – 14 (cf. Rom 6:4). God's "glory" (δόξα) includes both his Shekinah glory (the glory "dwelling" among his people) and the ineffable glory, majesty, and splendor of the enthroned God of Isa 6 and Ezek 1. The heavenly host in one sense would be heaven's armies, expected by the Jewish people at the eschaton, but they are also agents of judgment and eschatological heralds. This imagery is frequent in Matthew (13:41; 24:30 – 31; 25:31) and part of his strong apocalyptic undercurrents.

16:27 ... and then I will reward each one on the basis of their deed (καὶ τότε ἀποδώσει ἑκάστῳ κατὰ τὴν πρᾶξιν αὐτοῦ). Once more eschatology is the mother of ethics. This theme of "judged/rewarded by works" is frequent in the OT (2 Chr 6:23; Job 34:11; Ps 28:4; 62:12; Prov 24:12; Jer 17:10; Ezek 18:20; Hos 12:2), Jewish literature (*1 En.* 41:1 – 2; *Pss. Sol.* 2:16; 17:8; *4 Ezra* 7:35; 8:33; *2 Bar.* 14:12), and the NT (Matt 16:27; Rom 2:6; 14:12; 1 Cor 3:12 – 15; 2 Cor 5:10, 11:15; 2 Tim 4:14; 1 Pet 1:17; Rev 2:23; 11:18; 14:13; 18:6; 20:12, 13; 22:12). The language is especially close, probably an allusion to Ps 62:12 (and Prov 24:12).

It is interesting that the emphasis is on the singular "each one" and especially the singular "deed" (πρᾶξις), most likely a collective but still emphasizing that every person is responsible to God for each and every thing done. The doctrine sums up vv. 25 – 26 in the sense that those who choose the earthly will be judged, but here the emphasis is on those who choose God's way and receive his reward for those choices.

16:28 I tell you the truth, there are some standing here who will not experience death until they see the Son of Man coming in his kingdom (ἀμὴν λέγω ὑμῖν ὅτι εἰσίν τινες τῶν ὧδε ἑστώτων οἵτινες οὐ μὴ γεύσωνται θανάτου ἕως ἂν ἴδωσιν τὸν υἱὸν τοῦ ἀνθρώπου ἐρχόμενον ἐν τῇ βασιλείᾳ αὐτοῦ). This is a well-known crux interpretum (with 10:23). The opening "amen" (ἀμήν) formula stresses the importance of the saying (see on 5:18). The problem, of course, is the association of the "coming of the Son of Man" with the promise that some will still be alive. This has given rise to several solutions, with many opting for the parousia because of the connection between vv. 27 and 28 (Schlatter, Hill, Schweizer, Grundmann, Luz, Gnilka, Gundry, Beare), others for the transfiguration in the next passage (Origen, Chrysostom, Blomberg, Wilkins, Keener, France), the resurrection (Luther, Calvin, McNeile, Meier), the fall of Jerusalem (Plummer, Hagner, Wright), or the missionary expansion of the church (Hill).

This is a bewildering number of possibilities, and the only solution is to allow the context to guide us. The "coming" certainly is parousia language, yet the added "some standing here who will not experience death" also limits this to the current generation of Jesus' and Matthew's day. Thus it is certainly best to see a combination of the above, perhaps transfiguration and resurrection (Senior), or resurrection and parousia (Davies and Allison), or the resurrection, Pentecost, and mission of the church (Carson, Morris), or the cross and ensuing events (Nolland).

The transfiguration, however, must be added as a proleptic anticipation of these kingdom events that then exhibit the power and glory of the coming Son of Man and themselves are a foretaste of the second coming. It cannot be the sole thrust, because "not experience death" would make little sense if used of the next event. Nevertheless, it does inaugurate the series (and is even more explicit in Mark 9:1).

Theology in Application

Where should we begin with so rich a passage, truly the crisis node of the narrative this far. So many themes coalesce on this section — Christology, ecclesiology, discipleship, eschatology. We will simply begin at the top.

1. Perceptions

The perceptions of people will to an extent define your ministry, but you must go God's way, not their way. The people were always trying to make Jesus conform to their idea of a holy man/prophet, as in 16:13 – 14 and in John 6:15 (yet note some of his followers in John 6:60 – 66). Every man and woman of God faces similar pressures from well-meaning people. It is critical, as Jesus did, to know God and follow his path rather than allow others to force you on the wrong path.

2. Following the God-Given Path

Make certain your true followers understand the God-given path for your ministry. Jesus' entire ploy at Caesarea Philippi was to confront the disciples with his messianic reality and to correct any misunderstanding they had. The true test was about to occur as they moved along the road of destiny and faced many obstacles, moving ever closer to Jerusalem and the cross. Jesus wanted them on the same wavelength as much as possible as they faced the certain dread of that destiny. Such communication of purpose is essential for a united movement.

3. Leaders Chosen

God chooses certain leaders to be linchpins in his kingdom. Such, of course, was Peter. There have been so many throughout history — Paul, Irenaeus, Origen, Jerome, Augustine, Athanasius, Aquinus, Luther, Calvin, et al. They have become salvation-historical markers in a sense, standing at the turning points of church movements as bulwarks of God. In our passage, Peter was "the rock" and foundation of the church, its spokesman and chief actor. In all his brash imperfections, God chose him. He was the representative disciple and stood for the Twelve, indeed for the church. Jesus gave his incredible promises and authority to the church through Peter, who first wielded them for the church. His "keys of the kingdom" opened the door to the Gentile mission in Acts 10, and the power of death was eradicated in the church.

4. The Church's Authority in This World

Through Peter Jesus has imparted an eschatological power to the church beyond the disciples' comprehension. The three elements — power over death, the keys to open the kingdom reality, the authority to bind and loose — were explained above, but together they constitute a new messianic community that participates in the glory and power of the Godhead over both the cosmic forces and the powers of this world.

But what does that look like for the average Christian today? Primarily, this is meant to be lived out in the gospel message and teaching authority of the church, both horizontally (to a lost world that is under the power of death) and vertically (to a church that desperately needs to commit itself fully to Christ). One example of this authority is discipline in the church (e.g., 1 Cor 5:4 – 5; 1 Tim 1:20, where Paul uses that authority in "handing over to Satan" those who commited serious sin).

5. Christ as Lord

No Christian dare dictate to Christ what kind of Lord he is to be. Most of us at one time or another have sought to fashion Christ in our own image, to make him amenable to what we would prefer. To paraphrase J. B. Phillips' famous work, "Your Jesus is too small." Peter and the disciples wanted to mold Jesus after their image of the conquering Messiah and refused to accept his insistence that he was the suffering Servant who must die. This type of mistake has been repeated throughout history. We must submit to his will and refuse to impose our will and desires on him.

6. The Path of Self-Denial and Suffering

Jesus could not be more clear on this. To follow the human rather than the divine way is antithetical to discipleship. God demands that we seek the things that are above, not the things on earth (Col 3:1 – 2). This means a radical surrender and a radical abrogation of the world's ways and priorities. To "gain/find" the one, we must "lose/forfeit" the other. This involves living for the eternal future reality, not the temporary present desires. This distinctly involves wealth, possessions, and status ("gain the whole world"), a major concern of all three Synoptics but especially Luke (Luke 1:51 – 53; 3:7 – 14; 4:18 – 19; 6:20 – 26; etc.). Every Christian must come to grips with worldly possessions vs. serving God.

7. A Final Reckoning

While the stress on the second coming with its "reward" is positive here, it sums up the warning of vv. 25 – 26 and so also involves judgment on those who choose the finite world. Both judgment and reward in one sense are "on the basis of . . . deed[s]." Yet this does not contradict the doctrine of salvation by grace through faith alone (Eph 2:8 – 9). It reflects the classic Paul/James tension between faith and works, and the solution is fairly straightforward. We are saved only by the grace of God, but true salvation will always result in works (Eph 2:10; Jas 2:14 – 26). Therefore we must remain cognizant that our actions have eternal ramifications.

8. The Return of Christ

The return of Christ is characterized by imminence and delay, anticipated by the entire succession of salvation-historical moments inaugurated by the Christ-event. There is a real possibility that each one of the options noted under v. 28 are actually intended by Jesus as the powerful coming of the kingdom, all pointing forward to their finalization in the parousia. The emphasis is on the imminent events in v. 28, but v. 27 as connected to vv. 18 – 19, 25 – 26 points to a significant time lapse in which the church is inaugurated and acts in power.

CHAPTER 73

Matthew 17:1 – 13

Literary Context

The christological movement in 16:13 – 17:27 is powerful, proceeding from the misperception of the Jewish people (16:13 – 14) to Peter's initial confession of his messianic office (16:15 – 16) to Jesus' critical clarification of the meaning of his office (16:21) and Peter's inability to handle it (16:22 – 23). The present section now moves to the revelation of the true glory behind Jesus the Messiah. The basic premise is similar to the theme statement of 1 Pet 1:11: suffering is the path to glory. In this again there is a blend of Christology and discipleship, as the inner circle are still unable to comprehend its significance fully.

V. Rejection, Suffering, and Glory (13:54 – 18:35)
- **A. Jesus' Deeds: Rejection, Discipleship, and Glory (13:54 – 17:27)**
  - **2. The Movement to the Cross (16:21 – 17:27)**
    - a. First Passion Prediction and Discipleship (16:21 – 28)
    - ➡ **b. Transfiguration (17:1 – 13)**

Main Idea

This whole section is tied up with Jesus' identity as Messiah and Son of God.[1] Peter's confession is the basic christological claim, and Jesus then clarifies this in

1. There has always been great debate regarding the historicity of this event. In the eighteenth and early nineteenth centuries, Reimarus called it an OT miracle placed in a NT setting; and Schleiermacher said it was the power of Christ's "God-consciousness" shining through. David F. Strauss (1840) believed the conviction of Jesus' messiahship and OT stories (especially Exod 34 on glowing face of Moses) led to the creation of a "myth" so Jesus would surpass Moses and Elijah. Rudolf Bultmann called this and Peter's confession Easter stories projected back into the earthly ministry, and Martin Dibelius called it a Christ-myth involving his epiphany in glory to the disciples. However, the early church believed the gospel stories were not "cleverly devised stories" (2 Pet 1:16 – 18), and this should be taken seriously. This could not have been Hellenistic, for the parallels are all Jewish; the misplaced resurrection hypothesis is much too speculative; and if God is personal and involved in this world, the story makes perfect sense. See Robert H. Stein, "Is the Transfiguration (Mark 9:2 – 8) a Misplaced Resurrection-Account?" *JBL* 95 (1976): 79 – 96, as well as Hagner, Carson, Keener.

two directions: first, that he is to be the Isaianic suffering Messiah (16:21 – 23), and now that he is also the Messiah of glory, the new eschatological Moses.[2] At the same time a discipleship emphasis emerges, in keeping with the disciples' continuous struggle with faith seeking understanding and with the confusion segueing into dawning comprehension (v. 13).

Translation

Matthew 17:1-13

1a		After six days
b	Introduction/Setting	**Jesus took with him Peter and James and John his brother and**
c	Place	**led them up a high mountain by themselves,**
2a	Action	and **he was transfigured in front of them,**
b	Description	and **his face shone like the sun,**
c		and **his clothes became as white as the light.**
3a	Action	And **look! Moses and Elijah appeared with him, speaking to him.**
4a	Response	**Peter answered Jesus,**
b		*"Lord, it is good for us to be here.*
c		*If you desire,*
d		*I will make three tabernacles,*
e		*one each for you, for Moses, and for Elijah."*
5a		While he was still speaking,
b	Action	**look, a bright cloud enveloped them.**
c	Epiphany/Identification	And **behold, a voice out of the cloud said,**
d		*"This is my Son,*
		the beloved,
e		*in whom I am well pleased.*
f	Exhortation	*Listen to him."*
6a	Reaction to 5c-f	When the disciples heard this,
b		**they fell on their faces, completely terrified.**
7a	Response to 6a-b	But **Jesus came, touched them, and said,**
b		*"Get up, don't be afraid."*
8a		When they raised their eyes,
b	Conclusion	**they saw no one but Jesus alone.**

Continued on next page.

2. See Davies and Allison, *Matthew*, 2:686 – 88; France, *Gospel of Matthew*, 644 – 45. Witherington, *Matthew*, 324, believes that the main idea is of "Jesus as the one greater than Moses," and this certainly is a main theme with the transfigured visage (like the sun), the (bright) cloud, and the voice from heaven all paralleling, yet at the same time transcending, Moses on Sinai. Also, he is the one greater than Elijah.

Continued from previous page.

9a	Setting	While they were coming down the mountain,
b		**Jesus was commanding them,**
c	Exhortation/Command	*"Tell no one about the vision*
d	Time	*until the Son of Man has been raised from the dead."*
10a	Question	And **the disciples asked him,**
b		*"Why then do the teachers of law say Elijah must come first?"*
11a	Answer	**Jesus responded,**
b		*"Indeed, Elijah is going to come and will restore all things.*
12a		*But I tell you, Elijah has already come,*
b		*and they did not recognize him but*
c		*did to him whatever they wanted.*
d	Comparison/Prophecy	*So also the Son of Man is about to suffer at their hands."*
13a	Conclusion	**Then the disciples understood that he had spoken to them about John the Baptist.**

Structure and Literary Form

This is an epiphany story in which the divinity of Jesus breaks through and "manifests" itself, with Matthew highlighting that glory in the details added. Matthew builds on Mark 9:2 – 8 with a few important differences, such as adding "his face shone like the sun" (v. 2b), "Lord" rather than "rabbi" (v. 4), a "bright" cloud (v. 5), adding vv. 6 – 7 on the disciples' terror, and putting the messianic secret command into direct speech (v. 9). There is a slight antithetical structure as the story is framed by ascending and descending the mountain (vv. 1, 9) and by Jesus conversing with Moses and Elijah (v. 4) then alone with the disciples (v. 8), with the climax of the story being God's voice from the Shekinah cloud (v. 5).[3]

Exegetical Outline

➦ **I. Setting (17:1)**
  - A. The inner circle
  - B. Ascending the mountain

II. The Transfiguration (17:2)
  - A. Face like the sun
  - B. Clothes like light

III. Two Conversations (17:3 – 4)
  - A. Speaking with Moses and Elijah (v. 3)
  - B. Peter's confused request (v. 4)

3. Luz, *Matthew 8 – 20*, 394. Davies and Allison, *Matthew*, 2:684, and their more detailed chiasm do not quite fit the structure of the text.

IV. The Voice from the Cloud (17:5 – 7)
   A. The Shekinah cloud (v. 5a)
   B. The voice from the cloud (v. 5b)
   C. The disciples' fear assuaged (vv. 6 – 7)

V. Conclusion of Transfiguration (17:8 – 10)
   A. They are alone (v. 8)
   B. Command to tell no one (v. 9)

VI. Question about Elijah (17:11 – 13)
   A. Query about the Elijah forerunner (v. 10)
   B. Jesus' response (vv. 11 – 13)
      1. Elijah is coming (v. 11)
      2. Elijah has in fact come but unrecognized (v. 12)
      3. Interpretation of Elijah (vv. 12b – 13)
         a. Elijah rejected and afflicted (v. 12b)
         b. Jesus to be rejected and afflicted (v. 12c)
   C. Disciples understand (v. 13)

Explanation of the Text

17:1 After six days Jesus took with him Peter and James and John his brother (Καὶ μεθ' ἡμέρας ἓξ παραλαμβάνει ὁ Ἰησοῦς τὸν Πέτρον καὶ Ἰάκωβον καὶ Ἰωάννην τὸν ἀδελφὸν αὐτοῦ). The present tense "taking" (παραλαμβάνει), as so often in Matthew, stresses the ongoing action of the event. Though it is possible that the "six days" is nothing more that a temporal note, it is better to see it as reflecting a Sinai motif, reflecting Exod 24:15 – 16, where the Shekinah cloud covered the mountain for six days and then Moses entered and heard the voice of God speaking.[4] Jesus is the new, glorified Moses. Moreover, he takes his inner core of disciples, as Moses took Aaron, Nadab, and Abihu (Exod 24:1, 9). These three disciples were especially close to Jesus (cf. 26:37; Mark 5:37; 13:3 [with Andrew]).

17:1 ... and led them up a high mountain by themselves (καὶ ἀναφέρει αὐτοὺς εἰς ὄρος ὑψηλὸν κατ' ἰδίαν). It is difficult to be sure which "high mountain" (ὄρος ὑψηλόν) Jesus visits. Tradition says Mount Tabor, but it is only 1,900 feet high and had a Roman garrision at its summit (Josephus, *War* 2.20.6). Thus, some posit Mount Hermon, but at 9,232 feet it is cold and in Gentile territory. As a result, a popular alternative is Mount Meron, the highest in Palestine at 3,926 feet.[5] There is no way to be certain.

4. See Gundry, Hagner, Davies and Allison, Blomberg. Hauerwas, *Matthew*, 154, sees a creation motif, with the transfiguration itself "the seventh day, when God rested, bringing to completion the work of the previous six days." Connected with this, he sees the Sabbath as "a day of brightness in which Jesus shines with the brightness of the sun." This latter is a little too allegorical.

5. See Walter Liefeld, "Theological Motifs in the Transfiguration Narratives," in *New Dimensions in New Testament Study* (ed. R. N. Longenecker and M. C. Tenney; Grand Rapids: Zondervan, 1974), 167 – 68; Carson, "Matthew," 384; Hagner, *Matthew 14 – 28*, 492; France, *Gospel of Matthew*, 646 – 47.

In Matthew the mountain as a place of revelation is heightened (cf. 4:8; 5:1; 8:1; 14:23; 15:29; 28:16), and there may be an antithesis to the "high mountain" Satan used in the temptation narrative, when he promised Jesus "all the kingdoms of the world." Jesus chose the path of suffering rather than that of conquering. Donaldson shows that the Moses imagery is heightened in Matthew's account vis-à-vis Mark and sees in this account a blend of Moses and "Son" categories. Jesus is enthroned as the final Moses and especially as the "Son of God."[6]

17:2 And he was transfigured in front of them (καὶ μετεμορφώθη ἔμπροσθεν αὐτῶν). From the two present tense verbs in v. 1, Matthew now switches to aorist tense main verbs in the next few verses to describe the individual aspects of the action. μεταμορφόω means literally to "transform, change in form" and connotes not just a change externally visible but one that proceeds from inside and changes the whole person. Moses reflected the glory of God in his "radiance" when he descended the mountain (Exod 34:29, 33 – 35), but here Jesus' true preincarnate glory shines through his humanity. The disciples were the intended recipients of this glorious event ("in front of them" [ἔμπροσθεν αὐτῶν]).

17:2 ... and his face shone like the sun (καὶ ἔλαμψεν τὸ πρόσωπον αὐτοῦ ὡς ὁ ἥλιος). This is so much more elaborate than Mark 9:3, which mentions only the "dazzling white" clothes. Matthew is probably emphasizing the parallels with Moses on Sinai (see also below). In Ps 74:16; 136:7 – 9 God is creator of the heavenly lights, and in Jewish tradition the priestly Messiah shines with the light of the sun (*1 En.* 38:4; *4 Ezra* 7:97; *2 Bar.* 51:3). Moses' face was so "radiant" that he had to veil it (Exod 34:30 – 35); yet this person is greater than Moses (a frequent emphasis in Matthew). In Matt 13:43 "the righteous will shine like the sun," so the transfiguration is also a foretaste of what is in store for those faithful to God.

17:2 ... and his clothes became as white as the light (τὰ δὲ ἱμάτια αὐτοῦ ἐγένετο λευκὰ ὡς τὸ φῶς). Mark 9:3 adds "whiter than anyone in the world could bleach them." Matthew continues the imagery of light. The supernatural radiance of the clothes are not mentioned in Exod 24 or 34, but it is common in apocalyptic writings like Dan 7:9 (clothing of the Ancient of Days), 10:6 (an angel); 12:3 (the wise); *1 En.* 14:20 (the gown of God); *1 En.* 62:15 – 16 (clothes of the righteous); and 2 Cor 3:18 (the righteous in worship). This is also a precursor to the "white as snow" garment of the angel at the tomb in Matt 28:3. Matthew struggles for words to depict the glory[7] of the Son of God here.

17:3 And look! Moses and Elijah appeared with him, speaking to him (καὶ ἰδοὺ ὤφθη αὐτοῖς Μωϋσῆς καὶ Ἠλίας συλλαλοῦντες μετ' αὐτοῦ). "Look" (ἰδού) is often used in Matthew for dramatic detail and to move the action along (1:20; 2:9; 3:16; etc.). Scholars debate whether Moses and Elijah represent the law and the prophets or whether they appear as the forerunners of the Messiah (Deut 18:18; Mal 4:5 – 6). Yet surely these are not antithetical but supplemental. They were the two great miracle-working prophets, and the two witnesses of Rev 11:3 – 6 are modeled after them, where the first two miracles of 11:5 – 6a (fire from heaven, the drought) replicate Elijah, and the second two of 11:6b (water into blood, plagues) replicate Moses. It is also possible that Moses and

6. Donaldson, *Jesus on the Mountain*, 149 – 51.

7. S. Williams, "The Transfiguration of Jesus Christ," *Them* 28 (2002): 13 – 25, believes glory is the core motif of this event, as the disciples see the glory of God both in Jesus' transfigured appearance and in the cloud.

Elijah prefigure Jesus' rejection by the nation and vindication by God.[8] Only Luke 9:30 – 31 gives a hint of the content behind their conversation ("spoke about his departure [*exodos*]"), but the eschatological flavor is dominant here as well.[9]

17:4 Peter answered Jesus, "Lord, it is good for us to be here" (ἀποκριθεὶς δὲ ὁ Πέτρος εἶπεν τῷ Ἰησοῦ, Κύριε, καλόν ἐστιν ἡμᾶς ὧδε εἶναι). Matthew uses "Lord" in place of Mark and Luke's "rabbi/master," probably because of his strong rebuke of "rabbis" in 23:7 – 8; 26:25. κύριε is often used when addressing Jesus (e.g., 7:21 – 22; 8:2, 6, 21, 25; 9:28; et al.), and often connotes more respectful address than christological affirmation, but still there is usually "a serious level of engagement with him" involved.[10] Peter begins on a clumsy note, as "good" (καλόν) means "pleasant, profitable, desirable" and fits more a nice stroll in the park than a theophany.

17:4 If you desire, I will make three tabernacles, one each for you, for Moses, and for Elijah (εἰ θέλεις, ποιήσω ὧδε τρεῖς σκηνάς, σοὶ μίαν καὶ Μωϋσεῖ μίαν καὶ Ἠλίᾳ μίαν). It is difficult to know for certain the significance of the three "tabernacles" (σκηναί). They could refer to the tabernacle itself, called σκηνή from Exod 25:9 on. But Peter's desire to build three of them mitigates against such a theme, since there was never to have been more than one. More likely, this relates to the Feast of Tabernacles, when people built "booths" of branches and straw, then lived in these shelters throughout the seven-day festival. This festival celebrated the Exodus but also had eschatological connotations (Zech 14:16 – 20). So Peter wants to prolong the event[11] and be part of what he interprets a sign of the last days.

17:5 While he was still speaking, look, a bright cloud enveloped them (ἔτι αὐτοῦ λαλοῦντος ἰδοὺ νεφέλη φωτεινὴ ἐπεσκίασεν αὐτούς). Matthew uses another of his characteristic genitive absolutes (cf. 8:1, 5, 16, 28; 9:32, 33; et al.) temporally to link one part of a scene to another. The Shekinah cloud appears during Peter's speech. With his typical "look" (ἰδού, 1:20; 2:9, 3:16, 4:11; etc.) Matthew stresses the vividness of the scene (see on 17:3).

The cloud could have several associations: the Shekinah cloud where God manifests his presence on the mountain (Exod 24:15) or as he delivers his people in the wilderness (Exod 13:21 – 22), or the chariot clouds of the divine warrior with the hosts of heaven. Of these the Shekinah who delivers is certainly best, with the added "bright" (φωτεινή) stressing the Shekinah glory. ἐπεσκίασεν probably means "enveloped" rather than "overshadowed," since the cloud at the tabernacle first stood at the entrance (Exod 33:9) and at its dedication the cloud of glory "filled the temple" (Exod 40:34). The image here is likewise that of "filling" the site.

17:5 And behold, a voice out of the cloud said, "This is my Son, the beloved, in whom I am well pleased. Listen to him" (καὶ ἰδοὺ φωνὴ ἐκ τῆς νεφέλης λέγουσα, Οὗτός ἐστιν ὁ υἱός μου ὁ ἀγαπητός, ἐν ᾧ εὐδόκησα· ἀκούετε αὐτοῦ). As at Sinai (Exod 24:16), God speaks from the cloud

8. See M. Pamment, "Moses and Elijah in the Story of the Transfiguration," *ExpTim* 92 (1981): 338 – 39; contra J. Moiser, "Moses and Elijah," *ExpTim* 96 (1985), 216 – 17, who says the theme is not rejection but their testimony to Jesus (both listened to God on the mountain and now hear Jesus). Both are viable.

9. Herbert W. Basser, "The Jewish Roots of the Transfiguration," *BR* 14 (1998): 30 – 35, believes the major background is the Jewish midrash on Ps 43 that connects Moses and Elijah with the Messiah.

10. Nolland, *Matthew*, 339.

11. R. E. Otto, "The Fear Motivation in Peter's Offer to Build Τρεῖς Σκηνάς," *WTJ* 59 (1997): 101 – 12, argues it is not worship but fear that drives Peter, and he wishes to build them more for protection from the ineffable glory of God. While interesting, this does not fit the scene well. It is valid for Mark 9:6, but in Matthew the fear occurs after the divine voice speaks.

with all the eschatological overtones of the cloud at the parousia (Matt 24:30; 26:64; Acts 1:9; Rev 1:7). The divine voice speaks the same words as at the baptism (see on 3:17), then adds "Listen to him" from Deut 18:15, where Moses prophesied of a coming "prophet like me" and demanded that the people listen carefully to that messianic figure. Jesus is the suffering Servant (Isa 42:1), made all the more dramatic with his passion predictions as the centerpoint here.

17:6 When the disciples heard[12] this, they fell on their faces, completely terrified (καὶ ἀκούσαντες οἱ μαθηταὶ ἔπεσαν ἐπὶ πρόσωπον αὐτῶν καὶ ἐφοβήθησαν σφόδρα). It is common at a theophany for people to fall on their faces in terror (Ezek 1:28; 44:4; Dan 8:17; cf. John 18:6). "They were terrified" (ἐφοβήθησαν) could have double meaning, connoting not only fear but worship ("filled with awe," cf. Gen 17:3; Ezek 3:23), but the emphasis is on their fear. It is interesting that each gospel places the fear at a different place — Mark 9:6 as the reason for Peter's confusing suggestion, Luke 9:34 when they entered the cloud, and Matthew as part of their worship of Jesus. All the attention of every figure — the three disciples, Moses and Elijah, the cloud, the divine voice — centers on Jesus.

17:7 But Jesus came, touched[13] them, and said, "Get up, don't be afraid" (καὶ προσῆλθεν ὁ Ἰησοῦς καὶ ἁψάμενος αὐτῶν εἶπεν, Ἐγέρθητε καὶ μὴ φοβεῖσθε). Only here and in 28:18 does Jesus "come to" his disciples, and in both cases it is the exalted Lord addressing them. When Jesus "touches," the purpose is usually in a healing context (e.g., 8:3, 15; 9:29). In one sense he is healing their spiritual illness, but that seems more Markan than Matthean (cf. Mark 7:31 – 37, 8:22 – 26 surrounding Mark 8:17 – 18); here he is healing their terror. As always at a theophany or angelophany, the first thing is to calm one's fears (14:27; Mark 16:6 par; Acts 23:11).

17:8 When they raised their eyes, they saw no one but Jesus alone (ἐπάραντες δὲ τοὺς ὀφθαλμοὺς αὐτῶν οὐδένα εἶδον εἰ μὴ αὐτὸν Ἰησοῦν μόνον). Another temporal participle (see v. 5), this time aorist ("after they raised"), shows the effect of Jesus' soothing touch and words. With dramatic flourish, the visitors have disappeared at the twinkling of an eye, and we are left with the glorified Lord who is at the heart of the story. In Matthew more than the others, Jesus has the undivided attention of every aspect of the plot. This sets the tone for this entire section of Matthew, with Jesus at center stage directing the action. The success of the disciples will be completely connected to the extent that they center on Jesus "alone" (μόνον).

17:9 While they were coming down the mountain, Jesus was commanding them (Καὶ καταβαινόντων αὐτῶν ἐκ τοῦ ὄρους ἐνετείλατο αὐτοῖς ὁ Ἰησοῦς λέγων). A further temporal genitive absolute (see on v. 5) places Jesus' instructions as the final part of the new Sinai scene. Again, the transfiguration is seen as a Sinai-type revelation scene (see on v. 1), framed by the ascent/descent motif in vv. 1, 9. Moses ascended the mountain in Exod 19:3 and descended in Exod 19:14; 32:15.

17:9 "Tell no one about the vision until the Son of Man has been raised from the dead" (Μηδενὶ εἴπητε τὸ ὅραμα ἕως οὗ ὁ υἱὸς τοῦ ἀνθρώπου ἐκ νεκρῶν ἐγερθῇ). The aorist subjunctive in prohibition ("tell" [εἴπητε]) stresses the force of the command as a whole, making this a forceful

12. This is the third temporal participle and functions like the first two (vv. 1, 5).

13. This is a circumstantial participle but partakes of the force of the main verb and is often best translated as a main verb (see on 4:20). The three actions (coming, touching, speaking) are closely connected.

injunction.[14] The use of "the vision" (τὸ ὅραμα; Mark 9:9 has "what they had seen") does not indicate Matthew was thinking of an apocalyptic vision (like most of the uses in Daniel or the NT), for it can also refer to something actually seen.

This is the last of the "messianic secret" passages in Matthew (see 8:4; 9:30; 12:16; 16:20), and it highlights the fact that the true significance of Jesus can only be understood in light of the cross and the resurrection.[15] The transfiguration is at one and the same time a glimpse of his preincarnate glory and a harbinger of the passion events. The two are interdependent. It is like the two sides of his nature — the divine and the human. He is the God-man, and the two aspects cannot be separated from one another. Thus it is impossible for anyone to understand the transfiguration without the cross and the empty tomb.

17:10 And the disciples asked him, "Why then do the teachers of law say Elijah must come first?" (καὶ ἐπηρώτησαν αὐτὸν οἱ μαθηταὶ λέγοντες, Τί οὖν οἱ γραμματεῖς λέγουσιν ὅτι Ἠλίαν δεῖ ἐλθεῖν πρῶτον;). "Then" (οὖν) normally draws an inference from the preceding, and in this case it is the presence of Elijah talking with Jesus, reminding the disciples of the Elijah-forerunner prophecy in Mal 4:5 – 6. The disciples center on the teaching of the "scribes" (see on 2:4) because they were the legal experts of that day.

In Mal 4:5 Elijah would inaugurate "that great and dreadful day of the Lord," and in their query the disciples assume this is a divine "must" (δεῖ).[16] The disciples have interpreted the transfiguration as the inauguration of that day and wonder how the Malachi prophecy fits into the equation. Jesus has already told them that the Baptist fulfills the Malachi expectation (11:14), but their question is not "who" but "how" it will come to pass.

17:11 Jesus responded,[17] "Indeed, Elijah is going to come and will restore all things" (ὁ δὲ ἀποκριθεὶς εἶπεν, Ἠλίας μὲν ἔρχεται καὶ ἀποκαταστήσει πάντα). Jesus affirms the reality of their question, drawing the language directly from Mal 3:23 LXX (= 4:6), though in the LXX it is "restore the heart of a father to a child," while Jesus expands the family reconciliation into a universal restoration. The use of the prophetic present "is going to come" (ἔρχεται) followed by the future "will restore" seems strange in light of the fact that the Baptist has already finished his ministry, which leads some interpreters (e.g., Gundry, Blomberg) to posit a future coming of Elijah before the parousia (perhaps Rev 11:3 – 6). While possible, it is better to take the tenses rhetorically as a reference to the prophecy fulfilled in John the Baptist (stressing the certainty of its fulfillment in John), as the next verse shows. As Hagner says, the restoration of "all things" is thus not the final restoration at the eschaton but "a preparatory work of repentance and renewal (as in the Malachi passage . . .)."[18]

17:12 "But I tell you, Elijah has already come" (λέγω δὲ ὑμῖν ὅτι Ἠλίας ἤδη ἦλθεν). The "indeed . . . but" (μέν . . . δέ) construction in vv. 11 – 12 shows that Jesus places the emphasis on this statement. In other words, the scribes are right about Elijah coming before the Messiah but wrong

14. Wallace, 717; Porter, *Idioms*, 53 – 54.

15. Note the divine passive "has been raised" (ἐγερθῇ), indicating that God will raise him from the dead. See Grudem, *Systematic Theology*, 613 – 14, for the fact that both Father and Son took part in Jesus' resurrection.

16. It has been debated whether there is enough evidence for such an expectation in the first century, e.g., Joseph A. Fitzmyer, "More about Elijah Coming First," *JBL* 104 (1985): 295 – 96; but see Dale C. Allison, "Elijah Must Come First," *JBL* 103 (1984): 256 – 58, who shows it is Jewish and not Christian in origin.

17. For "answering, he said" (ἀποκριθεὶς εἶπεν) see on 4:4.

18. Hagner, *Matthew 14 – 28*, 499.

because they have failed to realize that the Baptist already was that forerunner. Their understanding of the future was correct, but their understanding of the present fulfillment of that future was fatally flawed.

17:12 "... and they did not recognize him but did to him whatever they wanted" (καὶ οὐκ ἐπέγνωσαν αὐτὸν ἀλλὰ ἐποίησαν ἐν αὐτῷ ὅσα ἠθέλησαν). The leaders refused to recognize the true significance of the Baptist as the Elijah forerunner. In a context like this, "did not recognize" (οὐκ ἐπέγνωσαν, with the aorist looking at their rejection as a whole) does not mean simply passive ignorance (i.e., a failure to understand), but rather an active rejection of a truth they should have known. "Whatever they wanted," of course, refers to the terrible events related in 14:6 – 12.

17:12 "So also the Son of Man is about to suffer at their hands" (οὕτως καὶ ὁ υἱὸς τοῦ ἀνθρώπου μέλλει πάσχειν ὑπ' αὐτῶν). There is a double typology ("so also" [οὕτως]) here, with the Baptist the antitype of Elijah as messianic forerunner and Jesus the antitype of the Baptist as suffering Servant. For both John and Jesus the messianic path is one of suffering, with "to suffer" (πάσχειν) used in the first passion prediction (16:21) and with "is about" (μέλλει) here having the same force of divine necessity as "must" (δεῖ) in v. 10.

17:13 Then the disciples understood that he had spoken to them about John the Baptist (τότε συνῆκαν οἱ μαθηταὶ ὅτι περὶ Ἰωάννου τοῦ βαπτιστοῦ εἶπεν αὐτοῖς). Matthew continues his theme regarding the gradual coming to understanding of the disciples (this verse is found only in Matthew). Matthew has been chronicling the vacillation of the disciples between "little faith" (6:30; 8:26; 14:31; 16:8) and the gradual understanding that has dawned as a result of the patient instruction and presence of Jesus (13:11 – 12, 16, 23, 43, 44 – 45, 52; 14:33; 16:12). Once again, the disciples have grown in their newfound realm of discipleship understanding, though the process is far from finished, for throughout the Passion Narrative their ignorance will be evident. Still, they have taken another positive step, this time regarding the Baptist's place in God's plan.[19]

Theology in Application

The transfiguration is part of a chain of salvation-historical events linked theologically, and it is impossible to restrict it to any one.

1. Exodus imagery predominates here; Jesus fulfills the exodus event, which was the basis for Israel's concept of deliverance/salvation, and instigates a new exodus.
2. Incarnation theology is seen in the preexistence motif in the story (i.e., in the supernatural glory manifest); more than a proleptic promise of glory to come, it is the divine essence that was always there suddenly radiating forth (note Matthew's special stress on the divine radiance).
3. Jesus' baptism is paralleled by the presence and message of the divine voice

19. For the negative side of this, see Carson, "Matthew," 389; for the positive side, see Wilkins, *Matthew*, 595; Hauerwas, *Matthew*, 157.

that inaugurated the first half of Jesus' ministry and now instigates the second half.

4. In Luke the prophets speak to Jesus regarding his passion (*exodus*, "departure"), and the placement of this with the Caesarea Philippi incident points to the true significance of the suffering Messiah theme.
5. The resurrection and ascension, of course, are part of the passion but should be mentioned separately, for they vindicate the passion; the glory of the transfiguration was the earnest of the exaltation in the resurrection/ascension.
6. The transfiguration also anticipated the glory of the parousia and final kingdom (cf. 16:28); Peter's reminiscence in 2 Pet 1:16 – 18 also looks to the final glory prefigured here.

1. Sharing His Glory

Jesus wants to share his glory with his most intimate followers. He chose to take the inner circle with him and give them a glimpse of his true preincarnate glory. The theme here — suffering is the path to glory — is also the theme of 1 Peter (cf. 1 Pet 1:10 – 12) and much of the rest of the NT. To share Jesus' exaltation, we must be willing to walk with him on the path of suffering (cf. 16:24, "take up their cross").

2. Jesus' Transcendent Glory

Three parts of this episode show the extent of Jesus' exaltation: the dazzling brightness of his face and clothes, the presence of the Shekinah cloud, and the divine voice. Without stating it explicitly (as does John in his "I am" sayings), it is clear that for Matthew Jesus shares the glory of Yahweh. The only proper response is worship.[20] Peter later ruminates, "We were eyewitnesses of his majesty. He received honor and glory from God the Father" (2 Pet 1:16 – 17). Jesus fulfills and transcends the ministries of the two great miracle-working prophets, Moses and Elijah. Peter's attempt to build three booths, inadequate though it was, still constituted one such worshipful reply. It is our privilege to share in the majesty and glory as Christ's followers.

3. Transfiguration and Cross

The transfiguration and the cross are connected as antithetical and yet interdependent events. Davies and Allison demonstrate the parallels:

> In the one, a private epiphany, an exalted Jesus, with garments glistening, stands on a high mountain and is flanked by two religious giants from the past. All is light.

20. H. F. Knight, "The Transfigured Face of Post-Shoah Faith: Critical Encounters with Root Experiences — Exod 24:12 – 18 and Matt 17:1 – 9," *Encounter* 58 (1997): 125 – 49, stresses the christological implications, with Jesus as the "God with us" encountering the disciples with a second Sinai experience.

In the other, a public spectacle, a humiliated Jesus, whose clothes have been torn from him and divided, is lifted upon a cross and flanked by two common, convicted criminals. All is darkness.[21]

The context of the Caesarea Philippi confession and Jesus' correction of Peter's failure to understand the true significance of his messianic work bring these two aspects — suffering and glory — together. The true majesty of Jesus lies in his humiliation and suffering, and the great victory over sin and death takes place on the cross, with the glory of the transfiguration anticipating the vindication of that great redeeming act. This is clarified especially in vv. 11 – 13, where the parallels between the Baptist as messianic forerunner and Jesus as the Messiah are especially drawn along lines of suffering.

4. The True Disciple

The discipleship implications are critical. Since Jesus is indeed the Son of God, the true follower will listen and obey. He is the fulfillment and authoritative interpreter of Torah (7:29), and the disciples are scribes trained for the kingdom truths (13:52). There are three stages in this story: first, Peter's feeble attempt to grasp the significance of the event through invoking the festival of tabernacles imagery (v. 4), then God's command from the cloud to "listen" (v. 5), and finally partial understanding (v. 13). The key is the second step, careful listening that implies obedience.

21. Davies and Allison, *Matthew*, 2:706.

CHAPTER 74

Matthew 17:14 – 21

Literary Context

This story follows the transfiguration in all three Synoptic accounts and centers on the discipleship/faith aspects of that narrative.[1] There is a tight interweaving of themes throughout this narrative (13:54 – 17:27) as the passion predictions take center stage and the action moves downward to the cross. In this Jesus turns from the crowds to center on the disciples, and this pericope shows why. The disciples have a smattering of understanding (17:13) but a real deficiency of faith (17:20a) and need the presence of Jesus more than ever. In fact, the incredible contrast between Jesus' preincarnate glory (v. 2) and the disciples' unbelief (v. 17a) shows the sad state of affairs.[2]

V. Rejection, Suffering, and Glory (13:54 – 18:35)
- **A. Jesus' Deeds: Rejection, Discipleship, and Glory (13:54 – 17:27)**
  - **2. The Movement to the Cross (16:21 – 17:27)**
    - a. First Passion Prediction and Discipleship (16:21 – 28)
    - b. Transfiguration (17:1 – 13)
    - ➦ **c. Healing of the Epileptic Child (17:14 – 21)**
    - d. Second Passion Prediction and Temple Tax (17:22 – 27)

Main Idea

By abbreviating Mark by nearly two-thirds, Matthew centers squarely on the disciples and their deficient faith. The spiritual warfare theme of Mark (Mark 9:18,

1. For arguments regarding the authenticity of this story, see Gregory E. Sterling, "Jesus as Exorcist: An Analysis of Matthew 17:14 – 20; Mark 9:14 – 29; Luke 9:37 – 43a," *CBQ* 55 (1993): 467 – 93.

2. Pregeant, *Matthew*, 127 – 28, shows that this movement from the transfiguration to the failure to exorcize the demon, "a 'high' moment followed by a 'low,'" repeats the pattern found in 16:13 – 28, thereby emphasizing the "duality" of discipleship from faith and understanding to "little faith."

20, 22, 26) retreats to the background (noted only in Matt 17:18a), and this becomes a lesson on the danger of unbelief and the power of faith to accomplish great things.

Translation

Matthew 17:14-21

14a	Setting	As they came to the crowd,
b	Action	**a man ran up and knelt before him, and said,**
15a	Request	*"Lord, have mercy on my son,*
b	Basis for 15b	*because he has epileptic seizures and suffers terribly.*
c		*He often falls into the fire and frequently into water.*
16a	Clarification	*I brought him to your disciples,*
b		*but they were unable to heal him."*
17a	Response	**Jesus answered,**
b		*"O unbelieving and depraved generation!*
c		*How long must I be with you?*
d		*How long must I put up with you?*
e		*Bring him here to me."*
18a	Action	**Then Jesus rebuked the demon,**
b	Result/Healing	and **it came out of the boy,**
c		and **he was healed from that very moment.**
19a	Question	**Then his disciples came to Jesus in private and asked,**
b		*"Why weren't we able to cast it out?"*
20a	Answer	**Jesus replied,**
b		*"It is because you have so little faith.*
c	Promise	*I tell you the truth,*
d		*if you have faith as small as a mustard seed, you can tell this mountain, 'Move from here to there,' and it will be moved.*
e		*Nothing will be impossible for you!"*

Structure and Literary Form

This narrative is both a healing story and a pronouncement story, as all the action moves toward Jesus' climactic statement on faith. Matthew's extensive abbreviation of Mark 9:14 – 29 has the effect of removing the debate between the crowds and disciples, the effects of the demon-possession on the boy, and the interaction between Jesus and the father, while adding the saying in v. 20 on the power of faith to move mountains. The simple structure consists of the healing story (vv. 14 – 18) followed by the discourse on faith (vv. 19 – 20).

Exegetical Outline

→ **I. The Healing of the Child (17:14 – 18)**
- A. The request for healing (vv. 14 – 16)
  - 1. The symptoms of epilepsy (v. 15)
  - 2. The inability of the disciples (v. 16)
- B. Jesus' response (vv. 17 – 18)
  - 1. Diatribe against the crowds and his disciples (v. 17)
  - 2. Healing of the child (v. 18)

II. Discourse on the Power of Faith (17:19 – 20)
- A. The disciples' query (v. 19)
- B. Jesus' response regarding faith (v. 20)

Explanation of the Text

17:14 As they came to the crowd, a man ran up and knelt before him (Καὶ ἐλθόντων πρὸς τὸν ὄχλον προσῆλθεν αὐτῷ ἄνθρωπος γονυπετῶν αὐτόν). Another temporal participle (vv. 1, 5, 6, 8) shows this event begins after the disciples and Jesus have descended the mountain. At that time Jesus and the inner circle see a crowd gathered near the place where they left the rest of the disciples. The somewhat rare "knelt" (γονυπετῶν) has the idea of kneeling in petition or entreaty rather than worship; as a circumstantial participle, it is best translated as another main verb.

17:15 ... and said, "Lord, have mercy on my son" (καὶ λέγων, Κύριε, ἐλέησόν μου τὸν υἱόν). Matthew often couples "Lord" (κύριος) with "have mercy" (ἐλεέω, cf. 15:22; 20:30 – 31) in healing contexts to stress Jesus' sovereign lordship coupled with his merciful compassion. Yet this also shows the basic faith of the man who parallels the Syro-Phoenician woman and blind Bartimaeus in their trust in Jesus. This is also the more remarkable in light of the failure of Jesus' disciples to effect the healing. As in Mark, this father is one of the "little people" who appear only once and yet show the way to true discipleship as placing one's trust wholly in Jesus rather than in self (contra the disciples). The placement of "my" (μου) before the noun emphasizes that the one ill is "*my* son."

17:15 "... because he has epileptic seizures and suffers terribly. He often falls into the fire and frequently into water" (ὅτι σεληνιάζεται καὶ κακῶς πάσχει· πολλάκις γὰρ πίπτει εἰς τὸ πῦρ καὶ πολλάκις εἰς τὸ ὕδωρ). In Mark 9:22 it is the demon who throws the child into fire and water, but Matthew stresses the epileptic seizures used by the demon. There is no contradiction; the two are together in the list in 4:24, and illness and demon-possession were often connected in the ancient world. Matthew knows of the presence of the demon (v. 18) but simply wishes to center on the discipleship aspects rather than the cosmic war aspects of the story. The child's plight is terrible, for he has lost control of his body and is in constant danger of death by falling into cooking fires or ponds.

17:16 "I brought him to your disciples, but they were unable to heal him" (καὶ προσήνεγκα αὐτὸν τοῖς μαθηταῖς σου, καὶ οὐκ ἠδυνήθησαν αὐτὸν θεραπεῦσαι). The disciples had already been given authority over the demonic realm and illness (10:1, 8) and had been involved in several miracles (14:13 – 21, 29; 15:29 – 39; cf. Mark 6:13). Thus, this is another instance of discipleship failure along with their "little faith" (6:30; 8:26; 14:31; 16:8) and spiritual dullness (15:15; 16:23). Some see a parallel with Gehazi, Elisha's disciple, who in 2 Kgs 4:31 was unable to raise the Shunnamite's son; only Elisha was able to do so. While possible, the differences make it difficult to prove such an allusion.

17:17 Jesus answered, "O unbelieving and depraved generation!" (ἀποκριθεὶς δὲ ὁ Ἰησοῦς εἶπεν, Ὦ γενεὰ ἄπιστος καὶ διεστραμμένη). It is debated whether the "depraved generation" is mainly the crowds (seen in the second person plurals and in "generation" [γενεά], referring to the continued rejection by the crowds)[3] or the disciples, the nearest antecedent and the focus of this pericope.[4] However, it is best to see this as a both-and situation, since both groups are in the immediate context.[5] In their failure, the disciples have joined the rest of the Jewish people in their unbelief and perversity.

It is interesting that this pericope follows immediately after the disciples have partly "understood" (v. 13). This represents the vacillation between belief and unbelief represented in the disciples as "little-faith ones" who are slowly growing. There is a likely allusion to the Song of Moses and the "warped and crooked generation" of Deut 32:5, 20, namely, Israel's failure in the wilderness. In other words, the disciples in their unbelief are replicating a long line of God's people who have "perverted" his commands.

17:17 "How long must I be with you? How long must I put up with you? Bring him here to me" (ἕως πότε μεθ' ὑμῶν ἔσομαι; ἕως πότε ἀνέξομαι ὑμῶν; φέρετέ μοι αὐτὸν ὧδε). The twice-repeated "how long" (ἕως πότε) has been called "prophetic exasperation" (Hill) or "prophetic lament" (Hagner) and expresses Jesus' upset and sorrow at their failure, reminiscent of 16:8 – 11. The two-part rebuke centers first on his continual presence with them ("I will be" [ἔσομαι]) and then on his endurance of them ("I will put up with" [ἀνέξομαι]). Implicit in both is his imminent departure from this earthly sphere. Jesus' followers do not have long to get their act together! In light of this persistent failure, Jesus takes the matter in his own hands and commands that the boy be brought to him.

17:18 Then Jesus rebuked the demon, and it came out of the boy, and he was healed from that very moment (καὶ ἐπετίμησεν αὐτῷ ὁ Ἰησοῦς καὶ ἐξῆλθεν ἀπ' αὐτοῦ τὸ δαιμόνιον, καὶ ἐθεραπεύθη ὁ παῖς ἀπὸ τῆς ὥρας ἐκείνης). The antecedent of "him" (αὐτῷ) is not specified, but from context as well as the Markan parallel it is certainly the demon rather than the boy that is rebuked. It is first the object of Jesus' castigation ("rebuked him") and then the subject of the exorcism ("it came out"). Until this point the reader has been unaware of the cosmic powers behind the epileptic seizures, but Jesus' authority over the demonic realm is once again absolute, and the demon exits the child immediately. Matthew also likes to stress the instantaneous, permanent effects; thus, the healing takes effect "from that very moment" (cf. 8:13; 9:22; 15:28).

3. See Gundry, *Matthew*, 350; Hagner, *Matthew 14 – 28*, 504; Luz, *Matthew 8 – 20*, 408; France, *Gospel of Matthew*, 660.

4. See Held, *Tradition and Interpretation*, 191; Schnackenburg, *Matthew*, 168; Nolland, *Matthew*, 712.

5. So Carson, "Matthew," 391; Davies and Allison, *Matthew*, 2:724; Blomberg, *Matthew*, 267.

17:19 Then his disciples came to Jesus in private and asked, "Why weren't we able to cast it out?" (Τότε προσελθόντες οἱ μαθηταὶ τῷ Ἰησοῦ κατ' ἰδίαν εἶπον, Διὰ τί ἡμεῖς οὐκ ἠδυνήθημεν ἐκβαλεῖν αὐτό;). Needless to say, the disciples are nonplussed at their stark inability to drive out the demon. In their acute embarrassment, they come to Jesus "in private" and ask how this could have happened. The basis of their defeat seems pretty clear from the emphatic pronoun, "Why couldn't *we* (ἡμεῖς)...?"

While the inner circle was with Jesus on the mountaintop in worship, the other disciples were in the valley strutting their stuff. Yet there may also be a double meaning here. "In private" (κατ' ἰδίαν) occurs six times in Matthew, always at key junctures for Jesus' desire for privacy (14:13, 23) or his private teaching of the "mysteries" (13:11) to his followers (17:1; 20:17; 24:3). Such truths were not meant for outsiders but for the inner core of followers. So at one level the privacy is due to their embarrassment, at another level it leads to the pronouncement of another kingdom truth.

17:20 Jesus replied, "It is because you have so little faith" (ὁ δὲ λέγει αὐτοῖς, Διὰ τὴν ὀλιγοπιστίαν ὑμῶν). The disciples have frequently been chided for their "little faith" (6:30; 8:26; 14:31; 16:8). In those passages we decided this does not refer to total disbelief but rather to a vacillating, struggling faith. Moreover, "faith" does not simply mean certitude that God will grant the request but rather a total dependence on the God who watches after his children. That is the case here. They likely believed their newfound power over illness and the demonic realm gave them status, and they may have been showing off rather than centering on the God who alone has true power. Such self-centeredness guarantees failure.

17:20 "I tell you the truth, if you have faith as small as a mustard seed" (ἀμὴν γὰρ λέγω ὑμῖν, ἐὰν ἔχητε πίστιν ὡς κόκκον σινάπεως). Jesus couches his pronouncement as an ἀμήν-saying that guarantees the veracity and importance of the point. As the smallest seed to produce a large plant (ten to twelve feet high), the mustard seed was proverbial for one's potential greatness (13:31 – 32).

17:20 "... you can tell this mountain, 'Move from here to there,' and it will be moved. Nothing will be impossible for you!" (ἐρεῖτε τῷ ὄρει τούτῳ, Μετάβα ἔνθεν ἐκεῖ, καὶ μεταβήσεται· καὶ οὐδὲν ἀδυνατήσει ὑμῖν).[6] The saying on moving the mountain has no parallel in Mark, which has, "This kind can come out only by prayer" (Mark 9:29), though there is a doublet of the mountain saying in Matt 21:21 = Mark 11:23 (cf. also Luke 17:6).

The idea of moving mountains is a frequent proverb for overcoming obstacles or doing the impossible, possibly stemming from its use in Isa 40:3 – 4 in the famous "voice ... in the wilderness prepar[ing] the way for the LORD" passage (cf. Ps 46:2; Isa 49:11; 54:10; *b. Ber.* 63b; *T. Sol.* 23:1; 1 Cor 13:2). The inner circle of disciples could not help but think of the very mountain on which they just witnessed the transfiguration take place, with its Sinai ramifications. "Nothing" can be "impossible" for such a faith![7] This will prove true in ensuing years and centuries, as Christianity first conquered the Roman empire and then spread throughout the world. The key, of course, is the presence of God in even a miniscule faith. It is not we who accomplish great things but God in us.

6. Several ancient manuscripts (ℵ [2] C D L W TR etc.) add a sentence here from Mark 9:29, "This kind can only come out by prayer and fasting." However, an impressive group of witnesses omits this passage (ℵ * B Θ 33 syr[s,c] etc.), and it is most likely a scribal assimilation from Mark.

7. J. D. M. Derrett speaks for some in his "Moving Mountains and Uprooting Trees (Mark 11:22; Matt 17:20; 21:21; Luke 17:6)," *BibOr* 30 (1988): 231 – 44, in taking this image as apocalyptic and a reference to uprooting the old order at the parousia. This could be part of the meaning in an inaugurated sense, but the emphasis in this context is on the realized side, the power of kingdom faith in the present.

Theology in Application

This pericope continues several important themes already established in Matthew, primarily Christology and discipleship. Jesus is sovereign Lord with authority over both the physical and the cosmic, i.e., illness and the demonic. In spite of the failure of the disciples, it is clear that this authority has been passed on to the disciples, for the very fact that it was a failure on their part shows that they should have been able to cast out the demon.

1. The "Unbelieving" Generation

Even God's chosen people can be part of the "unbelieving and depraved generation." The entire Godhead undergirds his followers and both loves and strengthens them (Isa 40:29, 31; John 20:21 – 23). However, believers must take that strength and depend on it at all times, or they will fail like the nine disciples in this story. Matthew wants us to realize that Jesus' presence is a promise but not a guarantee of victory. Paul said it well in Phil 2:12 – 13: you must "continue to work out your salvation with fear and trembling, for it is God who works in you to will and to act in order to fulfill his good purpose." Our responsibility is to put his power to work in our lives.

2. True Faith

True faith is not seen in the amount it attempts but in the degree of its absolute dependence on God. The focus in this story is on Jesus and the power of God available to those who trust completely in him. Even the smallest amount of this kind of God-awareness can remove great obstacles. The question is clear: Is it self or God in whom our reliance is based? Even the smallest amount of God-centered living can accomplish incredible things.

3. Accomplishing the Impossible

Matthew has a great interest in the power of faith (5:8; 7:7 – 11; 8:10, 13; 9:2, 22; 15:28; 21:21 – 22), but by faith he does not mean that we can control God simply by believing. While faith in one sense is trusting God to do great things in our lives, it is even more a total dependence and reliance on God accompanied by a dedication to live by his will and purposes. As in John 14:12 – 14, power in prayer is prayer "in [his] name," i.e., in union with Christ's person and purpose.

CHAPTER 75

Matthew 17:22 – 27

Literary Context

The purpose of this second prophecy regarding the passion and resurrection of Christ keeps the attention riveted on the primary theme of this section, the movement of Jesus to the cross. Every detail is deepened by its connection to the coming passion event. The third passion prediction (fourth if one counts 17:12) will occur in 20:17 – 19 and with this prediction draws these final two narrative portions of Matthew (13:54 – 17:27; 19:1 – 22:46) together as preparing for the decisive events in Jerusalem. The temple tax incident shows Jesus' faithfulness to (and at the same time freedom from) the very system that has turned against him and prepares for the corporate emphasis in ch. 18 on the church, the "royal children" of God.

- **V. Rejection, Suffering, and Glory (13:54 – 18:35)**
  - **A. Jesus' Deeds: Rejection, Discipleship, and Glory (13:54 – 17:27)**
    - **2. The Movement to the Cross (16:21 – 17:27)**
      - a. First Passion Prediction and Discipleship (16:21 – 28)
      - b. Transfiguration (17:1 – 13)
      - c. Healing of the Epileptic Child (17:14 – 21)
      - ➦ **d. Second Passion Prediction and Temple Tax (17:22 – 27)**

Main Idea

The Christlike path is that of suffering (16:24), but that path leads to glory and vindication. The theme of death preceding life is the great Christian paradox but is also the cycle of nature, as the death of the seed produces the living plant (John 12:24). The temple tax centers on freedom and responsibility, the freedom of God's children from earthly obligations and yet their responsibility as members of the current world order to fulfill these same obligations to the authorities.[1]

Translation

Matthew 17:22-27

22a	Setting	As they were gathered around him in Galilee,
b	Assertion/Prophecy	**Jesus said to them,**
c		*"The Son of Man is going to be delivered into human hands,*
23a		and *they will kill him,*
b		and *he will be raised on the third day."*
c	Response	**And they were filled with grief.**
24a	Setting	When they came to Capernaum,
b	Action/Question	**those who collect the two-drachma temple tax came to Peter and asked,**
c		*"Your teacher pays the temple tax, doesn't he?"*
25a	Answer	**Peter said,**
b		*"Yes."*
c	Setting	When Peter had entered the house,
d	Action/Question	**Jesus came to him and said,**
e		*"What do you think, Simon?*
f		*From whom do the kings of the earth receive their customs duty and taxes?*
g		*From their children or from others?"*
26a	Answer	**Peter replied,**
b		*"From others."*
c	Answer/Inference	**Jesus told him,**
d		*"So the children are exempt.*
27a	Purpose of 27b-f	*But* *so that we might not offend them,*
b	Exhortation	*go to the lake and throw out a fishing hook.*
c		*Take the first fish that comes up,*
d		*open its mouth,*
e		and *you will find there a four-drachma coin.*
f		*Take that and give it to them on behalf of me as well as you."*

1. David Garland, "Matthew's Understanding of the Temple Tax," in *Treasures New and Old: Recent Contributions to Matthean Studies,* ed. D. R. Bauer and M. A. Powell (SBLSS 1; Atlanta: Scholar's Press, 1996), 69 – 98 (esp. 90 – 91), calls this story a "theological object lesson" on surrendering one's rights and going the extra mile to avoid offending others and as part of witness to the community.

Structure and Literary Form

Jesus' prophecy of his God-ordained destiny follows Mark 9:30–32 and is the shortest of the three predictions, containing three terse clauses that foretell his betrayal, death, and resurrection. The disciple's continued failure to understand is seen in the fact that they "grieve" rather than rejoice, since they fail to understand the reason for his death. The temple tax incident is a dialogue story and is unique to Matthew. It partakes of two scenes, Peter's interaction with the temple authorities (vv. 24–25a) and then his interaction with Jesus (vv. 25b–27).

Exegetical Outline

- **I. The Setting in Galilee (17:22a)**
- **II. The Prophecy (17:22b–23)**
  - A. Betrayal, death, and resurrection on the third day (vv. 22b–23a)
  - B. The disciples' response: grief (v. 23b)
- **III. The Temple Tax (17:24–27)**
  - A. Arrival of temple tax collectors (vv. 24–25a)
  - B. Jesus' query and response (vv. 25–27)
    1. Question: Do the kings tax their children or others? (v. 25b)
    2. Peter's response: from others (v. 26a)
    3. Jesus' response: free but responsible to give anyway (vv. 26b–27)

Explanation of the Text

17:22 As they were gathered around[2] him in Galilee, Jesus said to them (Συστρεφομένων δὲ αὐτῶν ἐν τῇ Γαλιλαίᾳ εἶπεν αὐτοῖς ὁ Ἰησοῦς). This is probably another private meeting (after v. 19), with Jesus wanting to help his disciples understand the reality of his passion predictions in 16:21 and 17:12. It is hard to know why Galilee is emphasized. It is taken from Mark 9:30 but also prepares for the salvation-historical movement of 19:1, when Jesus "went away from Galilee and came into the region of Judea" to face his destiny. The time of kingdom proclamation in Galilee is almost at an end.

17:22b–23a "The Son of Man is going to be delivered into human hands, and they will kill him, and he will be raised on the third day" (Μέλλει ὁ υἱὸς τοῦ ἀνθρώπου παραδίδοσθαι εἰς χεῖρας ἀνθρώπων, καὶ ἀποκτενοῦσιν αὐτόν, καὶ τῇ τρίτῃ ἡμέρᾳ ἐγερθήσεται). This is the shortest of the three passion predictions and was meant to remind the disciples of what Jesus had told them at Caesarea Philippi (16:21). For the meaning of "Son of Man" in the predictions, see 16:21. The important terms here are "is going to" (μέλλει; like "must" [δεῖ] in 16:21 this speaks of divine necessity) and "to be delivered" (παραδίδοσθαι),

2. This is another temporal genitive absolute like those in 17:5, 9.

used throughout the NT (Acts 3:13; Rom 4:25, 1 Cor 11:23) and fifteen times in Matt 26–27 with the idea that God has "handed over" his Son to sinful human beings to fulfill prophecy (Isa 53:6, 12) and to accomplish redemption. The "human hands" are certainly the Jewish leaders and Roman authorities. For the "third day" theme, see on 16:21.

17:23b And they were filled with grief (καὶ ἐλυπήθησαν σφόδρα). Deep ("exceedingly" [σφόδρα]) sorrow (cf. 26:22, 37) is the natural response for those who do not truly understand the import of Jesus' prophecy. The disciples understand the fact of his death but not the import. Yet at the same time they refuse to accept that death and cannot begin to comprehend his coming resurrection. However, at another level their sorrow is valid, for it is the sins of humankind that place Christ on the cross. In fact, the major reason for their sorrow is likely the loss of the kingdom glory it will entail (they want to be princes under Jesus, as we will see in 20:20–22).

17:24 When they came to Capernaum (Ἐλθόντων δὲ αὐτῶν εἰς Καφαρναούμ). During the period covered by this narrative section (13:54–17:27), Jesus and the disciples have crossed the lake to the area of the Decapolis and returned (ch. 14), then traveled northwest to Tyre and Sidon and east to Gentile territory along the Sea of Galilee (ch. 15). Since then they have remained in the area of the lake, first at Magadan near Tiberias (15:39) and then twenty miles north of Galilee to the region of Caesarea Philippi (16:13–17:23) and now back to Jesus' and Peter's hometown of Capernaum.

17:24 ... those who collect the two-drachma temple tax came to Peter and asked, "Your teacher pays the temple tax, doesn't he?" (προσῆλθον οἱ τὰ δίδραχμα λαμβάνοντες τῷ Πέτρῳ καὶ εἶπαν, Ὁ διδάσκαλος ὑμῶν οὐ τελεῖ τὰ δίδραχμα;). The identity of these collectors depends on the decision as to which kind of tax is indicated in the "two-drachma tax." Cassidy argues it is not the temple tax but a Roman civil tax similar to those collected in Egypt (where such taxes were also two drachmas).[3] Since Jesus responds by referencing secular rulers, Cassidy argues, this is more likely a civil tax.

However, most commentators accept the traditional view because the entire setting is Jewish and Jesus is simply using a secular metaphor (Roman rulers) for a religious issue (the temple tax).[4] The half-shekel tax (= two drachmas) stemmed from the tax imposed in Neh 10:32–33 (where it was one-third of a shekel) and was to be paid[5] by every Jewish male over twenty years old (*m. Šeqal.* 1:3–4). Yet the practice was apparently late in the Second Temple period,[6] and there was considerable debate over it. Qumran understood Exod 30:11–16 as requiring one payment in a lifetime (4Q159:6–7), and the Sadducees believed it was to be paid voluntarily. This was the lone exception to the Roman rule that foreign temples could not collect taxes from their people. After the destruction of the temple in AD 70, the Romans required the temple tax to be given to the temple of Jupiter Capitolinus.

Thus, these were likely local Jewish collectors who visited the residents of Capernaum (like Peter and Jesus) and then sent the money to Jerusalem. The collection was taken in the month of Adar

3. Richard J. Cassidy, "Matthew 17:24–27 — A Word on Civil Taxes," *CBQ* 41 (1979): 571–80.

4. See esp. Davies and Allison, *Matthew*, 2:739–41; Richard Bauckham, "The Coin in the Fish's Mouth," in *Gospel Perspectives* (ed. D. Wenham and C. L. Blomberg; Sheffield: JSOT Press, 1986), 6:219–52.

5. Garland, "Temple Tax," 74, shows it was not compulsory, and some groups (see below) refused to pay it.

6. Luz, *Matthew 8–20*, 415, believes it began during the period of the Maccabean Alexandra Salome (76–67 BC), when the Pharisees sought to have the temple expenses paid by the people themselves.

(February-March) and sent to Jerusalem in time for Passover. So much money was collected that the temple authorities had to find ways to use it, "eventually constructing a massive golden vine (cf. Josephus, *War* 5.210)."[7]

17:25 Peter said, "Yes" (λέγει, Ναί). It is difficult to know why these men approach Peter rather than Jesus himself. Some believe it is out of respect for his status as a teacher/rabbi, but just as easily it could be due to the tension between Jesus and the Jewish leaders. They refer to Jesus as "your teacher" (17:24, normal in Matthew for nonfollowers, cf. 9:11; 12:38; etc.), and their question assumes an affirmative answer (with οὐ). Peter obligingly answers, "Yes," meaning he is sure Jesus will pay the tax.

17:25 When Peter had entered the house, Jesus came to him and said, "What do you think, Simon? From whom do the kings of the earth receive their customs duty and taxes?"(καὶ ἐλθόντα εἰς τὴν οἰκίαν προέφθασεν αὐτὸν ὁ Ἰησοῦς λέγων, Τί σοι δοκεῖ, Σίμων; οἱ βασιλεῖς τῆς γῆς ἀπὸ τίνων λαμβάνουσιν τέλη ἢ κῆνσον;). Jesus has either overheard the conversation or supernaturally knew what it was about. He decides to give Simon (using his given Aramaic name, "Simon") a lesson about relationships with government, Roman and Jewish (see 18:12 for the rhetorical question). The analogy centers on pagan "kings of the earth" (first for emphasis) but clearly the point is paying taxes in general and not just Roman taxes.[8]

17:25 "From their children or from others?" (ἀπὸ τῶν υἱῶν αὐτῶν ἢ ἀπὸ τῶν ἀλλοτρίων;). The "children" (υἱοί) are certainly the literal children of a king, and the analogy behind Jesus' question does fit that. It could also refer to the citizens of Rome who were exempt from the head tax collected only from the Jews and other subject peoples. But there is no example in literature of citizens being called "children" (υἱοί), so that is unlikely. Jesus' point is that kings never raise revenue from their own family but only from the rest of the people.

17:26 Peter replied, "From others." Jesus told him, "So the children are exempt." (εἰπόντος δέ, Ἀπὸ τῶν ἀλλοτρίων, ἔφη αὐτῷ ὁ Ἰησοῦς, Ἄρα γε ἐλεύθεροί εἰσιν οἱ υἱοί). Jesus' conclusion is that the royal family is therefore "free" of any obligation to pay the taxes. The major issue is the identity of the "children" (υἱοί) in relation to the true "King," God. Some argue this is totally christological and a reference to Christ the Son (Carson), others that it is the Israelites (Pregeant, cf. 8:12) as called by God to enter their destiny (Horbury, Bauckham, Luz), but the majority and most natural view is that it refers to Jesus and his followers. As God's "children" they are exempt from paying the temple tax. Most assume this also means they are "free" from the Jewish system as a whole, which has been superseded and fulfilled by Christ (cf. 12:5 – 6, 41 – 42; Mark 7:19).

17:27 "But so that we might not offend them" (ἵνα δὲ μὴ σκανδαλίσωμεν αὐτούς). Here we are at the core of the pericope, with "so that" (ἵνα) having its usual force as the purpose for the command that follows. The disciples are "free" of obligation to the Jewish authorities and even to the central cultus of the temple. Yet at the same time they live among their Jewish compatriots and are part of the system. Therefore the mission

7. Keener, *Matthew*, 443.

8. The τέλος refers to "customs duties" paid on goods, the κῆνσος to the "poll or head tax" and possibly to property taxes. For background information see especially William Horbury, "The Temple Tax," in *Jesus and the Politics of His Day* (ed. E. Bammel and C. F. D. Moule; Cambridge: Cambridge Univ. Press, 1984), 265 – 86.

statement behind their relationship is defined by the principle of "not giving offense." σκανδαλίζω in this context does not mean "fall away" or "fall into sin" (as in 5:29, 30; 11:6; 13:21) but the more general "give offense."

Jesus does not wish to give the impression that he is rejecting the temple or the Jewish people. This is a similar principle to Paul's in 1 Cor 9:22b, "I have become all things to all people so that by all possible means I might save some" (cf. 1 Cor 8:13; 9:3 – 23). All decisions are made on the basis of what enhances the gospel, and Christ's ambassadors are to surrender their "rights" for its sake.

17:27 "Go[9] to the lake and throw out a fishing hook. Take the first fish that comes up, open its mouth, and you will find there a four-drachma coin. Take that and give it to them on behalf of me as well as you" (πορευθεὶς εἰς θάλασσαν βάλε ἄγκιστρον καὶ τὸν ἀναβάντα πρῶτον ἰχθὺν ἆρον, καὶ ἀνοίξας τὸ στόμα αὐτοῦ εὑρήσεις στατῆρα· ἐκεῖνον λαβὼν δὸς αὐτοῖς ἀντὶ ἐμοῦ καὶ σοῦ). This is the strangest miracle in the gospels, not only because it is never reported as happening[10] but also because it seems to be "performed for relatively trivial and self-serving purposes,"[11] namely, for paying the temple tax for Jesus and Peter. The purpose is undoubtedly to show that the royal Father continues to provide for the needs of his children.

Jesus' command would be quite appealing to Simon, a professional fisherman. The reason for a "fishhook" rather than a net is the intention to catch just a single fish. The image of the fish "coming up" is part of the miracle; the fish, having swallowed a shiny coin on the bottom, arises from the depths and takes the hook.[12] The coin is probably Tyrian silver, the exact amount for paying the temple tax for Jesus and Peter ("on behalf of me as well as you," two shekels or drachmas each).[13]

Theology in Application

The application of this passage to the life of the church depends on whether one sees it restricted to the temple tax, thus having primarily a christological significance (so Carson, Luz), or sees both the temple tax and the civil tax included, thus seeing it as the precursor to "submission to the government" passages (France, Davies and Allison). In light of the presence of both in the text (the temple tax the basis of the story, the civil tax noted in Jesus' metaphorical question), I believe both aspects are intended here.

9. As in 2:8; 9:13; 11:4; 28:19, the circumstantial participle πορευθείς followed by a command becomes part of that command, "Go and...." The aorist tenses stress the fact of the command, "Do it now."

10. Interestingly, France, *Matthew* (TNTC), 268, interprets the absence of a report of an actual miracle as evidence that Jesus' statement was nothing more than a "playful comment on their lack of ready money." However, this is unlikely in light of the detail on Jesus' part.

11. Blomberg, *Matthew*, 271.

12. So Nolland, *Matthew*, 728.

13. Witherington, *Matthew*, 331, discusses the history of this. The Jews hated to use Seleucid coins with their idolatrous images on them and were drawn to use silver coins from Tyre (just north of Galilee in Syria, see 15:21) with a purer quality of silver and the exact weight of shekels, even though they too had the image of the patron god of Tyre, Heracles, on them. This was even called "sacred money" and was the official coinage for the temple tax, though it still had to be exchanged for silver without images.

1. The Father/Son Metaphor

The Father/Son metaphor is central to the God/Christian relationship. The fatherhood of God is an essential component of Matthean theology, with "Father" (πατήρ) occurring sixty-three times in his gospel, half of them on the lips of Jesus (*EDNT*, 3:53). In the Lord's Prayer (6:9 – 13), we begin our prayer with meditation on God as our "Abba." We are his beloved children, and he both watches over us and expects our obedience. Our sonship is based on the relationship between Jesus and his Father (cf. 11:27) and has connotations of both election and privilege. The believer belongs to God and is part of his family.

2. Exemption

As citizens of heaven, God's children are exempt from earthly obligations. This principle cannot be applied without the next one. Still, the followers of Christ do not belong to this world but are members of God's family and therefore while "part of" the world must live "apart from" it. Therefore technically, they are not bound to the strictures of the world system. For Jesus and the disciples this meant he was in process of fulfilling the law and its system.

3. Foregoing Rights

Nevertheless, as part of God's mission to the world, believers will forego their "rights" and place themselves under obligation to the world's system. For Jesus and his followers this meant paying the temple tax. For Paul and Peter this meant submission to government (Rom 13:1 – 7; 1 Pet 2:13 – 17). In all cases the mission of the church is the key element. As God's representatives, believers are his agents in the world and must surrender their privileges for the sake of the message they proclaim and exemplify in their lives. In addition, some interpret this as love and concern for serving others, i.e., doing good when such is not demanded.

4. God's Care

God will take care of his children, and so they must entrust themselves to his care. The purpose of the command of Jesus to Peter in v. 27 is both to show that God provides for the needs of his children and to tell Peter to be dependent on God to meet his needs. This is the meaning of the fourth petition of the Lord's Prayer, "Give us today our daily needs" (6:11). It is not a consumer demand for God to give more and more but an expression of our reliance on God to meet our needs.

CHAPTER 76

Matthew 18:1 – 4

Introduction to Jesus' Discourse on Relationships in the Community

It has been common to liken 18:1 – 35 to Qumran's "Manual of Discipline" (1QS) as a type of manual on church order. However, this discourse is not filled with regulations guiding the life of the community, as at Qumran. Rather, Jesus' teaching here relates to relationships in the community of his followers (as in 16:18; 18:17). Even the central section (vv. 15 – 20) deals not so much with regulations for church order as a pattern for reconciliation and forgiveness in the corporate community; its purpose is more redemptive than punitive. So it centers on humility (vv. 1 – 4), not causing others to sin (vv. 5 – 9), concern that none be lost (vv. 10 – 14), discipline and reconciliation (vv. 15 – 20), and forgiveness (vv. 21 – 35). All are ecclesiastical and pastoral concerns dealing with life in the community.[1]

Literary Context

Matthew turns from the external to the internal connections of his disciples — from persecution and rejection to humility and reconciliation. The key words in this context are "little child" (vv. 2, 3, 4, 5) / "little ones" (vv. 6, 10, 14), which together describe Jesus' followers as the downtrodden and despised of the world. So the first section relates how these "little ones" interact with each other in the midst of the pressure the world has placed on them. Jesus deals with this first positively (vv. 1 – 4) and then negatively (vv. 5 – 9).

1. It is probably best to see two major subdivisions: vv. 1 – 14 and 15 – 35 (so Gnilka, Davies and Allison, Blomberg; Luz and France divide it into vv. 1 – 20 and 21 – 35, Turner into vv. 1 – 14, 15 – 20, 21 – 35). It is also common (e.g., Carson, Hagner, Keener, Nolland) simply to divide it into its five component parts (vv. 1 – 4, 5 – 9, 10 – 14, 15 – 20, 21 – 35).

V. Rejection, Suffering, and Glory (13:54 – 18:35)
- A. Jesus' Deeds: Rejection, Discipleship, and Glory (13:54 – 17:27)
- **B. Fourth Discourse: Life and Relationships in the Community (18:1 – 35)**
  - **1. Relationships in the Community (18:1 – 14)**
    - ➦ **a. The Greatest in the Kingdom (18:1 – 4)**
    - b. Warning against Causing Others to Sin (18:5 – 9)
    - c. The Problem of Wandering Sheep (18:10 – 14)

Main Idea

Jesus begins by defining greatness in terms of humility; the model for true discipleship is the simple humility of a child. In the same way that a child exemplifies a lack of pride and concern for status, the faithful follower must adopt humility in all relationships. At the same time, the section begins with the issue of power and greatness and establishes a tone for the rest of the chapter; this humble use of power will enable the church to overcome sin and find forgiveness.[2]

Translation

Matthew 18:1-4

1a	Setting (Temporal)	At that time
b	Question	**the disciples came to Jesus and said,**
c		*"Who then is greatest in the kingdom of heaven?"*
2a	Answer	**He called a little child,**
b		whom he placed in their midst, **and said,**
3a	Warning	*"I tell you the truth . . .* *you will never enter the kingdom of heaven*
b		*if you do not turn your lives around and* *become like little children.*
4a	Conclusion	So *whoever will humble themselves like this little child is the* ⮒ *greatest in the kingdom of heaven."*

2. See E. J. Ramshaw, "Power and Forgiveness in Matthew 18," *WW* 18 (1998): 397 – 404.

Structure and Literary Form

This passage parallels Mark 9:33 – 38 but with several changes. The dispute of Mark 9:33 – 34 and Jesus' discernment of their thoughts in Luke 9:46 – 48 are replaced with their direct question here.[3] In addition, Jesus' response in vv. 3 – 4 is added to the Markan rendition, with v. 3 taken from the Mark 10:15 tradition (omitted in Matt 19:13 – 15) and v. 4 being M material. As a result, it is not a correction to the disciples' misunderstanding (like Mark) but paraenetic instruction on the true source of kingdom greatness. There are two main aspects framed by the question of greatness (vv. 1, 4), the disciple's question (v. 1) and Jesus' response (vv. 2 – 4), with the latter having two parts, the demand to become like children (vv. 2 – 3) and the definition of the childlike quality needed, humility (v. 4).

Exegetical Outline

➡ **I. The Disciples' Query about Greatness (18:1)**

II. Jesus' Response (18:2 – 4)

- A. Become like a child (vv. 2 – 3)
  1. Placing a child among them (v. 2)
  2. The command: change and become childlike (v. 3a)
  3. The warning: never enter the heavenly kingdom (v. 3b)
- B. Humble yourself like a child (v. 4)

Explanation of the Text

18:1 At that time the disciples came to Jesus and said (Ἐν ἐκείνῃ τῇ ὥρᾳ προσῆλθον οἱ μαθηταὶ τῷ Ἰησοῦ λέγοντες). "At that time" (ἐν ἐκείνῃ τῇ ὥρᾳ) and similar phrases (26:55; cf. 11:25; 12:1; 13:1; 14:1; 22:23; 26:55) are used in Matthew to connect action with the preceding material, in this case Jesus' discussions with his disciples in ch. 17, in particular his claims that the disciples as "sons" have a special status in their relationship with the royal God of heaven (17:25 – 26).[4]

18:1 "Who then is greatest in the kingdom of heaven?" Τίς ἄρα μείζων ἐστὶν ἐν τῇ βασιλείᾳ τῶν οὐρανῶν;). Note the focus of their question, "Who then?" (τίς ἄρα). While the question is posed in general terms, the preoccupation of the disciples with their own greatness is noted in 17:19; 20:20 – 21. It is clear that they are not so much interested in the qualities that lead to greatness or the kingdom realities behind such greatness. Their question, "Who then is the 'greatest' [the comparative μείζων for the superlative]?" shows their primary interest is in status, power, and authority — in particular, their own future power position (as will be demonstrated in 20:20 – 21).

3. This does not have to mean an absence of historical veracity, as if Matthew reworked the story. As Carson brings out, "Matthew," 396, it could be that "Jesus detected their rivalry (Luke), challenged them, and thereby silenced them (Mark), and that they then blurted out their question (Matthew). Alternatively Matthew uses this brief question to summarize what was truly on their minds."

4. Thompson, *Matthew's Advice*, 96.

The presence of "the kingdom of heaven" could mean this is eschatological, i.e., "is" (ἐστίν) as a futuristic present pointing to status in heaven.[5] However, this is too disjunctive, for the context is in the present, and "kingdom" in Matthew also refers to the new kingdom reality Christ has inaugurated in his messianic ministry ("kingdom of heaven" in present in 11:11).[6] The question likely stems from the present rivalry of the disciples, a contention that will explode in 20:20 – 28. Thus there is an inaugurated thrust and their question relates both to their present status and their future potential.

18:2 He called a little child, whom he placed in their midst (καὶ προσκαλεσάμενος παιδίον ἔστησεν αὐτὸ ἐν μέσῳ αὐτῶν). From the context we know they are back in Capernaum (17:24), so they could have been in Peter's home with Peter's child. The use of "little child" (παιδίον) does not indicate age, for the diminutive form had lost much of its force; in general it refers to a child under the age of puberty.[7] The major points are the low status of children in the first century and their lack of interest in power and prestige. So Jesus uses a child as an object lesson. As Wilkins says, "Jesus celebrates the humility that comes from the child's weakness, defenselessness, and vulnerability. The child can really do nothing for himself or herself and will die if left alone. It is this kind of humility that Jesus uses as a visual aid."[8]

18:3 … and said, "I tell you the truth, if you do not turn your lives around and become like little children" (καὶ εἶπεν, Ἀμὴν λέγω ὑμῖν, ἐὰν μὴ στραφῆτε καὶ γένησθε ὡς τὰ παιδία). As often in Matthew, the "amen" (ἀμήν) formula points to a particularly important saying (see on 5:18). "If" (ἐάν) has its basic force as a hypothetical situation presenting a logical connection and could be translated, "unless you do … this will never happen." "Turn" (στραφῆτε) connotes a repentance or change of behavior, a turning from sin to follow God's way.[9] In this case the change is a choice to become childlike, to refuse the adult mania for greatness and adopt the simple faith of a child.

18:3 "… you will never enter the kingdom of heaven" (οὐ μὴ εἰσέλθητε εἰς τὴν βασιλείαν τῶν οὐρανῶν). Unless that change occurs they can "never [οὐ μή has its full emphatic force here][10] enter the kingdom of heaven." Here "kingdom" is again probably both present and future, that is, become a part of the kingdom community now and inherit the heavenly kingdom for eternity. There are three passages on entering the kingdom, and all center on ethical responsibility — in 5:20 it is a superior "righteousness" (= "right" living before God); in 7:21 it is "do[ing] the will of the Father," and here it is living in childlike humility.

18:4 "So whoever will humble themselves like this little child is the greatest in the kingdom of heaven" (ὅστις οὖν ταπεινώσει ἑαυτὸν ὡς τὸ παιδίον τοῦτο, οὗτός ἐστιν ὁ μείζων ἐν τῇ βασιλείᾳ τῶν οὐρανῶν). οὖν draws a conclusion from v. 3, and Jesus now defines what becoming

5. So Davies and Allison, *Matthew*, 2:756; Luz, *Matthew 8 – 20*, 426; Schnackenburg, *Matthew*, 171. Thompson, *Matthew's Advice*, 75, points out that "kingdom of heaven" is used "most often" in Matthew in a future setting (5:19; 8:11; 13:43; 16:28; 20:21; 26:29).

6. See Hagner, *Matthew 14 – 28*, 517; Beare, *Matthew*, 375.

7. See Louw and Nida, *Greek-English Lexicon*, 110.

8. Wilkins, *Matthew*, 613.

9. Jeremias, *Theology*, 155 – 56, takes this as equivalent to the Hebrew verb *šûb* (Aramaic *tûb*), often translated in the LXX as "again." While possible (so Thompson, Davies and Allison), that is too weak for this passage, where the "turn around" seems emphatic (so Pregeant, who says it is synonymous with "repent" [μετανοέω]).

10. It is debated whether "never' (οὐ μή) has retained its emphatic force in Koine Greek; but though it is primarily in quotes from the LXX and sayings of Jesus, it is generally recognized that it does, see Porter, *Idioms*, 283; Wallace, 468.

"childlike" entails. Some explain "humility" entirely in terms of low status in society, a willingness to take the inferior position.[11] Certainly that is an important (probably the central) connotation of "to be humble" (ταπεινόω), but that does not exhaust its meaning. Luz shows that while its core import is the condition of lowliness, it also involves "the practice of lowliness," as in hospitality to children/little ones (v. 5), accepting them (vv. 10 – 14), forgiving them (vv. 21 – 22), loving others as neighbor's (19:16 – 21), renouncing honors (23:8 – 10), and serving (20:26 – 28; 23:11).[12]

Humility is a major theme in Matthew (see on 11:29) as exemplified by Jesus (11:28 – 29; 12:17 – 21; 21:5), and here we discover the essence of discipleship. This defines true "greatness" in accord with the disciples' question of v. 1. As we will see later in 20:26 – 27, the "great" are those who make themselves servants and slaves, who take the lowest place. Then God exalts them (see 5:3, 5).

Theology in Application

1. Discipleship and Lowliness

Discipleship means reversing the world's standards of greatness and embracing the position of lowliness. This is a difficult principle for Christians in modern society, for far more than was true in the first century, it is possible for the lowly today to rise above their upbringing. Thus the desire for status and power may be more widespread today than ever before, and so it is hard to embrace this principle. Moreover, the "American way" is to make the best of yourself that you can, believing that "you can be anything you want to be." Yet in this "upward mobility," you are required by Christ to maintain humility and an attitude of service to others. Wilkins applies this to the problem of competition and its destructive effect on relationships because it involves "promotion of self at the expense of others."[13] Believers must depend on God and his mercy, not themselves.

2. Humility

Humility is an attitude and a lifestyle that alone defines the true kingdom community. In 7:21 – 23 Jesus made it clear that mere affirmation will not be sufficient to enter God's kingdom; one must have "fruit" (7:20) or the deeds that prove the confession was real. In Matthew, kingdom living is necessary in order to be kingdom people. Here that means a life of humility or gentle servitude toward others.

11. So France and Hagner. T. Raymond Hobbs, "Crossing Cultural Bridges: The Biblical World," *McMaster Journal of Theology* 1 (1990): 1 – 21, centers on powerlessness and total dependence of children on their parents. They had no rights.

12. Luz, *Matthew 8 – 20*, 429. See also R. N. Brown, "Jesus and the Child as a Model of Spirituality," *IBS* 4 (1982): 178 – 92, who stresses the model of childlike trust in God the Abba, who loves his children.

13. Wilkins, *Matthew*, 630 – 31.

Paul defined this well in Phil 2:2 – 3, "in humility value others above yourselves, not looking to your own interests but each of you to the interests of the others." Some scholars separate Matthew and Paul here, arguing that Matthew was interested only in the concept of lowly status. But in the rest of ch. 18 humility is defined in terms of action toward others and not just status in society. Both are part of the concept here.

CHAPTER 77

Matthew 18:5 – 9

Literary Context

From the positive example of humility in vv. 1 – 4, Jesus now turns to the negative example of causing others in the community to sin. Relationships among God's people must be defined by what strengthens others, not by what brings others down.

- **V. Rejection, Suffering, and Glory (13:54 – 18:35)**
  - **B. Fourth Discourse: Life and Relationships in the Community (18:1 – 35)**
    - **1. Relationships in the Community (18:1 – 14)**
      - a. The Greatest in the Kingdom (18:1 – 4)
      - ➦ **b. Warning against Causing Others to Sin (18:5 – 9)**
      - c. The Problem of Wandering Sheep (18:10 – 14)

Main Idea

The problem dealt with is Christians who become "stumbling blocks" to others in the community, i.e., who lead them into sin and even cause them to lose their faith (see below). This warns the community that such will bring severe judgment from God, and so the community had better discipline such members before it is too late.

Translation

Matthew 18:5-9

5a	Assertion	*"Whoever receives one such little child in my name receives me.*	
6a	Warning #1/ Condition	*[1] But*	*whoever causes one of these little ones* ↲ *who believes in me to fall away into sin,*
b	Result	*it would be better for*	*that person to have a large millstone* ↲ *hung around their necks and be drowned in the depths of the sea.*
7a		*Woe to the world because of its stumbling blocks.*	
b	Warning #2	*[2] For though such stumbling blocks must come,*	
c		*woe to that person on account of whom it comes.*	
8a	Exhortation	*Now if your hand or your foot causes you to stumble,*	
b		*cut them off and throw them away from you.*	
c	Basis for 8b	*It is better for you*	*to enter into life lame or crippled than*
d			*having two hands or two feet to be thrown into eternal fire.*
9a	Exhortation	*And if your eye causes you to stumble,*	
b		*pluck it out and throw it away from you.*	
c	Basis for 9a	*It is better for you*	*to enter into life with one eye than*
d			*to have two eyes but be thrown into fiery Gehenna."*

Structure and Literary Form

Matthew draws his material primarily from Mark 9:37a (= v. 5), 42 – 50 (= vv. 6, 8 – 9) but also from Q (Luke 17:1 – 2 = v. 7). It can be called a woe oracle, a warning of judgment on those who commit such a heinous sin. The structure utilizes v. 5 as a positive command set in contrast to the negative warning of vv. 6 – 9, which consist of four sayings, subdivided into (1) absolute judgment on the one causing another to stumble (vv. 5 – 6), (2) judgment on the world for producing such people (v. 7), and (3) a warning to the church to deal severely with such people (vv. 8 – 9).

Exegetical Outline

➡ **I. Encouragement to Accept Other Believers (18:5)**
   A. Welcome others
   B. To welcome others is to welcome Christ

II. Warning against Causing Others to Sin (18:6 – 9)
   A. The warning of serious judgment on the person (v. 6)
   B. Serious judgment on the world system as the source of such (v. 7)
   C. The church commanded to deal harshly with such people (vv. 8 – 9)
      1. The command to cast such people out
      2. The warning of eternal punishment

Explanation of the Text

18:5 Whoever receives one such little child in my name receives me (καὶ ὃς ἐὰν δέξηται ἓν παιδίον τοιοῦτο ἐπὶ τῷ ὀνόματί μου, ἐμὲ δέχεται). The major issue here is whether this belongs with vv. 1 – 4 or 6 – 9. The arguments for taking it with the former seem compelling — the use of "little child" (παιδίον; the text switches to "little one" [μικρός] in vv. 6 – 14), the positive orientation of v. 5, and the possibility that this is a specific type of lowly humility. However, it is better to take it with the following (see Thompson, Carson, Hagner), since (1) v. 4 has already concluded the paragraph by framing it with the issue of "greatness"; (2) the "whoever" opening of vv. 5 – 6 parallel each other; and (3) vv. 5 – 6 form a natural promise - warning proverb. The "little child" is now a fellow follower of Christ and not just children per se (hinted at in v. 4).

"Receive" (δέξηται) involves welcome, loving reception, and acceptance. Hagner takes it especially of hospitality shown to disciples in missionary work (cf. 10:42),[1] but more likely it is intended of community life in general. A good example would be Rom 14:1 – 15:13, where Jewish and Gentile Christians in conflict are told to accept one another. This is to be done "in my name," i.e., as part of his community and under his authority (cf. 7:22; 10:22; 18:20; 19:29; 24:5, 9; 28:19). To do so is to receive Jesus himself and to experience his blessing. Since Jesus is one with each of his followers, the one showing mercy experiences Christ's presence in the one they are helping.

18:6 But whoever causes one of these little ones who believes in me to fall away into sin (Ὃς δ' ἂν σκανδαλίσῃ ἕνα τῶν μικρῶν τούτων τῶν πιστευόντων εἰς ἐμέ). Some have connected "to fall away into sin" (σκανδαλίσῃ) with the use of the same verb in 17:27, where the Jerusalem authorities would have been "offended" if Jesus had refused to pay the temple tax. But the present situation is far more serious and is similar to the use of the verb in 5:29, 30; 11:6; 13:21; 24:10, where it means "fall into sin" and even to "fall away from the faith," thus apostasy (Luz, Blomberg, France, contra Carson). This is in keeping with the severity of the warning here.

This is especially serious because the "little

1. Hagner, *Matthew 14 – 28*, 522.

ones," the lowly and insignificant disciples, are those who "believe in me"[2] or continue (present tense) to place their faith in Jesus. The use of "whoever" (ὃς ἄν) means there is a potential for anyone to become a stumbling block, though Matthew may have in mind especially false prophets/teachers discussed by Jesus in 7:15 – 23; still, anyone can become a false prophet.

18:6 ... it would be better for that person to have[3] a large millstone hung around their necks and be drowned in the depths of the sea (συμφέρει αὐτῷ ἵνα κρεμασθῇ μύλος ὀνικὸς περὶ τὸν τράχηλον αὐτοῦ καὶ καταποντισθῇ ἐν τῷ πελάγει τῆς θαλάσσης). The "large millstone" (μύλος ὀνικός) was not the small millstone worked by hand but the large stone (probably the upper stone of two used for grinding) turned by a "donkey" (ὀνικός = "pertaining to a donkey," so BAGD, Turner). It could have weighed several tons and if attached to a neck would render drowning absolutely certain. Execution by drowning was a frequent Roman punishment and was terrifying because there could be no burial and therefore no peaceful afterlife (in a Hellenistic sense). Jesus' point is that this would be preferable to the punishment God would render such a person.

18:7 Woe to the world because of its stumbling blocks (οὐαὶ τῷ κόσμῳ ἀπὸ τῶν σκανδάλων). For "woe" (οὐαί), see on 11:21. Jesus is saying that divine judgment will fall on the world because its system is the true source of the stumbling that will destroy the faith of too many "little ones." This also means that the false teachers and others who cause such spiritual catastrophes are truly of the world.

18:7 For though such stumbling blocks must come, woe to that person[4] on account of whom it comes (ἀνάγκη γὰρ ἐλθεῖν τὰ σκάνδαλα, πλὴν οὐαὶ τῷ ἀνθρώπῳ δι' οὗ τὸ σκάνδαλον ἔρχεται). "Must" (ἀνάγκη) refers to the necessity (= "must" [δεῖ]) of such stumbling, undoubtedly referring to the evil world that will prevail until the eschaton. The presence of sin (an invading army in Rom 6) is part of the current world order and will exert its evil influence until Christ returns. Yet as throughout the book of Revelation, God is sovereign and uses even the evil forces to perform his will (cf. Rev 6:1 – 8, 13:5 – 8, 17:17). Still, those individuals who become part of the world system and lead the saints astray will come under particular judgment ("woe" [οὐαί] is a woe oracle in the OT and signifies imminent judgment).

18:8 Now if your hand or your foot causes you to stumble, cut them off and throw them away from you (Εἰ δὲ ἡ χείρ σου ἢ ὁ πούς σου σκανδαλίζει σε, ἔκκοψον αὐτὸν καὶ βάλε ἀπὸ σοῦ). εἰ is a condition of fact and assumes that such false teachers (the leaders in Jesus' day, heretical teachers in Matthew's time) are present. Yet this is strongly debated, for the majority of scholars take this in the same sense it had in 5:29 – 30, namely, sinful parts of the disciples' own "body" or self that lead them into sin. In 5:29 – 30 it was temptation to sexual lust, while here it is sin committed in the Christian assembly.[5]

However, Thompson argues (1) that the causative force of the key word "stumble" (σκανδαλίζω) must be respected, so that it means "cause *others* to stumble," and (2) that the condition of fact in "if" (εἰ) implies a real situation in

2. "Believe in" (πιστεύω εἰς) is strong and emphasizes the content of the faith, see Wallace, 359. This is the only place this expression is found in the Synoptics; it is a key motif in John's gospel.

3. "That" (ἵνα) in a context like this is virtually equivalent to an infinitive.

4. "That person" (τῷ ἀνθρώπῳ) generically refers to a person (man or woman) and the article is demonstrative in force, "that."

5. See, e.g., Basser, "The Meaning of '*Shtuth*,'" 148 – 51, who assumes it is the "offending member" of the body that leads the individual into sin in both ch. 5 and ch. 18.

the community.[6] Moreover, the context is corporate, and vv. 6 – 7 have warned the church against this very activity, namely, individuals who cause "the little ones" to fall spiritually. Thus the terms "your hand/foot" are personified to depict false teachers and others who are detrimental to the life of the church.

The absence of body language and the presence of singular pronouns σου/σε have led many (e.g., Carson, Davies and Allison, Hagner, Witherington) to doubt the corporate nature of these verses. Still, it makes a great deal of sense, and the pronouns could easily be collective singulars highlighting the nature of the church. This makes more sense than vv. 6 – 7 and vv. 10 – 14 being corporate while vv. 8 – 9 are an oasis of individual emphasis. So Jesus takes the personal metaphors of 5:29 – 30 and applies them corporately here to life in the church. The imagery of amputation parallels 18:17 and refers to the excommunication of offending members.[7] As such this is a call to church discipline.

18:8 It is better for you to enter into life lame or crippled than having two hands or two feet to be thrown into eternal fire (καλόν σοί ἐστιν εἰσελθεῖν εἰς τὴν ζωὴν κυλλὸν ἢ χωλόν, ἢ δύο χεῖρας ἢ δύο πόδας ἔχοντα βληθῆναι εἰς τὸ πῦρ τὸ αἰώνιον). At the individual level of 5:29 – 30 this refers to the danger of eternal punishment for those who yield to a life of sin and fail to control themselves. At the corporate level it applies the imagery of apostasy corporately to a church (though again most take this of individual sins rather than corporate sin). This is in keeping with the warning to the church of Ephesus that Christ would "come to you and remove your lampstand from its place" (Rev 2:5), or to Sardis that "I will come like a thief, and you will not know at what time I will come to you" (Rev 3:3). So interpreting this of corporate apostasy and judgment is possible and, I believe, likely.

Yet there is another aspect as well, fitting the discipline section of vv. 15 – 20, namely, the emphasis on the redemptive side. The reason for the harsh discipline of offending members is not so much punitive as redemptive, i.e., to bring such people to repentance and forgiveness in order that they may "enter[8] into life" rather than "be thrown[9] into eternal fire."

18:9 And if your eye causes you to stumble, pluck it out and throw it away from you. It is better for you to enter into life with one eye than to have two eyes but be thrown into fiery Gehenna (καὶ εἰ ὁ ὀφθαλμός σου σκανδαλίζει σε, ἔξελε αὐτὸν καὶ βάλε ἀπὸ σοῦ· καλόν σοί ἐστιν μονόφθαλμον εἰς τὴν ζωὴν εἰσελθεῖν ἢ δύο ὀφθαλμοὺς ἔχοντα βληθῆναι εἰς τὴν γέενναν τοῦ πυρός). This repeats the teaching of v. 8, adding the metaphor of the eye (reversing the order of 5:29 – 30). The teaching is exactly the same as v. 8, with the hand/foot symbolizing action in the church and the eye the visionary aspect of leadership. Again those individuals who lead others astray are to be harshly disciplined for the sake of the life of the church and for their own sake, lest they face eternal punishment. Thompson brings out the chiastic arrangement here of "into life to enter"/"to be thrown into the Gehenna of fire," thereby contrasting reward and punishment.[10] There is too much at stake for churches to ignore the critical aspect of church discipline!

6. Thompson, *Matthew's Advice*, 112, 116 – 18; see also Hauerwas, *Matthew*, 163.

7. See Luz, *Matthew 8 – 20*, 436, who agrees with Thompson but is more cautious.

8. The aorist "to enter" (εἰσελθεῖν) refers to the moment at the eschaton when God decides who is to "enter" heaven and who is not (cf. 7:21 – 23).

9. A divine passive referring to the same moment as the previous footnote (the great white throne judgment of Rev 20:11 – 15), when God casts the unsaved into the lake of fire.

10. Thompson, *Matthew's Advice*, 115.

Theology in Application

1. A Community of Caring Members

The church is intended to be a community of caring members. When Jesus commanded that discipleship involves "receiving" and "welcoming" one another, he was turning an "assembly" (ἐκκλησία) of disciples into a community of believers who share and care for each another. When this happens, the church evolves further into a family of deeply involved "brothers and sisters," who encourage and love one another "deeply from the heart" (1 Pet 1:22).

2. Protection from Spiritual Predators

The church is also responsible to protect its members from spiritual predators who will destroy their walk with God. Paul warned the Ephesian elders of "savage wolves" who would "not spare the flock," comprising some "even from your own number" (Acts 20:29 – 30), a prophecy that came true about five years later (Eph 4:14; 1 Tim 4). The church must respond swiftly and firmly to such dangerous people, and Jesus demands excommunication for such unless they repent (18:17; cf. 1 Cor 5:3 – 5; 1 Tim 1:20).

Yet in our day we must also be careful not to overreact to doctrinal differences among us. The key is that the "heresy" implied here deals with cardinal doctrines and serious practices like idolatry or immorality (cf. the Nicolaitan heresy of Rev 2), not with issues like Jewish food laws or holy days (cf. Rom 14:1 – 15:13). On the latter we practice tolerance.[11]

11. On this see Osborne, *Hermeneutical Spiral*, 399 – 402.

CHAPTER 78

Matthew 18:10 – 14

Literary Context

In the corporate context centering on the church, this parable concerns not those lost outside the church but those wandering and lost inside the church. Thus it reverses the focus of vv. 6 – 9, which centered on the person leading the sheep astray, while this passage centers on the sheep that are going astray.

- **V. Rejection, Suffering, and Glory (13:54 – 18:35)**
  - **B. Fourth Discourse: Life and Relationships in the Community (18:1 – 35)**
    - **1. Relationships in the Community (18:1 – 14)**
      - a. The Greatest in the Kingdom (18:1 – 4)
      - b. Warning against Causing Others to Sin (18:5 – 9)
      - ➦ **c. The Problem of Wandering Sheep (18:10 – 14)**

Main Idea

The central thrust is the importance of every single member of the church to God. Even though the "little ones" are despised and beaten down in this world, God watches over each one, and as such he demands that all the members watch out for each other (v. 10). The church must emulate God in its spiritual vigilance to make certain its members do not stray from their spiritual walk (cf. Gal 6:1; Heb 3:13).

Translation

(See next page.)

Structure and Literary Form

Matthew draws from his special M source (v. 10, 14) and possibly from Q (vv. 12 – 13 = Luke 15:3 – 7). Moreover, in the parable the central term is "go astray"

Matthew 18:10-14

10a	Exhortation	"See that you do not hold one of these little ones in contempt.	
b	Basis for 10a	For I tell you that their angels in heaven always look	
			on the face of my Father who is in heaven.
12a	Rhetorical Question	What do you think?	
b	Condition		If some person has a hundred sheep and one of them wanders astray,
c	Result/ Rhetorical Question	won't that person	leave the ninety-nine on the hills and go searching for the one that wandered off?
13a		And	if that person finds it,
b	Assertion	I tell you the truth, he rejoices over that sheep	more than over the ninety-nine that did not wander astray.
14a	Conclusion	Thus it is not the	will of your Father in heaven that one of these little ones perish."

rather than Luke's "lost." This and the altered ending gives the parable a different thrust (see below),[1] with the emphasis on wandering sheep from within God's flock rather than lost sheep outside his flock.

There are three sections. An introductory logion (v. 10) consists of a command not to have contempt for any of God's "little ones," followed by the reason — their guardian angels look on the face of God. Then comes the parable proper (vv. 12 – 13), formed around two "if" (ἐάν) clauses telling a story — a man with a single sheep that goes astray. The first is followed by a rhetorical question, the second by a declarative statement, but both tell what the shepherd will do — search for that sheep and then rejoice over it. Finally, a conclusion (v. 14) provides the moral of the story: God the supreme shepherd does not want a single sheep to perish.

Exegetical Outline

➦ I. Introduction: the Church's Responsibility (18:10)

A. The required action: no contempt for any of God's "little ones" (v. 10a)

B. The reason: their guardian angels see God's face (v. 10b)

1. See Carson, "Matthew," 400, for a strong argument that Matthew's and Luke's versions do not go back to an original but represent two different occasions and uses of the parable by Jesus. This makes a great deal of sense in light of the different forms and context between the two gospels.

II. The Parable of the Wandering Sheep (18:12 – 13)
- A. First act: the wandering sheep (v. 12)
  1. One of a herd of a hundred sheep wanders off
  2. The shepherd leaves the ninety-nine to search for the missing sheep
- B. Second act: the joy of finding (v. 13)
  1. He finds the sheep
  2. His great joy — more than over the ninety-nine

III. Conclusion: God Unwilling to Allow Any to Perish (v. 14)

Explanation of the Text

18:10 See that you do not hold one of these little ones in contempt (Ὁρᾶτε μὴ καταφρονήσητε ἑνὸς τῶν μικρῶν τούτων). "See" (ὁρᾶτε) is a strong command (present tense for the need for continual vigilance), which often is tantamount to "be on your guard against" (BAGD) and here warns the church of a serious expectation from God. "Hold in contempt" (καταφρονήσητε) connotes both the attitude of despising a person and the contemptuous actions that result (so Gundry).

Who are the "little ones" here? Throughout Matthew the "little ones" are disciples. Yet there may also be double meaning: they are all believers as despised by the world (so it refers to all relationships in the community) and also those of lower status in the community (thus referring also to economic and ethnic prejudice in the community). It may also be the leaders of the church looking down on those under them (so Luz).

18:10 For I tell you that their angels in heaven always look on the face of my Father who is in heaven (λέγω γὰρ ὑμῖν ὅτι οἱ ἄγγελοι αὐτῶν ἐν οὐρανοῖς διὰ παντὸς βλέπουσι τὸ πρόσωπον τοῦ πατρός μου τοῦ ἐν οὐρανοῖς). "For I say" (λέγω γάρ) is a shortened form of an ἀμήν-saying and points to a serious truth. The reason for respecting all fellow believers and treating them well is somewhat enigmatic. There is not a lot of material on guardian angels in Scripture, although there is supplementary teaching in Jewish literature. On this basis Carson follows Warfield in arguing that these are not angels but the departed spirits after death that see the Father's face.[2] Yet few have followed this because the language speaks of a present beholding rather than a future glory in God's presence and because it would be an unusual use of "angel" (though see Acts 12:15 with the same debate; most there too see a "guardian angel").

There is not much in Scripture to support the idea of guardian angels for each child of God — in the OT perhaps Gen 24:7, 40; 48:16; Ps 91:11 – 12 (cf. 34:7) and the idea of angels over nations (Dan 10:13; 12:1); and in the NT Acts 12:15; Heb 1:14 in addition to this passage. In Jewish literature the idea of guardian angels is more widespread (*1 En.* 100:5; Tob 5:4 – 15; *Jub.* 35:17; *3 Bar.* 12 – 13; *T. Jacob* 2:5; *T. Jos.* 6:7; *b. Šabb* 119b; *Gen. Rab.* 44:3). Since theirs is an earthly ministry, the idea of their "beholding the face of God" may refer to the access to God these angels have on behalf of their charges.[3] The special

2. Carson, "Matthew," 401, from B. B. Warfield, *Selected Shorter Writings*, 1:253 – 66.

3. See Witherington, *Matthew*, 348, who points out that "only some angels see the face of God" (cf. Isa 6:2; *1 En.* 14:21; and the references to the angels of the Presence in *Jub.* 2:2, 18 and *1 En.* 40). Thus the sense is that so important are these little ones that they have the top angels representing them in heaven, who have direct access to the 'face' of God." France,

glory they have is shared by the believers to whom they are assigned. The point is that each follower is special to God, and there is no place for disdain on the part of anyone.[4]

18:12 What do you think? If some person has a hundred sheep and one of them wanders astray, won't that person leave the ninety-nine on the hills and go[5] searching for the one that wandered off? (Τί ὑμῖν δοκεῖ; ἐὰν γένηταί τινι ἀνθρώπῳ ἑκατὸν πρόβατα καὶ πλανηθῇ ἓν ἐξ αὐτῶν, οὐχὶ ἀφήσει τὰ ἐνενήκοντα ἐννέα ἐπὶ τὰ ὄρη καὶ πορευθεὶς ζητεῖ τὸ πλανώμενον;). The opening "What do you think?" is frequent in Matthew (17:25; 21:28; 22:17, 42; 26:66) and invites the listener to ponder the message carefully. The parable, as Jesus does often, centers on a rhetorical question expecting the answer yes (οὐχί).

The herd of a hundred sheep is rather large and means a wealthy owner. The idea of God's people as a flock of sheep is frequent in the OT (Ps 77:20; Jer 3:15; 10:21), and Ezek 34 is especially intended, as seen in several parallels — "hills" = 34:6, "looks after" = 34:12, "strays" = 34:4, 16 (so Hagner, Luz). As Ezek 34 details the false shepherds of Israel, this is in part a poignant warning to the readers not to desert God's sheep.

There is double meaning in the concept of the shepherd here, as in Ezek 34. (1) God and Christ are the ones who shepherd their flock and search assiduously for straying followers (cf. Heb 13:20 – 21; 1 Pet 1:5). (2) The leaders of the church are responsible to care for the flock and must remain vigilant over it (cf. John 21:15 – 17; Heb 13:17; 1 Pet 5:2 – 4; remember that the imagery behind "pastor" is that of "shepherd"). (3) Every believer is warned in vv. 6 – 14 not to lead other "little ones" astray but rather to bring them back from wandering. (4) The "wandering" sheep are those in danger of falling away from their faith (vv. 6, 7 – 9 = Jas 5:19). The image here is powerful; would shepherds actually leave their flock helpless as they searched for a stray? The possible hyperbole strengthens the picture — God would![6]

18:13 And if that person finds it (καὶ ἐὰν γένηται εὑρεῖν αὐτό). Matthew has greatly simplified the ending of the parable (cf. Luke 15:5 – 7) and centers on the joy of finding it. The "if it may be" (ἐὰν γένηται) means "if he truly finds it," recognizing the fact that sheep were often killed by predators or fell into ravines and were lost (so Morris).

18:13 … I tell you the truth, he rejoices over that sheep more than over the ninety-nine that did not wander astray (ἀμὴν λέγω ὑμῖν ὅτι χαίρει ἐπ' αὐτῷ μᾶλλον ἢ ἐπὶ τοῖς ἐνενήκοντα ἐννέα τοῖς μὴ πεπλανημένοις). The emphasis is on the extent of the rejoicing (introduced by another "amen" [ἀμήν] saying to stress its importance, see 5:18). The μᾶλλον indicates God rejoices over the returned sheep "more than" those believers who remain in the fold. This hardly means he has no

Gospel of Matthew, 686 – 87, states that there is little evidence of general Jewish belief in guardian angels in the first century and prefers to think of angels representing the people of God as a whole before the throne of God.

4. Verse 11 ("For the Son of Man came to save the lost") is added in several manuscripts (D L^c TR lat et al.) but missing in others (ℵ B L* Θ 33 et al.) and most likely was added in assimilation to Luke 19:10 and because it aptly fits the imagery of v. 12.

5. As a circumstantial participle ("going, search") πορευθείς becomes almost a quasi-verb, "go searching."

6. See Paul J. Achtemeier, "It's the Little Things That Count (Mark 14:17 – 21; Luke 4:1 – 13; Matthew 18:10 – 14)," *BA* 46 (1983): 30 – 31, who points to the "not" (οὐχί) here to indicate God will always pursue his flock. See also J. M. Trau, "The Lost Sheep: A Living Metaphor," *TBT* 28 (1990): 277 – 83. Luke's parallel (Luke 15:7) refers to "ninety-nine righteous persons who do not need to repent" (alluding to the self-righteous Pharisees; cf. 15:2 and the older brother in 15:25 – 30). Matthew's whole stress is on God's compassion and the joy of reconciliation. Luke contrasts this joy with the contempt of the religious leaders.

joy in the faithful but rather highlights the importance of restoration. Parallel passages are found in Gal 6:1 (the "Spirit-led" restoration of those caught in sin) and especially Jas 5:19 – 20 (those who "bring them back" will "save them from death and cover over a multitude of sins"). The latter passage provides further reasons for the joy.[7]

18:14 Thus it is not the will of your Father in heaven that[8] one of these little ones perish (οὕτως οὐκ ἔστιν θέλημα ἔμπροσθεν τοῦ πατρὸς ὑμῶν τοῦ ἐν οὐρανοῖς ἵνα ἀπόληται ἓν τῶν μικρῶν τούτων). The importance of every single one of the "little ones," stated clearly in v. 6 and repeated in vv. 10, 12 – 13, is now finalized. God the supreme shepherd (for "Father in heaven," see 5:16, 45) does not want a single one to be lost. "Will before" (θέλημα ἔμπροσθεν) is a Semitism for the genitive (BDF §21.6, Davies and Allison) and adds emphasis to the idea of "the will of God." God's sovereign will is for the security of the believer, as in 2 Pet 3:9, "not wanting anyone to perish, but everyone to come to repentance." From this standpoint, it is inconceivable that the church and its leaders would fail to do the same, seeking always to protect the sheep both from predators and from the tendency to wander off. The mention of "perish" raises the stakes, for the end result is not just loss of reward but destruction.

Theology in Application

1. God's Love and Vigilance

God loves each member of his flock and is always vigilant over them. This whole section has centered on the compassion and mercy of God for each of the "little ones." The love of God is a frequent emphasis in Romans (Rom 5:5, 8; 8:31 – 39) and in the rest of the NT (2 Cor 13:14; 2 Thess 3:5; 1 John 2:5, 3:17, 4:9). The security of the believer is centered on God's love and concern for his children (e.g., Heb 13:5; 1 Pet 1:5, 5:7).

2. Emulating God's Concern

God's people must emulate God's concern by caring for and watching out for each other. In 5:48 Jesus said, "Be perfect ... as your heavenly Father is perfect." This means we are to be like God in every aspect of our lives; here that includes shepherding God's flock. God's deep-seated and active vigilance over even the weakest of his sheep must become the pattern for the church. The greatest joy a church will experience comes when a wandering member gets right with God. Moreover, every member should actively seek those who are failing spiritually and "restore" (Gal 6:1) them to Christ, the good Shepherd.

7. A version of this parable is found in *Gospel of Thomas* 107, probably a reworking of this Q story. In it the wandering sheep is the "largest," and there is no mention of the joy, just the shepherd's greater love for that sheep than for the others. The result is a quite different emphasis on God's playing favorites with his flock.

8. "That" (ἵνα) is virtually synonymous with "that" (ὅτι) in this instance and gives the content of God's "will."

CHAPTER 79

Matthew 18:15 – 20

Literary Context

The emphasis on relationships in 18:1 – 14 concluded with the centrality of bringing wandering sheep back into the fold. Here the method of doing so is described, i.e., discipline in the community. In vv. 6 – 9 the focus was on the danger of leading the "little ones" astray. Now we turn to another aspect, namely, offenses committed against other members of the community. Verus 10–14 centered on restoring those who strayed, here on disciplining those who sin.

V. Rejection, Suffering, and Glory (13:54 – 18:35)
- **B. Fourth Discourse: Life and Relationships in the Community (18:1 – 35)**
  1. Relationships in the Community (18:1 – 14)
  2. **Discipline and Forgiveness (18:15 – 35)**
     - ➦ **a. Discipline and Reconciliation (18:15 – 20)**
     - b. The Absolute Need for Forgiveness (18:21 – 35)

Main Idea

The process of discipline centers on those who refuse to "turn [their] lives around" (v. 3) and repent. In this instance, it covers what to do when a member sins and refuses to repent and return to the community; the goal is still redemptive, for at every stage the way is marked for reconciliation. There are three stages (private confrontation, challenge from two "witnesses," and judgment by the whole community); if at any stage the offending individual repents, full reconciliation will occur.

Translation

(See next page.)

Matthew 18:15-20

15a	Circumstance	*"If your brother or sister sins [against you],*
b	Exhortation	*go and reprove the person just between the two of you.*
c	Circumstance #1	*[1] If that person listens,*
d	Result of 15c	*you have won them over.*
16a	Circumstance #2	*[2] But*
		if they refuse to listen,
b	Exhortation	*take one or two others with you*
c	Purpose	*so that "every matter might be established*
		by the mouth of two or three witnesses."
17a	Circumstance	*But*
		if the person still refuses to listen to them,
b	Exhortation	*tell it to the church.*
c	Circumstance	*But*
		if they refuse to listen even to the church,
d	Result of 17c	*let them be to you as a Gentile or a tax collector.*
18a	Assertion/Promise	*I tell you the truth,*
		whatever you bind on earth will have been bound
		in heaven,
b	Assertion/Promise	*and whatever you loose on earth will have been loosed*
		in heaven.
19a	Assertion	*Again I tell you [the truth] . . .*
		it will be done for them by my Father in heaven
b	Condition	*if two of you agree on earth*
		about any matter you ask for.
20a	Basis for 19a-b	*For*
		where two or three are gathered together in my name,
20b	Assertion/Result	*there am I in the midst of them."*

Structure and Literary Form

This paraenetic passage centers on corporate responsibility and is similar to Qumran's *Manual of Discipline*, for it establishes the rules of the community for dealing with members who sin. It is loosely connected to Luke 17:3 ("If [any] brother or sister sins against you, rebuke them; and if they repent, forgive them"), which leads some to conclude that Q material lies behind it. But the differences are great, and it is M material on the whole. There are three parts to this passage: (1) the threefold pattern for discipline (vv. 15 – 17); (2) the authority of the church in discipline (v. 18); and (3) the presence of Christ with the church when disciplining (vv. 19 – 20). In the act of discipline Christ is especially present in the community.

Exegetical Outline

- **I. The Pattern for Church Discipline (18:15 – 17)**
  - A. Private confrontation (v. 15)
  - B. Judgment by two witnesses (v. 16)
  - C. Judgment by the whole community (v. 17)
- **II. Authority of the Church to Bind or Loose (18:18)**
- **III. The Presence of Christ with the Church (18:19 – 20)**
  - A. Confirmation of the decision by the Father (v. 19)
  - B. The presence of Christ during the decision (v. 20)

Explanation of the Text

18:15 If your brother or sister sins [against you][1] (Ἐὰν δὲ ἁμαρτήσῃ [εἰς σὲ] ὁ ἀδελφός σου). The presence of "your brother or sister" (ὁ ἀδελφός σου) means church relationships are in view. Whether "against you" is original in the Greek text or not, the immediate context indicates that the major idea is a sin committed against another believer, though if the phrase was added later, the basic teaching covers any type of sin committed. It is also clear from the whole context of vv. 15 – 17 that these are substantial and not just trivial sins. The conditional "if" (ἐάν) shows Jesus is discussing the possibility of such a sin occurring. When it does happen, however, action is mandatory (cf. 2 Cor 2:5 – 7; Gal 6:1; Heb 3:13).

18:15 . . . go and reprove the person just between the two of you (ὕπαγε ἔλεγξον αὐτὸν μεταξὺ σοῦ καὶ αὐτοῦ μόνου). ἐλέγχω means to "reprove and convict" someone, to "show them their fault" (BAGD). The goal obviously is to get such a person to repent and change his or her ways (cf. Lev 19:17b – 18a ("rebuke" without "bear[ing] a grudge"). This is not judgmentalism (cf. 7:1 – 5) but a desire to bring a wandering sheep (18:10 – 14) back into God's fold. The confrontation, moreover, must be private between the sinner and the one sinned against.

18:15 If that person listens, you have won them over (ἐάν σου ἀκούσῃ, ἐκέρδησας τὸν ἀδελφόν σου). It is between only that person and God at the initial stage. Therefore "listens" (ἀκούσῃ) means not just to hear what you have to say but to act on it and repent (it often contains the nuance of obedience). The idea of "winning" them (κερδαίνω) goes beyond the personal restoring of a brotherly or sisterly relationship but connotes also bringing them back into a right relationship with God (cf. 1 Cor 9:19 – 22; Phil 3:8; 1 Pet 3:1) — thus, reconciliation

1. While "against you" (εἰς σε) is found in DK LW Θ f[13] TR et al., it is missing in ℵ B f[1] et al. It may have been added to conform to v. 21, but it may have also been omitted to generalize the application to all types of sin. Most readings include them in brackets to indicate doubt. Still, as Gundry, *Matthew*, 367, and Davies and Allison, *Matthew*, 2:782, state, the presence of "just between the two of you" in the next clause favors its inclusion.

with the wounded party, with the church, and with God. The purpose of church discipline from the start is redemptive.

18:16 But if they refuse to listen, take one or two others with you (ἐὰν δὲ μὴ ἀκούσῃ, παράλαβε μετὰ σοῦ ἔτι ἕνα ἢ δύο). If the private confrontation is rejected, the next step comes into play, namely, the presence of others from the community. With the person who originally confronted the person, it becomes "two or three witnesses." This would likely be leaders in the community.[2]

18:16 ... so that "every matter might be established by the mouth of two or three witnesses" (ἵνα ἐπὶ στόματος δύο μαρτύρων ἢ τριῶν σταθῇ πᾶν ῥῆμα). Jesus now quotes Deut 19:15 (cf. Deut 17:6; 2 Cor 13:1; 1 Tim 5:19), the passage that establishes the legal precedent of two or three witnesses for any judicial situation. In Deuteronomy the context deals with criminal activity, but the passage applies also to community issues (so Carson, Luz). The primary purpose of the witnesses here is to affirm the "matter"[3] to the guilty party and help him or her realize the seriousness of the situation. Keener adds that the witnesses should gather evidence and ascertain the guilt of the person.[4] But if the person again refuses, the witnesses will have the additional duty of giving testimony at the trial before the whole community.[5] As in the private confrontation, the purpose of the second stage is primarily redemptive, to reconcile the sinner with the one they hurt and then to bring them back to God.

18:17 But if the person still refuses to listen to them, tell it to the church (ἐὰν δὲ παρακούσῃ αὐτῶν, εἰπὲ τῇ ἐκκλησίᾳ). παρακούω means "ignore, disobey, listen without heeding" (BAGD), and the plural "them" (αὐτῶν) refers to the three witnesses of v. 16. Only here and in 16:18 (see on that passage) is "church" (ἐκκλησία) found in the gospels. "The church" here is the local community, not the universal church. Discipline is always to be done in the local body and not to involve outsiders, even Christian outsiders.

The body as a whole is the final stage of appeal, the third time the offender is given the opportunity to admit wrong, repent, and be reconciled to the offended party, the local church, and God. Certainly the purpose of the local assembly is not just to declare the person guilty and render judgment, but to appeal to the offender as a corporate group and seek to bring about repentance.

18:17 But if they refuse to listen even to the church, let them be to you as a Gentile or a tax collector (ἐὰν δὲ καὶ τῆς ἐκκλησίας παρακούσῃ, ἔστω σοι ὥσπερ ὁ ἐθνικὸς καὶ ὁ τελώνης). The intensive καί ("even") draws this to a climax. They have "ignored" the pleas of the one they hurt, of the witnesses, and now even of the local church as a whole. The only recourse now is judgment. "Let him/her be to you" (ἔστω σοι) with the singular pronoun means that each member is part of the whole (the corporate view)[6] in carrying out the sentence.

2. Dennis C. Duling, "Matthew 18:15 – 17: Conflict, Confrontation, and Conflict Resolution in a 'Fictive Kin' Association," *BTB* 29 (1999): 4 – 22, describes the Christian community here as a "fictive kin" association by comparing the practice here with other groups like Qumran.

3. Thompson, *Matthew's Advice*, 182 – 83; and Luz, *Matthew 8 – 20*, 452, see the primary purpose of the witnesses to be warning and convincing the fellow disciple of the guilt, and thus "matter" (ῥῆμα) is not so much the content of the charges but the "word" of admonition.

4. Keener, *Matthew*, 454.

5. McNeile, *Matthew*, 266, says that both efforts at reconciliation and witness before the church if those efforts are rejected are part of the thrust here.

6. Contra Thompson, *Matthew's Advice*, 185, who says the singular refers not to the community but to the individuals who failed in their attempt to correct the brother. This is unlikely, for vv. 18 – 20 show the context is that of the church body as a whole.

The simile "as a Gentile or a tax collector" shows further that Matthew is writing primarily for Jewish Christians. The Gentiles were deeply despised by the Jews and completely shunned. The vision to Peter in the Cornelius story of Acts 10 shows that Peter had no problem converting a Gentile but had a great problem in entering a Gentile's home, where he would become unclean. The same is true of a tax collector (see on 5:46), who because of graft and conspiring with the hated Romans was also considered the lowest sort of person. So Christ here is talking about excommunication,[7] total ostracism and expulsion from the community (cf. Gen 17:14; Lev 17:4; Rom 16:17; 1 Cor 5:9 – 13; 2 Thess 3:14 – 15; 1 Tim 1:19 – 20; Titus 3:1 – 10).

This likely means to treat such a person as an unbeliever, someone outside the community. Senior, in fact, says that since Gentiles and tax collectors are objects of Jesus' ministry in Matthew (cf. 8:5 – 13; 9:9 – 13; 11:16 – 19) and are part of the subsequent ministry of the apostles (28:19), this may "suggest that the community's pastoral concern for the errant member does not end, even after the painful step of expulsion has taken place"[8]

18:18 I tell you the truth, whatever you bind on earth will have been bound in heaven, and whatever you loose on earth will have been loosed in heaven (Ἀμὴν λέγω ὑμῖν, ὅσα ἐὰν δήσητε ἐπὶ τῆς γῆς ἔσται δεδεμένα ἐν οὐρανῷ, καὶ ὅσα ἐὰν λύσητε ἐπὶ τῆς γῆς ἔσται λελυμένα ἐν οὐρανῷ). This is a virtually verbatim repetition of 16:19 (see the discussion of grammar and theological possibilities there), where it was part of the "keys of the kingdom" speech of Jesus after Peter's confession, with the major difference that the plurals here make it evident that the church as a whole has this authority, while the singular in 16:19 centers on Peter as the representative of the disciples. Also, the context makes this specifically applied to church discipline situations.

Thus the primary meaning here likely parallels John 20:23 in terms of retaining (= "binding") or forgiving (= "loosing") sins. The passive verbs used here are divine passives, which means that God is behind the community's decisions regarding forgiveness or condemnation of its wandering sheep/members. Behind this is the further aspect of church decisions as to which types of conduct are allowed and which are forbidden (so Morris).

18:19 Again I tell you [the truth][9] that if two of you agree on earth about any matter you ask for, it will be done for them by my Father in heaven (Πάλιν [ἀμὴν] λέγω ὑμῖν ὅτι ἐὰν δύο συμφωνήσωσιν ἐξ ὑμῶν ἐπὶ τῆς γῆς περὶ παντὸς πράγματος οὗ ἐὰν αἰτήσωνται, γενήσεται αὐτοῖς παρὰ τοῦ πατρός μου τοῦ ἐν οὐρανοῖς). "Again" (πάλιν) links this closely with the "I tell you the truth" of v. 18, so that even though some say this is a disconnected saying on prayer, it is not intended as such[10] but as a further statement regarding the authority of the church and its leaders in discipline situations. So

7. Some (e.g., Morris, Beare, France) believe this is not excommunication but personal ostracism by the offended brother or sister. However, this reads too much into the singular "to you" (σοι), for it occurs in the context of the whole community and more likely means each member of the community. It is also common to read too much into the absence of any mention of church leaders, as if Matthew's church was composed of equals, with no leadership. As Thompson, *Matthew's Advice*, 184, says, the presence of "church" implies organizational structure, but the text is not interested in such questions. We dare not read too much into the silence of the text.

8. Senior, *Matthew*, 210.

9. While B Θ TR include "amen" (ἀμήν), some (N W Δ) have "and" (δέ) instead, and ℵ D L omit it altogether. Therefore the UBS committee has placed it in brackets as doubtful.

10. Many popular preachers misuse this as a prayer promise and teach that our prayers control God, who has to give us "whatever we ask for." As Blomberg, *Matthew*, 280, says, "It ought to be obvious that God regularly does *not* fulfill a promise like that of v. 19 if it is interpreted as his response to any kind of request."

while "ask for" (αἰτέω) is often used of prayer in the NT, here it is specifically a prayer for wisdom and the Spirit's guidance in decisions regarding discipline.[11] Thus "any matter" (παντὸς πράγματος) is virtually synonymous with πᾶν ῥῆμα in v. 16, "every matter" that the church is facing in issues of discipline. The phrase here was commonly used in legal/judicial "matters" (so Hill, Carson).

The earth/heaven contrast is pivotal. The "heavenly Father" is in sovereign control of all earthly matters, and the only guarantee that earthly concerns will work out occurs when they are placed under God's control. That is especially true in discipline issues, when God's guidance must be behind the church's decision. Finally, the "two agreeing" refers back to the two or three witnesses of v. 16 (cf. v. 20).[12] The agreement is the church verdict regarding the case of vv. 15 – 17.

18:20 For where two or three are gathered together in my name, there am I in the midst of them (οὗ γάρ εἰσιν δύο ἢ τρεῖς συνηγμένοι εἰς τὸ ἐμὸν ὄνομα, ἐκεῖ εἰμι ἐν μέσῳ αὐτῶν). "For" (γάρ) provides the theological basis for v. 19. As there this seems to be a prayer promise and in a different context would have that connotation. Yet in this context it again refers mainly to the decision of a church regarding a discipline situation. The "two or three" as in vv. 16, 19 are the witnesses confronting the guilty person. As they make their decision, certainly while in prayer, Jesus wants them to understand that he is with them, and the "heavenly Father" is guiding their verdict.

The omnipresence of Jesus in the church is a central concept in Matthew (cf. 1:23; 28:20), and as Luz says, is "the christological center of the entire chapter."[13] Jesus is virtually declaring his divinity, for such a claim is possible only for God himself.[14] To gather "in my name" (εἰς τὸ ἐμὸν ὄνομα) means to be in union with Jesus, part of his community, and under his authority (cf. 7:22; 10:22; 18:5).[15] So Jesus is especially present among them, not just metaphorically but through the Spirit of Christ in their midst. This does not mean Jesus is with us only corporately and not individually, for as in 1 Cor 5:4 we can know that "the power of the Lord Jesus is present" with us.

Theology in Application

1. Address Sin

Sin, and in particular sinful actions between members of the community, must be addressed. Every member of the community is responsible for the reconciliation

11. The οὗ ἐάν does broaden the scope, "any matter *whatever* you ask for," but the context centers the focus on church discipline.

12. This could refer to the judges who preside in the church court looking into disciplinary situations (so Carson, Hagner, J. D. M. Derrett, "'Where Two or Three Are Convened in My Name . . .': A Sad Misunderstanding," *ExpTim* 91 [1979]: 83 – 86). The "two or three" of vv. 16, 20 would be legal witnesses or judges. However, this is not just a legal situation where the "two" litigants agree regarding the verdict, but any and all local disputes, legal or otherwise.

13. Luz, *Matthew 8 – 20*, 458.

14. Several (Davies and Allison, Hagner, Nolland) link this with the rabbinic saying that where two study the Torah together, the Shekinah glory is in their midst (*b. Sanh.* 39a; *b. Ber.* 5b). Thus Jesus is claiming to be the divine presence in the church.

15. Thompson, *Matthew's Advice*, 197 – 98, sees a parallel with Rev 16:14; 19:19; 20:7 – 8 and believes the "in" (εἰς) gives the purpose or reason for the church gathering, "to invoke the name of Jesus." S. von Dobbeler, "Die Versammlung 'auf meinem Namen hin' (Matt 18:20) as Identitäts und Differenzkriterium," *NovT* 44 (2002): 209 – 30, sees the name as a sign and identity marker for the community life of the church.

and restoration of saints who fail. Most Christians assume that the leaders of the church are the only ones responsible for discipline. Yet note that Jesus carefully refrains from even mentioning the leaders as having special responsibility in this. It is clear that every believer is responsible before God for maintaining the purity of the flock. As Hauerwas says,

> A community capable of protecting the little ones, a community who cares for the lost sheep, is a community that cannot afford to overlook one another's sins because doing so keeps the community from embodying the life of grace determined by God's forgiveness through the sacrifice of his Son.[16]

2. The Threefold Pattern of Discipline

The escalating pattern of discipline outlined here — individual confrontation followed by challenge from two or three and then from the whole church — shows common sense and should be the model for church discipline in our day. Again, the purpose is redemptive, bringing the guilty party back into right relationship with God and the church.

I used to say that the final stage, excommunication, needs to be replaced because it no longer works in a culture when the person can simply go down the street to another church.[17] But then I realized that this is indeed Christ's pattern, and the need is to turn our churches into families, so that it does matter when one is cut off from fellowship. Moreover, Paul's "hand [them] over to Satan" (1 Cor 5:5; 1 Tim 1:20) is critical alongside vv. 19 – 20, for they must understand that the church is reflecting God's decision, and God is going to allow Satan to do his terrible work in their lives so their "spirit may be saved on the day of the Lord" (1 Cor 5:5).

3. Discipline and Prayer

God guides the church in disciplinary decisions, and so the church must approach all such issues via deep prayer. The clear message of the passage is that the community will reflect God's verdict in all such decisions, and both vv. 19 and 20 apply prayer theology to the process. Therefore, the fact is that every step of the procedure must be bathed in prayer. The church has enormous authority to forgive and retain sins (cf. John 20:23), but it is not a unilateral power. Rather, it is mandatory that at all times the leaders and members render such verdicts off their knees in complete submission to God.

16. Hauerwas, *Matthew*, 165.

17. It is fairly common for scholars to believe this is no longer applicable in our day because of its "inconsistency" (so Luz) and because it has little effect in a church setting where the ostracized can just begin attending another church (so Hagner). We must remember that the basic OT text on rebuke, Lev 19:17, leads into the basic text on "love your neighbor" (Lev 19:18). These are two sides of the same coin.

CHAPTER 80

Matthew 18:21 – 35

Literary Context

The whole passage thus far (18:1 – 20) has recognized the redemptive side of discipline in the church. That aspect now comes into prominence with the parable of the unforgiving servant. Relationships in the community demand both discipline (vv. 6 – 9, 15 – 20) and reconciliation (vv. 10 – 14, 21 – 35). Yet even discipline has as its major purpose the restoration of the sinner to God and the community. This message is highlighted in this parable. The parable provides a theological underpinning to Jesus' command in v. 22 that the disciples must exercise boundless forgiveness (cf. 5:48, "Therefore, you must be perfect as your heavenly Father is perfect").

V. Rejection, Suffering, and Glory (13:54 – 18:35)
- **B. Fourth Discourse: Life and Relationships in the Community (18:1 – 35)**
  - 1. Relationships in the Community (18:1 – 14)
  - **2. Discipline and Forgiveness (18:15 – 35)**
    - a. Discipline and Reconciliation (18:15 – 20)
    - ➦ **b. The Absolute Need for Forgiveness (18:21 – 35)**
      - **(1) Introduction — The Need for Forgiveness (18:21 – 22)**
      - **(2) The Parable of the Unmerciful Slave (18:23 – 34)**
      - **(3) Conclusion — A Warning on the Necessity of Forgiveness (18:35)**

Main Idea

When one has experienced forgiveness from God (vv. 24 – 27), it is incumbent on them to forgive others (vv. 28 – 29); the forgiven must in turn be forgiving. If they refuse, they can expect to be judged in turn by God (vv. 31 – 34; cf. 6:14 – 15). When the disciplined person repents (vv. 15 – 20), the church must forgive (vv. 21 – 35).

Translation

Matthew 18:21-35

21a	Question	**Then Peter came to Jesus and asked,**
b		*"Lord, how many times should I forgive my brother or sister*
		who sins against me?
c		*As many as seven times?"*
22a	Answer	**Jesus said to him,**
b		*"I tell you, not just seven times, but*
		as many as seventy-seven times.
	Episode: Parable	
23a	Comparison	*Therefore, the kingdom of heaven is like a king*
		who wants to settle accounts with his slaves.
24a		*As he began this process,*
b	Scene #1	*a man was brought to him*
c	Problem	*who owed ten thousand talents.*
25a		*Since he was unable to pay it back,*
b	Command	*his lord commanded that he be sold,*
		along with his wife and
		children and
		all his possessions,
c	Purpose	*so that the debt could be repaid.*
26a	Request	*So the slave fell down on his knees, saying,*
b		*'Be patient with me, and I will repay everything to you.'*
27a	Result	*Then that slave's lord had compassion,*
		let him go, and
		cancelled his debt.
28a	Scene #2	*Then that slave went and found one of his fellow slaves,*
b	Parallel 24c	*who owed him a hundred denarii,*
c		*and he grabbed the fellow and began to choke him, saying,*
d		*'Pay what you owe!'*
29a		*So his fellow slave fell down and begged him,*
b	Parallel 26b	*'Be patient with me, and I will repay you.'*
30a	Contrast 27a	*But he did not want to do so.*
b	Result	*Instead, he went and*
		had the man thrown into prison
c		*until he could pay back what was owed.*

Continued on next page.

Continued from previous page.

31a	Scene #3	So when his fellow slaves saw what happened,
b	Reaction	they were greatly distressed,
c	Action	and they went and reported to the lord everything that had happened.
32a	Response	Then his lord summoned him and said,
b		[1] 'Wicked slave, I cancelled your whole debt for you because you begged me to.
33a	Question/Accusation	[2] Shouldn't you also have shown the same mercy to your fellow slave
b		as I had shown you?'
34a		And filled with wrath,
b	Result	his lord handed him over to the torturers
c		until he could repay all that was owed.
35a	Comparison	In the same way my heavenly Father will also do this to you unless each of you forgives your brother or sister from your heart."

Structure and Literary Form

The parable comes from Matthew's own special material, though the introduction (vv. 21 – 22) is similar to Luke 17:4 and may come from Q material. There are three parts: the introduction on forgiving not seven but seventy-seven times (vv. 21 – 22), the parable proper (vv. 23 – 34), and a conclusion on the necessity of heartfelt forgiveness (vv. 35). The parable can be broken into three scenes: (1) the king and his slave, centering on the cancellation of an incredible debt (vv. 23 – 27); (2) the slave and a fellow slave, centering on the refusal to cancel a relatively small debt (vv. 28 – 30); and (3) the king's reversal of his prior decision, forcing the first slave to pay the ultimate debt because of his folly (vv. 31 – 34).

Exegetical Outline

➡ **I. Introduction: The Need for Forgiveness (18:21 – 22)**

A. Peter's question on the extent of forgiveness (v. 21)

B. Jesus' response regarding the universality of forgiveness (v. 22)

II. The Parable of the Unmerciful Slave (18:23 – 34)

A. The king and his slave (vv. 23 – 27)

1. The king's decision to settle accounts (v. 23)
2. The impossible debt and the terrible payment (vv. 24 – 25)

3. The plea for mercy is granted (vv. 26 – 27)

B. The slave and his fellow slave (vv. 28 – 30)

1. The small debt and the harsh response (v. 28)
2. The plea for mercy is rejected (vv. 29 – 30)

C. The king reverses his decision (vv. 31 – 34)

1. The other slaves report the incident to the king (v. 31)
2. The king confronts the wicked slave for his harsh decision (vv. 32 – 33)
3. The king demands the ultimate penalty — torture (v. 34)

III. Conclusion: A Warning on the Necessity of Forgiveness (18:35)

Explanation of the Text

18:21 Then Peter came to Jesus and asked (Τότε προσελθὼν ὁ Πέτρος εἶπεν αὐτῷ). Peter acts for the final time (in chs. 14 – 18) as the spokesman for the disciples. Forgiveness is a major emphasis in Matthew's ethical teaching. In 6:12, 14 the willingness to forgive others is essential to experiencing God's forgiveness; it is the only element of the Lord's Prayer that Jesus elaborated. In 9:2, 6 the healing of the paralytic established Jesus' divine authority to forgive sins (cf. 12:31 – 32 on God's authority to forgive or withhold forgiveness). Then in 26:28 Jesus' eucharistic cup signifies his atoning sacrifice for "forgiveness of sins."

18:21 "Lord, how many times should I forgive my brother or sister who sins against[1] me? As many as seven times?" (Κύριε, ποσάκις ἁμαρτήσει εἰς ἐμὲ ὁ ἀδελφός μου καὶ ἀφήσω αὐτῷ; ἕως ἑπτάκις;). Peter's question reflects the rabbinic discussion regarding the limits of forgiveness, which they said was three times (*b. Yoma* 86b – 87a; the use of the future tense means Peter is thinking of later possibilities). Peter's extension[2] of that to a sevenfold pattern of forgiveness may reflect OT precedents, e.g., the sevenfold vengeance on anyone murdering Cain (Gen 4:15); the blood sprinkled seven times for atonement (Lev 26:18, 21); the sevenfold punishment for sin (Lev 26:18). It is possible Peter uses a traditional symbol for themes of "vengeance, expiation, and forgiveness."[3] At the same time, since seven symbolizes perfection, Peter could be asking whether he must forgive perfectly (so Luz).

18:22 Jesus said to him, "I tell you, not just seven times, but as many as seventy-seven times" (λέγει αὐτῷ ὁ Ἰησοῦς, Οὐ λέγω σοι ἕως ἑπτάκις ἀλλὰ ἕως ἑβδομηκοντάκις ἑπτά). This seemingly reflects the LXX of Gen 4:24 on Lamech's "seventy-seven"-fold vengeful spirit, establishing a contrast between the two. Lamech celebrated his vengeance; Jesus here abrogates it altogether. ἑβδομηκοντάκις can mean "seventy-seven" (NRSV, NIV, NJB) or "seventy times seven" (KJV, NASB, NLT);[4] but either way the emphasis is not on the number but on the boundless nature of the forgiveness. Blomberg quotes McNeile's excellent summary: "The unlimited revenge of primitive man has given place to the unlimited forgiveness of Christians."[5]

Jesus' point is not a limit of the times forgiveness must occur (a total of seventy-seven times)

1. As in v. 15, εἰς here is used in a hostile sense, "against" (BAGD, 229c).

2. Note the intensive καί, "do I *even* have to forgive the person?"

3. Davies and Allison, *Matthew*, 2:792.

4. BAGD, 213, says it could be either but is more likely "seventy-seven" (as in Gen 4:24).

5. McNeile, *Matthew*, 268, in Blomberg, *Matthew*, 281.

but the boundless nature of forgiveness, beyond perfection (as "seventy-seven" is beyond "seven"). As God's mercy is without limit, so the forgiveness of the saints must be infinite.

18:23 Therefore, the kingdom of heaven is like[6] a king who wants to settle accounts with his slaves (Διὰ τοῦτο ὡμοιώθη ἡ βασιλεία τῶν οὐρανῶν ἀνθρώπῳ βασιλεῖ, ὃς ἠθέλησεν συνᾶραι λόγον μετὰ τῶν δούλων αὐτοῦ). The parable begins with "therefore" (διὰ τοῦτο), a favorite introductory phrase in Matthew (eleven times), used to show that forgiveness is a kingdom characteristic. "King" (βασιλεύς) is found only here, with "lord" (ὁ κύριος) used in the rest of the parable, probably to stress the connection with God, the "Lord" of all.

This king makes a decision ("wants" [θέλω]) to "settle accounts" or work out the debts of all his δοῦλοι, a term normally meaning "slaves" rather than "servants."[7] In a context like this the term often refers to the civil servants under the king, who in the ancient world were considered virtual slaves of the king. That makes sense in this parable with the huge amount of the debt. It is also generally acknowledged that Jesus is using the image of a Gentile court here, with absolute royal authority and officials in the court. Galilean listeners would be familiar with such practices through the rule of the Herodian family, which often followed Hellenistic patterns.[8] A parable centering on debts makes sense here, since in 6:12 (the Lord's Prayer), Matthew has "Forgive our sins."

18:24 As he began this process, a man was brought to him who owed ten thousand talents (ἀρξαμένου δὲ αὐτοῦ συναίρειν προσηνέχθη αὐτῷ εἷς ὀφειλέτης μυρίων ταλάντων). This verse begins with another of Matthew's many temporal genitive absolutes (see on 8:1). The man[9] must have been the treasurer of the kingdom or a major governor, for the debt was incalculably high. A "talent" was the highest monetary standard, and a "myriad" was the highest number that could be stated. Since a "talent" was the amount of weight a soldier could carry on his back, it referred to 75 to 100 pounds of gold or silver, depending on which standard was used (= 6,000 denarii, with a denarius the pay for a day's work by the average laborer, thus 20 years of work).[10] If you multiply $1,000 (the approximate cost of an ounce of gold today) by 16 (ounces in a pound), then by 75 (pounds), then by 10,000 (talents), the equivalent worth today is twelve billion dollars (if gold is worth $600 an ounce and 100 pounds, it is 9.6 billion dollars)![11]

David and the leaders of Israel respectively gave 3,000/5,000 talents of gold and 7,000/10,000 talents of silver for the building of the temple (1 Chr

6. As stated in 13:24, "it is like" (ὡμοιώθη) connotes the idea "it is the case with the kingdom as with this story."

7. See *EDNT*, 1:350. Hagner, *Matthew 14 – 28*, 538, brings out the eschatological overtones of judgment in this phrase, cf. 25:19 (the parable of the talents, where the phrase is repeated). Eschatological judgment is hardly found in this verse, but there is an underpinning of this concept in the parable as a whole.

8. See Keener, *Matthew*, 457, who follows Derrett, *Law in the New Testament*, 30. Both think these are tax farmers whose profit is dependent on everyone paying and so are ruthless in collecting the tax debts. While interesting, it is not as likely as royal officials. Both amounts are too high for taxes.

9. The use of "one" (εἷς) for a single person (= indefinite article) is common, cf. BDF §247 (2).

10. Turner, "Matthew," 242 – 43, calculates the total at 193,000 years of labor by the average person and points out that BAGD, 661, translates it "zillions."

11. This is so astronomical that many believe it is a Matthean addition and that Jesus originally had a much lower number, cf. Davies and Allison, *Matthew*, 2:796; and M. C. DeBoer, "Ten Thousand Talents? Matthew's Interpretation and Redaction of the Parable of the Unforgiving Servant (Matt, 18:23 – 35)" *CBQ* 50 (1988): 214 – 32, who suggests it originally was 10,000 denarii. Yet Jesus frequently used shocking hyperbole (cf. 5:29 – 30; 18:8 – 9), and this is no different.

29:3 – 7), and Josephus said a total of 600 talents were collected in taxes from Judea and Samaria in 4 BC (*Ant.* 17.320). No reader could conceive of such an amount as in this parable, and Jesus' hearers would simply have thought of an impossibly large debt, like a child saying "a million gadzillions."

18:25 Since he was unable to pay it back, his[12] lord commanded that he be sold,[13] along with his wife and children and all his possessions, so that the debt could be repaid (μὴ ἔχοντος δὲ αὐτοῦ ἀποδοῦναι ἐκέλευσεν αὐτὸν ὁ κύριος πραθῆναι καὶ τὴν γυναῖκα καὶ τὰ τέκνα καὶ πάντα ὅσα ἔχει, καὶ ἀποδοθῆναι). The causal participle "having" (ἔχοντος) in a genitive absolute construction states the ironic fact that this "slave" (δοῦλος) could not pay back such an enormous sum. Very few people in the history of this world could ever have paid such a debt, and it is no wonder that this slave was not able to do so. So his "master" ordered that all his possessions be confiscated and his whole family sold into slavery.

This was commonplace in the OT, where the Torah allowed it (Exod 21:2 – 11; 22:2; 2 Kgs 4:1; Neh 5:5, 8; Amos 2:6; 8:6). In the Roman world, it has been estimated that the majority of slaves were due to debt (since the Roman world had been largely conquered and there were not as many captives in battle as before). Certainly the amount recovered from the sale would not begin to cover the amount owed, but it would serve justice by the standards of that day.

18:26 So the slave fell down on his knees, saying, "Be patient with me, and I will repay everything to you" (πεσὼν οὖν ὁ δοῦλος προσεκύνει αὐτῷ λέγων, Μακροθύμησον ἐπ' ἐμοί, καὶ πάντα ἀποδώσω σοι). The strong imagery of "falling down" and "prostrating"[14] himself before the king shows how desperate the man was. He begs for mercy and "patience" (with "be patient" [μακροθυμέω] often used of God's "long-suffering" toward Israel in the LXX). The very same plea will be made by the fellow slave in v. 29. Obviously the man could never "pay back everything" with such a huge debt. So the king's mercy is given even greater emphasis by this patently ridiculous pledge.

18:27 Then that slave's lord had compassion,[15] let him go, and cancelled his debt (σπλαγχνισθεὶς δὲ ὁ κύριος τοῦ δούλου ἐκείνου ἀπέλυσεν αὐτόν, καὶ τὸ δάνειον ἀφῆκεν αὐτῷ). The king responded to the official's pleas. "Have compassion" (σπλαγχνίζομαι) is used elsewhere in Matthew of Jesus' compassion (cf. 9:36; 14:14) and points to divine compassion for sinners. The king's heart was moved, and he "cancelled" (ἀφίημι, the term for forgiveness in v. 21) the "debt" (δάνειον, meaning the "loan" itself). A "debt" was a metaphor for sin in the first century (6:12; cf. Luke 7:41 – 43). This would surprise the audience and readers, who would assume the king would see through the false bravado of the servant and realize there was no hope of repaying the loan. In this sense it is a perfect picture of God, who shows grace and mercy to undeserving sinners.

18:28 Then that slave went and found one of his fellow slaves, who owed him a hundred denarii (ἐξελθὼν δὲ ὁ δοῦλος ἐκεῖνος εὗρεν ἕνα

12. This is another example of the article standing for the possessive pronoun, see Wallace, 215 – 16.

13. The passive infinitive for the action to be carried out is common with "command" (κελεύω, BAGD, 427).

14. The imperfect "fell down on his knees" (προσεκύνει) is graphic, dramatically picturing the man in total submission on the ground before the king. It is doubtful that "worship" is connoted, rather begging in total surrender to the king's mercy.

15. Matthew likes circumstantial participles (as here and in vv. 26, 28), which tell action that is linked closely with the main verb.

τῶν συνδούλων αὐτοῦ, ὃς ὤφειλεν αὐτῷ ἑκατὸν δηνάρια). The amount owed by the fellow slave is significant, representing a hundred days of earnings by a common laborer, but it is nothing compared to the previous loan that was 600,000 times as great.[16] The difference corresponds to the issue of forgiveness — God has forgiven us at least 600,000 sins in our lives, and we are unwilling to forgive one sin committed against us?!

18:28 ... and he grabbed the fellow and began to choke him, saying, "Pay what you owe" (καὶ κρατήσας αὐτὸν ἔπνιγεν λέγων, Ἀπόδος εἴ τι ὀφείλεις). The contrast between the king's mercy and the slave's violent reaction could not be more stark. The same person who prostrated himself on the ground now begins to choke his debtor (ingressive imperfect ἔπνιγεν) in a way similar to the violence of the wicked servant in 24:49a. The one who begged, "Be patient ... and I will repay you," now demands immediate repayment.

18:29 So his fellow slave fell down and begged him, "Be patient with me, and I will repay you" (πεσὼν οὖν ὁ σύνδουλος αὐτοῦ παρεκάλει αὐτὸν λέγων, Μακροθύμησον ἐπ' ἐμοί, καὶ ἀποδώσω σοι). The language closely resembles v. 26, showing the similarities between the two slave's reactions to their dangerous predicaments. The major difference is that this second fellow doesn't promise specifically to repay "everything," probably because the relatively small debt could be repaid fully. The first slave's promise was false bravado, while this slave's pledge could be fulfilled. This brings to mind the Golden Rule of 7:12; one would expect the first slave to "do to the other" as he would "like people to do to him." But that is not to be!

18:30 But he did not want to do so. Instead, he went and had the man thrown into prison until he could pay back what was owed (ὁ δὲ οὐκ ἤθελεν ἀλλὰ ἀπελθὼν ἔβαλεν αὐτὸν εἰς φυλακὴν ἕως ἀποδῷ τὸ ὀφειλόμενον). The harsh refusal of the first slave stands in total contrast to the undeserved compassion and mercy of the king in v. 27. The man had learned nothing from his experience of grace earlier. Note first the complete act of the will ("want" [ἤθελεν]) in refusing to hear the poor man's pleas, as well as the fact that he walked away (ἀπελθών, "went away") from the situation and had others do his bidding.

By using the passive participle "what was owed" (τὸ ὀφειλόμενον), the emphasis is also on the process of repaying the debt in full as well as the fact that his family and friends would have to pay it for him as he languished in prison.[17] Imprisonment was often done in cases of heavy debt as a way to force the family to pay it. But what is stressed here is the terrible hypocrisy of one who was forgiven so much and yet refused to forgive so little. The lesson is directly applicable to the kind of forgiveness Peter asked about in v. 21.

18:31 So when his fellow slaves saw what happened, they were greatly distressed, and they went and reported to the lord everything that had happened (ἰδόντες οὖν οἱ σύνδουλοι αὐτοῦ τὰ γενόμενα ἐλυπήθησαν σφόδρα καὶ ἐλθόντες διεσάφησαν τῷ κυρίῳ ἑαυτῶν πάντα τὰ γενόμενα). The other slaves "saw" it all (temporal participle ἰδόντες) and had an intense reaction. "Distressed" (ἐλυπήθησαν) has overtones of both grief and indignation, and the depth of their reaction at the man's harsh hypocrisy led them to report it all to the king, with διασαφέω meaning to

16. Luz, *Matthew 8 – 20*, 473, figures this on the basis of the Attic talent that was worth 6,000 drachmae/denarii.

17. Luz, *Matthew 8 – 20*, 473, points out that the first slave could not sell the man because Jewish law forbid selling a person into slavery unless the debt was at least as much as the slave price (*Meh. Exod.* 22:2; *b. Qidd.* 18a). Since that was not the case, he had to have his fellow slave thrown into prison.

"tell in detail" or "explain fully" the events to the king.

18:32 Then his lord summoned him and said, "Wicked slave, I cancelled your whole debt for you because you begged me to" (τότε προσκαλεσάμενος αὐτὸν ὁ κύριος αὐτοῦ λέγει αὐτῷ, Δοῦλε πονηρέ, πᾶσαν τὴν ὀφειλὴν ἐκείνην ἀφῆκά σοι, ἐπεὶ παρεκάλεσάς με). This verse is framed with -καλέω verbs, with the king "summoning" the former "beggar." The "wicked slave" will appear again in the parable of the talents (25:26) and refers to those who refuse to live by God's rules but follow their own dictates. The king reminds him of the great mercy he had received when the king had "forgiven" (ἀφῆκα) the whole massive debt he had accrued.

18:33 "Shouldn't you also have shown the same mercy to your fellow slave as I had shown you?" (οὐκ ἔδει καὶ σὲ ἐλεῆσαι τὸν σύνδουλόν σου, ὡς κἀγὼ σὲ ἠλέησα;). The repetition of ἐλεέω in both clauses shows that the primary thrust here is on "showing mercy." Since the first slave had experienced mercy from the king, he should have followed that model and shown mercy in turn to his own debtor (cf. Luke 6:36 in the Sermon on the Plain, "Be merciful, just as your Father is merciful"). The use of "should" (ἔδει) here makes this a necessity, not an option. It was required of the man (and of us!). This is the basic message of the parable: Once we have experienced God's merciful forgiveness, it is mandatory that we show that same forgiveness to others (cf. 6:14 – 15).

18:34 And filled with wrath, his lord handed him over to the torturers until he could repay all that was owed (καὶ ὀργισθεὶς ὁ κύριος αὐτοῦ παρέδωκεν αὐτὸν τοῖς βασανισταῖς ἕως οὗ ἀποδῷ πᾶν τὸ ὀφειλόμενον). This is the principle of *lex talionis*, the "law of retribution." What we do to others, God will do to us (a major theme in the book of Revelation, cf. Rev 16:5 – 7; 20:12 – 13; 22:12). The wrathful refusal to forgive has led the first slave to experience his king's wrath in turn. For his folly the man receives a more harsh punishment than he would have at the first. Moreover, the debt is so great that "all that was owed" could never be repaid, so this amounts to a lifelong punishment. Torture was not practiced in Judaism but was used by the Romans and the Herodian dynasty (cf. Josephus, *War* 1.548). The eschatological overtones are clear: God will be "filled with wrath" and will punish those who refuse to show mercy and forgiveness in the church.

18:35 In the same way my heavenly Father will also do this to you unless each of you forgives your brother or sister from your heart (οὕτως καὶ ὁ πατήρ μου ὁ οὐράνιος ποιήσει ὑμῖν, ἐὰν μὴ ἀφῆτε ἕκαστος τῷ ἀδελφῷ αὐτοῦ ἀπὸ τῶν καρδιῶν ὑμῶν). This verse makes the allegory behind the parable clear and frames it with vv. 21 – 22 on forgiveness. "In the same way" (οὕτως) defines the connection, providing the "moral of the story" as well as a serious warning. Forgiveness and mercy are essential aspects of kingdom living, and those who refuse to do so will not be shown forgiveness or mercy by God (cf. 5:7; 6:14; 9:13; 12:7; Jas 2:13).

The future "will do" (ποιήσει) likely has an inaugurated thrust: for the rest of our lives as well as at the final judgment we will receive what we have earned with our ethical decisions. ἕκαστος means it is not just a corporate responsibility of the church as a whole but a requirement for "each" of its members. Both in the corporate aspect of church discipline and in the individual aspect of forgiveness, judgment will occur if God's mercy is not extended to the repentant sinner. Moreover, this mercy must stem "from your heart," meaning with all sincerity and not through pretension or due to legalistic requirements (so France, Davies and Allison).

Theology in Application

This concludes Jesus' discourse on relationships in the church community and as such sums up the themes discussed throughout this chapter. Yet it still has a point of its own, namely, that God's demands that every believer emulate what he or she has experienced in terms of mercy and forgiveness from God, and that forgiveness is a community responsibility and not just that of the individual.[18]

1. Unbounded Mercy and Undeserved Forgiveness

In the parable, as was pointed out, the first slave's debt to the king was 600,000 times as great as his fellow slave's debt to him was. That percentage is probably close to our own situations. God has likely forgiven each of us at least 600,000 sins over our lifetime. Think about it this way: say you are forty years old, which means you have lived 14,600 days and 350,400 hours. How many sins do you suppose you committed in that time? At least two per hour? Because Christ gave himself as the atoning sacrifice on the cross, all of those sins have been forgiven, not because of who you are or what you have accomplished but because of his infinite love and forgiveness. Of course this has been only an illustration; it is not about counting our sins but about the incredibly great debt our sins have produced.

2. Forgiveness Reciprocated

God expects us to apply our experience of divine forgiveness to our relationships and to show mercy and forgiveness to others even when they don't deserve it. After having been forgiven of at least 600,000 sins, to refuse to forgive one sin against us by another member of the community is a serious transgression. A willingness to forgive must be labeled a basic characteristic of true discipleship. Christ is unequivocal on this point.

Clearly those who are bitter and refuse to forgive a wrong they have experienced are under indictment from God and will be punished. Yet it must also be admitted that forgiveness is not an easy thing to do, especially when one has undergone serious wrongs like physical or sexual abuse. Christ is not saying that forgiveness must be instantaneous. It is a process often demanding a great deal of time and counseling. Still, mercy and forgiveness should at all times be the goal for which we strive. Moreover, this is a community and not just an individual responsibility; reconciliation must be the goal of all, and when we are deeply hurt, we need the counsel and help of our brothers and sisters in the church family.

18. On the community implications, see S. E. Hylen, "Forgiveness and Life in the Community," *Int* 54 (2000): 146 – 57.

CHAPTER 81

Matthew 19:1 – 12

Introduction to the Movement to the Cross (Matthew 19:1 – 25:46)

The fifth and final combination of narrative (19:1 – 22:46) and discourse (23:1 – 25:46) prepares the reader for the final events of Jesus life — his passion and resurrection. We will make some comments on the narrative section here and on the Olivet Discourse later. The narrative falls into two distinct sections, the road to Jerusalem (19:1 – 20:34) and the beginning events of Passion Week (21:1 – 22:46). In both sections Matthew largely follows Mark 10 – 12, but with some significant redactional changes and additions.

The debate is whether ch. 23 belongs with the narrative material[1] or with the discourse material.[2] There are strengths to both sides, since ch. 23 has clear structural ties to 19:1 – 22:46 (guilt and judgment) as well as to 24:1 – 25:46 (it functions like ch. 5 in the Sermon on the Mount, with the woes of ch. 23 balancing the beatitudes in ch. 5). It is probably best to steer a middle course, viewing ch. 23 as a discourse but separate from the Olivet Discourse (so Hagner). Its negative tone and seven woes both provide an indictment against the leaders whose constant opposition is a feature of chs. 19 – 22 and an introduction to chs. 24 – 25. If you think of it as a courtroom setting, ch. 23 is the evidence and chs. 24 – 25 the verdict for the nation's (and its leaders') rejection of its Messiah. Therefore the solution is to see the fifth discourse as a two-part literary work, chs. 23 and 24 – 25.

Literary Context

The new narrative section begins on a geographical note, with Jesus starting his final trip to Jerusalem by leaving Galilee for Judea. Then vv. 3 – 12 renew the hostilities between Jesus and the Pharisees as the latter try to "test" Jesus with their question on divorce. This continues the emphasis on relationships from ch. 18 by

1. So Carson, Gnilka, Davies and Allison, Nolland, Witherington, Turner, France, primarily due to the different tone and audiences of 23:1 (the crowds and disciples) and 24:3 (the disciples alone).

2. So Gundry, Blomberg, Keener, since 13:36 also has a shift from crowds to disciples.

discussing the central relationship of all, marriage and family (see on children in vv. 13 – 15). Jesus has just talked about forgiveness, and the marriage relationship is the most intense example of that need. In fact, Carter believes that family and household structures provide the coherence to chs. 19 – 20 as a whole.[3] Finally, Jesus' response continues the theme of Jesus as the final interpreter of Torah (cf. 5:17 – 20) when Jesus corrects his enemies' misunderstanding of Gen 1:27 and 2:24 (vv. 4 – 5).

V. Rejection, Suffering, and Glory (13:54 – 18:35)
VI. The Movement to the Cross (19:1 – 25:46)
A. Jesus' Deeds: Opposition and Discipleship (19:1 – 22:46)
1. The Road to Jerusalem (19:1 – 20:34)
➦ **a. The Question on Divorce (19:1 – 12)**
b. Blessing the Children (19:13 – 15)

Main Idea

There are three major points here: (1) the movement of Jesus to his destiny in Jerusalem (signified in the passion predictions but here found in the geographical movement); (2) continuing opposition from the Pharisees, who try to trap Jesus in a point of Torah; and (3) important teaching on both marriage/divorce (vv. 3 – 9) and celibacy (vv. 10 – 12), with the reality of the kingdom demanding a stronger view of the sanctity of marriage and a recognition that both marriage and celibacy are valid kingdom realities.

Translation

Matthew 19:1-12

1a	Introduction	And it happened that
		when Jesus had finished saying these things,
b		**he went away from Galilee and**
c	Setting	**came into the region of Judea across the Jordan.**
2a	Action	And **large crowds followed him,**
b	Result of 2a/Healing	and **he healed them there.**

3. Warren Carter, *Households and Discipleship: A Study of Matthew 19 – 20* (JSNTSup 103; Sheffield: JSOT Press, 1994), 18.

3a	Question/Test	**Some Pharisees came in order to test him, saying,**
b		*"Is it lawful for a man to divorce his wife*
		for any reason whatever?"
4a	Response	But **Jesus replied,**
b		*"You have read, haven't you,*
c	OT Quotation	*that from the beginning*
		the Creator 'made them male and female?'"
		(Gen 1:27)
5a		And **he said,**
b	OT Quotation	*[1] "'For this reason*
		a man will leave his father and mother and
		be united with his wife,
c		*[2] and the two will be one flesh.'* (Gen 2:24)
6a	Assertion	*So they are no longer two, but one flesh.*
b	Inference	*Therefore, what God has joined together, let no one separate."*
7a	Question	**They asked him,**
b		*"Why then did Moses command the husband*
		to give a certificate of divorce and
		release her?"
8a		**Jesus told them,**
b	Answer/Assertion	*"Moses permitted you to divorce your wives*
		because of the hardness of your hearts.
c	Assertion	*But it was not like this from the beginning.*
9a	Warning	*Now I am telling you that whoever divorces his wife, except*
		for immorality, and marries another commits adultery."
10a	Response	**His disciples said to him,**
b		*"If the relationship between a husband and wife is like this,*
c		*it is better not to marry."*
11a	Response	But **he told them,**
b		*"Not everyone can grasp this word, but*
c		*only those to whom it has been given.*
12a	Option #1	*For there are eunuchs who have been born this way*
		from the mother's womb,
b	Option #2	*and there are eunuchs who have been made eunuchs by people.*
c	Option #3	*And there are eunuchs who have made themselves eunuchs*
		for the sake of the kingdom of heaven.
d	Exhortation	*Let the one who is able to grasp it do so."*

Structure and Literary Form

Verses 1 – 2, 3 – 9 follow Mark (= Mark 10:1, 2 – 12)[4] while vv. 10 – 12 stem from Matthew's special material (M). Essentially, this passage centers on questions of Torah and is usually called a controversy dialogue. After the introductory vv. 1 – 2, each section is introduced by a question, vv. 3 – 6 on the legality of unlimited divorce, vv. 7 – 9 on the limits of divorce permitted, and vv. 10 – 12 (an implied question) on celibacy.

Exegetical Outline

➦ **Introduction: Jesus Begins His Journey (19:1 – 2)**
   A. Jesus leaves Galilee for Judea (v. 1)
   B. Jesus heals many among the following crowds (v. 2)

I. The Legality of Unlimited Divorce (19:3 – 6)
   A. The Pharisees test Jesus with a question (v. 3)
   B. Jesus quotes Torah (Gen 1:27; 2:24) (vv. 4 – 5)
   C. Conclusion: the indissolubility of marriage (v. 6)

II. The Limits of Divorce (19:7 – 9)
   A. The question regarding Moses allowing divorce (v. 7)
   B. The basis of divorce — hardness of heart (v. 8)
   C. The limits — only one exception, immorality (v. 9)

III. The Place of Celibacy (19:10 – 12)
   A. The disciples' reaction: better not to marry (v. 10)
   B. The division over celibacy (v. 11)
   C. The types of celibacy (v. 12)

Explanation of the Text

19:1 And it happened that when Jesus had finished saying these things, he went away from Galilee and came into the region of Judea across the Jordan (Καὶ ἐγένετο ὅτε ἐτέλεσεν ὁ Ἰησοῦς τοὺς λόγους τούτους, μετῆρεν ἀπὸ τῆς Γαλιλαίας καὶ ἦλθεν εἰς τὰ ὅρια τῆς Ἰουδαίας πέραν τοῦ Ἰορδάνου). The first clause is Matthew's formula for ending a discourse (cf. 7:28; 11:1; 13:53; 26:1) and introduces the first of the comments on the travel narrative in Matthew. Jesus has spent his entire ministry thus far in Galilee (in Matthew at least; cf. John 2:1 – 13; 4:1 – 5:47; 7:1 – 52; 10:22 – 42

4. Matthew makes Mark 10:2 – 9 more explicit by adding "for any reason whatsoever" to the Pharisees' question in v. 3, by having them call Moses' statement of divorce a "command" in v. 7, and by altering the structure to give a logical progression from basic scriptural principle (vv. 4 – 6) to objection on the basis of another OT passage (v. 7) to Jesus' explanation of how the first Scripture passage relates to the second (v. 8) to a final pronouncement of the truth (v. 9) (for the latter, see France, *Matthew* [TNTC], 280).

with several trips to Judea for the feasts) and now begins his final journey.

There is considerable debate on the meaning of "across the Jordan" (πέραν τοῦ Ἰορδάνου), which in 4:15, 25 referred to the Transjordan area where Gentiles predominated. So it is best to posit Jesus avoiding Samaria by crossing the Jordan on his way south and then recrossing it at Jericho (20:29) into Judea.[5]

19:2 And large crowds followed him, and he healed them there (καὶ ἠκολούθησαν αὐτῷ ὄχλοι πολλοί, καὶ ἐθεράπευσεν αὐτοὺς ἐκεῖ). This type of summary passage occurs often in Matthew (4:23 – 25; 9:35 – 36; 12:15; 15:29 – 30), and the latter two are similar, with the crowds "following" and Jesus conducting a healing ministry. Here Jesus performs the same ministry in Judea as he did in Galilee. Jesus' compassion for the needy was a prime characteristic of his messianic ministry.

19:3 Some Pharisees came in order to test him, saying (Καὶ προσῆλθον αὐτῷ Φαρισαῖοι πειράζοντες αὐτὸν καὶ λέγοντες). The Pharisees often "test"[6] Jesus (16:1; 22:18, 35; cf. 12:14, 24, 38; 15:1 – 2, 11). This is not a test to see whether he is a true or false prophet; they have already decided that and now are seeking anything at all to turn the people against him. It is indeed possible they were hoping that like John the Baptist, he will say something to anger Herod (see 14:3 – 12).

19:3 "Is it lawful for a man to divorce his wife for any reason whatever?" (Εἰ ἔξεστιν ἀνθρώπῳ ἀπολῦσαι τὴν γυναῖκα αὐτοῦ κατὰ πᾶσαν αἰτίαν;). The question with "is it lawful" (ἔξεστιν) makes this a legal issue of Torah (see 12:2, 4, 10, 12; 14:4), called later "Halakah" (questions of conduct). There were two schools of the Pharisees, Shammai (slightly earlier and at first more influential) and Hillel (dominant in Jesus' day and especially after AD 70). In general Shammai was more stringent and Hillel more lenient.[7] That is the case regarding divorce. The question centered on the interpretation of "something indecent" in the divorce text of Deut 24:1. Shammai understood it applied only to sexual immorality, while Hillel (the predominant view) extended it to "any reason whatever," even trivial things like bad cooking or a prettier woman (*m. Giṭ.* 9:10; *m. Ketub.* 7:6). The Pharisees' question came from this perspective (on the issue of women seeking divorce, see on 5:31).[8]

19:4 But Jesus replied, "You have read, haven't you[9] (ὁ δὲ ἀποκριθεὶς εἶπεν, Οὐκ ἀνέγνωτε). Jesus responds with a "weightier" quote from Genesis. In Jewish hermeneutics the further back one went in the Torah the more authority it possessed. So Jesus brings in the creation principle, which trumps the Pharisees' quote from the Deuteronomy. "You have read, haven't you" (οὐκ ἀνέγνωτε) goes back to Matt 12:3, 5, where Jesus also challenged the Pharisees' understanding of the Word of God. They have read it but don't realize the implications.

19:4 "... that from the beginning the Creator 'made them male and female?' " (ὅτι ὁ κτίσας ἀπ' ἀρχῆς ἄρσεν καὶ θῆλυ ἐποίησεν αὐτούς;). "From the beginning" (ἀπ' ἀρχῆς) recalls "in the beginning" that starts the Torah in Gen 1:1, and

5. So Hagner, France, Blomberg, Morris. But see H. D. Slingerland, "The Transjordanian Origin of St. Matthew's Gospel," *JSNT* 3 (1979): 18 – 28, who posits that Matthew writes from a Syrian perspective west of the Jordan and so considers Judea to be "across the Jordan."

6. This is a participle stating purpose, with the present tense picturing the process as it developed.

7. However, in 20 percent of the material Hillel is narrower; see Evans, "Hillel" and "Shammai," *DNTB*, 496 – 97, 1106 – 7.

8. Carter, *Households*, 59 – 60, argues that their question is both androcentric and patriarchal in that it assumes the husband's domination of the wife.

9. Another example of "not" (οὐκ) in a question expecting the answer yes (cf. 18:33).

"made them male and female" (quoting the LXX) describes the creation of humankind in Gen 1:27. Jesus' point is that God created men and women to be together, not to be divorced.

19:5 And he said (καὶ εἶπεν). "And he said" refers not to Jesus but to the Creator God of v. 4, who is seen as speaking the words of Gen 2:24.

19:5 "For this reason a man will leave his father and mother and be united with his wife, and the two will be one flesh" (Ἕνεκα τούτου καταλείψει ἄνθρωπος τὸν πατέρα καὶ τὴν μητέρα καὶ κολληθήσεται τῇ γυναικὶ αὐτοῦ, καὶ ἔσονται οἱ δύο εἰς σάρκα μίαν). This second creation ordinance shows that marriage was from the beginning the will of God, not divorce. God's purpose was the union ("one flesh")[10] of a man and a woman in marriage. "For this reason" (ἕνεκα τούτου) in Genesis refers to the creation of woman in 2:19 – 23, but here is meant to refer to the creation of both man and woman in Gen 1:27. Genesis 2:24 is used again in Mal 2:14 – 16, which says, "I [God] hate divorce."[11] Jesus' point is that while divorce is allowed in the Torah, it is not really God's actual will. The "two" were to be "one," end of point!

19:6 So they are no longer two, but one flesh (ὥστε οὐκέτι εἰσὶν δύο ἀλλὰ σὰρξ μία). Jesus draws the natural conclusion from the Genesis quotes. By centering only on the Deut 24 passage, the Pharisees have missed the true teaching of the Torah. The purpose of creation is the God-given union of "male and female."

19:6 Therefore, what God has joined together, let no one separate (ὃ οὖν ὁ θεὸς συνέζευξεν ἄνθρωπος μὴ χωριζέτω). God has "yoked them together" (the literal meaning of συνέζευξεν) into oneness, and "therefore" (οὖν connoting result) no one should be allowed to "divide" them or break that union. Nolland says it well: " 'no longer two but one flesh' aligns divorce with the violence of something like mutilation, amputation, or dismemberment."[12] When sinful humanity "separates" what God has "joined," it can only point to sin, the antithesis of what God wants. It is not whether people have a "right" to divorce (the legal aspect) but rather whether such can ever be in accordance with God's will (the moral and spiritual aspect).

19:7 They asked him, "Why then did Moses command the husband to give a certificate of divorce and release her?" (λέγουσιν αὐτῷ, Τί οὖν Μωϋσῆς ἐνετείλατο δοῦναι βιβλίον ἀποστασίου καὶ ἀπολῦσαι αὐτήν;). The second part of this pericope begins with a further question from the Pharisees, built on the obvious implications of Jesus' use of the Genesis passages to say that divorce is not according to God's will. They obviously feel they have caught Jesus in a legal error in that Moses had indeed permitted divorce. Their query centers on the "certificate of divorce" that officially freed a woman from the marriage and allowed her to remarry. In fact ἀπολύω carries these ideas, meaning both to "dismiss" or "send her away" and to "release" or "set her free" (BAGD, 96)

The legal certificate is mentioned often in the OT of God "divorcing" Israel (Isa 50:1; Jer 3:8) and was considered by Joseph after finding out that Mary was pregnant before they were married (cf.

10. While the language of "one flesh" is built upon sexual union, it encompasses the total person and refers to a complete "oneness" of the married couple in every area of their lives.

11. Some have argued that the Malachi passage refers not to Deut 24:1 but to spiritual unfaithfulness toward Yahweh on the part of Israel. Yet that is unlikely since it would make Yahweh both "witness" (v. 14) and "the wife of [one's] youth" (v. 15). So the analogy of Mal 2 is apt (so Davies and Allison, Nolland).

12. Nolland, *Matthew*, 773.

1:19). By calling it a "command"[13] the Pharisees are assuming that it was required of God's people as part of his will. In v. 8 Jesus will show that this is their basic error, their assumption that what God merely permits is actually a command.

19:8 Jesus told them, "Moses permitted you to divorce your wives because of the hardness of your hearts. But it was not like this from the beginning" (λέγει αὐτοῖς ὅτι Μωϋσῆς πρὸς τὴν σκληροκαρδίαν ὑμῶν ἐπέτρεψεν ὑμῖν ἀπολῦσαι τὰς γυναῖκας ὑμῶν, ἀπ' ἀρχῆς δὲ οὐ γέγονεν οὕτως). Jesus proceeds to explain the basic misunderstanding of the Pharisees and relates the creation ordinance (vv. 4 – 5) to Moses' statement in Deut 24. "From the beginning" (ἀπ' ἀρχῆς) deliberately recalls the Genesis material quoted in v. 4. In light of the creation principle that God does not want divorce, Moses' statement becomes mere "permission" rather than command. As Keener points out, "To be able to exercise some degree of restraint over human injustice, Moses' civil laws regulated some human institutions rather than seeking to abolish them altogether: divorce, polygyny, the avengers of blood, and slavery."[14] So what is behind it is not God's will but "the hardness of your hearts."

The "indecency" clause of Deut 24:1 is the key; divorce is always the result of a series of sins that a couple commits against each other. It is effected by going against God's will time after time. It is the better of two terrible options — continuing acts of "indecency" against each other, or breaking the marriage vow. The fact is that divorce had attained epidemic proportions in the first century (as today!), and Jesus had to address the serious problem.

19:9 Now I am telling you that whoever divorces his wife, except for immorality, and marries another commits adultery[15] (λέγω δὲ ὑμῖν ὅτι ὃς ἂν ἀπολύσῃ τὴν γυναῖκα αὐτοῦ μὴ ἐπὶ πορνείᾳ καὶ γαμήσῃ ἄλλην μοιχᾶται). Many of the issues in this verse have already been discussed at 5:32.[16] The various options for understanding the exception clause are explained there.[17] The exception is given here (and assumed by Mark) because Jesus recognized that sexual unfaithfulness broke the marriage bond and freed the innocent spouse to remarry.[18] The point was that the new sexual

13. The aorist "command" (ἐνετείλατο) is probably global, looking at all their teaching in the past (= oral tradition) as part of Moses' command. The Pharisees believed the oral Torah came from Moses and was as binding as the written Torah.

14. Keener, *Matthew*, 465.

15. There are a number of different endings in various manuscripts, e.g., "except on the ground of unchastity" (B D f^1) or the ending "makes her commit adultery" (B C* f^1). Yet both are assimilations to 5:32 and the shorter reading is preferable (see Metzger, *Textual Commentary*, 47 – 48).

16. One other must be mentioned. Several have proposed a new thesis, that "except for immorality" (μὴ ἐπὶ πορνείᾳ) modifies only the preceding clause rather than the whole clause and so allows divorce but not remarriage; cf. William A. Heth and Gordon J. Wenham, *Jesus and Divorce: The Problem with the Evangelical Consensus* (Nashville: Nelson, 1984), 117; Gordon J. Wenham, "Matthew and Divorce: An Old Crux Revisited," *JSNT* 22 (1984): 95 – 107; Hagner, *Matthew 14 – 28*, 549; Carter, *Households*, 66 – 68; Allen R. Guenther, "The Exception Phrases: Except, Including, or Excluding? (Matthew 5:32; 19:9)," *TynBul* 53 (2002): 83 – 96. However, the grammatical arguments for restricting this to the preceding clause rather than the whole are unconvincing. Moreover, there is no evidence that divorce ever occurred without giving the person freedom to remarry. That was the very purpose of the divorce document. See Philip H. Wiebe, "Jesus' Divorce Exception," *JETS* 32 (1989): 327 – 33; S. E. Porter and P. Buchanan, "On the Logical Structure of Matthew 19:9," *JETS* 34 (1991): 335 – 39; and Keener, *Matthew*, 469.

17. For a lengthy discussion of the options, see Carson, "Matthew," 413 – 19.

18. Keener, *Matthew*, 467, states that both Jewish and Roman law "*mandated* divorce for these grounds." See also Marcus Bockmuehl, "Matthew 5:32; 19:9 in the Light of Prerabbinic Halakah," *NTS* 35 (1989): 291 – 95, who says that some rabbinic teaching held that sexual contact outside marriage rendered a union unclean and prohibited further conjugal union.

union invalidated the first union between husband and wife. However, apart from that one instance, marriage is a divinely ordained covenant, and remarriage following divorce otherwise constituted adultery in the eyes of God. So Jesus is upholding the divine covenant in marriage and opposing the freedom to divorce in the Jewish world while recognizing the one exception to that rule.

19:10 His disciples said to him, "If the relationship between a husband and wife is like this, it is better not to marry" (λέγουσιν αὐτῷ οἱ μαθηταὶ αὐτοῦ, Εἰ οὕτως ἐστὶν ἡ αἰτία τοῦ ἀνθρώπου μετὰ τῆς γυναικός, οὐ συμφέρει γαμῆσαι). The third section begins with an implied question ("Why marry?"), this time on the part of the disciples, probably in private apart from the Pharisees. The disciples generally held the same views that predominated in the Judaism of their day and so had quite liberal views on divorce and remarriage. For them Jesus' position, even more conservative than the Shammaite view, made marriage unattractive since they could easily be trapped in an unhappy relationship.

The word αἰτία could mean "situation, case" (closer to its basic meaning) but in this circumstance may well mean simply "relationship" (so BAGD, 26).[19] Davies and Allison take this to be the first of three consecutive misunderstandings on the part of the disciples (with 19:13, 25), as they take Jesus' "exaltation of monogamy" to be virtually an "exaltation of celibacy."[20]

19:11 But he told them, "Not everyone can grasp this[21] word" (ὁ δὲ εἶπεν αὐτοῖς, Οὐ πάντες χωροῦσιν τὸν λόγον τοῦτον). Jesus responds to the disciples' misunderstanding. There is some doubt as to whether "this word" (τὸν λόγον τοῦτον) refers to vv. 3 – 9 (Bonnard, Gundry, Luz), v. 10 (Schlatter, Hagner, Davies and Allison, Nolland), or v. 12 (Gnilka, Schnackenberg). While "this" (τοῦτον) can refer forward, it normally refers back (nearly always so with "word" [λόγος]), and this fits better here. The primary argument for taking τοῦτον with the teaching of vv. 3 – 9 is that the disciples' sayings are not given this much importance in Matthew (so Luz). However, v. 10 is the closer antecedent, and it is difficult to see why Jesus would say that his teaching regarding divorce is not for everyone.

In other words, Jesus is saying that not everyone can "accept" (χωροῦσιν meaning to "grasp, comprehend") what the disciples have said about celibacy. While Qumran emphasized celibacy, Judaism as a whole did not. So the disciples are speaking of something they do not truly comprehend, but Jesus will now clarify its true significance.

19:11 "... but only those to whom it has been given" (ἀλλ' οἷς δέδοται). The passive "it has been given" (δέδοται) is not a divine passive, though in part it does refer to the "gift" of celibacy, but Jesus' three examples from v. 12 refer to fate ("born" that way) and human action ("made eunuchs," "made themselves eunuchs"). Christ is referring to followers who are open to a call to celibacy for the sake of the kingdom (v. 12; cf. 1 Cor 7:7, 26 – 35).

19:12 For there are eunuchs who have been born this way from the mother's womb, and there are eunuchs who have been made eunuchs by people (εἰσὶν γὰρ εὐνοῦχοι οἵτινες ἐκ κοιλίας μητρὸς ἐγεννήθησαν οὕτως, καὶ εἰσὶν εὐνοῦχοι οἵτινες εὐνουχίσθησαν ὑπὸ τῶν ἀνθρώπων). This may be

19. τοῦ ἀνθρώπου refers to a husband with the article and is a genitive of reference, "regarding a husband with a wife."

20. Davies and Allison, *Matthew*, 3:19.

21. A few manuscripts (B f^1) omit the demonstrative pronoun, but several (א C D L W TR et al.) include it, and it may have been omitted due to the very ambiguity of "this word." Thus it is best to include it.

an example of Jesus' wisdom teaching, in which he uses two concrete realities of everyday existence (those born eunuchs and those made eunuchs) to support a third spiritual or moral truth (those eunuchs for the kingdom).[22] The first two described the two different types of eunuchs in the world, those born without sexual organs or impotent[23] and those "made eunuchs," either castrated (often for service in a royal court [e.g., the Ethiopian eunuch in Acts 8] or in a harem) or had become impotent due to disease or accident.

Eunuchs were not allowed to "enter the assembly of the Lord" (Deut 23:1; cf. Lev 21:20; 22:24), though Isa 56:3 – 5 allows eunuchs to be part of the procession of the nations to Zion, probably the basis of the Ethiopian eunuch coming to Jerusalem to worship in Acts 8:26 – 40. Still, eunuchs were definitely looked down upon in first-century Judaism, and Davies and Allison go so far as to posit that v. 12 "was originally an apologetic counter, a response to the jeer that Jesus was a eunuch" (because he was unmarried).[24]

19:12 ... and there are eunuchs who have made themselves eunuchs for the sake of the kingdom of heaven. Let the one who is able to grasp it do so (καὶ εἰσὶν εὐνοῦχοι οἵτινες εὐνούχισαν ἑαυτοὺς διὰ τὴν βασιλείαν τῶν οὐρανῶν. ὁ δυνάμενος χωρεῖν χωρείτω). Jesus' major emphasis is on the third category, metaphorically labeled those "who have made themselves eunuchs." Some link this with v. 9 and interpret it as a reference to those who have had to divorce their wives because of adultery and who willingly remain unmarried.[25] This is unlikely, for it ignores the influence of vv. 10 – 11 and the great likelihood that those divorced in v. 9 were allowed to remarry. Nor is Jesus referring to those, like Origen, who took this literally and castrated himself.[26]

In reality Jesus is referring to disciples who choose the life of celibacy "for the sake of the kingdom," i.e., to give themselves wholly to ministry. Since marriage and child-bearing were so essential to the Jewish way of life, this was a powerful metaphor. As Keener says, "a metaphor of such shame and sacrifice testifies to the value of the kingdom of God for which anyone would pay such a price."[27] Primary examples, of course, are Jesus, John the Baptist, and Paul. One caveat is necessary: neither Jesus here nor Paul in 1 Cor 7 is saying that celibacy is to be preferred or is a higher calling. The only point is that it is a valid calling and should be considered by disciples who serve the kingdom.

Theology in Application

There are three issues here: marriage, divorce, and celibacy. All need to be explored and the spiritual principles elucidated.

22. Davies and Allison, *Matthew*, 3:22. Nevertheless Witherington, *Women in the Ministry of Jesus* (Cambridge: Cambridge Univ. Press, 1984) believes it moves from the least objectionable (born that way) to more so (made that way) to most objectionable (self-made). However, the former option catches Jesus' movement of thought better.

23. See France, *Gospel of Matthew*, 724 – 25, against the view of some that "born a eunuch" applies to homosexuality.

24. Davies and Allison, *Matthew*, 3:25.

25. Gundry, *Matthew*, 382 – 83; Luz, *Matthew 8 – 20*, 500 – 501; F. J. Moloney, "Matthew 19, 3 – 12 and Celibacy: A Redactional and Form Critical Study," *JSNT* 2 (1979): 42 – 60. Senior, *Matthew*, 215, interestingly takes it of Christian wives divorced but not remarrying.

26. For the practice of this in the early church, see D. F. Caner, "The Practice and Prohibition of Self-Castration in Early Christianity," *VC* 51 (1997), 396 – 415.

27. Keener, *Matthew*, 472; Witherington, *Matthew*, 364 – 65.

1. The Sanctity of Marriage

Hagner states that the new kingdom reality in Jesus involves "the restoration of the perfection of the pre-fall creation," reflecting the new ethics of the kingdom.[28] In this there is a special covenantal aspect to marriage reflecting the God-man relationship. God is present in a special way in a marital situation, and the choice of a spouse should be a spiritual act and not just a search for an attractive person to show off to your friends. For Paul it reflects the special union between Christ and the church (Eph 5:25 – 27). Therefore, it is incumbent on churches today to bring a new sacred atmosphere to discussions of marriage and family. The spiritual aspect must be uppermost at every level.

2. Divorce

Divorce is never part of God's will. Even in Christian circles today divorce is becoming an accepted phenomenon simply taken for granted. Statistics show that the level of divorce is the same in the church as in the world. This is not to say that divorced people are second-class members in the church. I believe the NT recognizes three exceptions that allow divorce and remarriage — sexual immorality (here), the desertion of an unbelieving spouse (1 Cor 7:15 – 16), and divorce before one becomes a Christian (based on the principle established in 1 Cor 6:9 – 11).

However, this does not mean divorce is God's will, just that God allows it in accord with the sinfulness of human nature (v. 8 above). As Wilkins says, "As with God's allowance through Moses, Jesus allows divorce as an exception because some destructive sin has entered into the relationship and destroyed the union God established."[29] Yet even when something like immorality occurs within marriage, that does not mean divorce is mandated. Rather, repentance and reconciliation through forgiveness should be sought first.

3. The Gift of Celibacy

The gift of celibacy is a valid option in the church. The disciples made an ironic statement that it would be better to be single (v. 10), but Jesus turns that on its head and says they are right. For many in ministry, it would be better to remain single and thereby have more time for kingdom business (cf. 1 Cor 7: 7, 26 – 35). This is as valid today as it was in the time of Jesus or Paul. We are all aware of those leaders who have chosen the path of celibacy (e.g., John Stott) and of the ministries they had as a result. Pioneer missionaries, evangelists, itinerant teachers, and many others should consider this gift as part of their calling. Most importantly, it is a calling and is not for everyone; Jesus does not elevate single status above marriage but rather says it is a valid calling for those in ministry.

28. Hagner, *Matthew 14 – 28*, 550.

29. Wilkins, *Matthew*, 657.

CHAPTER 82

Matthew 19:13 – 15

Literary Context

The movement from husband-wife relations to children is a natural progression. Children here become a model for discipleship and an essential part of the kingdom community.

- **VI. The Movement to the Cross (19:1 – 25:46)**
  - **A. Jesus' Deeds: Opposition and Discipleship (19:1 – 22:46)**
    - **1. The Road to Jerusalem (19:1 – 20:34)**
      - a. The Question on Divorce (19:1 – 12)
      - ➦ **b. Blessing the Children (19:13 – 15)**
      - c. Wealth and Kingdom Rewards (19:16 – 30)

Main Idea

Far from nuisances to be avoided, children are God's special gift to the community and are to be embraced. Even more than that, they are the very embodiment of the kingdom in the church.[1]

1. See J. D. M. Derrett, "Why Jesus Blessed the Children (Mark 10:13 – 16)," *NovT* 25 (1983): 1 – 18 (esp. p. 17), who brings out both aspects.

Translation

Matthew 19:13-15

13a	Introduction	**Then little children were brought to Jesus**
b	Purpose	so that he might lay hands on them and pray.
c	Result of 13a	But **the disciples rebuked them.**
14a	Response	But **Jesus said,**
b	Exhortation	*"Let the children come to me and*
c	Exhortation	*do not forbid them,*
d	Basis	*for the kingdom of heaven belongs to such as these."*
15a	Conclusion	After he laid his hands on them,
b		**he departed from there.**

Structure and Literary Form

In this passage Matthew has shortened Mark 10:13 – 16 but kept the story basically intact. This second controversy story (this time the barrier to truth is the disciples, not the Pharisees!) is also a pronouncement story, since the disciples' rebuke leads to a dominical saying on the part of Jesus. It contains three parts: The introduction (v. 13) containing the presentation of the children for blessing and the disciples' rebuke; the pronouncement by Jesus (v. 14), containing the invitation to the children and the kingdom basis of it; and the conclusion (v. 15), containing the blessing and Jesus' departure.

Exegetical Outline

➦ **I. The Controversy over the Children (19:13)**
- A. The children brought to Jesus for a blessing
- B. Rebuke by the disciples

II. Jesus' Response (19:14)
- A. His invitation regarding the children
- B. The kingdom reality — children as models

III. The Blessing and Jesus' Departure (19:15)

Explanation of the Text

19:13 Then little children were brought to Jesus so that he might lay hands on them and pray (Τότε προσηνέχθησαν αὐτῷ παιδία ἵνα τὰς χεῖρας ἐπιθῇ αὐτοῖς καὶ προσεύξηται). There is some evidence that in Judaism children were often brought to teachers/rabbis for a blessing, especially on the Day of Atonement (*Sopherim* 18:5).[2] Here people (probably parents) bring children for Jesus to "lay hands and pray" over them.

This is the normal form for a blessing in the ancient world. Laying on of hands was used for parental blessing (Gen 48:14, 17 – 18), ordaining leaders (Num 27:18; Deut 34:9; Acts 6:6; 13:3), presenting sacrifices (Exod 29:10, 15; Lev 1:4), healing (Matt 9:18; Mark 6:5; 7:32), and giving the Holy Spirit (Acts 8:17; 19:6).[3] In Matthew the bringing of the children to Jesus recognizes his "authority as the one who determines human destiny" as well as his "mercy and compassion" for those who need his help.[4]

19:13 But the disciples rebuked them (οἱ δὲ μαθηταὶ ἐπετίμησαν αὐτοῖς). There is a distinct contrast between the positive motive of those who bring the children and the negative reaction of the disciples. Matthew does not tell us why they do so (nor does Mark 10:13), but most likely they are upset at having their trip to Jerusalem interrupted for a trivial reason. Jesus is no simple teacher to be spending time blessing children.[5] In 2 Kgs 4:27 Elisha's servant Gehazi also tried to protect his master from a woman's interruption and was rebuked for his efforts.

19:14 But Jesus said, "Let the children come to me and do not forbid them" (ὁ δὲ Ἰησοῦς εἶπεν, Ἄφετε τὰ παιδία καὶ μὴ κωλύετε αὐτὰ ἐλθεῖν πρός με). The clear emphasis in the order of the sentence is on "Let them ... do not forbid." The infinitive "to come" (ἐλθεῖν) is last and modifies both clauses. Jesus makes his open invitation to the children emphatic (Matthew omits Mark's notation in 10:14 regarding Jesus' indignation) by saying it positively ("permit [ἄφετε with this thrust as in 3:15; 8:22; 13:30] them to come")[6] and negatively ("do not forbid them to come").[7] Jesus could hardly be more firm in his resolve to welcome children into his presence and bless them. The priorities of the disciples were warped, and they had not assimilated what Jesus taught in 18:3 – 5 about the centrality of little children in the kingdom community.

19:14 "... for the kingdom of heaven belongs to such as these" (τῶν γὰρ τοιούτων ἐστὶν ἡ βασιλεία τῶν οὐρανῶν). There are two aspects to this saying. (1) The children are recipients of the kingdom blessings. In Matt 5:3, 10 two of the beatitudes have as their eschatological blessing, "the kingdom of heaven belongs to them," with a

2. See France, *Matthew*, 283; Strack-Billerbeck, 2:138. The problem is that the evidence is late and it is difficult to know whether it went on in Jesus' day (so Luz, *Matthew 8 – 20*, 504n).

3. See J. K. Parratt, "The Laying on of Hands in the New Testament," *ExpTim* 80 (1969): 210 – 14.

4. Carter, *Households*, 93.

5. Hill, *Matthew*, 282, posits that the disciples failed to understand Jesus' mission and were hoping they could get to Jerusalem quickly so that Jesus could "make a triumphant messianic display there." This is possible but cannot be proved.

6. Nolland, *Matthew*, 784, believes "come to me" may be an echo of 14:28 – 29, where Jesus tells Peter to "come to me" on the water, as well as of 12:28, "Come to me, all you weary and burdened people."

7. For an excellent refutation of the attempts of some to read infant baptism into this verb on the basis of its use in Acts 8:36; 10:47; 11:17, see Luz, *Matthew 8 – 20*, 504 – 5 and the bibliography found therein.

similar grammatical structure[8] and message. This could well be an allusion back to that.

(2) As stated in 18:3 – 5, little children model kingdom realities in their helpless state and vulnerability as well as their sense of total dependence.[9] Carter brings out the changing place of children in first-century society. While they were generally more treasured in Jewish than in Greco-Roman homes, there were still four "common themes": the dependence of children on their parents; the lifelong submission and obedience required, including caring for aging parents; their status as "marginal beings" perceived even as "a threat to the civic order" and so needing to know their place (the disciples' rebuke stems from this attitude); and their orientation and training entirely for the future so they could take their proper place as adults.[10]

At the same time, in Jewish homes especially but more and more among Gentiles as well, children received affection and worth and were perceived as gifts from God. There was growing respect and appreciation for the value of children, and parents wanted to care for their children in terms of their weakness and needs. In short, they were concerned for the well-being of children.[11]

Finally, Carter finds several characteristics in Jesus' use of children as models.[12] (1) Transition is a key to discipleship, as followers move to maturity and especially to "the new goal of the Parousia." (2) Dependency becomes not a temporary aspect of childhood but a permanent norm for a proper relation with the heavenly Father. (3) Following Jesus means a "marginalized way of life" by abandoning "power and security" and embracing "vulnerability."

19:15 After he laid his hands on them, he departed from there (καὶ ἐπιθεὶς τὰς χεῖρας αὐτοῖς ἐπορεύθη ἐκεῖθεν). Jesus has just told them why he will bless the children, now he does so by "laying hands" on the children (as he was asked). The notation regarding Jesus' departure continues the travel narrative and provides a transition to the encounter with the rich young man in the next story.

Theology in Application

Jesus had a special place in his heart and in the kingdom for the downtrodden and despised of the world — tax collectors, the poor, women, and children. With their simple faith, vulnerability, lowliness, and humility children are not only welcome in the kingdom but are also special models of the kingdom that all disciples must emulate in following Christ. All the disciples are "little ones" (Jesus' special term for them in 10:42; 18:6, 10, 14) as the lowest in society. Their greatness will be found not in their accomplishments but in their servanthood (18:4; 20:26 – 28).

8. The genitive with the verb "to be" is generally possessive and is best translated "belongs to."

9. See J. Bailey, "Experiencing the Kingdom as a Little Child: A Rereading of Mark 10:13 – 16," *WW* 15 (1995): 58 – 67.

10. Carter, *Households*, 98 – 101.

11. Ibid, 108 – 13. He adds a fourth — discipleship is egalitarian in that all disciples are children, so that the church embraces equality over hierarchy in universal obedience to the will of God. But this is an overstatement, for the church embraced equality and yet a hierarchy of leadership from the start. See I. Howard Marshall, "'Early Catholicism' in the New Testament," in *New Dimensions in New Testament Study* (ed. R. N. Longenecker and M. C. Tenney; Grand Rapids: Zondervan, 1974), 217 – 31.

12. Carter, *Households*, 113 – 14.

83 CHAPTER

Matthew 19:16 – 30

Literary Context

This passage on wealth reverses that of becoming like a child in vv. 13 – 15 and yet at the same time tells how to become "like a child." It turns to a major barrier against doing so — the riches and rewards of this world. The rich young man embodies this anti-kingdom perspective as he chooses wealth over following Christ. As Blomberg says, "The children turn out to be nearer to the kingdom than most might have suspected; the rich man demonstrates that he is further away than most would have guessed."[1] This passage also continues the emphasis on the household affairs of everyday life, now turning to the subject of money and its proper place. Finally, this story is in a sense an illustrative vignette of the saying in 6:19 – 21 (seek treasures in heaven, not treasures on earth).

- **VI. The Movement to the Cross (19:1 – 25:46)**
  - **A. Jesus' Deeds: Opposition and Discipleship (19:1 – 22:46)**
    - **1. The Road to Jerusalem (19:1 – 20:34)**
      - b. Blessing the Children (19:13 – 15)
      - ➦ **c. Wealth and Kingdom Rewards (19:16 – 30)**
        - **(1) Encounter with the Rich Young Man (19:16 – 22)**
        - **(2) The Difficulty for the Rich to Enter the Kingdom (19:23 – 26)**
        - **(3) The Rewards for Leaving All (19:27 – 30)**
      - d. Parable of Workers in the Vineyard (20:1 – 16)

Main Idea

Davies and Allison point out that this is a narrative illustration of important themes from the Sermon on the Mount, in particular treasure on earth/heaven

1. Blomberg, *Matthew*, 296.

(6:19 – 21), generosity (6:22 – 23), reversal of the earthly and the eschatological (5:2 – 12), and perfection (5:48). So the theme here is that every follower must choose between God and money (6:24; Luke 16:13). That choice will determine whether their rewards are earthly and perishable or heavenly and eternal.

Translation

Matthew 19:16-30

16a	Question #1	**[1] And look, a man came to him and said,**
b		*"Teacher,*
		what good thing must I do
		in order to have eternal life?"
17a	Answer	**Jesus said to him,**
b		*"Why are you asking me about what is good?*
c		*There is One who is good.*
d		*But if you want to enter life, keep the commandments."*
18a	Question #2	**[2] The man asked,**
b		*"Which ones?"*
c	Answer	**Jesus responded,**
d		*"These: 'you shall not murder,*
e		*you shall not commit adultery,*
f		*you shall not steal,*
g		*you shall not give false testimony,*
19a		*honor your father and your mother,*
b		*and love your neighbor as your self.'"*
		(Exod 20:12-16; Deut 5:16-20)
20a	Question #3	**[3] The young man said to him,**
b		*"I have kept all these.*
c		*What do I still lack?"*
21a	Answer	**Jesus responded,**
b	Condition	*"If you want to be perfect,*
c	Exhortation	*go, sell your possessions,*
		and give the proceeds to the poor.
d	Result	*Then you will have treasure in heaven.*
e	Exhortation	*And come, follow me.*
22a	Response/Conclusion	Now when the young man heard this saying,
b		**he went away grieving,**
c	Basis for 22b	for he had many possessions.
23a		**Then Jesus told his disciples,**
b	Assertion	*"I tell you the truth,*
		a wealthy person will enter the kingdom of heaven
		with difficulty.
24a	Illustration/Analogy	*Again I tell you,*
		it is easier for a camel to pass through the eye of a needle
b		*than for a wealthy person to enter the kingdom of God."*

25a		Now after his disciples heard this,
b	Reaction	**they were totally amazed and said,**
c	Question	*"Then who can be saved?"*
26a	Answer	**But Jesus looked at them and said,**
b	Assertion	*"For human beings this is impossible,*
c	Contrast to 26b	but *for God all things are possible."*
27a	Response	**Then Peter responded,**
b	Assertion	*"Look, we have left everything and followed you.*
c	Question	*What will there be then for us?"*
28a	Answer	**So Jesus said to them,**
b		*"I tell you the truth,*
		at the renewal of the world
c		*when the Son of Man sits upon his glorious throne*
d	Promise	*as for you who have followed me … you will also sit*
		on twelve thrones, judging the twelve tribes of Israel.
29a	Condition	And *everyone who has left homes or*
		brothers or
		sisters or
		father or
		mother or
		children or
		fields
		for my name'sake
		will receive a hundred times as much, and
b	Promise	*will inherit eternal life.*
30a	Warning/Promise	But *many who are first will be last, and the last will be first.*

Structure and Literary Form

Matthew generally follows Mark 10:17 – 22, abbreviating it in several places but with a few key changes, like the famous "good thing/good teacher" (Mark 10:17 – 18 vs. Matt 19:16 – 17); the added "Love your neighbor as yourself" in v. 19; identifying the man as "young" in vv. 20, 22; the emphasis on perfection in v. 21; and the throne saying of v. 28. There is general agreement on a three-part structure: Jesus' encounter with the rich young man (vv. 16 – 22), Jesus' teaching on the difficulty of entering the kingdom (vv. 23 – 26), and finally Jesus' teaching on the rewards for leaving all and following him (vv. 27 – 30).

Exegetical Outline

➦ **I. Encounter with the Rich Young Man (19:16 – 22)**
   A. First question: how to gain eternal life (vv. 16 – 17)
   B. Second question: which commandments must be kept (vv. 18 – 19)
   C. Third question: what he lacks: sell possessions (vv. 20 – 21)
   D. Conclusion: departs unwilling to surrender possessions (v. 22)

II. The Difficulty for the Rich to Enter the Kingdom (19:23 – 26)
   A. The difficulty illustrated: camel through a needle's eye (vv. 23 – 24)
   B. The disciples' question: can anyone be saved? (v. 25)
   C. Jesus' response: possible only with God (v. 26)

III. The Rewards for Leaving All (19:27 – 30)
   A. Peter's question: what's in it for us? (v. 27)
   B. Jesus' response regarding rewards (vv. 28 – 29)
      1. Sitting on thrones (v. 28)
      2. The hundredfold reward (v. 29)
   C. Ethical warning: the great reversal (v. 30)

Explanation of the Text

19:16 And look, a man[2] came to him and said, "Teacher, what good thing must I do in order to have eternal life?" (Καὶ ἰδοὺ εἷς προσελθὼν αὐτῷ εἶπεν, Διδάσκαλε, τί ἀγαθὸν ποιήσω ἵνα σχῶ ζωὴν αἰώνιον;). As often, "look" (ἰδού) points to a particularly dramatic event (1:20, 23; 2:1, 9, 13, 19; et al.), insofar as a man (19:20 tells us he is "young," Luke 18:18 that he is a "ruler," thus "the rich young ruler") comes to Jesus with a serious query. His question introduces one of the best-known examples of redaction criticism in the gospels, for Mark 10:17 has "Good teacher, what must I do?" and Matthew alters Mark's use of "good" (ἀγαθός) as a christological statement (Mark 10:18, "Why do you call me good?") to an ethical statement (v. 17, "Why are you asking me about what is good?").

But do these changes produce an irreconcilable contradiction between Mark and Matthew?[3] That is unlikely, for both versions say essentially the same thing. A wealthy man comes to Jesus and asks what kind of works he could do to guarantee eternal life, and Jesus turns him away from such considerations to center on God and his requirements. In Mark the "(good) works" are presupposed, and in Matthew the "(good) teacher" is presupposed. There is no true contradiction.[4] The man wants to know how to make his eternity with

2. "One" (εἷς) is often used as an indefinite article, equivalent to "a certain one" (τις), and should be translated "a man" (see BDF §2472).

3. An important key is to realize that the gospel writers provide the *ipsissima vox* (the "exact voice") of Jesus more than the *ipsissima verba* (the "exact words"). The evangelists under the inspiration of the Holy Spirit are summarizing and highlighting the longer speeches and sermons of Jesus as well as dialogues like this one. On this issue see Paul Feinberg, "The Meaning of Inerrancy," in *Inerrancy* (ed. Norman Geisler; Grand Rapids: Zondervan, 1979), 267 – 304, who brings out that inerrancy demands the former rather than the latter.

4. For a lengthy discussion, see Carson, "Matthew," 421 – 23, and especially his "Redaction Criticism: On the Legitimacy and Illegitimacy of a Literary Tool," in *Scripture and Truth* (ed. D. A. Carson and J. D. Woodbridge; Grand

God certain and what "good works" will suffice to do so. "Eternal life" is mentioned only here and in 19:29; 25:46 in Matthew, though "life" (ζωή) in v. 17 is paralleled in 7:14; 18:8–9.

19:17 Jesus said to him, "Why are you asking[5] me about what is good? There is One who is good" (ὁ δὲ εἶπεν αὐτῷ, Τί με ἐρωτᾷς περὶ τοῦ ἀγαθοῦ; εἷς ἐστιν ὁ ἀγαθός). Jesus answers the question with another, more powerful question. The man was centering on his own good works rather than centering on God, who alone can grant eternal life. The criterion for life is not in the works themselves[6] but in the only true "good" there is, the goodness of God (and here Matthew and Mark are surely in complete agreement). Until the man turns from self (including one's good works) to God, there is no hope. It is possible that Jesus is alluding to the Shema (Deut 6:4, "Hear, O Israel: The LORD our God, the LORD is one"). There too the oneness of God leads to an injunction to keep "these commandments … on your hearts" (Deut 6:6).

19:17 "But if you want to enter life, keep the commandments" (εἰ δὲ θέλεις εἰς τὴν ζωὴν εἰσελθεῖν, τήρησον τὰς ἐντολάς). As Bruner points out, Jesus changes the man's verb. He had wanted to "get" eternal life (like a possession), but Jesus tells him he rather must "enter" it (as a journey).[7] Turning to God demands not just good works but obedience to God's commandments. The "good" that God has made available to humankind is centered on the divine revelation, specifically for Jews the Torah. So to discover "life" one must begin with obedience. This entails "righteousness" in the Matthean sense of ethical righteousness, i.e., living life according to God's will (see on 3:15; 5:6; et al.).

19:18–19 The man asked, "Which ones?"[8] (λέγει αὐτῷ, Ποίας;). The man's question is similar to the one that will be asked by the scribe later (22:36) about the greatest commandment: which of the commandments are necessary for attaining eternal life?

19:18–19 Jesus responded, "These: 'you shall not murder,[9] you shall not commit adultery, you shall not steal, you shall not give false testimony, honor your father and mother'" (ὁ δὲ Ἰησοῦς εἶπεν, Τὸ Οὐ φονεύσεις, Οὐ μοιχεύσεις, Οὐ κλέψεις, Οὐ ψευδομαρτυρήσεις, Τίμα τὸν πατέρα καὶ τὴν μητέρα). Jesus then proceeds to name five ethical commandments from the second table of the Decalogue,[10] primarily because of the ethical issues being addressed (good works, possessions). Also, since the Jewish people believed the Ten Commandments embodied the whole Torah, Jesus is in effect saying the man must keep the whole law.

The order is the same as in the sixth through the ninth commandments but with the fifth appended last, probably as a transition to "love your neighbor" (Exod 20:12–16; Deut 5:16–20). Coveting,

Rapids: Zondervan, 1983), 131–37. See also John W. Wenham, "'Why Do You Ask Me about the Good?' A Study of the Relation between Text and Source Criticism," *NTS* 28 (1982): 116–25.

5. The use of the present tense by Jesus (the man used an aorist) places Jesus' response in the foreground for emphasis.

6. Matthew may have wished to avoid a misunderstanding of Mark's rendering, "Why do you call me good?" (10:18). Yet as stated above in v. 16, the two do not contradict each other but simply highlight different emphases in Jesus' dialogue with the wealthy young man.

7. F. D. Bruner, *The Churchbook: Matthew 13–28* (Grand Rapids: Eerdmans, 2004), 289.

8. Here "which" (ποίας) is equivalent to "which one" (τίς) for "which commandments?" (see BAGD, 684, 2).

9. Matthew uses "not" (οὐ) plus the future indicative, Mark "not" (μή) plus the aorist subjunctive, but the two forms are virtually interchangeable, see BDF §369 (2). Matthew's wording follows the LXX.

10. This hardly means that he denigrates the first table of the Decalogue as less important. Davies and Allison, *Matthew*, 3:43, note Calvin in his *Institutes* 2.8.52–53: "right action (as depicted by the second table) is proof of right religion (as outlined by the first table)."

the tenth, will be addressed in Jesus' challenge about possessions in v. 21, but it is also embodied in the "love your neighbor" quote. These define the practical outworking of the goodness of God in daily life.

19:19 "And love your neighbor as yourself" (καί, Ἀγαπήσεις τὸν πλησίον σου ὡς σεαυτόν). Matthew adds this from Lev 19:18 to Mark, probably as a summary of the second table of the Decalogue (as in 22:39; cf. also on 5:43). In v. 17 he turned the man's focus from self to God, now he turns that focus also from self to others. The basic problem is that he has lived only for himself and his possessions. The Decalogue makes it clear that one can only find "life" by centering first on God (the first table) and then on others (the second table). "As yourself" (ὡς σεαυτόν, see further on 22:39) means to love those around you as deeply and as sacrificially as you love yourself.

19:20 The young man said to him, "I have kept[11] all these. What do I still lack?" (λέγει αὐτῷ ὁ νεανίσκος, Πάντα ταῦτα ἐφύλαξα· τί ἔτι ὑστερῶ;). Here we learn he is a "young man," with νεανίσκος meaning most likely a young adult twenty-one to twenty-eight years of age.[12] His hubris continues as he falsely claims, "I have kept all these." Jesus will soon show him the error of his claim.

Yet this man still does not feel as if he has guaranteed future salvation, as is shown by his added, "What do I still lack?" Bruner shows the query can be seen as supreme self-confidence (Allen, Grundmann, Gnilka), youthful exaggeration (Lohmeyer), or despair (McNeile).[13] The truth is probably a mixture of the first two, with uncertainty rather than despair. He has an exaggerated sense of his own piety that has led to self-sufficiency. Yet at the same time he is unsure whether he has done enough and is hoping Jesus will be able to give him further insight.

19:21 Jesus responded, "If you want to be perfect, go, sell your possessions, and give the proceeds to the poor" (ἔφη αὐτῷ ὁ Ἰησοῦς, Εἰ θέλεις τέλειος εἶναι, ὕπαγε πώλησόν σου τὰ ὑπάρχοντα καὶ δὸς τοῖς πτωχοῖς). Jesus cuts to the heart of the issue. He assumes (condition of fact "if" [εἰ]) that the man wants to be "perfect" (τέλειος), for he has asked what will give him "life." The meaning of the term must be found in 5:48, "you must be perfect as your heavenly Father is perfect." There it means wholehearted (many see "wholeness" here) obedience to *all* Jesus has said (cf. Matt 28:19, "keep everything I have commanded") and sums up the ethical requirements of 5:21 – 48.

That fits this passage admirably.[14] The man needs ethical completeness, true obedience to all God has said in his revealed Word. So Jesus turns to the primary problem in the man's life. His possessions have clearly become his god and have thus replaced God in his life. Therefore, the only recourse is to do what must be done with all idols: get rid of them. Moreover, if he is truly to "love his neighbor," he must sell the idolatrous possessions and then give the money "to the poor." This does not mean he had never engaged in almsgiving; he could not have said he had kept "all" the commands if he had not. Jesus is not talking about almsgiving but about idolatry.

19:21 "Then you will have treasure in heaven" (καὶ ἕξεις θησαυρὸν ἐν οὐρανοῖς). Jesus continues to allude to the Sermon on the Mount, this time to

11. This could be a culminative aorist but is more likely global, summing up his life of obedience under a single whole.

12. Davies and Allison, *Matthew*, 3:43, argue this from Hippocrates.

13. Bruner, *Matthew 13 – 28*, 295.

14. It has also been suggested that Jesus develops a two-level discipleship, with the superior followers seeking "perfection" and others satisfied to live at a lower plane. But there is no basis for that here. As in 5:48, Jesus demands that all his followers seek "perfection" (see Carson, Luz).

6:19–21. To attain "treasure in heaven," you must surrender "treasure on earth." This reverberates throughout the NT, as in 1 Cor 3:12–15, where each person's work is tested by fire at the final judgment and only that grounded in Christ will survive.

19:21 "And come, follow me" (καὶ δεῦρο ἀκολούθει μοι). Jesus gives two commands, and they are intertwined: "go, sell your possessions" and "come, follow me" (each consists of a two-part command—"go and sell," "come and follow"). Discipleship begins with rejecting the world, and then one becomes a "follower" (cf. 4:20, 22; 8:19, 22; 9:9; 10:38; 16:24). Every aspect of life, including one's earthly goods, must be used for God rather than self.

19:22 Now when the young man heard this saying, he went away grieving, for he had many possessions (ἀκούσας δὲ ὁ νεανίσκος τὸν λόγον ἀπῆλθεν λυπούμενος, ἦν γὰρ ἔχων κτήματα πολλά). The wealthy young man cannot accept Jesus' challenge and so goes away "grieving" (λυπούμενος),[15] that is, with deep sadness or grief. The use of the present participle fits in with the imperfect periphrastic "he had" (ἦν ἔχων), for both stress durative action, looking at the hold of his possessions as an ongoing force controlling his life.

19:23 Then Jesus told his disciples, "I tell you the truth, a wealthy person will enter the kingdom of heaven with difficulty" (Ὁ δὲ Ἰησοῦς εἶπεν τοῖς μαθηταῖς αὐτοῦ, Ἀμὴν λέγω ὑμῖν ὅτι πλούσιος δυσκόλως εἰσελεύσεται εἰς τὴν βασιλείαν τῶν οὐρανῶν). Once again the "amen" (ἀμήν) saying points to an important, solemn truth that his disciples had better listen to carefully (see on 5:18). The wealthy have so much power and control over this life that they perceive little need for the heavenly realm, as exemplified in the young man in the previous encounter. It is "hard" for such a person to turn to God.

All of the Twelve came from the social class of the poor (Matthew as a tax collector was probably the wealthiest of them), and while some rich and powerful individuals joined the church (Zaccheus in Luke 19, Sergius Paulus in Acts 13), the vast majority of converts were the poor or slaves. Some think the future tense "will enter" (εἰσελεύσεται) connotes final eschatology (as in vv. 28–29), "entering" eternity, but the immediate context (v. 24) is realized, referring to conversion.

19:24 "Again I tell you, it is easier for a camel to pass through the eye of a needle than for a wealthy person to enter the kingdom of God" (πάλιν δὲ λέγω ὑμῖν, εὐκοπώτερόν ἐστιν κάμηλον διὰ τρυπήματος ῥαφίδος διελθεῖν ἢ πλούσιον εἰσελθεῖν εἰς τὴν βασιλείαν τοῦ θεοῦ). "Again" (πάλιν) points to v. 23; this is the second solemn truth in a row. The emphasis here, by virtue of repetition in vv. 23–24, is on "entering the kingdom."[16] a frequent metaphor in Matthew for experiencing salvation (5:20; 7:21; 18:3, 9; 19:17).

Jesus' analogy for the degree of difficulty has been long misunderstood. Many still say that it refers to the Needle's Eye Gate in Jerusalem, a low opening that would be hard for a camel to get through. However, no such gate existed in Jesus' time! Others have said "needle" simply refers to a low opening like the narrow door of 7:13–14 or they see it as a "rope" (κάμιλον as opposed to "camel" [κάμηλον] in the text). Such attempts to water down the imagery are unnecessary; this is rabbinic hyperbole (e.g., "straining the gnat but

15. The first clause is framed with participles, the temporal "having heard" and the circumstantial "grieving."

16. Note that the parallels between "kingdom of heaven" (v. 23) and "kingdom of God" (v. 24) at the end of each verse shows that the two are synonymous in Matthew (see on 12:28; cf. 21:31, 43—these are the only places in Matthew where "kingdom of God" is found).

swallowing the camel" in 23:24), a stylistic device Jesus uses often. It depicts the largest animal in Palestine (a camel) going through the smallest hole (the eye of a needle) to illustrate how "difficult" it is for the wealthy to know God.

19:25 Now after his disciples heard this, they were totally amazed and said (ἀκούσαντες δὲ οἱ μαθηταὶ ἐξεπλήσσοντο σφόδρα λέγοντες). Elsewhere the crowds are amazed (7:28; 13:54; 22:33), here the disciples, but the astonishment is always addressed to Jesus' teaching. In Mark it is frequently the result of his miraculous power (Mark 1:27; 7:37) as well, but Matthew centers more on amazement at his teaching and tends to remove the amazement from miracle stories (cf. Mark 2:12; 5:42; 6:51; 9:15). This is in keeping with Matthew's emphasis on Jesus as the teacher of eschatological wisdom and the final interpreter of Torah.

Here the astonishment is caused by the general Jewish belief that riches actually signified favor with God, who blessed the piety of the family with earthly rewards. So for them the rich young man with his superficial piety was in reality one of God's chosen. His wealth "provided the possibility of both deeds of charity (almsgiving) and leisure for the study of Torah and the pursuit of righteousness."[17] If it is impossible for such a one to enter the kingdom, who can?

19:25 "Then who can be saved?" (Τίς ἄρα δύναται σωθῆναι;). The question of the disciples is the natural response, "Is it possible for anyone to be saved?" σῴζω in the sense of eschatological salvation is found in 1:21; 10:22; 24:13. Matthew also uses it of healing as both physical and spiritual salvation (see on 9:21 – 22). If the wealthy, already blessed by God, cannot make it into heaven, then no one can. δύναται in this context means "by any power known to us." Like all Jews, the disciples assume salvation is theirs by divine right, i.e., by ancestry. They are totally confused at this point.

19:26 But Jesus looked at[18] them and said, "For human beings this is impossible, but for God all things are possible" (ἐμβλέψας δὲ ὁ Ἰησοῦς εἶπεν αὐτοῖς, Παρὰ ἀνθρώποις τοῦτο ἀδύνατόν ἐστιν, παρὰ δὲ θεῷ πάντα δυνατά). Jesus' steady gaze at his disciples is a dramatic touch; he seems to be looking deep into their very being. Humanly speaking, the rich cannot be moved away from their security and dependence on the world's goods. Of course, in reality the salvation of anyone at all is a virtual impossibility. It is only by the grace of God that any of us belong to him.

There is an echo here of Gen 18:14 ("Is anything too hard for the Lord?"); Job 42:2 ("I know that you can do all things"; cf. Isa 40:28, Jer 32:17). As Nolland says, this involves "the breaking of the mesmerizing effect through which riches control those who possess them."[19] God alone can break the barriers of sin and bring people to himself, and he is in process of doing just that through the kingdom message of Jesus and the disciples.

19:27 Then Peter responded, "Look, we have left everything and followed you" (Τότε ἀποκριθεὶς ὁ Πέτρος εἶπεν αὐτῷ, Ἰδοὺ ἡμεῖς ἀφήκαμεν πάντα καὶ ἠκολουθήσαμέν σοι). This verse provides a transition, concluding vv. 23 – 26 and introducing vv. 28 – 30. In typical fashion Peter speaks for the group (cf. 14:28; 15:15; 16:16, 22; 17:4; 18:21), and as usual he shows his misunderstanding. Note the emphasis on first person pronouns ("we" [ἡμεῖς] and "us" [ἡμῖν] frame Peter's statement). He claims that, unlike the young man, they have "left everything" (cf. vv. 21b, 22) and "followed" Jesus (cf. v. 21c). That is a delusion of grandeur,

17. Hagner, *Matthew 14 – 28*, 561.
18. Another circumstantial participle, see on 4:4.
19. Nolland, *Matthew*, 796.

for their ambition for power and glory is intact (cf. 18:1; 20:20–21).[20] As Bruner says, "If we are not careful, too, we can successfully avoid the idol of money only to find ourselves with the new idol of self-congratulation."[21]

19:27 What will there be then for us?" (τί ἄρα ἔσται ἡμῖν;). Jesus will build on and treat seriously their query, which in essence is, "What's in it for us?" It will lead into important teaching on the concept of rewards. As in the Sermon on the Mount, God knows that even though we do not serve him for the rewards, we are human and still ask the question deep down, just as Peter does here. So God and Jesus go on and tell us the answer to our human question.

19:28 So Jesus said to them, "I tell you the truth, as for you who have followed me, at the renewal of the world when the Son of Man sits upon his glorious[22] throne" (ὁ δὲ Ἰησοῦς εἶπεν αὐτοῖς, Ἀμὴν λέγω ὑμῖν ὅτι ὑμεῖς οἱ ἀκολουθήσαντές μοι ἐν τῇ παλιγγενεσίᾳ, ὅταν καθίσῃ ὁ υἱὸς τοῦ ἀνθρώπου ἐπὶ θρόνου δόξης αὐτοῦ). This second "amen" (ἀμήν) saying of the chapter (cf. v. 23) points once more to an important truth. The throne saying is found only in Matthew in this section (cf. Luke 22:30, where it is said after the Lord's Supper in a discussion of greatness that parallels Matt 20:24–28).

The "renewal of the world" (παλιγγενεσία) is found only here and Titus 3:5 in the NT.[23] In Titus it refers to regeneration and renewal at conversion,[24] while here it has a final sense for the cosmic renewal of God's creation in the sense of Matt 5:18; 24:34–35; 2 Pet 3:7, 10, 12; Rev 21:1.[25] The idea of the Son of Man on his throne (cf. 25:31) is rooted in the throne of the Ancient of Days and the universal dominion of the "one like a son of man" in Dan 7:9–10, 13–14 as well as "sit at my right hand" in Ps 110:1. There is also a close connection with the *Similitudes of Enoch* (*1 En.* 62:5, 29, both of which connect "the throne of his glory" with the Son of Man). He will share the throne of Yahweh for eternity (cf. Rev 4:2; 5:6; 22:1, 3).

19:28 You will also sit on twelve thrones judging the twelve tribes of Israel (καθήσεσθε καὶ ὑμεῖς ἐπὶ δώδεκα θρόνους κρίνοντες τὰς δώδεκα φυλὰς τοῦ Ἰσραήλ). "You who have followed me" (ὑμεῖς οἱ ἀκολουθήσαντές μοι) is emphatic, placed at the beginning of Jesus' statement in v. 28a and then picked up again here with a pleonastic or redundant second "you" (ὑμεῖς) in the main clause (see BDF 297). Jesus wants it clear what the future reward will be for those "following" him.

It has often been assumed that the "judging" of Israel by the Twelve would be a single event at the final judgment (connected with the event of the great white throne in Rev 20:11–15), and that is a distinct possibility in light of 25:31–46 (the

20. Some interpret this not of selfishness but uncertainty (Ridderbos, Blomberg, Morris), as the disciples hope they have followed Jesus properly but wonder. The fact that Jesus does not rebuke them may favor this somewhat, but the portrait of the disciples in this section militates against it. Jesus did not rebuke their statement in 19:10 that "it is better not to marry," but that did not make it a correct statement. It represented an aspect of truth (as here) and Jesus drew out that truth (as here), but it still was due to ignorance.

21. Bruner, *Matthew 13–28*, 311.

22. Is "glory" (δόξης) a descriptive genitive ("glorious throne") or epexegetical ("throne of his glory")? The anarthrous form favors the former.

23. For its Greco-Roman use, see J. D. M. Derrett, "*Palingenesia* (Matthew 19.28)," *JSNT* 20 (1984): 51–58 (esp. 51–52); and Nolland, *Matthew*, 798–99.

24. See the extensive discussion in Marshall, *Pastoral Epistles*, 319–20.

25. See David C. Sim, "The Meaning of παλιγγενεσία in Matthew 19.28," *JSNT* 50 (1993): 3–12 (esp. 7–10). Derrett's argument (also Luz) that it means "resurrection" is possible (see Marshall, *Pastoral Epistles*, 320) but does not fit the context of Matthew here.

judgment of the nations). However, the development in the rest of the NT as well as the present participle "judging" (κρίνοντες) here fits the view that it refers to an ongoing period of ruling/judging in the period leading up to the eschaton. In Eph 2:6 the believers at conversion are seated with God in Christ in the heavenlies.[26] In 1 Cor 6:2–3 the saints judge the world as well as angels, and in Rev 3:21; 20:4, 6; 22:5 the saints sit on thrones and "reign with [Christ]," first for the millennial period (however that is interpreted) and then for eternity. France sees this as an allusion to Dan 7:13–14, with the saints sharing in the kingship of the enthroned Son of Man, in keeping with the original meaning of Dan 7, in which the "son of man" is the people of God to whom "judgment was given, and they possessed the kingdom" (Dan 7:22).[27]

Another issue is whether this should be taken literally as the Twelve judging Israel itself for its unbelief (so Bonnard, Carson, Gundry) or as a symbol for all the saints judging the nations (so Hill, Carter, Blomberg). In light of all the NT evidence, the second is more likely. Are there to be two levels of saints at the eschaton, the Twelve and then everyone else? At several points throughout this commentary it has been pointed out that Peter and the Twelve are corporately identified with the church and so symbolize all the saints, and in 25:31–46 and 1 Cor 6:2 it is the world that is judged. So the literal understanding is doubtful, and v. 29 connects these promises with "everyone" in the church as the new Israel.

19:29 And everyone who has left homes or brothers or sisters or father or mother or children or fields for my name's sake will receive a hundred[28] times as much (καὶ πᾶς ὅστις ἀφῆκεν οἰκίας ἢ ἀδελφοὺς ἢ ἀδελφὰς ἢ πατέρα ἢ μητέρα ἢ τέκνα ἢ ἀγροὺς ἕνεκεν τοῦ ὀνόματός μου, ἑκατονταπλασίονα λήμψεται). There are three parts to vv. 28–29 (28, 29a, 29b) and as Matthew often does, he centers his teaching on final reward rather than present blessing. In Mark 10:30 the "hundred times as much" concerns present reward (Mark has "in this present age"), but Matthew centers on final reward by removing the present reference and surrounding it with final eschatology.[29]

Jesus expands the focus from the Twelve to "every" follower. Since Peter said they had "left everything," Jesus picks up on that and names two main types of things that various followers have had to surrender—loved ones (brothers, sisters, father, mother, children) and possessions ("fields"),[30] with "homes" referring to both. The promise is that in eternity they "will receive" (from God) a hundred times as much, referring to the incredible family and home in heaven (cf. John 14:2–3).

19:29 ... and will inherit eternal life (καὶ ζωὴν αἰώνιον κληρονομήσει). The greatest gift of all is the eternal life that the wealthy young man asked for in v. 16. He wanted to earn it by works, but Jesus makes it clear one can "inherit" it only from God. Only by turning to God and "following," i.e., living entirely for him, can anyone "enter" eternal

26. P. T. O'Brien, *The Letter to the Ephesians* (Grand Rapids: Eerdmans, 1999), 170–71.

27. France, *Gospel of Matthew*, 742–43.

28. Some manuscripts (e.g., B L) have "many times as much" (πολλαπλασίονα) rather than "a hundred times as much" (ἑκατονταπλασίονα, supported by ℵ C* L W Θ TR et al.), but it is generally agreed that this reading is an assimilation to Luke 18:29.

29. There could be an inaugurated thrust, with the "hundred fathers and mothers" referring partly to those who will be a father or mother (e.g., "brother Bob" or "sister Sue") in the church now (cf. 1 John 2:10–14 or the constant use of "brothers and sisters" in the NT) but Matthew's emphasis is on the eternal situation.

30. Thomas E. Schmidt, "Mark 10.29–30; Matthew 19.29: 'Leave Houses ... and Region?'" *NTS* 28 (1992): 617–20, argues that ἀγρούς here means not "lands" but "territory," thus forming the logical movement from house to family to territory. This is viable but perhaps not necessary. "Lands" catches the idea quite well.

life. It is by becoming part of God's family that inheritance becomes an option. Eternal reward is spoken of as an "inheritance" also in 5:5; 25:34.

19:30 But many who are first will be last, and the last will be first (πολλοὶ δὲ ἔσονται πρῶτοι ἔσχατοι καὶ ἔσχατοι πρῶτοι). This is often called "the reversal of roles" and is a frequent theme in Luke. It will be repeated at the end of the next pericope in reverse order (20:16), with the inclusion forming a chiasm. The parable of the workers in the vineyard (20:1 – 15) is intended as an illustration of this very principle, so it is a dominant theme here. Those like the wealthy young man who seek primacy in this life will suffer the greatest loss eternally, and those like the disciples (claimed in 19:27) who surrender everything will have the greatest reward. As in 18:1 – 5; 19:13 – 15, followers must be willing to take the lowly place and humble attitude of a child to be "greatest" (18:1, 4) in the kingdom.

Theology in Application

This passage centers on one of the most emphasized themes in Scripture, the denial of the world's riches and the use of one's resources to help others.[31] It revolves around the basic choice every person must make between self and God. The challenge to eschew possessions and live entirely for God is the basic question coming from the garden of Eden.

1. Not Works Righteousness

Jesus is not teaching a works righteousness within which we find eternal life by keeping the commandments. There are two aspects to keep in mind concerning Jesus' "keep the commandments" in v. 17. (1) He is drawing the rich young man into reflection on the reality of his life of piety, probably to get him to realize his sin. As Paul said, one cannot find salvation by observing the law (Rom 3:20, 28; Gal 3:2 – 3); rather, the law makes us conscious of our sin and drives us to Christ. (2) Jesus is serious regarding the necessity of a life of obedience. This is a constant theme in Matthew's portrayal of Jesus' teaching — righteousness means living life according to the commandments of God.

2. Rejection of "Idols"

To follow Jesus involves a total rejection of the idol of possessions. Jesus demands "perfection" (v. 21), and that does not mean two kinds of Christians, the strong (who seek it) and the weak (who cannot seek it). All followers must come to grips with the antithesis between God and possessions. At the same time this does not mean that all must sell all their possessions. Clearly the problem with the young man was one

31. For the biblical teaching on this issue, see Blomberg, *Neither Poverty Nor Riches.*

of idolatry, but Jesus did not demand that Zaccheus (Luke 19:1 – 10) sell everything. Wealth is not the problem; "love of money" (1 Tim 6:9 – 10) is the problem.

But virtually all of us rationalize away our fascination with the world's goods.[32] We say, "But I don't love it; it isn't an idol." However, our actions prove that we are deceiving ourselves. Christ demands to be first in our life, and when God blesses us financially, he is giving us an opportunity to minister to others who are less fortunate (see also "Theology in Application" on 6:19 – 24). John Wesley often preached that "if you make money and do not give all you can and do all the good you can with it, you may be a living person, but you are a dead person."[33]

3. The Wealthy and Their Wealth

The wealthy cannot buy their way into the kingdom; in fact, that very attitude makes it nearly impossible for them to find God. Bruner shows how the very attempts to "minimize" the power of the "camel/needle's eye" by turning it into a rope or a low gate demonstrates the danger; it stresses humility as a path to salvation and "teaches how to be covetous and Christian at the same time."[34] In other words, people today (including all too many preachers) want to sidestep the severity of Jesus' challenge to the wealthy. In many churches rich Christians control the church and its decisions through their giving. It is not piety but power that controls, and too few realize the barrier this places on their walk with God.

4. Rewards

While we do not serve the Lord for the reward we will get, Jesus wants us to know that God will indeed reward us for our life of piety. We do not want to fall into Peter's error of asking, "What's in it for us?" That is a veneer of piety turned into self-interest. Yet at the same time Jesus wants us to know that God will vindicate us for our sacrifices and suffering. In fact, "reward" occurs seven times in 6:1 – 18 (1, 2, 4, 5 , 6, 16, 18) and is a central theme of the entire Sermon on the Mount (e.g., the eschatological promise in each of the beatitudes of 5:1 – 12). The key is our motivation and priorities — earthly or heavenly (cf. 6:19 – 21). Do we live for the glory of God or for self? Do we strive for the things of this world or the things of God? That will determine our true destiny.

32. On this see France, *Gospel of Matthew*, 731, who says, "There is … an undeniable element of self-justification in such exegesis of this by the wealthy (a category which in comparative terms includes almost all Western readers of the gospel)." He argues that at the fundamental level "affluence is in essential opposition to the kingdom of heaven."

33. Witherington, *Matthew*, 372.

34. Bruner, *Matthew 13 – 28*, 305. He quotes Luz (*Matthew 8 – 20*, 516), "Even more interesting than this new interpretation itself (i.e., the city gate in Jerusalem rumor) is the question why it has remained so popular."

CHAPTER 84

Matthew 20:1 – 16

Literary Context

This is closely connected to the previous verse (19:30) on "the last shall be first" and in fact concludes with that verse in reverse order (20:16). Thus this parable centers on the concept of reward and God's reversal of human concepts of pay/reward on the basis of God's grace rather than human effort. As France says, ch. 19 is dominated by the way the kingdom of heaven reverses human mores (the little child, the rich young man), and this parable now reverses "human expectations" regarding rewards for discipleship.[1]

VI. The Movement to the Cross (19:1 – 25:46)
- **A. Jesus' Deeds: Opposition and Discipleship (19:1 – 22:46)**
  - **1. The Road to Jerusalem (19:1 – 20:34)**
    - c. Wealth and Kingdom Rewards (19:16 – 30)
    - ➦ **d. Parable of Workers in the Vineyard (20:1 – 16)**
    - e. Third Passion Prediction and Kingdom Honor (20:17 – 28)

Main Idea

According to Davies and Allison, this section is more about "the last will be first" than the other ("the first will be last") because in the parable both have an equal reward.[2] The primary theme is the grace of God who treats all equally, even

1. France, *Gospel of Matthew*, 747 – 48.

2. Davies and Allison, *Matthew*, 3, 67 – 68. However, they fall into the normal redaction-critical pitfall by assuming that the Matthean context is artificial and secondary (so also Gundry, Luz; Mary Ann Tolbert, *Perspectives on the Parables: An Approach to Multiple Interpretations* [Philadelphia: Fortress, 1979], 60), and they posit an original meaning as a parable about the last judgment and a warning against pride in assuming that one is "among the first." But such attempts are speculative at best, and the only context we know is the one in Matthew. There is no reason to separate the parable from its frame (19:30; 20:16) and larger context. Some also posit a setting in which this is addressed to the Pharisees who believe they will be "first," e.g., Christian Dietzfelbinger, "Das Gleichnis von den Arbeitern im Weinberg als Jesus-wort," *EvT* 43 (1983): 126 – 37.

those "hired" at the last minute. Whether one takes Jesus' intended point to be God's acceptance of tax collectors and sinners or of Gentiles or of all disciples from the first (the Twelve) to the last (the Gentiles — all three are probably correct),[3] the issue is God's grace and mercy toward all equally, both in the present (realized eschatology) and at the final reward (final eschatology).

Translation

Matthew 20:1-16

1a	Scene #1 Analogy	*"The kingdom of heaven is like a story about a landowner*
b		*who went out at sunrise*
		to hire workers
		for his vineyard.
2a	Group #1	*[1] So he agreed with the workers to pay them a denarius*
		per day and
		sent them into his vineyard.
3a	Group #2	*[2] At about the third hour he went out and*
		saw other workers
		standing idle
		in the marketplace.
4a		*He told them,*
b	Instruction	*'You also go into the vineyard,*
		and I will pay you whatever is just.'
5a	Action	*And they went.*
b	Group #3	*[3] Again at about the sixth and*
c	Group #4	*[4] ninth hour he did the same.*
6a	Group #5	*[5] About the eleventh hour*
		he went out and found still another group standing idle,
b		*and he asked them,*
c	Question	*'Why have you stood here idle the whole day?'*
7a		*They replied,*
b	Answer	*'Because no one has hired us.'*
c	Instruction	*So he said to them,*
d		*'You also go into the vineyard.'*
8a	Scene #2 Setting	*Now when evening had arrived,*
b		*the master of the vineyard said to his foreman,*
c	Instruction	*'Call the workers*
		and pay them their wage, from the last to the first.'

3. See France, *Matthew* (TNTC), 289 – 90, who also adds the penitent thief at the cross in Luke 23:39 – 43 as an example. M. L. Barré, "The Workers in the Vineyard," *BT* 24 (1986): 173 – 80, believes this is about disciples who are the "last" in terms of rejection by the world yet taken care of by the Father.

9a	Group #5 Action	And *those . . . received a denarius each*
		who came about the eleventh hour.
10a	Group #1 Action	So *when the first group came,*
b		*they expected to receive more pay.*
c		Yet *even they themselves received a denarius each.*
11a	Objection	*After they received it,*
b		*they complained against the landowner, saying,*
12a		*'Those who were last did work for one hour,*
b		yet *you made them equal to us*
c		*who have borne the burden of the day and its heat.'*
13a	Response	But *he answered one of them,*
b		*'Friend, I have not cheated you.*
c		*You agreed with me for a denarius, didn't you?*
14a		*Take what is yours and go.*
b		*I want to give this last person the same*
		as I also gave you.
15a		*I am permitted to do what I want with what is mine, right?*
b		Or *is your eye evil because I am good?'*
16a	Conclusion/Aphorism	*In this way the last will be first and the first last."*

Structure and Literary Form

This parable stems from Matthew's special material (M) and is found only here, but this does not make it wholly redactional.[4] It fits well into this context and makes a valid contribution to the whole. Structurally, there are two major sections, the hiring (vv. 1 – 7) and the paying (vv. 8 – 15), with each having a distinct structure, the first section on the hiring process (vv. 2, 3 – 4, 5, 6 – 7) and the second on the controversy over the equal pay to all (vv. 8 – 10, 11 – 12, 13 – 15). Verse 16 is the moral of the story, repeating 19:30 in reverse order for emphasis.

Exegetical Outline

➡ I. The Hiring of the Workers (20:1 – 7)

A. The setting — the hiring by the vineyard owner (v. 1)

B. The first group hired for a denarius a day (v. 2)

4. Most agree it goes back to Jesus himself, and Carter, *Households*, 146 – 48, answers objections that it is secondary (e.g., the absence of a "reversal" motif, the positive use of a wealthy landowner [in light of the context's negative evaluation of wealth]) and shows that it fits the context quite well.

C. The second group hired at the third hour (vv. 3 – 4)
D. Others hired at the sixth and ninth hours (v. 5)
E. Final group hired at the eleventh hour (vv. 6 – 7)

II. The Dispute over the Equal Pay (20:8 – 15)

A. The workers paid in reverse order (vv. 8 – 10)
1. The order to pay them "from last to first" (v. 8)
2. The eleventh hour workers given a denarius (v. 9)
3. The first-hour workers also given a denarius (v. 10)

B. The complaint about the equal pay (vv. 11 – 12)

C. The owner's reply (vv. 13 – 15)
1. The denarius was agreed upon (v. 2) (v. 13)
2. It was the owner's desire to be gracious to all (v. 14)
3. The owner is free to do what he wants (v. 15a)
4. The evil of envy (v. 15b)

III. Conclusion: The Great Reversal (20:16)

Explanation of the Text

20:1 The kingdom of heaven is like a story about a landowner (Ὁμοία γάρ ἐστιν ἡ βασιλεία τῶν οὐρανῶν ἀνθρώπῳ οἰκοδεσπότῃ). "It is like" (ὁμοία ἐστιν) occurs often in the parable chapter (13:31, 33, 44, 45, 47) and means "it is the case with the kingdom as with this story ..." (see on 13:24). For "landowner" (οἰκοδεσπότης) see on 13:52; here it is the owner of the vineyard. Some think the landowner to be Jesus, but with the echo of Isa 5 (the song of the vineyard) and the theme of divine reward, God is the more likely allusion.

20:1 ... who went out at sunrise to hire workers for his vineyard (ὅστις ἐξῆλθεν ἅμα πρωῒ μισθώσασθαι ἐργάτας εἰς τὸν ἀμπελῶνα αὐτοῦ). Vineyards were plentiful in the rich soil of Galilee and many of Jesus' parables reflect this setting (e.g., Matt 21:28 – 32; Mark 12:1 – 9; John 15:1 – 6), especially since vineyards symbolized the people of Israel (Ps 80:8 – 9; Isa 5:1, 7; 27:2; Jer 2:21). It was normal in the first century to work twelve-hour days during harvest (though it must be admitted that the same was true of sowing the seed — the text does not say), and so ἅμα πρωῒ refers to "sunrise," the beginning of the workday. So this reflects harvest season, when the owner would need to hire[5] extra workers to take the grapes off the vine and to do various other tasks (e.g., guard the crops, drive the donkeys).[6] Day laborers (the lowest social group outside of slaves) would gather in the marketplace of towns and wait to be hired. It was a precarious existence, but they had little choice. Many were "freedmen," former slaves.

20:2 So he agreed[7] with the workers to pay them a denarius per day and sent them into his

5. μισθώσασθαι may have double meaning, to "hire" in the story but also to "reward" the workers, the point of this section (including 19:28 – 30).

6. See Keener, *Matthew*, 481 – 82, for a good discussion of background.

7. Here and in v. 3 we have two more of Matthew's many circumstantial participles that become virtually another main verb (cf. 4:21, 23).

vineyard (συμφωνήσας δὲ μετὰ τῶν ἐργατῶν ἐκ δηναρίου τὴν ἡμέραν ἀπέστειλεν αὐτοὺς εἰς τὸν ἀμπελῶνα αὐτοῦ). A denarius per day was the normal rate for a day laborer,[8] and this amount will be critical in the last part of the story (vv. 11–13). So the first group of workers begins at the normal time, shortly after the sun arose (at about 6:00 a.m.).

20:3 At about[9] the third hour he went out and saw other workers standing idle in the marketplace (καὶ ἐξελθὼν περὶ τρίτην ὥραν εἶδεν ἄλλους ἑστῶτας ἐν τῇ ἀγορᾷ ἀργούς). While the Roman day started at midnight, the Jewish day began at 6:00 a.m., so this means 9:00 a.m. It was common to break a day into quarters of three hours each (see Mark 15:25, 33, 34, where Mark divides the crucifixion of Jesus into these same segments). It is difficult to know why some workers had not been hired yet. Some posit that "standing idle" (ἑστῶτας ἀργούς, a circumstantial participle modifying "found" rather than an adjectival participle) means that they were lazy or perhaps had worked their own fields first. However, vv. 6–7 say clearly that they had been in the marketplace all day but no one had hired them (so were "idle"), and that fits the emphasis on the "last" in 19:30; 20:16. They apparently were the least impressive workers.

20:4–5a He told them, "You also go into the vineyard, and I will pay you whatever is just." And they went (καὶ ἐκείνοις εἶπεν, Ὑπάγετε καὶ ὑμεῖς εἰς τὸν ἀμπελῶνα, καὶ ὃ ἐὰν ᾖ δίκαιον δώσω ὑμῖν. οἱ δὲ ἀπῆλθον). The landowner may have miscalculated how many workers he needed and found out he had to have more, although it could also be that in light of vv. 6–7 he did it for the workers' sake, to give them work (Nolland suggests not that he needs them but that he can use them). Still, it seems the former is better, since it explains why he kept going back to the marketplace. At any rate, when he gets there he finds more workers who have not yet been hired. He promises them a fair recompense, which the reader naturally assumes will be a percentage of the amount paid those hired earlier. It is possible to translate ἀπῆλθον as "they went away" from the landowner and did not go to the field, but it makes better sense to translate that "they went away" from the marketplace and worked in the field.[10]

20:5b Again at about the sixth and ninth hour he did the same (πάλιν δὲ ἐξελθὼν περὶ ἕκτην καὶ ἐνάτην ὥραν ἐποίησεν ὡσαύτως). The landowner still needed more workers, so at noon and 3:00 p.m. he went back to the marketplace and hired still more workers. There is one slight inconsistency — the implication seems to be that they had not been there earlier (implicitly, he hired all "standing idle" in vv. 3–4), so this favors the supposition that they had been working their own fields. Yet in v. 6 the final group has been standing idle all day. However, Jesus may not have cared about such details, and the five hirings may have been "local color" (see the discussion of "interpreting parables" in ch. 13), especially since the discussion in vv. 8–15 only concerns the "first and last" group of workers.[11] So in the story

8. See Nolland, *Matthew*, 806n, who points out that a scribe would earn twelve denarii a week, and some Roman sources say that in Italy the wage was even lower.

9. This is a temporal use of περί, "at about, at around."

10. See Anonymous, "The Translation of Matthew 20:4–5 — An Exchange of Views between a Translator and his Consultants," *BT* 35 (1984): 437–41.

11. But see F. C. Glover, "Workers for the Vineyard, Mt. 20, 4," *ExpTim* 86 (1975): 310–11, who argues that "they went" (ἀπῆλθον) in v. 5 means they refused the owner's offer and "left." However, this reads more into the context than is there. Carter, *Households*, 154n, adds that in 21:29 this same verb means acceptance of the invitation (contra 19:22; 22:5, where it is rejection), and that "from the last to the first" in v. 8 suggests a graduated set of payments to several groups.

there are five groups, hired at 6 a.m., 9 a.m., noon, 3 p.m., and 5 p.m.

20:6 About the eleventh hour he went out and found still another group standing idle, and he asked them, "Why have you stood here idle the whole day?" (περὶ δὲ τὴν ἑνδεκάτην ἐξελθὼν εὗρεν ἄλλους ἑστῶτας καὶ λέγει αὐτοῖς, Τί ὧδε ἑστήκατε ὅλην τὴν ἡμέραν ἀργοί;). This final group fits closely the old adage regarding "the eleventh hour" when help comes, meaning at the last minute (here = 5:00 p.m.). One would think they would have given up long before (note the emphasis on "standing idle," repeated twice), and in real life that probably would have happened. It is also hard to imagine why the landowner would have hired people with only an hour of work time to go, but that is part of the story form, and this is the critical group for the dialogue in vv. 11 – 13. By having the landowner address them particularly, Jesus gives them greater importance than the groups in vv. 3 – 5, as will be seen in the second half of the parable.

20:7 They replied, "Because[12] no one has hired us." So he said to them, "You also go into the vineyard" (λέγουσιν αὐτῷ, Ὅτι οὐδεὶς ἡμᾶς ἐμισθώσατο. λέγει αὐτοῖς, Ὑπάγετε καὶ ὑμεῖς εἰς τὸν ἀμπελῶνα). Clearly there were several farms that needed help for the harvest, but these poor day laborers had been rejected by everyone. They clearly wanted to work, or they would have gone home long before. The owner's reply to them is the exact wording as in v. 4 and prepares for the startling equality between the groups in terms of pay (vv. 8 – 10). Still, the reader would think that their pay would be rather minimal.

20:8 Now when evening had arrived,[13] the master of the vineyard said to his foreman, "Call the workers and pay them their wage, from the last to the first" (ὀψίας δὲ γενομένης λέγει ὁ κύριος τοῦ ἀμπελῶνος τῷ ἐπιτρόπῳ αὐτοῦ, Κάλεσον τοὺς ἐργάτας καὶ ἀπόδος αὐτοῖς τὸν μισθὸν ἀρξάμενος ἀπὸ τῶν ἐσχάτων ἕως τῶν πρώτων). It was natural to pay day laborers when the work was concluded, namely, in the evening (cf. Lev 19:13; Deut 24:15).[14] The use of "master" (κύριος) for the landowner heightens the allusion to God, "Lord of all," and to God's recompense to all people (cf. Rev 22:12). "Foreman" (ἐπίτροπος) refers to the one who gives the orders (from the verb "to order, permit") and could refer to the governor of a province or a steward, the foreman of an estate.

The one to distribute the pay would naturally be the foreman who had directed the workers in the field. There is no special reason why the "last" hired would be paid first, except that the story form demands it (and prepares for v. 16). It is this that makes the first group aware that they had been paid equally and leads to their complaint (they would naturally have left if they had been paid first).

20:9 And those who came about the eleventh hour received a denarius each[15] (καὶ ἐλθόντες οἱ περὶ τὴν ἑνδεκάτην ὥραν ἔλαβον ἀνὰ δηνάριον). When the master hired people at the last minute, that was surprising, but this pay time is even more so. This group has only worked for an hour (from 5:00 to 6:00 p.m.), yet they receive the very same payment (a denarius, a full day's wage) that was promised to the group who had worked for twelve hours (v. 2). Thus the reader is amazed at the generosity of the

12. In the context this is best seen as causal "because" (ὅτι) rather than ὅτι leading into direct address.

13. Here we have one of Matthew's temporal genitive absolutes, see on 8:1.

14. Davies and Allison, *Matthew*, 3:73, say the reference to evening reminds one of the last judgment. It is difficult to see why, but on the whole the entire context of 19:28 – 20:16 has final reward at the eschaton in mind.

15. This is the distributive use of "each" (ἀνά) with the accusative, see BDF §204.

"master" and would naturally expect the first group to be paid proportionately higher.

20:10 So when the first group came, they expected to receive more pay. Yet even they themselves received a denarius each (καὶ ἐλθόντες οἱ πρῶτοι ἐνόμισαν ὅτι πλεῖον λήμψονται· καὶ ἔλαβον τὸ ἀνὰ δηνάριον καὶ αὐτοί). Now comes the "reversal of expectation" (see on parables in ch. 13) intended by Jesus to shock the hearer. Everyone would expect those who worked far longer to "receive more pay." So the second clause would have the readers scratching their heads in consternation. When "even they"[16] receive the denarius promised in v. 2, it is not that this would be unfair, since that was the contract. Rather, it was the master's generosity to the final group that has everyone confused. As Nolland says, "Despite a dramatic contrast in work done, there is no difference in wage received. Not only in the ancient world would such behavior cause resentment but today as well."[17]

20:11 After they received it, they complained against the landowner (λαβόντες δὲ ἐγόγγυζον κατὰ τοῦ οἰκοδεσπότου). This first group complains "against" (κατά) the master. This may well mean that their unhappiness is expressed first to others (probably anyone who was around) and then (v. 12) taken to the owner himself. In Num 14:27 LXX this verb is used of Israel complaining against God in the wilderness (in 14:2, 36 it is also grumbling against Moses and Aaron).

20:12 ... saying, "Those who were last did work for one hour, yet you made them equal to us who have borne the burden of the day and its heat" (λέγοντες, Οὗτοι οἱ ἔσχατοι μίαν ὥραν ἐποίησαν, καὶ ἴσους ἡμῖν αὐτοὺς ἐποίησας τοῖς βαστάσασι τὸ βάρος τῆς ἡμέρας καὶ τὸν καύσωνα). Their complaint is natural in any work-related context. ποιέω can mean "work" with the accusative of time (BAGD, 682 [2c]); there is a contrast between what little they "did" and how much the owner "did" (a second use of ποιέω) for them. By paying the final group the same amount, the owner made them "equal,"[18] and by doing so the master who had promised to be "just" (v. 4) was unjust to the first group. After all, they are the ones who have suffered (βαστάζω often connotes the idea of "enduring" difficulties) the "burden" of the intense "heat" all day long (perhaps they are hoping for extra remuneration for their discomfort).[19]

20:13 But he answered[20] one of them, "Friend, I have not cheated you. You agreed with me for a denarius,[21] didn't you?" (ὁ δὲ ἀποκριθεὶς ἑνὶ αὐτῶν εἶπεν, Ἑταῖρε, οὐκ ἀδικῶ σε· οὐχὶ δηναρίου συνεφώνησάς μοι;). The owner's response consists of the next three verses and will address the complaint in two ways — first the legal situation (he has fulfilled the contract, v. 13) and then the moral situation (his right to do as he wishes out of goodness, vv. 14 – 15). With a series of three rhetorical questions (note the use of "not" [οὐχί], expecting

16. Note the emphatic "even they themselves" (καὶ αὐτοί), placed last in the clause for special effect.

17. Nolland, *Matthew*, 810. J. D. M. Derrett, "Workers in the Vineyard: A Parable of Jesus," *JJS* 25 (1974): 64 – 91, disagrees, arguing that the owner is giving the minimum wage to all the workers in order to convince those hired later to work in his vineyard. However, this does not really fit the development of the story and removes the element of surprise entirely, turning it into a normal event rather than a parable.

18. Luz, *Matthew 8 – 20*, 532n, says "equal" (ἴσος) is "a fundamental dimension of justice," and by using it here a note of irony is introduced.

19. Gundry, *Matthew*, 398, sees two aspects of the complaint: failure to note the difference between one hour of work and twelve hours, and failure to "note the difference between the heat of midday and the cool of the evening."

20. On this formulation, see 4:4.

21. "Denarius" (δηναρίου) is a genitive of price or value, cf. BDF §179.

the answer yes) he forces the complainers to reflect on the meaning of "what is right" from v. 4.

He addresses "one of them," probably to stress (to the reader as well) the individual responsibility in this.[22] He begins by calling him "friend, comrade" (ἑταῖρε), which could mean the owner does not know the man's name. In Matthew (22:12 [the man without wedding clothes]; 26:50 [Jesus' arrest]) this word is used with those in the wrong; note also the contrast with the complainers, who use no respectful address with the master in v. 12. In a context like this ἀδικέω can mean "wronged" in the sense of "I have not cheated you" (BAGD). The first question centers on the original agreement for the regular pay of a denarius (v. 2), and that is exactly what the men have been paid.[23] There are no legal grounds for complaint.

20:14 "Take what is yours and go. I want to give this last person the same as I also gave you" (ἆρον τὸ σὸν καὶ ὕπαγε· θέλω δὲ τούτῳ τῷ ἐσχάτῳ δοῦναι ὡς καὶ σοί). The master dismisses the complaining worker and in effect orders him out of the vineyard. As Harnish says, the scene is now "a tribunal in which the accuser becomes the accused."[24] So now "go" (ὕπαγε, used in vv. 4, 7 for entering the vineyard to work) becomes a command to leave.[25] "What is yours" (τὸ σόν) is, of course, the pay he (the emphasis is still on the individual) has earned.[26] The master (and God) is sovereign over his domain and has the moral right to do as he "wants" (θέλω, v. 15) with his money. His decision is to be gracious to the last workers and "give" them the same amount. The first group has no right to complain about that decision because it is his money to do with as he wants.

20:15 "I am permitted to do what I want with what is mine, right?" (οὐκ ἔξεστίν μοι ὃ θέλω ποιῆσαι ἐν τοῖς ἐμοῖς;). Harnish notes how the rhetorical structure of vv. 13 – 15 centers on this verse (with its two rhetorical questions) as the culmination.[27] The owner used the same legal phrase as the Pharisees in 19:3, here meaning, "Isn't it my right?" (again "not" [οὐκ] expecting the answer yes; cf. 18:33; 19:4). True justice (v. 4) is found in his decision. No one can dispute that he can do whatever his "will" is with his own property ("what is mine" [τοῖς ἐμοῖς]). If he wants to show mercy to one group, that is perfectly all right. In this light Jeremias calls this a parable of mercy and grace,[28] and the message is that it is not one's worthiness or amount of service that determines one's reward but rather the grace and will of God.[29]

22. Jeremias, *Parables*, 137, thinks this is the main one complaining, but there is no evidence for such.

23. J. D. Crossan, "The Servant Parables of Jesus," *Semeia* 1 (1974): 36, finds a chiasm between vv. 2, 4 and v. 13 (A agree for a denarius; B what is just: B' I am not unjust; A' you agreed about a denarius). While Crossan unnecessarily argues that vv. 14 – 15 are Matthean and not original, he is probably correct about the chiasm.

24. W. Harnish, "The Metaphorical Process in Matthew 20.1 – 15," in *SBL Seminar Papers 1977* (ed. P. J. Achtemeier; Missoula, MT: Scholars Press, 1977), 231 – 50, esp. 241 (in Davies and Allison).

25. It is possible to take this as a positive statement, "Go happily with your pay," so Nolland, *Matthew*, 811. This is an interesting possibility but does not fit the context as well; there is a judgment aspect here, in both the parable itself and the eschatological overtones.

26. The use of the more rare possessive adjective (this was disappearing in the Koine period) here (σός) and in v. 15 (ἐμός) places emphasis on the contrast between the complainer ("what is yours") and the generous owner ("what is mine").

27. Harnish, "Metaphorical Process," 241 – 42.

28. Jeremias, *Parables*, 139. As Keener says (*Matthew*, 484), the issue is one of a mercy vs. a merit theology.

29. Bruner, *Matthew 14 – 28*, 321, says the first question is "theological" and asks about the sovereignty of God while the second is "anthropological" and asks about the sinfulness of humankind. Together they demonstrate the truth of Isa 55:8 – 9, "For my thoughts are not your thoughts, neither are your ways my ways, declares the LORD. As the heavens are higher than the earth, so are my ways higher than your ways and my thoughts than your thoughts."

20:15 "Or is your eye evil because I am good?" (ἢ ὁ ὀφθαλμός σου πονηρός ἐστιν ὅτι ἐγὼ ἀγαθός εἰμι;). The second question gets right to the heart of the problem: God's goodness vs. human sin. The "evil eye"[30] was discussed in 6:23 and refers to an evil intention, which for the complainers could be envy (Hagner, Elliott, Luz), resentment (Nolland), or miserliness (Morris), and its use here could combine all three in pointing to the self-centered behavior of the first group. The "good" (ἀγαθός) generosity of the landowner is the antithesis of the jealous, angry heart of the complainers ("evil" [πονηρός]).

20:16 In this way the last will be first and the first last (Οὕτως ἔσονται οἱ ἔσχατοι πρῶτοι καὶ οἱ πρῶτοι ἔσχατοι). This reverses the order of 19:30 and so frames the parable with the principle of the great eschatological reversal. Those who make the world's values primary and place them above God will be "last" at the eschaton, but those who put Christ first and find themselves last in this world will receive all the kingdom rewards of 19:28 – 29.

Theology in Application

This parable has frequently been compared with the parable of the prodigal son (Luke 15:11 – 32). The prodigal son illustrates the "last" (= the tax collectors and sinners in Luke 15), the elder brother the "first" (= the Pharisees in Luke 15), and the father is analogous to the landowner (= God both there and here). The incredible mercy of God is central to both.

1. God's Grace Available to All Equally

Jesus came for the sick, not just the healthy (9:12); for sinners, not just the righteous (9:13). He geared his ministry to those who were rejected and despised by society. As stated above this is a parable of grace and mercy and demonstrates God's great love and compassion for sinners. He is "not wanting anyone to perish, but everyone to come to repentance" (2 Pet 3:9).

2. Acceptance

Christians must accept those whom God has brought into his family. Like the older brother in Luke 15 or the first group in this parable, many Christians often resent and look down on many whom God has accepted, whether on racial, ethnic, or economic (e.g., the homeless) grounds. There are no possible grounds for such prejudices; it is entirely the "evil eye" of pride and prejudice that is at fault.[31]

30. For background see John H. Elliott, "Mt. 20:1 – 15: A Parable of Invidious Comparison and Evil Eye Accusation," *BTB* 22 (1992): 52 – 65.

31. For this reading, see P. A. Lamoureux and P. Zilonka, "The Workers in the Vineyard: Insights for the Moral Life," *RR* 61 (2002): 57 – 69.

3. Reward on an Equal Basis

This is highly debated. Blomberg says, "Luke 12:47 – 48 teaches that there are degrees of punishment in hell; Matt 20:1 – 16, that there are no degrees of reward in heaven. Neither of these is commonly known or understood in Christian circles."[32] He takes this as evidence that there are not degrees of reward but only one reward for all, the crown of life (1 Cor 9:25; 2 Tim 4:8; Jas 1:12). However, this does not fit all the data. Another parable, the shrewd manager in Luke 16:1 – 13, commands Christians to be shrewd in using their resources to help others, "so that when it is gone, *they will welcome you* [in the Greek] into eternal dwellings" (v. 9). Most translate it "you will be welcomed" (a reference to God) but one can take it literally as those we have helped welcoming us into heaven.

Moreover, "judged by works" occurs at least twenty-four times in Scripture (e.g., Ps 28:4; 62:12; Prov 24:12; Jer 17:10; Matt 16:27; Rom 2:6; 1 Pet 1:17; Rev 2:23; 11:18; 14:13; 22:12) and points to degrees of reward — we will take into eternity what we have done for the Lord and for others. The equality here does not mean we all receive only the same reward (the crown of life) but rather that we will all equally stand before the Lord without any disadvantage and be rewarded for what we have done (see also Matt 5:3 – 12; 6:1, 4, 6, 18, 7:11; 10:41 – 42; 13:12, 43; 19:28 – 29; 25:20 – 21, 23, 34). God will be gracious to every one of us.[33]

32. Blomberg, *Matthew*, 304. See also his "Degrees of Reward in the Kingdom of Heaven," *JETS* 35 (1992): 159 – 72.

33. See also Bruner, *Matthew 13 – 28*, 322 – 23; and Charette, *Theme of Recompense*, 13 – 14, who says that an interpretation of 20:1 – 16 that places the theme of recompense in contrast with the unmerited grace of God has to ignore the Matthean context (especially 19:30; 20:16).

CHAPTER 85

Matthew 20:17 – 28

Literary Context

This narrative section deals with the road to Jerusalem and Jesus' passion, yet at the same time the issue of rewards continues, as Jesus here becomes the prime example of the "last" while the disciples want to be the "first" (cf. 19:30; 20:16). As France notes, "the egalitarian picture of the twelve thrones in 19:28 is now challenged by the brothers' concern for personal status."[1]

VI. The Movement to the Cross (19:1 – 25:46)
- **A. Jesus' Deeds: Opposition and Discipleship (19:1 – 22:46)**
  - **1. The Road to Jerusalem (19:1 – 20:34)**
    - c. Wealth and Kingdom Rewards (19:16 – 30)
    - d. Parable of Workers in the Vineyard (20:1 – 16)
    - ➦ **e. Third Passion Prediction and Kingdom Honor (20:17 – 28)**
      - **(1) Jesus' Passion Prediction (20:17 – 19)**
      - **(2) The Ambitious Request for Honor and Power (20:20 – 23)**
      - **(3) Jesus' Teaching about True Greatness (20:24 – 28)**
    - f. Healing of the Two Blind Men (20:29 – 34)

Main Idea

Jesus is aware of his destiny and deliberately chooses the cross, while the disciples, aware of nothing, are consumed with their own desire for greatness. Here we have a microcosm of true discipleship, the choice between God's will and our own desires. We will become "first" only by making ourselves "last," and that can happen only when we pattern ourselves after Jesus.

1. France, *Gospel of Matthew*, 758.

Translation

Matthew 20:17-28

17a	Setting	While Jesus was ascending to Jerusalem,
b	Action	**he took the twelve [disciples] aside privately and said to them on the road,**
18a		*"Look, we are ascending to Jerusalem,*
b		*and the Son of Man will be delivered to the chief priests and the teachers of the law,*
c		*and they will condemn him to death.*
19a		*And they will deliver him to the Gentiles to be mocked and scourged and crucified,*
b		*and on the third day he will be raised."*
20a	Action	**Then the mother of the sons of Zebedee came to him with her sons**
b	Request	**and, prostrating herself, asked something of him.**
21a		**He replied to her,**
b	Question	*"What do you want?"*
c		**She asked him,**
d	Answer	*"Say that these my two sons might sit, . . . in your kingdom one at your right and the other at your left."*
22a	Response	**Jesus responded,**
b		*"You do not know what you are asking.*
c	Question	*Are you able to drink the cup that I am about to drink?"*
d	Answer	**They told him,**
e	Assertion	*"We are able!"*
23a	Response	**He told them,**
b		*"You will indeed drink my cup,*
c		*but to sit at my right and my left is not mine to give but*
d		*is only for those for whom it has been prepared by my Father."*
24a		When the ten heard about this,
b	Result	**they were angry at the two brothers.**
25a	Response	**So Jesus called them together and said,**
b		*"You know that the rulers of the Gentiles exercise lordship over them,*
c		*and their great leaders have authority over them.*
26a	Contrast 25b-c	*It must not be this way among you.*
b	Contrast 25b-c	*Instead, whoever wants to become great among you will be your servant,*
27a		*and whoever wants to be first among you must be your slave.*
28a	Example/ Pronouncement	*In the same way the Son of Man did not come to be served but to serve,*
b		*namely, to give his life as a ransom for many."*

Structure and Literary Form

This section, containing a prediction, a story about ambition, and paradigmatic teaching, again follows Mark (Mark 10:32 – 45), abbreviating it in Matt 20:17 – 19 and 24 – 28 but altering the story in vv. 20 – 23 by having the mother of James and John make the astounding request (see below for details). Several (Harrington, Carter, Senior, Nolland) recognize this as a unified pericope with three sections, the passion prediction (vv. 17 – 19), the misunderstanding and ambition of the mother and her sons (vv. 20 – 23), and the instruction of Jesus' about true greatness (vv. 24 – 28).

Exegetical Outline

➡ **I. Jesus' Passion Prediction (20:17 – 19)**
- A. The setting: journey to Jerusalem (v. 17)
- B. Delivery to chief priests and scribes for condemnation (v. 18)
- C. Delivery to the Gentiles for scourging and crucifixion (v. 19a)
- D. Resurrection on the third day (v. 19b)

II. The Ambitious Request for Honor and Power (20:20 – 23)
- A. The mother's request: sit at Jesus' right and left in the kingdom (vv. 20 – 21)
- B. The dialogue about the cup (vv. 22 – 23)
    1. The necessity of drinking the cup (vv. 22 – 23a)
    2. The right of God to decide (v. 23b)

III. Jesus' Teaching about True Greatness (20:24 – 28)
- A. The anger of the other disciples (v. 24)
- B. The reverse values of true greatness (vv. 25 – 27)
    1. The erroneous values of the Gentiles (v. 25)
    2. The correct value for disciples (vv. 26 – 27)
        - a. Greatness through servanthood (v. 26)
        - b. Primacy through becoming a slave (v. 27)
- C. Jesus as the model (v. 28)

Explanation of the Text

20:17 While Jesus was ascending[2] to Jerusalem, he took the twelve [disciples][3] aside privately and said to them on the road (Καὶ ἀναβαίνων ὁ Ἰησοῦς εἰς Ἱεροσόλυμα παρέλαβεν τοὺς δώδεκα [μαθητὰς] κατ' ἰδίαν καὶ ἐν τῇ ὁδῷ εἶπεν αὐτοῖς). The centrality of the journey to Jesus' destiny (note

2. Matthew likes to begin sentences with a temporal participle, cf. v. 8.

3. "Disciples" (μαθητάς) is found in B C W TR et al. but missing from ℵ D L Θ et al. It could have been omitted due to assimilation to Mark and Luke, but it could also have been added by later scribes to the simple "the Twelve." So most place it in brackets (see Metzger, *Textual Commentary*, 51), but Nolland, *Matthew*, 814, argues that as in 26:20 it probably was not original to this passage.

this only relates to "Jesus," not the Twelve) continues (as in Mark and Luke). It is stated twice that Jesus is "ascending" (see v. 18), and they are "on the road [way]" (cf. Mark 9:33–34; 10:32, 52; Luke 9:51–53, 57) to his appointed hour. The "way" (ὁδός) defines the journey to true discipleship as well, and here it is implied (as in 16:24) that Jesus is on the road to the cross; the passage is framed with the model of Jesus (20:17–19, 28).

This is the first time the disciples are called "the Twelve" (cf. 26:14, 20, 47), and apparently they are traveling with a larger group, because Jesus "takes [them] aside privately" to give them his third passion prediction (a brief fourth prediction occurs in 26:2).

20:18 "Look, we are ascending to Jerusalem" (Ἰδοὺ ἀναβαίνομεν εἰς Ἱεροσόλυμα). This third prediction is the most detailed of the three (cf. 16:21; 17:22–23) and becomes virtually a table of contents for the passion narrative—the delivery to the leaders (26:47–56), verdict (27:57–68), handing over to Pilate (27:1–14), mockery (27:29, 31, 41), scourging (27:26), crucifixion (27:33–50), and resurrection (28:1–20). The repetition of "ascend" (ἀναβαίνω) in vv. 17–18 makes emphatic the imagery of ascension to the cross, and the present tenses place this in the foreground of the action.[4] The switch to the first plural "we" shows that the disciples must go through it with him. This will make their failure (when they desert Jesus) all the more poignant.

20:18 ... and the Son of Man will be delivered to the chief priests and teachers of the law, and they will condemn him to death" (καὶ ὁ υἱὸς τοῦ ἀνθρώπου παραδοθήσεται τοῖς ἀρχιερεῦσιν καὶ γραμματεῦσιν, καὶ κατακρινοῦσιν αὐτὸν θανάτῳ). For "Son of Man" see excursus after 8:20–22. "Will be delivered" (παραδοθήσεται) is a divine passive reflecting the divine "must" of 16:21 (see on 17:22); God is handing his Son over to his destiny. The "chief priests and teachers of the law" are also found in 16:21 (with the elders there) and stand for the Jewish leadership that made up the Sanhedrin. All the gospels agree that it was the leaders who actually took Jesus to the cross and "condemned him to death," implying an actual judicial process ("condemned" [κατακρινοῦσιν]).

20:19 "And they will deliver him to the Gentiles to be mocked and scourged and crucified, and on the third day he will be raised" (καὶ παραδώσουσιν αὐτὸν τοῖς ἔθνεσιν εἰς τὸ ἐμπαῖξαι καὶ μαστιγῶσαι καὶ σταυρῶσαι, καὶ τῇ τρίτῃ ἡμέρᾳ ἐγερθήσεται). The Romans did not allow the Jews to execute anyone, so they will have to give Jesus over to Pilate before he can be crucified (this is the first time Jesus has mentioned delivery to the Gentiles). Jesus is aware not just of the fact of his death but sees ahead to the details as well. Mocking (27:29, 31, 41) and scourging (27:26; cf. John 19:1) were part of the crucifixion process. For his death and resurrection on the third day, see on 16:21.

20:20 Then the mother of the sons of Zebedee came to him with her sons and, prostrating herself, asked something of him (Τότε προσῆλθεν αὐτῷ ἡ μήτηρ τῶν υἱῶν Ζεβεδαίου μετὰ τῶν υἱῶν αὐτῆς προσκυνοῦσα καὶ αἰτοῦσά τι ἀπ' αὐτοῦ). In Mark 10:35 James and John themselves (for "sons of Zebedee," see 4:21; 10:2) make the request, while Matthew has their mother come in a remarkable series of actions involving her sons tagging along, and her obeisance (the feminine "prostrating" [προσκυνοῦσα, circumstantial participle]) has only her doing this before Jesus.

It has been common to suppose that Matthew introduced the mother to soften the image of

4. See Porter, *Idioms*, 23–25.

James and John, to make them look better by having their mother make the request. But that doesn't make a lot of sense. For one thing, Jesus addresses them directly in v. 22; it seems clear they put their mother up to it. That also makes sense with Mark, who omits the mother in order to show directly where the guilt lies (Mark's style). They have probably reasoned, "We have been messing up a lot lately, and Jesus has been exasperated with us, so we shouldn't ask directly. How can Jesus say no to Mom?"

This is especially true because she is not just their mother; she is likely Jesus' aunt (named Salome; for her name see Matt 27:55; Mark 15:40; for her as sister of Mary, Jesus' mother, see John 19:25).[5] The grammar of "something from him" [τι ἀπ' αὐτοῦ] means, "asks for a favor *from* him." There may well be some reflection of the Canaanite woman in 15:21–25, who prostrated herself before Jesus and asked help for her daughter.[6]

20:21 He replied to her, "What do you want?" (ὁ δὲ εἶπεν αὐτῇ, Τί θέλεις;). Jesus' "What do you want?" [τί θέλεις] asks Salome to explain the "something" (note τι) of v. 20. In 19:28 Jesus promised that the disciples would sit on twelve thrones, so Salome wants to make certain that her sons are granted the two primary places of honor and authority among the others.[7] She was one of the women who accompanied the apostolic band (27:55–56; cf. Luke 8:1–3) and may well have heard the promise of 19:28.

20:21 She asked him, "Say that[8] these my two sons might sit, one at your right and the other at your left, in your kingdom" (λέγει αὐτῷ, Εἰπὲ ἵνα καθίσωσιν οὗτοι οἱ δύο υἱοί μου εἷς ἐκ δεξιῶν σου καὶ εἷς ἐξ εὐωνύμων σου ἐν τῇ βασιλείᾳ σου). The two verbs ("say" [εἰπέ] and "might sit" [καθίσωσιν]) are aorist, requesting a specific action on the part of Jesus, namely, giving her sons the two seats of honor and power in the kingdom. So she wants to make certain that when the Twelve sit on their thrones, her sons have the most important seats. There may well be a deliberate irony, since Matthew changes Mark's wording slightly (cf. Mark 10:37) to conform to 27:38 (the two thieves at the cross "on his right and on his left"). This produces a sense of irony; the place of honor they sought would be fulfilled in an entirely different way by the two criminals.

20:22 Jesus responded, "You do not know what you are asking" (ἀποκριθεὶς δὲ ὁ Ἰησοῦς εἶπεν, Οὐκ οἴδατε τί αἰτεῖσθε). For the rest of the dialogue the mother plays no part. Salome and her boys have no idea about what they are asking. James and John have delusions of grandeur about the glory and greatness ahead of them. They "know" (οἴδατε) nothing about what the coming of the kingdom actually entails and have turned a deaf ear to the passion prediction immediately preceding their request.

20:22 "Are you able to drink the cup that I am about to drink?" (δύνασθε πιεῖν τὸ ποτήριον ὃ ἐγὼ μέλλω πίνειν;). The "cup" is the cup of suffering as a result of God's wrath (Ps 75:8; Isa 51:17; Jer 51:7; et al.) and fulfilled in Jesus' death (called "the cup" in the Gethsemane prayer of 26:39),[9] but

5. Keener, *Matthew*, 485, says that in the ancient world older women were accorded a special respect (Judg 5:7; 14:2) and could make awkward requests men could not (2 Sam 14:11–21; 1 Kgs 1:11–16).

6. Davies and Allison, *Matthew*, 3:87, think there may also be an echo of 1 Kgs 1:15–21, where Bathsheba stands before David and to his "What is it you want?" asks for the throne for her son Solomon.

7. Some say these might also be the chief seats of honor at the messianic banquet, see Witherington, *Matthew*, 378.

8. "That" (ἵνα) like ὅτι can introduce indirect address, "say that."

9. See C. E. B. Cranfield, "The Cup Metaphor in Mark xiv. 36 and Parallels," *ExpTim* 59 (1947–48): 137–38.

they think it the golden goblet of glory and power. When Jesus says "I am about" (μέλλω) to drink it, this reflects the passion prediction of 17:22 and divine necessity ("about to" [μέλλω] = "it is necessary" [δεῖ] of 16:21; cf. BAGD 1c δ, 501) as well as the imminence of the event.

20:22 They told him, "We are able!" (λέγουσιν αὐτῷ, Δυνάμεθα). In their confident affirmation, "we are able," they are totally clueless about what they are saying. They will be "able" to drink his cup of suffering (next verse), but in their desire to be first, they have just made themselves last in the kingdom (19:30 = 20:16). Their false bravado will continue in 26:33 – 35, when Peter and the others swear they will never "disown" Jesus, proven wrong when Peter denies Jesus three times (26:69 – 75) and the disciples desert him (26:56).

20:23 He told them, "You will indeed drink my cup" (λέγει αὐτοῖς, Τὸ μὲν ποτήριόν μου πίεσθε). "My cup" (τὸ ποτήριόν μου) is a shortened form of Mark 10:39, "The cup I drink." To "share a cup" in Jewish thought means to share one's life and destiny. Again there is a sense of irony here, for they are thinking they will share his glory, while in reality they will share his suffering (cf. 10:16 – 25); note that eventually James is martyred (Acts 12:2) and John is exiled on the island of Patmos (Rev 1:9 – 11; cf. John 21:23). Only late tradition has John being martyred early, and Irenaeus is probably more correct when he says John died a natural death during the reign of Trajan (*Adv. Haer.* 2.22.5, 3.3.4).[10]

20:23 "But to sit at my right and my left is not mine to give but is only for those for whom it has been prepared[11] by my Father" (τὸ δὲ καθίσαι ἐκ δεξιῶν μου καὶ ἐξ εὐωνύμων οὐκ ἔστιν ἐμὸν τοῦτο δοῦναι, ἀλλ᾽ οἷς ἡτοίμασται ὑπὸ τοῦ πατρός μου). James and John will indeed partake of Jesus' glory through suffering (cf. 1 Pet 1:11), but Jesus does not have the authority to grant them the right to sit in the positions of honor. That authority belongs only to God the Father,[12] and the positions are under his sovereign will and are reserved for "those for whom it has been prepared" (see the similar phrase in 25:34).

Some think "the seat prepared" refers to the two thieves on the cross (Nolland), but it is better seen as an eschatological reality at the close of this age. Jesus is not saying that there will be two seats of leadership in heaven (with Abraham and Moses or David and Paul in them) but rather that all such rewards will be God's decision at the eschaton. We have no indication as to what such imagery connotes. Most doubt that there will be a hierarchy of position in eternity (on the issue of rewards in heaven, see "Theology in Application" on 11:20 – 24).

20:24 When the ten heard about this, they were angry at the two brothers (Καὶ ἀκούσαντες οἱ δέκα ἠγανάκτησαν περὶ τῶν δύο ἀδελφῶν). The aorist temporal participle "when they heard" (ἀκούσαντες) stresses the event of hearing the report taken as a whole. It is doubtful that "they were angry" (ἠγανάκτησαν, "they were aroused,

10. See the excellent discussion in Davies and Allison, *Matthew*, 3:90 – 92.

11. The perfect tense ("it has been prepared" [ἡτοίμασται]) normally describes a "complex state of affairs" (Porter, *Idioms*, 40) and often has the force of completed action with existing results (Wallace, 574). These aspects are not contradictory but complimentary. In this context it describes the state of the issue — God has already decided who will have the places of honor, but the results will not be known until the Great Assize.

12. This is another reference to the subordination of Jesus to his Father during his earthly sojourn (11:27; 24:36; John 5:19, 21 – 22). Jesus was the God-man, equal in his essence but subordinate in his person. He will receive his dominion and "all authority" at the resurrection (28:18, echoing Dan 7:13 – 14).

indignant") connotes a pious indignation from those who would "encourage" a fallen brother in light of the "sin's deceitfulness" (Heb 3:13; cf. Matt 18:6–20) and seek to "restore" them (Gal 6:1). Rather, it is a jealous anger on the part of those who are upset that James and John thought of it first and got to Jesus before they could. They are upset that the two are "acing them out" and getting ahead of them in the race for greatness (as also 18:1).

20:25 So Jesus called them together[13] **and said, "You know that the rulers of the Gentiles exercise lordship over them, and their great leaders have authority over them"** (ὁ δὲ Ἰησοῦς προσκαλεσάμενος αὐτοὺς εἶπεν, Οἴδατε ὅτι οἱ ἄρχοντες τῶν ἐθνῶν κατακυριεύουσιν αὐτῶν καὶ οἱ μεγάλοι κατεξουσιάζουσιν αὐτῶν). Every one of the disciples was in serious error about kingdom priorities; they have learned nothing from the Sermon on the Mount or the rest of Jesus' ethical teaching. So he summons them all and addresses them as a group. The ethical principles they represent are not kingdom values but the ways of the Gentile world.

So Jesus uses the analogy of Gentile leaders. The "rulers" (ἄρχοντες) and "great leaders" (μεγάλοι) probably refer to the kings and their high officials. "Have authority over" (κατακυριεύουσιν) does not have a negative connotation of abuse of power but rather a more general thrust in terms of the general authority they wielded over others,[14] though there is still an aspect of total power and control exerted (Nolland). "Them" (αὐτῶν) here refers not to the disciples but to other people under the absolute control of the Gentile rulers. Christ is saying the disciples are interested in authority rather than servanthood and have become just like the Gentiles they despise. Greatness in the kingdom is the polar opposite of greatness in the secular world (every bit as true today!).

20:26 "It must not be this way among you" (οὐχ οὕτως ἔσται ἐν ὑμῖν). "Must be" (ἔσται) is an example of the future with imperatival force (cf. 5:21, 27, 33, 43; 23:10).[15] The citizens of the kingdom must never be like the Gentiles in a lust for power.

20:26 "Instead, whoever wants to become great among you will be your servant" (ἀλλ' ὃς ἐὰν θέλῃ ἐν ὑμῖν μέγας γενέσθαι ἔσται ὑμῶν διάκονος). This and v. 27 restate 19:30 = 20:16. The "great reversal" is not just at the eschaton (see 19:30; 20:16) but must exemplify ethical values today as well. Note the use of "wants" (θέλω); it is obvious that all the energy of the disciples is focused on a self-centered wish for personal power. Jesus is telling them that their "will" is sadly misplaced, and their desire must be refocused on serving others. Only then can true greatness be achieved.

"Greatness" will be attained only through servanthood, as demonstrated by Jesus himself (Phil 2:6–11). A διάκονος was a "household servant," especially one who waited on tables (*EDNT*, 1:302). This became one of the basic terms for an early church "minister" because of the whole idea of servanthood leadership. Therefore, the disciples did eventually catch on to what Jesus was saying! But that was in the future.

20:27 "And whoever wants to be first among you must be your slave" (καὶ ὃς ἂν θέλῃ ἐν ὑμῖν εἶναι πρῶτος ἔσται ὑμῶν δοῦλος). This repeats the message of v. 26 ("great" [μέγας] and "first"

13. Another circumstantial participle (as 20:2–3; cf. on 16:4).

14. See Kenneth W. Clark, "The Meaning of [κατα] κυριεύειν," in *Studies in New Testament Language and Text* (ed. J. K. Elliott; NovTSup 44; Leiden: Brill, 1976), 100–105, who argues that the prefix does not have perfective force and the verb simply means to have authority over others.

15. See Porter, *Idioms*, 44; BDF §362.

[πρῶτος] are synonymous)[16] and at the same time intensifies it (a δοῦλος is a "slave"). It is difficult to imagine a greater antithesis than between the "great" or "first" in society and the slaves who did their bidding. Yet that characterizes the kingdom people, the exact opposite of the people of the world (10:38 – 39; 16:25; 18:2 – 5). In fact, these two titles — servant/minister and slave — became primary descriptions of Christian leaders in the early church (see their constant use by Paul). As Bruner says, "Jesus turns this aristocratic ideal on its head and in one of cultural history's dramatic reversals he asks, in effect, 'How can anyone be happy *unless* one is the slave of everyone else?' " (italics his).[17]

20:28 "In the same way the Son of Man did not come to be served but to serve" (ὥσπερ ὁ υἱὸς τοῦ ἀνθρώπου οὐκ ἦλθεν διακονηθῆναι ἀλλὰ διακονῆσαι). This passage is so well-known for its Christology (Jesus' self-conscious knowledge as to why he is going to the cross), its soteriology (the primary gospel passage on substitutionary atonement), and its use of the OT (Isa 43:3 – 4; 53:4, 10, 12) that its true purpose in the context is often ignored.[18] Primarily, Jesus is using himself as a model for servanthood ministry (cf. also Ph 2:6 – 8).

"In the same way" (ὥσπερ) leads into this, making Jesus the prime example of the servant/slave metaphor in vv. 26 – 27. Like Jesus, every Christian, especially its leaders, should "not come to be served but to serve." "Serve" (διακονέω) deliberately recalls v. 26, where Jesus tells the disciples that they must become "servants" (διάκονος) to be "great" in the kingdom.[19] Jesus exemplifies the new kingdom reality in which we want to "serve" others rather than manipulate them to serve us.

20:28 "... namely, to give his life as a ransom for many" (καὶ δοῦναι τὴν ψυχὴν αὐτοῦ λύτρον ἀντὶ πολλῶν). The epexegetical καί ("that is, namely") means that Jesus' selfless act of "giving his life" is the very definition of the new ethical stance of servanthood. The christological aspect is the best-known issue in this verse. "Ransom" (λύτρον) has its background in the OT idea of the kinsman-redeemer (Boaz and Ruth) but mainly in the idea of the payment made to redeem the firstborn (Num 3:46 – 47; 18:15) as well as the Hellenistic idea of freeing a slave or buying the freedom of a prisoner of war. It denotes a "ransom" payment and has two connotations here and in the parallel ἀπολύτρωσις passages ("redemption" — e.g., Gal 4:5; Eph 1:7, 14; cf. Rom 3:24; Heb 9:12): the payment (the "blood" of Jesus) and the freedom from sin that it purchases for people.[20]

As Harris brings out, "for" (ἀντί) could have the idea of equivalence ("for, as the equivalence

16. As Hagner brings out (*Matthew 14 – 28*, 581), the two correspond to the request of James and John to sit at the "right and left" of Jesus in the final kingdom (v. 21).

17. Bruner, *Matthew 13 – 28*, 333.

18. For the authenticity of this passage, see Sydney H. T. Page, "The Authenticity of the Ransom Logion (Mark 10:45b)," in *Gospel Perspective: Studies of History and Tradition in the Four Gospels* (ed. R. T. France and David Wenham; Sheffield: JSOT Press, 1980), 1:137 – 61; Carson, "Matthew," 432 – 33; Blomberg, *Historical Reliability*, 243 – 44.

19. For an excellent discussion of the social position and identity of slaves in the Roman empire, see Carter, *Households*, 172 – 89. He concludes that the disciples are "slaves" in terms of their "liminal identity," that is, their marginalization and alienation from society even as they participate in it. They are called "to a way of life of equality, humiliation, obedience, and suffering," as they serve their master and the people to whom he sends them. In so doing they become like their master, Jesus (pp. 189 – 92).

20. France, *Gospel of Matthew*, 761, follows many in stating that the idea in the "ransom" imagery is not on the payment made as on the deliverance from evil secured. However, that depends on whether the "blood" payment is mentioned in the context (e.g., in Rom 3:24 – 25; Heb 9:12). The one aspect of the metaphor never explained is the one to whom the payment is given.

of") or exchange ("in return for, in the place of") but in this context connotes substitution ("instead of, for the place of"). He says, "the life of Jesus, surrendered in a sacrificial death, brought about the release of forfeited lives. He acted on behalf of the many by taking their place."[21]

"Many" (πολλοί) refers to all who turn to God and his Messiah and accept the ransom payment, becoming part of the kingdom community. Many have found the background in Isa 52:13 – 53:12,[22] with the servant giving his life as a substititute "for many" (Jeremias, Moo, Carson, France, Hagner). There is also a possible parallel with Isa 43:3 – 4, with the language of Israel "ransomed" as God gives the people of Egypt, Cush, and Seba "in exchange for you,"[23] but it involves a stretch of the imagination as the idea of Gentiles (Egypt, Ethiopia) as a ransom for Israel would have to be transferred to the Son of Man here. Still, the presence of such language shows that Jesus is drawing from OT concepts.

Theology in Application

Much of the material has been discussed before. The passion predictions have been applied at both 16:21 and 17:22 – 23; the disciples' self-centered desire for greatness is applied at 18:1 – 4.

1. The Cup of Suffering

We must be willing to drink the cup of Jesus' suffering (see on 10:17 – 31), but the clear message here is that we seek no greatness but the path of Christ, which will often involve suffering and persecution. As Jesus said in 16:24, we must "take up [our] cross," and that means a willingness to die if God so wills. In Phil 3:10 Paul talked about "participation in his suffering," and in Col 1:24 Paul discussed filling up "what is still lacking in regard to Christ's afflictions." Paul meant that suffering was a participation in Christ's life and a special eschatological event connected with the eschaton (see discussion of "messianic woes" at 10:22).

21. Murray J. Harris, "Prepositions and Theology in the Greek New Testament," *NIDNTT*, 3:1179 – 80. He says substitution is the "prevailing sense" in the LXX (Gen 22:13; 44:33; 2 Sam 19:1) as well as in nonbiblical Greek, including the papyri.

22. This is opposed by C. K. Barrett, "The Background of Mark 10:45," in *New Testament Essays* (ed. A. J. B. Higgins; Manchester: University Press, 1959), 1 – 18; and Morna Hooker, *Jesus and the Servant* (London: SPCK, 1959), 92 – 96, who have argued against an Isa 53 background on the basis of the lack of verbal parallels with the text here and the LXX. But if this passage is taken directly from the MT, with "many" emphasized in 53:11 – 12, "ransom" a viable translation of *ʾāšām* in 53:10, and "give his life" fitting 53:10, 12 (see Carson, Davies and Allison), then the background is definitely there.

23. See W. Grimm, *Weil ich dich liebe: Die Verkündigung Jesu und Seutereojesaja* (Frankfurt am Main: Lang, 1976), 234 – 58. Witherington, *Matthew*, 380, shows that "the many" should not be taken as a technical term for "the elect" à la Qumran (1QS 6:1, 7 – 25; CD 13:7; 14:7), since Jewish readers probably were not that familiar with Essene theology, and even if they were, they would never have endorsed such a view.

2. Servanthood

Servanthood is the only path to greatness in the kingdom. Jesus makes absolutely clear that the kingdom values and lifestyle are the exact opposite of the surrounding pagan world. This is exemplified in Luke 16:1 – 13, in the parable of the shrewd manager (vv. 1 – 8a) and Jesus' interpretation of it (vv. 8b – 9, 10 – 13). The world "gets ahead" by taking, but the "people of light" by giving." Following Jesus, who was "in very nature God" but who in his incarnation took on "the very nature of a servant" (Phil 2:6 – 7), the disciple must seek humility but leave the glory up to God (the message of Phil 2:6 – 11).

Servanthood must exemplify every Christian leader, indeed every Christian. We will never be Christlike until we serve rather than manipulate others to serve us (cf. Phil 2:3 – 4). As Wilkins says, "Because of the impact of God's love in our lives, we can now love (1 John 4:19). And because of the transforming impact of God's gift of grace in our lives, we can now give ourselves to serve others."[24]

3. Jesus' Atoning Sacrifice

Jesus' atoning sacrifice provides the ultimate model of servanthood. Of the three terms for salvation in Rom 3:24 – 25 ("justification," "redemption," "sacrifice of atonement"), the key is the third, which is the basis of redemption/the *ransom* payment and is closely connected to the "mercy seat" in the Most Holy Place. The term used here occurs twenty-one times in the Pentateuch for the mercy seat, or cover over the ark. That was both where the blood was poured on the Day of Atonement (Lev 16:14) and where Yahweh was particularly present (Lev 16:2). Thus the mercy seat was the place of atonement, and Christ here is seen as the NT counterpart, the means of atonement for all humankind. His blood is the once-for-all sacrifice, the *ransom payment* for sin, the only way atonement can be effected for sinful humanity. Three things happened: the wrath of God was appeased, sins were forgiven, and freedom was purchased.

24. Wilkins, *Matthew*, 676.

CHAPTER 86

Matthew 20:29–34

Literary Context

Jesus continues on the road to Jerusalem (for the first time Matthew tells us how far he has come—to Jericho, the gateway to Jerusalem for pilgrims)[1] and performs a powerful messianic miracle in healing two blind men. The twofold cry to Jesus as "Son of David" centers attention on Jesus as the Davidic Messiah and will be used again at the triumphal entry (21:9). So the one who is about to die in Jerusalem as a "ransom for many" (v. 28) is seen once again as the royal Messiah who brings healing power into this world. Also, it provides a transition to ch. 21, where the Son of God title (21:9) and healing of the blind (21:14) are repeated.

VI. The Movement to the Cross (19:1–25:46)
- **A. Jesus' Deeds: Opposition and Discipleship (19:1–22:46)**
  - **1. The Road to Jerusalem (19:1–20:34)**
    - d. Parable of Workers in the Vineyard (20:1–16)
    - e. Third Passion Prediction and Kingdom Honor (20:17–28)
    - ➦ **f. Healing of the Two Blind Men (20:29–34)**

Main Idea

The previous passage was framed by the emphasis on Jesus' coming death (vv. 17–19, 28) and his unyielding demand for a rejection of worldly power, while the present passage "underlines that God's compassionate mercy and power are available for all disciples who, in the midst of difficult circumstances, recognize their

1. As Blomberg, *Matthew*, 309, and Turner, "Matthew," 263, point out, Jericho is on the west bank of the Jordan about fifteen miles northeast of Jerusalem. Walking from there involved an ascent of 3,500 feet, as Jericho is 846 feet below sea level near the Dead Sea, while Jerusalem is in the Judean hills 2,625 feet above sea level. Wilkins adds, "Jesus and the disciples have now finished the trek from Galilee with ministry in Perea and Judea and are ready to make the ascent to Jerusalem."

inadequacy and call for God's help."[2] At the same time, the central figure is Jesus, who as royal Messiah and "Lord" of all (vv. 30, 31, 33) has the power to restore sight.

Translation

Matthew 20:29-34

29a	Setting	As they were departing from Jericho,
b	Action	**a large crowd followed Jesus.**
30a	Action	And **look, two blind men sitting by the road heard that Jesus was passing by.**
b	Request	**So they shouted,**
c		*"Lord, Son of David, have mercy on us!"*
31a	Objection	But **the crowd rebuked them so that they would be silent.**
b	Restatement of 30b	Yet **they shouted all the louder,**
c		*"Lord, Son of David, have mercy on us!"*
32a	Response/Question	**Jesus stopped, called out to them, and said,**
b		*"What do you want me to do for you?"*
33a	Answer	**They replied,**
b		*"Lord, we desire that our eyes might be opened."*
34a	Description	Filled with compassion,
b	Action	**Jesus touched their eyes,**
c	Result: Healing	and **immediately they received their sight and followed him.**

Structure and Literary Form

Matthew continues to work with Mark (Mark 10:46 – 52) and edit it to fit his themes. Here the emphasis is more on the miraculous power and majesty of Jesus, with details removed (the identity of Bartimaeus, the crowd calling to him, the emphasis on his faith) and added (the presence of two blind men, the emphasis on "Lord" three times, Jesus' compassion) to center on the miracle as the result of Jesus' lordship. There are two parts to the story, the interaction with the crowd (vv. 29 – 31), with the negative tone of the crowd contrasted to the persistence of the blind men; and the interaction with Jesus (vv. 32 – 34), featuring his willingness and compassion leading to the miracle itself.

2. Carter, *Households*, 203; cf. Davies and Allison, *Matthew*, 3:105.

Exegetical Outline

➦ **I. The Interaction with the Crowd (20:29 – 31)**
   A. The setting: leaving Jericho (v. 29)
   B. Interaction with the crowd (vv. 30 – 31a)
      1. The plea for mercy (v. 30)
      2. The rebuke by the crowd (v. 31a)
   C. Louder plea for mercy (v. 31b)

II. The Interaction with Jesus (20:32 – 34)
   A. Determining their request (vv. 32 – 33)
   B. The healing and discipleship (v. 34)

Explanation of the Text

20:29 As they were departing[3] from Jericho, a large crowd followed Jesus (Καὶ ἐκπορευομένων αὐτῶν ἀπὸ Ἰεριχὼ ἠκολούθησεν αὐτῷ ὄχλος πολύς). This is another of the so-called "doublets" of Matthew, a second healing of two blind men (see "Structure and Literary Form" of 9:27 – 31 for reasons why these are not duplicate stories) and repeats the themes of that story. At this time Jesus is almost finished on his road to Jerusalem, drawing within fifteen miles just after crossing the Jordan.

One difficulty is that while Mark and Matthew have Jesus leaving the town when this miracle occurs, Luke 18:35 has Jesus "approaching" it. The best solution is the fact of two Jerichos, with Jesus leaving the old Jericho (largely in ruins but still somewhat inhabited because of a nearby spring) and entering the more recent Jericho, a Herodian town built around Herod's winter palace a mile south of the old city (so Blomberg, Morris, Wilkins). Moreover, Mark 10 has Jesus entering and leaving Jericho, and so Matthew and Luke simply center on one of these two aspects.

The "large crowd" is natural since huge numbers are flocking to Jerusalem for Passover. Jericho was a natural spot for people to cross the Jordan on the way to the festival. This group, however, is "following" Jesus, undoubtedly as a result of his fame in Galilee. Because of the inclusion with v. 34 (the healed blind men "follow" Jesus), the crowd is probably to be seen as potential disciples.

20:30 And look, two blind men sitting by the road heard that Jesus was passing by (καὶ ἰδοὺ δύο τυφλοὶ καθήμενοι παρὰ τὴν ὁδόν, ἀκούσαντες ὅτι Ἰησοῦς παράγει). The replacement of Bartimaeus (Mark, Luke) with "two blind men" is normally taken as a redactional addition on the part of Matthew; and while it probably is a redactional/editorial choice, that does not make it unhistorical (see on 8:28b). Matthew frequently uses "look" (ἰδού) to add a dramatic emphasis to a scene (see on 19:16). These men are "sitting alongside [παρά] the road," probably the trunk road to Jerusalem in order to beg alms from pilgrims passing by (quite lucrative at this time of year). The presence of "road" (ὁδός) continues the road to Jerusalem theme (cf. 20:17; 21:8, 19). The emphasis on "hearing" most likely refers both to the excited talk of

3. Another temporal participle, with the present tense stressing the process of the journey out of Jericho.

the crowd that Jesus is approaching and to the previous stories the two blind heard about Jesus.

20:30 So they shouted, "Lord,[4] Son of David, have mercy on us!" (ἔκραξαν λέγοντες, Ἐλέησον ἡμᾶς, κύριε, υἱὸς Δαυίδ). The double title is particularly dramatic. As in Mark, the two blind men seem to understand more than the disciples. It is obviously difficult to know how much they intend in their use of "Lord" (κύριε), but Matthew clearly means Jesus' lordship over illness, as the threefold repetition (vv. 30, 31, 33) demonstrates. "Son of David" is used in 9:27; 12:23; 15:22 in healing contexts and in Matthew points to Jesus as the royal Messiah who heals the nation's sick (see esp. on 9:27). "Have mercy" in such a situation obviously means "heal us," but there is also a connection with the poor of Israel seeking alms and with people in general seeking the grace of God in their lives.

20:31 But the crowd rebuked them so that they would be silent. Yet they shouted all the louder, "Lord, Son of David, have mercy on us!" (ὁ δὲ ὄχλος ἐπετίμησεν αὐτοῖς ἵνα σιωπήσωσιν· οἱ δὲ μεῖζον ἔκραξαν λέγοντες, Ἐλέησον ἡμᾶς, κύριε, υἱὸς Δαυίδ). It is difficult to know whether the rebuke comes because the crowd thinks that the two beggars are nuisances (Davies and Allison, France, Morris) or because, like the disciples in 19:13, they feel Jesus has more important things on his mind with Passover coming (Plummer, Hagner, Blomberg). Both may be aspects of their attempt to silence the two.[5] But it has the opposite effect on these resolute men, who start imploring Jesus all the louder (μεῖζον, "greater"). The persistent cry repeats that of v. 30, centering on Jesus as "master" over illness and as the royal Messiah.

20:32 Jesus stopped, called out to them, and said, "What do you want me to do[6] for you?" (καὶ στὰς ὁ Ἰησοῦς ἐφώνησεν αὐτοὺς καὶ εἶπεν, Τί θέλετε ποιήσω ὑμῖν;). Jesus is at all times open to the poor and needy, and out of the tumult he hears the men clearly. His "stopping"[7] shows that he is willing even to postpone the march to his destiny when the oppressed call out to him. In his reply Jesus implicitly accepts their acclamation, perhaps as prolegomena for the triumphal entry (21:1 – 11). It does not mean he fails to understand their request, but he wants to hear it directly from them (cf. his response to the mother's request in v. 21). So he asks them what their desire is, knowing what that will be.

20:33 They replied, "Lord, we desire that our eyes might be opened" (λέγουσιν αὐτῷ, Κύριε, ἵνα ἀνοιγῶσιν οἱ ὀφθαλμοὶ ἡμῶν). This parallels 9:30, where Jesus "opened the eyes" of the two blind men. They answer that their heartfelt desire (implicit in their response) is for their sight to be restored. As Hagner says, "although this pericope does not stress faith as does the similar story in 9:28 (or the parallel in Mark 10:52), it is clearly implied in the request."[8] Once more they center on Jesus' lordship, his messianic ability to heal the blind (stressed in 9:27 – 31; 11:5; 12:22; 15:30 – 31; 21:14). These are certainly seen as messianic fulfillment of Isa 35:5, "Then will the eyes of the blind be opened."

4. The presence of "Lord" (κύριε) here is attested in K L Z W TR et al., but it is missing in ℵ D Θ it et al. It could have been omitted under influence of 9:27 and Mark 10:47, but it could have been added to harmonize with vv. 31, 33 below. Since both the manuscript and external evidence are virtually equal, some leave it in brackets. The majority of the UBS committee favored its inclusion, see Metzger, *Textual Commentary*, 53 – 54 (as well as Nolland, NRSV, TNIV, NLT). Its inclusion is likely to be preferred.

5. Most translate the "in order to" (ἵνα) as indirect address (parallel to an infinitive) rather than purpose, "rebuked them to be silent" (BAGD, 377, 6, calls it "a virtual imperative"), but it is better to retain the purposive force. It tells why they rebuked the two.

6. "To do" (ποιήσω) is an example of a subjunctive for an understood "that" (ἵνα) or as an indirect deliberative question, "What do you want *that* I should do for you?"

7. The aorist form of ἵστημι means to "stop" (BAGD, 382 [II.1]).

8. Hagner, *Matthew 14 – 28*, 587 – 88.

20:34 Filled with compassion,[9] **Jesus touched their eyes** (σπλαγχνισθεὶς δὲ ὁ Ἰησοῦς ἥψατο τῶν ὀμμάτων αὐτῶν). Jesus' compassion and touching their eyes are not found in Mark and add to the centrality of the messianic miracle in Matthew. Jesus' compassion is also found in 9:36; 14:14; 15:32, all connected to his miraculous ministry to the crowds. Jesus had great pity for the human dilemma and always responded. Most busy teacher-rabbis, let alone messianic pretenders, would never have "stopped" in their rush to destiny to help the unfortunate, but Jesus does so every time. The use of "touch" for healing is also found in 8:3, 15; 9:29 (9:20 – 21; 14:36 of people touching Jesus) and stresses further the physicality of the miracle.

20:34 And immediately they received their sight and followed him (καὶ εὐθέως ἀνέβλεψαν καὶ ἠκολούθησαν αὐτῷ). Matthew does not use "immediately" (εὐθύς/εὐθέως) nearly as frequently as does Mark, and thus it retains its force here, stressing the immediacy of the results. As a result of the healing they "followed" (ἠκολούθησαν) Jesus, meaning they became Jesus' disciples. As in 9:2, 22, 29; 15:28 (with "faith" [πίστις]) and 9:21 – 22 (with "save" [σῴζω]), physical healing produces spiritual healing. Many commentators see an allegorical dimension here as the two men exemplify the path to discipleship:

> Being blind is a characteristic of all who are not disciples (cf. 13:13 – 17). The opponents of Jesus, the Jewish leaders, are blind (15:14; cf. 23:16, 17, 19, 24, 26).... Blindness, though, need not be a permanent condition; Jesus' presence and power to save extends to those who desire to see (cf. 9:27, 28; 12:22; 15:30 – 31; 21:14).[10]

Theology in Application

Hagner calls this story "the gospel in a microcosm"[11] because it is so closely connected to the passion event in which Jesus responds to the world's cry for mercy and heals its spiritual blindness. In one of Matthew's fulfillment quotations in 4:16, Jesus fulfills Isa 9:2, "The people walking in darkness have seen a great light; on those living in the land of deep darkness, a light has dawned." Jesus takes the blind living in darkness and gives them the light of God so they can see spiritual truth. In Jesus, God is ever open to bring sight to those who call out for divine mercy and open themselves up to his healing presence in their lives.

Moreover, this prepares for the passion also by centering on Jesus as the royal Messiah, Son of David, who will inherit the eternal throne of David in fulfillment of the Davidic covenant (2 Sam 7:16). In this sense there is direct continuity between this and the next episode, the triumphal entry. Bruner calls this (along with ch. 21) a "summary Christology" in the sense that it puts together Matthew's message about Christ "in a comprehensive way for the church."[12]

9. "Filled with compassion" (σπλαγχνισθείς) could be an adjectival participle, but because it lacks the article it is most likely adverbial, a circumstantial participle telling how Jesus felt as he healed them.

10. Carter, *Households*, 199. See also Gnilka, *Matthäusevangelium*, 2:195 – 96; and Luz, *Matthew 8 – 20*, 549 – 50, who correctly recognize that the metaphorical dimension has validity precisely because it "reports of something that happened in the life of Jesus."

11. Hagner, *Matthew 14 – 28*, 588.

12. Bruner, *Matthew 13 – 28*, 348.

CHAPTER 87

Matthew 21:1 – 11

Introduction to Beginning Events of Passion Week (Matthew 21:1 – 22:46)

We now begin Passion Week, the final seven days of Jesus' life. As throughout this gospel, Matthew organizes his material into narrative and discourse, with the first four days of Passion Week in 21:1 – 22:46 and the final period in 26:1 – 27:56. In between are the two parts of the final discourse, the woes on the leaders (23:1 – 39) and the Judgment Discourse on the Mount of Olives (24:1 – 25:46). Wilkins provides an excellent harmony of the events that take place during this week:[1]

Friday	Arrival in Bethany (John 12:1)
Saturday	Mary's anointing of Jesus (John 12:2 – 8; cf. Matt 26:6 – 13 par.)
Sunday	Triumphal entry (Matt 21:1 – 11 par.), surveying the temple (Mark 11:11), return to Bethany (Matt 21:17; Mark 11:11)
Monday	Cleansing the temple (21:12 – 13 par.); cursing the fig tree (21:18 – 22); miracles and challenge in the temple (21:14 – 16); return to Bethany (Mark 11:19)
Tuesday	Disciples' questions regarding the fig tree (Mark 11:20 – 21); debates with the leaders in the temple (Matt 21:23 – 22:46 par.); Olivet Discourse after return to Bethany (Matt 24 – 25)
Wednesday	Little recorded in the gospels — Jesus and disciples apparently remain in Bethany; Judas arranges for his betrayal (26:14 – 16 par.)
Thursday	Preparation for Passover (26:17 – 19 par.); after sundown, Passover meal and Last Supper (26:20 – 35); Farewell Discourse (John 13 – 17); Gethsemane (Matt 26:30 – 46 par.)
Friday	After midnight, the betrayal and arrest (26:47 – 56); Jewish trials — Annas (John 18:13 – 14), Caiaphas and partial Sanhedrin (Matt 26:57 – 75 par.), full Sanhedrin (27:1 – 2); Roman trial — Pilate (27:2 – 14 par.), Herod Antipas (Luke 23:6 – 12), Pilate (Matt 27:15 – 26 par.); crucifixion (9 a.m. to 3 p.m., 27:27 – 56); burial (27:57 – 61 par.); tomb sealed with guards (27:62 – 66)

1. Wilkins, *Matthew*, 709 – 10.

Literary Context

The journey to Jerusalem has taken all of chs. 19 – 20, and Jesus has now reached his destination and entered the place of his destiny. The passion events are ready to commence, and the powers of darkness are about to erupt. Yet the kingdom truths are also operating, signified in the two blind men of 20:29 – 34 and the crowds at his entry into Jerusalem. It is God's Messiah, the Son of David, who confronts the powers, and their temporary victory will presage their eternal defeat.

VI. The Movement to the Cross (19:1 – 25:46)
- **A. Jesus' Deeds: Opposition and Discipleship (19:1 – 22:46)**
  1. The Road to Jerusalem (19:1 – 20:34)
  2. **Beginning Events of Passion Week (21:1 – 22:46)**
     - **a. The Messiah Enters Jerusalem (21:1 – 22)**
       - **(1) The Lowly King in His Humble Entry (21:1 – 11)**
       - (2) Judgment on the Temple (21:12 – 17)
       - (3) Judgment Parable: Cursing the Fig Tree (21:18 – 22)

Main Idea

Jesus here begins the process of overturning his "messianic secret" (see on 8:4) and proclaims himself publicly as the Messiah. Yet Jesus enters Jerusalem in abject humility on a lowly donkey rather than on a warhorse, staging a prophetic symbolic action to proclaim his messianic intentions.[2] The acclamation of the crowd of Galilean pilgrims streaming into Jerusalem is ironic in the sense that they have no awareness or appreciation for the truth, i.e., that the primary messianic act is suffering and death; they seek deliverance and victory but not the way Jesus intends.

Translation

(See next page.)

2. Yet see W. B. Tatum, "Jesus' So-called Triumphal Entry: On Making an Ass of the Romans," *Forum* 1 (1998): 129 – 43, who says this is not so much a symbolic action as a direct declaration of Jesus' royal status, since he follows the normal style of Roman entrance processions, and the ass was a well-known animal used in royal processions. Yet it is hard to see why Jesus' act is not a symbolic action along with a royal statement. W. A. Visser 'T Hooft, "Triumphalism in the Gospels," *SJT* 38 (1985): 491 – 504, argues it was not an entry at all but rather a symbolic action against triumphalism and emphasized Jesus as the gentle Messiah.

Matthew 21:1-11

1a	Setting/Action	When they drew near to Jerusalem and came to Bethphage on the Mount of Olives,
b		**Jesus then sent two disciples, telling them,**
2a	Instructions	*"Go to the village opposite you,*
b		*and immediately you will find a donkey tied and a colt with her.*
c		*Untie them and bring them to me.*
3a		*And if anyone says anything to you, tell them,*
b		*'The Lord needs them.'*
c		*And he will immediately send them."*
4a	Fulfillment Formula	**This took place so that the word spoken through the prophet might be fulfilled, saying,**
5a	OT Quotation	*"Say to the daughter of Zion:* (Isa 62:11)
b		*'Look, your king is coming to you,*
c		*meek and riding on a donkey, and*
d		*on a colt, the foal of a donkey.'"* (Zech 9:9)
6a	Response	**So his disciples went and did just what Jesus ordered them to do.**
7a	Group #1 Action	**They brought the donkey and colt,**
b	Action	**placed garments on them,**
c	Action	and **Jesus sat on them.**
8a	Group #2 Action	**A very large crowd spread their own garments on the road,**
b	Action	and **others cut branches from the trees and spread them on the road.**
9a	Action	And **the crowd going ahead of him as well as those following were shouting,**
b		*"Hosanna to the Son of David!*
c		*Blessed be the one who comes in the name of the Lord.*
d		*Hosanna in the highest."* (Ps 118:25-26)
10a	Action	As he entered Jerusalem,
b		**The whole city was shaken and said,**
c		*"Who is this?"*
11a	Response	**The crowds replied,**
b		*"This is Jesus,*
c	Description	*the prophet from Nazareth in Galilee."*

Structure and Literary Form

Matthew again is dependant on Mark (Mark 11:1 – 10), editing in his normal fashion and adding two parts, the formula quotation from Zech 9:9 in vv. 4 – 5 and the concluding section on Jesus as the prophet from Nazareth in vv. 10 – 11. Virtually every scholar sees a different structure for this triumphal entry (like many parousia narratives of royalty or military conquerors in ancient literature), but the best may be the simplest, as there are two primary sections, each with two parts: (1)

Jesus' preparations (vv. 1 – 3) followed by a christological interpretation (the formula quotation, vv. 4 – 5); (2) the fulfillment of those preparations (vv. 6 – 8) followed by two christological interpretations by the crowd — their messianic acclamation (v. 9) and their affirmation of Jesus as the prophet from Nazareth (vv. 10 – 11).

Exegetical Outline

➡ **I. First Cycle: Preparation (21:1 – 5)**
- A. The setting at Bethphage (v. 1a)
- B. Instructions to two disciples (vv. 1b – 3)
  1. Find a donkey and colt and bring them to Jesus (vv. 1b – 2)
  2. If asked, say that the Lord needs them (v. 3)
- C. Fulfillment (Zech 9:9) (vv. 4 – 5)

II. Second Cycle: Execution (21:6 – 11)
- A. Carrying out Jesus' orders (vv. 6 – 8)
  1. The donkey and colt brought to Jesus (vv. 6 – 7)
  2. The crowd spreads garments and branches on the road (v. 8)
- B. Christological affirmation (vv. 9 – 11)
  1. The messianic acclamation of the crowds (v. 9)
  2. Affirmation of the crowd (vv. 10 – 11)

Explanation of the Text

21:1 When they drew near to Jerusalem and came to Bethphage on the Mount of Olives, Jesus then sent two disciples (Καὶ ὅτε ἤγγισαν εἰς Ἱεροσόλυμα καὶ ἦλθον εἰς Βηθφαγὴ εἰς τὸ Ὄρος τῶν Ἐλαιῶν, τότε Ἰησοῦς ἀπέστειλεν δύο μαθητάς). It was a rugged walk from Jericho, about fifteen miles and an ascent of 3,500 feet on a rugged road. Bethany and Bethphage (unknown but placed within a mile of the Holy City in rabbinic writings) were on the southeast side of the Mount of Olives, which contains three ridges east of Jerusalem, with the northern peak the highest at 3,000 feet above sea level and the middle at 2,700 feet, just a hundred feet higher looking down across the Kidron Valley at the temple area itself.[3]

It is difficult to know whether Jesus sent the two disciples to Bethphage (Carson) or Bethany (Hagner, Turner). The text could point to either. It is also difficult to know whether Jesus had made prior arrangements or knew supernaturally that the donkeys would be there. Either way, he deliberately plans the event as a messianic fulfillment, possibly connected with three passages: Zech 14:4, which prophesied Yahweh would stand on the Mount of Olives on the day of the Lord (see further on 24:3 and Jesus' ascension from there in Luke 24:51 – 52); the lion of Judah (Gen 49:10 – 11, a messianic figure within Judaism) who "tethers his donkey ... [and] colt" (so Nolland); and David's return to Jerusalem (after his son Absalom

3. Warren J. Heard Jr., "Olives, Mount of," *ABD*, 5:13.

forced him to flee) on a donkey in 2 Sam 15:30 – 31; 16:1 – 2 (so France, Hauerwas).

21:2 ... telling them, "Go to the village opposite you, and immediately you will find a donkey tied and a colt with her. Untie them and bring them to me" (λέγων αὐτοῖς, Πορεύεσθε εἰς τὴν κώμην τὴν κατέναντι ὑμῶν, καὶ εὐθέως εὑρήσετε ὄνον δεδεμένην καὶ πῶλον μετ᾽ αὐτῆς· λύσαντες ἀγάγετέ μοι). Regardless of whether prior preparations were made, the emphasis is on the divine control of the events, as seen in "immediately" (εὐθέως), pointing to omniscience. Mark 11:2 just has a colt, but Matthew has a donkey and a colt in fulfillment of Zech 9:9. This refers to a female donkey (ὄνος/αὐτῆς) and a young male donkey (πῶλος). Jesus' need of them shows he intends a deliberate prophetic acted parable to confront the Jewish people with his true messianic nature.

21:3 And if anyone says anything to you, tell[4] them, "The Lord needs them." And he will immediately send them (καὶ ἐάν τις ὑμῖν εἴπῃ τι, ἐρεῖτε ὅτι Ὁ κύριος αὐτῶν χρείαν ἔχει· εὐθὺς δὲ ἀποστελεῖ αὐτούς). It is possible that "the Lord needs them" is a prearranged signal (Morris calls it a "password"), but the text does not indicate such. Derrett prefers to speak here of the royal right of *angereia* or "requisitioning," in which a king makes use of needed property or animals.[5] The latter fits the emphasis in 20:29 – 21:11 on Jesus as royal Messiah and makes better sense of the passage.

"Lord" (κύριος) is not God but a self-designation for Jesus, who was called "Lord" by the blind men (20:30, 31, 33) and indeed has been repeatedly called "Lord" (8:2, 6, 8, 25; 9:28; 14:28, 30; 15:22, 25, 27; 17:4, 15). Jesus is "the Lord Messiah who recovers the lordship of Adam over the animals (cf. Gen 1:26 – 31)."[6] So Jesus can predict that the owner of the animals will "immediately" comply, for Jesus is the eschatological "Lord."

21:4 This took place so that the word spoken through the prophet might be fulfilled, saying (Τοῦτο δὲ γέγονεν ἵνα πληρωθῇ τὸ ῥηθὲν διὰ τοῦ προφήτου λέγοντος). For Matthew's fulfillment quotations and formula, see on 1:22; the formula here is similar to that passage. This is the ninth of the ten such passages (1:22; 2:15, 17, 23; 4:14; 8:17; 12:17; 13:35; 21:4; 27:9), all of which stress Jesus as the one prophesied in OT expectation, the one who reenacts the life of Israel. God's sovereign control (note the divine passive, which means, "that God might fulfill") denotes that Jesus is the centerpoint of history, bringing to completion God's plan of salvation and OT hope.

21:5 "Say to the daughter of Zion: 'Look, your king is coming to you' "(Εἴπατε τῇ θυγατρὶ Σιών, Ἰδοὺ ὁ βασιλεύς σου ἔρχεταί σοι). The opening words echo Isa 62:11 ("Say to Daughter Zion, 'See, your Savior comes'") while Zech 9:9 has "Rejoice greatly, Daughter Zion" (= "people of Jerusalem"). The Isaianic context deals with the coming of salvation (this points forward to that), and Zechariah prophesies judgment on Israel's enemies; here judgment is pronounced on Israel itself, as seen in the omission from Zech 9:9 of "righteous and having salvation." The opposition and rejection of Jerusalem will bring judgment on them (cf. 23:37) because they have rejected God's coming salvation in Jesus.

4. "Tell" (ἐρεῖτε) is a case of a future with imperatival force, normally used of divine commands such as in the Ten Commandments and here to portray Jesus' sovereign command of the situation.

5. J. D. M. Derrett, "Law in the New Testament: The Palm Sunday Colt," *NovT* 13 (1971): 241 – 58, states that "Lord" (κύριος) labels Jesus the true owner of the donkeys, but that is going beyond the scene.

6. Davies and Allison, *Matthew*, 3:117.

21:5 "... meek" (πραΰς). A great deal of emphasis falls on Jesus' πραΰς, his "meekness, gentleness, humility," continuing the theme of Jesus' humility from 11:29 ("meek and humble in heart," cf. 5:5; 12:18 – 21; 18:1 – 4; 19:13 – 15; 21:5; 23:12). Thus the entry into Jerusalem is the antithesis of "triumphal" in the way meant by the pilgrims who acclaim him Messiah. They are thinking of the conquering victor, while Jesus intends it of the suffering Servant of Isa 53 by riding a donkey rather than a warhorse. Jesus will become the Davidic Messiah on the cross, not on a battlefield.

21:5 "... and riding on a donkey, and on a colt, the foal of a donkey" (καὶ ἐπιβεβηκὼς ἐπὶ ὄνον καὶ ἐπὶ πῶλον υἱὸν ὑποζυγίου). Another big issue is the question of the two animals, the donkey and the colt, especially since in Zech 9:9 it is "on a donkey, (namely) on a colt." Many critical scholars believe Matthew has misinterpreted the parallelism of Zechariah (perhaps because of a literal reading of the LXX) and created two animals. But this is surely unnecessary, for Matthew would certainly be aware of Zechariah and probably altered it slightly to fit the historical facts.[7] As many have said, it would be natural for the mother to accompany an unbroken colt on such a journey, and so Matthew is pointing to literal fulfillment.[8]

21:6 So his disciples went[9] and did just what Jesus ordered them to do (πορευθέντες δὲ οἱ μαθηταὶ καὶ ποιήσαντες καθὼς συνέταξεν αὐτοῖς ὁ Ἰησοῦς). The obedience of the disciples is part of the fulfillment. They procure the animals and bring them to Jesus. We are never told if someone challenges them, but this is likely due to v. 3 (which probably would have been omitted if nothing had happened).

21:7 They brought the donkey and colt, placed garments on them, and Jesus sat on them (ἤγαγον τὴν ὄνον καὶ τὸν πῶλον, καὶ ἐπέθηκαν ἐπ' αὐτῶν τὰ ἱμάτια, καὶ ἐπεκάθισεν ἐπάνω αὐτῶν). Matthew stresses the literal fulfillment of Zech 9:9, with both "the donkey and colt" (twice using αὐτῶν to speak of "them") brought to Jesus. The image of garments placed on both donkeys with Jesus sitting on them (hardly on both at the same time but on the colt [Mark 11:7] with the donkey accompanying) is royal imagery alluding to Solomon's riding a mule to his coronation at Gihon in 1 Kgs 1:33, 38, 44.[10] Since pilgrims were expected to walk into Jerusalem, this is a powerful image indeed.

21:8 A very large crowd spread their own garments on the road, and others cut branches from the trees and spread them on the road (ὁ δὲ πλεῖστος ὄχλος ἔστρωσαν ἑαυτῶν τὰ ἱμάτια ἐν τῇ ὁδῷ, ἄλλοι δὲ ἔκοπτον κλάδους ἀπὸ τῶν δένδρων καὶ ἐστρώννυον ἐν τῇ ὁδῷ). "Very large" (πλεῖστος, elative in force) pictures a great number of pilgrims (many coming out of Jerusalem after hearing Jesus was coming, John 12:12) accompanying Jesus into Jerusalem. Jerusalem, a city of about

7. As Keener, *Matthew*, 491, shows, Matthew elsewhere demonstrates a keen knowledge of Hebrew and would hardly make such a grammatical error. More likely he deliberately changes the text to state how literally Jesus has fulfilled prophecy here.

8. So Gundry, Hagner, Senior, Blomberg. Wilkins, *Matthew*, 686 – 87, notes the possibility of a further secondary allusion to Gen 49:11, "He will tether his donkey to a vine, his colt to the choicest branch." This is Jacob's prophecy regarding the "lion from the tribe of Judah," a "permanent kingly line in his descendants."

9. Another circumstantial participle becomes part of the action of the main verb (see on 20:2).

10. Witherington, *Matthew*, 388, notes that the name "Solomon" stems from *šālôm*, "peace," and calls Solomon David's "peace child," saying, "if ever there was a royal figure who was meant to be both king of peace and also a sage of the Davidic line, this was the man."

70,000 (Rev 11:13 says one-tenth of the city was 7,000), swelled to about 250,000 for Passover.[11]

The garments and leafy branches (John 12:13 has palm branches) spread on the road picture this as a royal procession (cf. 2 Kgs 9:13 of Jehu after being anointed as king; 1 Macc 13:51; 2 Macc 10:7 of palms carried in celebration during the time of the Maccabees). The scene may picture the cloaks being laid first (aorist tense) followed by the branches cut and placed in Jesus' path (imperfect tense) after the garments were all laid (so Nolland). Either way, Matthew pictures the entry as a "red carpet" ride into Jerusalem. Truly the royal Messiah is coming, but not in the way the crowds think.

21:9 And the crowd going ahead of him as well as those following were shouting (οἱ δὲ ὄχλοι οἱ προάγοντες αὐτὸν καὶ οἱ ἀκολουθοῦντες ἔκραζον λέγοντες). The use of the present participles and the imperfect main verb are dramatic, depicting the ongoing acclamation. The note of the crowd behind as well as in front pictures the pilgrims surrounding Jesus on all sides as they cry out their messianic hopes (perhaps the pilgrims behind and the people from Jerusalem in front). France points out that Galileans were essentially foreigners in Jerusalem, so Jesus and his disciples would stand out. Yet the large crowd, almost all pilgrims, were probably also mainly Galileans, and so all these acclaiming Jesus would make his threat to the Jerusalem authorities all the greater.[12]

21:9 "Hosanna to the Son of David!" (Ὡσαννὰ τῷ υἱῷ Δαυίδ). Behind their cry is Ps 118:25 – 26, part of the "Hallel Psalms" (Pss 113 – 18) used in Sabbath worship and at festivals, including the Passover celebration that is just a week away. It is a natural passage for the pilgrims in procession to Jerusalem (118:27, "with boughs in hand, join in the festal procession"). "Hosanna" (ὡσαννά) is the transliteration of the Aramaic (the Hebrew would be *hošîʿānāʾ*) and in 118:25 LXX is translated as a prayer, "Save now."

Its force here is debated. Most believe that in the first century it had become a cry of praise,[13] though a few would retain the prayer form as a cry from Ps 118 for the kingdom to arrive.[14] The former is more likely, especially with the added "to the Son of David." This is a major motif because of the twofold "Son of David" in the previous episode (20:30 – 31); this is the coronation procession of the royal Messiah. The people are calling out divine blessings on their expected deliverer, but they will be delivered by the suffering Servant rather than a conquering king.

21:9 "Blessed be the one who comes in the name of the Lord" (Εὐλογημένος ὁ ἐρχόμενος ἐν ὀνόματι κυρίου). The central acclamation between the two "Hosanna" cries comes word-for-word from Ps 118:26, in which the "coming one" may be the individual pilgrim or perhaps the king coming to thank Yahweh for a military victory. In Jewish festivals it meant the former, but in this context the pilgrims are thinking of the latter as fulfilled in Jesus the conquering Messiah. There is also a question both in the psalm and here whether "in the name of the Lord" modifies "blessed" (the

11. The size of Jerusalem in the first century has been variously estimated over the years. Wolfgang Reinhardt, "The Population Size of Jerusalem and the Numerical Growth of the Jerusalem Church," in *The Book of Acts in Its Palestinian Setting* (ed. Richard Bauckham; Grand Rapids: Eerdmans, 1995), estimates that Jerusalem was 100,000 and grew to as much as 1,000,000 during festivals.

12. France, *Gospel of Matthew*, 771.

13. See Joseph A. Fitzmyer, "Aramaic Evidence Affecting the Interpretation of Hosanna in the New Testament," in *Tradition and Interpretation in the New Testament: Festschrift for E. E. Ellis* (ed. G. F. Hawthorne and O. Betz; Grand Rapids: Eerdmans, 1987), 110 – 18; Gundry, *Use of the Old Testament*; 40 – 43; Hagner, *Matthew 14 – 28*, 595.

14. See Marvin H. Pope, "Hosanna — What It Really Means," *BRev* 4 (1988): 16 – 25; Edwards, *Mark*, 336; Keener, *Matthew*, 494.

blessing coming from Yahweh) or "the coming one." The latter definitely makes best sense, with Jesus coming as the Agent of Yahweh.

21:9 "Hosanna in the highest" (Ὡσαννὰ ἐν τοῖς ὑψίστοις). The final acclamation calls for "the highest blessing" or praise to fall on Jesus Messiah. It may also call for the angels who inhabit the "highest" heaven to join in the acclamation.

21:10 As he entered Jerusalem, the whole city was shaken (καὶ εἰσελθόντος αὐτοῦ εἰς Ἱεροσόλυμα ἐσείσθη πᾶσα ἡ πόλις). Matthew records here the "seismic" shock Jerusalem feels as the royal Messiah enters the city (cf. 2:3, where Herod and "all Jerusalem" are disturbed). We must remember that Jerusalem at this time was filled with excited pilgrims, and word of a possible messianic figure would ignite the people. Especially those visitors from outside Palestine (in John, Jesus visited Jerusalem many times) would be mystified as to the identity of this figure.

21:10 ... and said, "Who is this?" (λέγουσα, Τίς ἐστιν οὗτος;). Everyone would be intensely interested in the reality behind the rumors. As Carson interprets, they are asking, "Who really is this about whom there is so much excitement?"[15] Matthew wants every reader to ask the question along with the people of Jerusalem. It is the key question of this gospel.

21:11 The crowds replied (οἱ δὲ ὄχλοι ἔλεγον). There are two issues that arise from vv. 10 – 11. First, are the "crowds" the same as the Galilean pilgrims who have accompanied Jesus to Jerusalem in vv. 1 – 9 (Schweizer, Hill), or are they those who were in Jerusalem (Blomberg, Nolland)? From the use of "the whole city" in v. 10, the latter is the more likely, though it is certainly possible that the Galilean crowds answer the question coming from the people of the city (Luz).

21:11 "This is Jesus, the prophet from Nazareth in Galilee" (Οὗτός ἐστιν ὁ προφήτης Ἰησοῦς ὁ ἀπὸ Ναζαρὲθ τῆς Γαλιλαίας). Second, by "prophet" do these people mean the "prophet like Moses" of Deut 18:15 (France, Davies and Allison, Morris) or a general prophet from Galilee (Hagner, Keener)? The latter is best in the context (there is no hint of a Moses connection here), yet it is clear that the people regard Jesus highly and are on his side, which will keep the leaders from arresting Jesus publicly (21:46 and parallels; cf. Mark 11:18 = Luke 19:47 – 48).

It does seem likely that Matthew wants to show a deficient understanding by noting the crowd only considers him a prophet. Yet there is also a christological point, that Jesus is prophet as well as Messiah, as seen in the times Jesus' prophetic office is noted — 13:57 (Jesus calls himself a "prophet without honor"); 16:14 (the people say he is "Jeremiah or one of the prophets"); and 21:46 (the people still consider him a "prophet"; cf. John 6:14; 7:40, 52). Jesus is a prophet and more.

Theology in Application

This is the proper introduction to Passion Week, centering not only on Jesus' messianic office but also on the reactions of all who encounter him. In this final week of his earthly ministry, the "messianic secret" (see 8:4; 9:30; 12:16; 16:20; 17:9) is no longer needed, and so Jesus unveils his messianic nature in three stages — here, 22:41 – 46; and 26:64.

15. Carson, "Matthew," 440.

1. A Humble Messiah

Jesus is not coming as conquering king but as the humble Messiah bringing peace through suffering. The crowds acclaim him king by strewing garments and leafy branches before him, turning his entry into a royal procession. But Jesus' lengthy preparations show he intends this as a prophetic-acted parable that fulfills Zech 9:9, as he rides a donkey (the symbol of peace) rather than a warhorse (signifying the sword).

Moreover, in Matthew's quotation of Zech 9:9 the emphasis is on Jesus' "meekness," or humility (John 12:15 is the only other gospel to quote Zech 9:9, but he omits "meek"). This is a christological point made often in Matthew (see above on v. 5) and points to Jesus as the lowly Messiah who has come to serve by dying as a "ransom" (20:28) and has brought salvation to humankind (see the use of Isa 62:11 in v. 5). Also, Jesus becomes the paradigm for disciples who are characterized by humility and place their interests last (16:24 – 26; 18:3 – 4; 20:26 – 27).

2. A "Proleptic Parousia"

At the same time, entering Jerusalem could constitute Jesus as the "eschatological king" and his entrance as a "proleptic parousia." These points are made by Davies and Allison,[16] who make this motif more central than it is but still may be right at a secondary level. With the presence of the Mount of Olives, associated with the day of Yahweh in prophecy (Zech 14:4 – 5, where it is split in two as the feet of Yahweh stand on it), and with the centrality of the "Son of David" title, with its royal expectations, this anticipation of the exaltation and return of Jesus could be echoed here. Thus the acclamation of the crowd with its basis in Ps 118:25 – 26 might well be an unconscious prophecy of this future event.

3. No Preconceived Categories

The crowds (as well as the disciples) could only think of the coming Messiah as a conquering king and had no category for the true reason for his coming — the suffering Servant, whose death would bring salvation. As a result they ended up rejecting him and placing themselves outside the kingdom. J. B. Phillips wrote his classic *Your God Is Too Small*, and he could have written a corresponding *Your Jesus Is Too Small*. Christians all too often think of Jesus in comfortable categories as their friend and helper and forget that he must be worshiped as Savior and Lord of all.

16. Davies and Allison, *Matthew*, 3:128 – 29. See also Wilkins, *Matthew*, 686, who says Jesus' descent from the Mount of Olives echoes Zech 14:3 – 21, prophesying the Lord placing his feet on the Mount of Olives and liberating Jerusalem.

CHAPTER 88

Matthew 21:12 – 17

Literary Context

The authority of Jesus Messiah, recognized at the entry into Jerusalem, is now demonstrated at the temple. The next two chapters center on this authority, seen first in cleansing the temple of evil practices,[1] portrayed as judgment in the parabolic act that follows (vv. 18 – 22), and second in the temple debates with the leaders (21:23 – 22:46).

VI. The Movement to the Cross (19:1 – 25:46)
- **A. Jesus' Deeds: Opposition and Discipleship (19:1 – 22:46)**
  - **2. Beginning Events of Passion Week (21:1 – 22:46)**
    - **a. The Messiah Enters Jerusalem (21:1 – 22)**
      - (1) The Lowly King in His Humble Entry (21:1 – 11)
      - ➦ **(2) Judgment on the Temple (21:12 – 17)**
      - (3) Judgment Parable — Cursing the Fig Tree (21:18 – 22)

Main Idea

Jesus, called a prophet by the people (21:11, 46), now acts like a prophet and condemns the leaders for corrupting God's temple. Via another prophetic symbolic action (as in 21:1 – 11) he purifies the temple of its false commercial activity (vv. 12 – 13) and then as the Son of David heals "the blind and the lame" (vv. 14 – 17).

Translation

(See next page.)

1. For the authenticity of this story, accepted by most today, see Victor Eppstein, "The Historicity of the Gospel Account of the Cleansing of the Temple," *ZNW* 55 (1964), 42 – 58.

Matthew 21:12-17

12a	Setting/Action	And **Jesus entered the temple,**
b	Scene #1 Action	and **he began to throw out all who were selling and buying in the temple.**
c	Action	**Then he overturned the tables of the moneychangers and the benches of those selling doves.**
13a	Basis	And **he said to them,**
b		*"It is written,*
c	OT Quotation	*'My house will be called a house of prayer,'* (Isa 56:7)
d	Accusation	*but you are making it 'a hideout for robbers.'"* (Jer 7:11)
14a	Scene #2/ Action: Entreaty	And **the blind and the crippled came to him in the temple,**
b	Action: Healing	and **he healed them.**
15a	Scene #3 Response	When the chief priests and teachers of the law saw the wonders he performed and
b		heard the children shouting in the temple,
c		*"Hosanna to the Son of David,"* (Ps 118:25)
d	Reaction/Result of 14b	**they were angry**
16a		and **they said to him,**
b	Question	*"Do you hear what they are saying?"*
c	Answer	**Jesus answered,**
d	Question	*"Yes. Haven't you ever read,*
e	OT Quotation	*'From the mouths of infants and those who nurse he will prepare praise'?"* (Ps 8:2)
17a	Conclusion	And **leaving them, he went outside the city to Bethany and spent the night there.**

Structure and Literary Form

Matthew abbreviates Mark 11:11, 15 – 17[2] by removing (1) the time note of v. 11 (Jesus going into Jerusalem and looking at the temple, then going to Bethany for the night), (2) Jesus' not allowing anyone carrying vessels through the temple of v.

2. It is common for scholars to hold to just one cleansing, meaning that John 2:13 – 22 is the same event. While that is certainly possible, there are good reasons for separating John's story from the Synoptic event. The differences between the Synoptic and Johannine stories are considerable, and there is good reason why he was not arrested after either incident (note his debates with the leaders in the temple in 21:23 – 22:46) — he was so popular that they could not do so, plus after the earlier cleansing he went back to Galilee. See Carson, "Matthew," 441; Morris, *Matthew*, 525; Wilkins, *Matthew*, 690.

16; and (3) the "for all nations" from the Isa 56:7 quote. Matthew then adds from his special material (M) Jesus' healing in the temple (v. 14) and the controversy story regarding his Son of David status (vv. 15 – 17). So there are three sections: the cleansing of the temple (vv. 12 – 13), his healing (v. 14), and his debate with the leaders regarding the children praising him as Son of David (vv. 15 – 17).

Exegetical Outline

➦ **I. The Purging of the Temple (21:12 – 13)**
- A. Throwing out the merchants and buyers (v. 12)
- B. The reason for the purging (v. 13)
  1. Supposed to be a house of prayer (Isa 56:7)
  2. Turned into a den of thieves

II. Healings in the Temple (21:14)

III. Controversy with the Leaders (21:15 – 17)
- A. The children's testimony that he is Son of David (v. 15a)
- B. The leaders' indignation (vv. 15b – 16a)
- C. Jesus' response from Ps 8:2 (v. 16b)
- D. Jesus' departure to Bethany (v. 17)

Explanation of the Text

21:12 And Jesus entered[3] the temple (Καὶ εἰσῆλθεν Ἰησοῦς εἰς τὸ ἱερόν). Matthew omits Mark's note that this occurred the following morning and gives the impression that it happened the same day, thereby drawing the events of the entry and the cleansing into virtually a single event. Jesus is acting as both prophet (21:11, 46) and Messiah (21:5, 8 – 9, 15b, 42) here. "The temple" (τὸ ἱερόν) refers to the whole complex, not just the "inner sanctuary" (ναός).

21:12 ... and he began to throw out all who were selling and buying in the temple (καὶ ἐξέβαλεν πάντας τοὺς πωλοῦντας καὶ ἀγοράζοντας ἐν τῷ ἱερῷ). The ingressive aorist (Wallace, 558 – 59) "began to throw out" (ἐξέβαλεν) was not just anger but a calculated act. Jesus obviously realizes this will not be a long-term solution but still considers the violent act a symbolic action aimed at the leaders for corrupting the temple with their mercantile activity.[4] Most likely the activity resumes almost immediately (note the present participles emphasizing the ongoing activity of "selling" and "buying").

There were shops immediately outside the temple year-round, and they did a thriving trade. However, Jesus' act was not addressed against

3. There are three ways "entered into" can be said: repeating the "into" (εἰς) from the verb (as here) or having the "into" (εἰς) either with the verb or as a preposition after the verb. The choice is stylistic, and all three options have the same force.

4. Turner, "Matthew," 268, notes three earlier "cleansings": that of Josiah (2 Kgs 23:1 – 7), of Hezekiah (2 Chr 29:3 – 11), and of Judah Maccabeus (1 Macc 4; 2 Macc 10). Cleansing the temple is a critical aspect of national revival, but in this case portends national judgment.

them but against the trade inside the temple. It took place in the Court of Gentiles, a large area (twenty-five acres) in the southeast quadrant of the temple mount. The temple itself was the largest structure in the Roman world, measuring 1,590 feet on the west, 1,035 feet on the north, 1,536 feet on the east, and 912 feet on the south, equal to thirty-five football fields in size and covering one-sixth the total area of Jerusalem itself.[5] The need for sacrificial animals and birds, especially at Passover, was immense, and since priests had to certify their purity, people would naturally purchase them at the temple itself rather than walk them through the streets of the city and take the chance of their being rendered impure somehow. All the bargaining in the buying and selling plus the movement of the animals made a lot of noise.

21:12 Then he overturned the tables of the moneychangers and the benches of those selling doves (καὶ τὰς τραπέζας τῶν κολλυβιστῶν κατέστρεψεν καὶ τὰς καθέδρας τῶν πωλούντων τὰς περιστεράς). Most of the pilgrims carried pagan coins with idolatrous likenesses of the emperor on them. These had to be exchanged for Tyrian silver (see on 17:27), a pure silver that was used to pay the required half-shekel temple tax (Exod 30:11 – 16) and to buy animals. Jesus was not opposed to the fact of these businesses but the place: the temple was not where such activity should occur. Money exchangers set up on Adar 25, a short time before Passover, to collect the tax. However, there is evidence that the practice of selling in the temple precincts was recent; the normal place was the Mount of Olives, where markets had been established under the Sanhedrin.

The temple markets may have been set up by Caiaphas about AD 30 in competition with others, and this was controversial, thought by many to be a desecration of the temple (bringing idolatrous coins into it) and a scandal because it was purely mercenary.[6] Doves were by far the most frequently purchased items, as they were the sacrifice of the poor (Lev 12:8, 14:21 – 22; cf. Luke 2:22 – 24), and there is rabbinic evidence that exorbitant prices were often charged (*m. Ker.* 1:7; *m. Pesaḥ* 57a).

21:13 And he said to them, "It is written, 'My house will be called a house of prayer' " (καὶ λέγει αὐτοῖς, Γέγραπται, Ὁ οἶκός μου οἶκος προσευχῆς κληθήσεται). Matthew makes certain that the reader catches the centrality of the theme of economic exploitation and so drops "for all nations" from Isa 56:7 and Mark 11:17. So the contrast between "house of prayer" and "hideout for robbers" (both subjective genitives, a "house where prayer is supposed to take place" and a "den where robbery is actually taking place") becomes all the more apparent.[7]

The context of Isa 56 centers on the coming of universal salvation to the nations as well as to Israel, and v. 7 centers on "joy" and "prayer" that all peoples will share with Israel. This is not as emphasized by Matthew, but it is probably still a part of the thrust. The sacrifices were often called "a pleasing aroma" (= a prayer of thanksgiving and trust, Gen 8:21;

5. See M. O. Wise, "Temple," *DJG*, 812.

6. See Eppstein, "The Historicity of the Gospel Account of the Cleansing of the Temple," 44 – 45; Craig A. Evans, "Jesus' Action in the Temple: Cleansing or Portent of Destruction?" *CBQ* 51 (1989): 237 – 70. William Lane, *Gospel of Mark* (NICNT; Grand Rapids: Eerdmans, 1974), 403; Davies and Allison, *Matthew*, 3:138; R. T. France, *Gospel of Mark* (NICNT; Grand Rapids: Eerdmans, 2002), 444. Witherington, *Matthew*, 397, says the priests allowed those selling animals to charge whatever they wished and let the moneychangers "juggle the exchange rate for the Tyrian shekels" because the priests received a cut of the profits.

7. So Gundry, *Matthew*, 412. Other options for the deletion of the phrase are that the temple will have no future significance for the Gentiles since it will be destroyed (Hagner), or that for Matthew and his community the Jerusalem temple is no longer "the house of prayer for all nations" (Luz).

Exod 29:18; et al.), and the temple incense was seen as a prayer (Ps 141:2; Rev 5:8; 8:3). The temple always signified prayer, but the leaders were in the process of changing (present tense "making" [ποιεῖτε]) that purpose through their mercantile actions.

21:13 "... but you are making it 'a hideout for robbers' " (ὑμεῖς δὲ αὐτὸν ποιεῖτε σπήλαιον λῃστῶν). Matthew takes "hideout for robbers" (i.e., "bandits," who often instigated an insurrection, see on 26:65) from Jer 7:11, where it describes the failed worship of the people of Israel rather than of the priests but still applies here. It is likely that the whole context of Jer 7 is in mind, and thus the condemnation is for worshipers who live in sin outside the temple and then enter the house of God to "hide" from their sin (so Beare).[8] σπήλαιον signifies a "cave, hideout, or den," and Jesus is virtually saying the leaders have turned the temple into a mafia-like stronghold, for a λῃστής is not a simple thief but a revolutionary bandit, probably pointing to the violent criminal activity of the leaders in turning God's house into a mercantile exchange.[9] Neusner goes so far as to say Jesus is challenging the whole sacrificial system.[10]

21:14 And the blind and the crippled came to him in the temple, and he healed them (Καὶ προσῆλθον αὐτῷ τυφλοὶ καὶ χωλοὶ ἐν τῷ ἱερῷ, καὶ ἐθεράπευσεν αὐτούς). This new material that Matthew adds lists the final healing miracles in Jesus' ministry. In Lev 21:18 "the blind and lame" cannot function as priests in the temple, and in 2 Sam 5:8 David said the "blind or lame will not enter the palace." The crippled were restricted from entering the sanctuary, lest their unclean crutches or mats defile the temple. Qumran went even further, not allowing them in the congregation at all (1QSa 2:8–9; CD 15:15–17; 1QM 7:4–5). So here they come into the Court of the Gentiles, paralleling the crippled beggars at the temple gates in Acts 3:2.

In the context, Jesus uses the healings to display what the temple should look like as a "house of prayer," in contrast to the leaders who have turned into a place of commerce. His authority over the temple and over issues of uncleanness continues; Jesus is not only the "final interpreter of Torah" (see "Theology in Application" on 5:17–20) but has authority over Torah and temple (cf. 12:8). He is greater than the temple, and in the temple precincts themselves he heals and makes the impure pure.

21:15 When the chief priests and teachers of the law saw[11] the wonders he performed and heard the children shouting in the temple, "Hosanna to the Son of David," they were angry (ἰδόντες δὲ οἱ ἀρχιερεῖς καὶ οἱ γραμματεῖς τὰ θαυμάσια ἃ ἐποίησεν καὶ τοὺς παῖδας τοὺς κράζοντας ἐν τῷ ἱερῷ καὶ λέγοντας, Ὡσαννὰ τῷ υἱῷ Δαυίδ, ἠγανάκτησαν). It is interesting that the leaders do not show their indignation at Jesus' act of judgment in the temple but at his healing ministry and especially at the acclamation by the children. The children function like the chorus in a Greek play, and their cry is certainly closely connected with the acclamation at Jesus' entry (v. 9) and is the

8. J. Frankovic, "Remember Shiloh!" *Jerusalem Perspective* 46 (1994): 31, believes this also is reminiscent of the incident of the Philistines capturing the ark from Shiloh (1 Sam 4:1–22) as a symbol for the destruction of the temple in Jer 7:12–14.

9. Many (e.g., Hagner, Senior, Nolland) say the point is not economic profiteering or corruption in the temple but rather a failure to recognize the true purpose of the temple. They say there is too little evidence that profiteering was present. Yet there is a fair amount of evidence for economic corruption, see Evans, "Cleansing or Portent," 237–70; and U. Luz, *Matthew 21–28* (trans. W. C. Linns; Minneapolis: Augsburg, 2005), 12.

10. Jacob Neusner, "Money-Changers in the Temple: The Mishnah's Explanation," *NTS* 35 (1989): 287–90.

11. Here we have another aorist temporal participle (cf. 20:24) looking at the action as a single whole and governs both clauses. So they watch both Jesus and the children.

third straight affirmation of Jesus' Davidic status (20:30 – 31; 21:9).[12]

It also means that both the expelling of the people from the temple and the healings in the temple are aspects of Jesus' authority as Davidic Messiah (for healing as "Son of David," see 9:27; 12:23; 15:22; 20:30, 31). The leaders should have understood this, for they saw the "wonders" (θαυμάσια only here in the NT but echoing θαυμάζω in 8:27; 9:33; 15:31, always reactions to Jesus' "wondrous" works) but rejected their import. The children, however, saw them and echoed the truth of v. 9. So they sing Jesus' praise while the leaders become "angry."

21:16 And they said to him, "Do you hear what they are saying?" (καὶ εἶπαν αὐτῷ, Ἀκούεις τί οὗτοι λέγουσιν;). The depth of the Jewish leaders' refusal to accept Jesus as Messiah is now seen in their indignant question. They even expect him to castigate the children for daring to call him "Son of David"! The present tenses dramatically picture the children's christological cry as it continues throughout the scene.

21:16 Jesus answered, "Yes. Haven't you ever read, 'From the mouths of infants and those who nurse[13] he will prepare praise'?" (ὁ δὲ Ἰησοῦς λέγει αὐτοῖς, Ναί· οὐδέποτε ἀνέγνωτε ὅτι Ἐκ στόματος νηπίων καὶ θηλαζόντων κατηρτίσω αἶνον;). Jesus agrees that he has heard the children and then launches his own attack. In the first of two challenges to the leaders' scriptural knowledge (with 21:42; cf. 12:3; 19:4; 22:31), he asks why they have never noticed and understood Ps 8:2, a psalm of worship to the God of creation, thus implicitly giving Jesus adulation reserved for Yahweh alone.

In Jewish literature this verse was linked with the Song of Moses of Exod 15, and it was thought that at the crossing of the Red Sea even the babies raised their voices in praise to God.[14] The same supernatural revelation then is being reenacted in the children here. Keener notes the *qal wahomer* (the lesser to the greater) reasoning here: if children recognize and laud Jesus, how much more should the religious leaders know and worship him.[15]

21:17 And leaving them, he went outside the city to Bethany and spent the night there (Καὶ καταλιπὼν αὐτοὺς ἐξῆλθεν ἔξω τῆς πόλεως εἰς Βηθανίαν καὶ ηὐλίσθη ἐκεῖ). This could well be another symbolic action, as Jesus' withdrawal in Matthew is often a sign of rejection (cf. 12:15; 14:13; 15:21). Bethany is a suburb on the eastern slopes of the Mount of Olives, just two miles away. It was the home of Lazarus, Mary, and Martha; and Jesus spends nights there that final week (John 12:1). So many pilgrims crowded into Jerusalem at Passover that most had to stay outside the city, though the Torah required that they remain within the environs of Jerusalem.

12. Some say the children were doing little more than unknowingly mimicking the cry (so Hagner, Wilkins), but it is more likely that the children are used more positively as disciples, as in 18:3; 19:14. It is better to say that the children give "inspired revelation" to a divine truth (Davies and Allison). In 11:25 – 26 Jesus thanks the Father "that you have hidden these things from the wise and learned and revealed them to infants." That is what is taking place here.

13. This construction consists of a metaphorical noun followed by two subjective genitives, referring to the speech/message of infants and nursing babies.

14. *T. Soṭah* 6:4; *b. Soṭah* 30b; Wisd 10:21. See Martin McNamara, *Palestinian Judaism and the New Testament* (Wilmington, DE: Michael Glazier, 1983), 185 – 88; Davies and Allison, *Matthew*, 3:142; Luz, *Matthew 21 – 28*, 13; Nolland, *Matthew*, 848.

15. Keener, *Matthew*, 503.

Theology in Application

There is considerable debate regarding the purpose of Jesus' symbolic action at the temple, centering on whether it is a cleansing (i.e., a restoration of holiness) or a prophecy of the imminent judgment and destruction of the cultus and temple. Some believe it is indeed a "cleansing" or restoration of the temple in light of the corruption of the leaders and thus of the temple ritual itself.[16] According to this view Jesus was disturbed at the desecration of the temple by the rapacious business practices and wanted to bring back its sacred purpose (as in Zech 14:21; Mal 3:1–13).

Others believe it is primarily a curse on Israel and a portent of its coming doom.[17] Here Jer 7:11 as a prophecy of the temple's destruction and the cursing of the fig tree in vv. 18–22 are seen as a prophecy of divine judgment caused by the sin of the Jewish people (seen in the buyers and sellers). Moreover, if this is a judgment of coming destruction, did Jesus see the temple about to be replaced (by himself), or did he envision a new temple being built (so Sanders)?

These two primary options do not have to be seen as an either-or but are certainly a both-and. Jesus' symbolic action is both a cleansing and a curse.[18] Not only that, it is also a statement of his authority as Lord and Messiah over the temple.[19] On the final point, Matthew certainly saw Jesus replacing the temple with the new covenant.

1. Messiah and Judge

Jesus has revealed himself not only as Messiah but also as eschatological Judge of his people. As royal Davidic Messiah, Jesus is also Lord of all and has complete authority to stand in judgment over the nation and the temple. So Jesus is the humble King whose office is to die as the suffering Servant, yet also the great King who will sit on his judgment seat over all, including the church. He has come to humble the proud leaders and exalt the powerless and the children.

2. God Hates Sin

The entire OT is a testimony to the wrath and judgment of God when sin reigns among his people. In each instance—throughout the wilderness wanderings, the period of the judges, the exile—God turned his back on the apostate nation and

16. See Hill, *Matthew*, 293; Evans, "Cleansing or Portent," 237–70; Hagner, *Matthew 14–28*, 601; Schnackenburg, *Matthew*, 202. Hauerwas, *Matthew*, 183–84, calls it a virtual "jubilee," a return of true worship to the people.

17. See W. W. Watty, "Jesus and the Temple—Cleansing or Cursing?" *ExpTim* 93 (1982): 235–39; Sanders, *Jesus and Judaism*, 60–71; Senior, *Matthew*, 231–32.

18. See Morna D. Hooker, "Traditions about the Temple in the Sayings of Jesus," *BJRL* 70 (1988): 7–19; Davies and Allison, *Matthew*, 3:143; Keener, *Matthew*, 495–500.

19. France, *Matthew* (TNTC), 300–301; Morris, *Matthew*, 526. See also William R. Telford, *The Barren Temple and the Withered Tree* (Sheffield: JSOT Press, 1980), who makes this his thesis.

raised a new generation of those who would be faithful. In the present story two things have occurred: Jesus has symbolically proclaimed divine judgment on the nation for the desecration of the temple, and he has raised up a new Israel from their midst, symbolized in the blind and lame he heals and the children whose cry he accepts. In our day as well God will not countenance churches whose ministry centers on the profit motive. Too many churches like Laodicea in Rev 3:14 – 22 will experience God's wrath. As Bruner states,

> When a church exists for comfort to the exclusion of challenge, for grace and not ever for judgment, she becomes a hideout for thieves rather than a house of God. She also abandons the faithful exposition of Scripture, which regularly treats both grace *and* judgment.[20]

20. Bruner, *Matthew 13 – 28*, 361.

CHAPTER 89

Matthew 21:18 – 22

Literary Context

In his first twenty-four hours in Jerusalem, Jesus performs three prophetic symbolic actions (the humble entry, the cleansing, the cursing), with this third one (vv. 18 – 19) intended to interpret clearly the meaning of his cleansing of the temple. The second part of this pericope (vv. 20 – 22) is quite enigmatic but understandable when linked to the authority he has shown in all three actions — Jesus is passing on his authority to the disciples via the power of prayer.

VI. The Movement to the Cross (19:1 – 25:46)
A. Jesus' Deeds: Opposition and Discipleship (19:1 – 22:46)
2. Beginning Events of Passion Week (21:1 – 22:46)
a. The Messiah Enters Jerusalem (21:1 – 22)
(1) The Lowly King in His Humble Entry (21:1 – 11)
(2) Judgment on the Temple (21:12 – 17)
➦ **(3) Judgment Parable: Cursing the Fig Tree (21:18 – 22)**

Main Idea

Two primary themes are linked together because both flow out of the authority and spiritual power of Jesus. (1) The cursing of the fig tree is a parabolic enactment of the judgment Israel will soon face because the people have rejected God's Messiah and defiled his house, the temple. (2) Jesus promises that his followers will share his authority through prayer — with faith the disciple taps into the same power source as Jesus did.[1]

1. Mark Moulton, "Jesus' Goal for the Temple and Tree: A Thematic Revisit of Matt 21:12 – 17," *JETS* 41 (1998): 561 – 72, believes the demand for proper worship and prayer on the part of God's people is the controlling and unifying theme for the cleansing of the temple ("house of prayer") and the cursing of the fig tree. France, *Gospel of Matthew*, 791, goes so far as to say that the major purpose of this story is paraenetic, with the withering of the tree "as an example of powerful prayer."

Translation

Matthew 21:18-22

18a	Introduction	**Early the next morning ... he became hungry**
b		while he was returning to the city.
19a	Action	Seeing a single fig tree by the road,
b		**he went up to it, but**
c		**found nothing on it except only leaves.**
d		**So he told it,**
e	Curse	*"May no fruit ever come from you again!"*
f	Result	And **the fig tree withered at once.**
20a		When the disciples saw this,
b	Reaction	**they were amazed, asking,**
c	Question	*"How did the fig tree wither so suddenly?"*
21a	Answer	**Jesus answered them,**
b	Promise/Exhortation	*"I tell you the truth,*
		if you have faith and do not doubt
c		*you will not only do what happened to the fig tree,*
d		but *also*
		if you say to this mountain,
e		*'Be lifted up and thrown into the sea,'*
f		*it will take place.*
22a	Promise	And *everything, whatever you ask in prayer, believing, you will receive.*

Structure and Literary Form

This "miracle of destruction" (Blomberg; Davies and Allison — "penal miracle") abbreviates Mark 11:12–14, 20–26 and removes Mark's sandwiching technique, putting the whole story in one place. He omits Mark 11:18–19, 25 as well as "it was not the season for figs" and words here and there. There are two parts to the story, the cursing of the fig tree and the sayings on faith. Many critical scholars see little connection between them, yet the sayings are Jesus' response to the disciples' question regarding the fig tree, and it seems clear that Jesus is telling the disciples how they can possess such authority.

Exegetical Outline

- **I. The Cursing of the Fig Tree (21:18 – 19)**
  - A. The scene: Jesus' hunger as he returns to the city (v. 18)
  - B. The fig tree devoid of fruit (v. 19a)
  - C. Jesus curses it, and it withers (v. 19b)
- **II. The Sayings on Faith (21:20 – 22)**
  - A. The query by the disciples (v. 20)
  - B. Jesus' response — the power of faith (vv. 21 – 22)
    1. The twofold power (v. 21)
    2. The prayer promise (v. 22)

Explanation of the Text

21:18 Early the next morning, while he was returning[2] to the city, he became hungry (Πρωῒ δὲ ἐπανάγων εἰς τὴν πόλιν ἐπείνασεν).[3] In his hurry to get to Jerusalem, Jesus has apparently not taken time to eat breakfast and so becomes hungry as he and his disciples are going there early that morning (probably shortly after dawn — again we see his complete humanity as the God-man!). By his note that Jesus is "returning to the city" (cf. Mark 11:12, "came out of Bethany"), Matthew ties the action closely to the city and its future.

21:19 Seeing a single fig tree by the road, he went up to it, but found nothing on it except only leaves (καὶ ἰδὼν συκῆν μίαν ἐπὶ τῆς ὁδοῦ ἦλθεν ἐπ' αὐτήν καὶ οὐδὲν εὗρεν ἐν αὐτῇ εἰ μὴ φύλλα μόνον). Alongside the road Jesus sees a fig tree some distance away. Since leaves normally appear on fig trees after the fruit has come,[4] the presence of leaves would make one think a breakfast snack was available.[5] Yet when Jesus arrives, he finds there is no fruit.

21:19 So he told it, "May no fruit ever come from you again!" (καὶ λέγει αὐτῇ, Μηκέτι ἐκ σοῦ καρπὸς γένηται εἰς τὸν αἰῶνα). Jesus' reaction at first glance appears to be reprehensible, for seemingly in a fit of temper he curses the fig tree and kills it. How can this fit a compassionate Christ who has just healed the blind and lame and lauded the children? McNeile has the proper response: "If the narrative is historical, the tree fulfilled a more important function by dying than by living, and it is a false sentiment to think of it as badly treated." He thinks of it as more than a lesson about faith; it is primarily "a warning of punishment."[6]

2. Another temporal participle, as in vv. 15, 19.

3. In Mark this takes place over two days, with Jesus cursing the tree on the way to the temple. All the action, including cleansing the temple, occurs the second day. Yet the so-called contradiction is more apparent than real. Matthew gives the impression that the temple cleansing took place on the first day, but as we have seen, chronology is never a requirement in the gospels (e.g., see how Matthew scatters the events of Mark 1:21 – 44).

4. McNeile, *Matthew*, explains that while the main fruit does not appear until later, a small edible fruit-bud arrives in April and is even preferred by some natives today (though most find it fairly unpalatable). Keener, *Matthew*, 504, adds that such a fig tree with leaves but no early fruit would produce no fruit that season.

5. Mark 11:13 has "for it was not the season for figs," probably added to show that Jesus was deliberately enacting the curse as a sign of Israel, that also had promise of fruit but showed none (cf. France, *Mark*, 441).

6. McNeile, *Matthew*, 302 – 3.

Jesus is deliberately staging a symbolic act that uses an OT image in which the fig tree symbolizes Israel (Isa 28:4; Hos 9:10) and a barren fig tree symbolizes sin and corruption in the nation (Jer 8:13; 24:8, 29:17; Hos 9:10; Joel 1:12; Mic 7:1). He takes the opportunity afforded by the fruitless fig tree to signify the barrenness of Jerusalem and Israel and its imminent judgment.[7] Matthew often speaks of the fruitlessness of the nation and God's judgment on it (3:10; 7:16 – 20; 12:33; 13:4 – 7, 24 – 30; cf. 24:32 – 35), and this culminates that emphasis.

21:19 And the fig tree withered at once (καὶ ἐξηράνθη παραχρῆμα ἡ συκῆ). "At once" (παραχρῆμα) stresses the "immediate" and miraculous effects and also emphasizes the suddenness and imminence of the coming judgment, which will be spelled out in the Olivet Discourse as the destruction of Jerusalem and the temple.[8] So this symbolic action is intended by Jesus as a further explication of his actions in the temple the previous day.

21:20 When the disciples saw this, they were amazed, asking, "How did the fig tree wither so suddenly?" (καὶ ἰδόντες οἱ μαθηταὶ ἐθαύμασαν λέγοντες, Πῶς παραχρῆμα ἐξηράνθη ἡ συκῆ;). The disciples do not center on the meaning of Jesus' act but on the power demonstrated in it.[9] As in 8:27 they are filled with wonder at Jesus' miracle. The fact that the tree withered "at once" (παραχρῆμα) made it obvious this was a judgment miracle, and the disciples want to know "how" Jesus did it.

21:21 Jesus answered them, "I tell you the truth (ἀποκριθεὶς δὲ ὁ Ἰησοῦς εἶπεν αὐτοῖς, Ἀμὴν λέγω ὑμῖν). At first glance this "amen" (ἀμήν) saying (highlighting the importance of this truth, cf. 5:18) seems a strange thing to say after clearing the temple and cursing the fig tree, but when we realize the theology of authority that infused those two acted parables, this makes sense. Jesus is not only answering their question in a roundabout way but is also telling them how they can share that authority (cf. the authority he gave them "to drive out evil spirits and to heal every disease and sickness" in 10:1).

21:21 If you have faith and do not doubt (ἐὰν ἔχητε πίστιν καὶ μὴ διακριθῆτε). When the disciples failed to drive out demons (17:14 – 20), it was due to a lack of faith (17:17, 20). Faith and the absence of doubt (cf. Rom 4:20 of Abraham; Jas 1:6 of all believers), however, is not a magic formula for getting what one wants. "Doubt" (διακρίνομαι) refers not to a certainty that God will give anything one asks (see on v. 22) but rather to a "divided mind" that trusts God only partway and is centered more on self. Bruner says, "Doubt, in Jesus' teaching, is the decision to live as if God does not exist, and for disciples of Jesus this decision is disloyal. (In French, the word for doubt is *defiance.*)"[10]

21:21 You will not only do what happened to the fig tree, but also if you say to this mountain, 'Be lifted up and thrown into the sea,' it will take place" (οὐ μόνον τὸ τῆς συκῆς ποιήσετε, ἀλλὰ κἂν

7. See Telford, *Withered Tree*, who develops this symbolism at length.

8. Scholars often debate whether the image of judgment centers on the leaders, the temple, Jerusalem, or the nation as a whole. If we are to limit the image, Mark would center more on the temple and Matthew on Jerusalem, yet such discussions are too disjunctive. Any of the four would include the others, and in Matthew it is clear that all four levels are involved (e.g., see the parable of the wicked tenants [21:33 – 46] for the fruitlessness and judgment of all Israel).

9. Nolland, *Matthew*, 852, speaks of the "ironic inversion in the disciples' being amazed at this rather negative miracle while the chief priests and scribes become angry at the marvel of restored sight and limbs" in vv. 15 – 16.

10. Bruner, *Matthew 13 – 28*, 366.

τῷ ὄρει τούτῳ εἴπητε, Ἄρθητι καὶ βλήθητι εἰς τὴν θάλασσαν, γενήσεται). The "not only ... but also" (οὐ μόνον ... ἀλλὰ καί) format links this closely with the judgment miracle of vv. 18 – 19. With believing faith they could also pronounce judgment (see also 16:19b = John 20:23) and perform miracles. Matthew 17:20 (also an "amen" [ἀμήν] saying) is the basis for this saying, for there Jesus said that faith as small as "a mustard" seed could move a mountain "from here to there." As stated there, this was a common Jewish metaphor for overcoming great obstacles and doing the impossible.

The disciples could have been thinking of the Mount of Olives on which they were standing (though not of the Zech 14:4 prophecy of the coming of the day of the Lord,[11] which does not fit this context), though some interpret the mountain here as the Temple Mount and thus a prediction of the destruction of the temple.[12] But that too goes beyond the immediate context. This is simply a metaphor for accomplishing great things.

21:22 "And everything, whatever you ask in prayer, believing, you will receive" (καὶ πάντα ὅσα ἂν αἰτήσητε ἐν τῇ προσευχῇ πιστεύοντες λήμψεσθε). The accent here is on both "everything" (first for emphasis) and the dynamic present tense "believing" (which could be conditional ["if"] but is probably circumstantial ["believing" prayer]). Faith is frequently stressed in Matthew (5:8; 7:7 – 11; 8:10, 13; 9:2, 22; 15:28; 17:20), but again it is not an all-embracing promise that we can control God through prayer. As Hagner says, "Jesus does not offer the disciples magical power to do whatever they please or to perform extraordinary feats for their own sake.... All must relate to the purpose of God that is in process of being realized."[13]

John 14:12 – 14 relates to this issue: "You may ask me for anything *in my name*, and I will do it," where "in my name" means "in union with me and my purposes"; it is not a guarantee to get anything one wishes. So here believing once again means a total dependence on God and union with his will and purposes. It is not a formula for getting what we want but a God-centeredness for wanting what he wants.

Theology in Application

Both the major themes — a people of God who cease bearing fruit, become barren, and fall into judgment (cf. Isa 5:1 – 7; John 15:1 – 6) and the power of faith to accomplish great things — have been discussed in earlier passages (the first at 21:1 – 11; the second at 17:14 – 20). In particular, this is part of chs. 21 – 25 dealing with the divine judgment on Israel for rejecting God's Messiah and Son and for desecrating the temple with national sin.

11. So Lane, *Mark*, 410; Nolland, *Matthew*, 853 – 54; J. D. M. Derrett, "Moving Mountains," 231 – 44

12. Telford, *Withered Tree*, 109 – 17; Blomberg, *Matthew*, 318.

13. Hagner, *Matthew 14 – 28*, 606.

1. God's Antipathy to Sin

Many Christians fail to understand God's antipathy to sin and are perfectly satisfied to live in sin. They do not realize that in *every* case the one who sins must pay the consequences. There are several examples of tolerance toward sin in the NT (e.g., the Corinthians in 1 Cor 5:9 – 13 or the churches of Pergamum and Thyatira in Rev 2:14 – 16, 20 – 23). God is a forgiving God, but he is also a just God, and when sin is committed, there will be either *true* repentance (which includes a desire to overcome that sin and never commit it again) or judgment.

2. Prayer Changes Things

At the same time, prayer changes things. This is a debated area of Christian reflection. For those with a high sense of the sovereignty of God, prayer changes the one praying but not the event, since God has already foreordained it. That is a viable perspective, and I respect that position. That is not my view, however. I believe that prayer channels the presence of God into a situation, and so the more a person prays (cf. Luke 11:9 – 13; 18:1 – 8) and the more people who pray, the more God's presence enters the situation, and he makes a difference. We must all consider the issue of divine sovereignty and human prayer to be a mystery that will not be fully unlocked until we get to heaven. Yet we must also do our best to think through the question, and in this I believe that the prayer of faith does indeed accomplish great things, as Jesus says here.

Furthermore, faith is much more than a power that infuses our prayer life. Primarily, it is a perspective on life, a lifestyle that centers on God and immerses one's self in God. Faith is a way of thinking in which God is everything, the sphere within which we live, and this type of prayer is not just intercessory, a prayer life centered on getting God to do things for us. It is more a constant desire to do things for God, and such a life has great power because it centers on doing things for God. This is a true life of faith.

CHAPTER 90

Matthew 21:23 – 27

Introduction to Controversies in the Temple Court (Matthew 21:23 – 22:46)

The temple continues to be central as Jesus returns to debate the leaders in five controversial dialogues. His purpose is to carry out, via teaching, his prophetic act of clearing the temple. The temple becomes the scene of the controversies. The primary theme continues to be Jesus' authority, seen in the first question directed at him by the leaders and continued in the others. They are presented in a question-and-answer format in keeping with the Talmudic approach to controversies (so Hill).

The purpose of these controversies is to present both the messianic authority and teaching authority of Jesus in contrast to the growing rejection/apostasy of the leaders. In each of the episodes Jesus shows his superiority to the religious experts as he takes them on in rabbinic fashion and decimates them with his handling of Torah. Daube shows that the last four (22:15 – 46) correspond to the four main types of questions recognized by the rabbis: questions of wisdom, on a point of Torah (22:15 – 22); of mockery (scoffing at a belief), on the resurrection (22:23 – 33); of moral conduct, on the relationship between God and human beings (22:34 – 40); and of biblical exegesis, on a seeming contradiction between two passages (22:41 – 46).[1] Once again, Jesus is the final and authoritative interpreter of Torah (see on 5:17 – 20). The three parables between the first and second of the debates (21:28 – 22:14) center on the unbelief/opposition of the leaders and God's judgment of them.

Literary Context

The acclamation of the pilgrims and the children regarding Jesus as Davidic Messiah along with Jesus' symbolic actions has raised the issue of the source and meaning of his authority. The leaders ask him about this forthrightly, but not to ascertain the truth. They have opposed his authority from the start.

1. David Daube, "Four Types of Questions: Matt 22.15 – 46," *JTS* 2 n.s. (1951): 45 – 48.

VI. The Movement to the Cross (19:1 – 25:46)
A. Jesus' Deeds: Opposition and Discipleship (19:1 – 22:46)
2. Beginning Events of Passion Week (21:1 – 22:46)
a. The Messiah Enters Jerusalem (21:1 – 22)
b. Controversies in the Temple Court (21:23 – 22:46)
➦ **(1) The Question about Jesus' Authority (21:23 – 27)**
(2) The Parable of the Two Sons (21:28 – 32)
(3) The Parable of the Wicked Tenants (21:33 – 46)
(4) The Parable of the Wedding Banquet (22:1 – 14)

Main Idea

This unit contrasts (1) the authority of Jesus vs. the lack of authority on the part of the religious leaders, and (2) the faithfulness to God on the part of both Jesus and John the Baptist vs. the faithlessness of leaders who have lost their right to judge truth.

Translation

(See next page.)

Structure and Literary Form

This first conflict story closely follows Mark 11:27 – 33 with only minor changes that do not affect the story or message. The dialogue best falls into three parts: their question followed by Jesus' counter-question (vv. 23 – 25a), then their deliberations (vv. 25b – 26), and finally their response followed by Jesus' concluding statement (v. 27).

Exegetical Outline

➦ **I. The Controversy and Jesus' Counter-Question (21:23 – 25a)**
- A. The two questions from the leaders (v. 23)
  1. The meaning of his authority (v. 23a)
  2. The source of his authority (v. 23b)
- B. Jesus' counter-question (vv. 24 – 25a)
  1. Jesus' answer will depend on their answer (v. 24)
  2. The source of John's baptism — divine or human (v. 25a)

Matthew 21:23-27

23a	Setting/Action	When he had entered the temple,
b	Confrontation	**[A] the chief priests and the elders of the people came to him**
		while he was teaching, saying,
c	Question #1	[1] *"By what authority are you doing these things?*
d	Question #2	[2] *And who gave you this authority?"*
24a	Response	**[B] Jesus answered them,**
b		*"I will also ask you one thing.*
c	Condition	*If you tell me this,*
d		*I will also tell you by what authority I am doing these things.*
25a	Counter-Question	*From where does the baptism of John come?*
b	Options	*From heaven or from human beings?"*
c	Reaction	**[C] So they began discussing the issue among themselves, saying,**
d	Alternative #1 Condition	[1] *"If we respond,*
e		*'Of heavenly origin,'*
f	Result	*he will tell us,*
g		*'Then why didn't you believe him?'*
26a	Alternative #2 Condition	[2] *But if we say,*
b		*'Of human origin,'*
c	Result	*we are afraid of the crowd,*
d	Basis to 26c	*because they all regard John as a prophet."*
27a	Answer to 25a-b	**[B'] So they answered Jesus,**
b		*"We do not know."*
c	Answer to 23c-d	**[A'] He responded,**
d		*"Neither am I telling you by what authority I am doing these things."*

II. Their Deliberations (21:25b – 26)

A. If divine: should believe (v. 25b)

B. If human: afraid of the people (v. 26)

III. The Two Answers (21:27)

A. The leaders: Don't know (v. 27a)

B. Jesus: "Neither will I tell you" (v. 27b)

Explanation of the Text

21:23 When he had entered the temple, the chief priests and the elders of the people came to him while he was teaching (Καὶ ἐλθόντος αὐτοῦ εἰς τὸ ἱερὸν προσῆλθον αὐτῷ διδάσκοντι οἱ ἀρχιερεῖς καὶ οἱ πρεσβύτεροι τοῦ λαοῦ). There are two temporal participles here, the aorist in a genitive absolute ("when he had entered," ἐλθόντος) at the beginning, and the present "while he was teaching" (διδάσκοντι) going on at the end as the leaders come to him. This is probably the Tuesday of Passion Week, with Jesus clearing the temple and cursing the fig tree the day before. Luke 20:1 tells us that his teaching consisted of "proclaiming the good news" (εὐαγγελίζομαι) of the kingdom.

In light of the imminent judgment that is his central theme at this time (see chs. 24 – 25) Jesus is likely proclaiming the judgment side of the arrival of the kingdom and calling for repentance. Most likely he is teaching in one of the porticoes in the Court of the Gentiles, where most teaching occurred. The chief priests (see on 2:4) and elders (see on 16:21), together with the scribes and Pharisees, formed the Sanhedrin, the ruling council of the Jews. This could well be an official delegation.

21:23 ... saying, "By what authority are you doing these things? And who gave you this authority?" (λέγοντες, Ἐν ποίᾳ ἐξουσίᾳ ταῦτα ποιεῖς; καὶ τίς σοι ἔδωκεν τὴν ἐξουσίαν ταύτην;). Both questions center on the "authority" (ἐξουσία) that Jesus has shown in the events of the previous two days, with "what" (ποίᾳ) centering on the type of authority and "who" (τίς) on the person yielding that authority. From the Jewish leaders' perspective Jesus is teaching as a rabbi (but see on 12:2) in the temple courts with no official training and performing the miracles of a great prophet without any pedigree.

The first question challenges his presumption to both teach and perform miracles in the temple; how can he act as both rabbi and prophet? In so doing they are laying a trap for him, since if he answers "human authority" he will contradict his actions, and if "divine authority," he will be guilty of blasphemy. The second question assumes it could not have come from God, a possibility the leaders have long ago rejected. They are daring Jesus to incriminate himself by answering.

21:24 Jesus answered them, "I will also ask you one thing. If you tell me this, I will also tell you by what authority I am doing these things" (ἀποκριθεὶς δὲ ὁ Ἰησοῦς εἶπεν αὐτοῖς, Ἐρωτήσω ὑμᾶς κἀγὼ λόγον ἕνα, ὃν ἐὰν εἴπητέ μοι κἀγὼ ὑμῖν ἐρῶ ἐν ποίᾳ ἐξουσίᾳ ταῦτα ποιῶ). Jesus picks up on their first question, "by what authority" (ἐν ποίᾳ ἐξουσίᾳ), and turns it around on them. Sensing their true purpose, Jesus responds in good rabbinic fashion with a question of his own, promising them his answer after they respond to his own query. This is not just a way of avoiding giving an answer. The very question Jesus asks contains the answer to their two questions, for Jesus' mission and authority are tied closely to that of John the Baptist.

21:25 "From where does the baptism of John come? From heaven or from human beings?" (τὸ βάπτισμα τὸ Ἰωάννου πόθεν ἦν; ἐξ οὐρανοῦ ἢ ἐξ ἀνθρώπων;). Jesus' counter-question, especially "from where" (πόθεν), centering on origin, will reveal two things: (1) This is the very question they were asking Jesus, and now he turns the tables on them. Since John was the messianic forerunner, he and Jesus share the same source of authority ("baptism" [βάπτισμα] stands for John's entire ministry). (2) Moreover, the answer the leaders give regarding "one matter" (λόγον ἕνα) will show where the leaders stand as well. The two options — heavenly or human — fit Jesus as well as John, and their attitude toward the one will reveal their attitude toward the other. But now the tables are turned, and the Pharisees, not Jesus, are on the spot.

21:25 So they began discussing the issue among themselves, saying, "If we respond, 'Of heavenly origin,'[2] he will tell us, 'Then why didn't you believe him?'" (οἱ δὲ διελογίζοντο ἐν ἑαυτοῖς λέγοντες, Ἐὰν εἴπωμεν, Ἐξ οὐρανοῦ, ἐρεῖ ἡμῖν,

2. "From" (ἐξ) in both clauses (vv. 25 – 26) has its basic force of source or origin.

Διὰ τί οὖν οὐκ ἐπιστεύσατε αὐτῷ;). The chief priests and elders are in a quandary. The trap they have laid for Jesus has just sprung on them. However they answer, Jesus will have them. The imperfect "they began discussing" (διελογίζοντο) pictures dramatically their ongoing deliberations as they try to figure a way out so they do not lose face. Jesus has already stated that John is the divinely sent "messenger" of Mal 3:1, but they can hardly admit that. They know that Jesus' retort would be to "believe" (cf. 8:13; 9:28; 18:6, cf. 21:22) John's witness about Jesus (3:11 – 12, 14). Note once again that there is no search for the truth of the matter, only for how to protect themselves.

21:26 "But if we say, 'Of human origin,' we are afraid of the crowd, because they all regard John as a prophet" (ἐὰν δὲ εἴπωμεν, Ἐξ ἀνθρώπων, φοβούμεθα τὸν ὄχλον, πάντες γὰρ ὡς προφήτην ἔχουσιν τὸν Ἰωάννην). Herod was afraid to kill John for this very reason, that the people considered him a prophet (14:5; cf. 11:9). The leaders' dilemma is all too obvious. The use of πάντες shows just how popular the Baptist was; he was universally acclaimed a prophet. This same fear (present tense "we are afraid" [φοβούμεθα] to stress the ongoing nature of their fear) will soon keep them from arresting Jesus (21:46). At this Passover season, with thousands of zealous pilgrims filling the streets, many of them from Galilee, the leaders fear a riot more than any other thing, for a riot would bring the Romans down on them. In actual fact, they had long ago made their rejection of the Baptist apparent, and he had even called them a "brood of vipers" (echoed by Jesus in 12:34).

21:27 So they answered Jesus, "We do not know" (καὶ ἀποκριθέντες τῷ Ἰησοῦ εἶπαν, Οὐκ οἴδαμεν). The only response that could preserve their dignity and not give Jesus the upper hand was to say they did not know the origin of John's ministry. They could not admit the heavenly origin of John's ministry, and they did not dare call it merely human lest they antagonize the people.

21:27 "He responded, "Neither am I telling you by what authority I am doing these things" (ἔφη αὐτοῖς καὶ αὐτός, Οὐδὲ ἐγὼ λέγω ὑμῖν ἐν ποίᾳ ἐξουσίᾳ ταῦτα ποιῶ). This gives Jesus the perfect opportunity, "You won't tell me, so I won't tell you." Jesus leads the world cup match, 1 – 0. He will score four more goals in the ensuing debates. Jesus refuses to reveal heavenly secrets to those who have placed themselves deliberately outside the kingdom (as in 13:11 – 15).

Theology in Application

In terms of reader response, there are two major issues here: (1) the absolute authority of Jesus, confirmed by the Baptist, and (2) the danger of self-righteous rejection of Jesus' authority, as exemplified in the leaders. The first has been the message of Matthew throughout, the second is explored in 12:31 – 32; 13:11 – 15 and will dominate ch. 23. Rejection can go only so far, and then the opportunity to repent is gone, and only judgment remains (Heb 6:4 – 6; 10:26 – 31; 1 John 5:16. "It is a dreadful thing to fall into the hands of the living God" (Heb 10:31).

CHAPTER 91

Matthew 21:28 – 32

Literary Context

The three parables that ensue center on what is implicit in vv. 23 – 27, namely, the unbelief of the leaders and their judgment by God. Blomberg says of the three parables, "in sequence they depict God's indictment, sentence, and execution of the present Jewish leadership."[1]

- **VI. The Movement to the Cross (19:1 – 25:46)**
  - **A. Jesus' Deeds: Opposition and Discipleship (19:1 – 22:46)**
    - **2. Beginning Events of Passion Week (21:1 – 22:46)**
      - a. The Messiah Enters Jerusalem (21:1 – 22)
      - **b. Controversies in the Temple Court (21:23 – 22:46)**
        - (1) The Question about Jesus' Authority (21:23 – 27)
        - ➦ **(2) The Parable of the Two Sons (21:28 – 32)**
        - (3) The Parable of the Wicked Tenants (21:33 – 46)
        - (4) The Parable of the Wedding Banquet (22:1 – 14)

Main Idea

This is a parable[2] about rejection and unbelief, a reluctance and yet a final willingness to do the Father's will (the tax collectors and sinners) vs. an initial willingness and yet final refusal to follow his will (the leaders). It imparts the message that

1. Blomberg, *Matthew*, 320, building on Schweizer, *Matthew*, 402. Wesley G. Olmstead, *Matthew's Trilogy of Parables: The Nation, the Nations and the Reader in Matthew 21:28 – 22:14* (SNTSMS 127; Cambridge: Cambridge Univ. Press, 2003), 68, says that heretofore Matthew has implicated primarily the leaders as liable for judgment, but through these parables the people are seen as yielding to the leaders, joining in their plot against Jesus and being guilty as well.

2. The basic historical trustworthiness of this parable is widely accepted today (so Davies and Allison, Luz, in spite of the heavy redactional material they find in it), though see Gundry, *Matthew*, 421 – 22, who says Matthew "composed this parable" as a counterpart to the prodigal son parable of Luke 15:11 – 32. This is unnecessary. Throughout this gospel I have argued that redaction does not mean nonhistoricity (see Introduction).

it matters more "what one does" (the tax collectors and sinners) than what one is (the religious leaders).[3]

Translation

Matthew 21:28-32

Verse	Function	Text
28a	Rhetorical Question	*"What do you think?*
b		*A man had two sons.*
c	Action	*He came to the first and said,*
d	Exhortation	*'Son, go and work today in my vineyard.'*
29a	Response #1	*But he answered,*
b		*'I will not!'*
c		*Yet later he changed his mind and went.*
30a	Restatement of 28d	*Then the man went and said the same thing to the other son.*
b	Response #2	*But he answered,*
c		*'I will, sir,'*
d		*yet he did not go.*
31a	Question	*Which of the two did his father's will?"*
b		**They replied,**
c	Answer	*"The first."*
d		**Jesus said to them,**
e	Response	*"I tell you the truth, tax collectors and prostitutes are going to enter the kingdom of God before you.*
32a	Basis for 31e	*For John came to you in the way of righteousness*
b		*and you did not believe him.*
c		*But the tax collectors and prostitutes believed him.*
d		*Yet you yourselves saw this and still did not change your mind and believe him."*

Structure and Literary Form

This parable and its allegorical interpretation are unique to Matthew and the product of his special material. Only the second parable (the tenants) is found in Mark, and the third (the banquet) occurs at a different place in Luke. Both parable and interpretation here have two parts centering on the two sons.

3. See Witherington, *Matthew*, 401. W. E. Langley, "The Parable of the Two Sons (Matthew 21:28–32) against the Semitic and Rabbinic Backdrop," *CBQ* 58 (1996): 228–43, provides an interesting but in the end not quite as likely interpretation, that each son is partly right and partly wrong and that the parable says God's will is to combine both saying and doing.

Exegetical Outline

- **I. The Parable Presented (21:28–30)**
    - A. The father asks the first son to work in the vineyard (vv. 28–29)
        1. Initial refusal
        2. Later obedience
    - B. The father asks the second son to work in the vineyard (v. 30)
        1. Initial willingness
        2. Later refusal
- **II. The Parable Explained (21:31–32)**
    - A. The leaders admit the first son actually obeyed (v. 31a)
    - B. Jesus' explanation and contrast (vv. 31b–32)
        1. The first son: tax collectors and sinners will enter the kingdom (v. 31b)
        2. The second son: the leaders, guilty of unbelief (v. 32)

Explanation of the Text

21:28 "What do you think?" (Τί δὲ ὑμῖν δοκεῖ;). The introductory "What do you think" occurs often (17:25; 18:12; 22:17, 42; 26:66) and asks the listener (here the leaders) to ponder carefully what Jesus is saying. In this sense it is similar to an "amen" (ἀμήν) saying (e.g., 21:21, 31) in pointing to an important truth. Through it we the real readers are also invited to think carefully about the story's message.

21:28 A man had two sons. He came to the first and said, 'Son, go and work today in my[4] vineyard'"[5] (ἄνθρωπος εἶχεν τέκνα δύο. καὶ προσελθὼν τῷ πρώτῳ εἶπεν, Τέκνον, ὕπαγε σήμερον ἐργάζου ἐν τῷ ἀμπελῶνι). This is not the same parable as Luke 15:11–32 (the prodigal son), though both begin the same way.[6] The setting is a vineyard, as in the parable of the workers in a vineyard of 20:1–16, which symbolizes the people of Israel (cf. Ps 80:8–9; Isa 5:1; 27:2; Jer 2:21). This is clearly a family-owned vineyard, with the children expected to help care for the crop. It was common to have two sons who worked together (Simon and Andrew, James and John, the parable of the prodigal son).

21:29 "But he answered, 'I will not!'" (ὁ δὲ ἀποκριθεὶς εἶπεν, Οὐ θέλω). It is important to keep in mind that in the ancient Jewish world the respect and obedience of children was expected. So when the first (older?) son refused, it was quite shocking. "I will not" (οὐ θέλω) centers on his will, "I do not want to go." The picture indicates the son's rebellion and obstinate rejection.

4. This is an example of the definite article standing for the possessive pronoun, cf. Harris, *Jesus as God*, 304.

5. The textual history is difficult to unravel. Many manuscripts have the order of the two sons adopted here (ℵ * C* K W Δ Π et al.), but significant others reverse the two sons, with the second saying "No" then repenting (B Θ f 700 et al.). Several scholars (e.g., Carson, Schnackenburg, NEB) opt for the second reading, but we agree with those (e.g., Metzger, Hagner, Nolland, NRSV, NLT, TNIV) who take the traditional reading on the grounds that the second set was due to the desire to see the parable as addressing the salvation-historical switch from Jew vs. Gentile.

6. The presence of "son" (τέκνον) rather than "son" (υἱός) is probably due to the next two parables, in which Jesus is the "son." It thus avoids confusion (so Davies and Allison).

21:29 "Yet later he changed his mind and went" (ὕστερον δὲ μεταμεληθεὶς ἀπῆλθεν). μεταμέλομαι means not only a change of heart but also "regret" and "repentance." This would be in keeping with first-century expectations. So in the end this son showed respect and went to work in the vineyard.

21:30 "Then the man went and said the same thing to the other son. But he answered, 'I will, sir' " (προσελθὼν δὲ τῷ ἑτέρῳ εἶπεν ὡσαύτως. ὁ δὲ ἀποκριθεὶς εἶπεν, Ἐγώ, κύριε). This son is the polar opposite of the first. He shows the initial willingness to obey, with "I" (ἐγώ) a circumlocution for "I will do so" (perhaps to contrast himself with his brother, "As for me, yes") and with "sir" (κύριε) carrying a hint of "my lord," showing deep respect. So at first he seems the model son, unlike his brother, and makes a public display of acquiescence.

21:30 "Yet he did not go" (καὶ οὐκ ἀπῆλθεν). In the end this second son never shows up. Thus he is the perfect picture of the religious officials, who give God all the surface compliance one could ever ask for and yet refuse to follow God's Agent, Messiah, and Son into his vineyard. The contrast is complete. The first son says, "I will not"; the second, "I will"; the first repents and goes into the field, the second never shows up.

21:31 "Which of the two did his father's will?" (τίς ἐκ τῶν δύο ἐποίησεν τὸ θέλημα τοῦ πατρός;). Jesus used this ploy often, drawing the answer from his hearers (in addition to each of the controversies in this section, see 9:5; 12:48; 17:25; 21:25; Luke 10:36; 13:16). The combination of the second son's κύριος and "does his father's will" echoes 7:21 ("not everyone who says 'Lord, Lord' will enter the kingdom but only those who do my Father's will") and 12:50 ("the one who does my Father's will" is my family). Jesus is doing more than making a rhetorical point. He is summarizing his teaching on kingdom ethics. Those who claim to be God's people must show it by doing his will and obeying his commandments (cf. John 14:15, 21, 23).

21:31 They replied, "The first" (λέγουσιν, Ὁ πρῶτος). Only one answer suffices, and the leaders are forced to say truthfully that the first son is the one who has done his father's will.

21:31 Jesus said to them, "I tell you the truth, tax collectors and prostitutes are going to enter the kingdom of God before you" (λέγει αὐτοῖς ὁ Ἰησοῦς, Ἀμὴν λέγω ὑμῖν ὅτι οἱ τελῶναι καὶ αἱ πόρναι προάγουσιν ὑμᾶς εἰς τὴν βασιλείαν τοῦ θεοῦ). Jesus' interpretation must have shocked them.[7] The leaders were the second son and the despised tax collectors and prostitutes were the first son.[8] The "amen" (ἀμήν) saying stresses the solemn truth presented here (see on 5:18). The dregs of society (in 9:10 – 11; 11:19 it is the more common "tax collectors and sinners") will enter[9]

7. Davies and Allison, *Matthew*, 3:168 – 69, say it well after surveying all their responses in the five controversies of this section: "We are left with the impression that while Jesus' opponents were adept at laying traps, they were also good at falling into them.... Clearly Jesus' spiritual authority gives him a rhetorical sovereignty."

8. Keener, *Matthew*, 508 – 9, has an excellent excursus on prostitution in Palestine, pointing out that even though prostitution was forbidden in Deut 23:17, there were Jewish prostitutes who often consorted with Roman soldiers and others, and Rome regulated the practice at a profit. Inns and bars were especially notorious as virtual brothels. J. Gibson, "Hoi Telōnai kai hai Pornai," *JTS* 32 (1981): 429 – 33, believes the prostitutes are explicitly mentioned because both groups were in collusion with Rome.

9. προάγουσιν could be a durative present ("are entering," thus an inaugurated eschatology) or a futuristic present ("are going to enter," thus a final eschatology). In light of the centrality of final eschatology in Matthew (see on 13:24 – 30, 36 – 43, 47 – 52), the latter is better, although an inaugurated aspect is likely present as well, since the outcasts were coming to Jesus while the leaders were not. For entering the kingdom as a future event, see 5:20; 7:21; and for the inaugurated aspect, see 18:3; 19:23 – 24.

the kingdom that has arrived in Jesus "ahead of" the leaders.[10]

The allegorical elements are clear: the father is God, the vineyard is his kingdom community, the first son the outcasts, and the second son the leaders. The sinners turned against God for much of their lives but have now come back to God (and entered his vineyard) by turning to Jesus. The religious officials originally agreed to do God's will but have now turned their backs on God by rejecting his Son. The obvious turning point in both cases is Jesus.

21:32 "For John came to you in the way of righteousness, and you did not believe him. But the tax collectors and prostitutes believed him" (ἦλθεν γὰρ Ἰωάννης πρὸς ὑμᾶς ἐν ὁδῷ δικαιοσύνης, καὶ οὐκ ἐπιστεύσατε αὐτῷ, οἱ δὲ τελῶναι καὶ αἱ πόρναι ἐπίστευσαν αὐτῷ). This shows that indeed the leaders are not the first son who "changed his mind" but the second son. As in v. 24 Jesus uses John the Baptist as an example of their reaction to him. He had come "in the way of righteousness," which means both that he came according to God's will to fulfill his salvation-historical purpose and that he proclaimed the moral and ethical demands of God.[11] "Doing the father's will" in v. 31 is also the definition of "righteousness" in Matthew (see on 3:15; 5:6, 10, 20; 6:1, 33). Yet only the sinners had turned to him; the leaders had rejected him in the same way that they rejected Jesus.

21:32 "Yet you yourselves saw this and still did not change your mind and believe him" (ὑμεῖς δὲ ἰδόντες οὐδὲ μετεμελήθητε ὕστερον τοῦ πιστεῦσαι αὐτῷ). The Baptist's message and ministry gave the leaders an opportunity to "repent" (see on μεταμέλομαι in v. 29) and enter the kingdom, but they have rejected his message as well. Their "unbelief" regarding John echoes their rejection of Jesus. The tax collectors and sinners are the first son, for they were willing to "change their minds" and "believe" John's (and thus Jesus') message. The leaders rejected John (3:7 – 10; 21:25), but many among the tax collectors and crowds did believe and were baptized by John (Luke 3:7 – 15).

Theology in Application

It has long been supposed that this parable describes the switch from a Jewish to a Gentile church (Chrysostom, Origen, Luz). However, that is due more to a critical switch that says this reflects Matthew's community rather than the historical Jesus; there is no hint of that in this context, for the contrast is the unbelieving Jew vs. the believing Jew (see Hill, Blomberg).

Nor is it fair to say that the story is about salvation by works, for "doing the will of God" is completely linked with repentance and belief. The leaders and the sinners show the contrast between those who say they will follow God, yet never come to faith and obedience, vs. those who initially reject but find repentance and belief, then do the Father's will. The other aspect is that it is the despised members of society rather than the religious elite who are willing to do so.

10. We should not read into this that the leaders will eventually come to Jesus, though this certainly holds out the possibility that some of them, like Joseph of Arimathea and Nicodemus in John 19:38 – 39, will become believers.

11. Donald A. Hagner, "Righteousness in Matthew's Theology," in *Worship, Theology and Ministry in the Early Church: Essays in Honor of Ralph P. Martin* (ed. M. J. Wilkins and T. Paige; Sheffield, JSOT Press, 1992), 101 – 20, believes this and 3:15 are salvation-historical and refer to the new salvation brought in the ministries of John and Jesus. However, Olmstead, *Trilogy of Parables*, 102 – 3, challenges Hagner's contention and shows the centrality of ethics here. It is likely that as in 3:15, both are present.

CHAPTER 92

Matthew 21:33–46

Literary Context

This second of the three parables[1] centers on the guilt and judgment on the nation for rejecting and killing God's Son.

VI. The Movement to the Cross (19:1–25:46)

A. Jesus' Deeds: Opposition and Discipleship (19:1–22:46)

2. Beginning Events of Passion Week (21:1–22:46)

b. Controversies in the Temple Court (21:23–22:46)

(1) The Question about Jesus' Authority (21:23–27)

(2) The Parable of the Two Sons (21:28–32)

(3) The Parable of the Wicked Tenants (21:33–46)

(4) The Parable of the Wedding Banquet (22:1–14)

Main Idea

There are four major points in this parable: (1) the death of the Son of God at the hands of the nation; (2) the guilt of the leaders and the nation for rejecting, mistreating, and killing the prophets as well as the Son; (3) the judgment and terrible sentence on Israel and its leaders for turning against God and his representatives; and (4) the salvation-historical transfer of God's redemptive activity to a new movement, the church, made up of both Jew and Gentile.

1. For the authenticity of this parable, see Klyne Snodgrass, *The Parable of the Wicked Tenants* (WUNT 27; Tübingen: J. C. B. Mohr, 1983), 3–31; his "Recent Research on the Parable of the Wicked Tenants," *BBR* 8 (1998): 187–215; and Carson, "Matthew," 451–52. Part of the reason for doubting it is the heavy allegorizing and the centrality of the death of Jesus. Yet neither is a valid reason for doubting the parable, since Jesus' use of allegory has long been recognized, and Jesus has for some time been aware of his impending death (see on 16:21; 17:22–23; 20:17–19). On the view that *Gospel of Thomas* 65–66 is the original form, see Klyne Snodgrass, "The Parable of the Wicked Husbandmen: Is the Gospel of Thomas Version the Original?" *NTS* 21 (1975): 142–44 (also his *Tenants*, 52–71), who shows that *Thomas* is built on the Synoptic version rather than vice versa.

Translation

Matthew 21:33-46

33a	Introduction	*"Listen to another parable:*
b	Scene 1	*A man who was a landowner planted a vineyard.*
c	Action	*Then he put a fence around it,*
d	Action	*dug a winepress in it, and*
e	Action	*built a watchtower.*
f	Action	*Then he rented it to tenant farmers and moved away.*
34a	Scene 2	*So when the time for harvest drew near,*
b	Group #1	*he sent his slaves to the tenant farmers*
		to receive his share of the harvest.
35a	Result	*And the tenant farmers took his slaves,*
		beat one,
		killed another, and
		stoned a third.
36a	Group #2	*Again he sent other slaves, more than he did the first time,*
b	Result	*and they did the same things to them.*
37a	Group #3	*Finally, he sent to them his son, reasoning,*
b	Basis	*'They will respect my son.'*
38a		*But when the farmers saw the son,*
		they talked among themselves,
b	Scheme	*'This is the heir.*
c		*Come, let's kill him,*
d	Basis	*and then we can have his inheritance.'*
39a	Result	*So they took him, threw him out of the vineyard, and killed him.*
40a	Question	*Therefore,*
		when the Lord of the vineyard comes,
b		*what will he do to those tenant farmers?"*
41a		**They replied to him,**
b	Answer	*"He will destroy those evil people in an evil way, and*
c		*give the vineyard to other tenant farmers*
d		*who will give him the fruits of the harvest*
		in their season."
42a	Response	**Jesus told them,**
b		*"Have you never read in the Scriptures:*
c	OT Quotation	*'The stone . . . has become the cornerstone*
		that the builders rejected.
d		*This has come from the Lord,*
e		*and it is wondrous in our eyes'?* (Ps 118:22-23)
43a	Warning/Prophecy	*Therefore*
		I tell you that the kingdom of God will be taken away from you
b		*and given to a people*
		who will produce its fruit.

Continued on next page.

Continued from previous page.

44a		*And the one who falls on this stone will be broken to pieces,*
b		*but whoever it falls on will be crushed."*
45a	Reaction	When the chief priests and Pharisees heard his parables,
b		**they knew he was speaking about them.**
46a		Although they were seeking a way to arrest him,
b		**they were afraid of the crowds,**
c	Basis for 46b	since they held him to be a prophet.

Structure and Literary Form

This second allegorical parable[2] of judgment follows Mark 12:1 – 12 with the typical abbreviations (e.g., omitting Mark 12:5 – 6a) but also with some significant additions. (1) Matthew changes Marks "at harvest time" (τῷ καιρῷ) to "the time for harvest drew near" in keeping with his emphasis on fruitfulness elsewhere (21:19, 34b, 41, 43). (2) He has the leaders state the sentence on the wicked tenants (v. 41; in Mark 12:9b Jesus does so himself). (3) He adds the saying about the kingdom of God being taken away from the Jews and given to the Gentiles (v. 43), and possibly the judgment saying of v. 44 (see below).

The text consists of the parable proper (vv. 33 – 39), followed by an interpretation consisting of a question and answer (vv. 40 – 41) and Jesus' commentary on the parable (vv. 42 – 44) and concluded by the negative response of the leaders (vv. 45 – 46).

Exegetical Outline

➡ **I. The Parable of the Wicked Tenants (21:33 – 39)**

- A. The setting — vineyard built and leased (v. 33)
- B. The sending of servants to collect the owner's share (vv. 34 – 36)
  1. The beating and killing of the first group (vv. 34 – 35)
  2. The same mistreatment of the second group (v. 36)
- C. The sending and killing of the son (vv. 37 – 39)
  1. Reasoning of the owner — they will respect the son (v. 37)
  2. Reasoning of the tenants — kill him and get the inheritance (v. 38)
  3. Result — the son is killed (v. 39)

II. The Two Interpretations (21:40 – 44)

- A. First interpretation via question and answer (vv. 40 – 41)
  1. Jesus' question regarding the outcome (v. 40)

2. For rabbinic parallels to this parable form, see Snodgrass, *Tenants*, 22 – 24.

2. The leaders' response: execution and the vineyard given to others (v. 41)

B. Second interpretation via OT quotation (vv. 42 – 44)

1. Rejection and vindication of the Son via Ps 118:22 – 23 (v. 42)
2. The kingdom taken away from the Jews and given to the Gentiles (v. 43)
3. The wicked broken and crushed by the cornerstone (v. 44)

III. The Reaction of the Leaders (21:45 – 46)

A. Their realization that the parables were against them (v. 45)

B. Their desire to arrest Jesus yet fear of the people (v. 46)

Explanation of the Text

21:33 Listen to another parable: A man who was a landowner planted a vineyard (Ἄλλην παραβολὴν ἀκούσατε. Ἄνθρωπος ἦν οἰκοδεσπότης ὅστις ἐφύτευσεν ἀμπελῶνα). Jesus begins by commanding the leaders to listen[3] carefully to the parable that follows (cf. 13:18, 43); clearly it will speak of them. Like the previous parable (as well as 20:1 – 16), this centers on a vineyard (= the people of God) and a landowner (= God). As in 13:27, 52; 20:1, 11, οἰκοδεσπότης refers to a "landowner" who is also master of his house. Here he is building a vineyard on his property and planting vines, echoing the "Song of the Vineyard" in Isa 5:1 – 7, where the owner planted a vineyard (Isa 5:2).

In Isa 5 the vineyard produced bad fruit, prophesying the exile of the nation because of its sin.[4] Here the details differ, but the theme of national sin leading to judgment is the same. It normally took four years for the vines to mature and begin producing harvestable grapes, and it was not until the fifth year that crops and profits began.[5] The vineyard in Isa 5 and here refers to the people of God, chosen to serve him and produce fruit.[6] The master of the house, of course, is God.

21:33 Then he put a fence around it,[7] dug a winepress in it, and built a watchtower (καὶ φραγμὸν αὐτῷ περιέθηκεν καὶ ὤρυξεν ἐν αὐτῷ ληνὸν καὶ ᾠκοδόμησεν πύργον). These other aspects of constructing a vineyard also stem from Isa 5:1 – 2. The fence would be a wall of stones or perhaps a hedge to keep animals out, and the tower would be used by watchmen to warn of intruders and also to give shelter to the workers. The winepress would consist of two vats, an upper one in which the grapes

3. The aorist imperative "listen" (ἀκούσατε) is the basic command, ordering the action as a whole (Wallace, 485). Olmstead, *Trilogy of Parables*, 109, says this is intended to recall the conclusion of the parable of the sower (13:9) and of the weeds (13:43), "Whoever has ears, let them listen" (cf. also 13:18).

4. Olmstead, *Trilogy of Parables*, 110, points to *Targum Isaiah* 5:1b – 2, that identifies the tower with the temple and the wine vat with the altar, with the "Song of the Vineyard" seen as prophesying the destruction of the temple. Another passage providing background is 4Q500 1, which has a similar use of the vineyard story with Ps 118, see George J. Brooke, "4Q500 1 and the Use of Scripture in the Parable of the Vineyard," *DSD* 2 (1995): 268 – 94; W. J. C. Weren, "The Use of Isaiah 5:1 – 7 in the Parable of the Tenants (Mark 12, 1 – 12; Matthew 21, 33 – 46)," *Bib* 79 (1998): 1 – 26.

5. See J. D. M. Derrett, "Fresh Light on the Parable of the Wicked Vinedressers," in *Law in the New Testament*, 286 – 312 (esp. 290 – 91).

6. Snodgrass, *Tenants*, 73 – 76, shows the vineyard cannot be Israel per se, since "Israel" can hardly be taken away and given to others. Thus it refers to their privileges and status as the chosen people.

7. "Around it" (αὐτῷ) is similar to the classical dative of place (missing from the NT, BDF §199) and is best considered a locatival dative telling where the fence was built.

were placed and trampled by foot, and a lower one for collecting the juice. As in Isa 5 the emphasis is on the incredible effort the man put into his vineyard to make it productive and viable. The first-century problem with absentee patron landowners, virtually sucking the life out of their poor client tenants, is not a part of this story.

21:33 Then he rented it to tenant farmers and moved away (καὶ ἐξέδετο αὐτὸν γεωργοῖς καὶ ἀπεδήμησεν). This is not as unusual as some have supposed, since Galilee was beset by absentee landlords who bought huge properties and broke them up into tenant farms. It was common for the farmers to pay the owner half the crops. After leasing out the vineyard, the owner moved away, probably to a big city to enjoy its comforts.[8] There is a covenant perspective behind the arrangement that the farmer (God) had with his clients (especially the leaders who worked in God's vineyard). The owner would have subsidized the tenants in the four early unproductive years before crops appeared along the lines of Lev 19:23–25 (so Nolland).

21:34 So when the time for harvest drew near (ὅτε δὲ ἤγγισεν ὁ καιρὸς τῶν καρπῶν). "The time for harvest" (ὁ καιρὸς τῶν καρπῶν) is a Matthean phrase for the harvest time, the fifth year after the vineyard was planted. The idea of this time "drawing near" (ἤγγισεν) is reminiscent of the kingdom drawing near in 4:17. Here this issue is the "fruit" crop due to the owner, which refers to the fruitfulness and righteous deeds that God expected out of Israel (cf. 3:8, 10; 7:16–20; 12:33; 21:19, 41, 43).[9]

21:34 He sent his slaves to the tenant farmers to receive his share of the harvest (ἀπέστειλεν τοὺς δούλους αὐτοῦ πρὸς τοὺς γεωργοὺς λαβεῖν τοὺς καρποὺς αὐτοῦ). As stated above, the landowner in this story was not a robber baron but deserved his profits, as God deserved Israel's productive fruitfulness. Some (e.g., Gundry) have interpreted "to receive his share of harvest" (λαβεῖν τοὺς καρποὺς αὐτοῦ) to mean the whole crop would have belonged to the master, but that hardly fits first-century practice. Matthew and Mark are not really all that different in meaning here. The plural "slaves" (δούλους) refers to all the prophets (OT and NT) sent by God to Israel (in Mark they are sent one at a time). In this story the leaders have been given more than enough warning by God's emissaries to maintain the fruitfulness of the nation, but they have not done so.

21:35 And the tenant farmers took his slaves, beat one, killed another, and stoned a third (καὶ λαβόντες οἱ γεωργοὶ τοὺς δούλους αὐτοῦ ὃν μὲν ἔδειραν, ὃν δὲ ἀπέκτειναν, ὃν δὲ ἐλιθοβόλησαν). The growing intensity of opposition from beating to killing to stoning is simpler than Mark's movement (12:3–5) from beating to sending away empty-handed to wounding to shameful treatment to killing. Matthew's simple list of verbs is somehow more powerful in its messages and presupposes a list of prophetic denouements similar to Heb 11:32–38. All three of these verbal points were also experienced by Jesus and Paul. On stoning the prophets, see 2 Chr 24:21 (Zechariah); Matt 23:37; in addition, Jeremiah is beaten in Jer 20:2 and Uriah killed in Jer 26:21–23 (for NT emphasis

8. So Nolland, *Matthew*, 871, following W. Schottroff, "Das Gleichnis von den bösen Weingärtnern (Mark 12, 1–9 parr): Ein Beitrag zur Geschichte der Bodenpacht in Palästina," *ZDPV* 112 (1996): 18–48 (esp. 33). He points out that ἀπεδήμησεν means literally "to be away from one's home" and better presupposes a move than a long trip. See also Craig A. Evans, "Jesus' Parable of the Tenant Farmers in Light of Lease Agreements in Antiquity," *JSP* 14 (1996): 65–83, who argues that these were commercial farmers moderately well off in the ancient economy.

9. Turner, "Matthew," 275, calls "fruit" (καρπός) "a key Matthean metaphor for right living or obedience to God's law."

on killing the prophets, see Matt 23:31 – 33; Acts 7:52; 1 Thess 2:15; Heb 11:37 – 38).

21:36 Again he sent other slaves, more than he did the first time (πάλιν ἀπέστειλεν ἄλλους δούλους πλείονας τῶν πρώτων). These "other slaves" could refer to the latter prophets of future generations, or they could refer to the NT prophets and apostles (including John the Baptist, as in 21:24 – 26) sent to Israel. Most commentators opt for the former, but the latter does fit the many missions Jesus' disciples took by themselves or with him. This is not a Galilean peasant revolt, as some have pictured it, for they are killing unarmed messengers (so Keener).

21:36 . . . and they did the same things to them (καὶ ἐποίησαν αὐτοῖς ὡσαύτως). There is already a reversal of expectation here, for in real life the landowner would have sent soldiers after the first emissary was mistreated. The Romans would have executed or at least sent the offenders into slavery. The landowner's failure to act would have been mystifying to the hearers, and as such it pictures the long-suffering covenant patience of God, a theme that threads its way throughout the OT.

21:37 Finally, he sent to them his son, reasoning, "They will respect my son" (ὕστερον δὲ ἀπέστειλεν πρὸς αὐτοὺς τὸν υἱὸν αὐτοῦ λέγων, Ἐντραπήσονται τὸν υἱόν μου). The son comes with all the authority of the father as well as his love (Mark has "Son, whom he loved"). The reasoning seems valid — "even if they mistreated my messengers, they must[10] have regard for [respect, ἐντραπήσονται] my son." Slaves could be treated poorly, but not someone from the ruling class far above the farmers. For Jesus as "Son of God" in Matthew, see 3:17; 11:27; 17:5. For Jesus as "sent" from the Father, see 10:40; 15:24.

21:38 But when the farmers saw[11] the son, they talked among themselves, "This is the heir. Come, let's kill him, and then we can have his inheritance" (οἱ δὲ γεωργοὶ ἰδόντες τὸν υἱὸν εἶπον ἐν ἑαυτοῖς, Οὗτός ἐστιν ὁ κληρονόμος· δεῦτε ἀποκτείνωμεν αὐτὸν καὶ σχῶμεν τὴν κληρονομίαν αὐτοῦ). Several have attempted to make the reasoning of the evil tenant farmers legal, e.g., the point that if all the heirs were dead, the property would go to the residents,[12] or that the landowner was dead and had deeded the property over to the son, or that the owner will give up in light of the constant trouble the tenants have caused him.[13] But these arguments are based on needless speculation of a supposed mind-set of the evil tenants. The allegorical element demands that the tenant farmers kill the son in order to claim the inheritance. It doesn't have to fit "real life" since it is an allegorical parable based on what is going to happen to Jesus.

Moreover, it is clear enough as it stands. The tenant farmers are not thinking clearly and have not reckoned with the actions of the father after they kill his son. Criminals seldom plan as carefully as they think, and this is another instance of evil clouding the logic of its practitioners. With their previous murders and now the murder of the son, there will certainly be an investigation with the true facts brought to light. The parallels with the intention of the leaders to execute Jesus became obvious even to the leaders (see vv. 45 – 46), though not immediately (see vv. 40 – 41).

10. The verb used here is virtually an imperatival future telling what "must" happen.

11. "When they saw" (ἰδόντες) is a temporal participle as in vv. 15, 18, 19, 23.

12. Jeremias, *Parables*, 70 – 77; Hill, *Matthew*, 300.

13. Morris, *Matthew*, 542. Derrett, "Vinedressers," 300 – 308, believes that the tenants argued that they had right of possession because the owner owed them for the four years before the vine bore fruit. But Snodgrass, *Tenants*, 38, shows that rabbinic law did not allow seizure of property on such grounds.

21:39 So they took him,[14] threw him out of the vineyard, and killed him (καὶ λαβόντες αὐτὸν ἐξέβαλον ἔξω τοῦ ἀμπελῶνος καὶ ἀπέκτειναν). Matthew reverses Mark's order (Mark 12:8, "killed him, and threw him out"; Luke 20:15 agrees with Matthew) and in so doing makes clear the connection with Jesus being crucified "outside the camp" (Heb 13:11 – 12; cf. John 19:17, 20). At the same time, it represents the tenants' rejection of the son's mission from the father (so Nolland).

21:40 Therefore, when the Lord of the vineyard comes, what will he do to those tenant farmers? (ὅταν οὖν ἔλθῃ ὁ κύριος τοῦ ἀμπελῶνος, τί ποιήσει τοῖς γεωργοῖς ἐκείνοις;). In Mark 12:9 the question is rhetorical and Jesus answers it himself. Here he asks it of the leaders and gets them to supply the answer (and to indict themselves).[15] Jesus uses this rabbinic technique throughout the controversies in the temple (see 21:24 – 25, 31; 22:20 – 21, 42). The use of "Lord of the vineyard" coming in judgment has been interpreted as pointing to the destruction of Jerusalem (Davies and Allison, Harrington, Luz, Bruner) or to the parousia (Gundry), but the former is certainly the more likely.

21:41 They replied to him, "He will destroy those evil people in an evil way" (λέγουσιν αὐτῷ, Κακοὺς κακῶς ἀπολέσει αὐτούς). The TNIV has a particularly apt translation, "He will bring those wretches to a wretched end," catching Matthew's wordplay well (this was a common Greek idiom). The leaders possibly do not yet see the parable as addressed to them (otherwise, why would they be so direct?),[16] but they will soon do so (see v. 45). Their conclusion is to be expected. When a group of tenants beats and kills the messengers and then has the gall to execute even the son and heir of the estate, they should expect no mercy from the "master" of the estate. They have committed ultimate "evil" and should expect "evil" punishment in return (*lex talionis*, the Roman "law of retribution").[17]

21:41 "... and give the vineyard to other tenant farmers who will give him the fruits of the harvest in their season" (καὶ τὸν ἀμπελῶνα ἐκδώσεται ἄλλοις γεωργοῖς, οἵτινες ἀποδώσουσιν αὐτῷ τοὺς καρποὺς ἐν τοῖς καιροῖς αὐτῶν). Are the "other tenant farmers" (ἄλλοις γεωργοῖς, dative of indirect object) Gentiles, the church, or church leaders? These are not mutually exclusive. Certainly the Gentiles are part of this, signified in the "people" (ἔθνος) of v. 43, but they become part of the church, composed of Jews and Gentiles. Moreover, if the Jewish leaders are the "tenant farmers" (γεωργοί) of the parable, then the "other tenant farmers" (γεωργοί) here would be the church as established by the Gentile mission. So all three are the inheritors of the vineyard here.

The harvest fruits would be the fruitfulness and righteous deeds of the church (see on v. 34). Olmstead notes the concurrence of "season" (καιρός) with "fruit" (καρπός) in vv. 34, 41 and believes

14. "They took" (λαβόντες) is a circumstantial participle that partakes of the action of the main verb and is best translated as another main verb, see Zerwick, *Biblical Greek*, 127.

15. There is no reason to see the two as contradictory. Mark often brings details of a story together for dramatic effect.

16. Hagner, *Matthew 14 – 28*, 621 – 22, thinks they did not respond in this way since the answer reflects Jesus' purpose so well; rather, it was Matthew's redactional addition. But the answer at the same time is the natural (and legal) conclusion of the parable, and if they did not realize yet that it was addressed to them, it would make sense for them to respond in this fashion.

17. Scholars are often surprised that there is no hint of judicial process, and Nolland, *Matthew*, 876, thinks the "OT avenger of blood" may be in view. But that seeks too complete a story, and Jesus is uninterested in such questions and seeks ultimate effect. The father lost slaves and a son and so would be directly responsible for seeking justice, however it was achieved.

they constitute "the heart of the story," namely, the eschatological time when God collects his harvest fruit from his "tenants."[18]

21:42 Jesus told them, "Have you never read in the Scriptures" (λέγει αὐτοῖς ὁ Ἰησοῦς, Οὐδέποτε ἀνέγνωτε ἐν ταῖς γραφαῖς). Present tense "told" (λέγει) portrays Jesus in the process of challenging the people. The introductory formula is the second challenge to their understanding of Scripture (v. 16; cf. 22:29). Jesus is asking if they have realized the truth of this passage, namely, that it points to him as its typological fulfillment.

21:42 "'The stone that the builders rejected'" (Λίθον ὃν ἀπεδοκίμασαν οἱ οἰκοδομοῦντες). The rejection of the son in the parable leads Jesus to quote Ps 118:22 – 23 from the LXX on the rejected stone, perhaps based on a wordplay between the Hebrew *ben* ("son") and *ʾeben* ("stone").[19] The psalm itself is a thanksgiving hymn celebrating the deliverance of Israel by a supernatural military victory over Israel's enemies, so Israel is the cornerstone. Jesus and the early church understood this (Acts 4:11; Rom 9:33; 1 Pet 2:6 – 7) as typologically (see Introduction on the use of the OT) fulfilled in Jesus' rejection and vindication by God, also adding material from the stone imagery in Isa 8:14; 28:16. As the stone is Jesus, the "builders" are the leaders of Israel, especially since it was a frequent rabbinic designation for them.[20]

21:42 "'. . . has become the cornerstone'" (οὗτος ἐγενήθη εἰς κεφαλὴν γωνίας). It is debated whether the "cornerstone" (κεφαλὴν γωνίας) is the foundation stone of a building at its bottom corner (*EDNT*, 1:268; Morris) or the keystone at the top of an arch (Jeremias, Derrett, Carson, Hagner) or at the top of the wall holding two walls together (*NIDNTT*, 3:389 – 90, Luz, Cahill).[21] A growing number (France, Ridderbos, Wilkins, Keener, Nolland) believe it does not matter. The "stone of stumbling" image from Isa 8:14 and quoted in Rom 9:33; 1 Pet 2:8 (if the images are related, which is likely) would favor the first of the three (you do not "stumble" over the stone at the top of an arch or building), but in reality all three are viable and fit the image here. Charette summarizes it well: "The rejected son is himself restored and vindicated. He becomes the cornerstone of a new building, the restored people of God . . . the basis of the new nation which receives the inheritance."[22]

21:42 "'This has come from the Lord, and it is wondrous in our eyes'?" (παρὰ κυρίου ἐγένετο αὕτη καὶ ἔστιν θαυμαστὴ ἐν ὀφθαλμοῖς ἡμῶν;). The "wondrous" vindication of Jesus by divine intervention was a precious truth to the early church and accounts for the popularity of the stone passages in the NT (Acts 4:11; Rom 9:33; Eph 2:20; 1 Pet 2:7).

21:43 Therefore I tell you that the kingdom of God will be taken away from you (διὰ τοῦτο λέγω ὑμῖν ὅτι ἀρθήσεται ἀφ' ὑμῶν ἡ βασιλεία τοῦ θεοῦ). Verses 43 – 44 are found only in Matthew and provide a climax to both the ecclesiological (v. 43) and christological (v. 44) aspects of the parable; they restate v. 41 in reverse order, which this one recapitulates and expands v. 41b.

It is questionable whether the antecedent of "you" (ὑμῶν) in "taken away from you" refers to the religious leaders or the nation as a whole, but it is unnecessary to choose between them, as

18. Olmstead, *Trilogy of Parables*, 111 – 12. He sees an echo of Ps 1:3 with the doctrine of the "two ways" there (115).

19. See Snodgrass, *Tenants*, 113 – 18, who concludes that the stone quotation "is not illogical and disruptive; rather it is bound inextricably to the parable through the wordplay" (118). The anarthrous "stone" (λίθον) emphasizes the qualitative (theological) aspect, i.e., the christological import.

20. *B. Šabb.* 114a; *b. Ber.* 64a in Snodgrass, *Tenants*, 96.

21. M. Cahill, "Not a Cornerstone! Translating Ps 118,22 in the Jewish and Christian Scriptures." *RB* 106 (1999): 345 – 57.

22. Charette, *Theme of Recompense*, 138.

the leaders stand for the nation. This the fourth and last time that "kingdom of God" appears in Matthew (12:28; 19:24; 21:31), and as said in 3:2, it is synonymous with "the kingdom of heaven."

21:43 ... and given to a people who will produce its fruit (καὶ δοθήσεται ἔθνει ποιοῦντι τοὺς καρποὺς αὐτῆς). The salvation-historical move from the Jewish people to the Gentiles/church is seen in 8:11 – 12 (cf. 13:12) and is part of the universal mission theme in Matthew (see 1:3, 5 – 6; 2:1 – 12; 4:15 – 16; 8:5 – 13, 28 – 34; 12:21; 15:21 – 28; 24:14; 28:19). The singular "people" (ἔθνος, see 24:7) has double meaning[23] and at the secondary level could be the Gentiles, the church, or the leaders of the church. Still, as stated in v. 41, probably all three are intended in this image (see 1 Pet 2:9 for the church as "a holy nation").

God, the owner of the vineyard, will remove (note the future tense here) the wicked "tenants" from their privileged status and give the vineyard to new tenants, the church (Gentiles but also believing Jews) and its leaders. As in vv. 19, 34, 41, the "fruit" refers to the righteous behavior expected of the citizens of the kingdom (see also 5:6, 10, 20; 6:1, 33; 7:16 – 20). Many classical dispensationalists make this the classical text for Jesus withdrawing his offer of the kingdom from the Jewish people, inaugurating the church age. This in turn produces a replacement theology, where the church replaces Israel as the people of God. However, this does not fit Matthew or the rest of the NT.

It is clear that the Gentiles do not replace Israel but join Israel as the people of God. In Rom 11, only "some of" the Jewish people (i.e., those who reject the Messiah) are removed from the olive tree, and the Gentiles join the "remnant" (believing Jews as God's people). Moreover, Matthew has the Jewish people the focus of Jesus' mission (10:5 – 6; 15:24) and in 28:19 the Jews are part of the "nations" to be evangelized by his followers.

21:44 "And the one who falls on this stone will be broken to pieces" (Καὶ ὁ πεσὼν ἐπὶ τὸν λίθον τοῦτον συνθλασθήσεται). The inclusion of this verse is widely doubted, but on the whole it should probably be included as original.[24] This verse develops the first part of v. 41, the destruction of the evil tenants (the "outer darkness" of 8:12).[25] The opening part builds on the stone imagery of v. 42 and stems from Isa 8:14 – 15, the "stone that causes people to stumble." In Isaiah this warns of judgment against the nation for turning away from God, and the context is the same here.

21:44 "... but whoever it falls on will be crushed"[26] (ἐφ' ὃν δ' ἂν πέσῃ λικμήσει αὐτόν). The imagery in this verse switches from falling on the stone in the first part to the stone falling on the people in the second part ("fall" [πέσῃ] in both clauses is aorist, picturing the destruction as a whole). This is taken from Dan 2:34 – 35, 44 – 45, in which Daniel interprets Nebuchadnezzar's dream of the enormous statue shattered by the rock. Now the leaders and the nation will share Babylon's judgment. They will reject and kill the Messiah, but the Messiah will utterly destroy them.

23. The term was used often in the first century generally for "people," its primary meaning here ("people producing fruit"). But in the salvation-historical context of vv. 42 – 44, it also has a sense similar to 1 Pet 2:9 with the church as "a holy nation" composed of both believing Jews and Gentiles.

24. It is found in most of the better manuscripts (א B C K L f[1,13] Byz et al.) and omitted in some (D 33 it[b,d,e] et al.), but the reason it is bracketed by nearly everyone is that it seems an interpolation from Luke 20:18 (so Metzger, Gnilka, Davies and Allison, Hagner). Yet the manuscript evidence is strongly in favor of its inclusion, and it could be a Q reading. So it is better to include it in the text.

25. The primary reference of this destruction, as will be made explicit in ch. 24, is the destruction of Jerusalem. Yet as in 8:12, final judgment is also part of the image.

26. λικμήσει is an active future, meaning "it will crush them." The emphasis is on their utter destruction.

21:45 When the chief priests and Pharisees heard his parables, they knew he was speaking about them (Καὶ ἀκούσαντες οἱ ἀρχιερεῖς καὶ οἱ Φαρισαῖοι τὰς παραβολὰς αὐτοῦ ἔγνωσαν ὅτι περὶ αὐτῶν λέγει). It was the "chief priests and elders" who came to Jesus in v. 23, and it is "chief priests and Pharisees" who now react to his parables (vv. 28 – 44), so probably all three groups (who made up the Sanhedrin) were present the whole time. This prepares for their involvement in the Passion Narrative later (27:62); they were political enemies, so the fact they are working together here shows the extent of their opposition to Jesus.

Their reaction to the parable is particularly appropriate. Finally, after their summary (v. 41) and Jesus' interpretation of it (vv. 42 – 44) have cemented their own guilt and the proper judgment they deserve, they now recognize that they have pronounced the guilt and indictment on themselves (v. 41), that Jesus has been describing them all along.

21:46 Although they were seeking a way to arrest him (καὶ ζητοῦντες αὐτὸν κρατῆσαι). "Seeking" (ζητοῦντες) is a concessive participle, stressing that Jesus' freedom of movement has taken place in spite of their desire to arrest him (see Wallace, 634). The leaders then proceed to prove that Jesus was correct about them in the parable, for they want to arrest and execute him just as the wicked tenants plotted in the parable.

21:46 ... they were afraid of the crowds, since they held him to be a prophet (ἐφοβήθησαν τοὺς ὄχλους, ἐπεὶ εἰς προφήτην αὐτὸν εἶχον). The crowds have labeled Jesus a prophet in 16:14 and 21:11 and the Baptist a prophet in 21:26. This is especially connected with the triumphal entry of 21:11. The zealous, easily provoked pilgrims who came for Pentecost were intense in their piety and could erupt on a whim. So the leaders were justly afraid of them.

Theology in Application

Davies and Allison argue strongly that this parable does *not* refer to God's rejection of the Jews and turning to the Gentiles but to the Jewish leaders vs. the church.[27] However, this is not quite correct. It is true that the parable centers mainly on the leaders, but as Keener remarks,[28] the turning point comes in v. 43. The religious leaders have forfeited their right to guide the nation, and God's reign will be handed over to a "new nation," the people of a "new exodus." So this was an indictment and a judgment prophecy that will further point to the detailed judgment prophecy of the Olivet Discourse in ch. 24. There is heavy irony in the fact that the earlier parables were meant to conceal the message of the kingdom (Matt 13) from the religious leaders, while this one is meant to reveal it(!), thus provoking the crucifixion and fulfilling the parable.

27. Davies and Allison, *Matthew*, 3:189 – 90. They argue that the tenants are not Israel but the leaders and that the conflict is between Jesus and them, not Jesus and Judaism. The judgment is on the tenants/leaders, not on the vineyard/Israel, and the kingdom is given to an ἔθνος, not the Gentiles (which would be plural if it was the Gentiles) but the church. So it is not an ethnic issue but the salvation-historical transfer of the kingdom from the Jewish leaders to the church (composed of Jews and Gentiles).

28. Keener, *Matthew*, 515 – 16.

1. The Centerpoint of History Presented via Parable

The details of the story are incredible. The mistreatment and murder of the prophets was a major emphasis of NT apologetics, and the way Jesus is presented as not just the quintessential murdered prophet but the very Son of God killed by his own people provides a powerful picture of Jewish guilt. Yet before anyone labels the Jewish people "Christ-killers" and starts another anti-Semitic pogrom, look at this from the perspective of the book of Acts. There in the early preaching of the church, the message was *not* one of anti-Semitism but of "you put Christ on the cross, but he died for you, so come and accept him as your Savior" (Acts 2:23 – 24, 36 – 39; 3:13 – 20; 13:26 – 39). So the teaching is not due to rejection of the Jews but compassionate evangelism for them. Moreover, it is clear in Rom 3 and Heb 8 – 10 that he died for all of us, and we all, Gentiles as well as Jews, put Christ on the cross.

2. New Tenants for the Vineyard

This is the other great salvation-historical reality of this parable. The children of the kingdom now consist of the new kingdom community of the church. But this does not mean the Jewish people have no more hope. Paul clarifies this in Rom 9 – 11. God has not abandoned his covenant promises but even now has called a remnant from among the nation (Rom 11:1 – 10) and even has intended the Gentile mission to have as its main purpose making Israel jealous (Rom 10:19; 11:11 – 16), and the end result is intended that "all Israel will be saved" (Rom 11:25 – 32). Still, Jesus is prophesying divine judgment on a people and its leaders who have rejected and are about to kill the very Son of God.

3. God's Demand: Fruitfulness

Kingdom people (both Jew and Gentile) are required by God to live righteously before him and produce fruit (as in the fruitful branches of John 15:1 – 8 or the "fruit of the Spirit" of Gal 5:22 – 23) that will glorify God. In Matthew this certainly means the Gentile mission culminating in the Great Commission of 28:18 – 20. The Jewish people rejected that aspect of the Abrahamic covenant (blessing to the nations); now the church must take up and fulfill that divine mandate.

4. Jesus the Stone

Jesus as God's Son is the rejected stone who will become the head of the corner and destroy the enemies of God. The christological element is primary. Jesus is the Son[29] who will be killed and yet the rejected stone who will be vindicated. Especially

29. Jack D. Kingsbury, "The Parable of the Wicked Husbandmen and the Secret of Jesus' Divine Sonship in Matthew: Some Literary-Critical Observations," *JBL* 105 (1986): 643 – 55, says this is the first time in Matthew that Jesus' divine sonship is made public.

if v. 44 is original (likely), the vindication will take the form of Jesus as Judge, probably with an inaugurated thrust that begins with the imminent destruction of Jerusalem and ends with the eschatological Judge of the final Assize. There is a central theme of imminent judgment in the parable that points to the destruction of Jerusalem (ch. 24) for killing the prophets and the Son. Yet there is a redemptive side to the judgment as well. With the reign of God shifted to the church, the church becomes God's source of blessing for the nation by bringing the message of salvation back to the Jewish people.

CHAPTER 93

Matthew 22:1 – 14

Literary Context

This third of the triad of parables continues the themes of the wicked tenants in terms of God's gracious invitation to the guests, their refusal to respond, the king's judgment that fell on them as a result, and the extension of the invitation to others both "the bad and the good" (v. 10). The two primary differences are (1) the eschatological orientation to the messianic banquet at the end of history as well as the imminent judgment at the destruction of Jerusalem[1] (vv. 1 – 10, preparing for ch. 24); and (2) the demand that people allowed into the banquet come on God's terms rather than their own (vv. 11 – 14). With this final parable, the action then returns to the remaining four controversies (22:15 – 46).

VI. The Movement to the Cross (19:1 – 25:46)
- **A. Jesus' Deeds: Opposition and Discipleship (19:1 – 22:46)**
  - **2. Beginning Events of Passion Week (21:1 – 22:46)**
    - **b. Controversies in the Temple Court (21:23 – 22:46)**
      - (2) The Parable of the Two Sons (21:28 – 32)
      - (3) The Parable of the Wicked Tenants (21:33 – 46)
      - ➦ **(4) The Parable of the Wedding Banquet (22:1 – 14)**
      - (5) Paying Tribute Taxes to Caesar (22:15 – 22)
      - (6) Marriage in the Resurrection (22:23 – 33)

Main Idea

This moves from the centrality of the guilt of the leaders (the parable of the wicked tenants) to the guilt of the whole nation (building on v. 43). Two themes are

1. This fits the inaugurated eschatology of Matthew. Nolland, *Matthew*, 889, speaks of the interaction between "the provisional fulfillment and imminent expectation" and "a more open-ended futurity" in this parable.

uppermost — divine justice and divine grace. God is just in his wrath and judgment on those who flaunt his invitation and gracious in inviting both "the bad and the good" (v. 10) to the messianic banquet.

Translation

(See next page.)

Structure and Literary Form

There is some debate as to whether this judgment parable is M material (Davies and Allison, Luz, Nolland) or Q material (most others). There are actually three forms — *Gospel of Thomas* 64; Luke 14:15 – 24, and Matt 22:1 – 14. They are all sufficiently distinct to lead to the conclusion of three separate versions and therefore to M material here. Critical scholars spend a great deal of energy trying to go back to an original parable behind the three and to determine the Matthean redactional additions, but as we said before (see on ch. 13), such is not necessary. It is better to see these as uttered by Jesus on different occasions; as an itinerant preacher Jesus would naturally use a similar form to make different points at different times.[2] Not many today still argue that allegorizing means later additions, for Jesus used allegory in many of his parables.

There are three parts to this parable — the original invitation, its rejection, and the punishment meted out by the king (vv. 1 – 7), a second invitation and its acceptance by "the bad and the good" (vv. 8 – 10), and the guest who tries to enter the banquet dressed inappropriately along with his punishment by the king (vv. 11 – 13).[3]

Exegetical Outline

→ **I. The Wedding Banquet (Stage I) (22:1 – 7)**
- A. The banquet prepared (vv. 1 – 2)
- B. The invitations refused (vv. 3 – 6)
  1. The first invitation is rejected (v. 3)
  2. The second invitation is ignored (vv. 4 – 5)
  3. The messengers mistreated or killed (v. 6)
- C. The king's response: destruction (v. 7)

2. See Blomberg, *Parables*, 237 – 40; Carson, "Matthew," 455 – 56; Morris, *Matthew*, 546 – 47; Bock, *Luke 9:51 - 24:53*, 1269 – 70.

3. It is also viable to follow those (e.g., Davies and Allison, Luz) who combine the last two and find two parts (vv. 1 – 7, 8 – 13), with both involving an invitation, a reaction, and a punishment. However, the three parts better fit the themes of the parable.

Matthew 22:1-14

1a	Introduction	**Jesus answered and again spoke to them in parables, saying**
2a	Comparison	*"The kingdom of heaven is like a king*
		who made plans for a wedding banquet for his son.
3a	Scene #1 Invitation #1	*He sent his slaves to call those invited to the wedding feast,*
b	Result	*and yet they did not want to come.*
4a	Invitation #2	*Again, he sent other slaves, saying,*
b		*"Tell those invited:*
c	(Restatement)	*'Look, I have prepared my feast.*
d		*My oxen and fattened cattle are slain,*
e		*and everything is ready.*
f		*Come to the wedding feast.' "*
5a	Result	*But they paid no attention and*
		went away,
b		*one to his own field,*
		another to his business.
6a		*But the rest seized his slaves,*
		treated them shamefully, and
		killed them.
7a	Response	*So the king became angry and*
		sent his soldiers to destroy those murderers and
		burn their city
8a		*Then he said to his slaves,*
b		*'The wedding feast is ready,*
c		*but those invited were not worthy.*
9a	Invitation #3	*Therefore, go to exit points of the streets and*
		invite whoever you find to the banquet.'
10a		*So those slaves went out into the streets and*
		gathered together everyone they found,
b		*the bad and the good.*
c	Result	*And the wedding banquet was filled with guests.*
11a	Scene #2	*Now when the king entered and*
		observed those reclining at the tables,
b		*he saw there a man not dressed in proper wedding clothes.*
12a	Question	*And he said to him,*
b		*'Friend,*
		how did you get in here
		without proper wedding clothes?'
c	Answer	*And he was silent.*
13a	Result	*Then the king told his servants,*
b		*'Bind him hand and foot and*
		throw him out
		into outermost darkness,
c		*where there will be weeping and*
		grinding
		of teeth.'
14a	Basis	*For many are called, but few are chosen."*

II. The Wedding Banquet (Stage II) (22:8 – 10)
- A. The invitations go to anyone on the streets (vv. 8 – 9)
- B. The wedding filled with both "the bad and the good" (v. 10)

III. The Inappropriate Guest (22:11 – 14)
- A. The man without wedding clothes (vv. 11 – 12)
- B. The punishment: outer darkness (v. 13)
- C. Conclusion: few chosen (v. 14)

Explanation of the Text

22:1 Jesus answered and again spoke[4] to them in parables, saying (Καὶ ἀποκριθεὶς ὁ Ἰησοῦς πάλιν εἶπεν ἐν παραβολαῖς αὐτοῖς λέγων). This is Jesus' third parable here, and it is considered still a response to the chief priests, elders, and Pharisees with whom Jesus has been debating in this section (21:23 – 46). He has used three "parables" to challenge them regarding their unbelief and opposition to him as God's Messiah and Son, in particular their desire to arrest Jesus in 21:45 – 46. Like the other two parables (21:28 – 32, 33 – 46), this will also be heavily allegorical (see the "The Interpretation of Parables" at the beginning of ch. 13).

22:2 "The kingdom of heaven is like a king" (Ὡμοιώθη ἡ βασιλεία τῶν οὐρανῶν ἀνθρώπῳ βασιλεῖ). In 18:23 – 24 (the unforgiving servant) Jesus also centered a parable on the actions of a king, and in 9:15 he used the image of a wedding. Here he combines the two images to typify once more (for the formula intro, see on 13:24) the new reality established by the arrival of the kingdom with Jesus.

22:2 "... who made plans for a wedding banquet for his son"[5] (ὅστις ἐποίησεν γάμους τῷ υἱῷ αὐτοῦ). "Son" (υἱός) appears in all three parables (21:28 – 22:14), and clearly the theme that runs through them is the rejection of God's "Son." Today as well as then the wedding of the prince (and presumably heir) is a political as well as familial occasion, for it prepares for his accession to the throne (by establishing the future royal family). The background is certainly the messianic banquet (Isa 25:6; 62:1 – 5; Rev 19:6 – 9, cf. *1 En.* 58:4; *2 Bar.* 29:4 – 8), although it did not become a wedding banquet until Jesus. In Rev 19:7 – 9 the believers are both the bride and the invited guests; here the invited guests are first Israel (vv. 1 – 7) and then the Gentiles (vv. 8 – 10), and the invitation is the kingdom message. Obviously, the king is God and the son Jesus (as in the other two parables in this section).

22:3 He sent his slaves to call those invited to the wedding feast (καὶ ἀπέστειλεν τοὺς δούλους αὐτοῦ καλέσαι τοὺς κεκλημένους εἰς τοὺς γάμους). As in 21:34 (the same wording) the "slaves" are the OT and NT prophets,[6] this time summoning those invited (= the Jewish people) to the wedding banquet. As in the previous parable (21:34 – 36), he sends two groups of slaves to give the invitations. This was common in the ancient world, since the elaborate preparations required

4. For this Matthean formula of "answered and spoke" (ἀποκριθεὶς εἶπεν), see on 4:4. In this case with "again" (πάλιν) it is better to translate the two verbs separately.

5. "For his son" (τῷ υἱῷ) is a dative of advantage.

6. Olmstead, *Trilogy of Parables*, 122 – 23, makes a good case for seeing the servants here as NT messengers on the basis that they call the people to the messianic banquet.

meant that no definite date could be given at first. The first invitation informed them of the coming event (presupposed here), and the second tells them the exact date (the two of vv. 3 – 4). So they have already agreed to come.

22:3 ... but yet[7] they did not want to come (καὶ οὐκ ἤθελον ἐλθεῖν). In a patron-client society like the Roman world, attendance was virtually an obligation; it is possible that these are "established subordinates of the king, rather important people who are charged with implementing his policies in their spheres of influence,"[8] and thus they are especially obligated to attend. The fact that they changed their mind and now consciously "did not want to come" (with the imperfect "they did want" [ἤθελον] stressing repeated refusals) was a deliberate insult. Such "stubborn obstinacy" (Olmstead) would heap shame on the king, and reprisal (as in v. 7) would hardly be unexpected.[9] The language prepares for the "you were not willing" (οὐκ ἠθελήσατε) in the lament over Jerusalem in 23:37.

22:4 Again, he sent other slaves, saying, "Tell those invited:[10] 'Look, I have prepared my feast. My oxen and fattened cattle are slain, and everything is ready. Come to the wedding feast' " (πάλιν ἀπέστειλεν ἄλλους δούλους λέγων, Εἴπατε τοῖς κεκλημένοις, Ἰδοὺ τὸ ἄριστόν μου ἡτοίμακα, οἱ ταῦροί μου καὶ τὰ σιτιστὰ τεθυμένα, καὶ πάντα ἕτοιμα· δεῦτε εἰς τοὺς γάμους). The second set of emissaries now tells them "the feast is ready" (as stated in 21:36, these messengers could represent the Baptist and Jesus' disciples). Note that "prepare" (ἑτοιμάζω) frames the message in the rest of this verse. "Everything is ready" (here the adjective cognate is used) and it is time to come and enjoy the festivities. It is likely too that the king is giving them another chance to change their minds. The original listeners would be thinking he is very magnanimous in doing so; they deserve severe punishment.

The mention of the bulls and fattened cattle stresses the lavish nature of the feast, exemplified in the parable of the lost son, where the older brother complains, "You never gave me even a young goat" (Luke 15:29). Bulls and cattle were reserved for special guests. Such a lavish feast would remind the hearers of the messianic banquet (Isa 25:6, "the best of meats and the finest of wines"; cf. Prov 9:2 of wisdom). So the concluding "Come" is both a request and a virtual command.

22:5 But they paid no attention and went away (οἱ δὲ ἀμελήσαντες ἀπῆλθον). From rudeness they turn to indifference, just walking away (lit., "those who did not care walked away") from the king's emissaries. "Paid no attention" (ἀμελήσαντες) connotes not just inattention but also unconcern. They act as if no invitation has come at all and just return to their daily work.

22:5 ... one to his own field, another to his business (ὃς μὲν εἰς τὸν ἴδιον ἀγρόν, ὃς δὲ ἐπὶ τὴν ἐμπορίαν αὐτοῦ). ὃς μέν ... ὃς δέ is an idiom for "one ... another." The mention of "field" and "business" sums up the basic two categories, agriculture and commerce, which thus stand for all

7. καί is a general coordinating conjunction and can be used as a general connective (in the sense of the Hebrew ו) that can be translated many different ways. For its use indicating a surprising twist ("and yet, nevertheless"), see BAGD, 392 (g).

8. Luise Schottroff, *The Parables of Jesus* (trans. L. M. Maloney; Minneapolis: Fortress, 2006), 39, shows that Jesus is following rabbinic precedent, as the rabbis often used imperial practices in parables to describe God as king, absolute ruler, and judge.

9. See Keener, *Matthew*, 519 – 20. J. D. M. Derrett, "The Parable of the Great Supper," in *Law in the New Testament*, 139, says that allegiance to the king was part of the acceptance or rejection of the invitation; refusal would connote rebellion against his rule.

10. The perfect participle κεκλημένοις stresses the state of affairs — they are "the invited."

the different occupations. Luke 14:18 – 20 is similar, with the people providing excuses for not coming — buying a field, buying five oxen, and recently getting married. Again, the insult is far greater than we realize. These typify the reaction of the Jewish people to Jesus — rejection and apathy.

22:6 But the rest seized his slaves, treated them shamefully, and killed them (οἱ δὲ λοιποὶ κρατήσαντες τοὺς δούλους αὐτοῦ ὕβρισαν καὶ ἀπέκτειναν). The "rest" of the invited people (a group who did not return to their jobs) apparently decide the best response is armed rebellion, perhaps connoting political revolution. Jesus never explains why, but it accords with the actions of the wicked tenants (21:35 – 39) and likewise points forward to the passion events. ὑβρίζω means to "scoff at, insult," or to "arrogantly mistreat" someone (BAGD, 831). Needless to say, the rebuff and insult increase dramatically. Also, κρατέω is used elsewhere to describe the arrest of the Baptist (14:3) and Jesus (26:48; cf. 21:46). Josephus (*Ant.* 9:263 – 6) describes a similar rebellion against King Hezekiah involving the slaughter of prophets and the resultant execution of the rebels.

22:7 So the king became angry and sent[11] his soldiers to destroy those murderers and burn their city (ὁ δὲ βασιλεὺς ὠργίσθη καὶ πέμψας τὰ στρατεύματα αὐτοῦ ἀπώλεσεν τοὺς φονεῖς ἐκείνους καὶ τὴν πόλιν αὐτῶν ἐνέπρησεν). Apparently the rebels are all from the same city, and the reprisal is directed only at them ("those murderers") rather than at all who have rejected the invitation. Yet the others will face the king's displeasure as well. The rage of the king and his strong response pictures God's wrath at "the day of the Lord." Some have found it hard to imagine a king leading his army at the time of the wedding of his son, but to "send soldiers" at such a time is not so unusual.[12] The soldiers would hardly have been invited to the wedding.

The progression of the sending of soldiers to the destruction of the guilty rebels to the burning of the city pictures Rome's justice against its enemies,[13] in this case Israel. As in 21:44 this anticipates the destruction of Jerusalem,[14] with not "one stone upon another stone" (24:2). Some (Carson, Nolland) believe this is not an allusion to AD 70 because it is general OT imagery of judgment (so it is a reference to the final judgment), and Gundry sees an allusion to Isa 5:24 – 25 (5:1 – 7 is also behind the vineyard imagery of 21:33 – 34). Yet it is hard to see why both are not present, with Jesus' use of the OT imagery pointing to the specific judgment event of AD 70 as well as to final judgment.[15]

11. The verbal pattern of this verse has three main verbs and one circumstantial participle, "sent" (πέμψας), that becomes in effect another main verb (see on 4:4, 21, 23).

12. See Richard Bauckham, "The Parable of the Royal Wedding Feast (Matthew 22:1 – 14) and the Parable of the Lame Man and the Blind Man (Apocryphon of Ezekiel)," *JBL* 115 (1996): 471 – 88 (esp. 484), who shows the plausibility of this scenario and adduces a rabbinic parable (*Exod. Rab.* 18:10) as evidence.

13. Davies and Allison, *Matthew*, 3:202, say that this is a common *topos*, picturing the Roman army as an instrument of God's justice. See also Warren Carter, "Resisting and Imitating the Empire: Imperial Paradigms in Two Matthean Parables," *Int* 56 (2002): 260 – 72, who sees imperial imagery here and in 18:23 – 25.

14. Luz, *Matthew 21 – 28*, 54, says the leaders of Israel are here seen in a collective sense for Jerusalem, "the city of murderers." See also Blomberg, *Matthew*, 327 – 28; Witherington, *Matthew*, 409; and Turner, "Matthew," 280.

15. See Olmstead, *Trilogy of Parables*, 120 – 22. The concern of Gundry, *Matthew*, 436 – 37, is to avoid having Matthew "retrospect" the destruction of Jerusalem (a *vaticinium ex eventu* or "prophecy after the event"). But Matthew is actually saying that Jesus is "prophesying" the destruction *before* the event. For recent discussion of the importance of the destruction of Jerusalem in Matthew's "textual universe," see David Moffatt, "Righteous Bloodshed, " 299 – 320 (esp. 301 – 4).

22:8 Then he said[16] to his slaves, "The wedding feast is ready, but those invited were not worthy" (τότε λέγει τοῖς δούλοις αὐτοῦ, Ὁ μὲν γάμος ἕτοιμός ἐστιν, οἱ δὲ κεκλημένοι οὐκ ἦσαν ἄξιοι). We know from v. 4 that all the preparations have been completed. There is double meaning in "those invited" (κεκλημένοι, see on v. 4 for this form), referring not only to those "invited" to the banquet but also to the Jews and their sense of election as the special ("called") people of God, highlighted in v. 14 ("many are called, but few are chosen").

In 3:8 the Baptist told the leaders to "produce fruit *befitting* repentance" because the judgment of God was soon to come on the nation. The only "fruit" they were about to produce was the rejection and death of God's Son, and that made judgment certain. They are no longer "worthy" of divine mercy, and they are about to be replaced by those who are worthy (both from the Jews and the Gentiles).

22:9 "Therefore, go to the exit points of the streets" (πορεύεσθε οὖν ἐπὶ τὰς διεξόδους τῶν ὁδῶν). "The exit points of the streets" probably refers not to the "street corners" or "crossings" but to the point "where a street cuts *through* the city boundary and goes *out* into the open country."[17] This makes sense in this parable, because the city has been burned to the ground, and the emissaries will find people only out on the country roads where the town ends.

22:9 ". . . and invite whoever you find to the banquet" (καὶ ὅσους ἐὰν εὕρητε καλέσατε εἰς τοὺς γάμους). This continues the theme of the universal mission in Matthew (see on 21:43) and points first to the Gentiles and then to all who respond to the gospel, including many of the Jews (as in 28:19). The mention of "whoever you find" (ὅσος ἐάν is an idiom for "any person whosoever") is a natural reference to the mission beyond Israel, preparing the way from the restriction of the mission in 10:5 – 6; 15:24 to the "lost sheep of Israel" to the extension of the mission to all the world in 28:19.

In other words, this portrays the mission to all the nations that begins with Jesus' resurrection command. It does not begin after the destruction of Jerusalem, and to read chronology into "then" (τότε, v. 8) and see a contradiction with 28:19 are unnecessary.[18] This is a parable detailing the guilt of the people, God's judgment on them, and the worldwide mission, not a map of the timelines involved.

22:10 So those slaves went out into the streets and gathered together everyone they found (καὶ ἐξελθόντες οἱ δοῦλοι ἐκεῖνοι εἰς τὰς ὁδοὺς συνήγαγον πάντας οὓς εὗρον). Parallel to "whoever you find" in v. 9 is "everyone they found" in v. 10. The emphasis is clearly on the mission to the world. "Gathered together" (συνήγαγον) refers to the "gathering" of the multitudes who respond to the kingdom invitation, uniting all humankind via the gospel (cf. "every nation, tribe, people and language" in Rev 5:9; 7:9; 14:6; cf. 21:24, 26).[19] συνάγω

16. The historic present "says" (λέγει) is used here and in v. 12 dramatically to emphasize the action of the king/God.

17. BAGD, 194. See also W. Michaelis, *TDNT*, 5:108, who says they are "the points where the streets of the town give way to country roads."

18. The so-called "contradiction" is between the Gentile mission beginning after the destruction of Jerusalem (here) or after the resurrection command (28:19). This is hardly demanded by vv. 8 – 10, which depict salvation history rather than exact chronology.

19. At first glance, this seems a case of clear overallegorizing. Yet when you follow the principles for distinguishing between "local color" (details that are simply part of the story) and "theology-laden details" (those elements meant to carry theological meaning, see the discussion at the beginning of ch. 13), this becomes justified. Matthew has a clear theology of the universal mission, developed throughout his gospel; and in the immediate context the judgment of the Jewish people for unbelief and rejection of the Messiah plus the salvation-historical switch from the particularism of 10:5 – 6; 15:24 to the universalism of 28:18 – 20 are definitely signified (see 21:43 – 44; 22:8 – 10).

is used in 3:12; 13:30 for "gathering together" the wheat at the eschatological harvest and in 13:47 for "gathering" all the fish at the final judgment. It has this same eschatological sense here.

22:10 . . . the bad and the good. And the wedding banquet was filled with guests" (πονηρούς τε καὶ ἀγαθούς· καὶ ἐπλήσθη ὁ γάμος ἀνακειμένων). "The bad and the good" (πονηρούς τε καὶ ἀγαθούς, with "bad" placed first for emphasis) seems confusing at first, yet there may be a double meaning here. At one level (of the story itself) the mission of the church will net the disreputable (tax collectors and sinners) and the reputable (Pharisees like Nicodemus or Joseph of Arimathea).[20] At another level (of Matthean theology) it fits the two parables of 13:24 – 30 (36 – 43) and 13:47 – 52 quite well: there will be weeds/bad fish as well as wheat/good fish gathered at the harvest, and God alone will sort them out (as he does in vv. 11 – 13). God needs neither the Jews nor the Gentiles, and it is his grace that allows anyone into the kingdom (so Nolland). Finally, ὁ γάμος is specifically "the wedding hall" here, which is now "full" of guests.

22:11 Now when the king entered and observed those reclining at the tables, he saw there a man not dressed in proper wedding clothes (εἰσελθὼν δὲ ὁ βασιλεὺς θεάσασθαι τοὺς ἀνακειμένους εἶδεν ἐκεῖ ἄνθρωπον οὐκ ἐνδεδυμένον ἔνδυμα γάμου). The presence of "bad and good" at the banquet is now illustrated.[21] Olmstead argues that the focus shifts from Jewish rejection to the Christian community and paraenesis, i.e., ethical responsibility.[22] In the ancient setting clean, respectable (normally white) clothes at a feast were mandatory. Possibly garments were provided by the king,[23] but more likely he expected the guests to clean their garments before coming.[24] Either is possible, and the parable does not say. Jesus' point is that one guest insulted the king by not bothering to clean or change his garment.[25] Schottroff shows how rulers even employed spies to make certain that guests observed proper etiquette at such feasts and severely punished those who did not comply.[26]

22:12 And he said to him, "Friend, how did you get in here without proper wedding clothes?"

20. Schottroff, *Parables*, 40, points out that Roman rulers often provided feasts and celebrations for "the impoverished underclass of the city," with the entire populace invited. Derrett, "Great Supper," 140 – 41, discusses the normal distinction between classes of guests, with the poor given the "broken meats" at the back door. The grace of God here in this parable is especially evident.

21. Jeremias, *Parables*, 188, shows that Jesus here parallels a pre – AD 70 story told by Johanan ben Zakkai (*b. Šabb.* 153a) in which foolish guests continued to work until the banquet began (announced at the last minute) and thus could not attend due to their work-soiled clothes; they could only watch the "wise" who had prepared themselves as they enjoyed the feast.

22. Olmstead, *Trilogy of Parables*, 125. Charette, *Theme of Recompense*, 149, agrees, saying that the wedding garment symbolizes "the better righteousness and perfection which is demanded of all those who receive the call of God."

23. So Gundry, *Matthew*, 439; Blomberg, *Matthew*, 329, building on Klaus Haacker, "Das hochzeitliche Kleid von Mt. 22,11 – 13 und ein palästinisches Märchen," *ZDPV* 87 (1971): 95 – 97.

24. The one problem with this is the seeming haste because of the last-minute invitation to come to the wedding feast in v. 10. This has led David C. Sim, "The Man without the Wedding Garment (Matthew 22:11 – 13)," *HeyJ* 31 (1990): 165 – 78, to conclude he is not one of the "bad" in v. 10 but a separate guest representing all the wicked in the parable, including those rejecting the invitation in vv. 3 – 6. However, there is nothing in the parable to suggest sufficient time was not allowed for a change of clothing (so Blomberg, *Parables*, 238). It has also resulted in a near-universal consensus that this is a separate parable added by Matthew. Yet vv. 8 – 10 provide more than adequate background for this section, and it is easy to see why Jesus would zero in on such a detail. It provides an admirable conclusion to the parable.

25. Bauckham, "Wedding Feast," 484 – 86, shows the contempt that this would have indicated in the first century. The insult would have been great indeed.

26. Schottroff, *Parables*, 40 – 41.

And he was silent (καὶ λέγει αὐτῷ, Ἑταῖρε, πῶς εἰσῆλθες ὧδε μὴ ἔχων ἔνδυμα γάμου; ὁ δὲ ἐφιμώθη). The address of the guest as "friend" (ἑταῖρε, cf. 20:13; 26:50) is not condescending but shows the initial acceptance of the guest as one of those invited in v. 10. Again, the gracious lovingkindness of God is portrayed. The question assumes there were porters at the doors whose task it was to make certain only the deserving entered the feast (so Jeremias, Keener). It is disputed whether the wedding clothes signify repentance (3:2; 4:17, so Keener) or righteous conduct (Rev 19:8, so Derrett, Hagner, Luz).[27]

Yet these two options are closely intertwined and paralleled in the "faith without works" of Jas 2:14 – 26; the appropriate garment is not one or the other but "simply a life appropriate to one of God's new people."[28] The guilt of the man is shown in his "silence" ("to silence" [φιμόω] in Matthew only here and in v. 34, where Jesus "silences" the Sadducees); this man has no response but stands exposed and condemned.

22:13 Then the king told his servants (τότε ὁ βασιλεὺς εἶπεν τοῖς διακόνοις). The guest now becomes a condemned criminal, manacled with chains. Matthew switches from "slaves" or prophetic messengers (δοῦλοι, vv. 3, 4, 6, 8, 10) to "servants" or angelic beings (διάκονοι) who in 13:41, 49 throw the wicked into "the fiery furnace."

22:13 "Bind him hand and foot and throw him out into outermost darkness, where there will be weeping and grinding of teeth" (Δήσαντες αὐτοῦ πόδας καὶ χεῖρας ἐκβάλετε αὐτὸν εἰς τὸ σκότος τὸ ἐξώτερον· ἐκεῖ ἔσται ὁ κλαυθμὸς καὶ ὁ βρυγμὸς τῶν ὀδόντων). The punishment goes beyond the perspective of the story and clearly could be meted out only by God himself. The man is "cast out" just like the demons are expelled (ἐκβάλετε, used of exorcism in 7:22; 8:16, 31; 9:33, 34; 10:1, 8; et al.).[29]

The image of "outermost darkness" with "weeping and grinding teeth" is used frequently in Matthew for eternal punishment (8:12; 13:42, 50; 24:51; 25:30), paralleling the metaphor of Gehenna to describe the isolation, torment, and sorrow of everlasting judgment. Jesus' point is the same as in 7:21 – 23; those who try to enter the kingdom without repentance and the resultant righteous living will be rejected and be condemned to eternal torment at the final judgment.

22:14 For many are called, but few are chosen (πολλοὶ γάρ εἰσιν κλητοὶ, ὀλίγοι δὲ ἐκλεκτοί). This tells in a sense the "moral of the story" and provides a deeply theological conclusion to the parable.[30] "Many" (πολλοί) and "few" (ὀλίγοι) should be interpreted[31] in Semitic fashion as equivalent to "all/not all," meaning all Israel was called by God but only some (including the Gentiles) were actually chosen for the messianic banquet.

27. As Wilkins, *Matthew*, 717, points out, these would not be works that produce salvation but works that result from salvation. Davies and Allison, *Matthew*, 3:204 – 5, mention two other possibilities — a baptismal garment, which does not fit Matthew or the first-century church; and the resurrection body or luminous "garment of glory" (cf. 13:43, "the righteous will shine like the sun"). While possible, these do not make as much sense as the two options above, for it is difficult to imagine a person in the messianic banquet without the resurrection body.

28. France, *Matthew* (TNTC), 313.

29. Davies and Allison, *Matthew*, 3:206, sees literary influence from *1 En.* 10:4 – 5, where the fallen angel Azazel is bound "hand and foot and thrown into the darkness." See also David C. Sim, "Matthew 22.13a and 1 Enoch 10.4a: A Case of Literary Dependence?" *JSNT* 47 (1992): 3 – 19.

30. Carson, "Matthew," 457, following Zerwick, *Biblical Greek*, §§ 474 – 5, says γάρ "introduces a general, pithy conclusion explaining the parable."

31. So Joachim Jeremias, *TDNT,* 6:536 – 43; Ben F. Meyer, "Many (= All) Are Called, but Few (= Not All) Are Chosen," *NTS* 36 (1990): 89 – 97 (followed by Gnilka, Hagner, Wilkins, Olmstead, Nolland).

The play on words between "called" (κλητοί) and "chosen" (ἐκλεκτοί) is the key. The "called" are those "invited" (see the cognate καλέω in vv. 4, 8, 9) and refers to the sense of election Israel claimed as the special people of God. However, the leaders and those who followed them in rejecting God's Son were not the truly "elect"/"chosen" of God. Here there is both human responsibility and divine sovereignty at work, a fitting conclusion to the parable. "Called" (κλητοί) catches it well: the people must respond to God's summons with both repentance and right living to be part of God's elect!

Theology in Application

It is generally agreed that there are three aspects to this parable. The first two continue themes already presented in the two parables at the end of ch. 21 — the judgment on Israel and its leaders for rejecting their Messiah, and the movement to a new people who will enter the kingdom — not a Jew-Gentile antithesis but a universal mission to the entire world, Jews and Gentiles alike. As Rom 11 makes clear, the Jewish people have not lost their place. Only "some" have been replaced by Gentiles in the olive tree, but the Gentiles must be careful lest they too be rejected for unbelief (Rom 11:17 – 21).

In fact, that is what several (e.g., Davies and Allison, Luz, Bruner) see as the third theme in vv. 11 – 14, a warning to the church that they too will face judgment unless they live according to God's standards of righteousness. There is a salvation-historical movement in this parable from Israel to the Gentiles to the church composed of Jews and Gentiles who believe and live rightly according to the kingdom demands.

This latter theme is a critical message throughout Matthew's gospel — God demands of those who enter his kingdom a level of "right living" in discipleship that will determine their place in the kingdom (cf. 5:6, 10, 20; 6:1, 33; 7:21 – 23; 21:41, 43; 24:45 – 25:30). "It was the claim to belong without an appropriate change of life which characterized the old Israel and brought about its rejection; the new people of God must not fall into the same error."[32] Wilkins concludes that this is a call "to insiders to come inside." The leaders consider themselves the heirs of the prophets and yet reject Jesus' summons and will face swift judgment; so too Christians today must "take stock of our true membership within the kingdom," ascertaining whether we are truly living according to the standards of the new kingdom reality.[33]

32. France, *Matthew* (TNTC), 313.

33. Wilkins, *Matthew*, 734.

CHAPTER 94

Matthew 22:15 – 22

Literary Context

Matthew now returns to the controversies that are the core of this section. The three parables have established the guilt of the leaders and the nation for rejecting the summons of the Son of God to enter the new kingdom reality. In the four debates that follow the Pharisees and Sadducees prove their guilt by repeatedly "testing" Jesus and trying to gather evidence against him. As stated in the introduction to this larger unit (21:23 – 22:46), the four controversies relate to the major types of rabbinic questions: wisdom (22:15 – 22), mockery against a belief (22:23 – 33), moral conduct (22:34 – 40), and biblical contradictions (22:41 – 46).[1]

VI. The Movement to the Cross (19:1 – 25:46)
A. Jesus' Deeds: Opposition and Discipleship (19:1 – 22:46)
2. Beginning Events of Passion Week (21:1 – 22:46)
b. Controversies in the Temple Court (21:23 – 22:46)
(3) The Parable of the Wicked Tenants (21:33 – 46)
(4) The Parable of the Wedding Banquet (22:1 – 14)
➡ **(5) Paying Tribute Taxes to Caesar (22:15 – 22)**
(6) Marriage in the Resurrection (22:23 – 33)

Main Idea

Jesus' response to the Pharisees' attempt to trap him lies at the heart of all "submission to government" passages in the NT (e.g., Rom 13:1 – 7; 1 Tim 2:2; 1 Pet 2:13 – 17). The point is not that allegiance to God is the antithesis of allegiance to

1. See Daube, "Four Types," 45 – 48; reprinted in his *The New Testament and Rabbinic Judaism* (London: Athlone, 1956), 158 – 63.

government but that allegiance to government *is part of* allegiance to God. Yet at the same time God has the greater claim, and if a choice must be made, the believer must "obey God rather than human beings" (Acts 4:19; 5:29).

Translation

Matthew 22:15-22

15a	Setting/Scheme	**Then the Pharisees went and plotted how to entrap Jesus in his words.**
16a	Action	So **they were sending to him their disciples**
		along with the Herodians,
		saying,
b	Assertion	*"Teacher, we know that you are true and*
		teach the way of God in keeping with the truth.
c	Assertion	*Moreover, you are not concerned about the opinions of others,*
d	Basis of 16c	*for you are not swayed by the status of people.*
17a	Question	*So tell us what you think:*
		Is it lawful to pay taxes to Caesar or not?"
18a	Response #1	**[1]** But **Jesus, knowing their evil purpose, said,**
b		*"Why are you testing me, hypocrites?"*
19a	Response to 18b	*Show me the coin used for the tax."*
b	Response to 19a	And **they brought him a denarius.**
20a	Response #2	And **he asked them,**
b		*"Whose image and inscription are these?"*
21a	Answer to 20b	**They told him,**
b		*"Caesar's."*
c	Pronouncement/ Command	**Then he responded,**
d		*"Therefore,*
		give back to Caesar the things
		that belong to Caesar and
e		*to God the things*
		that belong to God."
22a	Reaction/Conclusion	When they heard this,
b		**they marveled,**
c		and leaving him,
d		**they went away.**

Structure and Literary Form

This controversy story[2] closely follows Mark 12:13 – 17 with no major changes. Matthew lengthens the narrative introduction to have the Pharisees plotting their

2. Witherington, *Matthew*, 410, calls this rather "a *chreia* focusing on a famous saying of Jesus." He quotes Gundry, *Mark*, 694: "In Jesus' universe of discourse, what counts as argumentatively persuasive is not logical validity, exegetical accuracy, or the like but cleverness, wordplay, one-upmanship."

strategy (vv. 15 – 16) and has them leaving in defeat at the end (v. 22b). Otherwise, the differences are merely verbal. Between the setting (vv. 15 – 16a) and the conclusion (v. 22), there are three parts to the interaction: (1) their hypocritical compliment and the entrapping question (vv. 16b – 17); (2) Jesus' exposure of their true intent and counter-request (vv. 18 – 19); and (3) Jesus' principial pronouncement (vv. 20 – 21).

Exegetical Outline

- **I. The Setting (22:15 – 16a)**
  - A. The plot to entrap Jesus (v. 15)
  - B. The sending of the Pharisees' disciples with some Herodians (v. 16a)
- **II. The Interaction with Jesus (22:16b – 21)**
  - A. Jesus questioned by the group (vv. 16b – 17)
    - 1. Their false flattery (v. 16b)
    - 2. The loaded question (v. 17)
  - B. Jesus first response (vv. 18 – 19)
    - 1. Exposing their true intention (v. 18)
    - 2. The request for the coin (v. 19)
  - C. Jesus' second response (vv. 20 – 21)
    - 1. The introductory question and their response (v. 20 – 21a)
    - 2. The principal pronouncement (v. 21b)
- **III. Conclusion: They Depart in Defeat (22:22)**

Explanation of the Text

22:15 Then the Pharisees went and plotted how to entrap Jesus in his words (Τότε πορευθέντες οἱ Φαρισαῖοι συμβούλιον ἔλαβον ὅπως αὐτὸν παγιδεύσωσιν ἐν λόγῳ). Literally, συμβούλιον ἔλαβον means "took council," but in this context it is certainly a hostile "plot" as to how to gather evidence against Jesus so they can arrest and convict him. The Pharisees are afraid of the thousands who are enamored with him (21:11, 46), so they seek something they can use to turn the people against him. Nolland[3] interestingly interprets ἐν λόγῳ as "with their words" due to the colorful παγιδεύσωσιν ("entrap"/"set a trap") here. However, that could go either way, and it seems better to follow Mark 12:13, "in his words" (λόγῳ). If Matthew was changing the thrust, one would expect that he would have made it more explicit by adding "their" (αὐτῶν). Again, there is no attempt to ascertain truth but only a studied "trap" to trick Jesus into incriminating himself.

22:16 So[4] they were sending to him their disciples along with the Herodians, saying (καὶ

3. Nolland, *Matthew*, 894.

4. For the loose connective "and yet" (καί) see on 22:3. For the use to indicate a result from what precedes, see BAGD, 392 (f).

ἀποστέλλουσιν αὐτῷ τοὺς μαθητὰς αὐτῶν μετὰ τῶν Ἡρῳδιανῶν λέγοντες). The dramatic use of a historic present (following Mark) shows Matthew moves this action to the forefront[5] as the Pharisees now unfold their plot. This is the only place "disciples" of the Pharisees are mentioned, but they are presumably followers who did the bidding of their rabbinic leadership. This is the only place in Matthew that "Herodians" (Ἡρῳδιανοί) are mentioned (he omitted them in 12:14 par. Mark 3:6). We know little about them, but most assume they were influential supporters of Herod and therefore of Rome, perhaps affiliated religiously and politically with the Sadducees[6] but mainly seeking full "Herodian" control of Palestine.

These two groups were not such "strange bedfellows" as some have assumed,[7] for in times of national crises unusual groups sometimes work together (see also Mark 3:6, where the Pharisees and Herodians plotted to take Jesus' life). The Herodians were there especially in case Jesus spoke against Roman taxation, which they would have viewed as sedition against Rome.

22:16 "Teacher, we know" (Διδάσκαλε, οἴδαμεν). These flattering words are reminiscent of the lawyer Tertullus's false praise of the Roman governor Felix at the trial of Paul in Acts 24:2 – 3. Such a canned speech oozes with hypocrisy and falsehood. The address διδάσκαλε (= "rabbi" but not in the sense we think, see on 12:2) is the normal address when outsiders address Jesus (8:19; 12:38; 19:16). This does not mean they accept Jesus as a valid rabbi; in fact, that is specifically what they are trying to disprove! The present tense "we know" (οἴδαμεν, a perfect stem that functions as a present) seems to be saying that they have always known this.

22:16 "... that you are true and teach the way of God in keeping with the truth" (ὅτι ἀληθὴς εἶ καὶ τὴν ὁδὸν τοῦ θεοῦ ἐν ἀληθείᾳ διδάσκεις). The statements they make are at the same time supremely ironic and true of Jesus. The key terms are "true/truth" (ἀληθής/ἀληθεία). Jesus is the opposite of the Pharisees, because he embodies "truth" (John 14:6) and is indeed the final interpreter of God's Torah (see on 5:17 – 20). He embodies all moral truth and everything he teaches is "in keeping with truth." τὴν ὁδὸν τοῦ θεοῦ should probably be interpreted ethically as "the way God demands," namely, righteous living (see on 21:32, 41, 43; 22:12). The Pharisees don't believe a word of what they are saying, but they are unconsciously stating absolute truth.

22:16 Moreover,[8] you are not concerned about the opinions of others,[9] for you are not swayed by the status of people (καὶ οὐ μέλει σοι περὶ οὐδενός· οὐ γὰρ βλέπεις εἰς πρόσωπον ἀνθρώπων). These enemies of Jesus are trying to force an answer from Jesus, and by decreeing his absolute integrity and fearless refusal to "show partiality" (lit., to "look upon the face," in other words, not swayed by the likes of Herod or Caesar), they are subtly hoping to goad him into making an anti-Roman statement.

22:17 "So tell us what you think: Is it lawful to pay taxes to Caesar or not?" (εἰπὲ οὖν ἡμῖν τί σοι δοκεῖ· ἔξεστιν δοῦναι κῆνσον Καίσαρι ἢ οὔ;). The leaders begin with the typical "what you think" (τί σοι δοκεῖ, see 17:25; 18:12; 21:28;

5. Porter, *Idioms*, 23 – 24, who calls this "foregrounding."

6. So Harold Hoener, "Herodian Dynasty," *DJG*, 325.

7. Keener, *Matthew*, 524 – 25, shows that the Pharisaic "populist theology" had much in common with the various revolutionary movements.

8. See on vv. 3, 16a for this broad use of καί ("moreover").

9. Lit., "it is not a concern for you about anyone."

22:42), asking Jesus to give a careful answer. There were three types of taxes for the Jews: the temple tax of 17:24 – 27; indirect taxes like customs duties, sales taxes, etc.; and the direct poll or head tax paid only by non-Roman citizens. This is the third type, and it became a form of tribute paid by all subject peoples. The amount was one denarius paid annually by all adults, women as well as men. It was controversial and opposed by many Jews. Judas the Galilean led a revolt against this tax in AD 6. So the Pharisees feel this will get Jesus in trouble however he responds, either with the Jews if he says yes or with the Romans if he says no.

22:18 But Jesus, knowing their evil purpose, said (γνοὺς δὲ ὁ Ἰησοῦς τὴν πονηρίαν αὐτῶν εἶπεν). There is real emphasis on Jesus' supernatural awareness ("knowing" [γνούς] of this in 12:15; 16:8) of the "evil" evident in their intention. This is the only use of the noun "evil" (πονηρία) in Matthew, but "evil" (πονηρός) is used of the leaders in 9:4; 12:34, 39; 16:4 and links them with the wilderness generation of Deut 1:35; 32:5, 20 in their rebellion and apostasy.

22:18 "Why are you testing me, hypocrites?" (Τί με πειράζετε, ὑποκριταί;). Jesus wants them to know he has seen behind their charade and is fully aware their question is not an honest one but a "test" (as in 16:1; 19:3; 22:35) designed not to ascertain truth but to entrap him. As a result of such dishonesty, they are "hypocrites" (on this see 6:2 and esp. 15:7 and throughout ch. 23), hiding their true purposes.

22:19 "Show me the coin used for the tax."[10] **And they brought him a denarius** (ἐπιδείξατέ μοι τὸ νόμισμα τοῦ κήνσου. οἱ δὲ προσήνεγκαν αὐτῷ δηνάριον). As Keener brings out,[11] copper coins minted locally did not have the emperor's likeness on them because the Jews were opposed to such images as idolatrous. However, silver and gold coins, required for paying the head tax, did have his portrait. This is why the leaders had such a coin, though the more scrupulous would have argued even then that any coin that contained the likeness of the emperor with the inscription, "Tiberius Caesar, son of the divine Augustus," was idolatrous and broke the Decalogue of Deut 5:8 (Exod 20:4, 23), "You shall not make for yourself an image in the form of anything in heaven above or on the earth beneath or in the waters below."

Jesus' reply says in effect that while a respectable Jew would not have such a coin on them, they would be able to get one when necessary, and "he did not believe that it was wicked to handle or display such a coin."[12] So the fact that they had such a coin readily on their person was itself somewhat of an indictment to the scrupulous and "cut the ground from under their feet — they were using Caesar's money, so let them also pay his taxes!"[13]

22:20 And he asked them, "Whose image and inscription are these?" (καὶ λέγει αὐτοῖς, Τίνος ἡ εἰκὼν αὕτη καὶ ἡ ἐπιγραφή;). As often in these controversy narratives (21:24 – 25, 31, 40 – 41; 22:42) Jesus uses a rhetorical question to involve the Pharisees in the answer. The image and title of Tiberias does not just signify the emperor himself but Roman hegemony in general, that is, the rights and authority of Rome as having political control over Palestine.[14] It is also possible that with

10. "For the tax" (τοῦ κήνσου) is a genitive of price or value, cf. BDF §179.

11. Keener, *Matthew*, 524 – 25.

12. Derrett, *Law in the New Testament*, 333 (cf. 329 – 33); cf. Keener, *Matthew*, 525.

13. France, *Matthew* (TNTC), 315.

14. Derrett, "Render to Caesar," 334.

"image" Jesus alludes to Gen 1:27, thus implying that we bear the image of God and so are loyal to him, while those bearing the coin (the leaders) owe a different kind of loyalty to Caesar.[15]

22:21 They told him, "Caesar's" (λέγουσιν αὐτῷ, Καίσαρος). Matthew uses two more historic presents ("they told, he responded" [λέγουσιν, λέγει]) to bring out the drama of the scene (see 22:8, 12, 20). The Pharisees have no response to Jesus; all they can do is acknowledge that Caesar's image is indeed on the coin, preparing for Jesus' brilliant riposte.

22:21 Then he responded, "Therefore, give back to Caesar the things that belong to Caesar and to God the things that belong to God" (τότε λέγει αὐτοῖς, Ἀπόδοτε οὖν τὰ Καίσαρος Καίσαρι καὶ τὰ τοῦ θεοῦ τῷ θεῷ). Jesus' pithy summation is memorable and capable of several interpretations.[16] In v. 17 the Pharisees' question was, "Is it lawful to pay [δοῦναι, 'give'] taxes to Caesar," but Jesus' reply here uses ἀπόδοτε, which can mean simply "give" (as in most translations) but is best rendered "give back" because it speaks of one's obligations both to government and to God (so McNeile, Gundry, Davies and Allison, Bruner; contra Carson, Luz, Nolland). Some believe the image of Caesar on the coin is paralleled by the divine image in humankind (Gen 1:26), which means we belong to him (so Giblin, Gundry, Bruner, Wilkins, Ball).[17] While this may be part of the meaning, it by no means is the major thrust. Others are led to the Lutheran two-kingdom view, that the Christian has two obligations, to the kingdom of Caesar (the secular realm) and to the kingdom of God (the spiritual realm). But it is unlikely that Jesus meant two distinct obligations or that the two were equal in force.

It is better to see the secular sphere as within the sacred sphere — in other words, that God is sovereign over Caesar. Jesus first agrees that it is right to pay the Roman head tax; we have a duty to Caesar. Yet he qualifies it carefully by hinting that the greater obligation is to God. The absence of the secular-sacred dichotomy in the ancient world means that Caesar's realm is actually part of God's realm.

The best way to flesh this out is to see how Paul and Peter built on Jesus' statement here. Goppelt shows how Rom 13:1 – 7 and 1 Pet 2:13 – 17 develop themes from Jesus' statement;[18] in fact, these two passages could be labeled midrashic developments of Jesus' teaching. (1) The obligation demands "submission" and loyalty. (2) All earthly rulers are put in place by God to serve its citizens and are answerable to him. (3) Submitting to Caesar is part of our submission to God; it is a mandate, not an option. (4) Paying taxes is a part of that obligation and an example of submission (Rom 13:6 – 7). When government turns evil, it is up to God to bring them down (Rev 13:10), and he will, often through other governments (as in World War II). Does this minimize the authority of the state completely, to the point that it has no place and should be opposed? That position goes much too far. Clearly, Jesus provides the basis for the later "submission" passages.

22:22 When they heard this, they marveled, and leaving him, they went away (καὶ ἀκούσαντες ἐθαύμασαν, καὶ ἀφέντες αὐτὸν ἀπῆλθον). Throughout the controversy narratives, Jesus'

15. So Witherington, *Matthew*, 413, following Larry Hurtado, *The Gospel of Mark* (New York: Harper and Row, 1980), 180 – 81.

16. For a list of options, see Charles H. Giblin, "'The Things of God' in the Question concerning Tribute to Caesar," *CBQ* 33 (1971): 510 – 27.

17. David T. Ball, "What Jesus Really Means by 'Render unto Caesar' (It's Not About Taxes)," *BRev* 19 (2003): 14 – 17.

18. Leonhard Goppelt, "The Freedom to Pay the Imperial Tax (Mark 12, 17)," *Studia Evangelica* 2 (1964): 185 – 94.

opponents again and again are forced to "hear" (with ἀκούσαντες a temporal participle) his wisdom (21:33, 45; 22:22, 33, 34), and they are struck silent and cannot help but be amazed (21:27, 42d; 22:22, 33, 46). There can be no response, and so they are forced to depart[19] in frustration once again. They cannot defeat him, and they cannot arrest him (21:46).

Theology in Application

As in all the controversy stories here — indeed, in both the infancy and resurrection narratives — a prevalent theme is the attempts of God's enemies to oppose his will. The more the leaders try to "test" Jesus and gather evidence against him, the more they fall on their own sword. The reason is that (as throughout Matthew) Jesus is the final interpreter of Torah, the archetypal teacher, and always speaks divine truth. So the hypocritical falsehoods of the Pharisees will always come to naught, as will always be the case in our time as well.

We too need not worry about the lies of the enemy. In 1 Pet 2:12 Peter says it well: "Live such good lives among the pagans that, though they accuse you of doing wrong, they may see your good deeds and glorify God on the day he visits us." Moreover, in the trial situation, when we are being attacked, the promise comes that "what you should say will be given you at that time. For it will not be you who speaks, but the Spirit of your Father who speaks through you" (Matt 10:19 – 20).

1. Giving the State Its Due

Give to the state its due, whether it is worthy or not. Jesus is clear that government is to be respected and taxes are to be paid. Rome was not a godly government, yet Jesus commanded his followers to submit (see above). The state is God's servant and should be accorded respect in that role. This means that the believer is to respect the fact of government even if the particular government is not worthy, which was certainly the case with the Roman emperors.

Moreover, there is no room for armed insurrection. Jesus was not a supporter of the revolutionaries of his day. The Zealots did not appear in full force until AD 67 – 68, but there were many visible revolutionary movements (cf. "Simon the Canaanean," 10:4) and messianic pretenders in the first century,[20] and these issues are partly in mind in this passage. Jesus did not countenance such movements and demanded respect for established government.[21] Yet this does not mean that protest of evil in government is wrong, as exemplified in Jesus and his early followers in their condemnation of the Jewish leaders. But there is a difference between prophetic

19. This is stated strongly with a circumstantial participle followed by a main verb (both synonyms), "leaving, they went away."

20. See *DNTB*, 936 – 47.

21. See Wilkins, *Matthew*, 735 – 37.

warning (as in the OT prophets) and armed rebellion. The former is part of respect for government (trying to remove evil and forestall divine judgment), the latter is taking God's judgment in our own hands.

2. God in Control

God is in control and deserves submission in every area of life. As Hagner puts it: "If one rendered to the state its restricted due, all the more is one to render to God his unrestricted due — the totality of one's being and substance, one's existence, is to be rendered to God and nothing less."[22] Submission to government takes place as part of one's complete submission to God in every area. If there is conflict, we must "obey God rather than human beings" (Acts 4:19; 5:29), for God is sovereign over government and over every aspect of one's being.

3. All Human Resources to be Submitted to God

By the use of the coin, Jesus in effect says it is good both to return Caesar's coin to him (via taxes) and to refuse to hold onto secular wealth at all. As Keener says, it was anathema to allow Caesar's image to enter Jerusalem on Roman standards, and the fact that they allowed it on coins shows that money was of supreme importance. So "surrendering to God 'what was God's' implied the surrender of all one was and possessed," i.e., "possessions have zero value."[23] God must have sovereignty over all secular resources, and the key to discipleship in Matthew (and even more in Luke) is the extent to which Jesus' followers have sacrificed all for him.

22. Hagner, *Matthew 14 – 28*, 637.

23. Keener, *Matthew*, 525 – 26.

CHAPTER 95

Matthew 22:23 – 33

Literary Context

This third debate with the leaders now concerns the Sadducees (the Pharisees have retreated in defeat), who now bring their own pet issue to the forefront in a further attempt to gain evidence against Jesus. This is not as serious publicly as the others, because it is an internal debate between the Pharisees and Sadducees over the doctrine of the afterlife. Still, they too hope to show the multitudes that Jesus is not a worthy teacher.

VI. The Movement to the Cross (19:1 – 25:46)
- **A. Jesus' Deeds: Opposition and Discipleship (19:1 – 22:46)**
  - **2. Beginning Events of Passion Week (21:1 – 22:46)**
    - **b. Controversies in the Temple Court (21:23 – 22:46)**
      - (4) The Parable of the Wedding Banquet (22:1 – 14)
      - (5) Paying Tribute Taxes to Caesar (22:15 – 22)
      - ➦ **(6) Marriage in the Resurrection (22:23 – 33)**
      - (7) The Greatest Commandment (22:34 – 40)
      - (8) Son of David and Lord of David (22:41 – 46)

Main Idea

The Sadducees probably use here a stock example that may have been successful against the Pharisees, developing Deut 25:5 (cf. Gen 38:8) on levirate marriage into a story of a woman who marries seven brothers in turn and still dies childless. Their point is that if there is a resurrection she will have to be a polygamist. The main point, then, is Jesus' teaching on the importance of resurrection both in Scripture and as pointing to "the power of God" (cf. 1 Cor 15).

Translation

Matthew 22:23-33

23a	Setting	On that day
b	Challenge	**Saddducees came to him, saying that there was no resurrection and asked him, saying,**
24a	Assertion	*"Teacher, Moses said,*
b	OT Quotation	*'If someone dies without having children,*
c		*his brother should marry that person's wife and*
d		*raise up offspring for him.'* (Deut 25:5 and Gen 38:8)
25a	Example	Now *there were seven brothers among us.*
b		*The first one married, then died,*
c		and *since he had no offspring,*
d		*he left his wife to his brother.*
26a		*The same thing happened to the second and the third brothers, right up to the seventh.*
27a		And *last of all the wife herself died.*
28a	Question	So *in the resurrection whose wife of the seven will she be?*
b	Basis for 28a	For *they all had her as a wife."*
29a	Response #1	**Jesus replied,**
b		*"You are deceived because you know neither the Scriptures nor the power of God.*
30a	Basis for 29b	For *in the resurrection neither will men marry nor will women be given in marriage,*
b		but *they will be like the angels in heaven.*
31a	Response #2	Now *concerning the resurrection of the dead,*
b	Question	*have you not read what was spoken to you by God, saying,*
32a	OT Quotation	*'I am the God of Abraham and the God of Isaac and the God of Jacob?'* (Exod 3:6)
b	Inference from 32a	*He is not the God of the dead but of the living."*
33a	Reaction/Conclusion	When the crowds heard this,
b		**they were amazed at his teaching.**

Structure and Literary Form

Matthew follows Mark 12:18 – 27 with only minor differences in this controversy story with its enclosed riddle and point of rabbinic law. It consists of two parts framed by an opening and closing (vv. 23, 33), first the story riddle presented by the Sadducees (vv. 24 – 28) and then Jesus' response (vv. 29 – 32), consisting of the refutation (vv. 29 – 30) and then the proof of it from Scripture (vv. 31 – 32).

Exegetical Outline

➡Opening: Sadducean Denial of Resurrection (22:23)

I. The Riddle (22:24 – 28)

A. Their use of Deut 25:5, Gen 38:8 on levirate marriage (v. 24)

B. The story of the widow with no children (vv. 25 – 28)

1. The seven brothers die without producing children, then the wife dies (vv. 25 – 27)
2. The question — whose wife in the resurrection? (v. 28)

II. Jesus' Response (22:29 – 32)

A. Challenge regarding their ignorance (vv. 29 – 30)

1. Their twofold ignorance (v. 29)
2. The truth regarding the resurrection (v. 30)

B. The proof from Exod 3:6 (vv. 31 – 32)

Closing: Reaction of the Crowd (22:33)

Explanation of the Text

22:23 On that day Sadducees came to him, saying that there was no resurrection, and asked him (Ἐν ἐκείνῃ τῇ ἡμέρᾳ προσῆλθον αὐτῷ Σαδδουκαῖοι, λέγοντες μὴ εἶναι ἀνάστασιν, καὶ ἐπηρώτησαν αὐτὸν). We cannot know whether or not the Sadducees overheard the earlier discussions, but they do come "on the same day." Their purpose is the same, to convince the people that Jesus is an unworthy teacher.

They begin by claiming (circumstantial participle λέγοντες) the resurrection is not in the true Scriptures. The Sadducees (see also on 3:7) accepted only the Torah/Pentateuch as canon and rejected any doctrine not found in it. There is no clear statement on the afterlife in the books of Moses, and the first teachings on resurrection are found in Hos 6:1 – 3; 13:14; Ezek 37:1 – 14 (corporate resurrection), and in Job 19:25 – 27; Isa 25:8, 26:19; and esp. Dan 12:1 – 3, 13 (individual resurrection),[1] with the doctrine developing in intertestamental literature (*1 En.* 22:13, 46:6; *4 Ezra* 4:41 – 43, 7:32 – 38; *T. Benj.* 10:6 – 9). The Sadducees rejected all this and often debated the Pharisees on the issue (see Acts 23:6 – 9).

22:24 ... saying, "Teacher, Moses said, 'If someone dies without having children, his brother should marry that person's wife and raise up offspring for him'" (λέγοντες, Διδάσκαλε, Μωϋσῆς εἶπεν, Ἐάν τις ἀποθάνῃ μὴ ἔχων τέκνα, ἐπιγαμβρεύσει ὁ ἀδελφὸς αὐτοῦ τὴν γυναῖκα αὐτοῦ καὶ ἀναστήσει σπέρμα τῷ ἀδελφῷ αὐτοῦ). This is a loose compilation of passages on levirate marriage from Deut 25:5 and Gen 38:8. As in Matt 22:16, 36 they call Jesus "rabbi" or "teacher" and

1. See Grant R. Osborne, "Resurrection," *DJG*, 673 – 74.

so address him on a point of law (for διδάσκαλε as an address only by those not following Jesus, see on 22:16).

The purpose of levirate marriage was to protect the name of a deceased brother without children and to guarantee that he would have legal heirs and thus the ancestral lands would continue in the family, as well as to take care of the widow who would often be left destitute. So when a man died childless, his brother was supposed to marry his wife and bear children in his name. In Deut 25:7 – 10 the brother could refuse but would be publicly shamed for doing so. We do not know how extensively this was practiced in Jesus' time (no instance is recorded), but the point of law was well known (discussed in Josephus, *Ant.* 4.254 – 56; *m. Yeb.*).

22:25 "Now there were seven brothers among us. The first one married, then died, and since he had[2] no offspring, he left his wife to his brother" (ἦσαν δὲ παρ' ἡμῖν ἑπτὰ ἀδελφοί· καὶ ὁ πρῶτος γήμας ἐτελεύτησεν, καὶ μὴ ἔχων σπέρμα ἀφῆκεν τὴν γυναῖκα αὐτοῦ τῷ ἀδελφῷ αὐτοῦ). The use of "seven" is due to its being the number of completion; this is a "perfect" example. So far this is a classic case of levirate marriage, a childless widow given to the deceased man's brother. By adding "among us" to the rendition of Mark 12:20, Matthew shows they are implying this is an actual situation. Note also the lack of concern for the widow herself; she is treated almost "as chattel to be transferred by inheritance."[3]

22:26 "The same thing happened to the second and the third brothers, right up to the seventh" (ὁμοίως καὶ ὁ δεύτερος καὶ ὁ τρίτος, ἕως τῶν ἑπτά). This goes way beyond the usual (it shortens Mark 12:21 – 22). All seven brothers ended up marrying the poor woman, none of them able to have children with her. It is possible that the Sadducees have taken the story form from the seven deceased husbands of Tob 3 or the seven brothers who become martyrs in 2 Macc 7.

22:27 "And last of all the wife herself died" (ὕστερον δὲ πάντων ἀπέθανεν ἡ γυνή). The poor widow now dies, and thus the key question arises: if there is a resurrection from the dead, what will happen to her in the next life if she has had seven husbands?

22:28 "So in the resurrection whose wife of the seven will she be? For they all had her as a wife" (ἐν τῇ ἀναστάσει οὖν τίνος τῶν ἑπτὰ ἔσται γυνή; πάντες γὰρ ἔσχον αὐτήν). "They had her" (ἔσχον[4] αὐτήν) means all seven husbands did in fact consummate the marriage sexually (unlike the seven in Tob 3:8). The question itself assumes a stance against polygamy, and the Sadducees are trying to force Jesus into a no-win situation. Either he denies the afterlife or accepts polygamy. It is clear that their entire purpose is to "ridicule the idea of life after death" and in so doing to "trap Jesus and discredit his teaching."[5]

22:29 Jesus replied, "You are deceived because you know neither the Scriptures nor the power of God" (ἀποκριθεὶς δὲ ὁ Ἰησοῦς εἶπεν αὐτοῖς, Πλανᾶσθε μὴ εἰδότες τὰς γραφὰς μηδὲ τὴν δύναμιν τοῦ θεοῦ). Jesus accuses the Sadducees of faulty theology, a self-deception caused (causal participle "know" [εἰδότες]) by failure to know the true teaching of Scripture. "The Scriptures" (τὰς γραφάς) refer to the whole inscripturated canon but in this case especially the five books of Moses (the only part the Sadducees accepted), as Jesus will demonstrate when he argues from Exod 3:6.

2. "Since he had" (ἔχων) is a causal participle.

3. Nolland, *Matthew*, 903.

4. The aorist "had" (ἔσχον) is global, considering the seven marriages as a single whole, see Wallace, 557.

5. Turner, "Matthew," 284.

Jesus' charge that the leaders do not know the Scriptures has been made before (21:16, 42). Their ignorance of "the power of God" (subjective genitive, the power that God wields) refers to their denial of his ability to raise the dead, indeed, to prepare a final harvest of eschatological blessing for his people in heaven. The Sadducees believed the messianic kingdom was earthly and had been fulfilled in the Maccabean victory over the Greeks.[6] Language of "power" for the resurrection is frequent in the NT, as in 1 Cor 15:43 ("raised in power") and Eph 1:19 ("his incomparably great power ... is the same as the mighty strength he exerted when he raised Christ from the dead").

22:30 "For in the resurrection neither will men marry nor will women be given in marriage" (ἐν γὰρ τῇ ἀναστάσει οὔτε γαμοῦσιν οὔτε γαμίζονται). The power of God is seen in the true reality of the resurrection existence. Jesus elaborates the situation with his two verbs so as to detail both men (marrying) and women (being given in marriage). ἐν τῇ ἀναστάσει means not "at the resurrection" (when it occurs) but "in the new resurrection life," i.e., heaven (so Davies and Allison). Jesus' point is that the analogy of the sevenfold widow is irrelevant because marriage and reproduction (the purpose of marriage, Gen 1:28) will not occur in the afterlife.

22:30 "But they will be like the angels in heaven" (ἀλλ' ὡς ἄγγελοι ἐν τῷ οὐρανῷ εἰσιν). "Like angels" (ὡς ἄγγελοι) draws on Jewish teaching (e.g., *1 En.* 104:1 – 4; *2 Bar.* 51:5 – 11; *T. Isaac* 4:43 – 48; that is, like the angels and sharing the glory of the angels in the age to come). Some also thought the human race was originally created as angels (*1 En.* 69:11).[7] Like the angels, the saints will dwell in heaven, worship God, and neither marry nor bear children.[8] In other words, there will be a new set of relationships in eternity, one in which husbands and wives will be closer to one another (and to all God's people) than they were in this life!

22:31 "Now concerning the resurrection of the dead,[9] have you not read what was spoken to you by God, saying" (περὶ δὲ τῆς ἀναστάσεως τῶν νεκρῶν οὐκ ἀνέγνωτε τὸ ῥηθὲν ὑμῖν ὑπὸ τοῦ θεοῦ λέγοντος). Now Jesus turns to the witness of Scripture itself and deliberately chooses a passage from the Pentateuch, the portion the Sadducees accept as canon. He begins with his typical challenge to their biblical understanding, "Have you not read?" (cf. 12:3; 19:4; 21:16, 42). By introducing Exod 3:6 with "what was spoken ... by God" (cf. 1:22; 2:15), Jesus emphasizes the divine inspiration behind the passage, thus a double indictment (ignorance of God as well as Scripture). In v. 24 they asserted "Moses said," so now Jesus trumps

6. This is the majority view, but it is debated. Others believe that the Maccabees (and their Sadduccean successors) gave tacit acknowledgment to Davidic hopes, but put off any messianic kingdom to the distant eschatological future (see 1 Macc 2:57). See John J. Collins, "Messianism in the Maccabean Period," in *Judaisms and Their Messiahs at the Turn of the Christian Era* (ed. Jacob Neusner et al.; New York: Cambridge Univ. Press, 1987), 104.

7. See Davies and Allison, *Matthew*, 3:227 – 29; Luz, *Matthew 21 – 28*, 70; Keener, *Matthew*, 527 – 28.

8. It is also often said that the Sadducees denied the existence of angels on the basis of Acts 23:8 ("The Sadducees say that there is no resurrection, and that there are neither angels nor spirits, but the Pharisees believe all these things") and so were guilty of a double error. The problem is there is no other evidence for such a belief, and angels are found often in the Pentateuch and would be difficult to deny. Therefore the recent (and more likely) view of Acts 23:8 is to take "angels and spirits" as in apposition to "resurrection," i.e. "there is no resurrection, namely, neither angels nor spirits," with both relating to the afterlife for human beings. See C. K. Barrett, *The Acts of the Apostles* (ICC; Edinburgh: T & T Clark, 1998), 2:1065 – 67; Joseph A. Fitzmyer, *The Acts of the Apostles* (AB; New York: Doubleday, 1998), 719. So the Sadducees did actually believe in the reality of angels.

9. This could be a genitive of source ("resurrection from the dead") but is much more likely to be an objective genitive (God will "raise the dead").

that by saying, "in actuality God said." The presence of "to you" (ὑμῖν) and the present tense participle "spoken" (λέγοντος) highlight the fact that through the OT passage God is speaking now directly to the Sadducees (so Bruner).

22:32 "'I am the God of Abraham and the God of Isaac and the God of Jacob'?" (Ἐγώ εἰμι ὁ θεὸς Ἀβραὰμ καὶ ὁ θεὸς Ἰσαὰκ καὶ ὁ θεὸς Ἰακώβ;). This is taken from Exod 3:6 LXX (omitting "your father"). Jesus is using a rabbinic argument[10] from grammar, with the present tense "I am" (εἰμι) demanding that in Moses' day Abraham, Isaac, and Jacob were still alive (or God would have had to say, "I was ..."). Since their deaths were recorded in the OT and yet they were alive in Moses' day, Jesus is arguing, they had to have been raised by God to heavenly life.

22:32 "He is not the God of the dead but of the living" (οὐκ ἔστιν ὁ θεὸς νεκρῶν ἀλλὰ ζώντων). This does not mean the patriarchs never died, for their deaths are recorded in Genesis (Gen 25:8; 35:29; 49:33). The argument that the patriarchs were still alive is found also in 4 Macc 7:19; 16:25; 18:19; *b. Sanh.* 90b; *Qoh. Rab.* 9:5, so Jesus is faithful to the first-century context and makes a valid point according to rabbinic logic. The Sadducees have no answer (see v. 34), which points to the effectiveness of Jesus' counter-argument.

22:33 When the crowds heard this, they were amazed at his teaching (καὶ ἀκούσαντες οἱ ὄχλοι ἐξεπλήσσοντο ἐπὶ τῇ διδαχῇ αὐτοῦ). The multitudes are often filled with wonder (ἐκπλήσσομαι, "overwhelmed with amazement") at Jesus' teaching (7:28; 13:54) and miracles (9:8, 33; 15:31), as are Jesus' disciples (8:27; 19:25; 21:20) and even the Pharisees (22:22). In this context it anchors Jesus as the great teacher of wisdom and interpreter of the law.

Theology in Application

It has always been the problem that we humans think we know more than we do and have little room for truths that go beyond our experience or challenge our commonly accepted axioms. This was true with the Sadducees of Jesus' day. They thought all truth began with their presuppositions regarding the five books of Moses, both in the extent of the canon and regarding their narrow interpretation of those books. Jesus showed them that they had little room for God's true Scripture or for his actual power.

Little has changed today. On the one hand, arrogant modernists and postmodernists make their solemn pronouncements regarding what God can or cannot do (or even whether there is a God!) with no regard whatever to the limits of their

10. D. M. Cohn-Sherbock, "Jesus' Defense of the Resurrection of the Dead," *JSNT* 11 (1981): 64 – 73, argues that Jesus is not following Taannaitic hermeneutical rules and believes his logic is "inadequate from a rabbinic point of view." While that may be true when compared with some later exegetical practices, it is similar to arguments for the resurrection found in *b. Sanh.* 90b (using Num 18:28 in a similar way) or in Philo, who also used Exod 3:6 in *Abraham* 50 – 55, see Davies and Allison, *Matthew*, 3:233; Keener, *Matthew*, 528 – 9; F. G. Downing, "The Resurrection of the Dead: Jesus and Philo," *JSNT* 15 (1982): 42 – 50. J. G. Janzen, "Resurrection and Hermeneutics: On Exodus 3.6 in Mark 12.26," *JSNT* 23 (1985): 43 – 58, argues that Jesus is faithful to Exod 3:6 in its context.

knowledge and for what God is doing and is going to do. The fact is that God has already raised people from the dead (as Jesus himself also did), and such events have occurred in our day in Indonesia and China. The resurrection is a reality and an essential component of true Christian belief (1 Cor 15:12 – 19).

On the other hand, some theologians have gone to war over the state of the resurrection body, arguing as to the extent it is material or immaterial. That is foolishness on the other side ("But someone will ask ... 'With what kind of body will they come?' How foolish!" 1 Cor 15:35 – 36). We know only that we will have an "imperishable [body] ... a spiritual body ... of heaven ... the image of the heavenly man" (1 Cor 15:42 – 49). It is not defined further.

The problem today is that too many theologians have no room for mystery. We must not pretend to know more than we do and fight over the wrong issues. Jesus here tells us two things. (1) There will be an entirely new set of relationships in eternity, one in which there will no longer be any need for marriage or procreation. I believe I will have a deeper love for and knowledge of my wife and children than I do now, and we will have that level of intimacy with all who are in heaven! That is true blessedness.

(2) This new relationship will remove all boundaries, creating a new union between the peoples of the world. When we combine 22:32 with 8:11 ("many from the east and the west will come sit down at the feast with Abraham and Isaac and Jacob in the kingdom of heaven"), we realize the barrier between Jew and Gentile, between racial and ethnic groups, will be broken once and for all. As Paul says in Eph 2:14, the present reality is that the cross has "destroyed the barrier, the dividing wall of hostility," and the future reality is that at the resurrection, "the glory and honor of the nations will be brought into" the Holy City (Rev 21:24, 26), so that there will be one people, one united heavenly culture.

CHAPTER 96

Matthew 22:34 – 40

Literary Context

Here Matthew provides a fourth (third in the series of ch. 22) and final confrontation and test of Jesus by the leaders. For Matthew (unlike Mark; see below on "Structure") this continues the series of hostile challenges. Jesus' victory here leads into the christological revelation of 22:41 – 46.

VI. The Movement to the Cross (19:1 – 25:46)
- **A. Jesus' Deeds: Opposition and Discipleship (19:1 – 22:46)**
  - **2. Beginning Events of Passion Week (21:1 – 22:46)**
    - **b. Controversies in the Temple Court (21:23 – 22:46)**
      - (5) Paying Tribute Taxes to Caesar (22:15 – 22)
      - (6) Marriage in the Resurrection (22:23 – 33)
      - ➦ **(7) The Greatest Commandment (22:34 – 40)**
      - (8) Son of David and Lord of David (22:41 – 46)

Main Idea

McKnight has called this "the Jesus creed," which he summarizes in this way: "A spiritually formed person loves God by following Jesus and loves others."[1] He believes it parallels the OT Shema (Deut 6:4 – 9) in its importance for NT Christianity, and he is correct. It lies at the heart of Christian spiritual ethics, defining one's relationship with God (the vertical) and others (the horizontal).

1. Scot McKnight, *The Jesus Creed: Loving God, Loving Others* (Brewster, MA: Paraclete, 2004), viii.

Translation

Matthew 22:34-40

34a	Introduction/Setting	When the Pharisees heard that he had silenced the Sadducees,
b	Action	**they gathered together in one place.**
35a	Challenge	And **one of them, a teacher of law, tested him:**
36a	Question	*"Teacher, what commandment in the law is greatest?"*
37a	Answer	And **Jesus said,**
b		*"'You shall love the Lord your God*
		with your whole heart and
c		*with your whole life and*
d		*with your whole mind.'* (Deut 6:5)
38a		*This is the great and first commandment.*
39a		*The second is like it:*
		'You shall love your neighbor as yourself.' (Lev 19:18)
40a		*All the law and the prophets hang on these two commandments."*

Structure and Literary Form

Matthew once more follows Mark (Mark 12:28–34) but now with significant differences. He omits Mark's "noticing that Jesus had given them a good answer" and adds "tested him" (Matt 22:35 = Mark 12:28) as well as the repetition of the Shema in Mark 12:29. He also omits Mark's positive ending (Mark 12:32–34), where the scribe admits Jesus is right and Jesus concludes, "You are not far from the kingdom of God." Mark makes this a preevangelistic story, and in it Jesus emerges "as the clear winner."[2] Matthew, however, continues the conflict setting, and the opposition develops further. There are two parts to this story, the question of the Pharisees (vv. 34–36) and Jesus' twofold answer (vv. 37–40).

Exegetical Outline

➡ **I. The Question Asked to Test Jesus (22:34–36)**
- A. The silence of the Sadducees (v. 34)
- B. The question regarding the greatest commandment (vv. 35–36)

II. Jesus' Response (22:37–40)
- A. Total love for God (Deut 6:5) (vv. 37–38)
- B. Love for one's neighbor (Lev 19:18) (v. 39)
- C. Conclusion: summarizes the Law and the Prophets (v. 40)

2. France, *Mark*, 476.

Explanation of the Text

22:34 When the Pharisees heard that he had silenced the Sadducees, they gathered together in one place[3] (Οἱ δὲ Φαρισαῖοι ἀκούσαντες ὅτι ἐφίμωσεν τοὺς Σαδδουκαίους συνήχθησαν ἐπὶ τὸ αὐτό). Mark 12:28 mentions only one scribe, while Matthew continues the centrality of the Pharisees in these hostile debates (cf. 21:45; 22:15). The scribe, or "teacher of law," is seen as "one of" the Pharisees in the next verse (which was common, see on 2:4). Matthew also notes that this question is occasioned by Jesus' having silenced the Sadducees, who have no answer to Jesus' brilliant response in the previous debate (preparing for 22:46).

There is some debate as to whether the Pharisees were pleased with Jesus' victory over the Sadducees (McNeile, Hill, Hagner) or not (Schweizer, Davies and Allison). The truth is probably in between: they were pleased that the Sadducean error on the resurrection had been proven, yet unhappy with yet another victory by Jesus. In "they gathered together" (συνήχθησαν) there is likely an intended echo of Ps 2:2, "The kings of the earth rise up and the rulers band together against the Lord and against his anointed."

22:35 And one of them, a teacher of law,[4] **tested him** (καὶ ἐπηρώτησεν εἷς ἐξ αὐτῶν [νομικὸς] πειράζων αὐτόν). Matthew normally uses γραμματεύς for "scribes" (e.g., 2:4; 5:20; 7:29) but here uses "teacher of the law" (νομικός) for the only time in his gospel, probably to emphasize the legal aspect (νομός) of the question. Once again the purpose is to "test" or "tempt" Jesus (as in 16:1; 19:3; 22:18, and for Satan using a similar ploy, 4:1); it is not designed to ascertain truth or to discover whether Jesus is truly of God but is meant to catch Jesus in a legal error. In this case it is difficult to know what the error might be. Such discussions were common (see below), so perhaps they are hoping Jesus will choose a poor answer and show his ignorance.[5]

22:36 "Teacher, what commandment in the law is greatest?" (Διδάσκαλε, ποία ἐντολὴ μεγάλη ἐν τῷ νόμῳ;). Again, they call Jesus "teacher" (cf. 22:16, 24) and want to demonstrate that he is anything but a valid "rabbi" (see on 12:2). On the whole rabbis considered all the commandments equal but still distinguished "light" from "heavy" laws (as Jesus charges in 23:23) and frequently asked which of them is "greatest"[6] or summarizes the others (cf. Mic 6:8; *m. Ḥag.* 1:8; *b. Mak. 24a; b. Ber.* 63a; *b. Šabb.* 31a), e.g., the Decalogue as a whole or obedience to parents or loving one's neighbor (see Keener).

22:37 And Jesus said, "You shall love[7] **the Lord your God"** (ὁ δὲ ἔφη αὐτῷ, Ἀγαπήσεις κύριον τὸν θεόν σου). Jesus quotes the beginning of the Shema (Deut 6:5; the first word of the creed, meaning "hear"). The Shema was recited every morning and evening and summed up Jewish faith and

3. τὸ αὐτό can mean "in the same way" or "at the same time" but in a context like this means "together" or "in one place" (cf. BAGD, 123 [4b]).

4. "Teacher of the law" (νομικός) is missing in f[1] it[e] syr[s] Origen et al., and while the great majority of manuscripts include it, some think it an assimilation to Luke 10:25. However, the strong manuscript evidence for its inclusion makes its presence in the text likely.

5. Davies and Allison, *Matthew*, 3:239, say the lawyer may have "expected Jesus to answer by annulling part of the law (cf. 5:17 – 20) or to denigrate certain statutes."

6. While most assume "greatest" (μεγάλη) is an example of the simple for the superlative, it is also possible that along with "what" (ποία) it means, "What sort of commandment is great in the Torah?" (so Davies and Allison, Luz). While the latter is possible, a superlative sense fits the context better.

7. The future tense here and in v. 39 expresses "the categorical injunctions and prohibitions (negative) in the legal language of the OT" (BDF §362).

practice. As McKnight says, "The Shema outlines a Torah lifestyle for spiritual formation: memorize, recite, instruct, and write out the Torah, and wear *tzitzit* (fringes) to remind themselves of Torah."[8]

22:37 "... with your whole heart and with your whole life and with your whole mind" (ἐν ὅλῃ τῇ καρδίᾳ σου καὶ ἐν ὅλῃ τῇ ψυχῇ σου καὶ ἐν ὅλῃ τῇ διανοίᾳ σου). Mark 12:30 has four nouns (heart, life, mind, strength), while the LXX has three (heart, life, strength). It is difficult to know why Matthew dropped "strength." Perhaps he felt the three presupposed the fourth.[9] All three (LXX, Mark, Matthew) mean that we should love God with our whole being, with every aspect of our life focused on that love. At the same time the rabbis emphasized each one, so that God must be loved with total obedience and devotion stemming from the "heart," with complete surrender of one's "life" to the point of martyrdom if necessary, and with all the thinking processes focused on him (so Luz, Nolland, Davies and Allison).

Notice that it is not just "love God" but "love *the Lord* your God." The object is Yahweh, the covenant God who never leaves or forsakes. Moreover, he is "your" God, so that one's love for him is simply the response of one who has already been loved completely and absolutely.

22:38 "This is the great and first commandment" (αὕτη ἐστὶν ἡ μεγάλη καὶ πρώτη ἐντολή). Loving God is not only the "greatest" commandment but also the most important, "first" in priority and the beginning of all Christian ethics. The command to love God is framed with "great" (μεγάλη, vv. 36, 38), and to it is now added "first" (πρώτη) for emphasis. This is the supreme commandment that has within it all the others. In fact, love for neighbor flows out of it.

22:39 "The second is like it: 'You shall love your neighbor as yourself'" (δευτέρα δὲ ὁμοία αὐτῇ, Ἀγαπήσεις τὸν πλησίον σου ὡς σεαυτόν). This follows Lev 19:18 LXX and is the companion aspect to loving God. One question is whether "second" (δευτέρα) connotes second in number or in importance. Most say unequivocally that it is the former, with "like" (ὁμοία) meaning "equally great or important, just as great as this one" (BAGD, 567). In one sense this is correct, for these are the two commandments that sum up the Torah, with the first fulfilling the first table of the Decalogue (the commands on loving and worshiping God), the second fulfilling the second table of the Decalogue (the ethical commands on relating to others). Yet at the same time, love for others flows out of and is made possible by love of God, both experiencing God's love and returning that love to God. Since that is true, in the previous "render to Caesar/God," loving God is the higher sphere that encompasses the other.

Leviticus 19:18 has been quoted twice before (5:43; 19:19, both only in Matthew) and so is an essential part of Matthean ethics. The followers of Christ cannot claim to love or serve God if they are not loving those around them. "As yourself" (ὡς σεαυτόν), as in 19:19, means to have as deep and sacrificial a love for those around you as you have for yourself. This is not a "self-disregard" or "other-centeredness" that involves denial of self (that is true of our relationship with God) but rather a consideration and care for others as being part of yourself (see Nolland).

22:40 "All the law and the prophets hang on these two commandments" (ἐν ταύταις ταῖς δυσὶν ἐντολαῖς ὅλος ὁ νόμος κρέμαται καὶ οἱ προφῆται). κρεμάννυμι means to "hang, depend"; "as a door hangs on its hinges, so the whole OT hangs on these

8. McKnight, *Jesus Creed*, 7.

9. Nolland, *Matthew*, 911, believes "all your energy" is omitted to focus on the "inner dispositions" so that the physical "energy" can be left to loving one's neighbor.

two commandments" (BAGD, 450). Donaldson calls "hang" a "rabbinic formulation" that means these two commands fulfill and provide a deeper understanding of Torah.[10] Love for God and others is thus the foundation of OT religion and ethics and the fulcrum that links OT and NT ethics.

It is commonly recognized that this is fulfillment language, and that these two complete and bring into fulfillment all of Scripture, "nothing less than a 'hermeneutic program' for the understanding and application of the law and the prophets."[11] In other words, following God in every area of life flows out of love for God, and that then makes it possible to love others, which itself is the basis for all relationships and ethical living on this earth.

Theology in Application

This is closely linked with the Sermon on the Mount, which itself is framed by "the Law and the Prophets" (5:17; 7:12, so Nolland). So Jesus here sums up what it means to know God and be his follower. As noted above, this provides the vertical (God-oriented) and horizontal (others-oriented) poles of the Christian life.

1. We Must Love God with Every Fiber of Our Being

To fulfill this principle involves knowing God, obeying all his commandments (cf. 28:20a), and committing totally to him. "Love" is much more than an emotion; it involves absolute surrender and selfless giving. Carson discusses five different ways the Bible describes God's love: (1) The Father's love for the Son and vice versa; (2) God's providential love for his creation; (3) his salvific love for the fallen world; (4) his special love for his elect; and (5) his conditional love for his people based on their obedience.[12] Our love for God is the result of experiencing him at all five levels.

2. Loving Our Neighbors as Part of Our Love for God

We cannot pretend that we love God if we harbor prejudice, bitterness, or resentment in our hearts toward others. The vertical love for God must be acted out in the horizontal love for others. As Bruner says, "whenever we are asked the *main* responsibility (of the church), Christians should usually give *two* answers. The spiritual and the social cannot be separated."[13] This means social concern for the poor, friendship for all around, as well as community love for fellow Christians. The lat-

10. Terence L. Donaldson, "The Law That Hangs (Matthew 22:40): Rabbinic Formulation and Matthean Social World," *CBQ* 57 (1995): 689 – 709.

11. Hagner, *Matthew 14 – 28*, 648, drawing from Birger Gerhardsson, "The Hermeneutic Program in Matthew 22:37 – 40," in *Jew, Greeks, and Christians* (ed. R. Hammerton-Kelly and R. Scroggs; Leiden: Brill, 1976), 129 – 50. Carson, "Matthew," 465, corrects an overstatement of this on the part of Gerhardsson and others that the love commandment virtually abrogates all the other laws. Rather, this demands a "heart religion" that makes obedience of the other laws possible.

12. D. A. Carson, *The Difficult Doctrine of the Love of God* (Wheaton: Crossway, 2000), 16 – 20.

13. Bruner, *Matthew 13 – 28*, 414.

ter two are represented well in Gal 6:10: "Let us do good to all people, especially to those who belong to the family of believers."

Luz traces the development of this idea in Jewish interpretation.[14] In the context of Leviticus "neighbor" meant the Jewish people, then with Israel in the land it was expanded to include the aliens living in Canaan. Then it was applied to proselytes, but only in Jesus is it used for love of one's enemy (Matt 5:43 – 48) and for all humanity (here). This is why we can say that all ethics flows out of this command.

14. Luz, *Matthew 21 – 28*, 83.

CHAPTER 97

Matthew 22:41 – 46

Literary Context

In the final pericope of the section (21:23 – 22:46), Jesus for the second time (after the triumphal entry) reveals himself as the Messiah and reverses the messianic secret. Jesus has shown himself to be the authoritative teacher, and now he turns the tables on the Pharisees, moving to the offensive. Before, they had asked him their trick questions; now he asks them a question that will illuminate the greatest truth of them all — his true identity.

VI. The Movement to the Cross (19:1 – 25:46)
- **A. Jesus' Deeds: Opposition and Discipleship (19:1 – 22:46)**
  - **2. Beginning Events of Passion Week (21:1 – 22:46)**
    - **b. Controversies in the Temple Court (21:23 – 22:46)**
      - (5) Paying Tribute Taxes to Caesar (22:15 – 22)
      - (6) Marriage in the Resurrection (22:23 – 33)
      - (7) The Greatest Commandment (22:34 – 40)
      - ➦ **(8) Son of David and Lord of David (22:41 – 46)**

Main Idea

Jesus is the Messiah and more; he is the royal Messiah, the Son of David, but he is also the Son of God, David's Lord. This is high Christology and climaxes the section with the nature of this Jesus who has so decimated his opponents on points of law. It constitutes the second time in which he overcomes his "messianic secret" and reveals himself to the public as "Lord" of all.

Translation

Matthew 22:41-46

41a	Introduction	Now when the Pharisees were gathered together,
b		**Jesus asked them a question, saying,**
42a	General Question	[1] *"What do you think about the Messiah?*
b	Specific Question	[2] *Whose son is he?"*
43a	Answer	**They responded,**
b		*"Of David"*
c	Question	**Jesus asked them,**
d	Riddle	*"How then does David by the Spirit call him 'Lord,' saying,*
44a	OT Quotation	*'The Lord said to my Lord,*
b		*'Sit at my right hand*
c		*until I place your enemies*
		under your feet.' (Ps 110:1)
45a	Restatement of 43d	*If therefore David calls him 'Lord,' how is he his son?"*
46a	Reaction/Conclusion	**No one was able to answer him even with a word,**
b		nor **from that day did anyone dare any longer to ask him anything.**

Structure and Literary Form

Again, we have a rabbinic dialogue on a point of exegesis, this time on Christology. Matthew once more follows Mark (Mark 12:35 – 37a) but with several points of difference. Only Matthew centers on the Pharisees (he omits the temple setting of Mark 12:35), and only he has the symmetry of the two double questions. Finally, Matthew adds the climactic statement that no one dared challenge Jesus again (found earlier in Mark 12:34 and Luke 20:40).

There are two main sections, each with a double question, with the τί questions introducing the question of the identity of the Messiah (vv. 41 – 42) and the πῶς questions providing the answer regarding his identity as David's Lord (vv. 43 – 45). Then there is the conclusion (actually to the whole division of controversy narratives) that Jesus' opponents dared not again ask him questions (v. 46).

Exegetical Outline

➦ **I. The Identity of the Messiah (22:41 – 42)**
- A. The general question regarding the Messiah (v. 42a)
- B. The specific question about sonship (v. 42b)

II. The Answer regarding the Messiah's Identity (22:43 – 45)
- A. David calls him "Lord" (Ps 110:1) (vv. 43 – 44)
- B. He is David's Lord and not just his son (v. 45)

III. Conclusion: No One Dared Ask Further Questions (22:46)

Explanation of the Text

22:41 Now when the Pharisees were gathered together, Jesus asked them a question (Συνηγμένων δὲ τῶν Φαρισαίων ἐπηρώτησεν αὐτοὺς ὁ Ἰησοῦς). Jesus uses a temporal genitive absolute ("when the Pharisees were gathered together") to tie this closely to 22:34 (also on the Pharisees "gathering together"). As there this is again a hostile council, but with a significant difference: now the Pharisees are on the defensive and have little to say. There they asked the legal question, but now Jesus goes on the offensive and asks his question.

22:42 ... saying, "What do you think about the Messiah?" (λέγων, Τί ὑμῖν δοκεῖ περὶ τοῦ Χριστοῦ;). Jesus begins with his typical "what do you think" (Τί ὑμῖν δοκεῖ; see 17:25; 18:12; 21:28), asking for a careful response on a serious issue. For Jewish messianic expectations, see on 1:1; 2:4. Jesus begins with the general issue. It is difficult to know how rife the messianic speculations were in Jesus' day, but the presence of all the messianic pretenders and the many references in intertestamental literature (see on 1:1) shows there was a great deal of interest.[1] So Jesus' question is a valid issue, and it would elicit real interest.

22:42 – 43a "Whose son is he?" They responded,[2] "Of David" (τίνος υἱός ἐστιν; λέγουσιν αὐτῷ, Τοῦ Δαυίδ). The most common aspect of first-century messianic belief was the Davidic overtones, with the Messiah a royal personage who would deliver Israel from her enemies after the pattern of David's victories.[3] This major theme stems from the OT (2 Sam 7:11b – 16; Ps 89:4, 36 – 37; Isa 9:6 – 7; 11:1 – 16; Jer 23:5; 33:15 – 16) and intertestamental literature (Sir 47:11; 48:15; *4 Ezra* 12:32; *Pss. Sol.* 17:21; 4QFlor 1:11 – 13) and is more frequent in Matthew (1:1, 20; 2:4; 9:27; 12:23; 15:22; 20:30 – 31; 21:9, 15) than in any other gospel. It is possible that Jesus had a double meaning, hinting that the answer was "Son of God" (so Davies and Allison). Still, the Pharisees' response was to be expected.

22:43b Jesus asked them, "How then does David by the Spirit call him 'Lord,' saying" (λέγει αὐτοῖς, Πῶς οὖν Δαυὶδ ἐν πνεύματι καλεῖ αὐτὸν κύριον λέγων). Jesus introduces a valid exegetical question, using "the rabbinic method of setting up an antinomy and then resolving it."[4] It was a common rabbinic ploy to harmonize two seemingly contradictory texts; here Jesus harmonizes two seemingly contradictory messianic ideas: Given that the Messiah is David's "son" (v. 42), how then can the great king David address him as "Lord"? In other words, how can his son at the same time be his Lord?

No patriarch, let alone the king, would call his son "my lord"; it would be the other way around. Moreover, David was speaking this "by the Spirit," i.e., under divine inspiration (cf. 2 Sam 23:2 at the last words of David, "The Spirit of the LORD spoke through me, his word was on my tongue"). Jesus is not denying that the Messiah is David's Son — that is attested too frequently in Matthew (see on the previous verse). Rather, he is saying that the Messiah, as well as being David's son, is more than David's son — he is David's Lord. As Carson says, "What Jesus does is synthesize the concept of a human Messiah in David's line with

1. See *DNTB*, 937 – 39.

2. Here and in v. 43 Matthew employs a historical present, used dramatically to make the action more vivid, see Wallace, 526 – 32.

3. See Bruce Chilton, "Jesus *ben David*: Reflections on the *Davidssohnfrage*," *JSNT* 14 (1982): 88 – 112, who adds overtones of wisdom, exorcism, and healing to the messianic aspects.

4. Blomberg, *Matthew*, 336.

the concept of a divine Messiah who transcends human limitations."[5]

22:44 "The Lord said to my Lord" (Εἶπεν κύριος τῷ κυρίῳ μου). Jesus' proof lies in his quote from Ps 110:1 (LXX 109:1)[6] that he introduced into Christian thought and became the most oft-quoted OT passage in the NT and the foundation passage for the exaltation of Jesus (cf. Mark 14:62 par.; Acts 2:33 – 35; 5:31; 7:55 – 56; Rom 8:34; 1 Cor 15:25; Eph 1:20; 2:6; Col 3:1; Heb 1:3, 13; 8:1; 10:12 – 13; 1 Pet 3:22; Rev 3:21).[7] Moreover, it was understood messianically in the time of Jesus; although most references come from a later time (*b. Sanh.* 38b; *Gen. Rab.* 85:9; *Num. Rab.* 18:23), it is likely that these references reflect pre – AD 70 ideas.[8] The use of "to my Lord" (τῷ κυρίῳ μου) in the text implies "Yahweh," speaking to the one seated next to him on the throne, suggesting Jesus' deity.

22:44 " 'Sit at my right hand until I place your enemies under your feet' " (Κάθου ἐκ δεξιῶν μου, ἕως ἂν θῶ τοὺς ἐχθρούς σου ὑποκάτω τῶν ποδῶν σου;). Jesus has just spoke of "the Lord your God" (22:37), and "your Lord" here as enthroned at God's right hand must partake of that transcendent status (so Gundry, Keener). If David is indeed the author of the psalm (as the superscription states, and there is no reason to doubt it), then "to my Lord" (τῷ κυρίῳ μου) cannot be David himself but must refer to the Messiah. So the quote establishes two things: the royal glory and power of the Messiah ("sit at my right hand") and the victory of the Messiah over his enemies (as demonstrated in Jesus' victory in the controversy narratives of 21:23 – 22:46).

22:45 "If therefore David calls him 'Lord,' how is he his son?" (εἰ οὖν Δαυὶδ καλεῖ αὐτὸν κύριον, πῶς υἱὸς αὐτοῦ ἐστιν;). Jesus then continues with the condition of fact "if" (εἰ, demonstrating the truth of the assertion), which is framed by questions making the same point that is proven by the Psalms passage — the Messiah is more than David's son, for as the one enthroned at Yahweh's side he is also David's Lord. Thus the concept of Messiah is elevated "from that of a special human being to one who uniquely manifests the presence of God," thereby justifying "the extravagant claims made by Jesus, or concerning him, earlier in the Gospel (e.g., 10:32 – 33, 40; 11:27; 14:33; 16:16)."[9] The two ideas come together in Peter's confession that Jesus is "the Messiah, the Son of the living God" (16:16). It is important to realize that the Pharisees can answer neither question posed by Jesus.

22:46 No one was able[10] to answer him even with a word (καὶ οὐδεὶς ἐδύνατο ἀποκριθῆναι αὐτῷ λόγον). Mark (Mark 12:34) and Luke (Luke 20:40) place this statement earlier, but Matthew wants to conclude the entire controversy narrative (21:33 – 22:46) with this. Not only are Jesus' opponents unable to answer his question of vv. 44 – 45, they, like the Sadducees in v. 34, have been silenced entirely.

22:46 ... nor from that day did anyone dare[11] any longer to ask him anything (οὐδὲ ἐτόλμησέν

5. Carson, "Matthew," 468.

6. This differs from the LXX only in the absence of the article before "Lord" (κύριος) and the replacement of ὑποπόδιον ("footstool") with ὑποκάτω ("under").

7. For full discussion see David M. Hay, *Glory at the Right Hand: Psalm 110 in Early Christian Literature* (SBLMS 18; Nashville: Abingdon, 1973).

8. See Hay, *Glory at the Right Hand*, 27 – 33; Davies and Allison, *Matthew*, 3:254 contra Luz, *Matthew 21 – 28*, 89.

9. Hagner, *Matthew 14 – 28*, 651.

10. The imperfect "was able" (ἐδύνατο) is used dramatically to continue the vivid picture of an ongoing debate between Jesus and his adversaries.

11. The switch to aorists in this clause looks at the time following as a single whole and places this action in the background (see Porter, *Idioms*, 23 – 25) as the result of Jesus' victories.

τις ἀπ' ἐκείνης τῆς ἡμέρας ἐπερωτῆσαι αὐτὸν οὐκέτι). The Pharisees cannot even "answer ... with a word." The debates are over, and only Jesus is standing at the end; the leaders are figuratively "under his feet." "From that day" on, the leaders disappear from the narrative and only reappear at Jesus' trial. The discourse of chs. 23 – 25 is addressed to the crowds and the disciples, though the leaders certainly provide the subject matter of ch. 23.

Theology in Application

This is one of the climactic points of Matthean Christology. Jesus is now uncovering the "messianic secret" in a public setting and going beyond the triumphal entry by showing that he transcends his earthly role as descendent of David and embraces his heavenly role as Son of God and "Lord," stated clearly in the early creed of Rom 1:3 – 4, "who as to his earthly life was a descendant of David, and who through the Spirit of holiness was appointed the Son of God in power by his resurrection from the dead." Critical scholars at times have hesitated to ascribe deity to this passage, for there is separation between Lord/Yahweh and Lord/Messiah in the Ps 110:1 passage. However, Bruner rightly quotes Luther on this:[12]

> "'Sit,' says God to him, not at my feet, not over my head, but next to me, as high as I sit.... [But] sitting next to God, what else is that than being also God? For God is so jealous for his honor that as He said himself, Isa 42:8, he will give it to no other.... And yet here, says the Psalmist, sits one who is like Him. From this it follows that He must be God.

The problem today is slightly different. It is not so much in our churches that members deny the deity of Christ[13] as that they ignore it in their lives. One of the sad results of the denigration of theology in the popular church is the tendency to lower Jesus to the status of friend and companion rather than of cosmic Lord and "very God of very God" (the Christology of the Nicene Creed). It is time to worship Jesus as Lord with a new depth.

12. Bruner, *Matthew 13 – 28*, 424.

13. Though see Wilkins, *Matthew*, 740, where he notes the book he helped edit, *Jesus Under Fire: Modern Scholarship Reinvents the Historical Jesus* (ed. M. J. Wilkins and J. P. Moreland; Grand Rapids: Zondervan, 1995), which responds to the attempt of the Jesus Seminar to challenge the historical veracity of the gospels.

CHAPTER 98

Matthew 23:1 – 12

Introduction to Woes upon the Leaders (Matthew 23)

The issue as to whether ch. 23 belongs to the previous or following section has already been discussed (see at 19:1). There it was decided that this chapter serves as a transition, both concluding chs. 19 – 22 (indicting the leaders for their opposition) and introducing chs. 24 – 25 (providing the evidence for the verdict against the nation and its leaders in the Olivet Discourse). As such it forms the first of two parts to the discourse of chs. 23 – 25. There is a certain symmetry between 23:1 – 25:46 and the Sermon on the Mount. These two frame Matthew and are of similar length, with the woes of ch. 23 balancing the beatitudes of 5:3 – 12. Some go so far as to say that in Q these may have been together (cf. Luke 6:20 – 26, so Keener), but these differ significantly from the woes of Luke 6:24 – 26 and are closer to Luke 11:37 – 54.

The strongly negative cast of the chapter has led some to believe the historical Jesus could not have delivered such a scathing rebuke (Hill, Beare). It has indeed fueled some of the anti-Semitic tragedies of history like the pogroms and the Holocaust. Luz says, "With its woes and its unjust wholesale judgments about scribes and Pharisees, Matthew 23 is 'the unloveliest chapter in the Gospel' … we share the shame for what has taken place in the history of Christian-Jewish relations, of which the history of the interpretation of Matthew 23 is also part."[1] While Luz is correct in the second part of his statement, it is a *misuse* of this text that accounts for anti-Semitism.

It is important to recognize how conventional Jesus' language is here. Parallels are shown by L. T. Johnson and Davies and Allison, who provide an illuminating chart of every critical comment Jesus makes in ch. 23, showing parallels in ancient Jewish and Greco-Roman literature.[2] The hypocrisy of many Pharisees, for instance, is discussed in *b. Soṭah* 22b; *y. Ber.* 9:5; and 4QpNah. This would not have

1. Luz, *Matthew 21 – 28*, 94, with the quote from Claude G. Montefiore, *The Synoptic Gospels*, 2 vols. (New York: Ktav, 1968), 2:96.

2. See Luke Timothy Johnson, "The New Testament's Anti-Jewish Slander and Conventions of Ancient Rhetoric," *JBL* 108 (1989): 419 – 41; Davies and Allison, *Matthew*, 3:258 – 60.

startled the original readers as being overly critical, nor would it have been taken as invective against all Pharisees. As Albright and Mann say,

> This chapter does not deny at all that there were many — probably most — Pharisees who were devout, God-fearing men, devoted to Israel, its religion, and its Lord. Nevertheless the chapter stands as clear warning that there are varieties of impiety and idolatry which are not confined to those who fashion graven images.[3]

Hauerwas rightly calls this the result of Jesus' "unrelenting concern for holiness" that makes him "the sworn enemy of hypocrisy."[4]

In short there is little reason to doubt that Jesus could have said these words. It is common to believe Matthew created much of this as part of his polemic against Judaism in his post – AD 70 situation, yet it is hard to see why this is necessary or what this accomplishes. Everything in Matthew is meant to speak to the church in his day, yet that does not mean he created the material. As Carson says:

> To read Matthew 23 as little more than Matthew's pique about A.D. 85 is not only without adequate historical and literary justification but also fails dismally to understand the historical Jesus, who not only taught his followers to love their enemies ... but proclaimed that he came not to bring peace but a sword (10:34) and presented himself as eschatological judge (e.g., 7:21 – 23; 25:31 – 46).[5]

It is widely recognized that there are three parts to this chapter, each with a distinctive audience and direction in mind: vv. 1 – 12 (to the crowds and disciples, warning them about the scribes and Pharisees), vv. 13 – 36 (to the leaders, denouncing them with seven woes), and vv. 37 – 39 (to Jerusalem, lamenting her imminent judgment).

Literary Context

Jesus has been opposed by the Pharisees and scribes throughout Matthew, and he has just sparred with them over rabbinic issues as they have tried to trick him into revealing his inadequacy as a teacher. Now Jesus begins a section in which he reveals their failure before God. Here he shows their hypocrisy and pride and contrasts that with the humility God demands from his people.

3. Albright and Mann, *Matthew*, 283.
4. Hauerwas, *Matthew*, 195.
5. Carson, "Matthew," 470.

Main Idea

The major thrust in this section is the contrast between the pride (and resultant hypocrisy) of the leaders and the humility (and resultant servanthood) demanded of Jesus' followers. The key is how each group conducts itself before others, the one to be seen and glorified by all, the other to serve and leave the exaltation up to God.

Translation

(See next page.)

Structure and Literary Form

This polemical discourse is unique to Matthew, with three parallels: v. 4 with Luke 11:46 (a Q saying), vv. 6 – 7a with Mark 12:38 – 39 (and Luke 20:46 – 47, thus a triple tradition saying), and v. 12 with Luke 14:11; 18:14 (a Q saying). This does not mean that Jesus could not have delivered this message himself (see Carson), but still, for Matthew it is more than a diatribe against Judaism; it is a warning against hypocrisy in the church.[6] There are two sections here, vv. 1 – 7 (warning about the hypocrisy and pride of the leaders), and vv. 8 – 12 (a call to a life of servanthood and humility).

Exegetical Outline

➡ **I. Warning about the Deeds of the Scribes and Pharisees (23:1 – 7)**
   A. What they have done right (vv. 1 – 3a)
   B. What they have done wrong (vv. 3b – 7)

6. See Benedict T. Viviano, "Social World and Community Leadership: The Case of Matthew 23:1 – 12, 34," *JSNT* 39 (1990): 3 – 21; Luz, *Matthew 21 – 28*, 110 – 11; Bruner, *Matthew 13 – 28*, 429; Keener, *Matthew*, 537.

Matthew 23:1-12

1a	Introduction	**Then Jesus spoke to the crowds and his disciples, saying,**
2a	Assertion	*"The teachers of law and the Pharisees sit on Moses' seat.*
3a	Exhortation	*So practice and keep everything they tell you,*
b	Warning	*but do not practice what they do,*
c	Basis #1	*[1] for they do not practice what they say.*
4a	Basis #2	*[2] They bind heavy burdens and*
		place them on people's shoulders,
b		*but they themselves are not willing*
		to lift even their finger
		to move them.
5a	Basis #3	*[3] They perform all their deeds in order to be seen by people,*
b	Basis #1 for 5a	*(i) for they make their phylacteries wide and their tassels long.*
6a	Basis #2 for 5a	*(ii) And they love the seats of honor at banquets and*
b		*the important seats in the synagogues,*
7a	Basis #3 for 5a	*(iii) as well as greetings in the marketplaces and*
b		*to be called 'rabbi' by people.*
8a	Exhortation (Contrast 7b)	*[A] But you should not be called 'rabbi,'*
b	Basis	*[B] for there is only one who is your teacher,*
		and you are all brothers and sisters.
9a	Exhortation	*[A] And do not call anyone 'father' on earth,*
b	Basis	*[B] for there is only one, your heavenly Father.*
10a	Exhortation	*[A] Nor should you be called 'instructor,'*
b	Basis	*[B] because there is one*
		who is your instructor, the Christ.
11a	Exhortation	*But the greatest among you must be your servant.*
12a	Basis/Aphorism	*Those who exalt themselves will be humbled,*
b		*and those who humble themselves will be exalted."*

1. Hypocrisy (v. 3b)
2. The heavy burden of their teaching (v. 4)
3. Love for the praise of others (vv. 5 – 7)
   a. The size of their religious dress (v. 5)
   b. Demand for the seats of honor (v. 6)
   c. Love for respectful address by others (v. 7)

II. Admonition for Proper Behavior (23:8 – 12)

A. Titles to avoid: rabbi, father, teacher (vv. 8 – 10)

B. Lifestyle to embrace (vv. 11 – 12)
   1. Servanthood (v. 11)
   2. Humility (v. 12)

Explanation of the Text

23:1 Then Jesus spoke to the crowds and his disciples (Τότε ὁ Ἰησοῦς ἐλάλησεν τοῖς ὄχλοις καὶ τοῖς μαθηταῖς αὐτοῦ). As in the Sermon on the Mount (5:1) and the Parable Discourse (13:2, 10), Jesus addresses the crowds (to warn them against the leaders) and his disciples (to warn them against committing similar sins). It is common to see them as symbolizing various groups,[7] but it is best to see simply the original historical groups (Davies and Allison).

23:2 ... saying, "The teachers of law and the Pharisees sit on Moses' seat" (λέγων, Ἐπὶ τῆς Μωϋσέως καθέδρας ἐκάθισαν οἱ γραμματεῖς καὶ οἱ Φαρισαῖοι). Jesus begins with a positive statement. The scribes and Pharisees are often lumped together in Matthew (5:20; 12:38; 15:1; 23:13), probably because they often acted in concert and many belonged to both groups. The Pharisees held considerable influence in first-century Judaism and were considered the legal experts of the day (cf. Josephus, *Ant.* 13:288 – 98; 400 – 432; 17:41 – 45).[8]

There have been many interpretations of "Moses' seat,"[9] three of which stand out. (1) They could be stone seats on which synagogue presidents and authoritative interpreters sat,[10] but the examples are after the NT period. (2) They could be stone receptacles for Scripture scrolls, but no one ever "sat" on those. (3) This could be a figurative image for the authority the Pharisees claimed as interpreters of the Torah of Moses (see Davies and Allison, Nolland, France).

Complicating this is the aorist tense "sit" (ἐκάθισαν); all attempts to see this as a past tense (as if this relates an authority that has now passed) fail, and it is best to label it a gnomic aorist stating a general claim by the leaders (see Garland, Nolland).[11] Of the three options, the third is definitely correct, but it could be combined with one of the two other options (e.g., Witherington takes one and three). The meaning is that the Pharisees considered themselves to be the successors of Moses as official interpreters of Torah.

23:3 So practice and keep everything they tell you (πάντα οὖν ὅσα ἐὰν εἴπωσιν ὑμῖν ποιήσατε καὶ τηρεῖτε). This is another difficult statement, for it seems to contradict the rest of the chapter as well as earlier criticisms of the Pharisees (e.g., 15:1 – 20; 16:6, 11 – 12). The language is strong. The two verbs[12] relate to everyday practice and to ongoing obedience, and the strong "everything" (πάντα ὅσα ἐὰν) seems to mean "every" area of life. There are several options:

1. this statement recognizes the claim of authority by the ordained teachers, but vv. 3b – 4 proceed to dispute that claim (Hill)

7. For instance, Gundry, *Matthew*, 453 — Jewish Christians and Gentile converts; Garland, *Matthew 23*, 36 – 37 — non-Christian Jews and Christian leaders.

8. See Steven Mason, "Pharisaic Dominance Before 70 CE and the Gospels' Hypocrisy Charge (Matt 23:2 – 3)," *HTR* 83 (1990): 363 – 81; Stephen Westerholme, "Pharisees," *DJG*, 610 – 11.

9. Mark A. Powell, "Do and Keep What Moses Says (Matthew 23:2 – 7)," *JBL* 114 (1995): 419 – 35, lists ten options, believing that it refers to their authority as those who controlled access to the Torah scrolls and interpreted them for the people. The genitive "of Moses" (τῆς Μωϋσέως, placed before the noun for emphasis) could be subjective ("Moses sat on it") but is most likely a simple possessive as in the translation.

10. See E. L. Sukenik, *Ancient Synagogues in Palestine and Greece* (London: Oxford, 1934), 57 – 61.

11. Wallace, 562, agrees, calling this a "timeless, general fact."

12. Note the aorist "practice" (ποιήσατε) followed by the present "keep" (τηρεῖτε). Likely the aorist "practice" refers to the general reality and the present "keep" to the ongoing action that defines the practice. The aorist could also be a dramatic use with present force (see Porter, *Idioms*, 36).

2. people are to obey only to the extent that the teachers truly interpret the Torah (Schlatter, Plummer, Gundry, Morris)
3. it is sarcasm or irony, intended to show the futility of following their teaching (France, Carson)
4. it reflects only earlier tradition, not the time of Matthew's church (Beare)
5. it reflects Matthew's day and was intended to satisfy Jewish opponents and avoid a Jewish-Christian split (Schweizer, Hummel)
6. the purpose is to read v. 3a in light of v. 3b — the teachers talk the talk (v. 3a, so approval only in principle) but do not walk the walk (v. 3b) (McNeile, Garland, Hagner, Blomberg)

The two best options are the third and sixth, for the others do not fit the language of v. 3; of these the last is probably the best. The Pharisees and scribes know the truth (v. 3a) but fail to live it (v. 3b).

23:3 But do not practice what they do, for they do not practice what they say (κατὰ δὲ τὰ ἔργα αὐτῶν μὴ ποιεῖτε· λέγουσιν γὰρ καὶ οὐ ποιοῦσιν). TNIV says it well, "they do not practice what they preach." They handle the law correctly, but their understanding goes no further than head knowledge. It is not followed by the way they live. The present tense prohibition "do not practice" (μὴ ποιεῖτε) means "at no time" follow their practices (lit., "on the basis of their works"). In the Sermon on the Mount Jesus demanded that the citizens of the kingdom let their "light shine" in "good works" (5:16; cf. 15:7 – 9; Rom 2:19 – 23).

23:4 They bind heavy[13] burdens and place them on people's shoulders (δεσμεύουσιν δὲ φορτία βαρέα καὶ ἐπιτιθέασιν ἐπὶ τοὺς ὤμους τῶν ἀνθρώπων). Not only are the deeds of the Pharisees out of keeping with their teaching, but they also go beyond Moses in placing "heavy burdens" (the present tenses again stress the continuous nature of their actions) on the shoulders of their followers (δεσμεύουσιν, to "tie up" in bundles or with a load, BAGD). The image is similar to that of the "yoke" (placed on oxen) in 11:28 – 30, and indeed there is an implied contrast between the "easy yoke" of Jesus in 11:30 and the "heavy burden" of the Pharisees here.

This is almost certainly a reference to the oral tradition developed by the Pharisees. They tried to "build a fence around the law" and protect it by adding further rules so that people would not inadvertently break the Torah regulations (so Grundmann, Garland, Hagner, Schnackenburg; contra Gundry, who takes this of attempts to win praise from people). The Pharisees add rule after rule on purity laws or Sabbaths or holy days, and they become a real "yoke" or "burden" around the shoulders of the people who have to follow these complex rules.[14] Davies and Allison say these are not "heavy" because they are harder or more numerous (cf. 5:20, which says our "righteousness" must "surpass" theirs) but because their system was deficient in justice and mercy and because of the contrast with Jesus' "easy yoke."[15] Yet they admit that the purity laws of the Pharisees were especially toilsome on the people, and it seems that

13. "And difficult to bear" (καὶ δυσβάστακτα) is present in B D K W Θ Byz et al. but missing in L f^1 892 $it^{a,b,e,h}$ $syr^{h,pal}$ et al. While it could have been omitted due to homoioteleuton (where the eye skips a phrase between two καί connectives), it is probably best to follow Metzger (*Textual Commentary*, 59 – 60) in seeing this as a later assimilation to Luke 11:46 and so not original to Matthew (so also Carson, Hagner, Davies and Allison, Nolland; contra Morris).

14. Interestingly, Qumran had the opposite complaint, calling the Pharisees "the seekers of smooth things" (CD 1:18; 4QpNah 3 – 4.1.2) because in light of the Essenic monastic approach to life, they made the Torah too easy and were too accommodating to change! See Anthony J. Saldarini, "Pharisees," *ABD*, 5:301.

15. Davies and Allison, *Matthew*, 3:272.

both the number and the difficulty of these oral laws are part of the equation.

23:4 ... but they themselves are not willing to lift even their finger to move them (αὐτοὶ δὲ τῷ δακτύλῳ αὐτῶν οὐ θέλουσιν κινῆσαι αὐτά). Emphatic "themselves" (αὐτοί) emphasizes their guilt. This contrasts further with 11:28 – 30, where the gentle Jesus asks the burdened to "come to me ... and I will give you rest." With the present tense "willing" (θέλουσιν) Jesus is saying their unwillingness to help is an ongoing problem. As Luz points out, this takes on a moral dimension: "the Lord intentionally does not say, 'they cannot,' but 'they will not.' "[16] The imagery is that of a taskmaster who places load after load on the shoulders of his workmen but then does nothing to ease their load or help move the burden. The Pharisees will not do even the smallest thing ("lift their finger") to ease the burden. "They have multiplied 'the number of ways in which a man may offend God,' but they have failed in helping him to please God."[17] The rest of the chapter will elaborate on this.

23:5 They perform all their deeds in order to be seen by people (πάντα δὲ τὰ ἔργα αὐτῶν ποιοῦσιν πρὸς τὸ θεαθῆναι τοῖς ἀνθρώποις). Nolland points out the linguistic similarities between this and 6:1 ("Take care that you don't do your righteous deeds before others in order to be seen by them"), which introduces the problem of "ostentatious almsgiving, prayer, and fasting" in 6:1 – 18.[18] "All" (πάς) dominates (vv. 3, 5) as Jesus uses rabbinic hyperbole to emphasize the serious problem of hypocrisy. Everything the scribes and Pharisees do (vv. 5 – 7 provide illustrations) is calculated to produce (with "in order" [πρὸς τό] introducing a purpose clause) the praise of others. This develops further "they do not practice what they say" from v. 3. Instead of providing a model to ease the burdens they have imposed on others, the leaders orchestrate "all their deeds" for attention.

23:5 For they make their phylacteries wide and their tassels long (πλατύνουσιν γὰρ τὰ φυλακτήρια αὐτῶν καὶ μεγαλύνουσιν τὰ κράσπεδα). Their ostentatious self-concern is exemplified in the way they dress, making their adherence to Torah obvious by enlarging the accoutrements of piety. The phylacteries were small leather boxes (called *tefellin*) containing passages of Scripture (usually Exod 13:1 – 16; Deut 6:4 – 9; 11:13 – 21) and worn on the forehead and left arm (cf. Exod 13:9, 16; Deut 6:8; 11:18) to remind the people of their faithfulness to Torah.[19] The tassels were blue or white cords worn at the four corners of the hem of the outer robe (in accordance with Num 15:37 – 41; Deut 22:12), also as a reminder to obey the commands of Torah (Jesus likely wore them in 9:20; 14:36). The leaders often made the boxes larger (some think it means they wore them more often than required) and the tassels longer so their piety would be noticed and lauded by others. So these actually cause them to disobey Torah (by elevating themselves) rather than obeying it.

23:6 And they love the seats of honor at banquets and the important seats in the synagogues (φιλοῦσιν δὲ τὴν πρωτοκλισίαν ἐν τοῖς δείπνοις καὶ τὰς πρωτοκαθεδρίας ἐν ταῖς συναγωγαῖς). In

16. Luz, *Matthew 21 – 28*, 103.

17. Garland, *Matthew 23*, 51, quote from T. W. Manson, *Sayings of Jesus* (London: SCM, 1949), 101. He notes the many (e.g., Bornkamm, Grundmann, Schweizer) who try to avoid the implication that the Pharisees don't try to help others by interpreting this to say the scribes do not follow their own injunctions but find loopholes to avoid the implications. However, this does not fit the wording ("moving" a burden), the context, or the contrast with 11:28 – 30.

18. Nolland, *Matthew*, 925.

19. For background see Jeffrey H. Tigay, "On the Term Phylacteries (Matt 23:5)," *HTR* 72 (1979): 45 – 53.

the ancient world the order of seating had important social implications, as those nearer the host had greater status. The chief seats (or benches) in the synagogues are those up front near the speaker and the Torah scrolls. Again, the point is status in the community. Things are not that different in our day. Such things as power dressing, placement of furniture in the office, etc., are all designed with the same thing in mind: power and authority over others.

23:7 ... as well as greetings in the marketplaces and to be called "rabbi" by people (καὶ τοὺς ἀσπασμοὺς ἐν ταῖς ἀγοραῖς καὶ καλεῖσθαι ὑπὸ τῶν ἀνθρώπων, Ῥαββί). These are not friendly greetings in the spirit of comradeship but signs of respect by those who consider the Pharisees to be superior. In all these the issue is to be considered by everyone around as being important. "Rabbi" (ῥαββί) was not a technical title of sacred office until the second century, but it was emerging as a title of respect in the time of Jesus.[20] The term indicated a revered teacher, and the whole village was expected to show deference to such an elevated personage, even greater respect than to their parents (see Keener). The scribes and Pharisees were guilty of pride and wanted everyone to acknowledge how important they were.

23:8 But you should not be called "rabbi" (ὑμεῖς δὲ μὴ κληθῆτε, Ῥαββί). In the next five verses, Jesus turns from the leaders to his followers, telling them how they should conduct themselves. Schlatter sees this as the church's constitution.[21] In contrast to v. 7, titles of respect and deference ("rabbi" in Hebrew means "my great one") are not for Christian leaders. Jesus' followers should at all times avoid honorific nomenclature.

Again, this is a big problem today; witness the scramble of Christian leaders to be awarded an honorary DD (or to earn a DMin), often not to better serve the Lord but in order to be called "Doctor so and so." Such is a sin. As France says, "It is not difficult for a modern reader to think of similar honorifics in use today, and to discern behind the titles an excessive deference to academic or ecclesiastical qualifications."[22]

23:8 For there is only one who is your teacher, and you are all brothers and sisters (εἷς γάρ ἐστιν ὑμῶν ὁ διδάσκαλος, πάντες δὲ ὑμεῖς ἀδελφοί ἐστε). Jesus gives a simple reason: there is only "one" (note the emphatic position of εἷς) true rabbi/teacher (cf. John 1:38), Jesus himself. Jesus had called his disciples "teachers of the law" in his kingdom (cf. 13:52), and he now clarifies that role as not being one of status but one of servanthood. In short, there is no place for teachers in the church to jostle and compete for who is the best (cf. Jas 3:1); there is only one true "teacher," and all of us serve him not ourselves.

It has been pointed out that Jesus is called "teacher" only by those uncommitted to him, and that Jesus' teaching office is connected in Matthew with his position as Son of God and Lord (so Kingsbury, Garland). Moreover, there should be an egalitarian perspective in the church, as every one of us (the third use of "all" [πάς], cf. vv. 3, 5) should consider one another "brothers" (ἀδελφοί) or members of the same family; no one is superior to or more important than anyone else. There dare not be any distinction of status levels between teachers in the church.

23:9 And do not call anyone "father" on earth (καὶ πατέρα μὴ καλέσητε ὑμῶν ἐπὶ τῆς γῆς). The family metaphor continues. If everyone is "brother or sister," then no one is to be "father."

20. See Herschel Shanks, "Is the Title 'Rabbi' Anachronistic in the Gospels?" *JQR* 53 (1962 – 63): 337 – 45.

21. Schlatter, *Matthäus*, 670 – 71.

22. France, *Gospel of Matthew*, 863.

In one sense this seems to contradict the use of "fathers" in 1 Cor 4:15; 1 Thess 2:11; 1 John 2:13 – 14 as a term for Christian relationships. Yet in this context it is clearly related to the teaching office, though some have seen a reference to the patriarchs here.[23] There is some evidence that Jewish teachers were called by the honorific term "father," and Jesus is saying he does not want such elevated titles to be used among his followers.

23:9 For there is only one, your heavenly Father (εἷς γάρ ἐστιν ὑμῶν ὁ πατὴρ ὁ οὐράνιος). In v. 8 there was only one "teacher," Jesus, and now there is only one "father," God. He is "the heavenly Father" (cf. 5:48; 6:14, 26, 32; 15:13; 18:35), so there is no place for elevating earthly Christian leaders to any semblance of equality with him.

23:10 Nor should you be called "instructor," because there is one who is your instructor, the Christ (μηδὲ κληθῆτε καθηγηταί, ὅτι καθηγητὴς ὑμῶν ἐστιν εἷς ὁ Χριστός). This forms an ABA pattern in vv. 8 – 10, with Jesus as the one "teacher" framing God as the one "father." "Instructor" (καθηγητής, only here in either the LXX or the NT) is fairly synonymous with "teacher/rabbi" above. It stems from a verb meaning "to guide, explain" and so means a "teacher, instructor, tutor."[24] So again, Jesus wants to make certain that there are no attention-grabbers and status-seekers in the church.

Of course, these are not absolute prescriptions, for both "father" and "teacher" are used often in the NT for Christian leaders, and the teaching office was highly prized (Acts 13:1; 1 Cor 12:29; Eph 4:11; 1 Tim 3:2). Jesus is saying such an office should never be sought for the self-glory it will give (cf. Phil 2:3; Jas 3:1). As Blomberg says, there is nothing inherently wrong with Christian leaders today being called "Father," Reverend," or "Doctor," but still it can lead to "an unbiblical pride from all the plaudits. It is probably best to abolish most uses of such titles and look for equalizing terms to show that we are all related as family."[25]

23:11 But the greatest among you must be your servant (ὁ δὲ μείζων ὑμῶν ἔσται ὑμῶν διάκονος). As in 20:27 (cf. 5:21, 27, 33, 43) the future ἔσται functions a strong imperative, "must be" (so Hagner). This is the heart of the Christian paradox of discipleship, greatness through making one's self the least (10:38 – 39; 16:25; 18:2 – 5), and it virtually repeats 20:26 – 27.

23:12 Those who exalt themselves will be humbled, and those who humble themselves will be exalted (ὅστις δὲ ὑψώσει ἑαυτὸν ταπεινωθήσεται καὶ ὅστις ταπεινώσει ἑαυτὸν ὑψωθήσεται). The future passives here point to eschatological reversals, meaning that those who exalt (or humble) themselves in this life *will be* humbled (or exalted) by God at the last judgment. This is similar to 18:4 (see also Prov 3:34; 29:23; Job 22:29; Isa 57:15; Ezek 21:26; 2 Cor 11:7; Jas 4:6; 1 Pet 5:5; *b. ʿErub.* 3b). Moreover, these are divine passives and mean that God will reward or judge accordingly, following the *lex talionis* ("law of retribution") principle of "judged by works" (see on 16:27). In Phil 2:3 (cf. 3:1 – 11) Paul provides a powerful example of pride vs. humility in leadership.

23. See John C. Townsend, "Matthew XXIII. 9," *JTS* 12 (1961): 56 – 59.

24. Louw and Nida, *Greek-English Lexicon*, 33.245). See Bruce W. Winter, "The Messiah as Tutor: The Meaning of καθηγητής in Matthew 23:10," *TynBul* 42 (1991): 151 – 57, who argues that the term specifically refers to a tutor here, a person who instructs outside formal instruction (with Jesus the only tutor they need).

25. Blomberg, *Matthew*, 343, pointing to R. S. Barbour, "Uncomfortable Words: VIII. Status and Titles," *ExpTim* 82 (1970 – 71): 137 – 42.

Theology in Application

Davies and Allison say it well, "Christian history has demonstrated that … all the vices here attributed to the scribes and Pharisees have attached themselves to Christians, and in abundance."[26] Like the scribes and Pharisees, Christians must make certain that they do not just know the Word and teach it but live it in their lives. Hypocrisy can be defined as pretending to be something that you are not; in other words, you "walk the walk but don't talk the talk," or "you don't practice what you preach" (23:3b).

1. Keeping Oneself from Hypocrisy

Make certain that you are not guilty of hypocrisy (v. 3), ostentatious parading of the self (vv. 4 – 6) or pride (v. 7). It is clear that such people are not serving God but their true god, self. There is a certain idolatry in exalting oneself rather than serving God and others. To want to impress those around us by your knowledge, dress, office, and degrees is the height of hubris.

To ask others to do something when we are not doing it ourselves is the height of hypocrisy. We must all recognize that no matter what our gifts or accomplishments, we are superior to no one. Rather, the one God is so superior to us all that this fact evens us out and makes us all "brothers and sisters." It is not the privilege of others to listen to us; it is our privilege to share with them in some small way *what we have been given by Christ, our one teacher.*

2. Seeking Humility and Servanthood

Seek humility and servanthood, leaving the glory up to God. This is the message of the Philippians hymn (Phil 2:5 – 11), using the incarnation and life of Christ as a paradigm (2:5) for Christians; like Jesus we should seek a life of humility (Phil 2:6 – 8) and let God glorify us in his own time (2:9 – 11). Therefore, Jesus is saying that we must refuse to go by titles that appeal to our pride (23:8, 10) or elevate anyone else to glorified status (23:9).

These things happen all too often in successful churches and ministries. Sadly, all too many well-known Christian leaders begin to believe the plaudits of others and become virtual demigods in their own fiefdom! This is one of the most disobeyed and ignored passages of the Bible. As so often before (cf. 10:38 – 39; 16:25; 18:2 – 5; 20:26 – 27) true discipleship is defined not by human achievement but by service to God and his people, by taking the road of servanthood and living a life of

26. Davies and Allison, *Matthew*, 3:262. See also Viviano, "Social World and Community Leadership," 3 – 21, who says Matthew especially has Christian "prophets, sages, and teachers" (v. 34) in mind.

humility. Those guilty of self-glory (Gal 5:26; Phil 2:3) can expect no reward from God.

Again, this does not mean that one must eschew a fruitful ministry that results in becoming well known (Paul was certainly famous, cf. 2 Pet 3:15 – 16). Rather, it means that fame and attention must never be a goal. Our goal is not to create sacred listeners or readers who cannot wait to hear what we have to say but rather to create lovers of Jesus and the Word, who enjoy our exposition of God's truth. As Bruner says, this is not "a going down into a paralyzing self-negation or self-abasement (but) an active, free, and *con brio* decision for service.... There is a joyful look to the future in this Gospel's 'law' of humility."[27]

27. Bruner, *Matthew 13 – 28*, 442.

CHAPTER 99

Matthew 23:13 – 36

Literary Context

These verses flow nicely from the foundation piece of 23:11 – 12. The hypocrisy stated in v. 3 is now expanded and becomes the centerpiece of the discourse. In fact, these expand on the basic charges made in v. 3b, "They do not practice what they say." The woes provide the reason for the divine judgment that is coming, while the Olivet Discourse (chs. 24 – 25) tells what form that judgment will take.

VI. The Movement to the Cross (19:1 – 25:46)
- A. Jesus' Deeds: Opposition and Discipleship (19:1 – 22:46)
- **B. Fifth Discourse: Guilt and Judgment of Israel (23:1 – 25:46)**
  - **1. Guilt: Woes upon the Leaders (23:1 – 39)**
    - a. Warning and Humility (23:1 – 12)
    - ➦ **b. The Seven Woes (23:13 – 36)**
      - **(1) Woes on the Negative Effect They Have on Others (23:13 – 15)**
        - **(a) Judgment for Closing the Kingdom to Others (23:13)**
        - **(b) Judgment for Leading Proselytes to Gehenna (23:15)**
      - **(2) Woes on the Misleading Effect of Their Teaching and Conduct (23:16 – 24)**
        - **(a) Judgment for Their False Teaching on Oaths and the Temple (23:16 – 22)**
        - **(b) Judgment for Their False Teaching on Tithing While Ignoring Mercy (23:23 – 24)**
      - **(3) Woes on Their External Religion (23:25 – 32)**
        - **(a) Judgment for Their Ritual Cleanliness Yet Unclean Hearts (23:25 – 26)**
        - **(b) Judgment for Their Self-Righteous Exterior Yet Wicked Interior (23:27 – 28)**
      - **(4) Woe for Participating in the Sins of Their Ancestors (23:29 – 32)**
      - **(5) Conclusion — Judgment Coming (23:33 – 36)**
    - c. Lament over Jerusalem (23:37 – 39)
  - 2. Judgment — Olivet Discourse (24:1 – 25:46)

Main Idea

This "woes" section builds on the woe oracles of the prophets (Isa 5:8 – 24; Amos 5:18 – 20; Mic 2:1 – 4; Hab 2:6 – 20) and *1 Enoch* (94:6 – 9; 95:5 – 7; 96:4 – 8; 99:11 – 15). Such judgment prophecies utilize *hôy*, followed by a series of participles describing the transgression and judgment levied by God. All seven woes here relate to the religious sins of the scribes and Pharisees, and especially their basic "hypocrisy" (found in all the woes except the third) of knowing the Scripture but twisting it to their own ends. As elsewhere this functions at two levels: Matthew intends this as a denunciation of the sins of the Jewish leaders who brought about God's judgment on the nation, but he also intends this as a warning to Christians not to commit the same sins, lest they also be judged.

Translation

Matthew 23:13-36

13a	Warning #1 (A)	*[1] "Woe to you, teachers of the law and Pharisees,*
b	Rebuke (B)	*hypocrites!*
c	Basis for 13a (C)	*because you shut the kingdom of heaven to people.*
d		For *you neither enter it yourselves nor allow those who would enter it to do so.*
15a	Warning #2 (A)	*[2] Woe to you, teachers of the law and Pharisees,*
b	Rebuke (B)	*hypocrites!*
c	Basis for 15a (C)	*because you travel over sea and land to make one proselyte,*
d		and *when you do so*
e		*you make that person twice the child meant for Gehenna than you are.*
16a	Warning #3 (A)	*[3] Woe to you, blind guides who say,*
b	Error #1 (D)	*(i) 'Whoever swears by the temple, it is nothing,*
c	(E)	but *whoever swears . . . is bound by it by the gold of the temple.'*
17a	Rebuke (B)	*You fools and blind people!*
b	Rhetorical Question (F) (Basis for 16a-17a)	For *what is greater, the gold or the temple that makes the gold holy?*

Continued on next page.

Continued from previous page.

18a	Error #2 (D)	*(ii) Also, 'Whoever swears by the altar, it is nothing,*
b	(E)	*But whoever swears . . . is bound by it*
		by the gift that is on it.'
19a	Rebuke (B)	*You blind people!*
b	Rhetorical Question (F) (Basis for 18a-19a)	*What is greater, the gift or the altar that makes the gift holy?*
20a	Conclusion	*(x) Therefore, anyone who swears by the altar swears*
		by it and
		by everything on it,
21a		*(x') and anyone who swears by the temple swears*
		by it and
		by the One who dwells in it.
22a		*(x") And anyone who swears by heaven swears*
		by the throne of God and
		by the One who sits on it.
23a	Warning #4 (A)	*[4] Woe to you, teachers of the law and*
		Pharisees,
b	Rebuke (B)	*hypocrites!*
c	Basis for 23a (C)	*because you tithe mint, dill, and cumin,*
d		*yet you have neglected the more important matters of the law—*
		justice, mercy, and faithfulness.
e	Conclusion	*Now you should have done these things*
		without neglecting the others.
24a		*You are blind guides who strain the gnat but swallow the camel.*
25a	Warning #5 (A)	*[5] Woe to you, teachers of the law and*
		Pharisees,
b	Rebuke (B)	*hypocrites!*
c	Basis for 25a (C)	*because you clean the outside of the cup and dish,*
d		*but inside they are full of greed and*
		self-indulgence.
26a	Rebuke	*Blind Pharisees!*
b	Exhortation	*First cleanse the inside of the cup*
c	Purpose	*so that its outside might also be clean.*
27a	Warning #6 (A)	*[6] Woe to you, teachers of the law and*
		Pharisees,
b	Rebuke (B)	*hypocrites!*

c	Basis for 27a (C)	*because you resemble whitewashed tombs*
d		*which appear beautiful on the outside, but*
e		*on the inside are filled*
		with the bones of the dead
		and all kinds
		of impurity.
28a	Explanation of 27c-e	*In this way you yourselves also appear righteous to people*
		on the outside,
b		*but inside you are full of hypocrisy and wickedness.*
29a	Warning #7 (A)	*[7] Woe to you, teachers of the law and*
		Pharisees,
b	Rebuke (B)	*hypocrites!*
c	Basis #1 for 29a	*(i) because you construct the tombs of the prophets and*
d		*decorate the monuments of the righteous.*
30a	Basis #2 for 29a	*(ii) And you say,*
b		*'. . . we would not have shared with them*
		in shedding the blood of the prophets.
c		*if we had lived in the days of our fathers,*
31a	Result of 30a-c	*As a result, you bear witness*
		against yourselves
		that you are the children
		of those who murdered the prophets.
32a		*So as for you, fill up the measure of your fathers!*
33a	Rebuke	*Snakes!*
b	Rebuke	*Offspring of vipers!*
c	Rhetorical Question	*How will you escape from the judgment of Gehenna?*
34a	Basis	*Look, because of this I am sending you prophets and*
		sages and
		scribes.
b	Prediction	*You will kill and crucify some of them,*
c	Prediction	*and you will have some of them scourged*
		in your synagogues and
		persecuted from city to city,
35a	Result of 34b-c	*with the result that all the righteous blood . . . will come upon you*
		poured out on the earth,
b		*from the blood of righteous Abel*
		to the blood of Zechariah son of Berachiah,
c		*whom you murdered between the sanctuary and the altar.*
36a	Summary and Conclusion	*I tell you the truth,*
		all these things will come on this generation."

Structure and Literary Form

The seven woes definitely parallel the six woes of Luke 11:37 – 54, but the order and wording are strikingly different (Matthew's first [23:13] = Luke's sixth [Luke 11:52]; his fourth [23:23] = Luke's first [Luke 11:42]; his fifth [23:25 – 26] = Luke's introduction [Luke 11:39 – 41]; his sixth (23:27] = Luke's third [Luke 11:44]; his seventh [23:29] = Luke's fifth [Luke 11:47]). The wording and length of each is also so strikingly different that any attempt to reconstruct a so-called "Q original" is doomed to failure, and it is likely that Jesus, the itinerant teacher, delivered the woes on at least two different occasions (cf. Luke 6:24 – 26).

The structure is also heavily debated, with several distinct possibilities suggested:

1. they are individual, related by code words and increasing in length and intensity (Luz)
2. the first three center on scribal teaching, the next three on Pharisaic conduct, the last on national sin (McNeile)
3. there is a 2 – 3 – 2 pattern (Nolland)
4. there is a chiasm (1 = 7, 2 = 6, 3 = 5, with the fourth the centerpiece (Carson)
5. the first two relate to 23:4, the next four to 23:5 – 7, and the last forms a climax (Witherington)
6. there are three pairs of judgments (1 – 2, 3 – 4, 5 – 6), with the seventh forming a climax (Sabourin, Davies and Allison, Hagner, Blomberg).

This final one is the simplest and fits the organization best, as this commentary will seek to demonstrate.

Exegetical Outline

➡ **I. Woes on the Negative Effect They Have on Others (23:13 – 15)**
  A. Judgment for closing the kingdom to others (v. 13)
  B. Judgment for leading proselytes to Gehenna (v. 15)

II. Woes on the Misleading Effect of Their Teaching and Conduct (23:16 – 24)
  A. Judgment for false teaching on oaths and the temple (vv. 16 – 22)
    1. First error — oaths based on the temple vs. its gold (vv. 16 – 17)
    2. Second error — oaths based on the altar vs. gifts on it (vv. 18 – 19)
    3. Conclusion — the validity of oaths based on temple and altar (vv. 20 – 21)
    4. Final point — validity of oaths based on heaven (v. 22)
  B. Judgment for false teaching on tithing while ignoring mercy (vv. 23 – 24)

III. Woes on Their External Religion (23:25 – 28)
  A. Judgment for their ritual cleanliness yet unclean hearts (vv. 25 – 26)
  B. Judgment for their self-righteous exterior yet wicked interior (vv. 27 – 28)

IV. Woe for Participating in the Sins of Their Ancestors (23:29 – 32)
- A. Their pious acts and claim: revere the prophets (v. 29 – 30)
- B. The reality: participate with those who murdered the prophets (vv. 31 – 32)

V. Conclusion (23:33 – 36)
- A. Proclamation of judgment (v. 33)
- B. Reason for judgment (v. 34)
- C. Severity of judgment (vv. 35 – 36)

Explanation of the Text

23:13 "Woe to you, teachers of the law and Pharisees, hypocrites!" (Οὐαὶ δὲ ὑμῖν, γραμματεῖς καὶ Φαρισαῖοι ὑποκριταί). "Woe" (οὐαί) has already occurred in 11:21 and 18:7 and generally means divine judgment is on the people.[1] Garland provides a lengthy discussion and generally follows Bonnard in seeing two types of woe sayings in Matthew — one centering on lamentation (18:7; 24:19; 26:24), the other on condemnation (11:21; 23:13 – 14). He notes a strong imprecatory aspect stemming from the woe oracles of the OT. Thus Jesus is pronouncing prophetic judgment on the leaders and the planned vengeance of God on them for their sins.[2]

For "teachers of the law and Pharisees," see on v. 2. Jesus' discussion of "hypocrisy" has occurred frequently (6:2, 5, 16; 7:5; 15:7; 22:18), is featured in all but the third woe in this chapter, and describes those who "put on a false face" and pretend to be what they are not, seeking approval from others more than from God.[3] Garland adds that it must also include a false interpretation and misuse of the Torah, thus constituting an attack on their biblical understanding as well as their character.[4] As we will see, this fits well the context of ch. 23.

23:13 "... because you shut the kingdom of heaven to people" (ὅτι κλείετε τὴν βασιλείαν τῶν οὐρανῶν ἔμπροσθεν τῶν ἀνθρώπων). ἔμπροσθεν is strong here, meaning normally "in front of, before" and having the idea of slamming the door of heaven "right in the face of" their followers. The purpose of the Pharisees in "building a fence around the law" should have been to shepherd God's flock through the gate or door to the kingdom. Their teaching should have made the reign of God (for "kingdom" see on 3:2; 4:8) more apparent and meaningful in the lives of the people. Instead, they have closed the door to God.

Earlier Jesus had taught about the narrow and wide gates (7:13 – 14) and had given Peter (and the church) the "keys of the kingdom of heaven" (16:19), meaning the authority to open the doors of heaven. The binding/loosing metaphor that followed referred to the authority to open the kingdom truths by properly interpreting God's Word (see on 16:19). The Pharisees have rejected the final authority of Jesus as interpreter of Torah and so have fallen into false teaching.

23:13 "For you neither enter it yourselves nor

1. But see K. C. Hanson, "How Honorable! How Shameful! A Cultural Analysis of Matthew's Makarisms and Reproaches," *Semeia* 68 (1994): 81 – 111, who points out that in an honor-shame culture as in both Jewish and Greco-Roman worlds, οὐαί should be seen as an utterance of shame. This is certainly part of the meaning but does not exhaust its semantic range here.

2. Garland, *Matthew 23*, 64 – 90; cf. Bonnard, *Matthieu*, 338, 452.

3. Luz (*Matthew 21 – 28*, 137) tells how after the Reformation and the advent of printing, the Bible could be read by common people and the woes began to have great influence. At that time the metaphorical use of "Pharisee" as "hypocrite" became widespread.

4. Garland, *Matthew 23*, 111 – 12.

allow those who would enter it to do so" (ὑμεῖς γὰρ οὐκ εἰσέρχεσθε οὐδὲ τοὺς εἰσερχομένους ἀφίετε εἰσελθεῖν). Christ has brought the true kingdom into this world, but the Jewish leaders have rejected it and therefore have closed the door for themselves and their followers, not only by their false teaching but even more so by their rejection of the Messiah. The use of present tenses in the participles and imperative emphasizes the constant negation of the reality of the kingdom that this rejection entails.

The idea of "entering" the kingdom also occurs in 5:20; 7:21; 18:3 (8 – 9); 19:(17), 23, 24 and refers both to conversion and to acceptance by God. There is an inaugurated thrust referring to the present stance before God and the final judgment. The opposition by these leaders to God's Messiah has made it impossible not only for themselves but also for all who hope to enter the kingdom by following their teaching. The presence of ἀφίετε means they do not inadvertently make it difficult but actively refuse to "allow" their followers access to God's true kingdom.[5]

23:15 Woe to you, teachers of the law and Pharisees, hypocrites! because you travel over sea and land to make one proselyte (Οὐαὶ ὑμῖν, γραμματεῖς καὶ Φαρισαῖοι ὑποκριταί, ὅτι περιάγετε τὴν θάλασσαν καὶ τὴν ξηρὰν ποιῆσαι ἕνα προσήλυτον). This makes the same point as v. 13 but another way. To keep a person from entering the kingdom is to send them to eternal hellfire. The ὅτι clause has been much discussed. Previously, scholars thought it indicated extensive missionary activity by the Jews among the Gentiles.[6] "Proselyte" (προσήλυτος) does refer to a pagan convert to Judaism, and "over sea and land" means travel to lands outside the borders of Palestine where Jews lived. However, McKnight has shown that little actual proselytizing occurred outside the synagogues. Therefore, this probably refers to travel to Diaspora synagogues by Jewish sages to convince God-fearers (Gentiles who worshiped as Jews but were unwilling to undergo circumcision) to become full proselytes.[7]

23:15 And when you do so you make that person twice the child meant for Gehenna than you are (καὶ ὅταν γένηται ποιεῖτε αὐτὸν υἱὸν γεέννης διπλότερον ὑμῶν). In this context "child" (υἱός) with the genitive means "worthy of" or "meant for" (BAGD, 834, δ). "Gehenna" (γεέννα) is a metaphor for eternal torment (see on 5:22). "Twice" (διπλότερον) probably means that the followers of the Pharisees go even further into the false teaching and rejection of Jesus than their teachers did. It is rabbinic hyperbole for the dedication of the followers.

23:16 Woe to you, blind guides who say (Οὐαὶ ὑμῖν, ὁδηγοὶ τυφλοὶ οἱ λέγοντες). Only in this third of the seven woes does Jesus alter his opening formula and insert "blind guides," undoubtedly because he calls them "blind" again in vv. 17, 19. This emphasizes they are not only "hypocrites" but also "blind" to the truth. They were also "blind guides" in 15:14 (see there).

23:16 "Whoever swears by the temple, it is nothing, but whoever swears by the gold of the temple is bound by it" (ὃς ἂν ὀμόσῃ ἐν τῷ ναῷ, οὐδέν ἐστιν· ὃς δ' ἂν ὀμόσῃ ἐν τῷ χρυσῷ τοῦ ναοῦ, ὀφείλει). On "oaths" see 5:33 – 37, where the

5. Verse 14 ("Woe to you, teachers of the law and Pharisees, hypocrites. You devour widow's houses and for show make lengthy prayers. Therefore you will be judged more severely") is missing in most earlier manuscripts (ℵ B D L Z Θ vg et al.) from a wide variety of traditions (Alexandrian, Western et al.). Those who do include it place it either after v. 12 or v. 13. It almost certainly is an interpolation from Mark 12:40; Luke 20:47.

6. See Jeremias, *Promise to the Nations*, 11 – 19; L. H. Feldman, *Jew and Gentile in the Ancient World* (Princeton: Princeton Univ. Press, 1993).

7. Scot McKnight, *A Light among the Gentiles*, 106 – 8; Witherington, *Matthew*, 428 – 29.

centrality of oaths in the ancient Jewish world was discussed.[8] The Pharisees would shallowly anchor even casual statements by calling on the name of God or angels or OT saints to provide witness to the veracity of what they said or promised. One of the distinctions the Pharisees made between valid and invalid oaths is used by Jesus here. The problem is that this particular distinction occurs nowhere in Jewish literature; yet this *type* of distinction appears often. As stated in 5:33 oaths had proliferated and become such a part of everyday life that teachers began to develop a gradation of forms of oath and to ask which types had true legal force (so Nolland). To "be nothing" means to be not binding, while "to be bound" means to be legally binding on the one making the oath.

But why is an oath made on the temple invalid while one made on its gold (there were many gold accoutrements — the golden vine, censers, utensils, and plates, the gold leaf around the Most Holy Place, the gold in the treasury) is valid? Some (Gundry, Keener) say that creditors cannot place liens on the temple or altar but can claim the gold of the temple or the gifts placed on the altar. A better explanation, however, relates to the principle of *korban* (cf. Mark 7:11 = Matt 15:5 – 6). As Garland explains, oaths were terribly misused by the ignorant for any and all occasions in the first century. Oaths using God's name or sacred objects were avoided because it was felt they were binding; the Jews then would swear an oath by peripheral objects, like "the temple" or "the altar" in the temple, so they would not be totally bound (cf. 5:33 – 37).

In other words, rabbis spent a great deal of time distinguishing valid from invalid oaths, concluding that only those based on the divine name and attributes were binding — with one exception, namely, things dedicated to the temple as *korban*, a "(temple) gift devoted to God" (e.g., the temple treasure is called *korban*). "It can ... be inferred that in vv. 16 and 18 the Temple gold and the altar gift were binding as part of an oath because they were connected with the term *korban*, while the Temple and altar, though holy objects, were illegitimate substitutes in an oath formula."[9]

23:17 You fools and blind people! For what is greater, the gold or the temple that makes the gold holy? (μωροὶ καὶ τυφλοί, τίς γὰρ μείζων ἐστίν, ὁ χρυσὸς ἢ ὁ ναὸς ὁ ἁγιάσας τὸν χρυσόν;). This opening could almost be translated, "blind morons" (with epexegetical καί and transliteration of μωροί). The Pharisees call themselves the teachers of the blind and yet make such ridiculous distinctions. The temple sanctuary (ναός) was the place of holiness, and the gold had sacred value only because it was part of the temple instruments, not the other way around. So Jesus asks (interrogative "what" [τίς]): since the temple is infinitely greater than its gold, on what basis could anyone elevate the gold above the sanctuary?

23:18 Also, "Whoever swears by the altar, it is nothing. But whoever swears by the gift that is on it is bound by it" (καί, Ὃς ἂν ὀμόσῃ ἐν τῷ θυσιαστηρίῳ, οὐδέν ἐστιν· ὃς δ᾽ ἂν ὀμόσῃ ἐν τῷ δώρῳ τῷ ἐπάνω αὐτοῦ, ὀφείλει). This virtually repeats vv. 16 – 17, substituting "altar" and "the gift on it" for the temple and gold in vv. 16 – 17. It makes the same point. The teachers/rabbis considered the altar "gift" as *korban* and so made an oath based on it binding, while the altar was invalid as the basis for an oath.

8. This is often taken as a contradiction to 5:33 – 37, where Jesus seems to say that all oaths are wrong. Yet as Carson says ("Matthew," 479) this provides the rationale or basis for 5:33 – 37, as Jesus shows that all oaths actually relate to God and are binding (here), and at the same time says that the core of the issue is telling the truth (there). The point in both passages is that a person is responsible for the promises uttered.

9. Garland, *Matthew 23*, 134 – 35. See also Davies and Allison, *Matthew*, 3:290 – 91; Nolland, *Matthew*, 935.

23:19 You blind people! What is greater, the gift or the altar that makes the gift holy? (τυφλοί, τί γὰρ μεῖζον, τὸ δῶρον ἢ τὸ θυσιαστήριον τὸ ἁγιάζον τὸ δῶρον;). Jesus' counter-argument is that the altar makes the gift holy, not vice versa, so the altar is the greater. It must be remembered that this is not really a discussion of oaths so much as a further example of the casuistry of the scribes and Pharisees. Keener's title for this section is a propos: "Inconsistency in evaluating standards of holiness dishonors God."[10]

23:20 Therefore, anyone who swears by the altar swears by it and by everything on it (ὁ οὖν ὀμόσας ἐν τῷ θυσιαστηρίῳ ὀμνύει ἐν αὐτῷ καὶ ἐν πᾶσι τοῖς ἐπάνω αὐτοῦ). By reversing the order of vv. 16 – 19, Jesus here creates a kind of chiasm (temple/altar:altar/temple), thereby making his point all the more emphatic. Yet there is also an intensifying force, as v. 20 makes the point that when one swears by the altar, the oath includes "everything on it," including the gifts of vv. 18 – 19. The two cannot be separated.

23:21 And anyone who swears by the temple swears by it and by the One who dwells in it (καὶ ὁ ὀμόσας ἐν τῷ ναῷ ὀμνύει ἐν αὐτῷ καὶ ἐν τῷ κατοικοῦντι αὐτόν). Verse 21 also goes beyond the point to conclude that an oath based on the sanctuary includes the God who indwells it. This is the ultimate point — making oaths means standing before God himself. The Shekinah (*šākan*, "to dwell") presence of God in his temple is a central truth of the OT.

23:22 And anyone who swears by heaven swears[11] by the throne of God and by the One who sits on it (καὶ ὁ ὀμόσας ἐν τῷ οὐρανῷ ὀμνύει ἐν τῷ θρόνῳ τοῦ θεοῦ καὶ ἐν τῷ καθημένῳ ἐπάνω αὐτοῦ). God is described in successive verses as the One who indwells the temple and the One who sits on the eternal throne. For the Jewish people the throne of God was at the point where the wings of the seraphim meet above the ark in the Most Holy Place, so these two ideas belong together. Again the second idea intensifies the first.

Here the point made in 23:16 – 22 comes full circle. Every oath, from the least to the greatest, involves God and his throne and so is binding. In this sense Jesus' point in 5:34 – 37 is in full agreement. Since every oath by nature centers on God and is made in relation to God, there is no need to swear by anything, but instead a "yes" is a "yes" and a "no" is a "no" because all promises are made before the throne of God and will be judged by God (so also Davies and Allison, Morris, Nolland).

23:23 Woe to you, teachers of the law and Pharisees, hypocrites! because you tithe mint, dill, and cumin (Οὐαὶ ὑμῖν, γραμματεῖς καὶ Φαρισαῖοι ὑποκριταί, ὅτι ἀποδεκατοῦτε τὸ ἡδύοσμον καὶ τὸ ἄνηθον καὶ τὸ κύμινον). The fourth "woe"[12] concerns tithing, which appears first in Gen 14:17 – 20 (Abraham to Melchizedek) and 28:18 – 22 (Jacob at Bethel). The legislation occurs in Deut 12:11 – 18; 14:22 – 29; Num 18:21 – 29, where God's people are to tithe grain, wine, oil, fruit, and the first harvests of herds and flocks (Deut 14:23), every tenth animal (Lev 27:30 – 33), with each family consuming the tithe in a sacred meal shared with the Levites (Deut 12:15 – 19). Moreover, tithes were to go to the Levites as their "inheritance" (Num 18:21), and they in turn would return to the Lord a tenth of that for the priests (Num 18:27 – 28). Every third year the tithes were stored up not only for the Levites but also for the orphans and widows (Deut 14:28 – 29).

10. Keener, *Matthew*, 549.

11. The aorist participle "swears" ὀμόσας) considers the oath-taking as a complete whole, and the present main verb "swears" (ὀμνύει) centers on the repeated oaths that result.

12. Verse 23 is a slightly expanded version of Luke 11:42 (Q), while v. 24 is an added saying.

It has been estimated that the actual amount given in tithes was 17 to 20 percent of the farmer's income.[13] The Pharisees again were overscrupulous[14] in observing this, tithing not just main crops (the original intention) but every kind of food, even spices and medicinal herbs like cumin (tithed according to *m. Demai* 2:P1), and dill (tithed according to *m. Maʿaś* 4:5) or mint (not mentioned in any text). It needs to be noted that Jesus does not condemn this practice but instead what they neglect, namely, concern for others.

23:23 Yet you have neglected the more important matters of the law (καὶ ἀφήκατε τὰ βαρύτερα τοῦ νόμου). In one sense this verse could parallel the two great commandments of 22:37 – 39, with tithing (present tense to emphasize current activity) directed to God and their neglect (global aorist to sum up their basic activity) of justice and mercy directed to the neighbor, but Jesus does not have this in mind.

23:23 ... justice, mercy, and faithfulness (τὴν κρίσιν καὶ τὸ ἔλεος καὶ τὴν πίστιν). The "weightier matters," meaning the truly central aspects of the law as in 22:36, are here threefold, with the first two neighbor-related and the third ("faithfulness" [πίστις]) God-related, and so these three sum up the twofold "greatest commandment" of 22:37 – 38. Lack of "justice" (κρίσις) is one of the basic sins condemned by the prophets (Isa 1:16 – 18; Jer 22:3; Amos 5:14 – 15) and is a basic characteristic of God (Ps 9:8, 16; 89:14). "Mercy" (ἔλεος) is closely connected and is the way justice occurs in this world; Jesus demands "mercy" in the Hos 6:6 quote in 9:13; 12:7.

"Faithfulness" (πίστις) most likely has its OT connotation of "faithfulness" to God and his commandments (though it does not have this thrust elsewhere in Matthew). It is possible that Mic 6:8 is in Jesus' mind ("What does the Lord require of you? To act justly and to love mercy and to walk humbly with your God"), with the third item here the equivalent of "walking humbly." The Pharisees, as in 9:13, 12:7, have not fulfilled these "more important matters."

23:23 Now you should have done these things without neglecting the others (ταῦτα δὲ ἔδει ποιῆσαι κἀκεῖνα μὴ ἀφιέναι). ἔδει often refers to divine necessity but here connotes "the compulsion of duty," so "ought" or "should" (BAGD, 172). Jesus is not opposed to the zealous tithing on behalf of the Pharisees. However, they should make certain that they center on the essentials and not just the peripherals.

23:24 You are blind guides who strain the gnat but swallow the camel (ὁδηγοὶ τυφλοί, οἱ διϋλίζοντες τὸν κώνωπα, τὴν δὲ κάμηλον καταπίνοντες). Jesus now uses a rabbinic hyperbole reminiscent of 19:24 (a camel through a needle's eye), using a pun on the "gnat" (Aramaic *qlmʾ*) and the "camel" (Aramaic *qmlʾ*). He repeats the "blind guides" of v. 16 to highlight their misuse of the law. The image of "straining"[15] stems from the ancient practice of filtering wine through a cloth to remove unclean insects (Lev 11:23, 41) like gnats (as in Amos 6:6 LXX; *m. Šabb.* 20:2) that would easily enter open containers. Broadus says that gnats are known to sip at wine and then fall into it and that the larvae of gnats are known to swarm in the water.[16] While avoiding unclean minutiae, however, they would

13. Keener, *Matthew*, 550, from E. P. Sanders, *Jewish Law from Jesus to the Mishnah: Five Studies* (Philadelphia: Trinity Press International, 1990), 44 – 45.

14. Turner, "Matthew," 297, explains that the Pharisees believed "only food that had been tithed was ritually pure and lawful to eat. Cf. *m.*, *ʾAbot.* 1:16; *m. Demai* 2:1."

15. Once more the present tense participles speak of ongoing practice.

16. Broadus, *Matthew*, 473.

end up "swallowing" a much larger unclean animal, the camel (the largest animal in Palestine). Obviously, the Pharisees center on the lesser and ignore the greater.

23:25 Woe to you, teachers of the law and Pharisees, hypocrites! (Οὐαὶ ὑμῖν, γραμματεῖς καὶ Φαρισαῖοι ὑποκριταί). The fifth woe[17] repeats the characteristic opening formula and gets back to the issue of hypocrisy, denigrating the concern of the Pharisees for outward cleanliness to the detriment of inward purity.

23:25 Because you clean the outside of the cup and dish, but inside they are full of greed and self-indulgence (ὅτι καθαρίζετε τὸ ἔξωθεν τοῦ ποτηρίου καὶ τῆς παροψίδος, ἔσωθεν δὲ γέμουσιν ἐξ ἁρπαγῆς καὶ ἀκρασίας). The next four verses are dominated by the "outside-inside" (ἔξωθεν-ἔσωθεν) distinction, forming the perfect definition of hypocrisy as stemming from the dichotomy between "outward" appearance and "inward" reality. Jesus uses as his example the care with which the scribes wash the outside surface of cups and plates.

There is a difference of opinion as to the thrust of Jesus' statement here. Some take this literally as reflecting a debate between the schools of Shammai (one had to cleanse both the inside and the outside of the vessel, thus washing one's hands before using it) and of Hillel (the outside did not effect the inside, and so immersing the vessel was sufficient); Jesus in this sense would be criticizing the Shammaite view.[18] Others see this as primarily metaphorical because such fine legal distinctions are not indicated in the language of the text, which centers only on the washing of the vessels. Therefore, this is simple imagery for hypocrisy, namely, that the Pharisees[19] appeared clean on the outside but were actually unclean on the inside.[20]

This latter makes better sense here, especially in light of ἐξ ἁρπαγῆς καὶ ἀκρασίας, which some take as "because of (causal ἐκ) greed and self-indulgence," thereby accusing the scribes and Pharisees of economic and sexual sin (in 1 Cor 7:5, 9 it refers to sexual urges).[21] Yet this does not have to be taken in this way. Blomberg sees this as hendiadys for "violence and selfishness," referring to their mistreatment of others.[22] It could even more easily be seen as "greedy selfishness" (epexegetical καί), referring to economic sins like Mark 12:40 = Luke 20:47 ("devour widow's houses," see Nolland).

23:26 Blind Pharisees! First cleanse the inside of the cup so that its outside might also be clean (Φαρισαῖε τυφλέ, καθάρισον πρῶτον τὸ ἐντὸς τοῦ ποτηρίου, ἵνα γένηται καὶ τὸ ἐκτὸς αὐτοῦ καθαρόν). Jesus reverses the outside-inside order of v. 25 and so produces another chiasm (see 23:20 – 21). The metaphorical nature of this is demonstrated by what Jesus says here. The Pharisees[23] centered on cleansing the inside of vessels. So Jesus is saying that they should extend their ritual concerns to matters of inner purity. Being

17. Verse 25 is similar to Luke 11:39, but v. 26 differs from Luke 11:40 – 41 (though the resultant message is similar), which calls on the Pharisees to give a clean heart back to God as alms (probably a separate saying from Matthew's version).

18. So Jacob Neusner, "'First Cleanse the Inside': The Halakhic Background of a Controversy-Saying," *NTS* 22 (1976): 486 – 95; Schweizer, *Matthew*, 434; Keener, *Matthew*, 552.

19. Note the switch from second person "you" in the first clause to third person "they" in the second clause. This is a rhetorical ploy to address the Pharisees themselves first and then tell the crowds about them in the second. It makes the denunciation all the more powerful.

20. So Hyam Maccoby, "The Washing of Cups," *JSNT* 14 (1982): 3 – 15; Carson, "Matthew," 481 – 82; Luz, *Matthew 21 – 28*, 127; Blomberg, *Matthew*, 347; France, *Gospel of Matthew*, 874 – 75.

21. Garland, *Matthew 23*, 148 – 49. McNeile, *Matthew*, 336, sees it in a similar way as result. Carson, "Matthew," 482, rejects this because of the abstemious nature of the Pharisees in food and drink.

22. Blomberg, *Matthew*, 347.

23. Jesus has the singular "blind Pharisee," which Gundry

ritually clean is negated by the internal sins noted in v. 25b.

23:27 Woe to you, teachers of the law and Pharisees, hypocrites! because you resemble whitewashed tombs (Οὐαὶ ὑμῖν, γραμματεῖς καὶ Φαρισαῖοι ὑποκριταί, ὅτι παρομοιάζετε τάφοις κεκονιαμένοις). The sixth woe[24] restates the fifth, but with a very different metaphor for the outside-inside distinction. This image would have been quite familiar—the tombs of family ancestors "whitewashed" or "plastered" during the month of Adar before Passover to render them recognizable for pilgrims, lest they inadvertently touch them and become unclean for the seven days of the feast (Num 19:16).

23:27 ... which appear beautiful on the outside but on the inside are filled with the bones of the dead and all kinds of impurity (οἵτινες ἔξωθεν μὲν φαίνονται ὡραῖοι, ἔσωθεν δὲ γέμουσιν ὀστέων νεκρῶν καὶ πάσης ἀκαθαρσίας). This is where the complications start. Tombs were not whitewashed for the sake of their "beauty" (ὡραῖοι) but because they were places to be avoided. In fact, the whitewash was the color of "the bones of the dead" and so was not meant to attract admiration but repulsion. How do we resolve this discrepancy?

1. Some simply say this is due to the ignorance of the author to the purity laws and so he wrote simply to highlight the metaphor.[25] But this is hardly necessary in light of the evidence below.
2. Others have argued that the image refers not to tombs but to whitened urns or ossuaries.[26]
3. The image refers "not to whitewashing but to the ornamental plastering of the walls of the sepulchers."[27]
4. Possibly the best such explanation is that of Garland, who says the "beauty" stems from the ornamental structure of the tomb rather than the whitewashing.[28]

However we understand the connection between the whitewashing and however we take the image of beauty, Jesus' point stands. The scribes and Pharisees resemble tombs in terms of their outward respectability and inward corruption.

23:28 In this way you yourselves[29] also appear righteous to people on the outside, but inside you are full of hypocrisy and wickedness (οὕτως καὶ ὑμεῖς ἔξωθεν μὲν φαίνεσθε τοῖς ἀνθρώποις δίκαιοι, ἔσωθεν δέ ἐστε μεστοὶ ὑποκρίσεως καὶ ἀνομίας). The comparison is drawn by "in this way" (οὕτως). When others look at them, they "appear" on the "outside" to be paragons of legal righteousness. But that goes no more than skin-deep. Underneath that righteous exterior they are filled on the "inside" with the kind of "wickedness" that produces ultimate "hypocrisy" (see on v. 25). "Wickedness" (ἀνομία) has a double meaning, referring not only to inner impurity but to "lawlessness." Their overly scrupulous adherence to the legalities of "the law" (ὁ νόμος) has led to "lawlessness" (ἀνομία).

23:29 Woe to you, teachers of the law and Pharisees, hypocrites, because you construct the

(*Matthew*, 465) explains is intended to match them with the "cup and dish" (singular in v. 25) and thereby make the referent of the metaphor more clear.

24. Luke 11:44 is much shorter and makes a different point ("you are like unmarked graves, which people walk over without knowing it"). If both stem from the same original saying (it is also possible that they come from different teaching events), Matthew and Luke take Jesus' saying in slightly different directions.

25. Luz, *Matthew 21–28*, 130.

26. Samuel T. Lachs, "On Matthew 23:27–28," *HTR* 68 (1975): 385–88. See also his list of suggested options.

27. McNeile, *Matthew*, 337. So also Gundry, *Matthew*, 466.

28. Garland, *Matthew 23*, 155–57. Davies and Allison, *Matthew*, 3:302, believe this may be correct, but the finished plastered façade could still be magnificent, shining in the sun.

29. The emphatic ὑμεῖς stresses the diatribe against "you" Pharisees.

tombs of the prophets and decorate the monuments of the righteous (Οὐαὶ ὑμῖν, γραμματεῖς καὶ Φαρισαῖοι ὑποκριταί, ὅτι οἰκοδομεῖτε τοὺς τάφους τῶν προφητῶν καὶ κοσμεῖτε τὰ μνημεῖα τῶν δικαίων). This seventh and last of the woes[30] flows out of the sixth with the catchword "tomb" (τάφος) and accuses the Pharisees of constructing elaborate tombs for the saints while negating their significance by participating in the persecution of God's latter-day prophets. On the "prophets" and "righteous" see 10:41; 13:17. Garland notes how Herod led the way in constructing elaborate tombs, possibly to atone for his atrocities (Josephus, *Ant.* 16:179 – 82, 18:108),[31] and Acts 2:29 mentions the tomb of David. Jesus' point is the great effort not only to build the tombs but to beautify them; however, he is not really criticizing this practice but rather the negation of these acts of piety by their opposition to him and his followers.

23:30 And you say, "If we had lived in the days of our fathers, we would not have shared with them in shedding the blood of the prophets" (καὶ λέγετε, Εἰ ἤμεθα ἐν ταῖς ἡμέραις τῶν πατέρων ἡμῶν, οὐκ ἂν ἤμεθα αὐτῶν κοινωνοὶ ἐν τῷ αἵματι τῶν προφητῶν). εἰ ... ἄν is a contrary-to-fact condition that says, "If we had lived then (but we didn't)." Their claim here is part of their action in v. 29. They honor the prophets by constructing elaborate tombs and deny any guilt or complicity for the action of their ancestors in killing the prophets (see Heb 11:35 – 37). However, their actions against Jesus put the lie to their claim.

23:31 As a result, you bear witness against yourselves that you are the children of those who murdered the prophets (ὥστε μαρτυρεῖτε ἑαυτοῖς ὅτι υἱοί ἐστε τῶν φονευσάντων τοὺς προφήτας). The present tense "you bear witness" (μαρτυρεῖτε) continues the string of presents in the woes, emphasizing the continuous nature of their actions. The dative of disadvantage (Wallace, 142 – 43) "against yourselves" (ἑαυτοῖς) pictures the Pharisees standing in the witness box and testifying "against" their very own claims. In the very claim they make in v. 30, they admit that it was their ancestors who murdered God's servants, so they are already guilty by being the "descendants" of the murderers of the prophets. There is double meaning in "children" (υἱοί), for these children "descend" from them and at the same time inherit the same tendencies ("son of" is a Semitic idiom for partaking of the same character, cf. "son of Gehenna" in 23:15) — as will be shown in v. 34.

23:32 So as for you, fill up the measure of your fathers! (καὶ ὑμεῖς πληρώσατε τὸ μέτρον τῶν πατέρων ὑμῶν). There are two levels of meaning here. On the one level, "you fill up" (πληρώσατε, an aorist imperative looking at their actions now as a complete whole) tells the Pharisees to "finish" what their fathers started, namely, the murder of God's servants. "Measure" (μέτρον, followed by a partitive genitive, i.e., the whole of which their actions are a part, cf. BDF §164) means "the measure of sin," with the image of a measuring vessel that slowly fills to the brim. When it is full (note "full of" in vv. 25, 27), God will act in judgment.

30. Matthew 23:29 – 32 expands Luke 11:47 – 48 (vv. 29b – 30, 32 are not in Luke), which centers only on building the tombs and "consenting" to the deeds of their ancestors. Virtually everyone considers Matthew's version a redactional expansion, but Luke could also have easily abbreviated the original form. Bock (*Luke 9:51 – 24:53*, 1120n), in fact, takes the two versions as stemming from two different events.

31. Garland, *Matthew 23*, 163 – 64. See also J. D. M. Derrett, "'You Build the Tombs of the Prophets' (Lk. 11, 47 – 51; Mt. 23, 229 – 31)," *SE* 4 (Berlin: Akademie-Verlag, 1968), 187 – 93; and "Receptacles and Tombs (Matt 23.24 – 30)," *ZNW* 77 (1986), 255 – 66, says the Pharisees forbade the erection of such tombs, but his evidence is unconvincing.

This leads to the second level, namely, that God's mercy extends only so far. There is a level of evil after which God must act. When that level has "reached its full measure," the wrath of God must be released (see Gen 15:16; 1 Thess 2:16). This is akin to the "messianic woes" in which God has established a certain amount of suffering; and when that limit is reached, the eschaton will come (see *1 En.* 47:1 – 4; *4 Ezra* 4:35 – 37; Col 1:24; Rev 6:11).

23:33 Snakes! Offspring of vipers! (ὄφεις, γεννήματα ἐχιδνῶν).[32] Jesus repeats the judgment of the Baptist in 3:7 ("Offspring of vipers, who warned you to flee from the wrath soon to come"), meaning they are a spreading poison[33] (cf. Isa 14:29; Matt 12:34) like the serpent in the garden (Gen 3).

23:33 How will you escape from the judgment of Gehenna? (πῶς φύγητε ἀπὸ τῆς κρίσεως τῆς γεέννης;). This is an example of "how" (πῶς) used "in questions of deliberation with a deliberative subjunctive" (BAGD, 732e; BDF §366), with the aorist subjunctive "escape" (φύγητε) equivalent to a future. It is used here rhetorically to force the readers to confront the certain judgment to come. The message is that the Pharisees have virtually completed storing up wrath, and there will now be no escape. In 23:15 they make their proselytes "child[ren] of Gehenna," and now they in turn will suffer eternal punishment, with "Gehenna" (τῆς γεέννης) an epexegetical genitive, "the judgment which is Gehenna," the eternal lake of fire (see on 5:22).

23:34 Look, because of this I am sending you (διὰ τοῦτο ἰδοὺ ἐγὼ ἀποστέλλω πρὸς ὑμᾶς).[34] διὰ τοῦτο can mean "because of this, for this reason, therefore" (Carson, Morris, Blomberg) or "accordingly, in keeping with this" (Hagner). The former makes slightly better sense, but to what does τοῦτο refer, the whole of vv. 29 – 33 or the "filling up the measure" of v. 32 or the judgment of v. 33? In each of these v. 32 is central. The Pharisees are completing their ministry of evil, so in light of this Jesus will give them the opportunity to do so by sending them (note present tense "send" [ἀποστέλλω] for the ongoing mission of the church) other servants of God to persecute and kill,[35] beginning with himself!

"Look" (ἰδού), as throughout Matthew (see 1:20, 19:16), highlights a dramatic, critical point. This idea of sending his followers out is used twice in the Mission Discourse, at 9:38 ("Pray to the Lord of the harvest that he send out workers") and at 10:16 ("I am sending you as sheep in the midst of wolves"). Jesus as royal Messiah echoes the work of God in sending out his agents in mission.

23:34 ... prophets and sages and scribes (προφήτας καὶ σοφοὺς καὶ γραμματεῖς). These are certainly Christian "prophets and sages and scribes." Does this refer to the office of prophet (Acts 13:1; 1 Cor 12:28 – 29; Eph 4:11) or in a more general sense to Christian missionaries as sent to bring his kingdom message? Probably the latter, for the three categories are not separate but together describe the disciples as God's emissaries; moreover, all three nouns are anarthrous and are probably qualitative (Wallace, 244 – 45), not looking at NT prophets but at all disciples as the new class of prophets and sages. The use of "prophets"

32. There is some debate as to whether v. 33 concludes vv. 13 – 33 (so Hagner, Davies Allison, Luz) or begins the conclusion of the woes (vv. 33 – 36, so Carson, Keener). As a transition verse, it functions both ways, but it is slightly more intimately connected with v. 34 (note "because of this" [διὰ τοῦτο] there). Interestingly, Gnilka takes 32 – 39 together as the conclusion.

33. Not their shrewdness, contra Blomberg, *Matthew*, 77.

34. This parallels Luke 11:49, and there is debate about the original form of Q, as to whether Luke or Matthew is closer (most say Luke, so Luz), but both versions are redactional at the core, i.e., paraphrases of what Jesus originally said (see the discussion of the Beatitudes in 5:3 – 12).

35. Here they are not being sent to warn the leaders of judgment to come, see France, *Gospel of Matthew*, 878.

establishes continuity with the persecution of the OT prophets by the ancestors of the Pharisees.

Up this point Luke 11:49 has "prophets and apostles."[36] The "wise men" are the teachers of the church (so Garland) who are controlled by divine wisdom (Luke has, "God in his wisdom said, 'I will send ...'"). The use of "scribes" points back to Matt 13:52 ("every teacher of the law [scribe] who becomes trained as a disciple in the kingdom of heaven") and describes the disciples again as Jesus' sanctioned interpreters of holy law.

23:34 You will kill and crucify some of them, and you will have some of them scourged in your synagogues and persecuted from city to city (ἐξ αὐτῶν ἀποκτενεῖτε καὶ σταυρώσετε καὶ ἐξ αὐτῶν μαστιγώσετε ἐν ταῖς συναγωγαῖς ὑμῶν καὶ διώξετε ἀπὸ πόλεως εἰς πόλιν). Jesus has already experienced the last of these and will soon experience the others, but here he predicts that his followers will share them with him. The first three (kill, crucify, and scourge) occur in the passion prediction of 20:18 – 19, and all parallel the persecution predicted for missionaries in 10:17, 23, 28. The suffering of Jesus will be echoed in the suffering of his followers, and all will have their source in the rejection and rabid opposition of the leaders.

23:35 ... with the result that all the righteous blood poured out on the earth will come upon you (ὅπως ἔλθῃ ἐφ' ὑμᾶς πᾶν αἷμα δίκαιον ἐκχυννόμενον ἐπὶ τῆς γῆς). "With the result" (ὅπως) can denote purpose or result, but in the context of vv. 33 – 34 result fits better. The leaders did not intend to bring judgment down on themselves, but it is the natural result of their many sins that have piled up to heaven and "filled the measure" of God's wrath, especially their rejection and opposition against Jesus and his followers. The idea of "blood coming upon you" is an OT idiom for responsibility and guilt for the death of others (Jer 26:15; Jonah 1:14; so Nolland). Because these people have joined their ancestors in such nefarious activities, they join in the guilt (by ancestry and by action) of all the innocent blood shed from the beginning to the end.

23:35 ... from the blood of righteous Abel to the blood of Zechariah son of Berachiah, whom you murdered between the sanctuary and the altar (ἀπὸ τοῦ αἵματος Ἅβελ τοῦ δικαίου ἕως τοῦ αἵματος Ζαχαρίου υἱοῦ Βαραχίου, ὃν ἐφονεύσατε μεταξὺ τοῦ ναοῦ καὶ τοῦ θυσιαστηρίου). "Righteous Abel" was the first martyr (Gen 4:8), but the identity of this Zechariah is difficult to establish.[37] At first glance one thinks of the prophet Zechariah son of Berekiah in Zech 1:1, but there is no hint that he was ever killed. Still, some believe it was indeed this Zechariah, with some late Jewish texts alluding to it (so Blomberg).

Two others named Zechariah are mentioned in this regard: a Zechariah son of Baris who was murdered by Zealots in the temple area before AD 70 (but no evidence he was a priest and could have been "between the sanctuary and the altar"), and the priest Zechariah who was stoned in the courtyard of the temple in 2 Chr 24:20 – 21. This latter would fit well because 2 Chronicles is the last book in the Hebrew Bible, so the two (Abel and Zechariah) would frame the biblical period. But this latter Zechariah is the son of Jehoiada (2 Chr 24:20). There are two ways of harmonizing this — that Jehoiada was actually the grandfather of this

36. Taking this and Luke 11:49 (where "God in his wisdom" sends out the messengers) as Q sayings, Witherington, *Matthew*, 432, says that Matthew envisions Jesus as the Wisdom of God sending out his sages. However, Gench, *Wisdom*, 75 – 79, shows that here Jesus is not assuming the prerogatives of Sophia but of God in sending out his emissaries.

37. Some believe this is an unknown Zechariah, lost in the ancient records, e.g., Albright and Mann, *Matthew*, 282; John M. Ross, "Which Zechariah?" *IBS* 9 (1987): 70 – 73.

Zechariah (Broadus, Carson) or Matthew makes a deliberate conflation of the two Zechariahs (Gundry, Keener, Nolland, France). This second option fits the situation, is quite plausible, and probably provides the best solution.

23:36 I tell you the truth, all these things will come on this generation (ἀμὴν λέγω ὑμῖν, ἥξει ταῦτα πάντα ἐπὶ τὴν γενεὰν ταύτην). This further "amen" (ἀμήν) saying (see on 5:18) highlights a key point of the narrative, in this case the extension of the imminent judgment to "this generation." The leaders typify the people as a whole, and they have followed in the footsteps of their religious leaders and so share in the indictment. Thus, just as the blood guilt "came on" the scribes and Pharisees (v. 35), so "all these things" (ταῦτα πάντα) will "come on" the people of the current generation with Jesus. They share in the rejection of Jesus and his messengers, and they will share in the judgment it engenders. As such this prepares for the lament over Jerusalem in vv. 37 – 39 and the prophecy about imminent judgment on the nation in chs. 24 – 25. Similar statements are found in 11:16; 12:39 – 45; 16:4; 24:34.

Theology in Application

There are two primary aspects to these seven "woes," the diatribe and warning to the historical generation of Jesus about the religious sins of the leaders,[38] and the warning to Christians of every generation regarding the danger of hypocrisy. It is the latter that we explore here. In addition, there are two further general nuances that must be noted, since the errors are also twofold: misusing Scripture to justify false religious practices, and the hypocrisy that results. So let us apply each of the woes in turn:

1. Teaching the Word of God

Do not teach the Word of God falsely and in this way close the door of the kingdom to people. The first woe addressed the claim of the Pharisees to build a fence around the law and enable people to obey Torah. However, in reality they twisted God's truth and rejected his Messiah. For us this applies to a proper use of God's Word to bring people to Christ and to enable them to live the new truths of the kingdom (e.g., the Sermon on the Mount). This is especially true when we allow our systems to triumph over the text, thus "binding people to human traditions rather than to God's true law and obscuring the pure center with trivia and minutiae."[39] We need to become Berean Christians, who "examined the Scriptures every day to see if what Paul said was true" (Acts 17:11), and to remember Paul's injunction to Timothy,

38. At the same time, the summary of Hagner, *Matthew 14 – 28*, 672 – 73, must also be taken into consideration: this was not universal denunciation of all Pharisees and should not be used to describe the whole movement (as it was until recent times). Rather, it should be used to challenge ourselves not to commit these religious sins.

39. Bruner, *Matthew 13 – 28*, 444.

"Do your best to present yourself to God as one approved, a worker who does not need to be ashamed and who correctly handles the word of truth" (2 Tim 2:15).

2. Making Proselytes

Those who make converts had better make certain they are teaching the true gospel. It is easy to proclaim a religious truth and create fervent followers who exhibit even more zeal than we do. But what happens if it turns out that it is our own truth and not God's that we are proclaiming? That was the case with the Pharisees, and that is often the case today with a Joseph Smith, a Jim Jones, a David Koresh, but also with those who have shallow teaching ministries. God will hold each of us accountable for what we are feeding our flock (Heb 13:17; Jas 3).

3. Distinctions

Do not make meaningless legalistic distinctions to support false religious views. The shallow multiplication of oaths to support vapid promises in the first century was a sign of the false religion Judaism had become to Jesus. Everything was external rather than a true commitment to God, and Jesus did not want God's name attached to such hypocritical practices. When a religion descends into arcane details and strange rules involving teaching that clearly does not come from Scripture, it proves itself to be false. "Tricky, convoluted, casuistic teaching is not the teaching of the Holy Spirit."[40] Such casuistic legalism was found at Colosse (Col 2:16 – 19) and is too often seen in the church today.

4. Don't Major in Minors

These leaders tithed scrupulously, even on things not demanded in the Torah, but they did not care for the unfortunate or live lives faithful to God. That is true in many different denominations and Christian groups, who demand all kinds of legalistic trivia but harshly judge others and fail to exhibit God's mercy to outsiders. As Blomberg says, "a scandal of the contemporary church is its unparalleled fragmentation into hundreds of denominations … (divided) over issues nonessential to salvation."[41] The Corinthian enthusiasts elevated their spiritual gifts over everyone else (1 Cor 12 – 14), and Jewish and Gentile Christians frequently fought over issues like food or drink or holy days (Rom 14:1 – 15:13; 1 Cor 8 – 10). We must learn to agree to disagree and respect each other's right to differ over the noncardinal issues.

40. Ibid, 446.

41. Blomberg, *Matthew*, 346.

5. Looks Are Deceiving

Avoid looking pious while living lives of greedy self-indulgence. The fifth and sixth woes describe a life of hypocrisy and typify much of Western Christianity, building huge luxurious churches whose members on Sunday look worshipful while they live lives of extravagance. The members live above their means, yet give little to God in terms of both time and money. It has been estimated that only 25 to 30 percent of the average evangelical church is actually involved in that church's ministry. The rest attend regularly but live self-centered lives. There are only two possible destinies for them: to squeak into heaven "as one escaping through the flames" (1 Cor 3:12 – 15) or to have Christ say, "I never knew you" (Matt 7:21 – 23, see discussion of that passage). It is a terrible thing to play games with one's eternal destiny!

6. Avoid Hostility

Make certain you are not hostile to a movement that God is behind. At one level this is history specific, for it addresses primarily the Jewish leaders and their participation in the sins of their fathers who killed the prophets. At another level this has been repeated in the inquisition and similar Christian movements, where believers rejected, persecuted, and even killed fellow believers. Romans 14:1 – 15:13 makes clear that Christians must tolerate differences among themselves so long as heresy is not at stake.

Yet the term "heretic" has been terribly misused in history, as minor issues (e.g., Reformed vs. Anabaptist in the sixteenth century or debates over predestination, charismatic doctrine, or the rapture in our day) have been elevated to cardinal doctrines. It is critical to recognize issues that fall under God's wrath and those that God accepts and uses for his glory (again, see Rom 14). In vv. 34 – 36, Israel is guilty and headed for judgment. When a Christian group becomes arrogant and narrow and persecutes another group that God is also using, they too will have to give account to the ultimate Judge.

CHAPTER 100

Matthew 23:37 – 39

Literary Context

The lament flows right out of the preceding context. Jesus had to indict first the leaders for their hypocrisy and sin, and then in the previous verse had to extend that judgment to the whole nation. This caused Jesus deep sorrow, and he wants them to know the deep love of both God and himself for them.

VI. The Movement to the Cross (19:1 – 25:46)
- **B. Fifth Discourse: Guilt and Judgment of Israel (23:1 – 25:46)**
  - **1. Guilt: Woes upon the Leaders (23:1 – 39)**
    - a. Warning and Humility (23:1 – 12)
    - b. The Seven Woes (23:13 – 36)
    - ➦ **c. Lament over Jerusalem (23:37 – 39)**
  - 2. Judgment — Olivet Discourse (24:1 – 25:46)

Main Idea

By using the metaphor of a hen and her chicks, Jesus reveals his tender concern to see the people of Jerusalem get right with God. At the same time, they have already rejected his offer, and so their future is "desolate." Yet one thing is certain: he will return as the royal Messiah.

Translation

(See next page.)

Matthew 23:37-39

37a	Address	*"O Jerusalem, Jerusalem,*
b	Description	*who kills the prophets and stones those sent to her,*
c	Desire	*how often I have wanted to gather your children together,*
d	Analogy	*as a hen gathers her young under her wings,*
e	Response	*but you were not willing.*
38a	Prediction/Judgment	*Look, your house is going to be left to you desolate.*
39a	Promise/Warning	*For I tell you, you will never see me again until you say,*
b	OT Quotation	*'Blessed is the One who comes in the name of the Lord.'* (Ps 118:26)

Structure and Literary Form

This lament is a Q passage, nearly in verbatim agreement with Luke 13:34 – 35 (but a different place in Luke). Most agree that Matthew is likely the more original setting. There are three natural segments: the lament itself (v. 37), the certainty of judgment (v. 38), and a promise and warning (v. 39).

Exegetical Outline

- **I. Jesus' Deep Sorrow over Jerusalem (23:37)**
  - A. His desire to gather them to himself
  - B. Their rejection and murder of God's ambassadors
- **II. The Certainty of the Judgment (23:38)**
- **III. The Promise and Warning (23:39)**
  - A. Jesus' departure
  - B. Jesus' return

Explanation of the Text

23:37 "O Jerusalem, Jerusalem, who kills the prophets and stones those sent to her" (Ἰερουσαλὴμ Ἰερουσαλήμ, ἡ ἀποκτείνουσα τοὺς προφήτας καὶ λιθοβολοῦσα τοὺς ἀπεσταλμένους πρὸς αὐτήν). There is an ABA pattern in this verse, with murder and rejection framing Jesus' desire to gather his Jewish kinspeople to himself. The result is an incredible contrast between the deep love of Jesus and the absolute rejection of him by the Jewish people. The double vocative and the

Hebrew spelling "Jerusalem" (Ἰερουσαλήμ) echo OT divine address (Gen 46:2; Exod 3:4; 1 Sam 3:10, so Nolland). "Jerusalem" is personified and stands for the nation.

The description of Jerusalem "killing" and "stoning" ties this closely with vv. 30 – 31 (killing), 34b, 35 (Zechariah stoned in 2 Chr 24:21) and the murder of both OT and NT prophets and messengers. Jerusalem is now an apostate city that has turned against God and rejected his Son. Indeed, Jerusalem is the "great city" amalgamated with Rome in Rev 11:8.

23:37 "How often I have wanted to gather your children together, as a hen gathers her young under her wings" (ποσάκις ἠθέλησα ἐπισυναγαγεῖν τὰ τέκνα σου, ὃν τρόπον ὄρνις ἐπισυνάγει τὰ νοσσία αὐτῆς ὑπὸ τὰς πτέρυγας). The image of a hen "gathering her young under her wings" highlights the great love of God and Jesus for the Jewish people and connotes a mother's love especially in protecting her young (cf. Deut 32:11; Ps 17:8; 36:7; 63:7; Isa 34:15; Jer 48:40). In fact, there is a further contrast, as Jerusalem is also described as a mother with her "children." Jesus longs to protect and love her children, but Jerusalem is training them to reject Jesus, as is to be expected with an apostate city (see on previous verse). "How often" (ποσάκις) refers to the many missions Jesus and his disciples have taken both in Galilee (Matthew) and in Judea (John).[1]

23:37 "But you were not willing" (καὶ οὐκ ἠθελήσατε). Adversative "but" (καί) in Semitic contexts like this is fairly common. There is an interesting development from all the second singulars earlier in v. 37 to the second plural of "you were willing" (ἠθελήσατε),[2] continued in vv. 38 – 39. As Carson says, "The effect is to move from the abstraction of the city to the concrete reality of people."[3] Jerusalem is made up of people who have joined her in rejecting God's Messiah, and they personify the nation as a whole.

23:38 "Look, your house is going to be left to you desolate" (ἰδοὺ ἀφίεται ὑμῖν ὁ οἶκος ὑμῶν ἔρημος). As often in Matthew, "look" (ἰδού) is a dramatic formula pointing to a critical event (see 1:20; 19:16; 23:34), and it is also used often in prophetic judgment passages (Ps 73:12; Isa 7:14; Ezek 5:8). ἀφίεται is a prophetic or futuristic present ("is going to be left") and a divine passive expressing the certainty of the coming judgment.[4] It is debated whether "your house" is Israel as a whole (Hill), Jerusalem (McNeile, Manson, Senior), or the temple (France, Luz, Nolland; Davies and Allison say the latter two), but it is best to see not an either-or but all three as intended (Carson, Hagner).

Verse 38 points to Jerusalem and 24:1 – 2 to the temple, but throughout chs. 23 – 24 both personify the Jewish people as a whole. The idea of being left "desolate" (ἔρημος) pictures the absolute destruction of AD 70. The noun (and verb) are also used in Rev 17:16; 18:17, 19 to depict the "ruination" of the great prostitute and Babylon the Great; in Rev 18:2, 21 – 23 it is described as a virtual desert, a ghost town. Such is the picture of Jerusalem (and the temple) here, soon to become a wasteland, virtually uninhabitable (for OT background, see 2 Kgs

1. See Davies and Allison, *Matthew*, 3:321, for various explanations of the "awkward 'how many'" in light of the fact that in Matthew this is Jesus' first trip to Jerusalem. Yet if Jerusalem with "your children" personifies all the Jewish people (see below), the notion makes good sense, and John 2:13 – 3:16; 5:1 – 15; 7:1 – 52; 10:22 – 39 show the many trips Jesus made to Jerusalem and Judea before that final journey.

2. This is another global aorist looking at the ongoing rejection as a single whole (Porter, *Idioms*, 24, calls this "perfective" force, viewing the action "in its entirety as a single and complete whole"). "Willing" (θέλω) emphasizes the deliberate choice of the will.

3. Carson, "Matthew," 486.

4. See Moulton, *Grammar*, 63; BDF §323.

21:14; Jer 12:7; 22:5). This connotes both abandonment by God (Ezek 8:6, 11:23)[5] and destruction.

23:39 "For I tell you, you will not see me again" (λέγω γὰρ ὑμῖν, οὐ μή με ἴδητε ἀπ' ἄρτι). Jesus anchors ("for" [γάρ]) the prophecy of v. 38 in further revelation here. His solemn "I tell you" in Matthew (cf. 3:9; 5:20; et al.; in 5:28, 32, 34, 39, 44 it was part of the formula ["it was said ... but I am telling you"] behind the antitheses) builds on the "amen" (ἀμήν) formula in pointing to an important truth. His "you will never[6] see me again" is a prophetic pronouncement of Jesus' impending departure via his death and resurrection and states the fact that they will not encounter him again until his parousia. "From now" (ἀπ' ἄρτι), in fact, points forward to the parousia and the eschaton (26:29, 64).

23:39 "... until you say, 'Blessed is the One who comes in the name of the Lord' " (ἕως ἂν εἴπητε, Εὐλογημένος ὁ ἐρχόμενος ἐν ὀνόματι κυρίου). The quote stems from Ps 118:26 and was proclaimed by the crowds at the triumphal entry (21:9). The addition of the positive quotation to the negative context led to three possible interpretations. (1) It could be judgment and refer to the forced homage of defeated enemies (Manson, Gnilka, Garland, Luz). (2) It could refer to the ultimate repentance and salvation of Israel as seen in Rom 11:25–32 (Plummer, Schlatter, Schweizer, Gundry, Blomberg) or as taking place during the church's mission (Nolland). (3) It could be conditional ("until" [ἕως]) and mean Jesus will wait until the Jewish people repent (Davies and Allison). The third is unlikely since there is nothing in Scripture that hints Jesus is in heaven biding his time and waiting for the Jewish people to repent. The best is a combination of the first two—when Jesus comes, all humanity will either rejoice at his return or be forced to bow before him (cf. also Phil 2:10–11, so Carson).

Theology in Application

The application of this lament depends entirely on one's interpretation of v. 39, as to whether it proclaims judgment or possible salvation for Israel (contrast the concluding observations of Hagner and Davies and Allison). Yet one thing is certain—it demonstrates the deep love of Jesus for his own people, the desire to "gather [them] under [his] wings." Jesus' entire desire for Israel is that they may be saved, but the people will not accept his offer of salvation.

So there are two conclusions. The immediate future is "desolation" in the destruction of AD 66–70 (as will be prophesied in 24:2–28). Yet in the final analysis it will depend on the decision of each individual—a decision that will determine whether they will rejoice in the "coming" of Christ and be "blessed" or be forced to bow before him as they face judgment. In this the Jewish people stand for all the people of history who will share the same two possible destinies. Also, Christ is the model for all believers as they participate in his mission with compassion and love, yet at the same time with severe warning for those who have rejected the gospel. We too should lament the lost (cf. Phil 3:18, "I ... tell you again even with tears").

5. Garland, *Matthew 23*, 201–3, says it means more abandonment by Jesus as "God with us." Thus the Shekinah for Matthew is Jesus' presence, and he has abandoned the temple to judgment.

6. οὐ μή as emphatic future negation is less emphatic than in classical Greek, and whether it means "never" or "not" must be inferred from its context (see BDF §365; Porter, *Idioms*, 283).

CHAPTER 101

Matthew 24:1 – 3

Introduction to the Olivet Discourse (Matthew 24:1 – 25:46)

Impending judgment has been the dominant theme since the symbolic actions of the cleansing of the temple and cursing of the fig tree in 21:12 – 22. This theme culminates in the Olivet Discourse (named for the place it was presented), or the Apocalyptic Discourse (named for the content), the fifth and final discourse of Jesus in Matthew.[1] The reason for this judgment was presented in the woes and lament of the previous chapter. Now Jesus combines the imminent destruction of the temple and Jerusalem with the events of the eschaton.

It is generally agreed that this is apocalyptic material, though of course it is not pure apocalyptic characterized as being in a narrative framework.[2] But many qualities are indeed present, such as a revelatory stance, the use of predictive symbolism, the coming of the eschaton, a modified dualism in terms of God vs. the powers of evil, and an ethical perspective centering on the need for perseverance. The best approach is probably defined by George Ladd, who notes the blend of prophetic and apocalyptic styles in Revelation as well as this discourse.[3]

A major problem stems from source-critical comparisons of Matt 24 – 25 with Mark 13 and Luke 17 and 21. While most recognize the literary dependence of Mark 13, Matt 24, and Luke 17, it is often believed that Luke 21 is a "historicization" of the material largely from separate sources. The best solution is that of David Wenham, who argues that all the Synoptic writers used the same eschatological discourse.[4] As in all the Matthean discourses (chs. 5 – 7; 10; 13; 18), it is debated whether this was all uttered by Jesus on a single occasion (so Carson) or whether Matthew was

1. There is no need to posit a prophecy after the event or to doubt the basic historicity of this discourse. As Craig A. Evans shows ("Prediction of the Destruction of the Herodian Temple in the Pseudepigrapha, Qumran Scrolls, and Related Texts," *JSP* 10 [1992]: 89 – 147), there were other such prophecies in that era. See also Sanders, *Jesus and Judaism*, 71 – 90, for the authenticity of the prediction.

2. For a definition see John J. Collins, "Apocalypse: The Morphology of a Genre," *Semeia* 14 (1979): 1 – 20; David Aune, "The Apocalypse of John and the Problem of Genre," *Semeia* 36 (1986): 65 – 96; and Osborne, *Hermeneutical Spiral*, 222.

3. George Ladd, "Why Not Prophetic-Apocalyptic?" *JBL* 76 (1957): 192 – 200.

4. David Wenham, *The Rediscovery of Jesus' Eschatological Discourse* (Sheffield: JSOT Press, 1984). See also Blomberg, *Historical Reliability*, 142 – 43; Keener, *Matthew*, 560 – 62.

free to add other material from Jesus' teaching (most others). Either is possible, but the great amount of material found elsewhere in Mark and Luke (see below) would make the latter slightly more likely.

Another problem is the connection between the destruction of Jerusalem and the events at the parousia (e.g., the "great tribulation," Rev 7:14). How do we explain the seeming discrepancy between the historical perspective and the apocalyptic expectation/imminence? There are several suggested solutions:

1. Many classical dispensationalists assert that this passage is entirely future and 24:29–31 is not the rapture (before the tribulation) but the revelation (after it) as seen in the Jewish nature of the disciples; among critical scholars some also take it as entirely future (Schlatter, Zahn, Gnilka).
2. The parousia is not found here; instead the whole relates to the destruction of Jerusalem, with the shaking of the heavens symbolizing political disasters (Isa 13:10, 34:4) and with the parousia referring to Jesus coming to take his people back from exile (France, Wright, McKnight).
3. Jesus describes only the destruction in vv. 4–28, and the parousia is found in vv. 29–31 with the tribulation period in vv. 32–35 (Wenham, Gnilka, Carson).
4. This is apocalyptic language, in which the destruction of Jerusalem foreshadows the tribulation period in vv. 4–28, 32–35 (esp. vv. 8, 14, 15, 21–22, 27–28) and the parousia in vv. 29–31 (Hill, Ladd, Gundry, Turner,[5] Davies and Allison, Wilkins).

In light of the nature of apocalyptic language, the centrality of Daniel in the discourse, and the use of similar motifs in 2 Thess 2 and the book of Revelation, the fourth view is the most probable (hinted at in the question of the disciples in v. 3).

It is generally agreed that there are three parts to the structure: 24:1–35, 24:36–25:30, 25:31–46,[6] though there is some debate as to whether the first section ends at v. 31, 35, 36, or 41 (see Luz). This scheme makes the most sense, so the segments concern the destruction of Jerusalem and events of the end time (24:1–36), parables on readiness (24:37–25:30), and a parable on the final judgment (25:31–46).

Literary Context

Jesus has spent most of Passion Week in the temple, first cleansing it and then debating the leaders in it. Now he is about to cap the woes against the scribes and

5. David L. Turner, "The Structure and Sequence of Matthew 24:1–41: Interaction with Evangelical Treatments," *GTJ* 10 (1989): 3–27.

6. But Beare, *Matthew*, 461, 473; and Hagner, *Matthew 14–28*, 684, see two parts, 24:1–36; 25:37–25:46.

Pharisees by pronouncing imminent judgment on the temple. In 23:35 – 36 the people were guilty of "all the righteous blood" spilled, and in 23:38 her future was "desolate." Now that desolation is spelled out. The prophecy of this section will dominate the next two chapters.

VI. The Movement to the Cross (19:1 – 25:46)
- **B. Fifth Discourse: Guilt and Judgment of Israel (23:1 – 25:46)**
  - 1. Guilt: Woes upon the Leaders (23:1 – 39)
  - **2. Judgment — Olivet Discourse (24:1 – 25:46)**
    - **a. Destruction of Jerusalem and the Events of the End Time (24:1 – 35)**
      - ➦ **(1) Prophecy on the Destruction (24:1 – 3)**
      - (2) The Destruction and the End-Time Events (24:4 – 28)

Main Idea

The disciples point out the temple, and Jesus responds with the sad fact that God is soon to destroy it. This is followed by the question that the disciples (and all of us) have: what and when. The link on the part of the disciples between the destruction and the end of the age is an important hermeneutical key to Jesus' message in 24:4 – 28.

Translation

(See next page.)

Structure and Literary Form

These first three verses are built closely on Mark 13:1 – 4, with the main differences being the indirect discourse in v. 1 (plus the absence of the disciples' wonder at the beauty of the temple) and the twofold nature of the sign in Matthew (Jesus' coming and the end of the age). There are two parts, the prediction of the temple's destruction (vv. 1 – 2), and the question regarding when and what (v. 3).

Exegetical Outline

➦ **I. The Prophecy of Destruction (24:1 – 2)**
- A. The disciples point out the buildings (v. 1)

Matthew 24:1-3

1a	Introduction/Setting	And	when Jesus departed and was going away from the temple,
b	Action	**his disciples came to him to show him the buildings of the temple.**	
2a	Rhetorical Question	**But Jesus responded,**	
b		*"You do see all these things, don't you?*	
c	Prediction	*I tell you the truth, there will not be left here one stone upon another stone that will not be thrown down."*	
3a	Setting	Now	while he was sitting on the Mount of Olives,
b	Action	**his disciples came to him privately, saying,**	
c	Question #1	*"Tell us, [1] when will these things take place?*	
d	Question #2	*[2] And what will be the sign of your coming and of the end of the age?"*	

B. Jesus predicts its destruction (v. 2)

II. The Questions of the Disciples (24:3)

A. When will it happen? (v. 3a)

B. What will be the sign? (v. 3b)

Explanation of the Text

24:1 And when Jesus departed[7] and was going away from the temple (Καὶ ἐξελθὼν ὁ Ἰησοῦς ἀπὸ τοῦ ἱεροῦ ἐπορεύετο). It is difficult to reconstruct the time here, for the last mention of entering the temple is 21:23, but it is likely that the debates in the temple and this discourse occur on the same day (Tuesday; see the chart at the beginning of ch. 21). Thus, Jesus is apparently leaving the temple[8] after conducting the debates there. This ties the discourse closely to the debates of chs. 21 – 22 and the woes in ch. 23. France says, "He is abandoning it, never to return, and after that it has no future except to be destroyed."[9]

24:1 ... his disciples came to him to show him the buildings of the temple (καὶ προσῆλθον οἱ μαθηταὶ αὐτοῦ ἐπιδεῖξαι αὐτῷ τὰς οἰκοδομὰς τοῦ ἱεροῦ). Matthew does not have as strong a statement of wonder at the temple's beauty as Mark does, but that is implied. The disciples have not understood the meaning of the temple cleansing and cursing of the fig tree, nor of the woes and lament at the wickedness of the leaders and the city. They are still enamored with the wonder of the temple, which certainly deserved such exclamations on the face of it.

The temple was indeed considered, even by the

7. ἐξελθών is a temporal aorist participle that could be translated, "after Jesus departed."

8. In Matthew when Jesus "leaves" a group, it often is a prophetic action of rejection (see on 21:17), and that may be true here as well.

9. France, *Gospel of Matthew*, 886.

Romans, to be one of the most beautiful structures in the ancient world (Josephus, *J.W.* 6.267). The walls were made of huge stones, some up to forty feet long, and the top was adorned by pure white marble, with gold plates on the façade so numerous that people were almost blinded when the sun shone on it.[10]

24:2 But Jesus responded, "You do see all these things, don't you?" (ὁ δὲ ἀποκριθεὶς εἶπεν αὐτοῖς, Οὐ βλέπετε ταῦτα πάντα;). When "not" (οὐ) is used to introduce a question, it expects an affirmative answer (BDF §440). Jesus directs the disciples to all the incredible sights as they look over from the Mount of Olives to the next hill, Mount Zion, and see "all" the magnificence of the temple.[11]

24:2 I tell you the truth, there will not[12] be left here one stone upon another stone that will not be thrown down (ἀμὴν λέγω ὑμῖν, οὐ μὴ ἀφεθῇ ὧδε λίθος ἐπὶ λίθον ὃς οὐ καταλυθήσεται). Then Jesus proceeds to blow his disciples away, beginning his prophecy with the solemn "amen" (ἀμήν) saying (see on 5:18; 23:36 [also proclaiming judgment]). Jeremiah had predicted the destruction of the first temple (Jer 7:12 – 14; 26:6, 18; cf. 9:11, 22:1 – 5), as did Micah (Mic 3:12). Jesus likely has these prophecies in mind, for the cause, national apostasy, has occurred once more.

Jesus' description, not "one stone upon another stone," forecasts total destruction, which did take place as the Romans razed the temple in AD 70 (Josephus, *J.W.* 7.1.1). Of course, some of the massive stones of the retaining walls were left in place (see the Western Wall today), but the temple was thoroughly razed, and that is what Jesus is referring to. Nolland draws a parallel with Hag 2:15, where "one stone ... on another" was used in rebuilding the temple. Here the restoration is reversed and turned to destruction.[13]

24:3 Now while he was sitting[14] on the Mount of Olives, his disciples came to him privately (Καθημένου δὲ αὐτοῦ ἐπὶ τοῦ Ὄρους τῶν Ἐλαιῶν προσῆλθον αὐτῷ οἱ μαθηταὶ κατ' ἰδίαν). Matthew uses a genitive absolute to situate the dialogue on the Mount of Olives (thus the title "Olivet Discourse"), associated in Ezek 11:23; Zech 14:4 with the coming of Yahweh in judgment. Thus Jesus predicts judgment on the very mountain where that judgment is to begin. Moreover, mountain scenes are linked with divine revelation in Matthew (5:1; 15:29; 17:1; 28:16). As in the Sermon on the Mount (5:1) and the Parable Discourse (13:2), Jesus is "sitting," the normal posture for a rabbi teaching his disciples. His disciples do not doubt the veracity of his prediction, probably because they too are aware of the biblical precedents. They come to him "privately," away from the crowds and in keeping with 13:11, where Jesus said the kingdom "mysteries" are meant only for the insiders.

24:3 ... saying, "Tell us, when will these things take place?" (λέγοντες, Εἰπὲ ἡμῖν, πότε ταῦτα ἔσται;). The disciples clearly link the destruction of the temple with the arrival of the eschaton.

10. See Carol Meyers, "Temple, Jerusalem," *ABD*, 6:365; see also on 21:12,

11. Some have interpreted "see" as "understand" and believe Jesus is asking them to understand what he said in ch. 23 about the coming judgment of the temple. However, in the context this is unlikely, and Jesus is simply responding to their exclamation about the splendor of the buildings (see Carson, Bruner).

12. This is emphatic οὐ μή and means "never." It is debated whether this has retained its emphatic force, but though it is primarily in quotes from the LXX and sayings of Jesus, it is generally recognized that it does; see Porter, *Idioms*, 283; Wallace, 468.

13. Nolland, *Matthew*, 959.

14. This is another temporal genitive absolute (see on 8:1) and with the present tense looks at action contemporaneous to the main verb.

Moreover, since Jesus in 23:36 said the judgment was to take place during "this generation," the disciples assumed everything would happen soon. Their question is twofold, centering on the time ("when" [πότε]) of "these things," namely, the whole complex of events the disciples associated with the OT "day of the LORD" and in their minds would be inaugurated by the destruction of the temple; and the "sign" (σημεῖον) they should look for to herald those events. Jesus will answer the first question negatively when he tells them, "you do not know on what day your Lord is going to come" (24:42) and "you do not know the day or the hour" (25:13). The time is not for them to know.

24:3 "And what will be the sign of your coming and of the end of the age?" (καὶ τί τὸ σημεῖον τῆς σῆς παρουσίας καὶ συντελείας τοῦ αἰῶνος;). The second question is in fact addressed by Jesus. He will spend the first part of his address telling what are *not* the signs (vv. 4 – 14, 23 – 26), and then will elucidate what are, namely, the "abomination that causes desolation" of v. 15, the "great tribulation" of v. 21, and especially "the sign of the Son of Man" coming in v. 30. The coming and the eschaton are considered a single event by the disciples, as indicated by the article governing both.[15] They have also connected both of these to the destruction of the temple.

"Of your coming" (τῆς σῆς παρουσίας) is an objective genitive ("what will designate your coming"), and the term was often used for the arrival of a king or high official, so this expression became the primary term for the second "coming" of Christ (1 Cor 15:23; 1 Thess 4:15; 2 Thess 2:1, 8; mentioned also here in vv. 27, 37, 39). The disciples, of course, do not understand all this; they most likely are thinking of the expected moment when Jesus will become conquering Messiah. But they do link this with the final "consummation of the age" (found only in 13:39, 40, 49; 28:20 and here in the NT, though Heb 9:26 marks Jesus' sacrifice on the cross as inaugurating "the culmination of the ages"), when the enemies of the people of God will be destroyed.

It is debated whether Jesus corrected or accepted the implicit link between the destruction of the temple and the eschaton. Blomberg, for instance, says, "Jesus will make clear that the destruction of the temple and the end of the age are two separate events,"[16] while Bruner says, "I can believe that both Jesus and Matthew saw the destruction of Jerusalem and the end of the world as being almost contemporaneous ... the destruction of Jerusalem is everywhere in the sermon that end's classic precursor."[17] The issue is complex, but I believe the former is the best scenario, as the subsequent commentary will show. Bruner is correct to see a link between the two, but the apocalyptic language does not establish a chronological link but rather a salvation-historical connection. The term "precursor" is right, but that does not make the events simultaneous.

15. This is Granville Sharp's rule; cf. Moulton, *Grammar*, 181; Porter, *Idioms*, 110 – 11.

16. Blomberg, *Matthew*, 353; so also France, *Matthew* (TNTC), 337.

17. Bruner, *Matthew 13 – 28*, 473.

Theology in Application

These introductory verses establish the tone of the entire discourse, and every reader throughout the ages has asked the same questions. What is the connection between the destruction of the temple and the coming eschaton? When will these events take place? There are several lessons in this, such as the danger of being overly impressed by the earthly splendor of a man-made structure, even if it be a temple, cathedral, or beautiful church. Another danger is to be overly consumed by questions of timing, e.g., the exact date of the Lord's return (as several embarrassed "prophecy preachers" have discovered when they predicted the date of the parousia). It is not for us to know the timing, but it is not wrong to await the "signs" that God will provide, as the development of this discourse will show. The tension between these two perspectives has defined eschatological debates throughout the centuries.

CHAPTER 102

Matthew 24:4 – 14

Literary Context

Jesus begins his answer with the second question of the disciples, the signs that presage the end. As such he is also addressing the implicit assumption that these are connected to the destruction of the temple and Jerusalem, saying in effect that these troubles are not the end of the age (see Hagner).

VI. The Movement to the Cross (19:1 – 25:46)
- **B. Fifth Discourse: Guilt and Judgment of Israel (23:1 – 25:46)**
  - 1. Guilt: Woes upon the Leaders (23:1 – 39)
  - **2. Judgment — Olivet Discourse (24:1 – 25:46)**
    - **a. Destruction of Jerusalem and the Events of the End Time (24:1 – 35)**
      - (1) Prophecy on the Destruction (24:1 – 3)
      - **(2) The Destruction and the End-Time Events (24:4 – 28)**
        - ➦ **(a) Signs That Are Not the End (24:4 – 14)**
          - **(i) Great Deception and Great Travail (24:4 – 8)**
          - **(ii) Great Apostasy and the Great Mission (24:9 – 14)**
        - (b) Signs That Point to the End (24:15 – 28)

Main Idea

Do not listen to the false messiahs, for the normal calamities that are often taken as signs of the end — wars, earthquakes, etc. — are only the beginning of the travails and do not point to the end. During the interim period, there will be great suffering and even apostasy in the church, but it will also be a period in which the gospel will reach the whole world.[1]

1. For the extent to which this section stems from dominical tradition, see Keener, *Matthew*, 565 – 66.

Translation

Matthew 24:4-14

4a		**Jesus responded,**
b	Warning #1	*[1] "Watch out lest someone deceives you!*
5a	Basis	For *many will come in my name, saying, 'I am the Messiah,'*
b	Result	and *they will deceive many.*
6a	Warning #2	*[2]* Now *you are about to hear of wars and rumors of wars.*
b	Exhortation	*See that you are not alarmed,*
c	Basis for 6b	for *these things must take place,*
d	Clarification	but *the end is not yet.*
7a	Basis for 6a/Prediction	For *nation will rise up against nation, and kingdom against kingdom,*
b	Prediction	and *there will be famines and earthquakes in various places.*
8a	Clarification	But *all these things constitute the beginning of birth pains.*
9a	Warning #3/Prediction	*[3] Then they will deliver you up to tribulation,*
b	Prediction	and *they will kill you,*
c	Prediction	and *you will be hated by all nations because of my name.*
10a	Warning #4/Prediction	*[4]* And *then many will fall away,*
b	Prediction	and *they will betray one another and hate one another.*
11a	Prediction	And *many false prophets will rise up and deceive many.*
12a	Prediction	And *because wickedness increases, the love of many will grow cold.*
13a	Promise #1	But *the one who endures to the end will be saved.*
14a	Promise #2/Prediction	And *this gospel of the kingdom will be proclaimed in the entire world for a witness to all nations,*
b	Prediction	and *then the end will come."*

Structure and Literary Form

Matthew follows Mark 13:5 – 13, though more closely in vv. 4 – 8 than in vv. 9 – 14. Matthew has already reproduced Mark 13:9 – 13 in the Mission Discourse (10:17 – 22), so here in 24:9 – 14 he adds material from his M source (24:10 – 12). Mark's conclusion frames Matthew's second paragraph, with "hated by all" (cf. Mark 13:13a) beginning this section (24:9b), and "endures to the end" (cf. Mark 13:13b) coming toward the end (24:13). Finally, Mark 13:10 ("the gospel must first be preached") was omitted from 10:17 – 22 and is now used to conclude the paragraph here (24:14). This falls into two fairly equal parts, vv. 4 – 8 (great deception and great travail) and vv. 9 – 14 (great apostasy and the great mission).

Exegetical Outline

→ **I. Great Deception and Great Travail (24:4 – 8)**
- A. False Messiahs deceive many (vv. 4 – 5)
  1. The need for vigilance (v. 4)
  2. The great deception (v. 5)
- B. The travails come (vv. 6 – 8)
  1. Wars do not signify the end (v. 6)
  2. Wars, famines, and earthquakes are only the beginning (vv. 7 – 8)

II. Great Apostasy and the Great Mission (24:9 – 14)
- A. Great affliction (v. 9)
- B. Great apostasy (vv. 10 – 12)
  1. Apostasy, betrayal, and hatred (v. 10)
  2. False prophets deceive (v. 11)
  3. The disappearance of love (v. 12)
- C. Great endurance means salvation (v. 13)
- D. The great mission to the world (v. 14)

Explanation of the Text

24:4 Jesus responded, "Watch out lest someone deceives you!" (καὶ ἀποκριθεὶς ὁ Ἰησοῦς εἶπεν αὐτοῖς, Βλέπετε μή τις ὑμᾶς πλανήσῃ). Jesus calls out for unceasing vigilance (present tense "watch out" [βλέπετε], used at key points of Mark's discourse [Mark 13:5, 9, 23, 33] to call for spiritual watchfulness) in light of the great deception to come. "Deceive" (πλανάω) is used often in this discourse (24:4, 5, 11, 24) to signify false teachers who lead others astray into apostasy.[2]

24:5 "For many will come in my name, saying, 'I am the Messiah,' and they will deceive many" (πολλοὶ γὰρ ἐλεύσονται ἐπὶ τῷ ὀνόματί μου λέγοντες, Ἐγώ εἰμι ὁ Χριστός, καὶ πολλοὺς πλανήσουσιν). "In my name" (ἐπὶ τῷ ὀνόματί μου) has a twofold thrust — they will come using Jesus' personal name and also his "name" or office as Messiah. In terms of the latter, there were many false messiahs in the first century, several named in Acts (Theudas, 5:36; Judas the Galilean, 5:37; the Egyptian, 21:38) and more in Josephus (*J.W.* 2:261 – 63, 433 – 56; 6:285 – 87; 7:437 – 39; *Ant.* 17:271 – 85; 18:85 – 87; 20:97 – 99, 160 – 61, 167 – 72).[3] Jesus is also predicting the rise of Christian false teachers, as in 1 John 2:18, "even now many antichrists have come." Instead of proclaiming truth, they will "deceive many" (exactly what Jesus warns against in v. 4). This will be the "great apostasy" predicted in vv. 10 – 12, 23 – 24; 2 Thess 2:3.

2. Davies and Allison, *Matthew*, 3:338, point out the widespread teaching that in the last days many will be led astray — CD 5:20, 7:21; *T. Mos.* 7:4; Rev 2:20; 12:9; 13:14; 19:20; 20:3, 8, 10; *2 Bar.* 48:34; *T. Levi* 10:2; *Sib. Or.* 3:68; *Apoc. Elijah* 1:13.

3. See Richard A. Horsley, *Bandits, Prophets and Messiahs* (San Francisco: Harper and Row, 1985); and Martin Hengel, *The Zealots: Investigations into the Jewish Freedom Movement in the Period from Herod I until 70 AD* (trans. D. Smith; Edinburgh: T & T Clark, 1989).

24:6 Now you are about to hear of wars and rumors of wars (μελλήσετε δὲ ἀκούειν πολέμους καὶ ἀκοὰς πολέμων). The future tense "you are about to" (μελλήσετε) emphasizes the imminence of the event; the rumors "will soon" begin. There is also an aspect of inevitability with "be about to" (μέλλω, BAGD, 501β) and here this has an edge of prophecy about it. The first thing that comes to mind is the revolt of AD 66 – 70, but in the entire period leading up to that, the Jewish people were constantly hearing such reports of devastating possibilities as well as wars between Rome and Gaul, Spain, or Britain. They were never at peace.

24:6 See that you are not alarmed, for these things must take place, but the end is not yet (ὁρᾶτε, μὴ θροεῖσθε· δεῖ γὰρ γενέσθαι, ἀλλ' οὔπω ἐστὶν τὸ τέλος). The saints dare not allow themselves to become "frightened" or "alarmed" (the present tense means "at any time") by such reports, for the false teachers will use this information to scare the people into joining their cults. Instead they need to realize that such conflagrations are part of divine necessity, with "must" (δεῖ) pointing to God's sovereign control (see the same use of "must" for the divine control over the future in Rev 1:1; 4:1; 22:6) and possibly to the "messianic woes" or the amount of suffering God has established before the end of history (see "Theology in Application" on 13:36 – 43 and discussion of 23:32).

War is a necessary prelude to the end-time events (see Rev 6:1 – 8 for the cycle of war – civil war – famine – death), yet at the same time "the end is not yet" (cf. Luke 21:9, "the end will not come right away"). In other words, the calamities that occur in a sin-sick world will take place for the rest of history, but they are not the "sign" of the eschaton. While the destruction of the temple (and events of AD 66 – 70) is a harbinger of the end, it will not constitute the end itself.

24:7 For nation will rise up against[4] nation, and kingdom against kingdom, and there will be famines and earthquakes in various places (ἐγερθήσεται γὰρ ἔθνος ἐπὶ ἔθνος καὶ βασιλεία ἐπὶ βασιλείαν καὶ ἔσονται λιμοὶ καὶ σεισμοὶ κατὰ τόπους). Jesus now alludes to 2 Chr 15:6 in his "nation ... against nation" and Isa 19:2 in his "kingdom against kingdom," both contexts of the turmoil God caused among the nations. Here there are three aspects: war, famine, and earthquake — all part of the chaos and cataclysm that evil has brought upon this world.

In addition to the wars noted above (see on v. 6), there were earthquakes in Antioch (AD 37), Phrygia (AD 53), Asia (AD 61), the Lycus Valley (AD 61), and Jerusalem (AD 67, see Luz, France). There were numerous famines and food shortages in the first century (e.g., the one predicted by Agabus in Acts 11:28), and famine is one of the eschatological woes noted in Rev 6:8; 18:8. These latter two involve creation and not human depravity and are part of creation's "groaning" in Rom 8:19 – 22. All three are to be expected throughout human history. So the counting of earthquakes, tsunamis, and other disasters by prophecy preachers is erroneous, for Jesus explicitly says these do not signify the end.

24:8 But all these things constitute the beginning of birth pains (πάντα δὲ ταῦτα ἀρχὴ ὠδίνων). The image of labor pains at birth was a common metaphor for calamities like death (cf. 2 Sam 22:6; Ps 18:4) or national crises (Isa 13:8; Jer 6:24), and it was a natural image for eschatological cataclysm (Isa 26:17 – 18; *1 En.* 62:4). It normally referred to the messianic woes that would usher in the final events of history, but here it is the

4. ἐπί (like κατά) can mean "against."

"beginning" of that period Jesus is referring to. His point is the same as v. 6—wars, famines, and earthquakes do herald the start of the last days, but they do not constitute the eschaton itself, nor do they signify that it is near.

The disciples should not listen to anyone who says such things mean the close of history and urge the disciples to follow them. They are false prophets, and their premature warnings should not be given credence. In this sense such events are like false labor—"signs" that the last days are inaugurated (the entire time between the two advents is called the "last days" in the NT, cf. 1 Tim 4:1; 2 Tim 3:1) but not signifying the end itself.

24:9 Then they will deliver you up to tribulation (τότε παραδώσουσιν ὑμᾶς εἰς θλῖψιν). The focus now shifts from the external chaos of war and creation to internal troubles, as the world turns against the church. It is debated whether τότε means "that which follows in time" (Luz) or "at the same general time" (Carson, Hagner). At stake is whether this refers to persecution throughout the church age or specific persecution at the end of history. Complicating this is the doublet of this with 10:17–22, where "they will deliver you" (10:17) and "kill you" (10:21), and "you will be hated by all" (10:22). Is this the same time span as 10:17–22 or a final instance at the eschaton? The movement from Jewish persecution in ch. 10 to worldwide persecution here can fit either scenario.

Yet this may be too disjunctive. As stated above this is apocalyptic language and could easily fit both scenarios. The primary thrust is probably "during the time" of the birth pangs in v. 8,[5] but the persecution of the church in history is a harbinger of the final persecution, as indeed is the case in the book of Revelation, where the beast of ch. 13 refers to the "many antichrists" of history consummated in the final Antichrist at the end of history (cf. 1 John 2:18). "Tribulation" (θλῖψις) occurs also in Matt 24:21 (unequaled distress) and v.29 (the time "immediately" before the parousia), again moving from the "tribulation" of history to "the great tribulation" (Rev 7:14) of the final events of history.

24:9 And they will kill you, and you will be hated by all nations because of my name (καὶ ἀποκτενοῦσιν ὑμᾶς, καὶ ἔσεσθε μισούμενοι ὑπὸ πάντων τῶν ἐθνῶν διὰ τὸ ὄνομά μου). Both the martyrdom of the saints and the hatred "by all nations" function in the same way as "tribulation." There is irony in "you will be hated [with ἔσεσθε μισούμενοι a future periphrastic for emphasis] by all nations/Gentiles," for in v. 14 (= 28:19) the gospel will be preached to all the nations. The very people the church loves enough to evangelize will hate the very ones who bring the good news to them. "Because of my name" (διὰ τὸ ὄνομά μου) echoes 10:22; 18:5, 20; 19:29 and refers to the true followers who take the name of Jesus.

24:10 And then many will fall away, and they will betray one another and hate one another (καὶ τότε σκανδαλισθήσονται πολλοὶ καὶ ἀλλήλους παραδώσουσιν καὶ μισήσουσιν ἀλλήλους). "At that time" ("then" [τότε], the time of the "tribulation" of v. 9) there will be a great "falling away" or apostasy from the faith. "Fall away" (σκανδαλίζω) occurs also in 5:29–30; 11:6; and a close parallel in 13:21, where the seed on rocky soil "falls away" because of "trouble or persecution." It means to fall into sin and reject the faith. In 2 Thess 2:3 (built on the Olivet Discourse) this becomes the

5. In this sense vv. 9–14 are part of vv. 4–8. Persecution, apostasy, and false teachers will continue throughout the period of the church and are not a "sign" that the end is here. At the same time, they are proleptic of the final days of history and will be consummated in the events of the "great tribulation" of Rev 7:14.

"apostasy" or "rebellion" that accompanies the appearance of the "man of lawlessness."

Once again this is both a general falling away due to persecution and false teachers (vv. 9 – 11; cf. Dan 11:32 – 35; Acts 20:29; 1 Tim 4:1 – 5; 2 Tim 3:1 – 13; Jude 17 – 19) and a final falling away at the close of history (2 Thess 2:3; Rev 13:11 – 18; *1 En.* 93:9). As before the present danger is uppermost. The betrayal by other members of the church, even by one's own family, builds on 10:21, 35 – 36; and hostility toward each other expands 10:22 ("you will be hated by all"). Still, only here is this betrayal and hatred internal within the church itself. The three flow together — those who leave the faith will join the enemy and turn against their former fellow believers. The repeated "one another" (ἀλλήλους) emphasizes the previous relationship.

24:11 And many false prophets will rise up and deceive many (καὶ πολλοὶ ψευδοπροφῆται ἐγερθήσονται καὶ πλανήσουσιν πολλούς). Mentioned also in 7:15, "false prophets" (ψευδοπροφῆται) were Jewish opponents in Jesus' day and false teachers in Matthew's time. In 18:6 they "cause one of these little ones who believes in me to fall away into sin" (the same "fall away" [σκανδαλίζω] as in v. 10). Their teaching will turn many members of the church from Christ through "deception," also mentioned in 24:5 (false messiahs) and 24:24 (false messiahs and false prophets). As noted in the v. 10, this occurred often in the NT and will be finalized when the "false prophet" of Rev 13:11 – 18; 16:13 appears.

24:12 And because wickedness increases, the love of many will grow cold (καὶ διὰ τὸ πληθυνθῆναι τὴν ἀνομίαν ψυγήσεται ἡ ἀγάπη τῶν πολλῶν). "Wickedness" (ἀνομία), as elsewhere in Matthew (7:23; 13:41; 23:28, nowhere else in the gospels) carries a double sense of those who disregard God's law and therefore do evil acts. It "increases" ("multiplies") and as a result "causes" (διὰ τό, leading into a causal infinitival clause, Wallace, 596 – 97) "love" to decrease. "Wickedness" (ἀνομία) and "love" (ἀγάπη) cannot coexist; where one proliferates, the other must correspondingly disappear. The false prophets have developed a religion of discord and lovelessness (cf. 1 Tim 1:4 – 7; 2 Tim 3:1 – 5). This is the heart of apostasy, for it probably means both love of God and love of neighbor (cf. 22:37 – 40).[6] "Will grow cold" (ψυγήσεται), a future passive, connotes the image of a fire being extinguished (BAGD, 894). The fire of God has gone out of them and left them spiritually cold.

24:13 But the one who endures to the end will be saved (ὁ δὲ ὑπομείνας εἰς τέλος οὗτος σωθήσεται). The need for "endurance" or firm faithfulness to God is a prime emphasis in all apocalyptic writings (e.g., Dan 9:10, 14; 12:12 – 13; Rev 1:3; 13:9 – 10; 14:12; 16:15; 22:7, 9 [a major theme in Rev]). This verse is a doublet of 10:22, where it means "to the end of our life" in a similar context of persecution and hostility. Here there is double meaning, adding that the church will endure to the end of this age, and the hostility comes from inside the church (v. 10) as well as outside it (v. 9).

24:14 And this gospel of the kingdom will be proclaimed in the entire world for a witness to all nations (καὶ κηρυχθήσεται τοῦτο τὸ εὐαγγέλιον τῆς βασιλείας ἐν ὅλῃ τῇ οἰκουμένῃ εἰς μαρτύριον

6. Many (e.g., Schweizer, Hagner, Luz) take it mainly as love of neighbor in Matthew, but it is difficult to see why this must be so in this context of spiritual apostasy. It is better of both (Morris, Schnackenburg, Senior, France). S. Légasse, "Le refroidissement de l'amour avant la fin (Matt 24,12)," *SNTSU* 8 (1983): 91 – 102, in fact, considers this to be mainly love of God and faithfulness to Jesus.

πᾶσιν τοῖς ἔθνεσιν). In vv. 5 – 13 Jesus has told the events that do not mean the end; here he tells the first one that will indeed herald the end. Here we have a harbinger of 28:19 and the universal mission to "all nations" to be inaugurated by the Risen Lord. Yet both of these also sum up a theological composition from Matthew that is a masterpiece, namely, the universal mission, beginning with the Gentile women in the genealogy (1:3, 5 – 6) to the Magi who came to worship Jesus (2:1 – 12) to the beginning of Jesus' mission (4:14 – 16) to the centurion who had a faith greater than anyone in Israel (8:5 – 13; cf. 21:43) to Jesus' deliberate ministry to the Gentiles even though restricting his disciples' ministry to the Jews alone (8:28 – 34; 15:21 – 28, 29 – 39). God's intention was to use the Jewish mission to launch the Gentile mission, and everything has been preparing for 24:14 and 28:19.

"This gospel of the kingdom" (cf. 4:23; 9:35) likely parallels "this book of the law" in Deut 28:61; 29:21; 30:10; 31:26 (cf. Josh 1:8; 8:34) and points to Jesus' "new testament" as a fulfillment of the old.[7] The fact that the kingdom message "will be proclaimed" (κηρυχθήσεται, another future passive, cf. vv. 10, 11, 12, 13) points to the later Gentile mission following the resurrection command of 28:19, for until that time the mission of the disciples was restricted to Israel (10:5 – 6; 15:24). This mission is "in the entire world" (ἐν ὅλῃ τῇ οἰκουμένῃ), a phrase found only here in Matthew and meaning "in the entire inhabited earth" (cf. Luke 4:5; 21:26; Acts 11:28; Rom 10:18), emphasizing all the peoples of earth.[8] εἰς μαρτύριον plus the dative could be positive ("for a witness to") or negative ("for a witness against"). As in 10:18 ("led before governors and kings ... as a witness to them") it is more positive, but in this apocalyptic context there are probably overtones of both.[9]

24:14 **And then the end will come** (καὶ τότε ἥξει τὸ τέλος). This turns around v. 6, "the end is not yet." This does not mean that all the nations will be converted before the end can come but rather that the universal proclamation will continue until the end.[10] Romans 11:25 – 26 says that at the parousia of Christ the Gentile mission will be completed and "all Israel will be saved." This is another passage that shows Jesus expected a lengthy interim before his second advent. The primary activity of the church during the interim is to be mission to the lost.

Theology in Application

The return of Christ is the great moment the church awaits with all its heart as it prays, "May your kingdom come" (6:10). In fact, all three God-centered petitions in the Lord's Prayer center on that coming, because until that time God's name cannot "be kept sacred," nor can his "will be done." Yet Jesus is aware of the great danger this interim period brings, for with it comes all the tragedies of a sin-sick world (war, earthquakes, famine) and all the false teachers who will use those tragedies for their own ends. So he must begin with a series of warnings to the faithful.

7. See Joseph A. Grassi, "Matthew as a Second Testament Deuteronomy," *BTB* 19 (1989): 23 – 29.

8. See BAGD, 561; Louw and Nida, *Greek-English Lexicon*, 10.

9. Davies and Allison, *Matthew*, 3:344, quotes Cranfield (*Mark*, 397), "it is surely better to allow for the various ideas which are involved in the witness-imagery rather than to insist on choosing between 'witness to' and 'witness against.'"

10. Contra Nolland, *Matthew*, 967, who says, "Matthew gives such a central role to the universal mission that he can link the timing of the end to its completion."

1. False Teachers

Do not listen to false teachers who twist events in order to develop their own agenda. There are two levels here — leaders of cults like Charles Russell (Jehovah's Witnesses) and David Koresh (Branch Davidian), and prophecy preachers who continually twist Scripture into patterns that fit current events. The latter are not false teachers but just mistaken in their hermeneutic. The former are truly dangerous, for they lead their followers into apostasy with hearts cold to God. The answer in the New Testament is an aggressive stance that confronts the heretics head-on and warns the faithful of their errors (as in 2 Cor 10 – 13; Phil 3:1 – 4:1; the Pastorals; 1 John; 2 Pet 2; Jude; Rev 2).

2. Natural Disasters

Do not elevate natural disasters into apocalyptic portents. Wars and human tragedies like earthquakes, famines, tsunamis, hurricanes, and the like will happen throughout history, but they show only that the lasts days have begun, not that the end is here. Yet still today many are counting up these natural disasters as signifying that the Lord is coming soon. Such people mean well but have not read 24:4 – 8 closely enough. Jesus says here not to consider them signs of the end, only the beginning of the end. Wilkins says it well:

> The onset of childbirth is not steady but is a repeated phenomenon, coming in waves over and over again.... We do not know if the baby will come on the fifth, the fifteenth, the fiftieth, or the five hundredth.... Throughout the labor we must "remain on guard," but we should not read the "false labor" as the real thing.[11]

3. Expecting Persecution and Suffering

Throughout the NT the saints are told again and again that as the world turned against Jesus, we must expect it to turn against us as well (e.g., 10:17 – 39; John 3:19 – 20; 15:18 – 16:4; Rom 5:3 – 5; 2 Cor 5:1; Phil 3:10; Col 1:24). In the Western context there is not a great deal of suffering, and Christians do not know what to do with such passages. Yet we must realize that (1) Christians around the world are suffering greatly; (2) the way in which our secular society is developing, persecution may be around the corner for us as well; and (3) many of us are not experiencing opposition because we are not truly taking a stand for Christ in our workplace, schools, or neighborhoods.

11. Wilkins, *Matthew*, 773 – 74. He points to Conrad Gempf, "The Imagery of Birth Pangs in the New Testament," *TynBul* 45 (1994): 119 – 35 (esp. 132 – 34).

4. Proclaiming the Good News of Christ around the World

We are not all called to be missionaries, but we are called to be world Christians, to have a deep concern for the lost and to do our part in reaching unbelievers everywhere (as Jesus commanded in 28:18 – 20 and Acts 1:8). The proliferation of short-term missions has wonderful potential for making the members of our churches into mission-minded Christians. The downturn in giving as a result of the economic pressures of recent years is a tragedy, for it means we place our creature comforts ahead of the Lord's work. A recent study showed that the average church member gave only 2.1 percent, and many churches have 30 to 40 percent who gave nothing the year before. Mission giving should be at an all-time high, and we should all be in constant prayer for reaching the world.

CHAPTER 103

Matthew 24:15 – 28

Literary Context

Jesus has finished telling what will not constitute the end (vv. 4 – 14), and now he turns to those events that will inaugurate the end of history. As stated in the introduction to this chapter, Jesus describes first the destruction of Jerusalem and instructs his followers what to do when it comes. But he is also proleptically anticipating the events that will precede the eschaton.

- **VI. The Movement to the Cross (19:1 – 25:46)**
  - **B. Fifth Discourse: Guilt and Judgment of Israel (23:1 – 25:46)**
    - 1. Guilt: Woes upon the Leaders (23:1 – 39)
    - **2. Judgment — Olivet Discourse (24:1 – 25:46)**
      - **a. Destruction of Jerusalem and the Events of the End Time (24:1 – 35)**
        - (1) Prophecy on the Destruction (24:1 – 3)
        - **(2) The Destruction and the End-Time Events (24:4 – 28)**
          - (a) Signs That Are Not the End (24:4 – 14)
          - ➦ **(b) Signs That Point to the End (24:15 – 28)**
            - **(i) The Abomination and the Need to Flee (24:15 – 22)**
            - **(ii) The Speculations of the False Messiahs vs. the True Parousia (24:23 – 28)**
        - (3) The Parousia (24:29 – 31)

Main Idea

The first half of this passage (vv. 15 – 22) centers on the destruction of Jerusalem, and vv. 16 – 20 are instructions for the needed reaction of the saints when the disaster strikes. The second half restates the warning against false teachers and contrasts their false claims (vv. 23 – 26) with the true and lightning-quick coming of the Son of Man (vv. 27 – 28). Yet the whole also points forward to the final events just prior to the return of Christ, e.g., the "abomination" (v. 15), the terrible nature of the conflagration (v. 21), and the "cutting short" of those days (v. 22).

Translation

Matthew 24:15-28

15a	Prediction/ Circumstance	*"So when you see standing in the Holy Place 'the abomination that causes desolation,'*
b	Description	*which was spoken through the prophet Daniel*
c	Narrative Aside	*—let the reader understand—*
16a	Exhortation	*then those who are in Judea should flee to the mountains.*
17a	Circumstance #1	*[1] The one . . . should not go down to take anything* *who is on the rooftop* *from the house.*
18a	Circumstance #2	*[2] And one in the field should not turn back to get a cloak.*
19a	Circumstance #3	*[3] And woe to those who are pregnant and* *who are nursing in those days.*
20a	Circumstance #4	*[4] And pray that your flight might not have to occur* *in winter or* *on a Sabbath.*
21a	Warning	*For then there will be great tribulation,*
b	Description	*such as has not occurred* *from the beginning of the world* *until now,* *nor will it ever be.*
22a	Condition	*And if those days had not been shortened,*
b	Result	*not one person would be saved.*
c		*But for the elect's sake,*
d	Promise	*those days will be shortened.*
23a	Condition	*At that time* *if anyone says to you,*
b	Exhortation	*'Look, here is the Messiah,' or, 'There he is,'*
c		*do not believe it.*
24a	Basis of 23c	*For false messiahs and* *false prophets will arise and* *perform great signs and wonders*
b	Purpose of 24a	*in order to deceive, if possible, even the elect.*

Continued on next page.

Continued from previous page.

25a	Warning	*Look, I have told you this beforehand.*
b	Condition	*So if they tell you,*
26a		*'Look, he is in the desert,'*
b		*do not go there or,*
c		*"Look, he is in the inner rooms,'*
d		*do not believe it.*
27a	Basis/Comparison	*For just as the lightning comes from the east and*
		is visible in the west,
		so will be the coming of the Son of Man.
28a	Proverb	*Wherever the corpse is, there the vultures will gather together."*

Structure and Literary Form

This first half of this passage (vv. 15 – 22) closely follows Mark 13:14 – 20, but only vv. 23 – 25 of the second half parallels Mark 13:21 – 23. Verse 26 is from M material, v. 27 parallels Luke 17:24, and v. 28 parallels Luke 17:37b. It is possible that Matthew has put the material together, but it is equally viable to suppose that Luke put the material in different places. There are two major parts, the abomination and its terrifying results in vv. 15 – 22, and the contrast between the speculations of the false messiahs and the actual sudden coming of the true Messiah (vv. 23 – 28).

Exegetical Outline

➡ **I. The Abomination and the Need to Flee (24:15 – 22)**
- A. The abomination in the Holy Place (v. 15)
- B. The need to flee (vv. 16 – 20)
  1. The rooftop — don't enter the house (v. 17)
  2. The field — don't return for your cloak (v. 18)
  3. Pregnant women — run (v. 19)
  4. Pray it not be winter or the Sabbath (v. 20)
- C. Unequaled distress (v. 21)
- D. The days shortened for the elect's sake (v. 22)

II. The Speculations of the False Messiahs vs. the True Parousia (24:23 – 28)
- A. Do not believe the false speculations (vv. 23 – 26)
  1. False identifications of the Messiah (vv. 23 – 25)
     - a. The miracles of the false messiahs (v. 24)
     - b. Statement of prophecy (v. 25)
  2. False identification of the place of his appearing (v. 26)

B. The sudden appearing of the true Messiah (vv. 27 – 28)
   1. The lightning-fast parousia (v. 27)
   2. Visibility and inevitability of the return, like vultures to a corpse (v. 28)

Explanation of the Text

24:15 So when you see standing in the Holy Place "the abomination that causes desolation," which was spoken through the prophet Daniel (Ὅταν οὖν ἴδητε τὸ βδέλυγμα τῆς ἐρημώσεως τὸ ῥηθὲν διὰ Δανιὴλ τοῦ προφήτου ἑστὸς ἐν τόπῳ ἁγίῳ). "Of desolation" (τῆς ἐρημώσεως) is probably an objective genitive ("the sacrilege that produces desolation"), though it could also be a Hebraic genitive ("desolating sacrilege").[1] So the "desolating sacrilege" is that which is first of all "detestable, abominable" to God and his people (often of idolatry, as here) and second, it "lays waste" or "devastates" the worship of God. This phrase is drawn from Dan 9:27; 11:31; 12:11, where it is commonly understood as a prediction of Antiochus IV (Epiphanes), the Syrian king who in 167 BC slaughtered a pig on the altar of burnt offering and erected an idol of Olympian Zeus on the altar in the temple (see 1 Macc 1:54; 2 Macc 6:1 – 5, 8:17; Josephus, *Ant.* 18.3.1; 18.8.2 – 9).[2] The phrase "standing in the holy place" (ἑστὸς ἐν τόπῳ ἁγίῳ) replaces Mark 13:14, "standing where he [the masculine participle ἑστηκότα] does not belong," where it refers to the coming Antichrist.

With the formula "which was spoken through the prophet Daniel" (τὸ ῥηθὲν διὰ Δανιὴλ τοῦ προφήτου) Jesus explicitly sees a further fulfillment of that prophecy. The debate is how many fulfillments Jesus is intending here. Everyone agrees that he is predicting the destruction of the temple. In this sense the sacrilege would have occurred when the Zealots went into the Most Holy Place (see previous footnote) and when the Romans leveled the temple and its sanctuary. Nolland describes the event as the temple lay in flames, how the Roman army brought its standards into the temple court opposite the eastern gate, made sacrifices to the gods, and declared Titus imperator (Josephus, *J.W.* 6.316).[3]

Yet it is also likely that Jesus intends a further fulfillment of a future eschatological sacrilege at the hands of the Antichrist. Davies and Allison see three reasons for this: (1) 2 Thess 2:3 – 4 (stemming from this discourse) sees this as fulfilled in the "man of lawlessness," an Antichrist figure; (2) Mark 13:14 points to such a figure (see above); (3) *Did.* 16 ("which has so many close ties to Matthew") applies this to a "world deceiver" who declares himself a son of God.[4] This makes a great deal of sense not only here, but as the basis for the further teaching of Paul in 2 Thess 2 and of John in Rev 6 and 13.

1. Ernest Lucas, *Daniel* (Downers Grove, IL: IVP, 2002), 227, 244 – 45, translates Dan 9:27c, "Upon the wing of abominations there will be a desolator," taking "wing" as the altar with its four horns at the corners and "desolator" as equivalent to the Aramaic for *baʿal šamem* (= the altar to Olympian Zeus). There is a further wordplay in that another title for Baal is "lord of wing" or "winged one."

2. McNeile, *Matthew*, 348, lists the other interpretations of this sacrilege — the desecration by the Zealots who entered the Most Holy Place just before Titus laid siege to the city (Josephus, *J.W.* 4.3.6 – 8, 6.3); Pilate bringing the Roman standards bearing the image of Caesar into Jerusalem (Josephus, *J.W.* 2.9.2); Caligula's attempt to erect a statue of himself in the temple (Josephus, *Ant.* 18.8.8); Vespasian's equestrian statue erected in the Most Holy Place (Jerome); a statue of Titus erected on the site of the ruined temple (Chrysostom).

3. Nolland, *Matthew*, 971.

4. Davies and Allison, *Matthew*, 3:346. So also Bonnard, Gundry, Gnilka, Hagner (possible), Wilkins; contra Carson, France, Luz, Morris.

24:15 Let the reader understand (ὁ ἀναγινώσκων νοείτω). This[5] present tense imperative calls for ongoing wisdom on the part of the church in interpreting this apocalyptic prophecy; it echoes Dan 7:16; 8:17; 9:22 – 23 on the need for understanding (cf. Rev 13:18; 17:9, "This calls for wisdom"). The reader needs divine help in understanding the Daniel prophecy and its fulfillment. Jesus promised that the "knowledge of the mysteries" would be given to the disciples (13:11), and this refers to their responsibility to utilize that knowledge here.

24:16 Then those who are in Judea should flee to the mountains (τότε οἱ ἐν τῇ Ἰουδαίᾳ φευγέτωσαν εἰς τὰ ὄρη). Like v. 14 "then" (τότε) is chronological (unlike in vv. 9, 10) and means that when people see the events taking place, it is time to flee. Often in the OT flight from overwhelming foes is noted (Gen 19:15 – 22; Exod 2:15; Judg 6:2, 20:45; 1 Sam 21:10, 23:19; Jer 39:4), and in prophecy it typified the flight from evil in the last days (Amos 2:16; Zech 2:6, 14:5; Rev 12:6). The flight "to the hills" looks to the mountain crevices and caves as the place of safety, much like the desert in Rev 12:6, 14.

24:17 The one who is on the rooftop should not go down to take anything from the house (ὁ ἐπὶ τοῦ δώματος μὴ καταβάτω ἆραι τὰ ἐκ τῆς οἰκίας αὐτοῦ). The picture is one of dire straits, a life-and-death urgency. Palestinian homes were mostly one room with a flat, mud-packed roof (that functioned almost as a den — one often ate meals on the roof and entertained there) and a stairway up the back of the house. To get one's possessions would mean going down the stairs and then around the house and in the front door. The enemy is apparently so close that the time it would take to do so would mean one's death. So people must flee and leave all their possessions. It is "their things" or their life!

24:18 And one in the field should not turn back to get a cloak (καὶ ὁ ἐν τῷ ἀγρῷ μὴ ἐπιστρεψάτω ὀπίσω ἆραι τὸ ἱμάτιον αὐτοῦ). There is a certain punctiliar force here in the aorist imperative μὴ ἐπιστρεψάτω here ("let them not return," so also v. 17). The laborer in the field has apparently removed his outer garment because of heat or the needs of his work and has placed it on the other side of the field or left it at home. Again, the nearness of the danger will not allow time to return and retrieve it. He must flee for his life while there is time.

These two cases (vv. 17 – 18) apply both to the historical arrival of the Romans in AD 66 – 70 and to the imminent second coming of Christ (v. 27). Some scholars see in this the flight of Christians from Jerusalem in AD 70, many of them going to Pella in Transjordan (described in Eusebius, *Hist. Eccl.* 3.5.3).[6] This is indeed possible if Matthew wrote after AD 70 (see the "Introduction," pp. 864–65), but it was not a *vaticinium ex eventu* ("prophecy after the event") but an actual prophecy of Jesus. At the same time, it also goes beyond AD 70 to the events of Rev 13. As Nolland says, "it is hard to avoid the suspicion that even in Matthew and Mark the urgency is being given an ultimacy that has more to do with being in place for an eschatological denouement than with a realistic

5. It has long been thought that this is an aside on the part of Mark and Matthew, but Larry Perkins, "'Let the Reader Understand': A Contextual Interpretation of Mark 13:14," *BBR* 16 (2006): 95 – 104, argues that it is an authentic statement of Jesus in which he corrects the disciples' misunderstanding about the "abomination of desolation."

6. For debates over the veracity of Eusebius's account, see C. R. Koester, "The Origin and Significance of the Flight to Pella Tradition," *CBQ* 51 (1989): 90 – 106; Davies and Allison, *Matthew*, 3:347, for the viability of it; and Gerd Lüdemann, "The Successors of Earliest Jerusalem Christianity: An Analysis of the Pella Tradition," in *Opposition to Paul in Jewish Christianity* (trans. M. E. Boring; Minneapolis: Fortress, 1989), 200 – 213, against the tradition.

response to a particular political and military development."[7]

24:19 And woe to those who are pregnant and who are nursing in those days (οὐαὶ δὲ ταῖς ἐν γαστρὶ ἐχούσαις καὶ ταῖς θηλαζούσαις ἐν ἐκείναις ταῖς ἡμέραις). "And" (δέ) is not adversative but coordinating here. "Woe" (οὐαί) here does have the idea of sorrow or pity, "How sad for ..." (cf. 23:13–36, where the judgment aspect is paramount). Pregnant women and nursing mothers will be encumbered by their babies and will not be able to move fast, and their infants will be endangered by the flight. Here the "woe" is not of judgment (see on 11:21) but of compassion and pity, for they are in even greater danger as the swift enemy overtakes them.

24:20 And pray[8] that your flight might not have to occur in winter or on a Sabbath (προσεύχεσθε δὲ ἵνα μὴ γένηται ἡ φυγὴ ὑμῶν χειμῶνος μηδὲ σαββάτῳ). Verse 19 dealt with physical situations that made flight difficult, and this verse deals with external situations in which flight is difficult. Winter in Palestine means flooded wadis, a swollen Jordan difficult to cross, cold at night, and a relative scarcity of food.[9]

The "Sabbath" notation (added to Mark) has been debated. On the surface it seems to refer to the restrictions of movement on the Sabbath to 2,000 cubits, plus on the day of rest city gates and stores will be closed, making travel difficult. Yet from the time of the Maccabees, Jews felt that defensive warfare and thus movement was allowed in emergency situations, and this certainly fits the danger a military enemy posed and thus flight on the Sabbath. Still, the conservative view persisted,[10] and many Jewish Christians would have been hesitant to flee on the Sabbath.[11] That hesitancy could cost them their lives.

24:21 For then there will be great tribulation (ἔσται γὰρ τότε θλῖψις μεγάλη). Jesus now turns his attention to the oppression itself that will accompany the "abomination that causes desolation" of v. 15. As in v. 9 "then" (τότε) means "at the same general time." The terror-ridden flight is thus framed by the reason for it: the desolating sacrilege and the horrible oppression that will result from it. He adds "great" (μεγάλη) to Mark and has "great tribulation," a phrase paralleled in Rev 7:14, "those who have come out of the great tribulation," but with an article that is missing from Matthew. So here once more there is a double fulfillment in the destruction of Jerusalem and in the final "great tribulation" period.[12]

24:21 ... such as has not occurred from the beginning of the world until now, nor will it ever[13] be (οἵα οὐ γέγονεν ἀπ᾽ ἀρχῆς κόσμου ἕως τοῦ νῦν οὐδ᾽ οὐ μὴ γένηται). Daniel 12:1 is behind this, saying that in the end times "there will be a time

7. Nolland, *Matthew*, 973.

8. The switch to the present tense here probably means, "start praying now."

9. "Winter" (χειμών) can also mean "stormy weather," but since those are the winter conditions, the meaning is similar either way.

10. See Hengel, *Zealots*, 287–90. Most commentators are consumed by questions about whether Matthew's community still observed the Sabbath laws, but if this was a prophecy of Jesus (and there is little reason to doubt it), Matthew's community is not decisive here.

11. Graham Stanton, "Pray That Your Flight May Not Be in Winter or on a Sabbath (Matthew 24.20)," *JSNT* 37 (1989): 17–30, after a thorough review of the options, argues that this refers to flight from persecution and that the Sabbath addition has to do with antagonizing Jewish opponents of Matthew's community. However, Eric K.-C. Wong, "The Matthean Understanding of the Sabbath: A Response to G. N. Stanton," *JSNT* 44 (1991): 3–18, shows that conservative Jewish Christians could well have been reluctant to flee on the Sabbath and that this provides a better solution.

12. For this see Osborne, *Revelation*, 324–25.

13. This is emphatic οὐ μή and generally means "never." See on 24:2 for its force.

of distress such as has not happened from the beginning of nations until then." Jesus adds "nor will it ever be" (possibly echoing Exod 10:14; 11:6) to Daniel, thereby making it the worst slaughter in the history of humankind, past or future. As Hagner notes, this must be either (1) hyperbolic language for the fall of Jerusalem (see Josephus, *J.W.* 5.10.1; 5.11.3 – 4; 5.12.3 for the terrible suffering in that siege); (2) prediction of the events at the end of the age; or (3) the destruction of Jerusalem as a foreshadowing of the final events of history.[14] As we have argued throughout this section, the third is the most likely. Nolland also admits that the language here, while befitting the horrible nature of the Roman slaughter of the Jewish people, has a "heightening" that portrays an "eschatological horizon" that goes beyond the Jewish War.[15]

24:22 And if those days had not been shortened, not one person would be saved (καὶ εἰ μὴ ἐκολοβώθησαν αἱ ἡμέραι ἐκεῖναι, οὐκ ἂν ἐσώθη πᾶσα σάρξ). There are two themes here, God's absolute sovereign control over history and the severity of the tribulation suffered by the saints. Matthew uses the divine passives "had … been shortened" (ἐκολοβώθησαν) and "will be shortened" (κολοβωθήσονται) for Mark's more direct "If the Lord had not cut short … he has shortened" (Mark 13:20). God is in charge even of the forces of evil, and he will not allow "those days" of suffering to go too far (cf. "was given" in Rev 6:1 – 8, 13:5 – 8 for a similar theme).

"Those days" (αἱ ἡμέραι ἐκεῖναι) is debated. Some (e.g., Carson, Blomberg) see the use here as broader than the days of tribulation in vv. 15 – 21, namely, as a reference to the entire church age. Yet this phrase is repeated from v. 19, and it is difficult to see why it should be interpreted differently. Moreover, the unequaled suffering in v. 22 parallels that described in vv. 15 – 21. While the time of persecution in vv. 15 – 22 could be the church age, the discussion of this whole chapter favors it referring to the destruction of Jerusalem as a foreshadow of the final time of tribulation connected with the appearance of the Antichrist. For their sake God will shorten the time of suffering, or else "no person" (σάρξ as referring to a person of flesh and blood, a human being, see BAGD, 743, 3) would be "saved," with σῴζω here meaning "delivered" or "preserved" from death. In AD 70 the Romans took the city after five months of siege (three-and-a-half years total), and the final conflagration will be similar (Rev 13:5, forty-two months).

24:22 But for the elect's sake, those days will be shortened (διὰ δὲ τοὺς ἐκλεκτοὺς κολοβωθήσονται αἱ ἡμέραι ἐκεῖναι). "The elect" (τοὺς ἐκλεκτούς) are those "chosen" in 22:14, namely, the true believers (so also 24:24, 31). If God does not curtail the time of suffering, there would be no one to answer the trumpet call and be gathered by the angels (24:31).

24:23 At that time if[16] anyone says to you, "Look, here is the Messiah," or, "There he is," do not believe it (τότε ἐάν τις ὑμῖν εἴπῃ, Ἰδοὺ ὧδε ὁ Χριστός, ἤ, Ὧδε, μὴ πιστεύσητε). Jesus returns to the subject of false prophets and messiahs from vv. 4 – 5, 10 – 12. These impostors will use the conditions of suffering ("at that time" refers to the time of the desolating sacrilege, great persecution, and flight of vv. 15 – 21) to claim special knowledge of where the Messiah or deliverer may be found, undoubtedly with themselves as the Messiah. Jesus warns his followers not to "believe" these false claims; if they truly "believe" in Jesus, they cannot believe such lies.

14. Hagner, *Matthew 14 – 28*, 702.

15. Nolland, *Matthew*, 975 – 76.

16. "If" (ἐάν) is a possible condition; Wallace, 696, calls it "uncertain of fulfillment, but still likely."

24:24 For false messiahs and false prophets will arise and perform great signs and wonders (ἐγερθήσονται γὰρ ψευδόχριστοι καὶ ψευδοπροφῆται, καὶ δώσουσιν σημεῖα μεγάλα καὶ τέρατα). These pretenders appeared often in the first century (see on v. 5) and throughout the history of the church, but they will be consummated in the Antichrist, who will appear at the final period of history (1 John 2:18; 4:3; cf. Matt 24:15). The "signs and wonders" stem from the great "signs and wonders" at the Exodus (Deut 4:34; 6:22; 7:19; 29:3) and are mentioned in Heb 2:4 as evidence that God's salvation is proclaimed by the apostles; but here it is opposite, used by false messiahs (in Deut 13:1 – 3 false prophets use them to deceive Israel into idolatry) to proclaim themselves and "lead astray" any believers they can (the success of this is noted in vv. 10 – 12). In Rev 13:13 – 14; 16:13 – 14; 19:20 the second beast, the false prophet (16:13), uses such "signs" to "deceive" the earthdwellers into worshiping the Antichrist (cf. 2 Thess 2:9).

24:24 ... in order to deceive, if possible, even the elect (ὥστε πλανῆσαι, εἰ δυνατόν, καὶ τοὺς ἐκλεκτούς). "In order to" (ὥστε) can refer to purpose or result; here it is purpose and equivalent to an "in order to" (ἵνα) clause. "If possible" (εἰ δυνατόν, condition of fact) on the surface seems to contradict vv. 10 – 12. The natural connotation would be that it is not possible to deceive in any final sense the true "elect." Yet v. 10 says, "many will fall away," and v. 12 says, "the love of many will grow cold."

There are two possible answers, and both are viable depending on one's theological orientation. For those who hold to eternal security, those who "fall away" (vv. 10 – 12) prove in their apostasy that they were never true believers (cf. 1 John 2:19). For those who hold to the possibility of apostasy (and I would count myself among these), the "if possible" here means that God's power is indeed keeping them secure (cf. 1 Pet 1:5), but that in the end they must make choices to remain within his secure hold (John 15:1 – 6; Heb 6:2 – 4). As Nolland says, "once there is talk of that which might deceive, then the discussion is operating in the terms of human responsibility, and the possibility of being led astray must be taken fully seriously."[17]

24:25 Look, I have told you this beforehand (ἰδοὺ προείρηκα ὑμῖν). Jesus wants his disciples to know that by foretelling the false teachers and their message, he has prepared them "ahead of time" so that they will be ready and not succumb. One question is whether we should narrow this "telling beforehand" to vv. 23 – 24 or expand it to all of vv. 15 – 24 or perhaps the whole of ch. 24 thus far. Probably it refers to all of these. Jesus has predicted the destruction of Jerusalem as well as persecutions yet to come, the false prophets of the church age, and the events of the end times so that his followers will be prepared for all the contingencies.

24:26 So if they tell you, "Look, he is in the desert," do not go there (ἐὰν οὖν εἴπωσιν ὑμῖν, Ἰδοὺ ἐν τῇ ἐρήμῳ ἐστίν, μὴ ἐξέλθητε). "Do not believe" (μὴ πιστεύσητε) here (see v. 26b, below) and in v. 23 frames the warnings of vv. 24 – 26a with the prohibition[18] not to believe any lies these people tell. Here two more claims are added to the ones in v. 23. The idea of the Messiah coming out of the wilderness stems from the wilderness (miraculous) ministries of Moses and Elijah. In mind especially would be John the Baptist, who "arrived, preaching

17. Nolland, *Matthew*, 979.

18. The aorist in prohibitions looks at the action as a complete whole, see Wallace, 717.

in the desert of Judea" (3:1; cf. 3:1 – 12; 11:7). The idea of false prophets in the desert could stem from these traditions (the two witnesses of Rev 11:3 – 6 replicate the miracles of Moses and Elijah).

24:26 … or, "Look, he is in the inner rooms," do not believe it (Ἰδοὺ ἐν τοῖς ταμείοις, μὴ πιστεύσητε). The "inner room" is more mysterious and has several possible meanings: (1) Matthew Black thought this a mistranslation of the Aramaic *beᶜdidrayya*, "in the Sanhedrin,"[19] but that is unnecessary. (2) Others see this in light of 6:6 as the inner rooms in a house in contrast with the public appearance in the desert (Broadus, Gundry, Hagner, Turner, Witherington), a much more plausible view. (3) Or it could refer to a messiah hidden except to insiders who would reveal himself in time (Hill, France, Carson, Blomberg), also possible. (4) It might refer to the hidden meetings of urban revolutionary groups, like the sicarii or the later Zealots (Bruner), but that is too conjectural. (5) Still others think these are the "lecture rooms" of a synagogue, leading to a contrast between a desert prophet like the Baptist or like a great rabbi in the synagogue (Morris); this is interesting but difficult to prove.

Of these options, the most likely are the second or third, with the second probably best because it is the simplest reading (Occam's razor). The main thing is not to give any credence to false reports, whether they say the Messiah will have a public ministry or a hidden one.

24:27 For just as the lightning comes from the east and is visible in the west, so will be the coming of the Son of Man (ὥσπερ γὰρ ἡ ἀστραπὴ ἐξέρχεται ἀπὸ ἀνατολῶν καὶ φαίνεται ἕως δυσμῶν, οὕτως ἔσται ἡ παρουσία τοῦ υἱοῦ τοῦ ἀνθρώπου). This may be a Q passage, but Luke 17:24 is worded differently ("For the Son of Man in his day will be like the lightning, which flashes and lights up the sky from one end to the other"). The image here is of the visibility of lightning from one horizon to the other (cf. Job 36:30; Ps 97:4; Zech 9:14). In this same way the parousia of the true Messiah, the Son of Man (see pp. 307–8, above), will be sudden and visible to all. There will be no hiddenness, no doubt at all as to the meaning of the event, and all false messiahs will be shown for what they are. The second clause is repeated in vv. 37, 39, so Jesus is here answering the disciples' second question of v. 3, "What will be the sign of your coming?"

24:28 Wherever the corpse is, there the vultures will gather together (ὅπου ἐὰν ᾖ τὸ πτῶμα, ἐκεῖ συναχθήσονται οἱ ἀετοί). Another Q passage (= Luke 17:37), this uses a familiar image of carrion birds (οἱ ἀετοί) gathering to eat a carcass (Job 39:27 – 30; Ezek 39:17; Hab 1:8; Rev 19:17 – 18, 21). These could be vultures or eagles, both scavenger birds that feed on flesh. The meaning, however, is difficult, and Davies and Allison note eight options.

1. The parousia will be as "public and obvious" as the circling of vultures over carrion.
2. At the parousia the judgment of the wicked will be concluded by the carrion birds feasting on the corpses of God's enemies (Rev 19:17 – 21).
3. Just as vultures swoop down on a corpse, so the Son of Man and his angels will descend in judgment on the wicked.
4. The saints like eagles will ascend to the Son of Man (the body) when he comes (Irenaeus).
5. In *4 Bar.* 7:1 – 36, an eagle descends and brings to life a body buried by Jeremiah, so this could as a whole picture the general resurrection.

19. Matthew Black, "The Aramaic Dimension of Q with Notes on Luke 17.22 and Matthew 24.26 (Luke 17.23)," *JSNT* 40 (1990): 33 – 41 (esp. 38 – 39).

6. The corpse is spiritually dead Israel, and the eagles are the Son of Man with his angels coming in judgment.
7. The eagles are the Romans with their standards and the body the destroyed Jerusalem or the temple.
8. The eagles are the angels and the bodies are the saints gathered to the Son of Man.

We could narrow these to three: v. 28 is a picture of the public return of Christ, the judgment of his enemies, or the resurrection of the saints. All are possible, but the order of likelihood follows the order here. The first fits v. 27 well and is the consensus of most today, yet the second would make sense as God's response to the evils of the wicked in ch. 23 and 24:15 – 21, and the general resurrection of the saints is presented in vv. 29 – 31.

Theology in Application

After telling what will not constitute the consummation of history (vv. 4 – 14), Jesus tells what are the true signs for the end (vv. 15 – 28). He does so by relating the destruction of Jerusalem and the terrible suffering that will accompany that event, yet at the same time looking at that tragedy as a foreshadowing of the final "great tribulation" that will precede the parousia.

1. Suffering and Victory

Suffering is terrible, but at the same time it is a sharing in Christ's victory over evil. Josephus reports the unbelievable amount of suffering and slaughter that occurred at the siege and leveling of Jerusalem. The Assyrian and Babylonian exiles as well as the slaughter of the Jews by Antiochus IV were all summed up in the terrible events of AD 66 – 70. Yet even that was a precursor to the martyrdom of thousand of Christians down through the centuries, which itself will be completed in the coming final holocaust at the hands of the Antichrist. Yet the NT is firm on this point — the suffering of God's people is a sharing in the suffering of Christ (Phil 3:10; Col 1:24) and will end in a sharing in his victory (Rev 7:14; 19:14; 20:4).

2. Sovereign over All

As in the book of Revelation, God is in absolute control of evil and does not allow it to move beyond the patterns established by his messianic woes (see on v. 6). When the amount of suffering he has allowed has been reached (Rev 6:11), he will intercede, cut the time of the evil powers short (v. 22), and bring the eschaton. Evil will not, and cannot, win.

3. False Prophets

Do not believe the lies of the false prophets. This has already been discussed in the theology of the previous section, but more can be added here. Christ will unmask all the charlatans, but he has also stated our responsibility to do so here. The record of the church is not good. Most cult leaders of our time have not been noted and opposed until it was virtually too late and they had already established their power base. We dare not follow the bad example of Pergamum and Thyatira (Rev 2:12 – 29), whose tolerance allowed the heretics to subvert so many of their members.

For us it is not so much tolerance as theological ignorance and lack of concern. We do not even notice people are teaching heresy until it is too late. God will hold us accountable for our lack of vigilance (Heb 13:17; Rev 16:15). When Christ returns, such teachers will be made visible and judged for their evil deeds. How much better if we bring them back to Christ before it gets that far (Jas 5:19 – 20)!

CHAPTER 104

Matthew 24:29 – 31

Literary Context

After his discussion of the signs that will precede his return, Jesus now turns and replies in part to the first question of v. 3, the "when" of his return. He leaves the issue of the destruction of the temple and turns to the effects of his second coming. This will dominate the rest of the discourse.

VI. The Movement to the Cross (19:1 – 25:46)
- **B. Fifth Discourse: Guilt and Judgment of Israel (23:1 – 25:46)**
  - **2. Judgment — Olivet Discourse (24:1 – 25:46)**
    - **a. Destruction of Jerusalem and the Events of the End Time (24:1 – 35)**
      - (1) Prophecy on the Destruction (24:1 – 3)
      - (2) The Destruction and the End-Time Events (24:4 – 28)
      - ➦ **(3) The Parousia (24:29 – 31)**

Main Idea

There are two primary thrusts: the triumphant "coming" of the Son of Man, using OT language of theophany with the shaking of the heavens, and the glorious gathering up of the saints at the last trumpet.

Translation

(See next page.)

Structure and Literary Form

Matthew, as often in this discourse, follows Mark 13:24 – 27 fairly well, adding "the sign of the Son of Man" and "the tribes of the earth" mourning in v. 30 and

Matthew 24:29-31

29a	Setting	"But immediately after the tribulation of those days,
b	Sequential Events	the sun will be darkened,
c		and the moon will stop giving its light.
d		The stars will fall from the sky,
e		and the powers of heaven will be shaken.
30a		And then the sign of the Son of Man will appear in heaven.
b		And then all the tribes of the earth will mourn.
c		And they will see the Son of Man coming on the clouds of heaven with power and great glory.
31a		And he will send his angels with a loud trumpet call.
b		And they will gather his elect from the four winds,
c		from one end of heaven to the other."

the "trumpet call" in v. 31 (see commentary). This apocalyptic prophecy has three natural parts: the shaking of the heavens (v. 29), the parousia (v. 30), and the gathering of the elect (v. 31).

Exegetical Outline

→ **I. The Shaking of the Heavens (24:29)**
- A. The time note: immediately after the tribulation
- B. The cosmic signs

II. The Parousia (24:30)
- A. The sign and the mourning
- B. The coming on the clouds in power and glory

III. The Gathering of the Elect (24:31)
- A. The loud trumpet call
- B. The gathering from all over

Explanation of the Text

24:29 But immediately after the tribulation of those days (Εὐθέως δὲ μετὰ τὴν θλῖψιν τῶν ἡμερῶν ἐκείνων). Matthew's "but" (δέ) is probably adversative as a stylistic variation of Mark's "but" (ἀλλά). The debate on this is significant. (1) Some (France) believe this is a reference entirely to the destruction of Jerusalem, so that the return of Christ here is not his second coming but his vindication in the events of AD 66 – 70.

(2) Others (Carson, Blomberg, Morris) believe this goes back to the "tribulation" of vv. 9, 22 and not the "abomination" of vv. 15 – 21 (i.e.,

the destruction of Jerusalem), and "immediately after" means that the parousia follows the period of "tribulation" (θλῖψις) during the church age.

(3) Still others (Hagner) believe this is stated from Matthew's perspective as "immediately" following the destruction, but with "immediately" (εὐθέως) meaning "it is to be expected after" rather than "very soon after" because of the constant aspect of delay in chs. 24 – 25.

(4) However, to link this just with the destruction of AD 66 – 70 or with the suffering of the entire church age is to miss the whole context of vv. 4 – 28. The best understanding is to take "the tribulation of those days" (τὴν θλῖψιν τῶν ἡμερῶν ἐκείνων) as recapitulating "those days" of vv. 19, 22 and thus refers both to "those days" of the destruction of Jerusalem and of the final conflagration of the "great tribulation" (24:21; Rev 7:14) period. Here with εὐθέως (retaining its force as "immediately," unlike Mark) it especially refers to the final events of history, those "immediately" preceding the return of Christ (so McNeile, Grundmann, Hill, Gundry, Bruner, Wilkins, Witherington, Turner).

24:29 The sun will be darkened, and the moon will stop giving its light. The stars will fall from the sky (ὁ ἥλιος σκοτισθήσεται, καὶ ἡ σελήνη οὐ δώσει τὸ φέγγος αὐτῆς, καὶ οἱ ἀστέρες πεσοῦνται ἀπὸ τοῦ οὐρανοῦ). All of this is commonly called "the shaking of the heavens" and is most likely symbolic rather than a series of actual events. It was a common OT symbol for critical moments of history, stemming from the God of creation shaking the "powers of the heavens" at significant moments of history. These cosmic signs appear at major events (Ps 18:7 – 15 on the deliverance of David from Saul; Hag 2:6, 21, the rebuilding of the temple) or divine judgment on nations (Jer 4:23 – 28, on Israel; Ezek 32:7, on Pharaoh). But there are also apocalyptic texts where it signifies the coming day of the Lord (Isa 24:21, 23; Joel 2:10; Amos 5:20, 8:9; Zeph 1:15) or the eschaton (*1 En.* 80:4 – 7, 91:16; *Sib. Or.* 2:34 – 38, 196 – 203; 3:80 – 90; *4 Ezra* 5:4 – 5; 7:39 – 42; *T. Levi* 4:1).

For this text the question is whether the cosmic shaking describes the destruction of Jerusalem (so France), as Josephus did in *J.W.* 6:288 – 310, or the arrival of the end of the ages at the parousia (so most others) following OT and Jewish precedents. The description here in v. 29 is drawn from Isa 13:10 (the sun darkened and the moon not giving light, at the day of the Lord, 13:9) and 34:4 (the stars fall, at judgment on the nations). In the context the reference is almost certainly to the end of the age inaugurated by the return of Christ.

24:29 . . . and the powers of heaven will be shaken (καὶ αἱ δυνάμεις τῶν οὐρανῶν σαλευθήσονται). This final line is thought by some to refer to demonic cosmic powers (in line with Eph 1:21; 3:10; 6:12; Col 1:16; 1 Pet 3:22); this is possible, but there is nothing in the context to make it probable, and the heavenly bodies are more likely the "powers."

24:30 And then the sign of the Son of Man will appear in heaven (καὶ τότε φανήσεται τὸ σημεῖον τοῦ υἱοῦ τοῦ ἀνθρώπου ἐν οὐρανῷ). This is not found in Mark but clearly ties this with the disciple's question regarding the sign in v. 3. Yet what is the actual sign? Is it the cosmic portents of v. 29 (taking τοῦ υἱοῦ τοῦ ἀνθρώπου as an objective genitive, a "sign pointing to the Son of Man," so Nolland) or the actual appearing of the Son of Man in this verse (taking it as an appositional genitive, "the sign that is the Son of Man"; so Bonnard, Gundry, Schnackenburg, Luz, Bruner)? Or is it separate from both (Hagner), perhaps the resurrection of the saints or the enthronement of Jesus in heaven (France) or a standard (σημεῖον means both "sign" and "standard") or ensign of Christ in the heavens signaling that the end has arrived (Carson, Gnilka, Senior, Davies and Allison)?[1]

It is impossible to know for certain. Yet the cosmic portents and the return of Christ are unlikely because both are separated from the sign by "and then" (καὶ τότε). The last, a general "sign/standard" for the coming of the eschaton, is probably best.

24:30 And then all the tribes of the earth will mourn (καὶ τότε κόψονται πᾶσαι αἱ φυλαὶ τῆς γῆς). This stems from Zech 12:10 – 14 but with a significant difference (paralleling Rev 1:7). Zechariah 12:10, 12, 14 has "they [each clan in Israel] will mourn," so that "all the tribes of the earth" will do so. However, Matthew and Revelation universalize it to "all the tribes of the earth." Moreover, in Zechariah it is mourning for sin and getting right with God after "looking on ... the one they have pierced," while here it is mourning for the judgment about to fall on them (in Revelation both are connoted).[2] This judgment is spelled out in Rev 19:11 – 21, the final coming of Christ as a conquering king to destroy his enemies. Here this text draws together the crucifixion ("the one they have pierced") and the results of the parousia ("all will mourn" in judgment).

24:30 And they will see the Son of Man coming on the clouds of heaven with power and great glory (καὶ ὄψονται τὸν υἱὸν τοῦ ἀνθρώπου ἐρχόμενον ἐπὶ τῶν νεφελῶν τοῦ οὐρανοῦ μετὰ δυνάμεως καὶ δόξης πολλῆς). The image now turns from Zechariah to Dan 7:13 – 14, the coming of the Son of Man on the clouds. Revelation 1:7 also combines Daniel with Zechariah, showing this saying of Jesus was also the basis for Rev 1:7. It could be that Zech 12:10 ("they will look on ... the one they have pierced") is combined with Daniel in "they will see" (ὄψονται), as they see "the one they have pierced" "coming on the clouds."[3]

The "clouds" are not merely mentioned because of Dan 7:13; in Exod 13:21 – 22; 14:24 the Shekinah presence of God went ahead of Israel in a pillar of cloud by day and a pillar of fire at night. Then at the close of Exodus (Exod 40:34 – 38) the Shekinah glory appeared as a cloud and covered the tabernacle. In Ps 68:4 and Isa 19:1 God "rides on the clouds," in Ps 104:3 he "makes the clouds his chariot," and in Jer 4:13 he "advances like the clouds." In other words Jesus' return "on the clouds" is the coming of Yahweh himself, both in the image of the Shekinah arriving and in the judgment image of the clouds caused by the wheels of the chariots of the hosts of heaven. Finally, this coming is "with power and great glory" (probably from Dan 7:14 LXX "authority [or power; ἐξουσία] and all glory"),[4] meaning that in the parousia the divine "power" and the Shekinah "glory" will be manifest.

24:31 And he will send his angels with a loud trumpet call[5] (καὶ ἀποστελεῖ τοὺς ἀγγέλους αὐτοῦ μετὰ σάλπιγγος μεγάλης). The combination of the coming of the Son of Man and the trumpet

1. They all build on T. Francis Glasson, "The Ensign of the Son of Man (Matthew xxiv.30), *JTS* 15 (1964): 299 – 300. See also J. A. Draper, "The Development of 'the Sign of the Son of Man' in the Jesus Tradition," *NTS* 39 (1993): 1 – 21, who develops the idea of the standard along the lines of the call for battle, in this case the final battle. Davies and Allison, *Matthew*, 3:360 – 61, believe this sign or standard will be the cross, the view of church fathers like Chrysostom or Jerome and natural since the Hebrew *nēs* or "ensign" was a crossbar.

2. See Osborne, *Revelation*, 68 – 69.

3. It is also possible, with Davies and Allison, *Matthew*, 3:60, to see a pre-Matthean tradition behind both Matthew and Revelation.

4. G. D. Kirchhevel, "He That Cometh in Mark 1:7 and Matt 24:30," *BBR* 4 (1994): 105 – 11, believes the background is the swift coming of judgment in Isa 5:26 – 30.

5. Some manuscripts add "sound of" (B D K TR et al.) to make the meaning more clear, perhaps through the influence of Exod 19:16. However, the shorter reading is more likely and makes sense as it is.

blast plus angels and the resurrection of the saints links this with 1 Cor 15:52 and 1 Thess 4:15 – 16. The trumpet blast announcing the coming of the king (1 Kgs 1:34), a sacred event (Lev 25:9), a theophany (Exod 20:18; Heb 12:19), a call to war (Judg 6:34, 7:20; Isa 18:3), or the day of the Lord (Isa 27:13; Joel 2:1; Zech 9:14) was a royal call either from the ruler or from God himself. For the place of the angels in the gathering of the saints and final judgment, see also 13:41, 49; 16:27; 25:31 – 32.

24:31 And they will gather his elect from the four winds, from one end of heaven to the other (καὶ ἐπισυνάξουσιν τοὺς ἐκλεκτοὺς αὐτοῦ ἐκ τῶν τεσσάρων ἀνέμων ἀπ' ἄκρων οὐρανῶν ἕως τῶν ἄκρων αὐτῶν). In the OT the gathering of God's people ("the elect" [see on 22:14; 24:22], with "his" [αὐτοῦ] referring to the returning Christ) from all over the world occurs in Deut 30:4; Isa 27:12 – 13; 60:4; Jer 32:37; Ezek 34:13; Zech 2:6 – 7; cf. *4 Ezra* 13:39 – 40, 47 – 50; *Apoc. Elijah* 5:2 – 6. The resurrection of the saints occurs in Isa 26:19; Dan 12:1 – 3, 13; cf. *4 Ezra* 4:41 – 43; *T. Benj.* 10:6 – 9; *2 Bar.* 49:2 – 51:12.

Jesus states their being caught up from everywhere two ways for emphasis, "from the four winds" (= the four corners of the earth) and "from one end of heaven to the other" (looking at the heavens as a firmament encasing the earth).[6] The point is that every follower will be gathered from everywhere and will be caught up to be with the conquering King. The place of the angels as the divine agents or heralds of resurrection and judgment is found also in Zech 14:5; Matt 13:41, 49; 16:27; 25:31; 1 Thess 4:17; Jude 14.

Theology in Application

The cross is the central event in history, the parousia the final event in history. The entire Bible looks to both events as the heir to the exodus, effecting the salvation of God's people. We are looking at the consummation of all of history seen as salvation history. This passage extends the point of vv. 27 – 28: unlike the false teachers and their emphasis on a secret coming, the true Messiah will come with a public event that no one will be able to ignore. The conspicuous nature of the return is seen in the loud trumpet blast and in the arrival of the hosts of heaven to gather God's people to Christ.

1. When?

The return of the Lord is "immediately after" the tribulation period. One major doctrinal debate that centers on this passage is the so-called "rapture debate" within premillennialism. The issue is whether the Lord will return at the beginning (pretribulation position), in the middle (midtribulation), or at the end (posttribulation) of the "great tribulation" period (24:21; Rev 7:14). The pretribulation position (mostly dispensational scholars) believes that Jesus is addressing Jewish disciples

6. There is no need, as some have done, to separate believing Jews from Gentile Christians. Both are united to constitute the church. France, *Gospel of Matthew*, 927 – 28, in keeping with his view that 29 – 31 is not the parousia but the enthronement of Jesus, takes this of the mission to the world seen as a "gathering" of people to Jesus.

rather than members of the church, and so Jesus is not addressing the "rapture" at the beginning of the period (which is only for the church) but the "revelation" of Jesus in power and glory at the end of the period.

The midtribulation position argues that this is the same event as Rev 11:11 – 12 (the catching up of the two witnesses, who symbolize the church) and so the middle of the period described in Rev 6 – 19.

The posttribulation position asserts that there is only one return, not two; and so this must be the same event as Rev 19:11 – 21 (cf. 1 Thess 4:13 – 18; 5:1 – 12, which they say is also a single event) and must occur "immediately after" this period. Amillennialists would tend to agree with the posttribulation position on Matt 24:29 – 31. It is a difficult issue, and all three are viable, but I find the third position more in keeping with Matt 24 and the NT evidence.[7]

2. Glory for the Saints and Terrible Judgment for Sinners

Matthew is the only one of the Synoptic writers to add the image of people "mourning," and that is in keeping with his additions to the Parable Discourse in 13:24 – 30, 36 – 43, 47 – 52 (the weeds, the dragnet), both of which stress the final harvest, with the reward for the faithful and judgment for the unfaithful. Both of these themes have been explored often and do not need further comment here.

3. The Culmination of God's Plan of Salvation

The glorious appearing of the Son of Man will be the culmination of God's plan of salvation. This in many ways is the hinge on which all NT theology rests. All the promises and warnings of Scripture come to fruition at that future moment. The purpose of the first coming was to make the second coming a reality. When we pray "May your kingdom come," we are praying, "Marana tha" (1 Cor 16:22, "Come, Lord"), which is to say, "Amen. Come, Lord Jesus!" (Rev 22:20).

4. Christian Lives of Sacrifice

Paul already said this in 1 Cor 15:19, "If only for this life we have hope in Christ, we are to be pitied more than all others." The doctrine of the afterlife drives every believer, for it alone makes sense of this sin-sick world and its suffering. This is the theme of Rev 21:1 – 22:5, when the final reality will come true: "God's dwelling place is now among the people, and he will dwell with them. They will be his people, and God himself will be with them and be their God" (21:3).

7. See Robert H. Gundry, *The Church and the Tribulation* (Grand Rapids: Zondervan, 1973).

CHAPTER 105

Matthew 24:32 – 35

Literary Context

Jesus has finished responding to the disciples' question of v. 3 and now is giving the implications of the whole chapter. When the signs of vv. 15 – 28 appear, they will know the end is near (vv. 4 – 14; note those signs that do not herald the end). This is then followed by a series of parables on imminence and readiness.

VI. The Movement to the Cross (19:1 – 25:46)
- **B. Fifth Discourse: Guilt and Judgment of Israel (23:1 – 25:46)**
  - **2. Judgment — Olivet Discourse (24:1 – 25:46)**
    - **a. Destruction of Jerusalem and the Events of the End Time (24:1 – 35)**
      - (1) Prophecy on the Destruction (24:1 – 3)
      - (2) The Destruction and the End-Time Events (24:4 – 28)
      - (3) The Parousia (24:29 – 31)
      - ➦ **(4) The Nearness of the Day (24:32 – 35)**

Main Idea

The disciples in v. 3 asked when the eschaton would occur and what signs would mark its near arrival. Jesus is saying that the signs he has elucidated (the destruction of the temple, the desolating sacrilege of the Antichrist, the terrible suffering of AD 66 – 70 and of the church age, and finally the final suffering of the tribulation period) will provide signs that his second coming is "at the door." In fact, all the signs will have been fulfilled in "this generation."

Translation

Matthew 24:32-35

32a	Analogy	*"Learn the lesson about the fig tree:*
b	Circumstance	*When its branch becomes tender and its leaves start to grow,*
c	Inference	*you know that summer is near.*
33a	Circumstance	*In this same way, when you see all these things,*
b	Inference	*you know that he is near, at the very doors.*
34a	Promise	*I tell you the truth, this generation will not pass away*
b		*until all these things take place.*
35a	Promise/Contrast	*Heaven and earth may pass away,*
b		*but my words will never pass away."*

Structure and Literary Form

This is virtually a verbatim rendering of Mark 13:28 – 32, with only a couple of words different. The core is the parable of the fig tree (vv. 32 – 33), followed by an "amen" (ἀμήν) saying on the signs occurring during the present generation (v. 34) and an attestation of the eternal character of Jesus' words (v. 35).

Exegetical Outline

➦ **I. The Parable of the Fig Tree (24:32 – 33)**
- A. The parable presented (v. 32)
- B. The application made (v. 33)

II. The Near Fulfillment of the Signs (24:34)

III. The Eternal Truth of Jesus' Words (24:35)

Explanation of the Text

24:32 Learn the lesson about the fig tree (Ἀπὸ δὲ τῆς συκῆς μάθετε τὴν παραβολήν). "Learn" (μάθετε, the aorist imperative looks at the process as a single whole) designates learning the content "about [ἀπό, BAGD, 87, IV. 2b] the fig tree" (cf. learning as discipleship in 9:13; 11:29). This is more a metaphor than a pure parable and is often translated "lesson." Jesus wants his disciples to have the fig tree provide its lesson and to think carefully about its significance.

24:32 When its branch becomes tender and its leaves start to grow, you know that summer is near (ὅταν ἤδη ὁ κλάδος αὐτῆς γένηται ἁπαλὸς καὶ τὰ φύλλα ἐκφύῃ, γινώσκετε ὅτι ἐγγὺς τὸ θέρος). Now Jesus switches to the present "you know" (γινώσκετε), stressing the process of recognizing the signs. The fig tree was the harbinger of summer. It was somewhat unusual among trees of Palestine in that it lost its leaves when winter hit. That makes it easier to note the change in spring when the sap begins to flow and the branches become "soft" or "tender" and ready to sprout leaves. Since this is easy to see with the absence of leaves, fig trees were one of the primary signs of the approach of summer. As the leaves began to unfurl, people's hearts surged with joy because the warm days of summer were around the corner.

24:33 In this same way, when you see all these things, you know that he is near, at the very doors (οὕτως καὶ ὑμεῖς, ὅταν ἴδητε ταῦτα πάντα, γινώσκετε ὅτι ἐγγύς ἐστιν ἐπὶ θύραις). "All these things" (ταῦτα πάντα) refers to the events of vv. 15 – 26 that precede the parousia (the fall of Jerusalem, the suffering of the interim period, and the great apostasy, and the final suffering),[1] but not the parousia itself in vv. 27 – 31, for in that case there would be nothing left to be "near."

It is difficult to decide whether the understood subject of "is" (ἐστιν) is the end ("it is near") or the Son of Man ("he is near"). Most assume the latter (due to the image of a door), but Jesus may have left it deliberately ambiguous. Either way the emphasis is on imminence, stressed by the conjunction of "near" with "at the doors." However, as Blomberg says, "nearness simply implies that nothing more in God's plan of redemption must occur before the end can come."[2] The emphasis in the parables that follow is on an interval of time before the master appears, so Jesus did not mean by nearness an any-moment return.

24:34 I tell you the truth, this generation will not pass away until all these things take place (ἀμὴν λέγω ὑμῖν ὅτι οὐ μὴ παρέλθῃ ἡ γενεὰ αὕτη ἕως ἂν πάντα ταῦτα γένηται). Jesus here centers on the "signs" of his generation: the fall of Jerusalem, the abominating sacrilege, false teachers, and apostasy of the first century. Everything he said in vv. 4 – 26 would come to pass. He repeats "all these things" (πάντα ταῦτα) from v. 33, and it must mean the same thing, but Jesus here is thinking of the concrete historical events that "take place" (γένηται), not the future events they foreshadow.[3]

All the imminence sayings in Matthew are preceded by an "amen" (ἀμήν) saying (10:23; 16:28; 23:36) for emphasis (so Hagner). Moreover, "this generation" (ἡ γενεὰ αὕτη) in the gospels always means the people of Jesus' own time (11:16; 12:41 – 42; 23:36) not, as some have proposed, the generation of the last days in history, the Jewish

1. This is certainly how Paul read this section on the basis of 2 Thess 2:3, where he said the parousia would not come until the "apostasy" occurred and the appearance of the "man of lawlessness," or Antichrist.

2. Blomberg, *Matthew*, 363. He quotes C. E. B. Cranfield, "The Parable of the Unjust Judge and the Eschatology of Luke-Acts," *SJT* 16 (1963): 300 – 301, "since the decisive event of history has already taken place in the ministry, death, resurrection and ascension of Christ, all subsequent history is a kind of epilogue, an interval inserted by God's mercy in order to allow men time for repentance, and, as such an epilogue, necessarily in a real sense short, even though it may last a very long time."

3. Contra Davies and Allison, *Matthew*, 3:367 – 8, who take it as all the events, including the parousia, and then they have to admit that Jesus was wrong but say that "some of Jesus' contemporaries were perhaps alive when Matthew wrote, so he did not have the problem we do." This is unnecessary.

people, the human race in general, or the sinful people. As Nolland says:[4]

> The present and immediately future events were to be seen in the light of and somehow as participating in the reality of what would one day be fully true eschatologically.... The fundamental driving force for the sentiment expressed ... is the conviction that Jesus' Jewish contemporaries in Palestine ("this generation") were to find themselves at a climax point in the purposes of God in judgment (cf. esp. [Lk] 11:49 – 51), just as they had been experiencing a climax point of God's saving purposes in the ministry of Jesus.

24:35 Heaven and earth may pass away, but my words will never pass away (ὁ οὐρανὸς καὶ ἡ γῆ παρελεύσεται, οἱ δὲ λόγοι μου οὐ μὴ παρέλθωσιν). In 5:18 we were told that the smallest part of the Torah will not pass away "until heaven and earth disappear" (the same Greek formation). Yet Jesus' words transcend the eschaton and therefore have eternal weight. As the final interpreter of Torah (5:17 – 20) and the one who has brought the final Torah of the Messiah (chs. 5 – 7), Jesus is the final arbiter of truth. In one sense "my words" (οἱ λόγοι μου) go beyond this context to embrace all his teachings. In another sense it has special relevance for the eschatological truths Jesus has just uttered. When the prophets spoke prophecies of the future, they always prefaced those prophecies with, "Thus says the Lord." Jesus, however, speaks with the authority of Yahweh himself. He is God and his words are the Word of God.

Theology in Application

This passage is all about imminence. Yet we must understand imminence properly in our expectation of Jesus' soon return. As was said at 10:23, Jesus expected a lengthy period before the end (13:24 – 33; 19:28; 21:43; 23:32; 24:14; 28:19) and so cast his soon return in the light of the interim period between his advents. So "nearness" means it can occur in the near future, but God is the one who decides how near (see v. 36). The believer is to be ready at all times in light of the near and sudden (v. 27) return of Christ.

This will be the theme of the parables that will follow this. The signs will herald the end, but we must differentiate those that are not signs (vv. 4 – 14) from those that are (vv. 25 – 26). Moreover, we must realize that with our finite perspective we may not be reading the signs correctly. This is the problem with many who label themselves "prophecy preachers." We dare not apply certitude to our reading of current events; the only certain thing is the appearance of Antichrist (2 Thess 2:3), whom the church has often prematurely identified as the popes (Reformation period) or Mussolini or Hitler, etc. Still, Jesus encourages us to note the signs.

4. Nolland, *Matthew*, 989, quoting from his *Luke*, 3:1009 – 10.

CHAPTER 106

Matthew 24:36 – 44

Literary Context

This begins the next major section of the Olivet Discourse, the parables on watchfulness (24:36 – 25:30). This passage provides the thesis for the section, alert vigilance as we await the end, and leads into the parables that follow.[1]

- **VI. The Movement to the Cross (19:1 – 25:46)**
  - **B. Fifth Discourse: Guilt and Judgment of Israel (23:1 – 25:46)**
    - **2. Judgment — Olivet Discourse (24:1 – 25:46)**
      - a. Destruction of Jerusalem and the Events of the End Time (24:1 – 35)
      - **b. Parables on Readiness (24:36 – 25:30)**
        - ➦ **(1) The Need for Spiritual Vigilance (24:36 – 44)**
        - (2) The Parable of the Faithful and Wicked Slaves (24:45 – 51)
        - (3) The Parable of the Ten Bridesmaids (25:1 – 13)

Main Idea

God has not seen fit to reveal the time of the eschaton; not even Christ knows the date. As a result, people will be living lives unaware and unprepared; many of them will be left for judgment when the Lord comes. There is only one conclusion: be continually vigilant and live lives of readiness for the Master's return.

1. Blomberg, *Matthew*, 364, makes an interesting observation regarding the first three parables: in 24:43 – 44 Christ's return is wholly unexpected, in 24:45 – 51 it is sooner than expected, and in 25:1 – 13 it is later than expected. The meaning is: "Christians must remain prepared for him to come at any time." Wilkins, *Matthew*, 815, says that each parable stresses a further aspect of preparedness: "responsibility (24:45 – 51), readiness (25:1 – 13), productivity (25:14 – 30), and accountability (25:31 – 46)."

Translation

Matthew 24:36-44

36a		"Now concerning that day and hour,
b	Assertion	*no one knows except only the Father,*
c	Assertion	*not even heaven's angels or the Son.*
37a	Example #1/Analogy	*[1] For just as it was in the days of Noah,*
		so it will be at the parousia of the Son of Man.
38a		*For as people were in the days before the flood,*
b		*eating and drinking,*
		marrying and giving in marriage,
c		*until the day Noah entered the ark.*
39a		*And they did not know until the flood came and*
		took them all away.
b	Comparison	*This is how it will [also] be at the coming of the Son of Man.*
40a	Example #2 (A)	*[2] At that time two men will be in the field.*
b	(B)	*One is going to be taken away and one is going to be left.*
41a	(A')	*Two women will be grinding at the mill.*
b	(B')	*One is going to be taken and one left.*
42a	Exhortation	*So be constantly vigilant,*
b	Basis	*because you do not know on what day your Lord is going to come.*
43a	Example #3/Analogy	*[3] But know this:*
b		*If the householder had realized in which watch of the night the thief was coming,*
c		*he would have been vigilant and*
		would not have allowed him to break into his house.
44a	Comparison	*For this reason you yourselves should also be ready,*
b	Basis for 44a	*because at a time you do not expect,*
		the Son of Man is going to come."

Structure and Literary Form

Matthew departs somewhat from the order of Mark 13, with v. 32 following the next part of Mark (13:32), but vv. 37 – 44 as a pastiche of Q material (24:37 – 39a = Luke 17:26 – 27; 24:39b = Luke 17:30; 24:41 = Luke 17:35; 24:43 – 44 = Luke 12:39 – 40) and a little from Mark (24:42 = Mark 13:35). In this set of parables, v. 36 provides the thesis for this passage and the whole of 24:36 – 25:30: no one but the Father knows the time of the end. Then the section flows into three parables or extended metaphors related to watchfulness: (1) the example of the days of Noah, when people were unaware of impending judgment and as a result were swept away unprepared

(vv. 37 – 39); (2) two examples of the need for watchfulness (vv. 40 – 42); and (3) the parable of the unprepared householder who lost his possessions (vv. 43 – 44).

Exegetical Outline

➡ **I. Thesis: Only God Knows the Time (24:36)**

II. Examples of the Need for Watchfulness (24:37 – 44)

A. The days of Noah: living unaware of judgment (vv. 37 – 39)

1. Living normal lives but unaware of what was coming (vv. 37 – 38)
2. Sudden judgment sweeps them away (v. 39)

B. Examples of the need for watchfulness: only one taken (vv. 40 – 42)

1. In the field or at the mill, one taken, the other left (v. 40 – 41)
2. Conclusion: keep watch (v. 42)

C. Parable of the unprepared householder (vv. 43 – 44)

1. The parable: the householder not ready for the thief (v. 43)
2. Conclusion: be ready at all times (v. 44)

Explanation of the Text

24:36 Now concerning that day and hour, no one knows except only the Father, not even heaven's angels or the Son[2] (Περὶ δὲ τῆς ἡμέρας ἐκείνης καὶ ὥρας οὐδεὶς οἶδεν, οὐδὲ οἱ ἄγγελοι τῶν οὐρανῶν οὐδὲ ὁ υἱός, εἰ μὴ ὁ πατὴρ μόνος). This is an incredible statement, for after Jesus has given remarkably detailed prophecies regarding the signs of the times as they relate to the destruction of Jerusalem and his own second coming, he now admits ignorance regarding the disciples' first question from v. 3, the time of the eschaton! He begins with both "that day" (τῆς ἡμέρας ἐκείνης = the day of the Lord) and "hour" (ὥρας, cf. 24:50; 25:13) to highlight the issue of the "when" of v. 3.[3] The emphasis on "no one knows" (οὐδεὶς οἶδεν, a perfect stem used as a present [BAGD, 555] to emphasize "at any time") is made even more emphatic by the addition of "not even heaven's angels or the Son." It is a closely held heavenly secret known "only [by] the Father."

This becomes the thesis of the next sections, which center on the impossibility of knowing the exact time, yet the necessity of being ready at all times. The primary problem, of course, is the christological implications. Yet this makes perfect sense when placed in the context of NT teaching. Jesus is the God-man and as such is both fully God and fully human. This involves limitations when in his incarnate state. When walking Planet Earth he was not omnipresent and limited himself in his

2. Several manuscripts, mostly later (ℵ [a] L W 0133 TR et al.), omit "or the Son." While this could be an assimilation to Mark 13:32, it is more likely that this was dropped by scribes who were troubled by the christological implications of it. Moreover, a wide cross-section of manuscripts (ℵ B D Θ et al.) contain it.

3. The semantic quibbling by some who say that therefore it is all right to establish the "month" or the "year" of the Lord's return is so wrong as to be dangerous (see Carson, Hagner, Blomberg). This clearly says we are not to guess the time but be ready at all times. To tell people you know the time is against this passage and gives people a false security bound to lead them down the wrong path spiritually.

omnipotence and his omniscience.[4] His subordination to the Father is also found in 11:27; 20:23; John 5:19, 21–22.

24:37 For just as it was in the days of Noah, so it will be at the parousia of the Son of Man (ὥσπερ γὰρ αἱ ἡμέραι τοῦ Νῶε, οὕτως ἔσται ἡ παρουσία τοῦ υἱοῦ τοῦ ἀνθρώπου). This verse states the basic truth, while vv. 38–39 elaborate on it using the same format ("just as ... so it will be"). It is a type of Alpha (beginning) and Omega (end) comparison. The message centers on the unexpected event (the flood/the eschaton) resulting in judgment. In Jewish literature the people of Noah's day exemplified sinners who did not foresee the coming of divine wrath (Sir 16:7; *Jub.* 20:5–6; *1 En.* 67:10, 2 Macc 2:4, so Davies and Allison).[5] Sin in this sense produces a lack of awareness. Among the eschatological discourses in the gospels, "parousia" (παρουσία) is found only in Matthew (24:3, 27, 37, 39) and speaks of the arrival of a monarch; here the emphasis is not on the joy of the royal arrival but the judgment that will ensue for those unprepared.

24:38 For as people were in the[6] days before the flood, eating and drinking, marrying and giving in marriage, until the day Noah entered the ark (ὡς γὰρ ἦσαν ἐν ταῖς ἡμέραις ταῖς πρὸ τοῦ κατακλυσμοῦ τρώγοντες καὶ πίνοντες, γαμοῦντες καὶ γαμίζοντες, ἄχρι ἧς ἡμέρας εἰσῆλθεν Νῶε εἰς τὴν κιβωτόν). The flood was a common warning example in Judaism and the early church (see passages above as well as 1 Pet 3:20; 2 Pet 2:5; 3:6–7). The picture here is of normal life, eating and drinking at meals and parties, getting married and giving their children in marriage (with present participles stressing the continuous nature of the activity). In itself it is not a negative picture, but these were a people obsessed with their daily lives, giving no thought whatsoever to their obligations to God. All this was to change when "Noah entered the ark," but then it would be too late.

24:39 And they did not know until the flood came and took them all away (καὶ οὐκ ἔγνωσαν ἕως ἦλθεν ὁ κατακλυσμὸς καὶ ἦρεν ἅπαντας). The normal rhythms of life came to an abrupt end. "Did not know" (οὐκ ἔγνωσαν) often does not connote lack of knowledge but deliberate rejection, but it might also mean a failure to "comprehend" or "recognize" the signs of imminent judgment. With the emphasis on the unexpected nature of the judgment here, the latter is best. The people were going about their godless business until the flood arrived and "took them all away" to their doom (note the similar pattern with respect to business practices in Jas 4:13–14).

24:39 This is how it will [also][7] be at the coming of the Son of Man[8] (οὕτως ἔσται [καὶ] ἡ παρουσία τοῦ υἱοῦ τοῦ ἀνθρώπου). The same point is true with respect to "the parousia." As Luz says, "The knowledge about the nearness of the parousia keeps the statements about the uncertainty of the time from becoming the expression of a belief that the end is in such a distant future that it loses its

4. Many link this with Phil 2:7 and Jesus' "emptying" himself of many of the prerogatives of his Godhood. However, I agree with the TNIV translation, "made himself nothing," meaning he did not empty himself of anything. As an intransitive verb, κενόω means he "poured himself out" or "took the lower place" (see G. Fee, *Philippians* [IVPNTC; Downers Grove, IL: IVP, 1999], 210).

5. For an extended discussion of the Jewish background, see Jaques Schlosser, "Les jours de Noé et de Lot: À propos de Luc XVII, 26–30," *RB* 80 (1973): 13–36.

6. "Those" (ἐκείναις) is present in B D it sa but missing in most others, and it is probably best to leave it out.

7. "Also" (καί) is missing in B D it 892 et al. but present in ℵ L W Θ Byz. The manuscript evidence is fairly equal, but since καί is also added in v. 37 by D W Θ Byz, it is probably best to omit it from both.

8. As elsewhere the genitive "of the Son of Man" (τοῦ υἱοῦ τοῦ ἀνθρώπου) is subjective ("when the Son of Man comes").

ability to influence life."[9] The danger of becoming lackadaisical is simply too great, for judgment will be swift, sudden, and irrevocable.

24:40 At that time two men will be in the field. One is going to be taken away and one is going to be left (τότε δύο ἔσονται ἐν τῷ ἀγρῷ, εἷς παραλαμβάνεται καὶ εἷς ἀφίεται). For "at that time" (τότε) see on v. 9; here it means "at the same general time." The image of two in the field pictures members of the same family (father and son or two brothers) working their farm together. It is difficult to know which is the negative image and which the positive. It could be one is "taken" to be with Christ (the majority of commentators) or "taken away" to judgment. If the two verbs for "taken away" in vv. 39–40 are different, the former is the connotation. But they are not really different in meaning, so the more likely is "taken away to judgment," the same in v. 40 as in v. 39 (the context of vv. 37–39 is judgment). The two verbs here are futuristic or prophetic presents, "going to be taken/left." The main thrust is again on those engaged in the normal rhythms of life when the end unexpectedly comes.

24:41 Two women will be grinding at the mill. One is going to be taken and one left (δύο ἀλήθουσαι ἐν τῷ μύλῳ, μία παραλαμβάνεται καὶ μία ἀφίεται.). From the image of men in v. 49, Jesus turns to that of two women. Probably again they stem from the same family, sitting across from one another and turning a stone hand mill for grinding grain, with each pulling the circular stone 180 degrees (so Carson). The image is the same as v. 40, as one is taken away for judgment, the other "left" and so safe from danger.

24:42 So be constantly vigilant (γρηγορεῖτε οὖν). "So" (οὖν) draws a conclusion from vv. 40–41. The present tense imperative "be constantly vigilant" (γρηγορεῖτε) stresses the durative aspect, demanding constant watchfulness. The verb is active: "the watching involves an active dimension, namely, the faithful righteous conduct of the disciples (cf. v 46) that becomes the focus at the end of the discourse (cf. 25:14–46)."[10] Jesus' followers must remain in a state of total alertness in light of the serious repercussions of ignoring the imminent eschaton.

24:42 ... because you do not know on what day your Lord is going to come (ὅτι οὐκ οἴδατε ποίᾳ ἡμέρᾳ ὁ κύριος ὑμῶν ἔρχεται). The switch from "know" (γινώσκω) in v. 39 to "know" (οἶδα) here is probably not a shift from experiential knowledge to intellectual awareness; the two are synonymous here. Ignorance will be no excuse (see vv. 44, 50; 25:13). The Lord "is going to" return (another futuristic present), and every person will be accountable at that moment.

24:43 But know this: If the householder had realized in which watch of the night the thief was coming (ἐκεῖνο δὲ γινώσκετε ὅτι εἰ ᾔδει ὁ οἰκοδεσπότης ποίᾳ φυλακῇ ὁ κλέπτης ἔρχεται). Jesus turns to a brief parable (only one sentence long) to state the danger another way. The "master of the house" (cf. 10:25; 13:27, 52; 20:1, 11; 21:33) seeks home security, to protect the estate from burglary. This is a contrary-to-fact sentence ("if" [εἰ] in the protasis plus the particle ἄν in the apodosis) concerning a householder who has apparently received information that a thief is coming but does not have details as to exactly what time he is coming. So he has to set armed guards around the estate every "watch of the night" (Romans divided the period 6:00 p.m. to 6:00 a.m. into four night watches; the Jews divided it into three night watches [BAGD, 868, 4]).

9. Luz, *Matthew 21–28*, 213.

10. Hagner, *Matthew 14–28*, 720.

24:43 ... he would have been vigilant and would not have allowed him to break into his house (ἐγρηγόρησεν ἂν καὶ οὐκ ἂν εἴασεν διορυχθῆναι τὴν οἰκίαν αὐτοῦ). This man's purpose is to protect the home from the thief who wants to "break into" (διορύσσω, lit., "dig through" the mud-brick walls of) the house. The message once again is the need for constant spiritual vigilance in light of the soon return of Christ. As Blomberg says, there are two thrusts — the need for constant readiness for the return of Christ and Jesus' coming like a thief at an unexpected time.[11] This image of Jesus' return "like a thief" became a major NT metaphor for the unanticipated nature of the parousia (1 Thess 5:2; 2 Pet 3:10; Rev 3:3; 16:15).

24:44 For this reason you yourselves should also be ready (διὰ τοῦτο καὶ ὑμεῖς γίνεσθε ἕτοιμοι). "For this reason" (διὰ τοῦτο) and "because" (ὅτι) are synonyms; the "reason" we must be ready is "because" Christ is coming at an unexpected moment. Spiritual "readiness" is the stepchild of vigilance. The disciples do not want to be like the owner who seemingly is unprepared to protect his domicile. The emphatic "yourselves" (ὑμεῖς) drives home the importance of personal responsibility in light of Jesus' soon return. Just as the owner did not know when the thief was coming and so had to be "ready" (ἕτοιμος, "prepared") at all times, so disciples must at all times be prepared for the event.

24:44 ... because at a time you do not expect, the Son of Man is going to come (ὅτι ᾗ οὐ δοκεῖτε ὥρᾳ ὁ υἱὸς τοῦ ἀνθρώπου ἔρχεται). Since Jesus is "going to come" (another futuristic present, cf. vv. 40, 41, 42) "at a time you do not expect" (δοκέω, which means "seems best"), the only possible answer is to maintain readiness all the time.

Theology in Application

All three images used here center on the unexpected nature of Jesus' soon return and the necessity of being ready at all times for his parousia. The implication is that the consequences of being unprepared are far too serious to ignore. The only possible response is to maintain constant vigilance, to make certain that we are always "ready." Bruner says it well: "Our not knowing is necessary (v. 36) but dangerous (vv. 37ff.) because we might use not knowing as an excuse for not acting.... But disciples' not knowing when should make them alert lest they be unprepared for the knowable that of his coming."[12]

This theme of ethical responsibility stemming from the imminent return of Christ governs the ensuing parables and becomes a major theme in the rest of the NT. Every major passage on the Lord's return emphasizes right conduct on our part (cf. 1 Cor 15:58; 2 Cor 5:9 – 10; 1 Thess 5:8 – 11; 2 Thess 2:13 – 15; the perseverance theme in Revelation). In addition, in several places a statement that "the end is near" or some such saying is used to anchor ongoing ethical responsibility (cf. Rom 13:11; 1 Cor 7:29 – 31, 10:11 – 13; Jas 5:7 – 9; 1 Pet 4:7 – 11).

11. Blomberg, *Parables*, 278.

12. Bruner, *Matthew 13 – 28*, 523.

CHAPTER 107

Matthew 24:45 – 51

Literary Context

As explained in the introduction to the previous section, this is part of a series of parables on the need for readiness and proper ethical conduct in light of the soon and yet unexpected parousia. This parable speaks of the responsibility that the believer has in light of the fact that Christ's return may come sooner than we think. The rest of this section will build on this.

VI. The Movement to the Cross (19:1 – 25:46)
- **B. Fifth Discourse: Guilt and Judgment of Israel (23:1 – 25:46)**
  - **2. Judgment — Olivet Discourse (24:1 – 25:46)**
    - a. Destruction of Jerusalem and the Events of the End Time (24:1 – 35)
    - **b. Parables on Readiness (24:36 – 25:30)**
      - (1) The Need for Spiritual Vigilance (24:36 – 44)
      - ➦ **(2) The Parable of the Faithful and Wicked Slaves (24:45 – 51)**
      - (3) The Parable of the Ten Bridesmaids (25:1 – 13)

Main Idea

The primary theme is the necessity of proper conduct insofar as no one knows when Christ will return. A secondary theme is the certainty of judgment for those who are not ready. When Christ appears, everyone will be accountable for how they are living at that time.

Translation

Matthew 24:45-51

45a	Question	*"Who then is the faithful and wise servant*
b		*whom the master appoints*
		over his household servants
		to give them food
		at the proper time?
46a	Alternative #1	*Blessed is that servant*
		whose master finds him doing this
		when he comes back.
47a	Result	*I tell you the truth,*
		he will place him in charge of all he possesses.
48a	Alternative #2	But *if that wicked servant should say in his heart,*
b		*'My master is taking a long time,'*
49a		and *he begins to beat his fellow servants,*
b		and *he eats and drinks with drunkards.*
50a	Result	*The master of that servant will come on a day*
		when he does not expect and
		at an hour
		that he does not know
51a		and *he will cut him into pieces*
b		and *assign him a place with the hypocrites,*
c		*where there will be weeping and*
		grinding of teeth."

Structure and Literary Form

This is a Q passage paralleled closely by Luke 12:41 – 46, with only an isolated word here and there different[1] (the main addition is Matt 24:51c, "where there will be weeping and grinding of teeth"). It falls neatly into two contrasting parts, the faithful slave who earns a reward (vv. 45 – 47), and the wicked slave who earns judgment (vv. 48 – 51). Each can be divided into the actions of the slaves (vv. 46, 48 – 49) and their consequent fates (vv. 47, 50 – 51). The emphasis is on the wicked slave, whose actions and punishment are given in much greater detail.

1. At the same time there are sufficient differences (e.g., Matthew has "slave," Luke "steward") to cause numerous debates over which was original, Matthew or Luke. I would agree more with Wenham, *Rediscovery*, 15 – 49, that both Matthew and Luke were redactional in the sense of editing Jesus' original (though I am not so certain of an "Ur-Gospel" behind them). Any attempt to distinguish an "original" is too speculative to be of value.

Exegetical Outline

→ **I. The Faithful and Wise Slave (24:45 – 47)**

A. The basis of the parable: take care of the other slaves (v. 45)

B. His actions: faithful in carrying out the duties (v. 46)

C. His reward: given charge over all the master's possessions (v. 47)

II. The Wicked Slave (24:48 – 51)

A. His actions: beating the other slaves and getting drunk (vv. 48 – 49)

B. His punishment: dismembered, loss of inheritance, terrible sorrow (vv. 50 – 51)

Explanation of the Text

24:45 Who then is the faithful and wise servant (Τίς ἄρα ἐστὶν ὁ πιστὸς δοῦλος καὶ φρόνιμος;). "Then" (ἄρα) with a question draws an inference from preceding material, in this case from the demand for eschatological readiness in v. 44. The number of slaves (for δοῦλος see on 8:9) a person owned was a sign of status in the ancient world. Slaves were often highly educated and were doctors, teachers, accountants, and workers for every function in a home. Wealthy homes would have dozens of slaves (one senator had 400), some whose job was little more than doing the mistress's hair or folding napkins for dinner parties. Slaves were allowed to own property, earn wages, and even purchase their freedom.[2]

The theme of this parable is the search for a "faithful and wise" leader[3] who can be trusted as a head slave. Both are discipleship terms, with "faithful" (πιστός) found again in 25:21, 23 of the "good and faithful slaves" who used their "talents" for the benefit of their master, and "wise" (φρόνιμος, meaning "prudent, discerning") used in 7:24; 10:16 as a wisdom term for understanding the situation and doing what the master commands (cf. 25:2, 4, 8, 9).

24:45 ... whom the master appoints over his household servants to give them food at the proper time? (ὃν κατέστησεν ὁ κύριος ἐπὶ τῆς οἰκετείας αὐτοῦ τοῦ δοῦναι αὐτοῖς τὴν τροφὴν ἐν καιρῷ;). This parable pictures a wealthy householder with multiple slaves. He leaves on a lengthy journey with an indeterminate time for returning, and while he is gone he chooses one of the slaves (certainly a male in the first century) to be in charge of the others and to take care of them.[4]

24:46 Blessed is that servant whose master finds him doing this when he comes back (μακάριος ὁ δοῦλος ἐκεῖνος ὃν ἐλθὼν ὁ κύριος αὐτοῦ εὑρήσει οὕτως ποιοῦντα). There is double meaning in "blessed" (μακάριος). In the story it means "fortunate" or "it will be good" (as TNIV). In discipleship it means (as in the Beatitudes of 5:3 – 12) "God blesses the one who. ..." The point is that God's blessing lies on those who are found "faithful" in serving him and others when Christ "returns."

2. See S. Scott Bartchy, "Slavery, Greco-Roman," *ABD*, 6:69 – 70.

3. Many (e.g., Gundry, Keener) consider this mainly a challenge to Christian teachers and leaders, a viable position since the point of the parable is authority over other slaves. Yet at the same time, "slave" (δοῦλος) became a metaphor for all believers serving God, and the thrust was the responsibility of every Christian to serve others in the kingdom.

4. Some (e.g., Nolland) see this slave as merely in control of the food supplies, but it is more likely that the giving of food is symbolic for authority over every area of life (as in the "daily needs" of 6:11).

24:47 I tell you the truth, he will place him in charge of all he possesses (ἀμὴν λέγω ὑμῖν ὅτι ἐπὶ πᾶσιν τοῖς ὑπάρχουσιν αὐτοῦ καταστήσει αὐτόν). This is the third of six "amen" (ἀμήν) sayings in this discourse (24:2, 34, 47; 25:12, 40, 45), matched only by the six in the Sermon on the Mount. Jesus wants his disciples to realize the vast importance of these truths. Again, there are discipleship implications. As the faithful slave was given authority over the master's entire household, so the faithful disciple will be given even more authority in God's church.[5] This blessing will be spelled out in more detail in 25:10, 21b, 23b.

24:48 But if that wicked servant should say in his heart, "My master is taking a long time" (ἐὰν δὲ εἴπῃ ὁ κακὸς δοῦλος ἐκεῖνος ἐν τῇ καρδίᾳ αὐτοῦ, Χρονίζει μου ὁ κύριος). In Luke 12:42 – 46 it is the same slave who makes a choice to be good or bad (v. 45, "But suppose the servant says to himself..."). Here in Matt 24 it is more likely that there are two contrasting slaves (so Hagner, Nolland; contra Blomberg). The key to the use of the parable here is χρονίζει, which means to "delay, stay away a long time," or even "fail to come" (BAGD, 887; *EDNT*, 3:487). This is why Jesus tells this parable, for it speaks to the issue of the "delay of the parousia" (1 Thess 4:15 – 16; 2 Pet 3:4), vastly overstated by many critical scholars[6] but still a problem for the early church.

All the apostles (Paul included) expected Jesus to return soon, and when he did not, it certainly caused consternation. If anyone had told Matthew or Paul that Jesus would not return for at least two thousand years, they might well have called that person a false prophet! Knowing this, Jesus is warning the church about false reactions to that delay. Such is a type of unbelief, for they reject the possibility of Jesus' soon return.

24:49 ... and he begins to beat his fellow servants, and he eats and drinks with drunkards (καὶ ἄρξηται τύπτειν τοὺς συνδούλους αὐτοῦ, ἐσθίῃ δὲ καὶ πίνῃ μετὰ τῶν μεθυόντων). Believing that the master is long gone, this slave's true wicked nature takes over. The imagery of violence (see 18:28 – 30 for a similar wicked deed against a "fellow slave") and carousing was a common picture of depravity in the ancient world. There are stories of Nero going out with armed guards and beating strangers to death at random just for R and R.

The message for the reader is clear: the delay in Jesus' return dare not become an excuse for wicked behavior. Bruner speaks of a misuse of power when we who are nothing more than fellow servants begin to abuse our authority and act like the master: "Loss of faith in Christ's Return is always followed by some kind of violence in interpersonal relationships and by laxity in moral relationships. Where spiritual sensitivities die, social services wither."[7]

24:50 The master of that servant will come on a day when he does not expect and at an hour that he does not know (ἥξει ὁ κύριος τοῦ δούλου ἐκείνου ἐν ἡμέρᾳ ᾗ οὐ προσδοκᾷ καὶ ἐν ὥρᾳ ᾗ οὐ γινώσκει). The extremely detailed time note with its synonymous parallelism ("day when he does not expect"/"hour that he does not know," cf. v. 36) lays great stress on the unexpected nature of the return. Beginning with v. 36 this has been the

5. It is important to realize that the reward is more responsibility, not less. As Morris, *Matthew*, 616, says, "The reward for faithful service is the opportunity of serving in a higher and more responsible place (not ease and rest forevermore)." This is realized, not final, eschatology, centering on the present life in the church rather than eternal reward.

6. There is no need to say this is the result of a crisis in Matthew's community. All these parables show Jesus' awareness of the coming problem of the delay. Jesus was preparing his followers for the lengthy time before he came back.

7. Bruner, *Matthew 13 – 28*, 539 – 40.

major emphasis (vv. 39, 42, 44), and this will carry over to the rest of the discourse (25:5, 10, 13, 19, 31). Not only will Jesus return like a thief when least expected, but that return will bring judgment for those unprepared. The wicked slave thought he had plenty of time to get ready and set things right, but he was caught unprepared.

24:51 And he will cut him into pieces and assign him a place with the hypocrites, where there will be weeping and grinding of teeth (καὶ διχοτομήσει αὐτὸν καὶ τὸ μέρος αὐτοῦ μετὰ τῶν ὑποκριτῶν θήσει· ἐκεῖ ἔσται ὁ κλαυθμὸς καὶ ὁ βρυγμὸς τῶν ὀδόντων). This is the first of four straight severe judgments (cf. 25:10 – 12, 30, 41, 46). This punishment on the surface seems much too harsh for the crime. The second part seems reasonable: "a place [μέρος, 'part, share'] with the hypocrites" means he will suffer the same punishment as hypocrites will because he has pretended to be a trustworthy slave when he was not. However, remember that hypocrisy is the major sin of the leaders in ch. 23 (vv. 13, 14, 15, 23, 25, 27, 29), and so this is hinting that the leaders will share the same fate as the wicked servant.

The first aspect, however, seems way over the top. διχοτομέω literally means "cut in two" and was one of the worst ways to die (ultimate disgrace as well as filled with pain). So some have tried to water it down to "punish" (RSV, Phillips, LB) or "cut him off" (JB, probably = excommunication from the congregation). Yet hyperbole is common in Jesus' teaching (5:22, 29 – 30; 7:3 – 5; 10:9 – 10; 18:8 – 9, 22, 23 with 28) and is likely the case here.[8] Moreover, masters in the Roman world had life and death power over their slaves, and this was done on occasion with rebellious or runaway slaves. This is a metaphor for eternal punishment, as seen in "weeping and grinding of teeth," a reference to eternal damnation used by Jesus in 8:12; 13:42, 50; 22:13; 25:30.

Theology in Application

Throughout the history of the church this parable was applied mainly to church leaders and teachers. But this is unlikely, for certainly Jesus meant it for all believers who are tempted to mistreat and lord themselves over others (see 20:25 – 27). There are three messages here. (1) Jesus is going to return, and that return will be unexpected. (2) Every believer is responsible to be ready at all times, for we will all be held accountable for the way we live. (3) There will be severe judgment for those who live for themselves and refuse to serve others. The abuse of others and hedonism are more a part of the parable (local color, see introduction to ch. 13) than intended to be singled out, but both are viable illustrations of the self-centered living that is condemned here.

8. For this literal meaning of the metaphor, see T. A. Fredrichsen, "A Note on διχοτομήσει αὐτόν (Luke 12:46 and the Parallel in Matthew 24:51)," *CBQ* 63 (2001): 258 – 64, who sees a reference to the warning to the leaders of Israel in Jer 34:18 – 20, "I will treat (them) like the calf they cut in two and then walked between its pieces," the covenant ceremony from Gen 15:10, 17 – 18.

CHAPTER 108

Matthew 25:1 – 13

Literary Context

This is the next in the set of parables that center on readiness for the Lord's return. All have the same basic themes — ignorance of the time of the coming, importance of vigilance, being prepared for the sudden return, and accountability.

VI. The Movement to the Cross (19:1 – 25:46)
- **B. Fifth Discourse: Guilt and Judgment of Israel (23:1 – 25:46)**
  - **2. Judgment — Olivet Discourse (24:1 – 25:46)**
    - a. Destruction of Jerusalem and the Events of the End Time (24:1 – 35)
    - **b. Parables on Readiness (24:36 – 25:30)**
      - (1) The Need for Spiritual Vigilance (24:36 – 44)
      - (2) The Parable of the Faithful and Wicked Slaves (24:45 – 51)
      - ➦ **(3) The Parable of the Ten Bridesmaids (25:1 – 13)**
      - (4) The Parable of the Talents (25:14 – 30)

Main Idea

This is an allegorical parable in which the bridegroom is the Son of Man and the bridesmaids are the members of the messianic community, the church (the bride is not a part of this parable). The plot turns on the delay of the bridegroom and the preparedness of the bridesmaids; the five who are not ready are excluded from the wedding feast. Thus the message is the same as 24:36 – 51: Jesus demands readiness and those unprepared face judgment.

Translation

Matthew 25:1-13

1a	Illustration/Analogy	"Then the kingdom of heaven will be like ten young women
b		who took their torches and
		went out to meet the bridegroom.
2a	Description	Five of them were foolish and five wise
3a	Group #1	[1] For the foolish . . . failed to take oil with them
		while taking their torches.
4a	Group #2	[2] But the wise took oil
		in the containers
		with their own torches.
5a	Circumstance	Now when the bridegroom was delayed,
b	Result of 5a	they all became drowsy and fell asleep
6a	Setting	But in the middle of the night a cry came,
b	Exclamation	'Look!
c	Assertion	The bridegroom is here.
d	Exhortation	Come out to meet him.'
7a	Action	At that time all those young women arose and
		began to trim their torches.
8a	Request	But the foolish ones asked the wise,
b		"Give us some of your oil,
c	Basis for 8b	because our torches are going out.'
9a	Answer: Refusal	But the wise responded,
b		"There will hardly be enough for us and for you.
c		Go instead to the shops and buy some for yourselves.'
10a	Setting	Now when they went off to purchase it,
b	Action	the bridegroom came.
c	Result	Those who were ready entered the wedding banquet with him,
d		and the door was shut.
11a	Request	Later the rest of the young women came and said,
b		'Lord, lord, open the door for us.'
12a	Response	But he replied,
b		'I tell you the truth, I do not know you.'
13a	Exhortation	So be constantly vigilant,
b	Basis for 13a	because you do not know the day or the hour."

Structure and Literary Form

This parable stems from Matthew's own special source. There are stories with similar motifs in Mark 13:33 – 37 and Luke 12:35 – 38, 13:25 – 27, as well as in Matt

7:21 – 23, but no parallels.[1] The story is framed by a thematic introduction (v. 1) and the moral of the story (v. 13). In between are three parts: (1) The two sets of maidens go forth to meet the bridegroom, half of them prepared, half not (vv. 2 – 5). (2) After some time the bridegroom suddenly appears, but the foolish bridesmaids are not ready (vv. 6 – 9). (3) Those prepared enter the banquet, those not ready are denied entrance at the door (vv. 10 – 12).

Exegetical Outline

➡ **I. Thematic Introduction: The Ten Set Forth to Meet the Bridegroom (25:1)**

II. The Wise and Foolish Maidens (25:2 – 5)

- A. The foolish take torches but no oil (v. 3)
- B. The wise take oil with their torches (v. 4)
- C. The bridegroom is delayed, and the ten fall asleep (v. 5)

III. Chaos as the Bridegroom Approaches (25:6 – 9)

- A. The bridegroom comes, and they prepare the torches (vv. 6 – 7)
- B. The foolish try to borrow oil (v. 8)
- C. The wise tell them to go buy some oil (v. 9)

IV. Entrance to the Wedding Banquet (25:10 – 12)

- A. The wise enter the wedding banquet (v. 10)
- B. The foolish are denied entrance (vv. 11 – 12)

V. The Moral: Maintain Watchfulness (25:13)

Explanation of the Text

25:1 Then the kingdom of heaven will be like ten young women (Τότε ὁμοιωθήσεται ἡ βασιλεία τῶν οὐρανῶν δέκα παρθένοις). For the opening formula see 13:24. The primary difference is the future "will be like" (ὁμοιωθήσεται) because Jesus is looking to the arrival of the kingdom at his second coming. As stated in 13:24 the kingdom is not like the maidens, but rather the situation occasioned at the arrival of the kingdom will be like the story regarding the wise and foolish young women. The emphasis in "young women" (πάρθενοι) is not on the fact of their virginity (that is assumed) but on the fact that they were unmarried young women, probably between twelve and eighteen years old (by then most young women were married). Here they are obviously friends of the bride (like modern bridesmaids) sent out to meet her groom.

25:1 ... who took[2] their torches and went out to meet the bridegroom[3] (αἵτινες λαβοῦσαι τὰς

1. This parable has become somewhat of a battleground over authentic parable material. Some critical scholars believe the whole a fabrication of the early church due to the delay of the parousia (e.g., Bultmann, Bornkamm), but most today accept at least a nucleus of the story as authentic Jesus material. Yet there is huge debate as to what constitutes Matthean redaction (cf. Davies and Allison, Luz, Nolland). It is best not to engage overmuch in such speculations but to accept the basic historical veracity of the story as it stands.

2. "Took" (λαβοῦσαι) is another circumstantial participle that becomes virtually another main verb (see on 4:4; 11:4).

3. Several witnesses (D Θ f^1) add "and the bride," but most

λαμπάδας ἑαυτῶν ἐξῆλθον εἰς ὑπάντησιν τοῦ νυμφίου). Marriage celebrations lasted seven days, but this story centers on the first night, as the groom is on the way to the bride's home[4] in order to escort her back to his home. The bride sends out her friends to meet him halfway. Since it is night, they take torches[5] with them. Such torchlit processions at night are still practiced today, and they symbolize the glorious splendor of the wedding couple. Jesus probably chose the number "ten" because of its biblical implications as a symbol of fullness or completeness (ten commandments, ten plagues, ten percent tithe, see Davies and Allison).

25:2 Five of them were foolish and five wise (πέντε δὲ ἐξ αὐτῶν ἦσαν μωραὶ καὶ πέντε φρόνιμοι). This is a further statement of the "theme" of the story. φρόνιμος ("wise" or "prudent") stems from 24:45 ("the faithful and wise slave") and continues the wisdom motif of the discerning Christ-follower who understands the situation and does what is right, namely, being ready for the coming of the groom. μωρός ("foolish, stupid") occurs in 5:22; 23:17 and especially in 7:24 – 27 is contrasted also with the "wise" in terms of "hearing [Jesus'] words and putting them into practice." This is also a key wisdom contrast, and "fools" are those who ignore God in their lives (Prov 10:14; 12:15 – 16; 14:33; 17:12; etc.). Here it refers to those who make bad decisions and are not prepared to meet the groom/Christ when he comes.

25:3 For the foolish, while taking their torches, failed to take oil with them (αἱ γὰρ μωραὶ λαβοῦσαι τὰς λαμπάδας αὐτῶν οὐκ ἔλαβον μεθ' ἑαυτῶν ἔλαιον). Again the theme is being ready for the unexpected. The story will turn on having sufficient oil, as we will see in vv. 6 – 9. The foolish bridesmaids live only for the moment and give little thought to contingencies. They can hardly go out at night without torches, but they do not prepare for a lengthy wait. It is sometimes said that the torches would only burn for fifteen minutes without extra oil. With torches the "oil"[6] would be extra oil for dowsing the rags (or perhaps extra oil-soaked rags) wrapped around the torch to ensure they would keep burning.

25:4 But the wise took oil in the containers with their own torches (αἱ δὲ φρόνιμοι ἔλαβον ἔλαιον ἐν τοῖς ἀγγείοις μετὰ τῶν λαμπάδων ἑαυτῶν). These prudent bridesmaids have the wisdom to think ahead. They are to meet the groom at a certain spot at a certain time, but they are aware that something could hold him up and so take enough oil to last in case he is late.

texts (ℵ B L W et al.) omit it, and this appears nowhere else in the story; it may have been added to furnish the image of the church as the bride of Christ, see Metzger, *Textual Commentary*, 62; Witherington, *Matthew*, 459.

4. Another possible scenario is that they waited at the groom's home for him to bring the bride to the feast (Song 3:11; 1 Macc 9:37 – 42; Josephus, *Ant.* 13:20); see Turner, "Matthew," 323.

5. There is considerable discussion as to whether these are torches or oil lamps. One would not think torches would have oil, yet at the same time lamps were usually found inside the home. Probably these were torches with rags soaked in oil wrapped around them, see France, Luz, Keener; contra Davies and Allison.

6. Many have seen allegorical meaning in the oil, interpreting it as good works (most) or faith or love or joy, but it is more likely that this is local color rather than a theology-laden detail (see the introduction to ch. 13) and thus part of the story rather than a metaphor for some spiritual quality or such. An example of extensive allegorizing is J. M. Ford, "The Parable of the Foolish Scholars (Matt. xxv. 1 – 13)," *NovT* 9 (1967): 107 – 23, who takes the maidens as Jewish scholars, the lamps as the Torah, and the oil as good deeds. Similarly, Albright and Mann, *Matthew*, 301 – 2, interpret this as an adaptation of an OT theme in which Israel's custodians (the leaders) have failed, and as such it is a warning to the new custodians of the messianic community, the church. For the history of interpretation see the excellent discussion in Luz, *Matthew 21 – 28*, 235 – 44.

25:5 Now when the bridegroom was delayed[7] (χρονίζοντος δὲ τοῦ νυμφίου). Jeremias suggests that the delay was caused by negotiations between the groom and the bride's parents over the financial settlement (dowry, etc.).[8] This is plausible, but the reason is not specified by Jesus and thus cannot be known.

25:5 ... they all became drowsy and fell asleep (ἐνύσταξαν πᾶσαι καὶ ἐκάθευδον). ἐνύσταξαν is an ingressive aorist, "began to nod off," and graphically pictures the maidens on the ground starting to get sleepy as they wait. The bridegroom is late enough that they finally fall asleep. There is no negative connotation in "sleep," for the wise sleep as well as the foolish. While they sleep, their torches undoubtedly flicker, then go out. However, in v. 13 the contrast between "sleep" and "remaining watchful" will become apparent.

25:6 But in the middle of the night a cry came, "Look! The bridegroom is here. Come out to meet him"[9] (μέσης δὲ νυκτὸς κραυγὴ γέγονεν, Ἰδοὺ ὁ νυμφίος, ἐξέρχεσθε εἰς ἀπάντησιν αὐτοῦ). The young women have been asleep awhile, probably with the torches long extinguished. "Middle of the night" (μέσης δὲ νυκτός) could mean "at midnight," but such precision is unnecessary here. We do not know who raises the cry;[10] possibly one of the women wake up and see the groom's procession approaching. The cry parallels 1 Thess 4:16, where the Lord will descend "with a loud command, with the voice of the archangel and with the trumpet call of God." This is the heart of the story and corresponds to the arrival of the parousia. The question for the parable and for the reader is, "Who is ready to meet the bridegroom?"

25:7 At that time all those young women arose and began to trim their torches (τότε ἠγέρθησαν πᾶσαι αἱ παρθένοι ἐκεῖναι καὶ ἐκόσμησαν τὰς λαμπάδας ἑαυτῶν). Excitement reigns as the bridesmaids awake, jump off the ground, grab their torches, and start to get them ready for going out in the dark to meet the procession. This makes the rest of the story all the more poignant, for we know that half of them will not make it. "Began to trim" (ἐκόσμησαν) is another ingressive aorist and means to "adorn, decorate" — in this case, to get the torches ready by either putting on extra oil or replacing the burnt-out rags with new oil-soaked rags, then lighting them.

25:8 But the foolish ones asked the wise, "Give us some of your oil, because our torches are going out" (αἱ δὲ μωραὶ ταῖς φρονίμοις εἶπαν, Δότε ἡμῖν ἐκ τοῦ ἐλαίου ὑμῶν, ὅτι αἱ λαμπάδες ἡμῶν σβέννυνται). The five thoughtless maidens have no oil to add to their torches and so quickly realize they are in trouble. Their torches are "going out" (the present tense "are going out" [σβέννυνται] pictures the flickering torches as they try to light them, cf. Job 18:5; 21:17; Prov 13:9; 20:20; 24:20, for the "lamp of the wicked is snuffed out"). So they turn to the wise and beg them to share their oil.

25:9 But the wise responded, "There will hardly be enough for us and for you" (ἀπεκρίθησαν δὲ αἱ φρόνιμοι λέγουσαι, Μήποτε οὐ μὴ ἀρκέσῃ ἡμῖν καὶ ὑμῖν). The response of the wise is somewhat

7. Note the presence of another of Matthew's genitive absolutes, used temporally here.

8. Jeremias, *Parables*, 172 – 73. See also A. W. Argyle, "Wedding Custioms at the Time of Jesus" *ExpTim* 86 (1975), 214 – 15.

9. The use of "in" (εἰς) with a verbal noun becomes virtually a verbal clause like εἰς τό with the infinitive, "in order to meet." "Him" (αὐτοῦ) is an objective genitive that becomes the object of the verbal idea. Some manuscripts (א B Z 700) omit αὐτοῦ, but others (A D L W Byz) include it, and it is probably best to leave it in the text.

10. Note the dramatic perfect "came" (γέγονεν), stressing the effects of the cry (see BDF §342).

surprising, because sharing is an essential quality for the citizens of the kingdom. But this is not a parable about sharing, and the explanation of the wise clears it up. There will not be sufficient oil for all ten; neither group will make it through the torchlight procession to the groom's home if the wise do so. In that case, the bride and bridegroom will be shamed rather than honored.

25:9 Go instead to the shops and buy some for yourselves (πορεύεσθε μᾶλλον πρὸς τοὺς πωλοῦντας καὶ ἀγοράσατε ἑαυταῖς). With a festive celebration like this, shops for supplies would be open even late at night.[11] In fact, v. 11 tells us the foolish bridesmaids were indeed able to purchase the oil they needed. In terms of the parousia, this means that we are each responsible for ourselves before the Lord. We cannot depend on others for our spirituality.

25:10 Now when they went off to purchase it, the bridegroom came (ἀπερχομένων δὲ αὐτῶν ἀγοράσαι ἦλθεν ὁ νυμφίος). The tragedy begins here. The foolish bridesmaids have been unprepared and so must rush out to buy sufficient oil. But they do not have enough time to do so, for while they are gone the bridegroom arrives and the procession to the banquet takes place.[12]

25:10 Those who were ready entered the wedding banquet with him (καὶ αἱ ἕτοιμοι εἰσῆλθον μετ᾽ αὐτοῦ εἰς τοὺς γάμους). "Were ready" (ἕτοιμοι) goes back to 24:44 ("you yourselves should also be ready") and the basic theme of the Olivet Discourse, that in light of the sudden, unexpected nature of Christ's return, believers must be prepared at all times. This is also the primary thrust of this parable. The separation between the wise and the foolish begins here, with one moving away from the bridal party and the other joining the bridal party. This fits the image of "one … taken and one left" in 24:40–41.

25:10 … and the door was shut (καὶ ἐκλείσθη ἡ θύρα). The finality of "the door was shut" is tragic. In one sense it does not fit a village wedding atmosphere,[13] but Jesus often does this in his parables. This is the "reversal of expectation" (see intro to ch. 13) that leaves the audience open-mouthed in consternation. Unlike village weddings, there is a finality to the parousia. There will not be multiple chances.

25:11 Later the rest of the young women came and said, "Lord, lord, open the door for us" (ὕστερον δὲ ἔρχονται καὶ αἱ λοιπαὶ παρθένοι λέγουσαι, Κύριε κύριε, ἄνοιξον ἡμῖν). Note the difference between "the ready" in v. 10 and "the rest" in v. 11. The foolish have gotten their oil (though it is useless since the procession is finished), and they now arrive (historical present "came" [ἔρχονται]) and seek admission. The use of κύριε κύριε (= "lord, lord") takes us back to the same expression in 7:21, and the end of this parable intends to do so (so also v. 12). This is not what normal attendants of the bride say to a groom, so Jesus has departed from the world of the parable and is addressing the situation at the time of the eschaton, i.e., the time of 7:21–23. There Jesus warned, "Not everyone who says to me 'Lord, Lord,' will enter the kingdom of heaven." The similarities with these foolish maidens are clear.

11. Argyle, "Wedding Customs at the Time of Jesus," 214–15, believes shops were regularly open all night for such celebrations.

12. Nolland, *Matthew*, 1008, tells it another way, with the bridegroom arriving at the banquet itself rather than at a prearranged point to meet the bridesmaids. However, that would nullify the torchlight procession and minimize the centrality of torches in the story. Thus this version is not as likely.

13. One is to picture either the guest list complete or (better) an arrival that is so late as to insult the groom, so Keener, Nolland.

25:12 But he replied,[14] "I tell you the truth, I do not know you" (ὁ δὲ ἀποκριθεὶς εἶπεν, Ἀμὴν λέγω ὑμῖν, οὐκ οἶδα ὑμᾶς). The close connection to 7:21 – 23 continues, for in 7:23 Jesus says to the counterfeit followers, "I never knew you. Depart from me, workers of evil." This also parallels Luke 13:25, where Jesus says to those outside the narrow door, "I don't know you or where you come from." This is a "formula of renunciation" (Davies and Allison, Carson), and there are parallels with the wedding guest of 22:11 – 14 who did not have the proper attire.

As in v. 11, we have another "reversal of expectation," with the groom's harsh rejection endemic to the parousia more than to the normal wedding banquet (rejection of wedding guests did sometimes happen, though hardly ever for this type of reason). People do not enter the kingdom on their own terms but on God's terms, and it is clear from the whole of 24:36 – 25:30 that one of those terms is readiness for the parousia, i.e., a life of obedience to God.

25:13 So be constantly vigilant (γρηγορεῖτε οὖν). This repeats 24:42, "So be constantly vigilant [also a progressive present imperative], because you do not know on what day your Lord is going to come" (note the repetition of 24:44 in v. 10); as such it provides the moral of the parable story and sums up the basic message of the entire discourse. Vigilance is the way believers maintain readiness, and it entails right living as well as right thinking.

25:13 ... because you do not know the day or the hour (ὅτι οὐκ οἴδατε τὴν ἡμέραν οὐδὲ τὴν ὥραν). Ignorance of the time of the parousia (24:36, 42, 44, 50) means that Jesus' followers must be "ever watchful" and ready. Another parallel is Rev 16:15, "Look, I come like a thief [cf. Matt 24:43]. Blessed are those who stay awake [the literal meaning of γρηγορέω] and keep their clothes on, so that they may not go naked and be shamefully exposed."

Theology in Application

Luz says it well: "The goal of the Matthean parable is paraenesis for the church. Here the readers learn that not everyone who is called to the wedding of the bridegroom will actually share in it."[15] In a sense this pictures the visible and the invisible church, yet at the same time it is a warning to all of us. We do not know when the Lord is returning, and we dare not say, "Not today!" He will come at a time of his own choosing, and at that time we are all accountable for our lifestyle and priorities. For those who are not ready and miss it, it will be too late. There will be no second chance.

At the same time this is not a call to sinless perfection but to constant readiness. We do not have to be perfect, but we do have to be prepared. The consequences could not be more severe. The quasi-Christians in our churches (those who attend regularly and give lip service to affirming the key doctrines but do not live in obedience to God) must be aware that they are playing games with their eternal destiny

14. For the circumstantial participle "answering" (ἀποκριθείς) modifying a verb of saying, see on 4:4. It is best to translate the verbal unit "responded" or some such. This occurs also in 25:26, 40. The opposite, with "answered" the main verb with the participle "saying" (λέγων) occurs in 25:9, 37, 44, 45 and should be translated the same.

15. Luz, *Matthew 21 – 28*, 244.

(see also "Theology in Application" on 7:21 – 23). Charette provides an excellent summation:

> Presumption in the face of God's goodness, indifference to his call and unfaithfulness in his service place one in a position of danger. A terrible judgment had come upon Israel because of its failure to conform to the will of God ... the covenant relationship had been revoked and they had been cut off from the blessing of God. The church is warned that it too is not exempt from judgment, but must face a day of reckoning when it will be called upon to present fruit befitting the call and advantage it has received.[16]

16. Charette, *Theme of Recompense*, 154.

CHAPTER 109

Matthew 25:14 – 30

Literary Context

This is the final parable in the series of 24:36 – 25:30 centering on the delay of the parousia and the need for constant readiness on the part of every believer. This one adds the element of working for the kingdom as part of that readiness. Witherington calls this a twin parable with the wise and foolish virgins of 25:1 – 13, indicating that both men and women would be involved in the messianic banquet and would be alike in both honor and dishonor, in grace and disgrace.[1]

VI. The Movement to the Cross (19:1 – 25:46)

- **B. Fifth Discourse: Guilt and Judgment of Israel (23:1 – 25:46)**
  - **2. Judgment — Olivet Discourse (24:1 – 25:46)**
    - a. Destruction of Jerusalem and the Events of the End Time (24:1 – 35)
    - **b. Parables on Readiness (24:36 – 25:30)**
      - (1) The Need for Spiritual Vigilance (24:36 – 44)
      - (2) The Parable of the Faithful and Wicked Slaves (24:45 – 51)
      - (3) The Parable of the Ten Bridesmaids (25:1 – 13)
      - ➦ **(4) The Parable of the Talents (25:14 – 30)**

Main Idea

The connection of this parable to the others is the delay of the master's return, but the emphasis here is on the responsibility to serve the master with all one's worldly resources and abilities (here in terms of money but symbolizing every aspect of life).[2] The theme of judgment continues. Each one is accountable, and those who serve the Master well will have an abundant reward, while those who do not will be condemned.

1. Witherington, *Matthew*, 459.

2. France, *Gospel of Matthew*, 951, argues this is not about abilities God gives but about the responsibility every believer has to use every opportunity for the benefit of the kingdom.

Translation

Matthew 25:14-30

14a	Analogy	*"For it will be like a man*	
b	Description/Action	*who*	*was going on a journey and*
			called his own slaves and
			handed his money over to them.
15a	Person #1/Action	*[A] To the one he gave five talents,*	
b	Person #2/Action	*[B] to another two, and*	
c	Person #3/Action	*[C] to the other one,*	
d	Basis for 15a-c	*to each according to his own ability.*	
e	Action	*Then he went on his journey.*	
16a	Result of 15a	*[A] Immediately the one who had received five talents* ↵	
		went and	
		worked with his money and	
		gained five talents more.	
17a	Result of 15b	*[B] Likewise, the one with two talents gained two more.*	
18a	Result of 15c	*[C] But the one who had received one*	*went away and*
			dug a hole
			in the ground and
			hid his master's money.
19a	Setting		*After a long time away*
b	Action	*the master of those slaves*	*returned and*
			settled accounts with them.
20a	Person #1	*[A] And the one who had received five talents* ↵	
		came and brought the other five talents, saying,	
b		*(a) 'Master, you handed five talents over to me.*	
c	Result	*(b) Look, I have gained another five talents.'*	
21a	Result of 20a-c	*His master responded,*	
b		*(i) 'Well done, good and faithful slave.*	
c		*(ii) You were faithful over a little.*	
d		*(iii) I will place you in charge of much.*	
e		*(iv) Enter into the joy of your master.'*	
22a	Person #2	*[B] The one with two talents also came to him and said,*	
b		*(a) 'Master, you handed over to me two talents.*	
c	Result	*(b) Look, I have gained another two talents more.'*	
23a	Result of 22a-c	*His master responded,*	
b		*(i) 'Well done, good and faithful slave.*	
c		*(ii) You were faithful over a little.*	
d		*(iii) I will place you in charge of much.*	
e		*(iv) Enter into the joy of your master.'*	
24a	Person #3	*[C] But the one who had received one talent also* ↵	
		came to him and said,	
b		*'Master, I knew that you are a hard man,*	
c		*reaping harvest where you have not sown and*	

Continued on next page.

Continued from previous page.

d		*gathering crops where you have not scattered seed.*
25a		*And since I was afraid,*
b	Result	*I went and*
		hid your talent in the ground.
c		*Look, you have what is yours.'*
26a	Result of 24a-25c/ Rebuke	*But his master responded,*
b		*'Evil and lazy servant!*
c	Rhetorical Question	*Did you really know that I harvest*
		where I have not sown and
d		*gather*
		where I have not scattered?
27a	Rebuke	*You should have placed my money in with the bankers.*
b		*Then when I came*
		I could have received what is mine with interest.
28a	Consequence	*Therefore,*
		take the talent from him and
b		*give it to the one who has ten talents.*
29a	Basis of 28a-b	*For to everyone who has, more will be given,*
b		*and they will have abundance;*
c		*but as for the one who does not have,*
d		*even what they have will be taken away from them.*
30a	Judgment	*So throw this worthless slave out into outer darkness.*
b		*In that place there will be weeping and*
		grinding of teeth.'"

Structure and Literary Form

It is common for critical scholars to assume this parable stems from the same source as Luke 19:11 – 27 (the parable of ten minas), with the general consensus that Matthew is closer to the original. However, the differences are numerous enough (minas [= 100 denarii] rather than talents [= 6000 denarii], a king, the rebellion of his subjects, the giving of ten minas to each, the punishment of the king's enemies rather than the lazy servant) to justify the conclusion of many (Schlatter, Carson, France, Blomberg, Morris, Keener, Witherington) that these are separate (though similar) parables told by Jesus on separate occasions. Therefore this is M material.

The story has three parts: (1) the differing amounts of money entrusted to the slaves (vv. 14 – 15); (2) the work done by the slaves to make profit off the money (vv. 16 – 18); (3) the master settling accounts with each (vv. 19 – 30). The latter section can be subdivided into the rewarding of each in turn (vv. 19 – 28) and then the explanation of the rewards to the first two and the punishment of the third (vv. 29 – 30).

Exegetical Outline

- **I. Responsibilities Given on the Basis of Ability (25:14 – 15)**
- **II. The Work of Each to Increase the Yield on the Money (25:16 – 18)**
  - A. The first two doubled the money given them (vv. 16 – 17)
  - B. The third hid his in the ground (v. 18)
- **III. The Settling of Accounts with the Slaves (25:19 – 30)**
  - A. The rewards earned by each (vv. 19 – 28)
    1. The first two commended and given authority "over much" (vv. 19 – 23)
    2. The third condemned (vv. 24 – 28)
       a. His explanation — his fear of the master (vv. 24 – 25)
       b. His condemnation by the master (vv. 26 – 28)
  - B. The master's explanation of his actions (vv. 29 – 30)
    1. Giving to those who have, removing from those who have not (v. 29)
    2. The ultimate judgment of the lazy slave (v. 30)

Explanation of the Text

25:14 For it will be like a man who was going on a journey[3] (Ὥσπερ γὰρ ἄνθρωπος ἀποδημῶν). The setting of this parable is similar to the first in the series (24:45 – 51) as a story about slaves being given responsibilities while their master is away on a journey. As a result, the thrust is on the period of absence between the advents of Christ, the responsibility every believer has to be at work and ready for the Master's return, and the accountability they will have to him. This verse may build on Mark 13:34 (a man "going away" who "puts his servants in charge, each with an assigned task"), with Matthew deciding to replace Mark 13:35 – 37 with a more developed parable (so Nolland).

25:14 ... and called his own slaves and handed his money over to them (ἐκάλεσεν τοὺς ἰδίους δούλους καὶ παρέδωκεν αὐτοῖς τὰ ὑπάρχοντα αὐτοῦ). It appears incongruous today to think of a wealthy landowner entrusting all his money to slaves, but in 24:45 we discussed how slaves were teachers, accountants, and even treasurers of a kingdom (see 18:23 – 24). These were not just household slaves or agricultural workers but highly skilled business experts.[4] The amount of money the master gave them (v. 15) shows why he had three slaves just for this. He must have had a thriving business.

25:15 To the one he gave five talents, to another two, and to the other one (καὶ ᾧ μὲν ἔδωκεν πέντε τάλαντα, ᾧ δὲ δύο, ᾧ δὲ ἕν). "Talents" (τάλαντα) was already described in 18:24; it was the amount of weight a soldier could carry on his back and

3. This is another circumstantial participle. It could be translated, "he went on a journey and called."

4. Derrett, *Law in the New Testament*, 17 – 31 (esp. 18), who believes they were servants rather than slaves (but δοῦλος always means "slave," see BAGD, 205), states that they were virtually partners and may have shared some of the profits. This would be true of slaves as well, as they too could receive remuneration for their efforts. Luz, *Matthew 21 – 28*, 251, says no mention is made of profit in the story, but the whole progression of the story shows profit was the implicit expectation, and in ancient times slaves sharing in profits (at the master's whim, of course, but still common) happened often.

referred to seventy-five to a hundred pounds of gold or silver. By the calculations there, a talent is worth $800,000 in today's money ($960,000 when gold is worth $600 an ounce).[5] So the man gave his slaves a fortune in money, probably a large part of his net worth (ὑπάρχοντα in v. 14 refers to all a person's "possessions"; cf. 19:21; 24:47) in order to earn him profit.[6]

25:15 ... to each according to his own ability. Then he went on his journey (ἑκάστῳ κατὰ τὴν ἰδίαν δύναμιν, καὶ ἀπεδήμησεν). "His own ability" (with δύναμιν meaning "capability") refers to the master's evaluation of each one's prowess in economic affairs. It almost certainly symbolizes the spiritual gifts God gives his people, and Jesus' comments here may have become the basis for Paul in Rom 12:3 ("in accordance with the faith God has distributed to each of you") and v. 6 ("according to the grace given to each of us") as well as for Peter in 1 Pet 4:10 ("use whatever gift you have received ... as faithful stewards of God's grace").

The master is not taking as great a chance as people think. These slaves have probably long been a part of his business (probably some commercial enterprise). Yet to give them so much, especially if it is the whole net worth of his commercial enterprise, is surprising. The master leaving on a lengthy journey continues the delay of the parousia theme from the earlier parables of this section.

25:16 Immediately the one who had received five talents went[7] and worked with his money and gained five talents more (εὐθέως πορευθεὶς ὁ τὰ πέντε τάλαντα λαβὼν ἠργάσατο ἐν αὐτοῖς καὶ ἐκέρδησεν ἄλλα πέντε). "Immediately" (εὐθέως) from v. 15 belongs here. The first industrious slave gets started at once and puts a lot of energy into his task, earning 100 percent profit. The idea in "working with the money" is of great industry and initiative, as seen also in the results.[8] In terms of the eschatological message, Jesus expects his disciples to spend the same effort in working for the kingdom.

25:17 Likewise, the one with two talents gained two more (ὡσαύτως ὁ τὰ δύο ἐκέρδησεν ἄλλα δύο). The second replicates the efforts of the first slave, also earning 100 percent profit from his industrious work. Those who have lesser abilities in the church are still expected to use them for the glory of God and to expand the kingdom.

25:18 But the one who had received one went away and dug a hole in the ground and hid his master's money (ὁ δὲ τὸ ἓν λαβὼν ἀπελθὼν ὤρυξεν γῆν καὶ ἔκρυψεν τὸ ἀργύριον τοῦ κυρίου αὐτοῦ). The lazy servant decides to hide his money in the ground. This was considered a valid practice for safeguarding valuables (cf. 13:44; in Luke 19:20, where the servant hid the money "in a piece of cloth," the action was more disgraceful), but it was deliberate disobedience and an insult to the master, since he was supposed to use it to make a profit. He played it safe to avoid taking a loss, but that was distinctly against the master's wishes.

25:19 After a long time away the master of those slaves returned and settled accounts with them

5. While these talents were in silver rather than gold (v. 18), silver was worth as much as gold in the ancient world.

6. Luz, *Matthew 21–28*, 251–52, says the term for this money given to slaves was "peculium," and while the slave could use it as he wished, the money was always considered the property of the master. He adds, "The best way to make money quickly in antiquity was dealing in commodities or speculating in land."

7. On the circumstantial participle "went" (πορευθείς) with a main verb, see 11:4; 17:27; 18:12; 28:19.

8. On the other hand, Derrett, "Talents," 24, calls this "the minimum profit accepted under the law of Hammurabi" and says they did "what was expected of them." In Luke 19:16, 18, the first earned 1000 percent profit and the second 500 percent profit. Still, the tone here is that the first two slaves did very well.

(μετὰ δὲ πολὺν χρόνον ἔρχεται ὁ κύριος τῶν δούλων ἐκείνων καὶ συναίρει λόγον μετ᾽ αὐτῶν). The historic presents in this verse (after the aorists in previous verses) foreground the return of the master[9] and highlight the action (especially as symbolizing the delay of the parousia, cf. 24:48; 25:5). The emphasis here is not on the unexpected nature of the return but on both the length of the time away (further evidence Jesus was preparing them for the church age) and the accountability it entails. "Settled accounts" (συναίρει λόγον) is a commercial phrase for settling the books, both in terms of the extent to which each one has fulfilled his duty and the remuneration due each one.

25:20 And the one who had received five talents came and brought the other five talents, saying, "Master, you handed five talents over to me. Look, I have gained another five talents" (καὶ προσελθὼν ὁ τὰ πέντε τάλαντα λαβὼν προσήνεγκεν ἄλλα πέντε τάλαντα λέγων, Κύριε, πέντε τάλαντά μοι παρέδωκας· ἴδε ἄλλα πέντε τάλαντα ἐκέρδησα). The use of "to" (πρός) in both the opening verbs shows that everything done is oriented "to" pleasing his master. The second verb "brought" (προσφέρω) is a formal term often used for presenting a sacrifice to God. It adds the aspect of an offering "presented" to the master (so Nolland). ἄλλα in this context means "other" in the sense of "more" talents.

25:21 His master responded, "Well done, good and faithful slave. You were faithful over a little, I will place you in charge of much" (ἔφη αὐτῷ ὁ κύριος αὐτοῦ, Εὖ, δοῦλε ἀγαθὲ καὶ πιστέ, ἐπὶ ὀλίγα ἦς πιστός, ἐπὶ πολλῶν σε καταστήσω). The parable in Luke (Luke 19:17) is more specific. "Well done, my good servant.... Because you have been trustworthy in a very small matter, take charge of ten cities." In the present parable Jesus does not have as great a contrast, using "little" rather than "least" and having the "good (and faithful)" slave given charge simply "over much" (Luke 19:17, "take charge of ten cities").

Still the use of "little" and "much" is ironic, as the slave had been given the unheard of sum of five talents. It may be that the reader is supposed to link the reward with 24:47 in which the faithful slave was given "charge [over] all" his master "possesses." This is made more possible by "faithful" (πιστός, added here by Matthew) that links this with the "faithful and wise slave" of 24:45. The master's "well done" is unusual in the ancient world (approbation was more common), as many have noted, and it points to God's reward of the believer for faithfulness at the final judgment (cf. Isa 40:10; 62:11; Rev 22:12). The slave has shown he can be trusted with a great amount of money and deserves to be raised higher and given more responsibility in the business (equivalent to being made a vice president and given a corner office today).

25:21 "Enter into the joy of your master" (εἴσελθε εἰς τὴν χαρὰν τοῦ κυρίου σου). With "well done" this frames the reaction of the master and shows the great pleasure he has in the faithful slave's industry. There are few parallels to this response, and it likely means the master wants his slave to bask in his master's joy at a job well done and to enjoy the rewards his master is piling on him. It is possible that "of your master" (τοῦ κυρίου σου) is a subjective genitive and means "the joy your master will give you," or it could be a simple possessive, meaning, "share in your master's joy" (in a job well done). Either way the concept is that of eschatological reward. Many see a link with the parable of the bridesmaids, and this is God's invitation for his faithful people into the messianic banquet, with eternal reward the prospect.

9. See Porter, *Idioms*, 23 – 24.

25:22 The one with two talents also came to him and said, "Master, you handed over to me two talents. Look, I have gained another two talents more" (προσελθὼν δὲ καὶ ὁ τὰ δύο τάλαντα εἶπεν, Κύριε, δύο τάλαντά μοι παρέδωκας· ἴδε ἄλλα δύο τάλαντα ἐκέρδησα). This repeats v. 20 in abbreviated fashion. The second slave has used the same industry to earn the same 100 percent profit, thereby also fulfilling the task given him.

25:23 His master responded, "Well done, good and faithful slave. You were faithful over a little. I will place you in charge of much. Enter into the joy of your master" (ἔφη αὐτῷ ὁ κύριος αὐτοῦ, Εὖ, δοῦλε ἀγαθὲ καὶ πιστέ, ἐπὶ ὀλίγα ἦς πιστός, ἐπὶ πολλῶν σε καταστήσω· εἴσελθε εἰς τὴν χαρὰν τοῦ κυρίου σου). This repeats v. 21 verbatim and has the same thrust. The slave is commended for a job well done and is given essentially the same reward. The message may be similar to the parable of the workers in the vineyard in 20:1–16, that God will reward not on the basis of quantity accomplished but the quality of the Christian life. It is not that the first slave earned two and a half times as much profit but that both used all they had been given to the best of their abilities. Their reward is essentially the same.

25:24 But the one who had received one talent also came to him and said, "Master, I knew that you are a hard man" (προσελθὼν δὲ καὶ ὁ τὸ ἓν τάλαντον εἰληφὼς εἶπεν, Κύριε, ἔγνων σε ὅτι σκληρὸς εἶ ἄνθρωπος). It is clear that the third servant knows he has not fulfilled his responsibility and is purely defensive in response. He calls his master σκληρός, which means "hard, strict, harsh, cruel, merciless" (BAGD, 756), showing his fear of the man. He was afraid to fail and so took the easiest route of burying his money to keep it safe.

25:24 ... reaping harvest where you have not sown and gathering crops where you have not scattered seed (θερίζων ὅπου οὐκ ἔσπειρας καὶ συνάγων ὅθεν οὐ διεσκόρπισας). These circumstantial participles (telling why he is "hard") are two agricultural metaphors that mean the same thing—harvesting/gathering seed where you haven't sown/scattered means he takes the harvest from other people's fields for his own. He is virtually calling his master a vicious tyrant, a capitalist who takes for himself the harvest that others worked so hard on. In other words, he takes what he wants without caring who gets hurt in the process. Some think there is bitterness here on the servant's part,[10] but the next verse settles that. It is not bitterness but terror.

25:25 "And since I was afraid, I went[11] and hid your talent in the ground. Look, you have what is yours" (καὶ φοβηθεὶς ἀπελθὼν ἔκρυψα τὸ τάλαντόν σου ἐν τῇ γῇ· ἴδε ἔχεις τὸ σόν). The slave was afraid to take a chance on losing the money and so hid it. If he had put the money on the market and lost it, he would expect severe punishment and perhaps be sold anew into slavery. He is now returning the money intact, none of the worse for wear. The other two slaves never mentioned the original investment, just the capital gains. This third one has no profit and so notes only the original capital that he is now returning whole to the master.[12]

10. In fact, Richard L. Rohrbaugh, "A Peasant Reading of the Parable of the Talents/Pounds: A Gospel of Terror?" *BTB* 23 (1993): 32–39, believes that this parable takes the peasant's perspective (that of the third servant) and condemns the master. He believes this parallels the version found in the "Gospel of the Nazarenes" (in Eusebius, *Theophania*) in which the third servant is received with joy. This is interesting and has convinced several scholars, but it is not ultimately successful in light of the larger context here.

11. These two successive participles modifying "hid" are first causal (terror is the reason he hid the money) and then temporal (he "went and hid)."

12. The use of the possessive adjective σόν emphasizes that it is "your" money that is being returned. The slave feels

25:26 But his master responded, "Evil and lazy slave!" (ἀποκριθεὶς δὲ ὁ κύριος αὐτοῦ εἶπεν αὐτῷ, Πονηρὲ δοῦλε καὶ ὀκνηρέ). The master has a far different estimation of the situation than the slave did. It is not his terror but his indolence that has driven the man. Rather than "good and faithful" (vv. 21, 23), he is "evil and lazy." The "wicked" actions of the slave (cf. 24:48, "if that wicked servant should say in his heart") lay in his refusal to obey his master's instructions seriously. When the master "handed over" his investment "according to each one's ability," that did not mean each one's power to keep the money safe but ability to increase its value.

25:26 "Did you really know that I harvest where I have not sown and gather where I have not scattered?" (ᾔδεις ὅτι θερίζω ὅπου οὐκ ἔσπειρα καὶ συνάγω ὅθεν οὐ διεσκόρπισα;). In fact, the slave has shown he "knew" (pluperfect [= aorist] of οἶδα, connoting here "understand, recognize") this all along in his two images that the master now repeats — the master is one who always demands a profit. So the wicked slave indicts himself. Blomberg makes an important observation: "The master does not dispute the servant's characterization of him, but neither need v. 26 be read as agreeing with it. The master's words sound like biting sarcasm. He points out that, even if the servant were right, he should have realized that his inaction proved all the more inconsistent with his premise."[13]

25:27 "You should have placed my money in with the bankers" (ἔδει σε οὖν βαλεῖν τὰ ἀργύριά μου τοῖς τραπεζίταις). While the slave "should" (with ἔδει connoting "an inner necessity, growing out of a given situation," BAGD, 172 [4]) have put the money to work in a capital venture, yet given the man's terror and consequent inability to do so, he should at least have invested it in a bank where it could have earned interest. To fail to do so indicates a lack of responsibility.

25:27 "Then when I came[14] I could have received what is mine with interest" (καὶ ἐλθὼν ἐγὼ ἐκομισάμην ἂν τὸ ἐμὸν σὺν τόκῳ). The particle ἄν shows the unreality of the situation; the master should have received the interest but did not. Keener argues at length that banks in the ancient world were safe investments, and that temples (acting as banks) as well as moneylenders could return a fivefold or even a tenfold yield.[15] So the indolent slave took the easy way out and insulted his master through disobedience.

25:28 "Therefore, take the talent from him and give[16] it to the one who has[17] ten talents" (ἄρατε οὖν ἀπ' αὐτοῦ τὸ τάλαντον καὶ δότε τῷ ἔχοντι τὰ δέκα τάλαντα). By his wicked indolence the man has forfeited his right to any reward. Instead, the one most faithful receives the reward that would have belonged to the third slave. It is difficult to know how far to take the image. The talent actually was the original capital investment of the master himself. So in the story the master does not

little sense of ownership or responsibility for the task assigned him.

13. Blomberg, *Matthew*, 374. Nolland, *Matthew*, 1019, adds, "The parable places the spotlight on the behaviour of the third slave, not on the question of the validity of his image of his master. It is content to imply that the images are not entirely right, but they are not totally wrong either." As implying the character of God, Jesus is probably saying that God is severe and ruler of all, but he cannot take what does not belong to him because as the Creator God, everything does belong to him.

14. With ἐλθών a temporal aorist participle, "after I came."

15. Keener, *Matthew*, 601, appealing to Naphtali Lewis, *Life in Egypt under Roman Rule* (Oxford: Clarendon, 1983), 147 – 48.

16. Both verbs here are aorist imperatives, denoting simple action conceived as a whole (Wallace, 717).

17. Here ἔχοντι switches to a present participle (used substantivally, "the one having"), showing continuous possession of the reward and placing this fact in the foreground for emphasis (see Porter, *Idioms*, 23).

even receive back his own original investment but instead yields it to the first slave.[18]

Probably, this is a further example of "reversal of expectation" (see on v. 10) that demonstrates the bountiful grace of God in rewarding the faithful slave. Note that the first slave was given all "ten talents," both the original amount of the master and all the profit he had earned (by extension that was also the case with the second slave). This would never have happened in this world and relates entirely to the incredible grace of God, who rewards us far beyond all human reason!

25:29 "For to everyone who has,[19] more will be given, and they will have abundance; but as for the one who does not have, even what they have will be taken away from them" (τῷ γὰρ ἔχοντι παντὶ δοθήσεται καὶ περισσευθήσεται· τοῦ δὲ μὴ ἔχοντος καὶ ὃ ἔχει ἀρθήσεται ἀπ᾽ αὐτοῦ). This is not part of the parable but probably is Jesus' parenthetical explanation of v. 28. It repeats the logion in 13:12 (= Mark 4:25). These are divine passives, with God as the Judge who gives and takes away, and the future tense could refer to the final judgment but is probably inaugurated, meaning God's reward or judgment in this life as well.

In 13:12 (cf. Prov 9:9, 11:24, 15:6; 4 Ezra 7:25) this logion stressed the responsibility of those who have been given the "mysteries" of the kingdom. Those who have accepted Jesus' gift will receive revelation in abundance; those who have rejected it (the Jewish people) will lose even what they have, namely, their place as the recipients of divine truth. Here it has the broader sense of the reality of the kingdom. The followers of Jesus will have the kingdom in abundance, while the leaders and the Jewish people who have opposed Jesus will lose it.

25:30 "So throw this worthless slave out into outer darkness. In that place there will be weeping and grinding of teeth" (καὶ τὸν ἀχρεῖον δοῦλον ἐκβάλετε εἰς τὸ σκότος τὸ ἐξώτερον· ἐκεῖ ἔσται ὁ κλαυθμὸς καὶ ὁ βρυγμὸς τῶν ὀδόντων). This wicked, lazy slave has proven himself to be ἀχρεῖος, "useless, worthless, of no value." He has shown himself to be devoid of any redeeming value for the master and so is not just fired (the image in the modern world) but totally condemned. The punishment again is way out of keeping with the crime committed, but again that is due to the eschatological reality being pictured behind the story (another "reversal of expectation," see vv. 10, 12, 28). The image of "outer darkness" with "weeping and grinding of teeth" also concluded the parable of the wicked slave in 24:51 and is a favorite metaphor for eternal punishment (also 8:12; 13:42, 50; 22:13). For those who in the guise of serving Christ actually live for themselves, the payback has eternal ramifications. Such people lose not only their reward but their eternal destiny.

Theology in Application

Every point in this parable has been discussed earlier in 24:36 – 25:13. The themes flow out of the lengthy period of absence combined with the sudden unexpectedness

18. Another possibility is to take this with Luz, *Matthew 21 – 28*, 253, that the master gives it to the first slave "to do business with it," in other words, not as a reward but as further responsibility. This makes sense, but the theme of vv. 21 – 28 is on reward more than responsibility. Still, v. 29 may contain both responsibility and reward, so there could be both senses here. The talent is given to the first slave to work with it and earn reward.

19. This has the same grammatical configuration as v. 28 but with the added παντί, extending the image to "every" follower of Jesus.

of the master's return. The result is the necessity of spiritual vigilance and the continued effort to serve God with the whole heart in the interim period. Blomberg sums up the themes here.[20] (1) God, like the master, entrusts his resources to his people and expects them to be good stewards of it. (2) Those who faithfully work for the kingdom and enhance it will be both commended and rewarded for their efforts. (3) Those who do not use their gifts and the kingdom resources will be condemned and separated from the very presence of God.

1. Using Your Resources

Use all your resources and spiritual gifts to serve Christ in the interim between his two comings. The main addition to the other parables in this section is the necessity of using everything we have[21] to benefit the kingdom, to consider them all a gift from God and use them to glorify him. This is a further development of the aspect of spiritual vigilance and centers on the ethical side of that.[22]

2. At Work for the Kingdom

There is no place for lazy Christians among Christ's followers. Apathy is clearly a danger here. When Christ returns, every person will be accountable for how they have lived and how central the kingdom has been in their priorities. Those quasi-Christians who claim they are Christ's servants but have hidden all he has entrusted them with (and used everything only for themselves) will answer for their misuse of the kingdom resources.

20. Blomberg, *Parables*, 214.

21. Daniel J. Harrington, "Polemical Parables in Matthew 24 – 25," *USQR* 44 (1991): 287 – 98, believes the third servant symbolizes Jewish scoffers and opponents of the Matthean community rather than lazy followers. However, this demands that the parable be constructed by Matthew for his situation, while the consensus is that the nucleus of this parable at least goes back to Jesus, and it is unlikely given the whole context of 24:36 – 25:30 that Jesus is thinking of opponents. This is a parable on the return of Christ, not on the situation of the church.

22. Joel B. Carpenter, "The Parable of the Talents in Missionary Perspective: A Call for an Economic Spirituality," *Missiology* 25 (1997): 165 – 81, emphasizes the economic aspects of this and develops the particular significance of economic responsibility for discipleship.

CHAPTER 110

Matthew 25:31 – 46

Literary Context

This is the final section of the discourse and develops a slightly different aspect than 24:36 – 25:30. Here it is the nations who are to be judged, and the basis of that judgment is how they treat God's people. There is no atmosphere of delay or the unexpected timing of the parousia. Yet, similar to the parables of the wheat and the weeds or the good and bad fish of 13:24 – 30, 47 – 52, this final part of the discourse centers on the glorious appearing of the Son of Man and the judgment of the nations that will ensue.

VI. The Movement to the Cross (19:1 – 25:46)
- **B. Fifth Discourse: Guilt and Judgment of Israel (23:1 – 25:46)**
  - **2. Judgment — Olivet Discourse (24:1 – 25:46)**
    - a. Destruction of Jerusalem and the Events of the End Time (24:1 – 35)
    - b. Parables on Readiness (24:36 – 25:30)
    - ➦ **c. Teaching on the Final Judgment (25:31 – 46)**

Main Idea

The righteous will be rewarded because in showing mercy and taking care of Jesus' messengers they have cared for him. The wicked will be punished because they did not show mercy to Jesus' messengers (note the contrasts — come/depart, blessed/cursed, inherit the kingdom/eternal punishment/eternal life). The theme is first the unity of Jesus with his people and then the responsibility of the world to accept and minister to his followers in mission.

Translation

Matthew 25:31-46

31a Setting "Now
when the Son of Man comes in his glory and
all his angels with him,
b Prediction **then he will sit on the throne of his glory.**
32a **And all the nations will be gathered together before him,**
b **and he will separate them from one another**
c *just as a shepherd separates the sheep*
from the goats.
33a **And he will cause the sheep to stand on his right and**
the goats on the left.

34a Group #1 (A) ***Then the king will say to those on his right,***
b Reward (B) *Come, you who are blessed by my Father,*
c *inherit the kingdom*
that was prepared for you
since the creation
of the world.'
35a Basis #1 (C) *(i) For I was hungry and you gave me food to eat;*
b Basis #2 (D) *(ii) I was thirsty and you gave me drink;*
c Basis #3 (E) *(iii) I was a stranger and you welcomed me;*
36a Basis #4 (F) *(iv) I was naked and you clothed me;*
b Basis #5 (G) *(v) I was sick and you looked after me;*
c Basis #6 (H) *(vi) I was imprisoned and you came to me.*
37a **Then the righteous will respond,**
b Question #1 (C') [1] 'Lord, when did we see you hungry and feed you, or
c (D') thirsty and give you drink?
38a Question #2 (E') [2] And when did we see you a stranger
and welcome you
b (F')
or naked
and clothe you?
39a Question #3 (G') [3] And when did we see you sick or
b (H') in prison
and come to you?'
40a Answer (I) **And the king will respond,**
b 'I tell you the truth . . .
you did them to me
c inasmuch as you have done these things
for one of the least
of these brothers and sisters of mine.'

41a Group #2 (A) ***Then he will also say to those on the left,***
b Punishment (B) *'Depart from me, you who are cursed,*
into the eternal fire

Continued on next page.

Continued from previous page.

Verse	Label	Text
		that is prepared
		for the devil and
		his angels.
42a	Basis #1 (C)	*(i) For I was hungry and*
		you did not give me food;
b	Basis #2 (D)	*(ii) I was thirsty and*
		you did not give me anything to drink;
43a	Basis #3 (E)	*(iii) I was a stranger and*
		you did not welcome me;
b	Basis #4 (F)	*(iv) I was naked and*
		you did not clothe me;
c	Basis #5 (G/H)	*(v) I was sick and in prison and*
		you did not look after me.'
44a		***Then they will answer . . .***
b	Question (C')	*'Lord, when did we see you hungry* or
c	(D')	*thirsty* or
d	(E')	*a stranger* or
e	(F')	*naked* or
f	(G')	*sick* or
g	(H')	*in prison and*
		did not take care of you?'
45a	Answer (I)	***Then he will respond,***
b		*'I tell you the truth . . .*
		you refused to do them for me'
c		*inasmuch as you have refused to do these things*
		for one of the least of these.'
46a	Conclusion: Judgment	And ***these people will go away to eternal punishment,***
b	Reward	but ***the righteous to eternal life."***

Structure and Literary Form

This picture of judgment is often called a parable but technically is not. Instead, it is an extended metaphor using the analogy of separating the sheep and goats for the judgment of the nations.[1] It is unique to Matthew and thus from his special material. There are four parts to the teaching: (1) the setting at the return of Christ and the separation of the nations (vv. 31 – 33); (2) the reward to those on the right, who cared for Christ's followers and thus for Christ himself (vv. 34 – 40); (3) the judgment of those on the left, who refused to care for Christ's followers and thus rejected Christ as well (vv. 41 – 45); (4) conclusion on punishment and reward (v. 46).

1. Witherington, *Matthew*, 465, calls it "an apocalyptic prophecy with some parabolic elements." France, *Gospel of Matthew*, 960, says its genre is closer to "the majestic visions of divine judgment in the Book of Revelation" than to the parables.

Exegetical Outline

➡ **I. Setting of the Story (25:31 – 33)**
   - A. The glorious appearing of the Son of Man (v. 31)
   - B. The separation of the nations like sheep and goats (vv. 32 – 33)

II. The Reward of the Sheep on the Right (25:34 – 40)
   - A. The reward: inheritance of the kingdom (v. 34)
   - B. The basis: showing mercy to Christ (vv. 35 – 36)
   - C. The question: when (vv. 37 – 39)
   - D. The answer: you cared for the least of my family (v. 40)

III. The Punishment of the Goats on the Left (25:41 – 45)
   - A. The punishment: eternal fire (v. 41)
   - B. The basis: refused to show mercy to Christ (vv. 42 – 43)
   - C. The question: when (v. 44)
   - D. The answer: refused to care for the least of my family (v. 45)

IV. Conclusion: Punishment and Reward (25:46)

Explanation of the Text

25:31 Now when[2] the Son of Man comes in his glory (Ὅταν δὲ ἔλθῃ ὁ υἱὸς τοῦ ἀνθρώπου ἐν τῇ δόξῃ αὐτοῦ). The glorious appearing of the Son of Man is also found in 13:41, 49; 16:27; 24:30, building on Dan 7:14 ("given authority, glory and sovereign power") and Zech 14:5 ("Then the Lord my God will come, and all the holy ones with him"). What is spoken of Yahweh in the OT belongs to Christ; his "glory" (δόξα) is clearly emphasized in this verse. In the other Matthean passages, the term connotes both God's (and thus Christ's) Shekinah "glory" (the divine glory "dwelling" among his people) and the ineffable glory, majesty, and splendor of the enthroned God of Isa 6 and Ezek 1.

25:31 ... and all his angels with him (καὶ πάντες οἱ ἄγγελοι μετ' αὐτοῦ). Jesus' coming "with the angels"[3] refers to the hosts of heaven who at the eschaton will be the eschatological agents of resurrection and judgment (cf. Zech 14:5; Matt 13:41, 49; 16:27; 24:31; 1 Thess 4:15; 2 Thess 1:7; Jude 14).

25:31 ... then he will sit on the throne of his glory (τότε καθίσει ἐπὶ θρόνου δόξης αὐτοῦ). The idea of the Son of Man seated "on the throne of his glory" (with δόξης αὐτοῦ an epexegetical genitive, "which is his glory")[4] looks to Jesus as the eschatological Judge on his *bēma,* or judgment seat. It goes back to 19:28, where it also is rooted in the throne of the Ancient of Days, the universal dominion of the "one like a son of man" in Dan 7:9 – 10, 13 – 14 as well as the "sit at my right hand" in Ps 110:1. It is common to think of Christ sharing the throne of God as in Rev 4:2; 5:6; 22:1, 3.

2. In a similar context in v. 27 Matthew used a temporal participle. Here for variety's sake he switches to the temporal conjunction "when" (ὅταν).

3. The "holy ones" in Zechariah could be the resurrected saints (so Davies and Allison) but in Ps 89:6 – 7; Dan 4:13, 23; 8:13 they are the celestial council, so it is viable to suppose they are angelic beings in Zechariah as well.

4. It could be an adjectival genitive, "his glorious throne," but here it is more likely his Shekinah glory that is connoted.

However, Davies and Allison make a strong case for seeing a plurality of thrones, as in Ps 110:1 (the enthronement of "my Lord" [the Messiah?]) at the "right hand" of God and the "thrones" in Dan 7:9 – 10. So the Son of Man and God could sit on separate thrones judging the nations here (cf. 22:44; 26:64).[5] This may be correct in the large picture, but here the Son of Man is the sole judge.

25:32 And all the nations will be gathered together before him (καὶ συναχθήσονται ἔμπροσθεν αὐτοῦ πάντα τὰ ἔθνη). This is the last judgment, with the Judge (the Son of Man) on his throne. The gathering (the divine passive "will be gathered" [συναχθήσονται] is future for the last judgment) of the nations for judgment builds on Isa 66:18 ("I ... am about to come and gather the people of all nations and languages, and they will come and see my glory") and Joel 3:2 ("I will gather all nations and ... enter into judgment against them"; cf. Joel 3:11 – 12; Zeph 3:8; Zech 12:3; 14:2).

Gray in his excellent discussion of the interpretation of this passage throughout history lists various options for understanding "all the nations" (πάντα τὰ ἔθνη): (1) all people, (2) all Christians, (3) all non-Christians, (4) non-Jews who are not Christians, (5) all non-Jews (Gentiles), and (6) Christians still alive at the parousia.[6] The answer depends on one's interpretation of the parable as a whole, especially of "the least of these brothers and sisters of mine." If "nations" (ἔθνη) refers entirely to Gentiles or pagans, then the meaning must be (3), (4), or (5). If the parable is about how Christians treat the poor (thus an extension of the preceding parables), then it will be (2) or (6). However, both are unlikely because "the nations" contain both the righteous and the wicked, and this story is most likely about how the nations treat God's emissaries, the church. Therefore the first is almost certainly the correct understanding.

25:32 And he will separate them from one another (καὶ ἀφορίσει αὐτοὺς ἀπ' ἀλλήλων). The separation of the nations[7] parallels the parables of the wheat and the weeds and of the good and bad fish in 13:24 – 30, 36 – 43, 47 – 50 (cf. also Rom 2:14 – 16; 14:10 – 12; 2 Cor 5:10; Rev 14:14 – 20, 20:11 – 15). Throughout it is clear that one part will experience reward and the other part condemnation.[8]

25:32 ... just as a shepherd separates the sheep from the goats" (ὥσπερ ὁ ποιμὴν ἀφορίζει τὰ πρόβατα ἀπὸ τῶν ἐρίφων). Jesus is the good shepherd who will watch over his sheep (John 10:1 – 18) and judge between them (Ezek 34 and here). Since Palestinian villages had both sheep and goats, they often had to separate them in this way, perhaps to keep the goats warm at night (sheep prefer the open) or for milking (see Gnilka, Keener, Davies and Allison).[9] The closest parallel is Ezek 34:17, 20, where Yahweh judges between the fat sheep and the lean sheep and between the rams and the goats (namely, the males of both species). Since Ezek 34 centers on the failure of the leaders of Israel (the shepherds), these are to separate the self-serving leaders from the righteous whom they have failed.[10] The simile here is similar, as the

5. Davies and Allison, *Matthew*, 3:420 – 21.

6. Sherman W. Gray, *The Least of My Brothers: Matthew 25:31 – 46 — A History of Interpretation* (Atlanta: Scholars Press, 1989).

7. The presence of the masculine "them" (αὐτούς) after the neuter "nations" (ἔθνη) does not indicate a different group but points to the individuals among the nations.

8. See K. Wengst, "Wie aus Böcken Ziegen wurden (Matt 25,32f): Zur Entstehung und Verbreitung einer Forschungslegende oder: Wissenschaft als 'stille Post,'" *EvT* 54 (1994): 491 – 500, says the goats were "separated" in order to be slaughtered. This is likely and fits the parable well.

9. K. Weber, "The Image of the Sheep and Goats in Matthew 25:31 – 46," *CBQ* 59 (1997): 657 – 78, says this is somewhat surprising since at that time they often placed sheep and goats into a single flock. He believes the purpose is to stress the radical nature of divine judgment.

10. See Block, *Ezekiel 25 – 48*, 292 – 93.

sheep are the followers of Christ (for "sheep" as God's people, see 10:16; John 10:1 – 18; Acts 20:29).

25:33 And he will cause the sheep to stand on his right and the goats on the left (καὶ στήσει τὰ μὲν πρόβατα ἐκ δεξιῶν αὐτοῦ, τὰ δὲ ἐρίφια ἐξ εὐωνύμων). The right is always the place of honor (1 Kgs 2:19; Ps 45:9; 110:1), but sometimes the right and the left are not opposed (e.g., 1 Kgs 22:19). Here the one side is for reward, the other for judgment. Sheep had a relative worth much higher than goats, because of their wool (goat hair made a coarse cloth) and the fact that they were easier to care for.[11]

25:34 Then the king will say to those on his right (τότε ἐρεῖ ὁ βασιλεὺς τοῖς ἐκ δεξιῶν αὐτοῦ). Now the image switches from the Son of Man as Shepherd (v. 33) to him as King on his judgment seat (David and Christ are the shepherd kings; see 9:27; 12:23; 15:22; 20:29, 31; 21:9, 15; 22:42 for Jesus as "Son of David"). Jesus has brought the kingdom as inaugurated in his first coming (see on 3:2; 4:17) and as the royal Messiah is offering it to the righteous at the last judgment after his second coming.

25:34 "Come, you who are blessed by my Father" (Δεῦτε οἱ εὐλογημένοι τοῦ πατρός μου). Nolland states that the perfect participle "blessed" (εὐλογημένοι) in the LXX is predominantly futuristic, and that is likely here.[12] It is also a divine passive,[13] with the genitive of agency (Wallace, 126) "by my Father" (τοῦ πατρός) as the subject: God is blessing the righteous by giving them their inheritance. The idea of the fatherhood of God goes hand-in-hand with inheritance language, for it is as part of God's family that believers will have an inheritance (see 5:5; 19:29; Rom 8:17; 1 Cor 6:9, 10; Heb 1:4, 14; et al.).

25:34 "Inherit the kingdom that was prepared for you since the creation of the world" (κληρονομήσατε τὴν ἡτοιμασμένην ὑμῖν βασιλείαν ἀπὸ καταβολῆς κόσμου). "Kingdom" has connotations of "eternal life" in Matthew, as seen in 19:29, "inherit eternal life." The perfect tense of "was prepared" (ἡτοιμασμένην) is stative, as the kingdom, meaning it is at all times in a state of preparedness.[14] It is likely that the same implied subject for "blessed" ("my Father") governs this verb as well. The fact that it has been readied "since the creation of the world" rehearses 13:35, with parables as "hidden since the creation of this world" (cf. 24:21). The inheritance for the faithful was part of God's plan of salvation from the start.

25:35 – 36 "For I was hungry and you gave me food to eat; I was thirsty and you gave me drink; I was a stranger and you welcomed me; I was naked and you clothed me; I was sick and you looked after me; I was imprisoned and you came to me" (ἐπείνασα γὰρ καὶ ἐδώκατέ μοι φαγεῖν, ἐδίψησα καὶ ἐποτίσατέ με, ξένος ἤμην καὶ συνηγάγετέ με, γυμνὸς καὶ περιεβάλετέ με, ἠσθένησα καὶ ἐπεσκέψασθέ με, ἐν φυλακῇ ἤμην καὶ ἤλθατε πρός με). It is common to make this the key to the entire section and to read Jesus' challenge as directed to all humanity (Jeremias, Hill, Bonnard, Davies and Allison, France) or to the disciples (Witherington) in terms of social action; that is, Jesus will judge everyone on the basis of helping the poor and the needy.[15] Yet this is

11. See Jeremias, *Parables*, 206; Keener, *Matthew*, 603 – 4; Nolland, *Matthew*, 1026.

12. Nolland, *Matthew*, 1027.

13. Though see McNeile, *Matthew*, 369, who believes it is a substantival participle ("You blessed ones") and takes the genitive as possessive, "who belong to my Father." This is viable but not the most natural way to understand the construction.

14. See Porter, *Idioms*, 39 – 41.

15. For this understanding see also David R. Catchpole, "The Poor on Earth and the Son of Man in Heaven: A Reappraisal of Matthew xxv.31 – 46," *BJRL* 61 (1979): 355 – 97; Joseph A. Grassi, "'I Was Hungry and You Gave Me to Eat' (Matt. 25:35ff.): The Divine Identification Ethic in Matthew," *BTB* 11 (1981): 81 – 84; C. E. B. Cranfield, "Who Are Christ's

not the best understanding, for "the least of these brothers and sisters of mine" (v. 40) must refer to believers, not to all humanity (see on v. 40 below), and Jesus is not teaching a works righteousness form of salvation here.[16]

Six items are listed here, and they have a great number of connections with previous social lists. Nolland has done an excellent job of summarizing the background:[17] Job 22:6 – 7, 9 parallels the first, second, and fourth items; Isa 58:6 – 7 the first and fourth; Ezek 18:7 the first and fourth; *T. Jos.* 1:5 – 7 the first, fifth, and sixth; *T. Jacob* 2:23 the second, third, fourth, and fifth; *b. Soṭah* 14a the fourth and fifth; *Midr. Pss.* 118:17 the first, second and fourth; Heb 13:2 – 3 the third and sixth. We might add Rom 12:20 (quoting Prov 25:21 – 22), paralleling the first and second items. It is important to realize that all these lists (including Jesus' enumeration here) are meant to be representative, not exhaustive. All speak of works of compassion and mercy to hurting people.

These six examples of need are global aorists looking at human suffering as a single whole. Hunger and thirst are the most frequently noted in Scripture and the greatest need in the world today. Hospitality to strangers[18] became a major sign of loving compassion for the early church and was a requirement for leadership (Rom 12:13; 1 Tim 3:2, 5:10; Titus 1:8; Heb 13:2; 1 Pet 4:9; cf. Judg 19:15; Job 31:32). Providing clothing for those who had none[19] is noted in Deut 15:11; Ezek 18:7), and the wearing of sumptuous clothing was a major sign of depravity in Rev 17:4; 18:16. Visiting and caring for the sick was at the heart of Jesus' miraculous ministry, and no one exemplified this better. Then even more than now, caring for the sick was to take the risk of catching the disease oneself. There is no better proof of a compassionate ministry. Visiting those imprisoned is mentioned in Col 4:18; Heb 10:34; 13:3. Many believers were put in prison, and in the first century (as in the Third World today), prisons were terrible cesspools of filth and degradation. These six items represented a ministry of mercy to those in need, which will always be at the core of true kingdom living.

25:37 – 39 Then the righteous will respond, "Lord, when did we see you hungry and feed you, or thirsty and give you drink? And when did we see you a stranger and welcome you or naked and clothe you? And when did we see you sick or in prison and come to you?" (τότε ἀποκριθήσονται αὐτῷ οἱ δίκαιοι λέγοντες, Κύριε, πότε σε εἴδομεν πεινῶντα καὶ ἐθρέψαμεν, ἢ διψῶντα καὶ ἐποτίσαμεν; πότε δέ σε εἴδομεν ξένον καὶ συνηγάγομεν, ἢ γυμνὸν καὶ περιεβάλομεν; πότε δέ σε εἴδομεν ἀσθενοῦντα ἢ ἐν φυλακῇ καὶ ἤλθομεν πρός σε;). Those on the right (= "the righteous," a major term in Matthew for right ethical living, cf. 10:41; 13:43, 49; on the noun, see 5:6, 10, 20 et al.) are naturally perplexed by Jesus' statement. So they ask Jesus "when" they could have acted in these ways toward him.

Matthew divides the list into three pairs, each preceded by "when did we see you" (πότε σε εἴδομεν). There is no special significance in the pairs, except they are more easily remembered in that fashion. The major thing is that the list is repeated four times (vv. 35 – 36, 37 – 39, 42 – 43, 44)

Brothers? (Matthew 25.40)," *Metanoia* 4 (1994): 31 – 39; and John P. Heil, "The Double Meaning of the Narrative of Universal Judgment in Matthew 25.31 – 46," *JSNT* 69 (1998): 3 – 14.

16. Good works do not produce salvation but rather are proof that salvation has occurred. Where there is true salvation, there will be works of compassion. On this see Dan O. Via, "Ethical Responsibility and Human Wholeness in Matthew 25:31 – 46," *HTR* 80 (1987): 79 – 100.

17. Nolland, *Matthew*, 1028 – 29.

18. In fact, the Greek word for "hospitality" (φιλοξενία) means "love of strangers."

19. γυμνός means not only "naked" but an inability to buy clothes, to be "without an outer garment" or "poorly dressed." (BAGD, 167).

for emphasis. The ethical responsibility to show mercy to the oppressed is a serious requirement for kingdom living and to be accepted by God.

25:40 And the king will respond, "I tell you the truth, inasmuch as you have done these things" (καὶ ἀποκριθεὶς ὁ βασιλεὺς ἐρεῖ αὐτοῖς, Ἀμὴν λέγω ὑμῖν, ἐφ᾽ ὅσον ἐποιήσατε). This is the heart of this section, the "moral of the story." The king on his glorious throne responds to their incredulous query with another "amen" (ἀμήν) saying that highlights the importance of it. Jesus and his followers are one (John 6:56; 15:4 – 7; 1 John 2:24, 3:24, 4:15), so what people do to one of his disciples they do to him (Matt 10:40 – 42). Some see this as an extension of 10:40 – 42. This union between Jesus and his kingdom community is a family union; they are "brothers and sisters." In 12:48 – 50 (another important parallel) Jesus' true family is identified as "whoever does the will of my Father in heaven." That is also the definition of "the righteous" in 25:37, so this is a further extension of the true ethical conduct required of kingdom people.

25:40 "... for one of the least of these brothers and sisters of mine, you did them to me" (ἑνὶ τούτων τῶν ἀδελφῶν μου τῶν ἐλαχίστων, ἐμοὶ ἐποιήσατε). "One" (ἑνί) is a dative of advantage, designating "the person whose interest is effected" (BDF §188). The debate is over the identification of "the least of these brothers and sisters" (τῶν ἀδελφῶν μου τῶν ἐλαχίστων). Are they all people (supporting the social interpretation on helping the poor noted on v. 35) or Christian missionaries (those sent on mission) or all Christians or Jewish Christians? It is unlikely that unbelievers would be called "my brothers and sisters," so one of the last three are best. Some dispensationalists take the fourth option by applying this to the time following the rapture, but there is little in the context to support that. Likewise, there is nothing to narrow it to missionaries in particular.

Thus, it refers to the way the nations treat Christ's ἐλαχίστοι ("little ones" in 18:6, 10, 14) those who in the eyes of the world are "least" in importance. In 12:48 – 50 Jesus' followers are clearly his "brothers and sisters." Moreover, in ch. 10 all believers are part of Christ's mission. So Jesus' message is that the world will be judged on the basis of how it treats those "little people" whom God is sending to it (so also Gray, Carson, France. Hagner, Blomberg, Morris, Keener, Turner).[20]

25:41 Then he will also say to those on the left, "Depart from me, you who are cursed" (Τότε ἐρεῖ καὶ τοῖς ἐξ εὐωνύμων, Πορεύεσθε ἀπ᾽ ἐμοῦ οἱ κατηραμένοι). Jesus now turns to the other side, the goats "on the left." The language will parallel the righteous almost exactly except that it is entirely negative. So instead of "Come, you who are blessed by my Father" (v. 34), he speaks words of renunciation, "Depart from me, you who are cursed," reminiscent of 7:23, "Depart from me, workers of evil" (cf. Ps 6:8, 119:115, 139:19).

25:41 "... into the eternal fire that is prepared for the devil and his angels" (εἰς τὸ πῦρ τὸ αἰώνιον τὸ ἡτοιμασμένον τῷ διαβόλῳ καὶ τοῖς ἀγγέλοις αὐτοῦ). The "cursed" of God are those headed for eternal judgment (cf. Deut 27:15 – 26, 30:19; Rom 9:3; 1 Cor 16:22; Gal 1:8 – 9) as explicated in the following "into the eternal fire" (3:12; 18:8, along with "Gehenna" in 5:22, 29, 30; 10:28; 18:9; 23:15, 33). This, of course, is the "fiery lake" "prepared for the devil" in Rev 19:20; 20:10; cf. 14:10 – 11; 20:14 – 15. While the kingdom was "prepared" by

20. For excellent articles from this standpoint, see J.-C. Ingelaere, "La 'parabole' du jugement dernier (Matthieu 25/31 – 46)," *RHPR* 50 (1970): 23 – 60; and George E. Ladd, "The Parable of the Sheep and the Goats in Recent Literature," in *New Dimensions in New Testament Study* (ed. R. Longenecker and M. C. Tenney; Grand Rapids: Eerdmans, 1974), 191 – 99.

God from creation (v. 34), now "eternal fire … is prepared" (ἡτοιμασμένον, another stative perfect as in v. 34) for the sinners. There they will join "the devil and his angels," namely, that one-third of the starry host of God seduced by the dragon in Rev 12:3 – 4 and that fought and lost against Michael and his angels in Rev 12:7 – 9. In Rev 20:14, 15 human sinners join the cosmic powers in the fiery lake.

25:42 – 43 "For I was hungry and you did not give me food; I was thirsty and you did not give me anything to drink; I was a stranger and you did not welcome me; I was naked and you did not clothe me; I was sick and in prison and you did not look after me" (ἐπείνασα γὰρ καὶ οὐκ ἐδώκατέ μοι φαγεῖν, ἐδίψησα καὶ οὐκ ἐποτίσατέ με, ξένος ἤμην καὶ οὐ συνηγάγετέ με, γυμνὸς καὶ οὐ περιεβάλετέ με, ἀσθενὴς καὶ ἐν φυλακῇ καὶ οὐκ ἐπεσκέψασθέ με). As v. 41 negates v. 34, so these are the negative counterparts to vv. 35 – 36, with the same six items but here detailing what the nations refused to do for Jesus' followers. One could break these into two categories: acts of mercy for physical needs (hungry, thirsty, ill), and acts of charity toward social deprivation (stranger, naked, in prison). The unrighteous are unwilling to help in any way and so are condemned for this.

25:44 Then they will answer and say, "Lord, when did we see you hungry or thirsty or a stranger or naked or sick or in prison and did not take care of you?" (τότε ἀποκριθήσονται καὶ αὐτοὶ λέγοντες, Κύριε, πότε σε εἴδομεν πεινῶντα ἢ διψῶντα ἢ ξένον ἢ γυμνὸν ἢ ἀσθενῆ ἢ ἐν φυλακῇ καὶ οὐ διηκονήσαμέν σοι;). Once more this parallels the previous section (vv. 37 – 39), but it is shortened greatly and leaves the impression that the unrighteous do not care about any of these six categories (the righteous emphasized each one in detail). Matthew uses "take care of" (διακονέω) for the first time in the story; it means to care for someone else in terms of willing charitable service rendered (cf. 4:11; 8:15; 27:55; Acts 6:2; 1 Pet 4:11).

Note that these wicked people still address Jesus as "Lord" (κύριε), but in forced subjugation rather than in worship. They are in the midst of their trial and can only hope to avoid the condemnation and punishment they so richly deserve. Still, like the righteous they are confused by Jesus' statement. Carson has three conclusions to this:[21] (1) The sheep and the goats are not surprised at the judgment rendered but at the basis of it: the way they have treated Jesus. (2) This is not works righteousness — the actions reflected the heart attitude behind them. (3) The test here eliminates "the possibility of hypocrisy" in that the actions of each group has demonstrated the true condition of their hearts.

25:45 Then he will respond, "I tell you the truth, inasmuch as you have refused to do these things for one of the least of these, you refused to do them for me'" (τότε ἀποκριθήσεται αὐτοῖς λέγων, Ἀμὴν λέγω ὑμῖν, ἐφ' ὅσον οὐκ ἐποιήσατε ἑνὶ τούτων τῶν ἐλαχίστων, οὐδὲ ἐμοὶ ἐποιήσατε). The parallels continue, as this negates Jesus' reply to the righteous in v. 40. The group on the left refused acts of charity for Jesus' followers ('the least" are Jesus' "little ones," his disciples, see on v. 40), and because Jesus was one with them, their rejection and opposition to his followers constituted rejection of Christ; and as in 10:40 – 42, what they do to Jesus they do to his Father.

25:46 And these people will go away to eternal punishment, but the righteous to eternal life (καὶ ἀπελεύσονται οὗτοι εἰς κόλασιν αἰώνιον, οἱ δὲ δίκαιοι εἰς ζωὴν αἰώνιον). A slight chiasm

21. Carson, "Matthew," 522.

is produced when Matthew reverses the order of the righteous (vv. 34 – 40) and the unrighteous (vv. 41 – 45). Building on Dan 12:2 ("Multitudes who sleep in the dust of the earth will awake: some to everlasting life, others to shame and everlasting contempt"), Jesus sums up the implications of his extended metaphor/prophecy — the eternal "separation" (v. 32) of the wicked from the righteous. κόλασις is "punishment" especially in terms of divine retribution, often with a sense of the absolute justice of the judicial act.[22] This punishment has already been defined as "eternal fire" (v. 41).

The emphasis is on the eternal nature of the two opposite destinies. "Eternal life" (19:16, 29) throughout the NT is the motivation for a life of sacrificial service to God, the church, and the very world that rejects and persecutes God's people. It is clear here that there are no second chances after death. The decisions made by "the sheep and the goats" have eternal ramifications.

Theology in Application

This final extended metaphor concludes the Olivet Discourse and moves from the responsibility of the disciples (24:36 – 25:30) to the responsibility of all the world in light of the imminent appearing of the Son of Man and the final judgment he will bring. Both groups — the righteous and the wicked — are responsible for the decisions they have made and the conduct that resulted from those decisions. Moreover, those decisions have eternal consequences, and there will be no turning back.[23]

1. One with Christ

We are one with Christ and so share his power and presence. We saw aspects of this in 10:11 – 14 (we have a charismatic presence of Christ in our message and speak with his voice) and 10:40 – 42 (when the world welcomes or rejects us, they are actually receiving or rejecting Christ). See the "Theology in Application" section of each passage for more on this. Here we have the third aspect, that the way the world treats us is an essential part of their reaction to Christ, because we are an essential aspect of his presence in our community. Since Christ is in us (John 15:4 – 7), people's mercy toward us personifies the way they respond to Christ.

2. Works as Faith Response

There is no true antithesis between faith and works. While works cannot save us (Eph 2:8 – 9), works are the necessary response to and proof of faith (Gal 2:10; Jas 2:14 – 26). Further, this passage does not teach salvation by works but rather centers

22. See *TDNT*, 3:815 – 16.

23. Notice that the centrality of good works, especially in terms of caring for the poor and oppressed, is not part of this application. The reason is the interpretation of the meaning of the passage, namely, that it centers on the way the nations treat Jesus' followers rather than the responsibility to feed the poor. Application should always be tied to the meaning of the text rather than to other possible interpretations (contra Luz, *Matthew 21 – 28*, 283 – 84).

on the ethical implications of faith salvation (see also "Theology in Application" on 5:20; 7:21 – 23).

3. Only Two Kinds of People in the World

In our "seeker-sensitive" environment, we are often guilty of elevating seekers to a third type of humanity — those who reject Christ and are headed for eternal damnation, seekers who are almost there, and believers who are headed for heaven. This is wrong; seekers actually belong to the first group. We might add to this the "quasi-Christians," those who attend regularly but show no fruit of this in their lives. Some belong to the first group and some to the second. There is no middle ground. Every person on earth is going either to heaven or to hell. Moreover, the decision will be made in this life, so it is essential that every person be confronted by the gospel and challenged to make a decision. There is no neutrality, and nothing in life is as important as this question, because it determines every person's eternal destiny!

CHAPTER 111

Matthew 26:1 – 5

Introduction to the Passion and Resurrection of Jesus (Matthew 26:1 – 28:20)

The reason for the incarnation begins here. God became human flesh and walked Planet Earth in order to die as the atoning sacrifice for our sin. So this is the true climax of Matthew's gospel — not just the resurrection but the passion and resurrection as a single event in salvation history. Here, in fact, the climax of the entire Bible and of God's plan of salvation occurs. The metanarrative of all of Scripture centers on how God in his gracious mercy overcomes the sin of Adam and brings salvation to humankind. As Hagner says,

> The passion narrative is a literary masterpiece. It contains gripping drama that cannot but move the reader, yet there is nothing maudlin here.... Pervading the narrative is a deep sense of irony. Though sinful men do their best to thwart the mission of Jesus, they accomplish the very purpose for which he came and thus fulfill God's will.[1]

This sense of irony will be noted often in the succeeding pages.

Several theological themes dominate this passage.[2]

1. God is in sovereign control of the events; he has determined the necessity of Jesus' death and proves it by supernatural phenomena at the death and resurrection. Divine necessity is stressed in the δεῖ (the divine "must") of the passion prediction in 16:21 and of 26:54 ("it must happen in this way"). Moreover, Matthew stresses the supernatural intervention of God in 27:51 – 53 and 28:2 – 3.
2. Jesus dies voluntarily. He is in control, going forth to his destiny as an act of obedience to God. In 26:2, 18 the passion is the fulfillment of the hour chosen by God, and Jesus is in supreme control as he gives himself up to his destiny (see 26:42, 53).

1. Hagner, *Matthew 14 – 28*, 749 – 50.
2. The first three are from Barth in Bornkamm, Barth, and Held, *Tradition and Interpretation*, 143 – 47.

3. Jesus is seen as the Lord, Son of God, and royal Messiah, soon to fulfill his destiny. This acts as bold relief to his humility in suffering and death. His is the ultimate paradox, as Jesus' suffering and death reveal him as ruler and judge.
4. The guilt of the Jewish leaders becomes clear. They even use false witnesses against Jesus and coerce the people into demanding Jesus' death, and they cry out, "May his blood be upon us and upon our children!" (27:25).
5. Jesus gains victory over his opponents. Matthew sets up contrast scenes that show Jesus' power and authority over all opposition (seen esp. in the resurrection). Jesus does not need the hosts of heaven (26:53) and predicts that by his death he will sit "at the right hand of power [or God]" and come "on the clouds of heaven" (26:64).
6. In contrast to Jesus' victory, his disciples experience discipleship failure (this is more central to Mark but is found in Matthew as well). Not only does Judas betray him, but the rest of his disciples desert him in a virtual apostasy (26:31, fulfilled in 26:56) and fail to support Jesus at Gethsemane (26:40, 43, 45). Peter denies him three times (26:69–75).
7. All this fulfills Scripture, showing that God has both known of everything that would happen and has prepared for it in salvation history (see 26:21, 24, 31, 54, 56, 64; 27:5, 7, 9–10, 30, 34, 35, 46, 52–53).

Matthew follows Mark closely in this account, omitting a couple of bits (Mark 14:51–52; 15:21b) and adding a few more (27:3–10, 51–53, 62–66; 28:2–3, 11–15, 18–20). In the passion and resurrection Matthew is both historian and theologian. Scholars have long bifurcated these two and argued that if the gospel writers were theologians, they could not be historians. This has more and more been recognized as a false dichotomy. Matthew is a theological interpreter of the historical events that surrounded the life of Jesus and his passion.[3]

The structure of the passage follows conventional lines, though scholars disagree at some of the details (e.g., whether the Last Supper scene is a separate section or part of the preliminary events, whether the prediction of the disciples' falling away is part of the Last Supper or not, whether Gethsemane should be combined with the arrest or stand alone, whether 27:62–66 belongs with the crucifixion or resurrection). I will divide the passion material into six scenes: preliminary events (26:1–16), the Last Supper scene (26:17–30), events in Gethsemane (26:31–56), the Jewish and Gentile trials sandwiched around Peter's denials (26:57–27:26), the crucifixion and death of Jesus (27:27–50), events following his death (27:51–61). The resurrection has three scenes, centering on contrast: preparation (the setting of the

3. See Osborne, "History and Theology," 5–22; and "Historical Narrative," 673–88. See also Keener's excursus on "Historical Tradition in the Passion Narrative" in his *Matthew*, 607–11.

guard [27:62 – 66] vs. the going forth of the women [28:1]), reaction (the fear of the guard [28:2 – 4] vs. the joy of the women [28:5 – 10]); and the results (the spreading of lies [28:11 – 15] vs. the proclamation of truth [28:18 – 20]).

Literary Context

Matthew 26:1 – 5 provides a transition from the Olivet Discourse to the Passion Narrative. Jesus' earthly ministry has effectively ended, and he tells his disciples of the final event yet to take place. He has just told the disciples that he will be the eschatological judge at his second coming, and now he tells them what must yet happen in order for that to be accomplished, namely, his atoning sacrifice on the cross. The Jewish plot is part of that divine plan.

VI. The Movement to the Cross (19:1 – 25:46)
- A. Jesus' Deeds: Opposition and Discipleship (19:1 – 22:46)
- B. Fifth Discourse: Guilt and Judgment of Israel (23:1 – 25:46)

VII. The Passion and Resurrection of Jesus (26:1 – 28:20)
- **A. The Passion Narrative (26:1 – 27:61)**
  - **1. Preliminary Events (26:1 – 16)**
    - ➦ **a. Introduction — Plot to Kill Jesus (26:1 – 5)**
    - b. Anointing of Jesus (26:6 – 13)
    - c. Judas's Betrayal (26:14 – 16)

Main Idea

There are only two more days remaining in Jesus' life, and God is handing Jesus over to become the paschal sacrifice. Jesus is in control and tells his followers what must soon take place. We then see the part the leaders will play in this central drama of history as they plot Jesus' death; they only think they are in control!

Translation

(See next page.)

Structure and Literary Form

This prologue to the passion events expands Mark 14:1 – 2, with Matthew's text turning the time note on two days before the Passover into a prophecy regarding

Matthew 26:1-5

1a	Introduction/Setting	And it happened that
		when Jesus had finished all these words,
b		**he told his disciples,**
2a	Prediction	*"You know that after two days Passover is coming,*
b		*and the Son of Man is going to be handed over to be crucified."*
3a	Setting (Social)	**Then the chief priests and elders of the people**
		met together
		in the palace of the high priest,
b		named Caiaphas,
4a	Action	and **they plotted together**
b	Purpose of 4a	so that by deceit they might arrest Jesus and have him killed.
5a	Qualification of 4b	*"But,"* **they said,** *"not during the feast,*
b	Basis for 5a	*lest there be a riot among the people."*

Jesus' imminent death and elaborating the priests' plot by noting that the meeting took place in Caiaphas's palace. There are two scenes: Jesus' prediction of his near sacrifice on the cross (vv. 1 – 2) and the leaders' plot to kill him (vv. 3 – 5).

Exegetical Outline

➡ **I. Jesus' Prediction (26:1 – 2)**
- A. The Passover coming (vv. 1 – 2a)
- B. The destiny of the Son of Man (v. 2b)

II. The Plot of the Leaders (26:3 – 5)
- A. The meeting in Caiaphas's palace (v. 3)
- B. The evil plot to kill Jesus (v. 4)
- C. The hesitation due to the people (v. 5)

Explanation of the Text

26:1 And it happened that when Jesus had finished all these words, he told his disciples (Καὶ ἐγένετο ὅτε ἐτέλεσεν ὁ Ἰησοῦς πάντας τοὺς λόγους τούτους, εἶπεν τοῖς μαθηταῖς αὐτοῦ). This is a transition from the Olivet Discourse (thus, some scholars place vv. 1 – 5 with that discourse instead of the Passion Narrative), and Matthew wants his readers to understand that Jesus' death is intimately connected with his proclamation of his future role as judge. Matthew has ended all his other discourses with, "And it happened that when Jesus had finished" (7:28; 11:1; 13:53; 19:1), but here he adds "all these words" — with two likely implications: an allusion to Deut 31:1, 24; 32:45 and the final message of Moses,[4] and the extension of this to all the teaching of Jesus in Matthew.[5]

26:2 "You know that after two days Passover is coming, and the Son of Man is going to be handed over to be crucified" (Οἴδατε ὅτι μετὰ δύο ἡμέρας τὸ πάσχα γίνεται, καὶ ὁ υἱὸς τοῦ ἀνθρώπου παραδίδοται εἰς τὸ σταυρωθῆναι). It is possible that "you know" (οἴδατε) is imperatival (so Gnilka, Hagner), but it seems that Jesus is building on the obvious (the reason they have come to Jerusalem) to make his point regarding his impending death.[6] "Passover" (τὸ πάσχα) appears only here and in vv. 17 – 19 in Matthew, and its use here alongside the imminent crucifixion almost certainly enacts Jesus' coming death as the paschal lamb (see 26:26 – 28; John 1:29; 1 Cor 5:7; 1 Pet 1:19).

Since Passover began with the slaughter of the lamb on Thursday afternoon and the paschal meal that evening, this is likely Tuesday night (Wednesday by Jewish reckoning, so Carson). This in effect constitutes a fourth passion prediction. The passive "is going to be handed over" (παραδίδοται) could refer to Judas's betrayal but is better here seen as a divine passive pointing to God's giving Jesus over to his destiny (see on 20:18); it is also a futuristic present stressing the certainty of the event.

26:3 Then the chief priests and elders of the people met together in the palace of the high priest, named Caiaphas (Τότε συνήχθησαν οἱ ἀρχιερεῖς καὶ οἱ πρεσβύτεροι τοῦ λαοῦ εἰς τὴν αὐλὴν τοῦ ἀρχιερέως τοῦ λεγομένου Καϊάφα). "Then" (τότε) makes the action of the leaders virtually a fulfillment of Jesus' prediction (so Hagner). Mark 14:1 has "the chief priests and the teachers of the law" here, but Matthew notes "the elders"[7] in keeping with earlier practice (16:21; 21:23) as well as throughout the Passion Narrative (26:47; 27:1, 3, 12, 20, 41). This may have been an unofficial group from the Sanhedrin, which included all three as well as the Pharisees.

The meeting is held in the "palace" (αὐλή) or courtyard of the palace of the high priest in Jerusalem (cf. 26:58, 69). Caiaphas, son-in-law of Annas, the former high priest (from AD 6 – 15), was appointed by the Romans to this office in AD 18 and held it until AD 36 (he knew how to get along with the Romans — his is the longest of any first-century high priest). The palace (where Annas and Caiaphas may have lived in separate wings) was probably the Hasmonean palace on the west hill of the city (so Augustine, Plummer).

Annas was the first of his family line to be named high priest by the Romans (by the Quirinius of Luke 2:2), and five of his sons were named high priest in the first two-thirds of the first century, with Caiaphas being the only son-in-law and therefore under even greater influence by Annas (see John 18:13, 19 – 24, where Jesus is interrogated by Annas before Caiaphas at his "trial"). Qumran (1QpHab 9:4), Second Temple Jewish literature (*T. Levi* 14:1; *2 Bar.* 10:18), and Josephus (*Life* 216) complained of the corruption and collusion with the Romans on the part of this family that

4. Hauerwas, *Matthew*, 213, links the "all" here with Deut 32:44 – 47, when Moses finished "all the words of this song" (i.e., the Song of Moses) and then told the people to take "all the words" to heart and instruct their children to "obey carefully all the words of this law." Thus the disciples as well as every reader are to take to heart "all" that Jesus has taught.

5. See Donald P. Senior, *The Passion Narrative according to Matthew: A Redactional Study* (Leuven: Leuven Univ. Press, 1982), 12 – 13, who after discussing the possibility that the phrase concludes chs. 24 – 25 or chs. 23 – 25, concludes that as the last of the five uses of this expression and as the transition to the Passion Narrative, this "makes the Passion narrative the climax and clarification of all Jesus has taught." See also Davies and Allison, Luz, Blomberg, Turner.

6. Senior, *Passion Narrative*, calls it "a well-known fact."

7. Here as in 21:23; 26:47; 27:1, Matthew adds τοῦ λαοῦ to designate their position as lay aristocracy over "the people."

controlled the high priesthood for much of the first century.[8]

26:4 And they plotted together so that by deceit they might arrest Jesus and have him killed (καὶ συνεβουλεύσαντο ἵνα τὸν Ἰησοῦν δόλῳ κρατήσωσιν καὶ ἀποκτείνωσιν). The συν-compound verbs in vv. 3 – 4 ("met together," "plotted together") stress the semiformal nature of the evil machinations of the meeting. This was not the first time the Jewish leaders decided to kill Jesus (cf. 12:14 = Mark 3:6; John 5:18), and, as before, it was a group decision. There is a possible allusion to Ps 31:13 ("They conspire against me and plot to take my life"), where David, the righteous sufferer, pleads with God for deliverance (so Nolland). They want to take Jesus by stealth, with "by deceit" (δόλῳ) a negative concept implying deceit or even treachery; their reason is a fear of Jesus' popularity with the people (v. 5). They want to find a time and place of their choosing, far away from the crowds, where they can take him into custody secretly.

26:5 "But," they said,[9] "not during the feast, lest there be a riot among the people" (ἔλεγον δέ, Μὴ ἐν τῇ ἑορτῇ, ἵνα μὴ θόρυβος γένηται ἐν τῷ λαῷ). These leaders know the people, who are still enamored with Jesus (see 21:8 – 11); they know the people would riot if they attempted a public arrest "during the feast."[10] As stated in the triumphal entry passage (see on 21:8), Jerusalem swelled to almost four times its normal size with excitable, volatile pilgrims. News of the arrest of one whom the people saw as a messianic figure could cause a riot that would bring the wrath of Rome down on their heads (see Josephus, *J.W.* 2:223 – 27 for Roman preparations for Jewish festivals). So they feel they should wait until the feast is over (it lasted eight days) and the pilgrims return home. Judas, however, will soon change their plans.

Theology in Application

Jesus has now ended his preaching, teaching, and miraculous ministries. All that remains is to accomplish the real reason for his incarnation, the true purpose of his mission, his death on the cross as the atoning sacrifice for our sins. In this brief introductory section, all the themes mentioned in the introduction to the Passion Narrative have been set in motion.

1. God and Jesus in Sovereign Control

The death and resurrection of Jesus will reenact the theme of the infancy narratives — God turning aside the attempts of his enemies to stymie his will. Job 42:2 is nowhere so true as here: "no purpose of yours can be thwarted." Even the treacherous plots of the Sanhedrin cannot do anything but work out God's will. This message is critical in our times. We live in a society with unprecedented affluence and plenty. As a result, people do not know how to handle life's setbacks and so often

8. See Keener, *Matthew*, 612 – 13; Witherington, *Matthew*, 474.

9. "They said" (ἔλεγον) is a historic imperfect to depict them in the process of uttering the message. It also places this in the foreground as the natural conclusion to this section.

10. France, *Gospel of Matthew*, 972, notes Jeremias's translation, "not in the presence of the festival crowd" (*Eucharistic Words*, 71 – 73), and believes this captures the nuance well.

have the same complaints as Israel in Isa 40:27: "My way is hidden from the LORD [= he doesn't know where I am] and my cause is disregarded by my God [= he is an unjust judge]." We do not realize that God's power is all the greater in times of adversity, and Christ is nearer then than at any other time.

2. Watching God's Power

Every crisis is an opportunity to watch God's power at work. This is a major theme in Acts as well, as after each crisis the power of God caused the church to grow (Acts 6:7; 9:31; 12:24; 19:20). For the believer who is truly centered on the triune Godhead, times of affliction are times of growth as we "hope in the LORD" (Isa 40:31) and trust his omnipotence and omniscience in each and every situation. That does not mean we will get what we want. Jesus didn't (see 26:39, 42), but if it is best that we die, our death will be our victory (see Rev 12:11).

3. Lord of All, Even over His Enemies

It is clear from the movement from v. 2 to v. 3 that the plot of the leaders is actually a fulfillment of Jesus' prophecy. His enemies are under the control of God even in the midst of their evil plots and can only do their part in the salvation drama that is unfolding. This is true of the beast/Antichrist in Rev 13:5 – 8. Everything the Antichrist does there is "authorized" (ἐδόθη, "it was given" in vv. 5, 7a, 7b) by God. This theme will control the rest of the narrative and is even stronger in John. This is true today as well. It only seems as if Satan is in control as we see Christian leader after Christian leader falling into moral failure and as we see the forces against the church growing in seeming power. They are doomed, not we!

CHAPTER 112

Matthew 26:6–13

Literary Context

This pericope is deliberately placed here by Mark and Matthew to supply a contrast with Judas's betrayal.[1] Jesus takes the anointing as "preparation" of his body for burial (v. 12), so it is a natural next step after he has announced his coming death in v. 2.

VI. The Movement to the Cross (19:1–25:46)

VII. The Passion and Resurrection of Jesus (26:1–28:20)

A. The Passion Narrative (26:1–27:61)

1. Preliminary Events (26:1–16)

a. Introduction — Plot to Kill Jesus (26:1–5)

➦ **b. Anointing of Jesus (26:6–13)**

c. Judas's Betrayal (26:14–16)

Main Idea

Jesus is here presented as the suffering Messiah, "anointed" for his messianic destiny as the one who will die for our sins. The woman's worshipful act of anointing stands in contrast with both the leaders' decision to kill Jesus and Judas's decision to betray him. So her act has a twofold significance—a messianic anointing and a washing of his body beforehand for burial.

1. In terms of chronology it is generally agreed that John 12:1–8 has correctly placed this before the triumphal entry, and that Mark and Matthew have placed it here thematically in order to provide a contrast with Judas. This is only a problem if we demand chronological exactness of the gospel writers, but that is not the case since the gospels often arranged material topically. John 12 has more similarities than differences with this story and is likely the same event (see Blomberg, *Historical Reliability*, 127–30). Finally, all four gospels have an anointing, but Luke 7:36–50 is quite different and certainly a separate episode.

Translation

Matthew 26:6-13

6a	Setting	While Jesus was in Bethany at the home of Simon the Leper,
7a	Scene #1	**a woman came to him,**
b	Description	having an alabaster jar of very expensive perfume and
c	Action	poured it over his head
d	Circumstance	as he reclined at table.
8a	Scene #2	When the disciples saw this,
b		**they were indignant, saying,**
8c-9a	Objection/ Rhetorical Question	*"Why this waste?*
b	Basis	For *this could have been sold for a great deal and given to the poor."*
10a		But **knowing this, Jesus told them,**
b	Response/ Rhetorical Question	*"Why are you bothering this woman,*
c	Basis for 10a	for *she has done a good deed for me?*
11a	Basis #1 for 10b	*[1]* For *you always have the poor with you,*
b		but *you are not always going to have me.*
12a	Basis #2 for 10b	*[2]* For *when she poured this perfume on my body,*
b		*she did it in order to prepare me for burial.*
13a	Result/ Pronouncement	*I tell you the truth . . .* *what she has done will also be told in remembrance of her,*
b		*wherever this gospel is proclaimed in all the world."*

Structure and Literary Form

This anointing story follows Mark 14:3 – 9 closely and shows only occasional verbal differences, with nothing important either added ("as he reclined at table" [v. 7], "she did it in order to prepare" [12]) or omitted from Mark ("broke the jar" [Mark 14:3], "were saying indignantly" [14:4], "leave her alone" [14:6], "you can help them any time you want" [14:7], "she did what she could" [14:8]). There are three parts to the story: the anointing itself (Matt 26:6 – 7), the objection of the disciples (vv. 8 – 9), and Jesus' explanation of the significance of the event (vv. 10 – 13).

Exegetical Outline

➡ I. The Anointing by the Woman (26:6 – 7)

A. The setting (v. 6)

B. The pouring of the perfume over Jesus' head (v. 7)

II. The Objection of the Disciples (26:8 – 9)

A. Indignation at the waste (v. 8)

B. Reason: the money could have helped the poor (v. 9)

III. Jesus' Explanation of the Incident (26:10 – 13)

A. Her good deed toward Jesus (v. 10)

B. Reason: Jesus will not be here much longer (v. 11)

C. Meaning of the event: preparation for burial (v. 12)

D. Result: story told in her memory (v. 13)

Explanation of the Text

26:6 While Jesus was in Bethany at the home of Simon the Leper (Τοῦ δὲ Ἰησοῦ γενομένου ἐν Βηθανίᾳ ἐν οἰκίᾳ Σίμωνος τοῦ λεπροῦ). With another of his temporal genitive absolutes, Matthew designates the occasion for the anointing story. Bethany (21:17) was a suburb of Jerusalem just two miles away on the eastern slopes of the Mount of Olives and was the home of Lazarus, Mary, and Martha. Jesus probably stayed there for Passion Week (John 12:1) and had just raised Lazarus (John 11). There is a possible contradiction with John 12:1 – 2, which seems to say the meal took place at Lazarus's home. Some solve the discrepancy by saying Simon was the father of the three siblings (with the three living at Simon's home, so McNeile), but that cannot go beyond conjecture. It is better to say that John merely gives the impression it was there (to link it with the raising of Lazarus in ch. 11), while Mark and Matthew state the site explicitly (see Carson). Either way there is no contradiction.

Nothing is told about Simon. We assume he was healed of his leprosy (probably by Jesus himself), for no leper would be with his family and friends at such a meal. The use of previous disabilities as nicknames occurred occasionally in the ancient world (see Schlatter). Some have linked this Simon with Simon the Pharisee in Luke 7, but that was a popular name in the first century (after the Maccabean hero of that name), and such is too speculative (see Witherington).

26:7 A woman came to him having[2] an alabaster jar of very expensive perfume (προσῆλθεν αὐτῷ γυνὴ ἔχουσα ἀλάβαστρον μύρου βαρυτίμου). From John 12:3 the woman is Mary, sister of Lazarus and Martha, but Matthew leaves her unnamed to center on her worshipful act. An alabaster flask was itself expensive, made of a soft stone that looked like marble and imported from Egypt. The stone was shaped into a small flask with a lengthy thin neck and was thought to preserve the perfume better.

Mark 14:3 tells us (1) that the woman "broke the jar," the common way of using the contents; (2) that the "expensive" perfume was worth three hundred denarii or a year's wages for the average laborer (I've never even smelled a perfume that expensive!); and (3) that the perfume was "pure nard," an expensive perfume made from fragrant spikenard and imported from India (Keener). We do not know whether Mary, Martha, and

2. ἔχουσα is probably an adjectival participle ("a woman having") but it could also be circumstantial ("came having"). Due to the word order, the former is more likely.

Lazarus were a wealthy family or this was a family heirloom. Either way, it was an incredible act of devotion.

26:7 ... and poured it over his head as he reclined at table (καὶ κατέχεεν ἐπὶ τῆς κεφαλῆς αὐτοῦ ἀνακειμένου). Anointing honored guests with oil was common at special celebrations, but not to this extent. There may also be an echo of the anointing of kings on their heads (cf. 1 Sam 9:16; 2 Kgs 9:6), and so this could be seen as a messianic anointing (contra Luz, who denies any "messianic anointing" here, but Bruner rightly calls this a "coronation"). "Reclining at table" (another temporal participle as in v. 6) was the common practice at banquets (see on 9:10). Jesus was virtually drenched with the oil, perhaps recalling Ps 133:2, where it symbolizes the blessed state of unity among God's people as "like precious oil poured on the beard, running down on the head." This pictures Jesus at this moment as the entire contents of the flask are poured on Jesus' head.

26:8 When the disciples saw[3] this, they were indignant, saying, "Why this waste?" (ἰδόντες δὲ οἱ μαθηταὶ ἠγανάκτησαν λέγοντες, Εἰς τί ἡ ἀπώλεια αὕτη;). The "indignation" ("anger, displeasure," cf. 20:24; 21:15) of the disciples is directed not at Jesus but at the woman for the "loss" (perhaps also the "destruction" [ἀπώλεια] of the jar) of the perfume for a more important purpose, spelled out in the next verse.

26:9 "For this could have been sold for a great deal[4] and given to the poor" (ἐδύνατο γὰρ τοῦτο πραθῆναι πολλοῦ καὶ δοθῆναι πτωχοῖς). The final teaching of the Olivet Discourse (25:31 – 46) had centered on acts of charity for the "least," and the rich young ruler in 19:21 was told to "sell your possessions, and give the proceeds to the poor." So on the surface this was in keeping with Jewish ethics and Jesus' own teaching. Yet at the same time it signified a lack of spiritual perception regarding the importance of the moment, as Jesus will make clear. The disciples were thinking of the external ministry of their apostolic band rather than the internal reality of Jesus as he faced his destiny.

26:10 But knowing this, Jesus told them, "Why are you bothering this woman, for she has done a good deed for me?" (γνοὺς δὲ ὁ Ἰησοῦς εἶπεν αὐτοῖς, Τί κόπους παρέχετε τῇ γυναικί; ἔργον γὰρ καλὸν ἠργάσατο εἰς ἐμέ). "Knowing" (γνούς, a circumstantial participle) reflects not Jesus' overhearing their comment but his supernatural "knowledge" of the thinking that lay behind it (cf. 9:4; 12:15, 25; 16:8; 22:18). So he asks why they are "causing trouble" or "bringing hardship" (κόπους παρέχετε) to the woman for her good deed. He then defines the deed as "a good deed" (ἔργον καλόν), stressing the cognate "worked a good work" (cf. 5:16). She has not only done nothing wrong; she has actually done a "beautiful" (καλόν) thing, for her thoughts were on Jesus while the disciples' minds were on others. Hers was an act of love or piety rather than an act of almsgiving.[5]

26:11 "For you always have the poor with you, but you are not always going to have me" (πάντοτε γὰρ τοὺς πτωχοὺς ἔχετε μεθ' ἑαυτῶν, ἐμὲ δὲ οὐ πάντοτε ἔχετε). The meaning of the parallel statements is clear (the present tenses place this in the foreground of the action).[6] The poor have been around through the whole history of humankind

3. "When they saw" (ἰδόντες) is a temporal participle.

4. "For a great deal" (πολλοῦ) is a genitive of price or value, cf. BDF §179.

5. See Joachim Jeremias, "Mc 14.9," *ZNW* 44 (1952): 103 – 7, as well as Hagner, Davies and Allison. Senior, *Passion Narrative*, 33, brings out that the emphasis is not on almsgiving in the story but on personal good works.

6. See Porter, *Idioms*, 23 – 25.

and will always be present. Jesus, however, is soon to die (v. 2), and there will not be much longer to care for him. The primary emphasis continues to be on the approaching passion of Jesus.

"Always going to have the poor" alludes to Deut 15:11 but with a twist. There the emphasis is on almsgiving and acts of kindness toward the needy, while here the stress is on ministering to Jesus. As Senior says, "It is Jesus' interpretation of the woman's act of kindness that plays the major role in the scene, and, of course, offers the ultimate justification for the pericope's setting within the Passion narrative."[7]

26:12 "For when she poured this perfume on my body, she did it in order to prepare me for burial" (βαλοῦσα γὰρ αὕτη τὸ μύρον τοῦτο ἐπὶ τοῦ σώματός μου πρὸς τὸ ἐνταφιάσαι με ἐποίησεν). Jesus now provides an interpretation for Mary's act of devotion that she undoubtedly knew nothing about. She had anointed (temporal participle "when she poured" [βαλοῦσα]) his head as an act of love, but as the perfume ran down his face and probably "on [his] body," he saw a much more important implication. It was common at burials to spread aromatic oil over the body to hide the smell because the Jews did not embalm corpses. John 19:39 tells us that Joseph of Arimathea and Nicodemus used seventy-five pounds of myrrh and aloes on Jesus' body, turning their act virtually into a royal burial. Jesus is saying that the woman's anointing is a precursor of that. Matthew omits Jesus' burial anointing as well as Mark 16:1 (the women going to the tomb "to anoint Jesus' body") and so suggests that this is his official burial preparation.

26:13 "I tell you the truth, wherever this gospel is proclaimed in all the world, what she has done will also be told in remembrance of her" (ἀμὴν λέγω ὑμῖν, ὅπου ἐὰν κηρυχθῇ τὸ εὐαγγέλιον τοῦτο ἐν ὅλῳ τῷ κόσμῳ, λαληθήσεται καὶ ὃ ἐποίησεν αὕτη εἰς μνημόσυνον αὐτῆς). With another "amen" (ἀμήν) saying (see on 5:18; the three in ch. 26 are the last of thirty-one such sayings in Matthew), Jesus concludes the pericope with an affirmation of the woman's kind deed. On the basis of his belief that Jesus never proclaimed a worldwide mission, Jeremias interprets this as final eschatology — at the parousia the angels will triumphantly proclaim both the gospel and what she has done.[8] However, there is no reason to doubt Jesus' anticipation of a mission to the world (see 28:18 – 20), and this is another of the many references in Matthew to the Gentile mission (see on 8:10 – 11).

Further, some have interpreted "gospel" (εὐαγγέλιον) as "the events of the Passion which are evoked by the burial anointing of Jesus,"[9] but "this gospel" reflects 24:14, which says "this gospel of the kingdom will be preached in the whole world." It is certainly the kingdom message in general that is the meaning here. So Jesus is saying that this woman's deed will be remembered throughout the age of the church, yet he is also hinting that his death and burial will be an essential part of that "good news."

"Her" (αὐτῆς) could be a subjective genitive (her good deed will be a remembrance of Christ) or an objective genitive (the church will remember her good deed). The latter is almost certainly correct in light of the emphasis on the proclamation of the gospel. This had already come true in John 11:2, when John, writing sixty years or so after the event, was able to describe Mary as "the same one who poured perfume on the Lord and wiped his feet with her hair."

7. Senior, *Passion Narrative*, 36.

8. Jeremias, *Prayers*, 112 – 24.

9. Senior, *Passion Narrative*, who names McNeile, Schlatter, Schniewind, Strecker, and Stuhlmacher.

Theology in Application

This story functions at two levels: (1) the homely level of the woman's deep concern and love for Jesus, and (2) the theological level of Jesus' coming death. At the same time there is the valid concern for the poor, seen in both the disciples' rebuke and in the allusion to Deut 15:11. The anointing itself may also have two significances, a royal anointing (the anointing of the head, v. 7) and an anointing for burial (the anointing of the body, v. 12), with the latter the major thrust.

1. Love for Jesus as the Heart of Discipleship

Bruner calls this a "lived-out commentary on the double-Love commands that Jesus taught as the main commandment in the law (22:34 – 40)," with the woman loving the Lord completely and Jesus loving her as he would want to be loved.[10] The "memorial" to her is a testimony to the depth of her love and self-sacrificial service to Jesus when she gave the family heirloom as an act of devotion to Jesus. This self-giving love models what we each must feel and do as we serve Jesus.

2. Care for the Poor

When Jesus alluded to Deut 15:11 and the presence of the poor in the future, he meant that for us, care for the needy is a key obligation. The Bible mentions this issue more than any other in terms of the responsibilities of God's people,[11] yet it is still one of the most neglected areas of ministry for the average church.

3. The Death of Jesus

The death of Christ is the central moment of history. Past and future meet at this event, the culmination of God's salvific plan to bring his creation back to himself. It is this act of atoning sacrifice that has made the second coming and the last judgment (25:31 – 46) possible, an event that will allow any of us to enter eternity as the children of God. Here divine love has its defining moment, and the triune Godhead has acted with finality to bring humankind and creation (Rom 8:19 – 22) back to themselves. It is fitting that the moment of love and self-sacrifice on the part of the woman bridge from the Olivet Discourse to the events of Jesus' passion, and her love in contrast to the evil plots of the leaders and the betrayal of Judas sets in motion this final act in the life of the incarnate God-man.

10. Bruner, *Matthew 13 – 28*, 599.

11. See Blomberg, *Neither Poverty Nor Riches*, for a good discussion of the biblical evidence.

CHAPTER 113

Matthew 26:14 – 16

Literary Context

The leaders had been afraid to arrest Jesus and planned to wait until after the Passover week (vv. 4 – 5), but now Judas gives them the opportunity they desire. The contrast between his selfish act of treachery and the woman's act of love in the previous story is stressed.

- VI. The Movement to the Cross (19:1 – 25:46)
- **VII. The Passion and Resurrection of Jesus (26:1 – 28:20)**
  - **A. The Passion Narrative (26:1 – 27:61)**
    - **1. Preliminary Events (26:1 – 16)**
      - a. Introduction — Plot to Kill Jesus (26:1 – 5)
      - b. Anointing of Jesus (26:6 – 13)
      - ➦ **c. Judas's Betrayal (26:14 – 16)**
    - 2. The Last Supper/Passover (26:17 – 30)

Main Idea

Without Judas, the arrest and crucifixion would not have occurred during the Passover. Judas serves God's purpose as well as that of the chief priests when his willingness to betray Jesus for money sets in motion the passion events so that Jesus will die as the paschal lamb for our sins.

Translation

(See next page.)

Matthew 26:14-16

14a	Action	**Then one of the Twelve named Judas Iscariot went to the chief priests, and said,**
15a	Question	*"What are you willing to give me*
b	Purpose	*so I will hand him over to you?"*
c	Response/Action	And **they paid out thirty pieces of silver to him.**
16a	Result	And **from that time on he kept seeking a good time in order to betray him.**

Structure and Literary Form

Matthew follows Mark 14:10 – 11 but with his own rendition. He highlights Judas's mercenary interest by including his offer to the Jewish leaders (Mark simply tells the story) and mentions the exact amount they pay him (preparing for 27:9 and the fulfillment from Zech 11:13). There are three parts: Judas takes the initiative and goes to the chief priests (v. 14); they agree to pay him money to betray Jesus (v. 15); Judas looks for a chance to betray Jesus (v. 16).

Exegetical Outline

➡ **I. Judas Goes to the Chief Priests (26:14)**
II. They Agree to Pay Him Money to Betray Jesus (26:15)
III. Judas Looks for an Opportunity (26:16)

Explanation of the Text

26:14 Then one of the Twelve named Judas Iscariot went to the chief priests (Τότε πορευθεὶς εἷς τῶν δώδεκα, ὁ λεγόμενος Ἰούδας Ἰσκαριώτης, πρὸς τοὺς ἀρχιερεῖς). Matthew places "one of the Twelve" at the beginning to highlight the relationship between Jesus and Judas and to make his action all the more horrifying. The betrayer is one of the very group that had experienced Jesus' love at the deepest level. Judas is mentioned only in the list of the twelve disciples (10:4, see that verse for "Iscariot") elsewhere, but he is obviously included every time the disciples are noted as a group.

26:15 ... and said, "What are you willing to give me so I will hand him over to you?" And they paid out thirty pieces of silver to him (εἶπεν, Τί θέλετέ μοι δοῦναι, κἀγὼ ὑμῖν παραδώσω αὐτόν; οἱ δὲ ἔστησαν αὐτῷ τριάκοντα ἀργύρια). In 10:4 Judas was described as the one "who also betrayed him," and now the story of the betrayal is told. Matthew makes it clear that Judas is motivated by greed. Mark simply tells the story while Matthew relates Judas's actual offer to the chief priests. The priests do not find him; he takes the initiative of going to them. John 12:6 says Judas was a thief who, as treasurer of the apostolic band, often stole from the common purse. This story is completely in keeping with that fact.

It is amazing how down through the centuries people have tried to explain away Judas's actions as a zealot who wanted Jesus to become active against the Romans or as a faithful follower who wanted Jesus to become the conquering Messiah rather than a passive suffering Servant. The *Gospel of Judas*, an early fourth-century Gnostic Gospel,[1] says Judas did this act at Jesus' own request so as to sacrifice Jesus' body and complete his mission.

It is common today to say we cannot know Judas's true motivation (e.g., Hill, Hagner, Davies and Allison), yet Matthew and John make it quite clear — it was an act of avarice. True, it was more complex than that and probably greed mixed with disappointment that Jesus was not the nationalistic hero Judas expected, yet clearly Mammon was the primary reason. Note that Judas is willing to take whatever the leaders offer and settles for what is a decent amount of money though not a lot.

It is not known exactly how much "thirty pieces of silver" were worth, since all coins a denarius and above were minted in silver. Most assume this payment was either thirty denarii (= one month's wages) or thirty shekels (= 120 denarii). Still, for a Palestinian peasant it was a fair amount of money, yet at the same time is only one-tenth the worth of the perfume used to anoint Jesus.[2] Most likely Matthew records the exact amount to prepare for 27:9, where it will fulfill Zech 11:12–13. Since Zech 11:4–14 is about the flock's (= Israel) rejection of their Shepherd-King, this looks at Judas as reenacting that rejection. "Paid out" (ἔστησαν) means "to fix, establish" a price, then "to weigh out" the amount (BAGD, 382, 1c) agreed upon.

26:16 And from that time on he kept seeking a good time in order to betray him (καὶ ἀπὸ τότε ἐζήτει εὐκαιρίαν ἵνα αὐτὸν παραδῷ). Undoubtedly the pact was for Judas to let the leaders know when Jesus was away from the crowds in a private spot so they could arrest Jesus without antagonizing the people. For the next couple of days Judas was ever alert (dramatic imperfect tense "he keep seeking" [ἐζήτει]) for the "opportune time." For the leaders this was a perfect chance to get rid of Jesus before the feast, for they were afraid that he might electrify the crowds with messianic fervor during the feast. As we know, Judas will find his moment when Jesus leads the disciples late at night to the olive grove of Gethsemane.

1. See Rodolphe Kasser, Marvin Meyer, and Gregor Wurst, *The Gospel of Judas* (Washington, DC: National Geographic Society, 2006). For an excellent summary and critique, see Craig A. Evans, *Fabricating Jesus: How Modern Scholars Distort the Gospels* (Downers Grove, IL: IVP, 2006), 240–45, who concludes that this gospel will have no impact on either understanding the historical Judas or on our "understanding of the gospel story." On other attempts to portray Judas as not a betrayer but a well-intentioned but mistaken follower, see France, *Gospel of Matthew*, 977.

2. Davies and Allison, *Matthew*, 3:450, note that this is the price of a slave in Exod 21:32, so that "Judas reckons Jesus to be no more than a slave." Joseph was sold as a slave by his brothers for twenty pieces of silver (Gen 37:28).

Theology in Application

This scene is one of most tragic and at the same time one of the most evil moments in world history. It is difficult to imagine how someone could sit under the personification of divine love and hear messages that were the greatest truths ever uttered by humankind, then turn around and betray Jesus to death just for money. At the same time, however, we must all remember how often we have rejected Jesus for Mammon. We cannot know what led Judas to this moment, what made him willing to betray his Lord for merely a few dollars. Yet we can know what leads us to forget Jesus and turn against him in our lives. We must realize that there is a bit of Judas in us all and determine to exemplify the woman's love rather than Judas's greed in our lives.

CHAPTER 114

Matthew 26:17 – 30

Literary Context

The two issues of the preceding material — God's sovereign hand and the betrayal of Jesus by his closest followers — combine here. Added to this is the redemptive significance of Jesus' death as the suffering Servant and as the paschal sacrifice.

VII. The Passion and Resurrection of Jesus (26:1 – 28:20)
- **A. The Passion Narrative (26:1 – 27:61)**
  - **1. Preliminary Events (26:1 – 16)**
    - a. Introduction — Plot to Kill Jesus (26:1 – 5)
    - b. Anointing of Jesus (26:6 – 13)
    - c. Judas's Betrayal (26:14 – 16)
  - ➦ **2. The Last Supper/Passover (26:17 – 30)**
    - **a. Preparation for the Supper (26:17 – 19)**
    - **b. Prediction of Judas' Betrayal (26:20 – 25)**
    - **c. Words of Institution (26:26 – 30)**
  - 3. Events in Gethsemane (26:31 – 56)

Main Idea

In this rich pericope, Jesus' preparations (vv. 17 – 19) show his control over the situation and perhaps supernatural knowledge of what is about to transpire. His prophecy of the betrayal (vv. 20 – 25) distinctly shows supernatural awareness not only of Judas's betrayal but also its fulfillment of Scripture, and the words of institution (vv. 26 – 30) show his sovereignty and also interpret his coming death in its redemptive significance and in establishing a new covenant.

Translation

Matthew 26:17-30

17a Setting — On the first day of the Feast of Unleavened Bread,
b Scene #1 Action — **the disciples came to Jesus, saying,**
c Question — *"Where do you want us to make preparation for you*
to eat the Passover?"
18a Answer/Instruction — **And he said,**
b — *"Go into the city to a certain man and tell him,*
c — *'The teacher says,*
d — *"My time is near.*
e — *At your place I am going*
to celebrate the Passover
with my disciples.'"
19a Response/Action — **So the disciples did as Jesus had commanded them,**
b Action — and **they prepared the Passover.**

20a Setting — And when evening arrived,
b Scene #2 Action — **he reclined at table with the Twelve.**

21a Setting — While they were eating,
b — **he said,**
c Prediction — *"I am telling you the truth, one of you will betray me."*
22a Response — **They became greatly upset**
b — **and began to say to him one after the other,**
c Question — *"It isn't I, is it, Lord?"*
23a — But **Jesus responded,**
b Answer/Prediction — *"The one who has dipped his hand with me in the bowl—*
c — *he is the one who will betray me.*
24a — *On the one hand, the Son of Man is passing*
b — *just as it has been written about him.*

c Indictment — *But woe to that man through whom the Son of Man is betrayed.*
d — *It would be better for that man if he had not been born."*
25a — **Now Judas, the one who was to betray him, responded,**
b Question — *"I am not the one, am I, Rabbi?"*
c — **Jesus told him,**
d Answer — *"So you have said."*

26a Setting — Now while they were eating,
b Scene #3 — **Jesus took bread and gave thanks,**
c Action — **He broke it,**
d Action — **gave it to the disciples, and**
e — **said,**
f Command — *"Take, eat, this is my body."*

27a Setting — And when he had taken the cup and given thanks,
b Action — **he gave it to them, saying,**

Continued on next page.

Continued from previous page.

c	Command	*"All of you, drink from it.*
28a	Basis for 27b	For *this is my blood of the covenant*
		that is poured out
		for many
b	Purpose of 28a	*for the forgiveness of sins.*
29a	Prediction	And *I tell you, I will not drink*
		from this fruit of the vine
		from now on
b	Promise	*until I drink it new*
		with you
		in the kingdom
		of my Father."
30a	Conclusion/Setting	And after they sang a hymn,
b	Action	**they departed to the Mount of Olives.**

Structure and Literary Form

Matthew once more follows Mark 14:12 – 26 fairly closely, with some abbreviation and one significant addition (v. 25, where Judas says, "I am not the one, am I, Rabbi?"). Luke, however, has quite a few differences, including a different form for the words of institution that agrees with 1 Cor 11:23 – 25. There are three parts to this important section: preparation (vv. 17 – 19), prediction of Judas's betrayal (vv. 20 – 25), and words of institution (vv. 26 – 30).

Exegetical Outline

➡ **I. Preparation for the Supper (26:17 – 19)**
- A. The disciples' request (v. 17)
- B. Jesus' directions (vv. 18 – 19)

II. Prediction of Judas's Betrayal (26:20 – 25)
- A. The prediction (vv. 20 – 21)
- B. Interaction with the disciples (vv. 22 – 24)
- C. Interaction with Judas (v. 25)

III. Words of Institution (26:26 – 30)
- A. The bread saying (v. 26)
- B. The cup saying (vv. 27 – 29)
- C. Departure (v. 30)

The Chronology of the Last Supper

Critics are divided on the chronology of the Last Supper. (1) Many believe John places the Last Supper one day earlier than the Synoptic Gospels do. Mark 14:12 (= Matt 26:17) places it on "the first day of the Festival of Unleavened Bread [= Passover], when it was customary to sacrifice the Passover lamb," so that Jesus was crucified when the Passover lambs were being slaughtered on Thursday. John, however, calls the day of crucifixion the "day of Preparation of the Passover" (John 19:14, 31, 42; cf. 18:28), thus indicating Thursday. So some critics insist the difference between the Synoptics and John cannot be harmonized. Yet as we will see below, they can be harmonized.

(2) It is quite common to accept the Johannine date as the correct one and to harmonize the Synoptics with it, saying the Last Supper was not a Passover meal.[1] Jeremias believed this was not a Passover meal but another of the preparatory meals, perhaps a *Kiddush*/prayer meal or a *Habburah*/fellowship meal.[2] France, Keener, and McKnight say that Jesus held a secret meal a day early because "he knew he would be dead before the regular time for the meal."[3] Witherington believes this is not a Passover meal but a Greco-Roman banquet celebrated sometime during Passion Week.[4] While these views are possible, for the four evangelists this was a Passover celebration. Stein summarizes the evidence:[5]

a. The meal was eaten in Jerusalem proper, a Passover requirement.
b. Jesus and the disciples spent the night in the environs of Jerusalem (Gethsemane), a further requirement.
c. They reclined on couches, which means it was a festive occasion.
d. The meal was eaten after sunset, while ordinary meals were in the late afternoon.
e. The meal ended with a hymn (26:30), and Passover meals closed with part of the Hallel (Pss 115 – 118).
f. The interpretation of the elements was part of the ritual (Exod 12:26 – 27).
g. Giving to the poor was a custom (cf. Matt 26:9; John 13:29).

The fact that several parts (like the consuming of the paschal lamb) are not mentioned can be explained as a result of the abbreviated nature of the

1. Raymond E. Brown, *The Death of the Messiah: From Gethsemane to the Grave* (2 volumes; New York: Doubleday, 1994), 1371 – 73; Luz, *Matthew 21 – 28*, 354 – 57; Davies and Allison, *Matthew*, 3:456.

2. Jeremias, *Eucharistic Words*, 41 – 62.

3. France, *Matthew* (TNTC), 365; Keener, *Matthew*, 623; Scot McKnight, *Jesus and His Death: Historiography, the Historical Jesus, and Atonement Theory* (Waco, TX: Baylor Univ. Press, 2005), 259 – 73.

4. Ben Witherington III, *John's Wisdom: A Commentary on the Fourth Gospel* (Louisville: Westminster John Knox, 1995), 231; and his *Matthew*, 482.

5. Robert Stein, "The Last Supper," *DJG*, 446.

accounts. They center only on the actions and words of Jesus and assume the other details. Moreover, many of the details of the Jewish Seder developed after AD 70, so we should not expect them here (so Davies and Allison).

(3) Jaubert posited that John followed a sectarian solar calendar like the one used at Qumran rather than the lunar calendar of the Pharisees and so placed it a day earlier.[6] However, there is no evidence Jesus ever followed a sectarian calendar, and the sacrifices in the temple were offered on the official day (Thursday). Moreover, the events in all four evangelists follow the same sequence, so this theory is unlikely.

(4) It is best to follow those who point out that the "day of preparation" on which Christ was crucified was oriented to the "special Sabbath," namely, the Sabbath (Saturday) of Passover week, rather than Friday.[7] So the meal talked about in John 18:28 is not the Passover meal itself (which was done the previous day) but the *ḥagigah* meal of the following day, beginning the Feast of Unleavened Bread, which was also called a Passover celebration; these went on for seven days (cf. Deut 16:2 – 3; 2 Chr 35:17). So the "day of Preparation" of John 19:14 was also Friday, meaning that John and the Synoptics are in agreement that the Last Supper was on Thursday night and the crucifixion on Friday.

Explanation of the Text

26:17 On the first day of the Feast of Unleavened Bread, the disciples came to Jesus, saying, "Where do you want us to make preparation for you to eat the Passover?" (Τῇ δὲ πρώτῃ τῶν ἀζύμων προσῆλθον οἱ μαθηταὶ τῷ Ἰησοῦ λέγοντες, Ποῦ θέλεις ἑτοιμάσωμέν σοι φαγεῖν τὸ πάσχα;). The time note is confusing, for this should be Passover, the first of the seven-day feast (with the two feasts coalescing into one, namely, 15 Nisan or Friday).[8] But in popular usage,[9] the festival had evolved into an eight-day festival with 14 Nisan or Thursday added as the day of preparation when the lambs (one for each extended household) were sacrificed (Mark 14:12, "when it was customary to sacrifice the Passover lamb") and when people ritually went through their homes removing all leaven/yeast (thus the title "Feast of Unleavened Bread").[10] The men would take the

6. Annie Jaubert, *The Date of the Last Supper* (Staten Island: Alba House, 1965). So also Morris, *Matthew*, 654.

7. Carson, "Matthew," 528 – 32; Ridderbos, *Matthew*, 476 – 77; Blomberg, *Historical Reliability of John* (Downers Grove, IL: IVP, 2002), 187 – 88, 246 – 47; Wilkins, *Matthew*, 832 – 33.

8. The Feast of Unleavened Bread was a harvest feast celebrating the gathering of the barley crop (Deut 16:9), offering the firstfruits (barley was the first crop to be harvested) to God; it was intended to be a preparation for the Feast of Weeks, which ended the harvest time. It was gradually combined with Passover because the two occurred in the same month and the presence of unleavened bread at the Passover (in the Passover because it looked back to the haste of the exodus, when they had to make unleavened bread and leave quickly, Exod 12:34) made the connection natural. Therefore in the first century the two were celebrated together and in the popular thinking actually functioned as a single feast.

9. Robert Stein, "Last Supper," 445, says, "In the more popular understanding, this technical distinction was lost.... Mark (and Matthew), in his description, has done what individuals today do when they speak of celebrating Christmas on Christmas Eve when presents are exchanged."

10. Gundry, *Matthew*, 524, notes how often Josephus calls

lambs during the afternoon while the women prepared the bitter herbs, the wine, and the unleavened bread; then that evening they would celebrate the Passover meal (Num 9:11).

This was one of three pilgrimage festivals (with Pentecost and Tabernacles, Deut 16:16), and thousands of lambs would be sacrificed. So the disciples are asking Jesus what place he has chosen for them to begin the preparations. The meal itself was characterized by the same hope of eschatological salvation which the exodus came to signify for Judaism, looking to God's final intervention to redeem Israel. The meal then became liturgical, centering on the Father's Passover prayer and the recitation of the Hallel (Pss 113 – 118). There was the blessing of the festival and wine, then the ritual drinking of the wine and the partaking of the food, followed by the liturgical question-answer response on the significance of the event.

The history of the celebration is interesting. In the days of wandering, the Passover was a family meal. The Deuteronomic code (Deut 16) prepared for the placing of the tabernacle at Shiloh and therefore prepared for a centralized celebration centered around the temple. In the exilic period it returned to a family meal (still celebrated by families). After the return and rebuilding of the temple it returned to a pilgrimage festival, and the true Passover meal had to be eaten in Jerusalem (of course, those in the Diaspora were allowed to commemorate it but could not take part in the temple service and celebrated while looking toward Jerusalem and the true feast).

The people would gather in the outer temple court in companies to slaughter the Passover victims; the priests formed two rows with gold and silver basins, respectively. The blood was caught in the basins and passed from hand to hand to be thrown on the altar. All was done to the singing of the Hallel (Pss 113 – 118) — we do not know if Jesus was there. That evening families would celebrate the Passover meal. Notice also that the apostolic band (as a rabbi and his disciples) constituted a "family" (see 12:46 – 50) for celebrating the festival. A "family" could designate any integrally related group, and a rabbi-disciple "family" could celebrate together, with the rabbi acting as "father" to the group. Jesus and his disciples were all from Galilee and so did not have their nuclear families with them for the celebration.

26:18 And he said, "Go into the city to a certain man and tell him (ὁ δὲ εἶπεν, Ὑπάγετε εἰς τὴν πόλιν πρὸς τὸν δεῖνα καὶ εἴπατε αὐτῷ). Matthew simplifies Mark 14:13 – 15, which has Jesus sending two disciples surreptitiously (probably to avoid the authorities) to a man carrying a water jar and following him home.[11] Here they would find τὸν δεῖνα ("such and such a person," used when one does not know the name or wants to avoid using the name) with a little of Mark's furtive air. In the gospel accounts it is difficult to ascertain whether Jesus made prior arrangements or exhibited supernatural awareness — perhaps both (so Blomberg).

26:18 " 'The teacher says, "My time is near. At your place I am going to celebrate the Passover with my disciples" ' " (Ὁ διδάσκαλος λέγει, Ὁ καιρός μου ἐγγύς ἐστιν, πρὸς σὲ ποιῶ τὸ πάσχα μετὰ τῶν μαθητῶν μου). When "the teacher" says, "My 'time' (καιρός) is near," he refers to that decisive moment in salvation history that God has appointed for his sacrificial death (see 26:2), what Gal 4:4 has called "when the set time had fully come" (cf. the "hour" of destiny in John 7:30; 8:20; 12:23,

14 Nisan the first day of the feast and calls the entire festival "the Feast of Unleavened Bread."

11. Senior, *Passion Narrative*, 55, says the reason is so Matthew can center on the person and words of Jesus rather than the actions of the disciples.

27; 13:1; 17:1). After an extensive study of "time" (καιρός) in Matthew, Senior interprets it as "the critical moment of Jesus' Passion. Betrayal, suffering, and death become the opportune moment that invites Jesus' full obedience to the salvific plan of his father."[12] There is an eschatological dimension of the convergence of time to this moment with that "appointed time" being near.

"Do the Passover" (ποιῶ τὸ πάσχα) is a biblical idiom[13] referring to the slaughter of the lamb at the temple and the eating of the meal. With so many pilgrims in Jerusalem for the Passover, it would not be easy to find a place for Jesus and the disciples, and on this point Jesus may well have made previous arrangements. Carson notes the theory proposed by Zahn that John Mark's father made his home available, but this must remain conjecture.[14]

26:19 So the disciples did as Jesus had commanded them, and they prepared the Passover (καὶ ἐποίησαν οἱ μαθηταὶ ὡς συνέταξεν αὐτοῖς ὁ Ἰησοῦς καὶ ἡτοίμασαν τὸ πάσχα). Luz calls this an "execution formula," consisting of a command, its fulfillment, and the carrying out.[15] "To command, instruct" (συντάσσω; see 21:6) shows that Jesus is in complete command of the situation. The focus continues to be on Jesus. The disciples would have taken the lamb to be slaughtered, prepared the herbs, wine, and bread, and got the room ready for the feast.

26:20 And when evening arrived, he reclined at table with the Twelve (Ὀψίας δὲ γενομένης ἀνέκειτο μετὰ τῶν δώδεκα). The Passover meal (this temporal genitive absolute occurs seven times in Matthew) was eaten after sunset on Thursday evening, 15 Nisan (the new day began after sundown) and had to be eaten in Jerusalem itself. Since the Jews followed the Roman pattern for feasts, they reclined on *triclinia*, couches that held three people, in a U-shaped pattern (with Jesus at the center of the head couch), resting on their left elbows with their right hands free to take the food from a table placed between the couches.

Lane provides an excellent timeline description of the Passover meal.[16]

1. The festival and the wine is blessed, followed by the first cup.
2. The food is then brought in — unleavened bread, bitter herbs, greens, stewed fruit, roast lamb.
3. The son asks why this night is distinguished from others; the family head answers with the exodus story, followed by praise to God for past and future redemption from the first part of the Hallel (Pss 113 – 114/15).
4. The second cup of wine is drunk.
5. The unleavened bread is blessed, broken, and distributed; then it is eaten with the herbs and fruit, as the father explains the meaning of the bread.
6. This is followed by the meal proper, which was not to extend beyond midnight.
7. At the consummation of the meal, the head blesses a third cup, followed by singing the second part of the Hallel (Pss 115/16 – 118).
8. A fourth cup concludes the meal.

26:21 While they were eating, he said, "I am telling you the truth, one of you will betray me" (καὶ ἐσθιόντων αὐτῶν εἶπεν, Ἀμὴν λέγω ὑμῖν ὅτι εἷς ἐξ ὑμῶν παραδώσει με). This must have occurred

12. Ibid, 59.

13. Nolland, *Matthew*, 1063n, says it occurs twelve times in the OT and in Heb 11:28.

14. Carson, "Matthew," 533.

15. Luz, *Matthew 21 – 28*, 354, following Rudolf Pesch, "Eine alttestamentliche Ausfürungsformel im Matthäus-Evangelium: Redaktionsgeschichtliche und exegetische Beobachtungen, *BZ* 10 (1966): 220 – 45 (esp. 223 – 24).

16. Lane, *Mark*, 501.

at the beginning of the meal, before the ritual had begun. The "amen" (ἀμήν) formula (see on 5:18) makes this a solemn pronouncement. παραδίδωμι, which means "hand over, deliver" in 17:22; 20:18; 26:2, here means to "betray" Jesus to the authorities. Mark adds the "one who is eating with me," an allusion to Ps 41:9 (a lament psalm where David is betrayed by a "close friend"). It is hard to know why Matthew omits the fulfillment allusion, but it is possible he felt the parallel was indicated in the whole story.[17]

26:22 They became greatly upset and began to say to him one after the other, "It isn't I, is it, Lord?" (καὶ λυπούμενοι σφόδρα ἤρξαντο λέγειν αὐτῷ εἷς ἕκαστος, Μήτι ἐγώ εἰμι, κύριε;). As in 18:31, "greatly" (σφόδρα) with "grieve" (λυπέω) refers to intense distress (in 17:23 it connotes deep sorrow). The disciples are deeply shocked and react with immediate denial, with εἷς ἕκαστος meaning "one by one, one at a time." "Not" (μήτι) in a question expects the answer no. Yet they have seen Jesus' supernatural awareness before and probably wonder if he knows something they do not, perhaps in a prophetic sense. There is a sharp contrast between their acknowledgment of Jesus as "Lord" and Judas, who calls him "rabbi" in v. 25.

26:23 But Jesus responded,[18] "The one who has dipped his hand with me in the bowl — he is the one who will betray me" (ὁ δὲ ἀποκριθεὶς εἶπεν, Ὁ ἐμβάψας μετ' ἐμοῦ τὴν χεῖρα ἐν τῷ τρυβλίῳ οὗτός με παραδώσει). This is not really any more specific than "one of you" in v. 21, since all the disciples have been dipping (unlike John 13:26, where Jesus gives a piece of the bread directly to Judas). Matthew switches from Mark's present tense to the more specific aorist "has dipped," indicating the disciples who have just been dipping with Jesus — probably the first stage of the meal after the first cup of wine and benediction, when lettuce or green herbs were dipped in the sauce (made of fruit, nuts, and ginger mixed with wine) in a bowl (so Nolland).

26:24 "On the one hand, the Son of Man is passing just as it has been written about him" (ὁ μὲν υἱὸς τοῦ ἀνθρώπου ὑπάγει καθὼς γέγραπται περὶ αὐτοῦ). ὑπάγω means "go, depart, pass" and here is a euphemism for death, so we have another passion prediction here (see 26:2, 11; and for "Son of Man" in the predictions, see 17:22; 20:18; 26:2). Here the passion is the fulfillment of Scripture, not any single passage but all those used throughout the Passion Narrative (cf. 26:54, 56; e.g., Zech 13:7 in 26:31; Zech 11:12, 13 in 27:9 – 10; Ps 22:1 in 27:46; cf. Ps 22:18 in 27:35) as well as the suffering Servant of Isa 52 – 53.

26:24 "But woe to that man through whom the Son of Man is betrayed. It would be better for that man if he had not been born" (οὐαὶ δὲ τῷ ἀνθρώπῳ ἐκείνῳ δι' οὗ ὁ υἱὸς τοῦ ἀνθρώπου παραδίδοται· καλὸν ἦν αὐτῷ εἰ οὐκ ἐγεννήθη ὁ ἄνθρωπος ἐκεῖνος). Matthew has recorded "woes" (meaning the terror of coming judgment) on unrepentant towns in 11:21, on the person who leads others into sin in 18:7, and on the scribes and Pharisees in ch. 23. Now the judgment oracle is proclaimed against the one who will betray him. In 18:6 Jesus says it would be preferable to be thrown into the sea with a large millstone around the neck than to face God's judgment. This passage is even more serious, for now it "would be better" to have

17. Nolland, *Matthew*, 1065, thinks Matthew may have missed the allusion in Mark. McNeile, *Matthew*, 380 believes the clause may have been a later addition to Mark and so missing from Matthew's copy. Senior, *Passion Narrative*, 68, follows Lohmeyer in thinking that Matthew wants to build the dramatic tension by not identifying Judas until the end of the section. Several others (Bonnard, Grundmann, Davies and Allison) believe Matthew thought the phrase redundant and so omitted it.

18. For this idiom see 3:15; 4:4.

never been born than to face such terrible judgment (cf. *1 En.* 38:2; *2 Bar.* 10:6). For such horrible apostasy and betrayal the eternal punishment predicted in 25:46 must await.

26:25 Now Judas, the one who was to betray him, responded, "I am not the one, am I, Rabbi?" Jesus told him, "So you have said" (ἀποκριθεὶς δὲ Ἰούδας ὁ παραδιδοὺς αὐτὸν εἶπεν, Μήτι ἐγώ εἰμι, ῥαββί; λέγει αὐτῷ, Σὺ εἶπας). In contrast to the disciples (v. 22), Jesus is not the "Lord" to Judas, just another "rabbi" (the title is used elsewhere only by opponents [23:7 – 8], as is also the parallel address "teacher" in 8:19; 9:11; 12:38; 17:24; 19:16; 22:16, 24, 36). Undoubtedly, Judas is hoping that Jesus is not aware of his earlier evil betrayal (vv. 14 – 16). His query takes the same form as the eleven in v. 22, expecting a negative answer. However, Jesus' response makes it clear that he knows all (he will use the same form affirming the statement with the high priest in 26:64). Yet it is also enigmatic enough that the disciples do not catch the meaning (though perhaps it was at the same time a private exchange).

26:26 Now while they were eating, Jesus took bread and gave thanks. He broke it, gave it to the disciples, and said, "Take, eat, this is my body" (Ἐσθιόντων δὲ αὐτῶν λαβὼν ὁ Ἰησοῦς ἄρτον καὶ εὐλογήσας ἔκλασεν καὶ δοὺς τοῖς μαθηταῖς εἶπεν, Λάβετε φάγετε, τοῦτό ἐστιν τὸ σῶμά μου).[19] Matthew typically uses a genitive absolute to designate their partaking of the meal (also v. 21). This section from the start became the most precious sacrament of worship celebrated by the church. Davies and Allison correctly call it "an aetiological cult narrative" without judging its historicity.[20] This part occurs a little later in the meal, at the eating of the paschal lamb, i.e., after it is served but before it is eaten.

At that time the head of the family sat up from his reclining position, blessed the bread, then broke it piece by piece and passed it to the guests. As Lane (*Mark*) and Jeremias (*Eucharistic Words*) point out, this was normally done in silence but Jesus went against custom (which allowed interpretation but only liturgical) in interpreting the act in light of his impending death. Matthew characteristically adds "the disciples" to Mark to stress the true meaning of the Passover as seen in the participation of the disciples, who must "take" and "eat." The blessing and breaking of bread also reenact 14:19 and 15:36 (the two feeding miracles).

The first word of institution interprets the meaning of the unleavened bread. The symbolism of the original elements of the Seder represented Israel's departure or redemption from Egypt, and the unleavened bread was labeled "the bread of affliction" (Deut 16:3; cf. Exod 34:18). McKnight takes it this way: "If the bread is connected to the cup, and the cup to sacrificial death, then the bread of affliction Jesus shares is participation in his death. This can only mean that the bread, now identified with Jesus, is given to the followers in order that they share in the death of Jesus in order to accrue its benefits."[21]

19. Matt 26:26 – 29 and Mark 14:22 – 25 agree on the words, but Luke 22:15 – 20 agrees with 1 Cor 11:23 – 25, with several differences, e.g., Luke and 1 Cor 11 add "given for you" and "do this in remembrance of me" to the cup words and both have "new covenant in my blood" for Mark's/Matthew's "my blood of the covenant." Many (Jeremias, Schweizer, Hill) assume that one of the two must be original and debate which is more "primitive" (usually Mark/Matthew). This is unnecessary; for all are *ipsissima vox* (the "exact voice") rather than *ipsissima verba* (the "exact words") and therefore paraphrases of Jesus' original, with each making redactional choices as to which elements to highlight (I. Howard Marshall, *Last Supper and Lord's Supper* [Grand Rapids: Eerdmans, 1980]; Carson; Davies and Allison; Keener; McKnight).

20. Davies and Allison, *Matthew*, 3:465.

21. McKnight, *Jesus and His Death*, 281.

Jesus reinterprets these elements to represent the redemptive effects of his departure. Matthew adds "eat" to Mark's "take" and emphasizes even further the meaning of this as an active participation of each one in the Christ's death. Some see the significance of "this is my body" as coming in the connection between Jesus' "body" and the "broken" bread (this fits the interpretation of 1 Cor 11), therefore in the redemptive effects of Jesus' broken body. Others believe the connection is more with the distribution ("gave to them") than the brokenness; it then would be a promise or pledge of his continued presence in the Eucharist. The second makes good sense due to its setting in the meal, but we dare not discount the interpretation of the early church.

The solution is to see "this" as referring to the "bread" itself (cf. 1 Cor 10:16) more than in the action done (so Jeremias), and therefore it refers to both the distribution and the breaking — "the bread (body) is broken, and all must partake of it" (Carson). The sacrificial nature of Jesus' death is clear, and there is a vicarious aspect as well (note Luke 22:19, "given for you" as well as "for many" in v. 28; cf. Heb 9:28; 1 Pet 2:24). Debates over transubstantiation (Catholic) and consubstantiation (Lutheran) read too much into ἐστιν, which is a very elastic verb that can mean "represents" as well as "equals" (Witherington translates "This — my body" to show the absence of the verb in Aramaic).[22] In this context the nonliteral use is likely (note ἐστιν in the cup saying, v. 28, so Stein). The emphasis is on the fulfillment of Passover imagery, not an ontological description of the Eucharist (see Hagner, Davies and Allison).

26:27 And when he had taken the cup and given thanks,[23] he gave it to them, saying, "All of you, drink from it" (καὶ λαβὼν ποτήριον καὶ εὐχαριστήσας ἔδωκεν αὐτοῖς λέγων, Πίετε ἐξ αὐτοῦ πάντες). In v. 26 the bread saying was probably part of step 5 when the father explained the significance of the unleavened bread. The cup saying was most likely part of step 7, the cup of blessing, with the entire meal taking place between the two sayings.

Each saying has individual significance. The traditional prayer of thanksgiving was "Blessed be you, O Lord our God, King of the universe, Creator of the fruit of the vine," though we do not know if they used that prior to AD 70. "All" (πάντες) is last for emphasis and requires the participation of every disciple, even Judas. Matthew turns Mark's "they all drank from it" into a command with liturgical implications. We should also note that at the Seder everyone had their own cup, whereas Jesus has the disciples drink from the same cup, emphasizing the community in unity that has been formed. From this verse the participation of every believer in this sacrament has become part of every church's liturgy.

26:28 "For this is my blood of the covenant" (τοῦτο γάρ ἐστιν τὸ αἷμά μου τῆς διαθήκης). "This is my blood" parallels "this is my body," with much the same meaning, "this represents my blood" and with "my blood" looking forward to Jesus' death on the cross. Each of the four cups is connected to a line of Exod 6:6 – 7a, this one to "I will redeem you" in v. 6c; a new liberation is offered, this time from sin (Blomberg). At the same time there is again a connection between the pouring and the distribution; in the interpretation the death of Jesus comes to the fore and the distribution recedes into the background (but with both present in the theological significance of the "cup").

22. Witherington, *Matthew*, 484.

23. With two temporal participles, "taking" and "thanking."

The "blood of the covenant" alludes to Exod 24:8 (cf. Zech 9:11; Heb 9:19 – 22; 10:29; 13:20), where the covenant was sealed with half the blood poured around the altar and half sprinkled on the people.[24] Jesus is inaugurating a new covenant (cf. "new covenant in my blood" in Luke 22:20; 1 Cor 11:25), in which the expiatory blood of the Messiah is "poured out" for the liberation of the sins of God's people. Probably the "new covenant" prophecy of Jer 31:31 – 34 (quoted in Heb 8:8 – 13) is also intended (also used by Qumran in CD 6:19; 8:21). McKnight looks at the OT possibilities for the background of the cup saying (Exod 24:8; Isa 53:12; Jer 31:31; Zech 9:11) and believes that all are viable but the Exod 24 with its reestablishment of the covenant here especially so.[25]

26:28 "... that is poured out for many for the forgiveness of sins" (τὸ περὶ πολλῶν ἐκχυννόμενον εἰς ἄφεσιν ἁμαρτιῶν). The redemptive significance of the Passover Seder is seen as fulfilled in Jesus' blood. ἐκχυννόμενον (an adjectival participle, "the poured out [blood]") is OT sacrificial language especially connoting atonement (Lev 4:7, 18, 25; 9:9; 17:11 – 14). Through the sacrifice "poured out" at the altar the sins of the people are being "covered over" (the meaning of Hebrew word *kpr*, "atone"). This idea of vicarious atonement is especially seen in the added "for many" (περὶ πολλῶν), echoing Isa 53:12 ("he poured out his life unto death ... [and] bore the sin of many") and reflected in NT atonement imagery (Matt 20:28 par.; Rom 4:25; 1 Cor 15:3; 2 Cor 5:21; Gal 1:4; et al.). In fact, "ransom for many" from Matt 20:28 is certainly part of the meaning of "poured out for many" here. The use of *peri* (Mark has *hyper*) in "for many" is probably equivalent to the *anti* of 20:28 and connotes substitutionary atonement with a possible allusion to Isa 53:10, 12.

The purpose and result of his atoning death will be "for the forgiveness of sins" (εἰς ἄφεσιν ἁμαρτιῶν), echoing both the suffering Servant (Isa 53:11 – 12) and the new covenant passage (Jer 31:34). This provides the basis for the ethical righteousness that is so central to Matthew's portrayal. The believer is able to live rightly because Jesus' atoning sacrifice has made it possible for us to become part of God's family and find the strength in Christ to live an obedient life (see esp. Nolland, who speaks of "grace and demand" in Matthew's soteriology).

26:29 "And I tell you, I will not drink from this fruit of the vine from now on until I drink it new with you in the kingdom of my Father" (λέγω δὲ ὑμῖν, οὐ μὴ πίω ἀπ' ἄρτι ἐκ τούτου τοῦ γενήματος τῆς ἀμπέλου ἕως τῆς ἡμέρας ἐκείνης ὅταν αὐτὸ πίνω μεθ' ὑμῶν καινὸν ἐν τῇ βασιλείᾳ τοῦ πατρός μου). This is in accordance with the fourth cup that concludes the meal (step 8 at v. 20). Jesus' solemn vow of abstinence may have extended to the whole meal (so Jeremias) or may have just extended to the particular "cup" (so Hill). The latter is favored by its place in the meal (after the meal had been eaten), and it is unlikely that Jesus abstained from the entire meal (Hagner). So this is an eschatological statement of the future reality, and the emphasis is not on the vow of abstinence but on the prophecy of the imminent coming of the kingdom, in keeping with the OT longing for the final redemption of Israel (Isa 11:1 – 16; 25:6 – 9; 55:1 – 2) and with the Olivet Discourse.

Of course, the idea of "not drink any longer" implicitly acknowledges Jesus' imminent death,

24. Turner, "Matthew," 339, translates this, "blood, which confirms the covenant," bringing together the Passover imagery and the new covenant imagery of Jer 31.

25. McKnight, *Jesus and His Death*, 286 – 92.

and the "drink it new" anticipates the messianic banquet of Rev 19:6 – 8, foreshadowed in Matt 5:6; 8:11; 14:20; 15:37; 22:11 – 12; 25:10, 21, 23. "With you" (μεθ' ὑμῶν) points back to 1:23 (Immanuel, "God with us") and means the disciples have a part in the final eschatological blessing. Now is the time of their perseverance after Christ is taken from them, but there will be a future vindication. "The kingdom of my Father" stresses the critical place Jesus has vis-à-vis the kingdom. He has brought it (3:2; 4:17; 12:28), and he will consummate it.

26:30 And after they sang a hymn (Καὶ ὑμνήσαντες). It is possible to place this verse with the following paragraph, and as a transition verse that fits well; but in light of the Passover meal this hymn (another temporal participle) should be seen as the concluding part and therefore part of the elements of the meal. Some (e.g., Schweizer, Davies and Allison) think this referred to Christian hymns (Eph 5:19; Col 3:16), but it is much more likely this was the last part of the Hallel (Ps 115 – 18) that concluded the Seder celebration.

26:30 ... they departed to the Mount of Olives (ἐξῆλθον εἰς τὸ ὄρος τῶν ἐλαιῶν). This is the third time Jesus and his disciples have been on the Mount of Olives (21:1; 24:3), and it is common to see in this "departure" (note the Passover link) an allusion to 2 Sam 15:30 – 31, when David fled to the Mount of Olives, weeping and praying after he learned that Ahithophel, his trusted adviser, had joined the plot of his son Absolam in rebellion against his reign. The parallels are clear, especially since Ahithophel wanted to attack David at night (17:1 – 2) and, like Judas, hung himself when his plot did not work (17:23). The apostolic band has undoubtedly planned to spend the night in the olive grove, as the rules said they must stay in the environs of Jerusalem during Passover Week (Bethany was too far away). It was during this time that Jesus' Farewell Address recorded in John 13 – 17 was given.

Theology in Application

Stein concludes, "Clearly, Jesus does not see his passion as a tragedy or error, but the crowning act of his ministry in which he pours out his blood as the once-for-all sacrifice which secures redemption 'for many' and insures a glorious consummation in the future."[26] Like the feeding miracles, the Last Supper draws its power (1) from its fulfillment of the past — the typological fulfillment of the key redemptive event of the OT (the Exodus) and the literal fulfillment of messianic prophecy (the suffering Servant of Isaiah); (2) from its present meaning — the atoning sacrifice of Christ on the cross and its vicarious nature; and (3) from its future implications — foreshadowing the consummation of God's plan of salvation in the Parousia and the messianic banquet.

1. The New Covenant

Jesus inaugurated the new covenant with his body and blood sacrificed for the redemption of humankind. The implications of the Last Supper are behind the quotation of Jer 31:31 – 34 in Heb 8:8 – 13, where Jesus became the high priest of the new

26. Stein, "Last Supper," 449.

covenant, as well as behind the "lamb without blemish or defect" of 1 Pet 1:18 – 21 and the suffering Servant imagery of 1 Pet 2:21 – 23. As Hagner says, "Jesus was the new, eschatological Passover lamb (cf. 1 Cor 5:7), whose sacrificial death was the atonement for the sins of the world.... For this reason the celebration of the Lord's Supper is at the center of Christian worship. The Eucharist becomes a Christian Passover"[27]

2. A Sacrificial and Redemptive Understanding of Jesus' Death

The Last Supper provides the sacrificial and redemptive understanding of Jesus' death. This event with its words of institution has a hermeneutical function in interpreting the meaning of Christ's death anew for every generation of the church. Paul recognized this with his thesis paragraph in Rom 3:21 – 26 when he spoke of the atoning sacrifice of Christ ("propitiation") that became Jesus' ransom payment on the cross ("redemption") and provided the basis for God's judicial declaration that in Christ those who believe are now right with him ("justification").

3. The Eucharistic Celebration of the Lord's Supper

The Last Supper launched the major sacramental event in corporate worship. As the church participates in this renewal event, it reenacts and remembers (Luke 22:19 and 1 Cor 11:24, 25, "in remembrance of me") Jesus' sacrificial death and virtually becomes a "word-event." For the early church the Last Supper and the Lord's Supper were Christian Seder celebrations, with the "love feast" (Jude 12) connected with the Lord's Supper as a Christian Passover meal.

The language of Matthew's telling of this story is transparent in its implications for the later church; each part of this passage is meant to be retold in the life of worship as every member of the church relives the meaning of the death of Christ in corporate communion. Wilkins speaks of the Lord's Supper as "not simply a religious exercise but a schematic for our lives" in the sense that it helps us to look "backward" to the finished act of salvation on the cross that provides an anchor for our lives, "forward" to our future in the consummation of history, "inward" as we examine (1 Cor 11:27 – 28) our heart and lives and confess our sins before God, "upward" as we realize he is now at God's right hand, enabling us to "set [our] minds on things above" (Col 3:1 – 4), "around" as we realize the community that makes corporate worship possible, and "outward" as we "proclaim the Lord's death" (1 Cor 11:26) to a world dying in sin.[28]

27. Hagner, *Matthew 14 – 28*, 774.

28. Wilkins, *Matthew*, 851 – 52.

CHAPTER 115

Matthew 26:31 – 56

Literary Context

The order here is chronological as we follow the events of the last night of Jesus' life. At the close of the Passover meal, Jesus and his followers leave Jerusalem and go to the olive grove on the Mount of Olives (v. 30). There Jesus predicts the failure of the rest of the disciples (vv. 31 – 35), prays in Gethsemane (vv. 36 – 46), and then is arrested (vv. 47 – 56).[1]

VII. The Passion and Resurrection of Jesus (26:1 – 28:20)
- **A. The Passion Narrative (26:1 – 27:61)**
  1. Preliminary Events (26:1 – 16)
  2. The Last Supper/Passover (26:17 – 30)
  3. **Events in Gethsemane (26:31 – 56)**
     - **a. Jesus Predicts the Failure of His Disciples (26:31 – 35)**
     - **b. The Prayer of Victory at Gethsemane (26:36 – 46)**
     - **c. The Arrest of Jesus (26:47 – 56)**
  4. The Trials of Jesus and Peter's Denials (26:57 – 27:26)

Main Idea

Every aspect of this pair of episodes looks to the divinely ordained event of the cross. There are three primary themes: Jesus' sovereign control and triumph in the events transpiring, the fulfillment of Jesus' predictions as well as of Scripture in the coming events, and the failure of the disciples in those events. Jesus will face his destiny alone, and yet he will be the master of his situation (the contrast between

1. On the historical veracity of this scene in which Jesus' prayer is recorded even though the disciples have fallen asleep, see France, *Gospel of Matthew*, 1003. He notes that the other disciples could have heard what was transpiring, or that Jesus himself could have told them after the resurrection.

Jesus and the disciples is central here). Moreover, God is sovereign over it all, and each event occurs in fulfillment of Scripture (vv. 31, 54, 56).

Translation

Matthew 26:31-56

31a	Scene #1 (A)	**Then Jesus told them,**
b	Prediction #1	*"You all will fall away because of me this night.*
c	Basis	*For it has been written,*
d	OT Quotation	*'I will strike the shepherd,*
e		*and the sheep of the flock will be scattered.'* (Zech 13:7)
32a	Circumstance	*But after I am raised,*
b	Promise	*I will go before you to Galilee."*
33a	Response #1	**But Peter responded,**
b		*"Even if everyone falls away because of you,*
		I will never fall away."
34a	Prediction #2	**Jesus said to him,**
b		*"I tell you the truth . . . you will deny me three times,*
c	Time	*before the rooster crows*
		this very night."
35a	Response #2	**Peter said to him,**
b		*"Even if I should have to die with you, I will never deny you."*
c	Affirmation	**All the disciples said the same thing.**
36a	Scene #2 (B)	**Then Jesus went with his disciples to a place called Gethsemane and**
	Action/Setting	**told them,**
b	Command	*"Sit here while I go there and pray."*
37a	Action	**And he took Peter and the two sons of Zebedee and**
b	Description	**began to be sorrowful and distressed.**
38a		**Then he told them,**
b	Assertion	*"My soul is filled with sorrow to the point of death.*
c	Request	*Stay here and watch with me."*
39a	Action	**And going ahead a short distance, he fell on his face, praying,**
b	Entreaty	*"My Father,*
c		*if it is possible,*
d		*may this cup pass from me.*
e		*Yet not as I will, but*
f		*as you will."*
40a	Action	**And he came to the disciples and found them sleeping.**
b		**Then he said to Peter,**
c	Rhetorical Question/ Indictment	*"So aren't you strong enough to keep watch*
		with me
		for one hour?
41a	Exhortation	*Keep watching and praying*
b	Purpose	*so that you do not enter into temptation.*
c	Aphorism	*The spirit is willing but the flesh is weak."*

42a	Parallel 39a/Action	**He went away again a second time and prayed, saying,**
b	Entreaty	*"My Father,*
c		*if it is not possible for this to pass away*
		unless I drink it,
d		*may your will be done."*
43a		And when he went back,
b	Parallel 40a/Action	**he found them sleeping again,**
c		for their eyes had become heavy.
44a	Parallel 39a, 42a/Action	**Again he left them,**
		went away, and
		prayed a third time,
b		once more saying the same prayer.
45a	Parallel 40a, 43b/Action	**Then he came to the disciples and told them,**
b		*"Are you still sleeping and resting?*
c		*Look, the hour is approaching,*
d	Prediction	*and the Son of Man is going to be betrayed*
		into the hands of sinners.
46a	Command	*Get up,*
b	Command	*let's go!*
c	Prediction	*My betrayer is near.*
47a	Setting	And while he was still speaking,
b	Scene #3 (A')/Action	**look, Judas, one of the Twelve, arrived.**
c	Action	**With him came a large crowd**
		from the chief priests and elders of the people
		with swords and clubs.
48a	Instruction	**His betrayer had given them a sign, saying,**
b		*"The one I kiss is the man.*
c		*Seize him!"*
49a	Action	And immediately
		when he came to Jesus,
b	Greeting	**he said,**
c		*"Greetings, Rabbi!"*
d		**and kissed him.**
50a	Response to 49b-c	**But Jesus said to him,**
b		*"Friend, I know why you have come."*
c	Action	**Then they came forward,**
		placed their hands on Jesus, and
		arrested him.
51a	Response to 50b	**And look, one of those with Jesus stretched out his hand and**
		drew his sword.
b	Action	Striking the slave of the high priest,

Continued on next page.

Continued from previous page.

c		**he cut off his ear.**
52a	Response to 51a-c	**Then Jesus told him,**
b		*"Put your sword back in its place,*
c	Basis for 52b	for *all who take the sword will perish by the sword.*
53a	Rhetorical Question #1	*[1]* Or *do you suppose that I cannot call upon my Father,*
b		and *he will send me now more than twelve legions of angels?*
54a	Rhetorical Question #2	*[2] How then could the Scriptures be fulfilled that it must happen in this way?"*
55a		**At that time Jesus told the crowds,**
b	Rhetorical Question	*"Am I an armed bandit, that you have come out with swords and clubs to arrest me?*
c	Assertion	*I was sitting daily in the temple teaching,*
d		and *you did not arrest me.*
56a		But *this whole thing has happened*
b	Purpose of 50b	*so that the writings of the prophets might be fulfilled."*
c	Conclusion/Action	**Then all the disciples left him and fled.**

Structure and Literary Form

As throughout the Passion Narrative, Matthew parallels Mark with only a few differences. Matthew adds "because of me this night" to "fall away" in v. 31 (also in v. 33); removes the redundancy of Mark's twofold reference to "if possible," may the cup pass from him (v. 39 = Mark 14:35 – 36), but yet adds a second "may your will be done" in v. 42; omits Mark's "they did not know to say to him" in v. 43; then adds v. 50 ("Friend, I know why you have come") and mainly adds vv. 52 – 54 (about the sword, the legion of angels, fulfillment of Scripture).

There are three sections in this pericope with an ABA pattern: Jesus' prediction of the disciples falling away (vv. 31 – 35), Gethsemane (vv. 36 – 46), and the carrying out of the prediction as they flee at his arrest (vv. 47 – 56). The first section has two parts: the failure of all the disciples (vv. 31 – 32) and the particular failure of Peter (vv. 33 – 35). The second has three scenes linked to the three times Jesus prays to the Father while the disciples fall asleep (vv. 36 – 41, 42 – 43, 44 – 46), preparing for the three denials of Peter in vv. 69 – 75. The third has three parts, each containing a speech by Jesus: the betrayal by Judas (vv. 47 – 50), the cutting off of the ear with Jesus' rejoinder (vv. 51 – 54), and his concluding comments to the crowds (vv. 55 – 56).

Exegetical Outline

→ **I. Jesus Predicts The Failure Of His Disciples (26:31 – 35)**
- A. They all will fall away (vv. 31 – 32)
  - 1. Their "apostasy," fulfilling Zech 13:7 (v. 31)
  - 2. The post-resurrection promise (v. 32)
- B. Peter will deny Jesus (vv. 33 – 35)
  - 1. Peter's disavowal (v. 33)
  - 2. Jesus' prophecy (v. 34)
  - 3. All join Peter in denying this (v. 35)

II. The Prayer of Victory at Gethsemane (26:36 – 46)
- A. The first prayer and interaction (vv. 36 – 41)
  - 1. The setting: Jesus going for prayer (v. 36)
  - 2. Request for the inner circle to watch with him (vv. 37 – 38)
  - 3. Prayer of surrender to the Father's will (v. 39)
  - 4. Challenge to the sleeping disciples (vv. 40 – 41)
- B. Second prayer and interaction (vv. 42 – 43)
- C. Third prayer and interaction (vv. 44 – 46)
  - 1. Prayer (v. 44)
  - 2. Finds them asleep again (v. 45a)
  - 3. The hour has arrived (vv. 45b – 46)

III. The Arrest of Jesus (26:47 – 56)
- A. The betrayal by Judas (v. 47 – 50)
- B. The act of rebellion (vv. 51 – 54)
  - 1. The sword blow (v. 51)
  - 2. Jesus' response (vv. 52 – 54)
    - a. Put away the sword (v. 52)
    - b. The hosts of heaven at Jesus' disposal (v. 53)
    - c. The necessity of fulfilling Scripture (v. 54)
  - 3. Closing remarks to the crowd (vv. 55 – 56)

Explanation of the Text

26:31 Then Jesus told them, "You all will fall away because of me this night" (Τότε λέγει αὐτοῖς ὁ Ἰησοῦς, Πάντες ὑμεῖς σκανδαλισθήσεσθε ἐν ἐμοὶ ἐν τῇ νυκτὶ ταύτῃ). This apparently is delivered on the way up the mountain, for they "depart" in v. 30 and then arrive at Gethsemane in v. 36 (Luke 22:31 – 34 places the prediction of Peter's denial within the Last Supper).[2] Note the sequence of Jesus' predictions of failure and their fulfillment; all occur in order: (Judas, vv. 21 – 25, fulfilled in

2. Bock, *Luke 9:51 – 24:53*, 1730, says that Luke's narration "may reflect Lukan summarization and compression."

3. France, *Gospel of Matthew*, 997.

vv. 47 – 50; the Twelve, v. 31, fulfilled in v. 56; Peter, v. 34, fulfilled in vv. 69 – 75).[3] It will not be just Judas who fails; Jesus now expands his prediction to "you all," a revelation that must have shocked them to the core.

"Fall away" (σκανδαλίζω) has been used several times with respect to leading one to sin (5:29, 30; 18:6, 8, 9), being offended (13:57; 15:12; 17:27), and falling away from one's faith (11:6; 24:10). Here the first and third are intended, especially the "falling away." The disciples are going to desert Jesus completely (v. 56); and even when Jesus appears to them on the first night of his resurrection, they will still be cowering behind closed doors "for fear of the Jewish leaders" (John 20:19). That very night[4] they will fail "on account of me" (causal ἐν ["because"], see BAGD, 261, 3).[5] They will perceive that following Jesus is dangerous and run for their lives, leaving Jesus to face the fury of the Jewish leaders and of Rome.

26:31 "For it has been written, 'I will strike the shepherd, and the sheep of the flock will be scattered' " (γέγραπται γάρ, Πατάξω τὸν ποιμένα, καὶ διασκορπισθήσονται τὰ πρόβατα τῆς ποίμνης). Jesus sees the disciples' "falling away" as part of God's will as foretold in Zech 13:7. This hardly means they do not stand guilty for what they are about to do. Rather, it means that God has planned for this ahead of time and is in sovereign control even of their failure. In the MT and LXX the passage quoted here employs imperatives, while here it uses future indicatives, which could reflect an early recension of the LXX (Carson, Gundry, Davies and Allison) or perhaps Matthew's own rendition (Nolland). Either way, "I will strike" denotes God's control of the passion events.

In Zechariah God is calling on a "sword" to strike the "shepherd" of Israel (who is God's associate) and to scatter the "sheep" (= the nation). The messianic figure of the shepherd being rejected and killed is undoubtedly central for Jesus' understanding of the events to come (along with Isa 53). This is closely connected to Ezek 34 and the false "shepherds of Israel" (= Zech 11:4 – 17) behind Matt 9:36, where Jesus had compassion for the crowds "because they were harassed and helpless like sheep without a shepherd." The disciples will become one with the nation of Israel in being "scattered." When Jesus, the true shepherd of Israel, is struck and killed, the disciples will scatter to the winds and join Israel in "apostasy." Zechariah 13:7 centers on the apostasy of the nation in deserting God, and the disciples will reenact that "falling away." In one sense, Zech 13:7 functions as a superscription to the passion events — the fleeing of the disciples (scattering of the sheep), the arrest of Jesus (Matt 26:50), and the smiting of the shepherd.[6]

26:32 "But after I am raised,[7] I will go before you to Galilee" (μετὰ δὲ τὸ ἐγερθῆναί με προάξω ὑμᾶς εἰς τὴν Γαλιλαίαν). Jesus has spoken of his resurrection from the dead numerous times (16:21; 17:9, 23; 20:19), and now he applies this to the issue of the disciples' apostasy, implicitly saying that he will be reunited with them in Galilee and there they will find forgiveness and reinstatement. Note the progression from v. 31 to v. 32. God will strike Jesus and then "raise" him (divine passive ἐγερθῆναι), and the disciples will be scattered from their shepherd and then brought back together with him. As the Good Shepherd Jesus will "go ahead of" or lead the disciples (cf. John 10:4) to Galilee.

4. There is no symbolic meaning to "night" as in John (= the time of sin). It simply means their desertion is imminent (so Luz).

5. This is added twice to Mark (here, v. 33 = Mark 14:27, 29) and so should be stressed.

6. See Douglas J. Moo, "The Use of the Old Testament in the Passion Texts of the Gospels" (PhD diss., University of St. Andrews, 1979), 186.

7. μετὰ τό with an infinitive becomes a temporal clause indicating action "after."

This prophecy of going into Galilee is repeated in 28:7, 10 and fulfilled in 28:16 – 20. It is even more central in Mark 14:28; 16:7, for it is at the core of Mark's discipleship failure emphasis (a key theme in Mark 6 – 16). Especially if Mark ends at 16:8 (which is likely), Galilee is the place of revelation where Jesus will meet the disciples and give them victory over their failures. Matthew picks up this theme, although it is not as central here. As Davies and Allison say, "not in Jerusalem but in 'Galilee of the Gentiles,' where he first gathered his community, will Jesus reconstitute the flock that has been scattered and then inaugurate the world mission."[8]

26:33 But Peter responded, "Even if everyone falls away because of you, I will never fall away" (ἀποκριθεὶς δὲ ὁ Πέτρος εἶπεν αὐτῷ, Εἰ πάντες σκανδαλισθήσονται ἐν σοί, ἐγὼ οὐδέποτε σκανδαλισθήσομαι). Peter displays his typical false bravado once again (see 14:28 – 31; 16:22, 23; 17:4; 19:27) and impulsively declares an absolute confidence in himself that he will never join the others in apostasy; there is one exception to the prediction, and he is it! By adding "because of you" (ἐν σοί, with causal ἐν) to Mark for the second time (see v. 31a), Matthew stresses the fact that Jesus is the reason the disciples fall into danger (cf. 10:24 – 25; John 15:18 – 16:4). Peter thought he was ready for whatever opposition and suffering came his way.

26:34 Jesus said to him, "I tell you the truth, before the rooster crows this night, you will deny me three times" (ἔφη αὐτῷ ὁ Ἰησοῦς, Ἀμὴν λέγω σοι ὅτι ἐν ταύτῃ τῇ νυκτὶ πρὶν ἀλέκτορα φωνῆσαι τρὶς ἀπαρνήσῃ με). Jesus quickly disabuses Peter of his pretensions. By using the "amen" (ἀμήν) formula (see on 5:18), he stresses the solemn truth behind this. The prophecy that "all" the disciples will fall away "this night" (v. 31) is especially true of Peter, who will not just fail but will "deny" knowing his Lord three times. Peter says, "Never!" and Jesus responds, "This very night!" Moreover, Peter will not just desert Jesus; he will deny him.

The meaning of the rooster crowing is debated. Kosmala states that roosters crowed at 12:30 a.m., 1:30, and 2:30 and saw the second as fitting Mark (the second crowing)[9] and thus Matthew.[10] The Romans called the third watch of the night (midnight to 3:00 a.m.) "Cockcrow," and this may be the best option (there is little evidence for roosters crowing at those times). Raymond E. Brown quotes Cicero, "Is there any time, night or day, that cocks do not crow?" and says simply that it refers to "the early hours of the morning before dawn; nothing more definite can be concluded."[11] The three denials come literally true in vv. 69 – 75.[12]

26:35 Peter said to him, "Even if I should have to die with you, I will never deny you." All the disciples said the same thing (λέγει αὐτῷ ὁ Πέτρος, Κἂν δέῃ με σὺν σοὶ ἀποθανεῖν, οὐ μή σε ἀπαρνήσομαι. ὁμοίως καὶ πάντες οἱ μαθηταὶ εἶπαν). Peter's self-confidence still refuses to lag

8. Davies and Allison, *Matthew*, 3:486.

9. So France and Blomberg. John W. Wenham, "How Many Cock-Crowings? The Problem of Hellenistic Text-Variants," *NTS* 25 (1979): 523 – 25, argues that the "twice/second" of Mark 14:30, 72 was a later interpolation. While possible, it is better to see the omission as an attempt to harmonize Mark with Matthew (so France, *Mark*, 573).

10. Hans Kosmala, "The Time of the Cock-Crow," *Annual of the Swedish Theological Institute* 2 (1963): 118 – 20 (so also Carson).

11. Brown, *Death*, 607.

12. This is one of the key errors in the theology of "open theism." They have to assert that Jesus did not know what Peter's decision would be but just knew the kind of person he was and that he would probably do such a thing. But so detailed a prophecy could not be merely an educated guess. Jesus had supernatural knowledge of what Peter would do. In the same way, there is no reason to take this as a *vaticinium ex eventu* (prophecy after the event). If the God of the Bible is real, such prophecies make perfect sense.

even with this onslaught of prophetic power. "Even if I should have to die with you" does not speak of divine necessity. Peter recognizes that Jesus has been speaking of the possibility of his death (he never realized until after the events were over that it was divine necessity) and reflects that here. Hagner rightly calls this "dramatic irony" in that this was exactly what was to transpire,[13] and it would cause Peter like the others to do exactly what Jesus was predicting.

"Deny" (ἀπαρνέομαι, with intensifying ἀπ- prefix) also appears in 16:24, where Peter had just rebuked Jesus for predicting his passion and Jesus had called Peter a "stumbling block" (σκάνδαλον, see vv. 31, 33 above), then went on to say the true disciple must "deny" self (the very problem Peter is demonstrating!). In 10:33 Jesus had said, "Whoever denies me before people, I will also deny before my Father in heaven," so Peter will be in serious spiritual danger mere hours from now. Peter thinks he is willing to die with Jesus, but the opposite transpires. Finally, Matthew adds that all the rest of the disciples reiterate the same foolish claim, and all will fail in similar ways.

26:36 Then Jesus went with his disciples to a place called Gethsemane and told them, "Sit here while I go[14] there and pray" (Τότε ἔρχεται μετ' αὐτῶν ὁ Ἰησοῦς εἰς χωρίον λεγόμενον Γεθσημανί καὶ λέγει τοῖς μαθηταῖς, Καθίσατε αὐτοῦ ἕως οὗ ἀπελθὼν ἐκεῖ προσεύξωμαι). The historic presents here have been taken over from Mark, and Nolland comments, "Perhaps [Matthew] saw there the beginning of a pattern that he could develop: the historic presents could track the story in terms of the interchange between Jesus and the disciples, the aorists could track the story of Jesus alone and praying to God."[15]

The apostolic band crosses the Kidron Valley and ascends the western slope of the mountain to an olive grove ("Gethsemane" means "oil press," so this was an olive orchard possibly owned by a wealthy supporter who allowed Jesus to use it).[16] John 18:2 says that Judas knew the place "because Jesus had often met there with his disciples." So it was a common hideaway for Jesus and his followers, perhaps for R and R away from people. Luke 21:37 says that Jesus and the others spent the nights there during Passion Week (probably along with Bethany, see on Matt 21:17).

Jesus asks eight of the eleven (Judas has already departed on his nefarious task) to sit at the entrance to the grove while he goes into the garden. The wording here may be "a subtle allusion to Gen 22:5, where Abraham instructs his servants to stay back while he and Isaac go a distance away to pray."[17] Jesus becomes the embodiment of Abraham's faith and Isaac's sacrifice.

26:37 And he took Peter and the two sons of Zebedee and began to be sorrowful and distressed (καὶ παραλαβὼν τὸν Πέτρον καὶ τοὺς δύο υἱοὺς Ζεβεδαίου ἤρξατο λυπεῖσθαι καὶ ἀδημονεῖν). Jesus takes the inner circle (see 17:1; Peter with James and John, the "sons of Zebedee," cf. 4:21; 10:2, 20:20) with him into the olive grove. It is likely that Peter is the only disciple named because he is central in this part of the narrative.

We now see the depth of Jesus' emotions that he has kept under control until now. He knows this is his destiny and he has come for this purpose. But as the God-man, he still feels human emotions,

13. Hagner, *Matthew 14 – 28*, 777.

14. For this use of a circumstantial participle (here and vv. 37, 39, 42, 50) see on 2:4, 4:20.

15. Nolland, *Matthew*, 1095, following S. L. Black, "The Historic Present in Matthew: Beyond Speech Margins," in *Discourse Analysis and the New Testament: Approaches and Results* (ed. S. E. Porter and J. T. Reed; JSNTSup 170; Sheffield: Sheffield Academic, 1999), 135 – 39.

16. So Carson, *John*, 576.

17. Senior, *Matthew*, 303.

and now dread overwhelms him.[18] As many have noted, the anguish is not due so much to his approaching death as to the fact that he will bear the sins of all humanity and thereby be separated from God.[19] The two infinitives show the horror he feels, with "to be sorrowful" (λυπεῖσθαι) pointing to sorrow and grief (see also 17:23; 26:22) and "[to be] distressed" (ἀδημονεῖν) pointing to his deep distress (only here in Matthew).

26:38 Then he told them, "My soul is filled with sorrow to the point of death. Stay here and watch with me" (τότε λέγει αὐτοῖς, Περίλυπός ἐστιν ἡ ψυχή μου ἕως θανάτου· μείνατε ὧδε καὶ γρηγορεῖτε μετ' ἐμοῦ). "Filled with sorrow" (περίλυπος) intensifies the "to be sorrowful" (λυπεῖσθαι) from v. 37 (note perfective περί). Jesus becomes "the righteous sufferer of the psalms" (Witherington) and alludes to the repeated refrain in Ps 42:5, 11; 43:5, "Why, my soul, are you downcast?" with the language the same in the LXX. Both are lament psalms reflecting trust in "God my rock" (42:9) and "God my stronghold" (43:2) in times of great affliction.

Yet Jesus intensifies the psalmist's distress, as he feels this "to the point of death," meaning not "I would rather die than feel this way" but rather as a sign of the great intensity of the grief ("it feels as if I am dying"). In the midst of this he needs friends to be with him, so he asks the three to "remain" with him through the ordeal. "Watch" (γρηγορέω) was used in 24:42 – 43; 25:13 of spiritual vigilance in the light of the imminent parousia; here it means persevering prayer (perhaps also an echo of the Passover "vigil" of Exod 12:42). Jesus is not asking his disciples to protect him from intruders but to bear with him in prayer as he pours out his anguish to his Father.

26:39 And going ahead[20] a short distance, he fell on his face, praying, "My Father, if it is possible, may this cup pass from me. Yet not as I will, but as you will" (καὶ προελθὼν μικρὸν ἔπεσεν ἐπὶ πρόσωπον αὐτοῦ προσευχόμενος καὶ λέγων, Πάτερ μου, εἰ δυνατόν ἐστιν, παρελθάτω ἀπ' ἐμοῦ τὸ ποτήριον τοῦτο· πλὴν οὐχ ὡς ἐγὼ θέλω ἀλλ' ὡς σύ). Removing himself from the three disciples a "short distance" (μικρόν), Jesus goes to be alone with his Father. His prayer shows the depth of his relationship with God. "My Father" (πάτερ μου) is found often in Matthew (7:21; 11:25 – 27; 12:50; 16:17; 25:34) as a title of intimacy (Mark 14:36 has "Abba [see on 6:9], Father" to stress this).[21] The use of εἰ (condition of fact) for "if possible" stresses the fact that God could do so, but the end of the prayer shows it is not his will.

"Cup" (ποτήριον), as in 20:22 – 23, is the cup of suffering due to God's wrath (e.g., Ps 75:8; Isa 51:17, 22; Jer 51:7), further evidence that Jesus is conscious of the vicarious nature of his death. Jesus' deep personal desire is for God to take away the necessity of this vicarious sacrifice. However, his greater desire is to see God's will accomplished, and this is where Jesus' victory over himself occurs.[22] Jesus is aware of the significance of his death for God's plan of salvation and for the

18. Brown, *Death*, 234, affirms the historicity of the scene: "*That, in the last days of his life in Jerusalem as the leaders of his people showed unremitting hostility … Jesus would have struggled in prayer with God about how his death fitted into the inbreaking of God's kingdom is, in my judgment, so extremely plausible as to warrant certainty*" (italics his).

19. See C. J. Armbruster, "The Messianic Significance of the Agony in the Garden," *Scr* 16 (1964): 111 – 19 as well as Gundry, Hagner, Morris, Blomberg, Keener, Hauerwas; contra Hill.

20. Several manuscripts (p^{53} A C D L W TR et al.) have προσελθών, "going to," while the reading chosen here is supported by $p^{37,45}$ B lat et al. The latter makes more sense in the context. The former may have been a simple copying error.

21. France, *Gospel of Matthew*, says this "further emphasizes that it is the relationship between Father and Son which is being tested and reaffirmed."

22. Of course, this does not mean there was a moment when Jesus placed himself above God's will. That is seen in

salvation of humankind, so he surrenders himself to the greater will of the Father.

26:40 And he came to the disciples and found them sleeping. Then he said to Peter, "So aren't you strong enough to keep watch with me for one hour?" (καὶ ἔρχεται πρὸς τοὺς μαθητὰς καὶ εὑρίσκει αὐτοὺς καθεύδοντας, καὶ λέγει τῷ Πέτρῳ, Οὕτως οὐκ ἰσχύσατε μίαν ὥραν γρηγορῆσαι μετ᾽ ἐμοῦ;). Jesus had asked the disciples to maintain prayer "vigilance" with him, but when he returns he finds the opposite. Many who are poor sleepers like me will be jealous at their ability to fall asleep in any and all situations, but needless to say, this was a horrible time to fall asleep! If temple guards fell asleep on duty, they were sent home naked and in disgrace. We should not go too far and call the disciples remorseless in their lack of concern for Jesus (as some do), but clearly Jesus views them as spiritually weak ("Aren't you strong enough?"). While "one hour" need not be taken literally,[23] it is also certain that Jesus poured out his soul to his Father for a long period. The prayer of v. 39 is probably a summary of all Jesus said in his time of prayer.

26:41 "Keep watching and praying so that you do not enter into temptation" (γρηγορεῖτε καὶ προσεύχεσθε, ἵνα μὴ εἰσέλθητε εἰς πειρασμόν). Bruner translates this, "Keep alert and be saying your prayers so that you will not go headlong into temptation."[24] The present tense imperatives stress ongoing vigilance and prayer. It is difficult to know whether these two verbs should be interpreted as separate acts ("vigilance and prayer") or the same act ("vigilance in prayer"). The use of "watching" (γρηγορέω) in vv. 38, 40 might prefer the latter; but this is a new idea dealing with their future "temptation" and "testing" (both ideas present in πειρασμός, see on 4:1; 6:13),[25] so Jesus means spiritual vigilance in general and prayer in particular (the second is part of the first).

As the similar phrase in 6:13, μὴ εἰσενέγκῃς ... εἰς means "lest you yield, succumb to" temptation. Jesus has already prophesied that his disciples will flunk their first test at the arrest, but he does not want them to make such failure a regular practice. Calvin says, "A sure remedy is set before us, which is not far to seek, nor sought in vain. Christ promises that [people] earnest in prayer, who can fully put away the idleness of their flesh, will be victorious."[26]

26:41 "The spirit is willing but the flesh is weak" (τὸ μὲν πνεῦμα πρόθυμον ἡ δὲ σὰρξ ἀσθενής). This famous saying is clear in its meaning. The disciples want to obey Jesus and do what is right in the depths of their spirit, but their external flesh lacks the strength (note the "not strong"/"weak" development from v. 40 to v. 41). This and John 6:63 are the only instances of spirit vs. flesh dichotomy in the gospels, but it is developed further in Paul, who uses "spirit" (πνεῦμα) for the Holy Spirit in Rom 8, thereby contrasting life in the Spirit with life in one's own strength. Brown proceeds from the OT and intertestamental perspective in which spirit and flesh referred to the

---

the temptation narrative of 4:1 – 11. This is the old issue of "able not to sin"/"not able to sin" so often linked to Heb 4:15, and that is itself linked to discussions regarding the relationship of Jesus' human nature to his divine nature. Scripture never answers that question finally, but in the temptation narrative and here it seems the temptations are real, and I prefer "able not to sin." Jesus' "not my will" must be taken seriously.

23. However, Turner, "Matthew," 342, notes the possibility that "one hour" designates the amount of time Jesus had been in prayer (and the disciples had been asleep).

24. Bruner, *Matthew 13 – 28*, 657.

25. Some (e.g., Senior, Hagner, Davies and Allison) take this word to denote the final eschatological trial at the end of history. However, this is not likely in a context that centers on the present situation in Gethsemane.

26. Calvin, *Matthew*, 3:153, in Bruner, *Matthew 13 – 28*, 658.

"whole human being considered under two different aspects." πνεῦμα, then, is "the human spirit through which people can be moved to do what is harmonious with God's plan."

"Flesh" (σάρξ) is not satanic powers (as at Qumran) but represents "people in their tangible, perishable, and earthly aspect," yet still "the means through which Satan moves to distract people from God's plan; it represents the vulnerability of the human being."[27] Finally, πρόθυμον means to be "ready, eager, or desirous" to do something. It connotes goodwill and the willingness to do what God wants. So Jesus is saying that the disciples desire to stay awake and do what he is asking but lack the personal strength to do so.

26:42 He went away again a second time and prayed, saying, "My Father, if it is not possible for this to pass away unless I drink it, may your will be done" (πάλιν ἐκ δευτέρου ἀπελθὼν προσηύξατο λέγων, Πάτερ μου, εἰ οὐ δύναται τοῦτο παρελθεῖν ἐὰν μὴ αὐτὸ πίω, γενηθήτω τὸ θέλημά σου). In Jesus' second session with the Father, he restates his earlier prayer but with a significant shift. He has come to grips with his Father's will, so now instead of the positive "if it is possible," he states it negatively, "if it is not possible," and recognizes the fact that he must "drink" the cup of suffering. So his only request is "your will be done" (cf. 6:10b). He has overcome his own "flesh," and his "spirit" is not only "willing" but focused on his divinely mandated destiny. He will "drink" the cup and see his Father's "will" accomplished.

26:43 And when he went back,[28] he found them sleeping again, for their eyes had become heavy (καὶ ἐλθὼν πάλιν εὗρεν αὐτοὺς καθεύδοντας, ἦσαν γὰρ αὐτῶν οἱ ὀφθαλμοὶ βεβαρημένοι). For the disciples it is "business as usual." Their "flesh" has taken over, and their "spirit" was willing but unable to triumph (the opposite of Jesus). Matthew omits Mark 14:40b, "they did not know what to say to him." The perfect periphrastic "had become heavy" (ἦσαν βεβαρημένοι) provides a dramatic touch, what BDF (§352) calls "a rhetorically more forceful expression." Apparently Jesus woke them up this second time as well. Luke 22:45 explains why they had fallen asleep: they were "exhausted from sorrow." Apparently they began to realize the import of what Jesus had been telling them and are filled with grief at the prospect of his death. They probably wept and then fell asleep with exhaustion.

26:44 Again he left them, went away, and prayed a third time, once more saying the same prayer (καὶ ἀφεὶς αὐτοὺς πάλιν ἀπελθὼν προσηύξατο ἐκ τρίτου τὸν αὐτὸν λόγον εἰπὼν πάλιν). Verse 44 (like v. 43) contains "again" (πάλιν), showing that on the third occasion, Jesus repeats what he had done the first two times, withdrawing[29] a short distance from the disciples and focusing on communicating with his Father. In the ancient world, doing something a second time (e.g., John's double "amen" structure for Jesus' teaching, cf. John 5:19, 24, 25; 6:26; et al.) emphasizes it greatly, while a third time makes it superlative or ultimate (e.g., "holy, holy, holy" in Isa 6:3 and Rev 4:8 means ultimate holiness, and "666" in Rev 13:18 means ultimate finiteness or sinfulness). So Jesus becomes the ultimate model of intense, persevering prayer.[30]

27. Brown, *Death*, 198 – 99.

28. Here "went back" (ἐλθών) is a temporal participle (cf. vv. 37, 39, 42).

29. As some (e.g., Hagner) have said, "he went away" (ἀφείς) seems redundant and could mean Jesus "allowed" the disciples to sleep in keeping with v. 45, "Are you still sleeping?" This is possible, but it seems more likely that this parallels v. 42, "he went away again a second time." Moreover, in Mark Jesus wakes them up.

30. So Luz, *Matthew 21 – 28*, 397 – 98. Davies and Allison,

26:45 Then he came to the disciples and told them, "Are you still sleeping and resting?" (τότε ἔρχεται πρὸς τοὺς μαθητὰς καὶ λέγει αὐτοῖς, Καθεύδετε τὸ λοιπὸν καὶ ἀναπαύεσθε;). Jesus statement can be taken as a question ("Are you still sleeping?" so NASB, NRSV, TNIV, France, Gundry, Nolland), as a basic statement ("You are still asleep," so NJB, Beare), or as an ironic, perhaps even sarcastic imperative ("Go ahead and sleep!" so KJV, NLT, McNeile, Carson, Hagner, Morris). It is a difficult decision, for all three fit the situation. Two points favor taking it as a question — the use of a question in v. 40, and Jesus' "Get up" in the next verse, which would not be in keeping with the command to stay asleep. The disappointment and rebuke are obvious.

26:45 "Look, the hour is approaching, and the Son of Man is going to be betrayed into the hands of sinners" (ἰδοὺ ἤγγικεν ἡ ὥρα καὶ ὁ υἱὸς τοῦ ἀνθρώπου παραδίδοται εἰς χεῖρας ἁμαρτωλῶν). For Jesus the hour of the passion has arrived, and it begins at this point. For "is approaching" (ἤγγικεν) see on 3:2 (cf. 4:17; 10:7), where it means "come near and in process of arriving." "The hour" (ἡ ὥρα) has a thrust similar to John (see on v. 18) as the "hour" of destiny; that hour has begun, and Jesus is soon to become the atoning sacrifice for humankind. The betrayal of the Son of Man has already been predicted several times (17:12, 22; 20:18; 26:2, 24), and its fulfillment is soon to come to pass. It is hard to know whether the implied subject of "betrayed" is God (cf. 17:22) or Judas (as will occur in the next scene). In this context, Judas the betrayer is probably meant. Now "the human hands" of 17:22 and "the chief priests and teachers of law" of 20:18 are further identified as "the hands of sinners."

26:46 "Get up, let's go! My betrayer is near" (ἐγείρεσθε, ἄγωμεν· ἰδοὺ ἤγγικεν ὁ παραδιδούς με). The emphatic present tense commands "get up" (ἐγείρεσθε) and "let's go" (ἄγωμεν) place this in the foreground of the action. The time for sleep is over. The time has come for Jesus to meet his destiny, so he rouses the three (and possibly the others as well at the entrance to the olive grove) and sets off for the decisive moment in human history, what Cullmann has called "the mid-point of time." The betrayer "has come," and there is no more time for rest or prayer, only for action.

27:47 And while he was still speaking, look, Judas, one of the Twelve, arrived. With him came a large crowd from the chief priests and elders of the people with swords and clubs (Καὶ ἔτι αὐτοῦ λαλοῦντος ἰδοὺ Ἰούδας εἷς τῶν δώδεκα ἦλθεν καὶ μετ' αὐτοῦ ὄχλος πολὺς μετὰ μαχαιρῶν καὶ ξύλων ἀπὸ τῶν ἀρχιερέων καὶ πρεσβυτέρων τοῦ λαοῦ). The arrest scene is closely linked with Gethsemane via the typical Matthean genitive absolute "while he was still speaking." Jesus' supernatural awareness of v. 46[31] is already coming to pass. The contingent "from the chief priests and elders" means an official act of the Sanhedrin (see on 21:23), and the "large crowd" probably consisted mainly of the temple guards along with the auxiliary police sent to arrest Jesus.[32] John 18:3, 12 tells us that a company of Roman soldiers accompanied them, undoubtedly to make certain that no riot broke out. This could mean that Pilate was aware of the plot and the arrests and would explain why

Matthew, 3:500, give examples of thrice-repeated prayers expressing "earnestness": 2 Kgs 1:9 – 15; Ps 55:17; Dan 6:10; 2 Cor 12:8; *Did.* 10:6, *b. Yoma 87a*.

31. He could have been the only one who heard them approaching, but that is not the atmosphere (see also v. 18), and either way he knew it was Judas leading the crowd to him.

32. Keener, *Matthew*, 640, says, "Jewish soldiers did use swords (*m. Šabb.* 6:4), and the high priest's servants were notorious for their use of clubs in the temple, as was the use of clubs in quieting unrest." This shows the guards did not know Jesus, for they are treating them as common criminals and seem to expect armed resistance (see Jesus' point in v. 55).

his wife had her dream of 27:19 (so Carson). The arrival of Judas causes many to wonder how he could have known since he apparently left much earlier before Jesus took them to the olive grove. Yet Judas would have known since the apostolic band had been spending the nights on the Mount of Olives (see on v. 36).

26:48 His betrayer had given them a sign, saying, "The one I kiss is the man. Seize him!" (ὁ δὲ παραδιδοὺς αὐτὸν ἔδωκεν αὐτοῖς σημεῖον λέγων, Ὃν ἂν φιλήσω αὐτός ἐστιν· κρατήσατε αὐτόν). Since Jesus was being arrested in a private place after dark, the authorities did not want to take a chance of arresting the wrong man. They had paid Judas to identify him so as to cause the least amount of fuss possible. Police today use informers for the same reason. This also shows that they never had any intention of arresting the disciples with Jesus; if that were the case, they would not have needed Judas to identify Jesus. The flight of the disciples will be due to a sad misunderstanding. In their desire to arrest Jesus by stealth (26:4), we can picture the police holding their swords and clubs at their sides under their cloaks so as not to attract the curious to follow them.

In a monumental and tragic irony, Judas chose the kiss of greeting, of affection (φιλέω), and of reconciliation[33] to identify Jesus, thereby making "the kiss of betrayal" a universal symbol. The kiss could be on the mouth, the cheek, the hands, or even the feet; we do not know what Judas chose. Judas and the police may have thought this would seem a normal greeting and keep Jesus and the others from running in fright, but it is hard to see how Jesus and his disciples would fail to be aware of the large crowd close behind Judas (so Nolland).

26:49 And immediately when he came to Jesus, he said, "Greetings, Rabbi!" and kissed him (καὶ εὐθέως προσελθὼν τῷ Ἰησοῦ εἶπεν, Χαῖρε, ῥαββί, καὶ κατεφίλησεν αὐτόν). The only two times in Matthew "Rabbi" (ῥαββί) is used to address Jesus are on the lips of Judas (26:25, 49) in contrast to the disciples' "Lord"; it suggests proof of disbelief. This could also have been part of the signal to identify Jesus for the police. The switch here to the intensive "kiss" (καταφιλέω, "kiss" [φιλέω] in v. 48) is likely more than stylistic and either denotes a prolonged kiss to stress deep affection, to identify Jesus more certainly, or perhaps to show how heinous the act was (see McNeile, Davies and Allison, Nolland).

26:50 But Jesus said to him, "Friend, I know why you have come" (ὁ δὲ Ἰησοῦς εἶπεν αὐτῷ, Ἑταῖρε, ἐφ' ὃ πάρει). ἑταῖρε is found also in 20:13; 22:12 and means "friend, companion, comrade." Even knowing that Judas was there to "hand him over" to his enemies, Jesus still shows acceptance and love for the man.[34] ἐφ' ὃ πάρει can be translated as a question ("Why have you come?" so KJV, Davies and Allison), a statement ("[I know] why you have come," so Senior, Morris, Luz, Nolland), or an implicit command ("[do] what you have come for," so TNIV, NLT, NRSV, NASB, Hill, Hagner). The question is unlikely because Jesus does indeed know why Judas is there. Of the other two the statement causes the fewest difficulties. As Senior says, Matthew employs Judas for christological purposes, and so this should emphasize Jesus' knowledge of Judas' mission and purpose.[35]

33. France, *Matthew*, 375, says it was not regular for disciples to kiss their rabbi (indeed there is no instance of such in the gospels), and it was "a mark of special honor." This makes Judas' choice especially heinous.

34. Some (Gundry, France, Blomberg, Turner [="acquaintance"]) consider it a negative or distancing term, but that is to read too much into it. Brown, *Death*, 256 – 57, is closer when he sees it as ironic in the sense that one who has been his "companion" has turned and become his enemy. As Bruner, *Matthew 13 – 28*, 669, says, "he uses a word of friendship in an hour of betrayal."

35. Senior, *Passion Narrative*, 127.

26:50 Then they came forward, placed their hands on Jesus, and arrested him (τότε προσελθόντες ἐπέβαλον τὰς χεῖρας ἐπὶ τὸν Ἰησοῦν καὶ ἐκράτησαν αὐτόν). The arrest is quick and final. The police step forward and take Jesus into custody. To "lay hands on a person" often connotes physical harm (Gen 22:12; 2 Sam 18:12) and here has a hostile intent behind it (so Brown).

26:51 And look, one of those with Jesus stretched out his hand and drew his sword. Striking the slave of the high priest, he cut off his ear (καὶ ἰδοὺ εἷς τῶν μετὰ Ἰησοῦ ἐκτείνας τὴν χεῖρα ἀπέσπασεν τὴν μάχαιραν αὐτοῦ καὶ πατάξας τὸν δοῦλον τοῦ ἀρχιερέως ἀφεῖλεν αὐτοῦ τὸ ὠτίον). The arrest seemingly has gone well for a short while; then the unthinkable happens, the very thing that led the police to bring swords and clubs. Gundry says that the deliberate placement of "look" (ἰδού) before vv. 47, 51 links the actions of the betrayer and "the violent disciple," showing "that violent response to persecution is no better than betraying others to persecution (cf. 5:5, 38 – 48)."[36]

One of Jesus' disciples (John 18:10 says it was Peter) offers resistance by drawing his sword. Matthew tells the story dramatically, picturing the man reaching for his sword and then drawing it out and striking (probably) at the one nearest him. Brown discusses the precedent for carrying a sword, noting that people from Galilee were used to wearing swords for self-defense, and that during a major festival and with all the pilgrims around, it would be thought prudent.[37] Moreover, Luke 22:36 tells that at the Last Supper Jesus said, "If you don't have a sword, sell your cloak and buy one" (and in v. 38 the disciples respond that they have two swords with them). Peter undoubtedly carries one of them.

But this does not mean it was zealot activity, as some have surmised (v. 52 is anti-zealot).[38] My own conjecture is that Peter was thinking of Jesus as the conquering Messiah and believed that when he swung the sword, the twelve legions of angels (which Jesus will shortly mention, v. 53) were going to appear and inaugurate the final battle. The high priest's "slave" (named "Malchus" in John 18:10) may have been his personal representative to see that Caiaphas's wishes were carried out and as such could have been "the leader of the mob" (Davies and Allison). He could also have been one of the military police (called "slave" [δοῦλοι] at that time). Matthew leaves out the healing scene (added by Luke), probably to stress the contrast between human efforts and God's sovereign will.

26:52 Then Jesus told him, "Put your sword back in its place" (τότε λέγει αὐτῷ ὁ Ἰησοῦς, Ἀπόστρεψον τὴν μάχαιράν σου εἰς τὸν τόπον αὐτῆς). The next three verses are unique to Matthew, though John 18:11 somewhat parallels this verse.[39] Note that there is no immediate arrest of Peter, further proof

36. Gundry, *Matthew*, 538.

37. Brown, *Death*, 268 – 69.

38. Nor was the purpose to maim or disfigure in some way (and so render unclean) as some have said, e.g., Benedict T. Viviano, "The High Priest's Servant's Ear," *RB* 96 (1989): 71 – 80, who says the purpose was to disqualify this servant from functioning ritually in his priestly service. There is no hint that there was a deliberate thrust to cut off the man's ear. Instead, the emphasis was defensive, the attempt to protect Jesus from arrest. In that sense the sword thrust fortunately missed and did not kill the man.

39. See Carson, "Matthew," 547, for the authenticity of the passage. Brown, *Death*, 270 – 72, 275, accepts the basic veracity of the story even though he has doubts about details such as the naming of the perpetrators. But that is really a "development" of the legend or redactional choices, as Brown admits. John simply prefers "person-to-person" encounters" (272). He believes Jesus' response comes from Christian tradition, not from Matthew's own hand (contra Senior, *Passion Narrative*, 132, who believes Jesus made a statement but that Matthew's rendition stems from his own gospel material). Yet the command to return the sword in v. 52 is found in John 18:11 as well and should be considered authentic on the basis of the criterion of multiple attestation. See Brown's response to Senior in *Death*, 275 – 76.

that the disciples are in no real danger and do not have to flee. Still, Jesus acts immediately before the disciples' second sword is drawn and before the group of police retaliate against Peter (Rome was notorious for cutting down any resistance and the temple guards for clubbing down any disturbance). Jesus addresses his remark to Peter (singular σου), but probably his gaze sweeps the crowd applying it to everyone. In one sentence he has defused a dangerous situation, and again he takes control even of the temple police.

26:52 "... for all who take the sword will perish by the sword" (πάντες γὰρ οἱ λαβόντες μάχαιραν ἐν μαχαίρῃ ἀπολοῦνται). Keener says there are three reasons here against violence: it "destroys those who employ it (52); Jesus trusts the Father's ability to protect him (53); and Jesus recognizes that his Father's will for him includes suffering (54)."[40] This proverbial and poetic (note the chiasm in the Greek order) saying has long been construed as a call to pacifism (see Turner), and in this context that has some validity. Jesus is saying that all such violence has its inevitable return.

The OT has several such passages (Gen 4:14; 9:6; Exod 21:12; Prov 22:8; Eccl 10:8; Isa 50:11; Hos 10:13), as does the NT (Rev 13:9 – 10); Matthew has similar material as well (5:39; 10:39). Gundry sees here an allusion to *Tg. Isa.* 50:11, "Whoever sheds the blood of man, by man his blood will be shed."[41] Both in Judaism and in Jesus' teaching, violence was improper and dangerous, always bringing back on itself more violence.

26:53 "Or do you suppose that I cannot call upon my Father, and he will send me now more than twelve legions of angels?" (ἢ δοκεῖς ὅτι οὐ δύναμαι παρακαλέσαι τὸν πατέρα μου, καὶ παραστήσει μοι ἄρτι πλείω δώδεκα λεγιῶνας ἀγγέλων;). This is probably exactly what Peter was thinking when he drew his sword, though many think he was simply trying to protect Jesus. Yet Jesus rebukes him and tells him that his thinking is seriously wrong. If Jesus was inaugurating the final holy war against "sinners" (v. 45b), he didn't need Peter's help, for he had the hosts of heaven at his disposal (cf. John 12:27). If he wanted he could call a legion of angels for himself and each of his eleven followers, and even "more"!

This was an enormous army. A legion contained 6,000 soldiers, and in the first century the Roman army normally had twenty-five legions. So this was half the size Rome could muster, but "more than" (πλείω) should likely be taken to mean he had more angels at his disposal than all the armies of Rome. Angels often had a military function and fought on behalf of or at the side of human beings (Gen 32:1 – 2; 2 Kgs 6:15 – 17; Ps 34:7; Dan 10:13, 12:1; Jude 9; 2 Macc 3:22 – 23; 1QM 7:6; 12:8; 13:10; *2 Bar.* 63:5 – 7). But Jesus does not need them at this time, for his Father's will is that he face the cross and become the sacrifice for sins. The whole emphasis is on Jesus' sovereign control over the whole situation.

26:54 "How then could the Scriptures be fulfilled that it must happen in this way?" (πῶς οὖν πληρωθῶσιν αἱ γραφαὶ ὅτι οὕτως δεῖ γενέσθαι;). Not only is Jesus in charge, so is his Father, and these events are to fulfill Scripture. Matthew has especially been interested in this issue, with two such statements in this scene (this and v. 56) and with fourteen formula citations and several others like this one in his gospel (on the fulfillment passages, see 1:22 – 23).[42] The language of divine

40. Keener, *Matthew*, 644.

41. Gundry, *Use of the Old Testament*, 144, following Hans Kosmala, "Matthew 26.52 — A Quotation from the Targum," *NovT* 4 (1960): 3 – 5.

42. Senior, *Passion Narrative*, 143, may be correct that Matthew has taken this from Mark 14:49, but that does not mean that he failed to embrace it as his own theme.

necessity ("it must happen" [δεῖ γενέσθαι]) is found in the passion predictions (16:21) and related passages (17:10; 24:6) and governs all the passion events, with fulfillment passages frequently quoted. In this passage there is no specific OT text intended but all those related to the suffering Messiah (such as Ps 22; 69; Isa 52 – 53; Zech 13:7).

26:55 At that time Jesus told the crowds, "Am I an armed bandit, that you have come out with swords and clubs to arrest me? (Ἐν ἐκείνῃ τῇ ὥρᾳ εἶπεν ὁ Ἰησοῦς τοῖς ὄχλοις, Ὡς ἐπὶ λῃστὴν ἐξήλθατε μετὰ μαχαιρῶν καὶ ξύλων συλλαβεῖν με;). Jesus now turns from Peter to address the crowd assembled to arrest him, though everything said in vv. 52 – 54 is also meant for them. "At that time" is what he has been addressing since the Last Supper, namely, the time of his passion. They know he is no "armed insurrectionist"[43] (λῃστής, like Barabbas and his companions later); yet by bringing a mob of temple guards and police armed with swords and clubs (v. 47), they are treating him as such.

26:55 "I was sitting daily in the temple teaching, and you did not arrest me" (καθ' ἡμέραν ἐν τῷ ἱερῷ ἐκαθεζόμην διδάσκων καὶ οὐκ ἐκρατήσατέ με). During the preceding week Jesus sat teaching (with the imperfect "sitting" [ἐκαθεζόμην] emphasizing the lengthy time he was there) in the temple[44] (see esp. the controversy episodes of 21:23 – 22:46 and the woes on the leaders in ch. 23). In 21:45 – 46; 26:4 we heard that the authorities wanted to arrest Jesus but were afraid of his popularity with the people and so looked for a way to arrest him privately. But they were not planning on seizing him because he was a dangerous cutthroat but because they believed he was a false Messiah.

26:56 "But this whole thing has happened so that the writings of the prophets might be fulfilled" (τοῦτο δὲ ὅλον γέγονεν ἵνα πληρωθῶσιν αἱ γραφαὶ τῶν προφητῶν). This is the second fulfillment passage in three verses. "This whole thing" (τοῦτο δὲ ὅλον) might refer to Jesus' "whole" understanding to this point (so Hagner) or to the events of the arrest as a whole (Carson, Brown), or it could be an editorial comment of Matthew related to the events of ch. 26 (Senior, Davies and Allison). The second is most likely, for in Mark 14:49b it is also clearly the words of Jesus. The "writings of the prophets" should not be restricted to the prophetic books. Probably Jesus regarded the entire OT as the result of prophetic inspiration.

26:56 Then all the disciples left him and fled (Τότε οἱ μαθηταὶ πάντες ἀφέντες αὐτὸν ἔφυγον). Matthew likely intends his particular scene as a "fulfillment" of Jesus' prophecy in v. 31. In v. 35 they had vehemently promised that no matter what, they would never forsake Jesus. Now their true colors are revealed. Mark 14:51 – 52 adds the story of the young man (undoubtedly a follower) fleeing naked, showing the deep disgrace of the disciples. The "hour" has truly come and Jesus' growing isolation (from Gethsemane to now) is complete; he goes to face his destiny alone, yet in control.

43. Brown, *Death*, 686 – 88, has an excellent discussion, showing that in 30 AD they were not considered to be revolutionary fighters like Che Guevara, but were considered "violent, armed men ... bands of marauders and robbers in the countryside, and troublemakers in the cities who fomented riots" (687).

44. Hill, *Matthew*, 343, believes this indicates a long period of time and dates the entry to Jerusalem at the time of the Feast of Tabernacles (Jesus had then been in Jerusalem several months). This is unnecessary, and a reference to his teaching that week is more than sufficient to fit his language here.

Theology in Application

The primary emphasis here is Jesus and the control of these events by him and his Father. This is the time of destiny, but Jesus must go it alone. His disciples fail him at this most critical moment of his life, and Jesus is aware that even his Father will have to turn away as he vicariously takes on himself the sins of humankind and becomes the atoning sacrifice. Like the scapegoat on the Day of Atonement, Jesus will have to go to his destiny alone. This is when he wins the victory over himself and becomes "Lord" over his enemies and his failing disciples.

1. Fulfillment of Prophecy

Each aspect in this story transpires as a fulfillment of prophecy. God has prepared for these negative events from before the foundation of the world, and they take place under his sovereign eye as part of salvation history. There is a divine necessity behind them — all "must happen" to fulfill Scripture, even the falling away of the disciples (v. 31) and the seizure of Jesus by his enemies (vv. 54, 56).

2. Dealing with Failure

We will never be perfect before Christ returns, and we will pass through dark days just as Peter and the others did. Yet Jesus wants to meet us in our "Galilee" and give us the strength to overcome our times of defeat. Victory in the Christian life comes about as we yield to the Spirit (Rom 8) and find the strength in Christ to apply God's enabling power (1 Pet 1:5) to meet the difficulties we encounter (Rom 8:37 – 39). In Heb 2:17 – 18 the author says that Jesus "had to be made like his brothers and sisters in every way" so that through his suffering "when he was tempted" he might "help those who are being tempted." There is nothing we go through that Christ has not only gone through but promises to lead us through it as well.

3. Praying in the Midst of Trials

We should learn to pray in the midst of trials as Jesus did. Jesus asks God to "remove" his cup of suffering, and it is not wrong to desire that God will refrain from taking us through certain trials and afflictions. Yet also Jesus surrenders himself to his Father's will (vv. 39, 42) even though he knows that will mean his life. That level of faith is the model for each of us. None of us will have to go through what Jesus did, yet we can entrust ourselves to God's sovereign will in the same way as Jesus did.

The key to victorious prayer is "not as I will, but as you will." We must maintain spiritual vigilance and remain alert lest we "enter into temptation" (v. 41). We have all felt a sadness so deep we felt we were going to die (v. 38) and asked close friends to stand by us in our time of need. Many of us have also, like Jesus, been failed by those friends. Yet he models for us a God-centered trust that can help us to rise above our problems ("on wings like eagles," Isa 40:31) and the failures of our friends.

4. Violence

We should not greet opposition and persecution with a violent response. Jesus could not have been more clear in vv. 52 – 54. There is no place for violence in Christian mission. Revelation 13:10 states this perfectly, "If anyone is to go into captivity, into captivity they will go. If anyone is to be killed with the sword, with the sword they will be killed. This calls for patient endurance and faithfulness on the part of God's people." In Rev 11:3 – 7a, the two witnesses, symbolizing the church, react to the hatred of the evil empire not with violence but with bold witness.[45] Throughout the history of the church, the reaction of the beleaguered saints with love instead of hatred has been a major reason for evangelistic revivals, as stated in 1 Pet 2:12, "Live such good lives among the pagans that, though they accuse you of doing wrong, they may see your good deeds and glorify God on the day he visits us."

45. See Osborne, *Revelation*, 417 – 18, 422. I believe they are two individuals who will appear at the end of history and lead the church in bold "testimony" (v. 7) during that final period. As such they also symbolize the church in its reaction to the evil empire at the end of history (and during history as well, as exemplified today in the church in China). The "fire coming from their mouths" in v. 5 is a symbol for their proclamation of rebuke and judgment during that time.

CHAPTER 116

Matthew 26:57 – 75

Literary Context

The events in the Passion Narrative are both chronological and logical. Jesus has been arrested in the area of Gethsemane, and it is natural that the first stage of the legal proceedings takes place next. The trial of Jesus is a two-stage affair (a Jewish trial, followed by a Roman trial, which makes sense in the political environment of the first century; see below). The three denials of Peter conclude the series of failures by Judas (vv. 14 – 16, 21 – 25), the Twelve (vv. 31, 56), and Peter (v. 34, here).

VII. The Passion and Resurrection of Jesus (26:1 – 28:20)
- **A. The Passion Narrative (26:1 – 27:61)**
  1. Preliminary Events (26:1 – 16)
  2. The Last Supper/Passover (26:17 – 30)
  3. Events in Gethsemane (26:31 – 56)
  4. **The Trials of Jesus and Peter's Denials (26:57 – 27:26)**
     - ➦ **a. The Sanhedrin Trial and Peter's Denials (26:57 – 75)**
     - b. The Trial before Pilate (27:1 – 26)

Main Idea

The main theme is not the contrived "trial" when the wicked authorities had already decided what they were going to do to Jesus (26:4 – 5, 14 – 15) but rather the revelation of the Christ they had rejected — he is the Messiah and Son of God (v. 63) and at the same time the Son of Man at the right hand of God in fulfillment of Ps 110:1 (v. 64a) and the eschatological Judge (v. 64b). The secondary theme is indeed the leaders standing for the nation as they produce false witness and half-truths in condemning Jesus. The third theme is the failure of Peter, the only one to follow Jesus rather than run away but who in doing so fulfills Jesus' prediction (v. 34) by denying Jesus three times in contrast to his brave proclamation as to his true personhood (v. 64).

Translation

Matthew 26:57-75

57a	Scene #1 Action	So **they arrested Jesus and took him away to Caiaphas the high priest,**
b		where the teachers of law and the elders had gathered together.
58a	Action	But **Peter was following him at a distance so far as the courtyard of the high priest,**
b		and **he entered it and was sitting with the servants to see the outcome.**
59a	Action	And **the chief priests, indeed the whole Sanhedrin, were seeking false witness against Jesus**
b	Purpose of 59a	so they could have him put to death.
60a	Result #1 of 59a	And **they did not find any,**
b		though many false witnesses came forward.
c	Result #2 of 59a	But **later, two came forward and said,**
61a		*"This man said,*
b		*'I am able to destroy the temple of God and after three days to build it again.'"*
62a	Question	And **the high priest rose and said to him,**
b		*"Have you no answer at all for what these men are accusing you of saying?"*
63a	Response to 62a	But **Jesus was silent.**
b	Exhortation	And **the high priest said to him,**
c		*"I charge you by the living God*
d		*that you tell us whether you are the Messiah,*
e		*the Son of God."*
64a	Answer to 63b-e	**Jesus told him,**
b		*"It is as you say.*
c	Expansion of 64a	Nevertheless, *I am telling you, from now on you will see the Son of Man sitting at the right hand of power* and
d		*coming on the clouds of heaven."*

65a	Response to 64a-c/ Accusation	**Then the high priest ripped his garments, saying,**
b		*"He has blasphemed!*
c		*Why do we still need any more witnesses?*
d		*Look, you have heard the blasphemy just now.*
66a	Question	*What do you think?"*
b		And **they responded,**
c	Answer to 66a	*"He is guilty and should die."*
67a	Action	**Then they spit in his face, struck him, and slapped him, saying,**
68a	Taunt	*"Prophesy to us, Messiah.*
b		*Who is it who has hit you?"*
69a	Scene #2	Now **Peter was sitting outside in the courtyard.**
b		**A servant girl came to him and said,**
c	Accusation #1 (A)	*"You too were with Jesus of Galilee."*
70a		But **he denied it before them all, saying,**
b	Response to 69c (B)	*"I do not know what you are talking about."*
71a	Setting	And after he went out into the entranceway,
b		**another servant girl saw him and said to those there,**
c	Accusation #2 (A)	*"This man was with Jesus of Nazareth."*
72a		And **again he denied this with an oath,**
c	Response to 71c (B)	*"I do not know the man."*
73a		**A short time later those standing there came to Peter and said,**
b	Accusation #3 (A)	*"Truly you are one of them,*
c	Basis for 73b	*for your speech accent also makes your origins clear."*
74a		**Then he began to invoke a curse and to swear an oath,**
b	Response to 73b-c (B)	*"I do not know the man."*
c	Action	And **immediately the rooster crowed.**
75a	Result	And **Peter remembered the word Jesus had spoken:**
b		*"Before the rooster crows, you will deny me three times."*
c		And **he went outside and wept bitterly.**

Structure and Literary Form

As throughout this section, Matthew follows Mark on the Sanhedrin trial with minor changes, e.g., replacing Mark's "warmed himself at the fire" with "to see the outcome" in v. 58; adding "false" to the testimony the council sought in v. 59; removing "made with hands/not made with hands" from v. 61; adding "I charge you [under oath] by the living God, that you tell us whether" in v. 63; changing Jesus' answer to "It is as you say. Nevertheless, I am telling you, from now on" in v. 64; adding the high priest's statement, "He has blasphemed!" in v. 65; omitting "blindfolded" in v. 67; and adding "to us, Messiah" to "prophesy" in v. 68.

The story of Peter's denials is different, with all four gospels differing from one another. All four agree that the first questioner was a maid, but John has a group. Matthew and Mark have another maid in the second, while Luke says, "someone else," and John has a group of people. For the third, Mark and Matthew have bystanders, Luke "another" person, and John a relative of the man whose ear was cut off doing the questioning. How do we reconcile such seemingly disparate accounts? (1) John places a significant amount of time between the first (John 18:17) and the other two (18:25 – 27). And Luke 22:59 tells us that the third occurred "an hour" after the second. So the three denials were at different parts of the trial. (2) Peter was in a group of people, and the questions were probably coming from more than one person. So the evangelists were following different traditions about who asked the questions.[1]

The structure of this section has two major sections, the trial (vv. 57 – 68) and the three denials of Peter (vv. 69 – 75). As John shows, the two were intertwined (and the denials took place throughout the time of the trial), but Mark and Matthew relate the denials at the end of the trial for dramatic effect. The Sanhedrin trial has four parts: the setting in the courtyard of Caiaphas (vv. 57 – 58), the false witnesses (vv. 59 – 63a), the truth about who Jesus is (vv. 63b – 64), and the charge of blasphemy (vv. 65 – 68). The denials of Peter have four parts corresponding to the three denials (vv. 69 – 70, 71 – 72, 73 – 74) and Peter's remorse (v. 75).

Exegetical Outline

➦ **I. The Trial before the Sanhedrin (26:57 – 68)**

- A. The setting in the courtyard (vv. 57 – 58)
  1. Jesus led to Caiaphas (v. 57)
  2. Peter sitting in the courtyard (v. 58)
- B. The false witnesses gathered (vv. 59 – 63a)
  1. The fruitless search for false witnesses (vv. 59 – 60a)
  2. The evidence of two about destroying the temple (vv. 60b – 61)
  3. Jesus' refusal to respond to their charge (vv. 62 – 63a)
- C. The truth about Jesus (vv. 63b – 64)
  1. The high priest's question — are you the Messiah? (v. 63b)
  2. Jesus' response — I am the divine Son of Man (v. 64)
- D. The charge of blasphemy (vv. 65 – 68)
  1. The high priests' charge (vv. 65 – 66a)
  2. The decision of the Sanhedrin (v. 66b)
  3. The mocking of Jesus (vv. 67 – 68)

II. Peter's Three Denials (26:69 – 75)

- A. The denial before the servant girl (vv. 69 – 70)
  1. The girl's statement (v. 69)
  2. Peter's denial (v. 70)

1. See also Carson, "Matthew," 557 – 58; Morris, *Matthew*, 687.

B. The denial before another girl (vv. 71 – 72)
   1. The girl's statement (v. 71)
   2. Peter's denial (v. 72)

C. The denial before a group standing around (vv. 73 – 74)
   1. Their statement based on Peter's accent (v. 73)
   2. Peter's denial (v. 74)

D. Peter's remorse (v. 75)

The Historicity of the Sanhedrin Trial

Virtually everyone has noticed the discrepancies between the gospel accounts and the procedures found in the later Mishnah (*m. Sanh.* 4 – 7). Jesus' trial was held at night just eighteen hours before Passover began; it did not take place over two successive days but was concluded that night; it was held at the palace of the high priest rather than the temple courts; the proceedings did not seem to fit a formal trial, as it does not appear that all the council members were there and no witnesses spoke on behalf of Jesus; and there was no attempt to find out the truth, only to condemn Jesus, with false testimony admitted as evidence. For this reason several have concluded this was not a historical trial but a theological story intended to point to Jewish guilt.[2]

However, a great deal may be said in favor of the trustworthiness of the gospel accounts.[3]

1. Many mishnaic regulations were more theoretical and never regarded as mandatory laws.
2. The Mishnah represented a post – AD 70 situation, and we do not know how much actually represented the Second Temple period.
3. In times of emergency (e.g., the arrest of the dangerous Jesus the night before the Passover) there was precedent for bracketing laws for a critical situation.

2. See Hans Lietzmann, "Der Prozess Jesu," in *Kleine Schriften* (Berlin: Akademie-Verlag, 1958), 2:251 – 68; Hill, *Matthew*, 343 – 44; Paul Winter, *On the Trial of Jesus* (Berlin: de Gruyter, 1961), 44 – 50; Beare, *Matthew*, 519. Chaim Cohn, *The Trial and Death of Jesus* (New York: Harper & Row, 1971), 94 – 137, accepts many of the gospel details but reverses the gospels' basic tenor by saying the leaders sought to exonerate Jesus but were forced to condemn him on the basis of his messianic claims.

3. See A. N. Sherwin-White, "The Trial of Christ," *History and Chronology in the New Testament* (London: SPCK, 1965), 97 – 116; David Catchpole, "The Problem of the Historicity of the Sanhedrin Trial," in *The Trial of Jesus* (ed. E. Bammel; FS C. F. D. Moule; London: SCM, 1970), 47 – 65; Carson, "Matthew," 549 – 52; Brown, *Death*, 548 – 60; Hagner, *Matthew 14 – 28*, 796 – 97; Luz, *Matthew 21 – 28*, 438 – 46; Darrell L. Bock, *Blasphemy and Exaltation in Judaism and the Final Examination of Jesus* (Grand Rapids: Eerdmans, 2000), 184 – 95; Keener, *Matthew*, 644 – 46; France, *Gospel of Matthew*, 1017 – 21.

4. The mishnaic regulations were written in a Pharisaic setting, while the Sadducees controlled the situation here.
5. The gospels portray the leaders ignoring judicial procedure in their haste to prove Jesus guilty.
6. There is an immense amount of material held in common in the four gospels, and the primary difference is arrangement.
7. The whole scene in the four gospels might favor the view that this is an official but informal interrogation rather than a formal trial; it was legal but not an official trial. The leaders did not need to reach an official verdict but needed to find evidence they could use to convince Pilate to crucify Jesus. The Romans had taken the right of capital punishment from the Jews, so the only way to have Jesus executed was to take him to Pilate.

Still, the high priest persisted in leading the meeting to a conclusion of blasphemy, which would carry little weight with the Romans, so this may have been a capital trial (so Morris); we cannot know for certain. However, they had to be united and to present convincing evidence to get Pilate to condemn Jesus. In short, there is little reason to doubt the historicity of the Sanhedrin "trial" as related in the four gospels, and the differences between them stem from redactional choices rather than from the insertion of fictional material.

Explanation of the Text

26:57 So they arrested Jesus and took him away to Caiaphas the high priest, where the teachers of law and the elders had gathered together (Οἱ δὲ κρατήσαντες τὸν Ἰησοῦν ἀπήγαγον πρὸς Καϊάφαν τὸν ἀρχιερέα, ὅπου οἱ γραμματεῖς καὶ οἱ πρεσβύτεροι συνήχθησαν). It is clear that Caiaphas and leaders in the Sanhedrin had sent out the temple guards and police to arrest Jesus. When he was in custody, they delivered him directly to Caiaphas (on whom see 26:3). The scribes are mentioned here for the first time in the Passion Narrative (they last appeared in 23:34; for them see on 2:4), probably to add an aura of legal expertise to the proceedings. We cannot surmise anything from the fact that Matthew mentions neither the Pharisees nor the elders. His list is representative rather than exhaustive (Mark 14:53 mentions the elders, and 26:59 notes the presence of the chief priests there). We do not know where the Sanhedrin normally met (Josephus, *J.W.* 5:144, tells us there was a place but not where), but an informal hearing like this could easily be held at the high priest's residence.

26:58 But Peter was following him at a distance so far as the courtyard of the high priest, and he entered it and was sitting with the servants to see the outcome (ὁ δὲ Πέτρος ἠκολούθει αὐτῷ ἀπὸ μακρόθεν ἕως τῆς αὐλῆς τοῦ ἀρχιερέως καὶ εἰσελθὼν ἔσω ἐκάθητο μετὰ τῶν ὑπηρετῶν ἰδεῖν τὸ τέλος). In a prelude of the event in vv. 69 – 75, we are told that Peter had not fled far and then had followed (the imperfect "was following" [ἠκολούθει] stressing ongoing action)[4] the group taking Jesus "at a distance," i.e., close enough to see where they were going but not so close as to risk being arrested. John 18:15 – 16 tells us that John himself accompanied Peter and got him admitted to the courtyard "because [he] was known to the high priest" (possibly because as Jesus' cousin he had contacts among the priestly community through Zechariah).[5]

Peter's purpose was "to see the outcome," to find out what was going to happen to Jesus, and so he was sitting with "the servants," those who would question him in vv. 69 – 74. At this point he clearly intended to be with Jesus all the way, but his failure will precipitate his flight as well, and only the women are with Jesus at the end (27:55 – 56), though John was also at the cross (John 19:25 – 27). As Davies and Allison say, "The upshot is contrast between faithful Lord and unfaithful servant."[6]

26:59 And the chief priests, indeed the whole Sanhedrin, were seeking false witness against Jesus so they could have him put to death (οἱ δὲ ἀρχιερεῖς καὶ τὸ συνέδριον ὅλον ἐζήτουν ψευδομαρτυρίαν κατὰ τοῦ Ἰησοῦ ὅπως αὐτὸν θανατώσωσιν). The chief priests (the instigators of the plot, 26:14 – 15) were part of the Sanhedrin (i.e., the members now present), so "indeed" (καί) is epexegetical. It is possible that "the whole Sanhedrin" means a formal, official capital trial, but we cannot know for certain. Of the seventy members of the Sanhedrin (see on 5:22), twenty-three were required present for a capital trial (*m. Sanh.* 7:1). There may have been two, an unofficial interrogation here, and an official verdict later at dawn (27:1, with the two conflated in Luke 22:66 – 71).

Undoubtedly the Sanhedrin leaders had been "seeking" (ἐζήτουν, again the imperfect dramatizes the action as ongoing) for evidence since Judas had offered to hand Jesus over, but there had not been much time to gather witnesses, so they were willing to accept anyone. Moreover, they were not seeking truth but a guilty verdict, so such witnesses could not be anything but "false" (added here by Matthew for emphasis). There may be an echo of Ps 27:12, "false witnesses rise up against me" (cf. Prov 6:19, "a false witness who pours out lies"). Their purpose ("so" [ὅπως]) was to ensure that Jesus was "put to death" (cf. 12:14; 26:4).

26:60 And they did not find any, though many false witnesses came forward[7] (καὶ οὐχ εὗρον πολλῶν προσελθόντων ψευδομαρτύρων). Matthew presupposes Mark's explanatory comment, "but their statements did not agree" (Mark 14:55). The leaders had discovered many who were willing to testify but discovered that their statements contradicted each other. They were frustrated and stymied in their evil plans. The whole emphasis in Matthew is on the lies that were propounded. Obviously the chief priests were not telling people to lie, but they were also not looking for the truth. Keener brings out that the penalty for a false witness in a capital trial was execution (Deut 19:16 – 21), and Roman law did the same.[8] To an extent this was followed here, as the interrogation of witnesses produced contradictions, and the Sanhedrin refused to allow these testimonies. Still, they were only searching for evidence to condemn Jesus.

26:60b – 61 But later, two came forward and said, "This man said, 'I am able to destroy the temple

4. Those who see an aspect of discipleship in "was following" (ἠκολούθει) read too much into the term ("illegitimate totality transfer").

5. See Osborne, *John* (Cornerstone Biblical Commentary; Wheaton, IL: Tyndale, 2007), 257.

6. Davies and Allison, *Matthew*, 3:522.

7. "Came forward" (προσελθόντων) is a concessive participle in a genitive absolute construction that stresses the inability to find evidence "in spite of" the presence of false witness (see Wallace, 634).

8. Keener, *Matthew*, 647 – 48.

of God and after three days to build it again'" (ὕστερον δὲ προσελθόντες δύο εἶπαν, Οὗτος ἔφη, Δύναμαι καταλῦσαι τὸν ναὸν τοῦ θεοῦ καὶ διὰ τριῶν ἡμερῶν οἰκοδομῆσαι). The two (necessary in a court of law, cf. Num 35:30; Deut 17:6; 19:15) who finally come forward continue that false witness,[9] because we know what Jesus had originally said from John 2:19, "Destroy this temple, and I will raise it again in three days," and 2:21 tells us that by "temple" Jesus meant his body.[10] They take Jesus' metaphor literally but even more importantly change the second person imperative "(you) destroy" to a first person "I am able to destroy." So they and the leaders take this as intention to destroy a sacred place,[11] which everyone in the first century took to be a capital crime. The leaders hoped to impress Pilate with this charge, but they wanted more.

26:62 And the high priest rose[12] and said to him, "Have you no answer at all for what these men are accusing you of saying?" (καὶ ἀναστὰς ὁ ἀρχιερεὺς εἶπεν αὐτῷ, Οὐδὲν ἀποκρίνῃ τί οὗτοί σου καταμαρτυροῦσιν;). By law a prisoner was required to respond to the charges, so the high priest demands that Jesus do so. In addition, Caiaphas wants to hear Jesus utter these words himself so that all doubt will be removed. Speaking for the council, therefore, he demands that Jesus respond to the accusations.

26:63 But Jesus was silent (ὁ δὲ Ἰησοῦς ἐσιώπα). Hagner calls this "a sovereign silence," Brown sees this as "contempt for the hostile proceedings," and Nolland understands this as acceptance of the oppression and a refusal to fight back, echoing several psalms (Ps 38:13 – 15; 39:9).[13] A combination of the first and third (there are no hints of contempt) is best, along with an allusion to Isa 53:7, "He was oppressed and afflicted, yet he did not open his mouth." The imagery of Jesus as suffering Servant continues (see also 26:67).

26:63 And the high priest said to him, "I charge you by the living God" (καὶ ὁ ἀρχιερεὺς εἶπεν αὐτῷ, Ἐξορκίζω σε κατὰ τοῦ θεοῦ τοῦ ζῶντος). ἐξορκίζω is a legal term, to "cause someone to swear under oath." When the high priest adds "by the living God" he is making the most solemn charge possible,[14] with all the authority of his sacred office behind it. If a person is placed under

9. Contra Brown, *Death*, 435, who thinks the false witnesses end at v. 60a. However, Mark 14:57 says these men "gave this false testimony against them," and there is no reason to think Matthew disagrees with Mark just because he omits this. More likely, Matthew assumes that v. 60b continues 60a.

10. Many (Senior, Brown, Hagner, Luz, Nolland) take this as an actual statement of Jesus, an apocalyptic prophecy based on Matt 24:2 (cf. 12:6; 21:12 – 13; 23:38) that he "has the power to destroy the temple." But Jesus does not claim in 24:2 – 3 that *he* would destroy the temple, so this does not represent his actual "claim to power." Clearly the witnesses are twisting Jesus' teaching, perhaps by combining Jesus' two statements from John 2:19 and Matt 24:2. Davies and Allison take this as Jesus' original statement and interpret it as "I am able to lay down my life," a possible but unprovable theory. It is better to consider this either a garbled version due to poor memory (Blomberg) or a deliberately changed version to heighten Jesus' guilt (my view).

11. Brown, *Death*, 440 – 44, also discusses the second half of the statement, primarily in its Markan form, "In three days will build another, not made with hands" (14:58). He notes three options suggested for this new sanctuary: (1) the Christian community, the church, as the temple of God, exemplified at Qumran (1QS 9:6), but "not made with hands" is never used for this; (2) the heavenly sanctuary of Jewish apocalyptic, expected in *1 En.* 90:28 – 29; *4 Ezra* 10:54; Rev 21:10, but it is always God, not the Messiah, who does the building; (3) the resurrection of the glorified Christ, as in John 2:19, which best fits the NT data.

12. For this use of a circumstantial participle, see v. 37.

13. Hagner, *Matthew 14 – 28*, 799; Brown, *Death*, 464; Nolland, *Matthew*, 1129.

14. Some have seen the high priest as an exorcist due to similar language in exorcism passages like Mark 5:7; Acts 19:13. But as Gundry, *Matthew*, 544 says, this makes littler sense here.

oath by the divine name, one must respond (*m. Šeb.* 4:13, so Brown). He is demanding a response.

26:63 "... that you tell us whether you are the Messiah, the Son of God" (ἵνα ἡμῖν εἴπῃς εἰ σὺ εἶ ὁ Χριστὸς ὁ υἱὸς τοῦ θεοῦ). Jesus' messianic status was often discussed (e.g., 16:14; 21:9; John 4:29; 7:26, 31) and Jesus often commanded silence in light of this messianic expectation (the so-called "messianic secret," cf. 8:4; 9:30; 12:16; 17:9). The leaders had long concluded that he was a false messiah, and the words here recall 16:16 (cf. 14:33), where Peter confessed, "You are the Messiah, the Son of the living God." By "Son of God" the high priest was simply using another term for Messiah (in the OT the divine sonship of the Messiah is stated in 2 Sam 7:14; Ps 2:7; 89:26 – 27), but in Matthew Son of God goes beyond that (see 2:15; 3:17; 4:3, 6; 8:29; 14:33; 16:16; 17:5; 27:40, 43, 54).[15] Still, for the high priest the question is about Jesus' messianic status, a natural outgrowth of the testimony in v. 61 that Jesus claimed authority over the temple.

26:64 Jesus told him, "It is as you say" (λέγει αὐτῷ ὁ Ἰησοῦς, Σὺ εἶπας). In the process of overturning the "messianic secret" (see above), both Matthew and Mark have the same three stages — the triumphal entry (21:1 – 11), the christological affirmation of 22:43 – 45, and now this, which climaxes the three. Matthew has Jesus say "you have said" (σὺ εἶπας) for Mark's "I am" (Mark 14:62) and Luke's "You say that I am" (Luke 22:70), but it likely has the same affirmative force. It can be taken as contrast "You know I have said it," as a challenge, "You have said it but don't believe it," or as affirmation ("[It is as] you have said"). It parallels "You have said so" in 26:25 (to Judas) and 27:11 (to Pilate), and so affirmation is primary, but there is also qualification (Caiaphas asks if he is Messiah, Jesus answers that he is the Son of Man).

Davies and Allison give three reasons why the wording differs from Mark:[16] (1) to establish a parallel between the two trials before the high priest and Pilate; (2) to put the responsibility on Caiaphas ("you") who knows the answer; and (3) for Jesus to distance himself from Caiaphas' legal language on oaths (cf. 5:33 – 37).

26:64 "Nevertheless, I am telling you" (πλὴν λέγω ὑμῖν). πλήν could be a strong adversative ("nevertheless, but, however"), a strong affirmation ("in truth"), or a clarification ("furthermore"). There are aspects of each, for Jesus is clarifying his messianic office and also contrasting it with the high priest's understanding of that office. Moreover, with πλήν it is equivalent to an "amen" (ἀμήν) formula saying (see on 5:18) and constitutes a solemn truth.

26:64 "... from now on" (ἀπ' ἄρτι). This phrase has occasioned discussion. NIV had "in the future" because of the parousia orientation here, but that is not quite the correct nuance, and the TNIV correctly changed it to "from now on." There is an imminent and yet inaugurated (speaking of what will continue in the future) thrust, as it means Jesus will take his seat with God immediately at his death and resurrection, and in his resurrection his vindication will be immediately visible to all; yet at the same time he will be in the seat of "power" from his resurrection to the parousia and beyond (so Gundry, Brown, Hagner). Senior summarizes it well: "Jesus' messianic identity which is

15. France, *Gospel of Matthew*, 1025, notes the objection of some critics that there is no evidence for Jewish belief in Jesus as Son of God and then opposes such conclusions on the basis of evidence from Qumran: 4Q174 (Florilegium); 4Q246 (Aramaic Apocalypse) 2:1, perhaps 1QSa (28a) 2:11 – 12.

16. Davies and Allison, *Matthew*, 3:529. So also Luz, *Matthew 21 – 28*, 429.

recognized now (although only implicitly in the wording of his question) by the high priest will become awesomely transparent in the future."[17]

26:64 "... you will see the Son of Man sitting at the right hand of power" (ὄψεσθε τὸν υἱὸν τοῦ ἀνθρώπου καθήμενον ἐκ δεξιῶν τῆς δυνάμεως). The two statements of Jesus develop this inaugurated thrust. The first is a "going *to*" God in Jesus' exaltation, the second is a "coming *from*" God in his parousia.[18] The idea of the Son of Man "sitting" at God's right hand evokes not only Ps 110:1 but also Jesus' use of that passage in 22:44 as well as the Son of Man "sitting" on his throne in 25:31 and his disciples "sitting" on thrones with him in 19:28. In all four passages the idea is not only glory but the Son of Man as eschatological Judge sitting on his throne.

"Power" (δύναμις) is a circumlocution for "God" but also builds on the idea of the "power to destroy" implicit in the false testimony of the two witnesses in v. 61. It may catch the second part of Ps 110:1, "your enemies a footstool for your feet." Jesus in effect is saying, "You have falsely accused me of saying I will destroy the temple with my messianic power, but you are right about one thing, I will be the powerful Judge."

26:64 "... and coming on the clouds of heaven" (καὶ ἐρχόμενον ἐπὶ τῶν νεφελῶν τοῦ οὐρανοῦ). The second half uses Dan 7:13, "there before me was one like a son of man, coming with the clouds of heaven" and presupposes v. 14, "He was given authority, glory and sovereign power; all nations and peoples of every language worshiped him. His dominion is an everlasting dominion that will not pass away, and his kingdom is one that will never be destroyed." Jesus' identification of himself with the "Son of Man" stems primarily from Dan 7:13 – 14 (see excursus after 8:22), and this Danielic passage is also behind Matt 16:27; 24:30; 28:18 (cf. Rev 1:7). So the thrust is the universal dominion and glory the Son of Man/Judge will have at the second coming/end of history.

Yet how will the leaders "see" (ὄψεσθε) all this? They will not see the parousia, but it is proleptically present in the resurrection (on this apocalyptic language see the introduction to 24:1 – 25:46). Brown makes three observations.[19] (1) There is both a present and a future eschatology in Jesus and the NT on this issue (often called "inaugurated eschatology"); both his glory and his judgment are an already/not yet in force. (2) Jesus does not say he will glorify himself but that God will vindicate him over the leaders; they will see the beginning of this. (3) There is a supreme irony in their condemnation of Jesus; everything they accuse him of doing and being is actually true, and the Sanhedrin will see one thing and not realize they are seeing another. On these things Matthew is even more vivid and intense than is Mark.

26:65 Then the high priest ripped his garments, saying (τότε ὁ ἀρχιερεὺς διέρρηξεν τὰ ἱμάτια αὐτοῦ λέγων). The response of Caiaphas is immediate. This is exactly what he had been waiting for, Jesus' self-incrimination. Tearing one's garments occurs at deep mourning (Lev 10:6; Jer 41:5) or at blasphemy (Acts 14:14).

17. Senior, *Passion Narrative*, 178 – 79. He brings out (179 – 83) that the tone of v. 64 is not polemical against the false understanding of the high priest but affirmative and centers on Jesus' exaltation and majesty at the right hand of God. I would argue that it is both, affirming that Jesus is the Messiah but also polemical in the sense that Jesus is saying he will be the eschatological Judge (over Israel). There is glory and power here.

18. This builds on the language of Davies and Allison, *Matthew*, 3:531. They prefer the parousia orientation for Jesus' response here, but in truth both his present exaltation and his future coming are in the two statements of Jesus in v. 64.

19. Brown, *Death*, 499 – 500.

26:65 "He has blasphemed! Why do we still need any more witnesses? Look, you have heard the blasphemy just now" (Ἐβλασφήμησεν· τί ἔτι χρείαν ἔχομεν μαρτύρων; ἴδε νῦν ἠκούσατε τὴν βλασφημίαν). This is the key charge and is quite debated. *M. Sanh.* 7:5 builds on Lev 24:15–16 and says the name of God must be uttered for blasphemy to occur. Technically, the name is not mentioned in Mark 14:62/Matt 26:64 (it is in Luke 22:69), though "Power" is a circumlocution for God and would be taken as such in all likelihood. Brown notes the possible meanings behind the Jewish charge:[20]

1. His followers called him Messiah, but that would probably not be enough for the charge.
2. He called himself Son of God; Brown doubts Jesus or his disciples used that title, but the evidence shows otherwise, and it is certainly part of the solution.
3. He claimed to be Son of Man and to come on the clouds of heaven (Mark 14:62); but though part of the reason, this also is not enough in and of itself.
4. The destruction of the temple claim, but this was not linked with a charge of blasphemy.
5. He was a false prophet and as such deceived the people, but this is not centrally addressed in the trial.

Bock moves toward a solution:[21]

1. Blasphemy per se did center on an inappropriate use of the divine name, but there were also *acts* of blasphemy, such as idolatry or disrespect toward God.
2. Few were allowed to approach the holy God; even the archangel Michael is never depicted as seated before God; so for Jesus to claim to "sit at [God's] right hand," as in v. 64, would be blasphemous.
3. This was not a capital trial but a hearing before the Sanhedrin, so they did not have to be technically correct.
4. Sources for information regarding this trial were plentiful (e.g., Joseph of Arimathea, Nicodemus), so there is no reason to think this a later fiction.
5. One finds two levels of blasphemy here: Jesus' claim to have comprehensive authority from God, and his claim to be the future judge of the Jewish leaders themselves (violating Exod 22:28 on not cursing God's leaders). This latter could also be used as a socio-political challenge to Rome's authority.

26:66 "What do you think?" And they responded,[22] "He is guilty and should die" (τί ὑμῖν δοκεῖ; οἱ δὲ ἀποκριθέντες εἶπαν, Ἔνοχος θανάτου ἐστίν). The high priest knows it is time to act. The Sanhedrin has heard the blasphemous words for itself. So Caiaphas asks for the verdict. If this is an official trial, a great deal of legal steps lay behind the scene here. If it is a hearing (which is likely), then this is close to what happened. "Deserves death" (ἔνοχος θανάτου) is a euphemism for the two aspects — they find Jesus guilty and in accordance with the Torah demand the death penalty. The next step is Pilate and the execution of Jesus.

26:67 Then they spit in his face, struck him, and slapped him (Τότε ἐνέπτυσαν εἰς τὸ πρόσωπον αὐτοῦ καὶ ἐκολάφισαν αὐτόν, οἱ δὲ ἐράπισαν). The mocking of Jesus is a critical part of the proceedings. We do not know if the actual leaders did this or their servants and guards, but in light of the mocking by the leaders in 27:41–43, it is likely that both groups did these terrible things. There are three stages to the mockery — here, by the

20. Ibid., 534–44.
21. Bock, *Blasphemy*, 234–36.
22. For this construction, see on 3:15; 4:4.

soldiers after Pilate's verdict (27:27 – 31), and by all the bystanders, including the criminals crucified with Jesus, at the cross (27:39 – 44). Mark adds that they also blindfolded Jesus; Matthew's omission may be due to a desire to strengthen the allusion to Isa 50:6, which has the spitting and beating but not the blindfolding.[23] Their absolute contempt and hatred for Jesus is seen in this reaction. There is a supreme irony in their mockery and abuse of the one who will be their Judge at the final judgment. This one who now stands before them as the suffering Servant will come back as the conquering King.

26:68 ... saying, "Prophesy to us, Messiah. Who is it who has hit you?" (λέγοντες, Προφήτευσον ἡμῖν, Χριστέ, τίς ἐστιν ὁ παίσας σε;). To them Jesus called himself the Messiah, so now they were going to find out just how messianic he really is. You can almost hear the dripping sarcasm as they contemptuously utter, "Messiah" (χριστέ). In the blindfolding (assumed by Matthew) and the call to "prophesy," they may have been playing a cruel version of a "blind man's bluff"-type child's game. Three types have been noted: a game of tag where one shuts his eyes and the others cry "prophesy" as he gropes for them; a game where a player covers the eyes and then others slap as he guesses where they are; and one in which a blindfolded player is hit with papyrus fragments and tries to find the others. The first and third are close to the one here.[24]

26:69 Now Peter was sitting outside in the courtyard. A servant girl came to him and said, "You too were with Jesus of Galilee" (Ὁ δὲ Πέτρος ἐκάθητο ἔξω ἐν τῇ αὐλῇ· καὶ προσῆλθεν αὐτῷ μία παιδίσκη λέγουσα, Καὶ σὺ ἦσθα μετὰ Ἰησοῦ τοῦ Γαλιλαίου). Peter was last seen entering the courtyard of the high priest and "sitting with the servants" (v. 58), and the imperfect "was sitting" (ἐκάθητο) here means he has continued to sit there. Therefore, these events take place during the trial conducted in vv. 59 – 68. The contrast is powerful; as Jesus endures in isolated control and is victorious once more over the leaders of Israel, Peter is failing because of their servants. One of the servants, a woman (the diminutive "servant girl" [παιδίσκη] does not mean she was young), recognizes Peter (either she has seen him before or his accent gives him away, see v. 73) and challenges him. He is linked with Jesus from Galilee.

26:70 But he denied it before them all, saying, "I do not know what you are talking about" (ὁ δὲ ἠρνήσατο ἔμπροσθεν πάντων λέγων, Οὐκ οἶδα τί λέγεις). Jesus' sovereign silence before the high priest is paralleled by Peter's bombastic rejection of any knowledge of Jesus or his messianic claims. Keener calls this "the emphatic form standard in Jewish law 'for formal legal denial.'"[25] The passive apostasy of the other ten as they ran away is intensified by Peter's verbal denials. "He denied it before" (ἠρνήσατο ἔμπροσθεν) picks up the language of 10:33, where Jesus said, "Whoever denies me before people, I will also deny before my Father in heaven." Peter is in the process of saving his life and losing his soul!

26:71 And after he went out into the entranceway, another servant girl saw him and said to those there, "This man was with Jesus of Nazareth" (ἐξελθόντα δὲ εἰς τὸν πυλῶνα εἶδεν αὐτὸν ἄλλη καὶ λέγει τοῖς ἐκεῖ, Οὗτος ἦν μετὰ Ἰησοῦ

23. So Brown, *Death*, 578 – 79; Davies and Allison, *Matthew*, 3:535; Luz, *Matthew 21 – 28*, 448.

24. This is discussed often, see Willem C. van Unnik, "Jesu Verhöhnung vor dem Synedrium," *ZNW* 29 (1930): 310 – 11; D. L. Miller, "*Empaizein*: Playing the Mock Game (Luke 22:63 – 64)," *JBL* 90 (1971): 309 – 13; David Flusser, "Who Is It That Struck You?" *Immanuel* 20 (1986): 27 – 32; Brown, *Death*, 575; Luz, *Matthew 21 – 28*, 448.

25. Keener, *Matthew*, 654.

τοῦ Ναζωραίου). Peter apparently starts to walk out of the courtyard and goes to the gate at the entrance to it ("entranceway" [πυλῶνα], with "after he went out" [ἐξελθόντα], a temporal aorist participle). Mark 14:68 calls it the "entryway," the vestibule at the entrance to the street. Peter may have been seeking a less public spot to avoid confrontations.

It doesn't work. Another servant woman[26] spies him, and the pressure intensifies. The first girl's question was directed only to him, though his answer was to everyone around. This one tells all "those" in the vicinity that he is definitely one of Jesus' followers. "Of Nazareth" intensifies the slight tone of contempt in "of Galilee" in v. 69. As exemplified in John 1:46 ("Can anything good come from [Nazareth]") it was a little-known backwater town in Galilee, and something of that is likely in her comment. In light of 2:23 ("he will be called a Nazarene"), there may also be for Matthew's readers a note of messianic identity that further defines vv. 62, 64 (see Nolland).

26:72 And again he denied this with an oath, "I do not know the man" (καὶ πάλιν ἠρνήσατο μετὰ ὅρκου ὅτι Οὐκ οἶδα τὸν ἄνθρωπον). As the challenge intensifies, so does Peter's negative response. He now denies any knowledge of Jesus "with an oath," with "oath" (ὅρκος) a cognate of "charge under oath" (ἐξορκίζω), used by the high priest in v. 63 and referring to the very kind of "oath" Jesus rejected in 5:33–37 (cf. Herod's oath that led to the death of the Baptist in 14:7, 9). Jesus has lost his personhood; he is now nothing more than "a man." Peter has gone further along the road to apostasy (see on 26:31).

26:73 A short time later those standing there came to Peter and said, "Truly you are one of them, for your speech accent also makes your origins clear" (μετὰ μικρὸν δὲ προσελθόντες οἱ ἑστῶτες εἶπον τῷ Πέτρῳ, Ἀληθῶς καὶ σὺ ἐξ αὐτῶν εἶ, καὶ γὰρ ἡ λαλιά σου δῆλόν σε ποιεῖ). Luke 22:59 makes this an hour later, probably about when Jesus was being condemned for blasphemy. In total contrast Peter is about to fail a third time. In a completely public confrontation (in the first two it was just one servant woman), the whole group standing with Peter begins to challenge him. "Truly" (ἀληθῶς) shows the certitude they feel that he has to be a Galilean supporter of Jesus.

Just like a person's accent today shows whether they are from New England or New York or the South, so the northern province of Galilee had a distinct accent when speaking Aramaic, and this betrays the area from which Peter came.[27] They then conclude that the only reason a Galilean would be standing among them would be if he was a follower of Jesus. The present tense "you are" (εἶ) is a further challenge, hinting that Peter still is a follower, perhaps threatening that he too should be arrested (so Hagner).

26:74 Then he began to invoke a curse and to swear an oath, "I do not know the man" (τότε ἤρξατο καταθεματίζειν καὶ ὀμνύειν ὅτι Οὐκ οἶδα τὸν ἄνθρωπον). This third and final denial is the most severe of all, and Matthew tells us this with his emphatic "invoke a curse ... swear an oath," two halves of the same coin (probably with the prefix κατα- in "invoke a curse" [καταθεματίζειν] having intensifying force, so Luz). The oath formula in the ancient world was often some form of "may God do such-and-such to me if...." So Peter anchors his lie (repeating exactly his words

26. Mark 14:69 implies it is the same servant as in the first instance (probably for dramatic purposes), while Matthew clarifies it was another woman.

27. The Judean contempt for the Galilean accent is found in *b. ʿErub.* 53a, 53b.

of v. 72) by invoking a curse on himself[28] if his lie is not true (certainly not the smartest thing to do!). Not too many would wish to challenge God in this way. As Wilkins says, "The more likely to others that Peter is lying, the more emphatic becomes his attempts to dupe the crowd with his deceptive sincerity — a well-known tactic of flagrant liars."[29]

26:74 And immediately the rooster crowed (καὶ εὐθέως ἀλέκτωρ ἐφώνησεν). This dramatic conclusion to Peter's final denial recalls Jesus' prophecy of v. 34, repeated in the next verse. One can imagine the effect that hearing that rooster must have had on Peter. He had undoubtedly refused to allow the memory of Jesus' prediction to enter his consciousness during his cowardly capitulation to the pressure of the crowds and the fear of arrest. Now he can no longer do so. This may well have been the onset of dawn (see 27:1) when the night of trials (for Jesus *and* Peter!) is over.

26:75 And Peter remembered the word Jesus had spoken:[30] **"Before the rooster crows, you will deny me three times"** (καὶ ἐμνήσθη ὁ Πέτρος τοῦ ῥήματος Ἰησοῦ εἰρηκότος ὅτι Πρὶν ἀλέκτορα φωνῆσαι τρὶς ἀπαρνήσῃ με). Jesus' prediction has been fulfilled to the letter! The memory of that prediction now rushes back into Peter's conscience, and he is appalled at his weakness and at what he has done. On the surface, he may have thought he had committed the unpardonable sin of Mark 3:28 – 30 and described in Heb 6:4 – 6, "It is impossible for those who have been once enlightened ... and who have fallen away, to be brought back to repentance." He has not, and his deep repentance in the next sentence shows he has not.

26:75 And he went outside and wept bitterly (καὶ ἐξελθὼν ἔξω ἔκλαυσεν πικρῶς). In v. 58 Peter entered the courtyard, now he leaves it (another circumstantial participle [cf. v. 37], perhaps symbolically realizing he had left his walk with Christ?) and begins his process of repentance. Peter knows he does not deserve to be forgiven and so weeps bitter tears similar to Esau in Heb 12:17 (see Gen 27:30 – 40) and to God's enemies in Isa 15:3; 22:4; 33:7 (the latter two with the same wording in the LXX). This is the first stage of his repentance, not recorded but presupposed here. Jesus' reinstatement of Peter is related in John 21:15 – 17. There is a further contrast between Peter and Judas. Peter's remorse leads to repentance, while Judas's remorse leads to suicide (27:3 – 10). The one found forgiveness,[31] the other did not.

28. Some have suggested he is invoking a curse on Jesus, which would indeed have the effect of separating himself from Jesus. Later Pliny, *Epistles* 10:96 – 97, says Christians were to denounce Jesus by cursing him (so Davies and Allison, Luz; contra Nolland). However, Peter was invoking a curse on himself, so this does not truly fit.

29. Wilkins, *Matthew*, 867 – 68. Broadus, *Matthew*, 553, adds, "Alas! for human nature; the Word made flesh was rejected by the great mass of his own people, was betrayed by one of his own followers, and by the very leader of them was basely denied, again and again, with oaths and curses."

30. Verbalizing the subjective genitive "Jesus" (Ἰησοῦ).

31. He is included among the disciples in 28:7 – 8, 16 and is explicitly mentioned in Luke 24:12 and John 20:2 – 10 as involved in the empty tomb events. In John 21:15 – 17, 18 – 23 he is singled out as the key disciple (cf. Matt 16:17 – 19).

Theology in Application

The Sanhedrin trial has three foci — the splendid isolation and majestic demeanor of Jesus, the opposition of the leaders to the extent that they are willing to forego legal procedure in order to condemn Jesus, and the absolute failure of Peter. Both the leaders and Peter are set in contrast to Jesus, the suffering Servant of Yahweh. The great irony is that the very reasons for which they sought to kill Jesus are the greatest truths of history; by putting Jesus to trial and death they were fulfilling God's plan of salvation and establishing the very church they wished to eradicate from this earth.

1. False Witness

Those who engage in false witness against Jesus are actually testifying against themselves. The leaders had no interest in the actual facts and were not seeking the God-given truth and reality of the Christ-event. Like people throughout history and today, they were only hurting themselves. The fact is that God in his wisdom turned their act of evil on its head so that it accomplished the greatest good of any act in all of history: the death of God's Son and the atoning sacrifice for the sins of humanity. Evil intentions will always turn back upon themselves and self-destruct. They may seem good for the time being (as they did to the leaders for the rest of their lives), but they will have eternal consequences for their perpetrators.

2. Final Judge and Conquering King

Jesus will return as the final Judge and conquering King and will have eternal dominion over his creation. The single most important truth of human history is found right here in Jesus the Christ. In his earthly humiliation and subjection, he set in motion those divine forces that would bring him back in glory and power. Weakness would be turned to strength, and humiliation to exaltation. The judged would become Judge, and the conquered would conquer. In Rev 12:11, 13:7 another important truth is added to this: we will participate in his glory with him. In this world we are beaten down and subjected to ignominy, but that very defeat is our victory. When Satan takes the life of one of the saints, he is helping place another nail in his own coffin! In entering Judas and taking Christ to the cross, Satan participated in his own defeat. That is replicated whenever he martyrs one of God's children.

3. Blaspheming Divinity

In v. 64 Jesus shows himself to be one with God. The leaders called him a blasphemer, and another great irony is in that very charge, they themselves were blaspheming the divine Son of God. So it is ever with the "antichrists" (1 John 2:18) of history; the Christ they oppose in us is the final arbiter of history, and in rejecting us they reject the only hope of eternal salvation, Christ in us the hope of glory!

4. Simon Peter and Us

Simon Peter is Everyman, one time confessing Jesus and being told he is the "rock" on which God will erect his church, another time denying Jesus and saying he does not know him. Failure is something every human being endures, even if they be Abraham, Moses, or Paul. Peter exemplifies that as well as anyone in Scripture. Jesus renamed him Simon, the Rock. Yet throughout his time with Jesus he was sifting sand. He never became the rock until after Pentecost, when the Spirit filled him.

Yet that is the case with each one of us. Whenever we try to live the Christian life in our own strength, we fail and cry, "What a wretched man I am! Who will rescue me from this body of death?" (Rom 7:24). Only when we are filled with the Spirit and depend entirely on his strength (Rom 8) can we find victory. There is both warning and promise in the portrayal of Peter here. There is forgiveness and restoration inherent in this, yet at the same time Peter would have given anything for this never to have occurred. We don't want future forgiveness but rather future victory over our weaknesses.

CHAPTER 117

Matthew 27:1 – 26

Literary Context

The passion is proceeding logically, and after the trial before the Sanhedrin, it is necessary for Jesus to go to Pilate for trial and sentencing, since only the Romans could execute a person. In the midst of this comes the remorse of Judas, and even more than Peter there is an absolute contrast between Judas and Christ.

- **VII. The Passion and Resurrection of Jesus (26:1 – 28:20)**
  - **A. The Passion Narrative (26:1 – 27:61)**
    1. Preliminary Events (26:1 – 16)
    2. The Last Supper/Passover (26:17 – 30)
    3. Events in Gethsemane (26:31 – 56)
    4. **The Trials of Jesus and Peter's Denials (26:57 – 27:26)**
       - a. The Sanhedrin Trial and Peter's Denials (26:57 – 75)
       - ➦ **b. The Trial before Pilate (27:1 – 26)**
         - **(1) The Delivery of Jesus to Pilate (27:1 – 2)**
         - **(2) The Suicide of Judas (27:3 – 10)**
         - **(3) Interrogation by Pilate (27:11 – 14)**
         - **(4) The Barabbas Incident (27:15 – 23)**
         - **(5) The Verdict Is Rendered (27:24 – 26)**
    5. The Crucifixion and Death of Jesus (27:27 – 50)

Main Idea

As with Peter's denial told in the context of the Sanhedrin trial, this scene places Judas's remorse into the trial before Pilate. There are two contrasts: Jesus with Judas, and Pilate with Judas; the first contrast centers on victory vs. defeat, the second on remorse vs. resignation. Judas has betrayed Jesus and commits suicide in his sorrow; Pilate tries to free Jesus, but when the pressure comes, he sentences Jesus with barely a shrug.

Translation

Matthew 27:1-26

1a	Setting	When morning had arrived,
b	Scene #1 (A)	**all the chief priests and**
		elders of the people took counsel against Jesus
c	Purpose of 1b	that he should be put to death.
2a	Action	And **they bound him,**
		led him away, and
		delivered him to Pilate,
b		the governor.
3a	Scene #2 (B)	Then after Judas, who betrayed Jesus, saw that he was condemned,
b	Result #1 of 3a	**[1] he was filled with remorse**
c	Result #2 of 3a	**[2]** and **returned the thirty pieces of silver**
		to the chief priests and elders, saying,
4a		*"I have sinned in betraying innocent blood."*
b	Response to 4a	But **they responded,**
c		*"What is that to us?*
d		*See to it yourself."*
5a		And after he had thrown the silver coins into the temple,
b		**he departed.**
c	Result #3 of 3a	**[3] Then he went and hanged himself.**
6a	Result of 5a	And **the chief priests took the silver coins and said,**
b		*"The law does not allow us to put this into the treasury,*
c		*since it is blood money."*
7a		So after they had taken counsel,
b		**they used it to buy a potter's field as a burial place for foreigners.**
8a	Identification of 7b	Therefore **that field is called "Field of Blood" to this very day.**
9a	Purpose of 6a-7b/ Fulfillment Formula	**Then the word spoken through Jeremiah the prophet was fulfilled, saying,**
b	OT Quotation	*"And they took the thirty pieces of silver,*
c		*the price of the honored one set by the people of Israel.*
10a		*And they gave them for the potter's field,*
b		*just as the Lord commanded me."* (Zech 11:12-13)
11a	Scene #3 (A')	Now **Jesus stood in front of the governor,**
b	Question	and **the governor asked him, saying,**
c		*"Are you the king of the Jews?*
d	Answer	And **Jesus answered,**
e		*"So you say."*
12a	Accusation	And when he was accused by the chief priests and elders,
b	Response	**he answered nothing.**
13a	Question	**Then Pilate said to him,**

b		*"Aren't you hearing how many things they are testifying about against you?"*
14a	Response	And **Jesus refused to answer him, not even to a single charge,**
b	Result of 14a	with the result that the governor was astounded.
15a	Scene #4 (C)	Now **it was the custom at a festival for the governor to release to the crowd one prisoner whom they wanted.**
16a		Now **at that time they had a well-known prisoner named [Jesus] Barabbas.**
17a	Setting	So **after they had gathered, Pilate asked them,**
b	Question	*"Whom do you want me to release to you,*
c	Alternative #1	*(1) [Jesus] Barabbas or*
d	Alternative #2	*(2) Jesus, the one called Messiah?"*
18a	Basis for 17a-d	For **he knew that they had handed Jesus over because of envy.**
19a	Setting	Now while he was sitting on his judgment seat,
b	Action (D)	**his wife sent a note to him, saying,**
c	Exhortation	*"Have nothing to do with that innocent man,*
d	Basis for 19c	*for I have suffered greatly today with a dream because of him."*
20a	Result of 17a-d (C′)	But **the chief priests and the elders persuaded the crowds**
b	Purpose of 20a	that they should ask for Barabbas and have Jesus destroyed.
21a		But **the governor responded,**
b	Question (Restatement of 17b-d)	*"Which of the two men do you want me to release to you?"*
c	Answer to 21b	And **they said,**
d		*"Barabbas."*
22a		**Pilate said to them,**
b	Question	*"What then should I do with Jesus,*
c		*the one called Messiah?"*
d	Answer to 22b-c	**They all said,**
e		*"Let him be crucified!"*
23a		But **he said,**
b	Question	*"Why?*
c		*What evil thing has he done?"*
d	Answer to 23b-c	But **they shouted all the more,**
e	(Parallel 22e)	*"Let him be crucified!"*
24a	Scene #5	Now when Pilate saw that he was getting nowhere, but instead the clamor was getting worse,
b	Action	**he took water and washed in front of the crowd, saying,**
c	Assertion	*"I am innocent of this man's blood.*
d		*See to it yourself!"*
25a	Response to 24c-d	And **all the people responded,**
b		*"May his blood be upon us and upon our children."*
26a	Conclusion	**Then he released Barabbas to them,**
b		but **he had Jesus scourged and handed him over to be crucified.**

Structure and Literary Form

There is a mixture of Markan and free material in this. Verses 1 – 2 (the handover to Pilate) and vv. 11 – 23 (the trial) follow Mark closely, while vv. 3 – 10 (Judas's suicide) and vv. 24 – 26 stem from M material (though the Judas material has some affinity with Acts 1:15 – 20). There are five sections here: the delivery to Pilate (vv. 1 – 2), the death of Judas (with three subsections: vv. 3 – 5, 6 – 8, 9 – 10), interrogation by Pilate (vv. 11 – 14), the Barabbas incident (vv. 15 – 23), and the verdict (vv. 24 – 26).

Exegetical Outline

➡ **I. The Delivery of Jesus to Pilate (27:1 – 2)**
- A. The decision of the Sanhedrin (v. 1)
- B. Jesus handed over to Pilate (v. 2)

II. The Suicide of Judas (27:3 – 10)
- A. Judas's remorse (vv. 3 – 5)
  1. He returns the betrayal money (vv. 3 – 4)
  2. He commits suicide (v. 5)
- B. The purchase of the field (vv. 6 – 8)
  1. What to do with the blood money (v. 6)
  2. Purchase of the "Field of Blood" (vv. 7 – 8)
- C. Fulfillment of Scripture (vv. 9 – 10)

III. Interrogation by Pilate (27:11 – 14)
- A. Jesus as King (v. 11)
- B. Silence before his accusers (v. 12)
- C. Silence before Pilate (vv. 13 – 14)

IV. The Barabbas Incident (27:15 – 23)
- A. The custom of releasing a prisoner (vv. 15 – 16)
- B. The question regarding whom to release (vv. 17 – 18)
- C. The warning from Pilate's wife (v. 19)
- D. The demand to release Barabbas (vv. 20 – 23)
  1. The leaders persuade the crowds (v. 20)
  2. The demand to release Barabbas (v. 21)
  3. The demand to crucify Jesus (vv. 22 – 23)

V. The Verdict Is Rendered (27:24 – 26)
- A. Pilate washes his hands of guilt (v. 24)
- B. All the people accept the guilt (v. 25)
- C. Barabbas released and Jesus given over for crucifixion (v. 26)

Explanation of the Text

27:1 When morning had arrived, all the chief priests and elders of the people took counsel against Jesus that he should be put to death (Πρωΐας δὲ γενομένης συμβούλιον ἔλαβον πάντες οἱ ἀρχιερεῖς καὶ οἱ πρεσβύτεροι τοῦ λαοῦ κατὰ τοῦ Ἰησοῦ ὥστε θανατῶσαι αὐτόν). This presumably takes place just as the trial of Jesus ends and the rooster crows after Peter's three denials. As either the final act of the Sanhedrin trial or a separate meeting at dawn,[1] the council condemns Jesus to death, an act they have been plotting since 12:14. This is strongly debated: Is this verdict (and that of Mark 15:1) the end of a single trial[2] or a second separate trial some time after the earlier interrogation of 26:57 – 68?[3]

The issue is complicated by Luke 22, which has Jesus taken to the high priest (22:54), followed by the denials of Peter (22:55 – 62), and then a trial at daybreak (22:66 – 71). Is that trial the same as Matt 26:57 – 68; 27:1 or just 27:1? One factor is whether συμβούλιον ἔλαβον means "took counsel" or "held a [separate] council." In 12:14 and 22:15 the phrase means the former, as the leaders "plot" to get rid of Jesus, and 27:7 is the same as the Jewish leaders "decide" to use the blood money of Judas to buy a field. In 28:12 the phrase could be either, but more likely the chief priests simply met and "devised a plan" rather than held a formal meeting. In short, the phrase can fit either view but more often in Matthew it means to "take counsel" together (Grundmann and Luz call this *concilium capere* or "making a decision").

One major argument for a second session is that then the Sanhedrin members would fulfill the Jewish requirement for a two-session trial, but *m. Sanh.* 4:1 actually required trials on two separate days, and these two (26:57 – 68 and 27:1) occur on the same day (days in Palestine were from dusk to dusk, not from dawn to dawn). Most who consider a second trial as a necessity treat 26:58 – 27:1 as a chronological sequence: a first trial, the denials of Peter, and then a second trial. Yet in our exegesis of Peter's denials, it seemed clear that they took place *during* the first interrogation rather than *after* it. So then 27:1 would be a natural conclusion to 26:57 – 68. When all the data is considered, it is best to take 27:1 as the verdict at the end of the interrogation rather than a separate trial. Either way, of course, the Jewish leaders condemn Jesus to death and take him to Pilate's hall. The mention of the "chief priests and elders," as in 26:3, 47, 57, stands for all the leaders of the Sanhedrin.

27:2 And they bound him,[4] led him away, and delivered him to Pilate, the governor (καὶ δήσαντες αὐτὸν ἀπήγαγον καὶ παρέδωκαν Πιλάτῳ τῷ ἡγεμόνι). Since Jesus is now a condemned prisoner intended for execution, he is "bound" before being taken to Pilate.[5] As noted earlier, the Jewish

1. "When morning had arrived" (πρωΐας γενομένης) is another of Matthew's many temporal genitive absolutes (see 26:6, 20).

2. France, *Matthew* (TNTC), 384; Brown, *Death*, 630 – 32; Davies and Allison, *Matthew*, 3:553; Luz, *Matthew 21 – 28*, 463; Nolland, *Matthew*, 1146; Turner, "Matthew," 352. Senior, *Passion Narrative*, 211 – 12, believes Mark presents them as separate trials but Matthew as a continuous trial. However, the parallels between the two are too close for such a decision. Marshall, *Luke*, 847, believes there was only one meeting but that it occurred in the morning rather than during the night. Yet Mark and Matthew are clear on the night trial.

3. Hill, *Matthew*, 347; Grundmann, *Matthäus*, 548 – 49; Bock, *Luke 9:51 – 24:53*, 1791 – 92; Hagner, *Matthew 14 – 28*, 809; Blomberg, *Historical Reliability*, 136 – 38; Wilkins, *Matthew*, 868.

4. This is another of Matthew's circumstantial participles that borrow the force of the verb they modify (see on 2:4; 4:20).

5. See Ernst Bammel, "The Trial before Pilate," in *Jesus and the Politics of His Day* (ed. E. Bammel and C. F. D. Moule; Cambridge: Cambridge Univ. Press, 1984), 415 – 51 (esp. 415).

authorities did not have the right to execute someone (unless they desecrated the temple),[6] so the entire purpose of the interrogation was to find hard evidence to take to Pilate and convince him to execute Jesus.

Moreover, Pilate held his public morning sessions quite early, so they had to get Jesus to his residence shortly after dawn (this is the reason for the night trial). The Romans appointed the high priests, so Caiaphas owed his job to Rome. Matthew adds to Mark the fact that Pilate was "the governor" of the region (from AD 26 to 36). This was a general term for a "prefect" who commanded auxiliary troops of about a thousand (prefects governed smaller provinces, and Pilate answered to the legate in Syria).[7]

Pilate was a knight of the equestrian class, not of the senatorial class, and that was why he governed Judea and Samaria rather than having a more important post. He lived in Caesarea Maritima but came to Jerusalem with extra troops during festivals to maintain order. There is some discrepancy, for the Pilate of Josephus (*Ant.* 18:35, 55 – 64, 85 – 89, 177 – 78) was an anti-Semitic, cruel governor who brought the Roman standards into Jerusalem (with images of the emperor on them) and caused riots, minted pagan coins, stole money from the temple treasury to build aqueducts, slaughtered Galilean pilgrims with their sacrifices (Luke 13:1), dedicated golden shields in Jerusalem bearing the name of the "divine Augustus," and killed Samaritans at Mount Gerizim (this last led to his recall in disgrace in AD 36).[8] The accounts of the trial in the gospels, however, seem to portray him as weak, vacillating, and concerned to release innocent Jesus.

How do we reconcile such disparate portraits? Those who think the portrait here to be unhistorical emphasize the Pilate of Josephus, who freely executed non-Romans without trial. Yet he never did so at a major festival with thousands of volatile pilgrims present, nor did he ever do so in an official Roman trial like the one here. The gospels present Pilate yielding to pressure but also bring out his full guilt, as we will see below. The two pictures do not contradict one another (see Carson, Brown).

27:3 Then after Judas, who betrayed Jesus, saw that he was condemned, he was filled with remorse and returned the thirty pieces of silver to the chief priests and elders (Τότε ἰδὼν Ἰούδας ὁ παραδιδοὺς αὐτὸν ὅτι κατεκρίθη, μεταμεληθεὶς ἔστρεψεν τὰ τριάκοντα ἀργύρια τοῖς ἀρχιερεῦσιν καὶ πρεσβυτέροις). Participles control this verse. The aorist temporal participle "after [he] saw" (ἰδών) links the condemnation of Jesus with Judas's remorse. Then another circumstantial participle, "he was filled with remorse" (μεταμεληθείς, see v. 2), defines the emotions behind his return of the blood money. This event apparently does follow after the verdict, because Judas acts on the basis of the verdict.

Yet this event is here for structural reasons as well. (1) It functions dramatically the same way as did Peter's denial, providing a buffer and contrast to the majesty of Christ at the trial. (2) It shows the true meaning of the trial; Peter's denial connected it with human weakness, Judas's death with

6. See Keener, *Matthew*, 664 – 65, who says that before AD 30 Rome removed the right of capital punishment from "municipal aristocracies."

7. The historicity of Pilate as prefect has been confirmed by an inscription found at Caesarea Maritima in 1961, see Craig A. Evans, "Pilate Inscription," *DNTB*, 803 – 4.

8. See Brown, *Death*, 698 – 705 for an in-depth discussion of these six incidents that we know about from the decade of the rule of Pilate.

human guilt and the spiritual consequences of rejection. (3) It stresses further the total innocence of Christ and the fact that all the events fulfilled prophecy (cf. v. 9) as well as Jesus' "woe" (26:24).

Presumably Judas went back with the arresting party to the high priest's residence and actually "saw" (ἰδών) from a distance what transpired in the trial. He suddenly "regretted" his action and was "filled with remorse" (μεταμεληθείς, meaning literally "changed his mind," cf. 21:29, 32) about what he had done.[9] The reality of what he had done sunk in, and he deeply regretted his betrayal. He took the money the leaders had given him in 26:15 and gave it back to the leaders, not wanting the blood money.

27:4 ... saying, "I have sinned in betraying innocent blood" (λέγων, Ἥμαρτον παραδοὺς αἷμα ἀθῷον). Judas acknowledges what has been said all along, that he has seriously "sinned" because he has "betrayed" (probably a participle of means, see Wallace) Jesus, and that in the events to come, "innocent blood" will be shed. Deuteronomy 27:25 condemns a person who takes a bribe to shed "an innocent person," and there may be an echo of the murder of Abel by Cain (Gen 4:11) here as well as Saul's desire to slay David, which his son Jonathan calls "an innocent man" in 1 Sam 19:5.

27:4 But they responded, "What is that to us? See to it yourself" (οἱ δὲ εἶπαν, Τί πρὸς ἡμᾶς; σὺ ὄψῃ). The authorities implicitly accept that "innocent blood" would be shed but refuse to acknowledge any guilt on their part and absolve themselves with their brusque "What is that to us?" They don't care whether Jesus is "innocent" or not; they just want to get rid of the troublemaker. Their indifference to Judas's remorse is in keeping with the way they tried Jesus.

σὺ ὄψῃ (lit., "you will see") is a Latinism, meaning "See to it yourself" (BDF §362) or "The responsibility is yours." The careless unconcern of the Jewish leaders makes the responsibility even more theirs than Judas's.

27:5 And after he had thrown the silver coins into the temple, he departed (καὶ ῥίψας τὰ ἀργύρια εἰς τὸν ναὸν ἀνεχώρησεν). Clearly the chief priests refuse to accept the money, so Judas has to "throw" it into the temple precincts (with the temporal participle ῥίψας indicating a violent act), with "temple" (ναός) here probably meaning not the inner sanctuary but the temple treasury (so Brown, see v. 6). This alludes to Zech 11:13 (quoted below in vv. 9–10), where Zechariah takes the "thirty pieces of silver" he was paid and throws it into "the house of the LORD." Bruner talks about the sacrilegious nature of Judas's act and asks, "But isn't this action exactly what a sanctuary deserves when it is there for everything except justice and mercy?"[10]

27:5 Then he went and hanged himself (καὶ ἀπελθὼν ἀπήγξατο). With the fourth circumstantial participle of this section, Matthew shows that Judas's remorse is so great that he despairs of life itself and commits suicide. Suicide was looked down on by the Jews, but the Romans thought it an honorable death that in some way could atone for the serious errors made, and many Jews accepted this; but even with the Romans hanging was a dishonorable. In fact, hanging was the legal

9. Some (Brown, Davies and Allison, Luz, Witherington) argue that "change of mind" (μεταμέλομαι) is quite similar to "repent" (μετανοέω) and interpret this as true "repentance" on Judas's part, noting his return of the money and confession of sin. Yet there is no hint that Judas parallels Peter here (and even with Peter it is implicit), and indeed there is more likely a contrast between the two (26:24, "it would be better for that man if he had not been born"). Morris is probably correct when he says, "the context here makes it clear that Judas was motivated by remorse rather than genuine repentance."

10. Bruner, *Matthew 13–28*, 707.

penalty for capital offenses (Deut 21:22 – 23), and the guilty person was thought to be under God's curse (so Luz). In Judas's hanging himself there may also be an echo of 2 Sam 17:23, where Ahithophel, the companion of David who betrayed him, hung himself.[11]

There is a discrepancy with Acts 1:18 – 19 here. Matthew says Judas "hanged himself," while Acts states he committed suicide by throwing himself into the field and "bursting open." What may well have happened is that the rope broke and his body fell into the field[12] (or perhaps that his body was thrown into the field afterward). This is possible, for Luke in Acts 1 is explaining the name of the field and chose those details that fit his explanation. Note the contrast with Peter, who "went outside and wept bitterly," while Judas "went and hanged himself."

27:6 And the chief priests took[13] the silver coins and said, "The law does not allow us to put this into the treasury, since it is blood money" (οἱ δὲ ἀρχιερεῖς λαβόντες τὰ ἀργύρια εἶπαν, Οὐκ ἔξεστιν βαλεῖν αὐτὰ εἰς τὸν κορβανᾶν, ἐπεὶ τιμὴ αἵματός ἐστιν). Senior believes that the twin ideas of "innocent blood" (v. 4) and "blood money" (v. 6) provide the foundation for this whole pericope.[14] Judas has accepted "blood money" to betray his Master, and the leaders are about to shed "innocent blood." "It is not lawful" (οὐκ ἔξεστιν) also occurs in 12:2; 14:4 for what is not allowed in the Torah; Deut 23:18 says that money acquired in a sinful meanner[15] could not be brought into the house of God, and this is probably the passage the leaders have in mind.[16]

What makes this especially ironic is that the leaders have disregarded the law in condemning "innocent blood" to death, and now they are scrupulous about Judas's returning the "price of blood" (τιμὴ αἵματος) or "blood money." A second irony is that this money was given to Judas by the high priests, so it is their "thirty pieces" as much as it belongs to Judas. They still fail to realize they are every bit as guilty as Judas. As Keener says, "most ancient readers would still assume that its (the blood money) curse remained on them."[17]

27:7 So after they had taken counsel, they used it to buy a potter's field as a burial place for foreigners (συμβούλιον δὲ λαβόντες ἠγόρασαν ἐξ αὐτῶν τὸν ἀγρὸν τοῦ κεραμέως εἰς ταφὴν τοῖς ξένοις). As in 27:1 συμβούλιον λαβόντες means to "make a decision together." So after "counseling" together (a temporal participle) they decide to use the blood money to "purchase" a field. They reason that the best use of "blood money" was to purchase a cemetery for foreigners: an unclean cemetery for unclean pagans, purchased with unclean money — perfect! A further link with Zech 11 (see Matt 27:5, 9 – 10) occurs here, for it is "a potter's field," and in Zech 11:13 the thirty pieces of silver are to be thrown "to the potter" in the sanctuary. The "potter" in Zechariah could be an

11. So Schweizer, Gundry, Brown, Davies and Allison, Luz, Witherington; contra Carson, Gnilka). See also Douglas J. Moo, "Tradition and Old Testament in Matthew 27:3 – 10," in *Studies in Midrash and Historiography* (ed. R. T. France and D. Wenham; Sheffield: JSOT Press, 1983), 157 – 75.

12. See F. F. Bruce, *The Book of Acts* (NICNT; Grand Rapids: Eerdmans, 1956), 49.

13. Another circumstantial participle (see v. 5).

14. Senior, *Passion Narrative*, 386 – 87, from a reprint of his "The Fate of the Betrayer: A Redactional Study of Matthew XXVII, 3 – 10," *ETL* 48 (1972): 372 – 46.

15. Peter C. Craigie, *The Book of Deuteronomy* (NICOT; Grand Rapids: Eerdmans, 1976), 301 – 2.

16. Nolland, *Matthew*, 1154, disagrees that Deut 23 is behind this since the Deuteronomy passage centers on guilt rather than ritual purity. He prefers 1 Chr 22:8 – 9 (David, a man "who has shed much blood," cannot build the temple), where the issue is one of purity. Yet the Deut 23 passage better parallels this issue, and OT passages are seldom used with the level of exactness Nolland is demanding here.

17. Keener, *Matthew*, 661.

artisan making vessels for the temple[18] or perhaps a metalworker at the temple foundry,[19] but here the fact that a potter's field is purchased is seen as a fulfillment of Zech 11.

Another of the discrepancies with Acts 1:18 occurs here. There Judas buys the field, while here the priests buy it. Yet this can be easily harmonized: they purchased the field in his name and with his money.[20]

27:8 Therefore that field is called "Field of Blood" to this very day (διὸ ἐκλήθη ὁ ἀγρὸς ἐκεῖνος Ἀγρὸς Αἵματος ἕως τῆς σήμερον). Acts 1:19 says it was called "in their language Akeldama, that is, Field of Blood" (with "of blood" [αἵματος] a genitive of content), but there it is linked with Judas's bloody death (v. 18) rather than the blood money as here. Once again it is a both-and rather than an either-or. Matthew centers on one aspect, Acts on the other.

Critical scholars tend to say that the field's name was due to other reasons and the Christians are here giving their own version, e.g., it was called this because the blood of the temple sacrifices was channeled to it (Brown, Davies and Allison),[21] that Christians changed it from *ḥᵃkēl dᵉmāʾ* ("field of sleep," so Gnilka), that it originally was based on the bloody death of many of the foreigners interred there (Nolland), or that it echoes Jer 19:6, "people will ... call this place ... the Valley of Slaughter" (France). These are possible but speculative and to some extent unnecessary, for even if one of the suggestions were to be correct, the use of ἕως means that from the time of Judas's death "until" Matthew's day, the name of the field was linked with Judas's death. As Carson concludes,[22] this again emphasizes the tendency of the leaders to stress ceremonial purity in face of injustice (12:9 – 10; 15:1 – 2; 23:23; 28:12 – 13).

27:9 Then the word spoken through Jeremiah the prophet was fulfilled (τότε ἐπληρώθη τὸ ῥηθὲν διὰ Ἰερεμίου τοῦ προφήτου). This is the final of the ten fulfillment formula passages so familiar to Matthew (see on 1:22). Yet at the same time it is part of a major use of this fulfillment motif in the Passion Narrative (see 26:21, 24, 31, 54, 56, 64, 67; 27:5, 7, 9 – 10, 30, 34, 35, 46, 52 – 53), showing that every aspect of Jesus' passion is grounded in God's salvation-historical knowledge and control.

There is a special correspondence to 2:17, linking the two Jeremiah prophecies. A major problem is seen in the allusion to Jeremiah here,[23] for the quote is far closer to Zech 11:12 – 13 (though there are many differences) and the only connection to Jeremiah is the fact that he bought a field (32:6 – 15) and visited a potter (18:2 – 12). Most critical scholars assume an error on Matthew's part or (for some) a copyist's error and discuss the principle of historical fulfillment as the more important issue (i.e., how could you call this "fulfillment" when the circumstances are so different?).[24] Yet it is better to say Matthew fused the two together and simply mentioned Jeremiah as the earlier (rabbinic "weightier") of the two; from Jeremiah comes the "field" and the "purchase" idea.

18. Thomas E. McComiskey, "Zechariah," *The Minor Prophets* (ed. T. E. McComiskey; Grand Rapids: Baker, 1998), 3:1200.

19. C. C. Torrey, "The Foundry of the Second Temple at Jerusalem," *JBL* 55 (1936): 247 – 60, noted by Carson, Davies and Allison, Nolland.

20. Bruce, *Acts*, 49.

21. Following Yigael Yadin, *The Temple Scroll* (New York: Random House, 1985), 132 – 34.

22. Carson, "Matthew," 561.

23. For detailed discussion of the options, see Knowles, *Jeremiah in Matthew's Gospel*, 60 – 69.

24. Typical is Beare, *Matthew*, 526 – 27, who says "This is surely the most extravagant example of Matthew's handling of scriptures as proof-texts.... However he arrived at what he wrote, it must be agreed that he has botched it badly." We hope to show that this simply is not true.

Gundry may have the best solution.[25] He argues that it is actually taken from the acted parables of Jer 19. There we have the purchase of a potter's jar (v. 1), the valley of Ben-Hinnom (v. 2, which may be identical with the field Judas bought), the change of the name to "the Valley of Slaughter" (v. 6), and the breaking of the jar (vv. 10 – 11). So Matthew's quote here partakes of the imagery from Jer 19 (which can also be alluded to in Zech 11), though it is taken mainly from Zech 11. The main emphasis is on fulfillment, i.e., God's sovereign control and knowledge of all events in salvation history. Knowles says this constitutes " 'fulfilment' in verbal detail from Zechariah but 'fulfilment' in thematic substance from Jeremiah."[26]

27:9 ... saying, "And they took the thirty pieces of silver, the price of the honored one set by the people of Israel" (λέγοντος, Καὶ ἔλαβον τὰ τριάκοντα ἀργύρια, τὴν τιμὴν τοῦ τετιμημένου ὃν ἐτιμήσαντο ἀπὸ υἱῶν Ἰσραήλ). Matthew's rendition of Zech 11:12 – 13 is closer to the Hebrew than to the LXX, and it is common to conclude that Matthew provides a free rendering of the Hebrew.[27] The meaning of Zech 11:4 – 14 centers on the false shepherds of Israel, the leaders, who have misused the "flock marked for slaughter," namely, the afflicted nation. So Zechariah becomes the shepherd and names his two staffs "Favor" and "Union." He fires the three false shepherds, but when the people reject him he breaks Favor, signifying their breaking their covenant with God. He then asks them to give him his pay, thirty pieces of silver, the price for buying a slave. Then Yahweh tells him to throw it to the potter in the temple, either the artisan who made the pots or a metalworker who worked at the temple foundry (v. 13), perhaps so they can make a false idol of a god and complete their rejection of Yahweh and his shepherd. Then he breaks Union, namely, the bond between Israel and Judah (v. 14).[28]

Matthew sees a typological parallel (for typology, see on 1:22) between Zechariah and the Judas incident. The false shepherds still lead the nation and again have turned the people away from Yahweh, this time away from his Son. The thirty pieces have now become betrayal or "blood money," and they have now been thrown to the "potter," this time the potter's field. Note the threefold repetition of "price" (τιμή) and cognates. I agree with Hagner that translating the second of these "of the honored (or precious) One" makes sense. Christ's life was valued only at the level of a slave, and Judas has betrayed him for that paltry sum.

27:10 "And they gave them for the potter's field, just as the Lord commanded me" (καὶ ἔδωκαν αὐτὰ εἰς τὸν ἀγρὸν τοῦ κεραμέως, καθὰ συνέταξέν μοι κύριος). The choice of the chief priests to purchase the potter's field with the blood money is also seen as under divine impetus. They were doing what "the Lord commanded," even though they did not know that. The potter is the temple potter of Zech 11:13 but also the potter of Jer 18:1 – 11; 19:1, and the field stems from Jer 32:6 – 15 (so Nolland). In Jeremiah the potter symbolized Yahweh's sovereign control over his people. In Jer 32 the prophet buys a field to typify the

25. Gundry, *Use of the Old Testament*, 122 – 27. So also Moo, "Tradition and Old Testament," 159 – 60; Cope, *Matthew*, 88 – 89; Senior, *Passion Narrative*, 359 – 61.

26. Knowles, *Jeremiah in Matthew's Gospel*, 76.

27. Stendahl, *School of St. Matthew*, 124; Senior, *Passion Narrative*, 356; Knowles, *Jeremiah in Matthew's Gospel*, 54. Brown, *Death*, 648 – 49, says Matthew freely chooses between the LXX and the Hebrew on each section of the quote.

28. See McComiskey, "Zechariah," 1188 – 203; Carson, "Matthew." 564 – 65. France, *Gospel of Matthew*, 1043, sees a "mosaic of scriptural motifs" here, primarily with allusions to Jer 18:1 – 11 (Jeremiah preaching at a potter's house), 19:1 – 13 (Jeremiah using a potter's jug as a visual aid to denounce Jerusalem for shedding "innocent blood"), and ch. 32 (Jeremiah buying a field).

prosperity God would bring to his people when they were restored. In this sense the quote could symbolize the judgment on the nation and yet the promised restoration that would come from Jesus' atoning death (note "Field of Blood" in v. 8).

Brown notes four parallels between the Judas story and Pilate here. (1) Judas tries to rid himself of guilt by saying, "I have sinned by betraying innocent blood," Pilate by saying, "I am innocent of … blood." (2) Both the chief priests and Pilate say, "See to it yourself." (3) Judas throws the money away to get rid of guilt, Pilate washes his hands to do so. (4) Judas involves the authorities in blood guilt, Pilate involves all the people in blood guilt (v. 25).[29]

27:11 Now Jesus stood in front of the governor, and the governor asked him, saying, "Are you the king of the Jews?" (Ὁ δὲ Ἰησοῦς ἐστάθη ἔμπροσθεν τοῦ ἡγεμόνος· καὶ ἐπηρώτησεν αὐτὸν ὁ ἡγεμὼν λέγων, Σὺ εἶ ὁ βασιλεὺς τῶν Ἰουδαίων;). When we combine all four accounts of the trial, John 18:28 – 19:16 gives us the details of the dialogue between Jesus and Pilate inside the praetorium[30] and of Pilate and the people outside, and Luke 23:6 – 12 tells of the interview with Herod (perhaps in the same palace, with the incident coming after Matt 27:14), while Matt 27:19 tells us of Pilate's wife's dream and 27:24 – 25 of Pilate's claim to innocence and the people's willingness to have Jesus' blood on their heads. After the initial accusations had been presented and Pilate's first attempt to send Jesus back to the Sanhedrin for trial (John 18:29 – 32), Pilate went inside the praetorium and asked how Jesus saw the primary issue (Pilate didn't care about blasphemy but about any danger to Rome). Did Jesus really consider himself to be "the king of the Jews" (this is in all four gospels at this point)?

At the outset, the charges are laid before Pilate by the prosecutors (here the Sanhedrin), and the leaders have by necessity twisted their own verdict from blasphemy to high treason by centering on the royal aspects of the messianic claim, thereby making Jesus "King of the Jews" (for this title see also the Magi in 2:2) to make it sound as if Jesus is plotting sedition against Rome (ironically, the very aspect he had denied). Their charge of blasphemy would satisfy a Jewish court but not a Roman court, since it would be considered a Jewish problem and of no concern to Rome.

The charges are elucidated in detail in Luke 23:2: subverting the nation (i.e., inciting them to revolt, possibly portraying him as a revolutionary zealot, cf. Simon the zealot, 10:4); opposing taxes to Caesar, a major aspect of zealot revolt (see on 22:15 – 22 for the lie here); and claiming to be king (see Nolland on the many false prophets who had claimed such). Pilate's initial question here shows he has already heard the charges. Roman law consisted of hearing the charges, then hearing the accused defend himself and the eyewitness testimony, followed by retiring with his advisors, considering it, and rendering the verdict, which would be carried out immediately.

27:11 And Jesus answered, "So you say" (ὁ δὲ Ἰησοῦς ἔφη, Σὺ λέγεις). Jesus' "so you say" (σὺ λέγεις) is the third time Jesus has given this evasive answer (26:25, 64), which agrees with the statement but shows there are important differences (note that in the Sanhedrin trial Jesus went on to spell them out). Therefore, the prophecy of Judas's betrayal (26:25), the Sanhedrin trial

29. Brown, *Death*, 659.

30. The "praetorium" was the residence of the governor, which could have been the fortress Antonia on a hill at the NW corner of the Temple Mount (a Hasmonean fortress rebuilt by Herod the Great and named after Marc Antony), but it was more likely the luxurious palace of Herod the Great at the highest point of the city, a hill on the western side (see Brown, *Death*, 706 – 10).

(26:64), and the trial before Pilate are all connected by Jesus' answer, which shows he transcends the implications of all three. The sufferings of Jesus are linked to his true person and shed light on the reality of his messianic office; here the royal Messiah is seen first as suffering Servant. John 18:34 – 37 shows Jesus' answer was actually more extensive than this and explained his true kingship more completely. Pilate does not react to this and seems aware that Jesus is no threat to Rome, no revolutionary brigand who poses any danger to his office.

27:12 And when he was accused by the chief priests and elders, he answered nothing (καὶ ἐν τῷ κατηγορεῖσθαι αὐτὸν ὑπὸ τῶν ἀρχιερέων καὶ πρεσβυτέρων οὐδὲν ἀπεκρίνατο). By law the claimants were allowed to interact with the charges, and here the leaders press forward with their same charges, with the accusations undoubtedly the charges specified in 26:61 but especially in Luke 23:2 (see above). As in 26:62, there is here another allusion to Isa 53:7 and the suffering Servant whose silence is like a lamb led to the slaughter.

27:13 Then Pilate said to him, "Aren't[31] you hearing how many things they are testifying about against you?" (τότε λέγει αὐτῷ ὁ Πιλᾶτος, Οὐκ ἀκούεις πόσα σου καταμαρτυροῦσιν;). This is also linked to the Sanhedrin trial (26:62), where Jesus did not respond to the charges. Pilate does not understand his silence, and it is hard to know if he is impressed or angered, for Roman trials were built on the defendant answering the charges. Probably he is mystified and cannot understand why Jesus will not respond to such serious charges.

27:14 And Jesus refused to answer him, not even to a single charge, with the result that the governor was astounded (καὶ οὐκ ἀπεκρίθη αὐτῷ πρὸς οὐδὲ ἓν ῥῆμα, ὥστε θαυμάζειν τὸν ἡγεμόνα λίαν). Jesus' refusal to answer "a single charge" (again, alluding to Isa 53:7, the suffering Servant as a lamb led to slaughter that refuses to open his mouth, see also 26:62) amazes Pilate. The majestic dignity of Jesus is stressed in all four accounts, and it is likely Pilate is impressed in spite of himself. It may be that Jesus answered those questions that were official but refused to answer the allegations/false charges (so Morris).

The contrast between Jesus and his accusers is evident in every scene; the passively suffering Messiah awaits his destiny in total control. Yet if Jesus refused to answer, Pilate would have judged him guilty. At the trials of early martyrs who also maintained silence, the Roman judges allowed them three opportunities to speak up and then pronounced them guilty. However, in the context it seems clear that Pilate did not take Jesus' silence as proof of guilt but as cause for wonder (so Davies and Allison).

27:15 Now it was the custom at a festival for the governor to release to the crowd one prisoner whom they wanted (Κατὰ δὲ ἑορτὴν εἰώθει ὁ ἡγεμὼν ἀπολύειν ἕνα τῷ ὄχλῳ δέσμιον ὃν ἤθελον). The problem is that there is no evidence in Roman records or Josephus or anywhere else for a paschal amnesty, so many critical scholars doubt the historicity of this scene, calling it a literary composition intended to explain Jesus' sentence. However three things can be said in favor of the historicity of the event. (1) Roman law does show that an imperial magistrate could pardon prisoners on the basis of the shouts of the crowd (Josephus, *Ant.* 20:208 – 9, 215; Livy 5:13). (2) A Jewish provision in *m. Pesaḥ* 8:6a ("they may slaughter for one ... whom they have promised to bring out of prison") is among the oldest mishnaic traditions

31. "Not" (οὐκ) expects the answer yes. "You are not, are you?"

and points to the release of one or several prisoners at Passover time in Jerusalem. (3) Roman law allowed two types of amnesty—*abolitio*, acquittal before trial (a δέσμιον was a "prisoner" who had been arrested but not yet condemned by trial), and *indulgentia*, acquittal after conviction—Pilate had the authority for this type of amnesty.

So most believe it a trustworthy story (Lane, Hagner, Blomberg, Davies and Allison, Keener, Witherington, France; contra Brown), for there is no reason why the early church would make it up. It would be a natural as a sign of Roman goodwill, and some think Pilate may have initiated it himself, perhaps to atone for some of his bad judgments in the past. Pilate would use this to get a potentially difficult situation off his plate. As Keener says, "Roman officials were generally not inclined to execute (hence, perhaps, make martyrs of) those they saw as harmless fools (cf. Josephus, *J.W.* 6.305)."[32]

27:16 Now at that time they had a well-known prisoner named [Jesus] Barabbas (εἶχον δὲ τότε δέσμιον ἐπίσημον λεγόμενον ['Ιησοῦν][33] Βαραββᾶν). Barabbas was a "notorious" insurrectionist who had committed murder (Mark 15:7), possibly the leader of the two who will eventually be crucified with Jesus and perhaps the leader of the rebellion mentioned in Luke 23:18–19, 25. This may be another strategic error on Pilate's part; to the Romans Barabbas was a murderous terrorist, but to many Jews he would have been a folk hero, an ancient Robin Hood.

27:17 So after they had gathered,[34] Pilate asked them, "Whom do you want me to release to you, [Jesus] Barabbas or Jesus, the one called Messiah?" (συνηγμένων οὖν αὐτῶν εἶπεν αὐτοῖς ὁ Πιλᾶτος, Τίνα θέλετε ἀπολύσω ὑμῖν, ['Ιησοῦν τὸν] Βαραββᾶν ἢ 'Ιησοῦν τὸν λεγόμενον Χριστόν;). The irony of the scene is great, especially since the insurrectionist's name was "Jesus Barabbas." The crowd considers two men named "Jesus" (a name meaning "God saves"), with both being "the son of the father" (the meaning of Bar Abbas).[35] However, the kind of salvation each one offers is quite different: temporal deliverance by the sword vs. eternal deliverance by a Savior. Moreover, Jesus is the true "Son of the Father," not the pretentious "son of a father." The same choices have faced the church in every age, but it is especially poignant in our age of a liberation theology that has preferred the sword over the Spirit.

27:18 For he knew that they had handed Jesus over because of envy (ᾔδει γὰρ ὅτι διὰ φθόνον παρέδωκαν αὐτόν). Pilate is the center of Matthew's story. He had apparently been told of the events of Passion Week and of Jesus' popularity with the crowds. If the triumphal entry made as big a splash as it seems to have, then Pilate would have heard about it from his many informants. So he realizes here that the leaders were φθόνον or "jealous" of Jesus' success with them. He has seen through the façade of legality to the heart of the issue, that the leaders wanted to rid themselves of

32. Keener, *Matthew*, 669–70.

33. The name "Jesus" attached to Barabbas is somewhat questionable due to textual difficulties, yet it has an important meaning (see below). The better witnesses (ℵ A B D K L W 064 Origen Byz et al.) omit it, and only a few contain it (Θ 700 f[1]). But at the same time it is more likely that later scribes would delete it out of reverence for the name "Jesus." Perhaps because in v. 17 the abbreviated form of "Jesus" is IN (taking the first and last later of 'Ιησοῦν), coming after "to you" (ὑμῖν), later scribes in the uncial of Matthew would have the combined form YMININ, and so the IN was lost by haplography. Thus "Jesus" is generally accepted as original (so Metzger, Carson, Hagner).

34. This (and v. 19) forms another temporal genitive absolute, cf. v. 1.

35. Actually "Abbas" was a proper name, so he was "the son of Abbas." At the same time the name is similar to "Abba," meaning "father," so that like Jesus it is "the son of the father." This type of wordplay was common in the first century and would not have been missed.

someone who was a threat to their position with the people.

27:19 Now while he was sitting on his judgment seat (Καθημένου δὲ αὐτοῦ ἐπὶ τοῦ βήματος). The "judgment seat" (βῆμα, *bēma*) (cf. John 19:13; Acts 12:21; 18:12) was a raised platform with a judicial bench or seat on it on which legal decisions were made. The picture (it is more clear in John) is of Pilate dialoguing with Jesus inside the praetorium and then Pilate coming outside and sitting on his *bēma* to address the leaders and crowds.

27:19 ... his wife sent a note to him, saying, "Have nothing to do with that innocent man. For I have suffered greatly today with a dream because of him" (ἀπέστειλεν πρὸς αὐτὸν ἡ γυνὴ αὐτοῦ λέγουσα, Μηδὲν σοὶ καὶ τῷ δικαίῳ ἐκείνῳ· πολλὰ γὰρ ἔπαθον σήμερον κατ᾽ ὄναρ δι᾽ αὐτόν). Pilate's wife (the apocryphal *Acts of Pilate* names her "Procla") probably knew of the trial of Jesus and so sent her message to him shortly after she woke up that morning.[36] We must remember how superstitious the Romans (like all ancient peoples) were, and dreams were often taken as omens from the gods. That is certainly how Pilate's wife understood it. Most likely just before waking up (as the trial was beginning?) she had a nightmare about Jesus, and she felt this was important enough to interrupt Pilate's deliberations.

"With a dream" (κατ᾽ ὄναρ) in the Passion Narrative is found only in Matthew in the NT and elsewhere the expression refers to a divine revelation to Joseph about Mary's pregnancy (1:20), to the Magi about Herod (2:12), or to Joseph about going down to Egypt (2:12 – 13) and returning (2:19). We are certainly to take the dream as a message from God.

There is double meaning in δικαίῳ, referring to Jesus as both "innocent" and "righteous." For her and Pilate, the former is the likely thrust, but both are intended for the reader. Structurally, the emphasis is on "righteous," which adds force to Matthew's stress throughout on Jesus as the "righteous" sufferer. So Pilate is warned by God about the significance of his action; he cannot claim innocence (v. 24b), for he is about to judge a truly innocent man. With this incident Matthew heightens the tension of the scene and its implications. Jesus' enemies are trying the One whom God has already vindicated.

27:20 But the chief priests and the elders persuaded the crowds that they should ask for Barabbas and have Jesus destroyed (Οἱ δὲ ἀρχιερεῖς καὶ οἱ πρεσβύτεροι ἔπεισαν τοὺς ὄχλους ἵνα αἰτήσωνται τὸν Βαραββᾶν, τὸν δὲ Ἰησοῦν ἀπολέσωσιν). This is an important comment. Throughout the gospels the crowds are on Jesus' side, and even here they turn against him only because the leaders "persuade them." The guilt of the leaders is obvious. They have taken the initiative from the start and now have brainwashed the people into serving their own ends.

In 21:46; 26:5 the leaders were afraid to arrest Jesus because of the crowds, but no more. They have turned the crowds against the one they called "the Son of David" who "comes in the name of the Lord" in 21:9. This verse plus the note in Mark 15:8 tells us that they were actually neutral and had really come to see who would be released.

36. Many (e.g., Davies and Allison) have denied the historicity of this because it is only in Matthew, who has a preference for dreams (as in the birth narratives); and because it fits similar tales in Jewish folklore (cf. *b. Taʿan.* 24b, *b. Qidd.* 70b). But the OT and Acts show God uses dreams and such to warn rulers (Gen 37 – 41; Dan 1 – 6); in fact, one of the reasons for Matthew's inclusion of this would probably be the OT imagery it would evoke for his Jewish readers. It is a historically viable story.

Some persuasion by the legal rulers alone could explain why the crowd so cruelly reacted.[37] First they called for Barabbas' release, understandable in itself; but then they called for Jesus' crucifixion. Certainly they were told that he had committed the most heinous of sins to the Jew, blasphemy against God.

27:21 But the governor responded, "Which of the two men do you want me to release to you?" And they said, "Barabbas" (ἀποκριθεὶς δὲ ὁ ἡγεμὼν εἶπεν αὐτοῖς, Τίνα θέλετε ἀπὸ τῶν δύο ἀπολύσω ὑμῖν; οἱ δὲ εἶπαν, Τὸν Βαραββᾶν). This expands on v. 17 and gives the brainwashed crowd's response to Pilate's question. The first question led to the discussion of v. 20, in which the leaders convinced the people to demand Jesus' death. This second time Pilate asks,[38] they are ready. Brown believes this is the turning point, as Pilate turns to decision by *acclamatio populi*, that is, a legal decision made by the demands of the people.[39] Yet this is true only partially, for he continues to seek Jesus' release, yet increasingly involves the crowd in the decision.

27:22 Pilate said to them, "What then should I do with Jesus, the one called Messiah?" They all said, "Let him be crucified!" (λέγει αὐτοῖς ὁ Πιλᾶτος, Τί οὖν ποιήσω Ἰησοῦν τὸν λεγόμενον Χριστόν; λέγουσιν πάντες, Σταυρωθήτω). The brevity of Matthew here increases the dramatic power. The acclamation of the crowd cannot be more clear. They do not want Jesus merely to be stoned like a false prophet (Lev 20:27; 24:14). They "all" (emphasis on πάντες) want him crucified and put on a tree (Deut 21:23; Gal 3:13) outside the camp (Exod 29:14; Lev 4:12, 21; Heb 13:12), thus doubly cut off from the covenant (both aspects meant to be outside the covenant).

The people now fully leave their role as bystanders and intensify their judicial role. Previously they were saying they wanted Barabbas set free, and now they demand the life of Jesus. As Nolland says, "the people seem to be called on ... to be co-judges with Pilate in the case of Jesus ... a deliberate choice on the part of Pilate to involve the same crowd that has thwarted his purposes with Barabbas in determining the fate of Jesus."[40] Pilate is also deflecting his own sense of guilt for condemning an innocent man, preparing for his disclaimer in v. 24.

27:23 But he said, "Why? What evil thing has he done?" But they shouted all the more, "Let him be crucified!" (ὁ δὲ ἔφη, Τί γὰρ κακὸν ἐποίησεν; οἱ δὲ περισσῶς ἔκραζον λέγοντες, Σταυρωθήτω). Pilate leads them to demand crucifixion a second time. In one sense he still would like to free Jesus, for he asks "what evil" the man has done to deserve death, stressing even more the reality of Jesus' "innocence" (δίκαιος, see v. 19). Yet at the same time he continues to capitulate to the crowd as he realizes even further that he cannot do so.

So for a third time Pilate leads the crowd into taking part via *acclamatio populi* (see on v. 21). "All the more" (περισσῶς) with the imperfect tense "shouted" (ἔκραζον) powerfully pictures the crowd screaming out again and again and ever louder their demand for Jesus' crucifixion (note the further contrast with the triumphal entry,

37. Blomberg, *Matthew*, 412, posits that the crowds at the triumphal entry were mainly Galilean pilgrims, while those present at the trial were mainly citizens of Jerusalem and not as well disposed toward Jesus. This is speculative but possible. Nolland, *Matthew*, 1173 – 74, adds that nationalism may have played a role, as Barabbas was a popular figure who represented the revolt against Rome.

38. Senior, *Passion Narrative*, 249, shows how Matthew has filled the gap in Mark 15:12, where Mark simply presupposes and omits this question of Pilate to the crowd. Matthew wants to build the tension of which one the crowd wants released.

39. Brown, *Death*, 720 – 22.

40. Nolland, *Matthew*, 1175.

there with the "shout" of "Hosanna" in 21:9). Their shout becomes a scream of rage, beyond all reason. They cannot answer Pilate's question[41] and so follow the old adage, "When in doubt, shout!" As Ridderbos says, Pilate "abandoned justice to the whims of the crowd."[42]

27:24 Now when Pilate saw that he was getting nowhere, but instead the clamor was getting worse (ἰδὼν δὲ ὁ Πιλᾶτος ὅτι οὐδὲν ὠφελεῖ ἀλλὰ μᾶλλον θόρυβος γίνεται). There have been three successive cries of the crowd, one for freeing Barabbas and two for crucifying Jesus, and in each the "uproar" gets louder. Now Pilate capitulates to the crowd, an action that he probably has been leading up to for at least the last two interactions (vv. 21 – 23). For Matthew there is a further note, the guilt of the Jews for Jesus' death (for the charge of anti-Semitism see on v. 25).

27:24 ... he took[43] water and washed in front of the crowd, saying, "I am innocent of this man's blood. See to it yourself!" (λαβὼν ὕδωρ ἀπενίψατο τὰς χεῖρας ἀπέναντι τοῦ ὄχλου λέγων, Ἀθῷός εἰμι ἀπὸ τοῦ αἵματος τούτου· ὑμεῖς ὄψεσθε). Pilate's act of washing his hands to indicate that he wanted nothing to do with this crucifixion is also widely doubted. The problem is that this was a Jewish rather than Roman custom and so is judged by some to be a creation of Matthew rather than a historical incident.[44] The ritual is found in Deut 21:1 – 9, where it releases a town from bloodguilt in the case of an unsolved murder. It said the people had nothing to do with the murder and so became a gesture of innocence (cf. Ps 26:6; 73:13). However, Pilate could easily have done this in utter contempt for the Jewish demand (so Carson); and there is Hellenistic background for this practice (Virgil, *Aeneid* 2.719; Sophocles, *Ajax* 654, so Hagner, Wilkins).

Also, there is no hint that Matthew thought this exonerated Pilate; his guilt is obvious, so there is real irony in his attempt to declare his innocence. As Davies and Allison say, "he is no more free of responsibility than was Adam when he complained about Eve's advice."[45] So two aspects flow out of this — Jesus' supreme innocence and the guilt of both the Jews and the Romans for Jesus' death. Senior notes the connection between the "innocent blood" in Judas's cry of v. 4 and Pilate's "innocent of blood" here.[46] Judas took responsibility and Pilate did not. Both were guilty. "See to it yourself" (ὑμεῖς ὄψεσθε) is found also in 27:4 (σὺ ὄψῃ) of the chief priests to Judas, and so Pilate joins them in responsibility for Jesus' death.

27:25 And all the people responded,[47] "May his blood be upon us and upon our children" (καὶ ἀποκριθεὶς πᾶς ὁ λαὸς εἶπεν, Τὸ αἷμα αὐτοῦ ἐφ' ἡμᾶς καὶ ἐπὶ τὰ τέκνα ἡμῶν). The response of the crowd is shocking. Pilate may want to exonerate himself of responsibility, but the crowd is more than happy to see the bloodguilt shifted to themselves and even to their children! The presence of "all the people" (πᾶς ὁ λαός) may indicate national guilt, as Israel joins its leaders in repudiating Christ.[48]

41. As in Mark 3:4b (the "silence" of the leaders), there was an answer (blasphemy), but the obvious "righteousness/innocence" of Jesus meant they could not shout it. Moreover, Pilate would not have considered that answer valid in Roman law.

42. Ridderbos, *Matthew*, 521.

43. With "when he saw" (ἰδών) a temporal participle and "he took" (λαβών) a circumstantial participle in this verse.

44. See Hill, *Matthew*, 351; Beare, *Matthew*, 531; Luz, *Matthew 21 – 28*, 500.

45. Davies and Allison, *Matthew*, 3:590.

46. Senior, *Passion Narrative*, 255 – 56.

47. For this common Matthean idiom, see on 3:15, 4:4.

48. So Beare, *Matthew*, 531; Nolland, *Matthew*, 1178, who notes that Matthew has been using "crowds" and here switches to "all the people," used in Exod 19:8, 24:3; 1 Kgs 18:24 for Israel. Contra Joseph A. Fitzmyer, "Anti-Semitism and the Cry of 'All the People' (Matt 27:25)," *TS* 26 (1965): 667 – 71; Hans Kosmala, "His Blood on Us and Our Children

The idea of bloodguilt occurs often in the OT (cf. Lev 20:9; 2 Sam 1:16, 3:28; Jer 26:15) and the NT (Acts 5:28; 18:6; 20:26), and for guilt falling on the children see Exod 20:5, 34:7; 2 Sam 14:9; Josh 7:24 – 25; Jer 31:30 (and the Jewish idea of corporate solidarity). France brings out that "all the people" and "upon our children" means the whole of Israel, including future generations, takes on the guilt.[49] It is common to see this coming true with the destruction of Jerusalem a generation later (so Hill, Hagner, Luz, Turner). This is viable and fits the emphasis that flowed from the cursing of the fig tree/cleansing of the temple to the woes upon the leaders (ch. 23) and then concludes in the prediction of chs. 24 – 25.

But this does not constitute anti-Semitism, and the use of this passage in the Crusades, the pogroms, and the Holocaust was a terrible tragedy that has led to acts of horrible depravity. Matthew does not say anything that was not said often by the OT prophets, and he nowhere says that God and the church have rejected the Jews. While they are indeed guilty of the death of Jesus, so are the Romans — indeed, so are all of us! In 28:18 the Jews are part of the nations to whom the gospel will go (see also on 10:5 – 6; 15:24). This is also true of the Jewish sermons in Acts, which also stress Jewish guilt but say in effect, "You put Christ on the cross, but he died for you. Come to him and be saved!" (Acts 2:36 – 39; 3:17 – 20; 13:27 – 29, 38 – 39).[50]

27:26 Then he released Barabbas to them, but he had Jesus scourged[51] and handed him over to be crucified (τότε ἀπέλυσεν αὐτοῖς τὸν Βαραββᾶν, τὸν δὲ Ἰησοῦν φραγελλώσας παρέδωκεν ἵνα σταυρωθῇ). In keeping with the paschal amnesty and the crowd's demand (vv. 17, 21 – 23), Pilate frees the guilty "son of the father" and sends him back "to them" (the people of Israel) and then "delivers" (παρέδωκεν, the final of the fifteen times this key term is used in the Passion Narrative) the innocent "Son of the Father" to the executioners. When Pilate delivered Jesus up to be scourged, he was following the legal code, which demanded that scourging precede capital punishment. The purpose in the case of crucifixion was actually humane, for it weakened the prisoner and helped him die more quickly, lessening the terrible agonies of the cross.

Scourging, however, was a terrible punishment in itself; in fact, as with crucifixion, it could only be inflicted on a Roman citizen by direct edict of Caesar. There were three kinds of beatings: the *fustigatio*, a less severe form for light offenses; the *flagellatio*, a severe beating for hardened criminals; and the *verberatio*, the most severe of them, in which the victim was beaten by a succession of soldiers, often with a scourge, a whip made up of strips of leather onto which were tied pieces of metal or bone. After only a few strokes the person's back was torn apart; and a hard blow could tear out a person's internal organs. With Jesus it was most likely the *verberatio* and thus undoubtedly

(The Background of Matt. 27, 24 – 25)," *ASTI* 7 (1968 – 69): 94 – 126; and Davies and Allison, *Matthew*, 3:592, who take it as a subgroup within Israel who were there and were subverted by the leaders.

49. France, *Gospel of Matthew*, 1057. He believes this represents the end of the old regime of Israel swept away by the events of AD 66 – 70 and making way for a new people of God made up of believing Jews and non-Jews.

50. Several go a step further and posit a double meaning, that "the blood be on our heads" is actually the atoning blood of Christ for salvation: Reginald H. Smith, "Matthew 27:25: The Hardest Verse in Matthew's Gospel," *CurTM* 17 (1990): 421 – 28; Timothy B. Cargal, "His Blood Be upon Us and upon Our Children: A Matthean Double Entendre?" *NTS* 37 (1991): 101 – 12. While this is an interesting possibility, it is unlikely at this point of the Passion Narrative. The crowd is calling for the blood of Christ (his death), and there is no hint in the context of a double meaning.

51. As so often in Matthew, the circumstantial participle "scourged" (φραγελλώσας) is translated as a main verb.

terrible, but controlled sufficiently that he could go to the cross.[52] He was indeed the suffering Servant of Isa 53:10 – 12. The phrase "handed him over to be crucified" is a further allusion to the righteous suffering Servant, recalling Isa 53:6, 12 LXX (cf. 26:28, 62; 27:12).

Theology in Application

Senior summarizes the redactional themes of Matthew in this section:[53] (1) emphasis on "a deliberate choice" between Jesus and Barabbas; (2) movement from the " 'eyewitness' flavor" of Mark to a "more formalized tableau" for the development of his themes; (3) the Gentile governor and his wife centering on Jesus' innocence, contrasted with the Jewish people who increasingly reject Christ and demand his death; (4) the strong underlying emphasis on the divine will, as even the claim of innocence (v. 24) and guilt (v. 25) are "addressed to God."

1. Who Is Responsible?

The Jewish people are guilty for putting to death the Messiah. In vv. 1 – 2 it is the Jewish leaders who take Jesus to Pilate and demand his death, and in vv. 21 – 25 the people take the responsibility for his crucifixion squarely on their own shoulders, saying, "May his blood be upon us and upon our children." Pilate and his wife are presented as standing against them, declaring the innocence of Jesus. Matthew, second only to John, stresses the Jewish rejection of Jesus, and beginning with ch. 11 it is a major theme of his gospel.

Of course, there are two levels. (1) In actuality, Jesus' Jewish opponents in Jerusalem were liable for the death of the Messiah. (2) Matthew also wants to stress the guilt of the Jewish people as a whole, as often in Acts (Acts 2:36; 3:15, 17; 7:51 – 53; 13:27 – 29). But as stated on v. 25, this is not anti-Semitism, for Matthew's purpose (as also John and Acts) is evangelistic. He hopes that the fact of their guilt will drive them to repentance and salvation.

2. Judas

Judas represents all who reject the Messiah out of greed and self-serving ambition. Bruner studies recent attempts to make Judas a hero and to explain away his betrayal (some caused by the misuse of the recently discovered *Gospel of Judas*), and he concludes that Judas was neither hero nor demon but a deeply flawed human being who did in fact betray his Lord. In that sense any of us can fall into this

52. The outcry about Mel Gibson's movie *The Passion of the Christ* and its realism was misguided. In reality, the flogging scene, bloody though it was, was not as terrible as the real event would have been!

53. Senior, *Passion Narrative*, 262.

terrible error. Jesus said, "But whoever denies me before people, I will also deny before my Father in heaven" (10:33). There are degrees by which this is done, from being a "closet" Christian who tells no one about the faith, to denying Jesus in a moment of pressure, to being a passive apostate (Jas 5:19 – 20), to being an active apostate (Heb 6:4 – 6).

3. God's Sovereignty, Even over Evil

The one thing both the trial narratives and the Judas story have in common is the superintending will of God. This has already been emphasized (see introduction to 26:1 – 28:20; 26:17 – 30; and "Theology in Application" on 26:1 – 5, 31 – 56), so there is no need to discuss it in further detail. But the centrality of this in vv. 9 – 10, 19, continues this theme, so it must be noted. Jesus' sovereign majesty as he stands alone before all the forces of evil stems from his knowledge of that divine will. As Job said in the conclusion to his book, "I know that you can do all things; no plan of yours can be thwarted" (Job 42:2).

4. Wash Your Hands?

It is common in our day to believe that the mere statement or thought of guiltlessness is enough to absolve one of sin. But we do not control the final judgment, God does. Anyone who says, "As long as I am more good than bad, I can get into heaven," is engaging in flights of fancy that will have disastrous (and eternal) consequences. Like Pilate, you cannot be free of guilt just by declaring it so.

CHAPTER 118

Matthew 27:27 – 50

Literary Context

The Passion Narrative is moving to its inevitable conclusion. Jesus has been condemned first by the Jewish leadership and then by Pilate. All that remains is the carrying out of the sentence. He will be mocked and rejected in turn by the Roman soldiers, the leaders, the crowds, and the criminals crucified alongside him. He will suffer every indignity possible, but he will endure it with but one cry of agony, not at the pain or the mockery but by the sense of abandonment by his Father.

VII. The Passion and Resurrection of Jesus (26:1 – 28:20)
- **A. The Passion Narrative (26:1 – 27:61)**
  - 4. The Trials of Jesus and Peter's Denials (26:57 – 27:26)
    - a. The Sanhedrin Trial and Peter's Denials (26:57 – 75)
    - b. The Trial before Pilate (27:1 – 26)
  - ➦ **5. The Crucifixion and Death of Jesus (27:27 – 50)**
    - **a. Mockery by the Roman Soldiers (27:27 – 31)**
    - **b. The Crucifixion of Jesus (27:32 – 38)**
    - **c. Mockery by the Jews (27:39 – 44)**
    - **d. The Death of Jesus (27:45 – 50)**
  - 6. Events Following Jesus' Death (27:51 – 61)

Main Idea

The crucifixion scene fulfills the passion predictions of Jesus, especially the third one (20:19), where Jesus is to be "mocked and scourged" by the Gentiles and then killed. It also fulfills messianic prophecy regarding the righteous martyr of Ps 22 and 69 and the suffering Servant, who would be beaten and mocked (Isa 50:6), despised and rejected (Isa 53:3), yet who "bore our suffering" and "was pierced for our transgressions ... crushed for our iniquities" (53:4 – 5). Once again, God's sovereign will controls the action, and Jesus dies as the vicarious sacrifice for humanity.

Translation

Matthew 27:27-50

27a Scene #1 Setting/ Action **Then the soldiers of the governor took Jesus into the praetorium and**
b **gathered the whole cohort**
around him.

28a Actions And **they stripped him and**
b **placed a scarlet cloak around him.**
29a **They wove a crown of thorns and**
placed it on his head
b **as well as a wooden stick in his right hand.**
c And **they fell on their knees before him and mocked him, saying,**
d *"Hail, King of the Jews!"*
30a And **they spit on him,**
b **then took the stick and repeatedly hit him on his head.**

31a Actions After they had mocked him,
b **they stripped the cloak off him,**
c **put his garments back on him, and**
d **led him away to be crucified**

32a Scene #2 Setting As they were going out,
b **they found a man from Cyrene named Simon.**
c Action **They forced him to carry Jesus' cross.**

33a Setting After they had gone out to a place
called "Golgotha,"
b Identification that is,
called "The Place of the Skull,"
34a Action **they gave him wine to drink mixed with gall.**

b And when he tasted it,
c Result of 34a **he did not want to drink it.**

35a Time And after they put him on the cross,
b Action **they divided his garments,**
c Means of 35b throwing dice for them.

36a Action So **they sat and watched him there.**
37a Identification And **they placed the criminal charge in writing above his head,**
b *"This is Jesus, the King of the Jews."*
38a Action **Then they crucified with him two armed bandits,**
b one on his right and the other on his left.

39a Scene #3 (A) And **those who passed by kept on hurling abuse at him,**
shaking their heads, and
saying,

Continued on next page.

Continued from previous page.

40a	Taunts	*"You . . . save yourself*
		who are going to destroy the temple and
		rebuild it in three days.
b		*If you are the Son of God,*
		come down from that cross."
41a	Parallel 39a (A')/Action	**In the same way the chief priests with the teachers of law and elders**
		continued to mock him, saying,
42a	Taunts	*"He saved others but did not have the power to save himself.*
b		*He is the king of Israel!*
c		*Let him come down now from the cross and*
		then we will believe in him.
43a		*He has trusted in God.*
b		*Let God rescue him now if he wants him,*
c		*for he said,*
d		*'I am the Son of God.'"*
44a	Parallel 39a, 41a (A")	**In the same way**
		the armed bandits . . . taunted him as well
		who had been crucified with him.
45a	Time	And from the sixth hour
b	Event	**darkness came over the whole land,**
c		lasting until the ninth hour.
46a	Time	Now about the ninth hour
b	Action	**Jesus cried out in a loud voice, saying,**
c	Entreaty	*"Eli, eli, lema sabachthani?"*
d	Explanation	That is, *"My God, my God, why have you abandoned me?"*
e		
47a	Response #1 for 46c	But when some of those standing there heard this,
b		**[1] they said,**
c		*"He is calling for Elijah."*
48a	Response #2 for 46c	**[2] And immediately one of them ran,**
		took a sponge, and
		immersed it in sour wine.
b		**Then he put it on a reed and gave it to him to drink.**
49a	Response #3 for 46c	**[3] But the rest of the people said,**
b		*"Leave him alone.*
c		*Let's see if Elijah comes and delivers him."*
50a	Conclusion	**But Jesus again cried out with a loud voice and gave up his spirit.**

Structure and Literary Form

Matthew continues his practice of working closely with Mark (Mark 15:16 – 41) with some departures. He adds material in v. 29 (the reed and kneeling added to Mark 15:17), omits material on Simon of Cyrene in v. 32 as well as the time note on "third hour" in v. 36, adds "If you are the Son of God" in v. 40 and the material in v. 43 (with "Son of God"), has the cry of dereliction in Hebrew ("Eli" in v. 46) while

Mark has the Aramaic "Eloi" in 15:34, and has Jesus "giving up his spirit" in v. 50 (Mark 15:37, "breathed his last"). It is best to see four sections: the mockery by the Roman soldiers (vv. 27 – 31, presented in a chiasm), the placing of Jesus on the cross (vv. 32 – 38), the mockery by the Jewish groups (vv. 39 – 44: the people, the leaders, the criminals), and the death of Jesus (vv. 45 – 50).

Exegetical Outline

- **I. Mockery by the Roman Soldiers (27:27 – 31)**
  - A. Taken and stripped (vv. 27 – 28, 31)
  - B. Crown of thorns, hit with a reed (vv. 29a, 30)
  - C. Hailed as King of the Jews (v. 29b)
- **II. Crucifixion of Jesus (27:32 – 38)**
  - A. The conscription of Simon (v. 32)
  - B. Refusing the drink at Golgotha (vv. 33 – 34)
  - C. Dividing his garments (vv. 35 – 36)
  - D. The superscription on the cross (v. 37)
  - E. The two criminals crucified with him (v. 38)
- **III. Mockery by the Jews (27:39 – 44)**
  - A. By the crowds (vv. 39 – 40)
  - B. By the leaders (vv. 41 – 43)
  - C. By the thieves (v. 44)
- **IV. The Death of Jesus (27:45 – 50)**
  - A. Darkness for three hours (v. 45)
  - B. The cry of dereliction (v. 46)
  - C. Giving Jesus a drink in misunderstanding (vv. 47 – 49)
  - D. Jesus' death (v. 50)

Introduction to the Crucifixion of Jesus

This is the central point of salvation history, for the cross and resurrection (i.e., the humiliation and vindication/exaltation) form a single event in *Heilsgeschichte* ("history of salvation") viewed as the eschatological fulcrum moving the wall between the God-humanity relationship. Crucifixion was considered the ultimate in cruel, degrading punishments.[1] It can be traced back to the

1. See Martin Hengel, *Crucifixion in the Ancient World and the Folly of the Message of the Cross* (Philadelphia: Fortress, 1977).

Persians and other ancient Near Eastern groups, who would publicly humiliate vanquished foes by exhibiting their corpses on spikes. An earlier form of this is seen in Deut 21:23: "Anyone who is hung on a pole is under God's curse."

The Carthaginians and then Romans changed this by devising a cruel, inhumane torturous death upon a cross. This was done in two ways: For a particularly slow, excruciating death they would tie the person up on the cross and let him expire as his weight slowly cut off his blood circulation; those crucified would repeatedly lift themselves up for air then fall back down in exhaustion as their arms slowly turned to gangrene and they died of asphyxiation. For a quicker death the Romans would nail a victim to the tree so that he would also bleed to death; and they would sometimes aid the process by scourging beforehand and/or breaking the legs so shock would cause instant death to the weakened victim.

To the Romans, it was so degrading that a Roman citizen could only be crucified by direct edict of Caesar. To the Jews, crucifixion meant that the person was outside the covenant people; they demanded that crucifixions take place outside the walls of Jerusalem (imagery of the OT scapegoat). The early church preserved the theological meaning of the cross as degrading (Heb 12:2) and especially as a curse (Gal 3:13) but added further nuances. The cross as life-giving balm became the leading thrust and substitutionary atonement the result. The OT idea of the paschal lamb and the sin offering were used by Jesus and then taken up by the church as explication of the true meaning of the cross.

Finally, Jesus fused his priestly work with the Isa 53 imagery of the suffering Servant ("for us") and became both sacrificer and sacrifice (esp. in Hebrews). In its preaching (*kerygma*) the early church focused on the resurrection (the apologetic basis of the gospel, as seen in Acts) while in its teaching (*didachē*) it focused on the crucifixion (the theological basis of our salvation in the gospel, as seen in the NT letters).

The four gospels each stress different nuances of the meaning of the crucifixion, as seen in the way they orchestrate their scenes. (1) Mark and Matthew stress the horror of the scene, as contrasted with the sovereignty of Jesus and the victorious nature of his death (the differences will be pointed out below). They do so by dividing it into two major scenes—first the threefold taunts by the spectators and then the horror of the death scene. The second half progresses from the darkness to the cry of dereliction to a further taunt and then to death "with a loud cry."

(2) Luke 23:33–48 makes the crucifixion a scene of worship. There are two major emphases: Jesus as the innocent righteous martyr who forgives his enemies and by his very attitude converts his opponents; the major element is the

atmosphere of worship that predominates. This is seen in the omissions (the wine and myrrh, the cry of dereliction, the Elijah taunt — those very scenes that paint a picture of the horror of the event) as well as the additions (the prayer that God forgive Jesus' enemies [contrasts with the mockery scene in Mark], the promise to the good malefactor [in answer to his prayer], and the commitment of his spirit to the Father [replaces the "loud cry" of Mark]). Luke replaces horror with worship.

(3) John 19:17 – 37 goes even further than Luke in removing details suggesting the horror of the scene (he also omits the darkness and the taunts) and stresses Jesus' total control of the situation. The enthronement of the suffering Messiah is seen in several ways: (a) The inscription on the cross is in Latin, Greek, and Hebrew, which "turns the charge into a worldwide proclamation of enthronement." (b) Pilate continues the dialogue on kingship and unconsciously upholds it (19:21 – 22). (c) The two sayings, "I am thirsty" and "it is finished," fuse the suffering Servant and paschal lamb motifs (recalling Ps 69). (d) At the same time, we see the personal, tender Jesus, who turns the care of his mother over to the Beloved Disciple (19:25 – 27), thereby establishing family relationships at the heart of his new community, the church.[2]

Explanation of the Text

27:27 Then the soldiers of the governor took[3] Jesus into the praetorium and gathered the whole cohort around him (Τότε οἱ στρατιῶται τοῦ ἡγεμόνος παραλαβόντες τὸν Ἰησοῦν εἰς τὸ πραιτώριον συνήγαγον ἐπ' αὐτὸν ὅλην τὴν σπεῖραν). This opening scene describes the setting for the mockery. Pilate had condemned Jesus in the courtyard, and now guards take him back into the praetorium, probably the former palace of Herod the Great (see on v. 11). These were the auxiliary troops (probably from Syria) commanded by Pilate. A "cohort" was normally six hundred soldiers (a tenth of a legion), but this probably refers to a company of them who were stationed at the palace that day. "Gathered" (συνάγω) is used often in the Passion Narrative (26:3, 57; 27:17, 62), always in a context of plotting against Jesus. So we can translate ἐπ' as "assembled *against*" Jesus (so Davies and Allison).

27:28 And they stripped him and placed a scarlet cloak around him (καὶ ἐκδύσαντες αὐτὸν χλαμύδα κοκκίνην περιέθηκαν αὐτῷ). This second mockery scene (once more fulfilling 20:19 as well as Isa 53:7 – 8)[4] builds on the first (cf.

2. See Osborne, *John*, 275 – 76.

3. Here and in vv. 28, 29 (twice), 30 circumstantial participles are translated as main verbs (see on v. 26).

4. Normally scourging either directly preceded crucifixion (as stated earlier) or was done on the way while the victim carried his cross. Here, however, the mocking by the soldiers follows the scourging; this seems difficult to reconcile both with the usual place of scourging and with its normal effects. While the soldiers would be cruel enough to taunt one who had been scourged, it would be dangerous insofar as the loss of blood during the taunting might make the prisoner unable to bear his cross and get them in trouble. One solution

26:67–68), but now it is Roman soldiers rather than Jewish leaders. Many have doubted the historicity of this (asking why trained soldiers would do such a thing), but there are many historical parallels.

Brown offers several possible backgrounds for the scene:[5] (1) historical incidents, e.g., a mentally challenged man named Karabbas mocked by an anti-Semitic crowd with a mock royal robe and a reed as a scepter; a crowd mocking Agrippa I (who acted like a god) after his death; pirates mocking prisoners as if they were notables; (2) games of mockery, e.g., *basilinda*, with one selected as king everyone must obey, or mockery of the crucified (the picture of a donkey crucified with people worshiping it); (3) theatrical mimes, e.g., mimes of kings; (4) carnival festivals, e.g., the Sacaean feast of Persia, with a condemned prisoner made king of the feast and then scourged and killed; the Roman Saturnalia, in which a mock king gave orders within the orgies; and the Roman Kronia, with a Roman soldier playing the god Saturn (Greek Kronos) during the feasting. These parallels show a strong background to such royal mockery, and there is no reason to doubt the historical basis for the game played here.

Jesus must have had his robe placed back on him after the beating of v. 26, because they once more strip his clothes off (probably with his loin cloth kept on). Mark 15:20 has a "purple" garment, Matthew a "scarlet" or "crimson" cloak placed on him (the two most expensive dies and thus most luxurious colors).[6] The first would signify royalty, the second authority (it was probably a worn officer's cloak). Undoubtedly a combination of the games mentioned above drove them (they would have been well known), and the soldiers likely did this often with condemned prisoners to pass the time.

27:29 They wove a crown of thorns and placed it on his head as well as a wooden stick in his right hand (καὶ πλέξαντες στέφανον ἐξ ἀκανθῶν ἐπέθηκαν ἐπὶ τῆς κεφαλῆς αὐτοῦ καὶ κάλαμον ἐν τῇ δεξιᾷ αὐτοῦ). The crown of thorns could have been made from the "thorn bush" mentioned in Isa 34:13 or the date palm, which had thorns up to twelve inches in length. If the latter, there is further irony since the same palm tree yielded the branches used to hail Jesus as king at the triumphal entry just five days earlier. However, it is impossible to know for certain since there were numerous kinds of thorn bushes. We can be sure, however, that they were long thorns, for they were intended to symbolize the royal diadem with the light rays radiating from the heads of the emperors, as on numerous coins in the first century.[7] The reed imitated the royal scepter and could be the flimsy staff of a reed (see 11:7) or a wooden staff (so BAGD, 398; Hagner). Both the crown and the reed mocked Jesus' status as "King of the Jews," further irony given the fact that he is actually the ruler of the world.

---

is to note how Luke 23:11 places the mocking scene during the trial before Herod; Mark and Matthew then follow a topical rather than chronological format, placing it after Pilate's trial (John places both the scourging and the mockery into the middle of the trial scene as part of his chiastic arrangement; so Hill). Still, we cannot be certain, and this order is also historically possible. Mocking was a common practice among soldiers and even among magistrates, as seen in the Sanhedrin trial scene; it is possible that there was a mockery scene at each stage of Jesus' trial.

5. Brown, *Death*, 873–77.

6. BAGD, 694 (noted in Carson), notes that in Appian, *Civil Wars* 2.150, a soldier's cloak is called "purple," so there is no contradiction.

7. For this reason France, *Matthew* (TNTC), 394, and C. Bonner, "The Crown of Thorns," *HTR* 46 (1953): 47–48, argue that the thorns were not meant for torture but were decorative. This is indeed possible, but it is likely a both-and. They did represent the light rays on the coins but were also intended to cause as much pain as possible (in keeping with the larger scene).

27:29 And they fell on their knees before him and mocked him, saying, "Hail, King of the Jews!" (καὶ γονυπετήσαντες ἔμπροσθεν αὐτοῦ ἐνέπαιξαν αὐτῷ λέγοντες, Χαῖρε, βασιλεῦ τῶν Ἰουδαίων). In the presence of the emperor all supplicants were to fall on their knees in obeisance. So the soldiers mockingly copy this[8] and hail Jesus as king, mimicking the "Ave, Caesar" cry. Again, there is great irony as they hail the one person in the world who is truly their King. Note how often "King of the Jews" appears, with Pilate's question (v. 11), the inscription on the cross (v. 37), and the taunts of the leaders (v. 42) — four in all. There is major emphasis on Jesus as the royal Messiah who will conquer (see also 2:2; 21:5; 25:31, 34, 40), but this time by dying as the atoning sacrifice.

27:30 And they spit on him, then took the stick and repeatedly hit him on his head (καὶ ἐμπτύσαντες εἰς αὐτὸν ἔλαβον τὸν κάλαμον καὶ ἔτυπτον εἰς τὴν κεφαλὴν αὐτοῦ). Spitting and hitting Jesus repeats the actions of the leaders in 26:67–68 and recalls Isa 50:6 ("I did not hide my face from mocking and spitting"). The spitting and beating may have started with mock kisses (oriental custom) and salutes of homage but degenerated into pure cruelty. The imperfect in "[they] hit" (ἔτυπτον) could be durative (kept on striking Jesus) or ingressive (began to hit him). The former seems more in keeping with the imagery. It may also be that this imagery favors a stick or cane rather than a fragile reed (which would break with repeated hitting).

27:31 After they had mocked him, they stripped the cloak off him, put his garments back on him, and led him away to be crucified (καὶ ὅτε ἐνέπαιξαν αὐτῷ, ἐξέδυσαν αὐτὸν τὴν χλαμύδα καὶ ἐνέδυσαν αὐτὸν τὰ ἱμάτια αὐτοῦ καὶ ἀπήγαγον αὐτὸν εἰς τὸ σταυρῶσαι). The "mockery" here sums up the derisive actions of vv. 27–30. Normally, the prisoner went naked to the place of execution. This odd departure from custom may have been done because the soldiers were not going to scourge him further (perhaps to do so would kill him). Or, perhaps better, they were taking into account Jewish sensitivities against nakedness at Passover (France, Hagner, Nolland). During the feast Pilate would not want to anger the crowds unduly.

Pilate's patron, the anti-Semite Sejanus, was falling out of favor and was executed the next year (AD 31); Pilate's conciliatory attitude may have been due to fear for his political life. John 19:23 adds a historical note to the scene of v. 31b: an execution squad consisting of four soldiers under the command of a centurion placed the cross on Jesus' back and began the way to the execution site.

27:32 As they were going out,[9] they found a man from Cyrene named Simon. They forced him to carry Jesus' cross (Ἐξερχόμενοι δὲ εὗρον ἄνθρωπον Κυρηναῖον ὀνόματι Σίμωνα, τοῦτον ἠγγάρευσαν ἵνα ἄρῃ τὸν σταυρὸν αὐτοῦ). This does not say whether the conscription occurred upon their leaving the praetorium or the city confines. Mark's added note that he was "passing by on his way in from the country" (Mark 15:21) may favor the latter, since he was likely on the road into Jerusalem. The historicity of "Simon of Cyrene" (modern Libya) is supported by Mark's peripheral "father of Alexander and Rufus," which shows that

8. This is linked with the bowing of the Magi in 2:11 and the Canaanite woman in 15:25. They bow in worship, while here the soldiers bow in derision. The Magi gave the baby Jesus, the future king, magnificent gifts, while the soldiers give him a mock robe and scepter (so Davies and Allison).

9. The participles here and v. 33 are temporal, with the present tense "going out" (ἐξερχόμενοι) indicating contemporaneous action ("while, as") and the aorist "gone out" (ἐλθόντες, v. 33) indicating subsequent action ("after").

his children were well known to the early church ("Rufus" in Rom 16:13).[10]

Normally a prisoner carried his own crosspiece (at times being scourged on the way) to the execution site, where it was fixed to the vertical beam kept there for crucifixions (Keener). But Christ's loss of blood made it obvious that he could not bear his cross far, so they requisitioned a civilian (a legal prerogative of the Romans); Simon likely bore it himself rather than helped Jesus, as many old inscriptions hint (Simon with the cross and Jesus holding the bottom end). About this incident France says, there was a "need for a new Simon to take the place of the Simon who had so loudly protested his loyalty in 26:33, 35."[11]

27:33 After they had gone out to a place called "Golgotha," that is, called "The Place of the Skull" (Καὶ ἐλθόντες εἰς τόπον λεγόμενον Γολγοθᾶ, ὅ ἐστιν Κρανίου Τόπος λεγόμενος). "Golgotha" is the Greek transliteration of the Aramaic *Gulgultā,* "skull." It is not known whether the place was called that because the knoll resembled a skull or because it was the Roman site for executions. The popular modern site for that is Gordon's Calvary, but most scholars are convinced the Church of the Holy Sepulchre is the better option.[12] The main thing we know is that it was on the main highway coming into Jerusalem. The Romans always executed criminals on major thoroughfares as a warning to the citizens.

27:34 ... they gave him wine to drink mixed with gall. And when he tasted it, he did not want to drink it (ἔδωκαν αὐτῷ πιεῖν οἶνον μετὰ χολῆς μεμιγμένον· καὶ γευσάμενος οὐκ ἠθέλησεν πιεῖν). Mark 15:23 has "wine mixed with myrrh," a mild narcotic that would dull the pain of the cross (Prov 31:6, "Let beer be for those who are perishing, wine for those who are in anguish"). But Matthew has "poison" (χολή) for two reasons. (1) The term is used in the LXX of Ps 69:21 ("They put gall in my food and gave me vinegar for my thirst"), with Jesus typologically reenacting the righteous sufferer of that psalm. (2) It brings out the bitterness of the taste (another temporal participle) as part of the cruel mockery of the Roman soldiers. Jesus' refusal is noted because it gives further stress to the voluntary nature of his death. He chose to face his death fully conscious and in control of the events. Jesus' tasting it brings out the fact that he could not know what it contained until he tasted it (so McNeile).

27:35 And after they put him on the cross (σταυρώσαντες δὲ αὐτόν). At a crucifixion site the execution detail (usually four soldiers) would either tie or nail the victim's wrists to the crossbar, then lift him up to the post where they would either let him hang or nail his feet to the post (often with a small perch halfway on which he could periodically pull himself up to rest his body, probably to prolong the agony). They would use the nails when they needed to ensure a quick death, as was the case here because the bodies had to be buried by sundown (when Passover began).

There were four types of crosses: a stake in the ground, a cross in the shape of an "X" (St. Andrew's

10. He was probably a Diaspora Jew either living in or visiting Jerusalem. It is possible that this led to Simon's conversion, although not definitely; if he had been a convert, one might expect that the fame of having bore the cross would have made him known to the early church and thereby would not have necessitated Mark's aside. Lane points to a burial cave discovered in the Kidron Valley in 1941, belonging to Cyrenian Jews from the pre – AD 70 first century and bearing an ossuary inscribed "Alexander, son of Simon" in Greek.

11. France, *Gospel of Matthew,* 1065.

12. See Reiner Riesner, "Golgotha und die Archäologie," *BK* 40 (1985): 21 – 26; G. Barkay, "The Garden Tomb — Was Jesus Buried There?" *BAR* 12/2 (1986): 40 – 57; D. Baahat, "Does the Holy Sepulchre Church Mark the Burial of Jesus?" *BAR* 12/3 (1986): 26 – 45.

cross), a cross in the shape of a "T" (St. Anthony's cross), and a traditional cross. This last one must be the one on which Christ was crucified, for it was used when a tablet listing the crimes was to be placed above the criminal's head. The poles were about seven feet high, enough to get the feet off the ground; when the soldier gave him the vinegar, he placed the sponge on a reed and extended it a couple feet to Jesus' mouth (v. 48).[13]

27:35 ... they divided his garments, throwing dice for them (διεμερίσαντο τὰ ἱμάτια αὐτοῦ βάλλοντες κλῆρον). Once again Jesus is stripped so that he is crucified nude.[14] Legally, the prisoner's goods belonged to the soldiers, and if these were meager (as with Jesus), they would make a diversion out of it by throwing dice (a circumstantial participle) to see who got it. More importantly, this is presented in language reminiscent of Ps 22:18 (implicit fulfillment here, explicit in John 19:23 – 25), another psalm on the innocent righteous sufferer. In this psalm, it is a cry of despair over the powerlessness of David in the midst of personal defeat; to the early church this is seen as fulfilled in the similar experience of Jesus, powerless before his enemies.

27:36 So they sat and watched him there (καὶ καθήμενοι ἐτήρουν αὐτὸν ἐκεῖ). This is found only in Matthew and records the vigilance of the guards.[15] Some say Matthew added this to counter the later charge that Jesus was taken from the cross before he was actually dead (Hill, Carson), but this could also mean they already sensed something unusual and were enthralled, preparing for the centurion's cry in v. 54 (France, Hagner). In 26:36, 38, Jesus asks his disciples to "sit" and keep watch over him as he enters Gethsemane. The guards do the same (the imperfect "they watched" [ἐτήρουν] indicates ongoing activity), but they do not fall asleep and at the same time do not have the same level of interest as the disciples did.

Brown reports a comment by Petronius (*Satyricon* 111) regarding a soldier watching over crucified robbers to make sure their bodies were not taken down from the cross.[16] Crucifixion was a boring time for the execution detail, as all the soldiers could do was sit and wait for death to overtake the prisoners. They probably had no great interest in the proceedings, and it was doubtful they shared in the entertainment value of the proceedings for the general populace (as executions were in the Middle Ages or in the Wild West of the nineteenth century). Still, there may have been more than just the centurion who sensed something extraordinary happening.

27:37 And they placed the criminal charge in writing above his head, "This is Jesus, the King of the Jews" (καὶ ἐπέθηκαν ἐπάνω τῆς κεφαλῆς αὐτοῦ τὴν αἰτίαν αὐτοῦ γεγραμμένην· Οὗτός ἐστιν Ἰησοῦς ὁ βασιλεὺς τῶν Ἰουδαίων). The inscription (called a *titulus*) was common in capital crimes, either tied around the victim's neck or nailed to the cross and stating his crime. It is probable that Pilate wrote "King of the Jews" as deliberate mockery, and the three languages (John's

13. For more details, see Hengel, *Crucifixion*; Ernst Bammel. "Crucifixion as a Punishment in Palestine," in *The Trial of Jesus* (FS C. F. D. Moule; ed. E. Bammel; London: SCM, 1970), 162 – 65; Joseph A. Fitzmyer, "Crucifixion in Ancient Palestine, Qumran Literature, and the New Testament," *CBQ* 40 (1978): 493 – 513; and Brown, *Death*, 945 – 52.

14. Brown, *Death*, 952 – 53, discusses the possibility that in respect for Jewish sensitivities the Romans allowed Jesus to wear a loincloth, concluding that such cannot be known. Yet contempt and hatred of Jesus by the Jews could mean the normal state of nudity was followed in this instance.

15. There is an ABBA pattern in vv. 35 – 36 describing the action of the guards, with main verb, participle, participle, main verb. The two circumstantial participles (throwing dice, sitting) have the force of main verbs but have the effect of separating the action into two groups, dividing the clothes and maintaining vigilance over the dying Jesus.

16. Brown, *Death*, 962.

account) meant to simulate the empire's "approval" (further contempt).[17] To the early church it signified an unconscious prophecy of the true significance of the One who suffered as the righteous martyr (for "King of the Jews," see on v. 29).

27:38 Then they crucified with him two armed bandits, one on his right and the other on his left (Τότε σταυροῦνται σὺν αὐτῷ δύο λῃσταί, εἷς ἐκ δεξιῶν καὶ εἷς ἐξ εὐωνύμων). The two criminals (for λῃσταί, see 26:55) were undoubtedly insurrectionists like Barabbas; he was the leader, and Jesus was crucified in the central position in his place. It was virtually the only crime punishable this way (the same term is used of Barabbas in John 18:40). It probably alludes to Isa 53:12, "numbered with the transgressors." Ironically, the right and the left of Jesus is where James and John wished to be (20:20 – 23), but there is no glory or authority in those positions now (Davies and Allison).

27:39 And those who passed by kept on hurling abuse at him, shaking their heads (Οἱ δὲ παραπορευόμενοι ἐβλασφήμουν αὐτὸν κινοῦντες τὰς κεφαλὰς αὐτῶν). The "passersby" would be those who came out to watch the executions but especially those coming by the major road into Jerusalem (see on v. 33). The three taunts in both Matthew and Mark build on the superscription and elucidate its meaning. In Mark they center on the royal implications of Jesus' kingship, but in Matthew their implications go beyond and center on the Son of God Christology.[18] The large crowd was probably composed of peoples from all over, since this was the Passover.

However, those "hurling abuse" (lit., "blasphemy" or "slander," cf. 15:19) at Jesus were court followers of the Sanhedrin, as seen in the reference to the temple in v. 40 (used as evidence in the Sanhedrin trial, 26:61). "Shaking the head" was an oriental gesture of contempt and recalls the derision heaped on the righteous sufferer in Ps 22:7 (cf. 2 Kgs 19:21; Ps 109:25; Lam 2:15).[19] The imperfect "hurling abuse' (ἐβλασφήμουν) has durative force ("kept on" doing it) and is a key term full of further irony, as Jesus was convicted of blasphemy (9:3; 26:65 – 66), yet now the true "blasphemy" comes from his enemies.

27:40 ... and saying, "You who are going to destroy the temple and rebuild it in three days, save yourself (καὶ λέγοντες, Ὁ καταλύων τὸν ναὸν καὶ ἐν τρισὶν ἡμέραις οἰκοδομῶν, σῶσον σεαυτόν). This taunt almost verbally repeats the charge of 26:61 and sees the crucifixion as virtually a recreation of the trial, adding further irony, for the true temple (Jesus' body) of Jesus' true prophecy (John 2:19) was to be destroyed imminently, and Jesus will indeed "build it again in three days" when he is raised from the dead. So this becomes an unconscious prophecy of Jesus' death and resurrection (similar to Caiaphas's unconscious prophecy in John 11:49 – 52).

After the false charges were made, the news apparently spread widely, and now the people at the crucifixion site are hurling it into Jesus' face in rejection and disbelief. You can almost hear the derisive laughter behind these words. Mockingly they cry in effect, "Since you have the power to

17. For a picture of how this *titulus* may have looked with the inscription in Aramaic, Latin, and Greek, see Witherington, *Matthew*, 516.

18. See Kingsbury, *Matthew*, 74 – 76.

19. It is common to see Lam 2:15 as a deliberate allusion as well (Davies and Allison). David M. Moffatt, "Righteous Bloodshed, Matthew's Passion Narrative, and the Temple's Destruction: Lamentations as a Matthean Interest," *JBL* 125 (2006): 299 – 320, argues that Lamentations is an important intertext in Matthew, used "to portray Jesus' death as a primary act of righteous bloodshed by the hands of the religious authorities in Jerusalem that results in the destruction of Jerusalem and the temple" (300, cf. 319).

rebuild Herod's magnificent temple, show us by saving yourself!"

27:40 "... if you are the Son of God, [and][20] come down from that cross" (εἰ υἱὸς εἶ τοῦ θεοῦ, [καὶ] κατάβηθι ἀπὸ τοῦ σταυροῦ). "If you are the Son of God" (εἰ υἱὸς εἶ τοῦ θεοῦ, here and in v. 43) repeats the words of Satan at Jesus' temptation (4:3, 6) and the words of the high priest (26:63). "Son of God" theology is a major emphasis of Matthew and comes to a head here and with the centurion's confession of v. 54. The challenge of Jesus' enemies to him to "save himself" and "descend from the cross" would come true in a way they could not begin to imagine, but they said it here in total contempt, expecting nothing. The majority of these people would refuse to countenance the rumors that would come a few days later. Blomberg calls the challenge to "come down from that cross" the "last great temptation," and if Jesus had given in, "he would thereby have forfeited his divinely ordained role as the innocent sufferer for the sins of all humanity (cf. 2 Cor 5:21; Rom 3:21 – 26; Heb 9:26 – 28)."[21]

27:41 In the same way also the chief priests with the teachers of law and elders continued to mock him, saying (ὁμοίως καὶ οἱ ἀρχιερεῖς ἐμπαίζοντες μετὰ τῶν γραμματέων καὶ πρεσβυτέρων ἔλεγον). Now the three major groups that constituted the Sanhedrin (cf. 5:22; 26:59) are mentioned together. The only other place in the Passion Narrative they are together is 26:57; the first and third occur in 26:3, 47; 27:1, 3, 12, 20. Some (e.g., Brown, Hagner) doubt they would come on the verge of Passover, but in a case this important, it is reasonable that some of them would want to see the results of their handiwork (so Keener). This also fulfills Jesus' first passion prediction (16:21) that these very groups would cause him to "suffer many things."

27:42 "He saved others but did not have the power to save himself. He is the king of Israel! Let him come down now from the cross and then we will believe in him" (Ἄλλους ἔσωσεν, ἑαυτὸν οὐ δύναται σῶσαι· βασιλεὺς Ἰσραήλ ἐστιν, καταβάτω νῦν ἀπὸ τοῦ σταυροῦ καὶ πιστεύσομεν ἐπ' αὐτόν). The language of their taunt is filled with irony. "He saved others" is certainly built on Jesus' healing ministry, as σῴζω is used for healing in this gospel (9:21 – 22). Then when they added "he cannot[22] save himself," they were using another aspect, "deliver, rescue." Matthew and his Christian readers would see a third, as through not "saving himself" he was making the "salvation" of humankind possible.

The difference in the Synoptic Gospels with respect to the titles is interesting: Mark 15:32 has "Messiah ... king of Israel," Matt 27:42 – 43 has "king of Israel ... Son of God," and Luke 23:35 – 37 has "God's Messiah, the Chosen One ... king of the Jews." Mark draws "Messiah" from the Sanhedrin trial, and Luke takes "king of the Jews" from the Roman trial. However, Mark and Matthew switch to "king of Israel" as the more theologically loaded title and therefore a stronger taunt. "Israel" is the covenant term for the nation and hints that the Messiah will fulfill God's covenant with Israel, which ironically is indeed the case.

20. "And" (καί) is omitted from א [2] B L W Θ f[1,13] 33 Byz et al. and found in א * A D it syr. It could have been left out accidentally on the basis of the beginning of the following word or inserted by copyists who thought the "if" clause modified the previous verb. Thus most believe it is a 50-50 decision (see Metzger, *Textual Commentary*, 69). Either way the "and" at that point is mandated by the two imperatives, "save" and "come down."

21. Blomberg, *Matthew*, 417.

22. οὐ δύναται in this context means more than just "not able to" but has the nuance of "lacks the power to." They were taunting Jesus with his impotence to come off the cross and destroy the Romans, their view of a true (conquering) Messiah.

The challenge to "descend from the cross" mocks once again Jesus' so-called messianic power, but now they mockingly add, "we will believe in him," with this the only time "believe in" (πιστεύω ἐπί) appears in the gospels (except once in the resurrection narrative of Luke 24:25), though it is used often in Acts (Acts 9:42; 11:17; 16:31; 22:19) and Paul (Rom 4:5, 18, 24; 9:33; 10:11; et al.). So Jesus' enemies mockingly promise a conversion, while Matthew expects his readers to catch the supreme irony. Since Jesus will do more than "come down" but will "go up" from the cross, every reader should indeed "believe in" him.

27:43 "He has trusted in God. Let God rescue him now if he wants him, for he said, 'I am the Son of God' " (πέποιθεν ἐπὶ τὸν θεόν, ῥυσάσθω νῦν εἰ θέλει αὐτόν· εἶπεν γὰρ ὅτι Θεοῦ εἰμι υἱός). Senior says, "This verse is special to Matthew. It manages to concentrate in a few words the same unique emphasis that Matthew has consistently displayed in his more subtle re-working of the Markan material in parallel passages."[23] The taunt reflects Ps 22:8, where David's enemies mock him with "He trusts in the LORD ... let the LORD rescue him." This was undoubtedly inadvertent from the leaders but deliberate on Matthew's part.

As the suffering Messiah, everyone turns against him (cf. also Isa 52:5, 14; 53:3 – 4, 7 – 8). Many (Senior, Bonnard, Grundmann, France, Nolland) have noted Wis 2:10 – 24 here as well, where the wicked plot against the righteous man ("a son of God") and which also builds on Ps 22:8. As in v. 40 the "Son of God" taunt stems from Matt 26:63 and the Sanhedrin trial. Indeed, their taunt will bear fruit soon as the true "Son of God" is raised from the dead by the "God" who "wants" to do so!

27:44 In the same way the armed bandits who had been crucified with him taunted him as well (τὸ δ' αὐτὸ καὶ οἱ λῃσταὶ οἱ συσταυρωθέντες σὺν αὐτῷ ὠνείδιζον αὐτόν). Luke 23:39 – 43 expands this scene, as one of the criminals mocks Jesus and the other chides the first, then asks to be included in Jesus' coming glory. This completes the circle, as everyone involved in the scene has turned against Jesus. In 5:11 Jesus said, "God blesses you when people insult you (ὀνειδίζω; cf. 11:20)." Jesus becomes the archetype of those insulted or mocked.

27:45 And from the sixth hour darkness came over the whole land, lasting until the ninth hour (Ἀπὸ δὲ ἕκτης ὥρας σκότος ἐγένετο ἐπὶ πᾶσαν τὴν γῆν ἕως ὥρας ἐνάτης). Since the day (according to the Roman system) started at dawn or 6:00 a.m., this means that total darkness came over the area from noon to 3:00 p.m. It is Mark 15 that breaks the crucifixion into two stages governed by the third (Mark 15:25 = 9:00 a.m.), the sixth (15:33 = noon), and the ninth (15:34 = 3:00 p.m.) hours. We know that the taunts governed the first three hours, but we know nothing about the second half, unless some of the events in John 19:25 – 30 (the giving of Jesus' mother into the care of the Beloved Disciple, Jesus' accepting a drink) occurred then (the second definitely, the first a possibility).

The emphasis here is on the totality of the darkness "over the whole earth" (ἐπὶ πᾶσαν τὴν γῆν, most likely that whole area rather than all of Planet Earth). The "darkness" could have been a natural phenomenon (storm clouds or sandstorm),[24] but more likely it was a supernatural event in keeping

23. Senior, *Passion Narrative*, 287. He believes, along with McNeile, Bultmann, Grundmann, Beare, and Gundry, that Matthew has placed these words on the lips of the leaders. Yet it is something the leaders would have said. Whether unconscious or a deliberate paraphrase of the Davidic psalm, it would fit. They are saying, "He thinks he is Davidic Messiah; let him prove it!" (see Carson, Hagner, Wilkins).

24. See Urban Holzmeister, "Die Finsternis beim Tode Jesu," *Bib* 22 (1941), 404 – 11, for an exhaustive list of the possibilities.

with Matthew's predilection for divine intervention (cf. 1:18, 20 – 21; 2:12, 13, 19 – 20; 27:51 – 53; 28:2 – 3). It cannot be a sun eclipse, for Passover always occurred at the full moon, and eclipses occur only during a new moon (Luz names Origen, Augustine as recognizing this), and this phenomenon lasts exactly from noon until the death of Jesus.

In the OT darkness was one of the Egyptian plagues (Exod 10:21 – 23) and was a total darkness which lasted for three days and was thereby linked to the first Passover. In the prophets Amos 8:9 is an obvious parallel ("I will make the sun go down at noon and darken the earth in broad daylight"), but there are also parallels with Isa 59:9 – 10; Jer 13:16, 15:9; Joel 2:2, 10, 31; Zeph 1:15. In Hellenistic circles darkness often signified the death of famous people, but here it is more the OT idea of divine judgment and human mourning. This darkness is a harbinger of the coming final judgment (as in Amos, Joel, Zephaniah), and the judgment is vicariously on Jesus as the atoning sacrifice for sin. This will be reflected next in his cry of agony on the cross.

27:46 Now about the ninth hour Jesus cried out in a loud voice, saying, "Eli, eli, lema sabachthani?" That is, "My God, my God, why have you abandoned me?" (περὶ δὲ τὴν ἐνάτην ὥραν ἀνεβόησεν ὁ Ἰησοῦς φωνῇ μεγάλῃ λέγων, Ηλι ηλι λεμα σαβαχθανι; τοῦτ' ἔστιν, Θεέ μου θεέ μου, ἱνατί με ἐγκατέλιπες;). At the end of the time of darkness and the onset of Jesus' death (the ninth hour), Jesus cries out in agony of soul. Mark has the Aramaic form ("Eloi, eloi") while Matthew gives the Hebrew form of the cry, "Eli, eli." Some believe Matthew's is original because it would best be misunderstood as a call to Elijah,[25] while others think the Aramaic is original as a cry from the heart.[26] Either is possible; whichever is correct, the other gospel changed it in order to emphasize the deep emotions of Jesus (Mark) or the Scripture quote (Matthew). In fact, it is irrelevant as to which is original, for both are equally inspired!

Jesus' cry comes from Ps 22:1, with David the righteous sufferer crying out his deep sorrow to God. The thrust of the cry is also debated. Some interpret the cry from the standpoint of the psalm as a whole as a faith-statement placing trust in the God who will vindicate; therefore it looks beyond the suffering to the triumph that will result.[27] This has much to commend it, for certainly Jesus' trust in his Father reflects Ps 22 and is part of its thrust (it is the theme of 22:19 – 31). Yet this cry is one of agony and hardly one of triumph. It culminates a major theme of the Passion Narrative, in which Jesus is abandoned by his disciples (26:56) and Peter (26:69 – 75), then condemned by the high court of his own people (26:57 – 68) and taunted by his enemies — first the Roman soldiers (27:27 – 31) and then the Jewish people (27:39 – 40), the leaders (27:41 – 43), and the criminals crucified with him (27:44). Jesus stands alone, forsaken by all, and now he feels forsaken even by his Father. If Jesus meant this as a cry of faith and victory, he would not have quoted the first verse of the psalm.

Thus, there is an aspect of trust, but that element looks forward to the resurrection. Neither Matthew nor Mark (Luke and John omit this) explains why Jesus utters this cry of desolation, but most theological reflections center on Jesus' realization of his vicarious sacrifice. He has become the sin offering, and at this dark moment

25. See Jeremias, *TDNT*, 2:935; France; Davies and Allison.

26. See Carson, Hagner, Keener. Actually, the "my God" (ηλι) is Hebrew while the "why have you abandoned me" (λεμα σαβαχθανι) is Aramaic, so it is a mixed quotation.

27. Birger Gerhardsson, "Jésus livré et abandonné d'après la passion selon S. Matthieu," *RB* 76 (1969): 206 – 27 (esp. 222 – 23); L. P. Trudinger, "Eli, Eli, Lama Sabachthani? A Cry of Dereliction or Victory?" *JETS* 17 (1974): 235 – 38; Senior, *Passion Narrative*, 298 – 99.

God must turn away from sin. As in Gethsemane Jesus is experiencing the depths of pain in his very soul, but this in no way mitigates his victory there, and Ps 22 is a perfect source for his expression of agony. Beneath his real pain there is still a trust in God, and he knows his deliverance is coming.

27:47 But when some of those standing there heard this, they said, "He is calling for Elijah" (τινὲς δὲ τῶν ἐκεῖ ἑστηκότων ἀκούσαντες ἔλεγον ὅτι Ἠλίαν φωνεῖ οὗτος). Many bystanders standing some distance away heard his cry of "Eli" and thought he was calling for "Elijah," who was taken up to heaven in a whirlwind and a chariot of fire in 2 Kgs 2:1 – 12 and became a messianic figure (Mal 4:5 – 6). Here this reflects the belief by many Jews that Elijah was ready to appear from heaven in time of need.[28]

27:48 And immediately one of them ran, took a sponge, and immersed it in sour wine (καὶ εὐθέως δραμὼν εἷς ἐξ αὐτῶν καὶ λαβὼν σπόγγον πλήσας τε ὄξους). Figuring that Jesus was crying to Elijah for help, one bystander ran to get him something for his parched mouth. He took a sponge, soaked it in sour wine (looked upon as a good thirst quencher), and offered it to Jesus (= Ps 69:21; in John he accepts it). It is debated whether it is mockery (Carson, Gundry, Davies and Allison, Luz) or mercy (France, Morris, Blomberg). The echo of Ps 69 could favor the former, since the vinegary wine there is given in mockery by David's enemies. Yet this was a common drink carried by soldiers to refresh themselves, so it does not seem a negative gesture. The latter fits better.

27:48 Then he put it on a reed and gave it to him to drink (καὶ περιθεὶς καλάμῳ ἐπότιζεν αὐτόν). As in 27:29, 30, κάλαμος probably refers to a wooden staff or stick rather than a reed, and the sponge was "part of a soldier's standard kit," a normal way of getting something to drink in such a circumstance (Nolland). The scene is recorded because it provides further fulfillment of Scripture and deepens the picture of Jesus as the righteous sufferer.

27:49 But the rest of the people said, "Leave him alone. Let's see if Elijah comes and delivers him" (οἱ δὲ λοιποὶ ἔλεγον, Ἄφες ἴδωμεν εἰ ἔρχεται Ἠλίας σώσων αὐτόν). Apparently nearly everyone has misunderstood what Jesus said, and their mockery appears in contradistinction (δέ) to the act of mercy in v. 48. ἄφες can mean "let it go" or "wait." Here it asks the person to step back and see what happens. The people mockingly want to see if Jesus is a righteous person and will draw Elijah to help him.

27:50 But Jesus again cried out with a loud voice and gave up his spirit (ὁ δὲ Ἰησοῦς πάλιν κράξας φωνῇ μεγάλῃ ἀφῆκεν τὸ πνεῦμα). For the second time Jesus "cried in a loud voice" (also v. 46). Both were cries of an agonized soul, the first at being abandoned by God, now at the fulfillment of the divine will in salvation history with his death. This is the climactic moment of the ages. Some have seen this as a cry of triumph (Senior, Grundmann) or of judgment (LaCoque),[29] but it is best to take it simply as Jesus' giving over his spirit to his Father. Mark 15:37 and Luke 23:46 have "breathed his last," while John 19:30 has "bowed his head and gave up his spirit." All emphasize Jesus' sovereignty over his own life. He wasn't killed so much as he yielded his life in obedience to the divine will.

There has been a great deal of discussion regarding the cause of death, much of it stemming

28. See Jeremias, *TDNT*, 2:930 – 33; he is called "a Jewish St. Christopher" by Bruner (see 11:14; 16:14; 17:10 – 13).

29. André LaCoque, "The Great Cry of Jesus in Matt 27:50," in *Putting Body and Soul Together: Essays in Honor of Robin Scroggs* (ed. V. Wiles et al.; Valley Forge, PA: Trinity Press, 1997), 138 – 64.

from John 19:34, the blood and water flowing out when Jesus' side was pierced by the spear. Brown surveys the opinions, from early views that Jesus died of a ruptured (broken) heart (medically difficult) to a hemorrhage in the pleural cavity between the ribs and lungs to asphyxia and shock due to circulatory failure (the normal cause of death at crucifixion) to shock caused by dehydration and blood loss (Brown's preference).[30] Anything we say is speculative; whatever the medical reasons, the gospels (esp. John) stress the reality of Jesus' horrible death.

Theology in Application

The meaning and theology of the crucifixion narrative is widely known, as it depicts the central event in history, that which alone brings together salvation history (*Geschichte*) with human history (*Historie*). Jesus does not speak extensively about the meaning of his death on the cross. That is developed primarily by the later NT writers, especially Paul, Hebrews, and 1 Peter. Yet Jesus is fully cognizant of the vicarious nature of his death as an atoning sacrifice, as seen in 20:28; 26:28.

1. The True Significance of Jesus' Death

The taunts of Jesus' enemies provide unconscious testimony to the true significance of his death. The christological core of the crucifixion narrative is found in the mockery of the people, leaders, and soldiers in 27:27–31, 39–44. Through their taunts we learn the following:

1. Jesus is "king of the Jews/king of Israel" (vv. 29, 42, cf. also vv. 11, 37), a major emphasis in Matthew (see also 2:2; 21:5; 25:31, 34, 40). He is the royal Messiah who will conquer, but first his great victory is won through becoming the atoning sacrifice for sin. When the soldiers mockingly dressed Jesus as king, they had no idea that one day they would be forced to bow before him as the true King of the ages (Rom 14:11; Phil 2:10; Rev 1:5; 21:24, 26).
2. Jesus is the Son of God, the central affirmation of this section, seen in the direct taunt of vv. 40, 43, the confession of v. 54, and the supernatural portents of vv. 51–53.
3. Jesus is the only viable object for faith decision, as seen in the leaders' cry, "Let him come down now from the cross and then we will believe in him." As we know, he did indeed "come down," but in a way they could not foresee, and the reader is challenged to "believe." The core of the gospel is found here, with Jesus as the sacrifice for sin that demands belief (see also Matt 4:17 = Mark 1:15).

30. Brown, *Death*, 1088–92. The asphyxiation hypothesis stems from W. D. Edwards, W. J. Gabel, and Floyd E. Hosmer, "On the Physical Death of Jesus Christ," *Journal of the American Medical Association* 255 (1986): 1455–63; that of dehydration from F. T. Zubige, "Two Questions about Crucifixion: Does the Victim Die of Asphyxiation? Would Nails in the Hands Hold the Weight of the Body?" *BRev* 5 (1989): 34–43.

2. Jesus and God in Sovereign Control

Neither the Romans nor the Jewish leaders were in control of these events. It is clear that God and Jesus were in charge, for this event is the culmination of God's redemptive activity from the OT on. The theme fulfilling Scripture continues here, moving from vv. 9 – 10 to vv. 35, 48, 50. Every aspect is part of God's plan conceived from before the foundation of the world and coming to fruition here. The Romans do not so much place Jesus on the cross as he gives himself up to the cross. They do not take his life; he "gives up his spirit" to his Father.

3. The Divine Purpose of Salvation

Though not explicitly explained in the crucifixion scene, the true meaning of Jesus' death was atonement (cf. 1:21; 20:28; 26:28), and the cross is the one remedy for the sin that Adam brought on this world (cf. Rom 5:12 – 21). The emphasis throughout is on Jesus' obedience to the will of his Father. Gethsemane encompassed this, as Jesus placed God's will above his own, and the cross was the final act of a life of obedience. As "God with us" (1:23) Jesus took our sins on himself, was willing at that moment to become separate from God for the only time in all eternity (v. 46), and in that act brought forgiveness to humankind (26:28). God tells us as he did Joshua, "I will never leave you nor forsake you" (Josh 1:5), and in that sense Jesus was the only person completely "forsaken" by God. And he did it for us!

4. Judgment and Horror

Matthew and Mark center on the horror of putting to death the Son of God. The negative aspects are front and center in contrast to the more positive aspects highlighted in Luke's and John's crucifixion narratives.[31] As Davies and Allison say, "Vv. 32 – 50 do not encourage or inspire but rather depict human sin and its frightening freedom in the unfathomable divine silence. There is terror in this text. The mocking and torture of the innocent and righteous Son of God are not intended to make but to shatter sense, to portray the depths of irrational human depravity."[32] The mockery deserves judgment, and the judgment of God is depicted in the three hours of darkness seen as a reenactment of the Egyptian plague of Exod 10:21 – 23 and a harbinger of the final judgment (see on v. 45).

31. See Grant R. Osborne, "Redactional Trajectories in the Crucifixion Narrative," *EvQ* 51/2 (1979): 80 – 96.

32. Davies and Allison, *Matthew*, 3:638 – 39.

CHAPTER 119

Matthew 27:51 – 61

Literary Context

After Jesus' death, God attests to its significance via supernatural events, after which both the soldiers and the women add their witness. Finally, the burial adds further witness as Jesus is given a royal burial in a new tomb.

VII. The Passion and Resurrection of Jesus (26:1 – 28:20)
- **A. The Passion Narrative (26:1 – 27:61)**
  - 4. The Trials of Jesus and Peter's Denials (26:57 – 27:26)
  - 5. The Crucifixion and Death of Jesus (27:27 – 50)
  - ➦ **6. Events Following Jesus' Death (27:51 – 61)**
    - **a. The Incredible After-Events: The Curtain and the Raised Saints (27:51 – 53)**
    - **b. Witnesses to the Events: The Soldiers and the Women (27:54 – 56)**
    - **c. The Burial of Jesus (27:57 – 61)**

Main Idea

The mockery of the three groups — the people, the leaders, and the soldiers — is countered by the threefold witness of nature, the soldiers, and the women. The emphasis is on the divine sonship of Jesus and the results of his death in judgment, resurrection, and a new access to God made possible. Even his burial points to the extraordinary nature of his person.

Translation

Matthew 27:51-61

51a Scene #1/Events — And **look, the curtain of the temple was split**
in two
from top to bottom.
b — And **the ground shook,**
c — and **the rocks were split apart.**
52a — And **the tombs were opened.**
b — **Then many bodies of the saints who had died were raised.**

53a Expansion of 52b — And when they had come out of the tombs after his resurrection,
b — **they entered the holy city and appeared to many**

54a Scene #2 — Now when the centurion and
those guarding Jesus with him saw the earthquake and
the things
that happened,
b Response to 54a — **they were filled with great terror and said,**
c Identification — *"Truly this was the Son of God!"*
55a Action — Now **there were many women there watching from a distance,**
b Description — who had followed Jesus from Galilee,
serving him.

56a Identification of 55a — Among whom were Mary Magdalene and
b — Mary the mother of James and Joseph and
c — the mother of the sons of Zebedee.

57a Scene #3/Setting — Now when evening arrived,
b Action — **a rich man came from Arimathea named Joseph,**
c Description — who had also been discipled by Jesus.
58a Action — **He came to Pilate and asked for the body of Jesus.**
b Response — **Then Pilate commanded that it be given to him.**

59a — And taking the body,
b Action — **Joseph wrapped it in a clean linen cloth,**
60a Action — and **placed it in his own new tomb**
that he had cut in the rock.
c Action — After he rolled a large stone at the entrance to the tomb,
d — **he departed.**
61a Verification — **Mary Magdalene and**
the other Mary were there sitting opposite the tomb.

Structure and Literary Form

Matthew again adapts material from Mark (vv. 51a, 54, 55 – 56, 57 – 61) and inserts his own unique material about the tombs opening with the OT saints emerging (vv. 51b – 53). In using Mark, Matthew adds the soldiers and the supernatural portents they saw to v. 54 and greatly abbreviates (about half the length) the burial story from Mark 15:42 – 47.

Exegetical Outline

➦ **I. The Incredible After-Events (27:51 – 53)**
- A. The tearing of the temple curtain (v. 51a)
- B. The earthquake (v. 51b)
- C. The tombs open and the saints emerge (vv. 52 – 53)

II. The Witnesses to the Events (27:54 – 56)
- A. The centurion's confession (v. 54)
- B. The women witnesses (vv. 55 – 56)

III. The Burial of Jesus (27:57 – 61)
- A. The body given to Joseph of Arimathea (vv. 57 – 58)
- B. The burial of Jesus in a rich man's new tomb (vv. 59 – 60)
- C. The women witnesses (v. 61)

Explanation of the Text

27:51 And look, the curtain of the temple was split in two from top to bottom (Καὶ ἰδοὺ τὸ καταπέτασμα τοῦ ναοῦ ἐσχίσθη ἀπ' ἄνωθεν ἕως κάτω εἰς δύο). "And look" (καὶ ἰδού) separates vv. 51 – 54 as the aftermath of the death of Jesus. The splitting of the curtain from top to bottom shows it is an act of God rather than of people. There were two veils in the temple, one separating the Holy Place from the Most Holy Place and the other separating the sanctuary as a whole from the court. The imagery here and in Heb 6:19; 9:12 – 13; 10:19 – 20 favors the inner curtain, signifying opening up a new entrance to the presence of God (so Hill, Hagner, Wilkins, Keener). The outer veil (sixty feet high and thirty wide) fits the imagery of a public sign, and Josephus (*J.W.* 5.3) and several Jewish sources speak of the tearing of Herod's magnificent veil at the entrance (so Lane, Blomberg, Ridderbos, Davies and Allison). Yet the early church undoubtedly connected the two, and it seems that the latter historical sign was interpreted in terms of the former — there is no way to know which veil, and the imagery fits both (with Luz).

There are two interpretations (both are probably in Matthew — so Carson, France, Hagner, Nolland):[1] (1) a new access to God, signifying

1. Nolland, *Matthew*, 1211 – 13, notes four categories of interpretation: what has been achieved by Jesus' death; God's negative reaction to the death of his Son; a symbol of Jesus' death itself; and God breaking forth from his temple in acts of power. He finds the second and fourth to be the most likely, and believes both are probably correct.

the end of the sacrificial system and a direct relationship with God — connected with the Isaianic Servant imagery; (2) a portent of the coming destruction of the temple (so interpreted by the early church fathers) — connected with the Olivet Discourse. The imagery of the "splitting" of the veil suggests violence and fits the developing theme of divine judgment on temple and people. At the same time, it brings about the results of Jesus' death, namely, a new openness of relationship with God, signifying direct access as a result of the once-for-all sacrifice of Christ on our behalf. As France says, "access to God will no longer be through the old, discredited cultic system but through Jesus himself, and more specifically through his death as a ransom for many."[2]

27:51 And the ground shook, and the rocks were split apart (καὶ ἡ γῆ ἐσείσθη καὶ αἱ πέτραι ἐσχίσθησαν). Matthew, who has a predilection for supernatural vindication (cf. 28:2 – 4), adds the part about the earthquake and the rejuvenation of the dead (vv. 51b – 53). This scene serves to unite Jesus' death and resurrection into a single event in salvation history and to show him as the "firstfruits" (1 Cor 15:20) of the resurrection of the saints (see below).

The incredible apocalyptic nature of this event and the fact it is only here make many believe it is a theological piece shaped as history rather than an actual event. Some consider this to be Matthean midrash, a theological scene shaped by him to portray the effects of the death/resurrection (Senior, Gundry, Hagner). Others call it a displaced resurrection tradition, in which a Palestinian epiphany tradition is placed between the passion and resurrection to link the two events (McNeile, Hutton),[3] or a Jewish apocalyptic hymn on the resurrection of the just, adapted by Matthew (Schenk).[4] However, it is presented as history, and "appeared to many" in v. 53 functions like 1 Cor 15:6 as an apologetic note to corroborate the event.

The "and" construction links this closely with the death of Jesus (v. 50) and the centurion's cry (v. 54). Would Matthew switch back and forth from history to legend to history without some type of hint? In fact, the entire crucifixion scene — Jesus' remarkable serenity throughout the day, the darkness, the tearing of the curtain, the earthquake, the raising of the saints — transcends history and demonstrates the intersection of human history by divine power. If there is a supernatural God, there is no reason to deny the historicity of this scene.[5]

2. France, *Gospel of Matthew*, 1081.

3. D. D. Hutton, "The Resurrection of the Holy Ones (Matthew 27:51b – 53): A Study of the Theology of the Matthean Passion Narrative" (PhD diss.: Harvard University, 1970), 100 – 101.

4. W. Schenk, *Der Passionsbricht nach Markus: Untersuchungen zur Überlieferungsgeschichte der Passions-traditionen* (Gütersloh: Gerd Mohr, 1974), 77 – 78.

5. For arguments on behalf of its historicity see David Wenham, "The Resurrection Narratives in Matthew's Gospel," *TynBul* 24 (1973): 21 – 54 (esp. 42 – 3), Carson, Morris, Wilkins, Wright, *Resurrection*. Hill and Davies and Allison call it "a primitive tradition." Few today speak of a "displaced resurrection tradition" or a Jewish apocalyptic hymn, because neither fit the scene here. I reject the idea of creative midrash because (1) Jewish midrashic works embellished specific OT texts while this is the reverse, using OT themes drawn from several OT texts. (2) Moreover, midrashic works added details to existing OT traditions rather than creating new stories entirely, so there are no true parallels in works like *Jubilees*, *Genesis Apocryphon*, Philo, or Josephus. (3) Midrash centered on the distant past rather than recent history. (4) Actual midrashim comprised halakhic midrash (ethical concerns for the life of the community) and haggadic midrash (illustrative stories for homiletical purposes), but the latter parallel (the only one that fits) stems from as late as the fourth century and cannot be used for this passage. So this cannot be called creative midrash; see R. T. France, "Jewish Historiography, Midrash, and the Gospels," *Gospel Perspectives III: Studies in Midrash and Historiography* (ed. R. T. France and D. Wenham; Sheffield: JSOT Press, 1983), 101 – 3; Douglas J. Moo, "Tradition and Old Testament in Matthew 27:3 – 10," ibid., 166 – 68.

Matthew has conflated two traditions here — one that took place on Good Friday, with an earthquake at Jesus' death splitting the veil curtain and opening several tombs; and another "after the resurrection" (see on v. 53), when many of the dead "holy ones" were seen in Jerusalem. Matthew's major purpose in his several supernatural scenes peculiar to him (the visions/dreams to the Magi, Joseph, Pilate's wife, as well as these two and 28:2) is to demonstrate the supernatural affirmation of Jesus' true nature and its effect on the God-man relationship. Here he brings these traditions together to connect the death and resurrection of Jesus as a single salvation-historical event and to show the divine sonship of Jesus through both supernatural (vv. 51 – 53) and human (v. 54) witness.

The earthquake[6] comes after the tearing of the veil, so the earthquake is not the cause of the splitting of the curtain (a supernatural act) but a separate event. It too is a supernatural event, as seen in the divine passive ("were split apart") here. Matthew has three σεισμός ("earthquake") scenes (8:24; 27:54; 28:2; see on 8:24). It is a common Jewish symbol for God's activity in the OT (Judg 5:4; 2 Sam 22:8; Ps 18:7; 77:18; Isa 2:19, 21; Joel 3:16) and in the Apocalypse (Rev 6:12; 8:5; 11:13; 16:18), often used in the NT for delivering God's messengers (Acts 16:26, Rev. 6:12, 8:5).[7] Thus, it is possible that here Matthew indicates the ascension of Jesus' spirit to the Father via the earthquake motif and that at the tomb on the third day another earthquake indicates the resurrection of his body (28:2).

27:52 And the tombs were opened. Then many bodies of the saints who had died were raised (καὶ τὰ μνημεῖα ἀνεῴχθησαν καὶ πολλὰ σώματα τῶν κεκοιμημένων ἁγίων ἠγέρθησαν). Note the continuation of the divine passives, pointing to God as the agent. Senior calls this an apocalyptic discourse building on the dry bones story of Ezek 37 to show the meaning of Jesus' death.[8] The opening of the tombs and resurrection of the dead continue the eschatological motif from the earthquake in two ways. (1) In Jesus' death the inauguration of the last days is sealed, the power of death is broken, and the righteous are resurrected. (2) The inauguration of the new age of salvation occurs, when life is made available to all. Both aspects are combined in apocalyptic expectation and look forward to the cosmic portents that will precede the return of Christ (so Hill).

The opening of the graves alludes to Ezek 37:12 – 13. "This is what the Sovereign Lord Says, 'My people, I am going to open your graves and bring you up from them.'" In Ezekiel it is a metaphor for the return from exile, but here it is the resurrection from the dead. "Fallen asleep" (κεκοιμημένων) was a common metaphor for death (Acts 7:60; 1 Cor 15:6, 51; 1 Thess 4:13), and this refers to the physical resurrection of the OT "saints," certainly not all[9] the "holy ones" (Zech 14:5) of old but more likely some of the "heroes and martyrs from Israel's history selected to bear miraculous testimony to these events."[10] There are many questions about this; for example, how many were raised (probably just a few)? And was

6. Dennis Baly, *The Geography of the Bible* (New York: Harper and Row, 1974), 25, says of this, "Though Matthew's explanation may be a later development, it is true that the temple area is on a line of structural weakness.... Slight tremors occur fairly frequently, and the latest one of any severity was on September 13, 1954." So an earthquake followed by an aftershock (27:51; 28:2) would hardly be unlikely on scientific grounds.

7. Richard Bauckham, "The Eschatological Earthquake in the Apocalypse of John," *NovT* 19 (1977): 224 – 33, shows that these were often symbols denoting the coming of God to deliver his people.

8. Donald Senior, "The Death of Jesus and the Resurrection of the Holy Ones (Matt 27:51 – 53)," *CBQ* 38 (1977): 312 – 29; and *Passion Narrative*, 312 – 23.

9. So Gundry, *Matthew*, 576, on the grounds of the universal thrust in the Ezekiel and Daniel parallels.

10. Wilkins, *Matthew*, 906, from Davies and Allison, *Matthew*, 3:633.

this a resuscitation like Lazarus, so that they lived out a life on earth and died, or a resurrection into their glorified bodies, so that they were taken up with Christ to heaven (most prefer the latter)?

27:53 And when they had come out[11] **of the tombs after his resurrection, they entered the holy city and appeared to many** (καὶ ἐξελθόντες ἐκ τῶν μνημείων μετὰ τὴν ἔγερσιν αὐτοῦ εἰσῆλθον εἰς τὴν ἁγίαν πόλιν καὶ ἐνεφανίσθησαν πολλοῖς). There is a distinct movement of the action centering on "out" (ἐκ) and "into" (εἰς), each found with the verb and the noun for emphasis. The picture of OT saints raised at Jesus' death but not seen until "after his resurrection" has raised many questions. Why would they be raised yet not appear until thirty-six hours later?

The best solution is provided by John Wenham,[12] who places a period between vv. 52a and 52b – 53, meaning that the earthquake and opening of the tombs belong with the death of Jesus, while the raising of the saints and their appearance in Jerusalem belongs with the resurrection. This provides a satisfactory separation between the events at Jesus' death and at his resurrection, showing that Matthew's purpose is to bring the death and resurrection together as a single event in salvation history. While the tombs were opened at the earthquake, the OT heroes were not raised until "after Jesus' resurrection." It would be gratifying to know which ones appeared — Abraham or Joseph or David or Aaron or Jeremiah or Malachi? Probably many were names not mentioned in the OT, but we will never know until we get to heaven. Yet we can imagine the excitement as people met them and heard their stories.

Matthew does not wish to tell the details because he wants us to focus on the meaning of the event. Note the deliberate emphasis on "holy ones"/"holy city." Matthew stresses the "holy" nature of the events, even transforming the apostate city that "kills the prophets" (23:37) and is killing the Messiah into the "holy city" that it will not become again until the end of time (Rev 21:2, 10). Yet even here there is promise of a remnant to be preserved (so Blomberg).

This remarkable pericope is certainly a reflection on Ezek 37; the rabbis interpreted the dry bones passage in terms of resurrection (e.g., 4 Macc 18:7; *b. Sanh.*, 92b), especially in the Ezekiel panels of the synagogue at Dura-Europus (painted AD 245 – 56).[13] Yet other passages provide background, such as 1 Kgs 19:11 for the earthquake and splitting of the rocks or Isa 26:19; Hos 6:2; Dan 12:2; Zech 14:4 – 5 for the earthly cataclysm and raising of the saints. Allison argues that the north panel at Dura-Europus reflects Zechariah as well as Ezekiel and that Matthew has in mind a plethora of OT passages on the resurrection of the saints at the end of history. [14]

27:54 Now when the centurion and those guarding Jesus with him saw the earthquake and the things that happened, they were filled with great terror (Ὁ δὲ ἑκατόνταρχος καὶ οἱ μετ' αὐτοῦ τηροῦντες τὸν Ἰησοῦν ἰδόντες τὸν σεισμὸν καὶ τὰ γενόμενα ἐφοβήθησαν σφόδρα). God has provided supernatural witness through nature to Jesus' sonship in vv. 51 – 53, and now the centurion

11. Another temporal participle as in vv. 3, 4, 7, 32, 33, 54, 57.

12. John W. Wenham, "When Were the Saints Raised? A Note on the Punctuation of Matthew xxvii.51 – 53," *JTS* 32 (1981): 150 – 52.

13. See Harald Riesenfeld, *The Resurrection in Ezekiel xxxvii and in the Dura-Europus Paintings* (Upsala: Lundaquistilca Bokhandeln, 1948), 37 – 48; J. Grassi, "Ezekiel xxxvii.1 – 14 and the New Testament," *NTS* 11 (1964 – 65): 163.

14. Dale C. Allison Jr., *The End of the Ages Has Come: An Early Interpretation of the Passion and Resurrection of Jesus* (Philadelphia: Fortress, 1985), 43 – 44.

makes it explicit in his own testimony.[15] Matthew has modified Mark 15:39 in a couple directions. (1) Mark has the testimony coming just from the centurion while Matthew has "the centurion and those guarding Jesus with him," providing multiple witness in accordance with the Deuteronomic demand for two or three witnesses (so Brown) as well as to draw out a parallel with the transfiguration account in 17:6 (so Hagner, Davies and Allison, Nolland — see further below).

(2) Matthew stresses that the basis was their seeing "the earthquake and the things that happened," probably at least the earthquake and the splitting of tombs (the curtain of the temple would be out of sight, and the saints did not appear until after Jesus' resurrection). In other words, they experienced the power of God and recognized it for what it was, divine witness.

(3) "They were filled with great terror" (ἐφοβήθησαν σφόδρα) draws an explicit link (the exact wording) with 17:6 and the reaction of the disciples to Jesus' transfiguration. Matthew considered the transfiguration to be a proleptic anticipation of the glory of Jesus to be seen at his death and resurrection.[16] For him the cross is his throne (made more explicit in John's crucifixion scene), and here Jesus becomes the royal Messiah.

27:54 ... and said, "Truly this was the Son of God!" (λέγοντες, Ἀληθῶς θεοῦ υἱὸς ἦν οὗτος). There are two levels of meaning in this confession. It is uncertain whether the centurion and the soldiers originally meant this testimony in a Judeo-Christian sense of divine sonship. Luke 23:47 translates the testimony as "Surely this was a righteous man," and that would be in keeping with a Roman understanding of the concept. They may have thought of Jesus as a "divine man" but more likely thought of him as a righteous, innocent sufferer, so that they join Pilate in being convinced of Jesus' innocence.[17] Matthew emphasizes the Christian side of the confession with "the Son of God" (θεοῦ υἱός), which could have articular force in line with Colwell's rule, which says that a predicate noun that comes before the copulative verb lacks the article (but often intends it) in order to differentiate it from the subject (which has the article).[18] In other words, the soldiers "utter the full Christian confession (cf. 3:17; 14:33; 16:16; 17:5)."[19] This could well be another instance of the Gentiles confessing Jesus and an anticipation of the Gentile mission in 28:19 (so Hill, Hagner, Keener).

27:55 Now there were many women there watching from a distance, who had followed Jesus from Galilee, serving him (Ἦσαν δὲ ἐκεῖ γυναῖκες πολλαὶ ἀπὸ μακρόθεν θεωροῦσαι, αἵτινες ἠκολούθησαν τῷ Ἰησοῦ ἀπὸ τῆς Γαλιλαίας διακονοῦσαι αὐτῷ). Jesus' Jewish people have turned against him and mocked him, and his disciples have forsaken him and fled (26:56). Even Peter, who also "followed at a distance" (26:58), failed and denied Jesus three times. Only the women followers have stood by him, and even they

15. Nolland, *Matthew*, 1218, shows that the three groups of mockers in 27:39 – 44 are paralleled by three "affirmations" of the true significance of Jesus in 27:54, 55 – 56, 57 – 61. Since the first group provides "unconscious testimony" to the significance of Jesus, both sets are witnesses to him.

16. See the detailed discussion of this in Dale C. Allison Jr., "Anticipating the Passion," *CBQ* 54 (1994): 701 – 14.

17. Carson, "Matthew," 582 – 83, says that since these were non-Roman auxiliary troops from Syria (see 27:27), they could have understood the title in a messianic sense. Yet they were also non-Jewish and may have been Roman, and the Roman understanding is more likely.

18. For excellent discussion of this, see Harris, *Jesus as God*, 310 – 13. For the meaning of this title, see also Donald Verseput, "The Role and Meaning of the 'Son of God' Title in Matthew's Gospel," *NTS* 33 (1987): 532 – 56 (esp. 547 – 49). On the confession as a cry not just emphasizing Jesus' innocence but also the guilt of the Romans, see J. Pobee, "The Cry of the Centurion — A Cry of Defeat," in *The Trial of Jesus*, ed. E. Bammel (London: SCM, 1970), 91 – 102.

19. Davies and Allison, *Matthew*, 3:636.

watched (imperfect periphrastic "they were watching" [ἦσαν ... θεωροῦσαι] to portray dramatically their vigilance) "from a distance."[20]

Women accompanied Jesus and were patrons of the apostolic band (Luke 8:1 – 3; cf. Matt 20:20). The fact that they are mentioned in all four gospels and also are official witnesses of the empty tomb and resurrection (28:1, 5 – 10) shows their importance as remaining with Jesus to the end. The language of discipleship ("follow" [ἀκολουθέω], "serve" [διακονέω]) emphasizes them as faithful disciples. This is unusual, for women were marginalized in the ancient world and were not allowed to be disciples of rabbis (remember the Barbara Streisand movie on that theme, called *Yentl*). Yet the fact that they were patrons of the group shows that Jesus went beyond custom here.[21]

27:56 Among whom were Mary Magdalene and Mary the mother of James and Joseph and the mother of the sons of Zebedee (ἐν αἷς ἦν Μαρία ἡ Μαγδαληνὴ καὶ Μαρία ἡ τοῦ Ἰακώβου καὶ Ἰωσὴφ μήτηρ καὶ ἡ μήτηρ τῶν υἱῶν Ζεβεδαίου). Mary of Magdala, a Galilean town south of Capernaum on the shore of the lake, is always first in the lists of women and was likely a leader of the group. Luke 8:2 tells us that Jesus had cast seven demons out of her, and she then became a devoted disciple. She is most important as a witness of Jesus' death and resurrection, and Jesus appeared to her and made her the first official witness of the resurrection (John 20:11 – 18, probably as one of the group of women named in Matt 28:9 – 10). Later traditions linking her with the sinful woman of Luke 7:36 – 50 or with Mary of Bethany are historically unfounded. Moreover, the portrayal of her rivalry with Peter in the *Gospel of Thomas* and her special relationship with Jesus in the *Gospel of Mary*, and most of all as Jesus' wife in the recent *DaVinci Code*, are completely spurious.

In Mark 15:40 the second woman named is called "the mother of James the younger and of Joseph," probably identifying her as the mother of the second disciple named James in Matt 10:3 and the same person as "Mary the wife of Clopas" in John 19:25. Some believe this is Jesus' mother, who also had sons named "James" and "Joseph" in Matt 13:55, but that would be a strange way to name Jesus' mother (specifically named as present in John 19:25).

Another woman, the mother of James and John, the sons of Zebedee, could be the "Salome" of Mark 15:40. There is a link with 20:20 here, where "the mother of the sons of Zebedee" asks Jesus if her boys could sit on Jesus' right and left in his kingdom. Apparently she was one of the "other women" who accompanied Jesus in Luke 8:3.

So there were at least four women present at the cross: the mother of Jesus, Mary Magdalene, Mary the wife of Clopus and mother of one of the Twelve, and Salome, probably Mary's sister and mother of James and John.

27:57 Now when evening arrived, a rich man came from Arimathea named Joseph, who had also been discipled by Jesus (Ὀψίας δὲ γενομένης ἦλθεν ἄνθρωπος πλούσιος ἀπὸ Ἁριμαθαίας, τοὔνομα Ἰωσήφ, ὃς καὶ αὐτὸς ἐμαθητεύθη τῷ Ἰησοῦ). This is a transition story that both concludes the crucifixion and prepares for the resurrection. The emphasis is on the reality of Jesus' death and its significance as the death of the royal Messiah. It was common for the Romans to refuse burial to a crucified person, allowing his body to rot on the cross or to lie exposed as a warning to others. Because of Jewish sensitivities (Deut 21:23)

20. John 19:25 has the women "near the cross." It is likely that in the beginning they were some distance away and then drew nearer as the end drew near, leading to Jesus giving his mother into the care of John in John 19:26 – 27.

21. See Osborne, "Women in Jesus' Ministry": 159 – 91.

they would bury them, but in a mass grave (probably the fate of the two criminals crucified with Jesus). There would be no dignity or honor.[22]

That was not the case with Jesus. Friday evening was the beginning of the Sabbath as well as Passover, so the bodies had to be buried by then. Joseph of Arimathea[23] went to Pilate shortly after Jesus died, probably about 4:00 p.m., since the body had to be prepared for burial and buried by dusk. Mark 15:43 tells us Joseph[24] was a member of the Sanhedrin, Matthew that he was quite wealthy.[25] Some (e.g., Brown) believe Joseph was not yet a disciple of Jesus, but one has to wonder why he would risk the censure of his fellow council members for burying the "blasphemer" Jesus if he were not already a devoted follower. Matthew tells us he for some time "had also been discipled" (αὐτὸς ἐμαθητεύθη; see also John 19:38) by Jesus, similar to "trained as a disciple in the kingdom of heaven" in 13:52. He has sat at Jesus' feet.

27:58 He came[26] to Pilate and asked for the body of Jesus. Then Pilate commanded that it be given to him (οὗτος προσελθὼν τῷ Πιλάτῳ ᾐτήσατο τὸ σῶμα τοῦ Ἰησοῦ. τότε ὁ Πιλᾶτος ἐκέλευσεν ἀποδοθῆναι). Pilate was in charge, and the soldiers had undoubtedly been given orders to bury the three in a common grave before dusk. To change that would require permission from Pilate. Pilate was certainly surprised to see a member of the Sanhedrin (who had earlier demanded Jesus be crucified) ask for the body but saw no reason to deny the request.[27] Mark 15:44 – 45 has a lengthy description of Pilate's surprise that Jesus had already died and his summoning the centurion to ensure that the death had indeed occurred. However, Matthew likely thought this unnecessary information and so omitted it. The death of Jesus led to such guilt in this Joseph that it turned his life around and led to this courageous act.

27:59 And taking the body, Joseph wrapped it in a clean linen cloth (καὶ λαβὼν τὸ σῶμα ὁ Ἰωσὴφ ἐνετύλιξεν αὐτὸ ἐν σινδόνι καθαρᾷ). There were too many activities associated with burial for Joseph to handle alone. He probably used servants, since handling the body would render them unclean for seven days, ruining any possibility of participation in the Passover festivities. John 19:39 mentions Nicodemus, who helped prepare the body. The first act after removing the body was to wash it, an act so important that Jews were allowed to perform it on the Sabbath. While it is possible that they dispensed with this because of the little time they had to bury Jesus before dusk (so Nolland), it was so important an act that it is more likely the gospel writers assume it. Moreover, it would not take overly long.

Then the body was wrapped tightly in a lengthy linen cloth, with spices/perfumes poured in to

22. Against Crossan's view that this is what happened to Jesus (*The Historical Jesus*, 91 – 94), see Davies and Allison, *Matthew*, 3:647.

23. Interestingly, the personal name of the high priest Caiaphas was "Joseph." To the extent that Matthew's readers would be aware of that, he could intend a contrast between the one whose perfidy led to Jesus' death and the one whose faithfulness led to Jesus' noble burial.

24. Arimathea lay about twenty miles northwest of Jerusalem but probably was his hometown rather than his residence. As a member of the Sanhedrin he must have resided in Jerusalem (so Keener). For discussion of the options for identifying Arimathea (the most likely being Ramathaim-Zophim of 1 Sam 1:1), see Nolland, *Matthew*, 1228 – 29.

25. Note the contrast with the "young man" with "many possessions" of 19:16 – 22, who went away sadly because he was so tied to his riches. Joseph uses his wealth to give Jesus an honorable burial.

26. "Came" (προσελθών) is another of the many circumstantial participles that partake of the force of the verb they modify, cf. 20:2.

27. For more on burial details and the historicity of the scene, see Grant R. Osborne, "Jesus' Empty Tomb and His Appearance in Jerusalem," in *Key Events in the Life of the Historical Jesus* (ed. D. L. Bock and R. L. Webb; Tübingen: Mohr Siebeck, 2009), 783 – 84.

guard against the stench (John 19:39 notes that 75 pounds of it was used, making it a virtual royal burial!).[28] The singular "a clean linen cloth" here seems to contradict the plural "strips of linen" in John 19:40, but it is possible that John uses a generalizing plural for a single sheet, or that by "long sheets" or pieces John includes the face cloth (cf. John 11:44).[29] Most likely it was a single long sheet wrapped around the body several times to "shroud" Jesus' mutilated body, and with the spices added to stave off the developing stench of the decay. Then a face cloth would be wrapped around Jesus' face (John 20:7).

27:60 ... and placed it in his own new tomb that he had cut in the rock. After he rolled a large stone at the entrance to the tomb, he departed (καὶ ἔθηκεν αὐτὸ ἐν τῷ καινῷ αὐτοῦ μνημείῳ ὃ ἐλατόμησεν ἐν τῇ πέτρᾳ καὶ προσκυλίσας λίθον μέγαν τῇ θύρᾳ τοῦ μνημείου ἀπῆλθεν). John 19:42 tells us the tomb[30] was "nearby" the place of execution, a fact that helped Joseph and Nicodemus in the short time they had to complete their act of devotion. Tombs were usually found in abandoned stone quarries, where stonecutters had already cut their way into the hillside — cave tombs. They had several chambers for the generations of the deceased, with the front room having a two-to-three foot high doorway (John 20:5, 11, "bent over to look [inside]").

The typical Jewish tomb also had: (1) a heavy wheel-shaped stone four to six feet in diameter rolled into a shallow trough and kept in place by a short wall on both sides of the opening; (2) a burial chamber with a preparation room encircled with a stone bench on which the body was readied; (3) burial niches (six feet long and two feet high) cut into the wall either above the bench or in a separate chamber; (4) a decorated limestone "bone box" (ossurary) on the floor to gather the bones after the body had decomposed.[31] A wealthy tomb especially would have a groove sloping down into the doorway, with the heavy stone rolled into it; while it was easy to roll in, it would take several men to roll it up the slope. The "new" rich man's tomb echoes Isa 53:9, "assigned a grave with the wicked, and with the rich in his death."

27:61 Mary Magdalene and the other Mary were there sitting opposite the tomb (ἦν δὲ ἐκεῖ Μαρία ἡ Μαγδαληνὴ καὶ ἡ ἄλλη Μαρία καθήμεναι ἀπέναντι τοῦ τάφου). Two of the women in vv. 55 – 56 stayed (imperfect periphrastic "were sitting" [ἦν ... καθήμεναι] stresses the ongoing vigilance of the women) with the body as it lay on the cross and watched as Joseph and the others removed Jesus from the cross, prepared him for burial, and laid him in the tomb. The "other Mary" is certainly "Mary the mother of James and Joseph" from v. 56. All three Synoptic authors mention this, so it was an important part of the tradition and showed the faithfulness of the women, who remained true to Jesus at every stage of the Passion Narrative.

Thus when they return in 28:1 to anoint his body again (in Mark), they know exactly where to

28. For excellent discussion of the historical details see Josef Blinzler, "Die Grablegung Jesu in historischer Sicht," in *Resurrexit: Actes du symposium international sur la résurrection de Jésus* (ed. É. Dhanis; Vatican: Libreria Editrice Vaticana, 1974), 56 – 107.

29. See Osborne, *John*, 173.

30. For the likelihood that the site is at the Church of the Holy Sepulchre in Jerusalem rather than the traditional "Gordon's Calvary," see Brown, *Death*, 1279 – 83; Carson, "Matthew," 584; Keener, *Matthew*, 695. We must remember that the walls of the city in the first century were at a completely different spot than they are today.

31. See Byron R. McCane, "Burial Practices, Jewish," *DNTB*, 173 – 75; Gary Burge, *John* (NIVAC; Grand Rapids: Zondervan, 2000), 536.

come. The importance of the women as eyewitnesses is shown by the threefold mention of them in all the gospels (see 27:55 – 56, 61; 28:1, 5 – 10). They, like the supernatural events of 27:51 – 53; 28:2 – 4, tie together the death and resurrection as a whole event.

Theology in Application

The rejection and mockery of Jesus by the three groups of the soldiers, the leaders, and the people is countermanded by the witness of God in nature, of the centurion and the soldiers, and of the women. This leads to the noble, even royal, burial of the crucified one by a wealthy man named Joseph.

1. Spectacular Events

The day of the Lord dawns on Golgotha; the divine judgment descends, and the firstfruits of the resurrection are gathered.[32] There is an apocalyptic air about the supernatural portents of vv. 51 – 53. Clearly, God further intersects this world as he did at the birth, baptism, and transfiguration of Jesus. Such explosions of nature were often recorded at the death of great men, but this goes beyond such conventional images. Earthquakes as well as the splitting of the temple curtain signified God's judgment on a people who would take the life of his Son (see on v. 51). The terror of the final judgment is a key feature of Matthew's eschatology (cf. 5:22; 7:21 – 23; 13:41 – 42, 49 – 50; 24:27 – 28, 30 – 31, 39, 41, 51; 25:10 – 13, 30, 31 – 46; 27:64), and that final event is prefigured in these portents.

2. Assurance of Resurrection

In Jesus' death the final resurrection of the saints is assured. The negative imagery of judgment is paralleled by the positive aspect, as the splitting of the curtain also signified the new access to God that the cross has made possible. Then this new access was extended to encompass the final resurrection in the appearance of the OT saints after the resurrection of Jesus. In Jesus' death and resurrection the believer's death to sin and promise of final resurrection are guaranteed. The imagery of the dry bones now goes beyond the physical restoration of the people of God to signify the spiritual restoration of the saints in heavenly glory. The raising to life of the ancients "holy ones" depicts the future of all God's people in embryo. The idea of Jesus as "firstfruits" is explored further in 1 Cor 15:20, 23; and we are "firstfruits" in Jas 1:18; Rev 14:4.

32. Davies and Allison, *Matthew*, 3:639.

3. Jesus Is Indeed "Son of God."

As already stated in the last section, the emphasis throughout this section is on Jesus' divine sonship. This soldiers' confession comes as close to a declaration of full divinity as we get this side of the gospel of John (see also on 1:23). Jesus is more than Messiah and Servant of Yahweh; he is fully God, and in him God has entered this world in a new way to accomplish the salvation of mankind.

CHAPTER 120

Matthew 27:62 – 28:1

Introduction to the Resurrection Narrative (Matthew 27:62 – 28:20)

Nearly all commentaries and studies of the Resurrection Narrative begin the resurrection narrative with 28:1, viewing the posting of the guard at the tomb (27:62 – 66) as the final event of the transition from the Passion Narrative to the Resurrection Narrative. While viable, this is not the best way to view Matthew's structure. While vv. 51 – 61 relate to the crucifixion, vv. 62 – 66 contain material that connect it more closely to the resurrection (Jesus' promise to "rise again" after three days, the guards, and the sealing of the tomb).[1]

The Matthean account is structured beautifully, showing the contrast between Jesus/God and his opponents. It is structured in three episodes, each with two parts contrasting the efforts of Jesus' enemies with the victory of the Risen Lord/God over them (as in the infancy narratives):

Preparation: The setting of the guard (27:62 – 63) vs. the going forth of the women (28:1)
Reaction: The fear of the guard (28:2 – 4) vs. the joy of the women (vv. 5 – 10)
Results: The spreading of lies (vv. 11 – 15) vs. the proclamation of truth (vv. 18 – 20).[2]

In this way Matthew shows the exaltation and glory of the enthroned Lord whose enemies are "a footstool for [his] feet" (Ps 110:1). Also there is a contrast between the figures involved in the action, between the guards and the women and between the leaders and the supernatural actions of God (see Luz).

Matthew's Resurrection Narrative functions not only as a conclusion to the Passion Narrative but also as both the conclusion to the book as a whole and a summary of Matthew's theological emphases. In the case of all four gospels the evangelist has

1. A few see the resurrection account beginning at 27:57 and see a chiasm in the Resurrection Narrative: A (the burial, 27:57 – 61), B (the guards at the tomb, 27:62 – 66), C (angels reveal the resurrection, 28:1 – 8), C' (the risen Lord appears, 28:9 – 10), B' (the bribing of the guards, 28:11 – 15), A' (appearance to the eleven, 28:16 – 20), cf. C. H. Giblin, "Structural and Thematic Correlations in the Matthean Burial – Resurrection Narrative (Matt, xxxvii, 57 – xxviii, 20)," *NTS* 21 (1975): 406 – 20. However, the two A accounts are somewhat artificial, and the burial belongs more closely with Jesus' death on the cross.

2. See Grant R. Osborne, *The Resurrection Narratives: A Redactional Study* (Grand Rapids: Baker, 1984), 73 – 74.

arranged his material to provide an abstract or resumé of his major themes; this explains the vast differences between the accounts in the four. As a result the various Resurrection Narratives must be studied in light of the emphases seen throughout the individual gospel (this, of course, is true of each pericope, but in this case is especially essential). The Resurrection Narratives are the most highly redactional passages in the gospels, exhibiting greater differences from one another than any other part of the gospels. In my opinion, redaction criticism is the friend rather than foe[3] for a high view of the accuracy of the resurrection accounts.

The differences between the resurrection accounts do not have to be attributed to fictional creation of material but rather to the deliberate choice of the evangelists as to which stories from the tradition to include and which to omit. We know from Acts 1:3 that the appearances took place over a forty-day period. When we compile all the material in the gospels and 1 Cor 15, we find a total of eleven appearance traditions:

1. Mary Magdalene (John 20:14 – 18)
2. a group of women (Mark 16:5 – 7; Matt 28:9)
3. Peter (Luke 24:34; 1 Cor 15:5)
4. two disciples on the road to Emmaus (Luke 24:13 – 35)
5. the disciples in Jerusalem (Luke 24:36 – 43; John 20:19 – 23)
6. Thomas and the others eight days later (John 20:26 – 29)
7. seven disciples on the Sea of Galilee (John 21:1 – 23)
8. the Great Commission appearance on a mountain in Galilee (Matt 28:16 – 20)
9. five hundred believers (1 Cor 15:6)
10. James (1 Cor 15:7)
11. the disciples at the ascension (Luke 24:44 – 53; Acts 1:1 – 12).[4]

This means an average of one appearance every four days (though the first five were on that first Sunday, so the rest were an average of one every six and a half days), certainly not the total number of appearances Jesus made during that period. Each evangelist, including Matthew, chooses only those appearances that fit their purpose in drawing their respective gospel and its theology to a close.

Furthermore, there are seven different theories propounded through the centuries to explain what may have happened behind the resurrection story; let us consider each one in turn.

1. The early Jewish apologetic against its truthfulness said the disciples stole the body and made up a story about the resurrection (28:13); yet this is exactly what Matthew's account intends to refute.

3. See Grant R. Osborne, "The Evangelical and Redaction Criticism: Critique and Methodology," *JETS* 22 (1979): 305 – 22; and "History and Theology," 5 – 22.

4. See Philip W. Comfort and Wendell C. Hawley, *Opening the Gospel of John: A Fresh Resource for Teaching and Preaching the Fourth Gospel* (Wheaton: Tyndale, 1994), 311 – 12.

2. The political theory of Hermann Samuel Reimarus in the eighteenth century stated that the disciples concocted the resurrection story to establish a movement that would bring them fame and power.[5] However, this has never been widely accepted because of the high ethical content of the NT. The disciples could hardly be so base as to make up such a story for personal gain and then create a Christian movement based on selflessness and filled with persecution for them.
3. The swoon theory of Friedrich Schleiermacher and K. A. Hase asserted that Jesus fainted on the cross and revived in the tomb (also the theory in the Koran, which says Jesus later preached in India and died in Kashmir). The gospels themselves combat this theory by stressing the observers and the reality of Jesus' wounds. The Romans were expert executioners, and the team that put Christ on the cross would have done so numerous times. There is simply no way they would have mistaken someone who had fainted for a corpse.
4. The mythical view of David F. Strauss and Rudolf Bultmann, which hypothesizes that the stories were created by the early church along the lines of Greco-Roman myth in order to explain the existential (Bultmann) impact of Jesus on the lives of the disciples (i.e., he "still lives" in their hearts). There was insufficient time for this to develop (most accept that the tradition behind 1 Cor 15:3 – 8 was developed within five years of Jesus' ascension). The disciples would hardly have been so radically changed by a "myth," and the vast differences between pagan myths and the subdued resurrection narratives make this theory doubtful indeed.
5. The subjective vision theory of Ernst Renan and Willi Marxsen, who hold that the disciples (Peter first) had dreams of Jesus and interpreted these from a first-century perspective as being sent by God. But the appearances came to some who were not psychologically prepared (e.g., James and Paul), and it is difficult to explain all the changes merely on psychological grounds. A mass hallucination to "five hundred people at once" (1 Cor 15:6) is hardly a viable alternative, as if they were stoned on sacred mushrooms or something!
6. The objective vision theory of Eduard Schweizer, Günter Bornkamm, and C. F. D. Moule, who maintain that God sent the disciples visions rather than physical appearances and that these were interpreted along physical lines by the Jewish followers who had no concept of differences between a physical and spiritual body/resurrected form. But this is to force a Greek view of a spiritual body on historical evidence that attests otherwise. It is hard to conceive why God would restrict himself to mere visions of the glorified Jesus. The God who could do the one could also do the other, and there is little reason along these lines to deny the validity of the biblical claims.

5. See also Hugh Schonfeld's *Passover Plot*.

7. The corporeal view of Karl Barth, Emil Brunner, and most conservative critics fits the evidence as we have it and makes the best sense. Jesus was raised from the dead literally and bodily.[6] Gnilka notes the centrality of verbs for "seeing" in this final section (28:1, 6, 7, 17, plus the six uses of "look" (ἰδού) in the chapter) and concludes that Matthew stresses what one can see with the eyes as interpreted through the Word.[7] Matthew clearly believes that Jesus actually appeared and was "seen" by the disciples.

In terms of resurrection and history, Wright notes five ways "history" can be intended: (1) as event, namely, something that happened; (2) as significant event, something with "momentous consequences"; (3) as provable event, that which can be demonstrated as having occurred; (4) as writing-about-events-in-the-past, something that was committed to writing or to oral history; and (5) as a combination of the third and fourth, centering on what modern historians say "*within the post-Enlightenment worldview*" (italics his). Wright argues that each sense must be respected in the debate.[8]

When the data is examined and the question honestly asked, "What really happened?" there are significant reasons for affirming the historicity of Jesus' resurrection.

1. The disparate accounts are not really contradictory to one another, and it is indeed possible to harmonize them and show they supplement one another.[9]
2. Little else can explain the incredible change of the disciples from self-centered cowards who would desert Jesus in his moment of greatest need to world-changing moral and spiritual giants.
3. Anyone making up the stories about the resurrection would never have women (who could not serve as witnesses in a Jewish framework) as the first official witnesses of the resurrection news.
4. The empty tomb is a historically verifiable fact, and in spite of Jewish claims

6. N. T. Wright, *The Resurrection of the Son of God* (Minneapolis: Fortress, 2003), 15 – 28, presents these historical objections another way, dividing them into two groups. (1) Some think we cannot study the evidence because there is no access to the evidence, no analogy in our own experience, and no real evidence. But we have the same access to resurrection data as we have to any other historical event, and we do not have to experience something to know it is true, (e.g., space flight). Others hold a hermeneutic of suspicion (Crossan et al.) and they think that studying the resurrection is unnecessary and self-destructive. (2) Others think we should not study the resurrection historically, because it is the starting point of Christian belief and cannot be studied historically (Frei, but the resurrection is a historical as well as Christian issue), or because it is completely tied up with incarnational Christology, with God in Christ (but it provides historical grounds for such theological beliefs rather than being those beliefs itself), or because it is an eschatological event rather than a historical event (but in the NT such eschatological events occur within history, not outside it).

7. Gnilka, *Matthäusevangelium*, 2:490.

8. Wright, *Resurrection*, 12 – 15.

9. See George E. Ladd, *I Believe in the Resurrection of Jesus* (Grand Rapids: Eerdmans, 1975), 91 – 93; John W. Wenham *The Easter Enigma: Are the Resurrection Accounts in Conflict?* (Grand Rapids: Zondervan, 1984); Murray J. Harris, *From Grave to Glory: Resurrection in the New Testament* (Grand Rapids: Zondervan, 1990), 157 – 63; Osborne, *Three Crucial Questions,* 39 – 41; Wilkins, *Matthew*, 934 – 36.

that the disciples stole the body (Matt 28:13 – 15), there is no evidence they were able to produce the body of Jesus.

5. From the start the early church used the resurrection as a historically verifiable event (1 Cor 15:5 – 8; the sermons of Acts), and to them it actually happened.
6. Jesus did not appear just to his followers but also to unbelievers, such as his brother James (1 Cor 15:7; for him as an unbeliever see John 7:5).[10]

In conclusion, the resurrection as a historical event makes best sense of the data. Bruner notes essays by Raymond Brown and Wolfhart Pannenberg that cite "the difference between the *'symbolic' language* the NT writers used to denote the *effects* of the resurrection on the one hand and the bald, *unsymbolic historicity* of the resurrection *event* on the other." The conclusion of all three is that the resurrection is an event that really happened in history.[11]

Literary Context

The chronological movement of the death and resurrection stories is apparent. At the same time, there is thematic development as the action of the leaders and the guards in trying to stymie God's will is contrasted with the faithful actions of women who, in spite of their failure to realize what was about to transpire, still want to show their devotion to Jesus. They continue as witnesses. As France notes, "The sealing of the tomb and the placing of an armed guard … add to the dramatic triumph of Jesus' resurrection despite every human precaution."[12]

VII. The Passion and Resurrection of Jesus (26:1 – 28:20)
- A. The Passion Narrative (26:1 – 27:61)
  - 5. The Crucifixion and Death of Jesus (27:27 – 50)
  - 6. Events Following Jesus' Death (27:51 – 61)
- **B. The Resurrection Narrative (27:62 – 28:20)**
  - ➦ **1. Preparatory Events (27:62 – 28:1)**
  - 2. Reactions to the Resurrection (28:2 – 10)
  - 3. Results of the Resurrection (28:11 – 20)

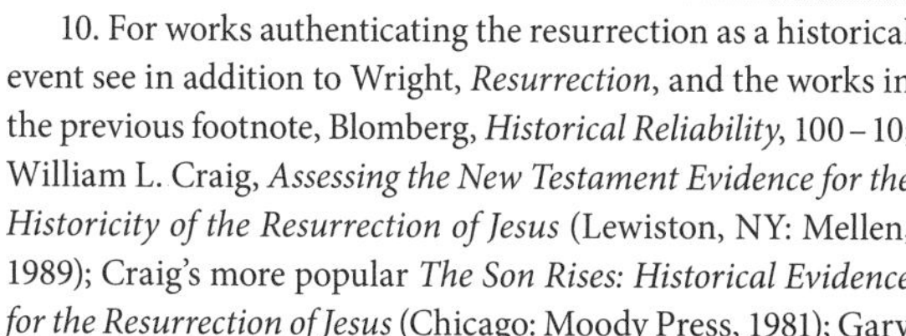

10. For works authenticating the resurrection as a historical event see in addition to Wright, *Resurrection*, and the works in the previous footnote, Blomberg, *Historical Reliability*, 100 – 10; William L. Craig, *Assessing the New Testament Evidence for the Historicity of the Resurrection of Jesus* (Lewiston, NY: Mellen, 1989); Craig's more popular *The Son Rises: Historical Evidence for the Resurrection of Jesus* (Chicago: Moody Press, 1981); Gary Habermas, *The Resurrection of Jesus: An Apologetic* (Grand Rapids: Baker, 1980); Osborne, "Jesus' Empty Tomb," 775–823.

11. Bruner, *Matthew 13 – 28*, 782, from Raymond E. Brown's "The Resurrection of Jesus," in *The New Jerome Biblical Commentary* (1990), 1374; and Wolfhart Pannenberg, "Did Jesus Really Rise from the Dead?" *Dialog* 4 (1965): 135.

12. France, *Gospel of Matthew*, 1092.

Main Idea

A major theme in both the infancy narratives and here is the desire of God's enemies to thwart his will and the actions they undertake to stand against him. Here the leaders ask Pilate for permission to make Jesus' tomb doubly secure by posting guards at it and sealing the rock in place in front of the entrance. This contrasts with the simple devoted act of the women as they come to the tomb to pay homage to the dead Jesus (yet in their own way are less aware than the Jewish leaders of Jesus' resurrection predictions).

Translation

Matthew 27:62-28:1

62a	Setting (Temporal)	Now on the next day,
b	Identification	namely, the day after the preparation,
c	Action	**the high priests and Pharisees gathered together before Pilate, saying,**
63a	Report	*"Lord, we remember that that deceiver said while he was still alive, 'After three days I will rise.'*
64a	Request	*So order that the tomb be made secure until the third day,*
b	Basis for 64a	*lest his disciples come, steal him, and tell the people that he was raised from the dead,*
c		*and the last deception will be worse than the first."*
65a	Response	**Pilate told them,**
b		*"Take a guard.*
c	Exhortation	*Go, make the tomb as secure as you know how."*
66a	Action	**So they came and made the tomb secure with a guard detail,**
b		sealing the stone.
1a	Setting	After the Sabbath at dawn on the first day of the week,
b	Event	**Mary Magdalene and the other Mary came to look at the tomb.**

Structure and Literary Form

This passage is unique, and it is debated whether this is Matthean (Gnilka, Luz) or from an independent tradition (Brown, Crossan, on the basis of parallels in the *Gospel of Peter*).[13] The story has two major parts: the action of the leaders (27:62 – 66, with three sections: the leaders telling Pilate of Jesus' prophecy [vv. 62 – 63], permission given to post the guards [vv. 64 – 65], and the tomb sealed and guards posted [v. 66]), and the action of the women (28:1).

Exegetical Outline

➡ **I. The Attempt of the Leaders to Keep Jesus in the Tomb (27:62 – 66)**
- A. The report to Pilate regarding Jesus' passion predictions (vv. 62 – 63)
  1. They go to Pilate in humble submission (v. 62)
  2. Their report of Jesus' prediction (v. 63)
- B. Permission to post a guard at the tomb (vv. 64 – 65)
  1. The request based on ensuring the disciples cannot steal the body (v. 64)
  2. Permission granted by Pilate (v. 65)
- C. Permission granted — the tomb sealed and guards posted (v. 66)

II. The Actions of the Women Who Come to the Tomb (28:1)

Explanation of the Text

27:62 Now on the next day, namely, the day after the preparation, the high priests and Pharisees gathered together before Pilate (Τῇ δὲ ἐπαύριον, ἥτις ἐστὶν μετὰ τὴν παρασκευήν, συνήχθησαν οἱ ἀρχιερεῖς καὶ οἱ Φαρισαῖοι πρὸς Πιλᾶτον). The "next day" refers to the day following the crucifixion, after Christ had been entombed through the night. By "day of preparation," Matthew meant Friday as the Jews prepared for the Sabbath (cf. Mark 15:42; John 19:14, 31, 42).[14] The chief priests and Pharisees were political opponents (see 21:45, the only other place they are mentioned together), so this may refer to a semiofficial delegation from the Sanhedrin. That this is done on the Sabbath is highly unusual (they would have to stay in the courtyard so as not to be rendered unclean by Pilate's residence) and shows they are still worried about the effects of Jesus on his followers and about the movement as a whole. Pilate is still the one who controls the situation, so they cannot post a guard at the tomb without his permission.

27:63 ... saying, "Lord, we remember that that deceiver said while he was still alive, 'After three

13. In reality it does not matter, for Matthew could have been writing from his own knowledge or from an oral or written tradition previously received. Either case, there is no reason to deny its historical base (contra Luz). See William L. Craig, "The Guard at the Tomb," *NTS* 30 (1984): 273 – 81.

14. No cooking or normal activities were allowed on the Sabbath, so everything had to be "prepared" before dusk on Friday.

days I will rise' " (λέγοντες, Κύριε, ἐμνήσθημεν ὅτι ἐκεῖνος ὁ πλάνος εἶπεν ἔτι ζῶν, Μετὰ τρεῖς ἡμέρας ἐγείρομαι). There is a deliberate emphasis here on the address to Pilate as "Lord" (κύριε), for elsewhere in Matthew the title (except in some parables) is restricted to Jesus. So the contrast is real; they have rejected their true Lord and have made the Romans their "Lord," reminiscent of John 19:15, where they say, "We have no king but Caesar" (so Nolland).

There is also a powerful irony in the fact that they "remember" Jesus' teaching about being raised on the third day, for his disciples have remembered *nothing* about Jesus' prediction. It is a strange quirk of history that the only ones who realize what Jesus really meant are his enemies, not his followers! The leaders place a guard at the tomb when they do not need to, for the disciples are too ignorant even to think of such a thing as stealing the body!

This is the only place Jesus is called "that deceiver," but it is in keeping with the trial narrative. The reference to Jesus' teaching on resurrection "on the third day" goes back to his teaching in 12:38 – 40 addressed to the scribes and Pharisees (regarding the sign of Jonah) and to the false witnesses at his trial (26:60 – 61), who remembered his teaching about destroying the temple. Of course, the chief priests as Sadducees do not believe in the possibility of resurrection from the dead, but they know the disciples and the people do, so they wish to prevent them from stealing the body.

27:64 "So order that the tomb be made secure until the third day" (κέλευσον οὖν ἀσφαλισθῆναι τὸν τάφον ἕως τῆς τρίτης ἡμέρας). The request is phrased the way it is to stress again the unconscious testimony of the priests to prophetic fulfillment and to anticipate the event recorded in the next section. Dramatically, the anticipation and tension are rising as events move to their inexorable climax. As we will state again on v. 65, the soldiers requested are probably Roman guards, since the Jewish leaders would not need permission for temple police; moreover, later the guards report to Pilate (28:11 – 15).

27:64 "... lest his disciples come, steal him, and tell the people that he was raised from the dead" (μήποτε ἐλθόντες οἱ μαθηταὶ αὐτοῦ κλέψωσιν αὐτὸν καὶ εἴπωσιν τῷ λαῷ, Ἠγέρθη ἀπὸ τῶν νεκρῶν). The Jewish leaders, of course, do not believe Jesus could ever rise from the dead, but they are asking that the tomb be both sealed and guarded to keep the disciples from stealing the body and propounding that very thing. Since Jesus' prediction was that it would happen after three days, they want the tomb guarded an extra day (three days from Saturday) to ensure that no such grave robbery could occur.

Pilate had commanded Jesus' death in 27:26 and also ordered that his body be given to Joseph in 26:58, so this will be his third order. All the earthly powers are working in concert to thwart the will of God (cf. Job 42:2). The fear of the Jewish leaders, however, is valid from their standpoint. The same zealous pilgrims who shouted out their acceptance of him as Messiah at the triumphal entry could be easily swayed by such news. They will take no chances.

27:64 "... and the last deception will be worse than the first" (καὶ ἔσται ἡ ἐσχάτη πλάνη χείρων τῆς πρώτης). The phrasing, "the last ... worse than the first" is similar to 12:45 (where the "final condition" of the one inhabited by seven demons is worse; cf. also 2 Pet 2:20) and constitutes further irony. The "worse deception" is their own rejection of Jesus as Messiah and Son of God! The "first" fraud is Jesus' messiahship and the "last" a belief in his resurrection (so Hill).

27:65 Pilate told them, "Take a guard. Go, make the tomb as secure as you know how" (ἔφη αὐτοῖς ὁ Πιλᾶτος, Ἔχετε κουστωδίαν· ὑπάγετε ἀσφαλίσασθε ὡς οἴδατε). There is some debate as to whether ἔχετε ("take") is imperative ("Take a guard," = Roman guards; so Morris, Hagner, Davies and Allison) or indicative ("You have guards," i.e., rejecting their request for Roman guards, Carson). Yet since those appointed are Roman soldiers in 28:11 – 15, the former is preferable. "Guard" (κουστωδία) is a Latin loanword and further favors the guards being Roman.

Thus, Pilate does the same as he did at the trial, seeking to please the leaders and avoiding controversy during the volatile period of the Passover. Even though he is filled with contempt for them, he does not want any further trouble from these Jewish diehards. His statement "as secure as you know how" is not a contemptuous dismissal (= "you know nothing") but simply a recognition of reality ("as secure as it can be made"), recognizing the prevalence of tomb robbery in the ancient world.

27:66 So they came and made the tomb secure with a guard detail, sealing the stone (οἱ δὲ πορευθέντες ἠσφαλίσαντο τὸν τάφον σφραγίσαντες τὸν λίθον μετὰ τῆς κουστωδίας). The twofold plan, "sealing the stone" and "setting the guard," prepares the reader for the overcoming power of God, who vindicates the simple purpose of the women. There is a deliberate and definite contrast between this double action and the devoted plan of the women in the next verse of coming to the tomb to pay their respects to dead Jesus.

The sealing of the tomb must have meant placing a wax seal on the stone that had been rolled in place at the entrance, probably between the stone and the façade of the tomb.[15] As on a legal document, this seal could not be legally broken by anyone except an authorized agent. The soldiers would easily dissuade a group of men planning to steal the body.[16]

28:1 After the Sabbath at dawn on the first day of the week (Ὀψὲ δὲ σαββάτων, τῇ ἐπιφωσκούσῃ εἰς μίαν σαββάτων). The time notes are more complex, for Matthew has "after (ὀψέ as a preposition, see BDF §164/4) the Sabbath at dawn," which seems to combine the separate notes of Mark 16, "When the Sabbath was over" (v. 1) and "very early on the first day of the week" (v. 2). Some see a contradiction, that Mark places the event on Sunday morning while Matthew changes it to Saturday evening (so Gundry), for ὀψέ can also mean "late." Yet if one takes ὀψέ as a preposition ("after") rather than an adverb ("late"), it is a general time note and the difficulty is removed (Osborne, Carson, Hagner, Davies and Allison, France). Matthew is stressing Sunday morning at dawn "after" the women have observed the Sabbath the day before.

Moreover, in Mark the first time note tells when the women bought spices to anoint Jesus' body and the second when they started for the tomb. Matthew has decided to omit the part about anointing Jesus' body (to simplify the story?) and so brings them together into a single reference. So at dawn the women walk to the tomb to show devotion to their slain Lord, expecting nothing and probably intending to continue their vigil of 26:61, to sit opposite the tomb and "look at" it. The desire to "see" continues the witness motif from 27:55 – 56, 61. The contrast between desire and reality is also heightened; they come to "view" the tomb but end up "seeing" the Risen Lord (28:9 – 10). In all four gospels this is a "new day" motif and signals a brand new period of salvation history.

15. So most, but McNeile, *Matthew*, 429, envisions "a cord with its ends fastened by seals to the stone and to the rock."

16. The *Gospel of Peter* has seven seals and a centurion with an entire company of soldiers accompanied by many Jewish leaders who spend the night with them.

28:1 Mary Magdalene and the other Mary came to look at the tomb (ἦλθεν Μαρία ἡ Μαγδαληνὴ καὶ ἡ ἄλλη Μαρία θεωρῆσαι τὸν τάφον). The same two Marys who witnessed the crucifixion and the burial of Jesus (27:56, 61) are featured in Matthew's opening scene of his empty tomb narrative. Mark 16:1 has these two plus Salome; Luke 24:10 adds Joanna and "the others with them"; and John 20:1 centers only on Mary Magdalene. Matthew may have omitted Salome because his readers were unfamiliar with her but more likely to conform this with 27:61.

Theology in Application

The major theme is the attempt of the enemies of God to thwart his will and the sovereignty of God over all things. This has been a theme throughout Matthew, also central in the infancy narratives with Herod trying to kill God's Messiah and God's supernatural intervention (see "Theology in Application" on 2:13 – 23). We will explore here God's providential and redemptive care of this world in light of the presence and opposition of evil. The doctrine of God's sovereign control of this world is firmly found in Scripture. In Heb 1:3 we are told that Christ in God "sustains all things by his powerful word," and in Col 1:17 it says "in him all things hold together."

Throughout Scripture the Word says that God created the universe and controls everything in his creation. In 2 Chr 20:6 that author states of the heavenly God "You rule over all the kingdoms of the nations ... and no one can withstand you," speaking of the victory of Judah over its enemies. Job 41:10 says in light of the trials of Job, "No one is fierce enough to rouse [God]. Who then is able to stand against [him]?" This theme is found again and again (Job 42:2; Ps 78:7; Isa 14:27; 46:5; Jer 32:27; 49:19; 50:44; Rev 6:17).

The message is clear. God is absolutely sovereign, and no actions of humankind can turn aside his divine will. Neither the opposition of the Jewish leaders and Roman soldiers nor the ignorance of the disciples can stop the resurrection from happening. God's control is especially seen in Rev 13:5 – 8, the description of the actions of the "beast" against God's people at the final period of history. Each one is preceded by the verb "it was given," a divine passive that says the beast could only do what God allowed or authorized him to do. God controls even the actions of the demonic powers.[17]

17. This does not mean God has created or caused evil (on this see Grudem, *Systematic Theology*, 322 – 23) but rather God has established the parameters within which evil can operate and will turn all it does around for good for his people (Rom 8:28). God did not create evil but created choice, which meant the possibility of evil. By our choices we bring evil into the world and participate in the results of sin (Rom 5:12).

CHAPTER 121

Matthew 28:2 – 10

Literary Context

The antithesis between the actions of God and those of human beings continues, as the guards and the women react to the reality of the resurrection. Both are filled with fear, but here the similarities cease. The guards faint, while the women become official witnesses to the disciples of the turning point of the ages.

VII. The Passion and Resurrection of Jesus (26:1 – 28:20)
- A. The Passion Narrative (26:1 – 27:61)
  - 5. The Crucifixion and Death of Jesus (27:27 – 50)
  - 6. Events Following Jesus' Death (27:51 – 61)
- **B. The Resurrection Narrative (27:62 – 28:20)**
  - 1. Preparatory Events (27:62 – 28:1)
  - ➦ **2. Reactions to the Resurrection (28:2 – 10)**
  - 3. Results of the Resurrection (28:11 – 20)

Main Idea

The empty tomb narrative is one of the two major aspects of the resurrection event, stressing the reality of the resurrection. The announcement is given to the guards and to the women, and in both it produces fear. This is the contrast: for the guards (and for all who stand against Jesus) the fear is all-encompassing, but for the women (and all followers) the fear turns to joy.

Translation

Matthew 28:2-10

2a	Scene #1 Event	And **look, there was a strong earthquake,**
b	Basis for 2a	for an angel of the Lord descended from heaven,
c		came to that place, and
		rolled back the stone and
		was sitting on it.
3a	Description of 2b	And **his appearance was like lightning**
b		and **his clothes as white as snow**
4a	Result of 2b	And because they were so afraid of him,
b	Result of 4a	**the guards shook and became like dead men.**
5a		Now **the angel answered and said to the women,**
b	Exhortation	*"Don't you be afraid,*
c	Basis for 5b	*for I know that you are seeking Jesus who was crucified.*
6a	Assertion	*He is not here,*
b	Basis for 6a	*for he has been raised just as he told you.*
c	Exhortation	*Come, see the place where he was lying.*
7a	Exhortation	*Go quickly and tell his disciples,*
b		*'He has been raised from the dead.'*
c	Promise	*And look, he is going before you into Galilee.*
d		*You will see him there.*
e		*Look, I have told you this."*
8a	Scene #3	And **they departed quickly from the tomb with fear and great joy**
b		**and ran to announce this to his disciples.**
9a	Event	And **look, Jesus met them and said,**
b		*"Greetings!"*
c	Response to 9a	And **they came to him, grabbed hold of his feet, and worshiped him.**
10a	Exhortation	**Then Jesus told them,**
b		*"Do not be afraid.*
c		*Go announce . . . that they should depart for Galilee*
		to my brothers and sisters.
d	Promise	*They will see me there."*

Structure and Literary Form

As throughout the passion and resurrection accounts Matthew here alters Mark on the basis of his own material. The earthquake, the descending of the angel, and the fainting of the guards are found only here. The commission of the women contains only minor changes. However, vv. 8 – 10 depend on the debate as to whether Mark's gospel ends at v. 8 or continues with an ending now lost. Even though I have argued strongly for such an ending,[1] I now believe such is unlikely since there is no evidence for such an ending and since Mark makes perfect sense as it is. Thus Matt 28:8 – 10 stems from his own special material. There are three parts to the empty tomb narrative: the coming of the angel to the tomb (vv. 2 – 4), the commissioning of the women (vv.5 – 7), and the appearance of Jesus to the women (vv.8 – 10).

Exegetical Outline

- **I. The Descent of the Angel to the Empty Tomb (28:2 – 4)**
  - A. The angel comes and rolls away the stone (v. 2)
  - B. The dazzling appearance of the angel (v. 3)
  - C. The fainting of the guards (v. 4)
- **II. The Commissioning of the Women (28:5 – 7)**
  - A. The rebuke of their search for a corpse (v. 5)
  - B. The triumphant announcement of the empty tomb and resurrection (v. 6)
  - C. The mission of the women to the disciples (v. 7)
- **III. The Appearance of Jesus to the Women (28:8 – 10)**
  - A. The fear and joy of the women as they go (v. 8)
  - B. The appearance of Jesus to them (v. 9)
  - C. The message to meet Jesus in Galilee (v. 10)

Explanation of the Text

28:2 And look, there was a strong earthquake (καὶ ἰδοὺ σεισμὸς ἐγένετο μέγας). "Look" (ἰδού), a common Matthean idiom to heighten the drama of a scene, occurs six times in ch. 28 (twice in v. 7). This is as close to a description of the actual resurrection as we have in the four gospels. The only more spectacular rendition is the apocryphal story in *Gospel of Peter* 8:35 – 45, in which two angels descend from heaven and roll away the stone, with the cross preceding Jesus and "the heads of the two reaching the heaven, but that of him who was led of them by the hand surpassing the heavens."

This is the second earthquake after the one following Jesus' death (27:51, 54), and together they connect the death and resurrection as a single event in salvation history. It is also the third apocalyptic *seismos* ("earthquake") scene and links this with the stilling of the storm (8:24) and passion events (27:51) in fulfillment of Zech 14:4 – 5.[2] The earthquake is not an earthly but rather a supernatural event, as Matthew says it occurred "for" or "because" (γάρ) the angel descended. Some say the earthquake and angel are apocalyptic symbols expressing the victory of God and drawn from the

1. Osborne, *Resurrection Narratives*, 59 – 65. See also Wright, *Resurrection*, 619 – 24; and Robert H. Gundry, *Mark: A Commentary on His Apology for the Cross* (Grand Rapids: Eerdmans, 1993), 1009 – 12.

2. Edward L. Bode, *The First Easter Morning: The Gospel Accounts of the Women's Visit to the Tomb of Jesus* (Rome: Biblical Institute Press, 1970), 57, says, "Matthew introduces a new motif through the apocalyptic earthquake. Jesus' work of redemption climaxed in his death and resurrection marks the beginning of the eschatological age, the signs and promise of the resurrection of all men."

portrait of the God of Sinai in Exod 19:18; Ps 114:7; Dan 10:5 – 6, *4 Ezra* 10:25 – 27.[3]

28:2 For an angel of the Lord descended from heaven, came[4] to that place, and rolled back the stone and was sitting on it (ἄγγελος γὰρ κυρίου καταβὰς ἐξ οὐρανοῦ καὶ προσελθὼν ἀπεκύλισεν τὸν λίθον καὶ ἐκάθητο ἐπάνω αὐτοῦ). The angel[5] apparently uses the "great earthquake" to move the "large stone" (27:60). The switch from the aorists to the imperfect ἐκάθητο pictures dynamically the triumphant action of the angel "sitting" on the rock, having participated in conquering death via resurrection (Keener).

28:3 And his appearance was like lightning and his clothes as white as snow (ἦν δὲ ἡ εἰδέα αὐτοῦ ὡς ἀστραπὴ καὶ τὸ ἔνδυμα αὐτοῦ λευκὸν ὡς χιών). The appearance of the angel draws on apocalyptic descriptions in Dan 10:6 (the man dressed in linen had "his face like lightning") and 7:9 (the clothing of "the Ancient of Days" was "as white as snow"). It also goes back to the transfiguration, where Jesus' face "shone like the sun" and his clothes became "as white as the light" (17:2). Since the transfiguration was a harbinger of the resurrection, this makes sense. The appearance of the angel depicts the glory of the Risen Lord. The "angel of the Lord" appears also in 1:20, 24; 2:13, 19 (in dreams), and angels are also observed by human beings in Dan 10:5 – 6; Rev 19:9 – 10 (cf. also *1 En.* 62:15 – 16; 71:1; 87:2).[6]

28:4 And because they were afraid of him,[7] the guards shook and became like dead men (ἀπὸ δὲ τοῦ φόβου αὐτοῦ ἐσείσθησαν οἱ τηροῦντες καὶ ἐγενήθησαν ὡς νεκροί). This is a causal use of this preposition (ἀπό, BAGD, 87 [V, 1]) and with a verbal noun becomes a virtual clause (see above). Fear is always the result of an angelophany (or theophany), so the guards are typically filled with fear (who wouldn't be?!). The imagery of "quaking" uses the language of the "earthquake" from v. 2; there was a shaking (σεισμός) of the earth and there is another shaking (vb. σείω) of the guards. They then fall into a "dead" faint. We must remember that these were Roman guards, trained never to fall down. They would easily have turned back anyone desiring to raid the tomb, but who can stand against God himself? Hagner says it well, "The irony is not to be missed: the ones assigned to guard the dead themselves appear dead while the dead now have been made alive."

28:5 Now the angel answered[8] and said to the women, "Don't you be afraid, for I know that you are seeking Jesus who was crucified" (ἀποκριθεὶς δὲ ὁ ἄγγελος εἶπεν ταῖς γυναιξίν, Μὴ φοβεῖσθε ὑμεῖς, οἶδα γὰρ ὅτι Ἰησοῦν τὸν ἐσταυρωμένον ζητεῖτε). In this context the women apparently have observed the angel as well as the fear and fainting of the guards, as the angel "answers" what is implicit in v. 4, the fact that their fear mirrors that of the guards (see Nolland). So the angel, as

3. Xavier Léon-Dufour, "The Easter Message according to Matthew," in *Resurrection and the Message of Easter* (trans. R. N. Wilson; New York: Holt, Rinehart and Winston, 1971), 139 – 40; B. Rigaux, *Dieu l'a ressuscité: Exégèse et théologie biblique* (Gembloux: Duculot, 1973), 202.

4. "Descended" (καταβάς) and "came" (προσελθών) are circumstantial participles that are so closely related to the main verb that they virtually become main verbs themselves, see on 4:20.

5. Here and in John 20:12 there are angels (John has two), while in Mark 16:5 ("a young man") and Luke 24:4 ("two men") the angels are described as they appeared to the women, as men. This is only an apparent contradiction, as angels are often described as men and throughout the gospels one narration will present a group while another will center on one member of the group for dramatic purposes (see Blomberg, *Historical Reliability*, 150 – 51).

6. See France, *Gospel of Matthew*, 1100.

7. αὐτοῦ is an objective genitive, "they feared him."

8. For this construction (which occurs fifty-six times in Matthew), see 3:15; 4:4.

always in Scripture, alleviates their fear and directs them to the truth about the situation.

The present tense prohibition "don't you be afraid" (μὴ φοβεῖσθε) in this context means "Stop being afraid."[9] There is a definite tone of rebuke (as in Mark) as the angel says in effect, "You are merely seeking a corpse, but he is not here. He is risen just as he said (and as you failed to note)." Their ongoing search (present tense "seeking" [ζητεῖτε]) is fruitless, for they want only to sit opposite the tomb and be in the presence of the crucified corpse. Jesus had told them and the disciples numerous times that his death would end in victory, but they had not understood.

28:6 "He is not here, for he has been raised just as he told you. Come, see the place where he was lying" (οὐκ ἔστιν ὧδε, ἠγέρθη γὰρ καθὼς εἶπεν· δεῦτε ἴδετε τὸν τόπον ὅπου ἔκειτο). The stone was rolled away from the tomb not so that Christ could emerge; he could pass through doors and walls (Luke 24:36; John 20:19) and did not need the stone removed. The stone was rolled away so that the women and others could see the tomb was empty. The triumphant "he has been raised" (ἠγέρθη) is a divine passive; God has raised Jesus from the grave.

"As he said," of course, refers to the passion predictions (12:40; 16:21; 17:23; 20:19; 26:32); if you add the three "lifted up" sayings of John 3:14; 8:28; 12:32, there are far more than the traditional three that are mentioned (16:21; 17:23; 20:19)! Jesus' followers should have expected something because of Jesus' repeated teaching, yet it was the leaders, the enemies and all they stood for, who alone realized what Jesus meant. When the angel added, "Come, see," he was emphasizing the reality of the empty tomb.[10]

28:7 "Go quickly and tell his disciples, 'He has been raised from the dead' " (καὶ ταχὺ πορευθεῖσαι εἴπατε τοῖς μαθηταῖς αὐτοῦ ὅτι Ἠγέρθη ἀπὸ τῶν νεκρῶν). "Quickly" (ταχύ) stresses eschatological urgency; this is the turning point of the ages, and it is a time for fast action. As in 28:19, the circumstantial participle "go" (πορευθεῖσαι) partakes of the imperatival force of the main verb. The message the women are commissioned to give the disciples[11] comes straight from God, who is the subject of the divine passive "he has been raised" (ἠγέρθη): God has raised Jesus from the dead! This is certainly one of the proofs for the historicity of the resurrection; no one would ever make up a story with women as the official witnesses, since women were not allowed to be witnesses in a legal sense.

28:7 "And look, he is going before you into Galilee. You will see him there. Look, I have told you this" (καὶ ἰδοὺ προάγει ὑμᾶς εἰς τὴν Γαλιλαίαν, ἐκεῖ αὐτὸν ὄψεσθε· ἰδοὺ εἶπον ὑμῖν). "Look" (ἰδού) occurs twice in v. 7 to emphasize the drama of this command (see also v. 2). The second part of the message fulfills the promise of 26:32, where Jesus told the disciples first that they would desert him (26:31) but then they would be restored when he met them in Galilee after he was raised. The fulfillment of that promise will take place in three stages — the message by the angel here, Jesus' repetition of it in v. 10, and the actual appearance in Galilee in vv. 16 – 20.

9. Many grammarians dispute this force and prefer "Don't at any time be afraid." This is often true. Yet in a context where their fear has been obvious, the force is to "stop" what they have been doing (Wallace, 724 – 25).

10. In Mark 16:5 (= Luke 24:3) they have already entered the tomb, a fact Matthew omits, possibly to signify the women as outsiders at this point.

11. Matthew omits "and Peter" here from Mark 16:7. Some (Plummer, McNeile) believe this is because Matthew is unaware of the appearance to Peter, but that is unlikely, given its predominance in 1 Cor 15:5 (first in the list). More likely, Matthew intends "disciples" to be inclusive of them all (Lohmeyer, Davies and Allison).

Galilee is the place where Jesus developed and trained his disciples, so Jesus has stressed that as the meeting place where the disciples will be reinstated.[12] With "I have told you" the angel adds his voice to that of Jesus from v. 6 ("as he told you"). This is a double commission, and there can be no greater proof of the divine authority behind the command.

28:8 And they departed quickly from the tomb with fear and great joy and ran to announce this to his disciples (καὶ ἀπελθοῦσαι ταχὺ ἀπὸ τοῦ μνημείου μετὰ φόβου καὶ χαρᾶς μεγάλης ἔδραμον ἀπαγγεῖλαι τοῖς μαθηταῖς αὐτοῦ). Mark ended his gospel with a note on fear and centered on their awe-filled silence as the women were probably struck dumb until they reached the eleven (Mark 16:8).[13] Matthew continues that sense of awe[14] and pictures them rushing breathlessly back[15] to Jerusalem, with the second use of "quickly" (ταχύ, v. 7) emphasizing their haste.

Yet for Matthew the fear turns to "great joy" (see 2:10, the joy of the Magi at seeing the star over the baby Jesus' home); this is an understatement to say the least, as the women realize Jesus was indeed risen and run to tell the disciples. Matthew uses the strong verb "announce" (ἀπαγγεῖλαι), which in the Resurrection Narratives (Matt 28:8, 10, 11; Luke 24:9; cf. John 20:18) "lifts up the special significance of the event for Christian faith"[16] and becomes an official announcement. These women thus become divinely commissioned heralds of the resurrection tidings from the King of kings.

28:9 And look, Jesus met them and said, "Greetings!" (καὶ ἰδοὺ Ἰησοῦς ὑπήντησεν αὐταῖς λέγων, Χαίρετε). A fourth "look" (ἰδού, see vv. 2, 7) highlights the dramatic turn to Jesus' first appearance; the reader's attention becomes riveted on Jesus as he physically proves he has risen from the dead.[17] There is double meaning in Jesus' "greetings" (χαίρετε), which on one level is a cheerful "Hello" (the Greek greeting) but at another level echoes the women's "great joy" (χαρᾶς μεγάλης) in v. 8; Jesus has now lifted their "joy" to a new magnitude.[18]

28:9 And they came to him, grabbed hold of his feet, and worshiped him (αἱ δὲ προσελθοῦσαι ἐκράτησαν αὐτοῦ τοὺς πόδας καὶ προσεκύνησαν αὐτῷ). The result is a scene reminiscent of theophany scenes throughout Scripture as the women (αἱ is another example of the definite article used as

12. Yet that is not the first appearance to the eleven. As we know from Luke 24:36 and John 20:19, Jesus appeared to them that very night in Jerusalem. They remained in Jerusalem for the seven days of the Passover celebration, and he appeared to them again at the end of that period (John 20:26). They then went up to Galilee, where the appearances of Matt 28 and John 21 took place.

13. Mark ends here in order to conclude his major emphasis on discipleship failure throughout his gospel (see esp. 6:30 – 52; 8:14 – 21, ch. 14 (*passim*); 16:1 – 8. Matthew, as we have seen, has that emphasis but shows how Jesus' presence allows the disciples to overcome failure and progress to understanding. It should be noted that several recent Markan commentaries (e.g., France, Stein, Garland) think that Mark's ending is not intentional, but is lost. That was my position in my PhD dissertation on the Resurrection Narratives, but now I see too little evidence for that view and believe Mark intended to end his gospel at 16:8 (there is no evidence for a further ending, and the two we have were added much later).

14. The women likely progressed from fear (v. 5) to awe (here), with both valid meanings of φοβός.

15. "Departed" (ἀπελθοῦσαι) is another circumstantial participle (see vv. 2, 9, 19).

16. I. Broer in *EDNT*, 1:13.

17. Adelbert Denaux, "Matthew's Story of Jesus' Burial and Resurrection (Matt 27,57 – 28, 20)," in *Resurrection in the New Testament: Festschrift J. Lambrecht* (ed. B. Bieranger et al.; Paris: Leuven Univ. Press, 2002), 131 (cf. 123 – 45), says this Christophany is "no superfluous doublet of the angelophany, but it forms the culmination of the entire pericope of 28, 1 – 10" and turns the promise of v. 7 into a command that will be carried out in vv. 16 – 20.

18. Nolland, *Matthew*, 1252, shows how this overturns the two previous uses of χαίρω in 26:49 (Judas's betrayal) and 27:29 (the soldiers' mockery).

the pronoun "they") fall prostrate and lay hold of his feet.

Grasping the feet is often used of petition (2 Kgs 4:27; *T. Abr.* 15:4) but here is an act of worship. It is reminiscent of the anointing of Jesus' feet in Luke 7:38; John 11:2, 12:3. Turner says, "In view of Jesus reminding Satan that only God is to be worshipped (4:9 – 10), the women's worship is indicative of Matthew's high Christology."[19] Throughout Matthew Jesus is to be "worshiped" as Lord (2:2, 8, 11; 8:2; 9:18; 14:33; 15:25), an act that centers on his divine glory as Son of God. Jesus is not a spirit but has been raised bodily — but with new meaning. Before there were resuscitations, but those raised had to die again. Jesus is raised for eternity.

28:10 Then Jesus told them, "Do not be afraid" (τότε λέγει αὐταῖς ὁ Ἰησοῦς, Μὴ φοβεῖσθε). Jesus echoes the commission given by the angel in v. 7. The women experienced the same kind of "fear" that they felt with the angel; after all, they have moved from an angelology to a theophany! So Jesus also begins by calming their fear.

28:10 "Go announce to my brothers and sisters" (ὑπάγετε ἀπαγγείλατε τοῖς ἀδελφοῖς μου). Jesus' calling his followers "brothers and sisters" (ἀδελφοί) is firmly in the tradition, found in John 20:17 as well (criterion of multiple attestation). This expression connotes acceptance and fellowship (cf. 12:48 – 50; 25:40), and in light of their desertion of him it connotes forgiveness and restoration. Jesus restores them before they have even repented! Moreover, it includes all Jesus' followers, as seen in the "more than five hundred ... at the same time" in 1 Cor 15:6. Jesus is creating a new family, the church.[20]

28:10 "... that they should depart for Galilee. They will see me there" (ἵνα ἀπέλθωσιν εἰς τὴν Γαλιλαίαν, κἀκεῖ με ὄψονται). The meeting in Galilee, as the angel's message in v. 7, goes back to Jesus' prediction in 26:32. There are two ways to understand the choice of Galilee (especially since Jesus would appear to them at least twice in Jerusalem before they get to Galilee). One is that of Ernst Lohmeyer, who took Galilee and Jerusalem symbolically as the places of revelation and rejection respectively.[21] This is viable, for in Matthew "Galilee" occurs sixteen times as the place of general acceptance where Jesus conducts his ministry and trains his disciples, and Jerusalem occurs twelve times as the "desolate" city of coming judgment (23:37 – 39). Yet most doubt this today because Jesus' ministry was to all of Israel (10:5 – 6; 15:24) and Jesus had followers in Jerusalem as well as Galilee.

Nevertheless, while Matthew (and Mark) do not have a symbolic meaning of Galilee in this way, Jesus probably does choose to emphasize the Galilee appearance both in the prediction of 26:32 and in the fulfillment of 28:7, 10, 16 because Galilee was the place the disciples were trained and spent most of their ministry. Furthermore, for Matthew there is another nuance; "Galilee of the Gentiles" (4:15) is a major theme of the great commission (28:19) and sums up the Gentile mission in Matthew (see 1:5, 6; 2:1 – 12; 4:14 – 16, 25; 8:5 – 13, 28 – 34; 10:18; 12:21, 42; 13:38; 15:21 – 28, 29 – 31; 24:14, 31; 25:31 – 46; 28:10, 19, building on Carson).

19. Turner, "Matthew," 371.

20. As Wilkins, *Matthew*, says, "There are still functional differences within the family of faith, especially with reference to positions of leadership (e.g., 16:16 – 19; 1 Tim 3:1 – 15; 5:17 – 20; Heb 13:17; 1 Pet 5:1 – 5). But emphasis is placed on the equality of all brothers and sisters in Christ."

21. Ernst Lohmeyer, *Galiläe und Jerusalem* (Göttingen: Vandenhoeck & Ruprecht, 1936), 36 – 37. This view dominated until the 70s and 80s.

Theology in Application

Victory and vindication are only two of the terms that describe the meaning of the resurrection of Jesus. Death is indeed the "last enemy," but in Jesus as the first-fruits death has been proleptically defeated for every follower of Christ. Paul said it well in 1 Cor 15:14, "if Christ has not been raised, our preaching is useless and so is your faith." On the reality of this event hangs everything that is Christian! The darkness that hung over the land for the last three hours of the crucifixion, symbolizing the death of hope, yielded to the life of the light of God, and Jesus the Risen Lord came forth from the tomb! In him and in this event lies the hope of humanity, and that hope has been realized. We have been lifted out of the depths of despair that the reality of this life must produce apart from the Jesus event. In his resurrection we enter a new potential and a new reality that replaces defeat with victory, despair with joy, the decay of death with life for eternity.

1. Victory despite Discipleship Failure

There will still be discipleship failure, but in the Risen Lord there is victory. The women coming to the tomb and expecting only to sit shivah with the corpse of their Lord (in Judaism a weeklong period of grief and mourning for a close relative who has died) conclude the theme of discipleship failure in Matthew. Yet it is not the same as in Mark, where the failure of the women is found in the last verse of the book (Mark 16:8). As elsewhere in Matthew (14:22 – 33; 16:8 – 12), the presence of Jesus enables the women to overcome their failures and grow in their understanding, however deficient it is. In Jesus we are all "teachers of the law who become trained ... in the kingdom of heaven" and so "bring out of [our] storehouse things new and old" (13:52). Like the women we are transformed into ambassadors of the resurrection news.

2. God's Supernatural Intervention

The supernatural events of chs. 2 and 28 do not occur often, and few of us are privileged to see angels descending. Yet the age-old debate in the church as to whether God still produces miracles must be answered with a resounding yes. It is impossible to read about events in China, for instance, without realizing that the book of Acts still takes place whenever God so wills. The resurrection power is more alive and well on Planet Earth than is the power of Satan or of evil.

Many of us would say we have never seen a miracle, yet most of us know someone who would say they have been miraculously healed. I ask this often in classes or services, and I have not seen a time when no one raised their hand. Moreover, when we get to heaven we will all discover the great number of times God intervened in our lives and we chalked it up to blind luck, saying, "Phew, that one sure worked out well!" Also, this is part of Jesus' authority over the cosmic powers that he has given to the church (10:1). Any seeming "victory" that the evil powers have in this world is under the strict control of God ("was given," Rev 13:5 – 8) and is both temporary and doomed to defeat in the final analysis.

3. The Marginal and the Despised

God chooses the marginal and the despised as the means by which he proclaims his great victories. The women would never have been accepted in Jewish circles as official witnesses of the greatest event in human history, but that is exactly how God determined to do it. The same is true with us; great corporations or governments would never make us their official spokespersons, but God has done so. Paul stated it perfectly in 2 Cor 11:30, "If I must boast, I will boast of the things that show my weakness," and the reason is "so that Christ's power may rest on me. That is why, for Christ's sake, I delight in weaknesses, in insults, in hardships, in persecutions, in difficulties. For when I am weak, then I am strong" (2 Cor 12:9 – 10).

4. The Defeat of Evil

The empty tomb is proof that in Jesus' resurrection, evil is defeated in the willing sacrifice of suffering and martyrdom. At the apologetic level, the empty tomb proves that Jesus was truly raised from the dead and defeated death for all God's people. At the spiritual level, the empty tomb shows the victory that all God's people enjoy when they enter "the participation in his sufferings" (Phil 3:10). In Africa, in Korea, in China, and elsewhere, the great mission stories of our century have centered on the victorious suffering of God's people. All over the world, the forces of evil in country after country are discovering that the more they persecute God's people, the more the church grows (cf. Acts 12:24).

CHAPTER 122

Matthew 28:11 – 20

Literary Context

The final event of Matthew and of the Jesus story (on earth) now occurs. As in the Passion Narrative, so here it follows chronologically from the previous events. The final contrast in the Resurrection Narrative takes place. As the leaders earlier tried to thwart God's will to raise his Son (27:62 – 66) and failed (28:2 – 4), so now they try again to spread their lies (vv. 11 – 15), but this time their defeat will be worldwide via the universal mission of the church (vv. 16 – 20). You could also entitle the two sections "the false commission" (vv. 11 – 15) and "the Great Commission" (vv. 16 – 20).

VII. The Passion and Resurrection of Jesus (26:1 – 28:20)
- A. The Passion Narrative (26:1 – 27:61)
  - 5. The Crucifixion and Death of Jesus (27:27 – 50)
  - 6. Events Following Jesus' Death (27:51 – 61)
- **B. The Resurrection Narrative (27:62 – 28:20)**
  - 1. Preparatory Events (27:62 – 28:1)
  - 2. Reactions to the Resurrection (28:2 – 10)
  - ➦ **3. Results of the Resurrection (28:11 – 20)**

Main Idea

There are three major themes here. (1) The continued efforts of the enemies of God to stand against his truths are shown in all their crass foolishness (vv. 11 – 15).[1] (2) The divine attributes of Jesus — his omnipotence (v. 18) and his omnipresence (v. 20) — are exercised on behalf of the church. (3) The church is commissioned to

1. France, *Gospel of Matthew*, 1104, says, "The chief priests and elders who have seemed to hold all the cards and who have so smugly celebrated their triumph over the northern prophet (27:41 – 43) are now in total disarray."

reach the world with the gospel (v. 19), a mission they conduct under the guidance and power of the Risen Lord.

Translation

Matthew 28:11-20

11a	Scene #1/Setting	And while the women were on their way,
b	Action	**look, some of the guard detail came into the city and**
		reported . . . all that had taken place
		to the chief priests.
12a		And after the chief priests had gathered together with the elders and
		took counsel together,
b	Action	**they gave a large sum of money to the soldiers, telling them,**
13a	Exhortation	*"You should say,*
b		*'His disciples came at night and*
		stole him
		while we were sleeping.'
14a		*And if this is reported to the governor,*
b		*we will satisfy him and keep you from blame."*
15a	Response to 12b-14b	So **they took the money and did as they were instructed.**
b	Conclusion	And **this story has spread among the Jews until this very day.**
16a	Action/Setting	**Then the eleven disciples went**
		into Galilee
		to the mountain
		where Jesus had ordered them.
17a		And when they saw him,
b	Response #1	**[1] they worshiped,**
c	Response #2	**[2]** but **some doubted.**
18a		**Jesus came and spoke to them, saying,**
b	Assertion	*"All authority in heaven and on earth has been given to me.*
19a	Exhortation	*Therefore go and*
		make disciples from all the nations,
b		*baptizing them*
		into the name
		of the Father and
c		*of the Son and*
d		*of the Holy Spirit,*
20a		*teaching them*
		to keep everything I have commanded you.
b	Promise	*And look, I am with you all the days,*
c		*even until the very end of the age."*

Structure and Literary Form

Verses 11 – 15 are M material, as is vv. 16 – 20. Though the Great Commission (v. 19) has parallels in Luke 24:47; John 20:21; and Acts 1:8,[2] they are likely separate traditions and show that Jesus launched the mission to the world several times in his resurrection appearances. There are two units here (vv. 11 – 15, 16 – 20). The first has three parts (vv. 11, 12 – 14, 15) and the second two parts (vv. 16 – 17, 18 – 20).

Exegetical Outline

➦ **I. The False Conspiracy of the Leaders and Guards (28:11 – 15)**
   A. The report of the guards to the chief priests (v. 11)
   B. The conspiracy to falsify the report (vv. 12 – 14)
      1. The bribe paid to the guards (v. 12)
      2. The false witness: the disciples stole the body (v. 13)
      3. The promise: protect the guards from Pilate's anger (v. 14)
   C. The false message begins to be proclaimed (v. 15)

II. Jesus Commissions the Disciples to Reach the World (28:16 – 20)
   A. Jesus appears to the disciples in Galilee (vv. 16 – 17)
      1. Appearance on a mountain (v. 16)
      2. They worship, but some doubt (v. 17)
   B. The Great Commission (vv. 18 – 20)
      1. The universal authority of Jesus (v. 18)
      2. The commission to disciple the world (v. 19)
      3. The universal presence of Jesus with the church (v. 20)

Explanation of the Text

28:11 And while the women were on their way, look, some of the guard detail came into the city and reported to the chief priests all that had taken place (Πορευομένων δὲ αὐτῶν ἰδού τινες τῆς κουστωδίας ἐλθόντες εἰς τὴν πόλιν ἀπήγγειλαν τοῖς ἀρχιερεῦσιν ἅπαντα τὰ γενόμενα). The temporal (present tense "while") genitive absolute ("they [the women] were on their way") (πορευομένων αὐτῶν) shows that the plot between the guards and the chief priests takes place simultaneous with the women's mission to the disciples. There is a further contrast — the joyful rush of the women is paralleled by the haste of the soldiers to tell the priests. The one is spreading the truth, the other will soon spread a lie. These Roman (see on 27:64 – 65) guards were devastated by their failure to "protect" the body in the tomb. They were in a delicate situation. They had failed

2. The longer ending in Mark also has a commissioning to a universal mission (Mark 16:15), but Mark 16:14 – 18 almost certainly is a reworking of Matt 28:16 – 20.

in their duty, and that could potentially cost them their lives. The fact that "some" rather than all of the guards went could reflect the fear that many of the guards felt.

It is interesting that Roman guards report to the priests rather than Pilate. But this is a necessity, for the soldiers had been "doing a favor for the high priests, who were the ones actually concerned about the matter,"[3] and the guards hope they will be protected by the priests (which does come to pass). They could expect little mercy from Pilate. All they could do is report truthfully "everything that had occurred" — the earthquake, the rolling back of the stone, and the brilliance of the descending angel (similar to the "glory" of the angels in Luke 2:9). So the guards become a further witness to the reality of the empty tomb! After that, they remember nothing since they fainted dead away, a fact that would not endear them to the authorities.

28:12 And after the chief priests had gathered together with the elders and took counsel together,[4] they gave a large sum of money to the soldiers (καὶ συναχθέντες μετὰ τῶν πρεσβυτέρων συμβούλιόν τε λαβόντες ἀργύρια ἱκανὰ ἔδωκαν τοῖς στρατιώταις). The conspiracy and the plot are hatched in another of the many hostile "council" meetings (2:4; 22:15, 34; 26:3 – 4, 57, 59; 27:1) that led to Jesus' death. Now God has intervened and foiled the plot of 27:62 – 66, so they have to hatch another false conspiracy to hide their defeat. Even though the guards reported the supernatural events perpetrated by God, that did not sway the chief priests at all; they were under the total control of the lie they believed and the rejection they conceived.

It is doubtful whether this is an official Sanhedrin assembly or an informal meeting of some of the leaders to figure out what to do. The "great amount of money" in the bribe parallels the money paid Judas to betray Jesus, "Whereas Judas had been bought (to make use of what he knew), these guards are to be bought off (to suppress what they knew)."[5]

28:13 ... telling them, "You should say, 'His disciples came[6] at night and stole him while we were sleeping' " (λέγοντες, Εἴπατε ὅτι Οἱ μαθηταὶ αὐτοῦ νυκτὸς ἐλθόντες ἔκλεψαν αὐτὸν ἡμῶν κοιμωμένων). The aorist imperative "you should say" (εἴπατε) commands the guards to spread a lie. In the same way that the guards paralleled the women, the deceptive lie the priests give the guards is the polar opposite of history's greatest truth that the angels gave the women. There is also an incredible irony in that the priests concoct the very thing they tried to prevent in 27:62 – 66 (the disciples stealing the body)! Note the parallels between the three scenes (vv. 1 – 7, 8 – 10, 11 – 15) — the haste of the travelers, the confrontation with the evidence, and the commission. There is also contrast, for the direction in the last two elements lies in opposite poles (the women accepting, the priests rejecting the truth).

There are several anomalies in this falsehood. How could they know it was the disciples who stole the body if they were asleep? And how could they fail to hear the stone being rolled away if they were only asleep? Note that the supernatural elements — the earthquake and the coming of the angel — are completely removed from the story. The priests want a completely human explanation.

3. Witherington, *Matthew*, 530.

4. "Gathered together" (συναχθέντες) and "took" (λαβόντες) are aorist temporal participles ("after," cf. vv. 11, 13). "And" (τε) is a coordinating conjunction that as in Heb 6:4 – 6 probably connects subordinating relationships within the main "and" (καί) clauses (see Turner, "Matthew," 338 – 39).

5. Nolland, *Matthew*, 1256.

6. Another circumstantial participle like vv. 11, 12.

28:14 "And if this is reported to the governor, we will satisfy him and keep you from blame" (καὶ ἐὰν ἀκουσθῇ τοῦτο ἐπὶ τοῦ ἡγεμόνος, ἡμεῖς πείσομεν αὐτὸν καὶ ὑμᾶς ἀμερίμνους ποιήσομεν). The message the guards are supposed to tell is dangerous, as they could be executed for falling asleep (not quite true — it was a dead faint) and failing at their post. So the promise of v. 14 was an absolute necessity if the guards were to accept the bribe and spread the lie. "Satisfy" (πείθω) in a context like this can mean "conciliate, pacify, set at ease"(BAGD 639, 1d).[7] The priests promise that if the true events come "before" (ἐπί) the governor, they will keep Pilate from taking action against them, so that legally they will be considered "blameless." There is no truth or justice left in the priests; they have become common criminals who have rationalized everything away.

28:15 So they took the money and did as they were instructed (οἱ δὲ λαβόντες τὰ ἀργύρια ἐποίησαν ὡς ἐδιδάχθησαν). The fact that guards "took the money" (still another circumstantial participle) is reminiscent of Judas in 26:14 – 16; the one was planning his death, here they are denying the reality of his resurrection. The lie goes forth and becomes the first attempt to explain away the resurrection.

28:15 And this story has spread among the Jews until this very day (Καὶ διεφημίσθη ὁ λόγος οὗτος παρὰ Ἰουδαίοις μέχρι τῆς σήμερον ἡμέρας). This narrative is undoubtedly based on an early Jerusalem tradition intended to form an apologetic answer to the Jewish claims that the body was stolen from the tomb and to provide a contrast whereby the resurrection vindication could predicate total victory over opponents of the gospel. So the "Jews" (Ἰουδαίοις) here refers not just to the "Jewish" people of Jesus' time but for the next decades "until" the time Matthew wrote this.[8]

Matthew has a twofold purpose in relating this material. For unbelievers this is an apologetic note that the soldiers function as witnesses of the reality of the empty tomb and the resurrection power, telling "all that had taken place" (v. 11). Matthew is saying that the rumors regarding the empty tomb are false. For the believer this story illustrates continuing opposition and slander (1 Pet 2:12) that Christians can expect as they promulgate the resurrection (persecution is part of Matthew's discipleship motif).

28:16 Then the eleven disciples went into Galilee (Οἱ δὲ ἕνδεκα μαθηταὶ ἐπορεύθησαν εἰς τὴν Γαλιλαίαν). Michel was the first to call this passage the conclusion and recapitulation of Matthew's major themes.[9] Since then, most have agreed with him. "Eleven" (ἕνδεκα) is found only here in the gospels (except for four times in Luke-Acts) and fits Matthew's stress on Judas's betrayal. The disciples follow Jesus' orders to return to Galilee after the seven days of the Passover celebration (see John 20:26).

7. Many believe that "satisfy" (πείθω) goes beyond conciliation to hint at a bribe to be paid Pilate to exonerate the guards (so Davies and Allison, Luz, Turner).

8. Luz, *Matthew 21 – 28*, 611 – 13, provides an excellent discussion of Matthew's use of "Jews" (Ἰουδαῖοι) here. It is true that the use of "Jews" rather than Israel speaks of the separation from the church and the rejection of the Messiah, but this does not mean the Jewish people have been replaced by the church as the new Israel. There is still hope for the Jewish people, and they are part of the mission inaugurated in 28:18 – 20. See also Hubert Frankemölle, "Zur Theologie der Mission im Matthäusevangelium," in *Mission im Neuen Testament* (ed. Karl Kertelge; Freiburg: Herder, 1982), 93 – 129.

9. Otto Michel, "The Conclusion of Matthew's Gospel," in *The Interpretation of Matthew* (ed. G. Stanton; Edinburgh: T & T Clark, 1995, originally 1950), 39 – 51. Turner, "Matthew," 377, says, "There may be no better way to summarize the theology of Matthew than by following up on the themes found in the Great Commission."

28:16 ... to the mountain where Jesus had ordered them (εἰς τὸ ὄρος οὗ ἐτάξατο αὐτοῖς ὁ Ἰησοῦς). Note the emphasis on "where Jesus had ordered them." This emphasizes the prediction of 26:32 and the commands of 28:7, 10. Jesus wanted to reconstitute his disciples as the apostolic band especially in the place where they had been trained and spent the major part of their ministry (see on v. 10). In "Galilee of the Gentiles" (4:15–16) Jesus will launch the universal mission (see on v. 10).

This, of course, is the final mountain scene in Matthew, and it both concludes his emphasis and sums up his theology on "the mountain" (τὸ ὄρος; see 4:8; 5:1; 14:23; 15:29; 17:1, 9; 21:1; 24:3). Donaldson argues that the primary motif is that of eschatological Zion (see on 4:8; 5:1): "As one who is greater than the temple, Jesus replaces Zion as the centre of eschatological fulfilment. He is the one around whom the people are to gather and to whom the Gentiles will make procession."[10]

Yet Sinai and the Moses tradition should be given even more weight. It is better to call this commissioning scene modeled on Moses; four of the OT commissioning passages (Exod 7:2; Josh 1:7; 1 Chr 22:13; Jer 1:7) center on Moses.[11] It is not that Jesus is a "new Moses" walking up Sinai but rather that as God gave Israel their marching orders through Moses at Sinai, Jesus gives his disciples their commission here on this mountain.

28:17 And when they saw him, they worshiped (καὶ ἰδόντες αὐτὸν προσεκύνησαν). When (temporal participle "saw" [ἰδόντες]) the women met the risen Jesus, they fell at his feet and worshiped him (v. 9). The disciples do so as well, and the message is clear—one cannot meet the Risen Lord without worshiping. This makes the next note difficult to understand.

28:17 ... but some doubted (οἱ δὲ ἐδίστασαν). There are three ways to take the "but some" (οἱ δέ) who doubt: "some" of the disciples doubt (Hill, Hubbard, Osborne, Gundry, Gnilka, Blomberg, Nolland, France); "all of them" doubt (Bonnard, Grundmann, Bruner, Hagnar, Pregeant); or "some others" (than the disciples) doubt (Allen, McNeile, Carson, Morris). Any of the three can fit "but some" (οἱ δέ), so the question is which fits the context best. Is "doubt" antithetical to worship, and so the same group cannot be included in both? What is the true meaning of "they doubted" (ἐδίστασαν)?

The latter needs to be answered first. διστάζω can mean to "hesitate" as well as "doubt" but does not really connote unbelief. When Peter failed to walk on the water and exhibited only a "little faith" in 14:31, Jesus asked him, "Why did you doubt?" It was not that he doubted Jesus' power but that he hesitated or was uncertain.[12] In fact, this summarizes the "little faith" motif in Matthew. "Hesitation in the midst of worship is a paradox well known to most believers; certainly Matthew's readers would identify with the problem."[13] Thus "but some" (οἱ δέ) could refer to "some" of those who worshiped or to all of them; it is impossible to be sure, but either would fit, though all of the disciples seem connoted here. The main thing is that this culminates the Matthean theme of "little faith." The disciples are still growing in their faith and understanding and have not yet reached maturity.

10. Donaldson, *Jesus on the Mountain*, 185.

11. See Benjamin J. Hubbard, *The Matthean Redaction of a Primitive Apostolic Commissioning: An Exegesis of Matthew 28:16–20* (SBLDS 19; Missoula, MT: Society of Biblical Literature, 1974), 92–93; Dale Allison, *The New Moses: A Matthean Typology* (Minneapolis: Fortress, 1993), 53–62; Davies and Allison, *Matthew*, 3:679–80.

12. See I. P. Ellis, "But Some Doubted," *NTS* 14 (1967–68): 574–80.

13. Osborne, *Resurrection Narratives*, 88.

28:18 Jesus came and spoke to them, saying (καὶ προσελθὼν ὁ Ἰησοῦς ἐλάλησεν αὐτοῖς λέγων). Some claim that the title "Great Commission" is inappropriate since the passage is an epiphany or exaltation story on the new status of the Risen One. Yet the early church would certainly and correctly read the universal mission into it, and the epiphany aspects "fore and aft" provide the encouragement and means of accomplishing the task; exaltation and mission are not contradictory but interdependent.

This section does have an ABA pattern, with the Christology of vv. 18, 20 surrounding the commission itself.[14] Is it a single whole delivered on one occasion or a composite of separate traditions (as many previous stories)? The majority of critical scholars argue for the latter (or for wholesale creation by the evangelist)[15] because it sums up so many previous themes: the language is so Matthean, and he habitually combines *logia Jesu*. Yet there are good reasons for seeing here a single tradition — the interdependence of each part, the homogeneous style, and the fact that Matthew's composite sections are normally much longer.

Did Jesus appear from heaven just to give a twenty-second sound-bite and then return to heaven? That is doubtful. As throughout the four gospels, Matthew has likely abbreviated a much longer speech and chosen those elements of Jesus' talk that fit his theological purposes. There is no need for fiction-like creation here.[16] This is a commissioning scene patterned after OT commissionings (Gen 12:1 – 4; Exod 3:1 – 10; Josh 1:1 – 11; Isa 6:1 – 13, so Hubbard) along with covenant renewal (Carson) and enthronement (Hagner).[17]

28:18 "All authority in heaven and on earth has been given to me" (Ἐδόθη μοι πᾶσα ἐξουσία ἐν οὐρανῷ καὶ ἐπὶ τῆς γῆς). The address itself could be called a Jewish midrash on the "Allness of Yahweh" applied to the church's mission, since "all" (πᾶς) is found in every section of the speech. Jesus "comes to" the disciples (probably from heaven) and begins first by establishing the basis for his command here, his absolute all-embracing authority as Risen Lord. The divine passive "has been given" (ἐδόθη) shows this authority/power comes from God himself, and it has been called the enthronement of the Messiah as eschatological ruler and judge.[18] This is an allusion to Dan 7:13 – 14 (with a similar wording and theme), where the "one like a son of man" is "given authority, glory and sovereign power.... His dominion is an everlasting dominion that will not pass away, and his kingdom is one that will never be destroyed."

14. David Hill, "The Conclusion of Matthew's Gospel: Some Literary-Critical Observations," *IBS* 8 (1986): 54 – 63, sees a chiasm here, with A (v. 18b), B (v. 19a), C (v. 19b), B' (v. 20a), A' (v. 20b), but this makes the baptism statement the center of the piece, and that is doubtful.

15. E.g., Pheme Perkins, *Resurrection: New Testament Witness and Contemporary Reflection* (Garden City, NY: Doubleday, 1984), 131.

16. On the historicity of this scene see Beasley-Murray, *Baptism in the New Testament*, 77 – 92; Carson, "Matthew," 591 – 92; Schnabel, *Early Christian Mission*, 1:349 – 51; Keener, *Matthew*, 715. Matthew is replete with redactional nuances and language (see Hubbard, Davies and Allison), but redaction does not mean wholesale creation but rather choices made to select and work with the traditional material. W. D. Davies and Dale C. Allison, "Matt. 28:16 – 20: Texts Behind the Text," *RHPR* 72 (1992): 89 – 98; and Davies and Allison, *Matthew*, 3:677 – 78, see it as stemming from tradition but redacted by Matthew. On the issue of history and narrative, see Osborne, "Historical Narrative," 673 – 88.

17. Denaux, "Burial and Resurrection," 140, seeks a middle ground between those who see 18 – 20 as an enthronement hymn and those who see it as a community rule, arguing that the "church-founding mission command only makes sense after the affirmation of the divine and universal power of the Risen Lord."

18. See Lohmeyer, *Matthäus*; Bornkamm, Barth, and Held, *Tradition and Interpretation*.

In Daniel the scene is that of an "investiture" of the one who will defeat the four beasts and the little horn of 7:2 – 8 and will be given both universal and everlasting dominion. In *1 Enoch* 48:10; 52:4; *4 Ezra* 13 this being is interpreted as the Messiah, and most modern interpreters take the figure either as angelic, perhaps Gabriel (9:21) or Michael (10:21), or as a symbol for the rule of God or for the people of God through whom he rules.[19] It is clear that for Jesus and the early church he fulfills that role, and this signifies his exaltation and enthronement. The "Son of Man" title is probably omitted because it would be misunderstood and given a parousia interpretation; Jesus wishes to teach that the parousia power and glory are his now and are given to his followers.

The "authority" (ἐξουσία) continues the astonishing statement of 11:27, "all things have been given to me by my Father." Jesus' authority has been emphasized often, seen in 4:23 – 24 and 9:35 (authority to heal all); 7:29 (authority of his words); 8:9 (authority to command); 8:29 – 32; 12:22; and 17:18 (authority over demons); 9:6, 8 (authority to forgive sins); 10:1 (passing his authority on to the disciples); 13:41 (authority to judge); 21:23 – 27 (authority from God to perform his deeds). ἐξουσία here "is a more comprehensive term than 'power' (*dynamis*), referring to position as well as function. The kingdom of heaven (a favorite Matthean phrase) is already present in Christ and thus his assertion of authority (v. 18) provides the foundation for the ecclesiastical command (vv. 19 – 20a)."[20] The Son of Man, once handed over to the power of others, now has power over them (Davies and Allison).

Moreover, the authority is "heavenly" as well as "earthly" (cf. 6:10; 16:19; 18:18), a sweeping concept that implies divine status; the major message here and in v. 20 is that Jesus as the Risen One has the authority of Yahweh, uniting the two spheres (cf. John 1:51, so Hubbard). This is not a new authority, for it is linked to the authority Jesus displayed throughout his earthly ministry. Yet at the same time it is a new level of authority, as Jesus receives from his Father his preexistent glory and authority (a further link to the transfiguration). As seen in 16:19; 18:18 this authority "in heaven and on earth" is linked to the authority to "bind and loose," given to the church, so it is intimately linked to the church's mission in v. 19.

28:19 "Therefore go and make disciples from all the nations" (πορευθέντες οὖν μαθητεύσατε πάντα τὰ ἔθνη). On the basis of ("therefore" [οὖν]) his authority, Jesus now commissions his disciples. The Risen Lord's universal authority makes possible the universal mission. This looks back to and universalizes the commissioning service of ch. 10. There Jesus told his followers what the mission constitutes and centered on the Jewish mission. Now he expands it and introduces a brand new element in salvation history, the universal mission. As Schnabel says, "Judaism had neither a missionary theory nor organized missionary activity before the first century A.D."[21]

Mission for Israel to the nations was to be centripetal; that is, Israel was to stay in the Holy Land and witness to the grace of God, so that the nations could come to them to be blessed (the Abrahamic covenant, Gen 12:3; 15:5; 18:18; 22:18; 26:4). The centrifugal mission, taking the message to the nations, would be a messianic act (Isa 11:9 – 10; 42:6; 49:6).[22] This passage is that messianic launch

19. See Ernest C. Lucas, *Daniel* (Apollos Old Testament Commentary; Downers Grove, IL: IVP, 2002), 185 – 87.

20. Osborne, *Resurrection Narratives*, 90.

21. Schnabel, *Early Christian Mission*, 1:173 (cf. 55 – 173). See also McKnight, *A Light among the Gentiles*.

22. Schnabel, *Early Christian Mission*, 1:90, where Schnabel summarizes the OT emphases: (1) as Creator, God is the Lord of nations; (2) "the nations will be admitted to God's salvation in the eschaton"; (3) Israel is to be a "passive witness of God's acts of salvation"; (4) Israel will have an active role

of that universal mission, and it constitutes "the final word of the exalted Jesus to the disciples" in Matthew.[23]

The circumstantial participle "go" (πορευθέντες) followed by the main verb is a common Matthean stylistic trait, and it becomes in effect another imperative, "Go and make disciples." In fact, the two participles that follow ("baptizing" and "teaching") are also circumstantial and are imperatival in force. Still, the main verb "make disciples" dominates, and all are aspects of that central part of the commission. "Go" is the operative act, as now God's people are no longer to stay in Jerusalem and be a kind of "show 'n' tell" for the nations[24] but they are actively to go and take the message to the nations. Matthew's emphasis on the universal mission is consummated here, with "all the nations" meaning Jewish (see 10:5 – 6; 15:24)[25] and Gentile mission (passages noted at 20:10). The coming of the Magi (2:1 – 12) plus Jesus' mission including the centurion (8:5 – 13), Gadarene demoniacs (8:28 – 34), and the Canaanite woman (15:21 – 28) have all prepared for this command.

The activity demanded is found in "make disciples" (μαθητεύσατε), found also in 13:52; 27:57 and summarizing the discipleship emphasis in Matthew. It is critical to note that the command is not to evangelize but to perform the broader and deeper task of "discipling" the nations. Many denominations and mission groups misunderstand this and spend all their effort winning new converts rather than anchoring them in the Christian faith (in spite of the many studies that show that too few are truly converted in that initial decision). Jesus mandates that all mission activity emulate his pattern of discipling followers as exemplified in this gospel. They must be brought to understanding and to that deep ethical commitment patterned in the Sermon on the Mount and the Community Discourse; then they will become "trained as disciples in the kingdom" (13:52).

28:19 "... baptizing them into the name of the Father and of the Son and of the Holy Spirit" (βαπτίζοντες αὐτοὺς εἰς τὸ ὄνομα τοῦ πατρὸς καὶ τοῦ υἱοῦ καὶ τοῦ ἁγίου πνεύματος). Not only does the postresurrection Jesus launch the universal mission; he also launches baptism as the primary sacrament of initiation into the Christian faith.[26] Jesus did not baptize (John 3:22, clarified in

and be sent to the nations in the "last days" when the Servant of Yahweh inaugurates that mission.

23. The title of the section in Gnilka, *Matthäusevangelium*, 2:501.

24. This is why the early Jewish Christians seemingly disobeyed the commission to go and remained in Jerusalem. They were misinterpreting Jesus' command on the basis of the OT centripetal mission strategy they had always assumed. Thus Acts 3 – 5 demonstrates that strategy. The Spirit led them in a series of "steps to the Gentile mission" in Acts 7 – 11 that forcefully launched them first to "Judea and Samaria" in Acts 8 and then to the "uttermost parts of the earth" in the rest of Acts, fulfilling Acts 1:8.

25. It has been fairly common to see 28:19 addressed only to the Gentiles, with the Jewish people excluded from the church's mission. In this way Matthew separates salvation history into two periods, the Jewish mission of Jesus and the Gentile mission of the church, so Joachim Lange, *Das Erscheinen des Auferstandenen im Evangelium nach Matthäus* (Würzburg: Echter, 1973), 300 – 305; Douglas R. A. Hare and Daniel J. Harrington, "Make Disciples of All the Gentiles," *CBQ* 37 (1975): 359 – 69. However, in Matthew both Jews and Gentiles are the object of evangelization and acceptance by Jesus, and it is better to speak not of Jewish vs. Gentile but of universal mission (see "nations" in 21:43; 24:9, 14; 25:32) in Matthew; see Kenzo Tagawa, "People and Community in the Gospel of Matthew," *NTS* 16 (19669 – 70): 149 – 62 (esp. 153); John P. Meier, "Nations or Gentiles in Matthew 28:19," *CBQ* 39 (1977): 94 – 102; and Hubbard, *Matthean Redaction*, 84 – 87.

26. However, France, *Gospel of Matthew*, 1116, believes that Christian baptism existed from the beginning, and that Jesus and his disciples followed the Baptist in baptizing followers (he argues it is assumed in John 3:22 – 26; 4:1 – 2). But this is insufficient evidence for such a practice. Why would the gospel writers omit every such reference?

John 4:1 – 2) during his ministry, and it is unlikely he and his disciples did so beyond that initial period. In Matthew it is only mentioned in connection with John the Baptist (3:6 – 16, metaphorically in 21:25). So Jesus here makes baptism an essential component of discipleship. Baptism and teaching "beautifully describe both the sacramental and experiential sides of discipleship which are essential aspects of ecclesiology."[27]

Jesus then adds the meaning of baptism, which brings the believer "into the name" (εἰς τὸ ὄνομα) of the triune Godhead. Some have interpreted "into" (εἰς) in a local sense and made it a formula for baptism ("in the name of") on the basis of the fact that "into" (εἰς) and "in" (ἐν) in the Koine period were sliding together. However, it is generally recognized that in Matthew "into" (εἰς) retains its classical force (see Zerwick §106), and it is better to see this as a baptism "into fellowship with" (Allen, Albright and Mann) or "into the Lordship of" (Carson) the Godhead, expressing a new relationship (Davies and Allison).[28]

The presence of the triune Godhead is only here in a baptism formula (though it is used also in *Did.* 7:1, 3). Most doubt the Trinitarian emphasis because of the absence of any such theology in Matthew. For instance, Luz says, "Of course, the triadic baptismal command does not yet imply the much later dogma of the Trinity, although later it was thusly interpreted."[29] Certainly this is not the Nicene Creed, but there is a Trinitarian theology in the NT, seen in 1 Cor 12:4 – 6; 2 Cor 13:14; Eph 4:4 – 6; 2 Thess 2:13 – 14; 1 Pet 1:2; Jude 20 – 21; Rev 1:4 – 5; and this is in line with the early beliefs in the deity of each member of the Godhead, the personhood of each member, and the fact that there is one God. We must speak of at least an incipient Trinitarian theology, and that this passage states that conversion and baptism bring us into a unity and community with that threefold Godhead.[30]

Moreover, Jesus is still bringing together his many statements on his Father (5:48; 6:1, 4; 11:25 – 27; 24:36), himself as the Son (16:27; 24:36), and the Holy Spirit (12:18, 28, 32); and Matthew is once again (as in all the discourses) abbreviating a lengthy teaching of Jesus on the mountain of revelation. The Great Commission is Matthew's summary of a much longer message, and the church was free to emphasize Jesus' name on other occasions.

28:20 "... teaching them to keep everything I have commanded you" (διδάσκοντες αὐτοὺς τηρεῖν πάντα ὅσα ἐνετειλάμην ὑμῖν). "Teaching" (διδάσκοντες) is based on Jesus' own "teaching" ministry (4:23; 5:2; 7:29; 9:35; 11:1; 13:54; 21:23; 22:16; 26:55), another key area of Matthean theology, and forms the *didachē,* the church's teaching ministry; since Jesus' words endure forever (24:35), the church must center on his commands. The discipleship of v. 19a is defined as ethical obedience; outreach (evangelism) must be balanced by inreach (teaching and living the Word).[31] Mark stresses the action side of Jesus as teacher[32] while

27. Osborne, *Resurrection Narratives*, 92.

28. In the rest of the NT three prepositions are used in baptism — "in" (ἐν, Acts 10:48); "into" (εἰς, Acts 8:16; 19:5; Rom 6:3; Gal 3:27); and "in" (ἐπί, Acts 2:38). There was no unitary formula.

29. Luz, *Matthew 21 – 28*, 632. He points to Tertullian, Vergilius, and Theophylactus.

30. The other issue is whether the original formula was monadic, since other references to baptism in the NT use variations of "in the name of Jesus Christ" and the only other triadic forms are in *Did.* 7:1, 3; so Hans Kosmala, "The Conclusion of Matthew," *ASTI* 4 (1965): 132 – 47. However, there is no reason to doubt the viability of this formula as authentic, and both the monadic and Trinitarian forms may well have existed side by side (see Carson, Morris, Keener).

31. See Blomberg, *Matthew*, 433.

32. See R. T. France, "Mark and the Teaching of Jesus," *Gospel Perspectives I* (ed. R. T. France and D. Wenham; Sheffield: JSOT Press, 1980), 101 – 36.

Matthew centers on the ethical content and demands of his teaching.

The emphasis on obeying "everything I have commanded you" shows that the discourse sections are not really didactic material to be learned but more importantly practical injunctions to be lived. In this sense Davies and Allison is right to call this a *nova lex* ("new law"), the "Torah of the Messiah" that constitutes the fulfillment of the Torah in Jesus' teaching (contra Carson), with "I have commanded" (ἐνετειλάμην) a global aorist that encapsulates all of Jesus' teaching as commands to be followed in life,[33] namely, the coming kingdom and our relation to it. At the same time, Jesus does not replace the Torah but transcends and "fulfills" it, taking it to a higher plane via radical demand for discipleship.

We are at the heart of Matthew's gospel here, with the five discourses centering on Jesus' ethical teaching as the basis here for the teaching ministry of the disciples. This culminates several passages: e.g., 5:18 – 19, where Jesus said even the smallest part of the "commandments" is intact in his teaching; 19:17, on obeying every commandment; 22:36 – 40, on the greatest commandment; and 23:10 (cf. 10:24 – 25; 26:18), on Jesus as the one "Teacher." Jesus passes this authority on to the disciples, who through the Spirit will share his teaching power under God. In 10:12 – 13, the very "greeting" (= the offer of the kingdom "peace") of the disciples on mission has charismatic power, and in 10:1 Jesus gave them his authority over demons and disease. In our teaching and our ministry, we partake of Jesus' authority "in heaven and on earth" (28:18). In other words, we disseminate the Lordship of Christ in this world as we proclaim his truths.

28:20 "And look, I am with you all the days, even until the very end of the age" (καὶ ἰδοὺ ἐγὼ μεθ' ὑμῶν εἰμι πάσας τὰς ἡμέρας ἕως τῆς συντελείας τοῦ αἰῶνος). The final of the six uses of "look" (ἰδού) in ch. 28 points to the dramatic truth that provides a proper conclusion to this commission and to the gospel as a whole. It completes one of the key christological themes of the book, namely, the omnipresence of Christ with his new kingdom community, seen in the beginning (1:23, "Immanuel ... God with us") and center (18:20, "there am I in the midst of them") of Matthew; and so it stresses the deity and divine glory of the Christ.[34] "The gospel ends with the 'Emmanuel' with which it began."[35] The Great Commission is thus framed by the omnipotence (v. 18) and omnipresence (v. 20b) of Christ. The theme partakes of the Shekinah glory of the OT and the divine comfort of Yahweh's presence among men (not just divine presence but divine assistance). So God's protection of his people throughout the ages is promised to the church.

There is strong stress on "all the days" (lit., "the whole of every day," i.e., each day as we live it);[36] the presence of Christ is with the believer at every moment throughout human history. In "the very end of the age" (τῆς συντελείας τοῦ αἰῶνος) the apocalyptic idea of the "consummation" (cf. 13:39 – 40, 49; 24:3; Heb 9:26) is made a present

33. Davies and Allison, *Matthew*, 3:686. But there is no "new Moses" typology here, see Nolland, *Matthew*, 1270 – 71.

34. Luz, *Matthew 21 – 28*, 634, shows that this "'being-with-us' of God in the Immanuel Jesus" is found throughout the gospel (9:15; 17:17; 18:20) but especially in the Passion Narrative (26:11, 18, 20, 23, 29, 36, 38, 50, 51, 69, 71) and in stories about Jesus helping the disciples via his presence (8:23 – 27; 14:13 – 21, 22 – 23; 15:29 – 39; 17:1 – 8; 26:26 – 29). So this encapsulates "the story of the earthly Jesus" and of the disciples' relationship with him.

35. Günther Bornkamm, "The Risen Lord and the Earthly Jesus: Matt 28, 16 – 20," in *The Future of Our Religious Past* (FS Rudolf Bultmann; ed. J. M. Robinson; New York: Harper and Row, 1971), 228 (cf. 203 – 29).

36. So Carson from Moule, *Idiom Book*.

hope (cf. 24:14). Eschatology once again is wedded to the present — the authority of the kingdom age will always be present.

So Matthew concludes with a blend of ecclesiology and eschatology — the church is God's chosen messenger during the interim before the consummation and as such is promised the continuous presence of the authoritative One in executing that task. The meaning of this is clarified in John 14:2 – 3, 16 – 17, 18, 23: Jesus will be in heaven "preparing a place" for us but will not "leave [us] as orphans." Rather, he and the Father will "make a home" in us by sending the Spirit to us, the Spirit of Christ and the Spirit of God. He will be the presence of the Father and of the Son in our hearts.

Theology in Application

1. Victory over Our Opponents

With the contrast between the lie that the priests and soldiers spread and the great truth Jesus gave the disciples, this pericope in one sense has the same emphasis as did 27:62 – 28:1 (see "Theology in Application" there) and 28:2 – 10, namely, the attempts of God's enemies to turn aside his will. Evil people will always spread lies and slander against God's people, but the saints have victory by living lives of goodness before their enemies (1 Pet 2:12), which heaps "burning coals [of conviction and judgment] on [their] heads" (Rom 12:20).

2. Doubt

Doubt is a universal experience of finite followers of Jesus. Every one of us has been a "doubting Thomas" at some time, and the tension between worship and doubt is with us as much as with the disciples. However, the great truth of Matthew in his discipleship emphasis is that Jesus is always present with us and gives us the strength to overcome the doubt and "little faith" in our lives (see 6:30; 8:26; 14:31; 16:8). Like the disciples we are on an upward pilgrimage of faith and discipleship throughout our time on earth, and like them we can overcome failure through radical surrender in the strength the Spirit supplies (John 16:12 – 15; 1 Pet 1:5).

3. Cosmic Authority

Christ has cosmic authority and gives this to his followers in mission. I believe we have little idea of just how much authority we possess in this world. In v. 18 we have the highest Christology to be found in the Bible. As God himself, Jesus has power over all the forces of heaven and over his creation, earth (John 1:3 – 4; 1 Cor 8:6; Col 1:16; Heb 1:3). Everything said of Yahweh in the creation theology of the OT (e.g., Job 38 – 41; Ps 89:11 – 13; Isa 40:26, 28; 42:5) applies to Jesus in his cosmic authority.

Yet this authority in this world is passed on to the church as it participates in Jesus' mission to the world. This is said very well in the mission theology of John as summarized in John 20:21 – 23.[37] God has sent his Son as a "Sent One" with his full authority to reach the world; then the Father and the Son send the Spirit with their authority (John 14 – 16); and finally the entire Godhead sends the disciples/the church with their authority. When we speak, we do not speak with our own authority but as the voice of the Godhead in this world!

4. To Evangelize and to Disciple

The task of the church is not just to evangelize but to *disciple* the world for Christ. A huge error has occurred over the last two hundred years in the missionary movement. Our task is, of course, to reach the world with the gospel message of salvation, but too many denominations and mission organizations have been content to give little more than salvation messages. The Great Commission makes it clear that this is not enough. Every single person who is won to Christ must be anchored in Christ and taught how to live for Christ in day-to-day decisions.

Christianity is a practical, ethical religion, and we cannot separate the secular from the sacred. Until the secular areas of our lives have been "baptized" with holiness, we are not truly disciples of Jesus. This is the mission of the church, and there is no excuse for shallowness. Consider many Third World churches with little opportunity often to find depth: the shallowness there is the fault of the mission organizations that have given too little priority to (1) the education and training of the leaders in those countries, and (2) the development and publication of good literature for those countries.

5. Baptism

Baptism is Christ's mandate for the church in the new covenant community. Some Christian movements believe baptism is not for today. This is not heresy, but it is serious error. The apostles would have been aghast at any such suggestion. At the same time many people in our churches have not been baptized and have just shrugged it off and rationalized it away. It is true that this will not endanger their salvation, but it is an act of serious disobedience. I do not believe that the mode of baptism is critical (though I personally think immersion is the best reading of the imagery), but the fact of baptism is treated as a necessity in the NT. In 1 Pet 3:20 – 21 baptism is a "pledge" (in a sense a signing of the contract/covenant with God)[38] and is thus a sacrament. Baptism does not save but is part of the salvation experience

37. See Köstenberger, *The Missions of Jesus and the Disciples*; and Grant R. Osborne, *John* (Cornerstone Biblical Commentary; Wheaton, IL: Tyndale, 2007), 290–91.

38. See Karen H. Jobes, *1 Peter* (BECNT; Grand Rapids: Baker, 2005), 255.

and is meant for every believer. Moreover, it is a Trinitarian experience because it brings us into union and relationship with the triune Godhead.

6. Teaching

In our teaching we share Jesus' authority by disseminating divine truths to the church and the world. There is no automatic authority that is wielded by the leaders of the church no matter what they say or do. Authority is not in the office but in the relationship, i.e., in the presence of Christ and the Spirit behind what is said and done. Our responsibility is to make certain that we are centered in him and his Word. It is critical to realize that Jesus said, "everything *I* have commanded you" (not whatever we feel like saying). This is entirely in keeping with 2 Tim 2:15, where Paul advised Timothy that he would only avoid "shame" when he stood before God if he "correctly handles the word of truth." Christian leaders will be judged (cf. Heb 13:17) by their faithfulness to the Word of God, i.e., by their desire to center at all times on what God has said in his Word and not on their own ideas. Moreover, Christian discipleship is ethical at the heart, at all times centered on Christian life and not just on right belief. Belief that is not lived out in every aspect of daily decisions is not true belief. It is heart and conduct, not just head knowledge.

7. Jesus' Presence with Us

The final emphasis of Matthew is that its truths are always a present reality and not just a past set of events. The Jesus of Matthew is omnipresent with his people and in every way at work in our lives. In the "Spirit of Christ" (Acts 16:7; Rom 8:9; Gal 4:6; Phil 1:19; 1 Pet 1:11) he is in our hearts and empowering our lives. It is this authority and presence, this "power" at work in us (1 Pet 1:5), that makes it possible for us to overcome (even rejoice in) our weaknesses (1 Cor 2:3 – 5; 2 Cor 12:5, 9 – 10) and accomplish great things for the kingdom.

The Theology of Matthew

Biblical theology is an important development over the past hundred years. Every book of the Bible has its own set of theological emphases, so that each of the four gospels contains different ideological messages. What we are seeking is a delineation of the theological threads Matthew has woven together to form his gospel. This is a descriptive task, accomplished by letting the themes "trickle up" out of the developing story. In the commentary we have sought to discuss those themes at the end of each pericope. Here we try to summarize them from the most extensive and important to the less dominating (but still important) themes.

Christology

All of Matthew's Christology is built on the *messianic role and nature* of Jesus. The first section, the genealogy, is framed with this theme, beginning with "This is a record of the genealogy of Jesus the Messiah" (1:1) and ending with "there were fourteen generations ... between the exile and the Messiah" (1:17). Then the next section begins with the origins of "Jesus Messiah" (1:18), and this is further clarified when Joseph is told in 1:23, "they will call his name Immanuel, which means, 'God with us,'" where Jesus' messianic work is seen as the presence of God accomplishing his salvation in this world. As Yahweh was ever-present with his people Israel, so Jesus is omnipresent with the new messianic community (cf. also 18:20; 28:20).

The story of Jesus Messiah is couched in OT fulfillment concepts (see below) and is presented in promise – fulfillment terms as the expected anointed figure who will finalize God's redemptive purposes for humankind. In some places Matthew elaborates Mark in explicating the meaning and further significance of Jesus as Messiah, e.g., in 16:16, where Peter confesses Jesus as "the Messiah, the Son of the living God" (cf. Mark 8:29, "Messiah").

The royal nature of Jesus' messianic nature is emphasized in the story of the Magi. They arrive in Jerusalem asking, "Where is the one born King of the Jews?" (2:2), and Herod's response is to ask the legal experts "where the Messiah was to be born" (2:4). The Jewish people expected the Messiah to be a conquering king who would defeat the Romans; thus, understandably, Herod took the birth of the messianic king to be a direct threat to his reign. This Jewish expectation of a conquering Messiah was a major factor in both the crowd's failure to embrace Jesus and his own disciples' continual failure to understand him. In 11:2 even John the Baptist expressed doubts, sending representatives after he was arrested to ask, "Are you the One who was to come?" He had proclaimed a message of apocalyptic judgment and could not understand Jesus' ministry of healing and forgiveness.

Simon Peter shows this same lack of awareness. First, his expansion of Jesus as not only "Messiah" but "Son of the living God" in 16:16 is the high point of discipleship in Matthew, yet Jesus tells the disciples not to tell others this (16:20) because of the Jewish false expectations. Second, when Jesus goes on to say in effect in the first passion prediction, "Yes, I am Messiah, but let me tell you what kind of Messiah I am to be — the suffering Servant," Peter refuses to accept this and in fact "rebukes" Jesus for saying such a thing! For Jesus the messianic work meant the cross, and he would fulfill his destiny by becoming the atoning sacrifice for sin. Yet neither the Jews nor the disciples could accept such a thing.

Finally, in the Passion Narrative Jesus as Messiah is central. Matthew, following the message in Mark but not as frequently, contains the "messianic secret" (see 8:4; 16:20; 17:9); Jesus requests people who were healed and his disciples not to tell others about his messianic identity because of the Jewish misunderstanding. Jesus eventually reverses this and makes public proclamation in three stages: (1) his triumphal entry (21:1 – 11) as he reveals himself as the humble Messiah in fulfillment of Zech 9:9; (2) the remarkable passage where he reveals himself as not only the Son of David but David's "Lord" (22:41 – 45); and (3) the even more remarkable passages where Jesus reveals himself as not only Messiah and Son of God but as the eschatological Judge, fulfilling Ps 110:1 and Dan 7:13 (26:64). Finally, during his arrest and trial the leaders and Pilate offer ironic, unconscious testimony to his true nature as Messiah (26:68; 27:17, 22).

As the Jewish gospel Matthew has more on the "Son of David" title than any of the others. In 1:1 Χριστός ("Christ") is closely linked with this. In Matthew's prologue (1:1 – 17) "David" (Δαυίδ) occurs five times, and with his name in Hebrew having the gematria of fourteen (*dwd*, with d = 4, w = 6; the genealogy is organized in three groups of fourteen) the emphasis is on Jesus as the expected Davidic Messiah, the anointed royal figure who will fulfill the divine promise in the Davidic covenant that David's throne will be eternal (2 Sam 7:16). In 1:20 Joseph, the righteous "son of David," adopts Jesus and brings him into the messianic line. The title "Son of David" is used often in the miracle stories (9:27; 12:23; 15:22; 20:30 – 31) to portray Jesus as the true Messiah of Israel, who heals the blindness and sickness of God's people; in fact, the healing and exorcism of the deaf-mute in 12:22 – 23 leads the crowds to ask if Jesus is the Son of David and the leaders to respond negatively, saying Jesus' power comes from Beelzebul/Satan.

In the Passion Narrative this title is far more predominant than in Mark. In the triumphal entry (21:9; cf. Mark 11:10) the crowd shouts, "Hosanna to the Son of David," showing that the crowd viewed this as a virtual coronation procession for the messianic king. On the children's lips in 21:15 (not in Mark), we have the third consecutive statement of this status (cf. 20:30 – 31; 21:9), and the children become a prophetic voice revealing who Jesus really is. This theme reaches a crescendo when Jesus affirms himself as David's "Lord" in 22:41 – 45 (par. Mark 12:35 – 37). As Luz concludes, the function of this title "is to characterize Jesus' coming as the fulfillment and transformation of Israel's messianic hopes and to help soften the blow of division between Christian community and synagogue."[1]

"Son of God" has often been called the primary christological title in Matthew.[2] This is an overstatement, but the title is important, signifying Jesus' unique filial relationship with his Father. Matthew uses this of Jesus in several key passages. In 2:15 Jesus typologically fulfills Hos 11:1 and reenacts Israel's exodus as God's Son and return from exile in "Egypt." God himself affirms Jesus' sonship both at the baptism (3:17, where he is anointed by the Holy Spirit) and the transfiguration (17:5, centering on God's Shekinah presence). Satan affirms his sonship but tries to tempt Jesus into misusing his authority for his own advantage (4:3, 6); Jesus, unlike Israel, refuses to yield (all three of Jesus' quotes in his temptations are from Deut 6 – 8, where Israel, "sons of God," failed in the same temptations).

During Jesus' ministry the demons acknowledge him as Son of God and are forced to succumb to his authority (8:29); and after they see his power over the storm, his disciples worship him as such (14:33). A significant explanation of Jesus' sonship is provided by him in 11:27, where he describes the unique mutual knowledge of one another by the Father and the Son. Jesus calls God his "Father" on numerous occasions (e.g., 6:9; 7:21; 10:32 – 33; 12:50; et al.), and the two are together in 24:36; 28:19. Jesus' sonship is further defined in the confession of Peter (16:16), which combines the titles of Messiah and Son of God, demonstrating the link between these key concepts. Two parables continue the revelation of this aspect — the wedding banquet (22:1 – 14), centering on the rejection of the Father and the Son, and the wicked tenants (21:33 – 46), centering on the murder of the Son by the Jews, God's tenants.

During Jesus' trial Caiaphas's cross-examination of Jesus echoes Peter's confession when he asks Jesus to affirm himself as "Messiah, the Son of God" (26:63), and the unconscious testimony of Jesus' enemies (27:40, 43) centers on his claim to be "Son of God." This theme culminates in the exclamation of the centurion and other soldiers at the cross, "Truly this was Son of God" (27:54). The special filial sonship

1. Ulrich Luz, *Studies in Matthew* (Grand Rapids: Eerdmans, 2005), 88.

2. Kingsbury, *Structure*, 78 – 83.

of Jesus in Matthew demonstrates the vertical dimension of Jesus' personhood and is virtually tantamount to an affirmation of deity.[3] Marshall says it well:

> Perhaps we are to see some development in the Gospel. At the outset Jesus is principally the messianic Son of David, thus emphasizing his role in relation to Israel, and his divine origin is stressed rather than his sonship. By the end of the Gospel, he is named in a Trinitarian formula as the Son of God, thus emphasizing his cosmic status for the world after the resurrection. But the difference is purely one of emphasis, and throughout the Gospel both lines of thought are held together.[4]

Jesus as "Son of Man" is also a major title in Matthew (30 of the 81 times in the gospels) and is only used by Jesus of himself.[5] Few aspects of Jesus' teaching have been more explored than this, and it has been common among critical scholars to assert that the historical Jesus used it only as a circumlocution for "I," perhaps building on the use in Ezekiel to signify that he was a mortal human being. However, most today would affirm the use in the glorified sense of Dan 7:13 – 14, where the "one like a son of man" has dominion over the whole earth.

In Matthew there are three types of "Son of Man" sayings: (1) the earthly work of the Son of Man (8:20; 9:6; 11:19; 12:32; 13:37; 16:13); (2) the suffering Son of Man (12:40; 17:9, 12, 22; 20:18, 28; 26:2, 24, 45); and (3) the apocalyptic and exalted Son of Man (10:23; 12:8; 13:41; 16:13, 27, 28; 19:28; 24:27, 30, 37, 39, 44; 25:31; 26:64). Luz brings out some interesting points:[6] (1) before 16:13 the sayings are addressed to the people, while after that all except 26:64 are given to the disciples. (2) Jesus' "present" sayings are public (mainly early in the narrative), while the latter two types are primarily for the disciples. (3) This title is not used to define who Jesus is but to narrate what he does (and suffers). The majority of the Son of Man sayings unique to Matthew concern the parousia (13:41; 16:28; 19:28?; 24:30a; 25:31). It is generally agreed that Jesus chose the title for its ambiguity, as it could connote both his humanity and his exaltation/glory. The irony of it is that the homeless One is the being who has dominion over this world and is Judge of all.

A debated aspect but one that is probably present as a secondary yet important theme is Jesus as a "new Moses" bringing a new exodus. Those who doubt this motif normally link it with Benjamin Bacon's thesis that the five discourses are a "new Pentateuch" with Jesus the "new Moses." The first is exceedingly unlikely, but that does not obviate the presence of Moses typology in Matthew. The primary voice for this is Dale Allison,[7] but many reject this on the grounds that Matthew is not comparing Jesus with Moses but contrasting the two: Jesus is greater than Moses. This is certainly correct, but the new Moses designation still stands. Note that Jesus

3. Blomberg, *Matthew*, 229.

4. Marshall, *New Testament Theology*, 113 – 14.

5. For the following see the excursus on this after 8:18 – 22.

6. Luz, *Studies*, 88 – 89.

7. Allison, *New Moses*; see also Davies and Allison, *Matthew*.

is Son of David, yet greater than David (22:41 – 46). In the same way, Jesus is the new Moses by fulfilling and transcending Moses.

In the infancy narrative, many (e.g., Gundry, Bruner, Keener, Nolland) note a Moses typology as God protects the baby Jesus (à la Moses) while their enemy Herod (à la Pharaoh) slaughters the innocents in Bethlehem. Like Moses, Jesus fled from his homeland (Exod 2:15), and Matt 2:15 quotes Hos 11:1, "Out of Egypt I have called my son," with the Hosea passage typologically showing how the return from exile in Egypt reenacted the exodus. So there is a double typology from exodus to exile to Jesus. In 2:20 the command to return from Egypt echoes Exod 4:19, where God told Moses to return from Midian, "for all those who wanted to kill you are dead." In the same way that Moses took his family back to Egypt (Exod 4:20), so Joseph took his family back to Israel.

We have space to highlight only a few others. In the testing of Jesus (4:1 – 11) Moses typology can be detected in the forty days and nights of fasting and in the three quotes from Deut 6 – 8. When Jesus ascends a mountain to deliver his "sermon" in 5:1, there is likely a parallel with Moses' ascent of Sinai to receive the law (see also mountain scenes in 14:23; 15:29; 17:1; 28:16). Moreover, I argued that Matt 5 – 7 is "the law of the new covenant," not so much a new Torah as a transformation of the Torah of the OT into the Torah of the Messiah. In 5:17 – 20 this fulfillment means Jesus is the final interpreter of Torah and so greater than Moses.

The Mission Discourse and especially the sending out of the Twelve in 9:35 – 10:5a may be partly built on the commissioning of Moses in Exod 3:1 – 4:17. There may also be several echoes of Exod 33 and Deut 34 in 11:25 – 30; and the two feeding miracles (14:13 – 21; 15:29 – 39) are certainly reminiscent of the manna miracle in the wilderness. The transfiguration (17:1 – 8) has several important parallels — the mountain, the radiant face, the presence of Moses, the Shekinah cloud, the voice from the cloud, and the fear of the disciples.

The climax of this theme comes at the Last Supper. First, as a Passover meal it was intended to be a celebration and reenactment of the exodus experience. Second, as one of the four cups of the celebration, the cup of 26:27 – 29 is connected to a line of Exod 6:6 – 7a, this one to "I will redeem you" in v. 6c, thereby producing a new redemption, this time from sin ("for the forgiveness of sins"). Moreover, the "blood of the covenant" is typologically connected to Exod 24:8, where Moses sprinkled "the blood of the covenant" on the people. Thielman concludes, "Jesus is like Moses, but he is greater than Moses and supersedes him."[8]

8. Frank Thielmann, *Theology of the New Testament: A Canonical and Synthetic Approach* (Grand Rapids: Zondervan, 2005), 93.

Several other aspects of Matthew's christology must be noted briefly. First, he is "Servant of Yahweh." As Marshall says, Jesus is identified as "the Servant of the Lord who works quietly and gently without raising his voice (Matt 12:18 – 21, citing Isa 42:1 – 4), and this is confirmed by the claim of Jesus to be gentle and humble (Matt 11:29, cf. Matt 21:5)."[9] The Isaianic Servant of Isa 53 is seen in the use of Isa 42:1 in God's affirmation of Jesus (3:15; 17:5), in interpreting Jesus' healing ministry in light of Isa 53:4, 11 in 8:17; in the "ransom for many" saying of 20:28 (see commentary); and in the addition of "for the forgiveness of sins" to the cup saying of 26:28, thereby centering on "the vicarious, atoning nature of the Servant's suffering."[10]

At the same time, Jesus is a teacher of ethical wisdom. Matthew does not use "teacher" (διδάσκαλος) as often as Mark, and when he does it is always on the mouth of his opponents (e.g., a scribe in 8:19; Pharisees in 9:11; 12:38; 22:16, 24, 36; Judas calls him "Rabbi" in 26:25, 49) or those not committed to Jesus (e.g., a tax collector in 17:24; the rich young ruler in 19:16). Still, in the five discourses Jesus centers on ethical teaching, and he calls himself a "teacher" on occasion (10:24 – 25, "no servant above his teacher"; 23:10, "you have one teacher, the Christ"; 26:18, "tell him, 'The teacher says, "My time is near" ' "). The crowds were often "astonished" at his teaching (7:28; 22:33). Witherington calls him "a sage who expressed his eschatological convictions in Wisdom forms."[11]

The Sermon on the Mount has a wisdom orientation, and 11:19 ("wisdom is vindicated by her deeds") identifies Jesus with the works of personified Wisdom. Then in 11:25 – 30 Jesus as God's Wisdom shares a unique mutual knowledge with his Father and becomes the source of revelation; those who come will find an easy yoke and rest in him.[12] Finally, in 23:34 Jesus sends "sages," most likely Christian teachers who bring the kingdom message and God's wisdom to the world. Jesus is the greater Moses and teacher of wisdom[13] who has brought final redemption to humankind.

Finally, Jesus in Matthew is also "King" and "Lord." Obviously, Jesus' kingly role is closely connected to Jesus as Messiah and Son of David. Jesus as the Davidic-King Messiah occurs first in the genealogy (1:1, 16, 17) and in a polemical context with the Magi (2:2) vs. Herod (2:4, 9, 13, 16). At the triumphal entry Matthew adds the quote from Zech 9:9 to Mark, especially "Look, your king is coming to you." At the trial and death of Jesus, Pilate asks Jesus about "the king of the Jews ... the one called Messiah" (27:11, 17, 22, 29, 37), and the leaders ironically taunt Jesus as king (26:63, 68; 27:41 – 42). The plaque on the cross said, "This is Jesus, the King of the

9. Marshall, *New Testament Theology*, 114.

10. Thielmann, *Theology of the New Testament*, 96 – 97.

11. Witherington, *Jesus the Sage*, 183.

12. See Thielman, *Theology of the New Testament*, 19, who sees this similar to the themes of God and wisdom in Sir 24.

13. This is not to say that Jesus is personified Wisdom in Matthew. As Marshall concludes (*New Testament Theology*, 115), "it is significant that there is no clear use of the term as a title, and it cannot be said to play a major role in the Gospel compared with the other Christological categories."

Jews" (27:37). Finally, in 25:34, 40 Jesus speaks of himself in the parable as the king sitting on his *bēma* in judgment.

Further, Jesus is seen as "Lord" in Matthew. While opponents and strangers call Jesus "teacher" (cf. above), his disciples call him "Lord" (8:21, 25; 14:28, 30; 16:22; 17:4; 18:21). He is also regularly called "Lord" in healing contexts (8:2, 6, 8; 9:28; 15:22, 25, 27; 17:15; 20:30, 31, 33). While certainly neither groups meant this in a cosmic sense, Kingsbury rightly notes its close connection to Son of God and Son of Man, recognizing Jesus as the exalted one who "wields divine authority."[14]

Turner notes how "Matthew applies other, less significant titles to Jesus." Among these are "shepherd" (2:6; 9:36; 25:32; 26:31), "bridegroom" (9:15; 25:1), "the coming one" (11:3; 21:9; 23:39), "prophet" (13:57; 16:14; 21:11, 46; cf. Deut 18:15), "stone" (21:42 – 44; cf. Ps 118:22 – 23; Dan. 2:44 – 45), and "rabbi" (26:25, 49).[15]

The Jewishness of Matthew

Everyone agrees that Matthew is the "Jewish Gospel." Hagner provides a good summary of the evidence, beginning with 5:17 – 18, that Jesus came to "fulfill," not "destroy" the law:

> The extensive quotation of the OT, especially the distinctive eleven quotations introduced with the fulfillment formula, "this happened to fulfill the words spoken by the prophet"; rabbinic-like patterns of argument, as in the antitheses of the Sermon on the Mount (5:21 – 48) and in the discussion of divorce (19:3 – 9); the repeated stress on righteousness; the preference for the language "kingdom of heaven" rather than "kingdom of God"; Matthew's omission of Mark's description of the practice of the Pharisees (cf. Mark 7:3 – 4 with Matt 15:2); Matthew's omission of Mark's editorial comment "Thus he declared all foods clean" (cf. Mark 7:19 with Matt 15:17); the reference to the limitation of Jesus and his disciples' mission to Israel (10:5 – 6; 15:24); the statement concerning the Pharisees sitting in "Moses' seat" (23:2); the mention of the Sabbath in 24:20; the explicit response to the Jewish allegation that the body of Jesus had been stolen (28:11 – 15).[16]

The major debate is over how Jewish his work is. Some scholars believe that Matthew's community is not Jewish Christian but a Jewish sect with Christian leanings.[17] They believe that the emphasis on the validity of Torah and the

14. Kingsbury, *Matthew*, 113 (cf. 103 – 13). He corrects the belief by Bornkamm and others that *kyrios* is the supreme title in Matthew but recognizes its exalted place as a confessional title.

15. Turner, "Matthew," 37.

16. Donald Hagner, "Matthew: Christian Judaism or Jewish Christianity?" in *The Face of New Testament Studies*, ed. Scot McKnight and Grant R. Osborne (Grand Rapids: Baker Book House, 2004), 263 – 64. On Matthew's use of the OT in a fulfillment sense, see also the discussion in the introduction to this commentary.

17. Overman, *Matthew's Gospel and Formative Judaism*; Anthony J. Saldarini, *Matthew's Christian-Jewish Community* (Chicago: Univ. of Chicago Press, 1994); David C. Sim, *The Gospel of Matthewand Christian Judaism: The History and Social Setting of the Matthean Community* (Edinburgh: T & T Clark, 1998).

centrality of righteousness fits the Jewish sectarian emphasis on legal righteousness. However, the issue in Matthew is not on the law per se but on Jesus as the fulfillment and final interpreter of the law. The central theme is on Christology, not on law. Moreover, as Bauckham argues, there is no Matthean community behind the book.[18] It is written for the church as a whole, and there is no sectarian atmosphere in the book. The church in Matthew is the new Israel providing the final stage in God's plan of salvation (see below), and salvation-history occurs in three stages — the OT, the time of Jesus, and the church age.

Matthew's gospel is set in a Jewish context only in the sense that Jesus and his disciples are Jewish set on a Jewish mission. It is true that in the Palestinian period after Pentecost the church considered itself to be "the Way" (Acts 9:2; 19:9, 23; 22:4; 24:14, 22), namely, the Jewish messianic sect, but they were followers of Jesus and not truly Jewish. Moreover, as we will see in the next section, Jesus several times deliberately ministered in Gentile contexts, probably to prepare the disciples for the future Gentile mission. So the Jewish and Gentile missions overlapped in the time of Jesus. This will also be seen in the universal mission theme in Matthew discussed in the next section; this theme reverberated through the whole of Jesus' ministry to the Jews. It is clear that Jewish and Gentile conversion was seen by Matthew as two interdependent parts of one overall mission of God to the whole world.

Still, Matthew is set in a Jewish context, and the centrality of the fulfillment theme (on this see the discussion of Matthew's use of the OT in the introduction to this commentary) and of Jesus' interaction with the Jews shows that the Jewish question is a dominating theme of Matthew's interest. In fact, Blomberg calls it "the most foundational or overarching theme of the book" on the grounds that Matthew centers on the fulfillment of God's promises to his chosen people and the path through them of the outpouring of his blessings/judgments on all humanity.[19]

Every part of his gospel is infused with this motif. In the genealogy (1:1 – 17) Jesus is son of Abraham and son of David. In 2:15 Jesus fulfills the return from exile (Hos 11:1) and becomes Israel bringing God's people into a new exodus. The Magi (2:1 – 11) fulfill Isa 60:1 – 6 and signify the Gentiles coming to Israel, bringing gifts for the Messiah. In the testing of God's Son (4:1 – 11) the three texts from Deut 6 – 8 relate to Israel's failing their test in the wilderness in contrast to Jesus succeeding as the new Israel.

One of the more debated issues in the book is particularism vs. universalism. In 10:5 – 6; 15:24 Jesus says he has come only for "the lost sheep of the house of Israel" and restricts his disciples' ministry only to the Jews; yet in 28:19 he tells them to go "make disciples from all nations." While some see these as two strands

18. See Bauckham, *The Gospel for All Christians.*

19. Blomberg, *Matthew*, 26.

of conflicting traditions,[20] that is unnecessary, for the first strand concerns the mission of the disciples during Jesus' life, the second their mission after his death. There is a distinct salvation-historical movement in Matthew's gospel (see above), and this is seen especially in the mission motif. Jesus' life and ministry culminated the old covenant concerns for Israel and at the same time began the new covenant ministry to the world as a whole.

Jesus' Jewishness and concern for his people is obvious throughout the first gospel, personified in his lament over Jerusalem, "O Jerusalem, Jerusalem ... how often I have wanted to gather your children together, as a hen gathers her young under her wings, but you were not willing" (23:37). Yet at the same time his conflict with the Jews, in particular with their leaders, is strongly emphasized in Matthew. Turner makes "Conflict over Authority" a primary section in his theology section and states, "The key motif in Matthew that moves the plot and portrays the struggle (cf. Matt. 11:12) involved in the advance of the kingdom is conflict."[21]

In the infancy material it is, of course, Herod who attempts to destroy his "rival," the baby Jesus (ch. 2). Then there is conflict between the Baptist and the leaders who are moving toward God's judgment (3:7 – 12; cf. 14:1 – 12), a foretaste of their conflict with Jesus (17:12). Jesus' troubles with the leaders begin with the crowds who notice Jesus' greater "authority" (7:28 – 29), and Jesus lauds the greater "faith" of the Roman officer and denounces the lack of faith in Israel (8:10 – 12). The actual conflict begins with the cost of following Jesus (8:19 – 20), debates over his forgiveness of sins (9:1 – 8), his association with notorious sinners (9:9 – 13), and the charge that his power comes from "the prince of demons" (9:34). In his Mission Discourse he warns his followers that they too can expect intense conflict and opposition as they take the message of the kingdom to the Jewish people and the nations (10:16 – 39).

This theme comes to the forefront in chs. 11 – 13 after Jesus' successful ministry in Galilee in chs. 8 – 9. In this section there are six pericopes on rejection and judgment (11:2 – 19, 20 – 24; 12:1 – 8, 9 – 14, 22 – 37, 38 – 42), beginning with the doubts of even John the Baptist (11:3). Then Matthew adds to his Markan source the parables of the weeds (13:24 – 30, 36 – 43) and of the net (13:47 – 52), both centering on the harvest that leads to final judgment. The section ends, then, with Jesus rejected even in his own hometown (13:53 – 58). This radical opposition continues and culminates in the cross.

Many (e.g., Luz) have accused Matthew of anti-Judaism because of the negative portrait found in so many places. In 8:10 – 12 he contrasts the Gentiles, who will participate in the messianic banquet, with the "children of the kingdom" (the Jews), who will be "thrown into outermost darkness, where there will be weeping and

20. See Schuyler Brown, "The Matthean Community and the Gentile Mission," *NovT* 22 (1980): 193 – 221.

21. Turner, "Matthew," 44.

grinding of teeth." In several passages Matthew refers to "*their* synagogue" (4:23; 9:35; 10:17; 12:9; 13:54), and in 27:25 at Jesus' trial the Jewish people cry out, "May his blood be upon us and upon our children." The leaders seek his life from the start (12:14), and at his trial they care nothing for justice (26:3 – 5) but allow false witnesses (26:59) and lies (28:11 – 15) to predominate. The parable of the wicked tenants (21:33 – 43) and the diatribe against the scribes and Pharisees (ch. 23) stress their guilt and coming judgment.

Yet does this constitute anti-Semitism, a Matthean rejection of Judaism? A growing number of scholars refuse to draw this conclusion.[22] For one thing, the "all the nations" of 28:19 includes Israel. On the whole, it is the leaders rather than the crowds who are condemned. When it is the people (e.g. 8:10 – 12; 27:5), the emphasis is on unbelieving Israel, not the people as a whole (13:53 – 58). Furthermore, the stress throughout is on Jesus' desire to bring the people to God, not on his wholesale rejection of them.

Thielman provides three arguments against the charge that Matthew is anti-Jewish. (1) Matthew belongs to a minority group and is responding to oppression (10:17; 23:34; cf. 5:11 – 12) rather than calling for it. (2) He does not just critique unbelieving Judaism but also speaks against unbelieving Gentiles (6:7 – 8), who will also "drag them before governors and kings" (10:17 – 18) and hate them (24:9). Even "hypocrites" in the church face "eschatological judgment and banishment from the kingdom" (cf. 24:51; also 7:5). (3) Matthew places Jesus' role against the background of Jeremiah, who spoke against the hypocrisy of the Jewish leaders who oppressed the powerless (Jer 7:6), violated the commandments (Jer 7:9), and practiced false religion (Jer 7:9, 16 – 18). Like Jeremiah Matthew shows Jesus trying to bring his people back to God.[23]

The entire Jewish nature of the book demonstrates a desire to make following Christ attractive to Jewish readers. When Jesus says, "I was not sent to anyone except to the lost sheep of the house of Israel" (15:24; cf. 10:5 – 6 for the disciples' mission), this is not the final statement of a past mission sense that is now in process of being replaced by the Gentile mission but a mission that is soon going to include the Gentiles in its focus. There is no replacement theology in Matthew but rather a universal mission to Jew and Gentile alike. France discusses the debate as to whether Matthew's church was "inside" or "outside" Judaism (dominant in the writings of Strecker, Borkmamm, Stendahl, [outside] or Davies, Goulder [inside]) and notes the artificiality of the debate. He believes (rightly) that Matthew and his Jewish Christian church viewed itself as both inside (as Jews) and outside (as Christians) Judaism.[24]

22. See Scot McKnight, "A Loyal Critic: Matthew's Polemic with Judaism in Theological Perspective," in *Anti-Semitism and Early Christianity: Issues of Polemic and Faith* (ed. C. A. Evans and D. A. Hagner; Minneapolis: Fortress, 1993), 55 – 79; James D. G. Dunn, "The Question of Anti-Semitism in the New Testament Writings of the Period," in *Jews and Christians: The Parting of the Ways, A.D. 70 – 135* (ed. J. D. G. Dunn; Grand Rapids: Eerdmans, 1999), 177 – 211. For a more complete list, see Turner, "Matthew," 46n.

23. Thielman, *Theology of the New Testament*, 103 – 4.

24. France, *Matthew: Evangelist and Teacher*, 98 – 102.

The Gentile Mission

Closely linked to the whole question of Matthew and the Jewish people is the movement to the universal mission in Matthew. To be sure, there have been some negative voices; Sim believes that there was an anti-Gentile bias and that Matthew wished to restrict the Christian mission to the Jews.[25] However, this is unlikely in light of all the passages noted below and has few adherents. The passages where the Gentiles are spoken of disparagingly (5:47; 6:7, 32; 18:17; 20:25) are all in contexts that make no statement about the Gentile mission and are intended only as behavioral contrasts.

The positive place the Gentiles have in God's economy is found even in the genealogy that begins Matthew's gospel. Jesus is called "son of Abraham" in 1:1, 17, a possible allusion to the Abrahamic covenant that contained the promise of "blessing to the nations" (Gen 12:3; 15:5; 18:18). Moreover, in 1:3, 5, 6 four women are named in the genealogical line (Tamar, Rahab, Ruth, Bathshebah) with Gentile connections (see on 1:3), hinting that Jesus was Messiah of the Gentiles as well as the Jews.[26] This is confirmed in 2:1 – 12, when pagan Magi (possibly from Persia or Babylon) represent Isaiah's "procession of the nations to Zion" (Isa 2:2 – 5; 11:10; 14:1; 26:2; 49:23; 56:6 – 7; 60:5, 10 – 11) and come bringing gifts from the nations to the infant messianic King. From the beginning Matthew portrays the nations coming to the Messiah.

Also, the Baptist's warning that God could "raise up children for Abraham" in 3:9 hints at the coming mission to the Gentiles; the emphasis there is on children coming from elsewhere, and in the Isaianic sense this would again be the procession of the nations to the Messiah. Finally, in the first ministry section of the book, Jesus opens in Capernaum, which is described in fulfillment of Isa 9:1 – 2 as taking place in "Galilee of the Gentiles," so that "people who sit in darkness have seen a great light" (4:15). In 4:25 crowds followed Jesus not only from Jewish Galilee but also from Gentile Decapolis and "the region across the Jordan." From the outset Jesus' salvific concern reaches out from the Jewish people to the nations beyond.

The second miracle enacted by Jesus in the book (8:5 – 13) concerns a Gentile centurion, and Jesus' response is amazing in the light of the fact that less than two chapters later he restricts the disciples' mission to the Jews, *not* the Gentiles (10:5 – 6). In 8:10 – 12 he expressed amazement at "such great faith" and then said that "many from the east and from the west" (Gentiles) would take part in the

25. Sim, *Christian Judaism*, 236 – 47. See the critique of this in Hagner, "Matthew: Christian Judaism or Jewish Christianity?" 273 – 74.

26. As Turner, "Matthew," 27 – 28, points out, while some reject this on the grounds that Jewish tradition considered these women "virtuous proselytes," this actually strengthens the point because "this would make them even better prototypes of Matthew's stress on gentile mission."

messianic feast while "the children of the kingdom" (the Jews) would be cast "into the outermost darkness" or final judgment. At first glance it seems a replacement theology, but we must note that (1) the miracle is preceded by the healing of the Jewish leper, (2) the Gentiles share the banquet with the patriarchs, and (3) in 8:10 the basis of participating in the banquet is not ethnicity but "faith in Jesus." So believing Gentiles will be sharing the banquet with believing Jews (like the patriarchs).

Then in 8:28 – 34 Jesus deliberately goes across the Jordan to the region of the Gadarenes, where he exorcizes two demon-possessed men, probably in part to prepare the disciples for their future mission to the nations (28:19). Jesus' intention for his disciples to eventually go beyond Israel in sharing the gospel is seen in the Mission Discourse at 10:18, where he prophesies that the coming persecution would result in their being "led before governors and kings for my sake as a witness to them and the Gentiles." This was fulfilled more fully by Paul, for Jesus was tried by Pilate while Paul went before Nero himself.

In the next section several passages show this purpose. Note 12:21, "the Gentiles will put their hope in his name." Chs. 11 – 12 exist in three triads, with two stories of opposition and rejection by the Jews followed by a third detailing Jesus and his redemptive purpose (see the introduction to that section). This occurs in the second triad and centers on Jesus the humble Servant who comes to bring hope not just to the Jewish people but to all Gentiles who "put their hope in his name." It is the last part of a quote from Isa 42:1 – 4 and shows that Jesus will bring about the Isaianic procession of the nations to Zion (see above). In 12:42 one of these Gentiles, "the Queen of the South" (Sheba), will condemn rejecting Israel at the last judgment, because like many Gentiles she "heard" (i.e., sought truth and accepted the wisdom of) Solomon while the Jewish people were unwilling to do so with the "one greater than Solomon." In the Parable Discourse at 13:38 Jesus interprets the parable of the weeds (13:24 – 30, 36 – 43) by saying, "The field is the world," referring to the worldwide mission of the church to Jew and Gentile as directed by God.

In 15:21 – 28 the Canaanite woman becomes a model of faith and humility to the disciples. Jesus tests her with his challenge, "I was not sent to anyone except to the lost sheep of the house of Israel." This has often been misunderstood as Matthean particularism, but France says rightly, "it is indicative in form, it functions in the dialogue more as a question, a test of faith, a statement of position which invites (and receives) a counter-proposal, and it is that counter-proposal which wins Jesus' assent and carries the day." Jesus has come for the Jews, "but there is plenty of bread for the 'dogs' as well."[27] The Gentiles are distinctly a part of Jesus' mission; this well fits Rom 2:9 – 10 (cf. Rom 1:16), where Paul says the gospel is "first for the Jew, then for the Gentile." If the feeding of the four thosuand in 15:29 – 31 takes place in Gentile territory (see Mark 7:31), it becomes an immediate example of the bread

27. France, *Matthew: Evangelist and Teacher*, 234.

for the Gentiles. Luz calls this whole scene "the power of God's love that bursts the borders of Israel."[28]

Then in the judgment section of the parable of the wicked tenants (21:33 – 46), Jesus tells the leaders, "The kingdom of God will be taken away from you and given to a people who will produce its fruit" (v. 43), with "people" (ἔθνος) meaning both the Gentiles and the church that will include them (see commentary). The new "tenants" of God's vineyard will be composed of both Gentiles and believing Jews. The fruit is the righteous conduct demanded of the kingdom people (cf. 5:6, 10, 20; 6:1, 33; 7:16 – 20).

The following parable of the wedding banquet (22:1 – 14) has the royal invitation being rejected by the (Jewish) people and then by royal edict being offered to those on the streets outside the city (vv. 8 – 9), an obvious reference to the mission outside Israel. This provides a natural transition from the restriction of the mission to Israel (10:5 – 6; 15:24) to the universal mission of 28:19. Once again, this is not a replacement theology, for believing Jews were also included and rejected by the rest of the nation, therefore being "outside" the city.

There are three passages in the Olivet Discourse that relate to this motif. (1) Matthew 24:14 is the famous passage that proclaims the universal mission as part of the last days, "And this gospel of the kingdom will be proclaimed in the entire world for a witness to all nations." This means that the universal proclamation of the gospel to all peoples of the earth (Jew and Gentile alike) will continue until the eschaton. (2) Matthew 24:31 says that "his elect" will be gathered "from the four winds" (= the four corners of the earth), a reference to all the nations as producing believers. The gospel will spread throughout the earth to all people. (3) Matthew 25:31 – 46 shows the result of the universal proclamation of the gospel, the responsibility of all peoples, Jew and Gentile, to stand before God and give account for their lives. There are only two kinds of people in the world: not Jew and Gentile but righteous and wicked. All will equally answer to God for their allegiance to Christ and for their conduct.

Finally, in the closing chapters there are three passages. (1) Matthew 27:54 is that well-known passage where the centurion and the other guards concluded, "Truly this was the Son of God." This is amazing christologically and demonstrates the ability of Gentiles (even hard-bitten soldiers) to understand and respond to Jesus. It provides one of the christological highlights of the book. (2) In 28:10 Jesus commissions the women to tell the disciples to meet him in Galilee, at once both a fulfillment of 26:32 and reminiscent of 4:15, "Galilee of the Gentiles," preparing them for the Great Commission they will receive there. (3) That commission in 28:19 launches the mission to all the world (Jew and Gentile), for which the entire gospel has been preparing. The Gentiles since the Abrahamic covenant have been part of

28. Luz, *Matthew 8 – 20*, 341.

God's plan, and in the disciples' (and the church's) mission that plan has now to come to fruition. The main point is that both the Jewish and Gentile people groups are the "nations" (24:14; 28:19) and part of the church's mission. Matthew would undoubtedly concur with Paul's strategy in Acts and the mission throughout the NT to both Jew and Gentile alike.

Eschatology

In eschatology there are three aspects: *realized eschatology*, where the stress is on the present reality of the kingdom blessings (emphasized in John); *inaugurated eschatology*, where the stress on the tension between the already and not yet as well as on the opening stages in the appearance of the last days (emphasized in Paul); and *final eschatology*, where the stress is on the consummation of history at the eschaton and last judgment (emphasized in Revelation). Matthew contains all three, with realized eschatology in the ethical teaching on righteousness in the Sermon on the Mount, inaugurated eschatology in the concept of reward in the Beatitudes and in the kingdom teaching of his gospel, and final eschatology in many of his parables and in portions of the Olivet Discourse.

(1) Let us deal with the most distinct emphasis first, his final eschatology. John the Baptist warns the leaders, "Who warned you to flee from the wrath soon to come?" (3:7). He goes on to state, "The ax is already laid at the root of the trees. So every tree that does not produce good fruit is going be cut down and thrown into the fire" (3:10). Then in 3:12 the Baptist concludes this scene by asserting that at the final harvest God will burn "the chaff with unquenchable fire," further evidence for the centrality of final judgment in Matthew's eschatology.

In the Sermon on the Mount (chs. 5 – 7) there are two consecutive statements on the danger of eternal hellfire: first concerning anger with a progressive series of judgments ending in "facing fiery Gehenna"[29] (5:22); then in Jesus' discussion of lust he says to pluck out the eye (which looks upon another) and to cut off the hand (which acts out the lust), lest "your whole body be thrown into Gehenna" (5:29 – 30; cf. also 18:8 – 9). In 7:13 Jesus says the gate is wide and the road long that leads to destruction, and in 7:19 he adds that fruitless trees are "cut down and thrown into the fire." Finally, in 7:21 – 23 many who claim to have done great things in his name will be excluded from the kingdom of heaven.

Then in the Mission Discourse of 10:14 – 15 Jesus warns that those towns who reject the messenger and the message of the kingdom will have a worse time even than Sodom and Gomorrah on the day of judgment. In 10:28 Christ declares we

29. "Gehenna" refers to the Hinnon Valley at the edge of Jerusalem, where in ancient times human sacrifices were offered to the pagan god Molech (2 Kgs 23:10) and where in Jesus' day garbage was burned day and night, making it a perfect metaphor for eternal fiery judgment. It is used seven times in Matthew.

should not fear those who can merely kill the body; rather, save our terror for "the one who has the power to destroy both soul and body in Gehenna." He emphasizes Gehenna in 5:22, 29 – 30; 10:28; 18:9; 23:15, 33 and the corresponding image of darkness with "weeping and grinding of teeth" in 8:12; 22:13; 24:51; 25:30. Both are metaphors that stress the eternal punishment enacted at the last judgment. In 8:12 Jesus contrasts the faith of the Gentiles to the obduracy of the Jewish people and states that the Gentiles will have their place in the messianic banquet while many Jews will "be thrown into outermost darkness" with "weeping and grinding of teeth." In 24:51 the evil servant will be cut up and experience "weeping and grinding of teeth," as will the one who buries his talent in 25:30. Thus Gehenna and outer darkness are images for eternal punishment in the lake of fire of Rev 20:13 – 15.

There is also a significant amount of material in Matt 12 – 13. In 12:33 – 37 Jesus warns of trees producing bad fruit and specifically says that we "will give account on the day of judgment for every careless word." In 12:41 – 42 (as noted in the previous section) the Queen of the South will condemn the current generation in Israel at the last judgment. Matthew adds a great deal of material to Mark in his parable chapter (ch. 13) and the Olivet Discourse (chs. 24 – 25). Two parables he adds especially develop this theme. The parables of the weeds (13:24 – 30, 36 – 43) and of the net (13:47 – 50) both end with the wicked "cast ... into the fiery furnace, where there will be weeping and grinding of teeth" (13:42, 50), in contrast to the righteous, who will "shine like the sun" (v. 43). It is clear that for Matthew the parable chapter is not just about the presence of the kingdom in this world but about the necessity of accepting the kingdom message (about the arrival of the Messiah and coming to faith in him) in light of the last judgment.

Further material is found in the material leading up to the Olivet Discourse of chs. 24 – 25. In the sayings on discipleship in 16:24 – 28 Jesus states that at the parousia he will give every person the reward they have earned with their deeds. In 19:28 – 29 the disciples are promised that "at the renewal of the world" they will sit on twelve thrones, judging the tribes of Israel. Moreover, everyone who has sacrificed for the Lord will "inherit eternal life." The parable of the wedding banquet in 22:1 – 14 depicts the messianic banquet and those "chosen" to participate; in v. 13 the person without a wedding garment is cast into outer darkness.

In the Olivet Discourse, the technical word for the "coming" of the Lord (παρουσία) is used four times (vv. 3, 27, 37, 39, only in Matthew) for the second coming of Christ, and vv. 29 – 31 detail the events — the shaking of the heavens, the appearance of the Son of Man on the clouds, and the gathering of the elect. The rest of Matt 24 – 25 centers on readiness and warning. Matthew 24:32 – 35 tell to watch the signs, namely, those he has given — the destruction of the temple, the desolating sacrilege of the Antichrist, the terrible suffering of AD 66 – 70 and of the church age, and the final suffering of the tribulation period. Then he provides a series of parables on watchfulness (24:36 – 25:30) that warn of the consequences of facing Christ unprepared. The consequences of not being ready for the parousia are terrible indeed — left behind (24:40, 41), cut to pieces (24:51), denied entrance to the messianic banquet (25:12), and cast into eternal darkness (24:51; 25:30). In each of these parables the readiness is emphasized in light of the eschaton that will be enacted at the final return of Christ.

(2) Realized eschatology is found in the concept of rewards for righteous conduct, to some extent in the Beatitudes of 5:1 – 12 (but see further below). The first beatitude uses the present tense, "the kingdom of heaven belongs to them" (5:3), meaning that the kingdom is the present possession of the poor in spirit. In 5:43 – 47 Jesus says that those who love their enemies are special children of the Father and are rewarded for that loving heart. In 6:25 – 34 the emphasis is on God's rewarding the trusting believer by taking care of his daily needs.

(3) But for the most part, the Sermon on the Mount contains inaugurated eschatology. The Beatitudes end with future promises, "they will (be) ..." and connote promises that begin in the present experiences of the faithful follower and are consummated at the eschaton. In 5:19 those who obey and teach Jesus' commandments "will be called great in the kingdom," with the emphasis on final reward but undoubtedly referring to present blessing as well. In the sections on almsgiving in 6:4, on prayer in 6:6, and in fasting in 6:18, Jesus says, "your Father ... will reward you," which is first earthly blessing and second eternal reward (see also 10:40 – 42; 20:1 – 16). Clearly, eschatology is used in service of ethical responsibility. Living "righteously" (see 3:15; 5:6, 10, 20; 6:1, 33; 21:32) will produce great reward; to fail to do so will result in condemnation.

There has been further debate regarding Matthew's eschatological structure in terms of salvation history, whether there are two periods (that of Israel and Jesus/the church — so Kingsbury), containing promise (the Law and the Prophets foretelling the Jesus event) and fulfillment (Jesus and the church as the new covenant age); three periods (Israel, Jesus, the church — so Strecker, Hagner), or four (Israel, Jesus, the church, the final consummation and beyond — so Carson). Scot McKnight sees six — anticipation and promise (the OT), transition (John the Baptist), the Messiah's inauguration of the kingdom, the time of Israel's decision, the time of the gospel going to all nations, and the consummation at the parousia.[30] With Matthew's emphasis on final eschatology, the fourfold view is best. The kingdom in Matthew is seen as inaugurated but not yet final. It is in process of being realized.

The Church

Matthew is the only gospel to contain the word "church" (ἐκκλησία; 16:18, twice in 18:17), both places centering on the great authority given to the new kingdom

30. Scot McKnight, "Matthew, Gospel of," *DJG*, 537 – 38.

community established by Jesus. The first occurs after Peter's confession and states that Jesus will build his community on Peter, the "rock." Peter is meant to be in corporate solidarity with the Twelve (when Christ chose them in 10:1 – 4, he constituted the new covenant community as the new Israel), so this means the disciples will be the nucleus and foundation of the kingdom movement Jesus has inaugurated.

As such, Peter typifies the eschatological authority that God is bestowing on the church. First, death itself ("the gates of Hades") has no power over it; the church will last forever and cannot be extinguished. Moreover, it has authority to "bind" the cosmic powers (10:1, 8; 12:29). The "keys of the kingdom" belong to the church, meaning that God has given her access to the doors of heaven and the powers of the heavenly realm. The motif of the doors of heaven opening means the last days have arrived, the age of fulfillment has come. This includes miracles (as in the book of Acts) and power in proclaiming the gospel, opening the doors of heaven to nation after nation in the ongoing mission of 24:14; 28:19.

The authority to "bind" and "loose" probably refers to the teaching office of the church as it interprets and proclaims Jesus' kingdom truths, thereby guiding the church in terms of what is forbidden (binding) and accepted (loosing) in the lives and conduct of the people. This is applied in 18:17 – 18 to church discipline. The final stage in correcting an erring member is to take the issue to the church as a whole and give the sinner a final chance to repent (18:17). It is the church as a whole that renders the final verdict under the leading of God (18:18 – 19) and Jesus (18:20). There binding and loosing parallel John 20:23, the authority of the church to "not forgive" and "forgive" sins.

Many of the passages dealing with Judaism in Matthew also pertain to the church. For instance, the condemnation of the scribes and Pharisees in Matt 23 becomes also a warning against hypocrisy and self-seeking in the church. Several passages warn against false teachers, beginning with 7:15 – 23 (beware those who come in "sheep's clothing" but are actually "rapacious wolves") and continuing through 24:4 – 5, 10 – 12, 23 – 24, the false messiahs who will "deceive many" and bring about a great apostasy (cf. 2 Thess 2:3; 1 John 2:18). Matthew stresses the unity and purity of the church, that at one and the same time the church must live without anger and dissension (e.g., 5:22 – 24) and protect itself against false teachers. In this enterprise of becoming the citizens of the new kingdom community and living out the new "Torah" or instructions Jesus brings for the new age, Jesus promises that God will oversee its growth and future greatness (13:31 – 33), but he also warns that in achieving that greatness, the members of the church must surrender everything they have and embrace that new reality in their lives (13:44 – 46; cf. 4:20 – 22).

The church is composed of Jew and Gentile (see above on "The Gentile Mission"), chosen by God and called by Jesus to become part of God's new people. The Baptist in 3:9 told the leaders that it is no longer sufficient to be able to "have Abraham" as their "father," for in the new messianic community God will demand more, specifically, belief in the Messiah. The only rule of this new divinely established community is to "follow" Jesus and join his new fishing ministry for souls (4:18 – 22). "Following" Jesus is the primary Matthean term for discipleship (8:19, 22 – 23; 9:9; 16:24; 19:21, 27 – 28; 20:34 — see further below) and signifies a radical commitment that places Jesus first in priority over all things.

Moreover, the members of the "church" are taken from those who know themselves to be sinners, not those who claim to be righteous (9:13b). Matthew warns of false prophets/teachers who have the appearance of being among the flock of God but in reality are ferocious wolves ready to destroy and devour the true sheep (7:15); they claim to be messiahs but are filled with lies and deception (24:4, 24). Many will be fooled by their pernicious words and counterfeit deeds and will be led into sin (7:22 – 23; 18:6 – 7; 24:24). Therefore it must be understood that in the Christian community there will be good and bad members, and this will continue until the final harvest (13:24 – 30, 36 – 43, 47 – 50).

The followers of Jesus are the citizens of the new kingdom community and are called to be "righteous" (3:15; 5:6, 10, 20; 6:1, 33; 21:32), a major term in Matthew for ethical responsibility, meaning to live one's life "rightly" before God. In a sense the five discourses of Matthew can be labeled a manual for church life; they are supremely ethical. In short, the church in Matthew is called to live its life "rightly" before God in such a way that it makes a difference in the world around it (5:13 – 16); it is a group of kingdom people concerned not just to believe but to follow in such a way that they live the ideals of the kingdom Christ has inaugurated on earth and are at all times prepared for the final kingdom he will bring with him when he comes back in his parousia.

Discipleship

The parallel issue to the church is naturally the growth and development of Jesus' disciples. Discussion on this issue began with Gerhardus Barth's seminal work in *Tradition and Interpretation in Matthew*, in which he argued that "faith" (πίστις) is placing trust in God and in the authority of Jesus but separated it from understanding, believing that the intellectual aspect of coming-to-understanding is restricted in Matthew to the one term for understanding (συνιέναι).[31] Ulrich Luz agrees but goes a step farther, arguing for a total separation between faith and understanding; he sees in the disciples a complete failure to understand until Jesus instructs them.[32]

Gundry, however, disagrees, maintaining that Matthew has deliberately removed the theme of misunderstanding from Mark and portrays the disciples as growing in their understanding and faith together; in this, "little faith" (ὀλιγόπιστοι; 6:30;

31. Barth, in Bornkamm, Barth, and Held, *Tradition and Interpretation*, 112 – 16.

32. Ulrich Luz, *Theology*, 92 – 94, 97 – 98.

8:26; 14:31; 16:8) refers not to an absence of understanding but to a basic confusion in their understanding.[33] Wilkins finds a consensus in redaction-critical studies that the disciples in the midst of their struggles with Jesus' teaching come to a basic understanding of them.[34] In a narrative sense, Edwards sees an uncertain faith that is inconsistent, yet an obedience that follows faithfully in the midst of doubting.[35]

Others modify this still further, arguing that the disciples understand only when Jesus teaches them and enables them to do so. They do not understand his passion predictions or his mission, and while they affirm him as Son of God (14:33), they misunderstand and refuse to let him become the suffering Messiah. They "stumble" in 18:6 – 9 and "fall away" by deserting him at his arrest (26:31). In other words, their understanding is partial at best and not that far removed from Mark's portrayal.[36]

Jeannine Brown sums up the discussion. The disciples do not fully understand. In their portrayal in Matthew, they misunderstand Jesus' mission and message, have an inadequate faith, and fall short of Jesus' intentions. She sees three dimensions of this portrayal — the role of the disciples in Matthew's story (textual world), their function in Matthew's community (concrete world), and their place in Matthew's concept of discipleship (symbolic world). In the textual world this is a foil to Jesus' teaching authority and effective presence. In the concrete world, they are transparent for similar problems in the Matthean community. In the symbolic world, discipleship is openness to and dependence on Jesus and his teaching.[37]

Let us trace this theme through Matthew.[38] We begin with the call to the first disciples (4:18 – 22). Mark has three stages, in which they are called (1:16 – 20), commissioned (3:13 – 19), and sent (6:7 – 13). Matthew has collapsed the latter two into 10:1 – 14 but also contains all three emphases. The teaching here is that discipleship demands absolute surrender to Jesus but entails great authority, indeed, sharing in the authority of Jesus. The ethical life of the disciple is set out in the Sermon on the Mount (chs. 5 – 7), in which Jesus establishes the laws of the new community, that standard of "righteousness" or ethical behavior (5:6, 10, 20; 6:1, 33) God demands. In 5:3 – 12 the basic ethical lifestyle is described, and in 5:20 we see the disciple must exceed the level attained by the scribes and Pharisees. In fact, in 5:48 the goal is the absolute "perfection" of God, which should probably be defined in OT terms as complete or wholehearted obedience to Jesus' teachings as given in the Sermon on the Mount (see commentary). The basic principles by which the disciple lives are

33. Gundry, *Matthew*, 156, 300, 624.

34. Michael Wilkins, "Named and Unnamed Disciples in Matthew: A Literary/Theological Study," in *1991 SBLSP* (Atlanta: Scholars Press, 1991), 419 – 22. See also his *Discipleship in the Ancient World and in Matthew's Gospel* (Grand Rapids: Baker, 1995), 143 – 48.

35. Richard A. Edwards, *Matthew's Narrative Portrait of the Disciples* (Valley Forge, PA: Trinity Press International, 1997). See also Verseput, "Faith of the Reader," 3 – 24.

36. Trotter, "Understanding and Stumbling"; Carson, "Matthew," 37 – 38.

37. Brown, *Disciples*, 51 – 54, 148 – 49.

38. Here I am indebted to my assistant Justin Fuhrmann, who gathered much of this together in a paper entitled, "Discipleship in Matthew," taught in my PhD seminar on the theology of Matthew.

found in 6:19 – 21, seeking treasures in heaven rather than earth; and in 6:24 – 34, trusting entirely in God to provide rather than trusting in earthly provisions. Finally, 7:13 – 27 shows that the disciples walk the narrow path and bear fruit for God rather than the broad path of worldly attainments.

There are two discipleship sections in the miracle section (8:18 – 22; 9:9 – 17), and they come between three triads of miracles that demonstrate Jesus' absolute authority. The message is that Jesus' authority demands absolute surrender to him. In 8:18 – 22 the cost of discipleship is described, as Jesus tells two would-be disciples that first, they will have to surrender a comfortable, settled life if they truly follow him (on the homeless nature of apostolic ministry, see 1 Cor 4:11; Heb 11:13 – 16); and second, that discipleship entails giving Jesus absolute priority even over the greatest of obligations (e.g., burying one's parents). Clearly, following Jesus entails great sacrifice and commitment. In 9:9 – 17 the emphasis is on discontinuity and newness. Societal boundaries are broken, and a new openness to every strata, including the disreputable, begins.

The "little faith" passages (6:30; 8:26; 14:31; 16:8; 17:20) are essential for the issue of discipleship in Matthew. Some believe this means the disciples have no faith (France, Luz, Blomberg) or that they have previously had faith but are now not utilizing it, so it is "bankrupt" (Wilkins). The majority, however, sees this as the beginning stages of a developing faith and understanding (Gundry, Carson, Davies and Allison, Bruner, Nolland). This latter view certainly fits Matthew best. The disciples have an insufficient faith but one that grows slowly into more and more understanding.

Two examples from this material will illustrate the point, from the sections following the two feeding miracles. In both sections Mark emphasizes the disciples' failure, noting that they had "hardened hearts" (Mark 6:52; 8:17) and ending the second episode with Jesus' challenge, "Do you still not understand?" (8:21). Matthew notes the failure but ends both episodes quite differently. In Jesus' walking on the water episode, Matthew adds to Mark the story of Peter walking on the water. After Jesus challenges them in 14:31 with their "little faith," the disciples "worship" him and say, "Truly you are the Son of God." In Mark the disciples never get beyond calling him "Messiah" (8:29), while Matthew shows their developing understanding. This is especially true in the parallel scene to Mark 8:21, where Matthew tells us, "Then they understood" (Matt 16:12). Clearly the "little faith" of 16:8 was faith seeking understanding. The emphasis is on the growth of faith and understanding as a result of the presence and help of Jesus.

This is seen especially in ch. 13, the Parable Discourse. In 13:11 Jesus told his disciples, "knowledge of the mysteries of the kingdom of heaven has been given to you," meaning that the kingdom has arrived in Jesus and its secrets made known to the disciples. In the following verse Jesus promises that they will be given even "more" insight into the kingdom truths. Then in v. 16 Jesus calls them "blessed" because they have "seen" and "heard" these kingdom realities. Clearly Jesus means that understanding is dawning. At the conclusion of his interpretation of the parable of the soils, Jesus tells them the fruitful soil refers to "the one who hears the message and understands it" (13:23). This is summed up in 13:51 – 52, where the disciples claim to have "understood" the parables, and then Jesus calls them teachers of the law "trained as disciples in the kingdom of heaven," meaning they are the new interpreters of the kingdom truths.

Yet Jesus seems to demur from this in 15:16 and 16:9. In the first Jesus has just told the crowds to "listen and understand" (15:10), and the disciples proceeded to demonstrate just the opposite by failing to understand the parable about the plants pulled up by the roots (v. 13). Jesus then calls them "dull" (uncomprehending, senseless), meaning they should have understood but have failed to do so (15:16). Next, in 16:9, after calling his disciples men of "little faith" (v. 8), Jesus challenges them, "Can't you yet understand?" Obviously the disciples waffle back and forth between understanding (ch. 13) and failure to do so (chs. 15 – 16).

Yet here too the presence of Jesus makes the difference, for after Jesus explains the meaning of the loaves, we are told, "then they understood" (v. 12). In some ways, Peter's confession in 16:16 represents a high point of understanding (see 16:17 – 19), yet even that was short-lived, as exemplified in Peter's unwillingness to accept the nature of Jesus' messianic work (16:21 – 28). Jesus even accuses Peter of being a tool of Satan who thinks in human rather than divine terms (v. 23). The high point is thus followed by a low point of discipleship misunderstanding.

On the road to Jerusalem after Peter's confession, Jesus turns from the crowds to center on the disciples. The action turns around the three passion predictions and the transfiguration, yet as Jesus discloses the "mysteries" (13:11) to them, they demonstrate a remarkable obtuseness and self-centeredness. Immediately after Jesus reveals his preincarnate glory to the inner circle (17:1 – 13), we see the rest of the disciples failing to heal an epileptic child, and Jesus calls them an "unbelieving ... generation" (see commentary on 17:17). Shortly after the second passion prediction (17:22 – 23), the disciples are arguing over who is the greatest (18:1); and after the third prediction (20:17 – 19), James and John send their mother (cf. Mark 10:35 – 41) to ask Jesus if her sons can sit at his right and left (the positions of power) in the kingdom. The hubris that this demands is astounding! It must be admitted that in this section there is little evidence of a growing understanding on the part of the disciples. This section would justify Brown's conclusion that "Matthew does not show the disciples to progress substantially in either their understanding or their faith."[39]

Yet when the whole picture is studied, Matthew is more positive than this. The failures of the disciples during the road to Jerusalem and the Passion Narrative

39. Brown, *Disciples*, 148.

(e.g., Gethsemane, their desertion at Jesus' arrest, Peter's denials) are overturned with the final scene. As Jesus meets them in Galilee (cf. 26:32), we see that "some doubted" (28:17, summing up their failures), but Jesus concludes the positive side of their discipleship process by commanding them to "teach [the nations] to keep everything I have commanded you," assuming the understanding of the disciples and restating 13:52.

When we consider the whole of Matthew, therefore, it is evident that realism pervades the picture of the disciples as we see the ebb and flow of their gradual progress. Matthew is more positive than Mark, showing the many failures of the disciples but portraying their growth as well. The basic message is that success is found only in Jesus, and his presence alone enables any development in faith and understanding. They are exemplified as having "little faith" but as slowly overcoming their failures when they depend on Jesus alone.

Scripture Index

Leviticus

Numbers

Deuteronomy

Joshua

Judges

Ruth

1 Samuel

2 Samuel

1 Kings

2 Kings

1 Chronicles

2 Chronicles

Ezra

Nehemiah

Proverbs

Ecclesiastes

Isaiah

Jeremiah

Lamentations

Ezekiel

Daniel

Malachi

Matthew

Mark

Luke

John

Acts

Romans

1 Corinthians

2 Corinthians

Galatians

Ephesians

Philippians

Colossians

1 Thessalonians

Subject Index

Author Index